Selected Works of
Virginia Woolf

Jacob's Room, Mrs Dalloway,
To the Lighthouse, Orlando,
A Room of One's Own,
The Waves, Three Guineas
&
Between the Acts

Wordsworth Editions

Readers who are interested in other titles from
Wordsworth Editions are invited to visit out website at
www.wordsworth-editions.com

For our latest list and a full mail-order service contact
Bibliophile Books, 5 Thomas Road, London E14 7BN
Tel: +44 0207 515 9222   Fax: +44 0207 538 4115
e-mail: orders@bibliophilebooks.com

This edition published 2005 by Wordsworth Editions Limited
8B East Street, Ware, Hertfordshire SG12 9HJ

ISBN 1 84022 058 9

Typeset by Antony Gray
Printed in Great Britain by
Mackays of Chatham, Chatham, Kent

Selected Works of Virginia Woolf

CONTENTS

JACOB'S ROOM

Jacob's Room

A novel by
VIRGINIA WOOLF
first published in 1922

Chapter One

'So of course,' wrote Betty Flanders, pressing her heels rather deeper in the sand, 'there was nothing for it but to leave.'

Slowly welling from the point of her gold nib, pale blue ink dissolved the full stop; for there her pen stuck; her eyes fixed, and tears slowly filled them. The entire bay quivered; the lighthouse wobbled; and she had the illusion that the mast of Mr Connor's little yacht was bending like a wax candle in the sun. She winked quickly. Accidents were awful things. She winked again. The mast was straight; the waves were regular; the lighthouse was upright; but the blot had spread.

' . . . nothing for it but to leave,' she read.

'Well, if Jacob doesn't want to play' (the shadow of Archer, her eldest son, fell across the notepaper and looked blue on the sand, and she felt chilly – it was the third of September already), 'if Jacob doesn't want to play' – what a horrid blot! It must be getting late.

'Where *is* that tiresome little boy?' she said. 'I don't see him. Run and find him. Tell him to come at once.' ' . . . but mercifully,' she scribbled, ignoring the full stop, 'everything seems satisfactorily arranged, packed though we are like herrings in a barrel, and forced to stand the perambulator which the landlady quite naturally won't allow . . . '

Such were Betty Flanders's letters to Captain Barfoot – many-paged, tear-stained. Scarborough is seven hundred miles from Cornwall: Captain Barfoot is in Scarborough: Seabrook is dead. Tears made all the dahlias in her garden undulate in red waves and flashed the glass house in her eyes, and spangled the kitchen with bright knives, and made Mrs Jarvis, the rector's wife, think at church, while the hymn-tune played and Mrs Flanders bent low over her little boys' heads, that marriage is a fortress and widows stray solitary in the open fields, picking up stones, gleaning a few golden straws, lonely, unprotected, poor creatures. Mrs Flanders had been a widow for these two years.

'Ja–cob! Ja–cob!' Archer shouted.

'Scarborough,' Mrs Flanders wrote on the envelope, and dashed a bold line beneath; it was her native town; the hub of the universe. But a stamp? She ferreted in her bag; then held it up mouth downwards; then fumbled in her lap, all so vigorously that Charles Steele in the Panama hat suspended his paintbrush.

Like the antennae of some irritable insect it positively trembled. Here was that woman moving – actually going to get up – confound her! He struck the canvas a hasty violet-black dab. For the landscape needed it. It was too pale – greys flowing into lavenders, and one star or a white gull suspended just so – too pale as usual. The critics would say it was too pale, for he was an unknown man exhibiting obscurely, a favourite with his landladies' children, wearing a cross on his watch chain, and much gratified if his landladies liked his pictures – which they often did.

'Ja–cob! Ja–cob!' Archer shouted.

Exasperated by the noise, yet loving children, Steele picked nervously at the dark little coils on his palette.

'I saw your brother – I saw your brother,' he said, nodding his head, as Archer lagged past him, trailing his spade, and scowling at the old gentleman in spectacles.

'Over there – by the rock,' Steele muttered, with his brush between his teeth, squeezing out raw sienna, and keeping his eyes fixed on Betty Flanders's back.

'Ja–cob! Ja–cob!' shouted Archer, lagging on after a second.

The voice had an extraordinary sadness. Pure from all body, pure from all passion, going out into the world, solitary, unanswered, breaking against rocks – so it sounded.

Steele frowned; but was pleased by the effect of the black – it was just *that* note which brought the rest together. 'Ah, one may learn to paint at fifty! There's Titian . . . ' and so, having found the right tint, up he looked and saw to his horror a cloud over the bay.

Mrs Flanders rose, slapped her coat this side and that to get the sand off, and picked up her black parasol.

The rock was one of those tremendously solid brown, or rather black, rocks which emerge from the sand like something primitive. Rough with crinkled limpet shells and sparsely strewn with locks of dry seaweed, a small boy has to stretch his legs far apart, and indeed to feel rather heroic, before he gets to the top.

But there, on the very top, is a hollow full of water, with a sandy bottom; with a blob of jelly stuck to the side, and some mussels. A fish darts across. The fringe of yellow-brown seaweed flutters, and out pushes an opal-shelled crab – 'Oh, a huge crab,' Jacob murmured – and begins his journey on weakly legs on the sandy bottom. Now! Jacob plunged his hand. The crab was cool and very light. But the water was thick with sand, and so, scrambling down, Jacob was about to jump, holding his bucket in front of him, when he saw, stretched entirely rigid, side by side, their faces very red, an enormous man and woman.

An enormous man and woman (it was early-closing day) were stretched motionless, with their heads on pocket-handkerchiefs, side by side, within a few feet of the sea, while two or three gulls gracefully skirted the incoming waves and settled near their boots.

The large red faces lying on the bandanna handkerchiefs stared up at Jacob. Jacob stared down at them. Holding his bucket very carefully, Jacob then jumped deliberately and trotted away very nonchalantly at first, but faster and faster as the waves came creaming up to him and he had to swerve to avoid them, and the gulls rose in front of him and floated out and settled again a little farther on. A large black woman was sitting on the sand. He ran towards her.

'Nanny! Nanny!' he cried, sobbing the words out on the crest of each gasping breath.

The waves came round her. She was a rock. She was covered with the seaweed which pops when it is pressed. He was lost.

There he stood. His face composed itself. He was about to roar when, lying among the black sticks and straw under the cliff, he saw a whole skull – perhaps a cow's skull, a skull, perhaps, with the teeth in it. Sobbing, but absent-mindedly, he ran farther and farther away until he held the skull in his arms.

'There he is!' cried Mrs Flanders, coming round the rock and covering the whole space of the beach in a few seconds. 'What has he got hold of? Put it down, Jacob! Drop it this moment! Something horrid, I know. Why didn't you stay with us? Naughty little boy! Now put it down. Now come along both of you,' and she swept round, holding Archer by one hand and fumbling for Jacob's arm with the other. But he ducked down and picked up the sheep's jaw, which was loose.

Swinging her bag, clutching her parasol, holding Archer's hand, and telling the story of the gunpowder explosion in which poor Mr Curnow had lost his eye, Mrs Flanders hurried up the steep lane, aware all the time in the depths of her mind of some buried discomfort.

There on the sand not far from the lovers lay the old sheep's skull without its jaw. Clean, white, wind-swept, sand-rubbed, a more unpolluted piece of bone existed nowhere on the coast of Cornwall. The sea holly would grow through the eye-sockets; it would turn to powder, or some golfer, hitting his ball one fine day, would disperse a little dust – No, but not in lodgings, thought Mrs Flanders. It's a great experiment coming so far with young children. There's no man to help with the perambulator. And Jacob is such a handful; so obstinate already.

'Throw it away, dear, do,' she said, as they got into the road; but Jacob squirmed away from her; and the wind rising, she took out her bonnet-pin, looked at the sea, and stuck it in afresh. The wind was rising. The waves showed that uneasiness, like something alive, restive, expecting the whip, of waves before a storm. The fishing-boats were leaning to the water's brim. A pale yellow light shot across the purple sea; and shut. The lighthouse was lit. 'Come along,' said Betty Flanders. The sun blazed in their faces and gilded the great blackberries trembling out from the hedge which Archer tried to strip as they passed.

'Don't lag, boys. You've got nothing to change into,' said Betty, pulling them along, and looking with uneasy emotion at the earth displayed so luridly, with sudden sparks of light from greenhouses in gardens, with a sort of yellow and black mutability, against this blazing sunset, this astonishing agitation and vitality of colour, which stirred Betty Flanders and made her think of responsibility and danger. She gripped Archer's hand. On she plodded up the hill.

'What did I ask you to remember?' she said.

'I don't know,' said Archer.

'Well, I don't know either,' said Betty, humorously and simply, and who shall deny that this blankness of mind, when combined with profusion, mother wit, old wives' tales, haphazard ways, moments of astonishing daring, humour and sentimentality – who shall deny that in these respects every woman is nicer than any man?

Well, Betty Flanders, to begin with.

She had her hand upon the garden gate.

'The meat!' she exclaimed, striking the latch down.

She had forgotten the meat.

There was Rebecca at the window.

The bareness of Mrs Pearce's front room was fully displayed at ten o'clock at night when a powerful oil lamp stood on the middle of the table. The harsh light fell on the garden; cut straight across the lawn; lit up a child's bucket and a purple aster and reached the hedge. Mrs Flanders had left her sewing on the table. There were her large reels of white cotton and her steel spectacles; her needle-case; her brown wool wound round an old postcard. There were the bulrushes and the *Strand* magazines; and the linoleum sandy from the boys' boots. A daddy-long-legs shot from corner to corner and hit the lamp globe. The wind blew straight dashes of rain across the window, which flashed silver as they passed through the light. A single leaf tapped hurriedly, persistently, upon the glass. There was a hurricane out at sea.

Archer could not sleep.

Mrs Flanders stooped over him. 'Think of the fairies,' said Betty Flanders. 'Think of the lovely, lovely birds settling down on their nests. Now shut your eyes and see the old mother bird with a worm in her beak. Now turn and shut your eyes,' she murmured, 'and shut your eyes.'

The lodging-house seemed full of gurgling and rushing; the cistern over-flowing; water bubbling and squeaking and running along the pipes and streaming down the windows.

'What's all that water rushing in?' murmured Archer.

'It's only the bathwater running away,' said Mrs Flanders.

Something snapped out of doors.

'I say, won't that steamer sink?' said Archer, opening his eyes.

'Of course it won't,' said Mrs Flanders. 'The captain's in bed long ago. Shut your eyes, and think of the fairies, fast asleep, under the flowers.'

'I thought he'd never get off – such a hurricane,' she whispered to Rebecca, who was bending over a spirit-lamp in the small room next door. The wind rushed outside, but the small flame of the spirit-lamp burnt quietly, shaded from the cot by a book stood on edge.

'Did he take his bottle well?' Mrs Flanders whispered, and Rebecca nodded and went to the cot and turned down the quilt, and Mrs Flanders bent over and looked anxiously at the baby, asleep, but frowning. The window shook, and Rebecca stole like a cat and wedged it.

The two women murmured over the spirit-lamp, plotting the eternal conspiracy of hush and clean bottles while the wind raged and gave a sudden wrench at the cheap fastenings.

Both looked round at the cot. Their lips were pursed. Mrs Flanders crossed over to the cot.

'Asleep?' whispered Rebecca, looking at the cot.

Mrs Flanders nodded.

'Good-night, Rebecca,' Mrs Flanders murmured, and Rebecca called her ma'm, though they were conspirators plotting the eternal conspiracy of hush and clean bottles.

Mrs Flanders had left the lamp burning in the front room. There were her spectacles, her sewing; and a letter with the Scarborough postmark. She had not drawn the curtains either.

The light blazed out across the patch of grass; fell on the child's green bucket with the gold line round it, and upon the aster which trembled violently beside it. For the wind was tearing across the coast, hurling itself at the hills, and leaping, in sudden gusts, on top of its own back. How it spread over the town in the hollow! How the lights seemed to wink and quiver in its fury, lights in the harbour, lights in bedroom windows high up! And rolling dark waves before it, it raced over the Atlantic, jerking the stars above the ships this way and that.

There was a click in the front sitting-room. Mr Pearce had extinguished the lamp. The garden went out. It was but a dark patch. Every inch was rained upon. Every blade of grass was bent by rain. Eyelids would have been fastened down by the rain. Lying on one's back one would have seen nothing but muddle and confusion – clouds turning and turning, and something yellow-tinted and sulphurous in the darkness.

The little boys in the front bedroom had thrown off their blankets and lay under the sheets. It was hot; rather sticky and steamy. Archer lay spread out, with one arm striking across the pillow. He was flushed; and when the heavy curtain blew out a little he turned and half-opened his eyes. The wind actually stirred the cloth on the chest of drawers, and let in a little light, so that the sharp edge of the chest of drawers was visible, running straight up, until a white shape bulged out; and a silver streak showed in the looking-glass.

In the other bed by the door Jacob lay asleep, fast asleep, profoundly unconscious. The sheep's jaw with the big yellow teeth in it lay at his feet. He had kicked it against the iron bed-rail.

Outside the rain poured down more directly and powerfully as the wind fell in the early hours of the morning. The aster was beaten to the earth. The child's bucket was half-full of rainwater; and the opal-shelled crab slowly circled round the bottom, trying with its weakly legs to climb the steep side; trying again and falling back, and trying again and again.

Chapter Two

'Mrs Flanders' – 'Poor Betty Flanders' – 'Dear Betty' – 'She's very attractive still' – 'Odd she don't marry again!' 'There's Captain Barfoot to be sure – calls every Wednesday as regular as clockwork, and never brings his wife.'

'But that's Ellen Barfoot's fault,' the ladies of Scarborough said. 'She don't put herself out for no one.'

'A man likes to have a son – that we know.'

'Some tumours have to be cut; but the sort my mother had you bear with for years and years, and never even have a cup of tea brought up to you in bed.'

(Mrs Barfoot was an invalid.)

Elizabeth Flanders, of whom this and much more than this had been said and would be said, was, of course, a widow in her prime. She was halfway between forty and fifty. Years and sorrow between them; the death of Seabrook, her husband; three boys; poverty; a house on the outskirts of Scarborough; her brother, poor Morty's, downfall and possible demise – for where was he? what was he? Shading her eyes, she looked along the road for Captain Barfoot – yes, there he was, punctual as ever; the attentions of the Captain – all ripened Betty Flanders, enlarged her figure, tinged her face with jollity, and flooded her eyes for no reason that anyone could see perhaps three times a day.

True, there's no harm in crying for one's husband, and the tombstone, though plain, was a solid piece of work, and on summer's days when the widow brought her boys to stand there one felt kindly towards her. Hats were raised higher than usual; wives tugged their husbands' arms. Seabrook lay six foot beneath, dead these many years; enclosed in three shells, the crevices sealed with lead; so that, had earth and wood been glass, doubtless his very face lay visible beneath, the face of a young man, whiskered, shapely, who had gone out duck-shooting and refused to change his boots.

'Merchant of this city,' the tombstone said; though why Betty Flanders had chosen so to call him when, as many still remembered, he had only sat behind an office window for three months, and before that had broken horses, ridden to hounds, farmed a few fields, and run a little wild – well, she had to call him something. An example for the boys.

Had he, then, been nothing? An unanswerable question, since even if it weren't the habit of the undertaker to close the eyes, the light so soon goes out of them. At first, part of herself; now one of a company, he had merged in the grass, the sloping hillside, the thousand white stones, some slanting, others upright, the decayed wreaths, the crosses of green tin, the narrow yellow paths, and the lilacs that drooped in April, with a scent like that of an invalid's bedroom, over the churchyard wall. Seabrook was now all that; and when, with her skirt hitched up, feeding the chickens, she heard the bell for service or funeral, that was Seabrook's voice – the voice of the dead.

The rooster had been known to fly on her shoulder and peck her neck, so that now she carried a stick or took one of the children with her when she went to feed the fowls.

'Wouldn't you like my knife, mother?' said Archer.

Sounding at the same moment as the bell, her son's voice mixed life and death inextricably, exhilaratingly.

'What a big knife for a small boy!' she said. She took it to please him. Then the rooster flew out of the hen-house, and, shouting to Archer to shut the door into the kitchen garden, Mrs Flanders set her meal down, clucked for the hens, went bustling about the orchard, and was seen from over the way by Mrs Cranch, who, beating her mat against the wall, held it for a moment suspended while she observed to Mrs Page next door that Mrs Flanders was in the orchard with the chickens.

Mrs Page, Mrs Cranch and Mrs Garfit could see Mrs Flanders in the orchard because the orchard was a piece of Dods Hill enclosed; and Dods Hill dominated the village. No words can exaggerate the importance of Dods Hill. It was the earth; the world against the sky; the horizon of how many glances can best be computed by those who have lived all their lives in the same village, only leaving it once to fight in the Crimea, like old George Garfit, leaning over his garden gate smoking his pipe. The progress of the sun was measured by it; the tint of the day laid against it to be judged.

'Now she's going up the hill with little John,' said Mrs Cranch to Mrs Garfit, shaking her mat for the last time, and bustling indoors. Opening the orchard gate, Mrs Flanders walked to the top of Dods Hill, holding John by the hand. Archer and Jacob ran in front or lagged behind; but they were in the Roman fortress when she came there, and shouting out what ships were to be seen in the bay. For there was a magnificent view – moors behind, sea in front, and the whole of Scarborough from one end to the other laid out flat like a puzzle. Mrs Flanders, who was growing stout, sat down in the fortress and looked about her.

The entire gamut of the view's changes should have been known to her; its winter aspect, spring, summer and autumn; how storms came up from the sea; how the moors shuddered and brightened as the clouds went over; she should have noted the red spot where the villas were building; and the criss-cross of lines where the allotments were cut; and the diamond flash of little glasshouses in the sun. Or, if details like these escaped her, she might have let her fancy play upon the gold tint of the sea at sunset, and thought how it lapped in coins of gold upon the shingle. Little pleasure boats shoved out into it; the black arm of the pier hoarded it up. The whole city was pink and gold; domed; mist-wreathed; resonant; strident. Banjoes strummed; the parade smelt of tar which stuck to the heels; goats suddenly cantered their carriages through crowds. It was observed how well the corporation had laid out the flower-beds. Sometimes a straw hat was blown away. Tulips burnt in the sun. Numbers of sponge-bag trousers were stretched in rows. Purple bonnets fringed soft, pink, querulous faces on pillows in bath chairs. Triangular hoardings were wheeled along by men in white coats. Captain George Boase had caught a monster shark. One side of the triangular hoarding said so in red, blue and yellow letters; and each line ended with three differently coloured notes of exclamation.

So that was a reason for going down into the Aquarium, where the sallow blinds, the stale smell of spirits of salt, the bamboo chairs, the tables with ashtrays, the revolving fish, the attendant knitting behind six or seven chocolate boxes (often she was quite alone with the fish for hours at a time) remained in the mind as part of the monster shark, he himself being only a flabby yellow receptacle, like an empty Gladstone bag, in a tank. No one had ever been cheered by the Aquarium; but the faces of those emerging quickly lost their dim, chilled expression when they perceived that it was only by standing in a queue that one could be admitted to the pier. Once through the turnstiles, everyone walked for a yard or two very briskly; some flagged at this stall; others at that. But it was the band that drew them all to it finally; even the fishermen on the lower pier taking up their pitch within its range.

The band played in the Moorish kiosk. Number nine went up on the board. It was a waltz tune. The pale girls, the old widow lady, the three Jews lodging in the same boarding-house, the dandy, the major, the horse-dealer, and the gentleman of independent means, all wore the same blurred, drugged expression, and through the chinks in the planks at their feet they could see the green summer waves, peacefully, amiably, swaying round the iron pillars of the pier.

But there was a time when none of this had any existence (thought the young man leaning against the railings). Fix your eyes upon the lady's skirt: the grey one will do – above the pink silk stockings. It changes: drapes her ankles – the nineties; then it amplifies – the seventies; now it's burnished red and stretched above a crinoline – the sixties; a tiny black foot wearing a white cotton stocking peeps out. Still sitting there? Yes – she's still on the pier. The silk now is sprigged with roses, but somehow one no longer sees so clearly. There's no pier beneath us. The heavy chariot may swing along the turnpike road, but there's no pier for it to stop at, and how grey and turbulent the sea is in the seventeenth century! Let's to the museum. Cannon-balls; arrow-heads; Roman glass and a forceps green with verdi-gris. The Reverend Jaspar Floyd dug them up at his own expense early in the forties in the Roman camp on Dods Hill – see the little ticket with the faded writing on it.

And now, what's the next thing to see in Scarborough?

Mrs Flanders sat on the raised circle of the Roman camp, patching Jacob's breeches; only looking up as she sucked the end of her cotton, or when some insect dashed at her, boomed in her ear, and was gone.

John kept trotting up and slapping down in her lap grass or dead leaves which he called 'tea', and she arranged them methodically but absent-mindedly, laying the flowery heads of the grasses together, thinking how Archer had been awake again last night; the church clock was ten or thirteen minutes fast; she wished she could buy Garfit's acre.

'That's an orchid leaf, Johnny. Look at the little brown spots. Come, my dear. We must go home. Ar-cher! Ja-cob!'

'Ar-cher! Ja-cob!' Johnny piped after her, pivoting round on his heel, and strewing the grass and leaves in his hands as if he were sowing seed. Archer and Jacob jumped up from behind the mound where they had been crouching with the intention of springing upon their mother unexpectedly, and they all began to walk slowly home.

'Who is that?' said Mrs Flanders, shading her eyes.

'That old man in the road?' said Archer, looking below.

'He's not an old man,' said Mrs Flanders. 'He's – no, he's not – I thought it was the Captain, but it's Mr Floyd. Come along, boys.'

'Oh, bother Mr Floyd!' said Jacob, switching off a thistle's head, for he knew already that Mr Floyd was going to teach them Latin, as indeed he did for three years in his spare time, out of kindness, for there was no other gentleman in the neighbourhood whom Mrs Flanders could have asked to do such a thing, and the elder boys were getting beyond her, and must be got ready for school, and it was more than most clergymen would have done, coming round after tea, or having them in his own room – as he could fit it in – for the parish was a very large one, and Mr Floyd, like his father before him, visited cottages miles away on the moors, and, like old Mr Floyd, was a great scholar, which made it so unlikely – she had never dreamt of such a thing. Ought she to have guessed? But let alone being a scholar he was eight years younger than she was. She knew his mother – old Mrs Floyd. She had tea there. And it was that very evening when she came back from having tea with old Mrs Floyd that she found the note in the hall and took it into the kitchen with her when she went to give Rebecca the fish, thinking it must be something about the boys.

'Mr Floyd brought it himself, did he? – I think the cheese must be in the parcel in the hall – oh, in the hall – ' for she was reading. No, it was not about the boys.

'Yes, enough for fish-cakes tomorrow certainly – Perhaps Captain Barfoot – ' she had come to the word 'love'. She went into the garden and read, leaning against the walnut tree to steady herself. Up and down went her breast. Seabrook came so vividly before her. She shook her head and was looking through her tears at the little shifting leaves against the yellow sky when three geese, half-running, half-flying, scuttled across the lawn with Johnny behind them, brandishing a stick.

Mrs Flanders flushed with anger.

'How many times have I told you?' she cried, and seized him and snatched his stick away from him.

'But they'd escaped!' he cried, struggling to get free.

'You're a very naughty boy. If I've told you once, I've told you a thousand times. I won't have you chasing the geese!' she said, and crumpling Mr Floyd's letter in her hand, she held Johnny fast and herded the geese back into the orchard.

'How could I think of marriage!' she said to herself bitterly, as she fastened the gate with a piece of wire. She had always disliked red hair in men, she thought, thinking of Mr Floyd's appearance, that night when the boys had gone to bed. And pushing her workbox away, she drew the blotting-paper towards her, and read Mr Floyd's letter again, and her breast went up and down when she came to the word 'love', but not so fast this time, for she saw Johnny chasing the geese, and knew that it was impossible for her to marry anyone – let alone Mr Floyd, who was so much younger than she was, but what a nice man – and such a scholar too.

'Dear Mr Floyd,' she wrote – 'Did I forget about the cheese?' she wondered, laying down her pen. No, she had told Rebecca that the cheese was in the hall. 'I am much surprised . . . ' she wrote.

But the letter which Mr Floyd found on the table when he got up early next morning did not begin 'I am much surprised', and it was such a motherly, respectful, inconsequent, regretful letter that he kept it for many years; long after his marriage with Miss Wimbush, of Andover; long after he had left the village. For he asked for a parish in Sheffield, which was given him; and, sending for Archer, Jacob and John to say goodbye, he told them to choose whatever they liked in his study to remember him by. Archer chose a paper-knife, because he did not like to choose anything too good; Jacob chose the works of Byron in one volume; John, who was still too young to make a proper choice, chose Mr Floyd's kitten, which his brothers thought an absurd choice, but Mr Floyd upheld him when he said: 'It has fur like you.' Then Mr Floyd spoke about the King's Navy (to which Archer was going); and about Rugby (to which Jacob was going); and next day he received a silver salver and went – first to Sheffield, where he met Miss Wimbush, who was on a visit to her uncle – then to Hackney – then to Maresfield House, of which he became the principal – and finally, becoming editor of a well-known series of ecclesiastical biographies, he retired to Hampstead with his wife and daughter, and is often to be seen feeding the ducks on Leg of Mutton Pond. As for Mrs Flanders's letter – when he looked for it the other day he could not find it, and did not like to ask his wife whether she had put it away. Meeting Jacob in Piccadilly lately, he recognised him after three seconds. But Jacob had grown such a fine young man that Mr Floyd did not like to stop him in the street.

'Dear me,' said Mrs Flanders, when she read in the *Scarborough and Harrogate Courier* that the Revd Andrew Floyd, etc., etc., had been made Principal of Maresfield House, 'that must be our Mr Floyd.'

A slight gloom fell upon the table. Jacob was helping himself to jam; the postman was talking to Rebecca in the kitchen; there was a bee humming at the yellow flower which nodded at the open window. They were all alive, that is to say, while poor Mr Floyd was becoming Principal of Maresfield House.

Mrs Flanders got up and went over to the fender and stroked Topaz on the neck behind the ears.

'Poor Topaz,' she said (for Mr Floyd's kitten was now a very old cat, a little mangy behind the ears, and one of these days would have to be killed).

'Poor old Topaz,' said Mrs Flanders, as he stretched himself out in the sun, and she smiled, thinking how she had had him gelded, and how she did not like red hair in men. Smiling, she went into the kitchen.

Jacob drew rather a dirty pocket-handkerchief across his face. He went upstairs to his room.

The stag-beetle dies slowly (it was John who collected the beetles). Even on the second day its legs were supple. But the butterflies were dead. A whiff of rotten eggs had vanquished the pale clouded yellows which came pelting across the orchard and up Dods Hill and away on to the moor, now lost behind a furze bush, then off again helter-skelter in a broiling sun. A fritillary basked on a white stone in the Roman camp. From the valley came the sound of church bells. They were all eating roast beef in Scarborough; for it was Sunday when Jacob caught the pale clouded yellows in the clover field, eight miles from home.

Rebecca had caught the death's-head moth in the kitchen.

A strong smell of camphor came from the butterfly boxes.

Mixed with the smell of camphor was the unmistakable smell of seaweed. Tawny ribbons hung on the door. The sun beat straight upon them.

The upper wings of the moth which Jacob held were undoubtedly marked with kidney-shaped spots of a fulvous hue. But there was no crescent upon the underwing. The tree had fallen the night he caught it. There had been a volley of pistol-shots suddenly in the depths of the wood. And his mother had taken him for a burglar when he came home late. The only one of her sons who never obeyed her, she said.

Morris called it 'an extremely local insect found in damp or marshy places'. But Morris is sometimes wrong. Sometimes Jacob, choosing a very fine pen, made a correction in the margin.

The tree had fallen, though it was a windless night, and the lantern, stood upon the ground, had lit up the still green leaves and the dead beech leaves. It was a dry place. A toad was there. And the red underwing had circled round the light and flashed and gone. The red underwing had never come back, though Jacob had waited. It was after twelve when he crossed the lawn and saw his mother in the bright room, playing patience, sitting up.

'How you frightened me!' she had cried. She thought something dreadful had happened. And he woke Rebecca, who had to be up so early.

There he stood pale, come out of the depths of darkness, in the hot room, blinking at the light.

No, it could not be a straw-bordered underwing.

The mowing-machine always wanted oiling. Barnet turned it under Jacob's window, and it creaked – creaked, and rattled across the lawn and creaked again.

Now it was clouding over.

Back came the sun, dazzlingly.

It fell like an eye upon the stirrups, and then suddenly and yet very gently rested upon the bed, upon the alarm clock, and upon the butterfly box stood open. The pale clouded yellows had pelted over the moor; they had zigzagged across the purple clover. The fritillaries flaunted along the hedgerows. The blues settled on little bones lying on the turf with the sun beating on them, and the painted ladies and the peacocks feasted upon bloody entrails dropped by a hawk. Miles away from home, in a hollow among teasles beneath a ruin, he had found the commas. He had seen a white admiral circling higher and higher round an oak tree, but he had never caught it. An old cottage woman living alone, high up, had told him of a purple butterfly which came every summer to her garden. The fox cubs played in the gorse in the early morning, she told him. And if you looked out at dawn you could always see two badgers. Sometimes they knocked each other over like two boys fighting, she said.

'You won't go far this afternoon, Jacob,' said his mother, popping her head in at the door, 'for the Captain's coming to say goodbye.' It was the last day of the Easter holidays.

Wednesday was Captain Barfoot's day. He dressed himself very neatly in blue serge, took his rubber-shod stick – for he was lame and wanted two fingers on the left hand, having served his country – and set out from the house with the flagstaff precisely at four o'clock in the afternoon.

At three Mr Dickens, the bath-chair man, had called for Mrs Barfoot.

'Move me,' she would say to Mr Dickens, after sitting on the esplanade for fifteen minutes. And again, 'That'll do, thank you, Mr Dickens.' At the first command he would seek the sun; at the second he would stay the chair there in the bright strip.

An old inhabitant himself, he had much in common with Mrs Barfoot – James Coppard's daughter. The drinking-fountain, where West Street joins Broad Street, is the gift of James Coppard, who was mayor at the time of Queen Victoria's jubilee, and Coppard is painted upon municipal watering-carts and over shop windows, and upon the zinc blinds of solicitors' consulting-room windows. But Ellen Barfoot never visited the Aquarium (though she had known Captain Boase who had caught the shark quite well), and when the men came by with the posters she eyed them super-ciliously, for she knew that she would never see the Pierrots, or the brothers Zeno, or Daisy Budd and her troupe of performing seals. For Ellen Barfoot in her bath-chair on the esplanade was a prisoner – civilisation's prisoner – all the bars of her cage falling across the esplanade on sunny days when the town hall, the drapery stores, the swimming-bath and the memorial hall striped the ground with shadow.

An old inhabitant himself, Mr Dickens would stand a little behind her, smoking his pipe. She would ask him questions – who people were – who now kept Mr Jones's shop – then about the season – and had Mrs Dickens tried, whatever it might be – the words issuing from her lips like crumbs of dry biscuit.

She closed her eyes. Mr Dickens took a turn. The feelings of a man had not altogether deserted him, though as you saw him coming towards you, you noticed how one knobbed black boot swung tremulously in front of the other; how there was a shadow between his waistcoat and his trousers; how he leant forward unsteadily, like an old horse who finds himself suddenly out of the shafts drawing no cart. But as Mr Dickens sucked in the smoke and puffed it out again, the feelings of a man were perceptible in his eyes. He was thinking how Captain Barfoot was now on his way to Mount Pleasant; Captain Barfoot, his master. For at home in the little sitting-room above the mews, with the canary in the window, and the girls at the sewing-machine, and Mrs Dickens huddled up with the rheumatics – at home where he was made little of, the thought of being in the employ of Captain Barfoot supported him. He liked to think that while he chatted with Mrs Barfoot on the front, he helped the Captain on his way to Mrs Flanders. He, a man, was in charge of Mrs Barfoot, a woman.

Turning, he saw that she was chatting with Mrs Rogers. Turning again, he saw that Mrs Rogers had moved on. So he came back to the bath-chair, and Mrs Barfoot asked him the time, and he took out his great silver watch and told her the time very obligingly, as if he knew a great deal more about the time and everything than she did. But Mrs Barfoot knew that Captain Barfoot was on his way to Mrs Flanders.

Indeed he was well on his way there, having left the tram, and seeing Dods Hill to the south-east, green against a blue sky that was suffused with dust colour on the horizon. He was marching up the hill. In spite of his lameness there was something military in his approach. Mrs Jarvis, as she came out of the Rectory gate, saw him coming, and her Newfoundland dog, Nero, slowly swept his tail from side to side.

'Oh, Captain Barfoot!' Mrs Jarvis exclaimed.

'Good-day, Mrs Jarvis,' said the Captain.

They walked on together, and when they reached Mrs Flanders's gate Captain Barfoot took off his tweed cap, and said, bowing very courteously, 'Good-day to you, Mrs Jarvis.'

And Mrs Jarvis walked on alone.

She was going to walk on the moor. Had she again been pacing her lawn late at night? Had she again tapped on the study window and cried: 'Look at the moon, look at the moon, Herbert!'

And Herbert looked at the moon.

Mrs Jarvis walked on the moor when she was unhappy, going as far as a certain saucer-shaped hollow, though she always meant to go to a more distant ridge; and there she sat down, and took out the little book hidden beneath her cloak and read a few lines of poetry, and looked about her. She was not very unhappy, and, seeing that she was forty-five, never perhaps would be very unhappy, desperately unhappy that is, and leave her husband, and ruin a good man's career, as she sometimes threatened.

Still there is no need to say what risks a clergyman's wife runs when she walks on the moor. Short, dark, with kindling eyes, a pheasant's feather in her hat, Mrs Jarvis was just the sort of woman to lose her faith upon the moors – to confound her God with the universal that is – but she did not lose her faith, did not leave her husband, never read her poem through, and went on walking the moors, looking at the moon behind the elm trees, and feeling as she sat on the grass high above Scarborough . . . Yes, yes, when the lark soars; when the sheep, moving a step or two onwards, crop the turf, and at the same time set their bells tinkling; when the breeze first blows, then dies down, leaving the cheek kissed; when the ships on the sea below seem to cross each other and pass on as if drawn by an invisible hand; when there are distant concussions in the air and phantom horsemen galloping, ceasing; when the horizon swims blue, green, emotional – then Mrs Jarvis, heaving a sigh, thinks to herself, 'If only someone could give me . . . if I could give someone . . . ' But she does not know what she wants to give, nor who could give it her.

'Mrs Flanders stepped out only five minutes ago, Captain,' said Rebecca. Captain Barfoot sat him down in the armchair to wait. Resting his elbows on the arms, putting one hand over the other, sticking his lame leg straight out, and placing the stick with the rubber ferrule beside it, he sat perfectly still. There was something rigid about him. Did he think? Probably the same thoughts again and again. But were they 'nice' thoughts, interesting thoughts? He was a man with a temper; tenacious, faithful. Women would have felt, 'Here is law. Here is order. Therefore we must cherish this man. He is on the bridge at night,' and, handing him his cup, or whatever it might be, would run on to visions of shipwreck and disaster, in which all the passengers come tumbling from their cabins, and there is the captain, buttoned in his pea-jacket, matched with the storm, vanquished by it but by none other. 'Yet I have a soul,' Mrs Jarvis would bethink her, as Captain Barfoot suddenly blew his nose in a great red bandanna handkerchief, 'and it's the man's stupidity that's the cause of this, and the storm's my storm as well as his' . . . so Mrs Jarvis would bethink her when the Captain dropped in to see them and found Herbert out, and spent two or three hours, almost silent, sitting in the armchair. But Betty Flanders thought nothing of the kind.

'Oh, Captain,' said Mrs Flanders, bursting into the drawing-room, 'I had to run after Barker's man . . . I hope Rebecca . . . I hope Jacob . . . '

She was very much out of breath, yet not at all upset, and as she put down the hearth-brush which she had bought of the oil-man, she said it was hot, flung the window farther open, straightened a cover, picked up a book, as if she were very confident, very fond of the Captain, and a great many years younger than he was. Indeed, in her blue apron she did not look more than thirty-five. He was well over fifty.

She moved her hands about the table; the Captain moved his head from side to side, and made little sounds, as Betty went on chattering, completely at his ease – after twenty years.

'Well,' he said at length, 'I've heard from Mr Polegate.'

He had heard from Mr Polegate that he could advise nothing better than to send a boy to one of the universities.

'Mr Floyd was at Cambridge . . . no, at Oxford . . . well, at one or the other,' said Mrs Flanders.

She looked out of the window. Little windows, and the lilac and green of the garden were reflected in her eyes.

'Archer is doing very well,' she said. 'I have a very nice report from Captain Maxwell.'

'I will leave you the letter to show Jacob,' said the Captain, putting it clumsily back in its envelope.

'Jacob is after his butterflies as usual,' said Mrs Flanders irritably, but was surprised by a sudden afterthought, 'Cricket begins this week, of course.'

'Edward Jenkinson has handed in his resignation,' said Captain Barfoot.

'Then you will stand for the council?' Mrs Flanders exclaimed, looking the Captain full in the face.

'Well, about that – ' Captain Barfoot began, settling himself rather deeper in his chair.

Jacob Flanders, therefore, went up to Cambridge in October, 1906.

Chapter Three

'This is not a smoking-carriage,' Mrs Norman protested, nervously but very feebly, as the door swung open and a powerfully built young man jumped in. He seemed not to hear her. The train did not stop before it reached Cambridge, and here she was shut up alone, in a railway carriage, with a young man.

She touched the spring of her dressing-case and ascertained that the scent-bottle and a novel from Mudie's were both handy (the young man was standing up with his back to her, putting his bag in the rack). She would throw the scent-bottle with her right hand, she decided, and tug the communication cord with her left. She was fifty years of age, and had a son at college. Nevertheless, it is a fact that men are dangerous. She read half a column of her newspaper; then stealthily looked over the edge to decide the question of safety by the infallible test of appearance . . . She would like to offer him her paper. But do young men read the *Morning Post*? She looked to see what he was reading – the *Daily Telegraph*.

Taking note of socks (loose), of tie (shabby), she once more reached his face. She dwelt upon his mouth. The lips were shut. The eyes bent down, since he was reading. All was firm, yet youthful, indifferent, unconscious – as for knocking one down! No, no, no! She looked out of the window, smiling slightly now, and then came back again, for he didn't notice her. Grave, unconscious . . . now he looked up, past her . . . he seemed so out of place, somehow, alone with an elderly lady . . . then he fixed his eyes – which were blue – on the landscape. He had not realised her presence, she thought. Yet it was none of *her* fault that this was not a smoking-carriage – if that was what he meant.

Nobody sees anyone as he is, let alone an elderly lady sitting opposite a strange young man in a railway carriage. They see a whole – they see all sorts of things – they see themselves . . . Mrs Norman now read three pages of one of Mr Norris's novels. Should she say to the young man (and after all he was just the same age as her own boy): 'If you want to smoke, don't mind me'? No: he seemed absolutely indifferent to her presence . . . she did not wish to interrupt.

But since, even at her age, she noted his indifference, presumably he was in some way or other – to her at least – nice, handsome, interesting, distinguished, well built, like her own boy? One must do the best one can with her report. Anyhow, this was Jacob Flanders, aged nineteen. It is no use trying to sum people up. One must follow hints, not exactly what is said, nor yet entirely what is done – for instance, when the train drew into the station, Mr Flanders burst open the door, and put the lady's dressing-case out for her, saying, or rather mumbling: 'Let me,' very shyly; indeed he was rather clumsy about it.

'Who . . . ' said the lady, meeting her son; but as there was a great crowd on the platform and Jacob had already gone, she did not finish her sentence. As this was Cambridge, as she was staying there for the weekend, as she saw nothing but young men all day long, in streets and round tables, this sight of her fellow-traveller was completely lost in her mind, as the crooked pin dropped by a child into the wishing-well twirls in the water and disappears for ever.

They say the sky is the same everywhere. Travellers, the shipwrecked, exiles and the dying draw comfort from the thought, and no doubt if you are of a mystical tendency, consolation, and even explanation, shower down from the unbroken surface. But above Cambridge – anyhow above the roof of King's College Chapel – there is a difference. Out at sea a great city will cast a brightness into the night. Is it fanciful to suppose the sky, washed into the crevices of King's College Chapel, lighter, thinner, more sparkling than the sky elsewhere? Does Cambridge burn not only into the night, but into the day?

Look, as they pass into service, how airily the gowns blow out, as though nothing dense and corporeal were within. What sculptured faces, what certainty, authority controlled by piety, although great boots march under the gowns. In what orderly procession they advance. Thick wax candles stand upright; young men rise in white gowns; while the subservient eagle bears up for inspection the great white book.

An inclined plane of light comes accurately through each window, purple and yellow even in its most diffused dust, while, where it breaks upon stone, that stone is softly chalked red, yellow and purple. Neither snow nor greenery, winter nor summer, has power over the old stained glass. As the sides of a lantern protect the flame so that it burns steady even in the wildest night – burns steady and gravely illumines the tree-trunks – so inside the Chapel all was orderly. Gravely sounded the voices; wisely the organ replied, as if buttressing human faith with the assent of the elements. The white-robed figures crossed from side to side; now mounted steps, now descended, all very orderly.

. . . If you stand a lantern under a tree every insect in the forest creeps up to it – a curious assembly, since though they scramble and swing and knock their heads against the glass, they seem to have no purpose – something senseless inspires them. One gets tired of watching them, as they amble round the lantern and blindly tap as if for admittance, one large toad being the most besotted of any and shouldering his way through the rest. Ah, but what's that? A terrifying volley of pistol-shots rings out – cracks sharply; ripples spread – silence laps smooth over sound. A tree – a tree has fallen, a sort of death in the forest. After that, the wind in the trees sounds melancholy.

But this service in King's College Chapel – why allow women to take part in it? Surely, if the mind wanders (and Jacob looked extraordinarily vacant, his head thrown back, his hymn-book open at the wrong place), if the mind wanders it is because several hat shops and cupboards upon cupboards of coloured dresses are displayed upon rush-bottomed chairs. Though heads and bodies may be devout enough, one has a sense of individuals – some like blue, others brown; some feathers, others pansies and forget-me-nots. No one would think of bringing a dog into church. For though a dog is all very well on a gravel path, and shows no disrespect to flowers, the way he wanders down an aisle, looking, lifting a paw, and approaching a pillar with a purpose that makes the blood run cold with horror (should you be one of a congregation – alone, shyness is out of the question), a dog destroys the service completely. So do these women – though separately devout, distinguished, and vouched for by the theology, mathematics, Latin and Greek of their husbands. Heaven knows why it is. For one thing, thought Jacob, they're as ugly as sin.

Now there was a scraping and murmuring. He caught Timmy Durrant's eye; looked very sternly at him; and then, very solemnly, winked.

'Waverley', the villa on the road to Girton was called, not that Mr Plumer admired Scott or would have chosen any name at all, but names are useful when you have to entertain undergraduates, and as they sat waiting for the fourth undergraduate, on Sunday at lunchtime, there was talk of names upon gates.

'How tiresome,' Mrs Plumer interrupted impulsively. 'Does anybody know Mr Flanders?'

Mr Durrant knew him; and therefore blushed slightly, and said, awkwardly, something about being sure – looking at Mr Plumer and hitching the right leg of his trouser as he spoke. Mr Plumer got up and stood in front of the fireplace. Mrs Plumer laughed like a straightforward friendly fellow. In short, anything more horrible than the scene, the setting, the prospect, even the

May garden being afflicted with chill sterility and a cloud choosing that moment to cross the sun, cannot be imagined. There was the garden, of course. Everyone at the same moment looked at it. Owing to the cloud, the leaves ruffled grey, and the sparrows – there were two sparrows.

'I think – ' said Mrs Plumer, taking advantage of the momentary respite, while the young men stared at the garden, to look at her husband, and he, not accepting full responsibility for the act, nevertheless touched the bell.

There can be no excuse for this outrage upon one hour of human life, save the reflection which occurred to Mr Plumer as he carved the mutton, that if no don ever gave a luncheon party, if Sunday after Sunday passed, if men went down, became lawyers, doctors, members of Parliament, businessmen – if no don ever gave a luncheon party –

'Now, does lamb make the mint sauce, or mint sauce make the lamb?' he asked the young man next him, to break a silence which had already lasted five minutes and a half.

'I don't know, sir,' said the young man, blushing very vividly.

At this moment in came Mr Flanders. He had mistaken the time.

Now, though they had finished their meat, Mrs Plumer took a second helping of cabbage. Jacob determined, of course, that he would eat his meat in the time it took her to finish her cabbage, looking once or twice to measure his speed – only he was infernally hungry. Seeing this, Mrs Plumer said that she was sure Mr Flanders would not mind – and the tart was brought in. Nodding in a peculiar way, she directed the maid to give Mr Flanders a second helping of mutton. She glanced at the mutton. Not much of the leg would be left for luncheon.

It was none of her fault – since how could she control her father begetting her forty years ago in the suburbs of Manchester? and once begotten, how could she do other than grow up cheese-paring, ambitious, with an instinctively accurate notion of the rungs of the ladder and an ant-like assiduity in pushing George Plumer ahead of her to the top of the ladder? What was at the top of the ladder? A sense that all the rungs were beneath one apparently; since by the time that George Plumer became Professor of Physics, or whatever it might be, Mrs Plumer could only be in a condition to cling tight to her eminence, peer down at the ground, and goad her two plain daughters to climb the rungs of the ladder.

'I was down at the races yesterday,' she said, 'with my two little girls.'

It was none of *their* fault either. In they came to the drawing-room, in white frocks and blue sashes. They handed the cigarettes. Rhoda had inherited her father's cold grey eyes. Cold grey eyes George Plumer had, but in them was an abstract light. He could talk about Persia and the Trade winds, the Reform Bill and the cycle of the harvests. Books were on his shelves by Wells and Shaw; on the table serious sixpenny weeklies written by pale men in muddy boots – the weekly creak and screech of brains rinsed in cold water and wrung dry – melancholy papers.

'I don't feel that I know the truth about anything till I've read them both!' said Mrs Plumer brightly, tapping the table of contents with her bare red hand, upon which the ring looked so incongruous.

'Oh God, oh God, oh God!' exclaimed Jacob, as the four undergraduates left the house. 'Oh, my God!'

'Bloody beastly!' he said, scanning the street for lilac or bicycle – anything to restore his sense of freedom.

'Bloody beastly,' he said to Timmy Durrant, summing up his discomfort at the world shown him at lunchtime, a world capable of existing – there was no doubt about that – but so unnecessary, such a thing to believe in – Shaw and Wells and the serious sixpenny weeklies! What were they after, scrubbing and demolishing, these elderly people? Had they never read Homer, Shakespeare, the Elizabethans? He saw it clearly outlined against the feelings he drew from youth and natural inclination. The poor devils had rigged up this meagre object. Yet something of pity was in him. Those wretched little girls –

The extent to which he was disturbed proves that he was already agog. Insolent he was and inexperienced, but sure enough the cities which the elderly of the race have built upon the skyline showed like brick suburbs, barracks and places of discipline against a red and yellow flame. He was impressionable; but the word is contradicted by the composure with which he hollowed his hand to screen a match. He was a young man of substance.

Anyhow, whether undergraduate or shop boy, man or woman, it must come as a shock about the age of twenty – the world of the elderly – thrown up in such black outline upon what we are; upon the reality; the moors and Byron; the sea and the lighthouse; the sheep's jaw with the yellow teeth in it; upon the obstinate irrepressible conviction which makes youth so intolerably disagreeable – 'I am what I am, and intend to be it,' for which there will be no form in the world unless Jacob makes one for himself. The Plumers will try to prevent him from making it. Wells and Shaw and the serious sixpenny weeklies will sit on its head. Every time he lunches out on Sunday – at dinner parties and tea parties – there will be this same shock – horror – discomfort – then pleasure, for he draws into him at every step as he walks by the river such steady certainty, such reassurance from all sides, the trees bowing, the grey spires soft in the blue, voices blowing and seeming suspended in the air, the springy air of May, the elastic air with its particles – chestnut bloom, pollen, whatever it is that gives the May air its potency, blurring the trees, gumming the buds, daubing the green. And the river too runs past, not at flood, nor swiftly, but cloying the oar that dips in it and drops white drops from the blade, swimming green and deep over the bowed rushes, as if lavishly caressing them.

Where they moored their boat the trees showered down, so that their topmost leaves trailed in the ripples and the green wedge that lay in the water being made of leaves shifted in leaf-breadths as the real leaves shifted.

Now there was a shiver of wind – instantly an edge of sky; and as Durrant ate cherries he dropped the stunted yellow cherries through the green wedge of leaves, their stalks twinkling as they wriggled in and out, and sometimes one half-bitten cherry would go down red into the green. The meadow was on a level with Jacob's eyes as he lay back; gilt with buttercups, but the grass did not run like the thin green water of the graveyard grass about to overflow the tombstones but stood juicy and thick. Looking up, backwards, he saw the legs of children deep in the grass, and the legs of cows. Munch, munch, he heard; then a short step through the grass; then again munch, munch, munch, as they tore the grass short at the roots. In front of him two white butterflies circled higher and higher round the elm tree.

'Jacob's off,' thought Durrant, looking up from his novel. He kept reading a few pages and then looking up in a curiously methodical manner, and each time he looked up he took a few cherries out of the bag and ate them abstractedly. Other boats passed them, crossing the backwater from side to side to avoid each other, for many were now moored, and there were now white dresses and a flaw in the column of air between two trees, round which curled a thread of blue – Lady Miller's picnic party. Still more boats kept coming, and Durrant, without getting up, shoved their boat closer to the bank.

'Oh–h–h–h,' groaned Jacob, as the boat rocked, and the trees rocked, and the white dresses and the white flannel trousers drew out long and wavering up the bank.

'Oh–h–h–h!' He sat up, and felt as if a piece of elastic had snapped in his face.

'They're friends of my mother's,' said Durrant. 'So old Bow took no end of trouble about the boat.'

And this boat had gone from Falmouth to St Ives Bay, all round the coast. A larger boat, a ten-ton yacht, about the twentieth of June, properly fitted out, Durrant said . . .

'There's the cash difficulty,' said Jacob.

'My people'll see to that,' said Durrant (the son of a banker, deceased).

'I intend to preserve my economic independence,' said Jacob stiffly. (He was getting excited.)

'My mother said something about going to Harrogate,' he said with a little annoyance, feeling the pocket where he kept his letters.

'Was that true about your uncle becoming a Mohammedan?' asked Timmy Durrant.

Jacob had told the story of his Uncle Morty in Durrant's room the night before.

'I expect he's feeding the sharks, if the truth were known,' said Jacob. 'I say, Durrant, there's none left!' he exclaimed, crumpling the bag which had held the cherries, and throwing it into the river. He saw Lady Miller's picnic party on the island as he threw the bag into the river.

A sort of awkwardness, grumpiness, gloom came into his eyes.
'Shall we move on . . . this beastly crowd . . . ' he said.
So up they went, past the island.

The feathery white moon never let the sky grow dark; all night the chestnut
blossoms were white in the green; dim was the cow-parsley in the meadows.

The waiters at Trinity must have been shuffling china plates like cards,
from the clatter that could be heard in the Great Court. Jacob's rooms,
however, were in Neville's Court; at the top; so that reaching his door one
went in a little out of breath; but he wasn't there. Dining in Hall, presumably.
It will be quite dark in Neville's Court long before midnight, only the pillars
opposite will always be white, and the fountains. A curious effect the gate has,
like lace upon pale green. Even in the window you hear the plates; a hum of
talk, too, from the diners; the Hall lit up, and the swing-doors opening and
shutting with a soft thud. Some are late.

Jacob's room had a round table and two low chairs. There were yellow
flags in a jar on the mantelpiece; a photograph of his mother; cards from
societies with little raised crescents, coats of arms, and initials; notes and
pipes; on the table lay paper ruled with a red margin – an essay, no doubt –
'Does History consist of the Biographies of Great Men?' There were
books enough; very few French books; but then anyone who's worth
anything reads just what he likes, as the mood takes him, with extravagant
enthusiasm. Lives of the Duke of Wellington, for example; Spinoza; the
works of Dickens; *The Faerie Queene*; a Greek dictionary with the petals of
poppies pressed to silk between the pages; all the Elizabethans. His slippers
were incredibly shabby, like boats burnt to the water's rim. Then there
were photographs from the Greeks, and a mezzotint from Sir Joshua – all
very English. The works of Jane Austen, too, in deference, perhaps, to
someone else's standard. Carlyle was a prize. There were books upon the
Italian painters of the Renaissance, a *Manual of the Diseases of the Horse*, and
all the usual textbooks. Listless is the air in an empty room, just swelling
the curtain; the flowers in the jar shift. One fibre in the wicker armchair
creaks, though no one sits there.

Coming down the steps a little sideways (Jacob sat on the window-seat
talking to Durrant; he smoked, and Durrant looked at the map), the old
man, with his hands locked behind him, his gown floating black, lurched,
unsteadily, near the wall; then, upstairs he went into his room. Then
another, who raised his hand and praised the columns, the gate, the sky;
another, tripping and smug. Each went up a staircase; three lights were lit
in the dark windows.

If any light burns above Cambridge, it must be from three such rooms;
Greek burns here; science there; philosophy on the ground floor. Poor old
Huxtable can't walk straight; Sopwith, too, has praised the sky any night

these twenty years; and Cowan still chuckles at the same stories. It is not simple, or pure, or wholly splendid, the lamp of learning, since if you see them there under its light (whether Rossetti's on the wall, or Van Gogh reproduced, whether there are lilacs in the bowl or rusty pipes), how priestly they look! How like a suburb where you go to see a view and eat a special cake! 'We are the sole purveyors of this cake.' Back you go to London; for the treat is over.

Old Professor Huxtable, performing with the method of a clock his change of dress, let himself down into his chair; filled his pipe; chose his paper; crossed his feet; and extracted his glasses. The whole flesh of his face then fell into folds as if props were removed. Yet strip a whole seat of an underground railway carriage of its heads and old Huxtable's head will hold them all. Now, as his eye goes down the print, what a procession tramps through the corridors of his brain, orderly, quick-stepping, and reinforced, as the march goes on, by fresh runnels, till the whole hall, dome, whatever one calls it, is populous with ideas. Such a muster takes place in no other brain. Yet sometimes there he'll sit for hours together, gripping the arm of the chair, like a man holding fast because stranded, and then, just because his corn twinges, or it may be the gout, what execrations, and, dear me, to hear him talk of money, taking out his leather purse and grudging even the smallest silver coin, secretive and suspicious as an old peasant woman with all her lies. Strange paralysis and constriction – marvellous illumination. Serene over it all rides the great full brow, and sometimes asleep or in the quiet spaces of the night you might fancy that on a pillow of stone he lay triumphant.

Sopwith, meanwhile, advancing with a curious trip from the fireplace, cut the chocolate cake into segments. Until midnight or later there would be undergraduates in his room, sometimes as many as twelve, sometimes three or four; but nobody got up when they went or when they came; Sopwith went on talking. Talking, talking, talking – as if everything could be talked – the soul itself slipped through the lips in thin silver disks which dissolve in young men's minds like silver, like moonlight. Oh, far away they'd remember it, and deep in dullness gaze back on it, and come to refresh themselves again.

'Well, I never. That's old Chucky. My dear boy, how's the world treating you?' And in came poor little Chucky, the unsuccessful provincial, Stenhouse his real name, but of course Sopwith brought back by using the other everything, everything, 'all I could never be' – yes, though next day, buying his newspaper and catching the early train, it all seemed to him childish, absurd; the chocolate cake, the young men; Sopwith summing things up; no, not all; he would send his son there. He would save every penny to send his son there.

Sopwith went on talking; twining stiff fibres of awkward speech – things young men blurted out – plaiting them round his own smooth garland, making the bright side show, the vivid greens, the sharp thorns, manliness. He loved it. Indeed to Sopwith a man could say anything, until perhaps he'd grown old, or gone under, gone deep, when the silver disks would tinkle hollow, and the inscription read a little too simple, and the old stamp look too pure, and the impress always the same – a Greek boy's head. But he would respect still. A woman, divining the priest, would, involuntarily, despise.

Cowan, Erasmus Cowan, sipped his port alone, or with one rosy little man, whose memory held precisely the same span of time; sipped his port, and told his stories, and without book before him intoned Latin, Virgil and Catullus, as if language were wine upon his lips. Only – sometimes it will come over one – what if the poet strode in? '*This* my image?' he might ask, pointing to the chubby man, whose brain is, after all, Virgil's representative among us, though the body gluttonise, and as for arms, bees, or even the plough, Cowan takes his trips abroad with a French novel in his pocket, a rug about his knees, and is thankful to be home again in his place, in his line, holding up in his snug little mirror the image of Virgil, all rayed round with good stories of the dons of Trinity and red beams of port. But language is wine upon his lips. Nowhere else would Virgil hear the like. And though, as she goes sauntering along the Backs, old Miss Umphelby sings him melodiously enough, accurately too, she is always brought up by this question as she reaches Clare Bridge: 'But if I met him, what should I wear?' – and then, taking her way up the avenue towards Newnham, she lets her fancy play upon other details of men's meeting with women which have never got into print. Her lectures, therefore, are not half so well attended as those of Cowan, and the thing she might have said in elucidation of the text for ever left out. In short, face a teacher with the image of the taught and the mirror breaks. But Cowan sipped his port, his exaltation over, no longer the representative of Virgil. No, the builder, assessor, surveyor, rather; ruling lines between names, hanging lists above doors. Such is the fabric through which the light must shine, if shine it can – the light of all these languages, Chinese and Russian, Persian and Arabic, of symbols and figures, of history, of things that are known and things that are about to be known. So that if at night, far out at sea over the tumbling waves, one saw a haze on the waters, a city illuminated, a whiteness even in the sky, such as that now over the Hall of Trinity where they're still dining, or washing up plates, that would be the light burning there – the light of Cambridge.

'Let's go round to Simeon's room,' said Jacob, and they rolled up the map, having got the whole thing settled.

All the lights were coming out round the court, and falling on the cobbles, picking out dark patches of grass and single daisies. The young men were now back in their rooms. Heaven knows what they were doing. What was it that could *drop* like that? And leaning down over a foaming window-box, one stopped another hurrying past, and upstairs they went and down they went, until a sort of fullness settled on the court, the hive full of bees, the bees home thick with gold, drowsy, humming, suddenly vocal; the Moonlight Sonata answered by a waltz.

The Moonlight Sonata tinkled away; the waltz crashed. Although young men still went in and out, they walked as if keeping engagements. Now and then there was a thud, as if some heavy piece of furniture had fallen, unexpectedly, of its own accord, not in the general stir of life after dinner. One supposed that young men raised their eyes from their books as the furniture fell. Were they reading? Certainly there was a sense of concentration in the air. Behind the grey walls sat so many young men, some undoubtedly reading magazines, shilling shockers, no doubt; legs, perhaps, over the arms of chairs; smoking; sprawling over tables, and writing while their heads went round in a circle as the pen moved – simple young men, these, who would – but there is no need to think of them grown old; others eating sweets; here they boxed; and, well, Mr Hawkins must have been mad suddenly to throw up his window and bawl: 'Jo–seph! Jo–seph!' and then he ran as hard as ever he could across the court, while an elderly man, in a green apron, carrying an immense pile of tin covers, hesitated, balanced, and then went on. But this was a diversion. There were young men who read, lying in shallow armchairs, holding their books as if they had hold in their hands of something that would see them through; they being all in a torment, coming from midland towns, clergymen's sons. Others read Keats. And those long histories in many volumes – surely someone was now beginning at the beginning in order to understand the Holy Roman Empire, as one must. That was part of the concentration, though it would be dangerous on a hot spring night – dangerous, perhaps, to concentrate too much upon single books, actual chapters, when at any moment the door opened and Jacob appeared; or Richard Bonamy, reading Keats no longer, began making long pink spills from an old newspaper, bending forward, and looking eager and contented no more, but almost fierce. Why? Only perhaps that Keats died young – one wants to write poetry too and to love – oh, the brutes! It's damnably difficult. But, after all, not so difficult if on the next staircase, in the large room, there are two, three, five young men all convinced of this – of brutality, that is, and the clear division between right and wrong. There was a sofa, chairs, a square table, and the window being open, one could see how they sat – legs issuing here, one there crumpled in a corner of the sofa; and, presumably, for you could not see him, somebody stood by the fender, talking. Anyhow, Jacob, who sat astride a chair and ate dates from a long box, burst out laughing. The answer came from the sofa corner; for his pipe was held in the air, then replaced. Jacob wheeled round. He had something to say to *that*, though the sturdy red-haired boy at the table seemed to deny it, wagging his head slowly from side to side; and then, taking out his penknife, he dug the point of it again and again into a knot in the table, as if affirming that the voice from the fender spoke the truth – which Jacob could not deny. Possibly, when he had done arranging the date-stones, he might find something to say to it – indeed his lips opened – only then there broke out a roar of laughter.

The laughter died in the air. The sound of it could scarcely have reached anyone standing by the Chapel, which stretched along the opposite side of the court. The laughter died out, and only gestures of arms, movements of bodies, could be seen shaping something in the room. Was it an argument? A bet on the boat races? Was it nothing of the sort? What was shaped by the arms and bodies moving in the twilight room?

A step or two beyond the window there was nothing at all, except the enclosing buildings – chimneys upright, roofs horizontal; too much brick and building for a May night, perhaps. And then before one's eyes would come the bare hills of Turkey – sharp lines, dry earth, coloured flowers, and colour on the shoulders of the women, standing naked-legged in the stream to beat linen on the stones. The stream made loops of water round their ankles. But none of that could show clearly through the swaddlings and blanketings of the Cambridge night. The stroke of the clock even was muffled; as if intoned by somebody reverent from a pulpit; as if generations of learned men heard the last hour go rolling through their ranks and issued it, already smooth and time-worn, with their blessing, for the use of the living.

Was it to receive this gift from the past that the young man came to the window and stood there, looking out across the court? It was Jacob. He stood smoking his pipe while the last stroke of the clock purred softly round him. Perhaps there had been an argument. He looked satisfied; indeed masterly; which expression changed slightly as he stood there, the sound of the clock conveying to him (it may be) a sense of old buildings and time; and himself the inheritor; and then tomorrow; and friends; at the thought of whom, in sheer confidence and pleasure, it seemed, he yawned and stretched himself.

Meanwhile behind him the shape they had made, whether by argument or not, the spiritual shape, hard yet ephemeral, as of glass compared with the dark stone of the Chapel, was dashed to splinters, young men rising from chairs and sofa corners, buzzing and barging about the room, one driving another against the bedroom door, which giving way, in they fell. Then Jacob was left there, in the shallow armchair, alone with Masham? Anderson? Simeon? Oh, it was Simeon. The others had all gone.

' . . . Julian the Apostate . . . ' Which of them said that and the other words murmured round it? But about midnight there sometimes rises, like a veiled figure suddenly woken, a heavy wind; and this now flapping through Trinity lifted unseen leaves and blurred everything. 'Julian the Apostate' – and then the wind. Up go the elm branches, out blow the sails, the old schooners rear and plunge, the grey waves in the hot Indian Ocean tumble sultrily, and then all falls flat again.

So, if the veiled lady stepped through the Courts of Trinity, she now drowsed once more, all her draperies about her, her head against a pillar.

'Somehow it seems to matter.'

The low voice was Simeon's.

The voice was even lower that answered him. The sharp tap of a pipe on the mantelpiece cancelled the words. And perhaps Jacob only said 'hum', or said nothing at all. True, the words were inaudible. It was the intimacy, a sort of spiritual suppleness, when mind prints upon mind indelibly.

'Well, you seem to have studied the subject,' said Jacob, rising and standing over Simeon's chair. He balanced himself; he swayed a little. He appeared extraordinarily happy, as if his pleasure would brim and spill down the sides if Simeon spoke.

Simeon said nothing. Jacob remained standing. But intimacy – the room was full of it, still, deep, like a pool. Without need of movement or speech it rose softly and washed over everything, mollifying, kindling, and coating the mind with the lustre of pearl, so that if you talk of a light, of Cambridge burning, it's not languages only. It's Julian the Apostate.

But Jacob moved. He murmured good-night. He went out into the court. He buttoned his jacket across his chest. He went back to his rooms, and being the only man who walked at that moment back to his rooms, his footsteps rang out, his figure loomed large. Back from the Chapel, back from the Hall, back from the Library, came the sound of his footsteps, as if the old stone echoed with magisterial authority: 'The young man – the young men – the young man – back to his rooms.'

Chapter Four

What's the use of trying to read Shakespeare, especially in one of those little thin paper editions whose pages get ruffled, or stuck together with sea-water? Although the plays of Shakespeare had frequently been praised, even quoted, and placed higher than the Greek, never since they started had Jacob managed to read one through. Yet what an opportunity!

For the Scilly Isles had been sighted by Timmy Durrant lying like mountain-tops almost a-wash in precisely the right place. His calculations had worked perfectly, and really the sight of him sitting there, with his hand on the tiller, rosy gilled, with a sprout of beard, looking sternly at the stars, then at a compass, spelling out quite correctly his page of the eternal lesson-book, would have moved a woman. Jacob, of course, was not a woman. The sight of Timmy Durrant was no sight for him, nothing to set against the sky and worship; far from it. They had quarrelled. Why the right way to open a tin of beef, with Shakespeare on board, under conditions of such splendour, should have turned them to sulky schoolboys, none can tell. Tinned beef is cold eating, though; and salt water spoils biscuits; and the waves tumble and lollop much the same hour after hour – tumble and lollop all across the horizon. Now a spray of seaweed floats past – now a log of wood. Ships have been wrecked here. One or two go past, keeping their own side of the road. Timmy knew where they were bound, what their cargoes were, and, by looking through his glass, could tell the name of the line, and even guess what dividends it paid its shareholders. Yet that was no reason for Jacob to turn sulky.

The Scilly Isles had the look of mountain-tops almost awash . . . Unfortunately, Jacob broke the pin of the Primus stove.

The Scilly Isles might well be obliterated by a roller sweeping straight across.

But one must give young men the credit of admitting that, though breakfast eaten under these circumstances is grim, it is sincere enough. No need to make conversation. They got out their pipes.

Timmy wrote up some scientific observations; and – what was the question that broke the silence – the exact time or the day of the month? anyhow, it was spoken without the least awkwardness; in the most matter-of-fact way in the world; and then Jacob began to unbutton his clothes and sat naked, save for his shirt, intending, apparently, to bathe.

The Scilly Isles were turning bluish; and suddenly blue, purple and green flushed the sea; left it grey; struck a stripe which vanished; but when Jacob had got his shirt over his head the whole floor of the waves was blue and white, rippling and crisp, though now and again a broad purple mark appeared, like a bruise; or there floated an entire emerald tinged with yellow. He plunged. He gulped in water, spat it out, struck with his right arm, struck with his left, was towed by a rope, gasped, splashed, and was hauled on board.

The seat in the boat was positively hot, and the sun warmed his back as he sat naked with a towel in his hand, looking at the Scilly Isles which – confound it! the sail flapped. Shakespeare was knocked overboard. There you could see him floating merrily away, with all his pages ruffling innumerably; and then he went under.

Strangely enough, you could smell violets, or if violets were impossible in July, they must grow something very pungent on the mainland then. The mainland, not so very far off – you could see clefts in the cliffs, white cottages, smoke going up – wore an extraordinary look of calm, of sunny peace, as if wisdom and piety had descended upon the dwellers there. Now a cry sounded, as of a man calling pilchards in a main street. It wore an extraordinary look of piety and peace, as if old men smoked by the door, and girls stood, hands on hips, at the well, and horses stood; as if the end of the world had come, and cabbage fields and stone walls, and coast-guard stations, and, above all, the white-sand bays with the waves breaking unseen by anyone, rose to heaven in a kind of ecstasy.

But imperceptibly the cottage smoke droops, has the look of a mourning emblem, a flag floating its caress over a grave. The gulls, making their broad flight and then riding at peace, seem to mark the grave.

No doubt if this were Italy, Greece, or even the shores of Spain, sadness would be routed by strangeness and excitement and the nudge of a classical education. But the Cornish hills have stark chimneys standing on them; and, somehow or other, loveliness is infernally sad. Yes, the chimneys and the coast-guard stations and the little bays with the waves breaking unseen by anyone make one remember the overpowering sorrow. And what can this sorrow be?

It is brewed by the earth itself. It comes from the houses on the coast. We start transparent, and then the cloud thickens. All history backs our pane of glass. To escape is vain.

But whether this is the right interpretation of Jacob's gloom as he sat naked, in the sun, looking at the Land's End, it is impossible to say; for he never spoke a word. Timmy sometimes wondered (only for a second) whether his people bothered him . . . No matter. There are things that can't be said. Let's shake it off. Let's dry ourselves, and take up the first thing that comes handy . . . Timmy Durrant's notebook of scientific observations.

'Now . . .' said Jacob.

It is a tremendous argument.

Some people can follow every step of the way, and even take a little one, six inches long, by themselves at the end; others remain observant of the external signs.

The eyes fix themselves upon the poker; the right hand takes the poker and lifts it; turns it slowly round, and then, very accurately, replaces it. The left hand, which lies on the knee, plays some stately but intermittent piece of march music. A deep breath is taken; but allowed to evaporate unused. The cat marches across the hearth-rug. No one observes her.

'That's about as near as I can get to it,' Durrant wound up.

The next minute is quiet as the grave.

'It follows . . . ' said Jacob.

Only half a sentence followed; but these half-sentences are like flags set on tops of buildings to the observer of external sights down below. What was the coast of Cornwall, with its violet scents, and mourning emblems, and tranquil piety, but a screen happening to hang straight behind as his mind marched up?

'It follows . . . ' said Jacob.

'Yes,' said Timmy, after reflection. 'That is so.'

Now Jacob began plunging about, half to stretch himself, half in a kind of jollity, no doubt, for the strangest sound issued from his lips as he furled the sail, rubbed the plates – gruff, tuneless – a sort of paean, for having grasped the argument, for being master of the situation, sunburnt, unshaven, capable into the bargain of sailing round the world in a ten-ton yacht, which, very likely, he would do one of these days instead of settling down in a lawyer's office, and wearing spats.

'Our friend Masham,' said Timmy Durrant, 'would rather not be seen in our company as we are now.' His buttons had come off.

'D'you know Masham's aunt?' said Jacob.

'Never knew he had one,' said Timmy.

'Masham has millions of aunts,' said Jacob.

'Masham is mentioned in Domesday Book,' said Timmy.

'So are his aunts,' said Jacob.

'His sister,' said Timmy, 'is a very pretty girl.'

'That's what'll happen to you, Timmy,' said Jacob.

'It'll happen to you first,' said Timmy.

'But this woman I was telling you about – Masham's aunt – '

'Oh, do get on,' said Timmy, for Jacob was laughing so much that he could not speak.

'Masham's aunt . . . '

Timmy laughed so much that he could not speak.

'Masham's aunt . . . '

'What is there about Masham that makes one laugh?' said Timmy.

'Hang it all – a man who swallows his tie-pin,' said Jacob.

'Lord Chancellor before he's fifty,' said Timmy.

'He's a gentleman,' said Jacob.

'The Duke of Wellington was a gentleman,' said Timmy.
'Keats wasn't.'
'Lord Salisbury was.'
'And what about God?' said Jacob.

The Scilly Isles now appeared as if directly pointed at by a golden finger issuing from a cloud; and everybody knows how portentous that sight is, and how these broad rays, whether they light upon the Scilly Isles or upon the tombs of crusaders in cathedrals, always shake the very foundations of scepticism and lead to jokes about God.

> 'Abide with me:
> Fast falls the eventide;
> The shadows deepen;
> Lord, with me abide,'

sang Timmy Durrant.
'At my place we used to have a hymn which began

> Great God, what do I see and hear?'

said Jacob.

Gulls rode gently swaying in little companies of two or three quite near the boat; the cormorant, as if following his long strained neck in eternal pursuit, skimmed an inch above the water to the next rock; and the drone of the tide in the caves came across the water, low, monotonous, like the voice of someone talking to himself.

> 'Rock of Ages, cleft for me,
> Let me hide myself in thee,'

sang Jacob.

Like the blunt tooth of some monster, a rock broke the surface; brown; overflown with perpetual waterfalls.

> 'Rock of Ages,'

Jacob sang, lying on his back, looking up into the sky at midday, from which every shred of cloud had been withdrawn, so that it was like something permanently displayed with the cover off.

By six o'clock a breeze blew in off an icefield; and by seven the water was more purple than blue; and by half-past seven there was a patch of rough gold-beater's skin round the Scilly Isles, and Durrant's face, as he sat steering, was of the colour of a red lacquer box polished for generations. By nine all the fire and confusion had gone out of the sky, leaving wedges of apple-green and plates of pale yellow; and by ten the lanterns on the boat were making twisted colours upon the waves, elongated or squab, as the waves stretched or humped themselves. The beam from the lighthouse strode rapidly across the water. Infinite millions of miles away powdered stars twinkled; but the waves slapped the boat, and crashed, with regular and appalling solemnity, against the rocks.

Although it would be possible to knock at the cottage door and ask for a glass of milk, it is only thirst that would compel the intrusion. Yet perhaps Mrs Pascoe would welcome it. The summer's day may be wearing heavy. Washing in her little scullery, she may hear the cheap clock on the mantel-piece tick, tick, tick . . . tick, tick, tick. She is alone in the house. Her husband is out helping Farmer Hosken; her daughter married and gone to America. Her elder son is married too, but she does not agree with his wife. The Wesleyan minister came along and took the younger boy. She is alone in the house. A steamer, probably bound for Cardiff, now crosses the horizon, while near at hand one bell of a foxglove swings to and fro with a bumble-bee for clapper. These white Cornish cottages are built on the edge of the cliff; the garden grows gorse more readily than cabbages; and for hedge, some primeval man has piled granite boulders. In one of these, to hold, an historian conjectures, the victim's blood, a basin has been hollowed, but in our time it serves more tamely to seat those tourists who wish for an uninterrupted view of the Gurnard's Head. Not that anyone objects to a blue print dress and a white apron in a cottage garden.
    'Look – she has to draw her water from a well in the garden.'
    'Very lonely it must be in winter, with the wind sweeping over those hills, and the waves dashing on the rocks.'
    Even on a summer's day you hear them murmuring.
    Having drawn her water, Mrs Pascoe went in. The tourists regretted that they had brought no glasses, so that they might have read the name of the tramp steamer. Indeed, it was such a fine day that there was no saying what a pair of field-glasses might not have fetched into view. Two fishing luggers, presumably from St Ives Bay, were now sailing in an opposite direction from the steamer, and the floor of the sea became alternately clear and opaque. As for the bee, having sucked its fill of honey, it visited the teasle and thence made a straight line to Mrs Pascoe's patch, once more directing the tourists' gaze to the old woman's print dress and white apron, for she had come to the door of the cottage and was standing there.
    There she stood, shading her eyes and looking out to sea.
    For the millionth time, perhaps, she looked at the sea. A peacock butterfly now spread himself upon the teasle, fresh and newly emerged, as the blue and chocolate down on his wings testified. Mrs Pascoe went indoors, fetched a cream pan, came out and stood scouring it. Her face was assuredly not soft, sensual or lecherous, but hard, wise, wholesome rather, signifying in a room full of sophisticated people the flesh and blood of life. She would tell a lie, though, as soon as the truth. Behind her on the wall hung a large dried skate. Shut up in the parlour she prized mats, china mugs and photographs, though

the mouldy little room was saved from the salt breeze only by the depth of a brick, and between lace curtains you saw the gannet drop like a stone, and on stormy days the gulls came shuddering through the air, and the steamers' lights were now high, now deep. Melancholy were the sounds on a winter's night.

The picture papers were delivered punctually on Sunday, and she pored long over Lady Cynthia's wedding at the Abbey. She, too, would have liked to ride in a carriage with springs. The soft, swift syllables of educated speech often shamed her few rude ones. And then all night to hear the grinding of the Atlantic upon the rocks instead of hansom cabs and footmen whistling for motor cars . . . So she may have dreamed, scouring her cream pan. But the talkative, nimble-witted people have taken themselves to towns. Like a miser, she has hoarded her feelings within her own breast. Not a penny piece has she changed all these years, and, watching her enviously, it seems as if all within must be pure gold.

The wise old woman, having fixed her eyes upon the sea, once more withdrew. The tourists decided that it was time to move on to the Gurnard's Head.

Three seconds later Mrs Durrant rapped upon the door.

'Mrs Pascoe?' she said.

Rather haughtily, she watched the tourists cross the field path. She came of a Highland race, famous for its chieftains.

Mrs Pascoe appeared.

'I envy you that bush, Mrs Pascoe,' said Mrs Durrant, pointing the parasol with which she had rapped on the door at the fine clump of St John's wort that grew beside it.

Mrs Pascoe looked at the bush deprecatingly.

'I expect my son in a day or two,' said Mrs Durrant. 'Sailing from Falmouth with a friend in a little boat . . . Any news of Lizzie yet, Mrs Pascoe?'

Her long-tailed ponies stood twitching their ears on the road twenty yards away. The boy, Curnow, flicked flies off them occasionally. He saw his mistress go into the cottage; come out again; and pass, talking energetically to judge by the movements of her hands, round the vegetable plot in front of the cottage. Mrs Pascoe was his aunt. Both women surveyed a bush. Mrs Durrant stooped and picked a sprig from it. Next she pointed (her movements were peremptory; she held herself very upright) at the potatoes. They had the blight. All potatoes that year had the blight. Mrs Durrant showed Mrs Pascoe how bad the blight was on her potatoes. Mrs Durrant talked energetically; Mrs Pascoe listened submissively. The boy Curnow knew that Mrs Durrant was saying that it is perfectly simple; you mix the powder in a gallon of water; 'I have done it with my own hands in my own garden,' Mrs Durrant was saying.

'You won't have a potato left – you won't have a potato left,' Mrs Durrant was saying in her emphatic voice as they reached the gate. The boy Curnow became as immobile as stone.

Mrs Durrant took the reins in her hands and settled herself on the driver's seat.

'Take care of that leg, or I shall send the doctor to you,' she called back over her shoulder; touched the ponies; and the carriage started forward. The boy Curnow had only just time to swing himself up by the toe of his boot. The boy Curnow, sitting in the middle of the back seat, looked at his aunt.

Mrs Pascoe stood at the gate looking after them; stood at the gate till the trap was round the corner; stood at the gate, looking now to the right, now to the left; then went back to her cottage.

Soon the ponies attacked the swelling moor road with striving forelegs. Mrs Durrant let the reins fall slackly, and leant backwards. Her vivacity had left her. Her hawk nose was thin as a bleached bone through which you almost see the light. Her hands, lying on the reins in her lap, were firm even in repose. The upper lip was cut so short that it raised itself almost in a sneer from the front teeth. Her mind skimmed leagues where Mrs Pascoe's mind adhered to its solitary patch. Her mind skimmed leagues as the ponies climbed the hill road. Forwards and backwards she cast her mind, as if the roofless cottages, mounds of slag, and cottage gardens overgrown with foxglove and bramble cast shade upon her mind. Arrived at the summit, she stopped the carriage. The pale hills were round her, each scattered with ancient stones; beneath was the sea, variable as a southern sea; she herself sat there looking from hill to sea, upright, aquiline, equally poised between gloom and laughter. Suddenly she flicked the ponies so that the boy Curnow had to swing himself up by the toe of his boot.

The rooks settled; the rooks rose. The trees which they touched so capriciously seemed insufficient to lodge their numbers. The tree-tops sang with the breeze in them; the branches creaked audibly and dropped now and then, though the season was midsummer, husks or twigs. Up went the rooks and down again, rising in lesser numbers each time as the sager birds made ready to settle, for the evening was already spent enough to make the air inside the wood almost dark. The moss was soft; the tree-trunks spectral. Beyond them lay a silvery meadow. The pampas grass raised its feathery spears from mounds of green at the end of the meadow. A breadth of water gleamed. Already the convolvulus moth was spinning over the flowers. Orange and purple, nasturtium and cherry pie, were washed into the twilight, but the tobacco plant and the passion flower, over which the great moth spun, were white as china. The rooks creaked their wings together on the tree-tops, and were settling down for sleep when, far off, a familiar sound shook and trembled – increased – fairly dinned in their ears – scared sleepy wings into the air again – the dinner bell at the house.

After six days of salt wind, rain and sun, Jacob Flanders had put on a dinner jacket. The discreet black object had made its appearance now and then in the boat among tins, pickles, preserved meats, and as the voyage went on had become more and more irrelevant, hardly to be believed in. And now, the world being stable, lit by candlelight, the dinner jacket alone preserved him. He could not be sufficiently thankful. Even so his neck, wrists and face were exposed without cover, and his whole person, whether exposed or not, tingled and glowed so as to make even black cloth an imperfect screen. He drew back the great red hand that lay on the tablecloth. Surreptitiously it closed upon slim glasses and curved silver forks. The bones of the cutlets were decorated with pink frills – and yesterday he had gnawn ham from the bone! Opposite him were hazy, semi-transparent shapes of yellow and blue. Behind them, again, was the grey-green garden, and among the pear-shaped leaves of the escallonia fishing-boats seemed caught and suspended. A sailing ship slowly drew past the women's backs. Two or three figures crossed the terrace hastily in the dusk. The door opened and shut. Nothing settled or stayed unbroken. Like oars rowing now this side, now that, were the sentences that came now here, now there, from either side of the table.

'Oh, Clara, Clara!' exclaimed Mrs Durrant, and Timothy Durrant adding, 'Clara, Clara,' Jacob named the shape in yellow gauze Timothy's sister, Clara. The girl sat smiling and flushed. With her brother's dark eyes, she was vaguer and softer than he was. When the laugh died down she said: 'But, mother, it was true. He said so, didn't he? Miss Eliot agreed with us . . . '

But Miss Eliot, tall, grey-headed, was making room beside her for the old man who had come in from the terrace. The dinner would never end, Jacob thought, and he did not wish it to end, though the ship had sailed from one corner of the window-frame to the other, and a light marked the end of the pier. He saw Mrs Durrant gaze at the light. She turned to him.

'Did you take command, or Timothy?' she said. 'Forgive me if I call you Jacob. I've heard so much of you.' Then her eyes went back to the sea. Her eyes glazed as she looked at the view.

'A little village once,' she said, 'and now grown . . . ' She rose, taking her napkin with her, and stood by the window.

'Did you quarrel with Timothy?' Clara asked shyly. 'I should have.'

Mrs Durrant came back from the window.

'It gets later and later,' she said, sitting upright, and looking down the table. 'You ought to be ashamed – all of you. Mr Clutterbuck, you ought to be ashamed.' She raised her voice, for Mr Clutterbuck was deaf.

'We *are* ashamed,' said a girl. But the old man with the beard went on eating plum tart. Mrs Durrant laughed and leant back in her chair, as if indulging him.

'We put it to you, Mrs Durrant,' said a young man with thick spectacles and a fiery moustache. 'I say the conditions were fulfilled. She owes me a sovereign.'

'Not *before* the fish – *with* it, Mrs Durrant,' said Charlotte Wilding.

'That was the bet; with the fish,' said Clara seriously. 'Begonias, mother. To eat them with his fish.'

'Oh dear,' said Mrs Durrant.

'Charlotte won't pay you,' said Timothy.

'How dare you . . . ' said Charlotte.

'That privilege will be mine,' said the courtly Mr Wortley, producing a silver case primed with sovereigns and slipping one coin on to the table. Then Mrs Durrant got up and passed down the room, holding herself very straight, and the girls in yellow and blue and silver gauze followed her, and elderly Miss Eliot in her velvet; and a little rosy woman, hesitating at the door, clean, scrupulous, probably a governess. All passed out at the open door.

'When you are as old as I am, Charlotte,' said Mrs Durrant, drawing the girl's arm within hers as they paced up and down the terrace.

'Why are you so sad?' Charlotte asked impulsively.

'Do I seem to you sad? I hope not,' said Mrs Durrant.

'Well, just now. You're *not* old.'

'Old enough to be Timothy's mother.' They stopped.

Miss Eliot was looking through Mr Clutterbuck's telescope at the edge of the terrace. The deaf old man stood beside her, fondling his beard, and reciting the names of the constellations: 'Andromeda, Bootes, Sidonia, Cassiopeia . . . '

'Andromeda,' murmured Miss Eliot, shifting the telescope slightly.

Mrs Durrant and Charlotte looked along the barrel of the instrument pointed at the skies.

'There are *millions* of stars,' said Charlotte with conviction. Miss Eliot turned away from the telescope. The young men laughed suddenly in the dining-room.

'Let *me* look,' said Charlotte eagerly.

'The stars bore me,' said Mrs Durrant, walking down the terrace with Julia Eliot. 'I read a book once about the stars . . . What are they saying?' She stopped in front of the dining-room window. 'Timothy,' she noted.

'The silent young man,' said Miss Eliot.

'Yes, Jacob Flanders,' said Mrs Durrant.

'Oh, mother! I didn't recognise you!' exclaimed Clara Durrant, coming from the opposite direction with Elsbeth. 'How delicious,' she breathed, crushing a verbena leaf.

Mrs Durrant turned and walked away by herself.

'Clara!' she called. Clara went to her.

'How unlike they are!' said Miss Eliot.

Mr Wortley passed them, smoking a cigar.

'Every day I live I find myself agreeing . . . ' he said as he passed them.

'It's so interesting to guess . . . ' murmured Julia Eliot.

'When first we came out we could see the flowers in that bed,' said Elsbeth.

'We see very little now,' said Miss Eliot.

'She must have been so beautiful, and everybody loved her, of course,' said Charlotte. 'I suppose Mr Wortley . . . ' she paused.

'Edward's death was a tragedy,' said Miss Eliot decidedly.

Here Mr Erskine joined them.

'There's no such thing as silence,' he said positively. 'I can hear twenty different sounds on a night like this without counting your voices.'

'Make a bet of it?' said Charlotte.

'Done,' said Mr Erskine. 'One, the sea; two, the wind; three, a dog; four...' The others passed on.

'Poor Timothy,' said Elsbeth.

'A very fine night,' shouted Miss Eliot into Mr Clutterbuck's ear.

'Like to look at the stars?' said the old man, turning the telescope towards Elsbeth.

'Doesn't it make you melancholy – looking at the stars?' shouted Miss Eliot.

'Dear me no, dear me no,' Mr Clutterbuck chuckled when he understood her. 'Why should it make me melancholy? Not for a moment – dear me no.'

'Thank you, Timothy, but I'm coming in,' said Miss Eliot. 'Elsbeth, here's a shawl.'

'I'm coming in,' Elsbeth murmured with her eye to the telescope. 'Cassiopeia,' she murmured. 'Where are you all?' she asked, taking her eye away from the telescope. 'How dark it is!'

Mrs Durrant sat in the drawing-room by a lamp winding a ball of wool. Mr Clutterbuck read *The Times*. In the distance stood a second lamp, and round it sat the young ladies, flashing scissors over silver-spangled stuff for private theatricals. Mr Wortley read a book.

'Yes; he is perfectly right,' said Mrs Durrant, drawing herself up and ceasing to wind her wool. And while Mr Clutterbuck read the rest of Lord Lansdowne's speech she sat upright, without touching her ball.

'Ah, Mr Flanders,' she said, speaking proudly, as if to Lord Lansdowne himself. Then she sighed and began to wind her wool again.

'Sit *there*,' she said.

Jacob came out from the dark place by the window where he had hovered. The light poured over him, illuminating every cranny of his skin; but not a muscle of his face moved as he sat looking out into the garden.

'I want to hear about your voyage,' said Mrs Durrant.

'Yes,' he said.

'Twenty years ago we did the same thing.'

'Yes,' he said.

She looked at him sharply.

'He is extraordinarily awkward,' she thought, noticing how he fingered his socks. 'Yet so distinguished-looking.'

'In those days . . . ' she resumed, and told him how they had sailed . . . 'my husband, who knew a good deal about sailing, for he kept a yacht before we married' . . . and then how rashly they had defied the fishermen, 'almost paid for it with our lives, but so proud of ourselves!' She flung the hand out that held the ball of wool.

'Shall I hold your wool?' Jacob asked stiffly.

'You do that for your mother,' said Mrs Durrant, looking at him again keenly, as she transferred the skein. 'Yes, it goes much better.'

He smiled; but said nothing.

Elsbeth Siddons hovered behind them with something silver on her arm.

'We want,' she said . . . 'I've come . . . ' she paused.

'Poor Jacob,' said Mrs Durrant, quietly, as if she had known him all his life. 'They're going to make you act in their play.'

'How I love you!' said Elsbeth, kneeling beside Mrs Durrant's chair.

'Give me the wool,' said Mrs Durrant.

'He's come – he's come!' cried Charlotte Wilding. 'I've won my bet!'

'There's another bunch higher up,' murmured Clara Durrant, mounting another step of the ladder. Jacob held the ladder as she stretched out to reach the grapes high up on the vine.

'There!' she said, cutting through the stalk. She looked semi-transparent, pale, wonderfully beautiful up there among the vine leaves and the yellow and purple bunches, the lights swimming over her in coloured islands. Geraniums and begonias stood in pots along planks; tomatoes climbed the walls.

'The leaves really want thinning,' she considered, and one green one, spread like the palm of a hand, circled down past Jacob's head.

'I have more than I can eat already,' he said, looking up.

'It does seem absurd . . . ' Clara began, 'going back to London . . . '

'Ridiculous,' said Jacob, firmly.

'Then . . . ' said Clara, 'you must come next year, properly,' she said, snipping another vine leaf, rather at random.

'If . . . if . . . '

A child ran past the greenhouse shouting. Clara slowly descended the ladder with her basket of grapes.

'One bunch of white, and two of purple,' she said, and she placed two great leaves over them where they lay curled warm in the basket.

'I have enjoyed myself,' said Jacob, looking down the greenhouse.

'Yes, it's been delightful,' she said vaguely.

'Oh, Miss Durrant,' he said, taking the basket of grapes; but she walked past him towards the door of the greenhouse.

'You're too good – too good,' she thought, thinking of Jacob, thinking that he must not say that he loved her. No, no, no.

The children were whirling past the door, throwing things high into the air.

'Little demons!' she cried. 'What have they got?' she asked Jacob.

'Onions, I think,' said Jacob. He looked at them without moving.

'Next August, remember, Jacob,' said Mrs Durrant, shaking hands with him on the terrace where the fuchsia hung, like a scarlet ear-ring, behind her head. Mr Wortley came out of the window in yellow slippers, trailing *The Times* and holding out his hand very cordially.

'Goodbye,' said Jacob. 'Goodbye,' he repeated. 'Goodbye,' he said once more.

Charlotte Wilding flung up her bedroom window and cried out: 'Goodbye, Mr Jacob!'

'Mr Flanders!' cried Mr Clutterbuck, trying to extricate himself from his beehive chair. 'Jacob Flanders!'

'Too late, Joseph,' said Mrs Durrant.

'Not to sit for me,' said Miss Eliot, planting her tripod upon the lawn.

Chapter Five

'I rather think,' said Jacob, taking his pipe from his mouth, 'it's in Virgil,' and pushing back his chair, he went to the window.

The rashest drivers in the world are, certainly, the drivers of post-office vans. Swinging down Lamb's Conduit Street, the scarlet van rounded the corner by the pillar box in such a way as to graze the kerb and make the little girl who was standing on tiptoe to post a letter look up, half frightened, half curious. She paused with her hand in the mouth of the box; then dropped her letter and ran away. It is seldom only that we see a child on tiptoe with pity – more often a dim discomfort, a grain of sand in the shoe which it's scarcely worthwhile to remove – that's our feeling, and so – Jacob turned to the bookcase.

Long ago great people lived here, and coming back from Court past midnight stood, huddling their satin skirts, under the carved door-posts while the footman roused himself from his mattress on the floor, hurriedly fastened the lower buttons of his waistcoat, and let them in. The bitter eighteenth-century rain rushed down the kennel. Southampton Row, however, is chiefly remarkable nowadays for the fact that you will always find a man there trying to sell a tortoise to a tailor. 'Showing off the tweed, sir; what the gentry wants is something singular to catch the eye, sir – and clean in their habits, sir!' So they display their tortoises.

At Mudie's corner in Oxford Street all the red and blue beads had run together on the string. The motor omnibuses were locked. Mr Spalding going to the city looked at Mr Charles Budgeon bound for Shepherd's Bush. The proximity of the omnibuses gave the outside passengers an opportunity to stare into each other's faces. Yet few took advantage of it. Each had his own business to think of. Each had his past shut in him like the leaves of a book known to him by heart; and his friends could only read the title, James Spalding or Charles Budgeon, and the passengers going the opposite way could read nothing at all – save 'a man with a red moustache', 'a young man in grey smoking a pipe'. The October sunlight rested upon all these men and women sitting immobile; and little Johnnie Sturgeon took the chance to swing down the staircase, carrying his large mysterious parcel, and so dodging a zigzag course between the wheels he reached the pavement, started to whistle a tune and was soon out of sight – for ever. The omnibuses jerked on, and every single person felt relief at being a little nearer to his journey's end, though some cajoled themselves past the immediate engagement by promise of indulgence beyond – steak and kidney pudding, drink or a game of dominoes in the smoky corner of a city restaurant. Oh yes, human life is very tolerable on the top of an omnibus in Holborn, when the policeman holds up his arm and the sun beats on your back, and if there is such a thing as a shell secreted by man to fit man himself here we find it, on the banks of the Thames, where the great streets join and St Paul's Cathedral, like the volute on the top of the snail shell, finishes it off. Jacob, getting off his omnibus, loitered up the steps, consulted his watch, and finally made up his mind to go in . . . Does it need an effort? Yes. These changes of mood wear us out.

Dim it is, haunted by ghosts of white marble, to whom the organ for ever chaunts. If a boot creaks, it's awful; then the order; the discipline. The verger with his rod has life ironed out beneath him. Sweet and holy are the angelic choristers. And for ever round the marble shoulders, in and out of the folded fingers, go the thin high sounds of voice and organ. For ever requiem – repose. Tired with scrubbing the steps of the Prudential Society's office, which she did year in year out, Mrs Lidgett took her seat beneath the great Duke's tomb, folded her hands and half closed her eyes. A magnificent place for an old woman to rest in, by the very side of the great Duke's bones, whose victories mean nothing to her, whose name she knows not, though she never fails to greet the little angels opposite, as she passes out, wishing the like on her own tomb, for the leathern curtain of the heart has flapped wide, and out steal on tiptoe thoughts of rest, sweet melodies . . . Old Spicer, jute merchant, thought nothing of the kind though. Strangely enough he'd never been in St Paul's these fifty years, though his office windows looked on the churchyard. 'So that's all? Well, a gloomy old place . . . Where's Nelson's tomb? No time now – come again – a coin to leave in the box . . . Rain or fine is it? Well, if it would only make up its mind!' Idly the children stray in – the verger dissuades them – and another and another . . . man, woman, man, woman, boy . . . casting their eyes up, pursing their lips, the same shadow brushing the same faces; the leathern curtain of the heart flaps wide.

Nothing could appear more certain from the steps of St Paul's than that each person is miraculously provided with coat, skirt and boots; an income; an object. Only Jacob, carrying in his hand Finlay's *Byzantine Empire*, which he had bought in Ludgate Hill, looked a little different; for in his hand he carried a book, which book he would at nine-thirty precisely, by his own fireside, open and study, as no one else of all these multitudes would do. They have no houses. The streets belong to them; the shops; the churches; theirs the innumerable desks; the stretched office lights; the vans are theirs, and the railway slung high above the street. If you look closer you will see that three elderly men at a little distance from each other run spiders along the pavement as if the street were their parlour, and here, against the wall, a woman stares at nothing, boot-laces extended, which she does not ask you to buy. The posters are theirs too; and the news on them. A town destroyed; a race won. A homeless people, circling beneath the sky whose blue or white is held off by a ceiling cloth of steel filings and horse dung shredded to dust.

There, under the green shade, with his head bent over white paper, Mr Sibley transferred figures to folios, and upon each desk you observe, like provender, a bunch of papers, the day's nutriment, slowly consumed by the industrious pen. Innumerable overcoats of the quality prescribed hung empty all day in the corridors, but as the clock struck six each was exactly filled, and the little figures, split apart into trousers or moulded into a single thickness, jerked rapidly with angular forward motion along the pavement; then dropped into darkness. Beneath the pavement, sunk in the earth, hollow drains lined with yellow light for ever conveyed them this way and that, and large letters upon enamel plates represented in the underworld the parks, squares and circuses of the upper. 'Marble Arch – Shepherd's Bush' – to the majority the Arch and the Bush are eternally white letters upon a blue ground. Only at one point – it may be Acton, Holloway, Kensal Rise, Caledonian Road – does the name mean shops where you buy things, and houses, in one of which, down to the right, where the pollard trees grow out of the paving stones, there is a square curtained window, and a bedroom.

Long past sunset an old blind woman sat on a camp-stool with her back to the stone wall of the Union of London and Smith's Bank, clasping a brown mongrel tight in her arms and singing out loud, not for coppers, no, from the depths of her gay wild heart – her sinful, tanned heart – for the child who fetches her is the fruit of sin, and should have been in bed, curtained, asleep, instead of hearing in the lamplight her mother's wild song, where she sits against the bank, singing not for coppers, with her dog against her breast.

Home they went. The grey church spires received them; the hoary city, old, sinful and majestic. One behind another, round or pointed, piercing the sky or massing themselves, like sailing ships, like granite cliffs, spires and offices, wharves and factories crowd the bank; eternally the pilgrims trudge; barges rest in midstream heavy laden; as some believe, the city loves her prostitutes.

But few, it seems, are admitted to that degree. Of all the carriages that leave the arch of the Opera House, not one turns eastward, and when the little thief is caught in the empty market-place no one in black-and-white or rose-coloured evening dress blocks the way by pausing with a hand upon the carriage door to help or condemn – though Lady Charles, to do her justice, sighs sadly as she ascends her staircase, takes down Thomas à Kempis, and does not sleep till her mind has lost itself tunnelling into the complexity of things. 'Why? Why? Why?' she sighs. On the whole it's best to walk back from the Opera House. Fatigue is the safest sleeping draught.

The autumn season was in full swing. Tristan was twitching his rug up under his armpits twice a week; Isolde waved her scarf in miraculous sympathy with the conductor's baton. In all parts of the house were to be found pink faces and glittering breasts. When a royal hand attached to an invisible body slipped out and withdrew the red and white bouquet reposing on the scarlet ledge, the Queen of England seemed a name worth dying for. Beauty, in its hothouse variety (which is none of the worst), flowered in box after box; and though nothing was said of profound importance, and though it is generally agreed that wit deserted beautiful lips about the time that Walpole died – at any rate when Victoria in her nightgown descended to meet her ministers, the lips (through an opera glass) remained red, adorable. Bald distinguished men with gold-headed canes strolled down the crimson avenues between the stalls, and only broke from intercourse with the boxes when the lights went down, and the conductor, first bowing to the queen, next to the bald-headed men, swept round on his feet and raised his wand.

Then two thousand hearts in the semi-darkness remembered, anticipated, travelled dark labyrinths; and Clara Durrant said farewell to Jacob Flanders, and tasted the sweetness of death in effigy; and Mrs Durrant, sitting behind her in the dark of the box, sighed her sharp sigh; and Mr Wortley, shifting his position behind the Italian ambassador's wife, thought that Brangaena was a trifle hoarse; and suspended in the gallery many feet above their heads, Edward Whittaker surreptitiously held a torch to his miniature score; and . . . and . . .

In short, the observer is choked with observations. Only to prevent us from being submerged by chaos, nature and society between them have arranged a system of classification which is simplicity itself: stalls, boxes, amphitheatre, gallery. The moulds are filled nightly. There is no need to distinguish details. But the difficulty remains – one has to choose. For though I have no wish to be Queen of England – or only for a moment – I would willingly sit beside her; I would hear the Prime Minister's gossip; the countess whisper, and share her memories of halls and gardens; the massive fronts of the respectable conceal after all their secret code; or why so impermeable? And then, doffing one's own headpiece, how strange to assume for a moment someone's – anyone's – to be a man of valour who has ruled the Empire; to refer while Brangaena sings to the fragments of Sophocles, or see in a flash, as the shepherd pipes his tune, bridges and aqueducts. But no – we must choose. Never was there a harsher necessity! or one which entails greater pain, more certain disaster; for wherever I seat myself, I die in exile: Whittaker in his lodging-house; Lady Charles at the Manor.

A young man with a Wellington nose, who had occupied a seven-and-sixpenny seat, made his way down the stone stairs when the opera ended, as if he were still set a little apart from his fellows by the influence of the music.

At midnight Jacob Flanders heard a rap on his door.

'By Jove!' he exclaimed. 'You're the very man I want!' and without more ado they discovered the lines which he had been seeking all day; only they come not in Virgil, but in Lucretius.

'Yes; that should make him sit up,' said Bonamy, as Jacob stopped reading. Jacob was excited. It was the first time he had read his essay aloud.

'Damned swine!' he said, rather too extravagantly; but the praise had gone to his head. Professor Bulteel, of Leeds, had issued an edition of Wycherley without stating that he had left out, disembowelled, or indicated only by asterisks, several indecent words and some indecent phrases. An outrage, Jacob said; a breach of faith; sheer prudery; token of a lewd mind and a disgusting nature. Aristophanes and Shakespeare were cited. Modern life was repudiated. Great play was made with the professional title, and Leeds as a seat of learning was laughed to scorn. And the extraordinary thing was that these young men were perfectly right – extraordinary, because, even as Jacob copied his pages, he knew that no one would ever print them; and sure enough back they came from the *Fortnightly*, the *Contemporary*, the *Nineteenth Century* – when Jacob threw them into the black wooden box where he kept his mother's letters, his old flannel trousers, and a note or two with the Cornish postmark. The lid shut upon the truth.

This black wooden box, upon which his name was still legible in white paint, stood between the long windows of the sitting-room. The street ran beneath. No doubt the bedroom was behind. The furniture – three wicker chairs and a gate-legged table – came from Cambridge. These houses (Mrs Garfit's daughter, Mrs Whitehorn, was the landlady of this one) were built, say, a hundred and fifty years ago. The rooms are shapely, the ceilings high; over the doorway a rose, or a ram's skull, is carved in the wood. The eighteenth century has its distinction. Even the panels, painted in raspberry-coloured paint, have their distinction . . .

'Distinction' – Mrs Durrant said that Jacob Flanders was 'distinguished-looking'. 'Extremely awkward,' she said, 'but so distinguished-looking.'

Seeing him for the first time that no doubt is the word for him. Lying back in his chair, taking his pipe from his lips, and saying to Bonamy: 'About this opera now' (for they had done with indecency). 'This fellow Wagner' . . . distinction was one of the words to use naturally, though, from looking at him, one would have found it difficult to say which seat in the opera house was his – stalls, gallery or dress circle. A writer? He lacked self-consciousness. A painter? There was something in the shape of his hands (he was descended on his mother's side from a family of the greatest antiquity and deepest obscurity) which indicated taste. Then his mouth – but surely, of all futile occupations this of cataloguing features is the worst. One word is sufficient. But if one cannot find it?

'I like Jacob Flanders,' wrote Clara Durrant in her diary. 'He is so unworldly. He gives himself no airs, and one can say what one likes to him, though he's frightening because . . . ' But Mr Letts allows little space in his shilling diaries. Clara was not the one to encroach upon Wednesday. Humblest, most candid of women! 'No, no, no,' she sighed, standing at the greenhouse door, 'don't break – don't spoil' – what? Something infinitely wonderful.

But then, this is only a young woman's language, one, too, who loves, or refrains from loving. She wished the moment to continue for ever precisely as it was that July morning. And moments don't. Now, for instance, Jacob was telling a story about some walking tour he'd taken, and the inn was called the Foaming Pot, which, considering the landlady's name . . . They shouted with laughter. The joke was indecent.

Then Julia Eliot said 'the silent young man', and as she dined with prime ministers, no doubt she meant: 'If he is going to get on in the world, he will have to find his tongue.'

Timothy Durrant never made any comment at all.

The housemaid found herself very liberally rewarded.

Mr Sopwith's opinion was as sentimental as Clara's, though far more skilfully expressed.

Betty Flanders was romantic about Archer and tender about John; she was unreasonably irritated by Jacob's clumsiness in the house.

Captain Barfoot liked him best of the boys; but as for saying why . . .

It seems then that men and women are equally at fault. It seems that a profound, impartial and absolutely just opinion of our fellow-creatures is utterly unknown. Either we are men, or we are women. Either we are cold, or we are sentimental. Either we are young, or growing old. In any case life is but a procession of shadows, and God knows why it is that we embrace them so eagerly, and see them depart with such anguish, being shadows. And why, if this – and much more than this – is true, why are we yet surprised in the window corner by a sudden vision that the young man in the chair is of all things in the world the most real, the most solid, the best known to us – why indeed? For the moment after we know nothing about him.

Such is the manner of our seeing. Such the conditions of our love.

('I'm twenty-two. It's nearly the end of October. Life is thoroughly pleasant, although unfortunately there are a great number of fools about. One must apply oneself to something or other – God knows what. Everything is really very jolly – except getting up in the morning and wearing a tail coat.')

'I say, Bonamy, what about Beethoven?'

('Bonamy is an amazing fellow. He knows practically everything – not more about English literature than I do – but then he's read all those Frenchmen.')

'I rather suspect you're talking rot, Bonamy. In spite of what you say, poor old Tennyson . . . '

('The truth is one ought to have been taught French. Now, I suppose, old Barfoot is talking to my mother. That's an odd affair to be sure. But I can't see Bonamy down there. Damn London!') for the market carts were lumbering down the street.

'What about a walk on Saturday?'

('What's happening on Saturday?')

Then, taking out his pocket-book, he assured himself that the night of the Durrants' party came next week.

But though all this may very well be true – so Jacob thought and spoke – so he crossed his legs – filled his pipe – sipped his whisky, and once looked at his pocket-book, rumpling his hair as he did so, there remains over something which can never be conveyed to a second person save by Jacob himself. Moreover, part of this is not Jacob but Richard Bonamy – the room; the market carts; the hour; the very moment of history. Then consider the effect of sex – how between man and woman it hangs wavy, tremulous, so that here's a valley, there's a peak, when in truth, perhaps, all's as flat as my hand. Even the exact words get the wrong accent on them. But something is always impelling one to hum vibrating, like the hawk moth, at the mouth of the cavern of mystery, endowing Jacob Flanders with all sorts of qualities he had not at all – for though, certainly, he sat talking to Bonamy, half of what he said was too dull to repeat; much unintelligible (about unknown people and Parliament); what remains is mostly a matter of guesswork. Yet over him we hang vibrating.

'Yes,' said Captain Barfoot, knocking out his pipe on Betty Flanders's hob, and buttoning his coat. 'It doubles the work, but I don't mind that.'

He was now town councillor. They looked at the night, which was the same as the London night, only a good deal more transparent. Church bells down in the town were striking eleven o'clock. The wind was off the sea. And all the bedroom windows were dark – the Pages were asleep; the Garfits were asleep; the Cranches were asleep – whereas in London at this hour they were burning Guy Fawkes on Parliament Hill.

Chapter Six

The flames had fairly caught.

'There's St Paul's!' someone cried.

As the wood caught the city of London was lit up for a second; on other sides of the fire there were trees. Of the faces which came out fresh and vivid as though painted in yellow and red, the most prominent was a girl's face. By a trick of the firelight she seemed to have no body. The oval of the face and hair hung beside the fire with a dark vacuum for background. As if dazed by the glare, her green-blue eyes stared at the flames. Every muscle of her face was taut. There was something tragic in her thus staring – her age between twenty and twenty-five.

A hand descending from the chequered darkness thrust on her head the conical white hat of a pierrot. Shaking her head, she still stared. A whiskered face appeared above her. They dropped two legs of a table upon the fire and a scattering of twigs and leaves. All this blazed up and showed faces far back, round, pale, smooth, bearded, some with billycock hats on; all intent; showed too St Paul's floating on the uneven white mist, and two or three narrow, paper-white, extinguisher-shaped spires.

The flames were struggling through the wood and roaring up when, goodness knows where from, pails flung water in beautiful hollow shapes, as of polished tortoiseshell; flung again and again; until the hiss was like a swarm of bees; and all the faces went out.

'Oh Jacob,' said the girl, as they pounded up the hill in the dark, 'I'm so frightfully unhappy!'

Shouts of laughter came from the others – high, low; some before, others after.

The hotel dining-room was brightly lit. A stag's head in plaster was at one end of the table; at the other some Roman bust blackened and reddened to represent Guy Fawkes, whose night it was. The diners were linked together by lengths of paper roses, so that when it came to singing 'Auld Lang Syne' with their hands crossed, a pink and yellow line rose and fell the entire length of the table. There was an enormous tapping of green wine-glasses. A young man stood up, and Florinda, taking one of the purplish globes that lay on the table, flung it straight at his head. It crushed to powder.

'I'm so frightfully unhappy!' she said, turning to Jacob, who sat beside her.

The table ran, as if on invisible legs, to the side of the room, and a barrel organ decorated with a red cloth and two pots of paper flowers reeled out waltz music.

Jacob could not dance. He stood against the wall smoking a pipe.

'We think,' said two of the dancers, breaking off from the rest, and bowing profoundly before him, 'that you are the most beautiful man we have ever seen.'

So they wreathed his head with paper flowers. Then somebody brought out a white and gilt chair and made him sit on it. As they passed, people hung glass grapes on his shoulders, until he looked like the figure-head of a wrecked ship. Then Florinda got upon his knee and hid her face in his waistcoat. With one hand he held her; with the other, his pipe.

'Now let us talk,' said Jacob, as he walked down Haverstock Hill between four and five o'clock in the morning of November the sixth arm in arm with Timmy Durrant, 'about something sensible.'

The Greeks – yes, that was what they talked about – how when all's said and done, when one's rinsed one's mouth with every literature in the world, including Chinese and Russian (but these Slavs aren't civilised), it's the flavour of Greek that remains. Durrant quoted Aeschylus – Jacob Sophocles. It is true that no Greek could have understood or professor refrained from pointing out – Never mind; what is Greek for if not to be shouted on Haverstock Hill in the dawn? Moreover, Durrant never listened to Sophocles, nor Jacob to Aeschylus. They were boastful, triumphant; it seemed to both that they had read every book in the world; known every sin, passion and joy. Civilisations stood round them like flowers ready for picking. Ages lapped at their feet like waves fit for sailing. And surveying all this, looming through the fog, the lamplight, the shades of London, the two young men decided in favour of Greece.

'Probably,' said Jacob, 'we are the only people in the world who know what the Greeks meant.'

They drank coffee at a stall where the urns were burnished and little lamps burnt along the counter.

Taking Jacob for a military gentleman, the stall-keeper told him about his boy at Gibraltar, and Jacob cursed the British army and praised the Duke of Wellington. So on again they went down the hill talking about the Greeks.

A strange thing – when you come to think of it – this love of Greek, flourishing in such obscurity, distorted, discouraged, yet leaping out, all of a sudden, especially on leaving crowded rooms, or after a surfeit of print, or when the moon floats among the waves of the hills, or in hollow, sallow, fruitless London days, like a specific; a clean blade; always a miracle. Jacob knew no more Greek than served him to stumble through a play. Of ancient history he knew nothing. However, as he tramped into London it seemed to him that they were making the flagstones ring on the road to the Acropolis, and that if Socrates saw them coming he would bestir himself and say 'my fine fellows', for the whole sentiment of Athens was entirely after his heart; free, venturesome, high-spirited . . . She had called him Jacob without asking his leave. She had sat upon his knee. Thus did all good women in the days of the Greeks.

At this moment there shook out into the air a wavering, quavering, doleful lamentation which seemed to lack strength to unfold itself, and yet flagged on; at the sound of which doors in back streets burst sullenly open; workmen stumped forth.

Florinda was sick.

Mrs Durrant, sleepless as usual, scored a mark by the side of certain lines in the *Inferno*.

Clara slept buried in her pillows; on her dressing-table dishevelled roses and a pair of long white gloves.

Still wearing the conical white hat of a pierrot, Florinda was sick.

The bedroom seemed fit for these catastrophes – cheap, mustard-coloured, half-attic, half-studio, curiously ornamented with silver-paper stars, Welsh-women's hats, and rosaries pendent from the gas brackets. As for Florinda's story, her name had been bestowed upon her by a painter who had wished it to signify that the flower of her maidenhood was still unplucked. Be that as it may, she was without a surname, and for parents had only the photograph of a tombstone beneath which, she said, her father lay buried. Sometimes she would dwell upon the size of it, and rumour had it that Florinda's father had died from the growth of his bones which nothing could stop; just as her mother enjoyed the confidence of a royal master, and now and again Florinda herself was a princess, but chiefly when drunk. Thus deserted, pretty into the bargain, with tragic eyes and the lips of a child, she talked more about virginity than women mostly do; and had lost it only the night before, or cherished it beyond the heart in her breast, according to the man she talked to. But did she always talk to men? No, she had her confidante: Mother Stuart. Stuart, as the lady would point out, is the name of a royal house; but what that signified, and what her business was, no one knew; only that Mrs Stuart got postal orders every Monday morning, kept a parrot, believed in the transmigration of souls, and could read the future in tea leaves. Dirty lodging-house wallpaper she was behind the chastity of Florinda.

Now Florinda wept, and spent the day wandering the streets; stood at Chelsea watching the river swim past; trailed along the shopping streets; opened her bag and powdered her cheeks in omnibuses; read love letters, propping them against the milk pot in the ABC shop; detected glass in the sugar bowl; accused the waitress of wishing to poison her; declared that young men stared at her; and found herself towards evening slowly sauntering down Jacob's street, when it struck her that she liked that man Jacob better than dirty Jews, and sitting at his table (he was copying his essay upon the Ethics of

Indecency), drew off her gloves and told him how Mother Stuart had banged her on the head with the tea-cosy.

Jacob took her word for it that she was chaste. She prattled, sitting by the fireside, of famous painters. The tomb of her father was mentioned. Wild and frail and beautiful she looked, and thus the women of the Greeks were, Jacob thought; and this was life; and himself a man and Florinda chaste.

She left with one of Shelley's poems beneath her arm. Mrs Stuart, she said, often talked of him.

Marvellous are the innocent. To believe that the girl herself transcends all lies (for Jacob was not such a fool as to believe implicitly), to wonder enviously at the unanchored life – his own seeming petted and even cloistered in comparison – to have at hand as sovereign specifics for all disorders of the soul Adonais and the plays of Shakespeare; to figure out a comradeship all spirited on her side, protective on his, yet equal on both, for women, thought Jacob, are just the same as men – innocence such as this is marvellous enough, and perhaps not so foolish after all.

For when Florinda got home that night she first washed her head; then ate chocolate creams; then opened Shelley. True, she was horribly bored. What on earth was it *about*? She had to wager with herself that she would turn the page before she ate another. In fact she slept. But then her day had been a long one, Mother Stuart had thrown the tea-cosy; there are formidable sights in the streets, and though Florinda was ignorant as an owl, and would never learn to read even her love letters correctly, still she had her feelings, liked some men better than others, and was entirely at the beck and call of life. Whether or not she was a virgin seems a matter of no importance whatever. Unless, indeed, it is the only thing of any importance at all.

Jacob was restless when she left him.

All night men and women seethed up and down the well-known beats. Late home-comers could see shadows against the blinds even in the most respectable suburbs. Not a square in snow or fog lacked its amorous couple. All plays turned on the same subject. Bullets went through heads in hotel bedrooms almost nightly on that account. When the body escaped mutilation, seldom did the heart go to the grave unscarred. Little else was talked of in theatres and popular novels. Yet we say it is a matter of no importance at all.

What with Shakespeare and Adonais, Mozart and Bishop Berkeley – choose whom you like – the fact is concealed and the evenings for most of us pass reputably, or with only the sort of tremor that a snake makes sliding through the grass. But then concealment by itself distracts the mind from the print and the sound. If Florinda had had a mind, she might have read with clearer eyes than we can. She and her sort have solved the question by turning it to a trifle of washing the hands nightly before going to bed, the only difficulty being whether you prefer your water hot or cold, which being settled, the mind can go about its business unassailed.

But it did occur to Jacob, halfway through dinner, to wonder whether she had a mind.

They sat at a little table in the restaurant.

Florinda leant the points of her elbows on the table and held her chin in the cup of her hands. Her cloak had slipped behind her. Gold and white with bright beads on her she emerged, her face flowering from her body, innocent, scarcely tinted, the eyes gazing frankly about her, or slowly settling on Jacob and resting there. She talked.

'You know that big black box the Australian left in my room ever so long ago? . . . I do think furs make a woman look old . . . That's Bechstein come in now . . . I was wondering what you looked like when you were a little boy, Jacob.' She nibbled her roll and looked at him.

'Jacob. You're like one of those statues . . . I think there are lovely things in the British Museum, don't you? Lots of lovely things . . . ' she spoke dreamily. The room was filling; the heat increasing. Talk in a restaurant is dazed sleep-walkers' talk, so many things to look at – so much noise – other people talking. Can one overhear? Oh, but they mustn't overhear *us*.

'That's like Ellen Nagle – that girl . . . ' and so on.

'I'm awfully happy since I've known you, Jacob. You're such a *good* man.'

The room got fuller and fuller; talk louder; knives more clattering.

'Well, you see what makes her say things like that is . . . '

She stopped. So did everyone.

'Tomorrow . . . Sunday . . . a beastly . . . you tell me . . . go then!' Crash! And out she swept.

It was at the table next them that the voice spun higher and higher. Suddenly the woman dashed the plates to the floor. The man was left there. Everybody stared. Then – 'Well, poor chap, we mustn't sit staring. What a go! Did you hear what she said? By God, he looks a fool! Didn't come up to the scratch, I suppose. All the mustard on the tablecloth. The waiters laughing.'

Jacob observed Florinda. In her face there seemed to him something horribly brainless – as she sat staring.

Out she swept, the black woman with the dancing feather in her hat.

Yet she had to go somewhere. The night is not a tumultuous black ocean in which you sink or sail as a star. As a matter of fact it was a wet November night. The lamps of Soho made large greasy spots of light upon the pavement. The by-streets were dark enough to shelter man or woman leaning against the doorways. One detached herself as Jacob and Florinda approached.

'She's dropped her glove,' said Florinda.

Jacob, pressing forward, gave it her.

Effusively she thanked him; retraced her steps; dropped her glove again. But why? For whom?

Meanwhile, where had the other woman got to? And the man?

The street lamps do not carry far enough to tell us. The voices, angry, lustful, despairing, passionate, were scarcely more than the voices of caged beasts at night. Only they are not caged, nor beasts. Stop a man; ask him the way; he'll tell it you; but one's afraid to ask him the way. What does one fear? – the human eye. At once the pavement narrows, the chasm deepens. There! They've melted into it – both man and woman. Farther on, blatantly advertising its meritorious solidity, a boarding-house exhibits behind uncurtained windows its testimony to the soundness of London. There they sit, plainly illuminated, dressed like ladies and gentlemen, in bamboo chairs. The widows of businessmen prove laboriously that they are related to judges. The wives of coal merchants instantly retort that their fathers kept coachmen. A servant brings coffee, and the crochet basket has to be moved. And so on again into the dark, passing a girl here for sale, or there an old woman with only matches to offer, passing the crowd from the tube station, the women with veiled hair, passing at length no one but shut doors, carved door-posts and a solitary policeman, Jacob, with Florinda on his arm, reached his room and, lighting the lamp, said nothing at all.

'I don't like you when you look like that,' said Florinda.

The problem is insoluble. The body is harnessed to a brain. Beauty goes hand in hand with stupidity. There she sat staring at the fire as she had stared at the broken mustard-pot. In spite of defending indecency, Jacob doubted whether he liked it in the raw. He had a violent reversion towards male society, cloistered rooms, and the works of the classics; and was ready to turn with wrath upon whoever it was who had fashioned life thus.

Then Florinda laid her hand upon his knee.

After all, it was none of her fault. But the thought saddened him. It's not catastrophes, murders, deaths, diseases, that age and kill us; it's the way people look and laugh, and run up the steps of omnibuses.

Any excuse, though, serves a stupid woman. He told her his head ached.

But when she looked at him, dumbly, half-guessing, half-understanding, apologising perhaps, anyhow saying as he had said, 'It's none of my fault,' straight and beautiful in body, her face like a shell within its cap, then he knew that cloisters and classics are no use whatever. The problem is insoluble.

Chapter Seven

About this time a firm of merchants having dealings with the East put on the market little paper flowers which opened on touching water. As it was the custom also to use finger-bowls at the end of dinner, the new discovery was found of excellent service. In these sheltered lakes the little coloured flowers swam and slid; surmounted smooth slippery waves, and sometimes foundered and lay like pebbles on the glass floor. Their fortunes were watched by eyes intent and lovely. It is surely a great discovery that leads to the union of hearts and foundation of homes. The paper flowers did no less.

It must not be thought, though, that they ousted the flowers of nature. Roses, lilies, carnations in particular, looked over the rims of vases and surveyed the bright lives and swift dooms of their artificial relations. Mr Stuart Ormond made this very observation; and charming it was thought; and Kitty Craster married him on the strength of it six months later. But real flowers can never be dispensed with. If they could, human life would be a different affair altogether. For flowers fade; chrysanthemums are the worst; perfect overnight; yellow and jaded next morning – not fit to be seen. On the whole, though the price is sinful, carnations pay best; it's a question, however, whether it's wise to have them wired. Some shops advise it. Certainly it's the only way to keep them at a dance; but whether it is necessary at dinner parties, unless the rooms are very hot, remains in dispute. Old Mrs Temple used to recommend an ivy leaf – just one – dropped into the bowl. She said it kept the water pure for days and days. But there is some reason to think that old Mrs Temple was mistaken.

The little cards, however, with names engraved on them, are a more serious problem than the flowers. More horses' legs have been worn out, more coachmen's lives consumed, more hours of sound afternoon time vainly lavished than served to win us the battle of Waterloo, and pay for it into the bargain. The little demons are the source of as many reprieves, calamities and anxieties as the battle itself. Sometimes Mrs Bonham has just gone out; at others she is at home. But, even if the cards should be superseded, which seems unlikely, there are unruly powers blowing life into storms, disordering sedulous mornings and uprooting the stability of the afternoon – dressmakers, that is to say, and confectioners' shops. Six yards of silk will cover one body; but if you have to devise six hundred shapes for it, and twice as many colours? – in the middle of which there is the urgent question of the pudding with tufts of green cream and battlements of almond paste. It has not arrived.

The flamingo hours fluttered softly through the sky. But regularly they dipped their wings in pitch black; Notting Hill, for instance, or the purlieus of Clerkenwell. No wonder that Italian remained a hidden art, and the piano always played the same sonata. In order to buy one pair of elastic stockings for Mrs Page, widow, aged sixty-three, in receipt of five shillings out-door relief, and help from her only son employed in Messrs Mackie's dye-works, suffering in winter with his chest, letters must be written, columns filled up in the same round, simple hand that wrote in Mr Letts's diary how the weather was fine, the children demons, and Jacob Flanders unworldly. Clara Durrant procured the stockings, played the sonata, filled the vases, fetched the pudding, left the cards, and when the great invention of paper flowers to swim in finger-bowls was discovered, was one of those who most marvelled at their brief lives.

Nor were there wanting poets to celebrate the theme. Edwin Mallett, for example, wrote his verses ending: 'And read their doom in Chloe's eyes', which caused Clara to blush at the first reading, and to laugh at the second, saying that it was just like him to call her Chloe when her name was Clara. Ridiculous young man! But when, between ten and eleven on a rainy morning, Edwin Mallett laid his life at her feet she ran out of the room and hid herself in her bedroom, and Timothy below could not get on with his work all that morning on account of her sobs.

'Which is the result of enjoying yourself,' said Mrs Durrant severely, surveying the dance programme all scored with the same initials, or rather they were different ones this time – R. B. instead of E. M.; Richard Bonamy it was now, the young man with the Wellington nose.

'But I could never marry a man with a nose like that,' said Clara.

'Nonsense,' said Mrs Durrant.

'But I am too severe,' she thought to herself. For Clara, losing all vivacity, tore up her dance programme and threw it in the fender.

Such were the very serious consequences of the invention of paper flowers to swim in bowls.

'Please,' said Julia Eliot, taking up her position by the curtain almost opposite the door, 'don't introduce me. I like to look on. The amusing thing,' she went on, addressing Mr Salvin, who, owing to his lameness, was accommodated with a chair, 'the amusing thing about a party is to watch the people – coming and going, coming and going.'

'Last time we met,' said Mr Salvin, 'was at the Farquhars. Poor lady! She has much to put up with.'

'Doesn't she look charming?' exclaimed Miss Eliot, as Clara Durrant passed them.

'And which of them . . . ?' asked Mr Salvin, dropping his voice and speaking in quizzical tones.

'There are so many . . . ' Miss Eliot replied. Three young men stood at the doorway looking about for their hostess.

'You don't remember Elizabeth as I do,' said Mr Salvin, 'dancing Highland reels at Banchorie. Clara lacks her mother's spirit. Clara is a little pale.'

'What different people one sees here!' said Miss Eliot.

'Happily we are not governed by the evening papers,' said Mr Salvin.

'I never read them,' said Miss Eliot. 'I know nothing about politics,' she added.

'The piano is in tune,' said Clara, passing them, 'but we may have to ask someone to move it for us.'

'Are they going to dance?' asked Mr Salvin.

'Nobody shall disturb you,' said Mrs Durrant peremptorily as she passed.

'Julia Eliot. It *is* Julia Eliot!' said old Lady Hibbert, holding out both her hands. 'And Mr Salvin. What is going to happen to us, Mr Salvin? With all my experience of English politics . . . My dear, I was thinking of your father last night – one of my oldest friends, Mr Salvin. Never tell me that girls of ten are incapable of love! I had all Shakespeare by heart before I was in my teens, Mr Salvin!'

'You don't say so,' said Mr Salvin.

'But I do,' said Lady Hibbert.

'Oh, Mr Salvin, I'm so sorry . . .'

'I will remove myself if you'll kindly lend me a hand,' said Mr Salvin.

'You shall sit by my mother,' said Clara. 'Everybody seems to come in here . . . Mr Calthorp, let me introduce you to Miss Edwards.'

'Are you going away for Christmas?' said Mr Calthorp.

'If my brother gets his leave,' said Miss Edwards.

'What regiment is he in?' said Mr Calthorp.

'The Twentieth Hussars,' said Miss Edwards.

'Perhaps he knows my brother?' said Mr Calthorp.

'I am afraid I did not catch your name,' said Miss Edwards.

'Calthorp,' said Mr Calthorp.

'But what proof was there that the marriage service was actually performed?' said Mr Crosby.

'There is no reason to doubt that Charles James Fox . . . ' Mr Burley began; but here Mrs Stretton told him that she knew his sister well; had stayed with her not six weeks ago; and thought the house charming, but bleak in winter.

'Going about as girls do nowadays – ' said Mrs Forster.

Mr Bowley looked round him, and catching sight of Rose Shaw moved towards her, threw out his hands, and exclaimed: 'Well!'

'Nothing!' she replied. 'Nothing at all – though I left them alone the entire afternoon on purpose.'

'Dear me, dear me,' said Mr Bowley. 'I will ask Jimmy to breakfast.'

'But who could resist her?' cried Rose Shaw. 'Dearest Clara – I know we mustn't try to stop you . . .'

'You and Mr Bowley are talking dreadful gossip, I know,' said Clara.

'Life is wicked – life is detestable!' cried Rose Shaw.

'There's not much to be said for this sort of thing, is there?' said Timothy Durrant to Jacob.

'Women like it.'

'Like what?' said Charlotte Wilding, coming up to them.

'Where have you come from?' said Timothy. 'Dining somewhere, I suppose.'

'I don't see why not,' said Charlotte.

'People must go downstairs,' said Clara, passing. 'Take Charlotte, Timothy. How d'you do, Mr Flanders.'

'How d'you do, Mr Flanders,' said Julia Eliot, holding out her hand. 'What's been happening to you?'

> 'Who is Silvia? what is she?
>   That all our swains commend her?'

sang Elsbeth Siddons.

Everyone stood where they were, or sat down if a chair was empty.

'Ah,' sighed Clara, who stood beside Jacob, halfway through.

> 'Then to Silvia let us sing,
>   That Silvia is excelling;
> She excels each mortal thing
>   Upon the dull earth dwelling.
> To her let us garlands bring,'

sang Elsbeth Siddons.

'Ah!' Clara exclaimed out loud, and clapped her gloved hands; and Jacob clapped his bare ones; and then she moved forward and directed people to come in from the doorway.

'You are living in London?' asked Miss Julia Eliot.

'Yes,' said Jacob.

'In rooms?'

'Yes.'

'There is Mr Clutterbuck. You always see Mr Clutterbuck here. He is not very happy at home, I am afraid. They say that Mrs Clutterbuck . . .' she dropped her voice. 'That's why he stays with the Durrants. Were you there when they acted Mr Wortley's play? Oh, no, of course not – at the last moment, did you hear – you had to go to join your mother, I remember, at Harrogate – At the last moment, as I was saying, just as everything was ready, the clothes finished and everything – Now Elsbeth is going to sing again. Clara is playing her accompaniment or turning over for Mr Carter, I think. No, Mr Carter is playing by himself – This is *Bach*,' she whispered, as Mr Carter played the first bars.

'Are you fond of music?' said Mrs Durrant.

'Yes. I like hearing it,' said Jacob. 'I know nothing about it.'

'Very few people do that,' said Mrs Durrant. 'I dare say you were never taught. Why is that, Sir Jasper? – Sir Jasper Bigham – Mr Flanders. Why is nobody taught anything that they ought to know, Sir Jasper?' She left them standing against the wall.

Neither of the gentlemen said anything for three minutes, though Jacob shifted perhaps five inches to the left, and then as many to the right. Then Jacob grunted, and suddenly crossed the room.

'Will you come and have something to eat?' he said to Clara Durrant.

'Yes, an ice. Quickly. Now,' she said.

Downstairs they went.

But halfway down they met Mr and Mrs Gresham, Herbert Turner, Sylvia Rashleigh, and a friend, whom they had dared to bring, from America, 'knowing that Mrs Durrant – wishing to show Mr Pilcher. Mr Pilcher from New York – This is Miss Durrant.'

'Whom I have heard so much of,' said Mr Pilcher, bowing low.

So Clara left him.

Chapter Eight

About half-past nine Jacob left the house, his door slamming, other doors slamming, buying his paper, mounting his omnibus, or, weather permitting, walking his road as other people do. Head bent down, a desk, a telephone, books bound in green leather, electric light . . . 'Fresh coals, sir?' . . . 'Your tea, sir.' . . . Talk about football, the Hotspurs, the Harlequins; six-thirty *Star* brought in by the office boy; the rooks of Gray's Inn passing overhead; branches in the fog thin and brittle; and through the roar of traffic now and again a voice shouting: 'Verdict – verdict – winner – winner,' while letters accumulate in a basket, Jacob signs them, and each evening finds him, as he takes his coat down, with some muscle of the brain new stretched.

Then, sometimes a game of chess; or pictures in Bond Street; or a long way home to take the air with Bonamy on his arm, meditatively marching, head thrown back, the world a spectacle, the early moon above the steeples coming in for praise, the seagulls flying high, Nelson on his column survey-ing the horizon, and the world our ship.

Meanwhile, poor Betty Flanders's letter, having caught the second post, lay on the hall table – poor Betty Flanders writing her son's name, Jacob Alan Flanders, Esq., as mothers do, and the ink pale, profuse, suggesting how mothers down at Scarborough scribble over the fire with their feet on the fender, when tea's cleared away, and can never, never say, whatever it may be – probably this – Don't go with bad women, do be a good boy; wear your thick shirts; and come back, come back, come back to me.

But she said nothing of the kind. 'Do you remember old Miss Wargrave, who used to be so kind when you had the whooping-cough?' she wrote; 'she's dead at last, poor thing. They would like it if you wrote. Ellen came over and we spent a nice day shopping. Old Mouse gets very stiff, and we have to walk him up the smallest hill. Rebecca, at last, after I don't know how long, went into Mr Adamson's. Three teeth, he says, must come out. Such mild weather for the time of year, the little buds actually on the pear trees. And Mrs Jarvis tells me – ' Mrs Flanders liked Mrs Jarvis, always said of her that she was too good for such a quiet place, and, though she never listened to her discontent and told her at the end of it (looking up, sucking her thread, or taking off her spectacles) that a little peat wrapped round the iris roots keeps them from the frost, and Parrot's great white sale is Tuesday next, 'do remember' – Mrs Flanders knew precisely how Mrs Jarvis felt; and how interesting her letters were, about Mrs Jarvis, could one read them year in, year out – the unpublished works of women, written by the fireside in pale profusion, dried by the flame, for the blotting-paper's worn to holes and the nib cleft and clotted. Then Captain Barfoot. Him she called 'the Captain', spoke of frankly, yet never without reserve. The Captain was enquiring for her about Garfit's acre; advised chickens; could promise profit; or had the sciatica; or Mrs Barfoot had been indoors for weeks; or the Captain says things look bad, politics that is, for as Jacob knew, the Captain would sometimes talk, as the evening waned, about Ireland or India; and then Mrs Flanders would fall musing about Morty, her brother, lost all these years – had the natives got him, was his ship sunk – would the Admiralty tell her? – the Captain knocking his pipe out, as Jacob knew, rising to go, stiffly stretching to pick up Mrs Flanders's wool which had rolled beneath the chair. Talk of the chicken farm came back and back, the women, even at fifty, impulsive at heart, sketching on the cloudy future flocks of Leghorns, Cochin Chinas, Orpingtons; like Jacob in the blur of her outline; but powerful as he was; fresh and vigorous, running about the house, scolding Rebecca.

The letter lay upon the hall table; Florinda coming in that night took it up with her, put it on the table as she kissed Jacob, and Jacob seeing the hand, left it there under the lamp, between the biscuit-tin and the tobacco-box. They shut the bedroom door behind them.

The sitting-room neither knew nor cared. The door was shut; and to suppose that wood, when it creaks, transmits anything save that rats are busy and wood dry is childish. These old houses are only brick and wood, soaked in human sweat, grained with human dirt. But if the pale blue envelope lying by the biscuit-box had the feelings of a mother, the heart was torn by the little creak, the sudden stir. Behind the door was the obscene thing, the alarming presence, and terror would come over her as at death or the birth of a child. Better, perhaps, burst in and face it than sit in the antechamber listening to the little creak, the sudden stir, for her heart was swollen, and pain threaded it. My son, my son – such would be her cry, uttered to hide her vision of him stretched with Florinda, inexcusable, irrational, in a woman with three children living at Scarborough. And the fault lay with Florinda. Indeed, when the door opened and the couple came out, Mrs Flanders would have flounced upon her – only it was Jacob who came first, in his dressing-gown, amiable, authoritative, beautifully healthy, like a baby after an airing, with an eye clear as running water. Florinda followed, lazily stretching; yawning a little; arranging her hair at the looking-glass – while Jacob read his mother's letter.

Let us consider letters – how they come at breakfast, and at night, with their yellow stamps and their green stamps, immortalised by the postmark – for to see one's own envelope on another's table is to realise how soon deeds sever and become alien. Then at last the power of the mind to quit the body is manifest, and perhaps we fear or hate or wish annihilated this phantom of ourselves, lying on the table. Still, there are letters that merely say how dinner's at seven; others ordering coal; making appointments. The hand in them is scarcely perceptible, let alone the voice or the scowl. Ah, but when the post knocks and the letter comes always the miracle seems repeated – speech attempted. Venerable are letters, infinitely brave, forlorn, and lost.

   Life would split asunder without them. 'Come to tea, come to dinner, what's the truth of the story? have you heard the news? life in the capital is gay; the Russian dancers . . . ' These are our stays and props. These lace our days together and make of life a perfect globe. And yet, and yet . . . when we go to dinner, when pressing fingertips we hope to meet somewhere soon, a doubt insinuates itself: is this the way to spend our days? the rare, the limited, so soon dealt out to us – drinking tea? dining out? And the notes accumulate. And the telephones ring. And everywhere we go wires and tubes surround us to carry the voices that try to penetrate before the last card is dealt and the days are over. 'Try to penetrate', for as we lift the cup, shake the hand, express the hope, something whispers, Is this all? Can I never know, share, be certain? Am I doomed all my days to write letters, send voices, which fall upon the tea-table, fade upon the passage, making appointments, while life dwindles, to come and dine? Yet letters are venerable; and the telephone valiant, for the journey is a lonely one, and if bound together by notes and telephones we went in company, perhaps – who knows? – we might talk by the way.

Well, people have tried. Byron wrote letters. So did Cowper. For centuries the writing-desk has contained sheets fit precisely for the communications of friends. Masters of language, poets of long ages, have turned from the sheet that endures to the sheet that perishes, pushing aside the tea-tray, drawing close to the fire (for letters are written when the dark presses round a bright red cave), and addressed themselves to the task of reaching, touching, penetrating the individual heart. Were it possible! But words have been used too often; touched and turned, and left exposed to the dust of the street. The words we seek hang close to the tree. We come at dawn and find them sweet beneath the leaf.

Mrs Flanders wrote letters; Mrs Jarvis wrote them; Mrs Durrant too; Mother Stuart actually scented her pages, thereby adding a flavour which the English language fails to provide; Jacob had written in his day long letters about art, morality and politics to young men at college. Clara Durrant's letters were those of a child. Florinda – the impediment between Florinda and her pen was something impassable. Fancy a butterfly, gnat, or other winged insect, attached to a twig which, clogged with mud, it rolls across a page. Her spelling was abominable. Her sentiments infantile. And for some reason when she wrote she declared her belief in God. Then there were crosses – tear stains; and the hand itself rambling and redeemed only by the fact – which always did redeem Florinda – by the fact that she cared. Yes, whether it was for chocolate creams, hot baths, the shape of her face in the looking-glass, Florinda could no more pretend a feeling than swallow whisky. Incontinent was her rejection. Great men are truthful, and these little prostitutes, staring in the fire, taking out a powder-puff, decorating lips at an inch of looking-glass, have (so Jacob thought) an inviolable fidelity.

Then he saw her turning up Greek Street upon another man's arm.

The light from the arc lamp drenched him from head to toe. He stood for a minute motionless beneath it. Shadows chequered the street. Other figures, single and together, poured out, wavered across, and obliterated Florinda and the man.

The light drenched Jacob from head to toe. You could see the pattern on his trousers; the old thorns on his stick; his shoe-laces; bare hands; and face.

It was as if a stone were ground to dust; as if white sparks flew from a livid whetstone, which was his spine; as if the switchback railway, having swooped to the depths, fell, fell, fell. This was in his face.

Whether we know what was in his mind is another question. Granted ten years' seniority and a difference of sex, fear of him comes first; this is swallowed up by a desire to help – overwhelming sense, reason, and the time of night; anger would follow close on that – with Florinda, with destiny; and then up would bubble an irresponsible optimism. 'Surely there's enough light in the street at this moment to drown all our cares in gold!' Ah, what's the use of saying it? Even while you speak and look over your shoulder towards Shaftesbury Avenue, destiny is chipping a dent in him. He has turned to go. As for following him back to his rooms, no – that we won't do.

Yet that, of course, is precisely what one does. He let himself in and shut the door, though it was only striking ten on one of the city clocks. No one can go to bed at ten. Nobody was thinking of going to bed. It was January and dismal, but Mrs Wagg stood on her doorstep, as if expecting something to happen. A barrel-organ played like an obscene nightingale beneath wet leaves. Children ran across the road. Here and there one could see brown panelling inside the hall door . . . The march that the mind keeps beneath the windows of others is queer enough. Now distracted by brown panelling; now by a fern in a pot; here improvising a few phrases to dance with the barrel-organ; again snatching a detached gaiety from a drunken man; then altogether absorbed by words the poor shout across the street at each other (so outright, so lusty) – yet all the while having for centre, for magnet, a young man alone in his room.

'Life is wicked – life is detestable,' cried Rose Shaw.

The strange thing about life is that though the nature of it must have been apparent to everyone for hundreds of years, no one has left any adequate account of it. The streets of London have their map; but our passions are uncharted. What are you going to meet if you turn this corner?

'Holborn straight ahead of you,' says the policeman. Ah, but where are you going if instead of brushing past the old man with the white beard, the silver medal, and the cheap violin, you let him go on with his story, which ends in an invitation to step somewhere, to his room, presumably, off Queen's Square, and there he shows you a collection of birds' eggs and a letter from the Prince of Wales's secretary, and this (skipping the inter-mediate stages) brings you one winter's day to the Essex coast, where the little boat makes off to the ship, and the ship sails and you behold on the skyline the Azores; and the flamingos rise; and there you sit on the verge of the marsh drinking rum-punch, an outcast from civilisation, for you have committed a crime, are infected with yellow fever as likely as not, and – fill in the sketch as you like. As frequent as street corners in Holborn are these chasms in the continuity of our ways. Yet we keep straight on.

Rose Shaw, talking in rather an emotional manner to Mr Bowley at Mrs Durrant's evening party a few nights back, said that life was wicked because a man called Jimmy refused to marry a woman called (if memory serves) Helen Aitken.

Both were beautiful. Both were inanimate. The oval tea-table invariably separated them, and the plate of biscuits was all he ever gave her. He bowed; she inclined her head. They danced. He danced divinely. They sat in the alcove; never a word was said. Her pillow was wet with tears. Kind Mr Bowley and dear Rose Shaw marvelled and deplored. Bowley had rooms in

Albany. Rose was reborn every evening precisely as the clock struck eight. All four were civilisation's triumphs, and if you persist that a command of the English language is part of our inheritance, one can only reply that beauty is almost always dumb. Male beauty in association with female beauty breeds in the onlooker a sense of fear. Often have I seen them – Helen and Jimmy – and likened them to ships adrift, and feared for my own little craft. Or again, have you ever watched fine collie dogs couchant at twenty yards' distance? As she passed him his cup there was that quiver in her flanks. Bowley saw what was up – asked Jimmy to breakfast. Helen must have confided in Rose. For my own part, I find it exceedingly difficult to interpret songs without words. And now Jimmy feeds crows in Flanders and Helen visits hospitals. Oh, life is damnable, life is wicked, as Rose Shaw said.

The lamps of London uphold the dark as upon the points of burning bayonets. The yellow canopy sinks and swells over the great four-poster. Passengers in the mail-coaches running into London in the eighteenth century looked through leafless branches and saw it flaring beneath them. The light burns behind yellow blinds and pink blinds, and above fanlights, and down in basement windows. The street market in Soho is fierce with light. Raw meat, china mugs and silk stockings blaze in it. Raw voices wrap themselves round the flaring gas-jets. Arms akimbo, they stand on the pavement bawling – Messrs Kettle and Wilkinson; their wives sit in the shop, furs wrapped round their necks, arms folded, eyes contemptuous. Such faces as one sees. The little man fingering the meat must have squatted before the fire in innumerable lodging-houses, and heard and seen and known so much that it seems to utter itself even volubly from dark eyes, loose lips, as he fingers the meat silently, his face sad as a poet's, and never a song sung. Shawled women carry babies with purple eyelids; boys stand at street corners; girls look across the road – rude illustrations, pictures in a book whose pages we turn over and over as if we should at last find what we look for. Every face, every shop, bedroom window, public-house and dark square is a picture feverishly turned – in search of what? It is the same with books. What do we seek through millions of pages? Still hopefully turning the pages – oh, here is Jacob's room.

He sat at the table reading the *Globe*. The pinkish sheet was spread flat before him. He propped his face in his hand, so that the skin of his cheek was wrinkled in deep folds. Terribly severe he looked, set and defiant. (What people go through in half an hour! But nothing could save him. These events are features of our landscape. A foreigner coming to London could scarcely miss seeing St Paul's.) He judged life. These pinkish and greenish newspapers are thin sheets of gelatine pressed nightly over the brain and heart of the world. They take the impression of the whole. Jacob cast his eye over it. A strike, a murder, football, bodies found; vociferation from all parts of England simultaneously. How miserable it is that the *Globe* newspaper offers nothing better to Jacob Flanders! When a child begins to read history one marvels, sorrowfully, to hear him spell out in his new voice the ancient words.

The Prime Minister's speech was reported in something over five columns. Feeling in his pocket, Jacob took out a pipe and proceeded to fill it. Five minutes, ten minutes, fifteen minutes passed. Jacob took the paper over to the fire. The Prime Minister proposed a measure for giving Home Rule to Ireland. Jacob knocked out his pipe. He was certainly thinking about Home Rule in Ireland – a very difficult matter. A very cold night.

The snow, which had been falling all night, lay at three o'clock in the afternoon over the fields and the hill. Clumps of withered grass stood out upon the hill-top; the furze bushes were black, and now and then a black shiver crossed the snow as the wind drove flurries of frozen particles before it. The sound was that of a broom sweeping – sweeping.

The stream crept along by the road unseen by anyone. Sticks and leaves caught in the frozen grass. The sky was sullen grey and the trees of black iron. Uncompromising was the severity of the country. At four o'clock the snow was again falling. The day had gone out.

A window tinged yellow about two feet across alone combated the white fields and the black trees . . . At six o'clock a man's figure carrying a lantern crossed the field . . . A raft of twig stayed upon a stone suddenly detached itself and floated towards the culvert . . . A load of snow slipped and fell from a fir branch . . . Later there was a mournful cry . . . A motor car came along the road shoving the dark before it . . . The dark shut down behind it . . .

Spaces of complete immobility separated each of these movements. The land seemed to lie dead . . . Then the old shepherd returned stiffly across the field. Stiffly and painfully the frozen earth was trodden under and gave beneath pressure like a treadmill. The worn voices of clocks repeated the fact of the hour all night long.

Jacob, too, heard them, and raked out the fire. He rose. He stretched himself. He went to bed.

Chapter Nine

The Countess of Rocksbier sat at the head of the table alone with Jacob. Fed upon champagne and spices for at least two centuries (four, if you count the female line), the Countess Lucy looked well fed. A discriminating nose she had for scents, prolonged, as if in quest of them; her underlip protruded a narrow red shelf; her eyes were small, with sandy tufts for eyebrows, and her jowl was heavy. Behind her (the window looked on Grosvenor Square) stood Moll Pratt on the pavement, offering violets for sale; and Mrs Hilda Thomas, lifting her skirts, preparing to cross the road. One was from Walworth; the other from Putney. Both wore black stockings, but Mrs Thomas was coiled in furs. The comparison was much in Lady Rocksbier's favour. Moll had more humour, but was violent; stupid too. Hilda Thomas was mealy-mouthed, all her silver frames aslant; egg-cups in the drawing-room; and the windows shrouded. Lady Rocksbier, whatever the deficiencies of her profile, had been a great rider to hounds. She used her knife with authority, tore her chicken bones, asking Jacob's pardon, with her own hands.

'Who is that driving by?' she asked Boxall, the butler.

'Lady Firtlemere's carriage, my lady,' which reminded her to send a card to ask after his lordship's health. A rude old lady, Jacob thought. The wine was excellent. She called herself 'an old woman' – 'so kind to lunch with an old woman' – which flattered him. She talked of Joseph Chamberlain, whom she had known. She said that Jacob must come and meet – one of our celebrities. And the Lady Alice came in with three dogs on a leash, and Jackie, who ran to kiss his grandmother, while Boxall brought in a telegram, and Jacob was given a good cigar.

A few moments before a horse jumps it slows, sidles, gathers itself together, goes up like a monster wave, and pitches down on the farther side. Hedges and sky swoop in a semicircle. Then as if your own body ran into the horse's body and it was your own forelegs grown with his that sprang, rushing through the air you go, the ground resilient, bodies a mass of muscles, yet you have command too, upright stillness, eyes accurately judging. Then the curves cease, changing to downright hammer strokes, which jar; and you draw up with a jolt; sitting back a little, sparkling, tingling, glazed with ice over pounding arteries, gasping: 'Ah! ho! Hah!' the steam going up from the horses as they jostle together at the crossroads, where the signpost is, and the woman in the apron stands and stares at the doorway. The man raises himself from the cabbages to stare too.

So Jacob galloped over the fields of Essex, flopped in the mud, lost the hunt, and rode by himself eating sandwiches, looking over the hedges, noticing the colours as if new scraped, cursing his luck.

He had tea at the inn; and there they all were, slapping, stamping, saying, 'After you,' clipped, curt, jocose, red as the wattles of turkeys, using free speech until Mrs Horsefield and her friend Miss Dudding appeared at the doorway with their skirts hitched up, and hair looping down. Then Tom Dudding rapped at the window with his whip. A motor car throbbed in the courtyard. Gentlemen, feeling for matches, moved out, and Jacob went into the bar with Brandy Jones to smoke with the rustics. There was old Jevons with one eye gone, and his clothes the colour of mud, his bag over his back, and his brains laid feet down in earth among the violet roots and the nettle roots; Mary Sanders with her box of wood; and Tom sent for beer, the half-witted son of the sexton – all this within thirty miles of London.

Mrs Papworth, of Endell Street, Covent Garden, did for Mr Bonamy in New Square, Lincoln's Inn, and as she washed up the dinner things in the scullery she heard the young gentlemen talking in the room next door. Mr Sanders was there again; Flanders she meant; and where an inquisitive old woman gets a name wrong, what chance is there that she will faithfully report an argument? As she held the plates under water and then dealt them on the pile beneath the hissing gas, she listened: heard Sanders speaking in a loud rather overbearing tone of voice: 'good', he said, and 'absolute' and 'justice' and 'punishment' and 'the will of the majority'. Then her gentleman piped up; she backed him for argument against Sanders. Yet Sanders was a fine young fellow (here all the scraps went swirling round the sink, scoured after by her purple, almost nailless hands). 'Women' – she thought, and wondered what Sanders and her gentleman did in *that* line, one eyelid sinking perceptibly as she mused, for she was the mother of nine – three still-born and one deaf and dumb from birth. Putting the plates in the rack she heard once more Sanders at it again ('He don't give Bonamy a chance,' she thought). 'Objective some-thing,' said Bonamy; and 'common ground' and something else – all very long words, she noted. 'Book learning does it,' she thought to herself, and, as she thrust her arms into her jacket, heard something – might be the little table by the fire – fall; and then stamp, stamp, stamp – as if they were having at each other – round the room, making the plates dance.

'Tomorrow's breakfast, sir,' she said, opening the door; and there were Sanders and Bonamy like two bulls of Bashan driving each other up and down, making such a racket, and all them chairs in the way. They never noticed her. She felt motherly towards them. 'Your breakfast, sir,' she said, as they came near. And Bonamy, all his hair tousled and his tie flying, broke off, and pushed Sanders into the armchair, and said Mr Sanders had smashed the coffee-pot and he was teaching Mr Sanders –

Sure enough, the coffee-pot lay broken on the hearthrug.

'Any day this week except Thursday,' wrote Miss Perry, and this was not the first invitation by any means. Were all Miss Perry's weeks blank with the exception of Thursday, and was her only desire to see her old friend's son? Time is issued to spinster ladies of wealth in long white ribbons. These they wind round and round, round and round, assisted by five female servants, a butler, a fine Mexican parrot, regular meals, Mudie's library, and friends dropping in. A little hurt she was already that Jacob had not called.

'Your mother,' she said, 'is one of my oldest friends.'

Miss Rosseter, who was sitting by the fire, holding the *Spectator* between her cheek and the blaze, refused to have a fire-screen, but finally accepted one. The weather was then discussed, for in deference to Parkes, who was opening little tables, graver matters were postponed. Miss Rosseter drew Jacob's attention to the beauty of the cabinet.

'So wonderfully clever in picking things up,' she said. Miss Perry had found it in Yorkshire. The North of England was discussed. When Jacob spoke they both listened. Miss Perry was bethinking her of something suitable and manly to say when the door opened and Mr Benson was announced. Now there were four people sitting in that room. Miss Perry aged 66; Miss Rosseter 42; Mr Benson 38; and Jacob 25.

'My old friend looks as well as ever,' said Mr Benson, tapping the bars of the parrot's cage; Miss Rosseter simultaneously praised the tea; Jacob handed the wrong plates; and Miss Perry signified her desire to approach more closely. 'Your brothers,' she began vaguely.

'Archer and John,' Jacob supplied her. Then to her pleasure she recovered Rebecca's name; and how one day 'when you were all little boys, playing in the drawing-room – '

'But Miss Perry has the kettle-holder,' said Miss Rosseter, and indeed Miss Perry was clasping it to her breast. (Had she, then, loved Jacob's father?)

'So clever' – 'not so good as usual' – 'I thought it most unfair,' said Mr Benson and Miss Rosseter, discussing the Saturday *Westminster*. Did they not compete regularly for prizes? Had not Mr Benson three times won a guinea, and Miss Rosseter once ten and sixpence? Of course Everard Benson had a weak heart, but still, to win prizes, remember parrots, toady Miss Perry, despise Miss Rosseter, give tea-parties in his rooms (which were in the style of Whistler, with pretty books on tables), all this, so Jacob felt without knowing him, made him a contemptible ass. As for Miss Rosseter, she had nursed cancer, and now painted watercolours.

'Running away so soon?' said Miss Perry vaguely. 'At home every afternoon, if you've nothing better to do – except Thursdays.'

'I've never known you desert your old ladies once,' Miss Rosseter was saying, and Mr Benson was stooping over the parrot's cage, and Miss Perry was moving towards the bell . . .

The fire burnt clear between two pillars of greenish marble, and on the mantelpiece there was a green clock guarded by Britannia leaning on her spear. As for pictures – a maiden in a large hat offered roses over the garden gate to a gentleman in eighteenth-century costume. A mastiff lay extended against a battered door. The lower panes of the windows were of ground glass, and the curtains, accurately looped, were of plush and green too.

Laurette and Jacob sat with their toes in the fender side by side, in two large chairs covered in green plush. Laurette's skirts were short, her legs long, thin, and transparently covered. Her fingers stroked her ankles.

'It's not exactly that I don't understand them,' she was saying thoughtfully. 'I must go and try again.'

'What time will you be there?' said Jacob.

She shrugged her shoulders.

'Tomorrow?'

No, not tomorrow.

'This weather makes me long for the country,' she said, looking over her shoulder at the back view of tall houses through the window.

'I wish you'd been with me on Saturday,' said Jacob.

'I used to ride,' she said. She got up gracefully, calmly. Jacob got up. She smiled at him. As she shut the door he put so many shillings on the mantelpiece.

Altogether a most reasonable conversation; a most respectable room; an intelligent girl. Only Madame herself seeing Jacob out had about her that leer, that lewdness, that quake of the surface (visible in the eyes chiefly), which threatens to spill the whole bag of ordure, with difficulty held together, over the pavement. In short, something was wrong.

Not so very long ago the workmen had gilt the final 'y' in Lord Macaulay's name, and the names stretched in unbroken file round the dome of the British Museum. At a considerable depth beneath, many hundreds of the living sat at the spokes of a cart-wheel copying from printed books into manuscript books; now and then rising to consult the catalogue; regaining their places stealthily, while from time to time a silent man replenished their compartments.

There was a little catastrophe. Miss Marchmont's pile overbalanced and fell into Jacob's compartment. Such things happened to Miss Marchmont. What was she seeking through millions of pages, in her old plush dress, and her wig of claret-coloured hair, with her gems and her chilblains? Sometimes one thing, sometimes another, to confirm her philosophy that colour is sound – or, perhaps, it has something to do with music. She could never quite say, though it was not for lack of trying. And she could not ask you back to her room, for it was 'not very clean, I'm afraid', so she must catch you in the passage, or take a chair in Hyde Park to explain her philosophy. The rhythm of the soul depends on it – ('how rude the little boys are!' she would say), and Mr Asquith's Irish policy, and Shakespeare comes in, 'and Queen Alexandra most graciously once acknowledged a copy of my pamphlet,' she would say, waving the little boys magnificently away. But she needs funds to publish her book, for 'publishers are capitalists – publishers are cowards'. And so, digging her elbow into her pile of books it fell over.

Jacob remained quite unmoved.

But Fraser, the atheist, on the other side, detesting plush, more than once accosted with leaflets, shifted irritably. He abhorred vagueness – the Christian religion, for example, and old Dean Parker's pronouncements. Dean Parker wrote books and Fraser utterly destroyed them by force of logic and left his children unbaptised – his wife did it secretly in the washing basin – but Fraser ignored her, and went on supporting blasphemers, distributing leaflets, getting up his facts in the British Museum, always in the same check suit and fiery tie, but pale, spotted, irritable. Indeed, what a work – to destroy religion!

Jacob transcribed a whole passage from Marlowe.

Miss Julia Hedge, the feminist, waited for her books. They did not come. She wetted her pen. She looked about her. Her eye was caught by the final letters in Lord Macaulay's name. And she read them all round the dome – the names of great men which remind us – 'Oh damn,' said Julia Hedge, 'why didn't they leave room for an Eliot or a Brontë?'

Unfortunate Julia! wetting her pen in bitterness, and leaving her shoe-laces untied. When her books came she applied herself to her gigantic labours, but perceived through one of the nerves of her exasperated sensibility how composedly, unconcernedly and with every consideration the male readers applied themselves to theirs. That young man for example. What had he got to do except copy out poetry? And she must study statistics. There are more women than men. Yes; but if you let women work as men work, they'll die off much quicker. They'll become extinct. That was her argument. Death and gall and bitter dust were on her pen-tip; and as the afternoon wore on, red had worked into her cheekbones and a light was in her eyes.

But what brought Jacob Flanders to read Marlowe in the British Museum?

Youth, youth – something savage – something pedantic. For example, there is Mr Masefield, there is Mr Bennett. Stuff them into the flame of Marlowe and burn them to cinders. Let not a shred remain. Don't palter with the second rate. Detest your own age. Build a better one. And to set that on foot read incredibly dull essays upon Marlowe to your friends. For which purpose one most collate editions in the British Museum. One must do the thing oneself. Useless to trust to the Victorians, who disembowel, or to the living, who are mere publicists. The flesh and blood of the future depends entirely upon six young men. And as Jacob was one of them, no doubt he looked a little regal and pompous as he turned his page, and Julia Hedge disliked him naturally enough.

But then a pudding-faced man pushed a note towards Jacob, and Jacob, leaning back in his chair, began an uneasy murmured conversation, and they went off together (Julia Hedge watched them), and laughed aloud (she thought) directly they were in the hall.

Nobody laughed in the reading-room. There were shiftings, murmurings, apologetic sneezes and sudden unashamed devastating coughs. The lesson hour was almost over. Ushers were collecting exercises. Lazy children wanted to stretch. Good ones scribbled assiduously – ah, another day over and so little done! And now and then was to be heard from the whole collection of human beings a heavy sigh, after which the humiliating old man would cough shamelessly, and Miss Marchmont hinnied like a horse.

Jacob came back only in time to return his books.

The books were now replaced. A few letters of the alphabet were sprinkled round the dome. Closely stood together in a ring round the dome were Plato, Aristotle, Sophocles and Shakespeare; the literature of Rome, Greece, China, India, Persia. One leaf of poetry was pressed flat against another leaf, one burnished letter laid smooth against another in a density of meaning, a conglomeration of loveliness.

'One does want one's tea,' said Miss Marchmont, reclaiming her shabby umbrella.

Miss Marchmont wanted her tea, but could never resist a last look at the Elgin Marbles. She looked at them sideways, waving her hand and muttering a word or two of salutation which made Jacob and the other man turn round. She smiled at them amiably. It all came into her philosophy – that colour is sound, or perhaps it has something to do with music. And having done her service, she hobbled off to tea. It was closing time. The public collected in the hall to receive their umbrellas.

For the most part the students wait their turn very patiently. To stand and wait while someone examines white discs is soothing. The umbrella will certainly be found. But the fact leads you on all day through Macaulay, Hobbes, Gibbon; through octavos, quartos, folios; sinks deeper and deeper through ivory pages and morocco bindings into this density of thought, this conglomeration of knowledge.

Jacob's walking-stick was like all the others; they had muddled the pigeon-holes perhaps.

There is in the British Museum an enormous mind. Consider that Plato is there cheek by jowl with Aristotle; and Shakespeare with Marlowe. This great mind is hoarded beyond the power of any single mind to possess it. Nevertheless (as they take so long finding one's walking-stick) one can't help thinking how one might come with a notebook, sit at a desk, and read it all through. A learned man is the most venerable of all – a man like Huxtable of Trinity, who writes all his letters in Greek, they say, and could have kept his end up with Bentley. And then there is science, pictures, architecture – an enormous mind.

They pushed the walking-stick across the counter. Jacob stood beneath the porch of the British Museum. It was raining. Great Russell Street was glazed and shining – here yellow, here, outside the chemist's, red and pale blue. People scuttled quickly close to the wall; carriages rattled rather helter-skelter down the streets. Well, but a little rain hurts nobody. Jacob walked off much as if he had been in the country; and late that night there he was sitting at his table with his pipe and his book.

The rain poured down. The British Museum stood in one solid immense mound, very pale, very sleek in the rain, not a quarter of a mile from him. The vast mind was sheeted with stone; and each compartment in the depths of it was safe and dry. The night-watchmen, flashing their lanterns over the backs of Plato and Shakespeare, saw that on the twenty-second of February neither flame, rat, nor burglar was going to violate these treasures – poor, highly respectable men, with wives and families at Kentish Town, do their best for twenty years to protect Plato and Shakespeare, and then are buried at Highgate.

Stone lies solid over the British Museum, as bone lies cool over the visions and heat of the brain. Only here the brain is Plato's brain and Shakespeare's; the brain has made pots and statues, great bulls and little jewels, and crossed the river of death this way and that incessantly, seeking some landing, now wrapping the body well for its long sleep; now laying a penny piece on the eyes; now turning the toes scrupulously to the East. Meanwhile, Plato continues his dialogue; in spite of the rain; in spite of the cab whistles; in spite of the woman in the mews behind Great Ormond Street who has come home drunk and cries all night long, 'Let me in! Let me in!'

In the street below Jacob's room voices were raised.

But he read on. For after all Plato continues imperturbably. And Hamlet utters his soliloquy. And there the Elgin Marbles lie, all night long, old Jones's lantern sometimes recalling Ulysses, or a horse's head; or sometimes a flash of gold, or a mummy's sunk yellow cheek. Plato and Shakespeare continue; and Jacob, who was reading the *Phaedrus*, heard people vociferating round the lamp-post, and the woman battering at the door and crying, 'Let me in!' as if a coal had dropped from the fire, or a fly, falling from the ceiling, had lain on its back, too weak to turn over.

The *Phaedrus* is very difficult. And so, when at length one reads straight ahead, falling into step, marching on, becoming (so it seems) momentarily part of this rolling, imperturbable energy, which has driven darkness before it since Plato walked the Acropolis, it is impossible to see to the fire.

The dialogue draws to its close. Plato's argument is done. Plato's argument is stowed away in Jacob's mind, and for five minutes Jacob's mind continues alone, onwards, into the darkness. Then, getting up, he parted the curtains, and saw, with astonishing clearness, how the Springetts opposite had gone to bed; how it rained; how the Jews and the foreign woman, at the end of the street, stood by the pillar-box, arguing.

Every time the door opened and fresh people came in, those already in the room shifted slightly; those who were standing looked over their shoulders; those who were sitting stopped in the middle of sentences. What with the light, the wine, the strumming of a guitar, something exciting happened each time the door opened. Who was coming in?

'That's Gibson.'

'The painter?'

'But go on with what you were saying.'

They were saying something that was far, far too intimate to be said outright. But the noise of the voices served like a clapper in little Mrs Withers's mind, scaring into the air blocks of small birds, and then they'd settle, and then she'd feel afraid, put one hand to her hair, bind both round her knees, and look up at Oliver Skelton nervously, and say: 'Promise, *promise*, you'll tell no one.' . . . so considerate he was, so tender. It was her husband's character that she discussed. He was cold, she said.

Down upon them came the splendid Magdalen, brown, warm, voluminous, scarcely brushing the grass with her sandalled feet. Her hair flew; pins seemed scarcely to attach the flying silks. An actress of course, a line of light perpetually beneath her. It was only 'My dear' that she said, but her voice went yodelling between Alpine passes. And down she tumbled on the floor, and sang, since there was nothing to be said, round ahs and ohs. Mangin, the poet, coming up to her, stood looking down at her, drawing at his pipe. The dancing began.

Grey-haired Mrs Keymer asked Dick Graves to tell her who Mangin was, and said that she had seen too much of this sort of thing in Paris (Magdalen had got upon his knees; now his pipe was in her mouth) to be shocked. 'Who is that?' she said, staying her glasses when they came to Jacob, for indeed he looked quiet, not indifferent, but like someone on a beach, watching.

'Oh, my dear, let me lean on you,' gasped Helen Askew, hopping on one foot, for the silver cord round her ankle had worked loose. Mrs Keymer turned and looked at the picture on the wall.

'Look at Jacob,' said Helen (they were binding his eyes for some game).

And Dick Graves, being a little drunk, very faithful, and very simple-minded, told her that he thought Jacob the greatest man he had ever known. And down they sat cross-legged upon cushions and talked about Jacob, and Helen's voice trembled, for they both seemed heroes to her, and the friendship between them so much more beautiful than women's friendships. Anthony Pollett now asked her to dance, and as she danced she looked at them, over her shoulder, standing at the table, drinking together.

The magnificent world – the live, sane, vigorous world . . . These words refer to the stretch of wood pavement between Hammersmith and Holborn in January between two and three in the morning. That was the ground beneath Jacob's feet. It was healthy and magnificent because one room, above a mews, somewhere near the river, contained fifty excited, talkative, friendly people. And then to stride over the pavement (there was scarcely a cab or policeman in sight) is of itself exhilarating. The long loop of Piccadilly, diamond-stitched, shows to best advantage when it is empty. A young man has nothing to fear. On the contrary, though he may not have said anything brilliant, he feels pretty confident he can hold his own. He was pleased to have met Mangin; he admired the young woman on the floor; he liked them all; he liked that sort of thing. In short, all the drums and trumpets were sounding. The street scavengers were the only people about at the moment. It is scarcely necessary to say how well disposed Jacob felt towards them; how it pleased him to let himself in with his latch-key at his own door; how he seemed to bring back with him into the empty room ten or eleven people whom he had not known when he set out; how he looked about for something to read, and found it, and never read it, and fell asleep.

Indeed, drums and trumpets is no phrase. Indeed, Piccadilly and Holborn, and the empty sitting-room and the sitting-room with fifty people in it are liable at any moment to blow music into the air. Women perhaps are more excitable than men. It is seldom that anyone says anything about it, and to see the hordes crossing Waterloo Bridge to catch the non-stop to Surbiton one might think that reason impelled them. No, no. It is the drums and trumpets. Only, should you turn aside into one of those little bays on Waterloo Bridge to think the matter over, it will probably seem to you all a muddle – all a mystery.

They cross the bridge incessantly. Sometimes in the midst of carts and omnibuses a lorry will appear with great forest trees chained to it. Then, perhaps, a mason's van with newly lettered tombstones recording how someone loved someone who is buried at Putney. Then the motor car in front jerks forward, and the tombstones pass too quick for you to read more. All the time the stream of people never ceases passing from the Surrey side to the Strand; from the Strand to the Surrey side. It seems as if the poor had gone raiding the town, and now trapesed back to their own quarters, like beetles scurrying to their holes, for that old woman fairly hobbles towards Waterloo, grasping a shiny bag, as if she had been out into the light and now made off with some scraped chicken bones to her hovel underground. On the other hand, though the wind is rough and blowing in their faces, those girls there, striding hand in hand, shouting out a song, seem to feel neither cold nor shame. They are hatless. They triumph.

The wind has blown up the waves. The river races beneath us, and the men standing on the barges have to lean all their weight on the tiller. A black tarpaulin is tied down over a swelling load of gold. Avalanches of coal glitter blackly. As usual, painters are slung on planks across the great riverside hotels, and the hotel windows have already points of light in them. On the other side the city is white as if with age; St Paul's swells white above the fretted, pointed, or oblong buildings beside it. The cross alone shines rosy-gilt. But what century have we reached? Has this procession from the Surrey side to the Strand gone on for ever? That old man has been crossing the bridge these six hundred years, with the rabble of little boys at his heels, for he is drunk, or blind with misery, and tied round with old clouts of clothing such as pilgrims might have worn. He shuffles on. No one stands still. It seems as if we marched to the sound of music; perhaps the wind and the river; perhaps these same drums and trumpets – the ecstasy and hubbub of the soul. Why, even the unhappy laugh, and the policeman, far from judging the drunk man, surveys him humorously, and the little boys scamper back again, and the clerk from Somerset House has nothing but tolerance for him, and the man who is reading half a page of *Lothair* at the bookstall muses charitably, with his eyes off the print, and the girl hesitates at the crossing and turns on him the bright yet vague glance of the young.

Bright yet vague. She is perhaps twenty-two. She is shabby. She crosses the road and looks at the daffodils and the red tulips in the florist's window. She hesitates, and makes off in the direction of Temple Bar. She walks fast, and yet anything distracts her. Now she seems to see, and now to notice nothing.

Chapter Ten

Through the disused graveyard in the parish of St Pancras, Fanny Elmer strayed between the white tombs which lean against the wall, crossing the grass to read a name, hurrying on when the grave-keeper approached, hurrying into the street, pausing now by a window with blue china, now quickly making up for lost time, abruptly entering a baker's shop, buying rolls, adding cakes, going on again so that any one wishing to follow must fairly trot. She was not drably shabby, though. She wore silk stockings and silver-buckled shoes, only the red feather in her hat drooped, and the clasp of her bag was weak, for out fell a copy of Madame Tussaud's programme as she walked. She had the ankles of a stag. Her face was hidden. Of course, in this dusk, rapid movements, quick glances and soaring hopes come naturally enough. She passed right beneath Jacob's window.

The house was flat, dark and silent. Jacob was at home engaged upon a chess problem, the board being on a stool between his knees. One hand was fingering the hair at the back of his head. He slowly brought it forward and raised the white queen from her square; then put her down again on the same spot. He filled his pipe; ruminated; moved two pawns; advanced the white knight; then ruminated with one finger upon the bishop. Now Fanny Elmer passed beneath the window.

She was on her way to sit to Nick Bramham the painter.

She sat in a flowered Spanish shawl, holding in her hand a yellow novel.

'A little lower, a little looser, so – better, that's right,' Bramham mumbled, who was drawing her, and smoking at the same time, and was naturally speechless. His head might have been the work of a sculptor, who had squared the forehead, stretched the mouth, and left marks of his thumbs and streaks from his fingers in the clay. But the eyes had never been shut. They were rather prominent, and rather bloodshot, as if from staring and staring, and when he spoke they looked for a second disturbed, but went on staring. An unshaded electric light hung above her head.

As for the beauty of women, it is like the light on the sea, never constant to a single wave. They all have it; they all lose it. Now she is dull and thick as bacon; now transparent as a hanging glass. The fixed faces are the dull ones. Here comes Lady Venice displayed like a monument for admiration, but carved in alabaster, to be set on the mantelpiece and never dusted. A dapper brunette complete from head to foot serves only as an illustration to lie upon the drawing-room table. The women in the streets have the faces of playing cards; the outlines accurately filled in with pink or yellow, and the line drawn tightly round them. Then, at a top-floor window, leaning out, looking down, you see beauty itself; or in the corner of an omnibus; or squatted in a ditch – beauty glowing, suddenly expressive, withdrawn the moment after. No one can count on it or seize it or have it wrapped in paper. Nothing is to be won from the shops, and Heaven knows it would be better to sit at home than haunt the plate-glass windows in the hope of lifting the shining green, the glowing ruby, out of them alive. Sea glass in a saucer loses its lustre no sooner than silks do. Thus if you talk of a beautiful woman you mean only something flying fast which for a second uses the eyes, lips or cheeks of Fanny Elmer, for example, to glow through.

She was not beautiful, as she sat stiffly; her underlip too prominent; her nose too large; her eyes too near together. She was a thin girl, with brilliant cheeks and dark hair, sulky just now, or stiff with sitting. When Bramham snapped his stick of charcoal she started. Bramham was out of temper. He squatted before the gas fire warming his hands. Meanwhile she looked at his drawing. He grunted. Fanny threw on a dressing-gown and boiled a kettle.

'By God, it's bad,' said Bramham.

Fanny dropped on to the floor, clasped her hands round her knees, and looked at him, her beautiful eyes – yes, beauty, flying through the room, shone there for a second. Fanny's eyes seemed to question, to commiserate, to be, for a second, love itself. But she exaggerated. Bramham noticed nothing. And when the kettle boiled, up she scrambled, more like a colt or a puppy than a loving woman.

Now Jacob walked over to the window and stood with his hands in his pockets. Mr Springett opposite came out, looked at his shop window, and went in again. The children drifted past, eyeing the pink sticks of sweetstuff. Pickford's van swung down the street. A small boy twirled from a rope. Jacob turned away. Two minutes later he opened the front door, and walked off in the direction of Holborn.

Fanny Elmer took down her cloak from the hook. Nick Bramham unpinned his drawing and rolled it under his arm. They turned out the lights and set off down the street, holding on their way through all the people, motor cars, omnibuses, carts, until they reached Leicester Square, five minutes before Jacob reached it, for his way was slightly longer, and he had been stopped by a block in Holborn waiting to see the King drive by, so that Nick and Fanny were already leaning over the barrier in the promenade at the Empire when Jacob pushed through the swing doors and took his place beside them.

'Hullo, never noticed you,' said Nick, five minutes later.

'Bloody rot,' said Jacob.

'Miss Elmer,' said Nick.

Jacob took his pipe out of his mouth very awkwardly.

Very awkward he was. And when they sat upon a plush sofa and let the smoke go up between them and the stage, and heard far off the high-pitched voices and the jolly orchestra breaking in opportunely, he was still awkward, only Fanny thought: 'What a beautiful voice!' She thought how little he said yet how firm it was. She thought how young men are dignified and aloof, and how unconscious they are, and how quietly one might sit beside Jacob and look at him. And how childlike he would be, come in tired of an evening, she thought, and how majestic; a little overbearing perhaps; 'But I wouldn't give way,' she thought. He got up and leant over the barrier. The smoke hung about him.

And for ever the beauty of young men seems to be set in smoke, however lustily they chase footballs, or drive cricket balls, dance, run, or stride along roads. Possibly they are soon to lose it. Possibly they look into the eyes of faraway heroes, and take their station among us half contemptuously, she thought (vibrating like a fiddle-string, to be played on and snapped). Anyhow, they love silence, and speak beautifully, each word falling like a disc new cut, not a hubble-bubble of small smooth coins such as girls use; and they move decidedly, as if they knew how long to stay and when to go – oh, but Mr Flanders was only gone to get a programme.

'The dancers come right at the end,' he said, coming back to them.

And isn't it pleasant, Fanny went on thinking, how young men bring out lots of silver coins from their trouser pockets, and look at them, instead of having just so many in a purse?

Then there she was herself, whirling across the stage in white flounces, and the music was the dance and fling of her own soul, and the whole machinery, rock and gear of the world was spun smoothly into those swift eddies and falls, she felt, as she stood rigid leaning over the barrier two feet from Jacob Flanders.

Her screwed-up black glove dropped to the floor. When Jacob gave it her, she started angrily. For never was there a more irrational passion. And Jacob was afraid of her for a moment – so violent, so dangerous is it when young women stand rigid; grasp the barrier; fall in love.

It was the middle of February. The roofs of Hampstead Garden Suburb lay in a tremulous haze. It was too hot to walk. A dog barked, barked, barked down in the hollow. The liquid shadows went over the plain.

The body after long illness is languid, passive, receptive of sweetness, but too weak to contain it. The tears well and fall as the dog barks in the hollow, the children skim after hoops, the country darkens and brightens. Beyond a veil it seems. Ah, but draw the veil thicker lest I faint with sweetness, Fanny Elmer sighed, as she sat on a bench in Judges Walk looking at Hampstead Garden Suburb. But the dog went on barking. The motor cars hooted on the road. She heard a faraway rush and humming. Agitation was at her heart. Up she got and walked. The grass was freshly green; the sun hot. All round the pond children were stooping to launch little boats; or were drawn back screaming by their nurses.

At midday young women walk out into the air. All the men are busy in the town. They stand by the edge of the blue pond. The fresh wind scatters the children's voices all about. My children, thought Fanny Elmer. The women stand round the pond, beating off great prancing shaggy dogs. Gently the baby is rocked in the perambulator. The eyes of all the nurses, mothers, and wandering women are a little glazed, absorbed. They gently nod instead of answering when the little boys tug at their skirts, begging them to move on.

And Fanny moved, hearing some cry – a workman's whistle perhaps – high in mid-air. Now, among the trees, it was the thrush trilling out into the warm air a flutter of jubilation, but fear seemed to spur him, Fanny thought; as if he too were anxious with such joy at his heart – as if he were watched as he sang, and pressed by tumult to sing. There! Restless, he flew to the next tree. She heard his song more faintly. Beyond it was the humming of the wheels and the wind rushing.

She spent tenpence on lunch.

'Dear, miss, she's left her umbrella,' grumbled the mottled woman in the glass box near the door at the Express Dairy Company's shop.

'Perhaps I'll catch her,' answered Milly Edwards, the waitress with the pale plaits of hair; and she dashed through the door.

'No good,' she said, coming back a moment later with Fanny's cheap umbrella. She put her hand to her plaits.

'Oh, that door!' grumbled the cashier.

Her hands were cased in black mittens, and the fingertips that drew in the paper slips were swollen as sausages.

'Pie and greens for one. Large coffee and crumpets. Eggs on toast. Two fruit cakes.'

Thus the sharp voices of the waitresses snapped. The lunchers heard their orders repeated with approval; saw the next table served with anticipation. Their own eggs on toast were at last delivered. Their eyes strayed no more.

Damp cubes of pastry fell into mouths opened like triangular bags.

Nelly Jenkinson, the typist, crumbled her cake indifferently enough. Every time the door opened she looked up. What did she expect to see?

The coal merchant read the *Telegraph* without stopping, missed the saucer, and, feeling abstractedly, put the cup down on the tablecloth.

'Did you ever hear the like of that for impertinence?' Mrs Parsons wound up, brushing the crumbs from her furs.

'Hot milk and scone for one. Pot of tea. Roll and butter,' cried the waitresses.

The door opened and shut.

Such is the life of the elderly.

It is curious, lying in a boat, to watch the waves. Here are three coming regularly one after another, all much of a size. Then, hurrying after them comes a fourth, very large and menacing; it lifts the boat; on it goes; somehow merges without accomplishing anything; flattens itself out with the rest.

What can be more violent than the fling of boughs in a gale, the tree yielding itself all up the trunk, to the very tip of the branch, streaming and shuddering the way the wind blows, yet never flying in dishevelment away? The corn squirms and abases itself as if preparing to tug itself free from the roots, and yet is tied down.

Why, from the very windows, even in the dusk, you see a swelling run through the street, an aspiration, as with arms outstretched, eyes desiring, mouths agape. And then we peaceably subside. For if the exaltation lasted we should be blown like foam into the air. The stars would shine through us. We should go down the gale in salt drops – as sometimes happens. For the impetuous spirits will have none of this cradling. Never any swaying or aimlessly lolling for them. Never any making believe, or lying cosily, or genially supposing that one is much like another, fire warm, wine pleasant, extravagance a sin.

'People are so nice, once you know them.'

'I couldn't think ill of her. One must remember – ' But Nick perhaps, or Fanny Elmer, believing implicitly in the truth of the moment, fling off, sting the cheek, are gone like sharp hail.

'Oh,' said Fanny, bursting into the studio three-quarters of an hour late because she had been hanging about the neighbourhood of the Foundling Hospital merely for the chance of seeing Jacob walk down the street, take out his latch-key, and open the door, 'I'm afraid I'm late'; upon which Nick said nothing and Fanny grew defiant.

'I'll never come again!' she cried at length.

'Don't, then,' Nick replied, and off she ran without so much as good-night.

How exquisite it was – that dress in Evelina's shop off Shaftesbury Avenue! It was four o'clock on a fine day early in April, and was Fanny the one to spend four o'clock on a fine day indoors? Other girls in that very street sat over ledgers, or drew long threads wearily between silk and gauze; or, festooned with ribbons in Swan and Edgar's, rapidly added up pence and farthings on the back of the bill and twisted the yard and three-quarters in tissue paper and asked, 'Your pleasure?' of the next comer.

In Evelina's shop off Shaftesbury Avenue the parts of a woman were shown separate. In the left hand was her skirt. Twining round a pole in the middle was a feather boa. Ranged like the heads of malefactors on Temple Bar were hats – emerald and white, lightly wreathed or drooping beneath deep-dyed feathers. And on the carpet were her feet – pointed gold, or patent leather slashed with scarlet.

Feasted upon by the eyes of women, the clothes by four o'clock were flyblown like sugar cakes in a baker's window. Fanny eyed them too. But coming along Gerrard Street was a tall man in a shabby coat. A shadow fell across Evelina's window – Jacob's shadow, though it was not Jacob. And Fanny turned and walked along Gerrard Street and wished that she had read books. Nick never read books, never talked of Ireland, or the House of Lords; and as for his fingernails! She would learn Latin and read Virgil. She had been a great reader. She had read Scott; she had read Dumas. At the Slade no one read. But no one knew Fanny at the Slade, or guessed how empty it seemed to her; the passion for ear-rings, for dances, for Tonks and Steer – when it was only the French who could paint, Jacob said. For the moderns were futile; painting the least respectable of the arts; and why read anything but Marlowe and Shakespeare, Jacob said, and Fielding if you must read novels?

'Fielding,' said Fanny, when the man in Charing Cross Road asked her what book she wanted.

She bought *Tom Jones*.

At ten o'clock in the morning, in a room which she shared with a school-teacher, Fanny Elmer read *Tom Jones* – that mystic book. For this dull stuff (Fanny thought) about people with odd names is what Jacob likes. Good people like it. Dowdy women who don't mind how they cross their legs read *Tom Jones* – a mystic book; for there is something, Fanny thought, about books which if I had been educated I could have liked – much better than ear-rings and flowers, she sighed, thinking of the corridors at the Slade and the fancy-dress dance next week. She had nothing to wear.

They are real, thought Fanny Elmer, setting her feet on the mantelpiece. Some people are. Nick perhaps, only he was so stupid. And women never – except Miss Sargent, but she went off at lunchtime and gave herself airs. There they sat quietly of a night reading, she thought. Not going to music-halls; not looking in at shop windows; not wearing each other's clothes, like Robertson who had worn her shawl, and she had worn his waistcoat, which Jacob could only do very awkwardly; for he liked *Tom Jones*.

There it lay on her lap, in double columns, price three and sixpence; the mystic book in which Henry Fielding ever so many years ago rebuked Fanny Elmer for feasting on scarlet, in perfect prose, Jacob said. For he never read modern novels. He liked *Tom Jones*.

'I do like *Tom Jones*,' said Fanny, at five-thirty that same day early in April when Jacob took out his pipe in the armchair opposite.

Alas, women lie! But not Clara Durrant. A flawless mind; a candid nature; a virgin chained to a rock (somewhere off Lowndes Square) eternally pouring out tea for old men in white waistcoats, blue-eyed, looking you straight in the face, playing Bach. Of all women, Jacob honoured her most. But to sit at a table with bread and butter, with dowagers in velvet, and never say more to Clara Durrant than Benson said to the parrot when old Miss Perry poured out tea, was an insufferable outrage upon the liberties and decencies of human nature – or words to that effect. For Jacob said nothing. Only he glared at the fire. Fanny laid down *Tom Jones*.

She stitched or knitted.

'What's that?' asked Jacob.

'For the dance at the Slade.'

And she fetched her head-dress; her trousers; her shoes with red tassels. What should she wear?

'I shall be in Paris,' said Jacob.

And what is the point of fancy-dress dances? thought Fanny. You meet the same people; you wear the same clothes; Mangin gets drunk; Florinda sits on his knee. She flirts outrageously – with Nick Bramham just now.

'In Paris?' said Fanny.

'On my way to Greece,' he replied.

For, he said, there is nothing so detestable as London in May.

He would forget her.

A sparrow flew past the window trailing a straw – a straw from a stack stood by a barn in a farmyard. The old brown spaniel snuffs at the base for a rat. Already the upper branches of the elm trees are blotted with nests. The chestnuts have flirted their fans. And the butterflies are flaunting across the rides in the forest. Perhaps the Purple Emperor is feasting, as Morris says, upon a mass of putrid carrion at the base of an oak tree.

Fanny thought it all came from *Tom Jones*. He could go alone with a book in his pocket and watch the badgers. He would take a train at eight-thirty and walk all night. He saw fire-flies, and brought back glow-worms in pill-boxes. He would hunt with the New Forest Staghounds. It all came from *Tom Jones*; and he would go to Greece with a book in his pocket and forget her.

She fetched her hand-glass. There was her face. And suppose one wreathed Jacob in a turban? There was his face. She lit the lamp. But as the daylight came through the window only half was lit up by the lamp. And though he looked terrible and magnificent and would chuck the forest, he said, and come to the Slade, and be a Turkish knight or a Roman emperor (and he let her blacken his lips and clenched his teeth and scowled in the glass), still – there lay *Tom Jones*.

Chapter Eleven

'Archer,' said Mrs Flanders with that tenderness which mothers so often display towards their eldest sons, 'will be at Gibraltar tomorrow.'

The post for which she was waiting (strolling up Dods Hill while the random church bells swung a hymn tune about her head, the clock striking four straight through the circling notes; the grass purpling under a storm-cloud; and the two dozen houses of the village cowering, infinitely humble, in company under a leaf of shadow), the post, with all its variety of messages, envelopes addressed in bold hands, in slanting hands, stamped now with English stamps, again with Colonial stamps, or sometimes hastily dabbed with a yellow bar, the post was about to scatter a myriad messages over the world. Whether we gain or not by this habit of profuse communication it is not for us to say. But that letter-writing is practised mendaciously nowadays, particularly by young men travelling in foreign parts, seems likely enough.

For example, take this scene.

Here was Jacob Flanders gone abroad and staying to break his journey in Paris. (Old Miss Birkbeck, his mother's cousin, had died last June and left him a hundred pounds.)

'You needn't repeat the whole damned thing over again, Cruttendon,' said Mallinson, the little bald painter who was sitting at a marble table, splashed with coffee and ringed with wine, talking very fast, and undoubtedly more than a little drunk.

'Well, Flanders, finished writing to your lady?' said Cruttendon, as Jacob came and took his seat beside them, holding in his hand an envelope addressed to Mrs Flanders, near Scarborough, England.

'Do you uphold Velasquez?' said Cruttendon.

'By God, he does,' said Mallinson.

'He always gets like this,' said Cruttendon irritably.

Jacob looked at Mallinson with excessive composure.

'I'll tell you the three greatest things that were ever written in the whole of literature,' Cruttendon burst out. ' "Hang there like fruit my soul," ' he began . . .

'Don't listen to a man who don't like Velasquez,' said Mallinson.

'Adolphe, don't give Mr Mallinson any more wine,' said Cruttendon.

'Fair play, fair play,' said Jacob judicially. 'Let a man get drunk if he likes. That's Shakespeare, Cruttendon. I'm with you there. Shakespeare had more guts than all these damned frogs put together. "Hang there like fruit my soul," ' he began quoting, in a musical rhetorical voice, flourishing his wine glass. 'The devil damn you black, you cream-faced loon!' he exclaimed as the wine washed over the rim.

' "Hang there like fruit my soul," ' Cruttendon and Jacob both began again at the same moment, and both burst out laughing.

'Curse these flies,' said Mallinson, flicking at his bald head. 'What do they take me for?'

'Something sweet-smelling,' said Cruttendon.

'Shut up, Cruttendon,' said Jacob. 'The fellow has no manners,' he explained to Mallinson very politely. 'Wants to cut off people's drink. Look here. I want grilled bone. What's the French for grilled bone? Grilled bone, Adolphe. Now, you juggins, don't you understand?'

'And I'll tell you, Flanders, the second most beautiful thing in the whole of literature,' said Cruttendon, bringing his feet down on to the floor, and leaning right across the table, so that his face almost touched Jacob's face.

' "Hey diddle diddle, the cat and the fiddle," ' Mallinson interrupted, strumming his fingers on the table. 'The most ex–qui–sitely beautiful thing in the whole of literature . . . Cruttendon is a very good fellow,' he remarked confidentially. 'But he's a bit of a fool.' And he jerked his head forward.

Well, not a word of this was ever told to Mrs Flanders; nor what happened when they paid the bill and left the restaurant, and walked along the Boulevard Raspaille.

Then here is another scrap of conversation; the time about eleven in the morning; the scene a studio; and the day Sunday.

'I tell you, Flanders,' said Cruttendon, 'I'd as soon have one of Mallinson's little pictures as a Chardin. And when I say that . . . ' he squeezed the tail of an emaciated tube . . . 'Chardin was a great swell . . . He sells 'em to pay his dinner now. But wait till the dealers get hold of him. A great swell – oh, a very great swell.'

'It's an awfully pleasant life,' said Jacob, 'messing away up here. Still, it's a stupid art, Cruttendon.' He wandered off across the room. 'There's this man, Pierre Louys now.' He took up a book.

'Now my good sir, are you going to settle down?' said Cruttendon.

'That's a solid piece of work,' said Jacob, standing a canvas on a chair.

'Oh, that I did ages ago,' said Cruttendon, looking over his shoulder.

'You're a pretty competent painter in my opinion,' said Jacob after a time.

'Now if you'd like to see what I'm after at the present moment,' said Cruttendon, putting a canvas before Jacob. 'There. That's it. That's more like it. That's . . . ' he squirmed his thumb in a circle round a lamp globe painted white.

'A pretty solid piece of work,' said Jacob, straddling his legs in front of it. 'But what I wish you'd explain . . . '

Miss Jinny Carslake, pale, freckled, morbid, came into the room.

'Oh Jinny, here's a friend. Flanders. An Englishman. Wealthy. Highly connected. Go on, Flanders . . . '

Jacob said nothing.

'It's *that* – that's not right,' said Jinny Carslake.

'No,' said Cruttendon decidedly. 'Can't be done.'

He took the canvas off the chair and stood it on the floor with its back to them.

'Sit down, ladies and gentlemen. Miss Carslake comes from your part of the world, Flanders. From Devonshire. Oh, I thought you said Devonshire. Very well. She's a daughter of the church too. The black sheep of the family. Her mother writes her such letters. I say – have you one about you? It's generally Sundays they come. Sort of church-bell effect, you know.'

'Have you met all the painter men?' said Jinny. 'Was Mallinson drunk? If you go to his studio he'll give you one of his pictures. I say, Teddy . . . '

'Half a jiff,' said Cruttendon. 'What's the season of the year?' He looked out of the window.

'We take a day off on Sundays, Flanders.'

'Will he . . . ' said Jinny, looking at Jacob. 'You . . . '

'Yes, he'll come with us,' said Cruttendon.

And then, here is Versailles. Jinny stood on the stone rim and leant over the pond, clasped by Cruttendon's arms or she would have fallen in.

'There! There!' she cried. 'Right up to the top!' Some sluggish, sloping-shouldered fish had floated up from the depths to nip her crumbs. 'You look,' she said, jumping down. And then the dazzling white water, rough and throttled, shot up into the air. The fountain spread itself. Through it came the sound of military music far away. All the water was puckered with drops. A blue air-ball gently bumped the surface. How all the nurses and children and old men and young crowded to the edge, leant over and waved their sticks! The little girl ran stretching her arms towards her air-ball, but it sank beneath the fountain.

Edward Cruttendon, Jinny Carslake and Jacob Flanders walked in a row along the yellow gravel path; got on to the grass; so passed under the trees; and came out at the summer-house where Marie Antoinette used to drink chocolate. In went Edward and Jinny, but Jacob waited outside, sitting on the handle of his walking-stick. Out they came again.

'Well?' said Cruttendon, smiling at Jacob.

Jinny waited; Edward waited; and both looked at Jacob.

'Well?' said Jacob, smiling and pressing both hands on his stick.

'Come along,' he decided; and started off. The others followed him, smiling.

And then they went to the little café in the by-street where people sit drinking coffee, watching the soldiers, meditatively knocking ashes into trays.

'But he's quite different,' said Jinny, folding her hands over the top of her glass. 'I don't suppose you know what Ted means when he says a thing like that,' she said, looking at Jacob. 'But I do. Sometimes I could kill myself. Sometimes he lies in bed all day long – just lies there . . . I don't want you right on the table,' she waved her hands. Swollen iridescent pigeons were waddling round their feet.

'Look at that woman's hat,' said Cruttendon. 'How do they come to think of it? . . . No, Flanders, I don't think I could live like you. When one walks down that street opposite the British Museum – what's it called? – that's what I mean. It's all like that. Those fat women – and the man standing in the middle of the road as if he were going to have a fit . . . '

'Everybody feeds them,' said Jinny, waving the pigeons away. 'They're stupid old things.'

'Well, I don't know,' said Jacob, smoking his cigarette. 'There's St Paul's.'

'I mean going to an office,' said Cruttendon.

'Hang it all,' Jacob expostulated.

'But you don't count,' said Jinny, looking at Cruttendon. 'You're mad. I mean, you just think of painting.'

'Yes, I know. I can't help it. I say, will King George give way about the peers?'

'He'll jolly well have to,' said Jacob.

'There!' said Jinny. 'He really knows.'

'You see, I would if I could,' said Cruttendon, 'but I simply can't.'

'I *think* I could,' said Jinny. 'Only, it's all the people one dislikes who do it. At home, I mean. They talk of nothing else. Even people like my mother.'

'Now if I came and lived here – ' said Jacob. 'What's my share, Cruttendon? Oh, very well. Have it your own way. Those silly birds, directly one wants them – they've flown away.'

And finally under the arc lamps in the Gare des Invalides, with one of those queer movements which are so slight yet so definite, which may wound or pass unnoticed but generally inflict a good deal of discomfort, Jinny and Cruttendon drew together; Jacob stood apart. They had to separate. Something must be said. Nothing was said. A man wheeled a trolley past Jacob's legs so near that he almost grazed them. When Jacob recovered his balance the other two were turning away, though Jinny looked over her shoulder, and Cruttendon, waving his hand, disappeared like the very great genius that he was.

No – Mrs Flanders was told none of this, though Jacob felt, it is safe to say, that nothing in the world was of greater importance; and as for Cruttendon and Jinny, he thought them the most remarkable people he had ever met – being of course unable to foresee how it fell out in the course of time that Cruttendon took to painting orchards; had therefore to live in Kent; and must, one would think, see through apple blossom by this time, since his wife, for whose sake he did it, eloped with a novelist; but no; Cruttendon still paints orchards, savagely, in solitude. Then Jinny Carslake, after her affair with Lefanu the American painter, frequented Indian philosophers, and now you find her in pensions in Italy cherishing a little jeweller's box containing ordinary pebbles picked off the road. But if you look at them steadily, she says, multiplicity becomes unity, which is somehow the secret of life, though it does not prevent her from following the macaroni as it goes round the table, and sometimes, on spring nights, she makes the strangest confidences to shy young Englishmen.

Jacob had nothing to hide from his mother. It was only that he could make no sense himself of his extraordinary excitement, and as for writing it down –

'Jacob's letters are so like him,' said Mrs Jarvis, folding the sheet.

'Indeed he seems to be having . . . ' said Mrs Flanders, and paused, for she was cutting out a dress and had to straighten the pattern, ' . . . a very gay time.'

Mrs Jarvis thought of Paris. At her back the window was open, for it was a mild night; a calm night; when the moon seemed muffled and the apple trees stood perfectly still.

'I never pity the dead,' said Mrs Jarvis, shifting the cushion at her back, and clasping her hands behind her head. Betty Flanders did not hear, for her scissors made so much noise on the table.

'They are at rest,' said Mrs Jarvis. 'And we spend our days doing foolish unnecessary things without knowing why.'

Mrs Jarvis was not liked in the village.

'You never walk at this time of night?' she asked Mrs Flanders.

'It is certainly wonderfully mild,' said Mrs Flanders.

Yet it was years since she had opened the orchard gate and gone out on Dods Hill after dinner.

'It is perfectly dry,' said Mrs Jarvis, as they shut the orchard door and stepped on to the turf.

'I shan't go far,' said Betty Flanders. 'Yes, Jacob will leave Paris on Wednesday.'

'Jacob was always my friend of the three,' said Mrs Jarvis.

'Now, my dear, I am going no farther,' said Mrs Flanders. They had climbed the dark hill and reached the Roman camp.

The rampart rose at their feet – the smooth circle surrounding the camp or the grave. How many needles Betty Flanders had lost there; and her garnet brooch.

'It is much clearer than this sometimes,' said Mrs Jarvis, standing upon the ridge. There were no clouds, and yet there was a haze over the sea, and over the moors. The lights of Scarborough flashed, as if a woman wearing a diamond necklace turned her head this way and that.

'How quiet it is!' said Mrs Jarvis.

Mrs Flanders rubbed the turf with her toe, thinking of her garnet brooch.

Mrs Jarvis found it difficult to think of herself tonight. It was so calm. There was no wind; nothing racing, flying, escaping. Black shadows stood still over the silver moors. The furze bushes stood perfectly still. Neither did Mrs Jarvis think of God. There was a church behind them, of course. The church clock struck ten. Did the strokes reach the furze bush, or did the thorn tree hear them?

Mrs Flanders was stooping down to pick up a pebble. Sometimes people do find things, Mrs Jarvis thought, and yet in this hazy moonlight it was impossible to see anything, except bones, and little pieces of chalk.

'Jacob bought it with his own money, and then I brought Mr Parker up to see the view, and it must have dropped – ' Mrs Flanders murmured.

Did the bones stir, or the rusty swords? Was Mrs Flanders's twopenny-halfpenny brooch for ever part of the rich accumulation? and if all the ghosts flocked thick and rubbed shoulders with Mrs Flanders in the circle, would she not have seemed perfectly in her place, a live English matron, growing stout?

The clock struck the quarter.

The frail waves of sound broke among the stiff gorse and the hawthorn twigs as the church clock divided time into quarters.

Motionless and broad-backed the moors received the statement, 'It is fifteen minutes past the hour,' but made no answer, unless a bramble stirred.

Yet even in this light the legends on the tombstones could be read, brief voices saying, 'I am Bertha Ruck,' 'I am Tom Gage.' And they say which day of the year they died, and the New Testament says something for them, very proud, very emphatic, or consoling.

The moors accept all that too.

The moonlight falls like a pale page upon the church wall, and illumines the kneeling family in the niche, and the tablet set up in 1780 to the squire of the parish who relieved the poor, and believed in God – so the measured voice goes on down the marble scroll, as though it could impose itself upon time and the open air.

Now a fox steals out from behind the gorse bushes.

Often, even at night, the church seems full of people. The pews are worn and greasy, and the hassocks in place, and the hymn-books on the ledges. It is a ship with all its crew aboard. The timbers strain to hold the dead and the living, the ploughmen, the carpenters, the fox-hunting gentlemen and the farmers smelling of mud and brandy. Their tongues join together in syllabling the sharp-cut words, which for ever slice asunder time and the broad-backed moors. Plaint and belief and elegy, despair and triumph, but for the most part good sense and jolly indifference, go trampling out of the windows any time these five hundred years.

Still, as Mrs Jarvis said, stepping out on to the moors, 'How quiet it is!' Quiet at midday, except when the hunt scatters across it; quiet in the afternoon, save for the drifting sheep; at night the moor is perfectly quiet.

A garnet brooch has dropped into its grass. A fox pads stealthily. A leaf turns on its edge. Mrs Jarvis, who is fifty years of age, reposes in the camp in the hazy moonlight.

'. . . and,' said Mrs Flanders, straightening her back, 'I never cared for Mr Parker.'

'Neither did I,' said Mrs Jarvis. They began to walk home.

But their voices floated for a little above the camp. The moonlight destroyed nothing. The moor accepted everything. Tom Gage cries aloud so long as his tombstone endures. The Roman skeletons are in safe keeping. Betty Flanders's darning needles are safe too and her garnet brooch. And sometimes at midday, in the sunshine, the moor seems to hoard these little treasures, like a nurse. But at midnight when no one speaks or gallops, and the thorn tree is perfectly still, it would be foolish to vex the moor with questions – what? and why?

The church clock, however, strikes twelve.

Chapter Twelve

The water fell off a ledge like lead – like a chain with thick white links. The train ran out into a steep green meadow, and Jacob saw striped tulips growing and heard a bird singing, in Italy.

A motor car full of Italian officers ran along the flat road and kept up with the train, raising dust behind it. There were trees laced together with vines – as Virgil said. Here was a station; and a tremendous leave-taking going on, with women in high yellow boots and odd pale boys in ringed socks. Virgil's bees had gone about the plains of Lombardy. It was the custom of the ancients to train vines between elms. Then at Milan there were sharp-winged hawks, of a bright brown, cutting figures over the roofs.

These Italian carriages get damnably hot with the afternoon sun on them, and the chances are that before the engine has pulled to the top of the gorge the clanking chain will have broken. Up, up, up, it goes, like a train on a scenic railway. Every peak is covered with sharp trees, and amazing white villages are crowded on ledges. There is always a white tower on the very summit, flat red-frilled roofs, and a sheer drop beneath. It is not a country in which one walks after tea. For one thing there is no grass. A whole hillside will be ruled with olive trees. Already in April the earth is clotted into dry dust between them. And there are neither stiles nor footpaths, nor lanes chequered with the shadows of leaves nor eighteenth-century inns with bow-windows, where one eats ham and eggs. Oh no, Italy is all fierceness, bareness, exposure, and black priests shuffling along the roads. It is strange, too, how you never get away from villas.

Still, to be travelling on one's own with a hundred pounds to spend is a fine affair. And if his money gave out, as it probably would, he would go on foot. He could live on bread and wine – the wine in straw bottles – for after doing Greece he was going to knock off Rome. The Roman civilisation was a very inferior affair, no doubt. But Bonamy talked a lot of rot, all the same. 'You ought to have been in Athens,' he would say to Bonamy when he got back. 'Standing on the Parthenon,' he would say, or, 'The ruins of the Coliseum suggest some fairly sublime reflections,' which he would write out at length in letters. It might turn to an essay upon civilisation. A comparison between the ancients and moderns, with some pretty sharp hits at Mr Asquith – something in the style of Gibbon.

A stout gentleman laboriously hauled himself in, dusty, baggy, slung with gold chains, and Jacob, regretting that he did not come of the Latin race, looked out of the window.

It is a strange reflection that by travelling two days and nights you are in the heart of Italy. Accidental villas among olive trees appear; and menservants watering the cactuses. Black victorias drive in between pompous pillars with plaster shields stuck to them. It is at once momentary and astonishingly intimate – to be displayed before the eyes of a foreigner. And there is a lonely hill-top where no one ever comes, and yet it is seen by me who was lately driving down Piccadilly on an omnibus. And what I should like would be to get out among the fields, sit down and hear the grasshoppers, and take up a handful of earth – Italian earth, as this is Italian dust upon my shoes.

Jacob heard them crying strange names at railway stations through the night. The train stopped and he heard frogs croaking close by, and he wrinkled back the blind cautiously and saw a vast strange marsh all white in the moonlight. The carriage was thick with cigar smoke, which floated round the globe with the green shade on it. The Italian gentleman lay snoring with his boots off and his waistcoat unbuttoned . . . And all this business of going to Greece seemed to Jacob an intolerable weariness – sitting in hotels by oneself and looking at monuments – he'd have done better to go to Cornwall with Timmy Durrant . . . 'O–h,' Jacob protested, as the darkness began breaking in front of him and the light showed through, but the man was reaching across him to get something – the fat Italian man in his dicky, unshaven, crumpled, obese, was opening the door and going off to have a wash.

So Jacob sat up, and saw a lean Italian sportsman with a gun walking down the road in the early morning light, and the whole idea of the Parthenon came upon him in a clap.

'By Jove!' he thought, 'we must be nearly there!' and he stuck his head out of the window and got the air full in his face.

It is highly exasperating that twenty-five people of your acquaintance should be able to say straight off something very much to the point about being in Greece, while for yourself there is a stopper upon all emotions whatsoever. For after washing at the hotel at Patras, Jacob had followed the tramlines a mile or so out; and followed them a mile or so back; he had met several droves of turkeys; several strings of donkeys; had got lost in back streets; had read advertisements of corsets and of Maggi's consommé; children had trodden on his toes; the place smelt of bad cheese; and he was glad to find himself suddenly come out opposite his hotel. There was an old copy of the *Daily Mail* lying among coffee-cups; which he read. But what could he do after dinner?

No doubt we should be, on the whole, much worse off than we are without our astonishing gift for illusion. At the age of twelve or so, having given up dolls and broken our steam engines, France, but much more probably Italy, and India almost for a certainty, draws the superfluous imagination. One's aunts have been to Rome; and everyone has an uncle who was last heard of – poor man – in Rangoon. He will never come back any more. But it is the governesses who start the Greek myth. Look at that for a head (they say) –

nose, you see, straight as a dart, curls, eyebrows – everything appropriate to manly beauty; while his legs and arms have lines on them which indicate a perfect degree of development – the Greeks caring for the body as much as for the face. And the Greeks could paint fruit so that birds pecked at it. First you read Xenophon; then Euripides. One day – that was an occasion, by God – what people have said appears to have sense in it: 'the Greek spirit'; the Greek this, that, and the other; though it is absurd, by the way, to say that any Greek comes near Shakespeare. The point is, however, that we have been brought up in an illusion.

Jacob, no doubt, thought something in this fashion, the *Daily Mail* crumpled in his hand; his legs extended; the very picture of boredom.

'But it's the way we're brought up,' he went on.

And it all seemed to him very distasteful. Something ought to be done about it. And from being moderately depressed he became like a man about to be executed. Clara Durrant had left him at a party to talk to an American called Pilchard. And he had come all the way to Greece and left her. They wore evening-dresses, and talked nonsense – what damned nonsense – and he put out his hand for the *Globe Trotter*, an international magazine which is supplied free of charge to the proprietors of hotels.

In spite of its ramshackle condition modern Greece is highly advanced in the electric-tramway system, so that while Jacob sat in the hotel sitting-room the trams clanked, chimed, rang, rang, rang imperiously to get the donkeys out of the way, and one old woman who refused to budge, beneath the windows. The whole of civilisation was being condemned.

The waiter was quite indifferent to that too. Aristotle, a dirty man, carnivorously interested in the body of the only guest now occupying the only armchair, came into the room ostentatiously, put something down, put something straight, and saw that Jacob was still there.

'I shall want to be called early tomorrow,' said Jacob, over his shoulder. 'I am going to Olympia.'

This gloom, this surrender to the dark waters which lap us about, is a modern invention. Perhaps, as Cruttendon said, we do not believe enough. Our fathers at any rate had something to demolish. So have we for the matter of that, thought Jacob, crumpling the *Daily Mail* in his hand. He would go into Parliament and make fine speeches – but what use are fine speeches and Parliament, once you surrender an inch to the black waters? Indeed there has never been any explanation of the ebb and flow in our veins – of happiness and unhappiness. That respectability and evening parties where one has to dress, and wretched slums at the back of Gray's Inn – something solid, immovable and grotesque – is at the back of it, Jacob thought probable. But then there was the British Empire which was beginning to puzzle him; nor was he altogether in favour of giving Home Rule to Ireland. What did the *Daily Mail* say about that?

For he had grown to be a man, and was about to be immersed in things – as indeed the chambermaid, emptying his basin upstairs, fingering keys, studs, pencils, and bottles of tabloids strewn on the dressing-table, was aware.

That he had grown to be a man was a fact that Florinda knew, as she knew everything, by instinct.

And Betty Flanders even now suspected it, as she read his letter, posted at Milan, 'Telling me,' she complained to Mrs Jarvis, 'really nothing that I want to know'; but she brooded over it.

Fanny Elmer felt it to desperation. For he would take his stick and his hat and would walk to the window, and look perfectly absent-minded and very stern too, she thought.

'I am going,' he would say, 'to cadge a meal of Bonamy.'

'Anyhow, I can drown myself in the Thames,' Fanny cried, as she hurried past the Foundling Hospital.

'But the *Daily Mail* isn't to be trusted,' Jacob said to himself, looking about for something else to read. And he sighed again, being indeed so profoundly gloomy that gloom must have been lodged in him to cloud him at any moment, which was odd in a man who enjoyed things so, was not much given to analysis, but was horribly romantic, of course, Bonamy thought, in his rooms in Lincoln's Inn.

'He will fall in love,' thought Bonamy. 'Some Greek woman with a straight nose.'

It was to Bonamy that Jacob wrote from Patras – to Bonamy who couldn't love a woman and never read a foolish book.

There are very few good books after all, for we can't count profuse histories, travels in mule carts to discover the sources of the Nile, or the volubility of fiction.

I like books whose virtue is all drawn together in a page or two. I like sentences that don't budge though armies cross them. I like words to be hard – such were Bonamy's views, and they won him the hostility of those whose taste is all for the fresh growths of the morning, who throw up the window, and find the poppies spread in the sun, and can't forbear a shout of jubilation at the astonishing fertility of English literature. That was not Bonamy's way at all. That his taste in literature affected his friendships, and made him silent, secretive, fastidious, and only quite at his ease with one or two young men of his own way of thinking, was the charge against him.

But then Jacob Flanders was not at all of his own way of thinking – far from it, Bonamy sighed, laying the thin sheets of notepaper on the table and falling into thought about Jacob's character, not for the first time.

The trouble was this romantic vein in him. 'But mixed with the stupidity which leads him into these absurd predicaments,' thought Bonamy, 'there is something – something' – he sighed, for he was fonder of Jacob than of anyone in the world.

Jacob went to the window and stood with his hands in his pockets. There he saw three Greeks in kilts; the masts of ships; idle or busy people of the lower classes strolling or stepping out briskly, or falling into groups and gesticulating with their hands. Their lack of concern for him was not the cause of his gloom; but some more profound conviction – it was not that he himself happened to be lonely, but that all people are.

Yet next day, as the train slowly rounded a hill on the way to Olympia, the Greek peasant women were out among the vines; the old Greek men were sitting at the stations, sipping sweet wine. And though Jacob remained gloomy he had never suspected how tremendously pleasant it is to be alone; out of England; on one's own; cut off from the whole thing. There are very sharp bare hills on the way to Olympia; and between them blue sea in triangular spaces. A little like the Cornish coast. Well now, to go walking by oneself all day – to get on to that track and follow it up between the bushes – or are they small trees? – to the top of that mountain from which one can see half the nations of antiquity –

'Yes,' said Jacob, for his carriage was empty, 'let's look at the map.'

Blame it or praise it, there is no denying the wild horse in us. To gallop intemperately; fall on the sand tired out; to feel the earth spin; to have – positively – a rush of friendship for stones and grasses, as if humanity were over, and as for men and women, let them go hang – there is no getting over the fact that this desire seizes us pretty often.

The evening air slightly moved the dirty curtains in the hotel window at Olympia.

'I am full of love for everyone,' thought Mrs Wentworth Williams ' – for the poor most of all – for the peasants coming back in the evening with their burdens. And everything is soft and vague and very sad. It is sad, it is sad. But everything has meaning,' thought Sandra Wentworth Williams, raising her head a little and looking very beautiful, tragic and exalted. 'One must love everything.'

She held in her hand a little book convenient for travelling – stories by Chekhov – as she stood, veiled, in white, in the window of the hotel at Olympia. How beautiful the evening was! and her beauty was its beauty. The tragedy of Greece was the tragedy of all high souls. The inevitable compromise. She seemed to have grasped something. She would write it down. And moving to the table where her husband sat reading she leant her chin in her hands and thought of the peasants, of suffering, of her own beauty, of the inevitable compromise, and of how she would write it down. Nor did Evan Williams say anything brutal, banal or foolish when he shut his book and put it away to make room for the plates of soup which were now being placed before them. Only his drooping bloodhound eyes and his heavy sallow cheeks expressed his melancholy tolerance, his conviction that though forced to live with circumspection and deliberation he could never possibly achieve any of those objects which, as he knew, are the only ones worth pursuing. His consideration was flawless; his silence unbroken.

'Everything seems to mean so much,' said Sandra. But with the sound of her own voice the spell was broken. She forgot the peasants. Only there remained with her a sense of her own beauty, and in front, luckily, there was a looking-glass.

'I am very beautiful,' she thought.

She shifted her hat slightly. Her husband saw her looking in the glass; and agreed that beauty is important; it is an inheritance; one cannot ignore it. But it is a barrier; it is in fact rather a bore. So he drank his soup; and kept his eyes fixed upon the window.

'Quails,' said Mrs Wentworth Williams languidly. 'And then goat, I suppose; and then . . . '

'Caramel custard presumably,' said her husband in the same cadence, with his toothpick out already.

She laid her spoon upon her plate, and her soup was taken away half finished. Never did she do anything without dignity; for hers was the English type which is so Greek, save that villagers have touched their hats to it, the vicarage reveres it; and upper-gardeners and under-gardeners respectfully straighten their backs as she comes down the broad terrace on Sunday morning, dallying at the stone urns with the Prime Minister to pick a rose – which, perhaps, she was trying to forget, as her eye wandered round the dining-room of the inn at Olympia, seeking the window where her book lay, where a few minutes ago she had discovered something – something very profound it had been, about love and sadness and the peasants.

But it was Evan who sighed; not in despair nor indeed in rebellion. But, being the most ambitious of men and temperamentally the most sluggish, he had accomplished nothing; had the political history of England at his finger-ends, and living much in company with Chatham, Pitt, Burke and Charles James Fox could not help contrasting himself and his age with them and theirs. 'Yet there never was a time when great men are more needed,' he was in the habit of saying to himself, with a sigh. Here he was picking his teeth in an inn at Olympia. He had done. But Sandra's eyes wandered.

'Those pink melons are sure to be dangerous,' he said gloomily. And as he spoke the door opened and in came a young man in a grey check suit.

'Beautiful but dangerous,' said Sandra, immediately talking to her husband in the presence of a third person. ('Ah, an English boy on tour,' she thought to herself.)

And Evan knew all that too.

Yes, he knew all that; and he admired her. Very pleasant, he thought, to have affairs. But for himself, what with his height (Napoleon was five feet four, he remembered), his bulk, his inability to impose his own personality (and yet great men are needed more than ever now, he sighed), it was useless. He threw away his cigar, went up to Jacob and asked him, with a simple sort of sincerity which Jacob liked, whether he had come straight out from England.

'How very English!' Sandra laughed when the waiter told them next morning that the young gentleman had left at five to climb the mountain. 'I am sure he asked you for a bath?' at which the waiter shook his head, and said that he would ask the manager.

'You do not understand,' laughed Sandra. 'Never mind.'

Stretched on the top of the mountain, quite alone, Jacob enjoyed himself immensely. Probably he had never been so happy in the whole of his life.

But at dinner that night Mr Williams asked him whether he would like to see the paper; then Mrs Williams asked him (as they strolled on the terrace smoking – and how could he refuse that man's cigar?) whether he'd seen the theatre by moonlight; whether he knew Everard Sherborn; whether he read Greek and whether (Evan rose silently and went in) if he had to sacrifice one it would be the French literature or the Russian?

'And now,' wrote Jacob in his letter to Bonamy, 'I shall have to read her cursed book' – her Chekhov, he meant, for she had lent it him.

Though the opinion is unpopular it seems likely enough that bare places, fields too thick with stones to be ploughed, tossing sea-meadows halfway between England and America, suit us better than cities.

There is something absolute in us which despises qualification. It is this which is teased and twisted in society. People come together in a room. 'So delighted,' says somebody, 'to meet you,' and that is a lie. And then: 'I enjoy the spring more than the autumn now. One does, I think, as one gets older.' For women are always, always, always talking about what one feels, and if they say 'as one gets older', they mean you to reply with something quite off the point.

Jacob sat himself down in the quarry where the Greeks had cut marble for the theatre. It is hot work walking up Greek hills at midday. The wild red cyclamen was out; he had seen the little tortoises hobbling from clump to clump; the air smelt strong and suddenly sweet, and the sun, striking on jagged splinters of marble, was very dazzling to the eyes. Composed, commanding, contemptuous, a little melancholy, and bored with an august kind of boredom, there he sat smoking his pipe.

Bonamy would have said that this was the sort of thing that made him uneasy – when Jacob got into the doldrums, looked like a Margate fisherman out of a job, or a British admiral. You couldn't make him understand a thing when he was in a mood like that. One had better leave him alone. He was dull. He was apt to be grumpy.

He was up very early, looking at the statues with his Baedeker.

Sandra Wentworth Williams, ranging the world before breakfast in quest of adventure or a point of view, all in white, not so very tall perhaps, but uncommonly upright – Sandra Williams got Jacob's head exactly on a level with the head of the Hermes of Praxiteles. The comparison was all in his favour. But before she could say a single word he had gone out of the museum and left her.

Still, a lady of fashion travels with more than one dress, and if white suits the morning hour, perhaps sandy yellow with purple spots on it, a black hat, and a volume of Balzac, suit the evening. Thus she was arranged on the terrace when Jacob came in. Very beautiful she looked. With her hands folded she mused, seemed to listen to her husband, seemed to watch the peasants coming down with brushwood on their backs, seemed to notice how the hill changed from blue to black, seemed to discriminate between truth and falsehood, Jacob thought, and crossed his legs suddenly, observing the extreme shabbiness of his trousers.

'But he is very distinguished looking,' Sandra decided.

And Evan Williams, lying back in his chair with the paper on his knees, envied them. The best thing he could do would be to publish, with Macmillans, his monograph upon the foreign policy of Chatham. But confound this tumid, queasy feeling – this restlessness, swelling and heat – it was jealousy! jealousy! jealousy! which he had sworn never to feel again.

'Come with us to Corinth, Flanders,' he said with more than his usual energy, stopping by Jacob's chair. He was relieved by Jacob's reply, or rather by the solid, direct, if shy manner in which he said that he would like very much to come with them to Corinth.

'Here is a fellow,' thought Evan Williams, 'who might do very well in politics.'

'I intend to come to Greece every year so long as I live,' Jacob wrote to Bonamy. 'It is the only chance I can see of protecting oneself from civilisation.'

'Goodness knows what he means by that,' Bonamy sighed. For as he never said a clumsy thing himself, these dark sayings of Jacob's made him feel apprehensive, yet somehow impressed, his own turn being all for the definite, the concrete and the rational.

Nothing could be much simpler than what Sandra said as she descended the Acro-Corinth, keeping to the little path, while Jacob strode over rougher ground by her side. She had been left motherless at the age of four; and the park was vast.

'One never seemed able to get out of it,' she laughed. Of course there was the library, and dear Mr Jones, and notions about things. 'I used to stray into the kitchen and sit upon the butler's knees,' she laughed, sadly though.

Jacob thought that if he had been there he would have saved her; for she had been exposed to great dangers, he felt, and, he thought to himself, 'People wouldn't understand a woman talking as she talks.'

She made little of the roughness of the hill; and wore breeches, he saw, under her short skirts.

'Women like Fanny Elmer don't,' he thought. 'What's-her-name Carslake didn't; yet they pretend . . . '

Mrs Williams said things straight out. He was surprised by his own knowledge of the rules of behaviour; how much more can be said than one thought; how open one can be with a woman; and how little he had known himself before.

Evan joined them on the road; and as they drove along uphill and downhill (for Greece is in a state of effervescence, yet astonishingly clean-cut, a treeless land, where you see the ground between the blades, each hill cut and shaped and outlined as often as not against sparkling deep blue waters, islands white as sand floating on the horizon, occasional groves of palm trees standing in the valleys, which are scattered with black goats, spotted with little olive trees and sometimes have white hollows, rayed and criss-crossed, in their flanks), as they drove uphill and down he scowled in the corner of the carriage, with his paw so tightly closed that the skin was stretched between the knuckles and the little hairs stood upright. Sandra rode opposite, dominant, like a Victory prepared to fling into the air.

'Heartless!' thought Evan (which was untrue).

'Brainless!' he suspected (and that was not true either). 'Still . . . !' He envied her.

When bedtime came the difficulty was to write to Bonamy, Jacob found. Yet he had seen Salamis, and Marathon in the distance. Poor old Bonamy! No; there was something queer about it. He could not write to Bonamy.

'I shall go to Athens all the same,' he resolved, looking very set, with this hook dragging in his side.

The Williamses had already been to Athens.

Athens is still quite capable of striking a young man as the oddest combination, the most incongruous assortment. Now it is suburban; now immortal. Now cheap continental jewellery is laid upon plush trays. Now the stately woman stands naked, save for a wave of drapery above the knee. No form can he set on his sensations as he strolls, one blazing afternoon, along the Parisian boulevard and skips out of the way of the royal landau which, looking indescribably ramshackle, rattles along the pitted roadway, saluted by citizens of both sexes cheaply dressed in bowler hats and continental costumes; though a shepherd in kilt, cap and gaiters very nearly drives his herd of goats between the royal wheels; and all the time the Acropolis surges into the air, raises itself above the town, like a large immobile wave with the yellow columns of the Parthenon firmly planted upon it.

The yellow columns of the Parthenon are to be seen at all hours of the day firmly planted upon the Acropolis; though at sunset, when the ships in the Piraeus fire their guns, a bell rings, a man in uniform (the waistcoat unbuttoned) appears; and the women roll up the black stockings which they are knitting in the shadow of the columns, call to the children, and troop off down the hill back to their houses.

There they are again, the pillars, the pediment, the Temple of Victory and the Erechtheum, set on a tawny rock cleft with shadows, directly you unlatch your shutters in the morning and, leaning out, hear the clatter, the clamour, the whip cracking in the street below. There they are.

The extreme definiteness with which they stand, now a brilliant white, again yellow, and in some lights red, imposes ideas of durability, of the emergence through the earth of some spiritual energy elsewhere dissipated in elegant trifles. But this durability exists quite independently of our admiration. Although the beauty is sufficiently humane to weaken us, to stir the deep deposit of mud – memories, abandonments, regrets, sentimental devotions – the Parthenon is separate from all that; and if you consider how it has stood out all night, for centuries, you begin to connect the blaze (at midday the glare is dazzling and the frieze almost invisible) with the idea that perhaps it is beauty alone that is immortal.

Added to this, compared with the blistered stucco, the new love songs rasped out to the strum of guitar and gramophone, and the mobile yet insignificant faces of the street, the Parthenon is really astonishing in its silent composure; which is so vigorous that, far from being decayed, the Parthenon appears, on the contrary, likely to outlast the entire world.

'And the Greeks, like sensible men, never bothered to finish the backs of their statues,' said Jacob, shading his eyes and observing that the side of the figure which is turned away from view is left in the rough.

He noted the slight irregularity in the line of the steps which 'the artistic sense of the Greeks preferred to mathematical accuracy', he read in his guide-book.

He stood on the exact spot where the great statue of Athena used to stand, and identified the more famous landmarks of the scene beneath.

In short he was accurate and diligent; but profoundly morose. Moreover he was pestered by guides. This was on Monday.

But on Wednesday he wrote a telegram to Bonamy, telling him to come at once. And then he crumpled it in his hand and threw it in the gutter.

'For one thing he wouldn't come,' he thought. 'And then I dare say this sort of thing wears off.' 'This sort of thing' being that uneasy, painful feeling, something like selfishness – one wishes almost that the thing would stop – it is getting more and more beyond what is possible – 'If it goes on much longer I shan't be able to cope with it – but if someone else were seeing it at the same time – Bonamy is stuffed in his room in Lincoln's Inn – oh, I say, damn it all, I say' – the sight of Hymettus, Pentelicus, Lycabettus on one side, and the sea on the other, as one stands in the Parthenon at sunset, the sky pink feathered, the plain all colours, the marble tawny in one's eyes, is thus oppressive. Luckily Jacob had little sense of personal association; he seldom thought of Plato or Socrates in the flesh; on the other hand his feeling for architecture was very strong; he preferred statues to pictures; and he was beginning to think a great deal about the problems of civilisation, which were solved, of course, so very remarkably by the ancient Greeks, though their solution is no help to us. Then the hook gave a great tug in his side as he lay in bed on Wednesday night; and he turned over with a desperate sort of tumble, remembering Sandra Wentworth Williams with whom he was in love.

Next day he climbed Pentelicus.

The day after he went up to the Acropolis. The hour was early; the place almost deserted; and possibly there was thunder in the air. But the sun struck full upon the Acropolis.

Jacob's intention was to sit down and read, and, finding a drum of marble conveniently placed, from which Marathon could be seen, and yet it was in the shade, while the Erechtheum blazed white in front of him, there he sat. And after reading a page he put his thumb in his book. Why not rule countries in the way they should be ruled? And he read again.

No doubt his position there overlooking Marathon somehow raised his spirits. Or it may have been that a slow capacious brain has these moments of flowering. Or he had, insensibly, while he was abroad, got into the way of thinking about politics.

And then looking up and seeing the sharp outline, his meditations were given an extraordinary edge; Greece was over; the Parthenon in ruins; yet there he was.

(Ladies with green and white umbrellas passed through the courtyard – French ladies on their way to join their husbands in Constantinople.)

Jacob read on again. And laying the book on the ground he began, as if inspired by what he had read, to write a note upon the importance of history – upon democracy – one of those scribbles upon which the work of a lifetime may be based; or again, it falls out of a book twenty years later, and one can't remember a word of it. It is a little painful. It had better be burnt.

Jacob wrote; began to draw a straight nose; when all the French ladies opening and shutting their umbrellas just beneath him exclaimed, looking at the sky, that one did not know what to expect – rain or fine weather?

Jacob got up and strolled across to the Erechtheum. There are still several women standing there holding the roof on their heads. Jacob straightened himself slightly; for stability and balance affect the body first. These statues annulled things so! He stared at them, then turned, and there was Madame Lucien Gravé perched on a block of marble with her kodak pointed at his head. Of course she jumped down, in spite of her age, her figure and her tight boots – having, now that her daughter was married, lapsed with a luxurious abandonment, grand enough in its way, into the fleshy grotesque; she jumped down, but not before Jacob had seen her.

'Damn these women – damn these women!' he thought. And he went to fetch his book which he had left lying on the ground in the Parthenon.

'How they spoil things,' he murmured, leaning against one of the pillars, pressing his book tight between his arm and his side. (As for the weather, no doubt the storm would break soon; Athens was under cloud.)

'It is those damned women,' said Jacob, without any trace of bitterness, but rather with sadness and disappointment that what might have been should never be.

(This violent disillusionment is generally to be expected in young men in the prime of life, sound of wind and limb, who will soon become fathers of families and directors of banks.)

Then, making sure that the Frenchwomen had gone, and looking cautiously round him, Jacob strolled over to the Erechtheum and looked rather furtively at the goddess on the left-hand side holding the roof on her head. She reminded him of Sandra Wentworth Williams. He looked at her, then looked away. He looked at her, then looked away. He was extraordinarily moved, and with the battered Greek nose in his head, with Sandra in his head, with all sorts of things in his head, off he started to walk right up to the top of Mount Hymettus, alone, in the heat.

That very afternoon Bonamy went expressly to talk about Jacob to tea with Clara Durrant in the square behind Sloane Street where, on hot spring days, there are striped blinds over the front windows, single horses pawing the macadam outside the doors, and elderly gentlemen in yellow waistcoats ringing bells and stepping in very politely when the maid demurely replies that Mrs Durrant is at home.

Bonamy sat with Clara in the sunny front room with the barrel-organ piping sweetly outside; the water-cart going slowly along spraying the pavement; the carriages jingling; and all the silver and chintz, brown and blue rugs and vases filled with green boughs, striped with trembling yellow bars.

The insipidity of what was said needs no illustration – Bonamy kept on gently returning quiet answers and accumulating amazement at an existence squeezed and emasculated within a white satin shoe (Mrs Durrant meanwhile enunciating strident politics with Sir Somebody in the back room) until the virginity of Clara's soul appeared to him candid; the depths unknown; and he would have brought out Jacob's name had he not begun to feel positively certain that Clara loved him – and could do nothing whatever.

'Nothing whatever!' he exclaimed, as the door shut, and, for a man of his temperament, got a very queer feeling, as he walked through the park, of carriages irresistibly driven; of flowerbeds uncompromisingly geometrical; of force rushing round geometrical patterns in the most senseless way in the world. 'Was Clara,' he thought, pausing to watch the boys bathing in the Serpentine, 'the silent woman? – would Jacob marry her?'

But in Athens in the sunshine, in Athens, where it is almost impossible to get afternoon tea, and elderly gentlemen who talk politics talk them all the other way round, in Athens sat Sandra Wentworth Williams, veiled, in white, her legs stretched in front of her, one elbow on the arm of the bamboo chair, blue clouds wavering and drifting from her cigarette.

The orange trees which flourish in the Square of the Constitution, the band, the dragging of feet, the sky, the houses, lemon and rose coloured – all this became so significant to Mrs Wentworth Williams after her second cup of coffee that she began dramatising the story of the noble and impulsive Englishwoman who had offered a seat in her carriage to the old American lady at Mycenae (Mrs Duggan) – not altogether a false story, though it said nothing of Evan, standing first on one foot, then on the other, waiting for the women to stop chattering.

'I am putting the life of Father Damien into verse,' Mrs Duggan had said, for she had lost everything – everything in the world, husband and child and everything – but faith remained.

Sandra, floating from the particular to the universal, lay back in a trance.

The flight of time which hurries us so tragically along; the eternal drudge and drone, now bursting into fiery flame like those brief balls of yellow among green leaves (she was looking at orange trees); kisses on lips that are to die; the world turning, turning in mazes of heat and sound – though to be sure there is the quiet evening with its lovely pallor, 'For I am sensitive to every side of it,' Sandra thought, 'and Mrs Duggan will write to me for ever, and I shall answer her letters.' Now the royal band marching by with the national flag stirred wider rings of emotion, and life became something that the courageous mount and ride out to sea on – the hair blown back (so she envisaged it, and the breeze stirred slightly among the orange trees), and she herself was emerging from silver spray – when she saw Jacob. He was standing in the square with a book under his arm looking vacantly about him. That he was heavily built and might become stout in time was a fact.

But she suspected him of being a mere bumpkin.

'There is that young man,' she said, peevishly, throwing away her cigarette, 'that Mr Flanders.'

'Where?' said Evan. 'I don't see him.'

'Oh, walking away – behind the trees now. No, you can't see him. But we are sure to run into him,' which, of course, they did.

But how far was he a mere bumpkin? How far was Jacob Flanders at the age of twenty-six a stupid fellow? It is no use trying to sum people up. One must follow hints, not exactly what is said, nor yet entirely what is done. Some, it is true, take ineffaceable impressions of character at once. Others dally, loiter, and get blown this way and that. Kind old ladies assure us that cats are often the best judges of character. A cat will always go to a good man, they say; but then, Mrs Whitehorn, Jacob's landlady, loathed cats.

There is also the highly respectable opinion that character-mongering is much overdone nowadays. After all, what does it matter – that Fanny Elmer was all sentiment and sensation, and Mrs Durrant hard as iron? that Clara, owing (so the character-mongers said) largely to her mother's influence, never yet had the chance to do anything off her own bat, and only to very observant eyes displayed deeps of feeling which were positively alarming; and would certainly throw herself away upon some one unworthy of her one of these days unless, so the character-mongers said, she had a spark of her mother's spirit in her – was somehow heroic. But what a term to apply to Clara Durrant! Simple to a degree, others thought her. And that is the very reason, so they said, why she attracts Dick Bonamy – the young man with the Wellington nose. Now *he's* a dark horse if you like. And there these gossips would suddenly pause. Obviously they meant to hint at his peculiar disposition – long rumoured among them.

'But sometimes it is precisely a woman like Clara that men of that temperament need . . . ' Miss Julia Eliot would hint.

'Well,' Mr Bowley would reply, 'it may be so.'

For however long these gossips sit, and however they stuff out their victims' characters till they are swollen and tender as the livers of geese exposed to a hot fire, they never come to a decision.

'That young man, Jacob Flanders,' they would say, 'so distinguished looking – and yet so awkward.' Then they would apply themselves to Jacob and vacillate eternally between the two extremes. He rode to hounds – after a fashion, for he hadn't a penny.

'Did you ever hear who his father was?' asked Julia Eliot.

'His mother, they say, is somehow connected with the Rocksbiers,' replied Mr Bowley.

'He doesn't overwork himself anyhow.'

'His friends are very fond of him.'

'Dick Bonamy, you mean?'

'No, I didn't mean that. It's evidently the other way with Jacob. He is precisely the young man to fall headlong in love and repent it for the rest of his life.'

'Oh, Mr Bowley,' said Mrs Durrant, sweeping down upon them in her imperious manner, 'you remember Mrs Adams? Well, that is her niece.' And Mr Bowley, getting up, bowed politely and fetched strawberries.

So we are driven back to see what the other side means – the men in clubs and Cabinets – when they say that character-drawing is a frivolous fireside art, a matter of pins and needles, exquisite outlines enclosing vacancy, flourishes and mere scrawls.

The battleships ray out over the North Sea, keeping their stations accurately apart. At a given signal all the guns are trained on a target which (the master gunner counts the seconds, watch in hand – at the sixth he looks up) flames into splinters. With equal nonchalance a dozen young men in the prime of life descend with composed faces into the depths of the sea; and there impassively (though with perfect mastery of machinery) suffocate uncomplainingly together. Like blocks of tin soldiers the army covers the cornfield, moves up the hillside, stops, reels slightly this way and that, and falls flat, save that, through field glasses, it can be seen that one or two pieces still agitate up and down like fragments of broken matchstick.

These actions, together with the incessant commerce of banks, laboratories, chancellories and houses of business, are the strokes which oar the world forward, they say. And they are dealt by men as smoothly sculptured as the impassive policeman at Ludgate Circus. But you will observe that far from being padded to rotundity his face is stiff from force of will, and lean from the efforts of keeping it so. When his right arm rises, all the force in his veins flows straight from shoulder to finger-tips; not an ounce is diverted into sudden impulses, sentimental regrets, wire-drawn distinctions. The buses punctually stop.

It is thus that we live, they say, driven by an unseizable force. They say that the novelists never catch it; that it goes hurtling through their nets and leaves them torn to ribbons. This, they say, is what we live by – this unseizable force.

'Where are the men?' said old General Gibbons, looking round the drawing-room, full as usual on Sunday afternoons of well-dressed people. 'Where are the guns?'

Mrs Durrant looked too.

Clara, thinking that her mother wanted her, came in; then went out again.

They were talking about Germany at the Durrants, and Jacob (driven by this unseizable force) walked rapidly down Hermes Street and ran straight into the Williamses.

'Oh!' cried Sandra, with a cordiality which she suddenly felt. And Evan added, 'What luck!'

The dinner which they gave him in the hotel which looks on to the Square of the Constitution was excellent. Plaited baskets contained fresh rolls. There was real butter. And the meat scarcely needed the disguise of innumerable little red and green vegetables glazed in sauce.

It was strange, though. There were the little tables set out at intervals on the scarlet floor with the Greek king's monogram wrought in yellow. Sandra dined in her hat, veiled as usual. Evan looked this way and that over his shoulder; imperturbable yet supple; and sometimes sighed. It was strange. For they were English people come together in Athens on a May evening. Jacob, helping himself to this and that, answered intelligently, yet with a ring in his voice.

The Williamses were going to Constantinople early next morning, they said.

'Before you are up,' said Sandra.

They would leave Jacob alone, then. Turning very slightly, Evan ordered something – a bottle of wine – from which he helped Jacob, with a kind of solicitude, with a kind of paternal solicitude, if that were possible. To be left alone – that was good for a young fellow. Never was there a time when the country had more need of men. He sighed.

'And you have been to the Acropolis?' asked Sandra.

'Yes,' said Jacob. And they moved off to the window together, while Evan spoke to the head waiter about calling them early.

'It is astonishing,' said Jacob, in a gruff voice.

Sandra opened her eyes very slightly. Possibly her nostrils expanded a little too.

'At half-past six then,' said Evan, coming towards them, looking as if he faced something in facing his wife and Jacob standing with their backs to the window.

Sandra smiled at him.

And, as he went to the window and had nothing to say, she added, in broken half-sentences: 'Well, but how lovely – wouldn't it be? The Acropolis, Evan – or are you too tired?'

At that Evan looked at them, or, since Jacob was staring ahead of him, at his wife, surlily, sullenly, yet with a kind of distress – not that she would pity him. Nor would the implacable spirit of love, for anything he could do, cease its tortures.

They left him and he sat in the smoking-room, which looks out on to the Square of the Constitution.

'Evan is happier alone,' said Sandra. 'We have been separated from the newspapers. Well, it is better that people should have what they want . . . You have seen all these wonderful things since we met . . . What impression . . . I think that you are changed.'

'You want to go to the Acropolis,' said Jacob. 'Up here then.'

'One will remember it all one's life,' said Sandra.

'Yes,' said Jacob. 'I wish you could have come in the daytime.'

'This is more wonderful,' said Sandra, waving her hand.

Jacob looked vaguely.

'But you should see the Parthenon in the daytime,' he said. 'You couldn't come tomorrow – it would be too early?'

'You have sat there for hours and hours by yourself?'

'There were some awful women this morning,' said Jacob.

'Awful women?' Sandra echoed.

'Frenchwomen.'

'But something very wonderful has happened,' said Sandra. Ten minutes, fifteen minutes, half an hour – that was all the time before her.

'Yes,' he said.

'When one is your age – when one is young. What will you do? You will fall in love – oh yes! But don't be in too great a hurry. I am so much older.'

She was brushed off the pavement by parading men.

'Shall we go on?' Jacob asked.

'Let us go on,' she insisted.

For she could not stop until she had told him – or heard him say – or was it some action on his part that she required? Far away on the horizon she discerned it and could not rest.

'You'd never get English people to sit out like this,' he said.

'Never – no. When you get back to England you won't forget this – or come with us to Constantinople!' she cried suddenly.

'But then . . . '

Sandra sighed.

'You must go to Delphi, of course,' she said. 'But,' she asked herself, 'what do I want from him? Perhaps it is something that I have missed . . . '

'You will get there about six in the evening,' she said. 'You will see the eagles.'

Jacob looked set and even desperate by the light at the street corner and yet composed. He was suffering, perhaps. He was credulous. Yet there was something caustic about him. He had in him the seeds of extreme disillusionment, which would come to him from women in middle life. Perhaps if one strove hard enough to reach the top of the hill it need not come to him – this disillusionment from women in middle life.

'The hotel is awful,' she said. 'The last visitors had left their basins full of dirty water. There is always that,' she laughed.

'The people one meets *are* beastly,' Jacob said.

His excitement was clear enough.

'Write and tell me about it,' she said. 'And tell me what you feel and what you think. Tell me everything.'

The night was dark. The Acropolis was a jagged mound.

'I should like to, awfully,' he said.

'When we get back to London, we shall meet . . . '

'Yes.'

'I suppose they leave the gates open?' he asked.

'We could climb them!' she answered wildly.

Obscuring the moon and altogether darkening the Acropolis the clouds passed from east to west. The clouds solidified; the vapours thickened; the trailing veils stayed and accumulated.

It was dark now over Athens, except for gauzy red streaks where the streets ran; and the front of the palace was cadaverous from electric light. At sea the piers stood out, marked by separate dots, the waves being invisible, and promontories and islands dark humps with a few lights.

'I'd love to bring my brother, if I may,' Jacob murmured.

'And then when your mother comes to London – ' said Sandra.

The mainland of Greece was dark; and somewhere off Euboea a cloud must have touched the waves and spattered them – the dolphins circling deeper and deeper into the sea. Violent was the wind now rushing down the Sea of Marmara between Greece and the plains of Troy.

In Greece and the uplands of Albania and Turkey, the wind scours the sand and the dust, and sows itself thick with dry particles. And then it pelts the smooth domes of the mosques, and makes the cypresses, standing stiff by the turbaned tombstones of Mohammedans, creak and bristle.

Sandra's veils were swirled about her.

'I will give you my copy,' said Jacob. 'Here. Will you keep it?'

(The book was the poems of Donne.)

Now the agitation of the air uncovered a racing star. Now it was dark. Now one after another lights were extinguished. Now great towns – Paris – Constantinople – London – were black as strewn rocks. Waterways might be distinguished. In England the trees were heavy in leaf. Here perhaps in some southern wood an old man lit dry ferns and the birds were startled. The sheep coughed; one flower bent slightly towards another. The English sky is softer, milkier than the Eastern. Something gentle has passed into it from the grass-rounded hills, something damp. The salt gale blew in at Betty Flanders's bedroom window, and the widow lady, raising herself slightly on her elbow, sighed like one who realises, but would fain ward off a little longer – oh, a little longer! – the oppression of eternity.

But to return to Jacob and Sandra.

They had vanished. There was the Acropolis; but had they reached it? The columns and the temple remain; the emotion of the living breaks fresh on them year after year; and of that what remains?

As for reaching the Acropolis who shall say that we ever do it, or that when Jacob woke next morning he found anything hard and durable to keep for ever? Still, he went with them to Constantinople.

Sandra Wentworth Williams certainly woke to find a copy of Donne's poems upon her dressing-table. And the book would be stood on the shelf in the English country house where Sally Duggan's *Life of Father Damien* in verse would join it one of these days. There were ten or twelve little volumes already. Strolling in at dusk, Sandra would open the books and her eyes would brighten (but not at the print), and subsiding into the armchair she would suck back again the soul of the moment; or, for sometimes she was restless, would pull out book after book and swing across the whole space of her life like an acrobat from bar to bar. She had had her moments. Meanwhile, the great clock on the landing ticked and Sandra would hear time accumulating, and ask herself, 'What for? What for?'

'What for? What for?' Sandra would say, putting the book back, and strolling to the looking-glass and pressing her hair. And Miss Edwards would be startled at dinner, as she opened her mouth to admit roast mutton, by Sandra's sudden solicitude: 'Are you happy, Miss Edwards?' – a thing Cissy Edwards hadn't thought of for years.

'What for? What for?' Jacob never asked himself any such questions, to judge by the way he laced his boots; shaved himself; to judge by the depth of his sleep that night, with the wind fidgeting at the shutters and half a dozen mosquitoes singing in his ears. He was young – a man. And then Sandra was right when she judged him to be credulous as yet. At forty it might be a different matter. Already he had marked the things he liked in Donne, and they were savage enough. However, you might place beside them passages of the purest poetry in Shakespeare.

But the wind was rolling the darkness through the streets of Athens, rolling it, one might suppose, with a sort of trampling energy of mood which forbids too close an analysis of the feelings of any single person, or inspection of features. All faces – Greek, Levantine, Turkish, English – would have looked much the same in that darkness. At length the columns and the temples whiten, yellow, turn rose; and the Pyramids and St Peter's arise, and at last sluggish St Paul's looms up.

The Christians have the right to rouse most cities with their interpretation of the day's meaning. Then, less melodiously, dissenters of different sects issue a cantankerous emendation. The steamers, resounding like gigantic tuning-forks, state the old old fact – how there is a sea coldly, greenly, swaying outside. But nowadays it is the thin voice of duty, piping in a white thread from the top of a funnel, that collects the largest multitudes, and night is nothing but a long-drawn sigh between hammer-strokes, a deep breath – you can hear it from an open window even in the heart of London.

But who, save the nerve-worn and sleepless, or thinkers standing with hands to the eyes on some crag above the multitude, see things thus in skeleton outline, bare of flesh? In Surbiton the skeleton is wrapped in flesh.

'The kettle never boils so well on a sunny morning,' says Mrs Grandage, glancing at the clock on the mantelpiece. Then the grey Persian cat stretches itself on the window-seat, and buffets a moth with soft round paws. And before breakfast is half over (they were late today), a baby is deposited in her lap, and she must guard the sugar basin while Tom Grandage reads the golfing article in *The Times*, sips his coffee, wipes his moustaches, and is off to the office, where he is the greatest authority upon the foreign exchanges and marked for promotion. The skeleton is well wrapped in flesh. Even this dark night when the wind rolls the darkness through Lombard Street and Fetter Lane and Bedford Square it stirs (since it is summertime and the height of the season) plane trees spangled with electric light and curtains still preserving the room from the dawn. People still murmur over the last word said on the staircase, or strain, all through their dreams, for the voice of the alarm clock. So when the wind roams through a forest innumerable twigs stir; hives are brushed; insects sway on grass blades; the spider runs rapidly up a crease in the bark; and the whole air is tremulous with breathing; elastic with filaments.

Only here – in Lombard Street and Fetter Lane and Bedford Square –

each insect carries a globe of the world in his head, and the webs of the forest are schemes evolved for the smooth conduct of business; and honey is treasure of one sort and another; and the stir in the air is the indescribable agitation of life.

But colour returns; runs up the stalks of the grass; blows out into tulips and crocuses; solidly stripes the tree trunks; and fills the gauze of the air and the grasses and pools.

The Bank of England emerges; and the Monument with its bristling head of golden hair; the dray horses crossing London Bridge show grey and strawberry and iron-coloured. There is a whir of wings as the suburban trains rush into the terminus. And the light mounts over the faces of all the tall blind houses, slides through a chink and paints the lustrous bellying crimson curtains; the green wine-glasses; the coffee-cups; and the chairs standing askew.

Sunlight strikes in upon shaving-glasses; and gleaming brass cans; upon all the jolly trappings of the day; the bright, inquisitive, armoured, resplendent, summer's day, which has long since vanquished chaos; which has dried the melancholy medieval mists; drained the swamp and stood glass and stone upon it; and equipped our brains and bodies with such an armoury of weapons that merely to see the flash and thrust of limbs engaged in the conduct of daily life is better than the old pageant of armies drawn out in battle array upon the plain.

Chapter Thirteen

'The height of the season,' said Bonamy.

The sun had already blistered the paint on the backs of the green chairs in Hyde Park; peeled the bark off the plane trees; and turned the earth to powder and to smooth yellow pebbles. Hyde Park was circled, incessantly, by turning wheels.

'The height of the season,' said Bonamy sarcastically.

He was sarcastic because of Clara Durrant; because Jacob had come back from Greece very brown and lean, with his pockets full of Greek notes, which he pulled out when the chair man came for pence; because Jacob was silent.

'He has not said a word to show that he is glad to see me,' thought Bonamy bitterly.

The motor cars passed incessantly over the bridge of the Serpentine; the upper classes walked upright, or bent themselves gracefully over the palings; the lower classes lay with their knees cocked up, flat on their backs; the sheep grazed on pointed wooden legs; small children ran down the sloping grass, stretched their arms, and fell.

'Very urbane,' Jacob brought out.

'Urbane' on the lips of Jacob had mysteriously all the shapeliness of a character which Bonamy thought daily more sublime, devastating, terrific than ever, though he was still, and perhaps would be for ever, barbaric, obscure.

What superlatives! What adjectives! How acquit Bonamy of sentimentality of the grossest sort; of being tossed like a cork on the waves; of having no steady insight into character; of being unsupported by reason, and of drawing no comfort whatever from the works of the classics?

'The height of civilisation,' said Jacob.

He was fond of using Latin words.

Magnanimity, virtue – such words when Jacob used them in talk with Bonamy meant that he took control of the situation; that Bonamy would play round him like an affectionate spaniel; and that (as likely as not) they would end by rolling on the floor.

'And Greece?' said Bonamy. 'The Parthenon and all that?'

'There's none of this European mysticism,' said Jacob.

'It's the atmosphere, I suppose,' said Bonamy. 'And you went to Constantinople?'

'Yes,' said Jacob.

Bonamy paused, moved a pebble; then darted in with the rapidity and certainty of a lizard's tongue.

'You are in love!' he exclaimed.

Jacob blushed.

The sharpest of knives never cut so deep.

As for responding, or taking the least account of it, Jacob stared straight ahead of him, fixed, monolithic – oh, very beautiful! – like a British admiral, exclaimed Bonamy in a rage, rising from his seat and walking off; waiting for some sound; none came; too proud to look back; walking quicker and quicker until he found himself gazing into motor cars and cursing women. Where was the pretty woman's face? Clara's – Fanny's – Florinda's? Who was the pretty little creature?

Not Clara Durrant.

The Aberdeen terrier must be exercised, and as Mr Bowley was going that very moment – would like nothing better than a walk – they went together, Clara and kind little Bowley – Bowley who had rooms in Albany, Bowley who wrote letters to *The Times* in a jocular vein about foreign hotels and the aurora borealis – Bowley who liked young people and walked down Piccadilly with his right arm resting on the boss of his back.

'Little demon!' cried Clara, and attached Troy to his chain.

Bowley anticipated – hoped for – a confidence. Devoted to her mother, Clara sometimes felt her a little, well, her mother was so sure of herself that she could not understand other people being – being – 'as ludicrous as I am,'

Clara jerked out (the dog tugging her forwards). And Bowley thought she looked like a huntress and turned over in his mind which it should be – some pale virgin with a slip of the moon in her hair, which was a flight for Bowley.

The colour was in her cheeks. To have spoken outright about her mother – still, it was only to Mr Bowley, who loved her, as everybody must; but to speak was unnatural to her, yet it was awful to feel, as she had done all day, that she *must* tell someone.

'Wait till we cross the road,' she said to the dog, bending down.

Happily she had recovered by that time.

'She thinks so much about England,' she said. 'She is so anxious – '

Bowley was defrauded as usual. Clara never confided in anyone.

'Why don't the young people settle it, eh?' he wanted to ask. 'What's all this about England?' – a question poor Clara could not have answered, since, as Mrs Durrant discussed with Sir Edgar the policy of Sir Edward Grey, Clara only wondered why the cabinet looked dusty, and Jacob had never come. Oh, here was Mrs Cowley Johnson . . .

And Clara would hand the pretty china teacups, and smile at the compliment – that no one in London made tea so well as she did.

'We get it at Brocklebank's,' she said, 'in Cursitor Street.'

Ought she not to be grateful? Ought she not to be happy?

Especially since her mother looked so well and enjoyed so much talking to Sir Edgar about Morocco, Venezuela, or some such place.

'Jacob! Jacob!' thought Clara; and kind Mr Bowley, who was ever so good with old ladies, looked; stopped; wondered whether Elizabeth wasn't too harsh with her daughter; wondered about Bonamy, Jacob – which young fellow was it? – and jumped up directly Clara said she must exercise Troy.

They had reached the site of the old Exhibition. They looked at the tulips. Stiff and curled, the little rods of waxy smoothness rose from the earth, nourished yet contained, suffused with scarlet and coral pink. Each had its shadow; each grew trimly in the diamond-shaped wedge as the gardener had planned it.

'Barnes never gets them to grow like that,' Clara mused; she sighed.

'You are neglecting your friends,' said Bowley, as someone, going the other way, lifted his hat. She started; acknowledged Mr Lionel Parry's bow; wasted on him what had sprung for Jacob.

('Jacob! Jacob!' she thought.)

'But you'll get run over if I let you go,' she said to the dog.

'England seems all right,' said Mr Bowley.

The loop of the railing beneath the statue of Achilles was full of parasols and waistcoats; chains and bangles; of ladies and gentlemen, lounging elegantly, lightly observant.

' "This statue was erected by the women of England . . . " ' Clara read out with a foolish little laugh. 'Oh, Mr Bowley! Oh!' Gallop – gallop – gallop – a horse galloped past without a rider. The stirrups swung; the pebbles spurted.

'Oh, stop! Stop it, Mr Bowley!' she cried, white, trembling, gripping his arm, utterly unconscious, the tears coming.

'Tut-tut!' said Mr Bowley in his dressing-room an hour later. 'Tut-tut!' – a comment that was profound enough, though inarticulately expressed, since his valet was handing his shirt studs.

Julia Eliot, too, had seen the horse run away, and had risen from her seat to watch the end of the incident, which, since she came of a sporting family, seemed to her slightly ridiculous. Sure enough the little man came pounding behind with his breeches dusty; looked thoroughly annoyed; and was being helped to mount by a policeman when Julia Eliot, with a sardonic smile, turned towards the Marble Arch on her errand of mercy. It was only to visit a sick old lady who had known her mother and perhaps the Duke of Wellington; for Julia shared the love of her sex for the distressed; liked to visit death-beds; threw slippers at weddings; received confidences by the dozen; knew more pedigrees than a scholar knows dates, and was one of the kindliest, most generous, least continent of women.

Yet five minutes after she had passed the statue of Achilles she had the rapt look of one brushing through crowds on a summer's afternoon, when the trees are rustling, the wheels churning yellow, and the tumult of the present seems like an elegy for past youth and past summers, and there rose in her mind a curious sadness, as if time and eternity showed through skirts and waistcoats, and she saw people passing tragically to destruction. Yet, heaven knows, Julia was no fool. A sharper woman at a bargain did not exist. She was always punctual. The watch on her wrist gave her twelve minutes and a half in which to reach Bruton Street. Lady Congreve expected her at five.

The gilt clock at Verrey's was striking five.

Florinda looked at it with a dull expression, like an animal. She looked at the clock; looked at the door; looked at the long glass opposite; disposed her cloak; drew closer to the table, for she was pregnant – no doubt about it, Mother Stuart said, recommending remedies, consulting friends; sunk, caught by the heel, as she tripped so lightly over the surface.

Her tumbler of pinkish sweet stuff was set down by the waiter; and she sucked, through a straw, her eyes on the looking-glass, on the door, now soothed by the sweet taste. When Nick Bramham came in it was plain, even to the young Swiss waiter, that there was a bargain between them. Nick hitched his clothes together clumsily; ran his fingers through his hair; sat down, to an ordeal, nervously. She looked at him; and set off laughing; laughed – laughed – laughed. The young Swiss waiter, standing with crossed legs by the pillar, laughed too.

The door opened; in came the roar of Regent Street, the roar of traffic, impersonal, unpitying; and sunshine grained with dirt. The Swiss waiter must see to the newcomers. Bramham lifted his glass.

'He's like Jacob,' said Florinda, looking at the newcomer.

'The way he stares.' She stopped laughing.

Jacob, leaning forward, drew a plan of the Parthenon in the dust in Hyde Park, a network of strokes at least, which may have been the Parthenon, or again a mathematical diagram. And why was the pebble so emphatically ground in at the corner? It was not to count his notes that he took out a wad of papers and read a long flowing letter which Sandra had written two days ago at Milton Dower House with his book before her and in her mind the memory of something said or attempted, some moment in the dark on the road to the Acropolis which (such was her creed) mattered for ever.

'He is,' she mused, 'like that man in Molière.'

She meant Alceste. She meant that he was severe. She meant that she could deceive him.

'Or could I not?' she thought, putting the poems of Donne back in the bookcase. 'Jacob,' she went on, going to the window and looking over the spotted flower-beds across the grass where the piebald cows grazed under beech trees, 'Jacob would be shocked.'

The perambulator was going through the little gate in the railing. She kissed her hand; directed by the nurse, Jimmy waved his.

'*He's* a small boy,' she said, thinking of Jacob.

And yet – Alceste?

'What a nuisance you are!' Jacob grumbled, stretching out first one leg and then the other and feeling in each trouser-pocket for his chair ticket.

'I expect the sheep have eaten it,' he said. 'Why do you keep sheep?'

'Sorry to disturb you, sir,' said the ticket-collector, his hand deep in the enormous pouch of pence.

'Well, I hope they pay you for it,' said Jacob. 'There you are. No. You can stick to it. Go and get drunk.'

He had parted with half a crown, tolerantly, compassionately, with considerable contempt for his species.

Even now poor Fanny Elmer was dealing, as she walked along the Strand, in her incompetent way with this very careless, indifferent, sublime manner he had of talking to railway guards or porters; or Mrs Whitehorn, when she consulted him about her little boy who was beaten by the schoolmaster.

Sustained entirely upon picture postcards for the past two months, Fanny's idea of Jacob was more statuesque, noble and eyeless than ever. To reinforce her vision she had taken to visiting the British Museum, where, keeping her eyes downcast until she was alongside of the battered Ulysses, she opened them and got a fresh shock of Jacob's presence, enough to last her half a day. But this was wearing thin. And she wrote now – poems, letters that were never posted – saw his face in advertisements on hoardings, and would cross the road to let the barrel-organ turn her musings to rhapsody. But at breakfast (she shared rooms with a teacher), when the butter was smeared about the plate, and the prongs of the forks were clotted with old egg yolk, she revised these visions violently; was, in truth, very cross; was losing her complexion, as Margery Jackson told her, bringing the whole thing down (as she laced her stout boots) to a level of mother-wit, vulgarity and sentiment, for she had loved too; and been a fool.

'One's godmothers ought to have told one,' said Fanny, looking in at the window of Bacon, the mapseller, in the Strand – told one that it is no use making a fuss; this is life, they should have said, as Fanny said it now, looking at the large yellow globe marked with steamship lines.

'This is life. This is life,' said Fanny.

'A very hard face,' thought Miss Barrett, on the other side of the glass, buying maps of the Syrian desert and waiting impatiently to be served. 'Girls look old so soon nowadays.'

The equator swam behind tears.

'Piccadilly?' Fanny asked the conductor of the omnibus, and climbed to the top. After all, he would, he must, come back to her.

But Jacob might have been thinking of Rome; of architecture; of jurisprudence; as he sat under the plane tree in Hyde Park.

The omnibus stopped outside Charing Cross; and behind it were clogged omnibuses, vans, motor cars, for a procession with banners was passing down Whitehall, and elderly people were stiffly descending from between the paws of the slippery lions, where they had been testifying to their faith, singing lustily, raising their eyes from their music to look into the sky, and still their eyes were on the sky as they marched behind the gold letters of their creed.

The traffic stopped, and the sun, no longer sprayed out by the breeze, became almost too hot. But the procession passed; the banners glittered far away down Whitehall; the traffic was released; lurched on; spun to a smooth continuous uproar; swerving round the curve of Cockspur Street; and sweeping past government offices and equestrian statues down Whitehall to the prickly spires, the tethered grey fleet of masonry, and the large white clock of Westminster.

Five strokes Big Ben intoned; Nelson received the salute. The wires of the Admiralty shivered with some faraway communication. A voice kept remarking that Prime Ministers and Viceroys spoke in the Reichstag; entered Lahore; said that the Emperor travelled; in Milan they rioted; said there were rumours in Vienna; said that the Ambassador at Constantinople had audience with the Sultan; the fleet was at Gibraltar. The voice continued, imprinting on the faces of the clerks in Whitehall (Timothy Durrant was one of them) something of its own inexorable gravity, as they listened, deciphered, wrote down. Papers accumulated, inscribed with the utterances of Kaisers, the statistics of ricefields, the growling of hundreds of work-people, plotting sedition in back streets, or gathering in the Calcutta bazaars, or mustering their forces in the uplands of Albania, where the hills are sand-coloured and bones lie unburied.

The voice spoke plainly in the square quiet room with heavy tables, where one elderly man made notes on the margin of typewritten sheets, his silver-topped umbrella leaning against the bookcase.

His head – bald, red-veined, hollow-looking – represented all the heads in the building. His head, with the amiable pale eyes, carried the burden of knowledge across the street; laid it before his colleagues, who came equally burdened; and then the sixteen gentlemen, lifting their pens or turning perhaps rather wearily in their chairs, decreed that the course of history should shape itself this way or that way, being manfully determined, as their faces showed, to impose some coherency upon Rajahs and Kaisers and the muttering in bazaars, the secret gatherings, plainly visible in Whitehall, of kilted peasants in Albanian uplands; to control the course of events.

Pitt and Chatham, Burke and Gladstone looked from side to side with fixed marble eyes and an air of immortal quiescence which perhaps the living may have envied, the air being full of whistling and concussions, as the procession with its banners passed down Whitehall. Moreover, some were troubled with dyspepsia; one had at that very moment cracked the glass of his spectacles; another spoke in Glasgow tomorrow; altogether they looked too red, fat, pale or lean, to be dealing, as the marble heads had dealt, with the course of history.

Timmy Durrant in his little room in the Admiralty, going to consult a Blue book, stopped for a moment by the window and observed the placard tied round the lamp-post.

Miss Thomas, one of the typists, said to her friend that if the Cabinet was going to sit much longer she should miss her boy outside the Gaiety.

Timmy Durrant, returning with his Blue book under his arm, noticed a little knot of people at the street corner; conglomerated as though one of them knew something; and the others, pressing round him, looked up, looked down, looked along the street. What was it that he knew?

Timothy, placing the Blue book before him, studied a paper sent round by the Treasury for information. Mr Crawley, his fellow-clerk, impaled a letter on a skewer.

Jacob rose from his chair in Hyde Park, tore his ticket to pieces, and walked away.

'Such a sunset,' wrote Mrs Flanders in her letter to Archer at Singapore.

'One couldn't make up one's mind to come indoors,' she wrote. 'It seemed wicked to waste even a moment.'

The long windows of Kensington Palace flushed fiery rose as Jacob walked away; a flock of wild duck flew over the Serpentine; and the trees were stood against the sky, blackly, magnificently.

'Jacob,' wrote Mrs Flanders, with the red light on her page, 'is hard at work after his delightful journey . . . '

'The Kaiser,' the faraway voice remarked in Whitehall, 'received me in audience.'

'Now I know that face – ' said the Reverend Andrew Floyd, coming out of Carter's shop in Piccadilly, 'but who the dickens – ?' and he watched Jacob, turned round to look at him, but could not be sure –

'Oh, Jacob Flanders!' he remembered in a flash.

But he was so tall; so unconscious; such a fine young fellow.

'I gave him Byron's works,' Andrew Floyd mused, and started forward, as Jacob crossed the road; but hesitated, and let the moment pass, and lost the opportunity.

Another procession, without banners, was blocking Long Acre. Carriages, with dowagers in amethyst and gentlemen spotted with carnations, intercepted cabs and motor cars turned in the opposite direction, in which jaded men in white waistcoats lolled, on their way home to shrubberies and billiard-rooms in Putney and Wimbledon.

Two barrel-organs played by the kerb, and horses coming out of Aldridge's with white labels on their buttocks straddled across the road and were smartly jerked back.

Mrs Durrant, sitting with Mr Wortley in a motor car, was impatient lest they should miss the overture.

But Mr Wortley, always urbane, always in time for the overture, buttoned his gloves, and admired Miss Clara.

'A shame to spend such a night in the theatre!' said Mrs Durrant, seeing all the windows of the coachmakers in Long Acre ablaze.

'Think of your moors!' said Mr Wortley to Clara.

'Ah! but Clara likes this better,' Mrs Durrant laughed.

'I don't know – really,' said Clara, looking at the blazing windows. She started.

She saw Jacob.

'Who?' asked Mrs Durrant sharply, leaning forward.

But she saw no one.

Under the arch of the Opera House large faces and lean ones, the powdered and the hairy, all alike were red in the sunset; and, quickened by the great hanging lamps with their repressed primrose lights, by the tramp, and the scarlet, and the pompous ceremony, some ladies looked for a moment into steaming bedrooms near by, where women with loose hair leaned out of windows, where girls – where children – (the long mirrors held the ladies suspended) but one must follow; one must not block the way.

Clara's moors were fine enough. The Phoenicians slept under their piled grey rocks; the chimneys of the old mines pointed starkly; early moths blurred the heather-bells; cartwheels could be heard grinding on the road far beneath; and the suck and sighing of the waves sounded gently, persistently, for ever.

Shading her eyes with her hand Mrs Pascoe stood in her cabbage-garden looking out to sea. Two steamers and a sailing-ship crossed each other; passed each other; and in the bay the gulls kept alighting on a log, rising high, returning again to the log, while some rode in upon the waves and stood on the rim of the water until the moon blanched all to whiteness.

Mrs Pascoe had gone indoors long ago.

But the red light was on the columns of the Parthenon, and the Greek women who were knitting their stockings and sometimes crying to a child to come and have the insects picked from its head were as jolly as sand-martins in the heat, quarrelling, scolding, suckling their babies, until the ships in the Piraeus fired their guns.

The sound spread itself flat, and then went tunnelling its way with fitful explosions among the channels of the islands.

Darkness drops like a knife over Greece.

'The guns?' said Betty Flanders, half asleep, getting out of bed and going to the window, which was decorated with a fringe of dark leaves.

'Not at this distance,' she thought. 'It is the sea.'

Again, far away, she heard the dull sound, as if nocturnal women were beating great carpets. There was Morty lost, and Seabrook dead; her sons fighting for their country. But were the chickens safe? Was that someone moving downstairs? Rebecca with the toothache? No. The nocturnal women were beating great carpets. Her hens shifted slightly on their perches.

Chapter Fourteen

'He left everything just as it was,' Bonamy marvelled. 'Nothing arranged. All his letters strewn about for anyone to read. What did he expect? Did he think he would come back?' he mused, standing in the middle of Jacob's room.

The eighteenth century has its distinction. These houses were built, say, a hundred and fifty years ago. The rooms are shapely, the ceilings high; over the doorways a rose or a ram's skull is carved in the wood. Even the panels, painted in raspberry-coloured paint, have their distinction.

Bonamy took up a bill for a hunting-crop.

'That seems to be paid,' he said.

There were Sandra's letters.

Mrs Durrant was taking a party to Greenwich.

Lady Rocksbier hoped for the pleasure . . .

Listless is the air in an empty room, just swelling the curtain; the flowers in the jar shift. One fibre in the wicker armchair creaks, though no one sits there.

Bonamy crossed to the window. Pickford's van swung down the street. The omnibuses were locked together at Mudie's corner. Engines throbbed, and carters, jamming the brakes down, pulled their horses sharp up. A harsh and unhappy voice cried something unintelligible. And then suddenly all the leaves seemed to raise themselves.

'Jacob! Jacob!' cried Bonamy, standing by the window. The leaves sank down again.

'Such confusion everywhere!' exclaimed Betty Flanders, bursting open the bedroom door.

Bonamy turned away from the window.

'What am I to do with these, Mr Bonamy?'

She held out a pair of Jacob's old shoes.

MRS DALLOWAY

Mrs Dalloway

A novel by
VIRGINIA WOOLF
first published in 1925

Mrs Dalloway said she would buy the flowers herself.

For Lucy had her work cut out for her. The doors would be taken off their hinges; Rumpelmayer's men were coming. And then, thought Clarissa Dalloway, what a morning – fresh as if issued to children on a beach.

What a lark! What a plunge! For so it had always seemed to her when, with a little squeak of the hinges, which she could hear now, she had burst open the French windows and plunged at Bourton into the open air. How fresh, how calm, stiller than this of course, the air was in the early morning; like the flap of a wave; the kiss of a wave; chill and sharp and yet (for a girl of eighteen as she then was) solemn, feeling as she did, standing there at the open window, that something awful was about to happen; looking at the flowers, at the trees with the smoke winding off them and the rooks rising, falling; standing and looking until Peter Walsh said, 'Musing among the vegetables?' – was that it? – 'I prefer men to cauliflowers' – was that it? He must have said it at breakfast one morning when she had gone out on to the terrace – Peter Walsh. He would be back from India one of these days, June or July, she forgot which, for his letters were awfully dull; it was his sayings one remembered; his eyes, his pocket-knife, his smile, his grumpiness and, when millions of things had utterly vanished – how strange it was! – a few sayings like this about cabbages.

She stiffened a little on the kerb, waiting for Durtnall's van to pass. A charming woman, Scrope Purvis thought her (knowing her as one does know people who live next door to one in Westminster); a touch of the bird about her, of the jay, blue-green, light, vivacious, though she was over fifty, and grown very white since her illness. There she perched, never seeing him, waiting to cross, very upright.

For having lived in Westminster – how many years now? over twenty – one feels even in the midst of the traffic, or waking at night, Clarissa was positive, a particular hush, or solemnity; an indescribable pause; a suspense (but that might be her heart, affected, they said, by influenza) before Big Ben strikes. There! Out it boomed. First a warning, musical; then the hour, irrevocable. The leaden circles dissolved in the air. Such fools we are, she thought, crossing Victoria Street. For Heaven only knows why one loves it so, how one sees it so, making it up, building it round one, tumbling it, creating it every moment afresh; but the veriest frumps, the most dejected of miseries sitting on doorsteps (drink their downfall) do the same; can't be dealt with, she felt positive, by Acts of Parliament for that very reason: they love life. In people's eyes, in the swing, tramp, and trudge; in the bellow and the uproar; the carriages, motor cars, omnibuses, vans, sandwich men shuffling and swinging; brass bands; barrel organs; in the triumph and the jingle and the strange high singing of some aeroplane overhead was what she loved; life; London; this moment of June.

For it was the middle of June. The War was over, except for someone like Mrs Foxcroft at the Embassy last night eating her heart out because that nice boy was killed and now the old Manor House must go to a cousin; or Lady Bexborough who opened a bazaar, they said, with the telegram in her hand, John, her favourite, killed; but it was over; thank Heaven – over. It was June. The King and Queen were at the Palace. And everywhere, though it was still so early, there was a beating, a stirring of galloping ponies, tapping of cricket bats; Lords, Ascot, Ranelagh and all the rest of it; wrapped in the soft mesh of the grey-blue morning air, which, as the day wore on, would unwind them, and set down on their lawns and pitches the bouncing ponies, whose forefeet just struck the ground and up they sprung, the whirling young men, and laughing girls in their transparent muslins who, even now, after dancing all night, were taking their absurd woolly dogs for a run; and even now, at this hour, discreet old dowagers were shooting out in their motor cars on errands of mystery; and the shopkeepers were fidgeting in their windows with their paste and diamonds, their lovely old sea-green brooches in eighteenth-century settings to tempt Americans (but one must economise, not buy things rashly for Elizabeth), and she, too, loving it as she did with an absurd and faithful passion, being part of it, since her people were courtiers once in the time of the Georges, she, too, was going that very night to kindle and illuminate; to give her party. But how strange, on entering the Park, the silence; the mist; the hum; the slow-swimming happy ducks; the pouched birds waddling; and who should be coming along with his back against the Government buildings, most appropriately, carrying a despatch box stamped with the Royal Arms, who but Hugh Whitbread; her old friend Hugh – the admirable Hugh!

'Good-morning to you, Clarissa!' said Hugh, rather extravagantly, for they had known each other as children. 'Where are you off to?'

'I love walking in London,' said Mrs Dalloway. 'Really, it's better than walking in the country.'

They had just come up – unfortunately – to see doctors. Other people came to see pictures; go to the opera; take their daughters out; the Whitbreads came 'to see doctors'. Times without number Clarissa had visited Evelyn Whitbread in a nursing home. Was Evelyn ill again? Evelyn was a good deal out of sorts, said Hugh, intimating by a kind of pout or swell of his very well-covered, manly, extremely handsome, perfectly upholstered body (he was almost too well dressed always, but presumably had to be, with his little job at Court) that his wife had some internal ailment, nothing serious, which, as an old friend, Clarissa Dalloway would quite understand without requiring him to specify. Ah yes, she did of course; what a nuisance;

and felt very sisterly and oddly conscious at the same time of her hat. Not the right hat for the early morning, was that it? For Hugh always made her feel, as he bustled on, raising his hat rather extravagantly and assuring her that she might be a girl of eighteen, and of course he was coming to her party tonight, Evelyn absolutely insisted, only a little late he might be after the party at the Palace to which he had to take one of Jim's boys – she always felt a little skimpy beside Hugh; schoolgirlish; but attached to him, partly from having known him always, but she did think him a good sort in his own way, though Richard was nearly driven mad by him, and as for Peter Walsh, he had never to this day forgiven her for liking him.

She could remember scene after scene at Bourton – Peter furious; Hugh not, of course, his match in any way, but still not a positive imbecile as Peter made out; not a mere barber's block. When his old mother wanted him to give up shooting or to take her to Bath he did it, without a word; he was really unselfish, and as for saying, as Peter did, that he had no heart, no brain, nothing but the manners and breeding of an English gentleman, that was only her dear Peter at his worst; and he could be intolerable; he could be impossible; but adorable to walk with on a morning like this.

(June had drawn out every leaf on the trees. The mothers of Pimlico gave suck to their young. Messages were passing from the Fleet to the Admiralty. Arlington Street and Piccadilly seemed to chafe the very air in the Park and lift its leaves hotly, brilliantly, on waves of that divine vitality which Clarissa loved. To dance, to ride, she had adored all that.)

For they might be parted for hundreds of years, she and Peter; she never wrote a letter and his were dry sticks; but suddenly it would come over her, If he were with me now what would he say? – some days, some sights bringing him back to her calmly, without the old bitterness; which perhaps was the reward of having cared for people; they came back in the middle of St James's Park on a fine morning – indeed they did. But Peter – however beautiful the day might be, and the trees and the grass, and the little girl in pink – Peter never saw a thing of all that. He would put on his spectacles, if she told him to; he would look. It was the state of the world that interested him; Wagner, Pope's poetry, people's characters eternally, and the defects of her own soul. How he scolded her! How they argued! She would marry a Prime Minister and stand at the top of a staircase; the perfect hostess he called her (she had cried over it in her bedroom), she had the makings of the perfect hostess, he said.

So she would still find herself arguing in St James's Park, still making out that she had been right – and she had too – not to marry him. For in marriage a little licence, a little independence there must be between peo- ple living together day in day out in the same house; which Richard gave her, and she him. (Where was he this morning, for instance? Some commit- tee, she never asked what.) But with Peter everything had to be shared; everything gone into. And it was intolerable, and when it came to that scene in the little garden by the fountain, she had to break with him or they would have been destroyed, both of them ruined, she was convinced; though she had borne about with her for years like an arrow sticking in her heart the grief, the anguish; and then the horror of the moment when someone told her at a concert that he had married a woman met on the boat going to India! Never should she forget all that! Cold, heartless, a prude, he called her. Never could she understand how he cared. But those Indian women did presumably – silly, pretty, flimsy nincompoops. And she wasted her pity. For he was quite happy, he assured her – perfectly happy, though he had never done a thing that they talked of; his whole life had been a failure. It made her angry still.

She had reached the Park gates. She stood for a moment, looking at the omnibuses in Piccadilly.

She would not say of anyone in the world now that they were this or were that. She felt very young; at the same time unspeakably aged. She sliced like a knife through everything; at the same time was outside, looking on. She had a perpetual sense, as she watched the taxi cabs, of being out, out, far out to sea and alone; she always had the feeling that it was very, very dangerous to live even one day. Not that she thought herself clever, or much out of the ordinary. How she had got through life on the few twigs of knowledge Fräulein Daniels gave them she could not think. She knew nothing; no language, no history; she scarcely read a book now, except memoirs in bed; and yet to her it was absolutely absorbing; all this; the cabs passing; and she would not say of Peter, she would not say of herself, I am this, I am that.

Her only gift was knowing people almost by instinct, she thought, walking on. If you put her in a room with someone, up went her back like a cat's; or she purred. Devonshire House, Bath House, the house with the china cockatoo, she had seen them all lit up once; and remembered Sylvia, Fred, Sally Seton – such hosts of people; and dancing all night; and the waggons plodding past to market; and driving home across the Park. She remembered once throwing a shilling into the Serpentine. But everyone remembered; what she loved was this, here, now, in front of her; the fat lady in the cab. Did it matter then, she asked herself, walking towards Bond Street, did it matter that she must inevitably cease completely; all this must go on without her; did she resent it; or did it not become consoling to believe that death ended absolutely? but that somehow in the streets of London, on the ebb and flow of things, here, there, she survived, Peter survived, lived in each other, she being part, she was positive, of the trees at home; of the house there, ugly, rambling all to bits and pieces as it was; part of people she had never met; being laid out like a mist between the people she knew best, who lifted her on their branches as she had seen the trees lift the mist, but it spread ever so far, her life, herself. But what was she dreaming as she looked into Hatchard's shop window? What was she trying to recover? What image of white dawn in the country, as she read in the book spread open:

Fear no more the heat o' the sun
Nor the furious winter's rages.

This late age of the world's experience had bred in them all, all men and women, a well of tears. Tears and sorrows; courage and endurance; a perfectly upright and stoical bearing. Think, for example, of the woman she admired most, Lady Bexborough, opening the bazaar.

There were *Jorrocks' Jaunts and Jollities*; there were *Soapy Sponge* and Mrs Asquith's *Memoirs* and *Big Game Shooting in Nigeria*, all spread open. Ever so many books there were; but none that seemed exactly right to take to Evelyn Whitbread in her nursing home. Nothing that would serve to amuse her and make that indescribably dried-up little woman look, as Clarissa came in, just for a moment cordial; before they settled down for the usual interminable talk of women's ailments. How much she wanted it – that people should look pleased as she came in, Clarissa thought and turned and walked back towards Bond Street, annoyed, because it was silly to have other reasons for doing things. Much rather would she have been one of those people like Richard who did things for themselves, whereas, she thought, waiting to cross, half the time she did things not simply, not for themselves; but to make people think this or that; perfect idiocy she knew (and now the policeman held up his hand) for no one was ever for a second taken in. Oh if she could have had her life over again! she thought, stepping on to the pavement, could have looked even differently!

She would have been, in the first place, dark like Lady Bexborough, with a skin of crumpled leather and beautiful eyes. She would have been, like Lady Bexborough, slow and stately; rather large; interested in politics like a man; with a country house; very dignified, very sincere. Instead of which she had a narrow pea-stick figure; a ridiculous little face, beaked like a bird's. That she held herself well was true; and had nice hands and feet; and dressed well, considering that she spent little. But often now this body she wore (she stopped to look at a Dutch picture), this body, with all its capacities, seemed nothing – nothing at all. She had the oddest sense of being herself invisible; unseen; unknown; there being no more marrying, no more having of children now, but only this astonishing and rather solemn progress with the rest of them, up Bond Street, this being Mrs Dalloway; not even Clarissa any more; this being Mrs Richard Dalloway.

Bond Street fascinated her; Bond Street early in the morning in the season, its flags flying; its shops; no splash; no glitter; one roll of tweed in the shop where her father had bought his suits for fifty years; a few pearls; salmon on an ice-block.

'That is all,' she said, looking at the fishmonger's. 'That is all,' she repeated, pausing for a moment at the window of a glove shop where, before the War, you could buy almost perfect gloves. And her old Uncle William used to say a lady is known by her shoes and her gloves. He had turned on his bed one morning in the middle of the War. He had said, 'I have had enough.' Gloves and shoes; she had a passion for gloves; but her own daughter, her Elizabeth, cared not a straw for either of then.

Not a straw, she thought, going on up Bond Street to a shop where they kept flowers for her when she gave a party. Elizabeth really cared for her dog most of all. The whole house this morning smelt of tar. Still, better poor Grizzle than Miss Kilman; better distemper and tar and all the rest of it than sitting mewed in a stuffy bedroom with a prayer book! Better anything, she was inclined to say. But it might be only a phase, as Richard said, such as all girls go through. It might be falling in love. But why with Miss Kilman? who had been badly treated of course; one must make allowances for that, and Richard said she was very able, had a really historical mind. Anyhow they were inseparable, and Elizabeth, her own daughter, went to Communion; and how she dressed, how she treated people who came to lunch she did not care a bit, it being her experience that the religious ecstasy made people callous (so did causes); dulled their feelings, for Miss Kilman would do anything for the Russians, starved herself for the Austrians, but in private inflicted positive torture, so insensitive was she, dressed in a green mackintosh coat. Year in year out she wore that coat; she perspired; she was never in the room five minutes without making you feel her superiority, your inferiority; how poor she was; how rich you were; how she lived in a slum without a cushion or a bed or a rug or whatever it might be, all her soul rusted with that grievance sticking in it, her dismissal from school during the War – poor embittered unfortunate creature! For it was not her one hated but the idea of her, which undoubtedly had gathered into itself a great deal that was not Miss Kilman; had become one of those spectres with which one battles in the night; one of those spectres who stand astride us and suck up half our life-blood, dominators and tyrants; for no doubt with another throw of the dice, had the black been uppermost and not the white, she would have loved Miss Kilman! But not in this world. No.

It rasped her, though, to have stirring about in her this brutal monster! to hear twigs cracking and feel hooves planted down in the depths of that leaf-encumbered forest, the soul; never to be content quite, or quite secure, for at any moment the brute would be stirring, this hatred, which, especially since her illness, had power to make her feel scraped, hurt in her spine; gave her physical pain, and made all pleasure in beauty, in friendship, in being well, in being loved and making her home delightful rock, quiver, and bend as if indeed there were a monster grubbing at the roots, as if the whole panoply of content were nothing but self love! this hatred!

Nonsense, nonsense! she cried to herself, pushing through the swing doors of Mulberry's the florists.

She advanced, light, tall, very upright, to be greeted at once by button-faced Miss Pym, whose hands were always bright red, as if they had been stood in cold water with the flowers.

There were flowers: delphiniums, sweet peas, bunches of lilac; and carnations, masses of carnations. There were roses; there were irises. Ah yes – so she breathed in the earthy garden sweet smell as she stood talking to Miss Pym who owed her help, and thought her kind, for kind she had been years ago; very kind, but she looked older, this year, turning her head from side to side among the irises and roses and nodding tufts of lilac with her eyes half closed, snuffing in, after the street uproar, the delicious scent, the exquisite coolness. And then, opening her eyes, how fresh, like frilled linen clean from a laundry laid in wicker trays the roses looked; and dark and prim the red carnations, holding their heads up; and all the sweet peas spreading in their bowls, tinged violet, snow white, pale – as if it were the evening and girls in muslin frocks came out to pick sweet peas and roses after the superb summer's day, with its almost blue-black sky, its delphiniums, its carnations, its arum lilies was over; and it was the moment between six and seven when every flower – roses, carnations, irises, lilac – glows; white, violet, red, deep orange; every flower seems to burn by itself, softly, purely in the misty beds; and how she loved the grey white moths spinning in and out, over the cherry pie, over the evening primroses!

And as she began to go with Miss Pym from jar to jar, choosing, nonsense, nonsense, she said to herself, more and more gently, as if this beauty, this scent, this colour, and Miss Pym liking her, trusting her, were a wave which she let flow over her and surmount that hatred, that monster, surmount it all; and it lifted her up and up when – oh! a pistol shot in the street outside!

'Dear, those motor cars,' said Miss Pym, going to the window to look, and coming back and smiling apologetically with her hands full of sweet peas, as if those motor cars, those tyres of motor cars, were all *her* fault.

The violent explosion which made Mrs Dalloway jump and Miss Pym go to the window and apologise came from a motor car which had drawn to the side of the pavement precisely opposite Mulberry's shop window. Passers-by who, of course, stopped and stared, had just time to see a face of the very greatest importance against the dove-grey upholstery, before a male hand drew the blind and there was nothing to be seen except a square of dove grey.

Yet rumours were at once in circulation from the middle of Bond Street to Oxford Street on one side, to Atkinson's scent shop on the other, passing invisibly, inaudibly, like a cloud, swift, veil-like upon hills, falling indeed with something of a cloud's sudden sobriety and stillness upon faces which a second before had been utterly disorderly. But now mystery had brushed them with her wing; they had heard the voice of authority; the spirit of religion was abroad with her eyes bandaged tight and her lips gaping wide. But nobody knew whose face had been seen. Was it the Prince of Wales's, the Queen's, the Prime Minister's? Whose face was it? Nobody knew.

Edgar J. Watkiss, with his roll of lead piping round his arm, said audibly, humorously of course: 'The Proime Minister's kyar.'

Septimus Warren Smith, who found himself unable to pass, heard him.

Septimus Warren Smith, aged about thirty, pale-faced, beak-nosed, wearing brown shoes and a shabby overcoat, with hazel eyes which had that look of apprehension in them which makes complete strangers apprehensive too. The world has raised its whip; where will it descend?

Everything had come to a standstill. The throb of the motor engines sounded like a pulse irregularly drumming through an entire body. The sun became extraordinarily hot because the motor car had stopped outside Mulberry's shop window; old ladies on the tops of omnibuses spread their black parasols; here a green, here a red parasol opened with a little pop. Mrs Dalloway, coming to the window with her arms full of sweet peas, looked out with her little pink face pursed in enquiry. Everyone looked at the motor car. Septimus looked. Boys on bicycles sprang off. Traffic accumulated. And there the motor car stood, with drawn blinds, and upon them a curious pattern like a tree, Septimus thought, and this gradual drawing together of everything to one centre before his eyes, as if some horror had come almost to the surface and was about to burst into flames, terrified him. The world wavered and quivered and threatened to burst into flames. It is I who am blocking the way, he thought. Was he not being looked at and pointed at; was he not weighted there, rooted to the pavement, for a purpose? But for what purpose?

'Let us go on, Septimus,' said his wife, a little woman, with large eyes in a sallow pointed face; an Italian girl.

But Lucrezia herself could not help looking at the motor car and the tree pattern on the blinds. Was it the Queen in there – the Queen going shopping?

The chauffeur, who had been opening something, turning something, shutting something, got on to the box.

'Come on,' said Lucrezia.

But her husband, for they had been married four, five years now, jumped, started, and said, 'All right!' angrily, as if she had interrupted him.

People must notice; people must see. People, she thought, looking at the crowd staring at the motor car; the English people, with their children and their horses and their clothes, which she admired in a way; but they were 'people' now, because Septimus had said, 'I will kill myself'; an awful thing to say. Suppose they had heard him? She looked at the crowd. Help, help! she wanted to cry out to butchers' boys and women. Help! Only last autumn she and Septimus had stood on the Embankment wrapped in the same cloak and, Septimus reading a paper instead of talking, she had snatched it from him and laughed in the old man's face who saw them! But failure one conceals. She must take him away into some park.

'Now we will cross,' she said.

She had a right to his arm, though it was without feeling. He would give her, who was so simple, so impulsive, only twenty-four, without friends in England, who had left Italy for his sake, a piece of bone.

The motor car with its blinds drawn and an air of inscrutable reserve proceeded towards Piccadilly, still gazed at, still ruffling the faces on both sides of the street with the same dark breath of veneration whether for Queen, Prince, or Prime Minister nobody knew. The face itself had been seen only once by three people for a few seconds. Even the sex was now in dispute. But there could be no doubt that greatness was seated within; greatness was passing, hidden, down Bond Street, removed only by a hand's breadth from ordinary people who might now, for the first and last time, be within speaking distance of the majesty of England, of the enduring symbol of the state which will be known to curious antiquaries, sifting the ruins of time, when London is a grass-grown path and all those hurrying along the pavement this Wednesday morning are but bones with a few wedding rings mixed up in their dust and the gold stoppings of innumerable decayed teeth. The face in the motor car will then be known.

It is probably the Queen, thought Mrs Dalloway, coming out of Mulberry's with her flowers; the Queen. And for a second she wore a look of extreme dignity standing by the flower shop in the sunlight while the car passed at a foot's pace, with its blinds drawn. The Queen going to some hospital; the Queen opening some bazaar, thought Clarissa.

The crush was terrific for the time of day. Lords, Ascot, Hurlingham, what was it? she wondered, for the street was blocked. The British middle classes sitting sideways on the tops of omnibuses with parcels and umbrellas, yes, even furs on a day like this, were, she thought, more ridiculous, more unlike anything there has ever been than one could conceive; and the Queen herself held up; the Queen herself unable to pass. Clarissa was suspended on one side of Brook Street; Sir John Buckhurst, the old Judge on the other, with the car between them (Sir John had laid down the law for years and liked a well-dressed woman) when the chauffeur, leaning ever so slightly, said or showed something to the policeman, who saluted and raised his arm and jerked his head and moved the omnibus to the side and the car passed through. Slowly and very silently it took its way.

Clarissa guessed; Clarissa knew of course; she had seen something white, magical, circular, in the footman's hand, a disc inscribed with a name, – the Queen's, the Prince of Wales's, the Prime Minister's? – which, by force of its own lustre, burnt its way through (Clarissa saw the car diminishing, disappearing), to blaze among candelabras, glittering stars, breasts stiff with oak leaves, Hugh Whitbread and all his colleagues, the gentlemen of England, that night in Buckingham Palace. And Clarissa, too, gave a party. She stiffened a little; so she would stand at the top of her stairs.

The car had gone, but it had left a slight ripple which flowed through glove shops and hat shops and tailors' shops on both sides of Bond Street. For thirty seconds all heads were inclined the same way – to the window. Choosing a pair of gloves – should they be to the elbow or above it, lemon or pale grey? – ladies stopped; when the sentence was finished something had happened. Something so trifling in single instances that no mathematical instrument, though capable of transmitting shocks in China, could register the vibration; yet in its fullness rather formidable and in its common appeal emotional; for in all the hat shops and tailors' shops strangers looked at each other and thought of the dead; of the flag; of Empire. In a public house in a back street a Colonial insulted the House of Windsor which led to words, broken beer glasses, and a general shindy, which echoed strangely across the way in the ears of girls buying white underlinen threaded with pure white ribbon for their weddings. For the surface agitation of the passing car as it sunk grazed something very profound.

Gliding across Piccadilly, the car turned down St James's Street. Tall men, men of robust physique, well-dressed men with their tail-coats and their white slips and their hair raked back who, for reasons difficult to discriminate, were standing in the bow window of White's with their hands behind the tails of their coats, looking out, perceived instinctively that greatness was passing, and the pale light of the immortal presence fell upon them as it had fallen upon Clarissa Dalloway. At once they stood even straighter, and removed their hands and seemed ready to attend their Sovereign, if need be, to the cannon's mouth, as their ancestors had done before them. The white busts and the little tables in the background covered with copies of the *Tatler* and bottles of soda water seemed to approve; seemed to indicate the flowing corn and the manor houses of England; and to return the frail hum of the motor wheels as the walls of a whispering gallery return a single voice expanded and made sonorous by the might of a whole cathedral. Shawled Moll Pratt with her flowers on the pavement wished the dear boy well (it was the Prince of Wales for certain) and would have tossed the price of a pot of beer – a bunch of roses – into St James's Street out of sheer light-heartedness and contempt of poverty had she not seen the constable's eye upon her, discouraging an old Irishwoman's loyalty. The sentries at St James's saluted; Queen Alexandra's policeman approved.

A small crowd meanwhile had gathered at the gates of Buckingham Palace. Listlessly, yet confidently, poor people all of them, they waited; looked at the Palace itself with the flag flying; at Victoria, billowing on her mound, admired her shelves of running water, her geraniums; singled out from the motor cars in the Mall first this one, then that; bestowed emotion, vainly, upon commoners out for a drive; recalled their tribute to keep it unspent while this car passed and that; and all the time let rumour accumulate in their veins and thrill the nerves in their thighs at the thought of Royalty looking at them; the Queen bowing; the Prince saluting; at the thought of the heavenly life divinely bestowed upon Kings; of the equerries and deep curtsies; of the Queen's old doll's house; of Princess Mary married to an Englishman, and the Prince – ah! the Prince! who took wonderfully, they said, after old King Edward, but was ever so much slimmer. The Prince lived at St James's; but he might come along in the morning to visit his mother.

So Sarah Bletchley said with her baby in her arms, tipping her foot up and down as though she were by her own fender in Pimlico, but keeping her eyes on the Mall, while Emily Coates ranged over the Palace windows and thought of the housemaids, the innumerable housemaids, the bed-rooms, the innumerable bedrooms. Joined by an elderly gentleman with an Aberdeen terrier, by men without occupation, the crowd increased. Little Mr Bowley, who had rooms in the Albany and was sealed with wax over the deeper sources of life but could be unsealed suddenly, inappropriately, sentimentally, by this sort of thing – poor women waiting to see the Queen go past – poor women, nice little children, orphans, widows, the War – tut-tut – actually had tears in his eyes. A breeze flaunting ever so warmly down the Mall through the thin trees, past the bronze heroes, lifted some flag flying in the British breast of Mr Bowley and he raised his hat as the car turned into the Mall and held it high as the car approached; and let the poor mothers of Pimlico press close to him, and stood very upright. The car came on.

Suddenly Mrs Coates looked up into the sky. The sound of an aeroplane bored ominously into the ears of the crowd. There it was coming over the trees, letting out white smoke from behind, which curled and twisted, actually writing something! making letters in the sky! Everyone looked up.

Dropping dead down the aeroplane soared straight up, curved in a loop, raced, sank, rose, and whatever it did, wherever it went, out fluttered behind it a thick ruffled bar of white smoke which curled and wreathed upon the sky in letters. But what letters? A C was it? an E, then an L? Only for a moment did they lie still; then they moved and melted and were rubbed out up in the sky, and the aeroplane shot further away and again, in a fresh space of sky, began writing a K, an E, a Y perhaps?

'Glaxo,' said Mrs Coates in a strained, awestricken voice, gazing straight up, and her baby, lying stiff and white in her arms, gazed straight up.

'Kreemo,' murmured Mrs Bletchley, like a sleep-walker. With his hat held out perfectly still in his hand, Mr Bowley gazed straight up. All down the Mall people were standing and looking up into the sky. As they looked the whole world became perfectly silent, and a flight of gulls crossed the sky, first one gull leading, then another, and in this extraordinary silence and peace, in this pallor, in this purity, bells struck eleven times, the sound fading up there among the gulls.

The aeroplane turned and raced and swooped exactly where it liked, swiftly, freely, like a skater –

'That's an E,' said Mrs Bletchley – or a dancer –

'It's toffee,' murmured Mr Bowley – (and the car went in at the gates and nobody looked at it), and shutting off the smoke, away and away it rushed, and the smoke faded and assembled itself round the broad white shapes of the clouds.

It has gone; it was behind the clouds. There was no sound. The clouds to which the letters E, G, or L had attached themselves moved freely, as if destined to cross from West to East on a mission of the greatest importance which would never be revealed, and yet certainly so it was – a mission of the greatest importance. Then suddenly, as a train comes out of a tunnel, the aeroplane rushed out of the clouds again, the sound boring into the ears of all people in the Mall, in the Green Park, in Piccadilly, in Regent Street, in Regent's Park, and the bar of smoke curved behind and it dropped down, and it soared up and wrote one letter after another – but what word was it writing?

Lucrezia Warren Smith, sitting by her husband's side on a seat in Regent's Park in the Broad Walk, looked up.

'Look, look, Septimus!' she cried. For Dr Holmes had told her to make her husband (who had nothing whatever seriously the matter with him but was a little out of sorts) take an interest in things outside himself.

So, thought Septimus, looking up, they are signalling to me. Not indeed in actual words; that is, he could not read the language yet; but it was plain enough, this beauty, this exquisite beauty, and tears filled his eyes as he looked at the smoke words languishing and melting in the sky and bestowing upon him in their inexhaustible charity and laughing goodness one shape after another of unimaginable beauty and signalling their intention to provide him, for nothing, for ever, for looking merely, with beauty, more beauty! Tears ran down his cheeks.

It was toffee; they were advertising toffee, a nursemaid told Rezia. Together they began to spell t . . . o . . . f . . .

'K . . . R . . . ' said the nursemaid, and Septimus heard her say 'Kay Arr' close to his ear, deeply, softly, like a mellow organ, but with a roughness in her voice like a grasshopper's, which rasped his spine deliciously and sent running up into his brain waves of sound which, concussing, broke. A marvellous discovery indeed – that the human voice in certain atmospheric conditions (for one must be scientific, above all scientific) can quicken trees into life! Happily Rezia put her hand with a tremendous weight on his knee so that he was weighted down, transfixed, or the excitement of the elm trees rising and falling, rising and falling with all their leaves alight and the colour thinning and thickening from blue to the green of a hollow wave, like plumes on horses' heads, feathers on ladies', so proudly they rose and fell, so superbly, would have sent him mad. But he would not go mad. He would shut his eyes; he would see no more.

But they beckoned; leaves were alive; trees were alive. And the leaves being connected by millions of fibres with his own body, there on the seat, fanned it up and down; when the branch stretched he, too, made that statement. The sparrows fluttering, rising, and falling in jagged fountains were part of the pattern; the white and blue, barred with black branches. Sounds made harmonies with premeditation; the spaces between them were as significant as the sounds. A child cried. Rightly far away a horn sounded. All taken together meant the birth of a new religion –

'Septimus!' said Rezia. He started violently. People must notice.

'I am going to walk to the fountain and back,' she said.

For she could stand it no longer. Dr Holmes might say there was nothing the matter. Far rather would she that he were dead! She could not sit beside him when he stared so and did not see her and made everything terrible; sky and tree, children playing, dragging carts, blowing whistles, falling down; all were terrible. And he would not kill himself; and she could tell no one. 'Septimus has been working too hard' – that was all she could say, to her own mother. To love makes one solitary, she thought. She could tell nobody, not even Septimus now, and looking back, she saw him sitting in his shabby overcoat alone, on the seat, hunched up, staring. And it was cowardly for a man to say he would kill himself, but Septimus had fought; he was brave; he was not Septimus now. She put on her lace collar. She put on her new hat and he never noticed; and he was happy without her. Nothing could make her happy without him! Nothing! He was selfish. So men are. For he was not ill. Dr Holmes said there was nothing the matter with him. She spread her hand before her. Look! Her wedding ring slipped – she had grown so thin. It was she who suffered – but she had nobody to tell.

Far was Italy and the white houses and the room where her sisters sat making hats, and the streets crowded every evening with people walking, laughing out loud, not half alive like people here, huddled up in Bath chairs, looking at a few ugly flowers stuck in pots!

'For you should see the Milan gardens,' she said aloud. But to whom?

There was nobody. Her words faded. So a rocket fades. Its sparks, having grazed their way into the night, surrender to it, dark descends, pours over the outlines of houses and towers; bleak hillsides soften and fall in. But though they are gone, the night is full of them; robbed of colour, blank of windows, they exist more ponderously, give out what the frank daylight fails to transmit – the trouble and suspense of things conglomerated there in the darkness; huddled together in the darkness; reft of the relief which dawn brings when, washing the walls white and grey, spotting each windowpane, lifting the mist from the fields, showing the red-brown cows peacefully grazing, all is once more decked out to the eye; exists again. I am alone; I am alone! she cried, by the fountain in Regent's Park (staring at the Indian and his cross), as perhaps at midnight, when all boundaries are lost, the country reverts to its ancient shape, as the Romans saw it, lying cloudy, when they landed, and the hills had no names and rivers wound they knew not where – such was her darkness; when suddenly, as if a shelf were shot forth and she stood on it, she said how she was his wife, married years ago in Milan, his wife, and would never, never tell that he was mad! Turning, the shelf fell; down, down she dropped. For he was gone, she thought – gone, as he threatened, to kill himself – to throw himself under a cart! But no; there he was; still sitting alone on the seat, in his shabby overcoat, his legs crossed, staring, talking aloud.

Men must not cut down trees. There is a God. (He noted such revelations on the backs of envelopes.) Change the world. No one kills from hatred. Make it known (he wrote it down). He waited. He listened. A sparrow perched on the railing opposite chirped Septimus, Septimus, four or five times over and went on, drawing its notes out, to sing freshly and piercingly in Greek words how there is no crime and, joined by another sparrow, they sang in voices prolonged and piercing in Greek words, from trees in the meadow of life beyond a river where the dead walk, how there is no death.

There was his hand; there the dead. White things were assembling behind the railings opposite. But he dared not look. Evans was behind the railings!

'What are you saying?' said Rezia suddenly, sitting down by him.

Interrupted again! She was always interrupting.

Away from people – they must get away from people, he said (jumping up), right away over there, where there were chairs beneath a tree and the long slope of the park dipped like a length of green stuff with a ceiling cloth of blue and pink smoke high above, and there was a rampart of far irregular houses, hazed in smoke, the traffic hummed in a circle, and on the right, dun-coloured animals stretched long necks over the Zoo palings, barking, howling. There they sat down under a tree.

'Look,' she implored him, pointing at a little troop of boys carrying cricket stumps, and one shuffled, spun round on his heel and shuffled, as if he were acting a clown at the music hall.

'Look,' she implored him, for Dr Holmes had told her to make him notice real things, go to a music hall, play cricket – that was the very game, Dr Holmes said, a nice out-of-door game, the very game for her husband.

'Look,' she repeated.

Look the unseen bade him, the voice which now communicated with him who was the greatest of mankind, Septimus, lately taken from life to death, the Lord who had come to renew society, who lay like a coverlet, a snow blanket smitten only by the sun, for ever unwasted, suffering for ever, the scapegoat, the eternal sufferer, but he did not want it, he moaned, putting from him with a wave of his hand that eternal suffering, that eternal loneliness.

'Look,' she repeated, for he must not talk aloud to himself out of doors.

'Oh look,' she implored him. But what was there to look at? A few sheep. That was all.

The way to Regent's Park Tube Station – could they tell her the way to Regent's Park Tube Station – Maisie Johnson wanted to know. She was only up from Edinburgh two days ago.

'Not this way – over there!' Rezia exclaimed, waving her aside, lest she should see Septimus.

Both seemed queer, Maisie Johnson thought. Everything seemed very queer. In London for the first time, come to take up a post at her uncle's in Leadenhall Street, and now walking through Regent's Park in the morning, this couple on the chairs gave her quite a turn; the young woman seeming foreign, the man looking queer; so that should she be very old she would still remember and make it jangle again among her memories how she had walked through Regent's Park on a fine summer's morning fifty years ago. For she was only nineteen and had got her way at last, to come to London; and now how queer it was, this couple she had asked the way of, and the girl started and jerked her hand, and the man – he seemed awfully odd; quarrelling, perhaps; parting for ever, perhaps; something was up, she knew; and now all these people (for she returned to the Broad Walk), the stone basins, the prim flowers, the old men and women, invalids most of them in Bath chairs – all seemed, after Edinburgh, so queer. And Maisie Johnson, as she joined that gently trudging, vaguely gazing, breeze-kissed company – squirrels perching and preening, sparrow fountains fluttering for crumbs, dogs busy with the railings, busy with each other, while the soft warm air washed over them and lent to the fixed unsurprised gaze with which they received life something whimsical and mollified – Maisie Johnson positively felt she must cry Oh! (for that young man on the seat had given her quite a turn. Something was up, she knew).

Horror! horror! she wanted to cry. (She had left her people; they had warned her what would happen.)

Why hadn't she stayed at home? she cried, twisting the knob of the iron railing.

That girl, thought Mrs Dempster (who saved crusts for the squirrels and often ate her lunch in Regent's Park), don't know a thing yet; and really it seemed to her better to be a little stout, a little slack, a little moderate in one's expectations. Percy drank. Well, better to have a son, thought Mrs Dempster. She had had a hard time of it, and couldn't help smiling at a girl like that. You'll get married, for you're pretty enough, thought Mrs Dempster. Get married, she thought, and then you'll know. Oh, the cooks, and so on. Every man has his ways. But whether I'd have chosen quite like that if I could have known, thought Mrs Dempster, and could not help wishing to whisper a word to Maisie Johnson; to feel on the creased pouch of her worn old face the kiss of pity. For it's been a hard life, thought Mrs Dempster. What hadn't she given to it? Roses; figure; her feet too. (She drew the knobbed lumps beneath her skirt.)

Roses, she thought sardonically. All trash, m'dear. For really, what with eating, drinking, and mating, the bad days and good, life had been no mere matter of roses, and what was more, let me tell you, Carrie Dempster had no wish to change her lot with any woman's in Kentish Town! But, she implored, pity. Pity, for the loss of roses. Pity she asked of Maisie Johnson, standing by the hyacinth beds.

Ah, but that aeroplane! Hadn't Mrs Dempster always longed to see foreign parts? She had a nephew, a missionary. It soared and shot. She always went on the sea at Margate, not out o' sight of land, but she had no patience with women who were afraid of water. It swept and fell. Her stomach was in her mouth. Up again. There's a fine young feller aboard of it, Mrs Dempster wagered, and away and away it went, fast and fading, away and away the aeroplane shot; soaring over Greenwich and all the masts; over the little island of grey churches, St Paul's and the rest, till, on either side of London, fields spread out and dark brown woods where adventurous thrushes, hopping boldly, glancing quickly, snatched the snail and tapped him on a stone, once, twice, thrice.

Away and away the aeroplane shot, till it was nothing but a bright spark; an aspiration; a concentration; a symbol (so it seemed to Mr Bentley, vigorously rolling his strip of turf at Greenwich) of man's soul; of his determination, thought Mr Bentley, sweeping round the cedar tree, to get outside his body, beyond his house, by means of thought, Einstein, speculation, mathematics, the Mendelian theory – away the aeroplane shot.

Then, while a seedy-looking nondescript man carrying a leather bag stood on the steps of St Paul's Cathedral, and hesitated, for within was what balm, how great a welcome, how many tombs with banners waving over them, tokens of victories not over armies, but over, he thought, that plaguy spirit of truth seeking which leaves me at present without a situation, and more than that, the cathedral offers company, he thought, invites you to membership of a society; great men belong to it; martyrs have died for it; why not enter in, he thought, put this leather bag stuffed with pamphlets before an altar, a cross, the symbol of something which has soared beyond seeking and questing and knocking of words together and has become all spirit, disembodied, ghostly – why not enter in? he thought and while he hesitated out flew the aeroplane over Ludgate Circus.

It was strange; it was still. Not a sound was to be heard above the traffic. Unguided it seemed; sped of its own free will. And now, curving up and up, straight up, like something mounting in ecstasy, in pure delight, out from behind poured white smoke looping, writing a T, an O, an F.

'What are they looking at?' said Clarissa Dalloway to the maid who opened her door.

The hall of the house was cool as a vault. Mrs Dalloway raised her hand to her eyes, and, as the maid shut the door to, and she heard the swish of Lucy's skirts, she felt like a nun who has left the world and feels fold round her the familiar veils and the response to old devotions. The cook whistled in the kitchen. She heard the click of the typewriter. It was her life, and, bending her head over the hall table, she bowed beneath the influence, felt blessed and purified, saying to herself, as she took the pad with the telephone message on it, how moments like this are buds on the tree of life, flowers of darkness they are, she thought (as if some lovely rose had blossomed for her eyes only); not for a moment did she believe in God; but all the more, she thought, taking up the pad, must one repay in daily life to servants, yes, to dogs and canaries, above all to Richard her husband, who was the foundation of it – of the gay sounds, of the green lights, of the cook even whistling, for Mrs Walker was Irish and whistled all day long – one must pay back from this secret deposit of exquisite moments, she thought, lifting the pad, while Lucy stood by her, trying to explain how.

'Mr Dalloway, ma'am' –

Clarissa read on the telephone pad, 'Lady Bruton wishes to know if Mr Dalloway will lunch with her today.'

'Mr Dalloway, ma'am, told me to tell you he would be lunching out.'

'Dear!' said Clarissa, and Lucy shared as she meant her to her disappointment (but not the pang); felt the concord between them; took the hint; thought how the gentry love; gilded her own future with calm; and, taking Mrs Dalloway's parasol, handled it like a sacred weapon which a Goddess, having acquitted herself honourably in the field of battle, sheds, and placed it in the umbrella stand.

'Fear no more,' said Clarissa. Fear no more the heat o' the sun; for the shock of Lady Bruton asking Richard to lunch without her made the moment in which she had stood shiver, as a plant on the river bed feels the shock of a passing oar and shivers; so she rocked: so she shivered.

Millicent Bruton, whose lunch parties were said to be extraordinarily amusing, had not asked her. No vulgar jealousy could separate her from Richard. But she feared time itself, and read on Lady Bruton's face, as if it had been a dial cut in impassive stone, the dwindling of life; how year by year her share was sliced; how little the margin that remained was capable any longer of stretching, of absorbing, as in the youthful years, the colours, salts, tones of existence, so that she filled the room she entered, and felt often as she stood hesitating one moment on the threshold of her drawing-room, an exquisite suspense, such as might stay a diver before plunging while the sea darkens and brightens beneath him, and the waves which threaten to break, but only gently split their surface, roll and conceal and encrust as they just turn over the weeds with pearl.

She put the pad on the hall table. She began to go slowly upstairs, with her hand on the banisters, as if she had left a party, where now this friend now that had flashed back her face, her voice; had shut the door and gone out and stood alone, a single figure against the appalling night, or rather, to be accurate, against the stare of this matter-of-fact June morning; soft with the glow of rose petals for some, she knew, and felt it, as she paused by the open staircase window which let in blinds flapping, dogs barking, let in, she thought, feeling herself suddenly shrivelled, aged, breastless, the grinding, blowing, flowering of the day, out of doors, out of the window, out of her body and brain which now failed, since Lady Bruton, whose lunch parties were said to be extraordinarily amusing, had not asked her.

Like a nun withdrawing, or a child exploring a tower, she went, upstairs, paused at the window, came to the bathroom. There was the green linoleum and a tap dripping. There was an emptiness about the heart of life; an attic room. Women must put off their rich apparel. At midday they must disrobe. She pierced the pincushion and laid her feathered yellow hat on the bed. The sheets were clean, tight stretched in a broad white band from side to side. Narrower and narrower would her bed be. The candle was half burnt down and she had read deep in Baron Marbot's *Memoirs*. She had read late at night of the retreat from Moscow. For the House sat so long that Richard insisted, after her illness, that she must sleep undisturbed. And really she preferred to read of the retreat from Moscow. He knew it. So the room was an attic; the bed narrow; and lying there reading, for she slept badly, she could not dispel a virginity preserved through childbirth which clung to her like a sheet. Lovely in girlhood, suddenly there came a moment – for example on the river beneath the woods at Cliveden – when, through some contraction of this cold spirit, she had failed him. And then at Constantinople, and again and again. She could see what she lacked. It was not beauty; it was not mind. It was something central which permeated; something warm which broke up surfaces and rippled the cold contact of man and woman, or of women altogether. For *that* she could dimly perceive. She resented it, had a scruple picked up Heaven knows where, or, as she felt, sent by Nature (who is invariably wise); yet she could not resist sometimes yielding to the charm of a woman, not a girl, of a woman confessing, as to her they often did, some scrape, some folly. And whether it was pity, or their beauty, or that she was older, or some accident – like a faint scent, or a violin next door (so strange is the power of sounds at certain moments), she did undoubtedly then feel what men felt. Only for a moment; but it was enough. It was a sudden revelation, a tinge like a blush which one tried to check and then, as it spread, one yielded to its expansion, and rushed to the farthest verge and there quivered and felt the world come closer, swollen with some astonishing significance, some pressure of rapture, which split its thin skin and gushed and poured with an extraordinary alleviation over the cracks and sores. Then, for that moment, she had an illumination; a match burning in a crocus; an inner meaning almost expressed. But the close withdrew; the hard softened. It was over – the moment. Against such moments (with women too) there contrasted (as she laid her hat down) the bed and Baron Marbot and the candle half-burnt. Lying awake, the floor creaked; the lit house was suddenly darkened, and if she raised her head she could just hear the click of the handle released as gently as possible by Richard, who slipped upstairs in his socks and then, as often as not, dropped his hot-water bottle and swore! How she laughed!

But this question of love (she thought, putting her coat away), this falling in love with women. Take Sally Seton; her relation in the old days with Sally Seton. Had not that, after all, been love?

She sat on the floor – that was her first impression of Sally – she sat on the floor with her arms round her knees, smoking a cigarette. Where could it have been? The Mannings'? The Kinloch-Joneses'? At some party (where, she could not be certain), for she had a distinct recollection of saying to the man she was with, 'Who is *that*?' And he had told her, and said that Sally's parents did not get on (how that shocked her – that one's parents should quarrel!). But all that evening she could not take her eyes off Sally. It was an extraordinary beauty of the kind she most admired, dark, large-eyed, with that quality which, since she hadn't got it herself, she always envied – a sort of abandonment, as if she could say anything, do anything; a quality much commoner in foreigners than in English women. Sally always said she had French blood in her veins, an ancestor had been with Marie Antoinette, had his head cut off, left a ruby ring. Perhaps that summer she came to stay at Bourton, walking in quite unexpectedly without a penny in her pocket, one night after dinner, and upsetting poor Aunt Helena to such an extent that she never forgave her. There had been some awful quarrel at home. She literally hadn't a penny that night when she came to them – had pawned a brooch to come down. She had rushed off in a passion. They sat up till all hours of the night talking. Sally it was who made her feel, for the first time, how sheltered the life at Bourton was. She knew nothing about sex – nothing about social problems. She had once seen an old man who had dropped dead in a field – she had seen cows just after their calves were born. But Aunt Helena never liked discussion of anything (when Sally gave her William Morris, it had to be wrapped in brown paper). There they sat, hour after hour, talking in her bedroom at the top of the house, talking about life, how they were to reform the world. They meant to found a society to abolish private property, and actually had a letter written, though not sent out. The ideas were Sally's, of course – but very soon she was just as excited – read Plato in bed before breakfast; read Morris; read Shelley by the hour.

Sally's power was amazing, her gift, her personality. There was her way with flowers, for instance. At Bourton they always had stiff little vases all the way down the table. Sally went out, picked hollyhocks, dahlias – all sorts of flowers that had never been seen together – cut their heads off, and made them swim on the top of water in bowls. The effect was extraordinary – coming in to dinner in the sunset. (Of course, Aunt Helena thought it wicked to treat flowers like that.) Then she forgot her sponge, and ran along the passage naked. That grim old housemaid, Ellen Atkins, went about grumbling – 'Suppose any of the gentlemen had seen?' Indeed she did shock people. She was untidy, Papa said.

The strange thing, on looking back, was the purity, the integrity, of her feeling for Sally. It was not like one's feeling for a man. It was completely disinterested, and besides, it had a quality which could only exist between women, between women just grown up. It was protective, on her side; sprang from a sense of being in league together, a presentiment of something that was bound to part them (they spoke of marriage always as a catastrophe), which led to this chivalry, this protective feeling which was much more on her side than Sally's. For in those days she was completely reckless; did the most idiotic things out of bravado; bicycled round the parapet on the terrace; smoked cigars. Absurd, she was – very absurd. But the charm was overpowering, to her at least, so that she could remember standing in her bedroom at the top of the house holding the hot-water can in her hands and saying aloud, 'She is beneath this roof . . . She is beneath this roof!'

No, the words meant absolutely nothing to her now. She could not even get an echo of her old emotion. But she could remember going cold with excitement, and doing her hair in a kind of ecstasy (now the old feeling began to come back to her, as she took out her hairpins, laid them on the dressing-table, began to do her hair), with the rooks flaunting up and down in the pink evening light, and dressing, and going downstairs, and feeling as she crossed the hall 'if it were now to die 'twere now to be most happy.' That was her feeling – Othello's feeling, and she felt it, she was convinced, as strongly as Shakespeare meant Othello to feel it, all because she was coming down to dinner in a white frock to meet Sally Seton!

She was wearing pink gauze – was that possible? She *seemed*, anyhow, all light, glowing, like some bird or air ball that has flown in, attached itself for a moment to a bramble. But nothing is so strange when one is in love (and what was this except being in love?) as the complete indifference of other people. Aunt Helena just wandered off after dinner; Papa read the paper. Peter Walsh might have been there, and old Miss Cummings; Joseph Breitkopf certainly was, for he came every summer, poor old man, for weeks and weeks, and pretended to read German with her, but really played the piano and sang Brahms without any voice.

All this was only a background for Sally. She stood by the fireplace talking, in that beautiful voice which made everything she said sound like a caress, to Papa, who had begun to be attracted rather against his will (he never got over lending her one of his books and finding it soaked on the terrace), when suddenly she said, 'What a shame to sit indoors!' and they all went out on to the terrace and walked up and down. Peter Walsh and Joseph Breitkopf went on about Wagner. She and Sally fell a little behind. Then came the most exquisite moment of her whole life passing a stone urn with flowers in it. Sally stopped; picked a flower; kissed her on the lips. The whole world might have turned upside down! The others disappeared; there she was alone with Sally. And she felt that she had been given a present, wrapped up, and told just to keep it, not to look at it – a diamond, something infinitely precious, wrapped up, which, as they walked (up and down, up and down), she uncovered, or the radiance burnt through, the revelation, the religious feeling! – when old Joseph and Peter faced them: 'Star-gazing?' said Peter.

It was like running one's face against a granite wall in the darkness! It was shocking; it was horrible!

Not for herself. She felt only how Sally was being mauled already, mal-treated; she felt his hostility; his jealousy; his determination to break into their companionship. All this she saw as one sees a landscape in a flash of lightning – and Sally (never had she admired her so much!) gallantly taking her way unvanquished. She laughed. She made old Joseph tell her the names of the stars, which he liked doing very seriously. She stood there: she listened. She heard the names of the stars.

'Oh this horror!' she said to herself, as if she had known all along that something would interrupt, would embitter her moment of happiness.

Yet how much she owed Peter Walsh later. Always when she thought of him she thought of their quarrels for some reason – because she wanted his good opinion so much, perhaps. She owed him words: 'sentimental', 'civilised'; they started up every day of her life as if he guarded her. A book was sentimental; an attitude to life sentimental. 'Sentimental', perhaps she was to be thinking of the past. What would he think, she wondered, when he came back?

That she had grown older? Would he say that, or would she see him thinking when he came back, that she had grown older? It was true. Since her illness she had turned almost white.

Laying her brooch on the table, she had a sudden spasm, as if, while she mused, the icy claws had had the chance to fix in her. She was not old yet. She had just broken into her fifty-second year. Months and months of it were still untouched. June, July, August! Each still remained almost whole, and, as if to catch the falling drop, Clarissa (crossing to the dressing-table) plunged into the very heart of the moment, transfixed it, there – the moment of this June morning on which was the pressure of all the other mornings, seeing the glass, the dressing-table, and all the bottles afresh, collecting the whole of her at one point (as she looked into the glass), seeing the delicate pink face of the woman who was that very night to give a party; of Clarissa Dalloway; of herself.

How many million times she had seen her face, and always with the same imperceptible contraction! She pursed her lips when she looked in the glass. It was to give her face point. That was her self – pointed; dartlike; definite. That was her self when some effort, some call on her to be her self, drew the parts together, she alone knew how different, how incompatible and composed so for the world only into one centre, one diamond, one woman who sat in her drawing-room and made a meeting-point, a radiancy no doubt in some dull lives, a refuge for the lonely to come to, perhaps; she had helped young people, who were grateful to her; had tried to be the same always, never showing a sign of all the other sides of her – faults, jealousies, vanities, suspicions, like this of Lady Bruton not asking her to lunch; which, she thought (combing her hair finally), is utterly base! Now, where was her dress?

Her evening dresses hung in the cupboard. Clarissa, plunging her hand into the softness, gently detached the green dress and carried it to the window. She had torn it. Someone had trod on the skirt. She had felt it give at the Embassy party at the top among the folds. By artificial light the green shone, but lost its colour now in the sun. She would mend it. Her maids had too much to do. She would wear it tonight. She would take her silks, her scissors, her – what was it? – her thimble, of course, down into the drawing-room, for she must also write, and see that things generally were more or less in order.

Strange, she thought, pausing on the landing, and assembling that diamond shape, that single person, strange how a mistress knows the very moment, the very temper of her house! Faint sounds rose in spirals up the well of the stairs; the swish of a mop; tapping; knocking; a loudness when the front door opened; a voice repeating a message in the basement; the chink of silver on a tray; clean silver for the party. All was for the party.

(And Lucy, coming into the drawing-room with her tray held out, put the giant candlesticks on the mantelpiece, the silver casket in the middle, turned the crystal dolphin towards the clock. They would come; they would stand; they would talk in the mincing tones which she could imitate, ladies and gentlemen. Of all, her mistress was loveliest – mistress of silver, of linen, of china, for the sun, the silver, doors off their hinges, Rumpelmayer's men, gave her a sense, as she laid the paper-knife on the inlaid table, of something achieved. Behold! Behold! she said, speaking to her old friends in the baker's shop, where she had first seen service at Caterham, prying into the glass. She was Lady Angela, attending Princess Mary, when in came Mrs Dalloway.)

'Oh, Lucy,' she said, 'the silver does look nice!'

'And how,' she said, turning the crystal dolphin to stand straight, 'how did you enjoy the play last night?' 'Oh, they had to go before the end!' she said. 'They had to be back at ten!' she said. 'So they don't know what happened,' she said. 'That does seem hard luck,' she said (for her servants stayed later, if they asked her). 'That does seem rather a shame,' she said, taking the old bald-looking cushion in the middle of the sofa and putting it in Lucy's arms, and giving her a little push, and crying: 'Take it away! Give it to Mrs Walker with my compliments! Take it away!' she cried.

And Lucy stopped at the drawing-room door, holding the cushion, and said, very shyly, turning a little pink, Couldn't she help to mend that dress?

But, said Mrs Dalloway, she had enough on her hands already, quite enough of her own to do without that.

'But, thank you, Lucy, oh, thank you,' said Mrs Dalloway, and thank you, thank you, she went on saying (sitting down on the sofa with her dress over her knees, her scissors, her silks), thank you, thank you, she went on saying in gratitude to her servants generally for helping her to be like this, to be what she wanted, gentle, generous-hearted. Her servants liked her. And then this dress of hers – where was the tear? and now her needle to be threaded. This was a favourite dress, one of Sally Parker's, the last almost she ever made, alas, for Sally had now retired, lived at Ealing, and if ever I have a moment, thought Clarissa (but never would she have a moment any more), I shall go and see her at Ealing. For she was a character, thought Clarissa, a real artist. She thought of little out-of-the-way things; yet her dresses were never queer. You could wear them at Hatfield; at Buckingham Palace. She had worn them at Hatfield; at Buckingham Palace.

Quiet descended on her, calm, content, as her needle, drawing the silk smoothly to its gentle pause, collected the green folds together and attached them, very lightly, to the belt. So on a summer's day waves collect, over-balance, and fall; collect and fall; and the whole world seems to be saying 'that is all' more and more ponderously, until even the heart in the body which lies in the sun on the beach says too, That is all. Fear no more, says the heart. Fear no more, says the heart, committing its burden to some sea, which sighs collectively for all sorrows, and renews, begins, collects, lets fall. And the body alone listens to the passing bee; the wave breaking; the dog barking, far away barking and barking.

'Heavens, the front-door bell!' exclaimed Clarissa, staying her needle. Roused, she listened.

'Mrs Dalloway will see me,' said the elderly man in the hall. 'Oh yes, she will see *me*,' he repeated, putting Lucy aside very benevolently, and running upstairs ever so quickly. 'Yes, yes, yes,' he muttered as he ran upstairs. 'She will see me. After five years in India, Clarissa will see me.'

'Who can – what can?' asked Mrs Dalloway (thinking it was outrageous to be interrupted at eleven o'clock on the morning of the day she was giving a party), hearing a step on the stairs. She heard a hand upon the door. She made to hide her dress, like a virgin protecting chastity, respecting privacy. Now the brass knob slipped. Now the door opened, and in came – for a single second she could not remember what he was called! so surprised she was to see him, so glad, so shy, so utterly taken aback to have Peter Walsh come to her unexpectedly in the morning! (She had not read his letter.)

'And how are you?' said Peter Walsh, positively trembling; taking both her hands; kissing both her hands. She's grown older, he thought, sitting down. I shan't tell her anything about it, he thought, for she's grown older. She's looking at me, he thought, a sudden embarrassment coming over him, though he had kissed her hands. Putting his hand into his pocket, he took out a large pocket-knife and half opened the blade.

Exactly the same, thought Clarissa; the same queer look; the same check suit; a little out of the straight his face is, a little thinner, dryer, perhaps, but he looks awfully well, and just the same.

'How heavenly it is to see you again!' she exclaimed. He had his knife out. That's so like him, she thought.

He had only reached town last night, he said; would have to go down into the country at once; and how was everything, how was everybody – Richard? Elizabeth?

'And what's all this?' he said, tilting his penknife towards her green dress.

He's very well dressed, thought Clarissa; yet he always criticises *me*.

Here she is mending her dress; mending her dress as usual, he thought; here she's been sitting all the time I've been in India; mending her dress; playing about; going to parties; running to the House and back and all that, he thought, growing more and more irritated, more and more agitated, for there's nothing in the world so bad for some women as marriage, he thought; and politics; and having a Conservative husband, like the admirable Richard. So it is, so it is, he thought, shutting his knife with a snap.

'Richard's very well. Richard's at a Committee,' said Clarissa.

And she opened her scissors, and said, did he mind her just finishing what she was doing to her dress, for they had a party that night?

'Which I shan't ask you to,' she said. 'My dear Peter!' she said.

But it was delicious to hear her say that – my dear Peter! Indeed, it was all so delicious – the silver, the chairs; all so delicious!

Why wouldn't she ask him to her party? he asked.

Now of course, thought Clarissa, he's enchanting! perfectly enchanting! Now I remember how impossible it was ever to make up my mind – and why did I make up my mind – not to marry him, she wondered, that awful summer?

'But it's so extraordinary that you should have come this morning!' she cried, putting her hands, one on top of another, down on her dress.

'Do you remember,' she said, 'how the blinds used to flap at Bourton?'

'They did,' he said; and he remembered breakfasting alone, very awkwardly, with her father, who had died; and he had not written to Clarissa. But he had never got on well with old Parry, that querulous, weak-kneed old man, Clarissa's father, Justin Parry.

'I often wish I'd got on better with your father,' he said.

'But he never liked anyone who – our friends,' said Clarissa; and could have bitten her tongue for thus reminding Peter that he had wanted to marry her.

Of course I did, thought Peter; it almost broke my heart too, he thought; and was overcome with his own grief, which rose like a moon looked at from a terrace, ghastly beautiful with light from the sunken day. I was more unhappy than I've ever been since, he thought. And as if in truth he were sitting there on the terrace he edged a little towards Clarissa; put his hand out; raised it; let it fall. There above them it hung, that moon. She too seemed to be sitting with him on the terrace, in the moonlight.

'Herbert has it now,' she said. 'I never go there now,' she said.

Then, just as happens on a terrace in the moonlight, when one person begins to feel ashamed that he is already bored, and yet as the other sits silent, very quiet, sadly looking at the moon, does not like to speak, moves his foot, clears his throat, notices some iron scroll on a table leg, stirs a leaf, but says nothing – so Peter Walsh did now. For why go back like this to the past? he thought. Why make him think of it again? Why make him suffer, when she had tortured him so infernally? Why?

'Do you remember the lake?' she said, in an abrupt voice, under the pressure of an emotion which caught her heart, made the muscles of her throat stiff, and contracted her lips in a spasm as she said 'lake.' For she was a child, throwing bread to the ducks, between her parents, and at the same time a grown woman coming to her parents who stood by the lake, holding her life in her arms which, as she neared them, grew larger and larger in her arms until it became a whole life, a complete life, which she put down by them and said, 'This is what I have made of it! This!' And what had she made of it? What, indeed? sitting there sewing this morning with Peter.

She looked at Peter Walsh; her look, passing through all that time and that emotion, reached him doubtfully; settled on him tearfully; and rose and fluttered away, as a bird touches a branch and rises and flutters away. Quite simply she wiped her eyes.

'Yes,' said Peter. 'Yes, yes, yes,' he said, as if she drew up to the surface something which positively hurt him as it rose. Stop! Stop! he wanted to cry. For he was not old; his life was not over; not by any means. He was only just past fifty. Shall I tell her, he thought, or not? He would like to make a clean breast of it all. But she is too cold, he thought; sewing, with her scissors; Daisy would look ordinary beside Clarissa. And she would think me a failure, which I am in their sense, he thought; in the Dalloways' sense. Oh yes, he had no doubt about that; he was a failure, compared with all this – the inlaid table, the mounted paper-knife, the dolphin and the candlesticks, the chair-covers and the old valuable English tinted prints – he was a failure! I detest the smugness of the whole affair, he thought; Richard's doing, not Clarissa's; save that she married him. (Here Lucy came into the room, carrying silver, more silver, but charming, slender, graceful she looked, he thought, as she stooped to put it down.) And this has been going on all the time! he thought; week after week; Clarissa's life; while I – he thought; and at once everything seemed to radiate from him; journeys; rides; quarrels; adventures; bridge parties; love affairs; work; work, work! and he took out his knife quite openly – his old horn-handled knife which Clarissa could swear he had had these thirty years – and clenched his fist upon it.

What an extraordinary habit that was, Clarissa thought; always playing with a knife. Always making one feel, too, frivolous; empty-minded; a mere silly chatterbox, as he used. But I too, she thought, and, taking up her needle, summoned, like a Queen whose guards have fallen asleep and left her unprotected (she had been quite taken aback by this visit – it had upset her) so that anyone can stroll in and have a look at her where she lies with the brambles curving over her, summoned to her help the things she did; the things she liked; her husband; Elizabeth; her self, in short, which Peter hardly knew now, all to come about her and beat off the enemy.

'Well, and what's happened to you?' she said. So before a battle begins, the horses paw the ground; toss their heads; the light shines on their flanks; their necks curve. So Peter Walsh and Clarissa, sitting side by side on the blue sofa, challenged each other. His powers chafed and tossed in him. He assembled from different quarters all sorts of things; praise; his career at Oxford; his marriage, which she knew nothing whatever about; how he had loved; and altogether done his job.

'Millions of things!' he exclaimed, and, urged by the assembly of powers which were now charging this way and that and giving him the feeling at once frightening and extremely exhilarating of being rushed through the air on the shoulders of people he could no longer see, he raised his hands to his forehead.

Clarissa sat very upright; drew in her breath.

'I am in love,' he said, not to her however, but to someone raised up in the dark so that you could not touch her but must lay your garland down on the grass in the dark.

'In love,' he repeated, now speaking rather dryly to Clarissa Dalloway; 'in love with a girl in India.' He had deposited his garland. Clarissa could make what she would of it.

'In love!' she said. That he at his age should be sucked under in his little bow-tie by that monster! And there's no flesh on his neck; his hands are red; and he's six months older than I am! her eye flashed back to her; but in her heart she felt, all the same; he is in love. He has that, she felt; he is in love.

But the indomitable egotism which for ever rides down the hosts opposed to it, the river which says on, on, on; even though, it admits, there may be no goal for us whatever, still on, on; this indomitable egotism charged her cheeks with colour; made her look very young; very pink; very bright-eyed as she sat with her dress upon her knee, and her needle held to the end of green silk, trembling a little. He was in love! Not with her. With some younger woman, of course.

'And who is she?' she asked.

Now this statue must be brought from its height and set down between them.

'A married woman, unfortunately,' he said; 'the wife of a Major in the Indian Army.'

And with a curious ironical sweetness he smiled as he placed her in this ridiculous way before Clarissa.

(All the same, he is in love, thought Clarissa.)

'She has,' he continued, very reasonably, 'two small children; a boy and a girl; and I have come over to see my lawyers about the divorce.'

There they are! he thought. Do what you like with them, Clarissa! There they are! And second by second it seemed to him that the wife of the Major in the Indian Army (his Daisy) and her two small children became more and more lovely as Clarissa looked at them; as if he had set light to a grey pellet on a plate and there had risen up a lovely tree in the brisk sea-salted air of their intimacy (for in some ways no one understood him, felt with him, as Clarissa did) – their exquisite intimacy.

She flattered him; she fooled him, thought Clarissa; shaping the woman, the wife of the Major in the Indian Army, with three strokes of a knife. What a waste! What a folly! All his life long Peter had been fooled like that; first getting sent down from Oxford; next marrying the girl on the boat going out to India; now the wife of a Major – thank Heaven she had refused to marry him! Still, he was in love; her old friend, her dear Peter, he was in love.

'But what are you going to do?' she asked him. Oh the lawyers and solicitors, Messrs Hooper and Grateley of Lincoln's Inn, they were going to do it, he said. And he actually pared his nails with his pocket-knife.

For Heaven's sake, leave your knife alone! she cried to herself in irrepressible irritation; it was his silly unconventionality, his weakness; his lack of the ghost of a notion what anyone else was feeling that annoyed her, had always annoyed her; and now at his age, how silly!

I know all that, Peter thought; I know what I'm up against, he thought, running his finger along the blade of his knife, Clarissa and Dalloway and all the rest of them; but I'll show Clarissa – and then to his utter surprise, suddenly thrown by those uncontrollable forces thrown through the air, he burst into tears; wept; wept without the least shame, sitting on the sofa, the tears running down his cheeks.

And Clarissa had leant forward, taken his hand, drawn him to her, kissed him – actually had felt his face on hers before she could down the brandishing of silver-flashing plumes like pampas grass in a tropic gale in her breast, which, subsiding, left her holding his hand, patting his knee, and feeling as she sat back extraordinarily at her ease with him and light-hearted, all in a clap it came over her, If I had married him, this gaiety would have been mine all day!

It was all over for her. The sheet was stretched and the bed narrow. She had gone up into the tower alone and left them blackberrying in the sun. The door had shut, and there among the dust of fallen plaster and the litter of birds' nests how distant the view had looked, and the sounds came thin and chill (once on Leith Hill, she remembered), and Richard, Richard! she cried, as a sleeper in the night starts and stretches a hand in the dark for help. Lunching with Lady Bruton, it came back to her. He has left me; I am alone for ever, she thought, folding her hands upon her knee.

Peter Walsh had got up and crossed to the window and stood with his back to her, flicking a bandanna handkerchief from side to side. Masterly and dry and desolate he looked, his thin shoulder-blades lifting his coat slightly; blowing his nose violently. Take me with you, Clarissa thought impulsively, as if he were starting directly upon some great voyage; and then, next moment, it was as if the five acts of a play that had been very exciting and moving were now over and she had lived a lifetime in them and had run away, had lived with Peter, and it was now over.

Now it was time to move, and, as a woman gathers her things together, her cloak, her gloves, her opera-glasses, and gets up to go out of the theatre into the street, she rose from the sofa and went to Peter.

And it was awfully strange, he thought, how she still had the power, as she came tinkling, rustling, still had the power as she came across the room, to make the moon, which he detested, rise at Bourton on the terrace in the summer sky.

'Tell me,' he said, seizing her by the shoulders. 'Are you happy, Clarissa? Does Richard – '

The door opened.

'Here is my Elizabeth,' said Clarissa, emotionally, histrionically, perhaps.

'How d'y do?' said Elizabeth coming forward.

The sound of Big Ben striking the half-hour struck out between them with extraordinary vigour, as if a young man, strong, indifferent, inconsiderate, were swinging dumb-bells this way and that.

'Hullo, Elizabeth!' cried Peter, stuffing his handkerchief into his pocket, going quickly to her, saying 'Goodbye, Clarissa' without looking at her, leaving the room quickly, and running downstairs and opening the hall door.

'Peter! Peter!' cried Clarissa, following him out on to the landing. 'My party! Remember my party tonight!' she cried, having to raise her voice against the roar of the open air, and, overwhelmed by the traffic and the sound of all the clocks striking, her voice crying, 'Remember my party tonight!' sounded frail and thin and very far away as Peter Walsh shut the door.

Remember my party, remember my party, said Peter Walsh as he stepped down the street, speaking to himself rhythmically, in time with the flow of the sound, the direct downright sound of Big Ben striking the half-hour. (The leaden circles dissolved in the air.) Oh these parties, he thought; Clarissa's parties. Why does she give these parties, he thought. Not that he blamed her or this effigy of a man in a tail-coat with a carnation in his button-hole coming towards him. Only one person in the world could be as he was, in love. And there he was, this fortunate man, himself, reflected in the plate-glass window of a motor-car manufacturer in Victoria Street. All India lay behind him; plains, mountains; epidemics of cholera; a district twice as big as Ireland; decisions he had come to alone – he, Peter Walsh; who was now really for the first time in his life, in love. Clarissa had grown hard, he thought; and a trifle sentimental into the bargain, he suspected, looking at the great motor cars capable of doing – how many miles on how many gallons? For he had a turn for mechanics; had invented a plough in his district, had ordered wheelbarrows from England but the coolies wouldn't use them, all of which Clarissa knew nothing whatever about.

The way she said 'Here is my Elizabeth!' – that annoyed him. Why not 'Here's Elizabeth' simply? It was insincere. And Elizabeth didn't like it either. (Still the last tremors of the great booming voice shook the air round him; the half-hour; still early; only half-past eleven still.) For he understood young people; he liked them. There was always something cold in Clarissa, he thought. She had always, even as a girl, a sort of timidity, which in middle age becomes conventionality, and then it's all up, it's all up, he thought, looking rather drearily into the glassy depths, and wondering whether by calling at that hour he had annoyed her; overcome with shame suddenly at having been a fool; wept; been emotional; told her everything, as usual, as usual.

As a cloud crosses the sun, silence falls on London; and falls on the mind. Effort ceases. Time flaps on the mast. There we stop; there we stand. Rigid, the skeleton of habit alone upholds the human frame. Where there is nothing, Peter Walsh said to himself; feeling hollowed out, utterly empty within. Clarissa refused me, he thought. He stood there thinking, Clarissa refused me.

Ah, said St Margaret's, like a hostess who comes into her drawing-room on the very stroke of the hour and finds her guests there already. I am not late. No, it is precisely half-past eleven, she says. Yet, though she is perfectly right, her voice, being the voice of the hostess, is reluctant to inflict its individuality. Some grief for the past holds it back; some concern for the present. It is half-past eleven, she says, and the sound of St Margaret's glides into the recesses of the heart and buries itself in ring after ring of sound, like something alive which wants to confide itself, to disperse itself, to be, with a tremor of delight, at rest – like Clarissa herself, thought Peter Walsh, coming downstairs on the stroke of the hour in white. It is Clarissa herself, he thought, with a deep emotion, and an extraordinarily clear, yet puzzling, recollection of her, as if this bell had come into the room years ago, where they sat at some moment of great intimacy, and had gone from one to the other and had left, like a bee with honey, laden with the moment. But what room? What moment? And why had he been so profoundly happy when the clock was striking? Then, as the sound of St Margaret's languished, he thought, She has been ill, and the sound expressed languor and suffering. It was her heart, he remembered; and the sudden loudness of the final stroke tolled for death that surprised in the midst of life, Clarissa falling where she stood, in her drawing-room. No! No! he cried. She is not dead! I am not old, he cried, and marched up Whitehall, as if there rolled down to him, vigorous, unending, his future.

He was not old, or set, or dried in the least. As for caring what they said of him – the Dalloways, the Whitbreads, and their set, he cared not a straw – not a straw (though it was true he would have, sometime or other, to see whether Richard couldn't help him to some job). Striding, staring, he glared at the statue of the Duke of Cambridge. He had been sent down from Oxford – true. He had been a Socialist, in some sense a failure – true. Still the future of civilisation lies, he thought, in the hands of young men like that; of young men such as he was, thirty years ago; with their love of abstract principles; getting books sent out to them all the way from London to a peak in the Himalayas; reading science; reading philosophy. The future lies in the hands of young men like that, he thought.

A patter like the patter of leaves in a wood came from behind, and with a rustling, regular thudding sound, which as it overtook him drummed his thoughts, strict in step, up Whitehall, without his doing. Boys in uniform, carrying guns, marched with their eyes ahead of them, marched, their arms stiff, and on their faces an expression like the letters of a legend written round the base of a statue praising duty, gratitude, fidelity, love of England.

It is, thought Peter Walsh, beginning to keep step with them, a very fine training. But they did not look robust. They were weedy for the most part, boys of sixteen, who might, tomorrow, stand behind bowls of rice, cakes of soap on counters. Now they wore on them unmixed with sensual pleasure or daily preoccupations the solemnity of the wreath which they had fetched from Finsbury Pavement to the empty tomb. They had taken their vow. The traffic respected it; vans were stopped.

I can't keep up with them, Peter Walsh thought, as they marched up Whitehall, and sure enough, on they marched, past him, past everyone, in their steady way, as if one will worked legs and arms uniformly, and life, with its varieties, its irreticences, had been laid under a pavement of monuments and wreaths and drugged into a stiff yet staring corpse by discipline. One had to respect it; one might laugh; but one had to respect it, he thought. There they go, thought Peter Walsh, pausing at the edge of the pavement; and all the exalted statues, Nelson, Gordon, Havelock, the black, the spectacular images of great soldiers stood looking ahead of them, as if they too had made the same renunciation (Peter Walsh felt he, too, had made it the great renunciation), trampled under the same temptations, and achieved at length a marble stare. But the stare Peter Walsh did not want for himself in the least; though he could respect it in others. He could respect it in boys. They don't know the troubles of the flesh yet, he thought, as the marching boys disappeared in the direction of the Strand – all that I've been through, he thought, crossing the road, and standing under Gordon's statue, Gordon whom as a boy he had worshipped; Gordon standing lonely with one leg raised and his arms crossed – poor Gordon, he thought.

And just because nobody yet knew he was in London, except Clarissa, and the earth, after the voyage, still seemed an island to him, the strangeness of standing alone, alive, unknown, at half-past eleven in Trafalgar Square overcame him. What is it? Where am I? And why, after all, does one do it? he thought, the divorce seeming all moonshine. And down his mind went flat as a marsh, and three great emotions bowled over him; understanding; a vast philanthropy; and finally, as if the result of the others, an irrepressible, exquisite delight; as if inside his brain by another hand strings were pulled, shutters moved, and he, having nothing to do with it, yet stood at the opening of endless avenues, down which if he chose he might wander. He had not felt so young for years.

He had escaped! was utterly free – as happens in the downfall of habit when the mind, like an unguarded flame, bows and bends and seems about to blow from its holding. I haven't felt so young for years! thought Peter, escaping (only of course for an hour or so) from being precisely what he was, and feeling like a child who runs out of doors, and sees, as he runs, his old nurse waving at the wrong window. But she's extraordinarily attractive, he thought, as, walking across Trafalgar Square in the direction of the Haymarket, came a young woman who, as she passed Gordon's statue, seemed, Peter Walsh thought (susceptible as he was), to shed veil after veil, until she became the very woman he had always had in mind; young, but stately; merry, but discreet; black, but enchanting.

Straightening himself and stealthily fingering his pocket-knife he started after her to follow this woman, this excitement, which seemed even with its back turned to shed on him a light which connected them, which singled him out, as if the random uproar of the traffic had whispered through hollowed hands his name, not Peter, but his private name which he called himself in his own thoughts. 'You,' she said, only 'you,' saying it with her white gloves and her shoulders. Then the thin long cloak which the wind stirred as she walked past Dent's shop in Cockspur Street blew out with an enveloping kindness, a mournful tenderness, as of arms that would open and take the tired –

But she's not married; she's young; quite young, thought Peter, the red carnation he had seen her wear as she came across Trafalgar Square burning again in his eyes and making her lips red. But she waited at the kerbstone. There was a dignity about her. She was not worldly, like Clarissa; not rich, like Clarissa. Was she, he wondered as she moved, respectable? Witty, with a lizard's flickering tongue, he thought (for one must invent, must allow oneself a little diversion), a cool waiting wit, a darting wit; not noisy.

She moved; she crossed; he followed her. To embarrass her was the last thing he wished. Still if she stopped he would say, 'Come and have an ice,' he would say, and she would answer, perfectly simply, 'Oh yes.'

But other people got between them in the street, obstructing him, blotting her out. He pursued; she changed. There was colour in her cheeks; mockery in her eyes; he was an adventurer, reckless, he thought, swift, daring, indeed (landed as he was last night from India) a romantic buccaneer, careless of all these damned proprieties, yellow dressing-gowns, pipes, fishing-rods, in the shop windows; and respectability and evening parties and spruce old men wearing white slips beneath their waistcoats. He was a buccaneer. On and on she went, across Piccadilly, and up Regent Street, ahead of him, her cloak, her gloves, her shoulders combining with the fringes and the laces and the feather boas in the windows to make the spirit of finery and whimsy which dwindled out of the shops on to the pavement, as the light of a lamp goes wavering at night over hedges in the darkness.

Laughing and delightful, she had crossed Oxford Street and Great Portland Street and turned down one of the little streets, and now, and now, the great moment was approaching, for now she slackened, opened her bag, and with one look in his direction, but not at him, one look that bade farewell, summed up the whole situation and dismissed it triumphantly, for ever, had fitted her key, opened the door, and gone! Clarissa's voice saying, Remember my party, Remember my party, sang in his ears. The house was one of those flat red houses with hanging flower-baskets of vague impropriety. It was over.

Well, I've had my fun; I've had it, he thought, looking up at the swinging baskets of pale geraniums. And it was smashed to atoms his fun, for it was half made up, as he knew very well; invented, this escapade with the girl; made up, as one makes up the better part of life, he thought – making oneself up; making her up; creating an exquisite amusement, and something more. But odd it was, and quite true; all this one could never share – it smashed to atoms.

He turned; went up the street, thinking to find somewhere to sit, till it was time for Lincoln's Inn – for Messrs Hooper and Grateley. Where should he go? No matter. Up the street, then, towards Regent's Park. His boots on the pavement struck out 'no matter'; for it was early, still very early.

It was a splendid morning, too. Like the pulse of a perfect heart, life struck straight through the streets. There was no fumbling – no hesitation. Sweeping and swerving, accurately, punctually, noiselessly, there, precisely at the right instant, the motor car stopped at the door. The girl, silk-stockinged, feathered, evanescent, but not to him particularly attractive (for he had had his fling), alighted. Admirable butlers, tawny chow dogs, halls laid in black and white lozenges with white blinds blowing, Peter saw through the opened door and approved of. A splendid achievement in its own way, after all, London; the season; civilisation. Coming as he did from a respectable Anglo-Indian family which for at least three generations had administered the affairs of a continent (it's strange, he thought, what a sentiment I have about that, disliking India, and empire, and army as he did), there were moments when civilisation, even of this sort, seemed dear to him as a personal possession; moments of pride in England; in butlers; chow dogs; girls in their security. Ridiculous enough, still there it is, he thought. And the doctors and men of business and capable women all going about their business, punctual, alert, robust, seemed to him wholly admirable, good fellows, to whom one would entrust one's life, companions in the art of living, who would see one through. What with one thing and another, the show was really very tolerable; and he would sit down in the shade and smoke.

There was Regent's Park. Yes. As a child he had walked in Regent's Park – odd, he thought, how the thought of childhood keeps coming back to me – the result of seeing Clarissa, perhaps; for women live much more in the past than we do, he thought. They attach themselves to places; and their fathers – a woman's always proud of her father. Bourton was a nice place, a very nice place, but I could never get on with the old man, he thought. There was quite a scene one night – an argument about something or other, what, he could not remember. Politics presumably.

Yes, he remembered Regent's Park; the long straight walk; the little house where one bought air-balls to the left; an absurd statue with an inscription somewhere or other. He looked for an empty seat. He did not want to be bothered (feeling a little drowsy as he did) by people asking him the time. An elderly grey nurse, with a baby asleep in its perambulator – that was the best he could do for himself; sit down at the far end of the seat by that nurse.

She's a queer-looking girl, he thought, suddenly remembering Elizabeth as she came into the room and stood by her mother. Grown big; quite grown-up, not exactly pretty; handsome rather; and she can't be more than eighteen. Probably she doesn't get on with Clarissa. 'There's my Elizabeth' – that sort of thing – why not 'Here's Elizabeth' simply? – trying to make out, like most mothers, that things are what they're not. She trusts to her charm too much, he thought. She overdoes it.

The rich benignant cigar smoke eddied coolly down his throat; he puffed it out again in rings which breasted the air bravely for a moment; blue, circular – I shall try and get a word alone with Elizabeth tonight, he thought – then began to wobble into hour-glass shapes and taper away; odd shapes they take, he thought. Suddenly he closed his eyes, raised his hand with an effort, and threw away the heavy end of his cigar. A great brush swept smooth across his mind, sweeping across it moving branches, children's voices, the shuffle of feet, and people passing, and humming traffic, rising and falling traffic. Down, down he sank into the plumes and feathers of sleep, sank, and was muffled over.

The grey nurse resumed her knitting as Peter Walsh, on the hot seat beside her, began snoring. In her grey dress, moving her hands indefatigably yet quietly, she seemed like the champion of the rights of sleepers, like one of those spectral presences which rise in twilight in woods made of sky and branches. The solitary traveller, haunter of lanes, disturber of ferns, and devastator of great hemlock plants, looking up suddenly, sees the giant figure at the end of the ride.

By conviction an atheist perhaps, he is taken by surprise with moments of extraordinary exaltation. Nothing exists outside us except a state of mind, he thinks; a desire for solace, for relief, for something outside these miserable pigmies, these feeble, these ugly, these craven men and women. But if he can conceive of her, then in some sort she exists, he thinks, and advancing down the path with his eyes upon sky and branches he rapidly endows them with womanhood; sees with amazement how grave they become; how majestically, as the breeze stirs them, they dispense with a dark flutter of the leaves charity, comprehension, absolution, and then, flinging themselves suddenly aloft, confound the piety of their aspect with a wild carouse.

Such are the visions which proffer great cornucopias full of fruit to the solitary traveller, or murmur in his ear like sirens lolloping away on the green sea waves, or are dashed in his face like bunches of roses, or rise to the surface like pale faces which fishermen flounder through floods to embrace.

Such are the visions which ceaselessly float up, pace beside, put their faces in front of, the actual thing; often overpowering the solitary traveller and taking away from him the sense of the earth, the wish to return, and giving him for substitute a general peace, as if (so he thinks as he advances down the forest ride) all this fever of living were simplicity itself; and myriads of things merged in one thing; and this figure, made of sky and branches as it is, had risen from the troubled sea (he is elderly, past fifty now) as a shape might be sucked up out of the waves to shower down from her magnificent hands compassion, comprehension, absolution. So, he thinks, may I never go back to the lamplight; to the sitting-room; never finish my book; never knock out my pipe; never ring for Mrs Turner to clear away; rather let me walk straight on to this great figure, who will, with a toss of her head, mount me on her streamers and let me blow to nothingness with the rest.

Such are the visions. The solitary traveller is soon beyond the wood; and there, coming to the door with shaded eyes, possibly to look for his return, with hands raised, with white apron blowing, is an elderly woman who seems (so powerful is this infirmity) to seek, over the desert, a lost son; to search for a rider destroyed; to be the figure of the mother whose sons have been killed in the battles of the world. So, as the solitary traveller advances down the village street where the women stand knitting and the men dig in the garden, the evening seems ominous; the figures still; as if some august fate, known to them, awaited without fear, were about to sweep them into complete annihilation.

Indoors among ordinary things, the cupboard, the table, the window-sill with its geraniums, suddenly the outline of the landlady, bending to remove the cloth, becomes soft with light, an adorable emblem which only the recollection of cold human contacts forbids us to embrace. She takes the marmalade; she shuts it in the cupboard.

'There is nothing more tonight, sir?'

But to whom does the solitary traveller make reply?

So the elderly nurse knitted over the sleeping baby in Regent's Park. So Peter Walsh snored. He woke with extreme suddenness, saying to himself, 'The death of the soul.'

'Lord, Lord!' he said to himself out loud, stretching and opening his eyes. 'The death of the soul.' The words attached themselves to some scene, to some room, to some past he had been dreaming of. It became clearer; the scene, the room, the past he had been dreaming of.

It was at Bourton that summer, early in the nineties, when he was so passionately in love with Clarissa. There were a great many people there, laughing and talking, sitting round a table after tea, and the room was bathed in yellow light and full of cigarette smoke. They were talking about a man who had married his housemaid, one of the neighbouring squires, he had forgotten his name. He had married his housemaid, and she had been brought to Bourton to call – an awful visit it had been. She was absurdly overdressed, 'like a cockatoo', Clarissa had said, imitating her, and she never stopped talking. On and on she went, on and on. Clarissa imitated her. Then somebody said – Sally Seton it was – did it make any real difference to one's feelings to know that before they'd married she had had a baby? (In those days, in mixed company, it was a bold thing to say.) He could see Clarissa now, turning bright pink; somehow contracting; and saying, 'Oh, I shall never be able to speak to her again!' Whereupon the whole party sitting round the tea-table seemed to wobble. It was very uncomfortable.

He hadn't blamed her for minding the fact, since in those days a girl brought up as she was, knew nothing, but it was her manner that annoyed him; timid; hard; arrogant; prudish. 'The death of the soul.' He had said that instinctively, ticketing the moment as he used to do – the death of her soul.

Everyone wobbled; everyone seemed to bow, as she spoke, and then to stand up different. He could see Sally Seton, like a child who has been in mischief, leaning forward, rather flushed, wanting to talk, but afraid, and Clarissa did frighten people. (She was Clarissa's greatest friend, always about the place, an attractive creature, handsome, dark, with the reputation in those days of great daring, and he used to give her cigars, which she smoked in her bedroom, and she had either been engaged to somebody or quarrelled with her family, and old Parry disliked them both equally, which was a great bond.) Then Clarissa, still with an air of being offended with them all, got up, made some excuse, and went off, alone. As she opened the door, in came that great shaggy dog which ran after sheep. She flung herself upon him, went into raptures. It was as if she said to Peter – it was all aimed at him, he knew – 'I know you thought me absurd about that woman just now; but see how extraordinarily sympathetic I am; see how I love my Rob!'

They had always this queer power of communicating without words. She knew directly he criticised her. Then she would do something quite obvious to defend herself, like this fuss with the dog – but it never took him in, he always saw through Clarissa. Not that he said anything, of course; just sat looking glum. It was the way their quarrels often began.

She shut the door. At once he became extremely depressed. It all seemed useless – going on being in love; going on quarrelling; going on making it up, and he wandered off alone, among outhouses, stables, looking at the horses. (The place was quite a humble one; the Parrys were never very well off; but there were always grooms and stable-boys about – Clarissa loved riding – and an old coachman – what was his name? – an old nurse, old Moody, old Goody, some such name they called her, whom one was taken to visit in a little room with lots of photographs, lots of bird-cages.)

It was an awful evening! He grew more and more gloomy, not about that only; about everything. And he couldn't see her; couldn't explain to her; couldn't have it out. There were always people about – she'd go on as if nothing had happened. That was the devilish part of her – this coldness, this woodenness, something very profound in her, which he had felt again this morning talking to her; an impenetrability. Yet Heaven knows he loved her. She had some queer power of fiddling on one's nerves, turning one's nerves to fiddle-strings, yes.

He had gone into dinner rather late, from some idiotic idea of making himself felt, and had sat down by old Miss Parry – Aunt Helena – Mr Parry's sister, who was supposed to preside. There she sat in her white Cashmere shawl, with her head against the window – a formidable old lady, but kind to him, for he had found her some rare flower, and she was a great botanist, marching off in thick boots with a black tin collecting box slung between her shoulders. He sat down beside her, and couldn't speak. Everything seemed to race past him; he just sat there, eating. And then halfway through dinner he made himself look across at Clarissa for the first time. She was talking to a young man on her right. He had a sudden revelation. 'She will marry that man,' he said to himself. He didn't even know his name.

For of course it was that afternoon, that very afternoon, that Dalloway had come over; and Clarissa called him 'Wickham'; that was the beginning of it all. Somebody had brought him over; and Clarissa got his name wrong. She introduced him to everybody as Wickham. At last he said, 'My name is Dalloway!' – that was his first view of Richard – a fair young man, rather awkward, sitting on a deckchair, and blurting out, 'My name is Dalloway!' Sally got hold of it; always after that she called him 'My name is Dalloway!'

He was a prey to revelations at that time. This one – that she would marry Dalloway – was blinding – overwhelming at the moment. There was a sort of – how could he put it? – a sort of ease in her manner to him; something maternal; something gentle. They were talking about politics. All through dinner he tried to hear what they were saying.

Afterwards he could remember standing by old Miss Parry's chair in the drawing-room. Clarissa came up, with her perfect manners, like a real hostess, and wanted to introduce him to someone – spoke as if they had never met before, which enraged him. Yet even then he admired her for it. He admired her courage; her social instinct; he admired her power of carrying things through. 'The perfect hostess,' he said to her, whereupon she winced all over. But he meant her to feel it. He would have done anything to hurt her, after seeing her with Dalloway. So she left him. And he had a feeling that they were all gathered together in a conspiracy against him – laughing and talking – behind his back. There he stood by Miss Parry's chair as though he had been cut out of wood, talking about wild flowers. Never, never had he suffered so infernally! He must have forgotten even to pretend to listen; at last he woke up; he saw Miss Parry looking rather disturbed, rather indignant, with her prominent eyes fixed. He almost cried out that he couldn't attend because he was in Hell! People began going out of the room. He heard them talking about fetching cloaks; about its being cold on the water, and so on. They were going boating on the lake by moonlight – one of Sally's mad ideas. He could hear her describing the moon. And they all went out. He was left quite alone.

'Don't you want to go with them?' said Aunt Helena – poor old lady! – she had guessed. And he turned round and there was Clarissa again. She had come back to fetch him. He was overcome by her generosity – her goodness.

'Come along,' she said. 'They're waiting.'

He had never felt so happy in the whole of his life! Without a word they made it up. They walked down to the lake. He had twenty minutes of perfect happiness. Her voice, her laugh, her dress (something floating, white, crimson), her spirit, her adventurousness; she made them all disembark and explore the island; she startled a hen; she laughed; she sang. And all the time, he knew perfectly well, Dalloway was falling in love with her; she was falling in love with Dalloway; but it didn't seem to matter. Nothing mattered. They sat on the ground and talked – he and Clarissa. They went in and out of each other's minds without any effort. And then in a second it was over. He said to himself as they were getting into the boat, 'She will marry that man,' dully, without any resentment; but it was an obvious thing. Dalloway would marry Clarissa.

Dalloway rowed them in. He said nothing. But somehow as they watched him start, jumping on to his bicycle to ride twenty miles through the woods, wobbling off down the drive, waving his hand and disappearing, he obviously did feel, instinctively, tremendously, strongly, all that; the night; the romance; Clarissa. He deserved to have her.

For himself, he was absurd. His demands upon Clarissa (he could see it now) were absurd. He asked impossible things. He made terrible scenes. She would have accepted him still, perhaps, if he had been less absurd. Sally thought so. She wrote him all that summer long letters; how they had talked of him; how she had praised him, how Clarissa burst into tears! It was an extraordinary summer – all letters, scenes, telegrams – arriving at Bourton early in the morning, hanging about till the servants were up; appalling tête-à-têtes with old Mr Parry at breakfast; Aunt Helena formidable but kind; Sally sweeping him off for talks in the vegetable garden; Clarissa in bed with headaches.

The final scene, the terrible scene which he believed had mattered more than anything in the whole of his life (it might be an exaggeration – but still, so it did seem now), happened at three o'clock in the afternoon of a very hot day. It was a trifle that led up to it – Sally at lunch saying something about Dalloway, and calling him 'My name is Dalloway'; whereupon Clarissa suddenly stiffened, coloured, in a way she had, and rapped out sharply, 'We've had enough of that feeble joke.' That was all; but for him it was as if she had said, 'I'm only amusing myself with you; I've an understanding with Richard Dalloway.' So he took it. He had not slept for nights. 'It's got to be finished one way or the other,' he said to himself. He sent a note to her by Sally asking her to meet him by the fountain at three. 'Something very important has happened,' he scribbled at the end of it.

The fountain was in the middle of a little shrubbery, far from the house, with shrubs and trees all round it. There she came, even before the time, and they stood with the fountain between them, the spout (it was broken) dribbling water incessantly. How sights fix themselves upon the mind! For example, the vivid green moss.

She did not move. 'Tell me the truth, tell me the truth,' he kept on saying. He felt as if his forehead would burst. She seemed contracted, petrified. She did not move. 'Tell me the truth,' he repeated, when suddenly that old man Breitkopf popped his head in carrying *The Times*; stared at them; gaped; and went away. They neither of them moved. 'Tell me the truth,' he repeated. He felt that he was grinding against something physically hard; she was unyielding. She was like iron, like flint, rigid up the backbone. And when she said, 'It's no use. It's no use. This is the end' – after he had spoken for hours, it seemed, with the tears running down his cheeks – it was as if she had hit him in the face. She turned, she left him, she went away.

'Clarissa!' he cried. 'Clarissa!' But she never came back. It was over. He went away that night. He never saw her again.

It was awful, he cried, awful, awful!

Still, the sun was hot. Still, one got over things. Still, life had a way of adding day to day. Still, he thought, yawning and beginning to take notice – Regent's Park had changed very little since he was a boy, except for the squirrels – still, presumably there were compensations – when little Elise Mitchell, who had been picking up pebbles to add to the pebble collection which she and her brother were making on the nursery mantelpiece, plumped her handful down on the nurse's knee and scudded off again full tilt into a lady's legs. Peter Walsh laughed out.

But Lucrezia Warren Smith was saying to herself, It's wicked; why should I suffer? she was asking, as she walked down the broad path. No; I can't stand it any longer, she was saying, having left Septimus, who wasn't Septimus any longer, to say hard, cruel, wicked things, to talk to himself; to talk to a dead man, on the seat over there; when the child ran full tilt into her, fell flat, and burst out crying.

That was comforting rather. She stood her upright, dusted her frock, kissed her.

But for herself she had done nothing wrong; she had loved Septimus; she had been happy; she had had a beautiful home, and there her sisters lived still, making hats. Why should *she* suffer?

The child ran straight back to its nurse, and Rezia saw her scolded, comforted, taken up by the nurse, who put down her knitting, and the kind-looking man gave her his watch to blow open to comfort her – but why should *she* be exposed? Why not left in Milan? Why tortured? Why?

Slightly waved by tears the broad path, the nurse, the man in grey, the perambulator, rose and fell before her eyes. To be rocked by this malignant torturer was her lot. But why? She was like a bird sheltering under the thin hollow of a leaf, who blinks at the sun when the leaf moves; starts at the crack of a dry twig. She was exposed; she was surrounded by the enormous trees, vast clouds of an indifferent world, exposed; tortured; and why should she suffer? Why?

She frowned; she stamped her foot. She must go back again to Septimus since it was almost time for them to be going to Sir William Bradshaw. She must go back and tell him, go back to him sitting there on the green chair under the tree, talking to himself, or to that dead man Evans, whom she had only seen once for a moment in the shop. He had seemed a nice quiet man; a great friend of Septimus's, and he had been killed in the War. But such things happen to everyone. Everyone has friends who were killed in the War. Everyone gives up something when they marry. She had given up her home. She had come to live here, in this awful city. But Septimus let himself think about horrible things, as she could too, if she tried. He had grown stranger and stranger. He said people were talking behind the bedroom walls. Mrs Filmer thought it odd. He saw things too – he had seen an old woman's head in the middle of a fern. Yet he could be happy when he chose. They went to Hampton Court on top of a bus, and they were perfectly happy. All the little red and yellow flowers were out on the grass, like floating lamps he said, and talked and chattered and laughed, making up stories. Suddenly he said, 'Now we will kill ourselves,' when they were standing by the river, and he looked at it with a look which she had seen in his eyes when a train went by, or an omnibus – a look as if something fascinated him; and she felt he was going from her and she caught him by the arm. But going home he was perfectly quiet – perfectly reasonable. He would argue with her about killing themselves; and explain how wicked people were; how he could see them making up lies as they passed in the street. He knew all their thoughts, he said; he knew everything. He knew the meaning of the world, he said.

Then when they got back he could hardly walk. He lay on the sofa and made her hold his hand to prevent him from falling down, down, he cried, into the flames! and saw faces laughing at him, calling him horrible disgusting names, from the walls, and hands pointing round the screen. Yet they were quite alone. But he began to talk aloud, answering people, arguing, laughing, crying, getting very excited and making her write things down. Perfect nonsense it was; about death; about Miss Isabel Pole. She could stand it no longer. She would go back.

She was close to him now, could see him staring at the sky, muttering, clasping his hands. Yet Dr Holmes said there was nothing the matter with him. What, then, had happened – why had he gone, then, why, when she sat by him, did he start, frown at her, move away, and point at her hand, take her hand, look at it terrified?

Was it that she had taken off her wedding ring? 'My hand has grown so thin,' she said; 'I have put it in my purse,' she told him.

He dropped her hand. Their marriage was over, he thought, with agony, with relief. The rope was cut; he mounted; he was free, as it was decreed that he, Septimus, the lord of men, should be free; alone (since his wife had thrown away her wedding ring; since she had left him), he, Septimus, was alone, called forth in advance of the mass of men to hear the truth, to learn the meaning, which now at last, after all the toils of civilisation – Greeks, Romans, Shakespeare, Darwin, and now himself – was to be given whole to . . . 'To whom?' he asked aloud. 'To the Prime Minister,' the voices which rustled above his head replied. The supreme secret must be told to the Cabinet; first, that trees are alive; next, there is no crime; next, love, universal love, he muttered, gasping, trembling, painfully drawing out these profound truths which needed, so deep were they, so difficult, an immense effort to speak out, but the world was entirely changed by them for ever.

No crime; love; he repeated, fumbling for his card and pencil, when a Skye terrier snuffed his trousers and he started in an agony of fear. It was turning into a man! He could not watch it happen! It was horrible, terrible to see a dog become a man! At once the dog trotted away.

Heaven was divinely merciful, infinitely benignant. It spared him, pardoned his weakness. But what was the scientific explanation (for one must be scientific above all things)? Why could he see through bodies, see into the future, when dogs will become men? It was the heat wave presumably, operating upon a brain made sensitive by eons of evolution. Scientifically speaking, the flesh was melted off the world. His body was macerated until only the nerve fibres were left. It was spread like a veil upon a rock.

He lay back in his chair, exhausted but upheld. He lay resting, waiting, before he again interpreted, with effort, with agony, to mankind. He lay very high, on the back of the world. The earth thrilled beneath him. Red flowers grew through his flesh; their stiff leaves rustled by his head. Music began clanging against the rocks up here. It is a motor horn down in the street, he muttered; but up here it cannoned from rock to rock, divided, met in shocks of sound which rose in smooth columns (that music should be visible was a discovery) and became an anthem, an anthem twined round now by a shepherd boy's piping (That's an old man playing a penny whistle by the public-house, he muttered) which, as the boy·stood still, came bubbling from his pipe, and then, as he climbed higher, made its exquisite plaint while the traffic passed beneath. This boy's elegy is played among the traffic, thought Septimus. Now he withdraws up into the snows, and roses hang about him – the thick red roses which grow on my bedroom wall, he reminded himself. The music stopped. He has his penny, he reasoned it out, and has gone on to the next public-house.

But he himself remained high on his rock, like a drowned sailor on a rock. I leant over the edge of the boat and fell down, he thought. I went under the sea. I have been dead, and yet am now alive, but let me rest still, he begged (he was talking to himself again – it was awful, awful!); and as, before waking, the voices of birds and the sound of wheels chime and chatter in a queer harmony, grow louder and louder, and the sleeper feels himself drawing to the shores of life, so he felt himself drawing towards life, the sun growing hotter, cries sounding louder, something tremendous about to happen.

He had only to open his eyes; but a weight was on them; a fear. He strained; he pushed; he looked; he saw Regent's Park before him. Long streamers of sunlight fawned at his feet. The trees waved, brandished. We welcome, the world seemed to say; we accept; we create. Beauty, the world seemed to say. And as if to prove it (scientifically) wherever he looked, at the houses, at the railings, at the antelopes stretching over the palings, beauty sprang instantly. To watch a leaf quivering in the rush of air was an exquisite joy. Up in the sky swallows swooping, swerving, flinging themselves in and out, round and round, yet always with perfect control as if elastics held them; and the flies rising and falling; and the sun spotting now this leaf, now that, in mockery, dazzling it with soft gold in pure good temper; and now and again some chime (it might be a motor horn) tinkling divinely on the grass stalks – all of this, calm and reasonable as it was, made out of ordinary things as it was, was the truth now; beauty, that was the truth now. Beauty was everywhere.

'It is time,' said Rezia.

The word 'time' split its husk; poured its riches over him; and from his lips fell like shells, like shavings from a plane, without his making them, hard, white, imperishable words, and flew to attach themselves to their places in an ode to Time; an immortal ode to Time. He sang. Evans answered from behind the tree. The dead were in Thessaly, Evans sang, among the orchids. There they waited till the War was over, and now the dead, now Evans himself –

'For God's sake don't come!' Septimus cried out. For he could not look upon the dead.

But the branches parted. A man in grey was actually walking towards them. It was Evans! But no mud was on him; no wounds; he was not changed. I must tell the whole world, Septimus cried, raising his hand (as the dead man in the grey suit came nearer), raising his hand like some colossal figure who has lamented the fate of man for ages in the desert alone with his hands pressed to his forehead, furrows of despair on his cheeks, and now sees light on the desert's edge which broadens and strikes the iron-black figure (and Septimus half rose from his chair), and with legions of men prostrate behind him he, the giant mourner, receives for one moment on his face the whole –

'But I am so unhappy, Septimus,' said Rezia, trying to make him sit down.

The millions lamented; for ages they had sorrowed. He would turn round, he would tell them in a few moments, only a few moments more, of this relief, of this joy, of this astonishing revelation –

'The time, Septimus,' Rezia repeated. 'What is the time?'

He was talking, he was starting, this man must notice him. He was looking at them.

'I will tell you the time,' said Septimus, very slowly, very drowsily, smiling mysteriously at the dead man in the grey suit. As he sat smiling, the quarter struck – the quarter to twelve.

And that is being young, Peter Walsh thought as he passed them. To be having an awful scene – the poor girl looked absolutely desperate – in the middle of the morning. But what was it about, he wondered; what had the young man in the overcoat been saying to her to make her look like that; what awful fix had they got themselves into, both to look so desperate as that on a fine summer morning? The amusing thing about coming back to England, after five years, was the way it made, anyhow the first days, things stand out as if one had never seen them before; lovers squabbling under a tree; the domestic family life of the parks. Never had he seen London look so enchanting – the softness of the distances; the richness; the greenness; the civilisation, after India, he thought, strolling across the grass.

This susceptibility to impressions had been his undoing, no doubt. Still at his age he had, like a boy or a girl even, these alternations of mood; good days, bad days, for no reason whatever, happiness from a pretty face, downright misery at the sight of a frump. After India, of course, one fell in love with every woman one met. There was a freshness about them; even the poorest dressed better than five years ago surely; and to his eye the fashions had never been so becoming; the long black cloaks; the slimness; the elegance; and then the delicious and apparently universal habit of paint. Every woman, even the most respectable, had roses blooming under glass; lips cut with a knife; curls of Indian ink; there was design, art, everywhere; a change of some sort had undoubtedly taken place. What did the young people think about? Peter Walsh asked himself.

Those five years – 1918 to 1923 – had been, he suspected, somehow very important. People looked different. Newspapers seemed different. Now, for instance, there was a man writing quite openly in one of the respectable weeklies about water-closets. That you couldn't have done ten years ago – written quite openly about water-closets in a respectable weekly. And then this taking out a stick of rouge, or a powder-puff, and making up in public. On board ship coming home there were lots of young men and girls – Betty and Bertie he remembered in particular – carrying on quite openly; the old mother sitting and watching them with her knitting, cool as a cucumber. The girl would stand still and powder her nose in front of everyone. And they weren't engaged; just having a good time; no feelings hurt on either side. As hard as nails she was – Betty Whatshername – but a thorough good sort. She would make a very good wife at thirty – she would marry when it suited her to marry; marry some rich man and live in a large house near Manchester.

Who was it now who had done that? Peter Walsh asked himself, turning into the Broad Walk – married a rich man and lived in a large house near Manchester? Somebody who had written him a long, gushing letter quite lately about 'blue hydrangeas'. It was seeing blue hydrangeas that made her think of him and the old days – Sally Seton, of course! It was Sally Seton – the last person in the world one would have expected to marry a rich man and live in a large house near Manchester, the wild, the daring, the romantic Sally!

But of all that ancient lot, Clarissa's friends – Whitbreads, Kindersleys, Cunninghams, Kinlock Jones's – Sally was probably the best. She tried to get hold of things by the right end anyhow. She saw through Hugh Whitbread anyhow – the admirable Hugh – when Clarissa and the rest were at his feet.

'The Whitbreads?' he could hear her saying. 'Who are the Whitbreads? Coal merchants. Respectable tradespeople.'

Hugh she detested for some reason. He thought of nothing but his own appearance, she said. He ought to have been a Duke. He would be certain to marry one of the Royal Princesses. And, of course, Hugh had the most extraordinary, the most natural, the most sublime respect for the British aristocracy of any human being he had ever come across. Even Clarissa had to own that. Oh, but he was such a dear, so unselfish, gave up shooting to please his old mother – remembered his aunts' birthdays, and so on.

Sally, to do her justice, saw through all that. One of the things he remembered best was an argument one Sunday morning at Bourton about women's rights (that antediluvian topic), when Sally suddenly lost her temper, flared up, and told Hugh that he represented all that was most detestable in British middle-class life. She told him that she considered him responsible for the state of 'those poor girls in Piccadilly' – Hugh, the perfect gentle-man, poor Hugh! – never did a man look more horrified! She did it on purpose, she said afterwards (for they used to get together in the vegetable garden and compare notes). 'He's read nothing, thought nothing, felt nothing,' he could hear her saying in that very emphatic voice which carried so much farther than she knew. The stable boys had more life in them than Hugh, she said. He was a perfect specimen of the public school type, she said. No country but England could have produced him. She was really spiteful, for some reason; had some grudge against him. Something had happened – he forgot what – in the smoking-room. He had insulted her – kissed her? Incredible! Nobody believed a word against Hugh, of course. Who could? Kissing Sally in the smoking-room! If it had been some Honourable Edith or Lady Violet, perhaps; but not that ragamuffin Sally without a penny to her name, and a father or a mother gambling at Monte Carlo. For of all the people he had ever met Hugh was the greatest snob – the most obsequious – no, he didn't cringe exactly. He was too much of a prig for that. A first-rate valet was the obvious comparison – somebody who walked behind carrying suit cases; could be trusted to send telegrams – indispensable to hostesses. And he'd found his job – married his Honourable Evelyn; got some little post at Court, looked after the King's cellars, polished the Imperial shoe-buckles, went about in knee-breeches and lace ruffles. How remorseless life is! A little job at Court!

He had married this lady, the Honourable Evelyn, and they lived here-abouts, so he thought (looking at the pompous houses overlooking the Park), for he had lunched there once in a house which had, like all Hugh's posses-sions, something that no other house could possibly have – linen cupboards it might have been. You had to go and look at them – you had to spend a great deal of time always admiring whatever it was – linen cupboards, pillow-cases, old oak furniture, pictures, which Hugh had picked up for an old song. But Mrs Hugh sometimes gave the show away. She was one of those obscure mouse-like little women who admire big men. She was almost negligible. Then suddenly she would say something quite unexpected – something sharp. She had the relics of the grand manner, perhaps. The steam coal was a little too strong for her – it made the atmosphere thick. And so there they lived, with their linen cupboards and their old masters and their pillow-cases fringed with real lace, at the rate of five or ten thousand a year presumably, while he, who was two years older than Hugh, cadged for a job.

At fifty-three he had to come and ask them to put him into some secretary's office, to find him some usher's job teaching little boys Latin, at the beck and call of some mandarin in an office, something that brought in five hundred a year; for if he married Daisy, even with his pension, they could never do on less. Whitbread could do it presumably; or Dalloway. He didn't mind what he asked Dalloway. He was a thorough good sort; a bit limited; a bit thick in the head; yes; but a thorough good sort. Whatever he took up he did in the same matter-of-fact sensible way; without a touch of imagination, without a spark of brilliancy, but with the inexplicable niceness of his type. He ought to have been a country gentleman – he was wasted on politics. He was at his best out of doors, with horses and dogs – how good he was, for instance, when that great shaggy dog of Clarissa's got caught in a trap and had its paw half torn off, and Clarissa turned faint and Dalloway did the whole thing; bandaged, made splints; told Clarissa not to be a fool. That was what she liked him for, perhaps – that was what she needed. 'Now, my dear, don't be a fool. Hold this – fetch that,' all the time talking to the dog as if it were a human being.

But how could she swallow all that stuff about poetry? How could she let him hold forth about Shakespeare? Seriously and solemnly Richard Dalloway got on his hind legs and said that no decent man ought to read Shakespeare's sonnets because it was like listening at keyholes (besides, the relationship was not one that he approved). No decent man ought to let his wife visit a deceased wife's sister. Incredible! The only thing to do was to pelt him with sugared almonds – it was at dinner. But Clarissa sucked it all in; thought it so honest of him; so independent of him; Heaven knows if she didn't think him the most original mind she'd ever met!

That was one of the bonds between Sally and himself. There was a garden where they used to walk, a walled-in place, with rose-bushes and giant cauliflowers – he could remember Sally tearing off a rose, stopping to exclaim at the beauty of the cabbage leaves in the moonlight (it was extraordinary how vividly it all came back to him, things he hadn't thought of for years), while she implored him, half laughing of course, to carry off Clarissa, to save her from the Hughs and the Dalloways and all the other 'perfect gentlemen' who would 'stifle her soul' (she wrote reams of poetry in those days), make a mere hostess of her, encourage her worldliness. But one must do Clarissa justice. She wasn't going to marry Hugh anyhow. She had a perfectly clear notion of what she wanted. Her emotions were all on the surface. Beneath, she was very shrewd – a far better judge of character than Sally, for instance, and with it all, purely feminine; with that extraordinary gift, that woman's gift, of making a world of her own wherever she happened to be. She came into a room; she stood, as he had often seen her, in a doorway with lots of people round her. But it was Clarissa one remembered. Not that she was striking; not beautiful at all; there was nothing picturesque about her; she never said anything specially clever; there she was, however; there she was.

No, no, no! He was not in love with her any more! He only felt, after seeing her that morning, among her scissors and silks, making ready for the party, unable to get away from the thought of her; she kept coming back and back like a sleeper jolting against him in a railway carriage; which was not being in love, of course; it was thinking of her, criticising her, starting again, after thirty years, trying to explain her. The obvious thing to say of her was that she was worldly; cared too much for rank and society and getting on in the world – which was true in a sense; she had admitted it to him. (You could always get her to own up if you took the trouble; she was honest.) What she would say was that she hated frumps, fogies, failures, like himself presumably; thought people had no right to slouch about with their hands in their pockets; must do something, be something and these great swells, these Duchesses, these hoary old Countesses one met in her drawing-room, unspeakably remote as he felt them to be from anything that mattered a straw, stood for something real to her. Lady Bexborough, she said once, held herself upright (so did Clarissa herself; she never lounged in any sense of the word; she was straight as a dart, a little rigid in fact). She said they had a kind of courage which the older she grew the more she respected. In all this there was a great deal of Dalloway, of course; a great deal of the public-spirited, British Empire, tariff-reform, governing-class spirit, which had grown on her, as it tends to do. With twice his wits, she had to see things through his eyes – one of the tragedies of married life. With a mind of her own, she must always be quoting Richard – as if one couldn't know to a tittle what Richard thought by reading the *Morning Post* of a morning! These parties, for example, were all for him, or for her idea of him (to do Richard justice he would have been happier farming in Norfolk). She made her drawing-room a sort of meeting-place; she had a genius for it. Over and over again he had seen her take some raw youth, twist him, turn him, wake him up; set him going. Infinite numbers of dull people conglomerated round her, of course. But odd unexpected people turned up; an artist sometimes; sometimes a writer; queer fish in that atmosphere. And behind it all was that network of visiting, leaving cards, being kind to people; running about with bunches of flowers, little presents; So-and-so was going to France – must have an air-cushion; a real drain on her strength; all that interminable traffic that women of her sort keep up; but she did it genuinely, from a natural instinct.

Oddly enough, she was one of the most thorough-going sceptics he had ever met, and possibly (this was a theory he used to make up to account for her, so transparent in some ways, so inscrutable in others), possibly she said to herself, As we are a doomed race, chained to a sinking ship (her favourite reading as a girl was Huxley and Tyndall, and they were fond of these nautical metaphors), as the whole thing is a bad joke, let us, at any rate, do our part; mitigate the sufferings of our fellow-prisoners (Huxley again); decorate the dungeon with flowers and air-cushions; be as decent as we possibly can. Those ruffians, the Gods, shan't have it all their own way – her notion being that the Gods, who never lost a chance of hurting, thwarting and spoiling human lives, were seriously put out if, all the same, you behaved like a lady. That phase came directly after Sylvia's death – that horrible affair. To see your own sister killed by a falling tree (all Justin Parry's fault – all his carelessness) before your very eyes, a girl too on the verge of life, the most gifted of them, Clarissa always said, was enough to turn one bitter. Later she wasn't so positive, perhaps; she thought there were no Gods; no one was to blame; and so she evolved this atheist's religion of doing good for the sake of goodness.

And of course she enjoyed life immensely. It was her nature to enjoy (though, goodness only knows, she had her reserves; it was a mere sketch, he often felt, that even he, after all these years, could make of Clarissa). Anyhow there was no bitterness in her; none of that sense of moral virtue which is so repulsive in good women. She enjoyed practically everything. If you walked with her in Hyde Park, now it was a bed of tulips, now a child in a perambulator, now some absurd little drama she made up on the spur of the moment. (Very likely she would have talked to those lovers, if she had thought them unhappy.) She had a sense of comedy that was really exquisite, but she needed people, always people, to bring it out, with the inevitable result that she frittered her time away, lunching, dining, giving these incessant parties of hers, talking nonsense, saying things she didn't mean, blunting the edge of her mind, losing her discrimination. There she would sit at the head of the table taking infinite pains with some old buffer who might be useful to Dalloway – they knew the most appalling bores in Europe – or in came Elizabeth and everything must give way to *her*. She was at a High School, at the inarticulate stage last time he was over, a round-eyed, pale-faced girl, with nothing of her mother in her, a silent stolid creature, who took it all as a matter of course, let her mother make a fuss of her, and then said, 'May I go now?' like a child of four; going off, Clarissa explained, with that mixture of amusement and pride which Dalloway himself seemed to rouse in her, to play hockey. And now Elizabeth was 'out', presumably; thought him an old fogy, laughed at her mother's friends. Ah well, so be it. The compensation of growing old, Peter Walsh thought, coming out of Regent's Park, and holding his hat in his hand, was simply this; that the passions remain as strong as ever, but one has gained – at last! – the power which adds the supreme flavour to existence – the power of taking hold of experience, of turning it round, slowly, in the light.

A terrible confession it was (he put his hat on again), but now, at the age of

fifty-three, one scarcely needed people any more. Life itself, every moment
of it, every drop of it, here, this instant, now, in the sun, in Regent's Park, was
enough. Too much, indeed. A whole lifetime was too short to bring out, now
that one had acquired the power, the full flavour; to extract every ounce of
pleasure, every shade of meaning; which both were so much more solid than
they used to be, so much less personal. It was impossible that he should ever
suffer again as Clarissa had made him suffer. For hours at a time (pray God
that one might say these things without being overheard!), for hours and days
he never thought of Daisy.

Could it be that he was in love with her, then, remembering the misery,
the torture, the extraordinary passion of those days? It was a different thing
altogether – a much pleasanter thing – the truth being, or course, that now
she was in love with *him*. And that perhaps was the reason why, when the
ship actually sailed, he felt an extraordinary relief, wanted nothing so much
as to be alone; was annoyed to find all her little attentions – cigars, notes, a
rug for the voyage – in his cabin. Everyone if they were honest would say the
same; one doesn't want people after fifty; one doesn't want to go on telling
women they are pretty; that's what most men of fifty would say, Peter Walsh
thought, if they were honest.

But then these astonishing accesses of emotion – bursting into tears this
morning, what was all that about? What could Clarissa have thought of him?
thought him a fool presumably, not for the first time. It was jealousy that
was at the bottom of it – jealousy which survives every other passion of
mankind, Peter Walsh thought, holding his pocket-knife at arm's length.
She had been meeting Major Orde, Daisy said in her last letter; said it on
purpose, he knew; said it to make him jealous; he could see her wrinkling her
forehead as she wrote, wondering what she could say to hurt him; and yet it
made no difference; he was furious! All this pother of coming to England
and seeing lawyers wasn't to marry her, but to prevent her from marrying
anybody else. That was what tortured him, that was what came over him
when he saw Clarissa so calm, so cold, so intent on her dress or whatever it
was; realising what she might have spared him, what she had reduced him
to – a whimpering, snivelling old ass. But women, he thought, shutting his
pocket-knife, don't know what passion is. They don't know the meaning of
it to men. Clarissa was as cold as an icicle. There she would sit on the sofa by
his side, let him take her hand, give him one kiss on the cheek – here he was
at the crossing.

A sound interrupted him; a frail quivering sound, a voice bubbling up
without direction, vigour, beginning or end, running weakly and shrilly and
with an absence of all human meaning into

> ee um fah um so
> foo swee too eem oo –

the voice of no age or sex, the voice of an ancient spring spouting from the earth; which issued, just opposite Regent's Park Tube Station, from a tall quivering shape, like a funnel, like a rusty pump, like a wind-beaten tree for ever barren of leaves which lets the wind run up and down its branches singing

> ee um fah um so
> foo swee too eem oo,

and rocks and creaks and moans in the eternal breeze.

Through all ages – when the pavement was grass, when it was swamp, through the age of tusk and mammoth, through the age of silent sunrise – the battered woman – for she wore a skirt – with her right hand exposed, her left clutching at her side, stood singing of love – love which has lasted a million years, she sang, love which prevails, and millions of years ago, her lover, who had been dead these centuries, had walked, she crooned, with her in May; but in the course of ages, long as summer days, and flaming, she remembered, with nothing but red asters, he had gone; death's enormous sickle had swept those tremendous hills, and when at last she laid her hoary and immensely aged head on the earth, now become a mere cinder of ice, she implored the Gods to lay by her side a bunch of purple heather, there on her high burial place which the last rays of the last sun caressed; for then the pageant of the universe would be over.

As the ancient song bubbled up opposite Regent's Park Tube Station, still the earth seemed green and flowery; still, though it issued from so rude a mouth, a mere hole in the earth, muddy too, matted with root fibres and tangled grasses, still the old bubbling, burbling song, soaking through the knotted roots of infinite ages, and skeletons and treasure, streamed away in rivulets over the pavements and all along the Marylebone Road, and down towards Euston, fertilising, leaving a damp stain.

Still remembering how once in some primeval May she had walked with her lover, this rusty pump, this battered old woman with one hand exposed for coppers, the other clutching her side, would still be there in ten million years, remembering how once she had walked in May, where the sea flows now, with whom it did not matter – he was a man, oh yes, a man who had loved her. But the passage of ages had blurred the clarity of that ancient May day; the bright-petalled flowers were hoar and silver frosted; and she no longer saw, when she implored him (as she did now quite clearly), 'look in my eyes with thy sweet eyes intently,' she no longer saw brown eyes, black whiskers or sunburnt face, but only a looming shape, a shadow shape, to which, with the bird-like freshness of the very aged, she still twittered, 'give me your hand and let me press it gently' (Peter Walsh couldn't help giving the poor creature a coin as he stepped into his taxi), 'and if someone should see, what matter they?' she demanded; and her fist clutched at her side, and she smiled, pocketing her shilling, and all peering inquisitive eyes seemed blotted out, and the passing generations – the pavement was crowded with bustling middle-class people – vanished, like leaves, to be trodden under, to be soaked and steeped and made mould of by that eternal spring –

ee um fah um so
foo swee too eem oo.

'Poor old woman,' said Rezia Warren Smith.
'Oh poor old wretch!' she said, waiting to cross.

Suppose it was a wet night? Suppose one's father, or somebody who had known one in better days, had happened to pass, and saw one standing there in the gutter? And where did she sleep at night?

Cheerfully, almost gaily, the invincible thread of sound wound up into the air like the smoke from a cottage chimney, winding up clean beech trees and issuing in a tuft of blue smoke among the topmost leaves. 'And if someone should see, what matter they?'

Since she was so unhappy, for weeks and weeks now, Rezia had given meanings to things that happened, almost felt sometimes that she must stop people in the street, if they looked good, kind people, just to say to them, 'I am unhappy'; and this old woman singing in the street, 'if someone should see, what matter they?' made her suddenly quite sure that everything was going to be right. They were going to Sir William Bradshaw; she thought his name sounded nice; he would cure Septimus at once. And then there was a brewer's cart, and the grey horses had upright bristles of straw in their tails; there were newspaper placards. It was a silly, silly dream, being unhappy.

So they crossed, Mr and Mrs Septimus Warren Smith, and was there, after all, anything to draw attention to them, anything to make a passer-by suspect here is a young man who carries in him the greatest message in the world, and is, moreover, the happiest man in the world, and the most miserable? Perhaps they walked more slowly than other people, and there was something hesitating, trailing, in the man's walk, but what more natural for a clerk, who has not been in the West End on a weekday at this hour for years, than to keep looking at the sky, looking at this, that and the other, as if Portland Place were a room he had come into when the family are away, the chandeliers being hung in holland bags, and the caretaker, as she lets in long shafts of dusty light upon deserted, queer-looking armchairs, lifting one corner of the long blinds, explains to the visitors what a wonderful place it is; how wonderful, but at the same time, he thinks, how strange.

To look at, he might have been a clerk, but of the better sort; for he wore brown boots; his hands were educated; so, too, his profile – his angular, big-nosed, intelligent, sensitive profile; but not his lips altogether, for they were loose; and his eyes (as eyes tend to be), eyes merely; hazel, large; so that he was, on the whole, a border case, neither one thing nor the other; might end with a house at Purley and a motor car, or continue renting apartments in back streets all his life; one of those half-educated, self-educated men whose education is all learnt from books borrowed from public libraries, read in the evening after the day's work, on the advice of well-known authors consulted by letter.

As for the other experiences, the solitary ones, which people go through alone, in their bedrooms, in their offices, walking the fields and the streets of London, he had them; had left home, a mere boy, because of his mother; she lied; because he came down to tea for the fiftieth time with his hands unwashed; because he could see no future for a poet in Stroud; and so, making a confidant of his little sister, had gone to London leaving an absurd note behind him, such as great men have written, and the world has read later when the story of their struggles has become famous.

London has swallowed up many millions of young men called Smith; thought nothing of fantastic Christian names like Septimus with which their parents have thought to distinguish them. Lodging off the Euston Road, there were experiences, again experiences, such as change a face in two years from a pink innocent oval to a face lean, contracted, hostile. But of all this what could the most observant of friends have said except what a gardener says when he opens the conservatory door in the morning and finds a new blossom on his plant: – It has flowered; flowered from vanity, ambition, idealism, passion, loneliness, courage, laziness, the usual seeds, which all muddled up (in a room off the Euston Road), made him shy, and stammering, made him anxious to improve himself, made him fall in love with Miss Isabel Pole, lecturing in the Waterloo Road upon Shakespeare.

Was he not like Keats? she asked; and reflected how she might give him a taste of *Antony and Cleopatra* and the rest; lent him books; wrote him scraps of letters; and lit in him such a fire as burns only once in a lifetime, without heat, flickering a red gold flame infinitely ethereal and insubstantial over Miss Pole; *Antony and Cleopatra*; and the Waterloo Road. He thought her beautiful, believed her impeccably wise; dreamed of her, wrote poems to her, which, ignoring the subject, she corrected in red ink; he saw her, one summer evening, walking in a green dress in a square. 'It has flowered,' the gardener might have said, had he opened the door; had he come in, that is to say, any night about this time, and found him writing; found him tearing up his writing; found him finishing a masterpiece at three o'clock in the morning and running out to pace the streets, and visiting churches, and fasting one day, drinking another, devouring Shakespeare, Darwin, *The History of Civilisation* and Bernard Shaw.

Something was up, Mr Brewer knew; Mr Brewer, managing clerk at Sibleys and Arrowsmiths, auctioneers, valuers, land and estate agents; something was up, he thought, and, being paternal with his young men, and thinking very highly of Smith's abilities, and prophesying that he would, in ten or fifteen years, succeed to the leather armchair in the inner room under the skylight with the deed-boxes round him, 'if he keeps his health,' said Mr Brewer, and that was the danger – he looked weakly; advised football, invited him to supper and was seeing his way to consider recommending a rise of salary, when something happened which threw out many of Mr Brewer's calculations, took away his ablest young fellows, and eventually, so prying and insidious were the fingers of the European War, smashed a plaster cast of Ceres, ploughed a hole in the geranium beds, and utterly ruined the cook's nerves at Mr Brewer's establishment at Muswell Hill.

Septimus was one of the first to volunteer. He went to France to save an England which consisted almost entirely of Shakespeare's plays and Miss Isabel Pole in a green dress walking in a square. There in the trenches the change which Mr Brewer desired when he advised football was produced instantly; he developed manliness, he was promoted; he drew the attention, indeed the affection of his officer, Evans by name. It was a case of two dogs playing on a hearth-rug; one worrying a paper screw, snarling, snapping, giving a pinch, now and then, at the old dog's ear; the other lying somnolent, blinking at the fire, raising a paw, turning and growling good-temperedly. They had to be together, share with each other, fight with each other, quarrel with each other. But when Evans (Rezia, who had only seen him once, called him 'a quiet man', a sturdy red-haired man, undemonstrative in the company of women), when Evans was killed, just before the Armistice, in Italy, Septimus, far from showing any emotion or recognising that here was the end of a friendship, congratulated himself upon feeling very little and very reasonably. The War had taught him. It was sublime. He had gone through the whole show, friendship, European War, death, had won promotion, was still under thirty and was bound to survive. He was right there. The last shells missed him. He watched them explode with indifference. When peace came he was in Milan, billeted in the house of an innkeeper with a courtyard, flowers in tubs, little tables in the open, daughters making hats, and to Lucrezia, the younger daughter, he became engaged one evening when the panic was on him – that he could not feel.

For now that it was all over, truce signed, and the dead buried, he had, especially in the evening, these sudden thunder-claps of fear. He could not feel. As he opened the door of the room where the Italian girls sat making hats, he could see them; could hear them; they were rubbing wires among coloured beads in saucers; they were turning buckram shapes this way and that; the table was all strewn with feathers, spangles, silks, ribbons; scissors were rapping on the table; but something failed him; he could not feel. Still, scissors rapping, girls laughing, hats being made protected him; he was assured of safety; he had a refuge. But he could not sit there all night. There were moments of waking in the early morning. The bed was falling; he was falling. Oh for the scissors and the lamplight and the buckram shapes! He asked Lucrezia to marry him, the younger of the two, the gay, the frivolous, with those little artist's fingers that she would hold up and say, 'It is all in them.' Silk, feathers, what not were alive to them.

'It is the hat that matters most,' she would say, when they walked out together. Every hat that passed, she would examine; and the cloak and the dress and the way the woman held herself. Ill-dressing, over-dressing she stigmatised, not savagely, rather with impatient movements of the hands, like those of a painter who puts from him some obvious well-meant glaring imposture; and then, generously, but always critically, she would welcome a shop-girl who had turned her little bit of stuff gallantly, or praise, wholly, with enthusiastic and professional understanding, a French lady descending from her carriage, in chinchilla, robes, pearls.

'Beautiful!' she would murmur, nudging Septimus, that he might see. But beauty was behind a pane of glass. Even taste (Rezia liked ices, chocolates, sweet things) had no relish to him. He put down his cup on the little marble table. He looked at people outside; happy they seemed, collecting in the middle of the street, shouting, laughing, squabbling over nothing. But he could not taste, he could not feel. In the tea-shop among the tables and the chattering waiters the appalling fear came over him – he could not feel. He could reason; he could read, Dante for example, quite easily ('Septimus, do put down your book,' said Rezia, gently shutting the *Inferno*), he could add up his bill; his brain was perfect; it must be the fault of the world then – that he could not feel.

'The English are so silent,' Rezia said. She liked it, she said. She respected these Englishmen, and wanted to see London, and the English horses, and the tailor-made suits, and could remember hearing how wonderful the shops were, from an Aunt who had married and lived in Soho.

It might be possible, Septimus thought, looking at England from the train window, as they left Newhaven; it might be possible that the world itself is without meaning.

At the office they advanced him to a post of considerable responsibility. They were proud of him; he had won crosses. 'You have done your duty; it is up to us – ' began Mr Brewer; and could not finish, so pleasurable was his emotion. They took admirable lodgings off the Tottenham Court Road.

Here he opened Shakespeare once more. That boy's business of the intoxication of language – *Antony and Cleopatra* – had shrivelled utterly. How Shakespeare loathed humanity – the putting on of clothes, the getting of children, the sordidity of the mouth and the belly! This was now revealed to Septimus; the message hidden in the beauty of words. The secret signal which one generation passes, under disguise, to the next is loathing, hatred, despair. Dante the same. Aeschylus (translated) the same. There Rezia sat at the table trimming hats. She trimmed hats for Mrs Filmer's friends; she trimmed hats by the hour. She looked pale, mysterious, like a lily, drowned, under water, he thought.

'The English are so serious,' she would say, putting her arms round Septimus, her cheeks against his.

Love between man and woman was repulsive to Shakespeare. The business of copulation was filth to him before the end. But, Rezia said, she must have children. They had been married five years.

They went to the Tower together; to the Victoria and Albert Museum; stood in the crowd to see the King open Parliament. And there were the shops – hat shops, dress shops, shops with leather bags in the window, where she would stand staring. But she must have a boy.

She must have a son like Septimus, she said. But nobody could be like Septimus; so gentle; so serious; so clever. Could she not read Shakespeare too? Was Shakespeare a difficult author? she asked.

One cannot bring children into a world like this. One cannot perpetuate suffering, or increase the breed of these lustful animals, who have no lasting emotions, but only whims and vanities, eddying them now this way, now that.

He watched her snip, shape, as one watches a bird hop, flit in the grass, without daring to move a finger. For the truth is (let her ignore it) that human beings have neither kindness nor faith, nor charity beyond what serves to increase the pleasure of the moment. They hunt in packs. Their packs scour the desert and vanish screaming into the wilderness. They desert the fallen. They are plastered over with grimaces. There was Brewer at the office, with his waxed moustache, coral tie-pin, white slip, and pleasurable emotions – all coldness and clamminess within – his geraniums ruined in the War – his cook's nerves destroyed; or Amelia Whatshername, handing round cups of tea punctually at five – a leering, sneering obscene little harpy; and the Toms and Berties in their starched shirt fronts oozing thick drops of vice. They never saw him drawing pictures of them naked at their antics in his notebook. In the street, vans roared past him; brutality blared out on placards; men were trapped in mines; women burnt alive; and once a maimed file of lunatics being exercised or displayed for the diversion of the populace (who laughed aloud), ambled and nodded and grinned past him, in the Tottenham Court Road, each half apologetically, yet triumphantly, inflicting his hopeless woe. And would *he* go mad?

At tea Rezia told him that Mrs Filmer's daughter was expecting a baby. *She* could not grow old and have no children! She was very lonely, she was very unhappy! She cried for the first time since they were married. Far away he heard her sobbing; he heard it accurately, he noticed it distinctly; he compared it to a piston thumping. But he felt nothing.

His wife was crying, and he felt nothing; only each time she sobbed in this profound, this silent, this hopeless way, he descended another step into the pit.

At last, with a melodramatic gesture which he assumed mechanically and with complete consciousness of its insincerity, he dropped his head on his hands. Now he had surrendered; now other people must help him. People must be sent for. He gave in.

Nothing could rouse him. Rezia put him to bed. She sent for a doctor – Mrs Filmer's Dr Holmes. Dr Holmes examined him. There was nothing whatever the matter, said Dr Holmes. Oh, what a relief! What a kind man, what a good man! thought Rezia. When he felt like that he went to the Music Hall, said Dr Holmes. He took a day off with his wife and played golf. Why not try two tabloids of bromide dissolved in a glass of water at bedtime? These old Bloomsbury houses, said Dr Holmes, tapping the wall, are often full of very fine panelling, which the landlords have the folly to paper over. Only the other day, visiting a patient, Sir Somebody Something, in Bedford Square –

So there was no excuse; nothing whatever the matter, except the sin for which human nature had condemned him to death; that he did not feel. He had not cared when Evans was killed; that was worst; but all the other crimes raised their heads and shook their fingers and jeered and sneered over the rail of the bed in the early hours of the morning at the prostrate body which lay realising its degradation; how he had married his wife without loving her; had lied to her; seduced her; outraged Miss Isabel Pole, and was so pocked and marked with vice that women shuddered when they saw him in the street. The verdict of human nature on such a wretch was death.

Dr Holmes came again. Large, fresh-coloured, handsome, flicking his boots, looking in the glass, he brushed it all aside – headaches, sleeplessness, fears, dreams – nerve symptoms and nothing more, he said. If Dr Holmes found himself even half a pound below eleven stone six, he asked his wife for another plate of porridge at breakfast. (Rezia would learn to cook porridge.) But, he continued, health is largely a matter in our own control. Throw yourself into outside interests; take up some hobby. He opened Shakespeare – *Antony and Cleopatra*; pushed Shakespeare aside. Some hobby, said Dr Holmes, for did he not owe his own excellent health (and he worked as hard as any man in London) to the fact that he could always switch off from his patients on to old furniture? And what a very pretty comb, if he might say so, Mrs Warren Smith was wearing!

When the damned fool came again, Septimus refused to see him. Did he indeed? said Dr Holmes, smiling agreeably. Really he had to give that charming little lady, Mrs Smith, a friendly push before he could get past her into her husband's bedroom.

'So you're in a funk,' he said agreeably, sitting down by his patient's side. He had actually talked of killing himself to his wife, quite a girl, a foreigner, wasn't she? Didn't that give her a very odd idea of English husbands? Didn't one owe perhaps a duty to one's wife? Wouldn't it be better to do something instead of lying in bed? For he had had forty years' experience behind him; and Septimus could take Dr Holmes's word for it – there was nothing whatever the matter with him. And next time Dr Holmes came he hoped to find Smith out of bed and not making that charming little lady his wife anxious about him.

Human nature, in short, was on him – the repulsive brute, with the blood-red nostrils. Holmes was on him. Dr Holmes came quite regularly every day. Once you stumble, Septimus wrote on the back of a postcard, human nature is on you. Holmes is on you. Their only chance was to escape, without letting Holmes know; to Italy – anywhere, anywhere, away from Dr Holmes.

But Rezia could not understand him. Dr Holmes was such a kind man. He was so interested in Septimus. He only wanted to help them, he said. He had four little children and he had asked her to tea, she told Septimus.

So he was deserted. The whole world was clamouring: Kill yourself, kill yourself, for our sakes. But why should he kill himself for their sakes? Food was pleasant; the sun hot; and this killing oneself, how does one set about it, with a table knife, uglily, with floods of blood – by sucking a gas-pipe? He was too weak; he could scarcely raise his hand. Besides, now that he was quite alone, condemned, deserted, as those who are about to die are alone, there was a luxury in it, an isolation full of sublimity; a freedom which the attached can never know. Holmes had won of course; the brute with the red nostrils had won. But even Holmes himself could not touch this last relic straying on the edge of the world, this outcast, who gazed back at the inhabited regions, who lay, like a drowned sailor, on the shore of the world.

It was at that moment (Rezia had gone shopping) that the great revelation took place. A voice spoke from behind the screen. Evans was speaking. The dead were with him.

'Evans, Evans!' he cried.

Mr Smith was talking aloud to himself, Agnes the servant girl cried to Mrs Filmer in the kitchen. 'Evans, Evans!' he had said as she brought in the tray. She jumped, she did. She scuttled downstairs.

And Rezia came in, with her flowers, and walked across the room, and put the roses in a vase, upon which the sun struck directly, and went laughing, leaping round the room.

She had had to buy the roses, Rezia said, from a poor man in the street. But they were almost dead already, she said, arranging the roses.

So there was a man outside; Evans presumably; and the roses, which Rezia said were half dead, had been picked by him in the fields of Greece. Communication is health; communication is happiness. Communication, he muttered.

'What are you saying, Septimus?' Rezia asked, wild with terror, for he was talking to himself.

She sent Agnes running for Dr Holmes. Her husband, she said, was mad. He scarcely knew her.

'You brute! You brute!' cried Septimus, seeing human nature, that is Dr Holmes, enter the room.

'Now what's all this about,' said Dr Holmes in the most amiable way in the world. 'Talking nonsense to frighten your wife?' But he would give him something to make him sleep. And if they were rich people, said Dr Holmes, looking ironically round the room, by all means let them go to Harley Street; if they had no confidence in him, said Dr Holmes, looking not quite so kind.

It was precisely twelve o'clock; twelve by Big Ben; whose stroke was wafted over the northern part of London; blent with that of other clocks, mixed in a thin ethereal way with the clouds and wisps of smoke and died up there among the seagulls – twelve o'clock struck as Clarissa Dalloway laid her green dress on her bed, and the Warren Smiths walked down Harley Street. Twelve was the hour of their appointment. Probably, Rezia thought, that was Sir William Bradshaw's house with the grey motor car in front of it. (The leaden circles dissolved in the air.)

Indeed it was – Sir William Bradshaw's motor car; low, powerful, grey with plain initials interlocked on the panel, as if the pomps of heraldry were incongruous, this man being the ghostly helper, the priest of science; and, as the motor car was grey, so to match its sober suavity, grey furs, silver grey rugs were heaped in it, to keep her ladyship warm while she waited. For often Sir William would travel sixty miles or more down into the country to visit the rich, the afflicted, who could afford the very large fee which Sir William very properly charged for his advice. Her ladyship waited with the rugs about her knees an hour of more, leaning back, thinking sometimes of the patient, sometimes, excusably, of the wall of gold, mounting minute by minute while she waited; the wall of gold that was mounting between them and all shifts and anxieties (she had borne them bravely; they had had their struggles) until she felt wedged on a calm ocean, where only spice winds blow; respected, admired, envied, with scarcely anything left to wish for, though she regretted her stoutness; large dinner-parties every Thursday night to the profession; an occasional bazaar to be opened; Royalty greeted; too little time, alas! with her husband, whose work grew and grew; a boy doing well at Eton; she would have liked a daughter too; interests she had, however, in plenty; child welfare; the after-care of the epileptic, and photography, so that if there was a church building, or a church decaying, she bribed the sexton, got the key and took photographs, which were scarcely to be distinguished from the work of professionals, while she waited.

Sir William himself was no longer young. He had worked very hard; he had won his position by sheer ability (being the son of a shopkeeper); loved his profession; made a fine figurehead at ceremonies and spoke well – all of which had by the time he was knighted given him a heavy look, a weary look (the stream of patients being so incessant, the responsibilities and privileges of his profession so onerous), which weariness, together with his grey hairs, increased the extraordinary distinction of his presence and gave him the reputation (of the utmost importance in dealing with nerve cases) not merely of lightning skill and almost infallible accuracy in diagnosis, but of sympathy; tact; understanding of the human soul. He could see the first moment they came into the room (the Warren Smiths they were called); he was certain directly he saw the man; it was a case of extreme gravity. It was a case of complete breakdown – complete physical and nervous breakdown, with every symptom in an advanced stage, he ascertained in two or three minutes (writing answers to questions, murmured discreetly, on a pink card).

How long had Dr Holmes been attending him?

Six weeks.

Prescribed a little bromide? Said there was nothing the matter? Ah yes (those general practitioners! thought Sir William. It took half his time to undo their blunders. Some were irreparable).

'You served with great distinction in the War?'

The patient repeated the word 'war' interrogatively.

He was attaching meanings to words of a symbolical kind. A serious symptom to be noted on the card.

'The War?' the patient asked. The European War – that little shindy of schoolboys with gunpowder? Had he served with distinction? He really forgot. In the War itself he had failed.

'Yes, he served with the greatest distinction,' Rezia assured the doctor; 'he was promoted.'

'And they have the very highest opinion of you at your office?' Sir William murmured, glancing at Mr Brewer's very generously worded letter. 'So that you have nothing to worry you, no financial anxiety, nothing?'

He had committed an appalling crime and been condemned to death by human nature.

'I have – I have,' he began, 'committed a crime –'

'He has done nothing wrong whatever,' Rezia assured the doctor. If Mr Smith would wait, said Sir William, he would speak to Mrs Smith in the next room. Her husband was very seriously ill, Sir William said. Did he threaten to kill himself?

Oh, he did, she cried. But he did not mean it, she said. Of course not. It was merely a question of rest, said Sir William; of rest, rest, rest; a long rest in bed. There was a delightful home down in the country where her husband would be perfectly looked after. Away from her? she asked. Unfortunately, yes; the people we care for most are not good for us when we are ill. But he was not mad, was he? Sir William said he never spoke of 'madness'; he called it not having a sense of proportion. But her husband did not like doctors. He would refuse to go there. Shortly and kindly Sir William explained to her the state of the case. He had threatened to kill himself. There was no alternative. It was a question of law. He would lie in bed in a beautiful house in the country. The nurses were admirable. Sir William would visit him once a week. If Mrs Warren Smith was quite sure she had no more questions to ask – he never hurried his patients – they would return to her husband. She had nothing more to ask – not of Sir William.

So they returned to the most exalted of mankind; the criminal who faced his judges; the victim exposed on the heights; the fugitive; the drowned sailor; the poet of the immortal ode; the Lord who had gone from life to death; to Septimus Warren Smith, who sat in the armchair under the skylight staring at a photograph of Lady Bradshaw in Court dress, muttering messages about beauty.

'We have had our little talk,' said Sir William.

'He says you are very, very ill,' Rezia cried.

'We have been arranging that you should go into a home,' said Sir William.

'One of Holmes's homes?' sneered Septimus.

The fellow made a distasteful impression. For there was in Sir William, whose father had been a tradesman, a natural respect for breeding and clothing, which shabbiness nettled; again, more profoundly, there was in Sir William, who had never had time for reading, a grudge, deeply buried, against cultivated people who came into his room and intimated that doctors, whose profession is a constant strain upon all the highest faculties, are not educated men.

'One of *my* homes, Mr Warren Smith,' he said, 'where we will teach you to rest.'

And there was just one thing more.

He was quite certain that when Mr Warren Smith was well he was the last man in the world to frighten his wife. But he had talked of killing himself.

'We all have our moment of depression,' said Sir William.

Once you fall, Septimus repeated to himself, human nature is on you. Holmes and Bradshaw are on you. They scour the desert. They fly screaming into the wilderness. The rack and the thumbscrew are applied. Human nature is remorseless.

'Impulses came upon him sometimes?' Sir William asked, with his pencil on a pink card.

That was his own affair, said Septimus.

'Nobody lives for himself alone,' said Sir William, glancing at the photograph of his wife in Court dress.

'And you have a brilliant career before you,' said Sir William. There was Mr Brewer's letter on the table. 'An exceptionally brilliant career.'

But if he confessed? If he communicated? Would they let him off then, Holmes, Bradshaw?

'I – I – ' he stammered.

But what was his crime? He could not remember it.

'Yes?' Sir William encouraged him. (But it was growing late.)

Love, trees, there is no crime – what was his message?

He could not remember it.

'I – I – ' Septimus stammered.

'Try to think as little about yourself as possible,' said Sir William kindly. Really, he was not fit to be about.

Was there anything else they wished to ask him? Sir William would make all arrangements (he murmured to Rezia) and he would let her know between five and six that evening.

'Trust everything to me,' he said, and dismissed them.

Never, never had Rezia felt such agony in her life! She had asked for help and been deserted! He had failed them! Sir William Bradshaw was not a nice man.

The upkeep of that motor car alone must cost him quite a lot, said Septimus, when they got out into the street.

She clung to his arm. They had been deserted.

But what more did she want?

To his patients he gave three-quarters of an hour; and if in this exacting science which has to do with what, after all, we know nothing about – the nervous system, the human brain – a doctor loses his sense of proportion, as a doctor he fails. Health we must have; and health is proportion; so that when a man comes into your room and says he is Christ (a common delusion), and has a message, as they mostly have, and threatens, as they often do, to kill himself, you invoke proportion; order rest in bed; rest in solitude; silence and rest; rest without friends, without books, without messages; six months' rest; until a man who went in weighing seven stone six comes out weighing twelve.

Proportion, divine proportion, Sir William's goddess, was acquired by Sir William walking hospitals, catching salmon, begetting one son in Harley Street by Lady Bradshaw, who caught salmon herself and took photographs scarcely to be distinguished from the work of professionals. Worshipping proportion, Sir William not only prospered himself but made England prosper, secluded her lunatics, forbade childbirth, penalised despair, made it impossible for the unfit to propagate their views until they, too, shared his sense of proportion – his, if they were men, Lady Bradshaw's if they were women (she embroidered, knitted, spent four nights out of seven at home with her son), so that not only did his colleagues respect him, his subordinates fear him, but the friends and relations of his patients felt for him the keenest gratitude for insisting that these prophetic Christs and Christesses, who prophesied the end of the world, or the advent of God, should drink milk in bed, as Sir William ordered; Sir William with his thirty years' experience of these kinds of cases, and his infallible instinct, this is madness, this sense; his sense of proportion.

But Proportion has a sister, less smiling, more formidable, a Goddess even now engaged – in the heat and sands of India, the mud and swamp of Africa, the purlieus of London, wherever in short the climate or the devil tempts men to fall from the true belief which is her own – is even now engaged in dashing down shrines, smashing idols and setting up in their place her own stern countenance. Conversion is her name and she feasts on the wills of the weakly, loving to impress, to impose, adoring her own features stamped on the face of the populace. At Hyde Park Corner on a tub she stands preaching; shrouds herself in white and walks penitentially disguised as brotherly love through factories and parliaments; offers help, but desires power; smites out of her way roughly the dissentient, or dissatisfied; bestows her blessing on those who, looking upward, catch submissively from her eyes the light of their own. This lady too (Rezia Warren Smith divined it) had her dwelling in Sir William's heart, though concealed, as she mostly is, under some plausible disguise; some venerable name; love, duty, self-sacrifice. How he would work – how toil to raise funds, propagate reforms, initiate institutions! But conversion, fastidious Goddess, loves blood better than brick, and feasts most subtly on the human will. For example, Lady Bradshaw. Fifteen years ago she had gone under. It was nothing you could put your finger on; there had been no scene, no snap; only the slow sinking, water-logged, of her will into his. Sweet was her smile, swift her submission; dinner in Harley Street, numbering eight or nine courses, feeding ten or fifteen guests of the professional classes, was smooth and urbane. Only as the evening wore on a very slight dullness, or uneasiness perhaps, a nervous twitch, fumble, stumble and confusion indicated, what it was really painful to believe – that the poor lady lied. Once, long ago, she had caught salmon freely: now, quick to minister to the craving which lit her husband's eye so oilily for dominion, for power, she cramped, squeezed, pared, pruned, drew back, peeped through; so that without knowing precisely what made the evening disagreeable, and caused this pressure on the top of the head (which might well be imputed to the professional conversation, or the fatigue of a great doctor whose life, Lady Bradshaw said, 'is not his own but his patients''), disagreeable it was: so that guests, when the clock struck ten, breathed in the air of Harley Street even with rapture; which relief, however, was denied to his patients.

There in the grey room, with the pictures on the wall, and the valuable furniture, under the ground glass skylight, they learnt the extent of their transgressions; huddled up in armchairs, they watched him go through, for their benefit, a curious exercise with the arms, which he shot out, brought sharply back to his hip, to prove (if the patient was obstinate) that Sir William was master of his own actions, which the patient was not. There some weakly broke down; sobbed, submitted; others, inspired by Heaven knows what intemperate madness, called Sir William to his face a damnable humbug; questioned, even more impiously, life itself. Why live? they demanded. Sir William replied that life was good. Certainly Lady Bradshaw in ostrich feathers hung over the mantelpiece, and as for his income it was quite twelve thousand a year. But to us, they protested, life has given no such bounty. He acquiesced. They lacked a sense of proportion. And perhaps, after all, there is no God? He shrugged his shoulders. In short, this living or not living is an affair of our own? But there they were mistaken. Sir William had a friend in Surrey where they taught, what Sir William frankly admitted was a difficult art – a sense of proportion. There were, moreover, family affection; honour; courage; and a brilliant career. All of these had in Sir

William a resolute champion. If they failed, he had to support him police and the good of society, which, he remarked very quietly, would take care, down in Surrey, that these unsocial impulses, bred more than anything by the lack of good blood, were held in control. And then stole out from her hiding-place and mounted her throne that Goddess whose lust is to override opposition, to stamp indelibly in the sanctuaries of others the image of herself. Naked, defenceless, the exhausted, the friendless received the impress of Sir William's will. He swooped; he devoured. He shut people up. It was this combination of decision and humanity that endeared Sir William so greatly to the relations of his victims.

But Rezia Warren Smith cried, walking down Harley Street, that she did not like that man.

Shredding and slicing, dividing and subdividing, the clocks of Harley Street nibbled at the June day, counselled submission, upheld authority, and pointed out in chorus the supreme advantages of a sense of proportion, until the mound of time was so far diminished that a commercial clock, suspended above a shop in Oxford Street, announced, genially and fraternally, as if it were a pleasure to Messrs Rigby and Lowndes to give the information gratis, that it was half-past one.

Looking up, it appeared that each letter of their names stood for one of the hours; subconsciously one was grateful to Rigby and Lowndes for giving one time ratified by Greenwich; and this gratitude (so Hugh Whitbread ruminated, dallying there in front of the shop window) naturally took the form later of buying off Rigby and Lowndes socks or shoes. So he ruminated. It was his habit. He did not go deeply. He brushed surfaces; the dead languages, the living, life in Constantinople, Paris, Rome; riding, shooting, tennis, it had been once. The malicious asserted that he now kept guard at Buckingham Palace, dressed in silk stockings and knee-breeches, over what nobody knew. But he did it extremely efficiently. He had been afloat on the cream of English society for fifty-five years. He had known Prime Ministers. His affections were understood to be deep. And if it were true that he had not taken part in any of the great movements of the time or held important office, one or two humble reforms stood to his credit; an improvement in public shelters was one; the protection of owls in Norfolk another; servant girls had reason to be grateful to him; and his name at the end of letters to *The Times*, asking for funds, appealing to the public to protect, to preserve, to clear up litter, to abate smoke, and stamp out immorality in parks, commanded respect.

A magnificent figure he cut too, pausing for a moment (as the sound of the half-hour died away) to look critically, magisterially, at socks and shoes; impeccable, substantial, as if he beheld the world from a certain eminence, and dressed to match; but realised the obligation which size, wealth, health entail, and observed punctiliously even when not absolutely necessary, little courtesies, old-fashioned ceremonies which gave a quality to his manner, something to imitate, something to remember him by, for he would never lunch, for example, with Lady Bruton, whom he had known these twenty years, without bringing her in his outstretched hand a bunch of carnations and asking Miss Brush, Lady Bruton's secretary, after her brother in South Africa, which, for some reason, Miss Brush, deficient though she was in every attribute of female charm, so much resented that she said 'Thank you, he's doing very well in South Africa,' when, for half a dozen years, he had been doing badly in Portsmouth.

Lady Bruton herself preferred Richard Dalloway, who arrived at the same moment. Indeed they met on the doorstep.

Lady Bruton preferred Richard Dalloway, of course. He was made of much finer material. But she wouldn't let them run down her poor dear Hugh. She could never forget his kindness – he had been really remarkably kind – she forgot precisely upon what occasion. But he had been – remarkably kind. Anyhow, the difference between one man and another does not amount to much. She had never seen the sense of cutting people up as Clarissa Dalloway did – cutting them up and sticking them together again; not at any rate when one was sixty-two. She took Hugh's carnations with her angular grim smile. There was nobody else coming, she said. She had got them there on false pretences, to help her out of a difficulty –

'But let us eat first,' she said.

And so there began a soundless and exquisite passing to and fro through swing doors of aproned white-capped maids, handmaidens not of necessity, but adepts in a mystery or grand deception practised by hostesses in Mayfair from one-thirty to two, when, with a wave of the hand, the traffic ceases, and there rises instead this profound illusion in the first place about the food – how it is not paid for; and then that the table spreads itself voluntarily with glass and silver, little mats, saucers of red fruit; films of brown cream mask turbot; in casseroles severed chickens swim; coloured, undomestic, the fire burns; and with the wine and the coffee (not paid for) rise jocund visions before musing eyes; gently speculative eyes; eyes to whom life appears musical, mysterious; eyes now kindled to observe genially the beauty of the red carnations which Lady Bruton (whose movements were always angular) had laid beside her plate, so that Hugh Whitbread, feeling at peace with the entire universe and at the same time completely sure of his standing, said, resting his fork: 'Wouldn't they look charming against your lace?'

Miss Brush resented this familiarity intensely. She thought him an underbred fellow. She made Lady Bruton laugh.

Lady Bruton raised the carnations, holding then rather stiffly with much the same attitude with which the General held the scroll in the picture behind her; she remained fixed, tranced. Which was she now, the General's great-grand-daughter? great-great-grand-daughter? Richard Dalloway asked himself. Sir Roderick, Sir Miles, Sir Talbot – that was it. It was remarkable how in that family the likeness persisted in the women. She should have been a general of dragoons herself. And Richard would have served under her, cheerfully; he had the greatest respect for her; he cherished these romantic views about well-set-up old women of pedigree, and would have liked, in his good-humoured way, to bring some young hot-heads of his acquaintance to lunch with her; as if a type like hers could be bred of amiable tea-drinking enthusiasts! He knew her country. He knew her people. There was a vine, still bearing, which either Lovelace or Herrick – she never read a word of poetry herself, but so the story ran – had sat under. Better wait to put before them the question that bothered her (about making an appeal to the public; if so, in what terms and so on), better wait until they have had their coffee, Lady Bruton thought; and so laid the carnations down beside her plate.

'How's Clarissa?' she asked abruptly.

Clarissa always said that Lady Bruton did not like her. Indeed, Lady Bruton had the reputation of being more interested in politics than people; of talking like a man; of having had a finger in some notorious intrigue of the eighties, which was now beginning to be mentioned in memoirs. Certainly there was an alcove in her drawing-room and a table in that alcove, and a photograph upon that table of General Sir Talbot Moore, now deceased, who had written there (one evening in the eighties) in Lady Bruton's presence, with her cognisance, perhaps advice, a telegram ordering the British troops to advance upon an historical occasion. (She kept the pen and told the story.) Thus, when she said in her offhand way 'How's Clarissa?' husbands had difficulty in persuading their wives and indeed, however devoted, were secretly doubtful themselves, of her interest in women who often got in their husbands' way, prevented them from accepting posts abroad, and had to be taken to the seaside in the middle of the session to recover from influenza. Nevertheless her inquiry, 'How's Clarissa?' was known by women infallibly to be a signal from a well-wisher, from an almost silent companion, whose utterances (half a dozen perhaps in the course of a lifetime) signified recognition of some feminine comradeship which went beneath masculine lunch parties and united Lady Bruton and Mrs Dalloway, who seldom met, and appeared when they did meet indifferent and even hostile, in a singular bond.

'I met Clarissa in the Park this morning,' said Hugh Whitbread, diving into the casserole, anxious to pay himself this little tribute, for he had only to come to London and he met everybody at once; but greedy, one of the greediest men she had ever known, Milly Brush thought, who observed men with unflinching rectitude, and was capable of everlasting devotion, to her own sex in particular, being knobbed, scraped, angular, and entirely without feminine charm.

'D'you know who's in town?' said Lady Bruton, suddenly bethinking her. 'Our old friend, Peter Walsh.'

They all smiled. Peter Walsh! And Mr Dalloway was genuinely glad, Milly Brush thought; and Mr Whitbread thought only of his chicken.

Peter Walsh! All three, Lady Bruton, Hugh Whitbread, and Richard Dalloway, remembered the same thing – how passionately Peter had been in love; been rejected; gone to India; come a cropper; made a mess of things; and Richard Dalloway had a very great liking for the dear old fellow too. Milly Brush saw that; saw a depth in the brown of his eyes; saw him hesitate; consider; which interested her, as Mr Dalloway always interested her, for what was he thinking, she wondered, about Peter Walsh?

That Peter Walsh had been in love with Clarissa; that he would go back directly after lunch and find Clarissa; that he would tell her, in so many words, that he loved her. Yes, he would say that.

Milly Brush once might almost have fallen in love with these silences; and Mr Dalloway was always so dependable; such a gentleman too. Now, being forty, Lady Bruton had only to nod, or turn her head a little abruptly, and Milly Brush took the signal, however deeply she might be sunk in these reflections of a detached spirit, of an uncorrupted soul whom life could not bamboozle, because life had not offered her a trinket of the slightest value; not a curl, smile, lip, cheek, nose; nothing whatever; Lady Bruton had only to nod, and Perkins was instructed to quicken the coffee.

'Yes; Peter Walsh has come back,' said Lady Bruton. It was vaguely flattering to them all. He had come back, battered, unsuccessful, to their secure shores. But to help him, they reflected, was impossible; there was some flaw in his character. Hugh Whitbread said one might of course mention his name to So-and-so. He wrinkled lugubriously, consequentially, at the thought of the letters he would write to the heads of Government offices about 'my old friend, Peter Walsh', and so on. But it wouldn't lead to anything – not to anything permanent, because of his character.

'In trouble with some woman,' said Lady Bruton. They had all guessed that *that* was at the bottom of it.

'However,' said Lady Bruton, anxious to leave the subject, 'we shall hear the whole story from Peter himself.'

(The coffee was very slow in coming.)

'The address?' murmured Hugh Whitbread; and there was at once a ripple in the grey tide of service which washed round Lady Bruton day in, day out, collecting, intercepting, enveloping her in a fine tissue which broke concussions, mitigated interruptions, and spread round the house in Brook Street a fine net where things lodged and were picked out accurately, instantly, by grey-haired Perkins, who had been with Lady Bruton these thirty years and now wrote down the address; handed it to Mr Whitbread, who took out his pocket-book, raised his eyebrows, and slipping it in among documents of the highest importance, said that he would get Evelyn to ask him to lunch.

(They were waiting to bring the coffee until Mr Whitbread had finished.)

Hugh was very slow, Lady Bruton thought. He was getting fat, she noticed. Richard always kept himself in the pink of condition. She was getting impatient; the whole of her being was setting positively, undeniably, domineeringly brushing aside all this unnecessary trifling (Peter Walsh and his affairs) upon that subject which engaged her attention, and not merely her attention, but that fibre which was the ramrod of her soul, that essential part of her without which Millicent Bruton would not have been Millicent Bruton; that project for emigrating young people of both sexes born of respectable parents and setting them up with a fair prospect of doing well in Canada. She exaggerated. She had perhaps lost her sense of proportion. Emigration was not to others the obvious remedy, the sublime conception. It was not to them (not to Hugh, or Richard, or even to devoted Miss Brush) the liberator of the pent egotism, which a strong martial woman, well nourished, well descended, of direct impulses, down-right feelings, and little introspective power (broad and simple – why could not everyone be broad and simple? she asked) feels rise within her, once youth is past, and must eject upon some object – it may be Emigration, it may be Emancipation; but whatever it be, this object round which the essence of her soul is daily secreted becomes inevitably prismatic, lustrous, half looking-glass, half precious stone; now carefully hidden in case people should sneer at it; now proudly displayed. Emigration had become, in short, largely Lady Bruton.

But she had to write. And one letter to *The Times*, she used to say to Miss Brush, cost her more than to organise an expedition to South Africa (which she had done in the war). After a morning's battle beginning, tearing up, beginning again, she used to feel the futility of her own womanhood as she felt it on no other occasion, and would turn gratefully to the thought of Hugh Whitbread who possessed – no one could doubt it – the art of writing letters to *The Times*.

A being so differently constituted from herself, with such a command of language; able to put things as editors liked them put; had passions which one could not call simply greed. Lady Bruton often suspended judgment upon men in deference to the mysterious accord in which they, but no woman, stood to the laws of the universe; knew how to put things; knew what was said; so that if Richard advised her, and Hugh wrote for her, she was sure of being somehow right. So she let Hugh eat his soufflé; asked after poor Evelyn; waited until they were smoking, and then said,

'Milly, would you fetch the papers?'

And Miss Brush went out, came back; laid papers on the table; and Hugh produced his fountain pen; his silver fountain pen, which had done twenty years' service, he said, unscrewing the cap. It was still in perfect order; he had shown it to the makers; there was no reason, they said, why it should ever wear out; which was somehow to Hugh's credit, and to the credit of the sentiments which his pen expressed (so Richard Dalloway felt) as Hugh began carefully writing capital letters with rings round them in the margin, and thus marvellously reduced Lady Bruton's tangles to sense, to grammar such as the editor of *The Times*, Lady Bruton felt, watching the marvellous transformation, must respect. Hugh was slow. Hugh was pertinacious. Richard said one must take risks. Hugh proposed modifications in deference to people's feelings, which, he said rather tartly when Richard laughed, 'had to be considered,' and read out, 'how, therefore, we are of opinion that the times are ripe . . . the superfluous youth of our ever-increasing population . . . what we owe to the dead . . . ' which Richard thought all stuffing and bunkum, but no harm in it, of course, and Hugh went on drafting sentiments in alphabetical order of the highest nobility, brushing the cigar ash from his waistcoat, and summing up now and then the progress they had made until, finally, he read out the draft of a letter which Lady Bruton felt certain was a masterpiece. Could her own meaning sound like that?

Hugh could not guarantee that the editor would put it in; but he would be meeting somebody at luncheon.

Whereupon Lady Bruton, who seldom did a graceful thing, stuffed all Hugh's carnations into the front of her dress, and flinging her hands out called him 'My Prime Minister!' What she would have done without them both she did not know. They rose. And Richard Dalloway strolled off as usual to have a look at the General's portrait, because he meant, whenever he had a moment of leisure, to write a history of Lady Bruton's family.

And Millicent Bruton was very proud of her family. But they could wait, they could wait, she said, looking at the picture; meaning that her family, of military men, administrators, admirals, had been men of action, who had done their duty; and Richard's first duty was to his country, but it was a fine face, she said; and all the papers were ready for Richard down at Aldmixton whenever the time came; the Labour Government she meant. 'Ah, the news from India!' she cried.

And then, as they stood in the hall taking yellow gloves from the bowl on the malachite table and Hugh was offering Miss Brush with quite unnecessary courtesy some discarded ticket or other compliment, which she loathed from the depths of her heart and blushed brick red, Richard turned to Lady Bruton, with his hat in his hand, and said,

'We shall see you at our party tonight?' whereupon Lady Bruton resumed the magnificence which letter-writing had shattered. She might come; or she might not come. Clarissa had wonderful energy. Parties terrified Lady Bruton. But then, she was getting old. So she intimated, standing at her doorway; handsome; very erect; while her chow stretched behind her, and Miss Brush disappeared into the background with her hands full of papers.

And Lady Bruton went ponderously, majestically, up to her room, lay, one arm extended, on the sofa. She sighed, she snored, not that she was asleep, only drowsy and heavy, drowsy and heavy, like a field of clover in the sunshine this hot June day, with the bees going round and about and the yellow butterflies. Always she went back to those fields down in Devonshire, where she had jumped the brooks on Patty, her pony, with Mortimer and

Tom, her brothers. And there were the dogs; there were the rats; there were her father and mother on the lawn under the trees, with the tea-things out, and the beds of dahlias, the hollyhocks, the pampas grass; and they, little wretches, always up to some mischief! stealing back through the shrubbery, so as not to be seen, all bedraggled from some roguery. What old nurse used to say about her frocks!

Ah dear, she remembered – it was Wednesday in Brook Street. Those kind good fellows, Richard Dalloway, Hugh Whitbread, had gone this hot day through the streets whose growl came up to her lying on the sofa. Power was hers, position, income. She had lived in the forefront of her time. She had had good friends; known the ablest men of her day. Murmuring London flowed up to her, and her hand, lying on the sofa back, curled upon some imaginary baton such as her grandfathers might have held, holding which she seemed, drowsy and heavy, to be commanding battalions marching to Canada, and those good fellows walking across London, that territory of theirs, that little bit of carpet, Mayfair.

And they went further and further from her, being attached to her by a thin thread (since they had lunched with her) which would stretch and stretch, get thinner and thinner as they walked across London; as if one's friends were attached to one's body, after lunching with them, by a thin thread, which (as she dozed there) became hazy with the sound of bells, striking the hour or ringing to service, as a single spider's thread is blotted with rain-drops, and, burdened, sags down. So she slept.

And Richard Dalloway and Hugh Whitbread hesitated at the corner of Conduit Street at the very moment that Millicent Bruton, lying on the sofa, let the thread snap; snored. Contrary winds buffeted at the street corner. They looked in at a shop window; they did not wish to buy or to talk but to part, only with contrary winds buffeting the street corner, with some sort of lapse in the tides of the body, two forces meeting in a swirl, morning and afternoon, they paused. Some newspaper placard went up in the air, gallantly, like a kite at first, then paused, swooped, fluttered; and a lady's veil hung. Yellow awnings trembled. The speed of the morning traffic slackened, and single carts rattled carelessly down half-empty streets. In Norfolk, of which Richard Dalloway was half thinking, a soft warm wind blew back the petals; confused the waters; ruffled the flowering grasses. Haymakers, who had pitched beneath hedges to sleep away the morning toil, parted curtains of green blades; moved trembling globes of cow parsley to see the sky; the blue, the steadfast, the blazing summer sky.

Aware that he was looking at a silver two-handled Jacobean mug, and that Hugh Whitbread admired condescendingly, with airs of connoisseurship, a Spanish necklace which he thought of asking the price of in case Evelyn might like it – still Richard was torpid; could not think or move. Life had thrown up this wreckage; shop windows full of coloured paste, and one stood stark with the lethargy of the old, stiff with the rigidity of the old, looking in. Evelyn Whitbread might like to buy this Spanish necklace – so she might. Yawn he must. Hugh was going into the shop.

'Right you are!' said Richard, following.

Goodness knows he didn't want to go buying necklaces with Hugh. But there are tides in the body. Morning meets afternoon. Borne like a frail shallop on deep, deep floods, Lady Bruton's great-grandfather and his memoir and his campaigns in North America were whelmed and sunk. And Millicent Bruton too. She went under. Richard didn't care a straw what became of Emigration; about that letter, whether the editor put it in or not. The necklace hung stretched between Hugh's admirable fingers. Let him give it to a girl, if he must buy jewels – any girl, any girl in the street. For the worthlessness of this life did strike Richard pretty forcibly – buying necklaces for Evelyn. If he'd had a boy he'd have said, Work, work. But he had his Elizabeth; he adored his Elizabeth.

'I should like to see Mr Dubonnet,' said Hugh in his curt worldly way. It appeared that this Dubonnet had the measurements of Mrs Whitbread's neck, or, more strangely still, knew her views upon Spanish jewellery and the extent of her possessions in that line (which Hugh could not remember). All of which seemed to Richard Dalloway awfully odd. For he never gave Clarissa presents, except a bracelet two or three years ago, which had not been a success. She never wore it. It pained him to remember that she never wore it. And as a single spider's thread after wavering here and there attaches itself to the point of a leaf, so Richard's mind, recovering from its lethargy, set now on his wife, Clarissa, whom Peter Walsh had loved so passionately; and Richard had had a sudden vision of her there at luncheon; of himself and Clarissa: of their life together; and he drew the tray of old jewels towards him, and taking up first this brooch, then that ring, 'How much is that?' he asked, but doubted his own taste. He wanted to open the drawing-room door and come in holding out something; a present for Clarissa. Only what? But Hugh was on his legs again. He was unspeakably pompous. Really, after dealing here for thirty-five years he was not going to be put off by a mere boy who did not know his business. For Dubonnet, it seemed, was out, and Hugh would not buy anything until Mr Dubonnet chose to be in; at which the youth flushed and bowed his correct little bow. It was all perfectly correct. And yet Richard couldn't have said that to save his life! Why these people stood that damned insolence he could not conceive. Hugh was becoming an intolerable ass. Richard Dalloway could not stand more than an hour of his society. And, flicking his bowler hat by way of farewell, Richard turned at the corner of Conduit Street eager, yes, very eager, to travel that spider's thread of attachment between himself and Clarissa; he would go straight to her, in Westminster.

But he wanted to come in holding something. Flowers? Yes, flowers, since he did not trust his taste in gold; any number of flowers, roses, orchids, to celebrate what was, reckoning things as you will, an event; this feeling about her when they spoke of Peter Walsh at luncheon; and they never spoke of it; not for years had they spoken of it; which, he thought, grasping his red and white roses together (a vast bunch in tissue paper), is the greatest mistake in the world. The time comes when it can't be said; one's too shy to say it, he thought, pocketing his sixpence or two of change, setting off with his great bunch held against his body to Westminster to say straight out in so many words (whatever she might think of him) holding out his flowers, 'I love you.' Why not? Really it was a miracle thinking of the war, and thousands of poor chaps, with all their lives before them, shovelled together, already half forgotten; it was a miracle. Here he was walking across London to say to Clarissa in so many words that he loved her. Which one never does say, he thought. Partly one's lazy; partly one's shy. And Clarissa – it was difficult to think of her; except in starts, as at luncheon, when he saw her quite distinctly; their whole life. He stopped at the crossing; and repeated – being simple by nature, and undebauched, because he had tramped, and shot; being pertinacious and dogged, having championed the down-trodden and followed his instincts in the House of Commons; being preserved in his simplicity yet at the same time grown rather speechless, rather stiff – he repeated that it was a miracle, that he should have married Clarissa; a miracle – his life had been a miracle, he thought; hesitating to cross. But it did make his blood boil to see little creatures of five or six crossing Piccadilly alone. The police ought to have stopped the traffic at once. He had no illusions about the London police. Indeed, he was collecting evidence of their malpractices; and those costermongers, not allowed to stand their barrows in the streets; and prostitutes, good Lord, the fault wasn't in them, nor in young men either, but in our detestable social system and so forth; all of which he considered, could be seen considering, grey, dogged, dapper, clean, as he walked across the Park to tell his wife that he loved her.

    For he would say it in so many words, when he came into the room. Because it is a thousand pities never to say what one feels, he thought, crossing the Green Park and observing with pleasure how in the shade of the trees whole families, poor families, were sprawling; children kicking up their legs; sucking milk; paper bags thrown about, which could easily be picked up (if people objected) by one of those fat gentlemen in livery; for he was of opinion that every park, and every square, during the summer months should be open to children (the grass of the park flushed and faded, lighting up the poor mothers of Westminster and their crawling babies, as if a yellow lamp were moved beneath). But what could be done for female vagrants like that poor creature, stretched on her elbow (as if she had flung herself on the earth, rid of all ties, to observe curiously, to speculate boldly, to consider the whys and the wherefores, impudent, loose-lipped, humorous), he did not know. Bearing his flowers like a weapon, Richard Dalloway approached her; intent he passed her; still there was time for a spark between them – she laughed at the sight of him, he smiled good-humouredly, considering the problem of the female vagrant; not that they would ever speak. But he would tell Clarissa that he loved her, in so many words. He had, once upon a time, been jealous of Peter Walsh; jealous of him and Clarissa. But she had often said to him that she had been right not to marry Peter Walsh; which, knowing Clarissa, was obviously true; she wanted support. Not that she was weak; but she wanted support.

As for Buckingham Palace (like an old prima donna facing the audience all in white) you can't deny it a certain dignity, he considered, nor despise what does, after all, stand to millions of people (a little crowd was waiting at the gate to see the King drive out) for a symbol, absurd though it is; a child with a box of bricks could have done better, he thought; looking at the memorial to Queen Victoria (whom he could remember in her horn spectacles driving through Kensington), its white mound, its billowing motherliness; but he liked being ruled by the descendant of Horsa; he liked continuity; and the sense of handing on the traditions of the past. It was a great age in which to have lived. Indeed, his own life was a miracle; let him make no mistake about it; here he was, in the prime of life, walking to his house in Westminster to tell Clarissa that he loved her. Happiness is this, he thought.

It is this, he said, as he entered Dean's Yard. Big Ben was beginning to strike, first the warning, musical; then the hour, irrevocable. Lunch parties waste the entire afternoon, he thought, approaching his door.

The sound of Big Ben flooded Clarissa's drawing-room, where she sat, ever so annoyed, at her writing-table; worried; annoyed. It was perfectly true that she had not asked Ellie Henderson to her party; but she had done it on purpose. Now Mrs Marsham wrote: 'She had told Ellie Henderson she would ask Clarissa – Ellie so much wanted to come.'

But why should she invite all the dull women in London to her parties? Why should Mrs Marsham interfere? And there was Elizabeth closeted all this time with Doris Kilman. Anything more nauseating she could not conceive. Prayer at this hour with that woman. And the sound of the bell flooded the room with its melancholy wave; which receded, and gathered itself together to fall once more, when she heard, distractingly, something fumbling, something scratching at the door. Who at this hour? Three, good Heavens! Three already! For with overpowering directness and dignity the clock struck three; and she heard nothing else; but the door handle slipped round and in came Richard! What a surprise! In came Richard, holding out flowers. She had failed him, once at Constantinople; and Lady Bruton, whose lunch parties were said to be extraordinarily amusing, had not asked her. He was holding out flowers – roses, red and white roses. (But he could not bring himself to say he loved her; not in so many words.)

But how lovely, she said, taking his flowers. She understood; she understood without his speaking; his Clarissa. She put them in vases on the mantelpiece. How lovely they looked! she said. And was it amusing, she asked? Had Lady Bruton asked after her? Peter Walsh was back. Mrs Marsham had written. Must she ask Ellie Henderson? That woman Kilman was upstairs.

'But let us sit down for five minutes,' said Richard.

It all looked so empty. All the chairs were against the wall. What had they been doing? Oh, it was for the party; no, he had not forgotten the party. Peter Walsh was back. Oh yes; she had had him. And he was going to get a divorce; and he was in love with some woman out there. And he hadn't changed in the slightest. There she was, mending her dress . . .

'Thinking of Bourton,' she said.

'Hugh was at lunch,' said Richard. She had met him too! Well, he was getting absolutely intolerable. Buying Evelyn necklaces; fatter than ever; an intolerable ass.

'And it came over me "I might have married you," ' she said, thinking of Peter sitting there in his little bow-tie; with that knife, opening it, shutting it. 'Just as he always was, you know.'

They were talking about him at lunch, said Richard. (But he could not tell her he loved her. He held her hand. Happiness is this, he thought.) They had been writing a letter to *The Times* for Millicent Bruton. That was about all Hugh was fit for.

'And our dear Miss Kilman?' he asked. Clarissa thought the roses absolutely lovely; first bunched together; now of their own accord starting apart.

'Kilman arrives just as we've done lunch,' she said. 'Elizabeth turns pink. They shut themselves up. I suppose they're praying.'

Lord! He didn't like it; but these things pass over if you let them.

'In a mackintosh with an umbrella,' said Clarissa.

He had not said 'I love you'; but he held her hand. Happiness is this, is this, he thought.

'But why should I ask all the dull women in London to my parties?' said Clarissa. And if Mrs Marsham gave a party, did *she* invite her guests?

'Poor Ellie Henderson,' said Richard – it was a very odd thing how much Clarissa minded about her parties, he thought.

But Richard had no notion of the look of a room. However – what was he going to say?

If she worried about these parties he would not let her give them. Did she wish she had married Peter? But he must go.

He must be off, he said, getting up. But he stood for a moment as if he were about to say something; and she wondered what? Why? There were the roses.

'Some Committee?' she asked, as he opened the door.

'Armenians,' he said; or perhaps it was, 'Albanians.'

And there is a dignity in people; a solitude; even between husband and wife a gulf; and that one must respect, thought Clarissa, watching him open the door; for one would not part with it oneself, or take it, against his will, from one's husband, without losing one's independence, one's self-respect – something, after all, priceless.

He returned with a pillow and a quilt.

'An hour's complete rest after luncheon,' he said. And he went.

How like him! He would go on saying 'An hour's complete rest after luncheon' to the end of time, because a doctor had ordered it once. It was like him to take what doctors said literally; part of his adorable, divine simplicity, which no one had to the same extent; which made him go and do the thing while she and Peter frittered their time away bickering. He was already halfway to the House of Commons, to his Armenians, his Albanians, having settled her on the sofa, looking at his roses. And people would say, 'Clarissa Dalloway is spoilt.' She cared much more for her roses than for the Armenians. Hunted out of existence, maimed, frozen, the victims of cruelty and injustice (she had heard Richard say so over and over again) – no, she could feel nothing for the Albanians, or was it the Armenians? but she loved her roses (didn't that help the Armenians?) – the only flowers she could bear to see cut. But Richard was already at the House of Commons; at his Committee, having settled all her difficulties. But no; alas, that was not true. He did not see the reasons against asking Ellie Henderson. She would do it, of course, as he wished it. Since he had brought the pillows, she would lie down . . . But – but – why did she suddenly feel, for no reason that she could discover, desperately unhappy? As a person who has dropped some grain of pearl or diamond into the grass and parts the tall blades very carefully, this way and that, and searches here and there vainly, and at last spies it there at the roots, so she went through one thing and another; no, it was not Sally Seton saying that Richard would never be in the Cabinet because he had a second-class brain (it came back to her); no, she did not mind that; nor was it to do with Elizabeth either and Doris Kilman; those were facts. It was a feeling, some unpleasant feeling, earlier in the day perhaps; something that Peter had said, combined with some depression of her own, in her bedroom, taking off her hat; and what Richard had said had added to it, but what had he said? There were his roses. Her parties! That was it! Her parties! Both of them criticised her very unfairly, laughed at her very unjustly, for her parties. That was it! That was it!

Well, how was she going to defend herself? Now that she knew what it was, she felt perfectly happy. They thought, or Peter at any rate thought, that she enjoyed imposing herself; liked to have famous people about her; great names; was simply a snob in short. Well, Peter might think so. Richard merely thought it foolish of her to like excitement when she knew it was bad for her heart. It was childish, he thought. And both were quite wrong. What she liked was simply life.

'That's what I do it for,' she said, speaking aloud, to life.

Since she was lying on the sofa, cloistered, exempt, the presence of this thing which she felt to be so obvious became physically existent; with robes of sound from the street, sunny, with hot breath, whispering, blowing out the blinds. But suppose Peter said to her, 'Yes, yes, but your parties – what's the sense of your parties?' all she could say was (and nobody could be expected to understand): 'They're an offering'; which sounded horribly vague. But who was Peter to make out that life was all plain sailing? – Peter always in love, always in love with the wrong woman? What's your love? she might say to him. And she knew his answer; how it is the most important thing in the world and no woman possibly understood it. Very well. But could any man understand what she meant either? about life? She could not imagine Peter or Richard taking the trouble to give a party for no reason whatever.

But to go deeper, beneath what people said (and these judgements, how superficial, how fragmentary they are!) in her own mind now, what did it mean to her, this thing she called life? Oh, it was very queer. Here was So-and-So in South Kensington; someone up in Bayswater; and somebody else, say, in Mayfair. And she felt quite continuously a sense of their existence; and she felt what a waste; and she felt what a pity; and she felt if only they could be brought together; so she did it. And it was an offering; to combine, to create; but to whom?

An offering for the sake of offering, perhaps. Anyhow, it was her gift. Nothing else had she of the slightest importance; could not think, write, even play the piano. She muddled Armenians and Turks; loved success; hated discomfort; must be liked; talked oceans of nonsense: and to this day, ask her what the Equator was, and she did not know.

All the same, that one day should follow another; Wednesday, Thursday, Friday, Saturday; that one should wake up in the morning; see the sky; walk in the park; meet Hugh Whitbread; then suddenly in came Peter; then these roses; it was enough. After that, how unbelievable death was! – that it must end; and no one in the whole world would know how she had loved it all; how, every instant . . .

The door opened. Elizabeth knew that her mother was resting. She came in very quietly. She stood perfectly still. Was it that some Mongol had been wrecked on the coast of Norfolk (as Mrs Hilbery said), had mixed with the Dalloway ladies, perhaps a hundred years ago? For the Dalloways, in general, were fair-haired; blue-eyed; Elizabeth, on the contrary, was dark; had Chinese eyes in a pale face; an Oriental mystery; was gentle, considerate, still. As a child, she had had a perfect sense of humour; but now at seventeen, why, Clarissa could not in the least understand, she had become very serious; like a hyacinth sheathed in glossy green, with buds just tinted, a hyacinth which has had no sun.

She stood quite still and looked at her mother; but the door was ajar, and outside the door was Miss Kilman, as Clarissa knew; Miss Kilman in her mackintosh, listening to whatever they said.

Yes, Miss Kilman stood on the landing, and wore a mackintosh; but had her reasons. First, it was cheap; second, she was over forty; and did not, after all, dress to please. She was poor, moreover; degradingly poor. Otherwise she would not be taking jobs from people like the Dalloways; from rich people, who liked to be kind. Mr Dalloway, to do him justice, had been kind. But Mrs Dalloway had not. She had been merely condescending. She came from the most worthless of all classes – the rich, with a smattering of culture. They had expensive things everywhere; pictures, carpets, lots of servants. She considered that she had a perfect right to anything that the Dalloways did for her.

She had been cheated. Yes, the word was no exaggeration, for surely a girl has a right to some kind of happiness? And she had never been happy, what with being so clumsy and so poor. And then, just as she might have had a chance at Miss Dolby's school, the war came; and she had never been able to tell lies. Miss Dolby thought she would be happier with people who shared her views about the Germans. She had had to go. It was true that the family was of German origin; spelt the name Kiehlman in the eighteenth century; but her brother had been killed. They turned her out because she would not pretend that the Germans were all villains – when she had German friends, when the only happy days of her life had been spent in Germany! And after all, she could read history. She had had to take whatever she could get. Mr Dalloway had come across her working for the Friends. He had allowed her (and that was really generous of him) to teach his daughter history. Also she did a little Extension lecturing and so on. Then Our Lord had come to her (and here she always bowed her head). She had seen the light two years and three months ago. Now she did not envy women like Clarissa Dalloway; she pitied them.

She pitied and despised them from the bottom of her heart, as she stood on the soft carpet, looking at the old engraving of a little girl with a muff. With all this luxury going on, what hope was there for a better state of things? Instead of lying on a sofa – 'My mother is resting,' Elizabeth had said – she should have been in a factory; behind a counter; Mrs Dalloway and all the other fine ladies!

Bitter and burning, Miss Kilman had turned into a church two years three months ago. She had heard the Revd Edward Whittaker preach; the boys sing; had seen the solemn lights descend, and whether it was the music, or the voices (she herself when alone in the evening found comfort in a violin; but the sound was excruciating, she had no ear); the hot and turbulent feelings which boiled and surged in her had been assuaged as she sat there, and she wept copiously, and had gone to call on Mr Whittaker at his private house in Kensington. It was the hand of God, he said. The Lord had shown her the way. So now, whenever the hot and painful feelings boiled within her, this hatred of Mrs Dalloway, this grudge against the world, she thought of God. She thought of Mr Whittaker. Rage was succeeded by calm. A sweet savour filled her veins, her lips parted, and, standing formidable upon the landing in her mackintosh, she looked with steady and sinister serenity at Mrs Dalloway, who came out with her daughter.

Elizabeth said she had forgotten her gloves. That was because Miss Kilman and her mother hated each other. She could not bear to see them together. She ran upstairs to find her gloves.

But Miss Kilman did not hate Mrs Dalloway. Turning her large gooseberry-coloured eyes upon Clarissa, observing her small pink face, her delicate body, her air of freshness and fashion, Miss Kilman felt, Fool! Simpleton! You who have known neither sorrow nor pleasure; who have trifled your life away! And there rose in her an overmastering desire to overcome her; to unmask her. If she could have felled her it would have eased her. But it was not the body; it was the soul and its mockery that she wished to subdue; make feel her mastery. If only she could make her weep; could ruin her; humiliate her; bring her to her knees crying, You are right! But this was God's will, not Miss Kilman's. It was to be a religious victory. So she glared; so she glowered.

Clarissa was really shocked. This a Christian – this woman! This woman had taken her daughter from her! She in touch with invisible presences! Heavy, ugly, commonplace, without kindness or grace, she know the meaning of life!

'You are taking Elizabeth to the Stores?' Mrs Dalloway said.

Miss Kilman said she was. They stood there. Miss Kilman was not going to make herself agreeable. She had always earned her living. Her knowledge of modern history was thorough in the extreme. She did out of her meagre income set aside so much for causes she believed in; whereas this woman did nothing, believed nothing; brought up her daughter – but here was Elizabeth rather out of breath, the beautiful girl.

So they were going to the Stores. Odd it was, as Miss Kilman stood there (and stand she did with the power and taciturnity of some prehistoric monster armoured for primeval warfare), how, second by second, the idea of her diminished, how hatred (which was for ideas, not people) crumbled, how she lost her malignity, her size, became second by second merely Miss Kilman, in a mackintosh, whom Heaven knows Clarissa would have liked to help.

At this dwindling of the monster, Clarissa laughed. Saying goodbye, she laughed.

Off they went together, Miss Kilman and Elizabeth, downstairs.

With a sudden impulse, with a violent anguish, for this woman was taking her daughter from her, Clarissa leant over the banisters and cried out, 'Remember the party! Remember our party tonight!'

But Elizabeth had already opened the front door; there was a van passing; she did not answer.

Love and religion! thought Clarissa, going back into the drawing-room, tingling all over. How detestable, how detestable they are! For now that the body of Miss Kilman was not before her, it overwhelmed her – the idea. The cruellest things in the world, she thought, seeing them clumsy, hot, domineering, hypocritical, eavesdropping, jealous, infinitely cruel and unscrupulous, dressed in a mackintosh coat, on the landing; love and religion. Had she ever tried to convert anyone herself? Did she not wish everybody merely to be themselves? And she watched out of the window the old lady opposite climbing upstairs. Let her climb upstairs if she wanted to; let her stop; then let her, as Clarissa had often seen her, gain her bedroom, part her curtains, and disappear again into the background. Somehow one respected that – that old woman looking out of the window, quite unconscious that she was being watched, There was something solemn in it – but love and religion would destroy that, whatever it was, the privacy of the soul. The odious Kilman would destroy it. Yet it was a sight that made her want to cry.

Love destroyed too. Everything that was fine, everything that was true went. Take Peter Walsh now. There was a man, charming, clever, with ideas about everything. If you wanted to know about Pope, say, or Addison, or just to talk nonsense, what people were like, what things meant, Peter knew better than anyone. It was Peter who had helped her; Peter who had lent her books. But look at the women he loved – vulgar, trivial, commonplace. Think of Peter in love – he came to see her after all these years, and what did he talk about? Himself. Horrible passion! she thought. Degrading passion! she thought, thinking of Kilman and her Elizabeth walking to the Army and Navy Stores.

Big Ben struck the half-hour.

How extraordinary it was, strange, yes touching to see the old lady (they had been neighbours ever so many years) move away from the window, as if she were attached to that sound, that string. Gigantic as it was, it had something to do with her. Down, down, into the midst of ordinary things the finger fell making the moment solemn. She was forced, so Clarissa imagined, by that sound, to move, to go – but where? Clarissa tried to follow her as she turned and disappeared, and could still just see her white cap moving at the back of the bedroom. She was still there moving about at the other end of the room. Why creeds and prayers and mackintoshes? when, thought Clarissa, that's the miracle, that's the mystery; that old lady, she meant, whom she could see going from chest of drawers to dressing-table. She could still see her. And the supreme mystery which Kilman might say she had solved, or Peter might say he had solved, but Clarissa didn't believe either of them had the ghost of an idea of solving, was simply this: here was one room; there another. Did religion solve that, or love?

Love – but here the other clock, the clock which always struck two minutes after Big Ben, came shuffling in with its lap full of odds and ends, which it dumped down as if Big Ben were all very well with his majesty laying down the law, so solemn, so just, but she must remember all sorts of little things besides – Mrs Marsham, Ellie Henderson, glasses for ices – all sorts of little things came flooding and lapping and dancing in on the wake of that solemn stroke which lay flat like a bar of gold on the sea. Mrs Marsham, Ellie Henderson, glasses for ices. She must telephone now at once.

Volubly, troublously, the late clock sounded, coming in on the wake of Big Ben, with its lap full of trifles. Beaten up, broken up by the assault of carriages, the brutality of vans, the eager advance of myriads of angular men, of flaunting women, the domes and spires of offices and hospitals, the last relics of this lap full of odds and ends seemed to break, like the spray of an exhausted wave, upon the body of Miss Kilman standing still in the street for a moment to mutter, 'It is the flesh.'

It was the flesh that she must control. Clarissa Dalloway had insulted her. That she expected. But she had not triumphed; she had not mastered the flesh. Ugly, clumsy, Clarissa Dalloway had laughed at her for being that; and had revived the fleshly desires, for she minded looking as she did beside Clarissa. Nor could she talk as she did. But why wish to resemble her? Why? She despised Mrs Dalloway from the bottom of her heart. She was not serious. She was not good. Her life was a tissue of vanity and deceit. Yet Doris Kilman had been overcome. She had, as a matter of fact, very nearly burst into tears when Clarissa Dalloway laughed at her. 'It is the flesh, it is the flesh,' she muttered (it being her habit to talk aloud), trying to subdue this turbulent and painful feeling as she walked down Victoria Street. She prayed to God. She could not help being ugly; she could not afford to buy pretty clothes. Clarissa Dalloway had laughed – but she would concentrate her mind upon something else until she had reached the pillar-box. At any rate she had got Elizabeth. But she would think of something else; she would think of Russia; until she reached the pillar-box.

How nice it must be, she said, in the country, struggling, as Mr Whittaker had told her, with that violent grudge against the world which had scorned her, sneered at her, cast her off, beginning with this indignity – the infliction of her unlovable body which people could not bear to see. Do her hair as she might, her forehead remained like an egg, bald, white. No clothes suited her. She might buy anything. And for a woman, of course, that meant never meeting the opposite sex. Never would she come first with anyone. Sometimes lately it had seemed to her that, except for Elizabeth, her food was all that she lived for; her comforts; her dinner, her tea; her hot-water bottle at night. But one must fight; vanquish; have faith in God. Mr Whittaker had said she was there for a purpose. But no one knew the agony! He said, pointing to the crucifix, that God knew. But why should she have to suffer when other women, like Clarissa Dalloway, escaped? Knowledge comes through suffering, said Mr Whittaker.

She had passed the pillar-box, and Elizabeth had turned into the cool brown tobacco department of the Army and Navy Stores while she was still muttering to herself what Mr Whittaker had said about knowledge coming through suffering and the flesh. 'The flesh,' she muttered.

What department did she want? Elizabeth interrupted her.

'Petticoats,' she said abruptly, and stalked straight on to the lift.

Up they went. Elizabeth guided her this way and that; guided her in her abstraction as if she had been a great child, an unwieldy battleship. There were the petticoats, brown, decorous, striped, frivolous, solid, flimsy; and she chose, in her abstraction, portentously, and the girl serving thought her mad.

Elizabeth rather wondered, as they did up the parcel, what Miss Kilman was thinking. They must have their tea, said Miss Kilman, rousing, collecting herself. They had their tea.

Elizabeth rather wondered whether Miss Kilman could be hungry. It was her way of eating, eating with intensity, then looking, again and again, at a plate of sugared cakes on the table next them; then, when a lady and a child sat down and the child took the cake, could Miss Kilman really mind it? Yes, Miss Kilman did mind it. She had wanted that cake – the pink one. The pleasure of eating was almost the only pure pleasure left her, and then to be baffled even in that!

When people are happy they have a reserve, she had told Elizabeth, upon which to draw, whereas she was like a wheel without a tyre (she was fond of such metaphors), jolted by every pebble – so she would say staying on after the lesson, standing by the fire-place with her bag of books, her 'satchel,' she called it, on a Tuesday morning, after the lesson was over. And she talked too about the war. After all, there were people who did not think the English invariably right. There were books. There were meetings. There were other points of view. Would Elizabeth like to come with her to listen to So-and-so? (a most extraordinary-looking old man). Then Miss Kilman took her to some church in Kensington and they had tea with a clergyman. She had lent her books. Law, medicine, politics, all professions are open to women of your generation, said Miss Kilman. But for herself, her career was absolutely ruined, and was it her fault? Good gracious, said Elizabeth, no.

And her mother would come calling to say that a hamper had come from Bourton and would Miss Kilman like some flowers? To Miss Kilman she was always very, very nice, but Miss Kilman squashed the flowers all in a bunch, and hadn't any small talk, and what interested Miss Kilman bored her mother, and Miss Kilman and she were terrible together; and Miss Kilman swelled and looked very plain, but Miss Kilman was frightfully clever. Elizabeth had never thought about the poor. They lived with every-thing they wanted – her mother had breakfast in bed every day; Lucy carried it up; and she liked old women because they were Duchesses, and being descended from some Lord. But Miss Kilman said (one of those Tuesday mornings when the lesson was over), 'My grandfather kept an oil and colour shop in Kensington.' Miss Kilman was quite different from anyone she knew; she made one feel so small.

Miss Kilman took another cup of tea. Elizabeth, with her oriental bearing, her inscrutable mystery, sat perfectly upright; no, she did not want anything more. She looked for her gloves – her white gloves. They were under the table. Ah, but she must not go! Miss Kilman could not let her go! this youth, that was so beautiful; this girl, whom she genuinely loved! Her large hand opened and shut on the table.

But perhaps it was a little flat somehow, Elizabeth felt. And really she would like to go.

But said Miss Kilman, 'I've not quite finished yet.'

Of course, then, Elizabeth would wait. But it was rather stuffy in here.

'Are you going to the party tonight?' Miss Kilman said. Elizabeth supposed she was going; her mother wanted her to go. She must not let parties absorb her, Miss Kilman said, fingering the last two inches of a chocolate éclair.

She did not much like parties, Elizabeth said. Miss Kilman opened her mouth, slightly projected her chin, and swallowed down the last inches of the chocolate éclair, then wiped her fingers, and washed the tea round in her cup.

She was about to split asunder, she felt. The agony was so terrific. If she could grasp her, if she could clasp her, if she could make her hers absolutely and for ever and then die; that was all she wanted. But to sit here, unable to think of anything to say; to see Elizabeth turning against her; to be felt repulsive even by her – it was too much; she could not stand it. The thick fingers curled inwards.

'I never go to parties,' said Miss Kilman, just to keep Elizabeth from going. 'People don't ask me to parties' – and she knew as she said it that it was this egotism that was her undoing; Mr Whittaker had warned her; but she could not help it. She had suffered so horribly. 'Why should they ask me?' she said. 'I'm plain, I'm unhappy.' She knew it was idiotic. But it was all those people passing – people with parcels who despised her – who made her say it. However, she was Doris Kilman. She had her degree. She was a woman who had made her way in the world. Her knowledge of modern history was more than respectable.

'I don't pity myself,' she said. 'I pity' – she meant to say, 'your mother,' but no, she could not, not to Elizabeth. 'I pity other people much more.'

Like some dumb creature who has been brought up to a gate for an unknown purpose, and stands there longing to gallop away, Elizabeth Dalloway sat silent. Was Miss Kilman going to say anything more?

'Don't quite forget me,' said Doris Kilman; her voice quivered. Right away to the end of the field the dumb creature galloped in terror.

The great hand opened and shut.

Elizabeth turned her head. The waitress came. One had to pay at the desk, Elizabeth said, and went off, drawing out, so Miss Kilman felt, the very entrails in her body, stretching them as she crossed the room, and then, with a final twist, bowing her head very politely, she went.

She had gone. Miss Kilman sat at the marble table among the éclairs, stricken once, twice, thrice by shocks of suffering. She had gone. Mrs Dalloway had triumphed. Elizabeth had gone. Beauty had gone; youth had gone.

So she sat. She got up, blundered off among the little tables, rocking slightly from side to side, and somebody came after her with her petticoat and she lost her way, and was hemmed in by trunks specially prepared for taking to India; next got among the accouchement sets and baby linen; through all the commodities of the world, perishable and permanent, hams, drugs, flowers, stationery, variously smelling, now sweet, now sour, she lurched; saw herself thus lurching with her hat askew, very red in the face, full length in a looking-glass; and at last came out into the street.

The tower of Westminster Cathedral rose in front of her, the habitation of God. In the midst of the traffic, there was the habitation of God. Doggedly she set off with her parcel to that other sanctuary, the Abbey, where, raising her hands in a tent before her face, she sat beside those driven into shelter too; the variously assorted worshippers, now divested of social rank, almost of sex, as they raised their hands before their faces; but once they removed them, instantly reverent, middle-class, English men and women, some of them desirous of seeing the wax works.

But Miss Kilman held her tent before her face. Now she was deserted; now rejoined. New worshippers came in from the street to replace the strollers, and still, as people gazed round and shuffled past the tomb of the Unknown Warrior, still she barred her eyes with her fingers and tried in this double darkness, for the light in the Abbey was bodiless to aspire above the vanities, the desires, the commodities, to rid herself both of hatred and of love. Her hands twitched. She seemed to struggle. Yet to others God was accessible and the path to Him smooth. Mr Fletcher, retired, of the Treasury, Mrs Gorham, widow of the famous KC, approached Him simply, and having done their praying, leant back, enjoyed the music (the organ pealed sweetly), and saw Miss Kilman at the end of the row, praying, praying, and, being still on the threshold of their underworld, thought of her sympathetically as a soul haunting the same territory; a soul cut out of immaterial substance; not a woman, a soul.

But Mr Fletcher had to go. He had to pass her, and being himself neat as a new pin, could not help being a little distressed by the poor lady's disorder; her hair down; her parcel on the floor. She did not at once let him pass. But, as he stood gazing about him, at the white marbles, grey window panes, and accumulated treasures (for he was extremely proud of the Abbey), her largeness, robustness, and power as she sat there shifting her knees from time to time (it was so rough the approach to her God – so tough her desires) impressed him, as they had impressed Mrs Dalloway (she could not get the thought of her out of her mind that afternoon), the Revd Edward Whittaker, and Elizabeth too.

And Elizabeth waited in Victoria Street for an omnibus. It was so nice to be out of doors. She thought perhaps she need not go home just yet. It was so nice to be out in the air. So she would get on to an omnibus. And already, even as she stood there, in her very well-cut clothes, it was beginning . . . People were beginning to compare her to poplar trees, early dawn, hyacinths, fawns, running water, and garden lilies; and it made her life a burden to her, for she so much preferred being left alone to do what she liked in the country, but they would compare her to lilies, and she had to go to parties, and London was so dreary compared with being alone in the country with her father and the dogs.

Buses swooped, settled, were off – garish caravans, glistening with red and yellow varnish. But which should she get on to? She had no preferences. Of course, she would not push her way. She inclined to be passive. It was expression she needed, but her eyes were fine, Chinese, oriental, and, as her mother said, with such nice shoulders and holding herself so straight, she was always charming to look at; and lately, in the evening especially, when she was interested, for she never seemed excited, she looked almost beautiful, very stately, very serene. What could she be thinking? Every man fell in love with her, and she was really awfully bored. For it was beginning. Her mother could see that – the compliments were beginning. That she did not care more about it – for instance for her clothes – sometimes worried Clarissa, but perhaps it was as well with all those puppies and guinea pigs about having distemper, and it gave her a charm. And now there was this odd friendship with Miss Kilman. Well, thought Clarissa about three o'clock in the morning, reading Baron Marbot for she could not sleep, it proves she has a heart.

Suddenly Elizabeth stepped forward and most competently boarded the omnibus, in front of everybody. She took a seat on top. The impetuous creature – a pirate – started forward, sprang away; she had to hold the rail to steady herself, for a pirate it was, reckless, unscrupulous, bearing down ruthlessly, circumventing dangerously, boldly snatching a passenger, or ignoring a passenger, squeezing eel-like and arrogant in between, and then rushing insolently all sails spread up Whitehall. And did Elizabeth give one thought to poor Miss Kilman who loved her without jealousy, to whom she had been a fawn in the open, a moon in a glade? She was delighted to be free. The fresh air was so delicious. It had been so stuffy in the Army and Navy Stores. And now it was like riding, to be rushing up Whitehall; and to each movement of the omnibus the beautiful body in the fawn-coloured coat responded freely like a rider, like the figure-head of a ship, for the breeze slightly disarrayed her; the heat gave her cheeks the pallor of white painted wood; and her fine eyes, having no eyes to meet, gazed ahead, blank, bright, with the staring incredible innocence of sculpture.

It was always talking about her own sufferings that made Miss Kilman so difficult. And was she right? If it was being on committees and giving up hours and hours every day (she hardly ever saw him in London) that helped the poor, her father did that, goodness knows – if that was what Miss Kilman meant about being a Christian, but it was so difficult to say. Oh, she would like to go a little farther. Another penny was it to the Strand? Here was another penny, then. She would go up the Strand.

She liked people who were ill. And every profession is open to the women of your generation, said Miss Kilman. So she might be a doctor. She might be a farmer. Animals are often ill. She might own a thousand acres and have people under her. She would go and see them in their cottages. This was Somerset House. One might be a very good farmer – and that, strangely enough, though Miss Kilman had her share in it, was almost entirely due to Somerset House. It looked so splendid, so serious, that great grey building. And she liked the feeling of people working. She liked those churches, like shapes of grey paper, breasting the stream of the Strand. It was quite different here from Westminster, she thought, getting off at Chancery Lane. It was so serious; it was so busy. In short, she would like to have a profession. She would become a doctor, a farmer, possibly go into Parliament if she found it necessary, all because of the Strand.

The feet of those people busy about their activities, hands putting stone to stone, minds eternally occupied not with trivial chatterings (comparing women to poplars – which was rather exciting, of course, but very silly), but with thoughts of ships, of business, of law, of administration, and with it all so stately (she was in the Temple), gay (there was the river), pious (there was the Church), made her quite determined, whatever her mother might say, to become either a farmer or a doctor. But she was, of course, rather lazy.

And it was much better to say nothing about it. It seemed so silly. It was the sort of thing that did sometimes happen, when one was alone – buildings without architects' names, crowds of people coming back from the city having more power than single clergymen in Kensington, than any of the books Miss Kilman had lent her, to stimulate what lay slumbrous, clumsy, and shy on the mind's sandy floor, to break surface, as a child suddenly stretches its arms; it was just that, perhaps, a sigh, a stretch of the arms, an impulse, a revelation, which has its effects for ever, and then down again it went to the sandy floor. She must go home. She must dress for dinner. But what was the time? – where was a clock?

She looked up Fleet Street. She walked just a little way towards St Paul's, shyly, like someone penetrating on tiptoe, exploring a strange house by night with a candle, on edge lest the owner should suddenly fling wide his bedroom door and ask her business, nor did she dare wander off into queer alleys, tempting by-streets, any more than in a strange house open doors which might be bedroom doors, or sitting-room doors, or lead straight to the larder. For no Dalloways came down the Strand daily; she was a pioneer, a stray, venturing, trusting.

In many ways, her mother felt, she was extremely immature, like a child still, attached to dolls, to old slippers; a perfect baby; and that was charming.

But then, of course, there was in the Dalloway family the tradition of public service. Abbesses, principals, head mistresses, dignitaries, in the republic of women – without being brilliant, any of them, they were that. She penetrated a little farther in the direction of St Paul's. She liked the geniality, sisterhood, motherhood, brotherhood of this uproar. It seemed to her good. The noise was tremendous; and suddenly there were trumpets (the unemployed) blaring, rattling about in the uproar; military music; as if people were marching; yet had they been dying – had some woman breathed her last, and whoever was watching, opening the window of the room where she had just brought off that act of supreme dignity, looked down on Fleet Street, that uproar, that military music would have come triumphing up to him, consolatory, indifferent.

It was not conscious. There was no recognition in it of one's fortune, or fate, and for that very reason even to those dazed with watching for the last shivers of consciousness on the faces of the dying, consoling.

Forgetfulness in people might wound, their ingratitude corrode, but this voice, pouring endlessly, year in year out, would take whatever it might be; this vow; this van; this life; this procession, would wrap them all about and carry them on, as in the rough stream of a glacier the ice holds a splinter of bone, a blue petal, some oak trees, and rolls them on.

But it was later than she thought. Her mother would not like her to be wandering off alone like this. She turned back down the Strand.

A puff of wind (in spite of the heat, there was quite a wind) blew a thin black veil over the sun and over the Strand. The faces faded; the omnibuses suddenly lost their glow. For although the clouds were of mountainous white so that one could fancy hacking hard chips off with a hatchet, with broad golden slopes, lawns of celestial pleasure gardens, on their flanks, and had all the appearance of settled habitations assembled for the conference of gods above the world, there was a perpetual movement among them. Signs were interchanged, when, as if to fulfil some scheme arranged already, now a summit dwindled, now a whole block of pyramidal size which had kept its station unalterably advanced into the midst or gravely led the procession to fresh anchorage. Fixed though they seemed at their posts, at rest in perfect unanimity, nothing could be fresher, freer, more sensitive superficially than the snow-white or gold-kindled surface; to change, to go, to dismantle the solemn assemblage was immediately possible; and in spite of the grave fixity, the accumulated robustness and solidity, now they struck light to the earth, now darkness.

Calmly and competently, Elizabeth Dalloway mounted the Westminster omnibus.

Going and coming, beckoning, signalling, so the light and shadow, which now made the wall grey, now the bananas bright yellow, now made the Strand grey, now made the omnibuses bright yellow, seemed to Septimus Warren Smith lying on the sofa in the sitting-room; watching the watery gold glow and fade with the astonishing sensibility of some live creature on the roses, on the wall-paper. Outside the trees dragged their leaves like nets through the depths of the air; the sound of water was in the room, and through the waves came the voices of birds singing. Every power poured its treasures on his head, and his hand lay there on the back of the sofa, as he had seen his hand lie when he was bathing, floating, on the top of the waves, while far away on shore he heard dogs barking and barking far away. Fear no more, says the heart in the body; fear no more.

He was not afraid. At every moment Nature signified by some laughing hint like that gold spot which went round the wall – there, there, there – her determination to show, by brandishing her plumes, shaking her tresses, flinging her mantle this way and that, beautifully, always beautifully, and standing close up to breathe through her hollowed hands Shakespeare's words, her meaning.

Rezia, sitting at the table twisting a hat in her hands, watched him; saw him smiling. He was happy then. But she could not bear to see him smiling. It was not marriage; it was not being one's husband to look strange like that, always to be starting, laughing, sitting hour after hour silent, or clutching her and telling her to write. The table drawer was full of those writings; about war; about Shakespeare; about great discoveries; how there is no death. Lately he had become excited suddenly for no reason (and both Dr Holmes and Sir William Bradshaw said excitement was the worst thing for him), and waved his hands and cried out that he knew the truth! He knew everything! That man, his friend who was killed, Evans, had come, he said. He was singing behind the screen. She wrote it down just as he spoke it. Some things were very beautiful; others sheer nonsense. And he was always stopping in the middle, changing his mind; wanting to add something; hearing something new; listening with his hand up. But she heard nothing.

And once they found the girl who did the room reading one of these papers in fits of laughter. It was a dreadful pity. For that made Septimus cry out about human cruelty – how they tear each other to pieces. The fallen, he said, they tear to pieces. 'Holmes is on us,' he would say, and he would invent stories about Holmes; Holmes eating porridge; Holmes reading Shakespeare – making himself roar with laughter or rage, for Dr Holmes seemed to stand for something horrible to him. 'Human nature,' he called him. Then there were the visions. He was drowned, he used to say, and lying on a cliff with the gulls screaming over him. He would look over the edge of the sofa down into the sea. Or he was hearing music. Really it was only a barrel organ or some man crying in the street. But, 'Lovely!' he used to cry, and the tears would run down his cheeks, which was to her the most dreadful thing of all, to see a man like Septimus, who had fought, who was brave, crying. And he would lie listening until suddenly he would cry that he was falling down, down into the flames! Actually she would look for flames, it was so vivid. But there was nothing. They were alone in the room. It was a dream, she would tell him, and so quiet him at last, but sometimes she was frightened too. She sighed as she sat sewing.

Her sigh was tender and enchanting, like the wind outside a wood in the evening. Now she put down her scissors; now she turned to take something from the table. A little stir, a little crinkling, a little tapping built up something on the table there, where she sat sewing. Through his eyelashes he could see her blurred outline; her little black body; her face and hands; her turning movements at the table, as she took up a reel, or looked (she was apt to lose things) for her silk. She was making a hat for Mrs Filmer's married daughter, whose name was – he had forgotten her name.

'What is the name of Mrs Filmer's married daughter?' he asked.

'Mrs Peters,' said Rezia. She was afraid it was too small, she said, holding it before her. Mrs Peters was a big woman; but she did not like her. It was only because Mr Filmer had been so good to them – 'She gave me grapes this morning,' she said – that Rezia wanted to do something to show that they were grateful. She had come into the room the other evening and found Mrs Peters, who thought they were out, playing the gramophone.

'Was it true?' he asked. She was playing the gramophone? Yes; she had told him about it at the time; she had found Mrs Peters playing the gramophone.

He began, very cautiously, to open his eyes, to see whether a gramophone was really there. But real things – real things were too exciting. He must be cautious. He would not go mad. First he looked at the fashion papers on the lower shelf, then gradually at the gramophone with the green trumpet. Nothing could be more exact. And so, gathering courage, he looked at the sideboard; the plate of bananas; the engraving of Queen Victoria and the Prince Consort; at the mantelpiece, with the jar of roses. None of these things moved. All were still; all were real.

'She is a woman with a spiteful tongue,' said Rezia.

'What does Mr Peters do?' Septimus asked.

'Ah,' said Rezia, trying to remember. She thought Mrs Filmer had said that he travelled for some company. 'Just now he is in Hull,' she said.

'Just now!' She said that with her Italian accent. She said that herself. He shaded his eyes so that he might see only a little of her face at a time, first the chin, then the nose, then the forehead, in case it were deformed, or had some terrible mark on it. But no, there she was, perfectly natural, sewing, with the pursed lips that women have, the set, the melancholy expression, when sewing. But there was nothing terrible about it, he assured himself, looking a second time, a third time at her face, her hands, for what was frightening or disgusting in her as she sat there in broad daylight, sewing? Mrs Peters had a spiteful tongue. Mr Peters was in Hull. Why then rage and prophesy? Why fly scourged and outcast? Why be made to tremble and sob by the clouds? Why seek truths and deliver messages when Rezia sat sticking pins into the front of her dress, and Mr Peters was in Hull? Miracles, revelations, agonies, loneliness, falling through the sea, down, down into the flames, all were burnt out, for he had a sense, as he watched Rezia trimming the straw hat for Mrs Peters, of a coverlet of flowers.

'It's too small for Mrs Peters,' said Septimus.

For the first time for days he was speaking as he used to do! Of course it was – absurdly small, she said. But Mrs Peters had chosen it.

He took it out of her hands. He said it was an organ grinder's monkey's hat.

How it rejoiced her that! Not for weeks had they laughed like this together, poking fun privately like married people. What she meant was that if Mrs Filmer had come in, or Mrs Peters or anybody, they would not have understood what she and Septimus were laughing at.

'There,' she said, pinning a rose to one side of the hat. Never had she felt so happy! Never in her life!

But that was still more ridiculous, Septimus said. Now the poor woman looked like a pig at a fair. (Nobody ever made her laugh as Septimus did.)

What had she got in her work-box? She had ribbons and beads, tassels, artificial flowers. She tumbled them out on the table. He began putting odd colours together – for though he had no fingers, could not even do up a parcel, he had a wonderful eye, and often he was right, sometimes absurd, of course, but sometimes wonderfully right.

'She shall have a beautiful hat!' he murmured, taking up this and that, Rezia kneeling by his side, looking over his shoulder. Now it was finished – that is to say the design; she must stitch it together. But she must be very, very careful, he said, to keep it just as he had made it.

So she sewed. When she sewed, he thought, she made a sound like a kettle on the hob; bubbling, murmuring, always busy, her strong little pointed fingers pinching and poking; her needle flashing straight. The sun might go in and out, on the tassels, on the wall-paper, but he would wait, he thought, stretching out his feet, looking at his ringed sock at the end of the sofa; he would wait in this warm place, this pocket of still air, which one comes on at the edge of a wood sometimes in the evening, when, because of a fall in the ground, or some arrangement of the trees (one must be scientific above all, scientific), warmth lingers, and the air buffets the cheek like the wing of a bird.

'There it is,' said Rezia, twirling Mrs Peters' hat on the tips of her fingers. 'That'll do for the moment. Later . . . ' her sentence bubbled away drip, drip, drip, like a contented tap left running.

It was wonderful. Never had he done anything which made him feel so proud. It was so real, it was so substantial, Mrs Peters' hat.

'Just look at it,' he said.

Yes, it would always make her happy to see that hat. He had become himself then, he had laughed then. They had been alone together. Always she would like that hat.

He told her to try it on.

'But I must look so queer!' she cried, running over to the glass and looking first this side, then that. Then she snatched it off again, for there was a tap at the door. Could it be Sir William Bradshaw? Had he sent already?

No! it was only the small girl with the evening paper.

What always happened, then happened – what happened every night of their lives. The small girl sucked her thumb at the door; Rezia went down on her knees; Rezia cooed and kissed; Rezia got a bag of sweets out of the table drawer. For so it always happened. First one thing, then another. So she built it up, first one thing and then another. Dancing, skipping, round and round the room they went. He took the paper. Surrey was all out, he read. There was a heat wave. Rezia repeated: Surrey was all out. There was a heat wave, making it part of the game she was playing with Mrs Filmer's grandchild, both of them laughing, chattering at the same time, at their game. He was very tired. He was very happy. He would sleep. He shut his eyes. But directly he saw nothing the sounds of the game became fainter and stranger and sounded like the cries of people seeking and not finding, and passing farther and farther away. They had lost him!

He started up in terror. What did he see? The plate of bananas on the sideboard. Nobody was there (Rezia had taken the child to its mother; it was bedtime). That was it: to be alone for ever. That was the doom pronounced in Milan when he came into the room and saw them cutting out buckram shapes with their scissors; to be alone for ever.

He was alone with the sideboard and the bananas. He was alone, exposed on this bleak eminence, stretched out — but not on a hill-top; not on a crag; on Mrs Filmer's sitting-room sofa. As for the visions, the faces, the voices of the dead, where were they? There was a screen in front of him, with black bulrushes and blue swallows. Where he had once seen mountains, where he had seen faces, where he had seen beauty, there was a screen.

'Evans!' he cried. There was no answer. A mouse had squeaked, or a curtain rustled. Those were the voices of the dead. The screen, the coal-scuttle, the sideboard remained to him. Let him then face the screen, the coal-scuttle and the sideboard . . . but Rezia burst into the room chattering.

Some letter had come. Everybody's plans were changed. Mrs Filmer would not be able to go to Brighton after all. There was no time to let Mrs Williams know, and really Rezia thought it very, very annoying, when she caught sight of the hat and thought . . . perhaps . . . she . . . might just make a little . . . Her voice died out in contented melody.

'Ah, damn!' she cried (it was a joke of theirs, her swearing); the needle had broken. Hat, child, Brighton, needle. She built it up; first one thing, then another, she built it up, sewing.

She wanted him to say whether by moving the rose she had improved the hat. She sat on the end of the sofa.

They were perfectly happy now, she said suddenly, putting the hat down.

For she could say anything to him now. She could say whatever came into her head. That was almost the first thing she had felt about him, that night in the café when he had come in with his English friends. He had come in, rather shyly, looking round him, and his hat had fallen when he hung it up. That she could remember. She knew he was English, though not one of the large Englishmen her sister admired, for he was always thin; but he had a beautiful fresh colour; and with his big nose, his bright eyes, his way of sitting a little hunched, made her think, she had often told him, of a young hawk, that first evening she saw him, when they were playing dominoes, and he had come in – of a young hawk; but with her he was always very gentle. She had never seen him wild or drunk, only suffering sometimes through this terrible war, but even so, when she came in, he would put it all away. Anything, anything in the whole world, any little bother with her work, anything that struck her to say she would tell him, and he understood at once. Her own family even were not the same. Being older than she was and being so clever – how serious he was, wanting her to read Shakespeare before she could even read a child's story in English! – being so much more experienced, he could help her. And she, too, could help him.

But this hat now. And then (it was getting late) Sir William Bradshaw.

She held her hands to her head, waiting for him to say did he like the hat or not, and as she sat there, waiting, looking down, he could feel her mind, like a bird, falling from branch to branch, and always alighting, quite rightly; he could follow her mind, as she sat there in one of those loose lax poses that came to her naturally, and, if he should say anything, at once she smiled, like a bird alighting with all its claws firm upon the bough.

But he remembered. Bradshaw said, 'The people we are most fond of are not good for us when we are ill.' Bradshaw said he must be taught to rest. Bradshaw said they must be separated.

'Must', 'must', why 'must'? What power had Bradshaw over him? 'What right has Bradshaw to say "must" to me?' he demanded.

'It is because you talked of killing yourself,' said Rezia. (Mercifully, she could now say anything to Septimus.)

So he was in their power! Holmes and Bradshaw were on him! The brute with the red nostrils was snuffing into every secret place! 'Must' I could say! Where were his papers? the things he had written?

She brought him his papers, the things he had written, things she had written for him. She tumbled them out on to the sofa. They looked at them together. Diagrams, designs, little men and women brandishing sticks for arms, with wings – were they? – on their backs; circles traced round shillings and sixpences – the suns and stars; zigzagging precipices with mountaineers ascending roped together, exactly like knives and forks; sea pieces with little faces laughing out of what might perhaps be waves: the map of the world. Burn them! he cried. Now for his writings; how the dead sing behind rhododendron bushes; odes to Time; conversations with Shakespeare;

Evans, Evans, Evans – his messages from the dead; do not cut down trees;
tell the Prime Minister. Universal love: the meaning of the world. Burn
them! he cried.

But Rezia laid her hands on them. Some were very beautiful, she thought.
She would tie them up (for she had no envelope) with a piece of silk.

Even if they took him, she said, she would go with him. They could not
separate them against their wills, she said.

Shuffling the edges straight, she did up the papers, and tied the parcel
almost without looking, sitting close, sitting beside him, he thought, as if all
her petals were about her. She was a flowering tree; and through her
branches looked out the face of a lawgiver, who had reached a sanctuary
where she feared no one; not Holmes; not Bradshaw; a miracle, a triumph,
the last and greatest. Staggering he saw her mount the appalling staircase,
laden with Holmes and Bradshaw, men who never weighed less than eleven
stone six, who sent their wives to Court, men who made ten thousand a year
and talked of proportion; who differed in their verdicts (for Holmes said one
thing, Bradshaw another), yet judges they were; who mixed the vision and
the sideboard; saw nothing clear, yet ruled, yet inflicted. Over them she
triumphed.

'There!' she said. The papers were tied up. No one should get at them.
She would put them away.

And, she said, nothing should separate them. She sat down beside him
and called him by the name of that hawk or crow which being malicious and
a great destroyer of crops was precisely like him. No one could separate
them, she said.

Then she got up to go into the bedroom to pack their things, but hearing
voices downstairs and thinking that Dr Holmes had perhaps called, ran
down to prevent him coming up.

Septimus could hear her talking to Holmes on the staircase.

'My dear lady, I have come as a friend,' Holmes was saying.

'No. I will not allow you to see my husband,' she said.

He could see her, like a little hen, with her wings spread barring his
passage. But Holmes persevered.

'My dear lady, allow me . . . ' Holmes said, putting her aside (Holmes was
a powerfully-built man).

Holmes was coming upstairs. Holmes would burst open the door.
Holmes would say, 'In a funk, eh?' Holmes would get him. But no; not
Holmes; not Bradshaw. Getting up rather unsteadily, hopping indeed from
foot to foot, he considered Mrs Filmer's nice clean bread-knife with 'Bread'
carved on the handle. Ah, but one mustn't spoil that. The gas fire? But it was
too late now. Holmes was coming. Razors he might have got, but Rezia, who
always did that sort of thing, had packed them. There remained only the
window, the large Bloomsbury lodging-house window; the tiresome, the
troublesome, and rather melodramatic business of opening the window and

throwing himself out. It was their idea of tragedy, not his or Rezia's (for she was with him). Holmes and Bradshaw liked that sort of thing. (He sat on the sill.) But he would wait till the very last moment. He did not want to die. Life was good. The sun hot. Only human beings? Coming down the stair-case opposite an old man stopped and stared at him. Holmes was at the door. 'I'll give it you!' he cried, and flung himself vigorously, violently down on to Mrs Filmer's area railings.

'The coward!' cried Dr Holmes, bursting the door open. Rezia ran to the window, she saw; she understood. Dr Holmes and Mrs Filmer collided with each other. Mrs Filmer flapped her apron and made her hide her eyes in the bedroom. There was a great deal of running up and down stairs. Dr Holmes came in – white as a sheet, shaking all over, with a glass in his hand. She must be brave and drink something, he said (What was it? Something sweet), for her husband was horribly mangled, would not recover consciousness, she must not see him, must be spared as much as possible, would have the inquest to go through, poor young woman. Who could have foretold it? A sudden impulse, no one was in the least to blame (he told Mrs Filmer). And why the devil he did it, Dr Holmes could not conceive.

It seemed to her as she drank the sweet stuff that she was opening long windows, stepping out into some garden. But where? The clock was striking – one, two, three: how sensible the sound was; compared with all this thumping and whispering; like Septimus himself. She was falling asleep. But the clock went on striking, four, five, six and Mrs Filmer waving her apron (they wouldn't bring the body in here, would they?) seemed part of that garden; or a flag. She had once seen a flag slowly rippling out from a mast when she stayed with her aunt at Venice. Men killed in battle were thus saluted, and Septimus had been through the War. Of her memories, most were happy.

She put on her hat, and ran through cornfields – where could it have been? – on to some hill, somewhere near the sea, for there were ships, gulls, butterflies; they sat on a cliff. In London, too, there they sat, and, half dreaming, came to her through the bedroom door, rain falling, whisperings, stirrings among dry corn, the caress of the sea, as it seemed to her, hollowing them in its arched shell and murmuring to her laid on shore, strewn she felt, like flying flowers over some tomb.

'He is dead,' she said, smiling at the poor old woman who guarded her with her honest light-blue eyes fixed on the door. (They wouldn't bring him in here, would they?) But Mrs Filmer pooh-poohed. Oh no, oh no! They were carrying him away now. Ought she not to be told? Married people ought to be together, Mrs Filmer thought. But they must do as the doctor said.

'Let her sleep,' said Dr Holmes, feeling her pulse. She saw the large outline of his body dark against the window. So that was Dr Holmes.

One of the triumphs of civilisation, Peter Walsh thought. It is one of the triumphs of civilisation, as the light high bell of the ambulance sounded. Swiftly, cleanly, the ambulance sped to the hospital, having picked up instantly, humanely, some poor devil; someone hit on the head, struck down by disease, knocked over perhaps a minute or so ago at one of these crossings, as might happen to oneself. That was civilisation. It struck him coming back from the East – the efficiency, the organisation, the communal spirit of London. Every cart or carriage of its own accord drew aside to let the ambulance pass. Perhaps it was morbid; or was it not touching rather, the respect which they showed this ambulance with its victim inside – busy men hurrying home, yet instantly bethinking them as it passed of some wife; or presumably how easily it might have been them there, stretched on a shelf with a doctor and a nurse . . . Ah, but thinking became morbid, sentimental, directly one began conjuring up doctors, dead bodies; a little glow of pleasure, a sort of lust, too, over the visual impression warned one not to go on with that sort of thing any more – fatal to art, fatal to friendship. True. And yet, thought Peter Walsh, as the ambulance turned the corner, though the light high bell could be heard down the next street and still farther as it crossed the Tottenham Court Road, chiming constantly, it is the privilege of loneliness; in privacy one may do as one chooses. One might weep if no one saw. It had been his undoing – this susceptibility – in Anglo-Indian society; not weeping at the right time, or laughing either. I have that in me, he thought, standing by the pillar-box, which could now dissolve in tears. Why, heaven knows. Beauty of some sort probably, and the weight of the day, which, beginning with that visit to Clarissa, had exhausted him with its heat, its intensity, and the drip, drip of one impression after another down into that cellar where they stood, deep, dark, and no one would ever know. Partly for that reason, its secrecy, complete and inviolable, he had found life like an unknown garden, full of turns and corners, surprising, yes; really it took one's breath away, these moments: there coming to him by the pillar-box opposite the British Museum one of them, a moment, in which things came together; this ambulance; and life and death. It was as if he were sucked up to some very high roof by that rush of emotion, and the rest of him, like a white shell-sprinkled beach, left bare. It had been his undoing in Anglo-Indian society – this susceptibility.

Clarissa once, going on top of an omnibus with him somewhere, Clarissa superficially at least, so easily moved, now in despair, now in the best of spirits, all aquiver in those days and such good company, spotting queer little scenes, names, people from the top of a bus, for they used to explore London and bring back bags full of treasures from the Caledonian market –

Clarissa had a theory in those days – they had heaps of theories, always theories, as young people have. It was to explain the feeling they had of dissatisfaction; not knowing people; not being known. For how could they know each other? You met every day; then not for six months, or years. It was unsatisfactory, they agreed, how little one knew people. But she said, sitting on the bus going up Shaftesbury Avenue, she felt herself everywhere; not 'here, here, here'; and she tapped the back of the seat; but everywhere. She waved her hand, going up Shaftesbury Avenue. She was all that. So that to know her, or anyone, one must seek out the people who completed them; even the places. Odd affinities she had with people she had never spoken to, some woman in the street, some man behind a counter – even trees, or barns. It ended in a transcendental theory which, with her horror of death, allowed her to believe, or say that she believed (for all her scepticism), that since our apparitions, the part of us which appears, are so momentary compared with the other, the unseen part of us, which spreads wide, the unseen might survive, be recovered somehow attached to this person or that, or even haunting certain places, after death. Perhaps – perhaps.

Looking back over that long friendship of almost thirty years her theory worked to this extent. Brief, broken, often painful as their actual meetings had been, what with his absences and interruptions (this morning, for instance, in came Elizabeth, like a long-legged colt, handsome, dumb, just as he was beginning to talk to Clarissa), the effect of them on his life was immeasurable. There was a mystery about it. You were given a sharp, acute, uncomfortable grain – the actual meeting; horribly painful as often as not; yet in absence, in the most unlikely places, it would flower out, open, shed its scent, let you touch, taste, look about you, get the whole feel of it and understanding, after years of lying lost. Thus she had come to him; on board ship; in the Himalayas; suggested by the oddest things (so Sally Seton, generous, enthusiastic goose! thought of *him* when she saw blue hydrangeas). She had influenced him more than any person he had ever known. And always in this way coming before him without his wishing it, cool, lady-like, critical; or ravishing, romantic, recalling some field or English harvest. He saw her most often in the country, not in London. One scene after another at Bourton . . .

He had reached his hotel. He crossed the hall, with its mounds of reddish chairs and sofas, its spike-leaved, withered-looking plants. He got his key off the hook. The young lady handed him some letters. He went upstairs – he saw her most often at Bourton, in the late summer, when he stayed there for a week, or fortnight even, as people did in those days. First on top of some hill there she would stand, hands clapped to her hair, her cloak blowing out, pointing, crying to them – She saw the Severn beneath. Or in a wood, making the kettle boil – very ineffective with her fingers; the smoke curtseying, blowing in their faces; her little pink face showing through; begging water from an old woman in a cottage, who came to the door to watch them go.

They walked always; the others drove. She was bored driving, disliked all animals, except that dog. They tramped miles along roads. She would break off to get her bearings, pilot him back across country; and all the time they argued, discussed poetry, discussed people, discussed politics (she was a Radical then); never noticing a thing except when she stopped, cried out at a view or a tree, and made him look with her; and so on again, through stubble fields, she walking ahead, with a flower for her aunt, never tired of walking for all her delicacy; to drop down on Bourton in the dusk. Then, after dinner, old Breitkopf would open the piano and sing without any voice, and they would lie sunk in armchairs, trying not to laugh, but always breaking down and laughing, laughing – laughing at nothing. Breitkopf was supposed not to see. And then in the morning, flirting up and down like a wagtail in front of the house . . .

Oh, it was a letter from her! This blue envelope; that was her hand. And he would have to read it. Here was another of those meetings, bound to be painful! To read her letter needed the devil of an effort. 'How heavenly it was to see him. She must tell him that.' That was all.

But it upset him. It annoyed him. He wished she hadn't written it. Coming on top of his thoughts, it was like a nudge in the ribs. Why couldn't she let him be? After all, she had married Dalloway, and lived with him in perfect happiness all these years.

These hotels are not consoling places. Far from it. Any number of people had hung up their hats on those pegs. Even the flies, if you thought of it, had settled on other people's noses. As for the cleanliness which hit him in the face, it wasn't cleanliness, so much as bareness, frigidity; a thing that had to be. Some arid matron made her rounds at dawn sniffing, peering, causing blue-nosed maids to scour, for all the world as if the next visitor were a joint of meat to be served on a perfectly clean platter. For sleep, one bed; for sitting in, one armchair; for cleaning one's teeth and shaving one's chin, one tumbler, one looking-glass. Books, letters, dressing-gown, slipped about on the impersonality of the horse-hair like incongruous impertinences. And it was Clarissa's letter that made him see all this. 'Heavenly to see you. She must say so!' He folded the paper; pushed it away; nothing would induce him to read it again!

To get that letter to him by six o'clock she must have sat down and written it directly he left her; stamped it; sent somebody to the post. It was, as people say, very like her. She was upset by his visit. She had felt a great deal; had for a moment, when she kissed his hand, regretted, envied him even, remembered possibly (for he saw her look it) something he had said – how they would change the world if she married him perhaps; whereas, it was this; it was middle age; it was mediocrity; then forced herself with her indomitable vitality to put all that aside, there being in her a thread of life which for toughness, endurance, power to overcome obstacles and carry her triumphantly through he had never known the like of. Yes; but there would come a reaction directly he left the room. She would be frightfully sorry for him; she would think what in the world she could do to give him pleasure (short always of the one thing), and he could see her with the tears running down her cheeks going to her writing-table and dashing off that one line which he was to find greeting him . . . 'Heavenly to see you!' And she meant it.

Peter Walsh had now unlaced his boots.

But it would not have been a success, their marriage. The other thing, after all, came so much more naturally.

It was odd; it was true; lots of people felt it. Peter Walsh, who had done just respectably, filled the usual posts adequately, was liked, but thought a little cranky, gave himself airs – it was odd that *he* should have had, especially now that his hair was grey, a contented look; a look of having reserves. It was this that made him attractive to women, who liked the sense that he was not altogether manly. There was something unusual about him, or something behind him. It might be that he was bookish – never came to see you without taking up the book on the table (he was now reading, with his bootlaces trailing on the floor); or that he was a gentleman, which showed itself in the way he knocked the ashes out of his pipe, and in his manners, of course, to women. For it was very charming and quite ridiculous how easily some girl without a grain of sense could twist him round her finger. But at her own risk. That is to say, though he might be ever so easy, and indeed with his gaiety and good-breeding fascinating to be with, it was only up to a point. She said something – no, no; he saw through that. He wouldn't stand that – no, no. Then he could shout and rock and hold his sides together over some joke with men. He was the best judge of cooking in India. He was a man. But not the sort of man one had to respect – which was a mercy; not like Major Simmons, for instance; not in the least, Daisy thought, when in spite of her two small children, she used to compare them.

He pulled off his boots. He emptied his pockets. Out came with his pocket-knife a snapshot of Daisy on the verandah; Daisy all in white, with a fox-terrier on her knee; very charming, very dark; the best he had ever seen of her. It did come, after all, so naturally; so much more naturally than Clarissa. No fuss. No bother. No finicking and fidgeting. All plain sailing. And the dark, adorably pretty girl on the verandah exclaimed (he could hear her), Of course, of course, she would give him everything! she cried (she had no sense of discretion), everything he wanted! she cried, running to meet him, whoever might be looking. And she was only twenty-four. And she had two children. Well, well!

Well indeed he had got himself into a mess at his age. And it came over him when he woke in the night pretty forcibly. Suppose they did marry? For him it would be all very well, but what about her? Mrs Burgess, a good sort and no chatterbox, in whom he had confided, thought this absence of his in England, ostensibly to see lawyers, might serve to make Daisy reconsider, think what it meant. It was a question of her position, Mrs Burgess said; the social barrier; giving up her children. She'd be a widow with a past one of these days, draggling about in the suburbs, or more likely, indiscriminate (you know, she said, what such women get like, with too much paint). But Peter Walsh pooh-poohed all that. He didn't mean to die yet. Anyhow, she must settle for herself; judge for herself, he thought, padding about the room in his socks, smoothing out his dress-shirt, for he might go to Clarissa's party, or he might go to one of the Halls, or he might settle in and read an absorbing book written by a man he used to know at Oxford. And if he did retire, that's what he'd do – write books. He would go to Oxford and poke about in the Bodleian. Vainly the dark, adorably pretty girl ran to the end of the terrace; vainly waved her hand; vainly cried she didn't care a straw what people said. There he was, the man she thought the world of, the perfect gentleman, the fascinating, the distinguished (and his age made not the least difference to her), padding about a room in an hotel in Bloomsbury, shaving, washing, continuing, as he took up cans, put down razors, to poke about in the Bodleian, and get at the truth about one or two little matters that interested him. And he would have a chat with whoever it might be, and so come to disregard more and more precise hours for lunch, and miss engagements; and when Daisy asked him, as she would, for a kiss, a scene, fail to come up to the scratch (though he was genuinely devoted to her) – in short it might be happier, as Mrs Burgess said, that she should forget him, or merely remember him as he was in August 1922, like a figure standing at the cross roads at dusk, which grows more and more remote as the dog-cart spins away, carrying her securely fastened to the back seat, though her arms are outstretched, and as she sees the figure dwindle and disappear, still she cries out how she would do anything in the world, anything, anything, anything . . .

He never knew what people thought. It became more and more difficult for him to concentrate. He became absorbed; he became busied with his own concerns; now surly, now gay; dependent on women, absent-minded, moody, less and less able (so he thought as he shaved) to understand why Clarissa couldn't simply find them a lodging and be nice to Daisy; introduce her. And then he could just – just do what? just haunt and hover (he was at the moment actually engaged in sorting out various keys, papers), swoop and taste, be alone, in short, sufficient to himself; and yet nobody, of course, was more dependent upon others (he buttoned his waistcoat); it had been his undoing. He could not keep out of smoking-rooms, liked colonels, liked golf, liked bridge, and above all women's society, and the fineness of their companionship, and their faithfulness and audacity and greatness in loving which, though it had its drawbacks, seemed to him (and the dark, adorably pretty face was on top of the envelopes) so wholly admirable, so splendid a flower to grow on the crest of human life, and yet he could not come up to the scratch, being always apt to see round things (Clarissa had sapped something in him permanently), and to tire very easily of mute devotion and to want variety in love, though it would make him furious if Daisy loved anybody else, furious! for he was jealous, uncontrollably jealous by temperament. He suffered tortures! But where was his knife; his watch; his seals, his note-case, and Clarissa's letter, which he would not read again but liked to think of, and Daisy's photograph? And now for dinner.

They were eating.

Sitting at little tables round vases, dressed or not dressed, with their shawls and bags laid beside them, with their air of false composure, for they were not used to so many courses at dinner; and confidence, for they were able to pay for it; and strain, for they had been running about London all day shopping, sightseeing; and their natural curiosity, for they looked round and up as the nice-looking gentleman in horn-rimmed spectacles came in; and their good nature, for they would have been glad to do any little service, such as lend a timetable or impart useful information; and their desire, pulsing in them, tugging at them subterraneously, somehow to establish connections if it were only a birthplace (Liverpool, for example), in common or friends of the same name; with their furtive glances, odd silences, and sudden withdrawals into family jocularity and isolation; there they sat eating dinner when Mr Walsh came in and took his seat at a little table by the curtain.

It was not that he said anything, for being solitary he could only address himself to the waiter; it was his way of looking at the menu, of pointing his forefinger to a particular wine, of hitching himself up to the table, of addressing himself seriously, not gluttonously to dinner, that won him their respect; which, having to remain unexpressed for the greater part of the meal, flared up at the table where the Morrises sat when Mr Walsh was heard to say at the end of the meal, 'Bartlett pears.' Why he should have spoken so moderately yet firmly, with the air of a disciplinarian well within his rights which are founded upon justice, neither young Charles Morris, nor old Charles, neither Miss Elaine nor Mrs Morris knew. But when he said, 'Bartlett pears', sitting alone at his table, they felt that he counted on their support in some lawful demand; was champion of a cause which immediately became their own, so that their eyes met his eyes sympathetically, and when they all reached the smoking-room simultaneously, a little talk between them became inevitable.

It was not very profound – only to the effect that London was crowded; had changed in thirty years; that Mr Morris preferred Liverpool; that Mrs Morris had been to the Westminster flower-show, and that they had all seen the Prince of Wales. Yet, thought Peter Walsh, no family in the world can compare with the Morrises; none whatever; and their relations to each other are perfect, and they don't care a hang for the upper classes, and they like what they like, and Elaine is training for the family business, and the boy has won a scholarship at Leeds, and the old lady (who is about his own age) has three more children at home; and they have two motor cars, but Mr Morris still mends the boots on Sunday: it is superb, it is absolutely superb, thought Peter Walsh swaying a little backwards and forwards with his liqueur glass in his hand among the hairy red chairs and ash-trays, feeling very well pleased with himself, for the Morrises liked him. Yes, they liked a man who said 'Bartlett pears'. They liked him, he felt.

He would go to Clarissa's party. (The Morrises moved off; but they would meet again.) He would go to Clarissa's party, because he wanted to ask Richard what they were doing in India – the conservative duffers. And what's being acted? And music . . . Oh, yes, and mere gossip.

For this is the truth about our soul, he thought, our self, who fish-like inhabits deep seas and plies among obscurities threading her way between the boles of giant weeds, over sun-flickered spaces and on and on into gloom, cold, deep, inscrutable; suddenly she shoots to the surface and sports on the wind-wrinkled waves; that is, has a positive need to brush, scrape, kindle herself, gossiping. What did the Government mean – Richard Dalloway would know – to do about India?

Since it was a very hot night and the paper boys went by with placards proclaiming in huge red letters that there was a heat-wave, wicker chairs were placed on the hotel steps and there, sipping, smoking, detached gentlemen sat. Peter Walsh sat there. One might fancy that day, the London day, was just beginning. Like a woman who had slipped off her print dress and white apron to array herself in blue and pearls, the day changed, put off stuff, took gauze, changed to evening, and with the same sigh of exhilaration that a woman breathes, tumbling petticoats on the floor, it too shed dust, heat, colour; the traffic thinned; motor cars, tinkling, darting, succeeded the lumber of vans; and here and there among the thick foliage of the squares an intense light hung. I resign, the evening seemed to say, as it paled and faded above the battlements and prominences, moulded, pointed, of hotel, flat, and block of shops, I fade, she was beginning, I disappear, but London would have none of it, and rushed her bayonets into the sky, pinioned her, constrained her to partnership in her revelry.

For the great revolution of Mr Willett's summer time had taken place since Peter Walsh's last visit to England. The prolonged evening was new to him. It was inspiriting, rather. For as the young people went by with their despatch-boxes, awfully glad to be free, proud too, dumbly, of stepping this famous pavement, joy of a kind, cheap, tinselly, if you like, but all the same rapture, flushed their faces. They dressed well too; pink stockings; pretty shoes. They would now have two hours at the pictures. It sharpened, it refined them the yellow-blue evening light; and on the leaves in the square shone lurid, livid – they looked as if dipped in sea water – the foliage of a submerged city. He was astonished by the beauty; it was encouraging too, for where the returned Anglo-Indian sat by rights (he knew crowds of them) in the Oriental Club biliously summing up the ruin of the world, here was he, as young as ever; envying young people their summer time and the rest of it, and more than suspecting from the words of a girl, from a housemaid's laughter – intangible things you couldn't lay your hands on – that shift in the whole pyramidal accumulation which in his youth had seemed immovable. On top of them it had pressed; weighed them down, the women especially, like those flowers Clarissa's Aunt Helena used to press between sheets of grey blotting-paper with Littré's dictionary on top, sitting under the lamp after dinner. She was dead now. He had heard of her, from Clarissa, losing the sight of one eye. It seemed so fitting – one of nature's masterpieces – that old Miss Parry should turn to glass. She would die like some bird in a frost gripping her perch. She belonged to a different age, but being so entire, so complete, would always stand up on the horizon, stone-white, eminent, like a lighthouse marking some past stage on this adventurous, long, long voyage, this interminable – (he felt for a copper to buy a paper and read about Surrey and Yorkshire; he had held out that copper millions of times – Surrey was all out once more) – this interminable life. But cricket was no mere game. Cricket was important. He could never help reading about cricket. He read the scores in the stop press first; then how it was a hot day; then about a murder case. Having done things millions of times enriched them, though it might be said to take the surface off. The past enriched, and experience, and having cared for one or two people, and so having acquired the power which the young lack, of cutting short, doing what one likes, not caring a rap what people say and coming and going without any very great expectations (he left his paper on the table and moved off), which however (and he looked for his hat and coat) was not altogether true of him, not tonight, for here he was starting to go to a party, at his age, with the belief upon him that he was about to have an experience. But what?

Beauty anyhow. Not the crude beauty of the eye. It was not beauty pure and simple – Bedford Place leading into Russell Square. It was straightness and emptiness of course; the symmetry of a corridor; but it was also windows lit up, a piano, a gramophone sounding; a sense of pleasure-making hidden, but now and again emerging when, through the uncurtained window, the window left open, one saw parties sitting over tables, young people slowly circling, conversations between men and women, maids idly looking out (a strange comment theirs, when work was done), stockings drying on top ledges, a parrot, a few plants. Absorbing, mysterious, of infinite richness, this life. And in the large square where the cabs shot and swerved so quick, there were loitering couples, dallying, embracing, shrunk up under the shower of a tree, that was moving; so silent, so absorbed, that one passed, discreetly, timidly, as if in the presence of some sacred ceremony to interrupt which would have been impious. That was interesting. And so on into the flare and glare.

His light overcoat blew open, he stepped with indescribable idiosyncrasy, leant a little forward, tripped, with his hands behind his back and his eyes still a little hawk-like; he tripped through London, towards Westminster, observing.

Was everybody dining out, then? Doors were being opened here by a footman to let issue a high-stepping old dame, in buckled shoes, with three purple ostrich feathers in her hair. Doors were being opened for ladies wrapped like mummies in shawls with bright flowers on them, ladies with bare heads. And in respectable quarters with stucco pillars through small front gardens, lightly swathed, with combs in their hair (having run up to see the children), women came; men waited for them, with their coats blowing open, and the motor started. Everybody was going out. What with these doors being opened, and the descent and the start, it seemed as if the whole of London were embarking in little boats moored to the bank, tossing on the waters, as if the whole place were floating off in carnival. And Whitehall was skated over, silver beaten as it was, skated over by spiders, and there was a sense of midges round the arc lamps; it was so hot that people stood about talking. And here in Westminster was a retired Judge, presumably, sitting four square at his house door dressed all in white. An Anglo-Indian presumably.

And here a shindy of brawling women, drunken women; here only a policeman and looming houses, high houses, domed houses, churches, parliaments, and the hoot of a steamer on the river, a hollow misty cry. But it was her street, this, Clarissa's; cabs were rushing round the corner, like water round the piers of a bridge drawn together, it seemed to him, because they bore people going to her party, Clarissa's party.

The cold stream of visual impressions failed him now as if the eye were a cup that overflowed and let the rest run down its china walls unrecorded. The brain must wake now. The body must contract now, entering the house, the lighted house, where the door stood open, where the motor cars were standing, and bright women descending: the soul must brave itself to endure. He opened the big blade of his pocket-knife.

Lucy came running full tilt downstairs, having just nipped into the drawing-room to smooth a cover, to straighten a chair, to pause a moment and feel whoever came in must think how clean, how bright, how beautifully cared for, when they saw the beautiful silver, the brass fire-irons, the new chair-covers, and the curtains of yellow chintz: she appraised each; heard a roar of voices; people already coming up from dinner; she must fly!

The Prime Minister was coming, Agnes said: so she had heard them say in the dining-room, she said, coming in with a tray of glasses. Did it matter, did it matter in the least, one Prime Minister more or less? It made no difference at this hour of the night to Mrs Walker among the plates, saucepans, cullenders, frying-pans, chicken in aspic, ice-cream freezers, pared crusts of bread, lemons, soup tureens, and pudding basins which, however hard they washed up in the scullery, seemed to be all on top of her, on the kitchen table, on chairs, while the fire blared and roared, the electric lights glared, and still supper had to be laid. All she felt was, one Prime Minister more or less made not a scrap of difference to Mrs Walker.

The ladies were going upstairs already, said Lucy; the ladies were going up, one by one, Mrs Dalloway walking last and almost always sending back some message to the kitchen, 'My love to Mrs Walker,' that was it one night. Next morning they would go over the dishes – the soup, the salmon; the salmon, Mrs Walker knew, as usual underdone, for she always got nervous about the pudding and left it to Jenny; so it happened, the salmon was always underdone. But some lady with fair hair and silver ornaments had said, Lucy said, about the entrée, was it really made at home? But it was the salmon that bothered Mrs Walker, as she spun the plates round and round, and pushed in dampers and pulled out dampers; and there came a burst of laughter from the dining-room; a voice speaking; then another burst of laughter – the gentlemen enjoying themselves when the ladies had gone. The tokay, said Lucy running in. Mr Dalloway had sent for the tokay, from the Emperor's cellars, the Imperial Tokay.

It was borne through the kitchen. Over her shoulder Lucy reported how Miss Elizabeth looked quite lovely; she couldn't take her eyes off her; in her pink dress, wearing the necklace Mr Dalloway had given her. Jenny must remember the dog, Miss Elizabeth's fox-terrier, which, since it bit, had to be shut up and might, Elizabeth thought, want something. Jenny must remember the dog. But Jenny was not going upstairs with all those people about. There was a motor at the door already! There was a ring at the bell – and the gentlemen still in the dining-room, drinking tokay!

There, they were going upstairs; that was the first to come, and now they would come faster and faster, so that Mrs Parkinson (hired for parties) would leave the hall door ajar, and the hall would be full of gentlemen waiting (they stood waiting, sleeking down their hair) while the ladies took their cloaks off in the room along the passage; where Mrs Barnet helped them, old Ellen Barnet, who had been with the family for forty years, and came every summer to help the ladies, and remembered mothers when they were girls, and though very unassuming did shake hands; said 'milady' very respectfully, yet had a humorous way with her, looking at the young ladies, and ever so tactfully helping Lady Lovejoy, who had some trouble with her underbodice. And they could not help feeling, Lady Lovejoy and Miss Alice, that some little privilege in the matter of brush and comb was awarded them having known Mrs Barnet – 'thirty years, milady,' Mrs Barnet supplied her. Young ladies did not use to rouge, said Lady Lovejoy, when they stayed at Bourton in the old days. And Miss Alice didn't need rouge, said Mrs Barnet, looking at her fondly. There Mrs Barnet would sit, in the cloakroom, patting down the furs, smoothing out the Spanish shawls, tidying the dressing-table, and knowing perfectly well, in spite of the furs and the embroideries, which were nice ladies, which were not. The dear old body, said Lady Lovejoy, mounting the stairs, Clarissa's old nurse.

And then Lady Lovejoy stiffened. 'Lady and Miss Lovejoy,' she said to Mr Wilkins (hired for parties). He had an admirable manner, as he bent and straightened himself, bent and straightened himself, and announced with perfect impartiality 'Lady and Miss Lovejoy . . . Sir John and Lady Needham . . . Miss Weld . . . Mr Walsh.' His manner was admirable; his family life must be irreproachable, except that it seemed impossible that a being with greenish lips and shaven cheeks could ever have blundered into the nuisance of children.

'How delightful to see you!' said Clarissa. She said it to everyone. How delightful to see you! She was at her worst – effusive, insincere. It was a great mistake to have come. He should have stayed at home and read his book, thought Peter Walsh; should have gone to a music hall; he should have stayed at home, for he knew no one.

Oh dear, it was going to be a failure; a complete failure, Clarissa felt it in her bones as dear old Lord Lexham stood there apologising for his wife who had caught cold at the Buckingham Palace garden party. She could see Peter out of the tail of her eye, criticising her, there, in that corner. Why, after all, did she do these things? Why seek pinnacles and stand drenched in fire? Might it consume her anyhow! Burn her to cinders! Better anything, better brandish one's torch and hurl it to earth than taper and dwindle away like some Ellie Henderson! It was extraordinary how Peter put her into these states just by coming and standing in a corner. He made her see herself; exaggerate. It was idiotic. But why did he come, then, merely to criticise? Why always take, never give? Why not risk one's one little point of view? There he was wandering off; and she must speak to him. But she would not get the chance. Life was that – humiliation, renunciation. What Lord

Lexham was saying was that his wife would not wear her furs at the garden party because 'my dears, you ladies are all alike' – Lady Lexham being seventy-five at least! It was delicious, how they petted each other, that old couple. She did like old Lord Lexham. She did think it mattered, her party, and it made her feel quite sick to know that it was all going wrong, all falling flat. Anything, any explosion, any horror was better than people wandering aimlessly, standing in a bunch at a corner like Ellie Henderson, not even caring to hold themselves upright.

Gently the yellow curtain with all the birds of Paradise blew out and it seemed as if there were a flight of wings into the room, right out, then sucked back. (For the windows were open.) Was it draughty, Ellie Henderson wondered? She was subject to chills. But it did not matter that she should come down sneezing tomorrow; it was the girls with their naked shoulders she thought of, being trained to think of others by an old father, an invalid, late vicar of Bourton, but he was dead now; and her chills never went to her chest, never. It was the girls she thought of, the young girls with their bare shoulders, she herself having always been a wisp of a creature, with her thin hair and meagre profile; though now, past fifty, there was beginning to shine through some mild beam, something purified into distinction by years of self-abnegation but obscured again, perpetually, by her distressing gentility, her panic fear, which arose from three hundred pounds income, and her weaponless state (she could not earn a penny) and it made her timid, and more and more disqualified year by year to meet well-dressed people who did this sort of thing every night of the season, merely telling their maids 'I'll wear so and so,' whereas Ellie Henderson ran out nervously and bought cheap pink flowers, half a dozen, and then threw a shawl over her old black dress. For her invitation to Clarissa's party had come at the last moment. She was not quite happy about it. She had a sort of feeling that Clarissa had not meant to ask her this year.

Why should she? There was no reason really, except that they had always known each other. Indeed, they were cousins. But naturally they had rather drifted apart, Clarissa being so sought after. It was an event to her, going to a party. It was quite a treat just to see the lovely clothes. Wasn't that Elizabeth, grown up, with her hair done in the fashionable way, in the pink dress? Yet she could not be more than seventeen. She was very, very handsome. But girls when they first came out didn't seem to wear white as they used. (She must remember everything to tell Edith.) Girls wore straight frocks, perfectly tight, with skirts well above the ankles. It was not becoming, she thought.

So, with her weak eyesight, Ellie Henderson craned rather forward, and it wasn't so much she who minded not having anyone to talk to (she hardly knew anybody there), for she felt that they were all such interesting people to watch; politicians presumably; Richard Dalloway's friends; but it was

Richard himself who felt that he could not let the poor creature go on standing there all the evening by herself.

'Well, Ellie, and how's the world treating *you*?' he said in his genial way, and Ellie Henderson, getting nervous and flushing, and feeling that it was extraordinarily nice of him to come and talk to her, said that many people really felt the heat more than the cold.

'Yes, they do,' said Richard Dalloway. 'Yes.'

But what more did one say?

'Hullo, Richard,' said somebody, taking him by the elbow, and, good Lord, there was old Peter, old Peter Walsh. He was delighted to see him – ever so pleased to see him! He hadn't changed a bit. And off they went together walking right across the room, giving each other little pats, as if they hadn't met for a long time, Ellie Henderson thought, watching them go, certain she knew that man's face. A tall man, middle aged, rather fine eyes, dark, wearing spectacles, with a look of John Burrows. Edith would be sure to know.

The curtain with its flight of birds of Paradise blew out again. And Clarissa saw – she saw Ralph Lyon beat it back, and go on talking. So it wasn't a failure after all! it was going to be all right now – her party. It had begun. It had started. But it was still touch and go. She must stand there for the present. People seemed to come in a rush.

Colonel and Mrs Garrod . . . Mr Hugh Whitbread . . . Mr Bowley . . . Mrs Hilbery . . . Lady Mary Maddox . . . Mr Quin . . . intoned Wilkins. She had six or seven words with each, and they went on, they went into the rooms; into something now, not nothing, since Ralph Lyon had beat back the curtain.

And yet for her own part, it was too much of an effort. She was not enjoying it. It was too much like being – just anybody, standing there; anybody could do it; yet this anybody she did a little admire, couldn't help feeling that she had, anyhow, made this happen, that it marked a stage, this post that she felt herself to have become, for oddly enough she had quite forgotten what she looked like, but felt herself a stake driven in at the top of her stairs. Every time she gave a party she had this feeling of being something not herself, and that everyone was unreal in one way; much more real in another. It was, she thought, partly their clothes, partly being taken out of their ordinary ways, partly the background; it was possible to say things you couldn't say anyhow else, things that needed an effort; possible to go much deeper. But not for her; not yet anyhow.

'How delightful to see you!' she said. Dear old Sir Harry! He would know everyone.

And what was so odd about it was the sense one had as they came up the stairs one after another, Mrs Mount and Celia, Herbert Ainsty, Mrs Dakers – oh, and Lady Bruton!

'How awfully good of you to come!' she said, and she meant it – it was odd how standing there one felt them going on, going on, some quite old, some . . .

What name? Lady Rosseter? But who on earth was Lady Rosseter?

'Clarissa!' That voice! It was Sally Seton! Sally Seton! after all these years! She loomed through a mist. For she hadn't looked like *that*, Sally Seton, when Clarissa grasped the hot water can. To think of her under this roof, under this roof! Not like that!

All on top of each other, embarrassed, laughing, words tumbled out – passing through London; heard from Clara Haydon; what a chance of seeing you! So I thrust myself in – without an invitation.

One might put down the hot water can quite composedly. The lustre had left her. Yet it was extraordinary to see her again, older, happier, less lovely. They kissed each other, first this cheek, then that, by the drawing-room door, and Clarissa turned, with Sally's hand in hers, and saw her rooms full, heard the roar of voices, saw the candlesticks, the blowing curtains, and the roses which Richard had given her.

'I have five enormous boys,' said Sally.

She had the simplest egotism, the most open desire to be thought first always, and Clarissa loved her for being still like that. 'I can't believe it!' she cried, kindling all over with pleasure at the thought of the past.

But alas, Wilkins; Wilkins wanted her; Wilkins was emitting in a voice of commanding authority, as if the whole company must be admonished and the hostess reclaimed from frivolity, one name: 'The Prime Minister,' said Peter Walsh.

The Prime Minister? Was it really? Ellie Henderson marvelled. What a thing to tell Edith!

One couldn't laugh at him. He looked so ordinary. You might have stood him behind a counter and bought biscuits – poor chap, all rigged up in gold lace. And to be fair, as he went his rounds, first with Clarissa, then with Richard escorting him, he did it very well. He tried to look somebody. It was amusing to watch. Nobody looked at him. They just went on talking, yet it was perfectly plain that they all knew, felt to the marrow of their bones, this majesty passing; this symbol of what they all stood for, English society. Old Lady Bruton, and she looked very fine too, very stalwart in her lace, swam up, and they withdrew into a little room which at once became spied upon, guarded, and a sort of stir and rustle rippled through everyone openly: the Prime Minister!

Lord, lord, the snobbery of the English! thought Peter Walsh, standing in the corner. How they loved dressing up in gold lace and doing homage! There! That must be – by Jove, it was – Hugh Whitbread, snuffing round the precincts of the great, grown rather fatter, rather whiter, the admirable Hugh!

He looked always as if he were on duty, thought Peter, a privileged but secretive being, hoarding secrets which he would die to defend, though it was only some little piece of tittle-tattle dropped by a court footman which would be in all the papers tomorrow. Such were his rattles, his baubles, in playing with which he had grown white, come to the verge of old age, enjoying the respect and affection of all who had the privilege of knowing this type of the English public school man. Inevitably one made up things like that about Hugh; that was his style; the style of those admirable letters which Peter had read thousands of miles across the sea in *The Times*, and had thanked God he was out of that pernicious hubble-bubble if it were only to hear baboons chatter and coolies beat their wives. An olive-skinned youth from one of the Universities stood obsequiously by. Him he would patronise, initiate, teach how to get on. For he liked nothing better than doing kindnesses, making the hearts of old ladies palpitate with the joy of being thought of in their age, their affliction, thinking themselves quite forgotten, yet here was dear Hugh driving up and spending an hour talking of the past, remembering trifles, praising the home-made cake, though Hugh might eat cake with a Duchess any day of his life, and, to look at him, probably did spend a good deal of time in that agreeable occupation. The All-judging, the All-merciful, might excuse. Peter Walsh had no mercy. Villains there must be, and, God knows, the rascals who get hanged for battering the brains of a girl out in a train do less harm on the whole than Hugh Whitbread and his kindness! Look at him now, on tiptoe, dancing forward, bowing and scraping, as the Prime Minister and Lady Bruton emerged, intimating for all the world to see that he was privileged to say something, something private, to Lady Bruton as she passed. She stopped. She wagged her fine old head. She was thanking him presumably for some piece of servility. She had her toadies, minor officials in Government offices who ran about putting through little jobs on her behalf, in return for which she gave them luncheon. But she derived from the eighteenth century. She was all right.

And now Clarissa escorted her Prime Minister down the room, prancing, sparkling, with the stateliness of her grey hair. She wore earrings, and a silver-green mermaid's dress. Lolloping on the waves and braiding her tresses she seemed, having that gift still; to be; to exist; to sum it all up in the moment as she passed; turned, caught her scarf in some other woman's dress, unhitched it, laughed, all with the most perfect ease and air of a creature floating in its element. But age had brushed her; even as a mermaid might behold in her glass the setting sun on some very clear evening over the waves. There was a breath of tenderness; her severity, her prudery, her woodenness were all warmed through now, and she had about her as she said goodbye to the thick gold-laced man who was doing his best, and good luck to him, to look important, an inexpressible dignity; an exquisite cordiality; as if she wished the whole world well, and must now, being on the very verge and rim of things, take her leave. So she made him think. (But he was not in love.)

Indeed, Clarissa felt, the Prime Minister had been good to come. And, walking down the room with him, with Sally there and Peter there and Richard very pleased, with all those people rather inclined, perhaps, to envy, she had felt that intoxication of the moment, that dilatation of the nerves of the heart itself till it seemed to quiver, steeped, upright – yes, but after all it was what other people felt, that; for, though she loved it and felt it tingle and sting, still these semblances, these triumphs (dear old Peter, for example, thinking her so brilliant), had a hollowness; at arm's length they were, not in the heart; and it might be that she was growing old, but they satisfied her no longer as they used; and suddenly, as she saw the Prime Minister go down the stairs, the gilt rim of the Sir Joshua picture of the little girl with a muff brought back Kilman with a rush; Kilman her enemy. That was satisfying; that was real. Ah, how she hated her – hot, hypocritical, corrupt; with all that power; Elizabeth's seducer; the woman who had crept in to steal and defile (Richard would say, What nonsense!). She hated her: she loved her. It was enemies one wanted, not friends – not Mrs Durrant and Clara, Sir William and Lady Bradshaw, Miss Truelock and Eleanor Gibson (whom she saw coming upstairs). They must find her if they wanted her. She was for the party!

There was her old friend Sir Harry.

'Dear Sir Harry!' she said, going up to the fine old fellow who had produced more bad pictures than any other two Academicians in the whole of St John's Wood (they were always of cattle, standing in sunset pools absorbing moisture, or signifying, for he had a certain range of gesture, by the raising of one foreleg and the toss of the antlers, 'the Approach of the Stranger' – all his activities, dining out, racing, were founded on cattle standing absorbing moisture in sunset pools).

'What are you laughing at?' she asked him. For Willie Titcomb and Sir Harry and Herbert Ainsty were all laughing. But no. Sir Harry could not tell Clarissa Dalloway (much though he liked her; of her type he thought her perfect, and threatened to paint her) his stories of the music-hall stage. He chaffed her about her party. He missed his brandy. These circles, he said, were above him. But he liked her; respected her, in spite of her damnable, difficult, upper-class refinement, which made it impossible to ask Clarissa Dalloway to sit on his knee. And up came that wandering will-o'-the-wisp, that vague phosphorescence, old Mrs Hilbery, stretching her hands to the blaze of his laughter (about the Duke and the Lady), which, as she heard it across the room, seemed to reassure her on a point which sometimes bothered her if she woke early in the morning and did not like to call her maid for a cup of tea: how it is certain we must die.

'They won't tell us their stories,' said Clarissa.

'Dear Clarissa!' exclaimed Mrs Hilbery. She looked tonight, she said, so like her mother as she first saw her walking in a garden in a grey hat.

And really Clarissa's eyes filled with tears. Her mother, walking in a garden! But alas! she must go.

For there was Professor Brierly, who lectured on Milton, talking to little Jim Hutton (who was unable even for a party like this to compass both tie and waistcoat or make his hair lie flat), and even at this distance they were quarrelling, she could see. For Professor Brierly was a very queer fish. With all those degrees, honours, lectureships between him and the scribblers, he suspected instantly an atmosphere not favourable to his queer compound; his prodigious learning and timidity; his wintry charm without cordiality; his innocence blent with snobbery; he quivered if made conscious, by a lady's unkempt hair, a youth's boots, of an underworld, very creditable doubtless, of rebels, of ardent young people, of would-be geniuses; and intimated with a little toss of the head, with a sniff – Humph! – the value of moderation; of some slight training in the classics in order to appreciate Milton. Professor Brierly (Clarissa could see) wasn't hitting it off with little Jim Hutton (who wore red socks, his black being at the laundry) about Milton. She interrupted.

She said she loved Bach. So did Hutton. That was the bond between them, and Hutton (a very bad poet) always felt that Mrs Dalloway was far the best of the great ladies who took an interest in art. It was odd how strict she was. About music she was purely impersonal. She was rather a prig. But how charming to look at! She made her house so nice, if it weren't for her Professors. Clarissa had half a mind to snatch him off and set him down at the piano in the back room. For he played divinely.

'But the noise!' she said. 'The noise!'

'The sign of a successful party.' Nodding urbanely, the Professor stepped delicately off.

'He knows everything in the whole world about Milton,' said Clarissa.

'Does he indeed?' said Hutton, who would imitate the Professor throughout Hampstead: the Professor on Milton; the Professor on moderation; the Professor stepping delicately off.

But she must speak to that couple, said Clarissa, Lord Gayton and Nancy Blow.

Not that *they* added perceptibly to the noise of the party. They were not talking (perceptibly) as they stood side by side by the yellow curtains. They would soon be off elsewhere, together; and never had very much to say in any circumstances. They looked; that was all. That was enough. They looked so clean, so sound, she with an apricot bloom of powder and paint, but he scrubbed, rinsed, with the eyes of a bird, so that no ball could pass him or stroke surprise him. He struck, he leapt, accurately, on the spot. Ponies' mouths quivered at the end of his reins. He had his honours, ancestral monuments, banners hanging in the church at home. He had his duties; his tenants; a mother and sisters; had been all day at Lords, and that was what they were talking about – cricket, cousins, the movies – when Mrs Dalloway came up. Lord Gayton liked her most awfully. So did Miss Blow. She had such charming manners.

'It is angelic – it is delicious of you to have come!' she said. She loved Lords; she loved youth, and Nancy, dressed at enormous expense by the greatest artists in Paris, stood there looking as if her body had merely put forth, of its own accord, a green frill.

'I had meant to have dancing,' said Clarissa.

For the young people could not talk. And why should they? Shout, embrace, swing, be up at dawn; carry sugar to ponies; kiss and caress the snouts of adorable chows; and then, all tingling and streaming, plunge and swim. But the enormous resources of the English language, the power it bestows, after all, of communicating feelings (at their age, she and Peter would have been arguing all the evening), was not for them. They would solidify young. They would be good beyond measure to the people on the estate, but alone, perhaps, rather dull.

'What a pity!' she said. 'I had hoped to have dancing.'

It was so extraordinarily nice of them to have come! But talk of dancing! The rooms were packed.

There was old Aunt Helena in her shawl. Alas! she must leave them – Lord Gayton and Nancy Blow. There was old Miss Parry, her aunt.

For Miss Helena Parry was not dead: Miss Parry was alive. She was past eighty. She ascended staircases slowly with a stick. She was placed in a chair (Richard had seen to it). People who had known Burma in the seventies were always led up to her. Where had Peter got to? They used to be such friends. For at the mention of India, or even Ceylon, her eyes (only one was glass) slowly deepened, became blue, beheld, no human beings – she had no tender memories, no proud illusions about Viceroys, Generals, Mutinies – it was orchids she saw, and mountain passes, and herself carried on the backs of coolies in the sixties over solitary peaks; or descending to uproot orchids (startling blossoms, never beheld before) which she painted in watercolour; an indomitable Englishwoman, fretful if disturbed by the war, say, which dropped a bomb at her very door, from her deep meditation over orchids and her own figure journeying in the sixties in India – but here was Peter.

'Come and talk to Aunt Helena about Burma,' said Clarissa.

And yet he had not had a word with her all the evening!

'We will talk later,' said Clarissa, leading him up to Aunt Helena, in her white shawl, with her stick.

'Peter Walsh,' said Clarissa.

That meant nothing.

Clarissa had asked her. It was tiring; it was noisy; but Clarissa had asked her. So she had come. It was a pity that they lived in London – Richard and Clarissa. If only for Clarissa's health it would have been better to live in the country. But Clarissa had always been fond of society.

'He has been in Burma,' said Clarissa.

Ah! She could not resist recalling what Charles Darwin had said about her little book on the orchids of Burma.

(Clarissa must speak to Lady Bruton.)

No doubt it was forgotten now, her book on the orchids of Burma, but it went into three editions before 1870, she told Peter. She remembered him now. He had been at Bourton (and he had left her, Peter Walsh remembered, without a word in the drawing-room that night when Clarissa had asked him to come boating).

'Richard so much enjoyed his lunch party,' said Clarissa to Lady Bruton.

'Richard was the greatest possible help,' Lady Bruton replied. 'He helped me to write a letter. And how are you?'

'Oh, perfectly well!' said Clarissa. (Lady Bruton detested illness in the wives of politicians.)

'And there's Peter Walsh!' said Lady Bruton (for she could never think of anything to say to Clarissa; though she liked her. She had lots of fine qualities; but they had nothing in common – she and Clarissa. It might have been better if Richard had married a woman with less charm, who would have helped him more in his work. He had lost his chance of the Cabinet). 'There's Peter Walsh!' she said, shaking hands with that agreeable sinner, that very able fellow who should have made a name for himself but hadn't (always in difficulties with women), and, of course, old Miss Parry. Wonderful old lady!

Lady Bruton stood by Miss Parry's chair, a spectral grenadier, draped in black, inviting Peter Walsh to lunch; cordial; but without small talk, re-membering nothing whatever about the flora or fauna of India. She had been there, of course; had stayed with three Viceroys; thought some of the Indian civilians uncommonly fine fellows; but what a tragedy it was – the state of India! The Prime Minister had just been telling her (old Miss Parry, huddled up in her shawl, did not care what the Prime Minister had just been telling her), and Lady Bruton would like to have Peter Walsh's opinion, he being fresh from the centre, and she would get Sir Sampson to meet him, for really it prevented her from sleeping at night, the folly of it, the wickedness she might say, being a soldier's daughter. She was an old woman now, not good for much. But her house, her servants, her good friend Milly Brush – did he remember her? – were all there only asking to be used if – if they could be of help, in short. For she never spoke of England, but this isle of men, this dear, dear land, was in her blood (without reading Shakespeare), and if ever a woman could have worn the helmet and shot the arrow, could have led troops to attack, ruled with indomitable justice barbarian hordes and lain under a shield noseless in a church, or made a green grass mound on some primeval hillside, that woman was Millicent Bruton. Debarred by her sex, and some truancy, too, of the logical faculty (she found it impossible to write a letter to *The Times*), she had the thought of Empire always at hand, and had acquired from her association with that armoured goddess her ramrod bearing, her robustness of demeanour, so that one could not figure her even in death parted from the earth or roaming territories over which, in some spiritual shape, the

Union Jack had ceased to fly. To be not English even among the dead – no, no! Impossible!

But was it Lady Bruton? (whom she used to know). Was it Peter Walsh grown grey? Lady Rosseter asked herself (who had been Sally Seton). It was old Miss Parry certainly – the old aunt who used to be so cross when she stayed at Bourton. Never should she forget running along the passage naked, and being sent for by Miss Parry! And Clarissa! oh Clarissa! Sally caught her by the arm.

Clarissa stopped beside them.

'But I can't stay,' she said. 'I shall come later. Wait,' she said, looking at Peter and Sally. They must wait, she meant, until all these people had gone.

'I shall come back,' she said, looking at her old friends, Sally and Peter, who were shaking hands, and Sally, remembering the past no doubt, was laughing.

But her voice was wrung of its old ravishing richness; her eyes not aglow as they used to be when she smoked cigars, when she ran down the passage to fetch her sponge bag without a stitch of clothing on her, and Ellen Atkins asked, What if the gentlemen had met her? But everybody forgave her. She stole a chicken from the larder because she was hungry in the night; she smoked cigars in her bedroom; she left a priceless book in the punt. But everybody adored her (except perhaps Papa). It was her warmth; her vitality – she would paint, she would write. Old women in the village never to this day forgot to ask after 'your friend in the red cloak who seemed so bright'. She accused Hugh Whitbread, of all people (and there he was, her old friend Hugh, talking to the Portuguese Ambassador), of kissing her in the smoking-room to punish her for saying that women should have votes. Vulgar men did, she said. And Clarissa remembered having to persuade her not to denounce him at family prayers – which she was capable of doing with her daring, her recklessness, her melodramatic love of being the centre of everything and creating scenes, and it was bound, Clarissa used to think, to end in some awful tragedy; her death; her martyrdom; instead of which she had married, quite unexpectedly, a bald man with a large buttonhole who owned, it was said, cotton mills at Manchester. And she had five boys!

She and Peter had settled down together. They were talking: it seemed so familiar – that they should be talking. They would discuss the past. With the two of them (more even than with Richard) she shared her past; the garden; the trees; old Joseph Breitkopf singing Brahms without any voice; the drawing-room wallpaper; the smell of the mats. A part of this Sally must always be; Peter must always be. But she must leave them. There were the Bradshaws, whom she disliked.

She must go up to Lady Bradshaw (in grey and silver, balancing like a sea-lion at the edge of its tank, barking for invitations, Duchesses, the typical successful man's wife), she must go up, to Lady Bradshaw and say . . .

But Lady Bradshaw anticipated her.

'We are shockingly late, dear Mrs Dalloway; we hardly dared to come in,' she said.

And Sir William, who looked very distinguished, with his grey hair and blue eyes, said yes; they had not been able to resist the temptation. He was talking to Richard about that Bill, probably, which they wanted to get through the Commons. Why did the sight of him, talking to Richard, curl her up? He looked what he was, a great doctor. A man absolutely at the head of his profession, very powerful, rather worn. For think what cases came before him – people in the uttermost depths of misery; people on the verge of insanity; husbands and wives. He had to decide questions of appalling difficulty. Yet – what she felt was, one wouldn't like Sir William to see one unhappy. No; not that man.

'How is your son at Eton?' she asked Lady Bradshaw.

He had just missed his eleven, said Lady Bradshaw, because of the mumps. His father minded even more than he did, she thought, 'being,' she said, 'nothing but a great boy himself'.

Clarissa looked at Sir William, talking to Richard. He did not look like a boy – not in the least like a boy.

She had once gone with someone to ask his advice. He had been perfectly right; extremely sensible. But Heavens – what a relief to get out to the street again! There was some poor wretch sobbing, she remembered, in the waiting-room. But she did not know what it was about Sir William; what exactly she disliked. Only Richard agreed with her, 'didn't like his taste, didn't like his smell'. But he was extraordinarily able. They were talking about this Bill. Some case Sir William was mentioning, lowering his voice. It had its bearing upon what he was saying about the deferred effects of shell shock. There must be some provision in the Bill.

Sinking her voice, drawing Mrs Dalloway into the shelter of a common femininity, a common pride in the illustrious qualities of husbands and their sad tendency to overwork, Lady Bradshaw (poor goose – one didn't dislike her) murmured how, 'just as we were starting, my husband was called up on the telephone, a very sad case. A young man (that is what Sir William is telling Mr Dalloway) had killed himself. He had been in the army.' Oh! thought Clarissa, in the middle of my party, here's death, she thought.

She went on, into the little room where the Prime Minister had gone with Lady Bruton. Perhaps there was somebody there. But there was nobody. The chairs still kept the impress of the Prime Minister and Lady Bruton, she turned deferentially, he sitting four-square, authoritatively. They had been talking about India. There was nobody. The party's splendour fell to the floor, so strange it was to come in alone in her finery.

What business had the Bradshaws to talk of death at her party? A young man had killed himself. And they talked of it at her party – the Bradshaws talked of death. He had killed himself – but how? Always her body went through it, when she was told, first, suddenly, of an accident; her dress flamed, her body burnt. He had thrown himself from a window. Up had flashed the ground; through him, blundering, bruising, went the rusty spikes. There he lay with a thud, thud, thud in his brain, and then a suffocation of blackness. So she saw it. But why had he done it? And the Bradshaws talked of it at her party!

She had once thrown a shilling into the Serpentine, never anything more. But he had flung it away. They went on living (she would have to go back; the rooms were still crowded; people kept on coming). They (all day she had been thinking of Bourton, of Peter, of Sally), they would grow old. A thing there was that mattered; a thing, wreathed about with chatter, defaced, obscured in her own life, let drop every day in corruption, lies, chatter. This he had preserved. Death was defiance. Death was an attempt to communicate, people feeling the impossibility of reaching the centre which, mystically, evaded them; closeness drew apart; rapture faded; one was alone. There was an embrace in death.

But this young man who had killed himself – had he plunged holding his treasure? 'If it were now to die, 'twere now to be most happy,' she had said to herself once, coming down, in white.

Or there were the poets and thinkers. Suppose he had had that passion, and had gone to Sir William Bradshaw, a great doctor, yet to her obscurely evil, without sex or lust, extremely polite to women, but capable of some indescribable outrage – forcing your soul, that was it – if this young man had gone to him, and Sir William had impressed him, like that, with his power, might he not then have said (indeed she felt it now), Life is made intolerable; they make life intolerable, men like that?

Then (she had felt it only this morning) there was the terror; the over-whelming incapacity, one's parents giving it into one's hands, this life, to be lived to the end, to be walked with serenely; there was in the depths of her heart an awful fear. Even now, quite often, if Richard had not been there reading *The Times*, so that she could crouch like a bird and gradually revive, send roaring up that immeasurable delight, rubbing stick to stick, one thing with another, she must have perished. She had escaped. But that young man had killed himself.

Somehow it was her disaster – her disgrace. It was her punishment to see sink and disappear here a man, there a woman, in this profound darkness, and she forced to stand here in her evening dress. She had schemed; she had pilfered. She was never wholly admirable. She had wanted success, Lady Bexborough and the rest of it. And once she had walked on the terrace at Bourton.

Odd, incredible; she had never been so happy. Nothing could be slow enough; nothing last too long. No pleasure could equal, she thought, straightening the chairs, pushing in one book on the shelf, this having done with the triumphs of youth, lost herself in the process of living, to find it, with a shock of delight, as the sun rose, as the day sank. Many a time had she gone, at Bourton when they were all talking, to look at the sky; or seen it between people's shoulders at dinner; seen it in London when she could not sleep. She walked to the window.

It held, foolish as the idea was, something of her own in it, this country sky, this sky above Westminster. She parted the curtains; she looked. Oh, but how surprising! – in the room opposite the old lady stared straight at her! She was going to bed. And the sky. It will be a solemn sky, she had thought, it will be a dusky sky, turning away its cheek in beauty. But there it was – ashen pale, raced over quickly by tapering vast clouds. It was new to her. The wind must have risen. She was going to bed, in the room opposite. It was fascinating to watch her, moving about, that old lady, crossing the room, coming to the window. Could she see her? It was fascinating, with people still laughing and shouting in the drawing-room, to watch that old woman, quite quietly, going to bed alone. She pulled the blind now. The clock began striking. The young man had killed himself; but she did not pity him; with the clock striking the hour, one, two, three, she did not pity him, with all this going on. There! the old lady had put out her light! the whole house was dark now with this going on, she repeated, and the words came to her, Fear no more the heat of the sun. She must go back to them. But what an extraordinary night! She felt somehow very like him – the young man who had killed himself. She felt glad that he had done it; thrown it away while they went on living. The clock was striking. The leaden circles dissolved in the air. But she must go back. She must assemble. She must find Sally and Peter. And she came in from the little room.

'But where is Clarissa?' said Peter. He was sitting on the sofa with Sally. (After all these years he really could not call her 'Lady Rosseter'.) 'Where's the woman gone to?' he asked. 'Where's Clarissa?'

Sally supposed, and so did Peter for the matter of that, that there were people of importance, politicians, whom neither of them knew unless by sight in the picture papers, whom Clarissa had to be nice to, had to talk to. She was with them. Yet there was Richard Dalloway not in the Cabinet. He hadn't been a success, Sally supposed. For herself, she scarcely ever read the papers. She sometimes saw his name mentioned. But then – well, she lived a very solitary life, in the wilds, Clarissa would say, among great merchants, great manufacturers, men, after all, who did things. She had done things too!

'I have five sons!' she told him.

Lord, lord, what a change had come over her! the softness of mother-hood; its egotism too. Last time they met, Peter remembered, had been among the cauliflowers in the moonlight, the leaves 'like rough bronze' she had said, with her literary turn; and she had picked a rose. She had marched him up and down that awful night, after the scene by the fountain; he was to catch the midnight train. Heavens, he had wept!

That was his old trick, opening a pocket-knife, thought Sally, always opening and shutting a knife when he got excited. They had been very, very intimate, she and Peter Walsh, when he was in love with Clarissa, and there was that dreadful, ridiculous scene over Richard Dalloway at lunch. She had called Richard 'Wickham'. Why not call Richard 'Wickham'? Clarissa had flared up! and indeed they had never seen each other since, she and Clarissa, not more than half a dozen times perhaps in the last ten years. And Peter Walsh had gone off to India, and she had heard vaguely that he had made an unhappy marriage, and she didn't know whether he had any children, and she couldn't ask him, for he had changed. He was rather shrivelled-looking, but kinder, she felt, and she had a real affection for him, for he was connected with her youth, and she still had a little Emily Brontë he had given her, and he was to write, surely? In those days he was to write.

'Have you written?' she asked him, spreading her hand, her firm and shapely hand, on her knee in a way he recalled.

'Not a word!' said Peter Walsh, and she laughed.

She was still attractive, still a personage, Sally Seton. But who was this Rosseter? He wore two camellias on his wedding day – that was all Peter knew of him. 'They have myriads of servants, miles of conservatories,' Clarissa wrote, something like that. Sally owned it with a shout of laughter.

'Yes, I have ten thousand a year' – whether before the tax was paid or after, she couldn't remember, for her husband, 'whom you must meet,' she said, 'whom you would like,' she said, did all that for her.

And Sally used to be in rags and tatters. She had pawned her great-grandfather's ring which Marie Antoinette had given him – had he got it right? – to come to Bourton.

Oh yes, Sally remembered; she had it still, a ruby ring which Marie Antoinette had given her great-grandfather. She never had a penny to her name in those days, and going to Bourton always meant some frightful pinch. But going to Bourton had meant so much to her – had kept her sane, she believed, so unhappy had she been at home. But that was all a thing of the past – all over now, she said. And Mr Parry was dead; and Miss Parry was still alive. Never had he had such a shock in his life! said Peter. He had been quite certain she was dead. And the marriage had been, Sally supposed, a success? And that very handsome, very self-possessed young woman was Elizabeth, over there, by the curtains, in red.

(She was like a poplar, she was like a river, she was like a hyacinth, Willie Titcomb was thinking. Oh how much nicer to be in the country and do what she liked! She could hear her poor dog howling, Elizabeth was certain.) She was not a bit like Clarissa, Peter Walsh said.

'Oh, Clarissa!' said Sally.

What Sally felt was simply this. She had owed Clarissa an enormous amount. They had been friends, not acquaintances, friends, and she still saw Clarissa all in white going about the house with her hands full of flowers – to this day tobacco plants made her think of Bourton. But – did Peter understand? – she lacked something. Lacked what was it? She had charm; she had extraordinary charm. But to be frank (and she felt that Peter was an old friend, a real friend – did absence matter? did distance matter? She had often wanted to write to him, but torn it up, yet felt he understood, for people understand without things being said, as one realises growing old, and old she was, had been that afternoon to see her sons at Eton, where they had the mumps), to be quite frank, then, how could Clarissa have done it? – married Richard Dalloway? a sportsman, a man who cared only for dogs. Literally, when he came into the room he smelt of the stables. And then all this? She waved her hand.

Hugh Whitbread it was, strolling past in his white waistcoat, dim, fat, blind, past everything he looked, except self-esteem and comfort.

'He's not going to recognise us,' said Sally, and really she hadn't the courage – so that was Hugh! the admirable Hugh!

'And what does he do?' she asked Peter.

He blacked the King's boots or counted bottles at Windsor, Peter told her. Peter kept his sharp tongue still! But Sally must be frank, Peter said. That kiss now, Hugh's.

On the lips, she assured him, in the smoking-room one evening. She went straight to Clarissa in a rage. Hugh didn't do such things! Clarissa said, the admirable Hugh! Hugh's socks were without exception the most beautiful she had ever seen – and now his evening dress. Perfect! And had he children?

'Everybody in the room has six sons at Eton,' Peter told her, except himself. He, thank God, had none. No sons, no daughters, no wife. Well, he didn't seem to mind, said Sally. He looked younger, she thought, than any of them.

But it had been a silly thing to do, in many ways, Peter said, to marry like that; 'a perfect goose she was,' he said, but, he said, 'we had a splendid time of it,' but how could that be? Sally wondered; what did he mean? and how odd it was to know him and yet not know a single thing that had happened to him. And did he say it out of pride? Very likely, for after all it must be galling for him (though he was an oddity, a sort of sprite, not at all an ordinary man), it must be lonely at his age to have no home, nowhere to go to. But he must stay with them for weeks and weeks. Of course he would; he would love to stay with them, and that was how it came out. All these years the Dalloways had never been once. Time after time they had asked them. Clarissa (for it was Clarissa of course) would not come. For, said Sally, Clarissa was at heart a snob – one had to admit it, a snob. And it was that that was between them, she was convinced. Clarissa thought she had married beneath her, her husband being – she was proud of it – a miner's son. Every penny they had he had earned. As a little boy (her voice trembled) he had carried great sacks.

(And so she would go on, Peter felt, hour after hour; the miner's son; people thought she had married beneath her; her five sons; and what was the other thing – plants, hydrangeas, syringas, very, very rare hybiscus lilies that never grow north of the Suez Canal, but she, with one gardener in a suburb near Manchester, had beds of them, positively beds! Now all that Clarissa had escaped, unmaternal as she was.)

A snob was she? Yes, in many ways. Where was she, all this time? It was getting late.

'Yet,' said Sally, 'when I heard Clarissa was giving a party, I felt I couldn't *not* come – must see her again (and I'm staying in Victoria Street, practically next door). So I just came without an invitation. But,' she whispered, 'tell me, do. Who is this?'

It was Mrs Hilbery, looking for the door. For how late it was getting! And, she murmured, as the night grew later, as people went, one found old friends; quiet nooks and corners; and the loveliest views. Did they know, she asked, that they were surrounded by an enchanted garden? Lights and trees and wonderful gleaming lakes and the sky. Just a few fairy lamps, Clarissa Dalloway had said, in the back garden! But she was a magician! It was a park . . . And she didn't know their names, but friends she knew they were, friends without names, songs without words, always the best. But there were so many doors, such unexpected places, she could not find her way.

'Old Mrs Hilbery,' said Peter; but who was that? that lady standing by the curtain all the evening, without speaking? He knew her face; connected her with Bourton. Surely she used to cut up underclothes at the large table in the window? Davidson, was that her name?

'Oh, that is Ellie Henderson,' said Sally. Clarissa was really very hard on her. She was a cousin, very poor. Clarissa *was* hard on people.

She was rather, said Peter. Yet, said Sally, in her emotional way, with a rush of that enthusiasm which Peter used to love her for, yet dreaded a little now, so effusive she might become – how generous to her friends Clarissa was! and what a rare quality one found it, and how sometimes at night or on Christmas Day, when she counted up her blessings, she put that friendship first. They were young; that was it. Clarissa was pure-hearted; that was it. Peter would think her sentimental. So she was. For she had come to feel that it was the only thing worth saying – what one felt. Cleverness was silly. One must say simply what one felt.

'But I do not know,' said Peter Walsh, 'what I feel.'

Poor Peter, thought Sally. Why did not Clarissa come and talk to them? That was what he was longing for. She knew it. All the time he was thinking only of Clarissa, and was fidgeting with his knife.

He had not found life simple, Peter said. His relations with Clarissa had not been simple. It had spoilt his life, he said. (They had been so intimate – he and Sally Seton, it was absurd not to say it.) One could not be in love twice, he said. And what could she say? Still, it is better to have loved (but he would think her sentimental – he used to be so sharp). He must come and stay with them in Manchester. That is all very true, he said. All very true. He would love to come and stay with them, directly he had done what he had to do in London.

And Clarissa had cared for him more than she had ever cared for Richard, Sally was positive of that.

'No, no, no!' said Peter (Sally should not have said that – she went too far). That good fellow – there he was at the end of the room, holding forth, the same as ever, dear old Richard. Who was he talking to? Sally asked, that very distinguished-looking man? Living in the wilds as she did, she had an insatiable curiosity to know who people were. But Peter did not know. He did not like his looks, he said, probably a Cabinet Minister. Of them all, Richard seemed to him the best, he said – the most disinterested.

'But what has he done?' Sally asked. Public work, she supposed. And were they happy together? Sally asked (she herself was extremely happy); for, she admitted, she knew nothing about them, only jumped to conclusions, as one does, for what can one know even of the people one lives with every day? she asked. Are we not all prisoners? She had read a wonderful play about a man who scratched on the wall of his cell, and she had felt that was true of life – one scratched on the wall. Despairing of human relationships (people were so difficult), she often went into her garden and got from her flowers a peace which men and women never gave her. But no; he did not like cabbages; he preferred human beings, Peter said. Indeed, the young are beautiful, Sally said, watching Elizabeth cross the room. How unlike Clarissa at her age! Could he make anything of her? She would not open her lips. Not much, not yet, Peter admitted. She was like a lily, Sally said, a lily by the side of a pool. But Peter did not agree that we know nothing. We know everything, he said; at least he did.

But these two, Sally whispered, these two coming now (and really she must go, if Clarissa did not come soon), this distinguished-looking man and his rather common-looking wife who had been talking to Richard – what could one know about people like that?

'That they're damnable humbugs,' said Richard, looking at them casually. He made Sally laugh.

But Sir William Bradshaw stopped at the door to look at a picture. He looked in the corner for the engraver's name. His wife looked too. Sir William Bradshaw was so interested in art.

When one was young, said Peter, one was too much excited to know people. Now that one was old, fifty-two to be precise (Sally was fifty-five, in body, she said, but her heart was like a girl's of twenty); now that one was mature then, said Peter, one could watch, one could understand, and one did not lose the power of feeling, he said. No, that is true, said Sally. She felt more deeply, more passionately, every year. It increased, he said, alas! perhaps, but one should be glad of it – it went on increasing in his experience. There was someone in India. He would like to tell Sally about her. He would like Sally to know her. She was married, he said. She had two small children. They must all come to Manchester, said Sally – he must promise before they left.

'There's Elizabeth,' he said, 'she feels not half what we feel, not yet.' 'But,' said Sally, watching Elizabeth go to her father, 'one can see they are devoted to each other.' She could feel it by the way Elizabeth went to her father.

For her father had been looking at her, as he stood talking to the Bradshaws, and he had thought to himself who is that lovely girl? And suddenly he realised that it was his Elizabeth, and he had not recognised her, she looked so lovely in her pink frock! Elizabeth had felt him looking at her as she talked to Willie Titcomb. So she went to him and they stood together, now that the party was almost over, looking at the people going, and the rooms getting emptier and emptier, with things scattered on the floor. Even Ellie Henderson was going, nearly last of all, though no one had spoken to her, but she had wanted to see everything, to tell Edith. And Richard and Elizabeth were rather glad it was over, but Richard was proud of his daughter. And he had not meant to tell her, but he could not help telling her. He had looked at her, he said, and he had wondered, who is that lovely girl? and it was his daughter! That did make her happy. But her poor dog was howling.

'Richard has improved. You are right,' said Sally. 'I shall go and talk to him. I shall say good-night. What does the brain matter,' said Lady Rosseter, getting up, 'compared with the heart?'

'I will come,' said Peter, but he sat on for a moment. What is this terror? what is this ecstasy? he thought to himself. What is it that fills me with extraordinary excitement?

It is Clarissa, he said.

For there she was.

TO THE LIGHTHOUSE

To the Lighthouse

A novel by
VIRGINIA WOOLF
first published in 1927

PART ONE
The Window

'Yes, of course, if it's fine tomorrow,' said Mrs Ramsay. 'But you'll have to be up with the lark,' she added.

To her son these words conveyed an extraordinary joy, as if it were settled the expedition were bound to take place, and the wonder to which he had looked forward, for years and years it seemed, was, after a night's darkness and a day's sail, within touch. Since he belonged, even at the age of six, to that great clan which cannot keep this feeling separate from that, but must let future prospects, with their joys and sorrows, cloud what is actually at hand, since to such people even in earliest childhood any turn in the wheel of sensation has the power to crystallise and transfix the moment upon which its gloom or radiance rests, James Ramsay, sitting on the floor cutting out pictures from the illustrated catalogue of the Army and Navy Stores, endowed the picture of a refrigerator as his mother spoke with heavenly bliss. It was fringed with joy. The wheelbarrow, the lawn-mower, the sound of poplar trees, leaves whitening before rain, rooks cawing, brooms knocking, dresses rustling – all these were so coloured and distinguished in his mind that he had already his private code, his secret language, though he appeared the image of stark and uncompromising severity, with his high forehead and his fierce blue eyes, impeccably candid and pure, frowning slightly at the sight of human frailty, so that his mother, watching him guide his scissors neatly round the refrigerator, imagined him all red and ermine on the Bench or directing a stern and momentous enterprise in some crisis of public affairs.

'But,' said his father, stopping in front of the drawing-room window, 'it won't be fine.'

Had there been an axe handy, a poker, or any weapon that would have gashed a hole in his father's breast and killed him, there and then, James would have seized it. Such were the extremes of emotion that Mr Ramsay excited in his children's breasts by his mere presence; standing, as now, lean as a knife, narrow as the blade of one, grinning sarcastically, not only with the pleasure of disillusioning his son and casting ridicule upon his wife, who was ten thousand times better in every way than he was (James thought), but also with some secret conceit at his own accuracy of judgement. What he said was true. It was always true. He was incapable of untruth; never tampered with a fact; never altered a disagreeable word to suit the pleasure or convenience of any mortal being, least of all of his own children, who, sprung from his loins, should be aware from childhood that life is difficult; facts uncompromising; and the passage to that fabled land where our brightest hopes are extinguished, our frail barks founder in darkness (here

Mr Ramsay would straighten his back and narrow his little blue eyes upon the horizon), one that needs, above all, courage, truth, and the power to endure.

'But it may be fine – I expect it will be fine,' said Mrs Ramsay, making some little twist of the reddish-brown stocking she was knitting, impatiently. If she finished it tonight, if they did go to the Lighthouse after all, it was to be given to the Lighthouse keeper for his little boy, who was threatened with a tuberculous hip; together with a pile of old magazines, and some tobacco, indeed whatever she could find lying about, not really wanted, but only littering the room, to give those poor fellows who must be bored to death sitting all day with nothing to do but polish the lamp and trim the wick and rake about on their scrap of garden, something to amuse them. For how would you like to be shut up for a whole month at a time, and possibly more in stormy weather, upon a rock the size of a tennis lawn? she would ask; and to have no letters or newspapers, and to see nobody; if you were married, not to see your wife, not to know how your children were – if they were ill, if they had fallen down and broken their legs or arms; to see the same dreary waves breaking week after week, and then a dreadful storm coming, and the windows covered with spray, and birds dashed against the lamp, and the whole place rocking, and not be able to put your nose out of doors for fear of being swept into the sea? How would you like that? she asked, addressing herself particularly to her daughters. So she added, rather differently, one must take them whatever comforts one can.

'It's due west,' said the atheist Tansley, holding his bony fingers spread so that the wind blew through them, for he was sharing Mr Ramsay's evening walk up and down, up and down the terrace. That is to say, the wind blew from the worst possible direction for landing at the Lighthouse. Yes, he did say disagreeable things, Mrs Ramsay admitted; it was odious of him to rub this in, and make James still more disappointed; but at the same time, she would not let them laugh at him. 'The atheist,' they called him; 'the little atheist.' Rose mocked him; Prue mocked him; Andrew, Jasper, Roger mocked him; even old Badger without a tooth in his head had bit him, for being (as Nancy put it) the hundred and tenth young man to chase them all the way up to the Hebrides when it was ever so much nicer to be alone.

'Nonsense,' said Mrs Ramsay, with great severity. Apart from the habit of exaggeration which they had from her, and from the implication (which was true) that she asked too many people to stay, and had to lodge some in the town, she could not bear incivility to her guests, to young men in particular, who were poor as church mice, 'exceptionally able', her husband said, his great admirers, and come there for a holiday. Indeed, she had the whole of the other sex under her protection; for reasons she could not explain, for their chivalry and valour, for the fact that they negotiated treaties, ruled India, controlled finance; finally for an attitude towards herself which no woman could fail to feel or to find agreeable, something trustful, childlike, reverential, which an old woman could take from a young man without loss of dignity, and woe betide the girl – pray heaven it was none of her daughters! – who did not feel the worth of it, and all that it implied, to the marrow of her bones.

She turned with severity upon Nancy. He had not chased them, she said. He had been asked.

They must find a way out of it all. There might be some simpler way, some less laborious way, she sighed. When she looked in the glass and saw her hair grey, her cheek sunk, at fifty, she thought, possibly she might have managed things better – her husband; money; his books. But for her own part she would never for a single second regret her decision, evade difficulties or slur over duties. She was now formidable to behold, and it was only in silence, looking up from their plates, after she had spoken so severely about Charles Tansley, that her daughters – Prue, Nancy, Rose – could sport with infidel ideas which they had brewed for themselves of a life different from hers: in Paris, perhaps; a wilder life; not always taking care of some man or other; for there was in all their minds a mute questioning of deference and chivalry, of the Bank of England and the Indian Empire, of ringed fingers and lace, though to them all there was something in this of the essence of beauty, which called out the manliness in their girlish hearts, and made them, as they sat at table beneath their mother's eyes, honour her strange severity, her extreme courtesy, like a queen's raising from the mud a beggar's dirty foot and washing it, when she thus admonished them so very severely about that wretched atheist who had chased them to – or, speaking accurately, been invited to stay with them in – the Isle of Skye.

'There'll be no landing at the Lighthouse tomorrow,' said Charles Tansley, clapping his hands together as he stood at the window with her husband. Surely, he had said enough. She wished they would both leave her and James alone and go on talking. She looked at him. He was such a miserable specimen, the children said, all humps and hollows. He couldn't play cricket; he poked; he shuffled. He was a sarcastic brute, Andrew said. They knew what he liked best – to be forever walking up and down, up and down, with Mr Ramsay, and saying who had won this, who had won that, who was a 'first-rate man' at Latin verses, who was 'brilliant but I think fundamentally unsound', who was undoubtedly the 'ablest fellow in Balliol', who had buried his light temporarily at Bristol or Bedford, but was bound to be heard of later when his Prolegomena, of which Mr Tansley had the first pages in proof with him if Mr Ramsay would like to see them, to some branch of mathematics or philosophy saw the light of day. That was what they talked about.

She could not help laughing herself sometimes. She said, the other day, something about 'waves mountains high'. Yes, said Charles Tansley, it was a little rough. 'Aren't you drenched to the skin?' she had said. 'Damp, not wet through,' said Mr Tansley, pinching his sleeve, feeling his socks.

But it was not that they minded, the children said. It was not his face; it was not his manners. It was him – his point of view. When they talked about something interesting, people, music, history, anything, even said it was a fine evening so why not sit out of doors, then what they complained of about Charles Tansley was that until he had turned the whole thing round and made it somehow reflect himself and disparage them, put them all on edge somehow with his acid way of peeling the flesh and blood off everything, he was not satisfied. And he would go to picture galleries, they said, and he would ask one, did one like his tie? God knows, said Rose, one did not.

Disappearing as stealthily as stags from the dinner-table directly the meal was over, the eight sons and daughters of Mr and Mrs Ramsay sought their bedrooms, their fastnesses in a house where there was no other privacy to debate anything, everything: Tansley's tie; the passing of the Reform Bill; seabirds and butterflies; people; while the sun poured into those attics, which a plank alone separated from each other so that every footstep could be plainly heard and the Swiss girl sobbing for her father who was dying of cancer in a valley of the Grisons, and lit up bats, flannels, straw hats, ink-pots, paintpots, beetles, and the skulls of small birds, while it drew from the long frilled strips of seaweed pinned to the wall a smell of salt and weeds, which was in the towels too, gritty with sand from bathing.

Strife, divisions, difference of opinion, prejudices twisted into the very fibre of being, oh that they should begin so early, Mrs Ramsay deplored. They were so critical, her children. They talked such nonsense. She went from the dining-room, holding James by the hand, since he would not go with the others. It seemed to her such nonsense – inventing differences, when people, heaven knows, were different enough without that. The real differences, she thought, standing by the drawing-room window, are enough, quite enough. She had in mind at the moment, rich and poor, high and low; the great in birth receiving from her, half grudging, some respect, for had she not in her veins the blood of that very noble, if slightly mythical, Italian house, whose daughters, scattered about English drawing-rooms in the nineteenth century, had lisped so charmingly, had stormed so wildly, and all her wit and her bearing and her temper came from them, and not from the sluggish English, or the cold Scotch; but more profoundly she ruminated the other problem, of rich and poor, and the things she saw with her own eyes, weekly, daily, here or in London, when she visited this widow, or that struggling wife in person with a bag on her arm, and a notebook and pencil with which she wrote down in columns carefully ruled for the purpose wages and spendings, employment and unemployment, in the hope that thus she would cease to be a private woman whose charity was half a sop to her own indignation, half a relief to her own curiosity, and become, what with her untrained mind she greatly admired, an investigator, elucidating the social problem.

Insoluble questions they were, it seemed to her, standing there, holding

James by the hand. He had followed her into the drawing-room, that young man they laughed at; he was standing by the table, fidgeting with something, awkwardly, feeling himself out of things, as she knew without looking round. They had all gone – the children; Minta Doyle and Paul Rayley; Augustus Carmichael; her husband – they had all gone. So she turned with a sigh and said: 'Would it bore you to come with me, Mr Tansley?'

She had a dull errand in the town; she had a letter or two to write; she would be ten minutes perhaps; she would put on her hat. And, with her basket and her parasol, there she was again, ten minutes later, giving out a sense of being ready, of being equipped for a jaunt, which, however, she must interrupt for a moment, as they passed the tennis lawn, to ask Mr Carmichael, who was basking with his yellow cat's eyes ajar, so that like a cat's they seemed to reflect the branches moving or the clouds passing but to give no inkling of any inner thoughts or emotion whatsoever, if he wanted anything.

For they were making the great expedition, she said, laughing. They were going to the town. 'Stamps, writing-paper, tobacco?' she suggested, stopping by his side. But no, he wanted nothing. His hands clasped themselves over his capacious paunch, his eyes blinked, as if he would have liked to reply kindly to these blandishments (she was seductive but a little nervous) but could not, sunk as he was in a grey-green somnolence which embraced them all, without need of words, in a vast and benevolent lethargy of well-wishing; all the house; all the world; all the people in it, for he had slipped into his glass at lunch a few drops of something, which accounted, the children thought, for the vivid streak of canary-yellow in moustache and beard that were otherwise milk-white. He wanted nothing, he murmured.

He should have been a great philosopher, said Mrs Ramsay, as they went down the road to the fishing village, but he had made an unfortunate marriage. Holding her black parasol very erect, and moving with an inde-scribable air of expectation, as if she were going to meet someone round the corner, she told the story: an affair at Oxford with some girl; an early marriage; poverty; going to India; translating a little poetry 'very beautifully, I believe,' being willing to teach the boys Persian or Hindustani, but what really was the use of that? – and then lying, as they saw him, on the lawn.

It flattered him; snubbed as he had been, it soothed him that Mrs Ramsay should tell him this. Charles Tansley revived. Insinuating, too, as she did the greatness of man's intellect, even in its decay, the subjection of all wives – not that she blamed the girl, and the marriage had been happy enough, she believed – to their husband's labours, she made him feel better pleased with himself than he had done yet, and he would have liked, had they taken a cab, for example, to have paid the fare. As for her little bag, might he not carry that? No, no, she said, she always carried *that* herself. She did too. Yes, he felt that in her. He felt many things, something in particular that excited him and disturbed him for reasons which he could not give. He would like her to see him, gowned and hooded, walking in a procession. A fellowship, a professorship – he felt capable of anything and saw himself – but what was she looking at? At a man pasting a bill. The vast flapping sheet flattened itself out, and each shove of the brush revealed fresh legs, hoops, horses, glistening reds and blues, beautifully smooth, until half the wall was covered with the advertisement of a circus: a hundred horsemen, twenty performing seals, lions, tigers . . . Craning forwards, for she was short-sighted, she read out how it . . . 'will visit this town'. It was terribly dangerous work for a one-armed man, she exclaimed, to stand on top of a ladder like that – his left arm had been cut off in a reaping machine two years ago.

'Let us all go!' she cried, moving on, as if all those riders and horses had filled her with childlike exultation and made her forget her pity.

'Let's go,' he said, repeating her words, clicking them out, however, with a self-consciousness that made her wince. 'Let us go to the Circus.' No. He could not say it right. He could not feel it right. But why not? she wondered. What was wrong with him then? She liked him warmly, at the moment. Had they not been taken, she asked, to circuses when they were children? Never, he answered, as if she asked the very thing he wanted to reply to; had been longing all these days to say, how they did not go to circuses. It was a large family, nine brothers and sisters, and his father was a working man; 'My father is a chemist, Mrs Ramsay. He keeps a shop.' He himself had paid his own way since he was thirteen. Often he went without a greatcoat in winter. He could never 'return hospitality' (those were his parched stiff words) at college. He had to make things last twice the time other people did; he smoked the cheapest tobacco: shag; the same the old men smoked on the quays. He worked hard – seven hours a day; his subject was now the influence of some-thing upon somebody – they were walking on and Mrs Ramsay did not quite catch the meaning, only the words, here and there . . . dissertation . . . fellowship . . . readership . . . lectureship. She could not follow the ugly academic jargon, that rattled itself off so glibly, but said to herself that she saw now why going to the circus had knocked him off his perch, poor little man, and why he came out, instantly, with all that about his father and mother and brothers and sisters, and she would see to it that they didn't laugh at him any more; she would tell Prue about it. What he would have liked, she supposed, would have been to say how he had been to Ibsen with the Ramsays. He was an awful prig – oh yes, an insufferable bore. For, though they had reached the town now and were in the main street, with carts grinding past on the cobbles, still he went on talking, about settlements, and teaching, and working men, and helping our own class, and lectures, till she gathered that he had got back entire self-confidence, had recovered from the circus, and was about (and now again she liked him warmly) to tell her – but here, the houses falling away on both sides, they came out on the quay, and the whole bay spread before them and Mrs Ramsay could not help exclaiming: 'Oh, how beautiful!' For the great plateful of blue water was before her; the hoary Lighthouse, distant, austere, in the midst; and on the right, as far as the eye could see, fading and falling, in soft low pleats, the green sand dunes with the wild flowing grasses on them, which always seemed to be running away into some moon country, uninhabited of men.

That was the view, she said, stopping, growing greyer-eyed, that her husband loved.

She paused a moment. But now, she said, artists had come here. There indeed, only a few paces off, stood one of them, in Panama hat and yellow boots, seriously, softly, absorbedly, for all that he was watched by ten little boys, with an air of profound contentment on his round red face, gazing, and then, when he had gazed, dipping; imbuing the tip of his brush in some soft mound of green or pink. Since Mr Paunceforte had been there, three years before, all the pictures were like that she said, green and grey, with lemon-coloured sailing-boats, and pink women on the beach.

But her grandmother's friends, she said, glancing discreetly as they passed, took the greatest pains; first they mixed their own colours, and then they ground them, and then they put damp cloths on them to keep them moist.

So Mr Tansley supposed she meant him to see that that man's picture was skimpy, was that what one said? The colours weren't solid? Was that what one said? Under the influence of that extraordinary emotion which had been growing all the walk, had begun in the garden when he had wanted to take her bag, had increased in the town when he had wanted to tell her everything about himself, he was coming to see himself and everything he had ever known gone crooked a little. It was awfully strange.

There he stood in the parlour of the poky little house where she had taken him, waiting for her, while she went upstairs a moment to see a woman. He heard her quick step above; heard her voice cheerful, then low; looked at the mats, tea-caddies, glass shades; waited quite impatiently; looked forward eagerly to the walk home, determined to carry her bag; then heard her come out; shut a door; say they must keep the windows open and the doors shut, ask at the house for anything they wanted (she must be talking to a child), when, suddenly, in she came, stood for a moment silent (as if she had been pretending up there, and for a moment let herself be now), stood quite motionless for a moment against a picture of Queen Victoria wearing the blue ribbon of the Garter; and all at once he realised that it was this: it was this – she was the most beautiful person he had ever seen.

With stars in her eyes and veils in her hair, with cyclamen and wild violets – what nonsense was he thinking? She was fifty at least; she had eight children. Stepping through fields of flowers and taking to her breast buds that had broken and lambs that had fallen; with the stars in her eyes and the wind in her hair – He took her bag.

'Goodbye, Elsie,' she said, and they walked up the street, she holding her parasol erect and walking as if she expected to meet someone round the corner, while for the first time in his life Charles Tansley felt an extraordinary pride; a man digging in a drain stopped digging and looked at her; let his arm fall down and looked at her; Charles Tansley felt an extraordinary pride; felt the wind and the cyclamen and the violets for he was walking with a beautiful woman for the first time in his life. He had hold of her bag.

II

'No going to the Lighthouse, James,' he said, as he stood by the window, speaking awkwardly, but trying in deference to Mrs Ramsay to soften his voice into some semblance of geniality at least.

Odious little man, thought Mrs Ramsay, why go on saying that?

III

'Perhaps you will wake up and find the sun shining and the birds singing,' she said compassionately, smoothing the little boy's hair, for her husband, with his caustic saying that it would not be fine, had dashed his spirits she could see. This going to the Lighthouse was a passion of his, she saw, and then, as if her husband had not said enough, with his caustic saying that it would not be fine tomorrow, this odious little man went and rubbed it in all over again.

'Perhaps it will be fine tomorrow,' she said, smoothing his hair.

All she could do now was to admire the refrigerator, and turn the pages of the Stores list in the hope that she might come upon something like a rake, or a mowing-machine, which, with its prongs and its handles, would need the greatest skill and care in cutting out. All these young men parodied her husband, she reflected; he said it would rain; they said it would be a positive tornado.

But here, as she turned the page, suddenly her search for the picture of a rake or a mowing-machine was interrupted. The gruff murmur, irregularly broken by the taking out of pipes and the putting in of pipes which had kept on assuring her, though she could not hear what was said (as she sat in the window), that the men were happily talking; this sound, which had lasted now half an hour and had taken its place soothingly in the scale of sounds pressing on top of her, such as the tap of balls upon bats, the sharp, sudden bark now and then, 'How's that? How's that?' of the children playing cricket, had ceased; so that the monotonous fall of the waves on the beach, which for the most part beat a measured and soothing tattoo to her thoughts and seemed consolingly to repeat over and over again as she sat with the children the words of some old cradle song, murmured by nature, 'I am guarding you – I am your support,' but at other times suddenly and unexpectedly, especially when her mind raised itself slightly from the task actually in hand, had no such kindly meaning, but like a ghostly roll of drums remorselessly beat the measure of life, made one think of the destruction of the island and its engulfment in the sea, and warned her whose day had slipped past in one quick doing after another that it was all ephemeral as a rainbow – this sound which had been obscured and concealed under the other sounds suddenly thundered hollow in her ears and made her look up with an impulse of terror.

They had ceased to talk; that was the explanation. Falling in one second from the tension which had gripped her to the other extreme which, as if to recoup her for her unnecessary expense of emotion, was cool, amused, and even faintly malicious, she concluded that poor Charles Tansley had been shed. That was of little account to her. If her husband required sacrifices (and indeed he did) she cheerfully offered up to him Charles Tansley, who had snubbed her little boy.

One moment more, with her head raised, she listened, as if she waited for some habitual sound, some regular mechanical sound; and then, hearing something rhythmical, half said, half chanted, beginning in the garden, as her husband beat up and down the terrace, something between a croak and a song, she was soothed once more, assured again that all was well, and looking down at the book on her knee found the picture of a pocket knife with six blades which could only be cut out if James was very careful.

Suddenly a loud cry, as of a sleep-walker, half roused, something about

Stormed at with shot and shell

sung out with the utmost intensity in her ear, made her turn apprehensively to see if anyone heard him. Only Lily Briscoe, she was glad to find; and that did not matter. But the sight of the girl standing on the edge of the lawn painting reminded her; she was supposed to be keeping her head as much in the same position as possible for Lily's picture. Lily's picture! Mrs Ramsay smiled. With her little Chinese eyes and her puckered-up face she would never marry; one could not take her painting very seriously; but she was an independent little creature, Mrs Ramsay liked her for it, and so remembering her promise, she bent her head.

IV

Indeed, he almost knocked her easel over, coming down upon her with his hands waving, shouting out: 'Boldly we rode and well,' but, mercifully, he turned sharp, and rode off, to die gloriously she supposed upon the heights of Balaclava. Never was anybody at once so ridiculous and so alarming. But so long as he kept like that, waving, shouting, she was safe; he would not stand still and look at her picture. And that was what Lily Briscoe could not have endured. Even while she looked at the mass, at the line, at the colour, at Mrs Ramsay sitting in the window with James, she kept a feeler on her surroundings lest someone should creep up, and suddenly she should find her picture looked at. But now, with all her senses quickened as they were, looking, straining, till the colour of the wall and the jacmanna beyond burnt into her eyes, she was aware of someone coming out of the house, coming towards her; but somehow divined, from the footfall, William Bankes, so that though her brush quivered, she did not, as she would have done had it been Mr Tansley, Paul Rayley, Minta Doyle, or practically anybody else, turn her canvas upon the grass, but let it stand. William Bankes stood beside her.

They had rooms in the village, and so, walking in, walking out, parting late on doormats, had said little things about the soup, about the children, about one thing and another which made them allies; so that when he stood beside her now in his judicial way (he was old enough to be her father too, a botanist, a widower, smelling of soap, very scrupulous and clean) she just stood there. He just stood there. Her shoes were excellent, he observed. They allowed the toes their natural expansion. Lodging in the same house with her, he had noticed too, how orderly she was, up before breakfast and off to paint, he believed, alone: poor, presumably, and without the complexion or the allurement of Miss Doyle certainly, but with a good sense which made her in his eyes superior to that young lady. Now, for instance, when Ramsay bore down on them, shouting, gesticulating, Miss Briscoe, he felt certain, understood.

Someone had blundered.

Mr Ramsay glared at them. He glared at them without seeming to see them. That did make them both vaguely uncomfortable. Together they had seen a thing they had not been meant to see. They had encroached upon a privacy. So, Lily thought, it was probably an excuse of his for moving, for getting out of earshot, that made Mr Bankes almost immediately say something about its being chilly and suggest taking a stroll. She could come, yes. But it was with difficulty that she took her eyes off her picture.

The jacmanna was bright violet; the wall staring white. She would not have considered it honest to tamper with the bright violet and the staring white, since she saw them like that, fashionable though it was, since Mr Paunceforte's visit, to see everything pale, elegant, semi-transparent. Then beneath the colour there was the shape. She could see it all so clearly, so commandingly, when she looked: it was when she took her brush in hand that the whole thing changed. It was in that moment's flight between the picture and her canvas that the demons set on her who often brought her to the verge of tears and made this passage from conception to work as dreadful as any down a dark passage for a child. Such she often felt herself – struggling against terrific odds to maintain her courage; to say: 'But this is what I see; this is what I see,' and so to clasp some miserable remnant of her vision to her breast, which a thousand forces did their best to pluck from her. And it was then too, in that chill and windy way, as she began to paint, that there forced themselves upon her other things, her own inadequacy, her insignificance, keeping house for her father off the Brompton Road, and had much ado to control her impulse to fling herself (thank heaven she had always resisted so far) at Mrs Ramsay's knee and say to her – but what could one say to her? 'I'm in love with you?' No, that was not true. 'I'm in love with this all,' waving her hand at the hedge, at the house, at the children? It was absurd, it was impossible. One could not say what one meant. So now she laid her brushes neatly in the box, side by side, and said to William Bankes: 'It suddenly gets cold. The sun seems to give less heat,' she said, looking about her, for it was bright enough, the grass still a soft deep green, the house starred in its greenery with purple passion flowers, and rooks dropping cool cries from the high blue. But something moved, flashed, turned a silver wing in the air. It was September after all, the middle of September, and past six in the evening. So off they strolled down the garden in the usual direction, past the tennis lawn, past the pampas grass, to that break in the thick hedge, guarded by red-hot pokers like braziers of clear burning coal, between which the blue waters of the bay looked bluer than ever.

They came there regularly every evening drawn by some need. It was as if the water floated off and set sailing thoughts which had grown stagnant on dry land, and gave to their bodies even some sort of physical relief. First, the pulse of colour flooded the bay with blue, and the heart expanded with it and the body swam, only the next instant to be checked and chilled by the prickly blackness on the ruffled waves. Then, up behind the great black rock, almost every evening spurted irregularly, so that one had to watch for it and it was a delight when it came, a fountain of white water; and then, while one waited for that, one watched, on the pale semicircular beach, wave after wave shedding again and again smoothly a film of mother-of-pearl.

They both smiled, standing there. They both felt a common hilarity, excited by the moving waves; and then by the swift cutting race of a sailing boat, which, having sliced a curve in the bay, stopped; shivered; let its sail drop down; and then, with a natural instinct to complete the picture, after this swift movement, both of them looked at the dunes far away, and instead of merriment felt come over them some sadness – because the thing was completed partly, and partly because distant views seem to outlast by a million years (Lily thought) the gazer and to be communing already with a sky which beholds an earth entirely at rest.

Looking at the far sandhills, William Bankes thought of Ramsay: thought of a road in Westmorland, thought of Ramsay striding along a road by himself hung round with that solitude which seemed to be his natural air. But this was suddenly interrupted, William Bankes remembered (and this must refer to some actual incident), by a hen, straddling her wings out in protection of a covey of little chicks, upon which Ramsay, stopping, pointed his stick and said, 'Pretty – pretty,' an odd illumination into his heart, Bankes had thought it, which showed his simplicity, his sympathy with humble things; but it seemed to him as if their friendship had ceased, there, on that stretch of road. After that, Ramsay had married. After that, what with one thing and another, the pulp had gone out of their friendship. Whose fault it was he could not say, only, after a time, repetition had taken the place of newness. It was to repeat that they met. But in this dumb colloquy with the sand dunes he maintained that his affection for Ramsay had in no way diminished; but there, like the body of a young man laid up in peat for a century, with the red fresh on his lips, was his friendship, in its acuteness and reality laid up across the bay among the sandhills.

He was anxious for the sake of this friendship and perhaps too in order to clear himself in his own mind from the imputation of having dried and shrunk – for Ramsay lived in a welter of children, whereas Bankes was childless and a widower – he was anxious that Lily Briscoe should not disparage Ramsay (a great man in his own way) yet should understand how things stood between them. Begun long years ago, their friendship had petered out on a Westmorland road, where the hen spread her wings before her chicks; after which Ramsay had married, and their paths lying different ways, there had been, certainly for no one's fault, some tendency, when they met, to repeat.

Yes. That was it. He finished. He turned from the view. And, turning to walk back the other way, up the drive, Mr Bankes was alive to things which would not have struck him had not those sandhills revealed to him the body of his friendship lying with the red on its lips laid up in peat – for instance, Cam, the little girl, Ramsay's youngest daughter. She was picking Sweet Alice on the bank. She was wild and fierce. She would not 'give a flower to the gentleman' as the nursemaid told her. No! no! no! she would not! She clenched her fist. She stamped. And Mr Bankes felt aged and saddened and somehow put into the wrong by her about his friendship. He must have dried and shrunk.

The Ramsays were not rich, and it was a wonder how they managed to contrive it all. Eight children! To feed eight children on philosophy! Here was another of them, Jasper this time, strolling past, to have a shot at a bird, he said, nonchalantly, swinging Lily's hand like a pump-handle as he passed, which caused Mr Bankes to say, bitterly, how *she* was a favourite. There was education now to be considered (true, Mrs Ramsay had something of her own perhaps), let alone the daily wear and tear of shoes and stockings which those 'great fellows', all well grown, angular, ruthless youngsters, must require. As for being sure which was which, or in what order they came, that was beyond him. He called them privately after the kings and queens of England: Cam the Wicked, James the Ruthless, Andrew the Just, Prue the Fair – for Prue would have beauty, he thought, how could she help it? – and Andrew brains. While he walked up the drive and Lily Briscoe said yes and no and capped his comments (for she was in love with them all, in love with this world), he weighed Ramsay's case, commiserated him, envied him, as if he had seen him divest himself of all those glories of isolation and austerity which crowned him in youth to cumber himself definitely with fluttering wings and clucking domesticities. They gave him something – William Bankes acknowledged that; it would have been pleasant if Cam had stuck a flower in his coat or clambered over his shoulder, as over her father's, to look at a picture of Vesuvius in eruption; but they had also, his old friends could not but feel, destroyed something. What would a stranger think now? What did this Lily Briscoe think? Could one help noticing that habits grew on him? eccentricities, weaknesses perhaps? It was astonishing that a man of his intellect could stoop so low as he did – but that was too harsh a phrase – could depend so much as he did upon people's praise.

'Oh but,' said Lily, 'think of his work!'

Whenever she 'thought of his work' she always saw clearly before her a large kitchen table. It was Andrew's doing. She asked him what his father's books were about. 'Subject and object and the nature of reality,' Andrew had said. And when she said Heavens, she had no notion what that meant, 'Think of a kitchen table then,' he told her, 'when you're not there.'

So she always saw, when she thought of Mr Ramsay's work, a scrubbed kitchen table. It lodged now in the fork of a pear tree, for they had reached the orchard. And with a painful effort of concentration, she focused her mind, not upon the silver-bossed bark of the tree, or upon its fish-shaped leaves, but upon a phantom kitchen table, one of those scrubbed board tables, grained and knotted, whose virtue seems to have been laid bare by years of muscular integrity, which stuck there, its four legs in air. Naturally, if one's days were passed in this seeing of angular essences, this reducing of lovely evenings, with all their flamingo clouds and blue and silver to a white deal four-legged table (and it was a mark of the finest minds so to do), naturally one could not be judged like an ordinary person.

Mr Bankes liked her for bidding him 'think of his work'. He had thought of it, often and often. Times without number, he had said: 'Ramsay is one of those men who do their best work before they are forty.' He had made a definite contribution to philosophy in one little book when he was only five and twenty; what came after was more or less amplification, repetition. But the number of men who make a definite contribution to anything whatsoever is very small, he said, pausing by the pear tree, well brushed, scrupulously exact, exquisitely judicial. Suddenly, as if the movement of his hand had released it, the load of her accumulated impressions of him tilted up, and down poured in a ponderous avalanche all she felt about him. That was one sensation. Then up rose in a fume the essence of his being. That was another. She felt herself transfixed by the intensity of her perception; it was his severity; his goodness. I respect you (she addressed him silently) in every atom; you are not vain; you are entirely impersonal; you are finer than Mr Ramsay; you are the finest human being that I know; you have neither wife nor child (without any sexual feeling, she longed to cherish that loneliness), you live for science (involuntarily, sections of potatoes rose before her eyes); praise would be an insult to you; generous, pure-hearted, heroic man! But simultaneously, she remembered how he had brought a valet all the way up here; objected to dogs on chairs; would prose for hours (until Mr Ramsay slammed out of the room) about salt in vegetables and the iniquity of English cooks.

How then did it work out, all this? How did one judge people, think of them? How did one add up this and that and conclude that it was liking one felt, or disliking? And to those words, what meaning attached, after all? Standing now, apparently transfixed, by the pear tree, impressions poured in upon her of those two men, and to follow her thought was like following a voice which speaks too quickly to be taken down by one's pencil, and the voice was her own voice saying without prompting undeniable, everlasting, contradictory things, so that even the fissures and humps on the bark of the pear tree were irrevocably fixed there for eternity. You have greatness, she continued, but Mr Ramsay has none of it. He is petty, selfish, vain, egotistical; he is spoilt; he is a tyrant; he wears Mrs Ramsay to death; but he has what you (she addressed Mr Bankes) have not; a fiery unworldliness; he knows nothing about trifles, he loves dogs and his children. He has eight. You have none. Did he not come down in two coats the other night and let Mrs Ramsay trim his hair into a pudding basin? All of this danced up and down, like a company of gnats, each separate, but all marvellously controlled in an invisible elastic net – danced up and down in Lily's mind, in and about the branches of the pear tree, where still hung in effigy the scrubbed kitchen table, symbol of her profound respect for Mr Ramsay's mind, until her thought which had spun quicker and quicker exploded of its own intensity; she felt released; a shot went off close at hand, and there came, flying from its fragments, frightened, effusive, tumultuous, a flock of starlings.

'Jasper!' said Mr Bankes. They turned the way the starlings flew, over the terrace. Following the scatter of swift-flying birds in the sky they stepped through the gap in the high hedge straight into Mr Ramsay, who boomed tragically at them: 'Someone had blundered!'

His eyes, glazed with emotion, defiant with tragic intensity, met theirs for a second, and trembled on the verge of recognition; but then, raising his hand halfway to his face as if to avert, to brush off, in an agony of peevish shame, their normal gaze, as if he begged them to withhold for a moment what he knew to be inevitable, as if he impressed upon them his own childlike resentment of interruption, yet even in the moment of discovery was not to be routed utterly, but was determined to hold fast to something of this delicious emotion, this impure rhapsody of which he was ashamed, but in which he revelled – he turned abruptly, slammed his private door on them; and, Lily Briscoe and Mr Bankes, looking uneasily up into the sky, observed that the flock of starlings which Jasper had routed with his gun had settled on the tops of the elm trees.

V

'And even if it isn't fine tomorrow,' said Mrs Ramsay, raising her eyes to glance at William Bankes and Lily Briscoe as they passed, 'it will be another day. And now,' she said, thinking that Lily's charm was her Chinese eyes, aslant in her white, puckered little face, but it would take a clever man to see it, 'and now stand up, and let me measure your leg,' for they might go to the Lighthouse after all, and she must see if the stocking did not need to be an inch or two longer in the leg.

Smiling, for an admirable idea had flashed upon her this very second – William and Lily should marry – she took the heather-mixture stocking, with its criss-cross of steel needles at the mouth of it, and measured it against James's leg.

'My dear, stand still,' she said, for in his jealousy, not liking to serve as measuring-block for the Lighthouse keeper's little boy, James fidgeted purposely; and if he did that, how could she see, was it too long, was it too short? she asked.

She looked up – what demon possessed him, her youngest, her cherished? – and saw the room, saw the chairs, thought them fearfully shabby. Their entrails, as Andrew said the other day, were all over the floor; but then what was the point, she asked herself, of buying good chairs to let them spoil up here all through the winter when the house, with only one old woman to see to it, positively dripped with wet? Never mind: the rent was precisely twopence halfpenny; the children loved it; it did her husband good to be three thousand, or if she must be accurate, three hundred miles from his library and his lectures and his disciples; and there was room for visitors. Mats, camp-beds, crazy ghosts of chairs and tables whose London life of service was done – they did well enough here; and a photograph or two, and books. Books, she thought, grew of themselves. She never had time to read them. Alas! even the books that had been given her, and inscribed by the hand of the poet himself: 'For her whose wishes must be obeyed' . . . 'The happier Helen of our days' . . . disgraceful to say, she had never read them. And Croom on the Mind and Bates on the Savage Customs of Polynesia ('My dear, stand still,' she said) – neither of those could one send to the Lighthouse. At a certain moment, she supposed, the house would become so shabby that something must be done. If they could be taught to wipe their feet and not bring the beach in with them – that would be something. Crabs, she had to allow, if Andrew really wished to dissect them, or if Jasper believed that one could make soup from seaweed, one could not prevent it; or Rose's objects – shells, reeds, stones; for they were gifted, her children, but all in quite different ways. And the result of it was, she sighed, taking in the whole room from floor to ceiling, as she held the stocking against James's leg, that things got shabbier and got shabbier summer after summer. The mat was fading; the wallpaper was flapping. You couldn't tell any more that those were roses on it. Still, if every door in a house is left perpetually open, and no lockmaker in the whole of Scotland can mend a bolt, things must spoil. What was the use of flinging a green Cashmere shawl over the edge of a picture frame? In two weeks it would be the colour of pea soup. But it was the doors that annoyed her; every door was left open. She listened. The drawing-room door was open; the hall door was open; it sounded as if the bedroom doors were open; and certainly the window on the landing was open for that she had opened herself. That windows should be open, and doors shut – simple as it was, could none of them remember it? She would go into the maids' bedrooms at night and find them sealed like ovens, except for Marie's, the Swiss girl, who would rather go without a bath than without fresh air, but then at home, she had said, 'the mountains are so beautiful'. She had said that last night looking out of the window with tears in her eyes. 'The mountains are so beautiful.' Her father was dying there, Mrs Ramsay knew. He was leaving them fatherless. Scolding and demonstrating (how to make a bed, how to open a window, with hands that shut and spread like a Frenchwoman's) all had folded itself quietly about her, when the girl spoke, as, after a flight through the sunshine the wings of a bird fold themselves quietly and the blue of its plumage changes from bright steel to soft purple. She had stood there silent for there was nothing to be said. He had cancer of the throat. At the recollection – how she had stood there, how the girl had said: 'At home the mountains are so beautiful,' and there was no hope, no hope whatever, she had a spasm of irritation, and speaking sharply said to James: 'Stand still. Don't be tiresome,' so that he knew instantly that her severity was real, and straightened his leg and she measured it.

The stocking was too short by half an inch at least, making allowance for the fact that Sorley's little boy would be less well grown than James.

'It's too short,' she said, 'ever so much too short.'

Never did anybody look so sad. Bitter and black, halfway down, in the darkness, in the shaft which ran from the sunlight to the depths, perhaps a tear formed; a tear fell; the waters swayed this way and that, received it, and were at rest. Never did anybody look so sad.

But was it nothing but looks? people said. What was there behind it – her beauty, her splendour? Had he blown his brains out, they asked, had he died the week before they were married – some other, earlier lover, of whom rumours reached one? Or was there nothing? nothing but an incomparable beauty which she lived behind, and could do nothing to disturb? For easily though she might have said at some moment of intimacy when stories of great passion – of love foiled, of ambition thwarted – came her way how she too had known or felt or been through it herself, she never spoke. She was silent always. She knew then – she knew without having learnt. Her simplicity fathomed what clever people falsified. Her singleness of mind made her drop plumb like a stone, alight exact as a bird, gave her, naturally, this swoop and fall of the spirit upon truth which delighted, eased, sustained – falsely perhaps.

('Nature has but little clay,' said Mr Bankes once, hearing her voice on the telephone, and much moved by it though she was only telling him a fact about a train, 'like that of which she moulded you.' He saw her at the end of the line, Greek, blue-eyed, straight-nosed How incongruous it seemed to be telephoning to a woman like that. The Graces assembling seemed to have joined hands in meadows of asphodel to compose that face. Yes, he would catch the 10.30 at Euston.

'But she's no more aware of her beauty than a child,' said Mr Bankes, replacing the receiver and crossing the room to see what progress the workmen were making with an hotel which they were building at the back of his house. And he thought of Mrs Ramsay as he looked at that stir among the unfinished walls. For always, he thought, there was something incongruous to be worked into the harmony of her face. She clapped a deerstalker's hat on her head; she ran across the lawn in goloshes to snatch a child from mischief. So that if it was her beauty merely that one thought of, one must remember the quivering thing, the living thing (they were carrying bricks up a little plank as he watched them), and work it into the picture; or if one thought of her simply as a woman, one must endow her with some freak of idiosyncrasy; or suppose some latent desire to doff her royalty of form as if her beauty bored her and all that men say of beauty, and she wanted only to be like other people, insignificant. He did not know. He did not know. He must go to his work.)

Knitting her reddish-brown hairy stocking, with her head outlined absurdly by the gilt frame, the green shawl which she had tossed over the edge of the frame, and the authenticated masterpiece by Michelangelo, Mrs Ramsay smoothed out what had been harsh in her manner a moment before, raised his head, and kissed her little boy on the forehead. 'Let's find another picture to cut out,' she said.

VI

But what had happened?

Someone had blundered.

Starting from her musing she gave meaning to words which she had held meaningless in her mind for a long stretch of time. 'Someone had blundered' – Fixing her short-sighted eyes upon her husband, who was now bearing down upon her, she gazed steadily until his closeness revealed to her (the jingle mated itself in her head) that something had happened, someone had blundered. But she could not for the life of her think what.

He shivered; he quivered. All his vanity, all his satisfaction in his own splendour, riding fell as a thunderbolt, fierce as a hawk at the head of his men through the valley of death, had been shattered, destroyed. Stormed at by shot and shell, boldly we rode and well, flashed through the valley of death, volleyed and thundered – straight into Lily Briscoe and William Bankes. He quivered; he shivered.

Not for the world would she have spoken to him, realising, from the familiar signs, his eyes averted, and some curious gathering together of his person, as if he wrapped himself about and needed privacy into which to regain his equilibrium, that he was outraged and anguished. She stroked James's head; she transferred to him what she felt for her husband, and, as she watched him chalk yellow the white dress shirt of a gentleman in the Army and Navy Stores catalogue, thought what a delight it would be to her should he turn out a great artist; and why should he not? He had a splendid forehead. Then, looking up, as her husband passed her once more, she was relieved to find that the ruin was veiled; domesticity triumphed; custom crooned its soothing rhythm, so that when stopping deliberately, as his turn came round again, at the window he bent quizzically and whimsically to tickle James's bare calf with a sprig of something, she twitted him for having dispatched 'that poor young man', Charles Tansley. Tansley had had to go in and write his dissertation, he said.

'James will have to write *his* dissertation one of these days,' he added ironically, flicking his sprig.

Hating his father, James brushed away the tickling spray with which in a manner peculiar to him, compound of severity and humour, he teased his youngest son's bare leg.

She was trying to get these tiresome stockings finished to send to Sorley's little boy tomorrow, said Mrs Ramsay.

There wasn't the slightest possible chance that they could go to the Lighthouse tomorrow, Mr Ramsay snapped out irascibly.

How did he know? she asked. The wind often changed.

The extraordinary irrationality of her remark, the folly of women's minds enraged him. He had ridden through the valley of death, been shattered and shivered; and now she flew in the face of facts, made his children hope what was utterly out of the question, in effect, told lies. He stamped his foot on the stone step. 'Damn you,' he said. But what had she said? Simply that it might be fine tomorrow. So it might.

Not with the barometer falling and the wind due west.

To pursue truth with such astonishing lack of consideration for other people's feelings, to rend the thin veils of civilisation so wantonly, so brutally, was to her so horrible an outrage of human decency that, without replying, dazed and blinded, she bent her head as if to let the pelt of jagged hail, the drench of dirty water, bespatter her unrebuked. There was nothing to be said.

He stood by her in silence. Very humbly, at length, he said that he would step over and ask the coastguards if she liked.

There was nobody whom she reverenced as she reverenced him.

She was quite ready to take his word for it, she said. Only then they need not cut sandwiches – that was all. They came to her, naturally, since she was a woman, all day long with this and that; one wanting this, another that; the children were growing up; she often felt she was nothing but a sponge sopped full of human emotions. Then he said, Damn you. He said, It must rain. He said, It won't rain; and instantly a heaven of security opened before her. There was nobody she reverenced more. She was not good enough to tie his shoe strings, she felt.

Already ashamed of that petulance, of that gesticulation of the hands when charging at the head of his troops, Mr Ramsay rather sheepishly prodded his son's bare legs once more, and then, as if he had her leave for it, with a movement which oddly reminded his wife of the great sea lion at the Zoo tumbling backwards after swallowing his fish and walloping off so that the water in the tank washes from side to side, he dived into the evening air which, already thinner, was taking the substance from leaves and hedges but, as if in return, restoring to roses and pinks a lustre which they had not had by day.

'Someone had blundered,' he said again, striding off, up and down the terrace.

But how extraordinarily his note had changed! It was like the cuckoo: 'in June he gets out of tune'; as if he were trying over, tentatively seeking, some phrase for a new mood, and having only this at hand, used it, cracked though it was. But it sounded ridiculous – 'Someone had blundered' – said like that, almost as a question, without any conviction, melodiously. Mrs Ramsay could not help smiling, and soon, sure enough, walking up and down, he hummed it, dropped it, fell silent.

He was safe, he was restored to his privacy. He stopped to light his pipe, looked once at his wife and son in the window, and as one raises one's eyes from a page in an express train and sees a farm, a tree, a cluster of cottages as an illustration, a confirmation of something on the printed page to which one returns, fortified and satisfied, so without his distinguishing either his son or his wife, the sight of them fortified him and satisfied him and consecrated his effort to arrive at a perfectly clear understanding of the problem which now engaged the energies of his splendid mind.

It was a splendid mind. For if thought is like the keyboard of a piano, divided into so many notes, or like the alphabet is ranged in twenty-six letters all in order, then his splendid mind had no sort of difficulty in running over those letters one by one, firmly and accurately, until it had reached, say, the letter Q. He reached Q. Very few people in the whole of England ever reach Q. Here, stopping for one moment by the stone urn which held the geraniums, he saw, but now far far away, like children picking up shells, divinely innocent and occupied with little trifles at their feet and somehow entirely defenceless against a doom which he perceived, his wife and son, together, in the window. They needed his protection; he gave it them. But after Q? What comes next? After Q there are a number of letters the last of which is scarcely visible to mortal eyes, but glimmers red in the distance. Z is only reached once by one man in a generation. Still, if he could reach R it would be something. Here at least was Q. He dug his heels in at Q. Q he was sure of. Q he could demonstrate. If Q then is Q – R . . . Here he knocked his pipe out, with two or three resonant taps on the ram's horn which made the handle of the urn, and proceeded. 'Then R . . . ' He braced himself. He clenched himself.

Qualities that would have saved a ship's company exposed on a broiling sea with six biscuits and a flask of water – endurance and justice, foresight, devotion, skill, came to his help. R is then – what is R?

A shutter, like the leathern eyelid of a lizard, flickered over the intensity of his gaze and obscured the letter R. In that flash of darkness he heard people saying – he was a failure – that R was beyond him. He would never reach R. On to R once more. R . . .

Qualities that in a desolate expedition across the icy solitudes of the Polar region would have made him the leader, the guide, the counsellor, whose temper, neither sanguine nor despondent, surveys with equanimity what is to be and faces it, came to his help again. R . . .

The lizard's eye flickered once more. The veins on his forehead bulged. The geranium in the urn became startlingly visible and, displayed among its leaves, he could see, without wishing it, that old, that obvious distinction between the two classes of men; on the one hand the steady goers of superhuman strength who, plodding and persevering, repeat the whole alphabet in order, twenty-six letters in all, from start to finish; on the other the gifted, the inspired who, miraculously, lump all the letters together in one flash – the way of genius. He had not genius; he laid no claim to that: but he had, or might have had, the power to repeat every letter of the alphabet from A to Z accurately in order. Meanwhile, he stuck at Q. On, then, on to R.

Feelings that would not have disgraced a leader who, now that the snow has begun to fall and the mountain-top is covered in mist, knows that he must lay himself down and die before morning comes, stole upon him, paling the colour of his eyes, giving him, even in the two minutes of his turn on the terrace, the bleached look of withered old age. Yet he would not die lying down; he would find some crag of rock, and there, his eyes fixed on the storm, trying to the end to pierce the darkness, he would die standing. He would never reach R.

He stood stock still, by the urn, with the geranium flowing over it. How many men in a thousand million, he asked himself, reach Z after all? Surely the leader of a forlorn hope may ask himself that, and answer, without treachery to the expedition behind him, 'One perhaps.' One in a generation. Is he to be blamed then if he is not that one? provided he has toiled honestly, given to the best of his power, till he has no more left to give? And his fame lasts how long? It is permissible even for a dying hero to think before he dies how men will speak of him hereafter. His fame lasts perhaps two thousand years. And what are two thousand years? (asked Mr Ramsay ironically, staring at the hedge). What, indeed, if you look from a mountain-top down the long wastes of the ages? The very stone one kicks with one's boot will outlast Shakespeare. His own little light would shine, not very brightly, for a year or two, and would then be merged in some bigger light, and that in a bigger still. (He looked into the darkness, into the intricacy of the twigs.) Who then could blame the leader of that forlorn party which after all has climbed high enough to see the waste of the years and the perishing of stars, if before death stiffens his limbs beyond the power of movement he does a little consciously raise his numbed fingers to his brow, and square his shoulders, so that when the search party comes they will find him dead at his post, the fine figure of a soldier? Mr Ramsay squared his shoulders and stood very upright by the urn.

Who shall blame him, if, so standing for a moment, he dwells upon fame, upon search parties, upon cairns raised by grateful followers over his bones? Finally, who shall blame the leader of the doomed expedition, if, having adventured to the uttermost, and used his strength wholly to the last ounce and fallen asleep not much caring if he wakes or not, he now perceives by some pricking in his toes that he lives, and does not on the whole object to live, but requires sympathy, and whisky, and someone to tell the story of his suffering to at once? Who shall blame him? Who will not secretly rejoice when the hero puts his armour off, and halts by the window and gazes at his wife and son, who very distant at first, gradually come closer and closer, till lips and book and head are clearly before him, though still lovely and unfamiliar from the intensity of his isolation and the waste of ages and the perishing of the stars, and finally putting his pipe in his pocket and bending his magnificent head before her – who will blame him if he does homage to the beauty of the world?

VII

But his son hated him. He hated him for coming up to them, for stopping and looking down on them; he hated him for interrupting them; he hated him for the exaltation and sublimity of his gestures; for the magnificence of his head; for his exactingness and egotism (for there he stood, commanding them to attend to him); but most of all he hated the twang and twitter of his father's emotion which, vibrating round them, disturbed the perfect simplicity and good sense of his relations with his mother. By looking fixedly at the page, he hoped to make him move on; by pointing his finger at a word, he hoped to recall his mother's attention, which, he knew angrily, wavered instantly his father stopped. But no. Nothing would make Mr Ramsay move on. There he stood, demanding sympathy.

Mrs Ramsay, who had been sitting loosely, folding her son in her arm, braced herself, and, half turning, seemed to raise herself with an effort, and at once to pour erect into the air a rain of energy, a column of spray, looking at the same time animated and alive as if all her energies were being fused into force, burning and illuminating (quietly though she sat, taking up her stocking again), and into this delicious fecundity, this fountain and spray of life, the fatal sterility of the male plunged itself, like a beak of brass, barren and bare. He wanted sympathy. He was a failure, he said. Mrs Ramsay flashed her needles. Mr Ramsay repeated, never taking his eyes from her face, that he was a failure. She blew the words back at him. 'Charles Tansley . . . ' she said. But he must have more than that. It was sympathy he wanted, to be assured of his genius, first of all, and then to be taken within the circle of life, warmed and soothed, to have his senses restored to him, his barrenness made fertile, and all the rooms of the house made full of life – the drawing-room; behind the drawing-room the kitchen; above the kitchen the bedrooms; and beyond them the nurseries; they must be furnished, they must be filled with life.

Charles Tansley thought him the greatest metaphysician of the time, she said. But he must have more than that. He must have sympathy. He must be assured that he too lived in the heart of life; was needed; not here only, but all over the world. Flashing her needles, confident, upright, she created drawing-room and kitchen, set them all aglow; bade him take his ease there, go in and out, enjoy himself. She laughed, she knitted. Standing between her knees, very stiff, James felt all her strength flaring up to be drunk and quenched by the beak of brass, the arid scimitar of the male, which smote mercilessly, again and again, demanding sympathy.

He was a failure, he repeated. Well, look then, feel then. Flashing her needles, glancing round about her, out of the window, into the room, at James himself, she assured him, beyond a shadow of a doubt, by her laugh, her poise, her competence (as a nurse carrying a light across a dark room assures a fractious child), that it was real; the house was full; the garden blowing. If he put implicit faith in her, nothing should hurt him; however deep he buried himself or climbed high, not for a second should he find himself without her. So boasting of her capacity to surround and protect, there was scarcely a shell of herself left for her to know herself by; all was so lavished and spent; and James, as he stood stiff between her knees, felt her rise in a rosy-flowered fruit tree laid with leaves and dancing boughs into which the beak of brass, the arid scimitar of his father, the egotistical man, plunged and smote, demanding sympathy.

Filled with her words, like a child who drops off satisfied, he said, at last, looking at her with humble gratitude, restored, renewed, that he would take a turn; he would watch the children playing cricket. He went.

Immediately, Mrs Ramsay seemed to fold herself together, one petal closed in another, and the whole fabric fell in exhaustion upon itself, so that she had only strength enough to move her finger, in exquisite abandonment to exhaustion, across the page of Grimm's fairy story, while there throbbed through her, like the pulse in a spring which has expanded to its full width and now gently ceases to beat, the rapture of successful creation.

Every throb of this pulse seemed, as he walked away, to enclose her and her husband, and to give to each that solace which two different notes, one high, one low, struck together, seem to give each other as they combine. Yet, as the resonance died, and she turned to the fairy tale again, Mrs Ramsay felt not only exhausted in body (afterwards, not at the time, she always felt this) but also there tinged her physical fatigue some faintly disagreeable sensation with another origin. Not that, as she read aloud the story of the Fisherman's Wife, she knew precisely what it came from; nor did she let herself put into words her dissatisfaction when she realised, at the turn of the page when she stopped and heard dully, ominously, a wave fall, how it came from this: she did not like, even for a second, to feel finer than her husband; and further, could not bear not being entirely sure, when she spoke to him, of the truth of what she said. Universities and people wanting him, lectures and books and their being of the highest importance – all that she did not doubt for a moment; but it was their relation, and his coming to her like that, openly, so that anyone could see, that discomposed her; for then people said he depended on her, when they must know that of the two he was infinitely the more important, and what she gave the world, in comparison with what he gave, negligible. But then again, it was the other thing too – not being able to tell him the truth, being afraid, for instance, about the greenhouse roof and the expense it would be, fifty pounds perhaps, to mend it; and then about his books, to be afraid that he might guess, what she a little suspected, that his last book was not quite his best book (she gathered that from William Bankes); and then to hide small daily things, and the children seeing it, and the burden it laid on them – all this diminished the entire joy, the pure joy, of the two notes sounding together, and let the sound die on her ear now with a dismal flatness.

A shadow was on the page; she looked up. It was Augustus Carmichael shuffling past, precisely now, at the very moment when it was painful to be reminded of the inadequacy of human relationships, that the most perfect was flawed, and could not bear the examination which, loving her husband, with her instinct for truth, she turned upon it; when it was painful to feel herself convicted of unworthiness, and impeded in her proper function by these lies, these exaggerations – it was at this moment, when she was fretted thus ignobly in the wake of her exaltation, that Mr Carmichael shuffled past, in his yellow slippers, and some demon in her made it necessary for her to call out, as he passed: 'Going indoors, Mr Carmichael?'

VIII

He said nothing. He took opium. The children said he had stained his beard yellow with it. Perhaps. What was obvious to her was that the poor man was unhappy, came to them every year as an escape; and yet every year, she felt the same thing; he did not trust her. She said: 'I am going to the town. Shall I get you stamps, paper, tobacco?' and she felt him wince. He did not trust her. It was his wife's doing. She remembered that iniquity of his wife's towards him, which had made her turn to steel and adamant there, in the horrid little room in St John's Wood, when with her own eyes she had seen that odious woman turn him out of the house. He was unkempt; he dropped things on his coat; he had the tiresomeness of an old man with nothing in the world to do; and she turned him out of the room. She said, in her odious way: 'Now, Mrs Ramsay and I want to have a little talk together,' and Mrs Ramsay could see, as if before her eyes, the innumerable miseries of his life. Had he money enough to buy tobacco? Did he have to ask her for it? half a crown? eighteen-pence? Oh, she could not bear to think of the little indignities she made him suffer. And always now (why, she could not guess, except that it came probably from that woman somehow) he shrank from her. He never told her anything. But what more could she have done? There was a sunny room given up to him. The children were good to him. Never did she show a sign of not wanting him. She went out of her way indeed to be friendly. Do you want stamps, do you want tobacco? Here's a book you might like and so on. And after all – after all (here insensibly she drew herself together, physically, the sense of her own beauty becoming, as it did so seldom, present to her) – after all, she had not generally any difficulty in making people like her; for instance, George Manning; Mr Wallace; famous as they were, they would come to her of an evening, quietly, and talk alone over her fire. She bore about with her, she could not help knowing it, the torch of her beauty; she carried it erect into any room that she entered; and after all, veil it as she might, and shrink from the monotony of bearing that it imposed on her, her beauty was apparent. She had been admired. She had been loved. She had entered rooms where mourners sat. Tears had flown in her presence. Men, and women too, letting go the multiplicity of things, had allowed themselves with her the relief of simplicity. It injured her that he should shrink. It hurt her. And yet not cleanly, not rightly. That was what she minded, coming as it did on top of her discontent with her husband; the sense she had now when Mr Carmichael shuffled past, just nodding to her question, with a book beneath his arm, in his yellow slippers, that she was suspected; and that all this desire of hers to give, to help, was vanity. For her own self-satisfaction was it that she wished so instinctively to help, to give, that people might say of her: 'O Mrs Ramsay! dear Mrs Ramsay . . . Mrs Ramsay, of course!' and need her and send for her and admire her? Was it not secretly this that she wanted, and therefore when Mr Carmichael shrank away from her, as he did at this moment, making off to some corner where he did acrostics endlessly, she did not feel merely snubbed back in her instinct, but made aware of the pettiness of some part of her, and of human relations, how flawed they are, how despicable, how self-seeking, at their best. Shabby and worn out, and not presumably (her cheeks were hollow, her hair was white) any longer a sight that filled the eyes with joy, she had better devote her mind to the story of the Fisherman and his Wife and so pacify that bundle of sensitiveness (none of her children was as sensitive as he was) her son James.

'The man's heart grew heavy,' she read aloud, 'and he would not go. He said to himself: "It is not right," and yet he went. And when he came to the sea the water was quite purple and dark blue, and grey and thick, and no longer so green and yellow, but it was still quiet. And he stood there and said – '

Mrs Ramsay could have wished that her husband had not chosen that moment to stop. Why had he not gone as he said to watch the children playing cricket? But he did not speak; he looked; he nodded; he approved; he went on. He slipped, seeing before him that hedge which had over and over again rounded some pause, signified some conclusion, seeing his wife and child, seeing again the urns with the trailing red geraniums which had so often decorated processes of thought, and bore, written up among their leaves, as if they were scraps of paper on which one scribbles notes in the rush of reading – he slipped, seeing all this, smoothly into speculation

SELECTED WORKS OF VIRGINIA WOOLF

suggested by an article in *The Times* about the number of Americans who visit Shakespeare's house every year. If Shakespeare had never existed, he asked, would the world have differed much from what it is today? Does the progress of civilisation depend upon great men? Is the lot of the average human being better now than in the time of the Pharaohs? Is the lot of the average human being, however, he asked himself, the criterion by which we judge the measure of civilisation? Possibly not. Possibly the greatest good requires the existence of a slave class. The liftman in the tube is an eternal necessity. The thought was distasteful to him. He tossed his head. To avoid it, he would find some way of snubbing the predominance of the arts. He would argue that the world exists for the average human being; that the arts are merely a decoration imposed on the top of human life; they do not express it. Nor is Shakespeare necessary to it. Not knowing precisely why it was that he wanted to disparage Shakespeare and come to the rescue of the man who stands eternally in the door of the lift, he picked a leaf sharply from the hedge. All this would have to be dished up for the young men at Cardiff next month, he thought; here, on his terrace, he was merely foraging and picnicking (he threw away the leaf that he had picked so peevishly), like a man who reaches from his horse to pick a bunch of roses, or stuffs his pockets with nuts as he ambles at his ease through the lanes and fields of a country known to him from boyhood. It was all familiar; this turning, that stile, that cut across the fields. Hours he would spend thus, with his pipe, of an evening, thinking up and down and in and out of the old familiar lanes and commons, which were all stuck about with the history of that campaign there, the life of this statesman here, with poems and with anecdotes, with figures too, this thinker, that soldier; all very brisk and clear; but at length the lane, the field, the common, the fruitful nut tree and the flowering hedge led him on to that further turn of the road where he dismounted always, tied his horse to a tree, and proceeded on foot alone. He reached the edge of the lawn and looked out on the bay beneath.

It was his fate, his peculiarity, whether he wished it or not, to come out thus on a spit of land which the sea is slowly eating away, and there to stand, like a desolate sea-bird, alone. It was his power, his gift, suddenly to shed all superfluities, to shrink and diminish so that he looked barer and felt sparer, even physically, yet lost none of his intensity of mind, and so to stand on his little ledge facing the dark of human ignorance, how we know nothing and the sea eats away the ground we stand on – that was his fate, his gift. But having thrown away, when he dismounted, all gestures and fripperies, all trophies of nuts and roses, and shrunk so that not only fame but even his own namë was forgotten by him, he kept even in that desolation a vigilance which spared no phantom and luxuriated in no vision, and it was in this guise that he inspired in William Bankes (intermittently) and in Charles Tansley (obsequiously) and in his wife now, when she looked up and saw him standing at the edge of the lawn, profound reverence, and pity, and gratitude too, as a stake driven into the bed of a channel upon which the gulls perch and the waves beat inspires in merry boatloads a feeling of gratitude for the duty it has taken upon itself of marking the channel out there in the floods alone.

'But the father of eight children has no choice . . . ' Muttering half aloud, so he broke off, turned, sighed, raised his eyes, sought the figure of his wife reading stories to the little boy; filled his pipe. He turned from the sight of human ignorance and human fate and the sea eating the ground we stand on, which, had he been able to contemplate it fixedly might have led to something; and found consolation in trifles so slight compared with the august theme just now before him that he was disposed to slur that comfort over, to deprecate it, as if to be caught happy in a world of misery was for an honest man the most despicable of crimes. It was true; he was for the most part happy; he had his wife; he had his children; he had promised in six weeks' time to talk 'some nonsense' to the young men of Cardiff about Locke, Hume, Berkeley, and the causes of the French Revolution. But this and his pleasure in it, in the phrases he made, in the ardour of youth, in his wife's beauty, in the tributes that reached him from Swansea, Cardiff, Exeter, Southampton, Kidderminster, Oxford, Cambridge – all had to be deprecated and concealed under the phrase 'talking nonsense', because, in effect, he had not done the thing he might have done. It was a disguise; it was the refuge of a man afraid to own his own feelings, who could not say, This is what I like – this is what I am; and rather pitiable and distasteful to William Bankes and Lily Briscoe, who wondered why such concealments should be necessary; why he needed always praise; why so brave a man in thought should be so timid in life; how strangely he was venerable and laughable at one and the same time.

Teaching and preaching is beyond human power, Lily suspected. (She was putting away her things.) If you are exalted you must somehow come a cropper. Mrs Ramsay gave him what he asked too easily. Then the change must be so upsetting, Lily said. He comes in from his books and finds us all playing games and talking nonsense. Imagine what a change from the things he thinks about, she said.

He was bearing down upon them. Now he stopped dead and stood looking in silence at the sea. Now he had turned away again.

IX

Yes, Mr Bankes said, watching him go. It was a thousand pities. (Lily had said something about his frightening her – he changed from one mood to another so suddenly.) Yes, said Mr Bankes, it was a thousand pities that Ramsay could not behave a little more like other people. (For he liked Lily Briscoe; he could discuss Ramsay with her quite openly.) It was for that reason, he said, that the young don't read Carlyle. A crusty old grumbler who lost his temper if the porridge was cold, why should he preach to us? was what Mr Bankes understood that young people said nowadays. It was a thousand pities if you thought, as he did, that Carlyle was one of the great teachers of mankind. Lily was ashamed to say that she had not read Carlyle since she was at school. But in her opinion one liked Mr Ramsay all the better for thinking that if his little finger ached the whole world must come to an end. It was not *that* she minded. For who could be deceived by him? He asked you quite openly to flatter him, to admire him, his little dodges deceived nobody. What she disliked was his narrowness, his blindness, she said, looking after him.

'A bit of a hypocrite?' Mr Bankes suggested, looking, too, at Mr Ramsay's back, for was he not thinking of his friendship, and of Cam refusing to give him a flower, and of all those boys and girls, and his own house, full of comfort, but, since his wife's death, quiet rather? Of course, he had his work . . . All the same, he rather wished Lily to agree that Ramsay was, as he said, 'a bit of a hypocrite'.

Lily Briscoe went on putting away her brushes, looking up, looking down. Looking up, there he was – Mr Ramsay – advancing towards them, swinging, careless, oblivious, remote. A bit of a hypocrite? she repeated. Oh no – the most sincere of men, the truest (here he was), the best; but, looking down, she thought, he is absorbed in himself, he is tyrannical, he is unjust; and kept looking down, purposely, for only so could she keep steady, staying with the Ramsays. Directly one looked up and saw them, what she called 'being in love' flooded them. They became part of that unreal but penetrating and exciting universe which is the world seen through the eyes of love. The sky stuck to them; the birds sang through them. And, what was even more exciting, she felt, too, as she saw Mr Ramsay bearing down and retreating, and Mrs Ramsay sitting with James in the window and the cloud moving and the tree bending, how life, from being made up of little separate incidents which one lived one by one, became curled and whole like a wave which bore one up with it and threw one down with it, there, with a dash on the beach.

Mr Bankes expected her to answer. And she was about to say something criticising Mrs Ramsay, how she was alarming, too, in her way, high-handed, or words to that effect, when Mr Bankes made it entirely unnecessary for her to speak by his rapture. For such it was considering his age, turned sixty, and his cleanliness and his impersonality, and the white scientific coat which seemed to clothe him. For him to gaze as Lily saw him gazing at Mrs Ramsay was a rapture, equivalent, Lily felt, to the loves of dozens of young men (and perhaps Mrs Ramsay had never excited the loves of dozens of young men). It was love, she thought, pretending to move her canvas, distilled and filtered; love that never attempted to clutch its object; but, like the love which mathematicians bear their symbols, or poets their phrases, was meant to be spread over the world and become part of the human gain. So it was indeed.

The world by all means should have shared it, could Mr Bankes have said why that woman pleased him so; why the sight of her reading a fairy tale to her boy had upon him precisely the same effect as the solution of a scientific problem, so that he rested in contemplation of it, and felt, as he felt when he had proved something absolute about the digestive system of plants, that barbarity was tamed, the reign of chaos subdued.

Such a rapture – for by what other name could one call it? – made Lily Briscoe forget entirely what she had been about to say. It was nothing of importance; something about Mrs Ramsay. It paled beside this 'rapture', this silent stare, for which she felt intense gratitude; for nothing so solaced her, eased her of the perplexity of life, and miraculously raised its burdens, as this sublime power, this heavenly gift, and one would no more disturb it, while it lasted, than break up the shaft of sunlight lying level across the floor.

That people should love like this, that Mr Bankes should feel this for Mrs Ramsay (she glanced at him musing) was helpful, was exalting. She wiped one brush after another upon a piece of old rag, menially, on purpose. She took shelter from the reverence which covered all women; she felt herself praised. Let him gaze; she would steal a look at her picture.

She could have wept. It was bad, it was bad, it was infinitely bad! She could have done it differently of course; the colour could have been thinned and faded; the shapes etherealised; that was how Paunceforte would have seen it. But then she did not see it like that. She saw the colour burning on a framework of steel; the light of a butterfly's wing lying upon the arches of a cathedral. Of all that only a few random marks scrawled upon the canvas remained. And it would never be seen; never be hung even, and there was Mr Tansley whispering in her ear, 'Women can't paint, women can't write . . . '

She now remembered what she had been going to say about Mrs Ramsay. She did not know how she would have put it; but it would have been something critical. She had been annoyed the other night by some high-handedness. Looking along the level of Mr Bankes's glance at her, she thought that no woman could worship another woman in the way he worshipped; they could only seek shelter under the shade which Mr Bankes extended over them both. Looking along his beam she added to it her different ray, thinking that she was unquestionably the loveliest of people (bowed over her book); the best perhaps; but also, different too from the perfect shape which one saw there. But why different, and how different? she asked herself, scraping her palette of all those mounds of blue and green which seemed to her like clods with no life in them now, yet she vowed, she would inspire them, force them to move, flow, do her bidding tomorrow. How did she differ? What was the spirit in her, the essential thing, by which, had you found a glove in the corner of a sofa, you would have known it, from its twisted finger, hers indisputably? She was like a bird for speed, an arrow for directness. She was wilful; she was commanding (of course,

Lily reminded herself, I am thinking of her relations with women, and I am much younger, an insignificant person, living off the Brompton Road). She opened bedroom windows. She shut doors. (So she tried to start the tune of Mrs Ramsay in her head.) Arriving late at night, with a light tap on one's bedroom door, wrapped in an old fur coat (for the setting of her beauty was always that – hasty, but apt), she would enact again whatever it might be – Charles Tansley losing his umbrella; Mr Carmichael snuffling and sniffing; Mr Bankes saying, 'the vegetable salts are lost'. All this she would adroitly shape; even maliciously twist; and, moving over to the window, in pretence that she must go – it was dawn, she could see the sun rising – half turn back, more intimately, but still always laughing, insist that she must, Minta must, they all must marry, since in the whole world, whatever laurels might be tossed to her (but Mrs Ramsay cared not a fig for her painting), or triumphs won by her (probably Mrs Ramsay had had her share of those), and here she saddened, darkened, and came back to her chair, there could be no disputing this: an unmarried woman (she lightly took her hand for a moment), an unmarried woman has missed the best of life. The house seemed full of children sleeping and Mrs Ramsay listening; of shaded lights and regular breathing.

Oh but, Lily would say, there was her father; her home; even, had she dared to say it, her painting. But all this seemed so little, so virginal, against the other. Yet, as the night wore on, and white lights parted the curtains, and even now and then some bird chirped in the garden, gathering a desperate courage she would urge her own exemption from the universal law; plead for it; she liked to be alone; she liked to be herself; she was not made for that; and so have to meet a serious stare from eyes of unparalleled depth, and confront Mrs Ramsay's simple certainty (and she was childlike now) that her dear Lily, her little Brisk, was a fool. Then, she remembered, she had laid her head on Mrs Ramsay's lap and laughed and laughed and laughed, laughed almost hysterically at the thought of Mrs Ramsay presiding with immutable calm over destinies which she completely failed to understand. There she sat, simple, serious. She had recovered her sense of her now – this was the glove's twisted finger. But into what sanctuary had one penetrated? Lily Briscoe had looked up at last, and there was Mrs Ramsay, unwitting entirely what had caused her laughter, still presiding, but now with every trace of wilfulness abolished, and in its stead, something clear as the space which the clouds at last uncover – the little space of sky which sleeps beside the moon.

Was it wisdom? Was it knowledge? Was it, once more, the deceptiveness of beauty, so that all one's perceptions, halfway to truth, were tangled in a golden mesh? or did she lock up within her some secret which certainly Lily Briscoe believed people must have for the world to go on at all? Everyone could not be as helter skelter, hand to mouth as she was. But if they knew, could they tell one what they knew? Sitting on the floor with her arms round

Mrs Ramsay's knees, close as she could get, smiling to think that Mrs Ramsay would never know the reason of that pressure, she imagined how in the chambers of the mind and heart of the woman who was, physically, touching her, were stood, like the treasures in the tombs of kings, tablets bearing sacred inscriptions, which if one could spell them out would teach one everything, but they would never be offered openly, never made public. What art was there, known to love or cunning, by which one pressed through into those secret chambers? What device for becoming, like waters poured into one jar, inextricably the same, one with the object one adored? Could the body achieve it, or the mind, subtly mingling in the intricate passages of the brain? or the heart? Could loving, as people called it, make her and Mrs Ramsay one? for it was not knowledge but unity that she desired, not inscriptions on tablets, nothing that could be written in any language known to men, but intimacy itself, which is knowledge, she had thought, leaning her head on Mrs Ramsay's knee.

Nothing happened. Nothing! Nothing! as she leant her head against Mrs Ramsay's knee. And yet, she knew knowledge and wisdom were stored in Mrs Ramsay's heart. How then, she had asked herself, did one know one thing or another thing about people, sealed as they were? Only like a bee, drawn by some sweetness or sharpness in the air intangible to touch or taste, one haunted the dome-shaped hive, ranged the wastes of the air over the countries of the world alone, and then haunted the hives with their murmurs and their stirrings; the hives which were people. Mrs Ramsay rose. Lily rose. Mrs Ramsay went. For days there hung about her, as after a dream some subtle change is felt in the person one has dreamt of, more vividly than anything she said, the sound of murmuring and, as she sat in the wicker armchair in the drawing-room window she wore, to Lily's eyes, an august shape; the shape of a dome.

This ray passed level with Mr Bankes's ray straight to Mrs Ramsay sitting reading there with James at her knee. But now while she still looked, Mr Bankes had done. He had put on his spectacles. He had stepped back. He had raised his hand. He had slightly narrowed his clear blue eyes, when Lily, rousing herself, saw what he was at, and winced like a dog who sees a hand raised to strike it. She would have snatched her picture off the easel, but she said to herself, One must. She braced herself to stand the awful trial of someone looking at her picture. One must, she said, one must. And if it must be seen, Mr Bankes was less alarming than another. But that any other eyes should see the residue of her thirty-three years, the deposit of each day's living, mixed with something more secret than she had ever spoken or shown in the course of all those days was an agony. At the same time it was immensely exciting.

Nothing could be cooler and quieter. Taking out a penknife, Mr Bankes tapped the canvas with the bone handle. What did she wish to indicate by the triangular purple shape, 'just there?' he asked.

It was Mrs Ramsay reading to James, she said. She knew his objection – that no one could tell it for a human shape. But she had made no attempt at likeness, she said. For what reason had she introduced them then? he asked. Why indeed? – except that if there, in that corner, it was bright, here, in this, she felt the need of darkness. Simple, obvious, commonplace, as it was, Mr Bankes was interested. Mother and child then – objects of universal veneration, and in this case the mother was famous for her beauty – might be reduced, he pondered, to a purple shadow without irreverence.

But the picture was not of them, she said. Or, not in his sense. There were other senses, too, in which one might reverence them. By a shadow here and a light there, for instance. Her tribute took that form, if, as she vaguely supposed, a picture must be a tribute. A mother and child might be reduced to a shadow without irreverence. A light here required a shadow there. He considered. He was interested. He took it scientifically in complete good faith. The truth was that all his prejudices were on the other side, he explained. The largest picture in his drawing-room, which painters had praised, and valued at a higher price than he had given for it, was of the cherry trees in blossom on the banks of the Kennet. He had spent his honeymoon on the banks of the Kennet, he said. Lily must come and see that picture, he said. But now – he turned, with his glasses raised to the scientific examination of her canvas. The question being one of the relations of masses, of lights and shadows, which, to be honest, he had never considered before, he would like to have it explained – what then did she wish to make of it? And he indicated the scene before them. She looked. She could not show him what she wished to make of it, could not see it even herself, without a brush in her hand. She took up once more her old painting position with the dim eyes and the absent-minded manner, subduing all her impressions as a woman to some-thing much more general; becoming once more under the power of that vision which she had seen clearly once and must now grope for among hedges and houses and mothers and children – her picture. It was a question, she remembered, how to connect this mass on the right hand with that on the left. She might do it by bringing the line of the branch across so; or break the vacancy in the foreground by an object (James perhaps) so. But the danger was that by doing that the unity of the whole might be broken. She stopped; she did not want to bore him; she took the canvas lightly off the easel.

But it had been seen; it had been taken from her. This man had shared with her something profoundly intimate. And, thanking Mr Ramsay for it and Mrs Ramsay for it and the hour and the place, crediting the world with a power which she had not suspected, that one could walk away down that long gallery not alone any more but arm in arm with somebody – the strangest feeling in the world, and the most exhilarating – she nicked the catch of her paintbox to, more firmly than was necessary, and the nick seemed to surround in a circle for ever the paintbox, the lawn, Mr Bankes, and that wild villain, Cam, dashing past.

X

For Cam grazed the easel by an inch; she would not stop for Mr Bankes and Lily Briscoe; though Mr Bankes, who would have liked a daughter of his own, held out his hand; she would not stop for her father, whom she grazed also by an inch; nor for her mother, who called, 'Cam! I want you a moment!' as she dashed past. She was off like a bird, bullet, or arrow, impelled by what desire, shot by whom, at what directed, who could say? What, what? Mrs Ramsay pondered, watching her. It might be a vision – of a shell, of a wheelbarrow, of a fairy kingdom on the far side of the hedge; or it might be the glory of speed; no one knew. But when Mrs Ramsay called, 'Cam!' a second time, the projectile dropped in mid career, and Cam came lagging back, pulling a leaf by the way, to her mother.

What was she dreaming about, Mrs Ramsay wondered, seeing her engrossed, as she stood there, with some thought of her own, so that she had to repeat the message twice – ask Mildred if Andrew, Miss Doyle and Mr Rayley have come back? – The words seemed to be dropped into a well, where, if the waters were clear, they were also so extraordinarily distorting that, even as they descended, one saw them twisting about to make heaven knows what pattern on the floor of the child's mind. What message would Cam give the cook? Mrs Ramsay wondered. And indeed it was only by waiting patiently, and hearing that there was an old woman in the kitchen with very red cheeks, drinking soup out of a basin, that Mrs Ramsay at last prompted that parrotlike instinct which had picked up Mildred's words quite accurately and could now produce them, if one waited, in a colourless singsong. Shifting from foot to foot, Cam repeated the words: 'No, they haven't, and I've told Ellen to clear away tea.'

Minta Doyle and Paul Rayley had not come back then. That could only mean, Mrs Ramsay thought, one thing. She must accept him or she must refuse him. This going off after luncheon for a walk, even though Andrew was with them – what could it mean? except that she had decided, rightly, Mrs Ramsay thought (and she was very, very fond of Minta), to accept that good fellow, who might not be brilliant, but then, thought Mrs Ramsay, realising that James was tugging at her to make her go on reading aloud the Fisherman and his Wife, she did in her own heart infinitely prefer boobies to clever men who wrote dissertations; Charles Tansley for instance. Anyhow it must have happened, one way or the other, by now.

But she read: 'Next morning the wife awoke first, and it was just daybreak, and from her bed she saw the beautiful country lying before her. Her husband was still stretching himself . . . '

But how could Minta say now that she would not have him? Not if she agreed to spend whole afternoons trapesing about the country alone – for

Andrew would be off after his crabs – but possibly Nancy was with them. She tried to recall the sight of them standing at the hall door after lunch. There they stood, looking at the sky, wondering about the weather, and she had said, thinking partly to cover their shyness, partly to encourage them to be off (for her sympathies were with Paul): 'There isn't a cloud anywhere within miles,' at which she could feel little Charles Tansley, who had followed them out, snigger. But she did it on purpose. Whether Nancy was there or not, she could not be certain, looking from one to the other in her mind's eye.

She read on: ' "Ah, wife," said the man, "why should we be King? I do not want to be King." "Well," said the wife, "if you won't be King, I will; go to the Flounder, for I will be King." '

'Come in or go out, Cam,' she said, knowing that Cam was attracted only by the word 'Flounder' and that in a moment she would fidget and fight with James as usual. Cam shot off. Mrs Ramsay went on reading, relieved, for she and James shared the same tastes and were comfortable together.

'And when he came to the sea it was quite dark grey, and the water heaved up from below, and smelt putrid. Then he went and stood by it and said:

> "Flounder, flounder, in the sea,
> Come, I pray thee, here to me;
> For my wife, good Ilsabil,
> Wills not as I'd have her will."

' "Well, what does she want then?" said the Flounder.' And where were they now? Mrs Ramsay wondered, reading and thinking, quite easily, both at the same time; for the story of the Fisherman and his Wife was like the bass gently accompanying a tune, which now and then ran up unexpectedly into the melody. And when should she be told? If nothing happened she would have to speak seriously to Minta. For she could not go trapesing about all over the country, even if Nancy were with them (she tried again, unsuccessfully, to visualise their backs going down the path, and to count them). She was responsible to Minta's parents – the Owl and the Poker. Her nicknames for them shot into her mind as she read. The Owl and the Poker – yes, they would be annoyed if they heard – and they were certain to hear – that Minta, staying with the Ramsays, had been seen etcetera, etcetera, etcetera. 'He wore a wig in the House of Commons and she ably assisted him at the head of the stairs,' she repeated, fishing them up out of her mind by a phrase which, coming back from some party, she had made to amuse her husband. Dear, dear, Mrs Ramsay said to herself, how did they produce this incongruous daughter? this tomboy Minta, with a hole in her stocking? How did she exist in that portentous atmosphere where the maid was always removing in a dustpan the sand that the parrot had scattered, and conversation was almost entirely reduced to the exploits – interesting perhaps, but limited after all – of that bird? Naturally, one had asked her to lunch, tea, dinner, finally to stay with them up at Finlay, which had resulted in some friction with the Owl, her mother, and more calling, and more conversation, and more sand, and really at the end of it, she had told enough lies about parrots to last her a lifetime (so she had said to her husband that night, coming back from the party). However, Minta came . . . Yes, she came, Mrs Ramsay thought, suspecting some thorn in the tangle of this thought; and disengaging it found it to be this: a woman had once accused her of 'robbing her of her daughter's affections'; some-thing Mrs Doyle had said made her remember that charge again. Wishing to dominate, wishing to interfere, making people do what she wished – that was the charge against her, and she thought it most unjust. How could she help being 'like that' to look at? No one could accuse her of taking pains to impress. She was often ashamed of her own shabbiness. Nor was she domineering, nor was she tyrannical. It was more true about hospitals and drains and the dairy. About things like that she did feel passionately, and would, if she had had the chance, have liked to take people by the scruff of their necks and make them see. No hospital on the whole island. It was a disgrace. Milk delivered at your door in London positively brown with dirt. It should be made illegal. A model dairy and a hospital up here – those two things she would have liked to do, herself. But how? With all these children? When they were older, then perhaps she would have time; when they were all at school.

Oh, but she never wanted James to grow a day older or Cam either. These two she would have liked to keep for ever just as they were, demons of wickedness, angels of delight, never to see them grow up into long-legged monsters. Nothing made up for the loss. When she read just now to James, 'and there were numbers of soldiers with kettledrums and trumpets,' and his eyes darkened, she thought, why should they grow up, and lose all that? He was the most gifted, the most sensitive of her children. But all, she thought, were full of promise. Prue, a perfect angel with the others, and sometimes now, at night especially, she took one's breath away with her beauty. Andrew – even her husband admitted that his gift for mathematics was extraordinary. And Nancy and Roger, they were both wild creatures now, scampering about over the country all day long. As for Rose, her mouth was too big, but she had a wonderful gift with her hands. If they had charades Rose made the dresses; made everything; liked best arranging tables, flowers, anything. She did not like it that Jasper should shoot birds; but it was only a stage; they all went through stages. Why, she asked, pressing her chin on James's head, should they grow up so fast? Why should they go to school? She would have liked always to have had a baby. She was happiest carrying one in her arms. Then people might say she was tyrannical, domineering, masterful, if they chose; she did not mind. And, touching his hair with her lips, she thought, he will never be so happy again, but stopped herself, remembering how it angered her husband that she should say that. Still, it was true. They were happier now than they would ever be again. A tenpenny tea-set made Cam happy for days. She heard them stamping and crowing on the floor above her head the moment they woke. They came bustling along the passage. Then the door sprang open and in they came, fresh as roses, staring, wide awake, as if this coming into the dining-room after breakfast, which they did every day of their lives, was a positive event to them; and so on, with one thing after another, all day long, until she went up to say good-night to them, and found them netted in their cots like birds among cherries and raspberries still making up stories about some little bit of rubbish – something they had heard, something they had picked up in the garden. They had all their little treasures . . . And so she went down and said to her husband, Why must they grow up and lose it all? Never will they be so happy again. And he was angry. Why take such a gloomy view of life? he said. It is not sensible. For it was odd; and she believed it to be true; that with all his gloom and desperation he was happier, more hopeful on the whole, than she was. Less exposed to human worries – perhaps that was it. He had always his work to fall back on. Not that she herself was 'pessimistic', as he accused her of being. Only she thought life – and a little strip of time presented itself to her eyes, her fifty years. There it was before her – life. Life: she thought but she did not finish her thought. She took a look at life, for she had a clear sense of it there, something real, something private, which she shared neither with her children nor with her husband. A sort of transaction went on between them, in which she was on one side, and life was on another, and she was always trying to get the better of it, as it was of her and sometimes they parleyed (when she sat alone); there were, she remembered, great reconciliation scenes; but for the most part, oddly enough, she must admit that she felt this thing that she called life terrible, hostile, and quick to pounce on you if you gave it a chance. There were the eternal problems: suffering; death; the poor. There was always a woman dying of cancer even here. And yet she had said to all these children: You shall go through with it. To eight people she had said relentlessly that (and the bill for the greenhouse would be fifty pounds). For that reason, knowing what was before them – love and ambition and being wretched alone in dreary places – she had often the feeling: Why must they grow up and lose it all? And then she said to herself, brandishing her sword at life, nonsense. They will be perfectly happy. And here she was, she reflected, feeling life rather sinister again, making Minta marry Paul Rayley; because whatever she might feel about her own transaction, and she had had experiences which need not happen to everyone (she did not name them to herself), she was driven on, too quickly she knew, almost as if it were an escape for her too, to say that people must marry; people must have children.

Was she wrong in this, she asked herself, reviewing her conduct for the past week or two, and wondering if she had indeed put any pressure upon Minta, who was only twenty-four, to make up her mind. She was uneasy.

Had she not laughed about it? Was she not forgetting again how strongly she influenced people? Marriage needed – oh all sorts of qualities (the bill for the greenhouse would be fifty pounds); one – she need not name it – that was essential; the thing she had with her husband. Had they that?

'Then he put on his trousers and ran away like a madman,' she read. 'But outside a great storm was raging and blowing so hard that he could scarcely keep his feet; houses and trees toppled over, the mountains trembled, rocks rolled into the sea, the sky was pitch black, and it thundered and lightened, and the sea came in with black waves as high as church towers and mountains, and all with white foam at the top.'

She turned the page; there were only a few lines more, so that she would finish the story, though it was past bedtime. It was getting late. The light in the garden told her that; and the whitening of the flowers and something grey in the leaves conspired together to rouse in her a feeling of anxiety. What it was about she could not think at first. Then she remembered: Paul and Minta and Andrew had not come back. She summoned before her again the little group on the terrace in front of the hall door, standing looking up into the sky. Andrew had his net and basket. That meant he was going to catch crabs and things. That meant he would climb out on to a rock; he would be cut off. Or coming back single file on one of those little paths above the cliff one of them might slip. He would roll and then crash. It was growing quite dark.

But she did not let her voice change in the least as she finished the story, and added, shutting the book, and speaking the last words as if she had made them up herself, looking into James's eyes: 'And there they are living still at this very time.

'And that's the end,' she said, and she saw in his eyes, as the interest of the story died away in them, something else take its place; something wondering, pale, like the reflection of a light, which at once made him gaze and marvel. Turning, she looked across the bay, and there, sure enough, coming regularly across the waves, first two quick strokes and then one long steady stroke, was the light of the Lighthouse. It had been lit.

In a moment he would ask her: 'Are we going to the Lighthouse?' And she would have to say: 'No: not tomorrow; your father says not.' Happily, Mildred came in to fetch them, and the bustle distracted them. But he kept looking back over his shoulder as Mildred carried him out, and she was certain that he was thinking, we are not going to the Lighthouse tomorrow; and she thought, he will remember that all his life.

XI

No, she thought, putting together some of the pictures he had cut out – a refrigerator, a mowing machine, a gentleman in evening dress – children never forget. For this reason it was so important what one said, and what one did, and it was a relief when they went to bed. For now she need not think about anybody. She could be herself, by herself. And that was what now she often felt the need of – to think; well not even to think. To be silent; to be alone. All the being and the doing, expansive, glittering, vocal, evaporated; and one shrunk, with a sense of solemnity, to being oneself, a wedge-shaped core of darkness, something invisible to others. Although she continued to knit, and sat upright, it was thus that she felt herself; and this self having shed its attachments was free for the strangest adventures. When life sank down for a moment, the range of experience seemed limitless. And to everybody there was always this sense of unlimited resources, she supposed; one after another, she, Lily, Augustus Carmichael, must feel, our apparitions, the things you know us by, are simply childish. Beneath it is all dark, it is all spreading, it is unfathomably deep; but now and again we rise to the surface and that is what you see us by. Her horizon seemed to her limitless. There were all the places she had not seen; the Indian plains; she felt herself pushing aside the thick leather curtain of a church in Rome. This core of darkness could go anywhere, for no one saw it. They could not stop it, she thought, exulting. There was freedom, there was peace, there was, most welcome of all, a summoning together, a resting on a platform of stability. Not as oneself did one find rest ever, in her experience (she accomplished here something dexterous with her needles), but as a wedge of darkness. Losing personality, one lost the fret, the hurry, the stir; and there rose to her lips always some exclamation of triumph over life when things came together in this peace, this rest, this eternity; and pausing there she looked out to meet that stroke of the Lighthouse, the long steady stroke, the last of the three, which was her stroke, for watching them in this mood always at this hour one could not help attaching oneself to one thing especially of the things one saw; and this thing, the long steady stroke, was her stroke. Often she found herself sitting and looking, sitting and looking, with her work in her hands until she became the thing she looked at – that light for example. And it would lift up on it some little phrase or other which had been lying in her mind like that – 'Children don't forget, children don't forget' – which she would repeat and begin adding to it, It will end, It will end, she said. It will come, it will come, when suddenly she added: We are in the hands of the Lord.

But instantly she was annoyed with herself for saying that. Who had said it? not she; she had been trapped into saying something she did not mean. She looked up over her knitting and met the third stroke and it seemed to her like her own eyes meeting her own eyes, searching as she alone could search into her mind and her heart, purifying out of existence that lie, any lie. She praised herself in praising the light, without vanity, for she was stern, she was searching, she was beautiful like that light. It was odd, she thought, how if one was alone, one leant to things, inanimate things; trees, streams, flowers; felt they expressed one; felt they became one; felt they knew one, in a sense were one; felt an irrational tenderness thus (she looked at that long steady light) as for oneself. There rose, and she looked and looked with her needles suspended, there curled up off the floor of the mind, rose from the lake of one's being, a mist, a bride to meet her lover.

What brought her to say that: 'We are in the hands of the Lord?' she wondered. The insincerity slipping in among the truths roused her, annoyed her. She returned to her knitting again. How could any Lord have made this world? she asked. With her mind she had always seized the fact that there is no reason, order, justice: but suffering, death, the poor. There was no treachery too base for the world to commit; she knew that. No happiness lasted; she knew that. She knitted with firm composure, slightly pursing her lips and, without being aware of it, so stiffened and composed the lines of her face in a habit of sternness that when her husband passed, though he was chuckling at the thought that Hume, the philosopher, grown enormously fat, had stuck in a bog, he could not help noting, as he passed, the sternness at the heart of her beauty. It saddened him, and her remoteness pained him, and he felt, as he passed, that he could not protect her, and, when he reached the hedge, he was sad. He could no nothing to help her. He must stand by and watch her. Indeed, the infernal truth was, he made things worse for her. He was irritable – he was touchy. He had lost his temper over the Lighthouse. He looked into the hedge, into its intricacy, its darkness.

Always, Mrs Ramsay felt, one helped oneself out of solitude reluctantly by laying hold of some little odd or end, some sound, some sight. She listened, but it was all very still; cricket was over; the children were in their baths; there was only the sound of the sea. She stopped knitting; she held the long reddish-brown stocking dangling in her hands a moment. She saw the light again. With some irony in her interrogation, for when one woke at all, one's relations changed, she looked at the steady light, the pitiless, the remorseless, which was so much her, yet so little her, which had her at its beck and call (she woke in the night and saw it bent across their bed, stroking the floor), but for all that she thought, watching it with fascination, hypnotised, as if it were stroking with its silver fingers some sealed vessel in her brain whose bursting would flood her with delight, she had known happiness, exquisite happiness, intense happiness, and it silvered the rough waves a little more brightly, as daylight faded, and the blue went out of the sea and it rolled in waves of pure lemon which curved and swelled and broke upon the beach and the ecstasy burst in her eyes and waves of pure delight raced over the floor of her mind and she felt, It is enough! It is enough!

He turned and saw her. Ah! She was lovely, lovelier now than ever he thought. But he could not speak to her. He could not interrupt her. He wanted urgently to speak to her now that James was gone and she was alone at last. But he resolved, no; he would not interrupt her. She was aloof from him now in her beauty, in her sadness. He would let her be, and he passed her without a word, though it hurt him that she should look so distant, and he could not reach her, he could do nothing to help her. And again he would have passed her without a word had she not, at that very moment, given him of her own free will what she knew he would never ask, and called to him and taken the green shawl off the picture frame, and gone to him. For he wished, she knew, to protect her.

XII

She folded the green shawl about her shoulders. She took his arm. His beauty was so great, she said, beginning to speak of Kennedy the gardener at once; he was so awfully handsome, that she couldn't dismiss him. There was a ladder against the greenhouse, and little lumps of putty stuck about, for they were beginning to mend the greenhouse roof. Yes, but as she strolled along with her husband, she felt that that particular source of worry had been placed. She had it on the tip of her tongue to say, as they strolled: 'It'll cost fifty pounds,' but instead, for her heart failed her about money, she talked about Jasper shooting birds, and he said, at once, soothing her instantly, that it was natural in a boy, and he trusted he would find better ways of amusing himself before long. Her husband was so sensible, so just. And so she said: 'Yes; all children go through stages,' and began considering the dahlias in the big bed, and wondering what about next year's flowers, and had he heard the children's nickname for Charles Tansley, she asked. The atheist, they called him, the little atheist. 'He's not a polished specimen,' said Mr Ramsay. 'Far from it,' said Mrs Ramsay.

She supposed it was all right leaving him to his own devices, Mrs Ramsay said, wondering whether it was any use sending down bulbs; did they plant them? 'Oh, he has his dissertation to write,' said Mr Ramsay. She knew all about *that*, said Mrs Ramsay. He talked of nothing else. It was about the influence of somebody upon something. 'Well, it's all he has to count on,' said Mr Ramsay. 'Pray heaven he won't fall in love with Prue,' said Mrs Ramsay. He'd disinherit her if she married him, said Mr Ramsay. He did not look at the flowers, which his wife was considering, but at a spot about a foot or so above them. There was no harm in him, he added, and was just about to say that anyhow he was the only young man in England who admired his – when he choked it back. He would not bother her again about his books. These flowers seemed creditable, Mr Ramsay said, lowering his gaze and noticing something red, something brown. Yes, but then these she had put in with her own hands, said Mrs Ramsay. The question was, what happened if she sent bulbs down; did Kennedy plant them? It was his incurable laziness, she added, moving on. If she stood over him all day long with a spade in her hand, he did sometimes do a stroke of work. So they strolled along, towards the red-hot pokers. 'You're teaching your daughters to exaggerate,' said Mr Ramsay, reproving her. Her Aunt Camilla was far worse than she was, Mrs Ramsay remarked. 'Nobody ever held up your Aunt Camilla as a model of virtue that I'm aware of,' said Mr Ramsay. 'She was the most beautiful woman I ever saw,' said Mrs Ramsay. 'Somebody else was that,' said Mr Ramsay. Prue was going to be far more beautiful than she was, said Mrs Ramsay. He saw no trace of it, said Mr Ramsay. 'Well, then, look tonight,' said Mrs Ramsay. They paused. He wished Andrew could be induced to work harder. He would lose every chance of a scholarship if he didn't. 'Oh scholarships!' she said. Mr Ramsay thought her foolish for saying that, about a serious thing, like a scholarship. He should be very proud of Andrew if he got a scholarship, he said. She would be just as proud of him if he didn't, she answered. They disagreed always about this, but it did not matter. She liked him to believe in scholarships, and he liked her to be proud of Andrew whatever he did. Suddenly she remembered those little paths on the edge of the cliffs.

Wasn't it late? she asked. They hadn't come home yet. He flicked his watch carelessly open. But it was only just past seven. He held his watch open for a moment, deciding that he would tell her what he had felt on the terrace. To begin with, it was not reasonable to be so nervous. Andrew could look after himself. Then, he wanted to tell her that when he was walking on the terrace just now – here he became uncomfortable, as if he were breaking into that solitude, that aloofness, that remoteness of hers . . . But she pressed him. What had he wanted to tell her, she asked, thinking it was about going to the Lighthouse; and that he was sorry he had said, 'Damn you.' But no. He did not like to see her look so sad, he said. Only wool gathering, she protested, flushing a little. They both felt uncomfortable, as if they did not know whether to go on or go back. She had been reading fairy tales to James, she said. No, they could not share that; they could not say that.

They had reached the gap between the two clumps of red-hot pokers, and there was the Lighthouse again, but she would not let herself look at it. Had she known that he was looking at her, she thought, she would not have let herself sit there, thinking. She disliked anything that reminded her that she had been seen sitting thinking. So she looked over her shoulder, at the town. The lights were rippling and running as if they were drops of silver water held firm in a wind. And all the poverty, all the suffering had turned to that, Mrs Ramsay thought. The lights of the town and of the harbour and of the boats seemed like a phantom net floating there to mark something which had sunk. Well, if he could not share her thoughts, Mr Ramsay said to himself, he would be off, then, on his own. He wanted to go on thinking, telling himself the story how Hume was stuck in a bog; he wanted to laugh. But first it was nonsense to be anxious about Andrew. When he was Andrew's age he used to walk about the country all day long, with nothing but a biscuit in his pocket and nobody bothered about him, or thought that he had fallen over a cliff. He said aloud he thought he would be off for a day's walk if the weather held. He had had about enough of Bankes and of Carmichael. He would like a little solitude. Yes, she said. It annoyed him that she did not protest. She knew that he would never do it. He was too old now to walk all day long with a biscuit in his pocket. She worried about the boys, but not about him. Years ago, before he had married, he thought, looking across the bay, as they stood between the clumps of red-hot pokers, he had walked all day. He had made a meal off bread and cheese in a public house. He had worked ten hours at a stretch; an old woman just popped her head in now and again and saw to the fire. That was the country he liked best, over there; those sandhills dwindling away into darkness. One could walk all day without meeting a soul. There was not a house scarcely, not a single village for miles on end. One could worry things out alone. There were little sandy beaches where no one had been since the beginning of time. The seals sat up and looked at you. It sometimes seemed to him that in a little house out there, alone – he broke off, sighing. He had no right. The father of eight children – he reminded himself. And he would have been a beast and a cur to wish a single thing altered. Andrew would be a better man than he had been. Prue would be a beauty, her mother said. They would stem the flood a bit. That was a good bit of work on the whole – his eight children. They showed he did not damn the poor little universe entirely, for on an evening like this, he thought, looking at the land dwindling away, the little island seemed pathetically small, half swallowed up in the sea.

'Poor little place,' he murmured with a sigh.

She heard him. He said the most melancholy things, but she noticed that directly he had said them he always seemed more cheerful than usual. All this phrase-making was a game, she thought, for if she had said half what he said, she would have blown her brains out by now.

It annoyed her, this phrase-making, and she said to him, in a matter-of-fact way, that it was a perfectly lovely evening. And what was he groaning about, she asked, half laughing, half complaining, for she guessed what he was thinking – he would have written better books if he had not married.

He was not complaining, he said. She knew that he did not complain. She knew that he had nothing whatever to complain of. And he seized her hand and raised it to his lips and kissed it with an intensity that brought the tears to her eyes, and quickly he dropped it.

They turned away from the view and began to walk up the path where the silver-green spear-like plants grew, arm in arm. His arm was almost like a young man's arm, Mrs Ramsay thought, thin and hard, and she thought with delight how strong he still was, though he was over sixty, and how untamed and optimistic, and how strange it was that being convinced, as he was, of all sorts of horrors seemed not to depress him, but to cheer him. Was it not odd, she reflected? Indeed he seemed to her sometimes made differently from other people, born blind, deaf and dumb to the ordinary things, but to the extraordinary things, with an eye like an eagle's. His understanding often astonished her. But did he notice the flowers? No. Did he notice the view? No. Did he even notice his own daughter's beauty, or whether there was pudding on his plate or roast beef? He would sit at table with them like a person in a dream. And his habit of talking aloud, or saying poetry aloud, was growing on him, she was afraid; for sometimes it was awkward –

Best and brightest, come away!

poor Miss Giddings, when he shouted that at her, almost jumped out of her skin. But then, Mrs Ramsay, though instantly taking his side against all the silly Giddingses in the world, then, she thought, intimating by a little pressure on his arm that he walked uphill too fast for her, and she must stop for a moment to see whether those were fresh molehills on the bank, then, she thought, stooping down to look, a great mind like his must be different in every way from ours. All the great men she had ever known, she thought, deciding that a rabbit must have got in, were like that, and it was good for young men (though the atmosphere of lecture-rooms was stuffy and depressing to her beyond endurance almost) simply to hear him, simply to look at him. But without shooting rabbits, how was one to keep them down? she wondered. It might be a rabbit; it might be a mole. Some creature anyhow was ruining her Evening Primroses. And looking up, she saw above the thin trees the first pulse of the full-throbbing star, and wanted to make her husband look at it; for the sight gave her such keen pleasure. But she stopped herself. He never looked at things. If he did, all he would say would be, Poor little world, with one of his sighs.

At that moment he said, 'Very fine,' to please her, and pretended to admire the flowers. But she knew quite well that he did not admire them, or even realise that they were there. It was only to please her . . . Ah, but was that not Lily Briscoe strolling along with William Bankes? She focused her short-sighted eyes upon the backs of a retreating couple. Yes, indeed it was. Did that not mean that they would marry? Yes, it must! What an admirable idea! They must marry!

XIII

He had been to Amsterdam, Mr Bankes was saying as he strolled across the lawn with Lily Briscoe. He had seen the Rembrandts. He had been to Madrid. Unfortunately, it was Good Friday and the Prado was shut. He had been to Rome. Had Miss Briscoe never been to Rome? Oh, she should – It would be a wonderful experience for her – the Sistine Chapel; Michelangelo; and Padua, with its Giottos. His wife had been in bad health for many years, so that their sightseeing had been on a modest scale.

She had been to Brussels; she had been to Paris, but only for a flying visit to see an aunt who was ill. She had been to Dresden; there were masses of pictures she had not seen; however, Lily Briscoe reflected, perhaps it was better not to see pictures: they only made one hopelessly discontented with one's own work. Mr Bankes thought one could carry that point of view too far. We can't all be Titians and we can't all be Darwins, he said; at the same time he doubted whether you could have your Darwin and your Titian if it weren't for humble people like ourselves. Lily would have liked to pay him a compliment; you're not humble, Mr Bankes, she would have liked to have said. But he did not want compliments (most men do, she thought), and she was a little ashamed of her impulse and said nothing while he remarked that perhaps what he was saying did not apply to pictures. Anyhow, said Lily, tossing off her little insincerity, she would always go on painting, because it interested her. Yes, said Mr Bankes, he was sure she would and as they reached the end of the lawn he was asking her whether she had difficulty in finding subjects in London when they turned and saw the Ramsays. So that is marriage, Lily thought, a man and a woman looking at a girl throwing a ball. That is what Mrs Ramsay tried to tell me the other night, she thought. For she was wearing a green shawl, and they were standing close together watching Prue and Jasper throwing catches. And suddenly the meaning which, for no reason at all, as perhaps they are stepping out of the tube or ringing a doorbell, descends on people, making them symbolical, making them representative, came upon them, and made them in the dusk standing, looking, the symbols of marriage, husband and wife. Then, after an instant, the symbolical outline which transcended the real figures sank down again, and they became, as they met them, Mr and Mrs Ramsay watching the children throwing catches. But still for a moment, though Mrs Ramsay greeted them with her usual smile (oh, she's thinking we're going to get married, Lily thought) and said, 'I have triumphed tonight,' meaning that for once Mr Bankes had agreed to dine with them and not run off to his own lodging where his man cooked vegetables properly; still, for one moment, there was a sense of things having been blown apart, of space, of irresponsibility as the ball soared high, and they followed it and lost it and saw the one star and the draped branches. In the failing light they all looked sharp-edged and ethereal and divided by great distances. Then, darting backwards over the vast space (for it seemed as if solidity had vanished altogether), Prue ran full tilt into them and caught the ball brilliantly high up in her left hand, and her mother said: 'Haven't they come back yet?' whereupon the spell was broken. Mr Ramsay felt free now to laugh out loud at Hume, who had stuck in a bog and an old woman rescued him on condition he said the Lord's Prayer, and chuckling to himself he strolled off to his study. Mrs Ramsay, bringing Prue back into the alliance of family life again, from which she had escaped, throwing catches, asked: 'Did Nancy go with them?'

XIV

(Certainly, Nancy had gone with them, since Minta Doyle had asked it with her dumb look, holding out her hand, as Nancy made off, after lunch, to her attic, to escape the horror of family life. She supposed she must go then. She did not want to go. She did not want to be drawn into it all. For as they walked along the road to the cliff Minta kept on taking her hand. Then she would let it go. Then she would take it again. What was it she wanted? Nancy asked herself. There was something, of course, that people wanted; for when Minta took her hand and held it, Nancy, reluctantly, saw the whole world spread out beneath her, as if it were Constantinople seen through a mist, and then, however heavy-eyed one might be, one must needs ask: 'Is that Santa Sofia?' 'Is that the Golden Horn?' So Nancy asked, when Minta took her hand: 'What is it that she wants? Is it that?' And what was that? Here and there emerged from the mist (as Nancy looked down upon life spread beneath her) a pinnacle, a dome; prominent things, without names. But when Minta dropped her hand, as she did when they ran down the hillside, all that, the dome, the pinnacle, whatever it was that had protruded through the mist, sank down into it and disappeared.

Minta, Andrew observed, was rather a good walker. She wore more sensible clothes than most women. She wore very short skirts and black knickerbockers. She would jump straight into a stream and flounder across. He liked her rashness, but he saw that it would not do – she would kill herself in some idiotic way one of these days. She seemed to be afraid of nothing – except bulls. At the mere sight of a bull in a field she would throw up her arms and fly screaming, which was the very thing to enrage a bull of course. But she did not mind owning up to it in the least; one must admit that. She knew she was an awful coward about bulls, she said. She thought she must have been tossed in her perambulator when she was a baby. She didn't seem to mind what she said or did. Suddenly now she pitched down on the edge of the cliff and began to sing some song about

Damn your eyes, damn your eyes.

They all had to join in and sing the chorus, and shout out together:

Damn your eyes, damn your eyes . . .

but it would be fatal to let the tide come in and cover up all the good hunting-grounds before they got on to the beach.

'Fatal,' Paul agreed, springing up, and as they went slithering down, he kept quoting the guidebook about 'these islands being justly celebrated for their park-like prospects and the extent and variety of their marine curiosities'. But it would not do altogether, this shouting and damning your eyes, Andrew felt, picking his way down the cliff, this clapping him on the back, and calling him 'old fellow' and all that; it would not altogether do. It was the worst of taking women on walks. Once on the beach they separated, he going out on to the Pope's Nose, taking his shoes off, and rolling his socks in them and letting that couple look after themselves; Nancy waded out to her own rocks and searched her own pools and let that couple look after themselves. She crouched low down and touched the smooth rubber-like sea anemones, who were stuck like lumps of jelly to the side of the rock. Brooding, she changed the pool into the sea, and made the minnows into sharks and whales, and cast vast clouds over this tiny world by holding her hand against the sun, and so brought darkness and desolation, like God himself, to millions of ignorant and innocent creatures, and then took her hand away suddenly and let the sun stream down. Out on the pale criss-crossed sand, high-stepping, fringed, gauntleted, stalked some fantastic leviathan (she was still enlarging the pool), and slipped into the vast fissures of the mountainside. And then, letting her eyes slide imperceptibly above the pool and rest on that wavering line of sea and sky, on the tree trunks which the smoke of steamers made waver upon the horizon, she became with all that power sweeping savagely in and inevitably withdrawing, hypnotised, and the two senses of that vastness and this tininess (the pool had diminished again) flowering within it made her feel that she was bound hand and foot and unable to move by the intensity of feelings which reduced her own body, her own life, and the lives of all the people in the world, for ever, to nothingness. So listening to the waves, crouched over the pool, she brooded.

And Andrew shouted that the sea was coming in, so she leapt splashing through the shallow waves on to the shore and ran up the beach and was carried by her own impetuosity and her desire for rapid movement right behind a rock and there oh heavens! in each other's arms were Paul and Minta! kissing probably. She was outraged, indignant. She and Andrew put on their shoes and stockings in dead silence without saying a thing about it. Indeed they were rather sharp with each other. She might have called him when she saw the crayfish or whatever it was, Andrew grumbled. However, they both felt, it's not our fault. They had not wanted this horrid nuisance to happen. All the same it irritated Andrew that Nancy should be a woman, and Nancy that Andrew should be a man and they tied their shoes very neatly and drew the bows rather tight.

It was not until they had climbed right up on to the top of the cliff again that Minta cried out that she had lost her grandmother's brooch – her grandmother's brooch, the sole ornament she possessed – a weeping willow, it was (they must remember it) set in pearls. They must have seen it, she said, with the tears running down her cheeks, the brooch which her grand-mother had fastened her cap with till the last day of her life. Now she had lost it. She would rather have lost anything than that! She would go back and look for it. They all went back. They poked and peered and looked. They kept their heads very low, and said things shortly and gruffly. Paul Rayley searched like a madman all about the rock where they had been sitting. All this pother about a brooch really didn't do at all, Andrew thought, as Paul told him to make a 'thorough search between this point and that'. The tide was coming in fast. The sea would cover the place where they had sat in a minute. There was not a ghost of a chance of their finding it now. 'We shall be cut off!' Minta shrieked, suddenly terrified. As if there were any danger of that! It was the same as the bulls all over again – she had no control over her emotions, Andrew thought. Women hadn't. The wretched Paul had to pacify her. The men (Andrew and Paul at once became manly, and different from usual) took counsel briefly and decided that they would plant Rayley's stick where they had sat and come back at low tide again. There was nothing more that could be done now. If the brooch was there it would still be there in the morning, they assured her, but Minta still sobbed, all the way up to the top of the cliff. It was her grandmother's brooch; she would rather have lost anything but that, and yet Nancy felt, though it might be true that she minded losing her brooch, she wasn't crying only for that. She was crying for something else. We might all sit down and cry, she felt. But she did not know what for.

They drew ahead together, Paul and Minta, and he comforted her, and said how famous he was for finding things. Once when he was a little boy he had found a gold watch. He would get up at daybreak, and he was positive he would find it. It seemed to him that it would be almost dark, and he would be alone on the beach, and somehow it would be rather dangerous. He began telling her, however, that he would certainly find it, and she said that she would not hear of his getting up at dawn: it was lost: she knew that: she had had a presentiment when she put it on that afternoon. And secretly he resolved that he would not tell her, but he would slip out of the house at dawn when they were all asleep and if he could not find it he would go to Edinburgh and buy her another, just like it but more beautiful. He would prove what he could do. And as they came out on the hill and saw the lights of the town beneath them, the lights coming out suddenly one by one seemed like things that were going to happen to him – his marriage, his children, his house; and again he thought, as they came out on to the high road, which was shaded with high bushes, how they would retreat into solitude together, and walk on and on, he always leading her, and she pressing close to his side (as she did now). As they turned by the crossroads he thought what an appalling experience he had been through, and he must tell someone – Mrs Ramsay, of course, for it took his breath away to think what he had been and done. It had been far and away the worst moment of his life when he asked Minta to marry him. He would go straight to Mrs Ramsay, because he felt somehow that she was the person who had made him do it. She had made him think he could do anything. Nobody else took him seriously. But she made him believe that he could do whatever he wanted. He had felt her eyes on him all day today, following him about (though she never said a word) as if she were saying: 'Yes, you can do it. I believe in you. I expect it of you.' She had made him feel all that, and directly they got back (he looked for the lights of the house above the bay) he would go to her and say: 'I've done it, Mrs Ramsay; thanks to you.' And so turning into the lane that led to the house he could see lights moving about in the upper windows. They must be awfully late then. People were getting ready for dinner. The house was all lit up, and the lights after the darkness made his eyes feel full, and he said to himself, childishly, as he walked up the drive, Lights, lights, lights, and repeated in a dazed way, Lights, lights, lights, as they came into the house, staring about him with his face quite stiff. (But, good heavens, he said to himself, putting his hand to his tie, I must not make a fool of myself.)

XV

'Yes,' said Prue, in her considering way, answering her mother's question, 'I think Nancy did go with them.'

XVI

Well then, Nancy had gone with them, Mrs Ramsay supposed, wondering, as she put down a brush, took up a comb, and said 'Come in' to a tap at the door (Jasper and Rose came in), whether the fact that Nancy was with them made it less likely or more likely that anything would happen; it made it less likely, somehow, Mrs Ramsay felt, very irrationally, except that after all holocaust on such a scale was not probable. They could not all be drowned. And again she felt alone in the presence of her old antagonist, life.

Jasper and Rose said that Mildred wanted to know whether she should wait dinner.

'Not for the Queen of England,' said Mrs Ramsay emphatically.

'Not for the Empress of Mexico,' she added, laughing at Jasper; for he shared his mother's vice: he, too, exaggerated.

And if Rose liked, she said, while Jasper took the message, she might choose which jewels she was to wear. When there are fifteen people sitting down to dinner, one cannot keep things waiting for ever. She was now beginning to feel annoyed with them for being so late; it was inconsiderate of them, and it annoyed her, on top of her anxiety about them, that they should choose this very night to be out late, when, in fact, she wished the dinner to be particularly nice, since William Bankes had at last consented to dine with them; and they were having Mildred's masterpiece – Boeuf en Daube. Everything depended upon things being served up the precise moment they were ready. The beef, the bayleaf, and the wine – all must be done to a turn. To keep it waiting was out of the question. Yet of course tonight, of all nights, out they went, and they came in late, and things had to be sent out, things had to be kept hot; the Boeuf en Daube would be entirely spoilt.

Jasper offered her an opal necklace; Rose a gold necklace. Which looked best against her black dress? Which did indeed? said Mrs Ramsay absent-mindedly, looking at her neck and shoulders (but avoiding her face), in the glass. And then, while the children rummaged among her things, she looked out of the window at a sight which always amused her – the rooks trying to decide which tree to settle on. Every time they seemed to change their minds and rose up into the air again, because, she thought, the old rook, the father rook, old Joseph was her name for him, was a bird of a very trying and difficult disposition. He was a disreputable old bird, with half his wing feathers missing. He was like some seedy old gentleman in a top hat she had seen playing the horn in front of a public house.

'Look!' she said, laughing. They were actually fighting. Joseph and Mary were fighting. Anyhow they all went up again, and the air was shoved aside by their black wings and cut into exquisite scimitar shapes. The movement of the wings beating out, out, out – she could never describe it accurately enough to please herself – was one of the loveliest of all to her. Look at that, she said to Rose, hoping that Rose would see it more clearly than she could. For one's children so often gave one's own perceptions a little thrust forwards.

But which was it to be? They had all the trays of her jewel-case open. The gold necklace, which was Italian, or the opal necklace, which Uncle James had brought her from India; or should she wear her amethysts?

'Choose, dearests, choose,' she said, hoping that they would make haste.

But she let them take their time to choose: she let Rose, particularly, take up this and then that, and hold her jewels against the black dress, for this little ceremony of choosing jewels, which was gone through every night, was what Rose liked best, she knew. She had some hidden reason of her own for attaching great importance to this choosing what her mother was to wear. What was the reason, Mrs Ramsay wondered, standing still to let her clasp the necklace she had chosen, divining, through her own past, some deep, some buried, some quite speechless feeling that one had for one's mother at Rose's age. Like all feelings felt for oneself, Mrs Ramsay thought, it made one sad. It was so inadequate, what one could give in return; and what Rose felt was quite out of proportion to anything she actually was. And Rose would grow up; and Rose would suffer, she supposed, with these deep feelings, and she said she was ready now, and they would go down, and Jasper, because he was the gentleman, should give her his arm, and Rose, as she was the lady, should carry her handkerchief (she gave her the handkerchief), and what else? oh, yes, it might be cold: a shawl. Choose me a shawl, she said, for that would please Rose, who was bound to suffer so. 'There,' she said, stopping by the window on the landing, 'there they are again.' Joseph had settled on another treetop. 'Don't you think they mind,' she said to Jasper, 'having their wings broken?' Why did he want to shoot poor old Joseph and Mary? He shuffled a little on the stairs, and felt rebuked, but not seriously, for she did not understand the fun of shooting birds; that they did not feel; and being his mother she lived away in another division of the world, but he rather liked her stories about Mary and Joseph. She made him laugh. But how did she know that those were Mary and Joseph? Did she think the same birds came to the same trees every night? he asked. But here, suddenly, like all grown-up people, she ceased to pay him the least attention. She was listening to a clatter in the hall.

'They've come back!' she exclaimed, and at once she felt much more annoyed with them than relieved. Then she wondered, had it happened? She would go down and they would tell her – but no. They could not tell her anything, with all these people about. So she must go down and begin dinner and wait. And, like some queen who, finding her people gathered in the hall, looks down upon them, and descends among them, and acknowledges their tributes silently, and accepts their devotion and their prostration before her (Paul did not move a muscle but looked straight before him as she passed), she went down, and crossed the hall and bowed her head very slightly, as if she accepted what they could not say: their tribute to her beauty.

But she stopped. There was a smell of burning. Could they have let the Boeuf en Daube overboil, she wondered? pray heaven not! when the great clangour of the gong announced solemnly, authoritatively, that all those scattered about, in attics, in bedrooms, on little perches of their own, reading, writing, putting the last smooth to their hair, or fastening dresses, must leave all that, and the little odds and ends on their washing-tables and dressing-tables, and the novels on the bed-tables, and the diaries which were so private, and assemble in the dining-room for dinner.

XVII

But what have I done with my life? thought Mrs Ramsay, taking her place
at the head of the table, and looking at all the plates making white circles
on it. 'William, sit by me,' she said. 'Lily,' she said, wearily, 'over there.'
They had that – Paul Rayley and Minta Doyle – she, only this – an
infinitely long table and plates and knives. At the far end, was her husband,
sitting down, all in a heap, frowning. What at? She did not know. She did
not mind. She could not understand how she had ever felt any emotion or
any affection for him. She had a sense of being past everything, through
everything, out of everything, as she helped the soup, as if there was an
eddy – there – and one could be in it, or one could be out of it, and she was
out of it. It's all come to an end, she thought, while they came in one after
another, Charles Tansley – 'Sit there, please,' she said – Augustus
Carmichael – and sat down. And meanwhile she waited, passively, for
someone to answer her, for something to happen. But this is not a thing,
she thought, ladling out soup, that one says.

Raising her eyebrows at the discrepancy – that was what she was thinking,
this was what she was doing – ladling out soup – she felt, more and more
strongly, outside that eddy; or as if a shade had fallen, and, robbed of colour,
she saw things truly. The room (she looked round it) was very shabby. There
was no beauty anywhere. She forebore to look at Mr Tansley. Nothing
seemed to have merged. They all sat separate. And the whole of the effort of
merging and flowing and creating rested on her. Again she felt, as a fact
without hostility, the sterility of men, for if she did not do it nobody would
do it, and so, giving herself the little shake that one gives a watch that has
stopped, the old familiar pulse began beating, as the watch begins ticking –
one, two, three, one, two, three. And so on and so on, she repeated, listening
to it, sheltering and fostering the still feeble pulse as one might guard a weak
flame with a newspaper. And so then, she concluded addressing herself by
bending silently in his direction to William Bankes – poor man! who had no
wife and no children, and dined alone in lodgings except for tonight; and in
pity for him, life being now strong enough to bear her on again, she began
all this business, as a sailor not without weariness sees the wind fill his sail
and yet hardly wants to be off again and thinks how, had the ship sunk, he
would have whirled round and round and found rest on the floor of the sea.

'Did you find your letters? I told them to put them in the hall for you,'
she said to William Bankes.

Lily Briscoe watched her drifting into that strange no man's land where
to follow people is impossible, and yet their going inflicts such a chill on
those who watch them that they always try at least to follow them with their

eyes as one follows a fading ship until the sails have sunk beneath the horizon.

How old she looks, how worn she looks, Lily thought, and how remote. Then when she turned to William Bankes, smiling, it was as if the ship had turned and the sun had struck its sails again, and Lily thought with some amusement because she was relieved, Why does she pity him? For that was the impression she gave, when she told him that his letters were in the hall. Poor William Bankes, she seemed to be saying, as if her own weariness had been partly pitying people, and the life in her, her resolve to live again, had been stirred by pity. And it was not true, Lily thought; it was one of those misjudgements of hers that seemed to be instinctive and to arise from some need of her own rather than of other people's. He is not in the least pitiable. He has his work, Lily said to herself. She remembered, all of a sudden as if she had found a treasure, that she too had her work. In a flash she saw her picture, and thought, Yes, I shall put the tree further in the middle; then I shall avoid that awkward space. That's what I shall do. That's what has been puzzling me. She took up the salt cellar and put it down again on a flower in the pattern in the tablecloth, so as to remind herself to move the tree.

'It's odd that one scarcely gets anything worth having by post, yet one always wants one's letters,' said Mr Bankes.

What damned rot they talk, thought Charles Tansley, laying down his spoon precisely in the middle of his plate, which he had swept clean, as if, Lily thought (he sat opposite to her with his back to the window precisely in the middle of view), he were determined to make sure of his meals. Everything about him had that meagre fixity, that bare unloveliness. But nevertheless, the fact remained, it was almost impossible to dislike anyone if one looked at them. She liked his eyes; they were blue, deep set, frightening.

'Do you write many letters, Mr Tansley?' asked Mrs Ramsay, pitying him too, Lily supposed; for that was true of Mrs Ramsay – she pitied men always as if they lacked something – women never, as if they had something. He wrote to his mother; otherwise he did not suppose he wrote one letter a month, said Mr Tansley, shortly.

For he was not going to talk the sort of rot these people wanted him to talk. He was not going to be condescended to by these silly women. He had been reading in his room, and now he came down and it all seemed to him silly, superficial, flimsy. Why did they dress? He had come down in his ordinary clothes. He had not got any dress clothes. 'One never gets anything worth having by post' – that was the sort of thing they were always saying. They made men say that sort of thing. Yes, it was pretty well true, he thought. They never got anything worth having from one year's end to another. They did nothing but talk, talk, talk, eat, eat, eat. It was the women's fault. Women made civilisation impossible with all their 'charm', all their silliness.

'No going to the Lighthouse tomorrow, Mrs Ramsay,' he said asserting himself. He liked her; he admired her; he still thought of the man in the drainpipe looking up at her; but he felt it necessary to assert himself.

He was really, Lily Briscoe thought, in spite of his eyes, but then look at his nose, look at his hands, the most uncharming human being she had ever met. Then why did she mind what he said? Women can't write, women can't paint – what did that matter coming from him, since clearly it was not true to him but for some reason helpful to him, and that was why he said it? Why did her whole being bow, like corn under a wind, and erect itself again from this abasement only with a great and rather painful effort? She must make it once more. There's the sprig on the tablecloth; there's my painting; I must move the tree to the middle; that matters – nothing else. Could she not hold fast to that, she asked herself, and not lose her temper, and not argue; and if she wanted a little revenge take it by laughing at him?

'Oh, Mr Tansley,' she said, 'do take me to the Lighthouse with you. I should so love it.'

She was telling lies he could see. She was saying what she did not mean to annoy him, for some reason. She was laughing at him. He was in his old flannel trousers. He had no others. He felt very rough and isolated and lonely. He knew that she was trying to tease him for some reason; she didn't want to go to the Lighthouse with him; she despised him: so did Prue Ramsay; so did they all. But he was not going to be made a fool of by women, so he turned deliberately in his chair and looked out of the window and said, all in a jerk, very rudely, it would be too rough for her tomorrow. She would be sick.

It annoyed him that she should have made him speak like that, with Mrs Ramsay listening. If only he could be alone in his room working, he thought, among his books. That was where he felt at his ease. And he had never run a penny into debt; he had never cost his father a penny since he was fifteen; he had helped them at home out of his savings; he was educating his sister. Still, he wished he had known how to answer Miss Briscoe properly; he wished it had not come out all in a jerk like that. 'You'd be sick.' He wished he could think of something to say to Mrs Ramsay, something which would show her that he was not just a dry prig. That was what they all thought him. He turned to her. But Mrs Ramsay was talking about people he had never heard of to William Bankes.

'Yes, take it away,' she said briefly, interrupting what she was saying to Mr Bankes to speak to the maid. 'It must have been fifteen – no, twenty years ago – that I last saw her,' she was saying, turning back to him again as if she could not lose a moment of their talk, for she was absorbed by what they were saying. So he had actually heard from her this evening! And was Carrie still living at Marlow, and was everything still the same? Oh, she could remember it as if it were yesterday – going on the river, feeling very cold. But if the Mannings made a plan they stuck to it. Never should she forget Herbert killing a wasp with a teaspoon on the bank! And it was still going on, Mrs Ramsay mused, gliding like a ghost among the chairs and tables of that drawing-room on the banks of the Thames where she had been so very, very cold twenty years ago; but now she went among them like a ghost; and it fascinated her, as if, while she had changed, that particular day, now become very still and beautiful, had remained there, all these years. Had Carrie written to him herself? she asked.

'Yes. She says they're building a new billiard room,' he said. No! No! That was out of the question! Building a billiard room! It seemed to her impossible.

Mr Bankes could not see that there was anything very odd about it. They were very well off now. Should he give her love to Carrie?

'Oh,' said Mrs Ramsay with a little start. 'No,' she added, reflecting that she did not know this Carrie who built a new billiard room. But how strange, she repeated, to Mr Bankes's amusement, that they should be going on there still. For it was extraordinary to think that they had been capable of going on living all these years when she had not thought of them more than once all that time. How eventful her own life had been, during those same years. Yet perhaps Carrie Manning had not thought about her either. The thought was strange and distasteful.

'People soon drift apart,' said Mr Bankes, feeling, however, some satisfaction when he thought that after all he knew both the Mannings and the Ramsays. He had not drifted apart, he thought, laying down his spoon and wiping his clean-shaven lips punctiliously. But perhaps he was rather unusual, he thought, in this; he never let himself get into a groove. He had friends in all circles . . . Mrs Ramsay had to break off here to tell the maid something about keeping food hot. That was why he preferred dining alone. All these interruptions annoyed him. Well, thought William Bankes, preserving a demeanour of exquisite courtesy and merely spreading the fingers of his left hand on the tablecloth as a mechanic examines a tool beautifully polished and ready for use in an interval of leisure, such are the sacrifices one's friends ask of one. It would have hurt her if he had refused to come. But it was not worth it for him. Looking at his hand he thought that if he had been alone dinner would have been almost over now; he would have been free to work. Yes, he thought, it is a terrible waste of time. The children were dropping in still. 'I wish one of you would run up to Roger's room,' Mrs Ramsay was saying. How trifling it all is, how boring it all is, he thought, compared with the other thing – work. Here he sat drumming his fingers on the tablecloth when he might have been – he took a flashing bird's-eye view of his work. What a waste of time it all was to be sure! Yet, he thought, she is one of my oldest friends. I am by way of being devoted to her. Yet now, at this moment, her presence meant absolutely nothing to him: her beauty meant nothing to him; her sitting with her little boy at the window – nothing, nothing. He wished only to be alone and to take up that book. He felt uncomfortable; he felt treacherous, that he could sit by her side and feel nothing for her. The truth was that he did not enjoy family life. It was in this sort of state that one asked oneself, What does one live for? Why, one asked oneself, does one take all these pains for the human race to go on? Is it so very desirable? Are we attractive as a species? Not so very, he thought, looking at those rather untidy boys. His favourite, Cam, was in bed, he supposed. Foolish questions, vain questions, questions one never asked if one was occupied. Is human life this? Is human life that? One never had time to think about it. But here he was asking himself that sort of question, because Mrs Ramsay was giving orders to servants, and also because it had struck him, thinking how surprised Mrs Ramsay was that Carrie Manning should still exist, that friendships, even the best of them, are frail things. One drifts apart. He reproached himself again. He was sitting beside Mrs Ramsay and he had nothing in the world to say to her.

'I'm so sorry,' said Mrs Ramsay, turning to him at last. He felt rigid and barren, like a pair of boots that has been soaked and gone dry so that you can hardly force your feet into them. Yet he must force his feet into them. He must make himself talk. Unless he were very careful, she would find out this treachery of his, that he did not care a straw for her, and that would not be at all pleasant, he thought. So he bent his head courteously in her direction.

'How you must detest dining in this bear garden,' she said, making use, as she did when she was distracted, of her social manner. So, when there is a strife of tongues at some meeting, the chairman, to obtain unity, suggests that everyone shall speak in French. Perhaps it is bad French; French may not contain the words that express the speaker's thoughts; nevertheless speaking French imposes some order, some uniformity. Replying to her in the same language, Mr Bankes said: 'No, not at all'; arid Mr Tansley, who had no knowledge of this language, even spoken thus in words of one syllable, at once suspected its insincerity. They did talk nonsense, he thought, the Ramsays; and he pounced on this fresh instance with joy, making a note which, one of these days, he would read aloud, to one or two friends. There, in a society where one could say what one liked, he would sarcastically describe 'staying with the Ramsays' and what nonsense they talked. It was worthwhile doing it once, he would say; but not again. The women bored one so, he would say. Of course Ramsay had dished himself by marrying a beautiful woman and having eight children. It would shape itself something like that, but now, at this moment, sitting stuck there with an empty seat beside him nothing had shaped itself at all. It was all in scraps and fragments. He felt extremely, even physically, uncomfortable. He wanted somebody to give him a chance of asserting himself. He wanted it so urgently that he fidgeted in his chair, looked at this person, then at that person, tried to break into their talk, opened his mouth and shut it again. They were talking about the fishing industry. Why did no one ask him his opinion? What did they know about the fishing industry?

Lily Briscoe knew all that. Sitting opposite him could she not see, as in an

X-ray photograph, the ribs and thigh bones of the young man's desire to impress himself lying dark in the mist of his flesh – that thin mist which convention had laid over his burning desire to break into the conversation? But, she thought, screwing up her Chinese eyes, and remembering how he sneered at women, 'can't paint, can't write', why should I help him to relieve himself?

There is a code of behaviour she knew, whose seventh article (it may be) says that on occasions of this sort it behoves the woman, whatever her own occupation may be, to go to the help of the young man opposite so that he may expose and relieve the thigh bones, the ribs, of his vanity, of his urgent desire to assert himself; as indeed it is their duty, she reflected, in her old-maidenly fairness, to help us, suppose the Tube were to burst into flames. Then, she thought, I should certainly expect Mr Tansley to get me out. But how would it be, she thought, if neither of us did either of these things? So she sat there smiling.

'You're not planning to go to the Lighthouse, are you, Lily?' said Mrs Ramsay. 'Remember poor Mr Langley; he had been round the world dozens of times, but he told me he never suffered as he did when my husband took him there. Are you a good sailor, Mr Tansley?' she asked.

Mr Tansley raised a hammer: swung it high in the air; but realising, as it descended, that he could not smite that butterfly with such an instrument as this, said only that he had never been sick in his life. But in that one sentence lay compact, like gunpowder, that his grandfather was a fisherman; his father a chemist; that he had worked his way up entirely himself; that he was proud of it; that he was Charles Tansley – a fact that nobody there seemed to realise; but one of these days every single person would know it. He scowled ahead of him. He could almost pity these mild cultivated people, who would be blown sky high, like bales of wool and barrels of apples, one of these days by the gunpowder that was in him.

'Will you take me, Mr Tansley?' said Lily, quickly, kindly, for, of course, if Mrs Ramsay said to her, as in effect she did, 'I am drowning, my dear, in seas of fire. Unless you apply some balm to the anguish of this hour and say something nice to that young man there, life will run upon the rocks – indeed I hear the grating and the growling at this minute. My nerves are taut as fiddle strings. Another touch and they will snap' – when Mrs Ramsay said all this, as the glance in her eyes said it, of course for the hundred and fiftieth time Lily Briscoe had to renounce the experiment – what happens if one is not nice to that young man there – and be nice.

Judging the turn in her mood correctly – that she was friendly to him now – he was relieved of his egotism, and told her how he had been thrown out of a boat when he was a baby; how his father used to fish him out with a boat hook; that was how he had learnt to swim. One of his uncles kept the light on some rock or other off the Scottish coast, he said. He had been there with him in a storm. This was said loudly in a pause. They had to listen to him when he said that he had been with his uncle in a lighthouse in a storm. Ah, thought Lily Briscoe, as the conversation took this auspicious turn, and she felt Mrs Ramsay's gratitude (for Mrs Ramsay was free now to talk for a moment herself), ah, she thought, but what haven't I paid to get it for you? She had not been sincere.

She had done the usual trick – been nice. She would never know him. He would never know her. Human relations were all like that, she thought, and the worst (if it had not been for Mr Bankes) were between men and women. Inevitably these were extremely insincere. Then her eye caught the salt cellar, which she had placed there to remind her, and she remembered that next morning she would move the tree further towards the middle, and her spirits rose so high at the thought of painting tomorrow that she laughed out loud at what Mr Tansley was saying. Let him talk all night if he liked it.

'But how long do they leave men on a lighthouse?' she asked. He told her. He was amazingly well informed. And as he was grateful, and as he liked her, and as he was beginning to enjoy himself, so now, Mrs Ramsay thought, she could return to that dream land, that unreal but fascinating place, the Mannings' drawing-room at Marlow twenty years ago; where one moved about without haste or anxiety, for there was no future to worry about. She knew what had happened to them, what to her. It was like reading a good book again, for she knew the end of that story, since it had happened twenty years ago, and life, which shot down even from this dining-room table in cascades, heaven knows where, was sealed up there, and lay, like a lake, placidly between its banks. He said they had built a billiard room – was it possible? Would William go on talking about the Mannings? She wanted him to. But no – for some reason he was no longer in the mood. She tried. He did not respond. She could not force him. She was disappointed.

'The children are disgraceful,' she said, sighing. He said something about punctuality being one of the minor virtues which we do not acquire until later in life.

'If at all,' said Mrs Ramsay merely to fill up space, thinking what an old maid William was becoming. Conscious of his treachery, conscious of her wish to talk about something more intimate, yet out of mood for it at present, he felt come over him the disagreeableness of life, sitting there, waiting. Perhaps the others were saying something interesting? What were they saying?

That the fishing season was bad; that the men were emigrating. They were talking about wages and unemployment. The young man was abusing the government. William Bankes, thinking what a relief it was to catch on to something of this sort when private life was disagreeable, heard him say something about 'one of the most scandalous acts of the present government'. Lily was listening; Mrs Ramsay was listening; they were all listening. But already bored, Lily felt that something was lacking; Mr Bankes felt that something was lacking. Pulling her shawl round her Mrs Ramsay felt that something was lacking. All of them bending themselves to listen thought: 'Pray heaven that the inside of my mind may not be exposed,' for each thought, 'The others are feeling this. They are outraged and indignant with the government about the fishermen. Whereas, I feel nothing at all.' But perhaps, thought Mr Bankes, as he looked at Mr Tansley, here is the man. One was always waiting for the man. There was always a chance. At any moment the leader might arise; the man of genius, in politics as in anything else. Probably he will be extremely disagreeable to us old fogies, thought Mr Bankes, doing his best to make allowances, for he knew by some curious physical sensation, as of nerves erect in his spine, that he was jealous, for himself partly, partly more probably for his work, for his point of view, for his science; and therefore he was not entirely open-minded or altogether fair, for Mr Tansley seemed to be saying: You have wasted your lives. You are all of you wrong. Poor old fogies, you're hopelessly behind the times. He seemed to be rather cocksure, this young man; and his manners were bad. But Mr Bankes bade himself observe: he had courage; he had ability; he was extremely well up in the facts. Probably, Mr Bankes thought, as Tansley abused the government, there is a good deal in what he says.

'Tell me now . . .' he said. So they argued about politics, and Lily looked at the leaf on the tablecloth; and Mrs Ramsay, leaving the argument entirely in the hands of the two men, wondered why she was so bored by this talk, and wished, looking at her husband at the other end of the table, that he would say something. One word, she said to herself. For if he said a thing, it would make all the difference. He went to the heart of things. He cared about fishermen and their wages. He could not sleep for thinking of them. It was altogether different when he spoke; one did not feel then, pray heaven you don't see how little I care, because one did care. Then, realising that it was because she admired him so much that she was waiting for him to speak, she felt as if somebody had been praising her husband to her and their marriage, and she glowed all over without realising that it was she herself who had praised him. She looked at him thinking to find this shown in his face; he would be looking magnificent . . . But not in the least! He was screwing his face up, he was scowling and frowning and flushing with anger. What on earth was it about? she wondered. What could be the matter? Only that poor old Augustus had asked for another plate of soup – that was all. It was unthinkable, it was detestable (so he signalled to her across the table) that Augustus should be beginning his soup over again. He loathed people eating when he had finished. She saw his anger fly like a pack of hounds into his eyes, his brow, and she knew that in a moment something violent would explode, and then – but thank goodness! she saw him clutch himself and clap a brake on the wheel, and the whole of his body seemed to emit sparks but not words. He sat there scowling. He had said nothing, he would have her observe. Let her give him the credit for that! But why after all should poor Augustus not ask for another plate of soup? He had merely touched Ellen's arm and said: 'Ellen, please, another plate of soup,' and then Mr Ramsay scowled like that.

And why not? Mrs Ramsay demanded. Surely they could let Augustus have his soup if he wanted it. He hated people wallowing in food, Mr Ramsay frowned at her. He hated everything dragging on for hours like this. But he had controlled himself, Mr Ramsay would have her observe, disgusting though the sight was. But why show it so plainly, Mrs Ramsay demanded (they looked at each other, down the long table sending these questions and answers across, each knowing exactly what the other felt). Everybody could see, Mrs Ramsay thought. There was Rose gazing at her father, there was Roger gazing at his father; both would be off in spasms of laughter in another second, she knew, and so she said promptly (indeed it was time): 'Light the candles,' and they jumped up instantly and went and fumbled at the sideboard.

Why could he never conceal his feelings? Mrs Ramsay wondered, and she wondered if Augustus Carmichael had noticed. Perhaps he had; perhaps he had not. She could not help respecting the composure with which he sat there, drinking his soup. If he wanted soup he asked for soup. Whether people laughed at him or were angry with him he was the same. He did not like her, she knew that; but partly for that very reason she respected him, and looking at him, drinking soup, very large and calm in the failing light, and monumental, and contemplative, she wondered what he did feel then, and why he was always content and dignified; and she thought how devoted he was to Andrew, and would call him into his room, and, Andrew said, 'show him things'. And there he would lie all day long on the lawn brooding presumably over his poetry, till he reminded one of a cat watching birds, and then he clapped his paws together when he had found the word, and her husband said: 'Poor old Augustus – he's a true poet,' which was high praise from her husband.

Now eight candles were stood down the table, and after the first stoop the flames stood upright and drew with them into visibility the long table entire, and in the middle a yellow and purple dish of fruit. What had she done with it, Mrs Ramsay wondered, for Rose's arrangement of the grapes and pears, of the horny pink-lined shell, of the bananas, made her think of a trophy fetched from the bottom of the sea, of Neptune's banquet, of the bunch that hangs with vine leaves over the shoulder of Bacchus (in some picture), among the leopard skins and the torches lolloping red and gold . . . Thus brought up suddenly into the light it seemed possessed of great size and depth, was like a world in which one could take one's staff and climb up hills, she thought, and go down into valleys, and to her pleasure (for it brought them into sympathy momentarily) she saw that Augustus too feasted his eyes on the same plate of fruit, plunged in, broke off a bloom there, a tassel here, and returned, after feasting, to his hive. That was his way of looking, different from hers. But looking together united them.

Now all the candles were lit, and the faces on both sides of the table were brought nearer by the candlelight, and composed, as they had not been in the twilight, into a party round a table, for the night was now shut off by panes of glass, which, far from giving any accurate view of the outside world, rippled it so strangely that here, inside the room, seemed to be order and dry land; there, outside, a reflection in which things wavered and vanished, waterily.

Some change at once went through them all, as if this had really happened, and they were all conscious of making a party together in a hollow, on an island; had their common cause against that fluidity out there. Mrs Ramsay, who had been uneasy, waiting for Paul and Minta to come in, and unable, she felt, to settle to things, now felt her uneasiness changed to expectation. For now they must come, and Lily Briscoe, trying to analyse the cause of the sudden exhilaration, compared it with that moment on the tennis lawn, when solidity suddenly vanished, and such vast spaces lay between them; and now the same effect was got by the many candles in the sparely furnished room, and the uncurtained windows, and the bright masklike look of faces seen by candlelight. Some weight was taken off them; anything might happen, she felt. They must come now, Mrs Ramsay thought, looking at the door, and at that instant, Minta Doyle, Paul Rayley, and a maid carrying a great dish in her hands came in together. They were awfully late; they were horribly late, Minta said, as they found their way to different ends of the table.

'I lost my brooch – my grandmother's brooch,' said Minta with a sound of lamentation in her voice, and a suffusion in her large brown eyes, looking down, looking up, as she sat by Mr Ramsay, which roused his chivalry so that he bantered her.

How could she be such a goose, he asked, as to scramble about the rocks in jewels?

She was by way of being terrified of him – he was so fearfully clever, and the first night when she had sat by him, and he talked about George Eliot, she had been really frightened, for she had left the third volume of *Middlemarch* in the train and she never knew what happened in the end; but afterwards she got on perfectly, and made herself out even more ignorant than she was, because he liked telling her she was a fool. And so tonight, directly he laughed at her, she was not frightened. Besides, she knew, directly she came into the room, that the miracle had happened; she wore her golden haze. Sometimes she had it; sometimes not. She never knew why it came or why it went, or if she had it until she came into the room and then she knew instantly by the way some man looked at her. Yes, tonight she had it, tremendously; she knew that by the way Mr Ramsay told her not to be a fool. She sat beside him, smiling.

It must have happened then, thought Mrs Ramsay; they are engaged. And for a moment she felt what she had never expected to feel again – jealousy. For he, her husband, felt it too – Minta's glow; he liked these girls, these golden-reddish girls, with something flying, something a little wild and harum-scarum about them, who didn't 'scrape their hair off', weren't, as he said about poor Lily Briscoe, 'skimpy'. There was some quality which she herself had not, some lustre, some richness, which attracted him, amused him, led him to make favourites of girls like Minta. They might cut his hair for him, plait him watch-chains, or interrupt him at his work, hailing him (she heard them), 'Come along, Mr Ramsay; it's our turn to beat them now,' and out he came to play tennis.

But indeed she was not jealous, only, now and then, when she made herself look in her glass, a little resentful that she had grown old, perhaps, by her own fault. (The bill for the greenhouse and all the rest of it.) She was grateful to them for laughing at him ('How many pipes have you smoked today, Mr Ramsay?' and so on), till he seemed a young man; a man very attractive to women, not burdened, not weighed down with the greatness of his labours and the sorrows of the world and his fame or his failure, but again as she had first known him, gaunt but gallant; helping her out of a boat, she remembered; with delightful ways, like that (she looked at him, and he looked astonishingly young, teasing Minta). For herself – 'Put it down there,' she said, helping the Swiss girl to place gently before her the huge brown pot in which was the Boeuf en Daube – for her own part she liked her boobies. Paul must sit by her. She had kept a place for him. Really, she sometimes thought she liked the boobies best. They did not bother one with their dissertations. How much they missed, after all, these very clever men! How dried up they did become, to be sure. There was something, she thought as he sat down, very charming about Paul. His manners were delightful to her, and his sharp cut nose and his bright blue eyes. He was so considerate. Would he tell her – now that they were all talking again – what had happened?

'We went back to look for Minta's brooch,' he said, sitting down by her. 'We' – that was enough. She knew from the effort, the rise in his voice to surmount a difficult word, that it was the first time he had said 'we'. 'We' did this, 'we' did that. They'll say that all their lives, she thought, and an exquisite scent of olives and oil and juice rose from the great brown dish as Marthe, with a little flourish, took the cover off. The cook had spent three days over that dish. And she must take great care, Mrs Ramsay thought, diving into the soft mass, to choose a specially tender piece for William Bankes. And she peered into the dish, with its shiny walls and its confusion of savoury brown and yellow meats, and its bay leaves and its wine, and thought: This will celebrate the occasion – a curious sense rising in her, at once freakish and tender, of celebrating a festival, as if two emotions were called up in her, one profound – for what could be more serious than the love of man for woman, what more commanding, more impressive, bearing in its bosom the seeds of death; at the same time these lovers, these people entering into illusion glittering eyed, must be danced round with mockery, decorated with garlands.

'It is a triumph,' said Mr Bankes, laying his knife down for a moment. He had eaten attentively. It was rich; it was tender. It was perfectly cooked. How did she manage these things in the depths of the country? he asked her. She was a wonderful woman. All his love, all his reverence had returned; and she knew it.

'It is a French recipe of my grandmother's,' said Mrs Ramsay, speaking with a ring of great pleasure in her voice. Of course it was French. What passes for cookery in England is an abomination (they agreed). It is putting cabbages in water. It is roasting meat till it is like leather. It is cutting off the delicious skins of vegetables. 'In which,' said Mr Bankes, 'all the virtue of the vegetable is contained.' And the waste, said Mrs Ramsay. A whole French family could live on what an English cook throws away. Spurred on by her sense that William's affection had come back to her, and that everything was all right again, and that her suspense was over, and that now she was free both to triumph and to mock, she laughed, she gesticulated, till Lily thought, How childlike, how absurd she was, sitting up there with all her beauty opened again in her, talking about the skins of vegetables. There was something frightening about her. She was irresistible. Always she got her own way in the end, Lily thought. Now she had brought this off – Paul and Minta, one might suppose, were engaged. Mr Bankes was dining here. She put a spell on them all, by wishing, so simply, so directly; and Lily contrasted that abundance with her own poverty of spirit, and supposed that it was partly that belief (for her face was all lit up – without looking young, she looked radiant) in this strange, this terrifying thing, which made Paul Rayley, the centre of it, all of a tremor, yet abstract, absorbed, silent. Mrs Ramsay, Lily felt, as she talked about the skins of vegetables, exalted that, worshipped that; held her hands over it to warm them, to protect it, and yet, having brought it all about, somehow laughed, led her victims, Lily felt, to the altar. It came over her too now – the emotion, the vibration of love. How inconspicuous she felt herself by Paul's side! He, glowing, burning; she, aloof, satirical; he, bound for adventure; she, moored to the shore; he, launched, incautious; she solitary, left out – and, ready to implore a share, if it were disaster, in his disaster, she said shyly: 'When did Minta lose her brooch?'

He smiled the most exquisite smile, veiled by memory, tinged by dreams. He shook his head. 'On the beach,' he said.

'I'm going to find it,' he said, 'I'm getting up early.' This being kept secret from Minta, he lowered his voice, and turned his eyes to where she sat, laughing, beside Mr Ramsay.

Lily wanted to protest violently and outrageously her desire to help him, envisaging how in the dawn on the beach she would be the one to pounce on the brooch half-hidden by some stone, and thus herself be included among the sailors and adventurers. But what did he reply to her offer? She actually said with an emotion that she seldom let appear: 'Let me come with you';

and he laughed. He meant yes or no – either perhaps. But it was not his meaning – it was the odd chuckle he gave, as if he had said, Throw yourself over the cliff if you like, I don't care. He turned on her cheek the heat of love, its horror, its cruelty, its unscrupulosity. It scorched her, and Lily, looking at Minta being charming to Mr Ramsay at the other end of the table, flinched for her exposed to those fangs, and was thankful. For at any rate, she said to herself, catching sight of the salt cellar on the pattern, she need not marry, thank heaven: she need not undergo that degradation. She was saved from that dilution. She would move the tree rather more to the middle.

Such was the complexity of things. For what happened to her, especially staying with the Ramsays, was to be made to feel violently two opposite things at the same time; that's what you feel, was one; that's what I feel, was the other; and then they fought together in her mind, as now. It is so beautiful, so exciting, this love, that I tremble on the verge of it, and offer, quite out of my own habit, to look for a brooch on a beach; also it is the stupidest, the most barbaric of human passions, and turns a nice young man with a profile like a gem (Paul's was exquisite) into a bully with a crowbar (he was swaggering, he was insolent) in the Mile End Road. Yet she said to herself, from the dawn of time odes have been sung to love; wreaths heaped and roses; and if you asked nine people out of ten they would say they wanted nothing but this; while the women, judging from her own experience, would all the time be feeling, This is not what we want; there is nothing more tedious, puerile and inhumane than love; yet it is also beautiful and necessary. Well then, well then? she asked, somehow expecting the others to go on with the argument, as if in an argument like this one threw one's own little bolt which fell short obviously and left the others to carry it on. So she listened again to what they were saying in case they should throw any light upon the question of love.

'Then,' said Mr Bankes, 'there is that liquid the English call coffee.'

'Oh coffee!' said Mrs Ramsay. But it was much rather a question (she was thoroughly roused, Lily could see, and talked very emphatically) of real butter and clean milk. Speaking with warmth and eloquence she described the iniquity of the English dairy system, and in what state milk was delivered at the door, and was about to prove her charges, for she had gone into the matter, when all round the table, beginning with Andrew in the middle, like a fire leaping from tuft to tuft of furze, her children laughed; her husband laughed; she was laughed at, fire-encircled, and forced to vail her crest, dismount her batteries, and only retaliate by displaying the raillery and ridicule of the table to Mr Bankes as an example of what one suffered if one attacked the prejudices of the British Public.

Purposely, however, for she had it on her mind that Lily, who had helped her with Mr Tansley, was out of things, she exempted her from the rest; said, 'Lily anyhow agrees with me,' and so drew her in, a little fluttered, a little startled. (For she was thinking about love.) They were both out of things, Mrs Ramsay had been thinking, both Lily and Charles Tansley. Both suffered from the glow of the other two. He, it was clear, felt himself utterly in the cold; no woman would look at him with Paul Rayley in the room. Poor fellow! Still, he had his dissertation, the influence of somebody upon something: he could take care of himself. With Lily it was different. She faded, under Minta's glow; became more inconspicuous than ever, in her little grey dress with her little puckered face and her little Chinese eyes. Everything about her was so small. Yet, thought Mrs Ramsay, comparing her with Minta, as she claimed her help (for Lily should bear her out she talked no more about her dairies than her husband did about his boots – he would talk by the hour about his boots), of the two Lily at forty will be the better. There was in Lily a thread of something; a flare of something; something of her own which Mrs Ramsay liked very much indeed, but no man would, she feared. Obviously not, unless it were a much older man, like William Bankes. But then he cared, well, Mrs Ramsay sometimes thought that he cared, since his wife's death, perhaps for her. He was not 'in love' of course; it was one of those unclassified affections of which there are so many. Oh, but nonsense, she thought; William must marry Lily. They have so many things in common. Lily is so fond of flowers. They are both cold and aloof and rather self-sufficing. She must arrange for them to take a long walk together.

Foolishly, she had set them opposite each other. That could be remedied tomorrow. If it were fine they should go for a picnic. Everything seemed possible. Everything seemed right. Just now (but this cannot last, she thought, dissociating herself from the moment while they were all talking about boots), just now she had reached security; she hovered like a hawk suspended; like a flag floated in an element of joy which filled every nerve of her body fully and sweetly, not noisily, solemnly rather, for it arose, she thought, looking at them all eating there, from husband and children and friends; all of which rising in this profound stillness (she was helping William Bankes to one very small piece more and peered into the depths of the earthenware pot) seemed now for no special reason to stay there like a smoke, like a fume rising upwards, holding them safe together. Nothing need be said; nothing could be said. There it was, all round them. It partook, she felt, carefully helping Mr Bankes to a specially tender piece, of eternity; as she had already felt about something different once before that afternoon; there is a coherence in things, a stability; something, she meant, is immune from change, and shines out (she glanced at the window with its ripple of reflected lights) in the face of the flowing, the fleeting, the spectral, like a ruby; so that again tonight she had the feeling she had had once today already, of peace, of rest. Of such moments, she thought, the thing is made that remains for ever after. This would remain.

'Yes,' she assured William Bankes, 'there is plenty for everybody.'

'Andrew,' she said, 'hold your plate lower, or I shall spill it.' (The Boeuf en Daube was a perfect triumph.) Here, she felt, putting the spoon down, was the still space that lies about the heart of things, where one could move or rest; could wait now (they were all helped) listening; could then, like a hawk which lapses suddenly from its high station, flaunt and sink on laughter easily, resting her whole weight upon what at the other end of the table her husband was saying about the square root of one thousand two hundred and fifty-three, which happened to be the number on his railway ticket.

What did it all mean? To this day she had no notion. A square root? What was that? Her sons knew. She leant on them; on cubes and square roots; that was what they were talking about now; on Voltaire and Madame de Staël; on the character of Napoleon; on the French system of land tenure; on Lord Rosebery; on Creevey's Memoirs: she let it uphold her and sustain her, this admirable fabric of the masculine intelligence, which ran up and down, crossed this way and that, like iron girders spanning the swaying fabric, upholding the world, so that she could trust herself to it utterly, even shut her eyes, or flicker them for a moment, as a child staring up from its pillow winks at the myriad layers of the leaves of a tree. Then she woke up. It was still being fabricated. William Bankes was praising the Waverley novels.

He read one of them every six months, he said. And why should that make Charles Tansley angry? He rushed in (all, thought Mrs Ramsay, because Prue will not be nice to him) and denounced the Waverley novels when he knew nothing about it, nothing about it whatsoever, Mrs Ramsay thought, observing him rather than listening to what he said. She could see how it was from his manner – he wanted to assert himself, and so it would always be with him till he got his professorship or married his wife, and so need not be always saying, 'I – I – I.' For that was what his criticism of poor Sir Walter, or perhaps it was Jane Austen, amounted to. 'I – I – I.' He was thinking of himself and the impression he was making, as she could tell by the sound of his voice, and his emphasis and his uneasiness. Success would be good for him. At any rate they were off again. Now she need not listen. It could not last she knew, but at the moment her eyes were so clear that they seemed to go round the table unveiling each of these people, and their thoughts and their feelings, without effort, like a light stealing under water so that its ripples and the reeds in it and the minnows balancing themselves, and the sudden silent trout are all lit up hanging, trembling. So she saw them; she heard them; but whatever they said had also this quality, as if what they said was like the movement of a trout when, at the same time, one can see the ripple and the gravel, something to the right, something to the left; and the whole is held together; for whereas in active life she would be netting and separating one thing from another; she would be saying she liked the Waverley novels or had not read them; she would be urging herself forward; now she said nothing. For the moment she hung suspended.

'Ah, but how long do you think it'll last?' said somebody. It was as if she had antennae trembling out from her, which, intercepting certain sentences, forced them upon her attention. This was one of them. She scented danger for her husband. A question like that would lead, almost certainly, to something being said which reminded him of his own failure. How long would he be read – he would think at once. William Bankes (who was entirely free from all such vanity) laughed, and said he attached no importance to changes in fashion. Who could tell what was going to last – in literature or indeed in anything else?

'Let us enjoy what we do enjoy,' he said. His integrity seemed to Mrs Ramsay quite admirable. He never seemed for a moment to think, But how does this affect me? But then if you had the other temperament, which must have praise, which must have encouragement, naturally you began (and she knew that Mr Ramsay was beginning) to be uneasy; to want somebody to say, Oh, but your work will last, Mr Ramsay, or something like that. He showed his uneasiness quite clearly now by saying, with some irritation, that, anyhow, Scott (or was it Shakespeare?) would last him his lifetime. He said it irritably. Everybody, she thought, felt a little uncomfortable, without knowing why. Then Minta Doyle, whose instinct was fine, said bluffly, absurdly, that she did not believe that anyone really enjoyed reading Shakespeare. Mr Ramsay said grimly (but his mind was turned away again) that very few people liked it as much as they said they did. But, he added, there is considerable merit in some of the plays nevertheless, and Mrs Ramsay saw that it would be all right for the moment anyhow; he would laugh at Minta, and she, Mrs Ramsay saw, realising his extreme anxiety about himself, would, in her own way, see that he was taken care of, and praise him, somehow or other. But she wished it was not necessary: perhaps it was her fault that it was necessary. Anyhow, she was free now to listen to what Paul Rayley was trying to say about books one had read as a boy. They lasted, he said. He had read some of Tolstoy at school. There was one he always remembered, but he had forgotten the name. Russian names were impossible, said Mrs Ramsay. 'Vronsky,' said Paul. He remembered that because he always thought it such a good name for a villain. 'Vronsky,' said Mrs Ramsay; 'Oh, *Anna Karenina*,' but that did not take them very far; books were not in their line. No, Charles Tansley would put them both right in a second about books, but it was all so mixed up with, Am I saying the right thing? Am I making a good impression? that, after all, one knew more about him than about Tolstoi, whereas what Paul said was about the thing simply, not himself. Like all stupid people he had a kind of modesty too, a consideration for what you were feeling, which, once in a way at least, she found attractive. Now he was thinking, not about himself or about Tolstoy, but whether she was cold, whether she felt a draught, whether she would like a pear.

No, she said, she did not want a pear. Indeed she had been keeping guard over the dish of fruit (without realising it) jealously, hoping that nobody would touch it. Her eyes had been going in and out among the curves and shadows of the fruit, among the rich purples of the lowland grapes, then over the horny ridge of the shell, putting a yellow against a purple, a curved shape against a round shape, without knowing why she did it, or why, every time she did it, she felt more and more serene; until, oh, what a pity that they should do it – a hand reached out, took a pear, and spoilt the whole thing. In sympathy she looked at Rose. She looked at Rose sitting between Jasper and Prue. How odd that one's child should do that!

How odd to see them sitting there, in a row, her children, Jasper, Rose, Prue, Andrew, almost silent, but with some joke of their own going on, she guessed, from the twitching at their lips. It was something quite apart from everything else, something they were hoarding up to laugh over in their own room. It was not about their father, she hoped. No, she thought not. What was it, she wondered, sadly rather, for it seemed to her that they would laugh when she was not there. There was all that hoarded behind those rather set, still, masklike faces, for they did not join in easily; they were like watchers, surveyors, a little raised or set apart from the grown-up people. But when she looked at Prue tonight, she saw that this was not now quite true of her. She was just beginning, just moving, just descending. The faintest light was on her face, as if the glow of Minta opposite, some excitement, some anticipation of happiness was reflected in her, as if the sun of the love of men and women rose over the rim of the tablecloth, and without knowing what it was she bent towards it and greeted it. She kept looking at Minta, shyly, yet curiously, so that Mrs Ramsay looked from one to the other and said, speaking to Prue in her own mind, You will be as happy as she is one of these days. You will be much happier, she added, because you are my daughter, she meant; her own daughters must be happier than other people's daughters. But dinner was over. It was time to go. They were only playing with things on their plates. She would wait until they had done laughing at some story her husband was telling. He was having a joke with Minta about a bet. Then she would get up.

She liked Charles Tansley, she thought, suddenly; she liked his laugh. She liked him for being so angry with Paul and Minta. She liked his awkwardness. There was a lot in that young man after all. And Lily, she thought, putting her napkin beside her plate, she always has some joke of her own. One need never bother about Lily. She waited. She tucked her napkin under the edge of her plate. Well, were they done now? No. That story had led to another story. Her husband was in great spirits tonight, and wishing, she supposed, to make it all right with old Augustus after that scene about the soup, had drawn him in – they were telling stories about someone they had both known at college. She looked at the window in which the candle flames burnt brighter now that the panes were black, and looking at that outside the voices came to her very strangely, as if they were voices at a service in a cathedral, for she did not listen to the words. The sudden bursts of laughter and then one voice (Minta's) speaking alone, reminded her of men and boys crying out the Latin words of a service in some Roman Catholic cathedral. She waited. Her husband spoke. He was repeating something, and she knew it was poetry from the rhythm and the ring of exaltation and melancholy in his voice:

> Come out and climb the garden path,
> Luriana Lurilee.
> The China rose is all abloom and buzzing with the yellow bee.

The words (she was looking at the window) sounded as if they were floating like flowers on water out there, cut off from them all, as if no one had said them, but they had come into existence of themselves.

> And all the lives we ever lived and all the lives to be
> Are full of trees and changing leaves.

She did not know what they meant, but, like music, the words seemed to be spoken by her own voice, outside herself, saying quite easily and naturally what had been in her mind the whole evening while she said different things. She knew, without looking round, that everyone at the table was listening to the voice saying:

> I wonder if it seems to you
> Luriana, Lurilee,

with the same sort of relief and pleasure that she had, as if this were, at last, the natural thing to say, this were their own voice speaking.

But the voice stopped. She looked round. She made herself get up. Augustus Carmichael had risen and, holding his table napkin so that it looked like a long white robe, he stood chanting:

> To see the Kings go riding by
> Over lawn and daisy lea
> With their palm leaves and cedar sheaves,
> Luriana, Lurilee,

and as she passed him he turned slightly towards her repeating the last words:

> Luriana, Lurilee,

and bowed to her as if he did her homage. Without knowing why she felt that he liked her better than he had ever done before; and with a feeling of relief and gratitude she returned his bow and passed through the door which he held open for her.

It was necessary now to carry everything a step further. With her foot on the threshold she waited a moment longer in a scene which was vanishing even as she looked, and then, as she moved and took Minta's arm and left the room, it changed, it shaped itself differently; it had become, she knew, giving one last look at it over her shoulder, already the past.

XVIII

As usual, Lily thought. There was always something that had to be done at that precise moment, something that Mrs Ramsay had decided for reasons of her own to do instantly, it might be with everyone standing about making jokes, as now, not being able to decide whether they were going into the smoking-room, into the drawing-room, up to the attics. Then one saw Mrs Ramsay, in the midst of this hubbub standing there with Minta's arm in hers, bethink her, 'Yes, it is time for that now,' and so make off at once with an air of secrecy to do something alone. And directly she went a sort of disintegration set in; they wavered about, went different ways, Mr Bankes took Charles Tansley by the arm and went off to finish on the terrace the discussion they had begun at dinner about politics, thus giving a turn to the whole poise of the evening, making the weight fall in a different direction, as if, Lily thought, seeing them go, and hearing a word or two about the policy of the Labour Party, they had gone up on to the bridge of the ship and were taking their bearings; the change from poetry to politics struck her like that; so Mr Bankes and Charles Tansley went off while the others stood looking at Mrs Ramsay going upstairs in the lamplight alone. Where, Lily wondered, was she going so quickly?

Not that she did in fact run or hurry; she went indeed rather slowly. She felt rather inclined just for a moment to stand still after all that chatter, and pick out one particular thing; the thing that mattered; to detach it; separate it off; clean it of all the emotions and odds and ends of things, and so hold it before her, and bring it to the tribunal where, ranged about in conclave, sat the judges she had set up to decide these things. Is it good, is it bad, is it right or wrong? Where are we going to? and so on. So she righted herself after the shock of the event, and quite unconsciously and incongruously, used the branches of the elm trees outside to help her to stabilise her position. Her world was changing: they were still. The event had given her a sense of movement. All must be in order. She must get that right and that right, she thought, insensibly approving of the dignity of the trees' stillness, and now again of the superb upward rise (like the beak of a ship up a wave) of the elm branches as the wind raised them. For it was windy (she stood a moment to look out). It was windy, so that the leaves now and then brushed open a star, and the stars themselves seemed to be shaking and darting light and trying to flash out between the edges of the leaves. Yes, that was done then, accomplished; and as with all things done, become solemn. Now one thought of it, cleared of chatter and emotion, it seemed always to have been, only was shown now, and so being shown struck everything into stability. They would, she thought, going on again, however long they lived, come back to this night; this moon; this wind, this house: and to her too. It flattered her, where she was most susceptible of flattery, to think how, wound about in their hearts, however long they lived, she would be woven; and this, and this, and this, she thought, going upstairs, laughing, but affectionately, at the sofa on the landing (her mother's) at the rocking-chair (her father's); at the map of the Hebrides. All that would be revived again in the lives of Paul and Minta; 'the Rayleys' – she tried the new name over, and she felt, with her hand on the nursery door, that community of feeling with other people which emotion gives as if the walls of partition had become so thin that practically (the feeling was one of relief and happiness) it was all one stream, and chairs, tables, maps, were hers, were theirs, it did not matter whose, and Paul and Minta would carry it on when she was dead.

She turned the handle, firmly, lest it should squeak, and went in, pursing her lips slightly, as if to remind herself that she must not speak aloud. But directly she came in she saw, with annoyance, that the precaution was not needed. The children were not asleep. It was most annoying. Mildred should be more careful. There was James wide awake and Cam sitting bolt upright, and Mildred out of bed in her bare feet, and it was almost eleven and they were all talking. What was the matter? It was that horrid skull again. She had told Mildred to move it but Mildred, of course, had forgotten, and now there was Cam wide awake and James wide awake quarrelling when they ought to have been asleep hours ago. What had possessed Edward to send them this horrid skull? She had been so foolish as to let them nail it up there. It was nailed fast, Mildred said, and Cam couldn't go to sleep with it in the room, and James screamed if she touched it.

Then Cam must go to sleep (it had great horns said Cam) – must go to sleep and dream of lovely palaces, said Mrs Ramsay, sitting down on the bed by her side. She could see the horns, Cam said, all over the room. It was true. Wherever they put the light (and James could not sleep without a light) there was always a shadow somewhere.

'But think, Cam, it's only an old pig,' said Mrs Ramsay, 'a nice black pig like the pigs at the farm.' But Cam thought it was a horrid thing, branching at her all over the room.

'Well then,' said Mrs Ramsay, 'we will cover it up,' and they all watched her go to the chest of drawers, and open the little drawers quickly one after another, and not seeing anything that would do, she quickly took her own shawl off and wound it round the skull, round and round and round, and then she came back to Cam and laid her head almost flat on the pillow beside Cam's and said how lovely it looked now, how the fairies would love it; it was like a bird's nest, it was like a beautiful mountain such as she had seen abroad, with valleys and flowers and bells ringing and birds singing and little goats and antelopes . . . She could see the words echoing as she spoke them rhythmically in Cam's mind, and Cam was repeating after her how it was like a mountain, a bird's nest, a garden, and there were little antelopes, and her eyes were opening and shutting, and Mrs Ramsay went on saying still more monotonously, and more rhythmically and more nonsensically, how she must shut her eyes and go to sleep and dream of mountains and valleys and stars falling and parrots and antelopes and gardens, and everything lovely, she said, raising her head very slowly and speaking more and more mechanically, until she sat upright and saw that Cam was asleep.

Now, she whispered, crossing over to his bed, James must go to sleep too, for see, she said, the boar's skull was still there; they had not touched it; they had done just what he wanted; it was there quite unhurt. He made sure that the skull was still there under the shawl. But he wanted to ask her something more. Would they go to the Lighthouse tomorrow?

No, not tomorrow, she said, but soon, she promised him; the next fine day. He was very good. He lay down. She covered him up. But he would never forget, she knew, and she felt angry with Charles Tansley, with her husband, and with herself for she had raised his hopes. Then feeling for her shawl and remembering that she had wrapped it round the boar's skull, she got up, and pulled the window down another inch or two, and heard the wind, and got a breath of the perfectly indifferent chill night air and murmured good-night to Mildred and left the room and let the tongue of the door slowly lengthen in the lock and went out.

She hoped he would not bang his books on the floor above their heads, she thought, still thinking how annoying Charles Tansley was. For neither of them slept well; they were excitable children, and since he said things like that about the Lighthouse, it seemed to her likely that he would knock a pile of books over, just as they were going to sleep, clumsily sweeping them off the table with his elbow. For she supposed that he had gone upstairs to work. Yet he looked so desolate; yet she would feel relieved when he went; yet she would see that he was better treated tomorrow; yet he was admirable with her husband; yet his manners certainly wanted improving; yet she liked his laugh – thinking this, as she came downstairs, she noticed that she could now see the moon itself through the staircase window – the yellow harvest moon – and turned, and they saw her, standing above them on the stairs.

'That's my mother,' thought Prue. Yes; Minta should look at her; Paul Rayley should look at her. That is the thing itself, she felt, as if there were only one person like that in the world; her mother. And, from having been quite grown up, a moment before, talking with the others, she became a child again, and what they had been doing was a game, and would her mother sanction their game, or condemn it, she wondered. And thinking what a chance it was for Minta and Paul and Lily to see her, and feeling what an extraordinary stroke of fortune it was for her to have her, and how she would never grow up and never leave home, she said, like a child: 'We thought of going down to the beach to watch the waves.'

Instantly, for no reason at all, Mrs Ramsay became like a girl of twenty, full of gaiety. A mood of revelry suddenly took possession of her. Of course they must go; of course they must go, she cried, laughing; and running down the last three or four steps quickly, she began turning from one to the other and laughing and drawing Minta's wrap round her and saying she only wished she could come too, and would they be very late, and had any of them got a watch?

'Yes, Paul has,' said Minta. Paul slipped a beautiful gold watch out of a little wash-leather case to show her. And as he held it in the palm of his hand before her, he felt, 'She knows all about it. I need not say anything.' He was saying to her as he showed her the watch: 'I've done it, Mrs Ramsay. I owe it all to you.' And seeing the gold watch lying in his hand, Mrs Ramsay felt, How extraordinarily lucky Minta is! She is marrying a man who has a gold watch in a wash-leather bag!

'How I wish I could come with you!' she cried. But she was withheld by something so strong that she never even thought of asking herself what it was. Of course it was impossible for her to go with them. But she would have liked to go, had it not been for the other thing, and tickled by the absurdity of her thought (how lucky to marry a man with a wash-leather bag for his watch) she went with a smile on her lips into the other room, where her husband sat reading.

XIX

Of course, she said to herself, coming into the room, she had to come here to get something she wanted. First she wanted to sit down in a particular chair under a particular lamp. But she wanted something more, though she did not know, could not think what it was that she wanted. She looked at her husband (taking up her stocking and beginning to knit), and saw that he did not want to be interrupted – that was clear. He was reading something that moved him very much. He was half smiling and then she knew he was controlling his emotion. He was tossing the pages over. He was acting it – perhaps he was thinking himself the person in the book. She wondered what book it was. Oh, it was one of old Sir Walter's, she saw, adjusting the shade of her lamp so that the light fell on her knitting. For Charles Tansley had been saying (she looked up as if she expected to hear the crash of books on the floor above) – had been saying that people don't read Scott any more. Then her husband thought: 'That's what they'll say of me'; so he went and got one of those books. And if he came to the conclusion 'That's true' what Charles Tansley said, he would accept it about Scott. (She could see that he was weighing, considering, putting this with that as he read.) But not about himself. He was always uneasy about himself. That troubled her. He would always be worrying about his own books – will they be read, are they good, why aren't they better, what do people think of me? Not liking to think of him so, and wondering if they had guessed at dinner why he suddenly became irritable when they talked about fame and books lasting, wondering if the children were laughing at that, she twitched the stocking out, and all the fine gravings came drawn with steel instruments about her lips and forehead, and she grew still like a tree which has been tossing and quivering and now, when the breeze falls, settles, leaf by leaf, into quiet.

It didn't matter, any of it, she thought. A great man, a great book, fame – who could tell? She knew nothing about it. But it was his way with him, his truthfulness – for instance at dinner she had been thinking quite instinctively, If only he would speak! She had complete trust in him. And dismissing all this, as one passes in diving now a weed, now a straw, now a bubble, she felt again, sinking deeper, as she had felt in the hall when the others were talking, There is something I want – something I have come to get, and she fell deeper and deeper without knowing quite what it was, with her eyes closed. And she waited a little, knitting, wondering, and slowly those words they had said at dinner, 'the China rose is all abloom and buzzing with the honey bee', began washing from side to side of her mind rhythmically, and as they washed, words, like little shaded lights, one red, one blue, one yellow, lit up in the dark of her mind, and seemed leaving their perches up there to fly across and across, or to cry out and to be echoed; so she turned and felt on the table beside her for a book.

> And all the lives we ever lived
> And all the lives to be,
> Are full of trees and changing leaves,

she murmured, sticking her needles into the stocking. And she opened the book and began reading here and there at random, and as she did so she felt that she was climbing backwards, upwards, shoving her way up under petals that curved over her, so that she only knew this is white, or this is red. She did not know at first what the words meant at all.

> Steer, hither steer your winged pines, all beaten Mariners!

she read and turned the page, swinging herself, zigzagging this way and that, from one line to another as from one branch to another, from one red and white flower to another, until a little sound roused her – her husband slapping his thighs. Their eyes met for a second; but they did not want to speak to each other. They had nothing to say, but something seemed, nevertheless, to go from him to her. It was the life, it was the power of it, it was the tremendous humour, she knew, that made him slap his thighs. Don't interrupt me, he seemed to be saying, don't say anything; just sit there. And he went on reading. His lips twitched. It filled him. It fortified him. He clean forgot all the little rubs and digs of the evening, and how it bored him unutterably to sit still while people ate and drank interminably, and his being so irritable with his wife and so touchy and minding when they passed his books over as if they didn't exist at all. But now, he felt, it didn't matter a damn who reached Z (if thought ran like an alphabet from A to Z). Somebody would reach it – if not he, then another. This man's strength and sanity, his feeling for straightforward simple things, these fishermen, the poor old crazed creature in Mucklebackit's cottage made him feel so vigorous, so relieved of something that he felt roused and triumphant and could not choke back his tears. Raising the book a little to hide his face he let them fall and shook his head from side to side and forgot himself completely (but not one or two reflections about morality and French novels and English novels and Scott's hands being tied but his view perhaps being as true as the other view), forgot his own bothers and failures completely in poor Steenie's drowning and Mucklebackit's sorrow (that was Scott at his best) and the astonishing delight and feeling of vigour that it gave him.

Well, let them improve upon that, he thought as he finished the chapter. He felt that he had been arguing with somebody, and had got the better of him. They could not improve upon that, whatever they might say; and his own position became more secure. The lovers were fiddlesticks, he thought, collecting it all in his mind again. That's fiddlesticks, that's first-rate, he thought, putting one thing beside another. But he must read it again. He could not remember the whole shape of the thing. He had to keep his judgement in suspense. So he returned to the other thought – if young men did not care for this, naturally they did not care for him either. One ought not to complain, thought Mr Ramsay, trying to stifle his desire to complain to his wife that young men did not admire him. But he was determined: he would not bother her again. Here he looked at her reading. She looked very peaceful, reading. He liked to think that everyone had taken themselves off and that he and she were alone. The whole of life did not consist in going to bed with a woman, he thought, returning to Scott and Balzac, to the English novel and the French novel.

Mrs Ramsay raised her head and like a person in a light sleep seemed to say that if he wanted her to wake she would, she really would, but otherwise, might she go on sleeping, just a little longer, just a little longer? She was climbing up those branches, this way and that, laying hands on one flower and then another.

Nor praise the deep vermilion in the rose,

she read, and so reading she was ascending, she felt, on to the top, on to the summit. How satisfying! How restful! All the odds and ends of the day stuck to this magnet; her mind felt swept, felt clean. And then there it was, suddenly entire shaped in her hands, beautiful and reasonable, clear and complete, the essence sucked out of life and held rounded here – the sonnet.

But she was becoming conscious of her husband looking at her. He was smiling at her, quizzically, as if he were ridiculing her gently for being asleep in broad daylight, but at the same time he was thinking, Go on reading. You don't look sad now, he thought. And he wondered what she was reading, and exaggerated her ignorance, her simplicity, for he liked to think that she was not clever, not book-learned at all. He wondered if she understood what she was reading. Probably not, he thought. She was astonishingly beautiful. Her beauty seemed to him, if that were possible, to increase.

> Yet seem'd it winter still, and, you away,
> As with your shadow I with these did play,

she finished.

'Well?' she said, echoing his smile dreamily, looking up from her book.

> 'As with your shadow I with these did play,'

she murmured putting the book on the table.

What had happened she wondered, as she took up her knitting, since she had last seen him alone? She remembered dressing, and seeing the moon; Andrew holding his plate too high at dinner; being depressed by something William had said; the birds in the trees; the sofa on the landing; the children being awake; Charles Tansley waking them with his books falling – oh no, that she had invented; and Paul having a wash-leather case for his watch. Which should she tell him about?

'They're engaged,' she said, beginning to knit, 'Paul and Minta.'

'So I guessed,' he said. There was nothing very much to be said about it. Her mind was still going up and down, up and down with the poetry; he was still feeling very vigorous, very forthright, after reading about Steenie's funeral. So they sat silent. Then she became aware that she wanted him to say something.

Anything, anything, she thought, going on with her knitting. Anything will do.

'How nice it would be to marry a man with a wash-leather bag for his watch,' she said, for that was the sort of joke they had together.

He snorted. He felt about this engagement as he always felt about any engagement; the girl is much too good for that young man. Slowly it came into her head, why is it then that one wants people to marry? What was the value, the meaning of things? (Every word they said now would be true.) Do say something, she thought, wishing only to hear his voice. For the shadow, the thing folding them in was beginning, she felt, to close round her again. Say anything, she begged, looking at him, as if for help.

He was silent, swinging the compass on his watch-chain to and fro, and thinking of Scott's novels and Balzac's novels. But through the crepuscular walls of their intimacy, for they were drawing together, involuntarily, coming side by side, quite close, she could feel his mind like a raised hand shadowing her mind; and he was beginning now that her thoughts took a turn he disliked – towards this 'pessimism' as he called it – to fidget, though he said nothing, raising his hand to his forehead, twisting a lock of hair, letting it fall again.

'You won't finish that stocking tonight,' he said, pointing to her stocking. That was what she wanted – the asperity in his voice reproving her. If he says it's wrong to be pessimistic probably it is wrong, she thought; the marriage will turn out all right.

'No,' she said, flattening the stocking out upon her knee, 'I shan't finish it.'

And what then? For she felt that he was still looking at her, but that his look had changed. He wanted something – wanted the thing she always found it so difficult to give him; wanted her to tell him that she loved him. And that, no, she could not do. He found talking so much easier than she did. He could say things – she never could. So naturally it was always he that said the things, and then for some reason he would mind this suddenly, and would reproach her. A heartless woman he called her; she never told him that she loved him. But it was not so – it was not so. It was only that she never could say what she felt. Was there no crumb on his coat? Nothing she could do for him? Getting up she stood at the window with the reddish-brown stocking in her hands, partly to turn away from him, partly because she did not mind looking now, with him watching, at the Lighthouse. For she knew that he had turned his head as she turned; he was watching her. She knew that he was thinking, You are more beautiful than ever. And she felt herself very beautiful. Will you not tell me just for once that you love me? He was thinking that, for he was roused, what with Minta and his book, and its being the end of the day and their having quarrelled about going to the Lighthouse. But she could not do it; she could not say it. Then, knowing that he was watching her, instead of saying anything she turned, holding her stocking, and looked at him. And as she looked at him she began to smile, for though she had not said a word, he knew, of course he knew, that she loved him. He could not deny it. And smiling she looked out of the window and said (thinking to herself, Nothing on earth can equal this happiness) –

'Yes, you were right. It's going to be wet tomorrow.' She had not said it, but he knew it. And she looked at him smiling. For she had triumphed again.

PART TWO
Time Passes

'Well, we must wait for the future to show,' said Mr Bankes, coming in from the terrace.

'It's almost too dark to see,' said Andrew, coming up from the beach.

'One can hardly tell which is the sea and which is the land,' said Prue.

'Do we leave that light burning?' said Lily as they took their coats off indoors.

'No,' said Prue, 'not if everyone's in.'

'Andrew,' she called back,' just put out the light in the hall.'

One by one the lamps were all extinguished, except that Mr Carmichael, who liked to lie awake a little reading Virgil, kept his candle burning rather longer than the rest.

So with the lamps all put out, the moon sunk, and a thin rain drumming on the roof, a downpouring of immense darkness began. Nothing, it seemed, could survive the flood, the profusion of darkness which creeping in at keyholes and crevices, stole round window blinds, came into bedrooms, swallowed up here a jug and basin, there a bowl of red and yellow dahlias, there the sharp edges and firm bulk of a chest of drawers. Not only was furniture confounded; there was scarcely anything left of body or mind by which one could say, 'This is he,' or, 'This is she.' Sometimes a hand was raised as if to clutch something or ward off something, or somebody groaned, or somebody laughed aloud as if sharing a joke with nothingness.

Nothing stirred in the drawing-room or in the dining-room or on the staircase. Only through the rusty hinges and swollen sea-moistened wood-work certain airs, detached from the body of the wind (the house was ramshackle after all), crept round corners and ventured indoors. Almost one might imagine them, as they entered the drawing-room, questioning and wondering, toying with the flap of hanging wallpaper, asking, would it hang much longer, when would it fall? Then smoothly brushing the walls, they passed on musingly as if asking the red and yellow roses on the wallpaper whether they would fade, and questioning (gently, for there was time at their disposal) the torn letters in the wastepaper basket, the flowers, the books, all of which were now open to them and asking: Were they allies? Were they enemies? How long would they endure?

So some random light directing them from an uncovered star, or wandering ship, or the Lighthouse even, with its pale footfall upon stair and mat, the little airs mounted the staircase and nosed round bedroom doors. But here surely, they must cease. Whatever else may perish and disappear what lies here is steadfast. Here one might say to those sliding lights, those fumbling airs, that breathe and bend over the bed itself, here you can neither touch nor destroy. Upon which, wearily, ghostlily, as if they had feather-light fingers and the light persistency of feathers, they would look, once, on the shut eyes and the loosely clasping fingers, and fold their garments wearily and disappear. And so, nosing, rubbing, they went to the window on the staircase, to the servants' bedrooms, to the boxes in the attics; descending, blanched the apples on the dining-room table, fumbled the petals of roses, tried the picture on the easel, brushed the mat and blew a little sand along the floor. At length, desisting, all ceased together, gathered together, all sighed together; all together gave off an aimless gust of lamentation to which some door in the kitchen replied; swung wide; admitted nothing; and slammed to.

[Here Mr Carmichael, who was reading Virgil, blew out his candle. It was past midnight.]

III

But what after all is one night? A short space, especially when the darkness dims so soon, and so soon a bird sings, a cock crows, or a faint green quickens, like a turning leaf, in the hollow of the wave. Night, however, succeeds to night. The winter holds a pack of them in store and deals them equally, evenly, with indefatigable fingers. They lengthen; they darken. Some of them hold aloft clear planets, plates of brightness. The autumn trees, ravaged as they are, take on the flash of tattered flags kindling in the gloom of cool cathedral caves where gold letters on marble pages describe death in battle and how bones bleach and burn far away in Indian sands. The autumn trees gleam in the yellow moonlight, in the light of harvest moons, the light which mellows the energy of labour, and smooths the stubble, and brings the wave lapping blue to the shore.

It seemed now as if, touched by human penitence and all its toil, divine goodness had parted the curtain and displayed behind it, single, distinct, the hare erect; the wave falling; the boat rocking, which, did we deserve them, should be ours always. But alas, divine goodness, twitching the cord, draws the curtain; it does not please him; he covers his treasures in a drench of hail, and so breaks them, so confuses them that it seems impossible that their calm should ever return or that we should ever compose from their fragments a perfect whole or read in the littered pieces the clear words of truth. For our penitence deserves a glimpse only; our toil respite only.

The nights now are full of wind and destruction; the trees plunge and bend and their leaves fly helter skelter until the lawn is plastered with them and they lie packed in gutters and choke rain-pipes and scatter damp paths. Also the sea tosses itself and breaks itself, and should any sleeper, fancying that he might find on the beach an answer to his doubts, a sharer of his solitude, throw off his bedclothes and go down by himself to walk on the sand, no image with semblance of serving and divine promptitude comes readily to hand bringing the night to order and making the world reflect the compass of the soul. The hand dwindles in his hand; the voice bellows in his ear. Almost it would appear that it is useless in such confusion to ask the night those questions as to what, and why, and wherefore, which tempt the sleeper from his bed to seek an answer.

[Mr Ramsay stumbling along a passage stretched his arms out one dark morning, but, Mrs Ramsay having died rather suddenly the night before, he stretched his arms out. They remained empty.]

IV

So with the house empty and the doors locked and the mattresses rolled round, those stray airs, advance guards of great armies, blustered in, brushed bare boards, nibbled and fanned, met nothing in bedroom or drawing-room that wholly resisted them but only hangings that flapped, wood that creaked, the bare legs of tables, saucepans and china already furred, tarnished, cracked. What people had shed and left – a pair of shoes, a shooting cap, some faded skirts and coats in wardrobes – those alone kept the human shape and in the emptiness indicated how once they were filled and animated; how once hands were busy with hooks and buttons; how once the looking-glass had held a face; had held a world hollowed out in which a figure turned, a hand flashed, the door opened, in came children rushing and tumbling; and went out again. Now, day after day, light turned, like a flower reflected in water, its clear image on the wall opposite. Only the shadows of the trees, flourishing in the wind, made obeisance on the wall, and for a moment darkened the pool in which light reflected itself; or birds, flying, made a soft spot flutter slowly across the bedroom floor.

So loveliness reigned and stillness, and together made the shape of loveliness itself, a form from which life had parted; solitary like a pool at evening, far distant, seen from a train window, vanishing so quickly that the pool, pale in the evening, is scarcely robbed of its solitude, though once seen. Loveliness and stillness clasped hands in the bedroom, and among the shrouded jugs and sheeted chairs even the prying of the wind, and the soft nose of the clammy sea airs, rubbing, snuffling, iterating, and reiterating their questions – 'Will you fade? Will you perish?' – scarcely disturbed the peace, the indifference, the air of pure integrity, as if the question they asked scarcely needed that they should answer: we remain.

Nothing it seemed could break that image, corrupt that innocence, or disturb the swaying mantle of silence which, week after week, in the empty room, wove into itself the falling cries of birds, ships hooting, the drone and hum of the fields, a dog's bark, a man's shout, and folded them round the house in silence. Once only a board sprang on the landing; once in the middle of the night with a roar, with a rupture, as after centuries of quiescence a rock rends itself from the mountain and hurtles crashing into the valley, one fold of the shawl loosened and swung to and fro. Then again peace descended; and the shadow wavered; light bent to its own image in adoration on the bedroom wall; when Mrs McNab, tearing the veil of silence with hands that had stood in the washtub, grinding it with boots that had crunched the shingle, came as directed to open all windows and dust the bedrooms.

V

As she lurched (for she rolled like a ship at sea) and leered (for her eyes fell on nothing directly, but with a sidelong glance that deprecated the scorn and anger of the world – she was witless, she knew it), as she clutched the banisters and hauled herself upstairs and rolled from room to room, she sang. Rubbing the glass of the long looking-glass and leering sideways at her swinging figure a sound issued from her lips – something that had been gay twenty years before on the stage perhaps, had been hummed and danced to, but now, coming from the toothless, bonneted, caretaking woman, was robbed of meaning, was like the voice of witlessness, humour, persistency itself, trodden down but springing up again, so that as she lurched, dusting, wiping, she seemed to say how it was one long sorrow and trouble, how it was getting up and going to bed again, and bringing things out and putting them away again. It was not easy or snug this world she had known for close on seventy years. Bowed down she was with weariness. How long, she asked, creaking and groaning on her knees under the bed, dusting the boards, how long shall it endure? but hobbled to her feet again, pulled herself up, and again with her sidelong leer which slipped and turned aside even from her own face, and her own sorrows, stood and gaped in the glass, aimlessly smiling, and began again the old amble and hobble, taking up mats, putting down china, looking sideways in the glass, as if, after all, she had her consolations, as if indeed there twined about her dirge some incorrigible hope. Visions of joy there must have been at the washtub, say with her children (yet two had been base-born and one had deserted her); at the public-house, drinking; turning over scraps in her drawers. Some cleavage of the dark there must have been, some channel in the depths of obscurity through which light enough issued to twist her face grinning in the glass and make her, turning to her job again, mumble out the old music-hall song. Meanwhile the mystic, the visionary, walked the beach, stirred a puddle, looked at a stone, and asked themselves: 'What am I?' 'What is this?' and suddenly an answer was vouchsafed them (what it was they could not say): so that they were warm in the frost and had comfort in the desert. But Mrs McNab continued to drink and gossip as before.

VI

The spring without a leaf to toss, bare and bright like a virgin fierce in her chastity, scornful in her purity, was laid out on fields wide-eyed and watchful and entirely careless of what was done or thought by the beholders.

[Prue Ramsay, leaning on her father's arm, was given in marriage that May. What, people said, could have been more fitting? And, they added, how beautiful she looked!]

As summer neared, as the evenings lengthened, there came to the wakeful, the hopeful, walking the beach, stirring the pool, imaginations of the strangest kind – of flesh turned to atoms which drove before the wind, of stars flashing in their hearts, of cliff, sea, cloud and sky brought purposely together to assemble outwardly the scattered parts of the vision within. In those mirrors, the minds of men, in those pools of uneasy water, in which clouds forever turn and shadows form, dreams persisted, and it was impossible to resist the strange intimation which every gull, flower, tree, man and woman and the white earth itself seemed to declare (but if questioned at once to withdraw), that good triumphs, happiness prevails, order rules; or to resist the extra-ordinary stimulus to range hither and thither in search of some absolute good, some crystal of intensity, remote from the known pleasures and familiar virtues, something alien to the processes of domestic life, single, hard, bright, like a diamond in the sand, which would render the possessor secure. Moreover, softened and acquiescent, the spring with her bees humming and gnats dancing threw her cloak about her, veiled her eyes, averted her head, and among passing shadows and flights of small rain seemed to have taken upon her a knowledge of the sorrows of mankind.

[Prue Ramsay died that summer in some illness connected with child-birth, which was indeed a tragedy, people said. They said nobody deserved happiness more.]

And now in the heat of summer the wind sent its spies about the house again. Flies wove a web in the sunny rooms; weeds that had grown close to the glass in the night tapped methodically at the window pane. When darkness fell, the stroke of the Lighthouse, which had laid itself with such authority upon the carpet in the darkness, tracing its pattern, came now in the softer light of spring mixed with moonlight gliding gently as if it laid its caress and lingered stealthily and looked and came lovingly again. But in the very lull of this loving caress, as the long stroke leant upon the bed, the rock was rent asunder; another fold of the shawl loosened; there it hung, and swayed. Through the short summer nights and the long summer days, when the empty rooms seemed to murmur with the echoes of the fields and the hum of flies, the long streamer waved gently, swayed aimlessly; while the sun so striped and barred the rooms and filled them with yellow haze that Mrs McNab, when she broke in and lurched about, dusting, sweeping, looked like a tropical fish oaring its way through sun-lanced waters.

But slumber and sleep though it might there came later in the summer ominous sounds like the measured blows of hammers dulled on felt, which, with their repeated shocks still further loosened the shawl and cracked the teacups. Now and again some glass tinkled in the cupboard as if a giant voice had shrieked so loud in its agony that tumblers stood inside a cupboard vibrated too. Then again silence fell; and then, night after night, and some-times in plain midday when the roses were bright and light turned on the wall, its shape clearly there seemed to drop into this silence, this indifference, this integrity, the thud of something falling.

[A shell exploded. Twenty or thirty young men were blown up in France, among them Andrew Ramsay, whose death, mercifully, was instantaneous.]

At that season those who had gone down to pace the beach and ask of the sea and sky what message they reported or what vision they affirmed had to consider among the usual tokens of divine bounty – the sunset on the sea, the pallor of dawn, the moon rising, fishing-boats against the moon and children pelting each other with handfuls of grass – something out of harmony with this jocundity, this serenity. There was the silent apparition of an ashen-coloured ship for instance, come, gone; there was a purplish stain upon the bland surface of the sea as if something had boiled and bled, invisibly, beneath. This intrusion into a scene calculated to stir the most sublime reflections and lead to the most comfortable conclusions stayed their pacing. It was difficult blandly to overlook them, to abolish their significance in the landscape; to continue, as one walked by the sea, to marvel how beauty outside mirrored beauty within.

Did nature supplement what man advanced? Did she complete what he began? With equal complacence she saw his misery, condoned his meanness and acquiesced in his torture. That dream, then, of sharing, completing, finding in solitude on the beach an answer, was but a reflection in a mirror, and the mirror itself was but the surface glassiness which forms in quiescence when the nobler powers sleep beneath? Impatient, despairing yet loth to go (for beauty offers her lures, has her consolations), to pace the beach was impossible; contemplation was unendurable; the mirror was broken.

[Mr Carmichael brought out a volume of poems that spring, which had an unexpected success. The war, people said, had revived their interest in poetry.]

VII

Night after night, summer and winter, the torment of storms, the arrow-like stillness of fine weather, held their court without interference. Listening (had there been anyone to listen) from the upper rooms of the empty house only gigantic chaos streaked with lightning could have been heard tumbling and tossing, as the winds and waves disported themselves, like the amorphous bulks of leviathans whose brows are pierced by no light of reason, and mounted one on top of another, and lunged and plunged in the darkness or the daylight (for night and day, month and year ran shapelessly together) in idiot games, until it seemed as if the universe were battling and tumbling, in brute confusion and wanton lust aimlessly by itself.

In spring the garden urns, casually filled with wind-blown plants, were gay as ever. Violets came and daffodils. But the stillness and the brightness of the day were as strange as the chaos and tumult of night, with the trees standing there, and the flowers standing there, looking before them, looking up, yet beholding nothing, eyeless, and thus terrible.

VIII

Thinking no harm, for the family would not come, never again, some said, and the house would be sold at Michaelmas perhaps, Mrs McNab stooped and picked a bunch of flowers to take home with her. She laid them on the table while she dusted. She was fond of flowers. It was a pity to let them waste. Suppose the house were sold (she stood arms akimbo in front of the looking-glass) it would want seeing to – it would. There it had stood all these years without a soul in it. The books and things were mouldy, for, what with the war and help being hard to get, the house had not been cleaned as she could have wished. It was beyond one person's strength to get it straight now. She was too old. Her legs pained her. All those books needed to be laid out on the grass in the sun; there was plaster fallen in the hall; the rain-pipe had blocked over the study window and let the water in; the carpet was ruined quite. But people should come themselves; they should have sent somebody down to see. For there were clothes in the cupboards; they had left clothes in all the bedrooms. What was she to do with them? They had the moth in them – Mrs Ramsay's things. Poor lady! She would never want *them* again. She was dead, they said; years ago, in London. There was the old grey cloak she wore gardening (Mrs McNab fingered it). She could see her, as she came up the drive with the washing, stooping over her flowers (the garden was a pitiful sight now, all run to riot, and rabbits scuttling at you out of the beds) – she could see her with one of the children by her in that grey cloak. There were boots and shoes; and a brush and comb left on the dressing-table, for all the world as if she expected to come back tomorrow. (She had died very sudden at the end, they said.) And once they had been coming, but had put off coming, what with the war, and travel being so difficult these days; they had never come all these years; just sent her money; but never wrote, never came, and expected to find things as they had left them, ah dear! Why, the dressing-table drawers were full of things (she pulled them open), handkerchiefs, bits of ribbon. Yes, she could see Mrs Ramsay as she came up the drive with the washing.

'Good-evening, Mrs McNab,' she would say.

She had a pleasant way with her. The girls all liked her. But dear, many things had changed since then (she shut the drawer); many families had lost their dearest. So she was dead; and Mr Andrew killed; and Miss Prue dead too, they said, with her first baby; but everyone had lost someone these years. Prices had gone up shamefully, and didn't come down again neither. She could well remember her in her grey cloak.

'Good-evening, Mrs McNab,' she said, and told cook to keep a plate of milk soup for her – quite thought she wanted it, carrying that heavy basket all the way up from town. She could see her now, stooping over her flowers (and faint and flickering, like a yellow beam or the circle at the end of a telescope, a lady in a grey cloak, stooping over her flowers, went wandering over the bedroom wall, up the dressing-table, across the washstand, as Mrs McNab hobbled and ambled, dusting, straightening).

And cook's name now? Mildred? Marian? – some name like that. Ah, she had forgotten – she did forget things. Fiery, like all red-haired women. Many a laugh they had had. She was always welcome in the kitchen. She made them laugh, she did. Things were better then than now.

She sighed; there was too much work for one woman. She wagged her head this side and that. This had been the nursery. Why, it was all damp in here; the plaster was falling. Whatever did they want to hang a beast's skull there for? gone mouldy too. And rats in all the attics. The rain came in. But they never sent; never came. Some of the locks had gone, so the doors banged. She didn't like to be up here at dusk alone neither. It was too much for one woman, too much, too much. She creaked, she moaned. She banged the door. She turned the key in the lock, and left the house shut up, locked, alone.

IX

The house was left; the house was deserted. It was left like a shell on a sandhill to fill with dry salt grains now that life had left it. The long night seemed to have set in; the trifling airs, nibbling, the clammy breaths, fumbling, seemed to have triumphed. The saucepan had rusted and the mat decayed. Toads had nosed their way in. Idly, aimlessly, the swaying shawl swung to and fro. A thistle thrust itself between the tiles in the larder. The swallows nested in the drawing-room; the floor was strewn with straw; the plaster fell in shovelfuls; rafters were laid bare; rats carried off this and that to gnaw behind the wainscots. Tortoiseshell butterflies burst from the chrysalis and pattered their life out on the windowpane. Poppies sowed themselves among the dahlias; the lawn waved with long grass; giant artichokes towered among roses; a fringed carnation flowered among the cabbages; while the gentle tapping of a weed at the window had become, on winters' nights, a drumming from sturdy trees and thorned briars which made the whole room green in summer.

What power could now prevent the fertility, the insensibility of nature? Mrs McNab's dream of a lady, of a child, of a plate of milk soup? It had wavered over the walls like a spot of sunlight and vanished. She had locked the door; she had gone. It was beyond the strength of one woman, she said. They never sent. They never wrote. There were things up there rotting in the drawers – it was a shame to leave them so, she said. The place was gone to rack and ruin. Only the Lighthouse beam entered the rooms for a moment, sent its sudden stare over bed and wall in the darkness of winter, looked with equanimity at the thistle and the swallow, the rat and the straw. Nothing now withstood them; nothing said no to them. Let the wind blow; let the poppy seed itself and the carnation mate with the cabbage. Let the swallow build in the drawing-room, and the thistle thrust aside the tiles, and the butterfly sun itself on the faded chintz of the armchairs. Let the broken glass and the china lie out on the lawn and be tangled over with grass and wild berries.

For now had come that moment, that hesitation when dawn trembles and night pauses, when if a feather alight in the scale it will be weighed down. One feather, and the house, sinking, falling, would have turned and pitched downwards to the depths of darkness. In the ruined room, picnickers would have lit their kettles; lovers sought shelter there, lying on the bare boards; and the shepherd stored his dinner on the bricks, and the tramp slept with his coat round him to ward off the cold. Then the roof would have fallen; briars and hemlocks would have blotted out path, step and window; would have grown, unequally but lustily over the mound, until some trespasser, losing his way, could have told only by a red-hot poker among the nettles, or a scrap of china in the hemlock, that here once someone had lived; there had been a house.

If the feather had fallen, if it had tipped the scale downwards, the whole house would have plunged to the depths to lie upon the sands of oblivion. But there was a force working; something not highly conscious; something that leered, something that lurched; something not inspired to go about its work with dignified ritual or solemn chanting. Mrs McNab groaned; Mrs Bast creaked. They were old; they were stiff; their legs ached. They came with their brooms and pails at last; they got to work. All of a sudden, would Mrs McNab see that the house was ready? one of the young ladies wrote: would she get this done?; would she get that done?; all in a hurry. They might be coming for the summer; had left everything to the last; expected to find things as they had left them. Slowly and painfully, with broom and pail, mopping, scouring, Mrs McNab, Mrs Bast stayed the corruption and the rot; rescued from the pool of Time that was fast closing over them now a basin, now a cupboard; fetched up from oblivion all the Waverley novels and a tea-set one morning; in the afternoon restored to sun and air a brass fender and a set of steel fire-irons. George, Mrs Bast's son, caught the rats, and cut the grass. They had the builders. Attended with the creaking of hinges and the screeching of bolts, the slamming and banging of damp-swollen woodwork, some rusty laborious birth seemed to be taking place, as the women, stooping, rising, groaning, singing, slapped and slammed, upstairs now, now down in the cellars. Oh, they said, the work!

They drank their tea in the bedroom sometimes, or in the study; breaking off work at midday with the smudge on their faces, and their old hands clasped and cramped with the broom handles. Flopped on chairs they contemplated now the magnificent conquest over taps and bath; now the more arduous, more partial triumph over long rows of books, black as ravens once, now white-stained, breeding pale mushrooms and secreting furtive spiders. Once more, as she felt the tea warm in her, the telescope fitted itself to Mrs McNab's eyes, and in a ring of light she saw the old gentleman, lean as a rake, wagging his head, as she came up with the washing, talking to himself, she supposed, on the lawn. He never noticed her. Some said he was dead; some said she was dead. Which was it? Mrs Bast didn't know for certain either. The young gentleman was dead. That she was sure. She had read his name in the papers.

There was the cook now, Mildred, Marian, some such name as that – a red-headed woman, quick-tempered like all her sort, but kind, too, if you knew the way with her. Many a laugh they had had together. She saved a plate of soup for Maggie; a bite of ham, sometimes; whatever was over. They lived well in those days. They had everything they wanted (glibly, jovially, with the tea hot in her, she unwound her ball of memories, sitting in the wicker armchair by the nursery fender). There was always plenty doing, people in the house, twenty staying sometimes, and washing up till long past midnight.

Mrs Bast (she had never known them; had lived in Glasgow at that time) wondered, putting her cup down, whatever they hung that beast's skull there for? Shot in foreign parts no doubt.

It might well be, said Mrs McNab, wantoning on with her memories; they had friends in eastern countries; gentlemen staying there, ladies in evening dress; she had seen them once through the dining-room door all sitting at dinner. Twenty she dared say in all their jewellery, and she asked to stay help wash up, might be till after midnight.

Ah, said Mrs Bast, they'd find it changed. She leant out of the window. She watched her son George scything the grass. They might well ask, what had been done to it? seeing how old Kennedy was supposed to have charge of it, and then his leg got so bad after he fell from the cart; and perhaps then no one for a year, or the better part of one; and then Davie Macdonald, and seeds might be sent, but who should say if they were ever planted? They'd find it changed.

She watched her son scything. He was a great one for work – one of those quiet ones. Well, they must be getting along with the cupboards, she supposed. They hauled themselves up.

At last, after days of labour within, of cutting and digging without, dusters were flicked from the windows, the windows were shut to, keys were turned all over the house; the front door was banged; it was finished.

And now as if the cleaning and the scrubbing and the scything and the mowing had drowned it there rose that half-heard melody, that intermittent music which the ear half catches but lets fall: a bark, a bleat, irregular, intermittent, yet somehow related; the hum of an insect, the tremor of cut grass, dissevered yet somehow belonging; the jar of a dor-beetle, the squeak of a wheel, loud, low, but mysteriously related; which the ear strains to bring together and is always on the verge of harmonising but they are never quite heard, never fully harmonised, and at last, in the evening, one after another the sounds die out, and the harmony falters, and silence falls. With the sunset sharpness was lost and, like mist rising, quiet rose, quiet spread, the wind settled; loosely the world shook itself down to sleep, darkly here without a light to it, save what came green suffused through leaves, or pale on the white flowers by the window.

[Lily Briscoe had her bag carried up to the house late one evening in September. Mr Carmichael came by the same train.]

X

Then indeed peace had come. Messages of peace breathed from the sea to the shore. Never to break its sleep any more, to lull it rather more deeply to rest and whatever the dreamers dreamt holily, dreamt wisely, to confirm – what else was it murmuring – as Lily Briscoe laid her head on the pillow in the clean still room and heard the sea. Through the open window the voice of the beauty of the world came murmuring, too softly to hear exactly what it said – but what mattered if the meaning were plain? – entreating the sleepers (the house was full again; Mrs Beckwith was staying there, also Mr Carmichael) if they would not actually come down to the beach itself at least to lift the blind and look out. They would see then night flowing down in purple; his head crowned; his sceptre jewelled; and how in his eyes a child might look. And if they still faltered (Lily was tired out with travelling and slept almost at once; but Mr Carmichael read a book by candlelight), if they still said no, that it was vapour this splendour of his, and the dew had more power than he, and they preferred sleeping; gently then without complaint, or argument, the voice would sing its song. Gently the waves would break (Lily heard them in her sleep); tenderly the light fell (it seemed to come through her eyelids). And it all looked, Mr Carmichael thought, shutting his book, falling asleep, much as it used to look years ago.

Indeed the voice might resume, as the curtains of dark wrapped themselves over the house, over Mrs Beckwith, Mr Carmichael and Lily Briscoe so that they lay with several folds of blackness on their eyes, why not accept this, be content with this, acquiesce and resign? The sigh of all the seas breaking in measure round the isles soothed them; the night wrapped them; nothing broke their sleep, until, the birds beginning and the dawn weaving their thin voices into its whiteness, a cart grinding, a dog somewhere barking, the sun lifted the curtains, broke the veil on their eyes, and Lily Briscoe stirring in her sleep clutched at her blankets as a faller clutches at the turf on the edge of a cliff. Her eyes opened wide. Here she was again, she thought, sitting bolt upright in bed. Awake.

PART THREE
The Lighthouse

I

What does it mean then, what can it all mean? Lily Briscoe asked herself, wondering whether, since she had been left alone, it behoved her to go to the kitchen to fetch another cup of coffee or wait here. What does it mean? – a catchword that was, caught up from some book, fitting her thought loosely, for she could not, this first morning with the Ramsays, contract her feelings, could only make a phrase resound to cover the blankness of her mind until these vapours had shrunk. For really, what did she feel, come back after all these years and Mrs Ramsay dead? Nothing, nothing – nothing that she could express at all.

She had come late last night when it was all mysterious, dark. Now she was awake, at her old place at the breakfast table, but alone. It was very early too, not yet eight. There was this expedition – they were going to the Lighthouse, Mr Ramsay, Cam and James. They should have gone already – they had to catch the tide or something. And Cam was not ready and James was not ready and Nancy had forgotten to order the sandwiches and Mr Ramsay had lost his temper and banged out of the room.

'What's the use of going now?' he had stormed.

Nancy had vanished. There he was, marching up and down the terrace in a rage. One seemed to hear doors slamming and voices calling all over the house. Now Nancy burst in, and asked, looking round the room, in a queer half-dazed, half-desperate way: 'What does one send to the Lighthouse?' as if she were forcing herself to do what she despaired of ever being able to do.

What does one send to the Lighthouse indeed! At any other time Lily could have suggested reasonably tea, tobacco, newspapers. But this morning everything seemed so extraordinarily queer that a question like Nancy's – What does one send to the Lighthouse? – opened doors in one's mind that went banging and swinging to and fro and made one keep asking, in a stupefied gape: What does one send? What does one do? Why is one sitting here after all?

Sitting alone (for Nancy went out again) among the clean cups at the long table she felt cut off from other people, and able only to go on watching, asking, wondering. The house, the place, the morning, all seemed strangers to her. She had no attachment here, she felt, no relations with it, anything might happen, and whatever did happen, a step outside, a voice calling ('It's not in the cupboard; it's on the landing,' someone cried), was a question, as if the link that usually bound things together had been cut, and they floated up here, down there, off, anyhow. How aimless it was, how chaotic, how unreal it was, she thought, looking at her empty coffee cup. Mrs Ramsay dead; Andrew killed; Prue dead too – repeat it as she might, it roused no feeling in her. And we all get together in a house like this on a morning like this, she said, looking out of the window – it was a beautiful still day.

II

Suddenly Mr Ramsay raised his head as he passed and looked straight at her, with his distraught wild gaze which was yet so penetrating, as if he saw you, for one second, for the first time, for ever; and she pretended to drink out of her empty coffee cup so as to escape him – to escape his demand on her, to put aside a moment longer that imperious need. And he shook his head at her, and strode on ('Alone' she heard him say, 'Perished' she heard him say) and like everything else this strange morning the words became symbols, wrote themselves all over the grey-green walls. If only she could put them together, she felt, write them out in some sentence, then she would have got at the truth of things. Old Mr Carmichael came padding softly in, fetched his coffee, took his cup and made off to sit in the sun. The extraordinary unreality was frightening; but it was also exciting. Going to the Lighthouse. But what does one send to the Lighthouse? Perished. Alone. The grey-green light on the wall opposite. The empty places. Such were some of the parts, but how bring them together? she asked. As if any interruption would break the frail shape she was building on the table she turned her back to the window lest Mr Ramsay should see her. She must escape somehow, be alone somewhere. Suddenly she remembered. When she had sat there last ten years ago there had been a little sprig or leaf pattern on the tablecloth, which she had looked at in a moment of revelation. There had been a problem about a foreground of a picture. Move the tree to the middle, she had said. She had never finished that picture. It had been knocking about in her mind all these years. She would paint that picture now. Where were her paints, she wondered? Her paints, yes. She had left them in the hall last night. She would start at once. She got up quickly, before Mr Ramsay turned.

She fetched herself a chair. She pitched her easel with her precise old maidish movements on the edge of the lawn, not too close to Mr Carmichael, but close enough for his protection. Yes, it must have been precisely here that she had stood ten years ago. There was the wall; the hedge; the tree. The question was of some relation between those masses. She had borne it in her mind all these years. It seemed as if the solution had come to her: she knew now what she wanted to do.

But with Mr Ramsay bearing down on her, she could do nothing. Every time he approached – he was walking up and down the terrace – ruin approached, chaos approached. She could not paint. She stooped, she turned; she took up this rag; she squeezed that tube. But all she did was to ward him off a moment. He made it impossible for her to do anything. For if she gave him the least chance, if he saw her disengaged a moment, looking his way a moment, he would be on her, saying, as he had said last night: 'You find us much changed.' Last night he had got up and stopped before her, and said that. Dumb and staring though they had all sat, the six children whom they used to call after the kings and queens of England – the Red, the Fair, the Wicked, the Ruthless – she felt how they raged under it. Kind old Mrs Beckwith said something sensible. But it was a house full of unrelated passions – she had felt that all the evening. And on top of this chaos Mr Ramsay got up, pressed her hand, and said: 'You will find us much changed,' and none of them had moved or had spoken; but had sat there as if they were forced to let him say it. Only James (certainly the Sullen) scowled at the lamp, and Cam screwed her handkerchief round her finger. Then he reminded them that they were going to the Lighthouse tomorrow. They must be ready, in the hall, on the stroke of half-past seven. Then, with his hand on the door, he stopped; he turned upon them. Did they not want to go? he demanded. Had they dared say No (he had some reason for wanting it) he would have flung himself tragically backwards into the bitter waters of despair. Such a gift he had for gesture. He looked like a king in exile. Doggedly James said yes. Cam stumbled more wretchedly. Yes, oh yes, they'd both be ready, they said. And it struck her, this was tragedy – not palls, dust, and the shroud; but children coerced, their spirits subdued. James was sixteen, Cam seventeen, perhaps. She had looked round for someone who was not there, for Mrs Ramsay, presumably. But there was only kind Mrs Beckwith turning over her sketches under the lamp. Then, being tired, her mind still rising and falling with the sea, the taste and smell that places have after long absence possessing her, the candles wavering in her eyes, she had lost herself and gone under. It was a wonderful night, starlit; the waves sounded as they went upstairs; the moon surprised them, enormous, pale, as they passed the staircase window. She had slept at once.

She set her clean canvas firmly upon the easel, as a barrier, frail, but she hoped sufficiently substantial to ward off Mr Ramsay and his exactingness. She did her best to look, when his back was turned, at her picture; that line there, that mass there. But it was out of the question. Let him be fifty feet away, let him not even speak to you, let him not even see you, he permeated, he prevailed, he imposed himself. He changed everything. She could not see the colour; she could not see the lines; even with his back turned to her, she could only think, But he'll be down on me in a moment, demanding – something she felt she could not give him. She rejected one brush; she chose another. When would those children come? When would they all be off? she fidgeted. That man, she thought, her anger rising in her, never gave; that man took. She, on the other hand, would be forced to give. Mrs Ramsay had given. Giving, giving, giving, she had died – and had left all this. Really, she was angry with Mrs Ramsay. With the brush slightly trembling in her fingers she looked at the hedge, the step, the wall. It was all Mrs Ramsay's doing. She was dead. Here was Lily, at forty-four, wasting her time, unable to do a thing, standing there, playing at painting, playing at the one thing one did not play at, and it was all Mrs Ramsay's fault. She was dead. The step where she used to sit was empty. She was dead.

But why repeat this over and over again? Why be always trying to bring up some feeling she had not got? There was a kind of blasphemy in it. It was all dry: all withered: all spent. They ought not to have asked her; she ought not to have come. One can't waste one's time at forty-four, she thought. She hated playing at painting. A brush, the one dependable thing in a world of strife, ruin, chaos – that one should not play with, knowingly even: she detested it. But he made her. You shan't touch your canvas, he seemed to say, bearing down on her, till you've given me what I want of you. Here he was, close upon her again, greedy, distraught. Well, thought Lily in despair, letting her right hand fall at her side, it would be simpler then to have it over. Surely she could imitate from recollection the glow, the rhapsody, the self-surrender she had seen on so many women's faces (on Mrs Ramsay's, for instance), when on some occasion like this they blazed up – she could remember the look on Mrs Ramsay's face – into a rapture of sympathy, of delight in the reward they had, which, though the reason of it escaped her, evidently conferred on them the most supreme bliss of which human nature was capable. Here he was, stopped by her side. She would give him what she could.

III

She seemed to have shrivelled slightly, he thought. She looked a little skimpy, wispy; but not unattractive. He liked her. There had been some talk of her marrying William Bankes once, but nothing had come of it. His wife had been fond of her. He had been a little out of temper too at breakfast. And then, and then – this was one of those moments when an enormous need urged him, without being conscious what it was, to approach any woman, to force them, he did not care how, his need was so great, to give him what he wanted: sympathy.

Was anybody looking after her? he said. Had she everything she wanted?

'Oh, thanks, everything,' said Lily Briscoe nervously. No; she could not do it. She ought to have floated off instantly upon some wave of sympathetic expansion: the pressure on her was tremendous. But she remained stuck. There was an awful pause. They both looked at the sea. Why, thought Mr Ramsay, should she look at the sea when I am here? She hoped it would be calm enough for them to land at the Lighthouse, she said. The Lighthouse! The Lighthouse! What's that got to do with it? he thought impatiently. Instantly, with the force of some primeval gust (for really he could not restrain himself any longer), there issued from him such a groan that any other woman in the whole world would have done something, said something – all except myself, thought Lily, girding at herself bitterly, who am not a woman, but a peevish, ill-tempered, dried-up old maid presumably.

Mr Ramsay sighed to the full. He waited. Was she not going to say anything? Did she not see what he wanted from her? Then he said he had a particular reason for wanting to go to the Lighthouse. His wife used to send the men things. There was a poor boy with a tuberculous hip, the lightkeeper's son. He sighed profoundly. He sighed significantly. All Lily wished was that this enormous flood of grief, this insatiable hunger for sympathy, this demand that she should surrender herself up to him entirely, and even so he had sorrows enough to keep her supplied for ever, should leave her, should be diverted (she kept looking at the house, hoping for an interruption) before it swept her down in its flow.

'Such expeditions,' said Mr Ramsay, scraping the ground with his toe, 'are very painful.' Still Lily said nothing. (She is a stock, she is a stone, he said to himself.) 'They are very exhausting,' he said, looking, with a sickly look that nauseated her (he was acting, she felt, this great man was dramatising himself), at his beautiful hands. It was horrible, it was indecent. Would they never come, she asked, for she could not sustain this enormous weight of sorrow, support these heavy draperies of grief (he had assumed a pose of extreme decrepitude; he even tottered a little as he stood there) a moment longer.

Still she could say nothing; the whole horizon seemed swept bare of objects to talk about; could only feel, amazedly, as Mr Ramsay stood there, how his gaze seemed to fall dolefully over the sunny grass and discolour it, and cast over the rubicund, drowsy, entirely contented figure of Mr Carmichael, reading a French novel on a deckchair, a veil of crape, as if such an existence, flaunting its prosperity in a world of woe, were enough to provoke the most dismal thoughts of all. Look at him, he seemed to be saying, look at me; and indeed, all the time he was feeling, Think of me, think of me. Ah, could that bulk only be wafted alongside of them, Lily wished; had she only pitched her easel a yard or two closer to him; a man, any man, would staunch this effusion, would stop these lamentations. A woman, she had provoked this horror; a woman, she should have known how to deal with it. It was immensely to her discredit, sexually, to stand there dumb. One said – what did one say? – Oh, Mr Ramsay! Dear Mr Ramsay! That was what that kind old lady who sketched, Mrs Beckwith, would have said instantly, and rightly. But no. They stood there, isolated from the rest of the world. His immense self-pity, his demand for sympathy poured and spread itself in pools at her feet, and all she did, miserable sinner that she was, was to draw her skirts a little closer round her ankles, lest she should get wet. In complete silence she stood there, grasping her paint brush.

Heaven could never be sufficiently praised! She heard sounds in the house. James and Cam must be coming. But Mr Ramsay, as if he knew that his time ran short, exerted upon her solitary figure the immense pressure of his concentrated woe: his age; his frailty; his desolation; when suddenly, tossing his head impatiently, in his annoyance – for, after all, what woman could resist him? – he noticed that his bootlaces were untied. Remarkable boots they were too, Lily thought, looking down at them: sculptured; colossal; like everything that Mr Ramsay wore, from his frayed tie to his half-buttoned waistcoat, his own indisputably. She could see them walking to his room of their own accord, expressive in his absence of pathos, surliness, ill-temper, charm.

'What beautiful boots!' she exclaimed. She was ashamed of herself. To praise his boots when he asked her to solace his soul; when he had shown her his bleeding hands, his lacerated heart, and asked her to pity them, then to say, cheerfully: 'Ah, but what beautiful boots you wear!' deserved, she knew, and she looked up expecting to get it, in one of his sudden roars of ill-temper, complete annihilation.

Instead, Mr Ramsay smiled. His pall, his draperies, his infirmities fell from him. Ah yes, he said, holding his foot up for her to look at, they were first-rate boots. There was only one man in England who could make boots like that. Boots are among the chief curses of mankind, he said. 'Bootmakers make it their business,' he exclaimed, 'to cripple and torture the human foot.' They are also the most obstinate and perverse of mankind. It had taken him the best part of his youth to get boots made as they should be made. He would have her observe (he lifted his right foot and then his left) that she had never seen boots made quite that shape before. They were made of the finest leather in the world, also. Most leather was mere brown paper and cardboard. He looked complacently at his foot, still held in the air. They had reached, she felt, a sunny island where peace dwelt, sanity reigned and the sun forever shone, the blessed island of good boots. Her heart warmed to him. 'Now let me see if you can tie a knot,' he said. He poohpoohed her feeble system. He showed her his own invention. Once you tied it, it never came undone. Three times he knotted her shoe; three times he unknotted it.

Why, at this completely inappropriate moment, when he was stooping over her shoe, should she be so tormented with sympathy for him that, as she stooped too, the blood rushed to her face, and, thinking of her callousness (she had called him a play-actor) she felt her eyes swell and tingle with tears? Thus occupied he seemed to her a figure of infinite pathos. He tied knots. He bought boots. There was no helping Mr Ramsay on the journey he was going. But now just as she wished to say something, could have said something, perhaps, here they were – Cam and James. They appeared on the terrace. They came, lagging, side by side, a serious, melancholy couple.

But why was it like *that* that they came? She could not help feeling annoyed with them; they might have come more cheerfully; they might have given him what, now that they were off, she would not have the chance of giving him. For she felt a sudden emptiness; a frustration. Her feeling had come too late; there it was ready; but he no longer needed it. He had become a very distinguished, elderly man, who had no need of her whatsoever. She felt snubbed. He slung a knapsack round his shoulders. He shared out the parcels – there were a number of them, ill tied, in brown paper. He sent Cam for a cloak. He had all the appearance of a leader making ready for an expedition. Then, wheeling about, he led the way with his firm military tread, in those wonderful boots, carrying brown-paper parcels, down the path, his children following him. They looked, she thought, as if fate had devoted them to some stern enterprise, and they went to it, still young enough to be drawn acquiescent in their father's wake, obediently, but with a pallor in their eyes which made her feel that they suffered something beyond their years in silence. So they passed the edge of the lawn, and it seemed to Lily that she watched a procession go, drawn on by some stress of common feeling which made it, faltering and flagging as it was, a little company bound together and strangely impressive to her. Politely, but very distantly, Mr Ramsay raised his hand and saluted her as they passed.

But what a face, she thought, immediately finding the sympathy which she had not been asked to give troubling her for expression. What had made it like that? Thinking, night after night, she supposed – about the reality of kitchen tables, she added, remembering the symbol which in her vagueness as to what Mr Ramsay did think about Andrew had given her. (He had been killed by the splinter of a shell instantly, she bethought her.) The kitchen table was something visionary, austere; something bare, hard, not ornamental. There was no colour to it; it was all edges and angles; it was uncompromisingly plain. But Mr Ramsay kept always his eyes fixed upon it, never allowed himself to be distracted or deluded, until his face became worn too and ascetic and partook of this unornamented beauty which so deeply impressed her. Then, she recalled (standing where he had left her, holding her brush), worries had fretted it – not so nobly. He must have had his doubts about that table, she supposed; whether the table was a real table; whether it was worth the time he gave to it; whether he was able after all to find it. He had had doubts, she felt, or he would have asked less of people. That was what they talked about late at night sometimes, she suspected; and then next day Mrs Ramsay looked tired, and Lily flew into a rage with him over some absurd little thing. But now he had nobody to talk to about that table, or his boots, or his knots; and he was like a lion seeking whom he could devour, and his face had that touch of desperation, of exaggeration in it which alarmed her, and made her pull her skirts about her. And then, she recalled, there was that sudden revivification, that sudden flare (when she praised his boots), that sudden recovery of vitality and interest in ordinary human things, which too passed and changed (for he was always changing, and hid nothing) into that other final phase which was new to her and had, she owned, made herself ashamed of her own irritability, when it seemed as if he had shed worries and ambitions, and the hope of sympathy and the desire for praise, had entered some other region, was drawn on, as if by curiosity, in dumb colloquy, whether with himself or another, at the head of that little procession out of one's range. An extraordinary face! The gate banged.

IV

So they're gone, she thought, sighing with relief and disappointment. Her sympathy seemed to fly back in her face, like a bramble sprung. She felt curiously divided, as if one part of her were drawn out there – it was a still day, hazy; the Lighthouse looked this morning at an immense distance; the other had fixed itself doggedly, solidly, here on the lawn. She saw her canvas as if it had floated up and placed itself white and uncompromising directly before her. It seemed to rebuke her with its cold stare for all this hurry and agitation, this folly and waste of emotion; it drastically recalled her and spread through her mind first a peace, as her disorderly sensations (he had gone and she had been so sorry for him and she had said nothing) trooped off the field; and then emptiness. She looked blankly at the canvas, with its uncompromising white stare; from the canvas to the garden. There was something (she stood screwing up her little Chinese eyes in her small puckered face), something she remembered in the relations of those lines cutting across, slicing down, and in the mass of the hedge with its green cave of blues and browns, which had stayed in her mind; which had tied a knot in her mind so that at odds and ends of time, involuntarily, as she walked along the Brompton Road, as she brushed her hair, she found herself painting that picture, passing her eye over it, and untying the knot in imagination. But there was all the difference in the world between this planning airily away from the canvas and actually taking her brush and making the first mark.

She had taken the wrong brush in her agitation at Mr Ramsay's presence, and her easel, rammed into the earth so nervously, was at the wrong angle. And now that she had put that right, and in so doing had subdued the impertinences and irrelevances that plucked her attention and made her remember how she was such and such a person, had such and such relations to people, she took her hand and raised her brush. For a moment it stayed trembling in a painful but exciting ecstasy in the air. Where to begin? – that was the question; at what point to make the first mark? One line placed on the canvas committed her to innumerable risks, to frequent and irrevocable decisions. All that in idea seemed simple became in practice immediately complex; as the waves shape themselves symmetrically from the clifftop but to the swimmer among them are divided by steep gulfs and foaming crests. Still the risk must be run; the mark made.

With a curious physical sensation, as if she were urged forward and at the same time must hold herself back, she made her first quick decisive stroke. The brush descended. It flickered brown over the white canvas; it left a running mark. A second time she did it – a third time. And so pausing and so flickering, she attained a dancing rhythmical movement, as if the pauses were one part of the rhythm and the strokes another, and all were related; and so, lightly and swiftly pausing, striking, she scored her canvas with brown running nervous lines which had no sooner settled there than they enclosed (she felt it looming out at her) a space. Down in the hollow of one wave she saw the next wave towering higher and higher above her. For what could be more formidable than that space? Here she was again, she thought, stepping back to look at it, drawn out of gossip, out of living, out of community with people into the presence of this formidable ancient enemy of hers – this other thing, this truth, this reality, which suddenly laid hands on her, emerged stark at the back of appearances and commanded her attention. She was half unwilling, half reluctant. Why always be drawn out and haled away? Why not left in peace, to talk to Mr Carmichael on the lawn? It was an exacting form of intercourse anyhow. Other worshipful objects were content with worship; men, women, God, all let one kneel prostrate; but this form, were it only the shape of a white lampshade looming on a wicker table, roused one to perpetual combat, challenged one to a fight in which one was bound to be worsted. Always (it was in her nature, or in her sex, she did not know which) before she exchanged the fluidity of life for the concentration of painting she had a few moments of nakedness when she seemed like an unborn soul, a soul reft of body, hesitating on some windy pinnacle and exposed without protection to all the blasts of doubt. Why then did she do it? She looked at the canvas, lightly scored with running lines. It would be hung in the servants' bedrooms. It would be rolled up and stuffed under a sofa. What was the good of doing it then, and she heard some voice saying she couldn't paint, saying she couldn't create, as if she were caught up in one of those habitual currents which after a certain time forms experience in the mind, so that one repeats words without being aware any longer who originally spoke them.

Can't paint, can't write, she murmured monotonously, anxiously considering what her plan of attack should be. For the mass loomed before her; it protruded; she felt it pressing on her eyeballs. Then, as if some juice necessary for the lubrication of her faculties were spontaneously squirted, she began precariously dipping among the blues and umbers, moving her brush hither and thither, but it was now heavier and went slower, as if it had fallen in with some rhythm which was dictated to her (she kept looking at the hedge, at the canvas) by what she saw, so that while her hand quivered with life, this rhythm was strong enough to bear her along with it on its current. Certainly she was losing consciousness of outer things. And as she lost consciousness of outer things, and her name and her personality and her appearance, and whether Mr Carmichael was there or not, her mind kept throwing up from its depths, scenes, and names, and sayings, and memories and ideas, like a fountain spurting over that glaring, hideously difficult white space, while she modelled it with greens and blues.

Charles Tansley used to say that, she remembered, women can't paint, can't write. Coming up behind her he had stood close beside her, a thing she hated, as she painted here on this very spot. 'Shag tobacco,' he said, 'fivepence an ounce,' parading his poverty, his principles. (But the war had drawn the sting of her femininity. Poor devils, one thought, poor devils of both sexes, getting into such messes.) He was always carrying a book about under his arm – a purple book. He 'worked'. He sat, she remembered, working in a blaze of sun. At dinner he would sit right in the middle of the view. And then, she reflected, there was that scene on the beach. One must remember that. It was a windy morning. They had all gone to the beach. Mrs Ramsay sat and wrote letters by a rock. She wrote and wrote. 'Oh,' she said, looking up at last at something floating in the sea, 'is it a lobster pot? Is it an upturned boat?' She was so short-sighted that she could not see, and then Charles Tansley became as nice as he could possibly be. He began playing ducks and drakes. They chose little flat black stones and sent them skipping over the waves. Every now and then Mrs Ramsay looked up over her spectacles and laughed at them. What they said she could not remember, but only she and Charles throwing stones and getting on very well all of a sudden and Mrs Ramsay watching them. She was highly conscious of that. Mrs Ramsay, she thought, stepping back and screwing up her eyes. (It must have altered the design a good deal when she was sitting on the step with James. There must have been a shadow.) Mrs Ramsay. When she thought of herself and Charles throwing ducks and drakes and of the whole scene on the beach, it seemed to depend somehow upon Mrs Ramsay sitting under the rock, with a pad on her knee, writing letters. (She wrote innumerable letters, and sometimes the wind took them and she and Charles just saved a page from the sea.) But what a power was in the human soul! she thought. That woman sitting there, writing under the rock resolved everything into simplicity; made these angers, irritations fall off like old rags; she brought together this and that and then this, and so made out of that miserable silliness and spite (she and Charles squabbling, sparring, had been silly and spiteful) something – this scene on the beach for example, this moment of friendship and liking – which survived, after all these years, complete, so that she dipped into it to refashion her memory of him, and it stayed in the mind almost like a work of art.

'Like a work of art,' she repeated, looking from her canvas to the drawing-room steps and back again. She must rest for a moment. And, resting, looking from one to the other vaguely, the old question which traversed the sky of the soul perpetually, the vast, the general question which was apt to particularise itself at such moments as these, when she released faculties that had been on the strain, stood over her, paused over her, darkened over her. What is the meaning of life? That was all – a simple question; one that tended to close in on one with years. The great revelation had never come. The great revelation perhaps never did come. Instead there were little daily miracles, illuminations, matches struck unexpectedly in the dark; here was one. This, that and the other; herself and Charles Tansley and the breaking wave; Mrs Ramsay bringing them together; Mrs Ramsay saying 'Life stand still here'; Mrs Ramsay making of the moment something permanent (as in another sphere Lily herself tried to make of the moment something permanent) – this was of the nature of a revelation. In the midst of chaos there was shape; this eternal passing and flowing (she looked at the clouds going and the leaves shaking) was struck into stability. Life stand still here, Mrs Ramsay said. 'Mrs Ramsay! Mrs Ramsay!' she repeated. She owed this revelation to her.

All was silence. Nobody seemed yet to be stirring in the house. She looked at it there sleeping in the early sunlight with its windows green and blue with the reflected leaves. The faint thought she was thinking of Mrs Ramsay seemed in consonance with this quiet house; this smoke; this fine early-morning air. Faint and unreal, it was amazingly pure and exciting. She hoped nobody would open the window or come out of the house, but that she might be left alone to go on thinking, to go on painting. She turned to her canvas. But impelled by some curiosity, driven by the discomfort of the sympathy which she held undischarged, she walked a pace or so to the end of the lawn to see whether, down there on the beach, she could see that little company setting sail. Down there among the little boats which floated, some with their sails furled, some slowly, for it was very calm, moving away, there was one rather apart from the others. The sail was even now being hoisted. She decided that there in that very distant and entirely silent little boat Mr Ramsay was sitting with Cam and James. Now they had got the sail up; now after a little flagging and hesitation the sails filled and, shrouded in profound silence, she watched the boat take its way with deliberation past the other boats out to sea.

V

The sails flapped over their heads. The water chuckled and slapped the sides of the boat, which drowsed motionless in the sun. Now and then the sails rippled with a little breeze in them, but the ripple ran over them and ceased. The boat made no motion at all. Mr Ramsay sat in the middle of the boat. He would be impatient in a moment, James thought, and Cam thought, looking at their father, who sat in the middle of the boat between them (James steered; Cam sat alone in the bow) with his legs tightly curled. He hated hanging about. Sure enough, after fidgeting a second or two, he said something sharp to Macalister's boy, who got out his oars and began to row. But their father, they knew, would never be content until they were flying along. He would keep looking for a breeze, fidgeting, saying things under his breath, which Macalister and Macalister's boy would overhear, and they would both be made horribly uncomfortable. He had made them come. He had forced them to come. In their anger they hoped that the breeze would never rise, that he might be thwarted in every possible way, since he had forced them to come against their wills.

All the way down to the beach they had lagged behind together, though he bade them, 'Walk up, walk up,' without speaking. Their heads were bent down, their heads were pressed down by some remorseless gale. Speak to him they could not. They must come; they must follow. They must walk behind him carrying brown-paper parcels. But they vowed, in silence, as they walked, to stand by each other and carry out the great compact – to resist tyranny to the death. So there they would sit, one at one end of the boat, one at the other, in silence. They would say nothing, only look at him now and then where he sat with his legs twisted, frowning and fidgeting, and pishing and pshawing and muttering things to himself, and waiting impatiently for a breeze. And they hoped it would be calm. They hoped he would be thwarted. They hoped the whole expedition would fail, and they would have to put back, with their parcels, to the beach.

But now, when Macalister's boy had rowed a little way out, the sails slowly swung round, the boat quickened itself, flattened itself, and shot off. Instantly, as if some great strain had been relieved, Mr Ramsay uncurled his legs, took out his tobacco pouch, handed it with a little grunt to Macalister, and felt, they knew, for all they suffered, perfectly content. Now they would sail on for hours like this, and Mr Ramsay would ask old Macalister a question – about the great storm last winter probably – and old Macalister would answer it, and they would puff their pipes together, and Macalister would take a tarry rope in his fingers, tying or untying some knot, and the boy would fish, and never say a word to anyone. James would be forced to keep his eye all the time on the sail. For if he forgot, then the sail puckered, and shivered, and the boat slackened, and Mr Ramsay would say sharply: 'Look out! Look out!' and old Macalister would turn slowly on his seat. So they heard Mr Ramsay asking some question about the great storm at Christmas. 'She comes driving round the point,' old Macalister said, describing the great storm last Christmas, when ten ships had been driven into the bay for shelter, and he had seen 'one there, one there, one there' (he pointed slowly round the bay. Mr Ramsay followed him, turning his head). He had seen three men clinging to the mast. Then she was gone. 'And at last we shoved her off,' he went on (but in their anger and their silence they only caught a word here and there, sitting at opposite ends of the boat, united by their compact to fight tyranny to the death). At last they had shoved her off, they had launched the lifeboat, and they had got her out past the point – Macalister told the story; and though they only caught a word here and there, they were conscious all the time of their father – how he leant forward, how he brought his voice into tune with Macalister's voice; how, puffing at his pipe, and looking there and there where Macalister pointed, he relished the thought of the storm and the dark night and the fishermen striving there. He liked that men should labour and sweat on the windy beach at night, pitting muscle and brain against the waves and the wind; he liked men to work like that, and women to keep house, and sit beside sleeping children indoors, while men were drowned, out there in a storm. So James could tell, so Cam could tell (they looked at him, they looked at each other), from his toss and his vigilance and the ring in his voice, and the little tinge of Scottish accent which came into his voice, making him seem like a peasant himself, as he questioned Macalister about the ten ships that had been driven into the bay in a storm. Three had sunk.

He looked proudly where Macalister pointed; and Cam thought, feeling proud of him without knowing quite why, had he been there he would have launched the lifeboat, he would have reached the wreck, Cam thought. He was so brave, he was so adventurous, Cam thought. But she remembered. There was the compact; to resist tyranny to the death. Their grievance weighed them down. They had been forced; they had been bidden. He had borne them down once more with his gloom and his authority, making them do his bidding, on this fine morning; come, because he wished it, carrying these parcels, to the Lighthouse; take part in those rites he went through for his own pleasure in memory of dead people, which they hated, so that they lagged after him, and all the pleasure of the day was spoilt.

Yes, the breeze was freshening. The boat was leaning, the water was sliced sharply and fell away in green cascades, in bubbles, in cataracts. Cam looked down into the foam, into the sea with all its treasure in it, and its speed hypnotised her, and the tie between her and James sagged a little. It slackened a little. She began to think, How fast it goes. Where are we going? and the movement hypnotised her, while James, with his eye fixed on the sail and on the horizon, steered grimly. But he began to think as he steered that he might escape; he might be quit of it all. They might land somewhere; and be free then. Both of them, looking at each other for a moment, had a sense of escape and exaltation, what with the speed and the change. But the breeze bred in Mr Ramsay too the same excitement, and, as old Macalister turned to fling his line overboard, he cried aloud: 'We perished,' and then again, 'each alone.' And then with his usual spasm of repentance or shyness, pulled himself up and waved his hand towards the shore.

'See the little house,' he said pointing, wishing Cam to look. She raised herself reluctantly and looked. But which was it? She could no longer make out, there on the hillside, which was their house. All looked distant and peaceful and strange. The shore seemed refined, far away, unreal. Already the little distance they had sailed had put them far from it and given it the changed look, the composed look, of something receding in which one has no longer any part. Which was their house? She could not see it.

'But I beneath a rougher sea,' Mr Ramsay murmured. He had found the house, and so seeing it, he had also seen himself there; he had seen himself walking on the terrace, alone. He was walking up and down between the urns; and he seemed to himself very old, and bowed. Sitting in the boat he bowed, he crouched himself, acting instantly his part – the part of a desolate man, widowed, bereft; and so called up before him in hosts people sympathising with him; staged for himself as he sat in the boat, a little drama; which required of him decrepitude and exhaustion and sorrow (he raised his hands and looked at the thinness of them, to confirm his dream); and then there was given him in abundance women's sympathy, and he imagined how they would soothe him and sympathise with him, and so getting in his dream some reflection of the exquisite pleasure women's sympathy was to him, he sighed and said gently and mournfully:

> But I beneath a rougher sea
> Was whelmed in deeper gulfs than he,

so that the mournful words were heard quite clearly by them all. Cam half started on her seat. It shocked her – it outraged her. The movement roused her father; and he shuddered, and broke off, exclaiming: 'Look! Look!' so urgently that James also turned his head to look over his shoulder at the island. They all looked. They looked at the island.

But Cam could see nothing. She was thinking how all those paths and the lawn, thick and knotted with the lives they had lived there, were gone; were rubbed out; were past; were unreal, and now this was real: the boat and the sail with its patch; Macalister with his earrings; the noise of the waves – all this was real. Thinking this, she was murmuring to herself: 'We perished, each alone,' for her father's words broke and broke again in her mind, when her father, seeing her gazing so vaguely, began to tease her. Didn't she know the points of the compass? he asked. Didn't she know the north from the south? Did she really think they lived right out there? And he pointed again, and showed her where their house was, there, by those trees. He wished she would try to be more accurate, he said: 'Tell me – which is east, which is west?' he said, half laughing at her, half scolding her, for he could not understand the state of mind of anyone, not absolutely imbecile, who did not know the points of the compass. Yet she did not know. And seeing her gazing, with her vague, now rather frightened, eyes fixed where no house was Mr Ramsay forgot his dream; how he walked up and down between the urns on the terrace; how the arms were stretched out to him. He thought, women are always like that; the vagueness of their minds is hopeless; it was a thing he had never been able to understand; but so it was. It had been so with her – his wife. They could not keep anything clearly fixed in their minds. But he had been wrong to be angry with her; moreover, did he not rather like this vagueness in women? It was part of their extraordinary charm. I will make her smile at me, he thought. She looks frightened. She was so silent. He clutched his fingers, and determined that his voice and his face and all the quick expressive gestures which had been at his command making people pity him and praise him all these years should subdue themselves. He would make her smile at him. He would find some simple easy thing to say to her. But what? For, wrapped up in his work as he was, he forgot the sort of thing one said. There was a puppy. They had a puppy. Who was looking after the puppy today? he asked. Yes, thought James pitilessly, seeing his sister's head against the sail, now she will give way. I shall be left to fight the tyrant alone. The compact would be left to him to carry out. Cam would never resist tyranny to the death, he thought grimly, watching her face, sad, sulky, yielding. And as sometimes happens when a cloud falls on a green hillside and gravity descends and there among all the surrounding hills is gloom and sorrow, and it seems as if the hills themselves must ponder the fate of the clouded, the darkened, either in pity or maliciously rejoicing in her dismay: so Cam now felt herself overcast, as she sat there among calm, resolute people and wondered how to answer her father about the puppy; how to resist his entreaty – forgive me, care for me; while James the lawgiver, with the tablets of eternal wisdom laid open on his knee (his hand on the tiller had become symbolical to her), said, Resist him. Fight him. He said so rightly; justly. For they must fight tyranny to the death, she thought. Of all human qualities she reverenced justice most. Her brother was most godlike, her father most suppliant. And to which did she yield, she thought, sitting between them, gazing at the shore whose points were all unknown to her, and thinking how the lawn and the terrace and the house were smoothed away now and peace dwelt there.

'Jasper,' she said sullenly. He'd look after the puppy.

And what was she going to call him? her father persisted. He had had a dog when he was a little boy, called Frisk. She'll give way, James thought, as he watched a look come upon her face, a look he remembered. They look down, he thought, at their knitting or something. Then suddenly they look up. There was a flash of blue, he remembered, and then somebody sitting with him laughed, surrendered, and he was very angry. It must have been his mother, he thought, sitting on a low chair, with his father standing over her. He began to search among the infinite series of impressions which time had laid down, leaf upon leaf, fold upon fold softly, incessantly upon his brain; among scents, sounds; voices, harsh, hollow, sweet; and lights passing, and brooms tapping; and the wash and hush of the sea; how a man had marched up and down and stopped dead, upright, over them. Meanwhile, he noticed Cam dabbled her fingers in the water, and stared at the shore and said nothing. No, she won't give way, he thought; she's different, he thought. Well, if Cam would not answer him, he would not bother her, Mr Ramsay decided, feeling in his pocket for a book. But she would answer him; she wished, passionately, to move some obstacle that lay upon her tongue and to say, Oh yes, Frisk. I'll call him Frisk. She wanted even to say, Was that the dog that found its way over the moor alone? But try as she might, she could think of nothing to say like that, fierce and loyal to the compact, yet passing on to her father, unsuspected by James, a private token of the love she felt for him. For she thought, dabbling her hand (and now Macalister's boy had caught a mackerel, and it lay kicking on the floor, with blood on its gills), for she thought, looking at James who kept his eyes dispassionately on the sail, or glanced now and then for a second at the horizon, you're not exposed to it, to this pressure and division of feeling, this extraordinary temptation. Her father was feeling in his pockets; in another second he would have found his book. For no one attracted her more; his hands were beautiful to her and his feet, and his voice, and his words, and his haste, and his temper, and his oddity, and his passion, and his saying straight out before everyone, we perish, each alone, and his remoteness. (He had opened his book.) But what remained intolerable, she thought, sitting upright, and watching Macalister's boy tug the hook out of the gills of another fish, was that crass blindness and tyranny of his which had poisoned her childhood and raised bitter storms, so that even now she woke in the night trembling with rage and remembered some command of his; some insolence: 'Do this,' 'Do that'; his dominance: his 'Submit to me.'

So she said nothing, but looked doggedly and sadly at the shore, wrapped in its mantle of peace; as if the people there had fallen asleep, she thought; were free like smoke, were free to come and go like ghosts. They have no suffering there, she thought.

VI

Yes, that is their boat, Lily Briscoe decided, standing on the edge of the lawn. It was the boat with greyish-brown sails, which she saw now flatten itself upon the water and shoot off across the bay. There he sits, she thought, and the children are quite silent still. And she could not reach him either. The sympathy she had not given him weighed her down. It made it difficult for her to paint.

She had always found him difficult. She had never been able to praise him to his face, she remembered. And that reduced their relationship to something neutral, without that element of sex in it which made his manner to Minta so gallant, almost gay. He would pick a flower for her, hand her his books. But could he believe that Minta read them? She dragged them about the garden, sticking in leaves to mark the place.

'D'you remember, Mr Carmichael?' she was inclined to ask, looking at the old man. But he had pulled his hat half over his forehead; he was asleep, or he was dreaming, or he was lying there catching words, she supposed.

'D'you remember?' she felt inclined to ask him as she passed him, thinking again of Mrs Ramsay on the beach; the cask bobbing up and down; and the pages flying. Why, after all these years had that survived, ringed round, lit up, visible to the last detail, with all before it blank and all after it blank, for miles and miles?

'Is it a boat? Is it a cork?' she would say, Lily repeated, turning back, reluctantly again, to her canvas. Heaven be praised for it, the problem of space remained, she thought, taking up her brush again. It glared at her. The whole mass of the picture was poised upon that weight. Beautiful and bright it should be on the surface, feathery and evanescent, one colour melting into another like the colours on a butterfly's wing; but beneath the fabric must be clamped together with bolts of iron. It was to be a thing you could ruffle with your breath; and a thing you could not dislodge with a team of horses. And she began to lay on a red, a grey, and she began to model her way into the hollow there. At the same time she seemed to be sitting beside Mrs Ramsay on the beach.

'Is it a boat? Is it a cask?' Mrs Ramsay said. And she began hunting round for her spectacles. And she sat, having found them, silent, looking out to sea. And Lily, painting steadily, felt as if a door had opened, and one went in and stood gazing silently about in a high cathedral-like place, very dark, very solemn. Shouts came from a world far away. Steamers vanished in stalks of smoke on the horizon. Charles threw stones and sent them skipping.

Mrs Ramsay sat silent. She was glad, Lily thought, to rest in silence, uncommunicative; to rest in the extreme obscurity of human relationships. Who knows what we are, what we feel? Who knows even at the moment of intimacy, This is knowledge? Aren't things spoilt then, Mrs Ramsay may have asked (it seemed to have happened so often, this silence by her side), by saying them? Aren't we more expressive thus? The moment at least seemed extraordinarily fertile. She rammed a little hole in the sand and covered it up, by way of burying in it the perfection of the moment. It was like a drop of silver in which one dipped and illumined the darkness of the past.

Lily stepped back to get her canvas – so – into perspective. It was an odd road to be walking, this of painting. Out and out one went, farther and farther, until at last one seemed to be on a narrow plank, perfectly alone, over the sea. And as she dipped into the blue paint, she dipped too into the past there. Now Mrs Ramsay got up, she remembered. It was time to go back to the house – time for luncheon. And they all walked up from the beach together, she walking behind with William Bankes, and there was Minta in front of them with a hole in her stocking. How that little round hole of pink heel seemed to flaunt itself before them! How William Bankes deplored it, without, so far as she could remember, saying anything about it! It meant to him the annihilation of womanhood, and dirt and disorder, and servants leaving and beds not made at midday – all the things he most abhorred. He had a way of shuddering and spreading his fingers out as if to cover an unsightly object, which he did now – holding his hand in front of him. And Minta walked on ahead, and presumably Paul met her and she went off with Paul in the garden.

The Rayleys, thought Lily Briscoe, squeezing her tube of green paint. She collected her impressions of the Rayleys. Their lives appeared to her in a series of scenes: one, on the staircase at dawn. Paul had come in and gone to bed early; Minta was late. There was Minta, weathered, tinted, garish on the stairs about three o'clock in the morning. Paul came out in his pyjamas carrying a poker in case of burglars. Minta was eating a sandwich, standing halfway up by a window, in the cadaverous early-morning light, and the carpet had a hole in it. But what did they say? Lily asked herself, as if by looking she could hear them. Something violent. Minta went on eating her sandwich, annoyingly, while he spoke. He spoke indignant, jealous words, abusing her, in a mutter so as not to wake the children, the two little boys. He was withered, drawn; she flamboyant, careless. For things had worked loose after the first year or so; the marriage had turned out rather badly.

And this, Lily thought, taking the green paint on her brush, this making up scenes about them, is what we call 'knowing' people, 'thinking' of them, 'being fond' of them! Not a word of it was true; she had made it up; but it was what she knew them by all the same. She went on tunnelling her way into her picture, into the past.

Another time, Paul said he 'played chess in coffee-houses'. She had built up a whole structure of imagination on that saying too. She remembered how, as he said it, she thought how he rang up the servant, and she said, 'Mrs Rayley's out, sir,' and he decided that he would not come home either. She saw him sitting in the corner of some lugubrious place where the smoke attached itself to the red plush seats, and the waitresses got to know you, playing chess with a little man who was in the tea trade and lived at Surbiton, but that was all Paul knew about him. And then Minta was out when he came home and then there was that scene on the stairs, when he got the poker in case of burglars (no doubt to frighten her too) and spoke so bitterly, saying she had ruined his life. At any rate, when she went down to see them at a cottage near Rickmansworth, things were horribly strained. Paul took her down the garden to look at the Belgian hares which he bred, and Minta followed them, singing, and put her bare arm on his shoulder, lest he should tell her anything.

Minta was bored by hares, Lily thought. But Minta never gave herself away. She never said things like that about playing chess in coffee-houses. She was far too conscious, far too wary. But to go on with their story – they had got through the dangerous stage by now. She had been staying with them last summer some time and the car broke down and Minta had to hand him his tools. He sat on the road mending the car, and it was the way she gave him the tools – businesslike, straightforward, friendly – that proved it was all right now. They were 'in love' no longer; no, he had taken up with another woman, a serious woman, with her hair in a plait and a case in her hand (Minta had described her gratefully, almost admiringly), who went to meetings and shared Paul's views (they had got more and more pronounced) about the taxation of land values and a capital levy. Far from breaking up the marriage, that alliance had righted it. They were excellent friends, obviously, as he sat on the road and she handed him his tools.

So that was the story of the Rayleys, Lily smiled. She imagined herself telling it to Mrs Ramsay, who would be full of curiosity to know what had become of the Rayleys. She would feel a little triumphant, telling Mrs Ramsay that the marriage had not been a success.

But the dead, thought Lily, encountering some obstacle in her design which made her pause and ponder, stepping back a foot or so, Oh the dead! she murmured, one pitied them, one brushed them aside, one had even a little contempt for them. They are at our mercy. Mrs Ramsay has faded and gone, she thought. We can override her wishes, improve away her limited, old-fashioned ideas. She recedes farther and farther from us. Mockingly she seemed to see her there at the end of the corridor of years saying, of all incongruous things, 'Marry, marry!' (sitting very upright early in the morning with the birds beginning to cheep in the garden outside). And one would have to say to her, It has all gone against your wishes. They're happy like that; I'm happy like this. Life has changed completely. At that all her being, even her beauty, became for a moment, dusty and out of date. For a moment Lily, standing there, with the sun hot on her back, summing up the Rayleys, triumphed over Mrs Ramsay, who would never know how Paul went to coffee-houses and had a mistress; how he sat on the ground and Minta handed him his tools; how she stood here painting, had never married, not even William Bankes.

Mrs Ramsay had planned it. Perhaps, had she lived, she would have compelled it. Already that summer he was 'the kindest of men'. He was 'the first scientist of his age, my husband says'. He was also 'poor William – it makes me so unhappy, when I go to see him, to find nothing nice in his house – no one to arrange the flowers'. So they were sent for walks together, and she was told, with that faint touch of irony that made Mrs Ramsay slip through one's fingers, that she had a scientific mind; she liked flowers; she was so exact. What was this mania of hers for marriage? Lily wondered, stepping to and fro her easel.

(Suddenly, as suddenly as a star slides in the sky, a reddish light seemed to burn in her mind, covering Paul Rayley, issuing from him. It rose like a fire sent up in token of some celebration by savages on a distant beach. She heard the roar and the crackle. The whole sea for miles round ran red and gold. Some winy smell mixed with it and intoxicated her, for she felt again her own headlong desire to throw herself off the cliff and be drowned looking for a pearl brooch on a beach. And the roar and the crackle repelled her with fear and disgust, as if while she saw its splendour and power she saw too how it fed on the treasure of the house, greedily, disgustingly, and she loathed it. But for a sight, for a glory it surpassed everything in her experience, and burnt year after year like a signal fire on a desert island at the edge of the sea, and one had only to say 'in love' and instantly, as happened now, up rose Paul's fire again. And it sank and she said to herself, laughing, 'The Rayleys'; how Paul went to coffee-houses and played chess.)

She had only escaped by the skin of her teeth though, she thought. She had been looking at the tablecloth, and it had flashed upon her that she would move the tree to the middle, and need never marry anybody, and she had felt an enormous exultation. She had felt, now she could stand up to Mrs Ramsay – a tribute to the astonishing power that Mrs Ramsay had over one. Do this, she said, and one did it. Even her shadow at the window with James was full of authority. She remembered how William Bankes had been shocked by her neglect of the significance of mother and son. Did she not admire their beauty? he said. But William, she remembered, had listened to her with his wise child's eyes when she explained how it was not irreverence: how a light there needed a shadow there and so on. She did not intend to disparage a subject which, they agreed, Raphael had treated divinely. She was not cynical. Quite the contrary. Thanks to his scientific mind he understood – a proof of disinterested intelligence which had pleased her and comforted her enormously. One could talk of painting then seriously to a man. Indeed, his friendship had been one of the pleasures of her life. She loved William Bankes.

They went to Hampton Court and he always left her, like the perfect gentleman he was, plenty of time to wash her hands, while he strolled by the river. That was typical of their relationship. Many things were left unsaid. Then they strolled through the courtyards, and admired, summer after summer, the proportions and the flowers, and he would tell her things, about perspective, about architecture, as they walked, and he would stop to look at a tree, or the view over the lake, and admire a child (it was his great grief – he had no daughter) in the vague aloof way that was natural to a man who spent so much time in laboratories that the world when he came out seemed to dazzle him, so that he walked slowly, lifted his hand to screen his eyes and paused, with his head thrown back, merely to breathe the air. Then he would tell her how his housekeeper was on her holiday; he must buy a new carpet for the staircase. Perhaps she would go with him to buy a new carpet for the staircase. And once something led him to talk about the Ramsays and he had said how when he first saw her she had been wearing a grey hat; she was not more than nineteen or twenty. She was astonishingly beautiful. There he stood looking down the avenue at Hampton Court, as if he could see her there among the fountains.

She looked now at the drawing-room step. She saw, through William's eyes, the shape of a woman, peaceful and silent, with downcast eyes. She sat musing, pondering (she was in grey that day, Lily thought). Her eyes were bent. She would never lift them. Yes, thought Lily, looking intently, I must have seen her look like that, but not in grey; nor so still, nor so young, nor so peaceful. The figure came readily enough. She was astonishingly beautiful, William said. But beauty was not everything. Beauty had this penalty – it came too readily, came too completely. It stilled life – froze it. One forgot the little agitations; the flush, the pallor, some queer distortion, some light or shadow, which made the face unrecognisable for a moment and yet added a quality one saw for ever after. It was simpler to smooth that all out under the cover of beauty. But what was the look she had, Lily wondered, when she clapped her deerstalker's hat on her head, or ran across the grass, or scolded Kennedy, the gardener? Who could tell her? Who could help her?

Against her will she had come to the surface, and found herself half out of the picture, looking, a little dazedly, as if at unreal things, at Mr Carmichael. He lay on his chair with his hands clasped above his paunch not reading, or sleeping, but basking like a creature gorged with existence. His book had fallen on to the grass.

She wanted to go straight up to him and say, 'Mr Carmichael!' Then he would look up benevolently as always, from his smoky vague green eyes. But one only woke people if one knew what one wanted to say to them. And she wanted to say not one thing, but everything. Little words that broke up the thought and dismembered it said nothing. 'About life, about death; about Mrs Ramsay' – no, she thought, one could say nothing to nobody. The urgency of the moment always missed its mark. Words fluttered sideways and struck the object inches too low. Then one gave it up; then the idea sank back again; then one became like most middle-aged people, cautious, fur- tive, with wrinkles between the eyes and a look of perpetual apprehension. For how could one express in words these emotions of the body? express that emptiness there? (She was looking at the drawing-room steps; they looked extraordinarily empty.) It was one's body feeling, not one's mind. The physical sensations that went with the bare look of the steps had become suddenly extremely unpleasant. To want and not to have sent all up her body a hardness, a hollowness, a strain. And then to want and not to have – to want and want – how that wrung the heart, and wrung it again and again! Oh Mrs Ramsay! she called out silently, to that essence which sat by the boat, that abstract one made of her, that woman in grey, as if to abuse her for having gone, and then having gone, come back again. It had seemed so safe, thinking of her. Ghost, air, nothingness, a thing you could play with easily and safely at any time of day or night, she had been that, and then suddenly she put her hand out and wrung the heart thus. Suddenly, the empty drawing-room steps, the frill of the chair inside, the puppy tumbling on the terrace, the whole wave and whisper of the garden became like curves and arabesques flourishing round a centre of complete emptiness.

'What does it mean? How do you explain it all?' she wanted to say, turning to Mr Carmichael again. For the whole world seemed to have dissolved in this early-morning hour into a pool of thought, a deep basin of reality, and one could almost fancy that had Mr Carmichael spoken, a little tear would have rent the surface of the pool. And then? Something would emerge. A hand would be shoved up, a blade would be flashed. It was nonsense of course.

A curious notion came to her that he did after all hear the things she could not say. He was an inscrutable old man, with the yellow stain on his beard, and his poetry, and his puzzles, sailing serenely through a world which satisfied all his wants, so that she thought he had only to put down his hand where he lay on the lawn to fish up anything he wanted. She looked at her picture. That would have been his answer, presumably – how 'you' and 'I' and 'she' pass and vanish; nothing stays; all changes; but not words, not paint. Yet it would be hung in the attics, she thought; it would be rolled up and flung under a sofa; yet even so, even of a picture like that, it was true. One might say, even of this scrawl, not of that actual picture, perhaps, but of what it attempted, that it 'remained for ever', she was going to say, or, for the words spoken sounded even to herself too boastful, to hint, wordlessly; when, looking at the picture, she was surprised to find that she could not see it. Her eyes were full of a hot liquid (she did not think of tears at first) which, without disturbing the firmness of her lips, made the air thick, rolled down her cheeks. She had perfect control of herself – Oh yes! – in every other way. Was she crying then for Mrs Ramsay, without being aware of any unhappiness? She addressed old Mr Carmichael again. What was it then? What did it mean? Could things thrust their hands up and grip one; could the blade cut; the fist grasp? Was there no safety? No learning by heart of the ways of the world? No guide, no shelter, but all was miracle, and leaping from the pinnacle of a tower into the air? Could it be, even for elderly people, that this was life? – startling, unexpected, unknown? For one moment she felt that if they both got up, here, now on the lawn, and demanded an explanation, why was it so short, why was it so inexplicable, said it with violence, as two fully equipped human beings from whom nothing should be hid might speak, then, beauty would roll itself up; the space would fill; those empty flourishes would form into shape; if they shouted loud enough Mrs Ramsay would return. 'Mrs Ramsay!' she said aloud, 'Mrs Ramsay!' The tears ran down her face.

VII

[Macalister's boy took one of the fish and cut a square out of its side to bait his hook with. The mutilated body (it was alive still) was thrown back into the sea.]

VIII

'Mrs Ramsay!' Lily cried, 'Mrs Ramsay!' But nothing happened. The pain increased. That anguish could reduce one to such a pitch of imbecility, she thought! Anyhow the old man had not heard her. He remained benignant, calm – if one chose to think it, sublime. Heaven be praised, no one had heard her cry that ignominious cry, stop pain, stop! She had not obviously taken leave of her senses. No one had seen her step off her strip of board into the waters of annihilation. She remained a skimpy old maid, holding a paintbrush on the lawn.

And now slowly the pain of the want, and the bitter anger (to be called back, just as she thought she would never feel sorrow for Mrs Ramsay again. Had she missed her among the coffee cups at breakfast? not in the least) lessened; and of their anguish left, as antidote, a relief that was balm in itself, and also, but more mysteriously, a sense of someone there, of Mrs Ramsay, relieved for a moment of the weight that the world had put on her, staying lightly by her side and then (for this was Mrs Ramsay in all her beauty) raising to her forehead a wreath of white flowers with which she went. Lily squeezed her tubes again. She attacked that problem of the hedge. It was strange how clearly she saw her, stepping with her usual quickness across fields among whose folds, purplish and soft, among whose flowers, hyacinths or lilies, she vanished. It was some trick of the painter's eye. For days after she had heard of her death she had seen her thus, putting her wreath to her forehead and going unquestioningly with her companion, a shadow, across the fields. The sight, the phrase, had its power to console. Wherever she happened to be, painting, here, in the country, or in London, the vision would come to her, and her eyes, half closing, sought something to base her vision on. She looked down the railway carriage, the omnibus; took a line from shoulder or cheek; looked at the windows opposite; at Piccadilly, lamp-strung in the evening. All had been part of the fields of death. But always something – it might be a face, a voice, a paper boy crying *Standard, News* – thrust through, snubbed her, waked her, required and got in the end an effort of attention, so that the vision must be perpetually remade. Now again, moved as she was by some instinctive need of distance and blue, she looked at the bay beneath her, making hillocks of the blue bars of the waves, and stony fields of the purpler spaces. Again she was roused as usual by something incongruous. There was a brown spot in the middle of the bay. It was a boat. Yes, she realised that after a second. But whose boat? Mr Ramsay's boat, she replied. Mr Ramsay; the man who had marched past her, with his hand raised, aloof, at the head of a procession, in his beautiful boots, asking her for sympathy which she had refused. The boat was now halfway across the bay.

So fine was the morning except for a streak of wind here and there that the sea and sky looked all one fabric, as if sails were stuck high up in the sky, or the clouds had dropped down into the sea. A steamer far out at sea had drawn in the air a great scroll of smoke which stayed there curving and circling decoratively, as if the air were a fine gauze which held things and kept them softly in its mesh, only gently swaying them this way and that. And as happens sometimes when the weather is very fine, the cliffs looked as if they were conscious of the ships and the ships looked as if they were conscious of the cliffs, as if they signalled to each other some secret message of their own. For sometimes quite close to the shore, the Lighthouse looked this morning in the haze an enormous distance away.

'Where are they now?' Lily thought, looking out to sea. Where was he, that very old man who had gone past her silently, holding a brown-paper parcel under his arm? The boat was in the middle of the bay.

IX

They don't feel a thing there, Cam thought, looking at the shore, which, rising and falling, became steadily more distant and more peaceful. Her hand cut a trail in the sea as her mind made the green swirls and streaks into patterns and, numbed and shrouded, wandered in imagination in that under-world of waters where the pearls stuck in clusters to white sprays, where in the green light a change came over one's entire mind and one's body shone half transparent enveloped in a green cloak.

Then the eddy slackened round her hand. The rush of the water ceased; the world became full of little creaking and squeaking sounds. One heard the waves breaking and flapping against the side of the boat as if they were anchored in harbour. Everything became very close to one. For the sail, upon which James had his eyes fixed until it had become to him like a person whom he knew, sagged entirely; there they came to a stop, flapping about waiting for a breeze, in the hot sun, miles from shore, miles from the Lighthouse. Everything in the whole world seemed to stand still. The Lighthouse became immovable, and the line of the distant shore became fixed. The sun grew hotter and everybody seemed to come very close together and to feel each other's presence, which they had almost forgotten. Macalister's fishing line went plumb down into the sea. But Mr Ramsay went on reading with his legs curled under him.

He was reading a little shiny book with covers mottled like a plover's egg. Now and again, as they hung about in that horrid calm, he turned a page. And James felt that each page was turned with a peculiar gesture aimed at him: now assertively, now commandingly; now with the intention of making people pity him; and all the time, as his father read and turned one after another of those little pages, James kept dreading the moment when he would look up and speak sharply to him about something or other. Why were they lagging about here? he would demand, or something quite unreasonable like that. And if he does, James thought, then I shall take a knife and strike him to the heart.

He had always kept this old symbol of taking a knife and striking his father to the heart. Only now, as he grew older, and sat staring at his father in an impotent rage, it was not him, that old man reading, whom he wanted to kill, but it was the thing that descended on him – without his knowing it perhaps: that fierce sudden black-winged harpy, with its talons and its beak all cold and hard, that struck and struck at you (he could feel the beak on his bare legs, where it had struck when he was a child) and then made off, and there he was again, an old man, very sad, reading his book. That he would kill, that he would strike to the heart. Whatever he did – (and he might do anything, he felt, looking at the Lighthouse and the distant shore) whether he was in a business, in a bank, a barrister, a man at the head of some enterprise, that he would fight, that he would track down and stamp out – tyranny, despotism, he called it – making people do what they did not want to do, cutting off their right to speak. How could any of them say, But I won't, when he said, Come to the Lighthouse. Do this. Fetch me that. The black wings spread, and the hard beak tore. And then next moment, there he sat reading his book; and he might look up – one never knew – quite reasonably. He might talk to the Macalisters. He might be pressing a sovereign into some frozen old woman's hand in the street, James thought; he might be shouting out at some fishermen's sports; he might be waving his arms in the air with excitement. Or he might sit at the head of the table dead silent from one end of dinner to the other. Yes, thought James, while the boat slapped and dawdled there in the hot sun; there was a waste of snow and rock very lonely and austere; and there he had come to feel, quite often lately, when his father said something which surprised the others, were two pairs of footprints only; his own and his father's. They alone knew each other. What then was this terror, this hatred? Turning back among the many leaves which the past had folded in him, peering into the heart of that forest where light and shade so chequer each other that all shape is distorted, and one blunders, now with the sun in one's eyes, now with a dark shadow, he sought an image to cool and detach and round off his feeling in a concrete shape. Suppose then that as a child sitting helpless in a perambulator, or on someone's knee, he had seen a wagon crush, ignorantly and innocently, someone's foot? Suppose he had seen the foot first, in the grass, smooth and whole; then the wheel; and the same foot, purple, crushed. But the wheel was innocent. So now, when his father came striding down the passage knocking them up early in the morning to go to the Lighthouse down it came over his foot, over Cam's foot, over anybody's foot. One sat and watched it.

But whose foot was he thinking of, and in what garden did all this happen? For one had settings for these scenes; trees that grew there; flowers; a certain light; a few figures. Everything tended to set itself in a garden where there was none of this gloom and none of this throwing of hands about; people spoke in an ordinary tone of voice. They went in and out all day long. There was an old woman gossiping in the kitchen; and the blinds were sucked in and out by the breeze; all was blowing, all was growing; and over all those plates and bowls and tall brandishing red and yellow flowers a very thin yellow veil would be drawn, like a vine leaf, at night. Things became stiller and darker at night. But the leaflike veil was so fine that lights lifted it, voices crinkled it; he could see through it a figure stooping, hear, coming close, going away, some dress rustling, some chain tinkling.

It was in this world that the wheel went over the person's foot. Something, he remembered, stayed and darkened over him; would not move; something flourished up in the air, something arid and sharp descended even there, like a blade, a scimitar, smiting through the leaves and flowers even of that happy world and making them shrivel and fall.

'It will rain,' he remembered his father saying. 'You won't be able to go to the Lighthouse.'

The Lighthouse was then a silvery, misty-looking tower with a yellow eye that opened suddenly and softly in the evening. Now –

James looked at the Lighthouse. He could see the whitewashed rocks; the tower, stark and straight; he could see that it was barred with black and white; he could see windows in it; he could even see washing spread on the rocks to dry. So that was the Lighthouse, was it?

No, the other was also the Lighthouse. For nothing was simply one thing. The other was the Lighthouse too. It was sometimes hardly to be seen across the bay. In the evening one looked up and saw the eye opening and shutting and the light seemed to reach them in that airy sunny garden where they sat.

But he pulled himself up. Whenever he said 'they' or 'a person', and then began hearing the rustle of someone coming, the tinkle of someone going, he became extremely sensitive to the presence of whoever might be in the room. It was his father now. The strain became acute. For in one moment if there was no breeze, his father would slap the covers of his book together, and say: 'What's happening now? What are we dawdling about here for, eh?' as, once before, he had brought his blade down among them on the terrace and she had gone stiff all over, and if there had been an axe handy, a knife, or anything with a sharp point he would have seized it and struck his father through the heart. His mother had gone stiff all over, and then, her arm slackening, so that he felt she listened to him no longer, she had risen somehow and gone away and left him there, impotent, ridiculous, sitting on the floor grasping a pair of scissors.

Not a breath of wind blew. The water chuckled and gurgled in the bottom of the boat where three or four mackerel beat their tails up and down in a pool of water not deep enough to cover them. At any moment Mr Ramsay (James scarcely dared look at him) might rouse himself, shut his book, and say something sharp; but for the moment he was reading, so that James stealthily, as if he were stealing downstairs on bare feet, afraid of waking a watchdog by a creaking board, went on thinking what was she like, where did she go that day? He began following her from room to room and at last they came to a room where in a blue light, as if the reflection came from many china dishes, she talked to somebody; he listened to her talking. She talked to a servant, saying simply whatever came into her head. 'We shall need a big dish tonight. Where is it – the blue dish?' She alone spoke the truth; to her alone could he speak it. That was the source of her everlasting attraction for him, perhaps; she was a person to whom one could say what came into one's head. But all the time he thought of her, he was conscious of his father following his thought, shadowing it, making it shiver and falter.

At last he ceased to think; there he sat with his hand on the tiller in the sun, staring at the Lighthouse, powerless to move, powerless to flick off these grains of misery which settled on his mind one after another. A rope seemed to bind him there, and his father had knotted it and he could only escape by taking a knife and plunging it . . . But at that moment the sail swung slowly round, filled slowly out, the boat seemed to shake herself, and then to move off half conscious in her sleep, and then she woke and shot through the waves. The relief was extraordinary. They all seemed to fall away from each other again and to be at their ease, and the fishing-lines slanted taut across the side of the boat. But his father did not rouse himself. He only raised his right hand mysteriously high in the air, and let it fall upon his knee again as if he were conducting some secret symphony.

X

[The sea without a stain on it, thought Lily Briscoe, still standing and looking out over the bay. The sea is stretched like silk across the bay. Distance had an extraordinary power; they had been swallowed up in it, she felt, they were gone for ever, they had become part of the nature of things. It was so calm; it was so quiet. The steamer itself had vanished, but the great scroll of smoke still hung in the air and drooped like a flag mournfully in valediction.]

XI

It was like that then, the island, thought Cam, once more drawing her fingers through the waves. She had never seen it from out at sea before. It lay like that on the sea, did it, with a dent in the middle and two sharp crags, and the sea swept in there, and spread away for miles and miles on either side of the island. It was very small; shaped something like a leaf stood on end. So we took a little boat, she thought, beginning to tell herself a story of adventure about escaping from a sinking ship. But with the sea streaming through her fingers, a spray of seaweed vanishing behind them, she did not want to tell herself seriously a story; it was the sense of adventure and escape that she wanted, for she was thinking, as the boat sailed on, how her father's anger about the points of the compass, James's obstinacy about the compact, and her own anguish, all had slipped, all had passed, all had streamed away. What then came next? Where were they going? From her hand, ice cold, held deep in the sea, there spurted up a fountain of joy at the change, at the escape, at the adventure (that she should be alive, that she should be there). And the drops falling from this sudden and unthinking fountain of joy fell here and there on the dark, the slumbrous shapes in her mind; shapes of a world not realised but turning in their darkness, catching, here and there, a spark of light: Greece, Rome, Constantinople. Small as it was, and shaped something like a leaf stood on end with the gold sprinkled waters flowing in and about it, it had, she supposed, a place in the universe – even that little island? The old gentlemen in the study she thought could have told her. Sometimes she strayed in from the garden purposely to catch them at it. There they were (it might be Mr Carmichael or Mr Bankes, very old, very stiff) sitting opposite each other in their low armchairs. They were crackling in front of them the pages of *The Times*, when she came in from the garden, all in a muddle, about something someone had said about

Christ; a mammoth had been dug up in a London street; what was the great Napoleon like? Then they took all this with their clean hands (they wore grey-coloured clothes; they smelt of heather) and they brushed the scraps together, turning the paper, crossing their knees, and said something now and then very brief. In a kind of trance she would take a book from the shelf and stand there, watching her father write, so equally, so neatly from one side of the page to another, with a little cough now and then, or something said briefly to the other old gentleman opposite. And she thought, standing there with her book open, here one could let whatever one thought expand like a leaf in water; and if it did well here, among the old gentlemen smoking and *The Times* crackling, then it was right. And watching her father as he wrote in his study, she thought (now sitting in the boat) he was most lovable, he was most wise; he was not vain, nor a tyrant. Indeed, if he saw she was there, reading a book, he would ask her, as gently as anyone could, Was there nothing he could give her?

Lest this should be wrong, she looked at him reading the little book with the shiny cover mottled like a plover's egg. No; it was right. Look at him now, she wanted to say aloud to James. (But James had his eye on the sail.) He is a sarcastic brute, James would say. He brings the talk round to himself and his books, James would say. He is intolerably egotistical. Worst of all, he is a tyrant. But look! she said, looking at him. Look at him now. She looked at him reading the little book with his legs curled; the little book whose yellow-ish pages she knew, without knowing what was written on them. It was small; it was closely printed; on the flyleaf, she knew, he had written that he had spent fifteen francs on dinner; the wine had been so much; he had given so much to the waiter; all was added up neatly at the bottom of the page. But what might be written in the book which had rounded its edges off in his pocket, she did not know. What he thought they none of them knew. But he was absorbed in it, so that when he looked up, as he did now for an instant, it was not to see anything; it was to pin down some thought more exactly. That done, his mind flew back again and he plunged into his reading. He read, she thought, as if he were guiding something, or wheedling a large flock of sheep, or pushing his way up and up a single narrow path; and sometimes he went fast and straight, and broke his way through the thicket, and sometimes it seemed a branch struck at him, a bramble blinded him, but he was not going to let himself be beaten by that; on he went, tossing over page after page. And she went on telling herself a story about escaping from a sinking ship, for she was safe, while he sat there; safe, as she felt herself when she crept in from the garden, and took a book down, and the old gentleman, lowering the paper suddenly, said something very brief over the top of it about the character of Napoleon.

She gazed back over the sea, at the island. But the leaf was losing its sharpness. It was very small; it was very distant. The sea was more important now than the shore. Waves were all round them, tossing and sinking, with a log wallowing down one wave; a gull riding on another. About here, she thought, dabbling her fingers in the water, a ship had sunk, and she murmured, dreamily, half asleep, how we perished, each alone.

XII

So much depends then, thought Lily Briscoe, looking at the sea which had scarcely a stain on it, which was so soft that the sails and the clouds seemed set in its blue, so much depends, she thought, upon distance: whether people are near us or far from us; for her feeling for Mr Ramsay changed as he sailed farther and farther across the bay. It seemed to be elongated, stretched out; he seemed to become more and more remote. He and his children seemed to be swallowed up in that blue, that distance; but here, on the lawn, close at hand, Mr Carmichael suddenly grunted. She laughed. He clawed his book up from the grass. He settled into his chair again puffing and blowing like some sea monster. That was different altogether, because he was so near. And now again all was quiet. They must be out of bed by this time, she supposed, looking at the house, but nothing appeared there. But then, she remembered, they had always made off directly a meal was over, on business of their own. It was all in keeping with this silence, this emptiness, and the unreality of the early-morning hour. It was a way things had sometimes, she thought, lingering for a moment and looking at the long glittering windows and the plume of blue smoke: they became unreal. So coming back from a journey, or after an illness, before habits had spun themselves across the surface, one felt that same unreality, which was so startling; felt something emerge. Life was most vivid then. One could be at one's ease. Mercifully one need not say, very briskly, crossing the lawn to greet old Mrs Beckwith, who would be coming out to find a corner to sit in, 'Oh good-morning, Mrs Beckwith! What a lovely day! Are you going to be so bold as to sit in the sun? Jasper's hidden the chairs. Do let me find you one!' and all the rest of the usual chatter. One need not speak at all. One glided, one shook one's sails (there was a good deal of movement in the bay, boats were starting off), between things, beyond things. Empty it was not, but full to the brim. She seemed to be standing up to the lips in some substance, to move and float and sink in it, yes, for these waters were unfathomably deep. Into them had spilled so many lives. The Ramsays'; the children's; and all sorts of waifs and strays of things besides. A washerwoman with her basket; a rook; a red-hot poker; the purples and grey-greens of flowers: some common feeling which held the whole together.

It was some such feeling of completeness perhaps which, ten years ago, standing almost where she stood now, had made her say that she must be in love with the place. Love had a thousand shapes. There might be lovers whose gift it was to choose out the elements of things and place them together and so, giving them a wholeness not theirs in life, make of some scene, or meeting of people (all now gone and separate), one of those globed compacted things over which thought lingers, and love plays.

Her eyes rested on the brown speck of Mr Ramsay's sailing boat. They would be at the Lighthouse by lunchtime she supposed. But the wind had freshened, and, as the sky changed slightly and the sea changed slightly and the boats altered their positions, the view, which a moment before had seemed miraculously fixed, was now unsatisfactory. The wind had blown the trail of smoke about; there was something displeasing about the placing of the ships.

The disproportion there seemed to upset some harmony in her own mind. She felt an obscure distress. It was confirmed when she turned to her picture. She had been wasting her morning. For whatever reason she could not achieve that razor edge of balance between two opposite forces; Mr Ramsay and the picture; which was necessary. There was something perhaps wrong with the design? Was it, she wondered, that the line of the wall wanted breaking, was it that the mass of the trees was too heavy? She smiled ironically; for had she not thought, when she began, that she had solved her problem?

What was the problem then? She must try to get hold of something that evaded her. It evaded her when she thought of Mrs Ramsay; it evaded her now when she thought of her picture. Phrases came. Visions came. Beautiful pictures. Beautiful phrases. But what she wished to get hold of was that very jar on the nerves, the thing itself before it has been made anything. Get that and start afresh; get that and start afresh; she said desperately, pitching herself firmly again before her easel. It was a miserable machine, an inefficient machine, she thought, the human apparatus for painting or for feeling; it always broke down at the critical moment; heroically, one must force it on. She stared, frowning. There was the hedge, sure enough. But one got nothing by soliciting urgently. One got only a glare in the eye from looking at the line of the wall, or from thinking – she wore a grey hat. She was astonishingly beautiful. Let it come, she thought, if it will come. For there are moments when one can neither think nor feel. And if one can neither think nor feel, she thought, where is one?

Here on the grass, on the ground, she thought, sitting down, and examining with her brush a little colony of plantains. For the lawn was very rough. Here sitting on the world, she thought, for she could not shake herself free from the sense that everything this morning was happening for the first time, perhaps for the last time, as a traveller, even though he is half asleep, knows, looking out of the train window, that he must look now, for he will never see that town, or that mule-cart, or that woman at work in the fields, again. The lawn was the world; they were up here together, on this exalted station, she thought, looking at old Mr Carmichael, who seemed (though they had not said a word all this time) to share her thoughts. And she would never see him again perhaps. He was growing old. Also, she remembered, smiling at the slipper that dangled from his foot, he was growing famous. People said that his poetry was 'so beautiful'. They went and published things he had written forty years ago. There was a famous man now called Carmichael, she smiled, thinking how many shapes one person might wear, how he was that in the newspapers, but here the same as he had always been. He looked the same – greyer, rather. Yes, he looked the same, but somebody had said, she recalled, that when he had heard of Andrew Ramsay's death (he was killed in a second by a shell; he should have been a great mathematician) Mr Carmichael had 'lost all interest in life'. What did it mean – that? she wondered. Had he marched through Trafalgar Square grasping a big stick? Had he turned pages over and over, without reading them, sitting in his room in St John's Wood alone? She did not know what he had done, when he heard that Andrew was killed, but she felt it in him all the same. They only mumbled at each other on staircases; they looked up at the sky and said it will be fine or it won't be fine. But this was one way of knowing people, she thought: to know the outline, not the detail, to sit in one's garden and look at the slopes of a hill running purple down into the distant heather. She knew him in that way. She knew that he had changed somehow. She had never read a line of his poetry. She thought that she knew how it went though, slowly and sonorously. It was seasoned and mellow. It was about the desert and the camel. It was about the palm tree and the sunset. It was extremely impersonal; it said something about death; it said very little about love. There was an aloofness about him. He wanted very little of other people. Had he not always lurched rather awkwardly past the drawing-room window with some newspaper under his arm, trying to avoid Mrs Ramsay whom for some reason he did not much like? On that account, of course, she would always try to make him stop. He would bow to her. He would halt unwillingly and bow profoundly. Annoyed that he did not want anything of her, Mrs Ramsay would ask him (Lily could hear her) wouldn't he like a coat, a rug, a newspaper? No, he wanted nothing. (Here he bowed.) There was some quality in her which he did not much like. It was perhaps her masterfulness, her positiveness, something matter-of-fact in her. She was so direct.

(A noise drew her attention to the drawing-room window – the squeak of a hinge. The light breeze was toying with the window.)

There must have been people who disliked her very much, Lily thought (Yes; she realised that the drawing-room step was empty, but it had no effect on her whatever. She did not want Mrs Ramsay now). – People who thought her too sure, too drastic. Also her beauty offended people probably. How monotonous, they would say, and the same always! They preferred another type – the dark, the vivacious. Then she was weak with her husband. She let him make those scenes. Then she was reserved. Nobody knew exactly what had happened to her. And (to go back to Mr Carmichael and his dislike) one could not imagine Mrs Ramsay standing painting, lying reading, a whole morning on the lawn. It was unthinkable. Without saying a word, the only token of her errand a basket on her arm, she went off to the town, to the poor, to sit in some stuffy little bedroom. Often and often Lily had seen her go silently in the midst of some game, some discussion, with her basket on her arm, very upright. She had noted her return. She had thought, half laughing (she was so methodical with the tea cups), half moved (her beauty took one's breath away), eyes that are closing in pain have looked on you. You have been with them there.

And then Mrs Ramsay would be annoyed because somebody was late, or the butter not fresh, or the teapot chipped. And all the time she was saying that the butter was not fresh one would be thinking of Greek temples, and how beauty had been with them there. She never talked of it – she went, punctually, directly. It was her instinct to go, an instinct like the swallows for the south, the artichokes for the sun, turning her infallibly to the human race, making her nest in its heart. And this, like all instincts, was a little distressing to people who did not share it; to Mr Carmichael perhaps, to herself certainly. Some notion was in both of them about the ineffectiveness of action, the supremacy of thought. Her going was a reproach to them, gave a different twist to the world, so that they were led to protest, seeing their own prepossessions disappear, and clutch at them vanishing. Charles Tansley did that too: it was part of the reason why one disliked him. He upset the proportions of one's world. And what had happened to him, she wondered, idly stirring the plantains with her brush. He had got his fellowship. He had married; he lived at Golder's Green.

She had gone one day into a hall and heard him speaking during the War. He was denouncing something: he was condemning somebody. He was preaching brotherly love. And all she felt was how could he love his kind who did not know one picture from another, who had stood behind her smoking shag ('fivepence an ounce, Miss Briscoe') and making it his business to tell her women can't write, women can't paint, not so much that he believed it, as that for some odd reason he wished it? There he was, lean and red and raucous, preaching love from a platform (there were ants crawling about among the plantains which she disturbed with her brush – red, energetic ants, rather like Charles Tansley). She had looked at him ironically from her seat in the half-empty hall, pumping love into that chilly space, and suddenly, there was the old cask or whatever it was bobbing up and down among the waves and Mrs Ramsay looking for her spectacle case among the pebbles. 'Oh dear! What a nuisance! Lost again. Don't bother, Mr Tansley. I lose thousands every summer,' at which he pressed his chin back against his collar, as if afraid to sanction such exaggeration, but could stand it in her whom he liked, and smiled very charmingly. He must have confided in her on one of those long expeditions when people got separated and walked back alone. He was educating his little sister, Mrs Ramsay had told her. It was immensely to his credit. Her own idea of him was grotesque, Lily knew well, stirring the plantains with her brush. Half one's notions of other people were, after all, grotesque. They served private purposes of one's own. He did for her instead of a whipping-boy. She found herself flagellating his lean flanks when she was out of temper. If she wanted to be serious about him she had to help herself to Mrs Ramsay's sayings, to look at him through her eyes.

She raised a little mountain for the ants to climb over. She reduced them to a frenzy of indecision by this interference in their cosmogony. Some ran this way, others that.

One wanted fifty pairs of eyes to see with, she reflected. Fifty pairs of eyes were not enough to get round that one woman with, she thought. Among them must be one that was stone blind to her beauty. One wanted most some secret sense, fine as air, with which to steal through keyholes and surround her where she sat knitting, talking, sitting silent in the window alone; which took to itself and treasured up like the air which held the smoke of the steamer, her thoughts, her imaginations, her desires. What did the hedge mean to her, what did the garden mean to her, what did it mean to her when a wave broke? (Lily looked up, as she had seen Mrs Ramsay look up; she too heard a wave falling on the beach.) And then what stirred and trembled in her mind when the children cried: 'How's that? How's that?' cricketing? She would stop knitting for a second. She would look intent. Then she would lapse again, and suddenly Mr Ramsay stopped dead in his pacing in front of her, and some curious shock passed through her and seemed to rock her in profound agitation on its breast when stopping there he stood over her, and looked down at her. Lily could see him.

He stretched out his hand and raised her from her chair. It seemed somehow as if he had done it before; as if he had once bent in the same way and raised her from a boat which, lying a few inches off some island, had required that the ladies should thus be helped on shore by the gentlemen. An old-fashioned scene that was, which required, very nearly, crinolines and peg-top trousers. Letting herself be helped by him, Mrs Ramsay had thought (Lily supposed) the time has come now. Yes, she would say it now. Yes, she would marry him. And she stepped slowly, quietly on shore. Probably she said one word only, letting her hand rest still in his. I will marry you, she might have said, with her hand in his; but no more. Time after time the same thrill had passed between them – obviously it had, Lily thought, smoothing a way for her ants. She was not inventing; she was only trying to smooth out something she had been given years ago folded up; something she had seen. For in the rough and tumble of daily life, with all those children about, all those visitors, one had constantly a sense of repetition – of one thing falling where another had fallen, and so setting up an echo which chimed in the air and made it full of vibrations.

But it would be a mistake, she thought, thinking how they walked off together, she in her green shawl, he with his tie flying, arm in arm, past the greenhouse, to simplify their relationship. It was no monotony of bliss – she with her impulses and quicknesses; he with his shudders and glooms. Oh no. The bedroom door would slam violently early in the morning. He would start from the table in a temper. He would whizz his plate through the window. Then all through the house there would be a sense of doors slamming and blinds fluttering as if a gusty wind were blowing and people scudded about trying in a hasty way to fasten hatches and make things shipshape. She had met Paul Rayley like that one day on the stairs. They had laughed and laughed, like a couple of children, all because Mr Ramsay, finding an earwig in his milk at breakfast had sent the whole thing flying through the air on to the terrace outside. 'An earwig,' Prue murmured, awestruck, 'in his milk.' Other people might find centipedes. But he had built round him such a fence of sanctity and occupied the space with such a demeanour of majesty that an earwig in his milk was a monster.

But it tired Mrs Ramsay, it cowed her a little – the plates whizzing and the doors slamming. And there would fall between them sometimes long rigid silences, when, in a state of mind which annoyed Lily in her, half plaintive, half resentful, she seemed unable to surmount the tempest calmly, or to laugh as they laughed, but in her weariness perhaps concealed something. She brooded and sat silent. After a time he would hang stealthily about the places where she was – roaming under the window where she sat writing letters or talking, for she would take care to be busy when he passed, and evade him, and pretend not to see him. Then he would turn smooth as silk, affable, urbane, and try to win her so. Still she would hold off, and now she would assert for a brief season some of those prides and airs, the due of her beauty, which she was generally utterly without; would turn her head; would look so, over her shoulder, always with some Minta, Paul or William Bankes at her side. At length, standing outside the group the very figure of a famished wolfhound (Lily got up off the grass and stood looking at the steps, at the window, where she had seen him), he would say her name, once only, for all the world like a wolf barking in the snow, but still she held back; and he would say it once more, and this time something in the tone would rouse her, and she would go to him, leaving them all of a sudden, and they would walk off together among the pear trees, the cabbages, and the raspberry beds. They would have it out together. But with what attitudes and with what words? Such a dignity was theirs in this relationship that, turning away, she and Paul and Minta would hide their curiosity and their discomfort, and begin picking flowers, throwing balls, chattering, until it was time for dinner, and there they were, he at one end of the table, she at the other, as usual.

'Why don't some of you take up botany? . . . With all those legs and arms why doesn't one of you . . . ?' So they would talk as usual, laughing, among the children. All would be as usual, save only for some quiver, as of a blade in the air, which came and went between them as if the usual sight of the children sitting round their soup plates had freshened itself in their eyes after that hour among the pears and the cabbages. Especially, Lily thought, Mrs Ramsay would glance at Prue. She sat in the middle between brothers and sisters, always so occupied, it seemed, seeing that nothing went wrong, that she scarcely spoke herself. How Prue must have blamed herself for that earwig in the milk! How white she had gone when Mr Ramsay threw his plate through the window! How she drooped under those long silences between them! Anyhow, her mother now would seem to be making it up to her; assuring her that everything was well; promising her that one of these days that same happiness would be hers. She had enjoyed it for less than a year, however.

She had let the flowers fall from her basket, Lily thought, screwing up her eyes and standing back as if to look at her picture, which she was not touching, however, with all her faculties in a trance, frozen over superficially but moving underneath with extreme speed.

She let her flowers fall from her basket, scattered and tumbled them on to the grass and, reluctantly and hesitatingly, but without question or complaint – had she not the faculty of obedience to perfection? – went too. Down fields, across valleys, white, flower-strewn – that was how she would have painted it. The hills were austere. It was rocky; it was steep. The waves sounded hoarse on the stones beneath. They went, the three of them together, Mrs Ramsay walking rather fast in front, as if she expected to meet someone round the corner.

Suddenly the window at which she was looking was whitened by some light stuff behind it. At last then somebody had come into the drawing-room; somebody was sitting in the chair. For heaven's sake, she prayed, let them sit still there and not come floundering out to talk to her. Mercifully, whoever it was stayed still inside; had settled by some stroke of luck so as to throw an odd-shaped triangular shadow over the step. It altered the composition of the picture a little. It was interesting. It might be useful. Her mood was coming back to her. One must keep on looking without for a second relaxing the intensity of emotion, the determination not to be put off, not to be bamboozled. One must hold the scene – so – in a vice and let nothing come in and spoil it. One wanted, she thought, dipping her brush deliberately, to be on a level with ordinary experience, to feel simply that's a chair, that's a table, and yet at the same time, It's a miracle, it's an ecstasy. The problem might be solved after all. Ah, but what had happened? Some wave of white went over the window pane. The air must have stirred some flounce in the room. Her heart leapt at her and seized her and tortured her.

'Mrs Ramsay! Mrs Ramsay!' she cried, feeling the old horror come back – to want and want and not to have. Could she inflict that still? And then, quietly, as if she refrained, that too became part of ordinary experience, was on a level with the chair, with the table. Mrs Ramsay – it was part of her perfect goodness to Lily – sat there quite simply, in the chair, flicked her needles to and fro, knitted her reddish-brown stocking, cast her shadow on the step. There she sat.

And as if she had something she must share, yet could hardly leave her easel, so full her mind was of what she was thinking, of what she was seeing, Lily went past Mr Carmichael holding her brush to the edge of the lawn. Where was that boat now? Mr Ramsay? She wanted him.

XIII

Mr Ramsay had almost done reading. One hand hovered over the page as if to be in readiness to turn it the very instant he had finished it. He sat there bareheaded with the wind blowing his hair about, extraordinarily exposed to everything. He looked very old. He looked, James thought, getting his head now against the Lighthouse, now against the waste of waters running away into the open, like some old stone lying on the sand; he looked as if he had become physically what was always at the back of both of their minds – that loneliness which was for both of them the truth about things.

He was reading very quickly, as if he were eager to get to the end. Indeed they were very close to the Lighthouse now. There it loomed up, stark and straight, glaring white and black, and one could see the waves breaking in white splinters like smashed glass upon the rocks. One could see lines and creases in the rocks. One could see the windows clearly; a dab of white on one of them, and a little tuft of green on the rock. A man had come out and looked at them through a glass and gone in again. So it was like that, James thought, the Lighthouse one had seen across the bay all these years; it was a stark tower on a bare rock. It satisfied him. It confirmed some obscure feeling of his about his own character. The old ladies, he thought, thinking of the garden at home, went dragging their chairs about on the lawn. Old Mrs Beckwith, for example, was always saying how nice it was and how sweet it was and how they ought to be so proud and they ought to be so happy, but as a matter of fact James thought, looking at the Lighthouse stood there on its rock, it's like that. He looked at his father reading fiercely with his legs curled tight. They shared that knowledge. 'We are driving before a gale – we must sink,' he began saying to himself, half aloud exactly as his father said it.

Nobody seemed to have spoken for an age. Cam was tired of looking at the sea. Little bits of black cork had floated past; the fish were dead in the bottom of the boat. Still her father read, and James looked at him and she looked at him, and they vowed that they would fight tyranny to the death, and he went on reading quite unconscious of what they thought. It was thus that he escaped, she thought. Yes, with his great forehead and his great nose, holding his little mottled book firmly in front of him, he escaped. You might try to lay hands on him, but then like a bird, he spread his wings, he floated off to settle out of your reach somewhere far away on some desolate stump. She gazed at the immense expanse of the sea. The island had grown so small that it scarcely looked like a leaf any longer. It looked like the top of a rock which some big wave would cover. Yet in its frailty were all those paths, those terraces, those bedrooms – all those innumerable things. But as, just before sleep, things simplify themselves so that only one of all the myriad details has power to assert itself, so, she felt, looking drowsily at the island, all those paths and terraces and bedrooms were fading and disappearing, and nothing was left but a pale blue censer swinging rhythmically this way and that across her mind. It was a hanging garden; it was a valley, full of birds, and flowers, and antelopes . . . She was falling asleep.

'Come now,' said Mr Ramsay, suddenly shutting his book.

Come where? To what extraordinary adventure? She woke with a start. To land somewhere, to climb somewhere? Where was he leading them? For after his immense silence the words startled them. But it was absurd. He was hungry, he said. It was time for lunch. Besides, look, he said. There's the Lighthouse. 'We're almost there.'

'He's doing very well,' said Macalister, praising James. 'He's keeping her very steady.'

But his father never praised him, James thought grimly.

Mr Ramsay opened the parcel and shared out the sandwiches among them. Now he was happy, eating bread and cheese with these fishermen. He would have liked to live in a cottage and lounge about in the harbour spitting with the other old men, James thought, watching him slice his cheese into thin yellow sheets with his penknife.

This is right, this is it, Cam kept feeling, as she peeled her hard-boiled egg. Now she felt as she did in the study when the old men were reading *The Times*. Now I can go on thinking whatever I like and I shan't fall over a precipice or be drowned, for there he is, keeping his eye on me, she thought.

At the same time they were sailing so fast along by the rocks that it was very exciting – it seemed as if they were doing two things at once; they were eating their lunch here in the sun and they were also making for safety in a great storm after a shipwreck. Would the water last? Would the provisions last? she asked herself, telling herself a story but knowing at the same time what was the truth.

They would soon be out of it, Mr Ramsay was saying to old Macalister; but their children would see some strange things. Macalister said he was seventy-five last March; Mr Ramsay was seventy-one. Macalister said he had never seen a doctor; he had never lost a tooth. And that's the way I'd like my children to live – Cam was sure that her father was thinking that, for he stopped her throwing a sandwich into the sea and told her, as if he were thinking of the fishermen and how they live, that if she did not want it she should put it back in the parcel. She should not waste it. He said it so wisely, as if he knew so well all the things that happened in the world, that she put it back at once, and then he gave her, from his own parcel, a gingerbread nut, as if he were a great Spanish gentleman, she thought, handing a flower to a lady at a window (so courteous his manner was). But he was shabby, and simple, eating bread and cheese; and yet he was leading them on a great expedition where, for all she knew, they would be drowned.

'That was where she sank,' said Macalister's boy suddenly.

'Three men were drowned where we are now,' said the old man. He had seen them clinging to the mast himself. And Mr Ramsay, taking a look at the spot, was about, James and Cam were afraid, to burst out:

But I beneath a rougher sea,

and if he did, they could not bear it; they would shriek aloud; they could not endure another explosion of the passion that boiled in him; but to their surprise all he said was 'Ah' as if he thought to himself, But why make a fuss about that? Naturally men are drowned in a storm, but it is a perfectly straightforward affair, and the depths of the sea (he sprinkled the crumbs from his sandwich paper over them) are only water after all. Then having lighted his pipe he took out his watch. He looked at it attentively; he made, perhaps, some mathematical calculation. At last he said, triumphantly: 'Well done!' James had steered them like a born sailor.

There! Cam thought, addressing herself silently to James. You've got it at last. For she knew that this was what James had been wanting, and she knew that now he had got it he was so pleased that he would not look at her or at his father or at anyone. There he sat with his hand on the tiller sitting bolt upright, looking rather sulky and frowning slightly. He was so pleased that he was not going to let anybody take away a grain of his pleasure. His father had praised him. They must think that he was perfectly indifferent. But you've got it now, Cam thought.

They had tacked, and they were sailing swiftly, buoyantly on long rocking waves which handed them on from one to another with an extraordinary lilt and exhilaration beside the reef. On the left a row of rocks showed brown through the water which thinned and became greener and on one, a higher rock, a wave incessantly broke and spurted a little column of drops which fell down in a shower. One could hear the slap of the water and the patter of falling drops and a kind of hushing and hissing sound from the waves rolling and gambolling and slapping the rocks as if they were wild creatures who were perfectly free and tossed and tumbled and sported like this for ever.

Now they could see two men on the Lighthouse, watching them and making ready to meet them.

Mr Ramsay buttoned his coat, and turned up his trousers. He took the large, badly packed, brown-paper parcel which Nancy had got ready and sat with it on his knee. Thus in complete readiness to land he sat looking back at the island. With his long-sighted eyes perhaps he could see the dwindled leaflike shape standing on end on a plate of gold quite clearly. What could he see? Cam wondered. It was all a blur to her. What was he thinking now? she wondered. What was it he sought, so fixedly, so intently, so silently? They watched him, both of them, sitting bareheaded with his parcel on his knee staring and staring at the frail blue shape which seemed like the vapour of something that had burnt itself away. What do you want? they both wanted to ask. They both wanted to say, Ask us anything and we will give it you. But he did not ask them anything. He sat and looked at the island and he might be thinking, We perished, each alone, or he might be thinking, I have reached it. I have found it, but he said nothing.

Then he put on his hat.

'Bring those parcels,' he said, nodding his head at the things Nancy had done up for them to take to the Lighthouse. 'The parcels for the Lighthouse men,' he said. He rose and stood in the bow of the boat, very straight and tall, for all the world, James thought, as if he were saying: 'There is no God,' and Cam thought, as if he were leaping into space, and they both rose to follow him as he sprang, lightly like a young man, holding his parcel, on to the rock

XIV

'He must have reached it,' said Lily Briscoe aloud, feeling suddenly completely tired out. For the Lighthouse had become almost invisible, had melted away into a blue haze, and the effort of looking at it and the effort of thinking of him landing there, which both seemed to be one and the same effort, had stretched her body and mind to the utmost. Ah, but she was relieved. Whatever she had wanted to give him, when he left her that morning, she had given him at last.

'He has landed,' she said aloud. 'It is finished.' Then, surging up, puffing slightly, old Mr Carmichael stood beside her, looking like an old pagan god, shaggy, with weeds in his hair and the trident (it was only a French novel) in his hand. He stood by her on the edge of the lawn, swaying a little in his bulk, and said, shading his eyes with his hand: 'They will have landed,' and she felt that she had been right. They had not needed to speak. They had been thinking the same things and he had answered her without her asking him anything. He stood there spreading his hands over all the weakness and suffering of mankind; she thought he was surveying, tolerantly, compassionately, their final destiny. Now he has crowned the occasion, she thought, when his hand slowly fell, as if she had seen him let fall from his great height a wreath of violets and asphodels which, fluttering slowly, lay at length upon the earth.

Quickly, as if she were recalled by something over there, she turned to her canvas. There it was – her picture. Yes, with all its greens and blues, its lines running up and across, its attempt at something. It would be hung in the attics, she thought; it would be destroyed. But what did that matter? she asked herself, taking up her brush again. She looked at the steps: they were empty; she looked at her canvas: it was blurred. With a sudden intensity, as if she saw it clear for a second, she drew a line there, in the centre. It was done; it was finished. Yes, she thought, laying down her brush in extreme fatigue, I have had my vision.

ORLANDO: A BIOGRAPHY

Orlando
A Biography

A novel by
VIRGINIA WOOLF
first published in 1928

ILLUSTRATIONS

TO
VITA SACKVILLE-WEST

Preface

Many friends have helped me in writing this book. Some are dead and so illustrious that I scarcely dare name them, yet no one can read or write without being perpetually in the debt of Defoe, Sir Thomas Browne, Sterne, Sir Walter Scott, Lord Macaulay, Emily Brontë, De Quincey, and Walter Pater – to name the first that come to mind. Others are alive, and though perhaps as illustrious in their own way, are less formidable for that very reason. I am specially indebted to Mr C. P. Sanger, without whose knowledge of the law of real property this book could never have been written. Mr Sydney-Turner's wide and peculiar erudition has saved me, I hope, some lamentable blunders. I have had the advantage – how great I alone can estimate – of Mr Arthur Waley's knowledge of Chinese. Madame Lopokova (Mrs J. M. Keynes) has been at hand to correct my Russian. To the unrivalled sympathy and imagination of Mr Roger Fry I owe whatever understanding of the art of painting I may possess. I have, I hope, profited in another department by the singularly penetrating, if severe, criticism of my nephew Mr Julian Bell. Miss M. K. Snowdon's indefatigable researches in the archives of Harrogate and Cheltenham were none the less arduous for being vain. Other friends have helped me in ways too various to specify. I must content myself with naming Mr Angus Davidson; Mrs Cartwright; Miss Janet Case; Lord Berners (whose knowledge of Elizabethan music has proved invaluable); Mr Francis Birrell; my brother, Dr Adrian Stephen; Mr F. L. Lucas; Mr and Mrs Desmond MacCarthy; that most inspiriting of critics, my brother-in-law, Mr Clive Bell; Mr G. H. Rylands; Lady Colefax; Miss Nellie Boxall; Mr J. M. Keynes; Mr Hugh Walpole; Miss Violet Dickinson; the Hon. Edward Sackville West; Mr and Mrs St John Hutchinson; Mr Duncan Grant; Mr and Mrs Stephen Tomlin; Mr and Lady Ottoline Morrell; my mother-in-law, Mrs Sidney Woolf; Mr Osbert Sitwell; Madame Jacques Raverat; Colonel Cory Bell; Miss Valerie Taylor; Mr J. T. Sheppard; Mr and Mrs T. S. Eliot; Miss Ethel Sands; Miss Nan Hudson; my nephew Mr Quentin Bell (an old and valued collaborator in fiction); Mr Raymond Mortimer; Lady Gerald Wellesley; Mr Lytton Strachey; the Viscountess Cecil; Miss Hope Mirrlees; Mr E. M. Forster; the Hon. Harold Nicolson; and my sister, Vanessa Bell – but the list threatens to grow too long and is already far too distinguished. For while it rouses in me memories of the pleasantest kind it will inevitably wake expectations in the reader which the book itself can only disappoint. Therefore I will conclude by thanking the officials of the British Museum and Record Office for their wonted courtesy; my niece Miss Angelica Bell, for a service which none but she could have rendered; and my husband for the patience with which he has invariably helped my researches and for the profound historical knowledge to which these pages owe whatever degree of accuracy they may attain. Finally, I would thank, had I not lost his name and address, a gentleman in America, who has generously and gratuitously corrected the punctuation, the botany, the entomology, the geography, and the chronology of previous works of mine and will, I hope, not spare his services on the present occasion.

He – for there could be no doubt of his sex, though the fashion of the time did something to disguise it – was in the act of slicing at the head of a Moor which swung from the rafters. It was the colour of an old football, and more or less the shape of one, save for the sunken cheeks and a strand or two of coarse, dry hair, like the hair on a cocoanut. Orlando's father, or perhaps his grandfather, had struck it from the shoulders of a vast Pagan who had started up under the moon in the barbarian fields of Africa; and now it swung, gently, perpetually, in the breeze which never ceased blowing through the attic rooms of the gigantic house of the lord who had slain him.

Orlando's fathers had ridden in fields of asphodel, and stony fields, and fields watered by strange rivers, and they had struck many heads of many colours off many shoulders, and brought them back to hang from the rafters. So too would Orlando, he vowed. But since he was sixteen only, and too young to ride with them in Africa or France, he would steal away from his mother and the peacocks in the garden and go to his attic room and there lunge and plunge and slice the air with his blade. Sometimes he cut the cord so that the skull bumped on the floor and he had to string it up again, fastening it with some chivalry almost out of reach so that his enemy grinned at him through shrunk, black lips triumphantly. The skull swung to and fro, for the house, at the top of which he lived, was so vast that there seemed trapped in it the wind itself, blowing this way, blowing that way, winter and summer. The green arras with the hunters on it moved perpetually. His fathers had been noble since they had been at all. They came out of the northern mists wearing coronets on their heads. Were not the bars of darkness in the room, and the yellow pools which chequered the floor, made by the sun falling through the stained glass of a vast coat of arms in the window? Orlando stood now in the midst of the yellow body of an heraldic leopard. When he put his hand on the window-sill to push the window open, it was instantly coloured red, blue, and yellow like a butterfly's wing. Thus, those who like symbols, and have a turn for the deciphering of them, might observe that though the shapely legs, the handsome body, and the well-set shoulders were all of them decorated with various tints of heraldic light, Orlando's face, as he threw the window open, was lit solely by the sun itself. A more candid, sullen face it would be impossible to find. Happy the mother who bears, happier still the biographer who records the life of such a one! Never need she vex herself, nor he invoke the help of novelist or poet. From deed to deed, from glory to glory, from office to office he must go, his scribe following after, till they reach whatever seat it may be that is the height of their desire. Orlando, to look at, was cut out

SELECTED WORKS OF VIRGINIA WOOLF

precisely for some such career. The red of the cheeks was covered with peach down; the down on the lips was only a little thicker than the down on the cheeks. The lips themselves were short and slightly drawn back over teeth of an exquisite and almond whiteness. Nothing disturbed the arrowy nose in its short, tense flight; the hair was dark, the ears small, and fitted closely to the head. But, alas, that these catalogues of youthful beauty cannot end without mentioning forehead and eyes. Alas, that people are seldom born devoid of all three; for directly we glance at Orlando standing by the window, we must admit that he had eyes like drenched violets, so large that the water seemed to have brimmed in them and widened them; and a brow like the swelling of a marble dome pressed between the two blank medallions which were his temples. Directly we glance at eyes and forehead, thus do we rhapsodise. Directly we glance at eyes and forehead, we have to admit a thousand disagreeables which it is the aim of every good biographer to ignore. Sights disturbed him, like that of his mother, a very beautiful lady in green walking out to feed the peacocks with Twitchett, her maid, behind her; sights exalted him – the birds and the trees; and made him in love with death – the evening sky, the homing rooks; and so, mounting up the spiral stairway into his brain – which was a roomy one – all these sights, and the garden sounds too, the hammer beating, the wood chopping, began that riot and confusion of the passions and emotions which every good biographer detests. But to continue – Orlando slowly drew in his head, sat down at the table, and, with the half-conscious air of one doing what they do every day of their lives at this hour, took out a writing book labelled 'Aethelbert: A Tragedy in Five Acts', and dipped an old stained goose quill in the ink.

Soon he had covered ten pages and more with poetry. He was fluent, evidently, but he was abstract. Vice, Crime, Misery were the personages of his drama; there were Kings and Queens of impossible territories; horrid plots confounded them; noble sentiments suffused them; there was never a word said as he himself would have said it, but all was turned with a fluency and sweetness which, considering his age – he was not yet seventeen – and that the sixteenth century had still some years of its course to run, were remarkable enough. At last, however, he came to a halt. He was describing, as all young poets are for ever describing, nature, and in order to match the shade of green precisely he looked (and here he showed more audacity than most) at the thing itself, which happened to be a laurel bush growing beneath the window. After that, of course, he could write no more. Green in nature is one thing, green in literature another. Nature and letters seem to have a natural antipathy; bring them together and they tear each other to pieces. The shade of green Orlando now saw spoilt his rhyme and split his metre. Moreover, nature has tricks of her own. Once look out of a window at bees among flowers, at a yawning dog, at the sun setting, once think 'how many more suns shall I see set', etc. etc. (the thought is too well known to be

Orlando as a boy

worth writing out) and one drops the pen, takes one's cloak, strides out of the room, and catches one's foot on a painted chest as one does so. For Orlando was a trifle clumsy.

He was careful to avoid meeting anyone. There was Stubbs, the gardener, coming along the path. He hid behind a tree till he had passed. He let himself out at a little gate in the garden wall. He skirted all stables, kennels, breweries, carpenters' shops, wash-houses, places where they make tallow candles, kill oxen, forge horseshoes, stitch jerkins – for the house was a town ringing with men at work at their various crafts – and gained the ferny path leading uphill through the park unseen. There is perhaps a kinship among qualities; one draws another along with it; and the biographer should here call attention to the fact that this clumsiness is often mated with a love of solitude. Having stumbled over a chest, Orlando naturally loved solitary places, vast views, and to feel himself for ever and ever and ever alone.

So, after a long silence, 'I am alone,' he breathed at last, opening his lips for the first time in this record. He had walked very quickly uphill through ferns and hawthorn bushes, startling deer and wild birds, to a place crowned by a single oak tree. It was very high, so high indeed that nineteen English counties could be seen beneath; and on clear days thirty or perhaps forty, if the weather was very fine. Sometimes one could see the English Channel, wave reiterating upon wave. Rivers could be seen and pleasure boats gliding on them; and galleons setting out to sea; and armadas with puffs of smoke from which came the dull thud of cannon firing; and forts on the coast; and castles among the meadows; and here a watch tower; and there a fortress; and again some vast mansion like that of Orlando's father, massed like a town in the valley circled by walls. To the east there were the spires of London and the smoke of the city; and perhaps on the very sky line, when the wind was in the right quarter, the craggy top and serrated edges of Snowdon herself showed mountainous among the clouds. For a moment Orlando stood counting, gazing, recognising. That was his father's house; that his uncle's. His aunt owned those three great turrets among the trees there. The heath was theirs and the forest; the pheasant and the deer, the fox, the badger, and the butterfly.

He sighed profoundly, and flung himself – there was a passion in his movements which deserves the word – on the earth at the foot of the oak tree. He loved, beneath all this summer transiency, to feel the earth's spine beneath him; for such he took the hard root of the oak tree to be; or, for image followed image, it was the back of a great horse that he was riding; or the deck of a tumbling ship – it was anything indeed, so long as it was hard, for he felt the need of something which he could attach his floating heart to; the heart that tugged at his side; the heart that seemed filled with spiced and amorous gales every evening about this time when he walked out. To the oak tree he tied it and as he lay there, gradually the flutter in and about him stilled itself; the little leaves hung, the deer stopped; the pale summer clouds stayed; his limbs grew heavy on the ground; and he lay so still that by degrees the deer stepped nearer and the rooks wheeled round him and the swallows dipped and circled and the dragonflies shot past, as if all the fertility and amorous activity of a summer's evening were woven weblike about his body.

After an hour or so – the sun was rapidly sinking, the white clouds had turned red, the hills were violet, the woods purple, the valleys black – a trumpet sounded. Orlando leapt to his feet. The shrill sound came from the valley. It came from a dark spot down there; a spot compact and mapped out; a maze; a town, yet girt about with walls; it came from the heart of his own great house in the valley, which, dark before, even as he looked and the single trumpet duplicated and reduplicated itself with other shriller sounds, lost its darkness and became pierced with lights. Some were small hurrying lights, as if servants dashed along corridors to answer summonses; others were high and lustrous lights, as if they burnt in empty banqueting-halls made ready to receive guests who had not come; and others dipped and waved and sank and rose, as if held in the hands of troops of serving men, bending, kneeling, rising, receiving, guarding, and escorting with all dignity indoors a great Princess alighting from her chariot. Coaches turned and wheeled in the courtyard. Horses tossed their plumes. The Queen had come.

Orlando looked no more. He dashed downhill. He let himself in at a wicket gate. He tore up the winding staircase. He reached his room. He tossed his stockings to one side of the room, his jerkin to the other. He dipped his head. He scoured his hands. He pared his finger nails. With no more than six inches of looking-glass and a pair of old candles to help him, he had thrust on crimson breeches, lace collar, waistcoat of taffeta, and shoes with rosettes on them as big as double dahlias in less than ten minutes by the stable clock. He was ready. He was flushed. He was excited. But he was terribly late.

By short cuts known to him, he made his way now through the vast congeries of rooms and staircases to the banqueting-hall, five acres distant on the other side of the house. But halfway there, in the back quarters where the servants lived, he stopped. The door of Mrs Stewkley's sitting-room stood open – she was gone, doubtless, with all her keys to wait upon her mistress. But there, sitting at the servants' dinner table with a tankard beside him and paper in front of him, sat a rather fat, rather shabby man, whose ruff was a thought dirty, and whose clothes were of hodden brown. He held a pen in his hand, but he was not writing. He seemed in the act of rolling some thought up and down, to and fro in his mind till it gathered shape or momentum to his liking. His eyes, globed and clouded like some green stone of curious texture, were fixed. He did not see Orlando. For all his hurry, Orlando stopped dead. Was this a poet? Was he writing poetry? 'Tell me,' he wanted to say, 'everything in the whole world' – for he had the wildest, most absurd, extravagant ideas about poets and poetry – but how speak to a man who does not see you? who sees ogres, satyrs, perhaps the depths of the sea instead? So Orlando stood gazing while the man turned his pen in his fingers, this way and that way; and gazed and mused; and then, very quickly, wrote half a dozen lines and looked up. Whereupon Orlando, overcome with shyness, darted off and reached the banqueting-hall only just in time to sink upon his knees and, hanging his head in confusion, to offer a bowl of rose water to the great Queen herself.

Such was his shyness that he saw no more of her than her ringed hand in water; but it was enough. It was a memorable hand; a thin hand with long fingers always curling as if round orb or sceptre; a nervous, crabbed, sickly hand; a commanding hand, too; a hand that had only to raise itself for a head to fall; a hand, he guessed, attached to an old body that smelt like a cupboard in which furs are kept in camphor; which body was yet caparisoned in all sorts of brocades and gems; and held itself very upright though perhaps in pain from sciatica; and never flinched though strung together by a thousand fears; and the Queen's eyes were light yellow. All this he felt as the great rings flashed in the water and then something pressed his hair – which, perhaps, accounts for his seeing nothing more likely to be of use to a historian. And in truth, his mind was such a welter of opposites – of the night and the blazing candles, of the shabby poet and the great Queen, of silent fields and the clatter of serving men – that he could see nothing; or only a hand.

By the same showing, the Queen herself can have seen only a head. But if it is possible from a hand to deduce a body, informed with all the attributes of a great Queen, her crabbedness, courage, frailty, and terror, surely a head can be as fertile, looked down upon from a chair of state by a lady whose eyes were always, if the waxworks at the Abbey are to be trusted, wide open. The long, curled hair, the dark head bent so reverently, so innocently before her, implied a pair of the finest legs that a young nobleman has ever stood upright upon; and violet eyes; and a heart of gold; and loyalty and manly charm – all qualities which the old woman loved the more the more they failed her. For she was growing old and worn and bent before her time. The sound of cannon was always in her ears. She saw always the glistening poison drop and the long stiletto. As she sat at table she listened; she heard the guns in the Channel; she dreaded – was that a curse, was that a whisper? Innocence, simplicity, were all the more dear to her for the dark background she set them against. And it was that same night, so tradition has it, when Orlando was sound asleep, that she made over formally, putting her hand and seal finally to the parchment, the gift of the great monastic house that had been the Archbishop's and then the King's to Orlando's father.

Orlando slept all night in ignorance. He had been kissed by a queen without knowing it. And perhaps, for women's hearts are intricate, it was his ignorance and the start he gave when her lips touched him that kept the memory of her young cousin (for they had blood in common) green in her mind. At any rate, two years of this quiet country life had not passed, and Orlando had written no more perhaps than twenty tragedies and a dozen histories and a score of sonnets when a message came that he was to attend the Queen at Whitehall.

'Here,' she said, watching him advance down the long gallery towards her, 'comes my innocent!' (There was a serenity about him always which had the look of innocence when, technically, the word was no longer applicable.)

'Come!' she said. She was sitting bolt upright beside the fire. And she held him a foot's pace from her and looked him up and down. Was she matching her speculations the other night with the truth now visible? Did she find her guesses justified? Eyes, mouth, nose, breast, hips, hands – she ran them over; her lips twitched visibly as she looked; but when she saw his legs she laughed out loud. He was the very image of a noble gentleman. But inwardly? She flashed her yellow hawk's eyes upon him as if she would pierce his soul. The young man withstood her gaze blushing only a damask rose as became him. Strength, grace, romance, folly, poetry, youth – she read him like a page. Instantly she plucked a ring from her finger (the joint was swollen rather) and as she fitted it to his, named him her Treasurer and Steward; next hung about him chains of office; and bidding him bend his knee, tied round it at the slenderest part the jewelled order of the Garter. Nothing after that was denied him. When she drove in state he rode at her carriage door. She sent him to Scotland on a sad embassy to the unhappy Queen. He was about to sail for the Polish wars when she recalled him. For how could she bear to think of that tender flesh torn and that curly head rolled in the dust? She kept him with her. At the height of her triumph when the guns were booming at the Tower and the air was thick enough with gunpowder to make one sneeze and the huzzas of the people rang beneath the windows, she pulled him down among the cushions where her women had laid her (she was so worn and old) and made him bury his face in that astonishing composition – she had not changed her dress for a month – which smelt for all the world, he thought, recalling his boyish memory, like some old cabinet at home where his mother's furs were stored. He rose, half suffocated from the embrace. 'This,' she breathed, 'is my victory!' – even as a rocket roared up and dyed her cheeks scarlet.

For the old woman loved him. And the Queen, who knew a man when she saw one, though not, it is said, in the usual way, plotted for him a splendid ambitious career. Lands were given him, houses assigned him. He was to be the son of her old age; the limb of her infirmity; the oak tree on which she leant her degradation. She croaked out these promises and strange domineering tendernesses (they were at Richmond now) sitting bolt upright in her stiff brocades by the fire which, however high they piled it, never kept her warm.

Meanwhile, the long winter months drew on. Every tree in the Park was lined with frost. The river ran sluggishly. One day when the snow was on the ground and the dark panelled rooms were full of shadows and the stags were barking in the Park, she saw in the mirror, which she kept for fear of spies always by her, through the door, which she kept for fear of murderers always open, a boy – could it be Orlando? – kissing a girl – who in the Devil's name was the brazen hussy? Snatching at her golden-hilted sword she struck violently at the mirror. The glass crashed; people came running; she was lifted and set in her chair again; but she was stricken after that and groaned much, as her days wore to an end, of man's treachery.

It was Orlando's fault perhaps; yet, after all, are we to blame Orlando? The age was the Elizabethan; their morals were not ours; nor their poets; nor their climate; nor their vegetables even. Everything was different. The weather itself, the heat and cold of summer and winter, was, we may believe, of another temper altogether. The brilliant amorous day was divided as sheerly from the night as land from water. Sunsets were redder and more intense; dawns were whiter and more auroral. Of our crepuscular half-lights and lingering twilights they knew nothing. The rain fell vehemently, or not at all. The sun blazed or there was darkness. Translating this to the spiritual regions as their wont is, the poets sang beautifully how roses fade and petals fall. The moment is brief they sang; the moment is over; one long night is then to be slept by all. As for using the artifices of the greenhouse or conservatory to prolong or preserve these fresh pinks and roses, that was not their way. The withered intricacies and ambiguities of our more gradual and doubtful age were unknown to them. Violence was all. The flower bloomed and faded. The sun rose and sank. The lover loved and went. And what the poets said in rhyme, the young translated into practice. Girls were roses, and their seasons were short as the flowers. Plucked they must be before night-fall; for the day was brief and the day was all. Thus, if Orlando followed the leading of the climate, of the poets, of the age itself, and plucked his flower in the window-seat even with the snow on the ground and the Queen vigilant in the corridor, we can scarcely bring ourselves to blame him. He was young; he was boyish; he did but as nature bade him do. As for the girl, we know no more than Queen Elizabeth herself did what her name was. It may have been Doris, Chloris, Delia, or Diana, for he made rhymes to them all in turn; equally, she may have been a court lady, or some serving maid. For Orlando's taste was broad; he was no lover of garden flowers only; the wild and the weeds even had always a fascination for him.

Here, indeed, we lay bare rudely, as a biographer may, a curious trait in him, to be accounted for, perhaps, by the fact that a certain grandmother of his had worn a smock and carried milk pails. Some grains of the Kentish or Sussex earth were mixed with the thin, fine fluid which came to him from Normandy. He held that the mixture of brown earth and blue blood was a good one. Certain it is that he had always a liking for low company, especially for that of lettered people whose wits so often keep them under, as if there were the sympathy of blood between them. At this season of his life, when his head brimmed with rhymes and he never went to bed without striking off some conceit, the cheek of an innkeeper's daughter seemed fresher and the wit of a gamekeeper's niece seemed quicker than those of the ladies at Court. Hence, he began going frequently to Wapping Old Stairs and the beer gardens at night, wrapped in a grey cloak to hide the star at his neck and the garter at his knee. There, with a mug before him, among the sanded alleys and bowling greens and all the simple architecture of such places, he listened to sailors' stories of hardship and horror and cruelty on the Spanish main; how some had lost their toes, others their noses – for the spoken story was never so rounded or so finely coloured as the written. Especially he loved to hear them volley forth their songs of the Azores, while the parrakeets, which they had brought from those parts, pecked at the rings in their ears, tapped with their hard acquisitive beaks at the rubies on their fingers, and swore as vilely as their masters. The women were scarcely less bold in their speech and less free in their manners than the birds. They perched on his knee, flung their arms round his neck and, guessing that something out of the common lay hid beneath his duffle cloak, were quite as eager to come at the truth of the matter as Orlando himself.

Nor was opportunity lacking. The river was astir early and late with barges, wherries, and craft of all description. Every day sailed to sea some fine ship bound for the Indies; now and again another blackened and ragged with hairy unknown men on board crept painfully to anchor. No one missed a boy or girl if they dallied a little on the water after sunset; or raised an eyebrow if gossip had seen them sleeping soundly among the treasure sacks safe in each other's arms. Such indeed was the adventure that befell Orlando, Sukey, and the Earl of Cumberland. The day was hot; their loves had been active; they had fallen asleep among the rubies. Late that night the Earl, whose fortunes were much bound up in the Spanish ventures, came to check the booty alone with a lantern. He flashed the light on a barrel. He started back with an oath. Twined about the cask two spirits lay sleeping. Superstitious by nature, and his conscience laden with many a crime, the Earl took the couple – they were wrapped in a red cloak, and Sukey's bosom was almost as white as the eternal snows of Orlando's poetry – for a phantom sprung from the graves of drowned sailors to upbraid him. He crossed himself. He vowed repentance. The row of almshouses still standing in the Sheen Road is the visible fruit of that moment's panic. Twelve poor old women of the parish today drink tea and tonight bless his Lordship for a roof above their heads; so that illicit love in a treasure ship – but we omit the moral.

Soon, however, Orlando grew tired, not only of the discomfort of this way of life, and of the crabbed streets of the neighbourhood, but of the primitive manners of the people. For it has to be remembered that crime and poverty had none of the attraction for the Elizabethans that they have for us. They had none of our modern shame of book learning; none of our belief that to be born the son of a butcher is a blessing and to be unable to read a virtue; no fancy that what we call 'life' and 'reality' are somehow connected with ignorance and brutality; nor, indeed, any equivalent for these two words at all. It was not to seek 'life' that Orlando went among them; not in quest of 'reality' that he left them. But when he had heard a score of times how Jakes had lost his nose and Sukey her honour – and they told the stories admirably, it must be admitted – he began to be a little weary of the repetition, for a nose can only be cut off in one way and maidenhood lost in another – or so it seemed to him – whereas the arts and the sciences had a diversity about them which stirred his curiosity profoundly. So, always keeping them in happy memory, he left off frequenting the beer gardens and the skittle alleys, hung his grey cloak in his wardrobe, let his star shine at his neck and his garter twinkle at his knee, and appeared once more at the Court of King James. He was young, he was rich, he was handsome. No one could have been received with greater acclamation than he was.

It is certain indeed that many ladies were ready to show him their favours. The names of three at least were freely coupled with his in marriage – Clorinda, Favilla, Euphrosyne – so he called them in his sonnets.

To take them in order; Clorinda was a sweet-mannered gentle lady enough – indeed Orlando was greatly taken with her for six months and a half; but she had white eyelashes and could not bear the sight of blood. A hare brought up roasted at her father's table turned her faint. She was much under the influence of the Priests too, and stinted her underlinen in order to give to the poor. She took it on her to reform Orlando of his sins, which sickened him, so that he drew back from the marriage, and did not much regret it when she died soon after of the smallpox.

Favilla, who comes next, was of a different sort altogether. She was the daughter of a poor Somersetshire gentleman; who, by sheer assiduity and the use of her eyes had worked her way up at court, where her address in horsemanship, her fine instep, and her grace in dancing won the admiration of all. Once, however, she was so ill-advised as to whip a spaniel that had torn one of her silk stockings (and it must be said in justice that Favilla had few stockings and those for the most part of drugget) within an inch of its life beneath Orlando's window. Orlando, who was a passionate lover of animals, now noticed that her teeth were crooked, and the two front turned inward, which, he said, is a sure sign of a perverse and cruel disposition in woman, and so broke the engagement that very night for ever.

The third, Euphrosyne, was by far the most serious of his flames. She was by birth one of the Irish Desmonds and had therefore a family tree of her own as old and deeply rooted as Orlando's itself. She was fair, florid, and a trifle phlegmatic. She spoke Italian well, had a perfect set of teeth in the upper jaw, though those on the lower were slightly discoloured. She was never without a whippet or spaniel at her knee; fed them with white bread from her own plate; sang sweetly to the virginals; and was never dressed before midday owing to the extreme care she took of her person. In short, she would have made a perfect wife for such a nobleman as Orlando, and matters had gone so far that the lawyers on both sides were busy with covenants, jointures, settlements, messuages, tenements, and whatever is needed before one great fortune can mate with another when, with the suddenness and severity that then marked the English climate, came the Great Frost.

The Great Frost was, historians tell us, the most severe that has ever visited these islands. Birds froze in midair and fell like stones to the ground. At Norwich a young countrywoman started to cross the road in her usual robust health and was seen by the onlookers to turn visibly to powder and be blown in a puff of dust over the roofs as the icy blast struck her at the street corner. The mortality among sheep and cattle was enormous. Corpses froze and could not be drawn from the sheets. It was no uncommon sight to come upon a whole herd of swine frozen immovable upon the road. The fields were full of shepherds, ploughmen, teams of horses, and little bird-scaring boys all struck stark in the act of the moment, one with his hand to his nose, another with the bottle to his lips, a third with a stone raised to throw at the raven who sat, as if stuffed, upon the hedge within a yard of him. The severity of the frost was so extraordinary that a kind of petrifaction sometimes ensued; and it was commonly supposed that the great increase of rocks in some parts of Derbyshire was due to no eruption, for there was none, but to the solidification of unfortunate wayfarers who had been turned literally to stone where they stood. The Church could give little help in the matter, and though some landowners had these relics blessed, the most part preferred to use them either as landmarks, scratching-posts for sheep, or, when the form of the stone allowed, drinking troughs for cattle, which purposes they serve, admirably for the most part, to this day.

But while the country people suffered the extremity of want, and the trade of the country was at a standstill, London enjoyed a carnival of the utmost brilliancy. The Court was at Greenwich, and the new King seized the opportunity that his coronation gave him to curry favour with the citizens. He directed that the river, which was frozen to a depth of twenty feet and more for six or seven miles on either side, should be swept, decorated and given all the semblance of a park or pleasure ground, with arbours, mazes, alleys, drinking booths, etc., at his expense. For himself and the courtiers, he reserved a certain space immediately opposite the Palace gates; which, railed off from the public only by a silken rope, became at once the centre of the most brilliant society in England. Great statesmen, in their beards and ruffs, despatched affairs of state under the crimson awning of the Royal Pagoda. Soldiers planned the conquest of the Moor and the downfall of the Turk in striped arbours surmounted by plumes of ostrich feathers. Admirals strode up and down the narrow pathways, glass in hand, sweeping the horizon and telling stories of the north-west passage and the

Spanish Armada. Lovers dallied upon divans spread with sables. Frozen roses fell in showers when the Queen and her ladies walked abroad. Coloured balloons hovered motionless in the air. Here and there burnt vast bonfires of cedar and oak wood, lavishly salted, so that the flames were of green, orange, and purple fire. But however fiercely they burnt, the heat was not enough to melt the ice which, though of singular transparency, was yet of the hardness of steel. So clear indeed was it that there could be seen, congealed at a depth of several feet, here a porpoise, there a flounder. Shoals of eels lay motionless in a trance, but whether their state was one of death or merely of suspended animation which the warmth would revive puzzled the philosophers. Near London Bridge, where the river had frozen to a depth of some twenty fathoms, a wrecked wherry boat was plainly visible, lying on the bed of the river where it had sunk last autumn, overladen with apples. The old bumboat woman, who was carrying her fruit to market on the Surrey side, sat there in her plaids and farthingales with her lap full of apples, for all the world as if she were about to serve a customer, though a certain blueness about the lips hinted the truth. 'Twas a sight King James specially liked to look upon, and he would bring a troupe of courtiers to gaze with him. In short, nothing could exceed the brilliancy and gaiety of the scene by day. But it was at night that the carnival was at its merriest. For the frost continued unbroken; the nights were of perfect stillness; the moon and stars blazed with the hard fixity of diamonds, and to the fine music of flute and trumpet the courtiers danced.

Orlando, it is true, was none of those who tread lightly the corantoe and lavolta; he was clumsy and a little absent-minded. He much preferred the plain dances of his own country, which he had danced as a child to these fantastic foreign measures. He had indeed just brought his feet together about six in the evening of the seventh of January at the finish of some such quadrille or minuet when he beheld, coming from the pavilion of the Muscovite Embassy, a figure, which, whether boy's or woman's, for the loose tunic and trousers of the Russian fashion served to disguise the sex, filled him with the highest curiosity. The person, whatever the name or sex, was about middle height, very slenderly fashioned, and dressed entirely in oyster-coloured velvet, trimmed with some unfamiliar greenish-coloured fur. But these details were obscured by the extraordinary seductiveness which issued from the whole person. Images, metaphors of the most extreme and extravagant twined and twisted in his mind. He called her a melon, a pineapple, an olive tree, an emerald, and a fox in the snow all in the space of three seconds; he did not know whether he had heard her, tasted her, seen her, or all three together. (For though we must pause not a moment in the narrative we may here hastily note that all his images at this time were simple in the extreme to match his senses and were mostly taken from things he had liked the taste of as a boy. But if his senses were simple they were at the same time extremely strong. To pause therefore and seek the reasons of things is out of the question.) . . . A melon, an emerald, a fox in the snow – so he raved, so he stared. When the boy, for alas, a boy it must be – no woman could skate with such speed and vigour – swept almost on tiptoe past him, Orlando was ready to tear his hair with vexation that the person was of his own sex, and thus all embraces were out of the question. But the skater came closer. Legs, hands, carriage, were a boy's, but no boy ever had a mouth like that; no boy had those breasts; no boy had eyes which looked as if they had been fished from the bottom of the sea. Finally, coming to a stop and sweeping a curtsey with the utmost grace to the King, who was shuffling past on the arm of some Lord-in-waiting, the unknown skater came to a standstill. She was not a handsbreadth off. She was a woman. Orlando stared; trembled; turned hot; turned cold; longed to hurl himself through the summer air; to crush acorns beneath his feet; to toss his arms with the beech trees and the oaks. As it was, he drew his lips up over his small white teeth; opened them perhaps half an inch as if to bite; shut them as if he had bitten. The Lady Euphrosyne hung upon his arm.

The stranger's name, he found, was the Princess Marousha Stanilovska Dagmar Natasha Iliana Romanovitch, and she had come in the train of the Muscovite Ambassador, who was her uncle perhaps, or perhaps her father, to attend the coronation. Very little was known of the Muscovites. In their great beards and furred hats they sat almost silent; drinking some black liquid which they spat out now and then upon the ice. None spoke English, and French with which some at least were familiar was then little spoken at the English Court.

It was through this accident that Orlando and the Princess became acquainted. They were seated opposite each other at the great table spread under a huge awning for the entertainment of the notables. The Princess was placed between two young Lords, one Lord Francis Vere and the other the young Earl of Moray. It was laughable to see the predicament she soon had them in, for though both were fine lads in their way, the babe unborn had as much knowledge of the French tongue as they had. When at the beginning of dinner the Princess turned to the Earl and said, with a grace which ravished his heart, 'Je crois avoir fait la connaissance d'un gentilhomme qui vous était apparenté en Pologne l'été dernier,' or 'La beauté des dames de la cour d'Angleterre me met dans le ravissement. On ne peut voir une dame plus gracieuse que votre reine, ni une coiffure plus belle que la sienne,' both Lord Francis and the Earl showed the highest embarrassment. The one helped her largely to horseradish sauce, the other whistled to his dog and made him beg for a marrow bone. At this the Princess could no longer contain her laughter, and Orlando, catching her eyes across the boars' heads and stuffed peacocks, laughed too. He laughed, but the laugh on his lips froze in wonder. Whom had he loved, what had he loved, he asked himself in a tumult of emotion, until now? An old woman, he answered, all skin and bone. Red-cheeked trulls too many to mention. A

The Russian princess as a child

puling nun. A hard-bitten cruel-mouthed adventuress. A nodding mass of lace and ceremony. Love had meant to him nothing but sawdust and cinders. The joys he had had of it tasted insipid in the extreme. He marvelled how he could have gone through with it without yawning. For as he looked the thickness of his blood melted; the ice turned to wine in his veins; he heard the waters flowing and the birds singing; spring broke over the hard wintry landscape; his manhood woke; he grasped a sword in his hand; he charged a more daring foe than Pole or Moor; he dived in deep water; he saw the flower of danger growing in a crevice; he stretched his hand – in fact he was rattling off one of his most impassioned sonnets when the Princess addressed him, 'Would you have the goodness to pass the salt?'

He blushed deeply.

'With all the pleasure in the world, Madame,' he replied, speaking French with a perfect accent. For, heaven be praised, he spoke the tongue as his own; his mother's maid had taught him. Yet perhaps it would have been better for him had he never learnt that tongue; never answered that voice; never followed the light of those eyes . . .

The Princess continued. Who were those bumpkins, she asked him, who sat beside her with the manners of stablemen? What was the nauseating mixture they had poured on her plate? Did the dogs eat at the same table with the men in England? Was that figure of fun at the end of the table with her hair rigged up like a Maypole (comme une grande perche mal fagotée) really the Queen? And did the King always slobber like that? And which of those popinjays was George Villiers? Though these questions rather discomposed Orlando at first, they were put with such archness and drollery that he could not help but laugh; and as he saw from the blank faces of the company that nobody understood a word, he answered her as freely as she asked him, speaking, as she did, in perfect French.

Thus began an intimacy between the two which soon became the scandal of the Court.

Soon it was observed Orlando paid the Muscovite far more attention than mere civility demanded. He was seldom far from her side, and their conversation, though unintelligible to the rest, was carried on with such animation, provoked such blushes and laughter, that the dullest could guess the subject. Moreover, the change in Orlando himself was extraordinary. Nobody had ever seen him so animated. In one night he had thrown off his boyish clumsiness; he was changed from a sulky stripling, who could not enter a ladies' room without sweeping half the ornaments from the table, to a nobleman, full of grace and manly courtesy. To see him hand the Muscovite (as she was called) to her sledge, or offer her his hand for the dance, or catch the spotted kerchief which she had let drop, or discharge any other of those manifold duties which the supreme lady exacts and the lover hastens to anticipate was a sight to kindle the dull eyes of age, and to make the quick pulse of youth beat faster. Yet over it all hung a cloud. The old men shrugged their shoulders. The young tittered between their fingers. All knew that Orlando was betrothed to another. The Lady Margaret O'Brien O'Dare O'Reilly Tyrconnel (for that was the proper name of Euphrosyne of the Sonnets) wore Orlando's splendid sapphire on the second finger of her left hand. It was she who had the supreme right to his attentions. Yet she might drop all the handkerchiefs in her wardrobe (of which she had many scores) upon the ice and Orlando never stooped to pick them up. She might wait twenty minutes for him to hand her to her sledge, and in the end have to be content with the services of her blackamoor. When she skated, which she did rather clumsily, no one was at her elbow to encourage her, and, if she fell, which she did rather heavily, no one raised her to her feet and dusted the snow from her petticoats. Although she was naturally phlegmatic, slow to take offence, and more reluctant than most people to believe that a mere foreigner could oust her from Orlando's affections, still even the Lady Margaret herself was brought at last to suspect that something was brewing against her peace of mind.

Indeed, as the days passed, Orlando took less and less care to hide his feelings. Making some excuse or other, he would leave the company as soon as they had dined, or steal away from the skaters, who were forming sets for a quadrille. Next moment it would be seen that the Muscovite was missing too. But what most outraged the Court, and stung it in its tenderest part, which is its vanity, was that the couple was often seen to slip under the silken rope, which railed off the Royal enclosure from the public part of the river and to disappear among the crowd of common people. For suddenly the Princess would stamp her foot and cry, 'Take me away. I detest your English mob,' by which she meant the English Court itself. She could stand it no longer. It was full of prying old women, she said, who stared in one's face, and of bumptious young men who trod on one's toes. They smelt bad. Their dogs ran between her legs. It was like being in a cage. In Russia they had rivers ten miles broad on which one could gallop six horses abreast all day long without meeting a soul. Besides, she wanted to see the Tower, the Beefeaters, the Heads on Temple Bar, and the jewellers' shops in the city. Thus, it came about that Orlando took her to the city, showed her the Beefeaters and the rebels' heads, and bought her whatever took her fancy in the Royal Exchange. But this was not enough. Each increasingly desired the other's company in privacy all day long where there were none to marvel or to stare. Instead of taking the road to London, therefore, they turned the other way about and were soon beyond the crowd among the frozen reaches of the Thames where, save for sea birds and some old country woman hacking at the ice in a vain attempt to draw a pailful of water or gathering what sticks or dead leaves she could find for firing, not a living soul ever came their way. The poor kept closely to their cottages, and the better sort, who could afford it, crowded for warmth and merriment to the city.

Hence, Orlando and Sasha, as he called her for short, and because it was the name of a white Russian fox he had had as a boy – a creature soft as snow, but with teeth of steel, which bit him so savagely that his father had it killed – hence, they had the river to themselves. Hot with skating and with love they would throw themselves down in some solitary reach, where the yellow osiers fringed the bank, and wrapped in a great fur cloak Orlando would take her in his arms, and know, for the first time, he murmured, the delights of love. Then, when the ecstasy was over and they lay lulled in a swoon on the ice, he would tell her of his other loves, and how, compared with her, they had been of wood, of sackcloth, and of cinders. And laughing at his vehemence, she would turn once more in his arms and give him, for love's sake, one more embrace. And then they would marvel that the ice did not melt with their heat, and pity the poor old woman who had no such natural means of thawing it, but must hack at it with a chopper of cold steel. And then, wrapped in their sables, they would talk of everything under the sun; of sights and travels; of Moor and Pagan; of this man's beard and that woman's skin; of a rat that fed from her hand at table; of the arras that moved always in the hall at home; of a face; of a feather. Nothing was too small for such converse, nothing was too great.

Then, suddenly Orlando would fall into one of his moods of melancholy; the sight of the old woman hobbling over the ice might be the cause of it, or nothing; and would fling himself face downwards on the ice and look into the frozen waters and think of death. For the philosopher is right who says that nothing thicker than a knife's blade separates happiness from melancholy; and he goes on to opine that one is twin fellow to the other; and draws from this the conclusion that all extremes of feeling are allied to madness; and so bids us take refuge in the true Church (in his view the Anabaptist), which is the only harbour, port, anchorage, etc., he said, for those tossed on this sea.

'All ends in death,' Orlando would say, sitting upright, his face clouded with gloom. (For that was the way his mind worked now, in violent see-saws from life to death, stopping at nothing in between, so that the biographer must not stop either, but must fly as fast as he can and so keep pace with the unthinking passionate foolish actions and sudden extravagant words in which, it is impossible to deny, Orlando at this time of his life indulged.)

'All ends in death,' Orlando would say, sitting upright on the ice. But Sasha who after all had no English blood in her but was from Russia where the sunsets are longer, the dawns less sudden, and sentences often left unfinished from doubt as to how best to end them – Sasha stared at him, perhaps sneered at him, for he must have seemed a child to her, and said nothing. But at length the ice grew cold beneath them, which she disliked, so pulling him to his feet again, she talked so enchantingly, so wittily, so wisely (but unfortunately always in French, which notoriously loses its flavour in translation) that he forgot the frozen waters or night coming or the old woman or whatever it was, and would try to tell her – plunging and splashing among a thousand images which had gone as stale as the women who inspired them – what she was like. Snow, cream, marble, cherries, alabaster, golden wire? None of these. She was like a fox, or an olive tree; like the waves of the sea when you look down upon them from a height; like an emerald; like the sun on a green hill which is yet clouded – like nothing he had seen or known in England. Ransack the language as he might, words failed him. He wanted another landscape, and another tongue. English was too frank, too candid, too honeyed a speech for Sasha. For in all she said, however open she seemed and voluptuous, there was something hidden; in all she did, however daring, there was something concealed. So the green flame seems hidden in the emerald, or the sun prisoned in a hill. The clearness was only outward; within was a wandering flame. It came; it went; she never shone with the steady beam of an Englishwoman – here, however, remembering the Lady Margaret and her petticoats, Orlando ran wild in his transports and swept her over the ice, faster, faster, vowing that he would chase the flame, dive for the gem, and so on and so on, the words coming on the pants of his breath with the passion of a poet whose poetry is half pressed out of him by pain.

But Sasha was silent. When Orlando had done telling her that she was a fox, an olive tree, or a green hilltop, and had given her the whole history of his family; how their house was one of the most ancient in Britain; how they had come from Rome with the Caesars and had the right to walk down the Corso (which is the chief street in Rome) under a tasselled palanquin, which he said is a privilege reserved only for those of imperial blood (for there was an orgulous credulity about him which was pleasant enough), he would pause and ask her, Where was her own house? What was her father? Had she brothers? Why was she here alone with her uncle? Then, somehow, though she answered readily enough, an awkwardness would come between them. He suspected at first that her rank was not as high as she would like; or that she was ashamed of the savage ways of her people, for he had heard that the women in Muscovy wear beards and the men are covered with fur from the waist down; that both sexes are smeared with tallow to keep the cold out, tear meat with their fingers and live in huts where an English noble would scruple to keep his cattle; so that he forbore to press her. But on reflection, he concluded that her silence could not be for that reason; she herself was entirely free from hair on the chin; she dressed in velvet and pearls, and her manners were certainly not those of a woman bred in a cattle-shed.

What, then, did she hide from him? The doubt underlying the tremendous force of his feelings was like a quicksand beneath a monument which shifts suddenly and makes the whole pile shake. The agony would seize him suddenly. Then he would blaze out in such wrath that she did not know how to quiet him. Perhaps she did not want to quiet him; perhaps his rages pleased her and she provoked them purposely – such is the curious obliquity of the Muscovitish temperament.

To continue the story – skating farther than their wont that day they reached that part of the river where the ships had anchored and been frozen in midstream. Among them was the ship of the Muscovite Embassy flying its double-headed black eagle from the main mast, which was hung with many-coloured icicles several yards in length. Sasha had left some of her clothing on board, and supposing the ship to be empty they climbed on deck and went in search of it. Remembering certain passages in his own past, Orlando would not have marvelled had some good citizens sought this refuge before them; and so it turned out. They had not ventured far when a fine young man started up from some business of his own behind a coil of rope and saying, apparently, for he spoke Russian, that he was one of the crew and would help the Princess to find what she wanted, lit a lump of candle and disappeared with her into the lower parts of the ship.

Time went by, and Orlando, wrapped in his own dreams, thought only of the pleasures of life; of his jewel; of her rarity; of means for making her, irrevocably and indissolubly his own. Obstacles there were and hardships to be overcome. She was determined to live in Russia, where there were frozen rivers and wild horses and men, she said, who gashed each other's throats open. It is true that a landscape of pine and snow, habits of lust and slaughter, did not entice him. Nor was he anxious to cease his pleasant country ways of sport and tree-planting; relinquish his office; ruin his career; shoot the reindeer instead of the rabbit; drink vodka instead of canary, and slip a knife up his sleeve – for what purpose, he knew not. Still, all this and more than all this he would do for her sake. As for his marriage with the Lady Margaret, fixed though it was for this day sennight, the thing was so palpably absurd that he scarcely gave it a thought. Her kinsmen would abuse him for deserting a great lady; his friends would deride him for ruining the finest career in the world for a Cossack woman and a waste of snow – it weighed not a straw in the balance compared with Sasha herself. On the first dark night they would fly. They would take ship to Russia. So he pondered; so he plotted as he walked up and down the deck.

He was recalled, turning westward, by the sight of the sun, slung like an orange on the cross of St Paul's. It was blood-red and sinking rapidly. It must be almost evening. Sasha had been gone this hour and more. Seized instantly with those dark forebodings which shadowed even his most confident thoughts of her, he plunged the way he had seen them go into the hold of the ship; and, after stumbling among chests and barrels in the darkness, was made aware by a faint glimmer in a corner that they were seated there. For one second, he had a vision of them; saw Sasha seated on the sailor's knee; saw her bend towards him; saw them embrace before the light was blotted out in a red cloud by his rage. He blazed into such a howl of anguish that the whole ship echoed. Sasha threw herself between them, or the sailor would have been stifled before he could draw his cutlass. Then a deadly sickness came over Orlando, and they had to lay him on the floor and give him brandy to drink before he revived. And then, when he had recovered and was sat upon a heap of sacking on deck, Sasha hung over him, passing before his dizzied eyes softly, sinuously, like the fox that had bit him, now cajoling, now denouncing, so that he came to doubt what he had seen. Had not the candle guttered; had not the shadows moved? The box was heavy, she said; the man was helping her to move it. Orlando believed her one moment – for who can be sure that his rage has not painted what he most dreads to find? – the next was the more violent with anger at her deceit. Then Sasha herself turned white; stamped her foot on deck; said she would go that night, and called upon her Gods to destroy her, if she, a Romanovitch, had lain in the arms of a common seaman. Indeed, looking at them together (which he could hardly bring himself to do) Orlando was outraged by the foulness of his imagination that could have painted so frail a creature in the paws of that hairy sea brute. The man was huge; stood six feet four in his stockings; wore common wire rings in his ears; and looked like a dray horse upon which some wren or robin has perched in its flight. So he yielded; believed her; and asked her pardon. Yet, when they were going down the ship's side, lovingly again, Sasha paused with her hand on the ladder, and called back to this tawny wide-cheeked monster a volley of Russian greetings, jests, or endearments, not a word of which Orlando could understand. But there was something in her tone (it might be the fault of the Russian consonants) that reminded Orlando of a scene some nights since, when he had come upon her in secret gnawing a candle-end in a corner, which she had picked from the floor. True, it was pink; it was gilt; and it was from the King's table; but it was tallow, and she gnawed it. Was there not, he thought, handing her on to the ice, something rank in her, something coarse flavoured, something peasant born? And he fancied her at forty grown unwieldy though she was now slim as a reed, and lethargic though she was now blithe as a lark. But again as they skated towards London such suspicions melted in his breast, and he felt as if he had been hooked by a great fish through the nose and rushed through the waters unwillingly, yet with his own consent.

It was an evening of astonishing beauty. As the sun sank, all the domes, spires, turrets, and pinnacles of London rose in inky blackness against the furious red sunset clouds. Here was the fretted cross at Charing; there the dome of St Paul's; there the massy square of the Tower buildings; there like a grove of trees stripped of all leaves save a knob at the end were the heads on the pikes at Temple Bar. Now the Abbey windows were lit up and burnt like a heavenly, many-coloured shield (in Orlando's fancy); now all the west seemed a golden window with troops of angels (in Orlando's fancy again) passing up and down the heavenly stairs perpetually. All the time they seemed to be skating on fathomless depths of air, so blue the ice had become; and so glassy smooth was it that they sped quicker and quicker to the city with the white gulls circling about them, and cutting in the air with their wings the very same sweeps that they cut on the ice with their skates.

Sasha, as if to reassure him, was tenderer than usual and even more delightful. Seldom would she talk about her past life, but now she told him how, in winter in Russia, she would listen to the wolves howling across the steppes, and thrice, to show him, she barked like a wolf. Upon which he told her of the stags in the snow at home, and how they would stray into the great hall for warmth and be fed by an old man with porridge from a bucket. And then she praised him; for his love of beasts; for his gallantry; for his legs. Ravished with her praises and shamed to think how he had maligned her by fancying her on the knees of a common sailor and grown fat and lethargic at forty, he told her that he could find no words to praise her; yet instantly bethought him how she was like the spring and green grass and rushing waters, and seizing her more tightly than ever, he swung her with him half across the river so that the gulls and the cormorants swung too. And halting at length, out of breath, she said, panting slightly, that he was like a million-candled Christmas tree (such as they have in Russia) hung with yellow globes; incandescent; enough to light a whole street by; (so one might translate it) for what with his glowing cheeks, his dark curls, his black and crimson cloak, he looked as if he were burning with his own radiance, from a lamp lit within.

All the colour, save the red of Orlando's cheeks, soon faded. Night came on. As the orange light of sunset vanished it was succeeded by an astonishing white glare from the torches, bonfires, flaming cressets, and other devices by which the river was lit up and the strangest transformation took place. Various churches and noblemen's palaces, whose fronts were of white stone showed in streaks and patches as if floating on the air. Of St Paul's, in particular, nothing was left but a gilt cross. The Abbey appeared like the grey skeleton of a leaf. Everything suffered emaciation and transformation. As they approached the carnival, they heard a deep note like that struck on a tuning-fork which boomed louder and louder until it became an uproar. Every now and then a great shout followed a rocket into the air. Gradually they could discern little figures breaking off from the vast crowd and spinning hither and thither like gnats on the surface of a river. Above and around this brilliant circle like a bowl of darkness pressed the deep black of a winter's night. And then into this darkness there began to rise with pauses, which kept the expectation alert and the mouth open, flowering rockets; crescents; serpents; a crown. At one moment the woods and distant hills showed green as on a summer's day; the next all was winter and blackness again.

By this time Orlando and the Princess were close to the Royal enclosure and found their way barred by a great crowd of the common people, who were pressing as near to the silken rope as they dared. Loth to end their privacy and encounter the sharp eyes that were on the watch for them, the couple lingered there, shouldered by apprentices; tailors; fishwives; horse dealers; cony catchers; starving scholars; maidservants in their whimples; orange girls; ostlers; sober citizens; bawdy tapsters; and a crowd of little ragamuffins such as always haunt the outskirts of a crowd, screaming and scrambling among people's feet – all the riff-raff of the London streets indeed was there, jesting and jostling, here casting dice, telling fortunes, shoving, tickling, pinching; here uproarious, there glum; some of them with mouths gaping a yard wide; others as little reverent as daws on a house-top; all as variously rigged out as their purse or stations allowed; here in fur and broadcloth; there in tatters with their feet kept from the ice only by a dish clout bound about them. The main press of people, it appeared, stood opposite a booth or stage something like our Punch and Judy show upon which some kind of theatrical performance was going forward. A black man was waving his arms and vociferating. There was a woman in white laid upon a bed. Rough though the staging was, the actors running up and down a pair of steps and sometimes tripping, and the crowd stamping their feet and whistling, or when they were bored, tossing a piece of orange peel on to the ice which a dog would scramble for, still the astonishing, sinuous melody of the words stirred Orlando like music. Spoken with extreme speed and a daring agility of tongue which reminded him of the sailors singing in the beer gardens at Wapping, the words even without meaning were as wine to him. But now and again a single phrase would come to him over the ice which was as if torn from the depths of his heart. The frenzy of the Moor seemed to him his own frenzy, and when the Moor suffocated the woman in her bed it was Sasha he killed with his own hands.

At last the play was ended. All had grown dark. The tears streamed down his face. Looking up into the sky there was nothing but blackness there too. Ruin and death, he thought, cover all. The life of man ends in the grave. Worms devour us.

> Methinks it should be now a huge eclipse
> Of sun and moon, and that the affrighted globe
> Should yawn –

Even as he said this a star of some pallor rose in his memory. The night was dark; it was pitch dark; but it was such a night as this that they had waited for; it was on such a night as this that they had planned to fly. He remembered everything. The time had come. With a burst of passion he snatched Sasha to him, and hissed in her ear 'Jour de ma vie!' It was their signal. At midnight they would meet at an inn near Blackfriars. Horses waited there. Everything was in readiness for their flight. So they parted, she to her tent, he to his. It still wanted an hour of the time.

Long before midnight Orlando was in waiting. The night was of so inky a blackness that a man was on you before he could be seen, which was all to the good, but it was also of the most solemn stillness so that a horse's hoof, or a child's cry, could be heard at a distance of half a mile. Many a time did Orlando, pacing the little courtyard, hold his heart at the sound of some nag's steady footfall on the cobbles, or at the rustle of a woman's dress. But the traveller was only some merchant, making home belated; or some woman of the quarter whose errand was nothing so innocent. They passed, and the street was quieter than before. Then those lights which burnt downstairs in the small, huddled quarters where the poor of the city lived moved up to the sleeping-rooms, and then, one by one, were extinguished. The street lanterns in these purlieus were few at most; and the negligence of the night watchman often suffered them to expire long before dawn. The darkness then became even deeper than before. Orlando looked to the wicks of his lantern, saw to the saddle girths; primed his pistols; examined his holsters; and did all these things a dozen times at least till he could find nothing more needing his attention. Though it still lacked some twenty minutes to midnight, he could not bring himself to go indoors to the inn parlour, where the hostess was still serving sack and the cheaper sort of canary wine to a few seafaring men, who would sit there trolling their ditties, and telling their stories of Drake, Hawkins, and Grenville, till they toppled off the benches and rolled asleep on the sanded floor. The darkness was more compassionate to his swollen and violent heart. He listened to every footfall; speculated on every sound. Each drunken shout and each wail from some poor wretch laid in the straw or in other distress cut his heart to the quick, as if it boded ill omen to his venture. Yet, he had no fear for Sasha. Her courage made nothing of the adventure. She would come alone, in her cloak and trousers, booted like a man. Light as her footfall was, it would hardly be heard, even in this silence.

So he waited in the darkness. Suddenly he was struck in the face by a blow, soft, yet heavy, on the side of his cheek. So strung with expectation was he, that he started and put his hand to his sword. The blow was repeated a dozen times on forehead and cheek. The dry frost had lasted so long that it took him a minute to realise that these were raindrops falling; the blows were the blows of the rain. At first, they fell slowly, deliberately, one by one. But soon the six drops became sixty; then six hundred; then ran themselves together in a steady spout of water. It was as if the hard and consolidated sky poured itself forth in one profuse fountain. In the space of five minutes Orlando was soaked to the skin.

Hastily putting the horses under cover, he sought shelter beneath the lintel of the door whence he could still observe the courtyard. The air was thicker now than ever, and such a steaming and droning rose from the downpour that no footfall of man or beast could be heard above it. The roads, pitted as they were with great holes, would be under water and perhaps impassable. But of what effect this would have upon their flight he scarcely thought. All his senses were bent upon gazing along the cobbled pathway – gleaming in the light of the lantern – for Sasha's coming. Sometimes, in the darkness, he seemed to see her wrapped about with rain strokes. But the phantom vanished. Suddenly, with an awful and ominous voice, a voice full of horror and alarm which raised every hair of anguish in Orlando's soul,

St Paul's struck the first stroke of midnight. Four times more it struck remorselessly. With the superstition of a lover, Orlando had made out that it was on the sixth stroke that she would come. But the sixth stroke echoed away, and the seventh came and the eighth, and to his apprehensive mind they seemed notes first heralding and then proclaiming death and disaster. When the twelfth struck he knew that his doom was sealed. It was useless for the rational part of him to reason; she might be late; she might be prevented; she might have missed her way. The passionate and feeling heart of Orlando knew the truth. Other clocks struck, jangling one after another. The whole world seemed to ring with the news of her deceit and his derision. The old suspicions subterraneously at work in him rushed forth from concealment openly. He was bitten by a swarm of snakes, each more poisonous than the last. He stood in the doorway in the tremendous rain without moving. As the minutes passed, he sagged a little at the knees. The downpour rushed on. In the thick of it, great guns seemed to boom. Huge noises as of the tearing and rending of oak trees could be heard. There were also wild cries and terrible inhuman groanings. But Orlando stood there immovable till Paul's clock struck two, and then, crying aloud with an awful irony, and all his teeth showing, 'Jour de ma vie!' he dashed the lantern to the ground, mounted his horse and galloped he knew not where.

Some blind instinct, for he was past reasoning, must have driven him to take the river bank in the direction of the sea. For when the dawn broke, which it did with unusual suddenness, the sky turning a pale yellow and the rain almost ceasing, he found himself on the banks of the Thames off Wapping. Now a sight of the most extraordinary nature met his eyes. Where, for three months and more, there had been solid ice of such thickness that it seemed permanent as stone, and a whole gay city had been stood on its pavement, was now a race of turbulent yellow waters. The river had gained its freedom in the night. It was as if a sulphur spring (to which view many philosophers inclined) had risen from the volcanic regions beneath and burst the ice asunder with such vehemence that it swept the huge and massy fragments furiously apart. The mere look of the water was enough to turn one giddy. All was riot and confusion. The river was strewn with icebergs. Some of these were as broad as a bowling green and as high as a house; others no bigger than a man's hat, but most fantastically twisted. Now would come down a whole convoy of ice blocks sinking everything that stood in their way. Now, eddying and swirling like a tortured serpent, the river would seem to be hurtling itself between the fragments and tossing them from bank to bank, so that they could be heard smashing against the piers and pillars. But what was the most awful and inspiring of terror was the sight of the human creatures who had been trapped in the night and now paced their twisting and precarious islands in the utmost agony of spirit. Whether they jumped into the flood or stayed on the ice their doom was certain. Sometimes quite a cluster of these poor creatures would come down together, some on their knees, others suckling their babies. One old man seemed to be reading aloud from a holy book. At other times, and his fate perhaps was the most dreadful, a solitary wretch would stride his narrow tenement alone. As they swept out to sea, some could be heard crying vainly for help, making wild promises to amend their ways, confessing their sins and vowing altars and wealth if God would hear their prayers. Others were so dazed with terror that they sat immovable and silent looking steadfastly before them. One crew of young watermen or post-boys, to judge by their liveries, roared and shouted the lewdest tavern songs, as if in bravado, and were dashed against a tree and sunk with blasphemies on their lips. An old nobleman – for such his furred gown and golden chain proclaimed him – went down not far from where Orlando stood, calling vengeance upon the Irish rebels, who, he cried with his last breath, had plotted this devilry. Many perished clasping some silver pot or other treasure to their breasts; and at least a score of poor wretches were drowned by their own cupidity, hurling themselves from the bank into the flood rather than let a gold goblet escape them, or see before their eyes the disappearance of some furred gown. For furniture, valuables, possessions of all sorts were carried away on the icebergs. Among other strange sights was to be seen a cat suckling its young; a table laid sumptuously for a supper of twenty; a couple in bed; together with an extraordinary number of cooking utensils.

Dazed and astounded, Orlando could do nothing for some time but watch the appalling race of waters as it hurled itself past him. At last, seeming to recollect himself, he clapped spurs to his horse and galloped hard along the river bank in the direction of the sea. Rounding a bend of the river, he came opposite that reach where, not two days ago, the ships of the Ambassadors had seemed immovably frozen. Hastily, he made count of them all; the French; the Spanish; the Austrian; the Turk. All still floated, though the French had broken loose from her moorings, and the Turkish vessel had taken a great rent in her side and was fast filling with water. But the Russian ship was nowhere to be seen. For one moment Orlando thought it must have foundered; but, raising himself in his stirrups and shading his eyes, which had the sight of a hawk's, he could just make out the shape of a ship on the horizon. The black eagles were flying from the mast head. The ship of the Muscovite Embassy was standing out to sea.

Flinging himself from his horse, he made, in his rage, as if he would breast the flood. Standing knee-deep in water he hurled at the faithless woman all the insults that have ever been the lot of her sex. Faithless, mutable, fickle, he called her; devil, adulteress, deceiver; and the swirling waters took his words, and tossed at his feet a broken pot and a little straw.

The biographer is now faced with a difficulty which it is better perhaps to confess than to gloss over. Up to this point in telling the story of Orlando's life, documents, both private and historical, have made it possible to fulfil the first duty of a biographer, which is to plod, without looking to right or left, in the indelible footprints of truth; unenticed by flowers; regardless of shade; on and on methodically till we fall plump into the grave and write *finis* on the tombstone above our heads. But now we come to an episode which lies right across our path, so that there is no ignoring it. Yet it is dark, mysterious, and undocumented; so that there is no explaining it. Volumes might be written in interpretation of it; whole religious systems founded upon the signification of it. Our simple duty is to state the facts as far as they are known, and so let the reader make of them what he may.

In the summer of that disastrous winter which saw the frost, the flood, the deaths of many thousands, and the complete downfall of Orlando's hopes – for he was exiled from Court; in deep disgrace with the most powerful nobles of his time; the Irish house of Desmond was justly enraged; the King had already trouble enough with the Irish not to relish this further addition – in that summer Orlando retired to his great house in the country and there lived in complete solitude. One June morning – it was Saturday the 18th – he failed to rise at his usual hour, and when his groom went to call him he was found fast asleep. Nor could he be awakened. He lay as if in a trance, without perceptible breathing; and though dogs were set to bark under his window; cymbals, drums, bones beaten perpetually in his room; a gorse bush put under his pillow; and mustard plasters applied to his feet, still he did not wake, take food, or show any sign of life for seven whole days. On the seventh day he woke at his usual time (a quarter before eight, precisely) and turned the whole posse of caterwauling wives and village soothsayers out of his room; which was natural enough; but what was strange was that he showed no consciousness of any such trance, but dressed himself and sent for his horse as if he had woken from a single night's slumber. Yet some change, it was suspected, must have taken place in the chambers of his brain, for though he was perfectly rational and seemed graver and more sedate in his ways than before, he appeared to have an imperfect recollection of his past life. He would listen when people spoke of the great frost or the skating or the carnival, but he never gave any sign, except by passing his hand across his brow as if to wipe away some cloud, of having witnessed them himself. When the events of the past six months were discussed, he seemed not so much distressed as puzzled, as if he were troubled by confused memories of some time long gone or were trying to recall stories told him by another. It was observed that if Russia was mentioned or Princesses or ships, he would fall into a gloom of an uneasy kind and get up and look out of the window or call one of the dogs to him, or take a knife and carve a piece of cedar wood. But the doctors were hardly wiser then than they are now, and after prescribing rest and exercise, starvation and nourishment, society and solitude, that he should lie in bed all day and ride forty miles between lunch and dinner, together with the usual sedatives and irritants, diversified, as the fancy took them, with possets of newt's slobber on rising, and draughts of peacock's gall on going to bed, they left him to himself, and gave it as their opinion that he had been asleep for a week.

But if sleep it was, of what nature, we can scarcely refrain from asking, are such sleeps as these? Are they remedial measures – trances in which the most galling memories, events that seem likely to cripple life for ever, are brushed with a dark wing which rubs their harshness off and gilds them, even the ugliest and basest, with a lustre, an incandescence? Has the finger of death to be laid on the tumult of life from time to time lest it rend us asunder? Are we so made that we have to take death in small doses daily or we could not go on with the business of living? And then what strange powers are these that penetrate our most secret ways and change our most treasured possessions without our willing it? Had Orlando, worn out by the extremity of his suffering, died for a week, and then come to life again? And if so, of what nature is death and of what nature life? Having waited well over half an hour for an answer to these questions, and none coming, let us get on with the story.

Now Orlando gave himself up to a life of extreme solitude. His disgrace at Court and the violence of his grief were partly the reason of it, but as he made no effort to defend himself and seldom invited anyone to visit him (though he had many friends who would willingly have done so) it appeared as if to be alone in the great house of his fathers suited his temper. Solitude was his choice. How he spent his time, nobody quite knew. The servants, of whom he kept a full retinue, though much of their business was to dust empty rooms and to smooth the coverlets of beds that were never slept in, watched, in the dark of the evening, as they sat over their cakes and ale, a light passing along the galleries, through the banqueting-halls, up the staircases, into the bedrooms, and knew that their master was per-ambulating the house alone. None dared follow him, for the house was haunted by a great variety of ghosts, and the extent of it made it easy to lose one's way and either fall down some hidden staircase or open a door which, should the wind blow it to, would shut upon one for ever – accidents of no uncommon occurrence, as the frequent discovery of the skeletons of men and animals in attitudes of great agony made evident. Then the light would be lost altogether, and Mrs Grimsditch, the housekeeper, would say to Mr Dupper, the chaplain, how she hoped his Lordship had not met with some bad accident. Mr Dupper would opine that his Lordship was on his knees, no doubt, among the tombs of his ancestors in the Chapel, which was in the Billiard Table Court, half a mile away on the south side. For he had sins on his conscience, Mr Dupper was afraid; upon which Mrs Grimsditch would retort, rather sharply, that so had most of us; and Mrs Stewkley and Mrs Field and old Nurse Carpenter would all raise their voices in his Lordship's praise; and the grooms and the stewards would swear that it was a thousand pities to see so fine a nobleman moping about the house when he might be hunting the fox or chasing the deer; and even the little laundry maids and scullery maids, the Judys and the Faiths, who were handing round the tankards and cakes, would pipe up their testimony to his Lordship's gallantry; for never was there a kinder gentleman, or one more free with those little pieces of silver which serve to buy a knot of ribbon or put a posy in one's hair; until even the Blackamoor whom they called Grace Robinson by way of making a Christian woman of her, understood what they were at, and agreed that his Lordship was a handsome, pleasant, darling gentleman in the only way she could, that is to say by showing all her teeth at once in a broad grin. In short, all his serving men and women held him in high respect, and cursed the foreign Princess (but they called her by a coarser name than that) who had brought him to this pass.

But though it was probably cowardice, or love of hot ale, that led Mr Dupper to imagine his Lordship safe among the tombs so that he need not go in search of him, it may well have been that Mr Dupper was right. Orlando now took a strange delight in thoughts of death and decay, and, after pacing the long galleries and ballrooms with a taper in his hand, looking at picture after picture as if he sought the likeness of somebody whom he could not find, would mount into the family pew and sit for hours watching the banners stir and the moonlight waver with a bat or death's head moth to keep him company. Even this was not enough for him, but he must descend into the crypt where his ancestors lay, coffin piled upon coffin, for ten generations together. The place was so seldom visited that the rats had made free with the lead work, and now a thigh bone would catch at his cloak as he passed, or he would crack the skull of some old Sir Malise as it rolled beneath his foot. It was a ghastly sepulchre; dug deep beneath the foundations of the house as if the first Lord of the family, who had come from France with the Conqueror, had wished to testify how all pomp is built upon corruption; how the skeleton lies beneath the flesh; how we that dance and sing above must lie below; how the crimson velvet turns to dust; how the ring (here Orlando, stooping his lantern, would pick up a gold circle lacking a stone, that had rolled into a corner) loses its ruby and the eye which was so lustrous shines no more. 'Nothing remains of all these Princes,' Orlando would say, indulging in some pardonable exaggeration of their rank, 'except one digit,' and he would take a skeleton hand in his and bend the joints this way and that. 'Whose hand was it?' he went on to ask. 'The right or the left?

The hand of man or woman, of age or youth? Had it urged the war-horse, or plied the needle? Had it plucked the rose, or grasped cold steel? Had it – ' but here either his invention failed him or, what is more likely, provided him with so many instances of what a hand can do that he shrank, as his wont was, from the cardinal labour of composition, which is excision, and he put it with the other bones, thinking how there was a writer called Thomas Browne, a Doctor of Norwich, whose writing upon such subjects took his fancy amazingly.

So, taking his lantern and seeing that the bones were in order, for though romantic, he was singularly methodical and detested nothing so much as a ball of string on the floor, let alone the skull of an ancestor, he returned to that curious, moody pacing down the galleries, looking for something among the pictures, which was interrupted at length by a veritable spasm of sobbing, at the sight of a Dutch snow scene by an unknown artist. Then it seemed to him that life was not worth living any more. Forgetting the bones of his ancestors and how life is founded on a grave, he stood there shaken with sobs, all for the desire of a woman in Russian trousers, with slanting eyes, a pouting mouth, and pearls about her neck. She had gone. She had left him. He was never to see her again. And so he sobbed. And so he found his way back to his own rooms; and Mrs Grimsditch, seeing the light in the window, put the tankard from her lips and said Praise be to God, his Lordship was safe in his room again; for she had been thinking all this while that he was foully murdered.

Orlando now drew his chair up to the table; opened the works of Sir Thomas Browne and proceeded to investigate the delicate articulation of one of the doctor's longest and most marvellously contorted cogitations.

For though these are not matters on which a biographer can profitably enlarge it is plain enough to those who have done a reader's part in making up from bare hints dropped here and there the whole boundary and circumference of a living person; can hear in what we only whisper a living voice; can see, often when we say nothing about it, exactly what he looked like; know without a word to guide them precisely what he thought – and it is for readers such as these that we write – it is plain then to such a reader that Orlando was strangely compounded of many humours – of melancholy, of indolence, of passion, of love of solitude, to say nothing of all those contortions and subtleties of temper which were indicated on the first page, when he slashed at a dead nigger's head; cut it down; hung it chivalrously out of his reach again and then betook himself to the window-seat with a book. The taste for books was an early one. As a child he was sometimes found at midnight by a page still reading. They took his taper away, and he bred glow-worms to serve his purpose. They took the glow-worms away, and he almost burnt the house down with a tinder. To put it in a nutshell, leaving the novelist to smooth out the crumpled silk and all its implications, he was a nobleman afflicted with a love of literature.

Many people of his time, still more of his rank, escaped the infection and were thus free to run or ride or make love at their own sweet will. But some were early infected by a germ said to be bred of the pollen of the asphodel and to be blown out of Greece and Italy, which was of so deadly a nature that it would shake the hand as it was raised to strike, cloud the eye as it sought its prey, and make the tongue stammer as it declared its love. It was the fatal nature of this disease to substitute a phantom for reality, so that Orlando, to whom fortune had given every gift – plate, linen, houses, menservants, carpets, beds in profusion – had only to open a book for the whole vast accumulation to turn to mist. The nine acres of stone which were his house vanished; one hundred and fifty indoor servants disappeared; his eighty riding horses became invisible; it would take too long to count the carpets, sofas, trappings, china, plate, cruets, chafing dishes and other movables often of beaten gold, which evaporated like so much sea mist under the miasma. So it was, and Orlando would sit by himself, reading, a naked man.

The disease gained rapidly upon him now in his solitude. He would read often six hours into the night; and when they came to him for orders about the slaughtering of cattle or the harvesting of wheat, he would push away his folio and look as if he did not understand what was said to him. This was bad enough and wrung the hearts of Hall, the falconer, of Giles, the groom, of Mrs Grimsditch, the housekeeper, of Mr Dupper, the chaplain. A fine gentleman like that, they said, had no need of books. Let him leave books, they said, to the palsied or the dying. But worse was to come. For once the disease of reading has laid hold upon the system it weakens it so that it falls an easy prey to that other scourge which dwells in the inkpot and festers in the quill. The wretch takes to writing. And while this is bad enough in a poor man, whose only property is a chair and a table set beneath a leaky roof – for he has not much to lose, after all – the plight of a rich man, who has houses and cattle, maidservant, asses and linen, and yet writes books, is pitiable in the extreme. The flavour of it all goes out of him; he is riddled by hot irons; gnawed by vermin. He would give every penny he has (such is the malignity of the germ) to write one little book and become famous; yet all the gold in Peru will not buy him the treasure of a well-turned line. So he falls into consumption and sickness, blows his brains out, turns his face to the wall. It matters not in what attitude they find him. He has passed through the gates of Death and known the flames of Hell.

Happily, Orlando was of a strong constitution and the disease (for reasons presently to be given) never broke him down as it has broken many of his peers. But he was deeply smitten with it, as the sequel shows. For when he had read for an hour or so in Sir Thomas Browne, and the bark of the stag and the call of the night watchman showed that it was the dead of night and all safe asleep, he crossed the room, took a silver key from his pocket and unlocked the doors of a great inlaid cabinet which stood in the corner.

Within were some fifty drawers of cedar wood and upon each was a paper neatly written in Orlando's hand. He paused, as if hesitating which to open. One was inscribed 'The Death of Ajax', another 'The Birth of Pyramus', another 'Iphigenia in Aulis', another 'The Death of Hippolytus', another 'Meleager', another 'The Return of Odysseus' – in fact there was scarcely a single drawer that lacked the name of some mythological personage at a crisis of his career. In each drawer lay a document of considerable size all written over in Orlando's hand. The truth was that Orlando had been afflicted thus for many years. Never had any boy begged apples as Orlando begged paper; nor sweetmeats as he begged ink. Stealing away from talk and games, he had hidden himself behind curtains, in priest's holes, or in the cupboard behind his mother's bedroom which had a great hole in the floor and smelt horribly of starling's dung, with an ink-horn in one hand, a pen in another, and on his knee a roll of paper. Thus had been written, before he was turned twenty-five, some forty-seven plays, histories, romances, poems; some in prose, some in verse; some in French, some in Italian; all romantic, and all long. One he had had printed by John Ball of the Feathers and Coronet opposite St Paul's Cross, Cheapside; but though the sight of it gave him extreme delight, he had never dared show it even to his mother, since to write, much more to publish, was, he knew, for a nobleman an inexpiable disgrace.

Now, however, that it was the dead of night and he was alone, he chose from this repository one thick document called 'Xenophila, A Tragedy' or some such title, and one thin one, called simply 'The Oak Tree' (this was the only monosyllabic title among the lot), and then he approached the ink-horn, fingered the quill, and made other such passes as those addicted to this vice begin their rites with. But he paused.

As this pause was of extreme significance in his history, more so, indeed, than many acts which bring men to their knees and make rivers run with blood, it behoves us to ask why he paused; and to reply, after due reflection, that it was for some such reason as this. Nature, who has played so many queer tricks upon us, making us so unequally of clay and diamonds, of rainbow and granite, and stuffed them into a case, often of the most incongruous, for the poet has a butcher's face and the butcher a poet's; nature, who delights in muddle and mystery, so that even now (the first of November 1927) we know not why we go upstairs, or why we come down again, our most daily movements are like the passage of a ship on an unknown sea, and the sailors at the mast-head ask, pointing their glasses to the horizon; Is there land or is there none? to which, if we are prophets, we make answer 'Yes'; if we are truthful we say 'No'; nature, who has so much to answer for besides the perhaps unwieldy length of this sentence, has further complicated her task and added to our confusion by providing not only a perfect rag-bag of odds and ends within us – a piece of a policeman's trousers lying cheek by jowl with Queen Alexandra's wedding veil – but has contrived that the whole assortment shall be lightly stitched together by a single thread. Memory is the seamstress, and a capricious one at that. Memory runs her needle in and out, up and down, hither and thither. We know not what comes next, or what follows after. Thus, the most ordinary movement in the world, such as sitting down at a table and pulling the inkstand towards one, may agitate a thousand odd, disconnected fragments, now bright, now dim, hanging and bobbing and dipping and flaunting, like the underlinen of a family of fourteen on a line in a gale of wind. Instead of being a single, downright, bluff piece of work of which no man need feel ashamed, our commonest deeds are set about with a fluttering and flickering of wings, a rising and falling of lights. Thus it was that Orlando, dipping his pen in the ink, saw the mocking face of the lost Princess and asked himself a million questions instantly which were as arrows dipped in gall. Where was she; and why had she left him? Was the Ambassador her uncle or her lover? Had they plotted? Was she forced? Was she married? Was she dead? – all of which so drove their venom into him that, as if to vent his agony somewhere, he plunged his quill so deep into the ink-horn that the ink spirted over the table, which act, explain it how one may (and no explanation perhaps is possible – Memory is inexplicable), at once substituted for the face of the Princess a face of a very different sort. But whose was it, he asked himself? And he had to wait, perhaps half a minute, looking at the new picture which lay on top of the old, as one lantern slide is half seen through the next, before he could say to himself, 'This is the face of that rather fat, shabby man who sat in Twitchett's room ever so many years ago when old Queen Bess came here to dine; and I saw him,' Orlando continued, catching at another of those little coloured rags, 'sitting at the table, as I peeped in on my way downstairs, and he had the most amazing eyes,' said Orlando, 'that ever were, but who the devil was he?' Orlando asked, for here Memory added to the forehead and eyes, first, a coarse, grease-stained ruffle, then a brown doublet, and finally a pair of thick boots such as citizens wear in Cheapside. 'Not a Nobleman; not one of us,' said Orlando (which he would not have said aloud, for he was the most courteous of gentlemen; but it shows what an effect noble birth has upon the mind and incidentally how difficult it is for a nobleman to be a writer), 'a poet, I dare say.' By all the laws, Memory, having disturbed him sufficiently, should now have blotted the whole thing out completely, or have fetched up something so idiotic and out of keeping – like a dog chasing a cat or an old woman blowing her nose into a red cotton handkerchief – that, in despair of keeping pace with her vagaries, Orlando should have struck his pen in earnest against his paper. (For we can, if we have the resolution, turn the hussy, Memory, and all her ragtag and bobtail out of the house.) But Orlando paused. Memory still held before him the image of a shabby man with big, bright eyes. Still he looked, still he paused. It is these pauses that are our undoing. It is then that sedition enters the fortress and our troops rise in insurrection. Once before he had paused, and love with its horrid rout, its shawms, its cymbals, and its heads with gory locks torn from the shoulders had burst in. From love he had suffered the tortures of the damned. Now, again, he paused, and into the breach thus made, leapt Ambition, the harridan, and Poetry, the witch, and Desire of Fame, the strumpet; all joined hands and made of his heart their dancing ground. Standing upright in the solitude of his room, he vowed that he would be the first poet of his race and bring immortal lustre upon his name. He said (reciting the names and exploits of his ancestors) that Sir Boris had fought and killed the Paynim; Sir Gawain, the Turk; Sir Miles, the Pole; Sir Andrew, the Frank; Sir Richard, the Austrian; Sir Jordan, the Frenchman; and Sir Herbert, the Spaniard. But of all that killing and campaigning, that drinking and lovemaking, that spending and hunting and riding and eating, what remained? A skull; a finger. Whereas, he said, turning to the page of Sir Thomas Browne, which lay open upon the table – and again he paused. Like an incantation rising from all parts of the room, from the night wind and the moonlight, rolled the divine melody of those words which, lest they should outstare this page, we will leave where they lie entombed, not dead, embalmed rather, so fresh is their colour, so sound their breathing – and Orlando, comparing that achievement with those of his ancestors, cried out that they and their deeds were dust and ashes, but this man and his words were immortal.

He soon perceived, however, that the battles which Sir Miles and the rest had waged against armed knights to win a kingdom, were not half so arduous as this which he now undertook to win immortality against the English language. Anyone moderately familiar with the rigours of composition will not need to be told the story in detail; how he wrote and it seemed good; read and it seemed vile; corrected and tore up; cut out; put in; was in ecstasy; in despair; had his good nights and bad mornings; snatched at ideas and lost them; saw his book plain before him and it vanished; acted his people's parts as he ate; mouthed them as he walked; now cried; now laughed; vacillated between this style and that; now preferred the heroic and pompous; next the plain and simple; now the vales of Tempe; then the fields of Kent or Cornwall; and could not decide whether he was the divinest genius or the greatest fool in the world.

It was to settle this last question that he decided, after many months of such feverish labour, to break the solitude of years and communicate with the outer world. He had a friend in London, one Giles Isham of Norfolk, who, though of gentle birth, was acquainted with writers and could doubtless put him in touch with some member of that blessed, indeed sacred, fraternity. For, to Orlando in the state he was now in, there was a glory about a man who had written a book and had it printed, which outshone all the glories of blood and state. To his imagination it seemed as if even the bodies of those instinct with such divine thoughts must be transfigured. They must have aureoles for hair, incense for breath, and roses must grow between their lips – which was certainly not true either of himself or Mr Dupper. He could think of no greater happiness than to be allowed to sit behind a curtain and hear them talk. Even the imagination of that bold and various discourse made the memory of what he and his courtier friends used to talk about – a dog, a horse, a woman, a game of cards – seem brutish in the extreme. He bethought him with pride that he had always been called a scholar, and sneered at for his love of solitude and books. He had never been apt at pretty phrases. He would stand stock still, blush, and stride like a grenadier in a ladies' drawing-room. He had twice fallen, in sheer abstraction, from his horse. He had broken Lady Winchilsea's fan once while making a rhyme. Eagerly recalling these and other instances of his unfitness for the life of society, an ineffable hope, that all the turbulence of his youth, his clumsiness, his blushes, his long walks, and his love of the country proved that he himself belonged to the sacred race rather than to the noble – was by birth a writer, rather than an aristocrat – possessed him. For the first time since the night of the great flood he was happy.

He now commissioned Mr Isham of Norfolk to deliver to Mr Nicholas Greene of Clifford's Inn a document which set forth Orlando's admiration for his works (for Nick Greene was a very famous writer at that time) and his desire to make his acquaintance; which he scarcely dared ask; for he had nothing to offer in return; but if Mr Nicholas Greene would condescend to visit him, a coach and four would be at the corner of Fetter Lane at whatever hour Mr Greene chose to appoint, and bring him safely to Orlando's house. One may fill up the phrases which then followed; and figure Orlando's delight when, in no long time, Mr Greene signified his acceptance of the Noble Lord's invitation; took his place in the coach and was set down in the hall to the south of the main building punctually at seven o'clock on Monday, April the twenty-first.

Many Kings, Queens, and Ambassadors had been received there; Judges had stood there in their ermine. The loveliest ladies of the land had come there; and the sternest warriors. Banners hung there which had been at Flodden and at Agincourt. There were displayed the painted coats of arms with their lions and their leopards and their coronets. There were the long tables where the gold and silver plate was stood; and there the vast fireplaces of wrought Italian marble where nightly a whole oak tree, with its million leaves and its nests of rook and wren, was burnt to ashes. Nicholas Greene, the poet stood there now, plainly dressed in his slouched hat and black doublet, carrying in one hand a small bag.

That Orlando as he hastened to greet him was slightly disappointed was inevitable. The poet was not above middle height; was of a mean figure; was lean and stooped somewhat, and, stumbling over the mastiff on entering, the dog bit him. Moreover, Orlando for all his knowledge of mankind was puzzled where to place him. There was something about him which belonged neither to servant, squire, or noble. The head with its rounded forehead and beaked nose was fine, but the chin receded. The eyes were brilliant, but the lips hung loose and slobbered. It was the expression of the face as a whole, however, that was disquieting. There was none of that stately composure which makes the faces of the nobility so pleasing to look at; nor had it anything of the dignified servility of a well-trained domestic's face; it was a face seamed, puckered, and drawn together. Poet though he was, it seemed as if he were more used to scold than to flatter; to quarrel than to coo; to scramble than to ride; to struggle than to rest; to hate than to love. This, too, was shown by the quickness of his movements; and by something fiery and suspicious in his glance. Orlando was somewhat taken aback. But they went to dinner.

Here, Orlando, who usually took such things for granted, was, for the first time, unaccountably ashamed of the number of his servants and of the splendour of his table. Stranger still, he bethought him with pride – for the thought was generally distasteful – of that great-grandmother Moll who had milked the cows. He was about somehow to allude to this humble woman and her milk-pails, when the poet forestalled him by saying that it was odd, seeing how common the name of Greene was, that the family had come over with the Conqueror and was of the highest nobility in France. Unfortunately, they had come down in the world and done little more than leave their name to the royal borough of Greenwich. Further talk of the same sort, about lost castles, coats of arms, cousins who were baronets in the north, intermarriage with noble families in the west, how some Greens spelt the name with an e at the end, and others without, lasted till the venison was on the table. Then Orlando contrived to say something of Grandmother Moll and her cows, and had eased his heart a little of its burden by the time the wild fowl were before them. But it was not until the Malmsey was passing freely that Orlando dared mention what he could not help thinking a more important matter than the Greens or the cows; that is to say the sacred subject of poetry. At the first mention of the word, the poet's eyes flashed fire; he dropped the fine gentleman airs he had worn; thumped his glass on the table, and launched into one of the longest, most intricate, most passionate, and bitterest stories that Orlando had ever heard, save from the lips of a jilted woman, about a play of his; another poet; and a critic. Of the nature of poetry itself, Orlando only gathered that it was harder to sell than prose, and though the lines were shorter took longer in the writing. So the talk went on with ramifications interminable, until Orlando ventured to hint that he had himself been so rash as to write – but here the poet leapt from his chair. A mouse had squeaked in the wainscot, he said. The truth was, he explained, that his nerves were in a state where a mouse's squeak upset them for a fortnight. Doubtless the house was full of vermin, but Orlando had not heard them. The poet then gave Orlando the full story of his health for the past ten years or so. It had been so bad that one could only marvel that he still lived. He had had the palsy, the gout, the ague, the dropsy, and the three sorts of fever in succession; added to which he had an enlarged heart, a great spleen, and a diseased liver. But, above all, he had, he told Orlando, sensations in his spine which defied description. There was one knob about the third from the top which burnt like fire; another about the second from the bottom which was cold as ice. Sometimes he woke with a brain like lead; at others it was as if a thousand wax tapers were alight and people were throwing fireworks inside him. He could feel a rose leaf through his mattress, he said; and knew his way almost about London by the feel of the cobbles. Altogether he was a piece of machinery so finely made and so curiously put together (here he raised his hand as if unconsciously, and indeed it was of the finest shape imaginable) that it confounded him to think that he had only sold five hundred copies of his poem, but that of course was largely due to the conspiracy against him. All he could say, he concluded, banging his fist upon the table, was that the art of poetry was dead in England.

How that could be with Shakespeare, Marlowe, Ben Jonson, Browne, Donne, all now writing or just having written, Orlando, reeling off the names of his favourite heroes, could not think.

Greene laughed sardonically. Shakespeare, he admitted, had written some scenes that were well enough; but he had taken them chiefly from Marlowe. Marlowe was a likely boy, but what could you say of a lad who died before he was thirty? As for Browne, he was for writing poetry in prose, and people soon got tired of such conceits as that. Donne was a mountebank who wrapped up his lack of meaning in hard words. The gulls were taken in; but the style would be out of fashion twelve months hence. As for Ben Jonson – Ben Jonson was a friend of his and he never spoke ill of his friends.

No, he concluded, the great age of literature is past; the great age of literature was the Greek; the Elizabethan age was inferior in every respect to the Greek. In such ages men cherished a divine ambition which he might call *La Gloire* (he pronounced it Glawr, so that Orlando did not at first catch his meaning). Now all young writers were in the pay of the booksellers and poured out any trash that would sell. Shakespeare was the chief offender in this way and Shakespeare was already paying the penalty. Their own age, he said, was marked by precious conceits and wild experiments – neither of which the Greeks would have tolerated for a moment. Much though it hurt him to say it – for he loved literature as he loved his life – he could see no good in the present and had no hope of the future. Here he poured himself out another glass of wine.

Orlando was shocked by these doctrines; yet could not help observing that the critic himself seemed by no means downcast. On the contrary, the more he denounced his own time, the more complacent he became. He could remember, he said, a night at the Cock Tavern in Fleet Street when Kit Marlowe was there and some others. Kit was in high feather, rather drunk, which he easily became, and in a mood to say silly things. He could see him now, brandishing his glass at the company and hiccoughing out,

'Stap my vitals, Bill' (this was to Shakespeare), 'there's a great wave coming and you're on the top of it,' by which he meant, Greene explained, that they were trembling on the verge of a great age in English literature, and that Shakespeare was to be a poet of some importance. Happily for himself, he was killed two nights later in a drunken brawl, and so did not live to see how this prediction turned out. 'Poor foolish fellow,' said Greene, 'to go and say a thing like that. A great age, forsooth – the Elizabethan a great age!'

'So, my dear Lord,' he continued, settling himself comfortably in his chair and rubbing the wineglass between his fingers, 'we must make the best of it, cherish the past and honour those writers – there are still a few left of 'em – who take antiquity for their model and write, not for pay but for Glawr.' (Orlando could have wished him a better accent.) 'Glawr', said Greene, 'is the spur of noble minds. Had I a pension of three hundred pounds a year paid quarterly, I would live for Glawr alone. I would lie in bed every morning reading Cicero. I would imitate his style so that you couldn't tell the difference between us. That's what I call fine writing,' said Greene; 'that's what I call Glawr. But it's necessary to have a pension to do it.'

By this time Orlando had abandoned all hope of discussing his own work with the poet; but this mattered the less as the talk now got upon the lives and characters of Shakespeare, Ben Jonson, and the rest, all of whom Greene had known intimately and about whom he had a thousand anecdotes of the most amusing kind to tell. Orlando had never laughed so much in his life. These, then, were his gods! Half were drunken and all were amorous. Most of them quarrelled with their wives; not one of them was above a lie or an intrigue of the most paltry kind. Their poetry was scribbled down on the backs of washing bills held to the heads of printer's devils at the street door. Thus Hamlet went to press; thus Lear; thus Othello. No wonder, as Greene said, that these plays show the faults they do. The rest of the time was spent in carousings and junketings in taverns and in beer gardens, when things were said that passed belief for wit, and things were done that made the utmost frolic of the courtiers seem pale in comparison. All this Greene told with a spirit that roused Orlando to the highest pitch of delight. He had a power of mimicry that brought the dead to life, and could say the finest things of books provided they were written three hundred years ago.

So time passed, and Orlando felt for his guest a strange mixture of liking and contempt, of admiration and pity, as well as something too indefinite to be called by any one name, but had something of fear in it and something of fascination. He talked incessantly about himself, yet was such good company that one could listen to the story of his ague for ever. Then he was so witty; then he was so irreverent; then he made so free with the names of God and Woman; then he was so full of queer crafts and had such strange lore in his head; could make salad in three hundred different ways; knew all that could be known of the mixing of wines; played half a dozen musical instruments, and was the first person, and perhaps the last, to toast cheese in the great

Italian fireplace. That he did not know a geranium from a carnation, an oak from a birch tree, a mastiff from a greyhound, a teg from a ewe, wheat from barley, plough land from fallow; was ignorant of the rotation of the crops; thought oranges grew under ground and turnips on trees; preferred any townscape to any landscape – all this and much more amazed Orlando, who had never met anybody of his kind before. Even the maids, who despised him, tittered at his jokes, and the manservant, who loathed him, hung about to hear his stories. Indeed, the house had never been so lively as now that he was there – all of which gave Orlando a great deal to think about, and caused him to compare this way of life with the old. He recalled the sort of talk he had been used to about the King of Spain's apoplexy or the mating of a bitch; he bethought him how the day passed between the stables and the dressing closet; he remembered how the Lords snored over their wine and hated anybody who woke them up. He bethought him how active and valiant they were in body; how slothful and timid in mind. Worried by these thoughts, and unable to strike a proper balance, he came to the conclusion that he had admitted to his house a plaguey spirit of unrest that would never suffer him to sleep sound again.

At the same moment, Nick Greene came to precisely the opposite conclusion. Lying in bed of a morning on the softest pillows between the smoothest sheets and looking out of his oriel window upon turf which for three centuries had known neither dandelion nor dock weed, he thought that unless he could somehow make his escape, he should be smothered alive. Getting up and hearing the pigeons coo, dressing and hearing the fountains fall, he thought that unless he could hear the drays roar upon the cobbles of Fleet Street, he would never write another line. If this goes on much longer, he thought, hearing the footman mend the fire and spread the table with silver dishes next door, I shall fall asleep and (here he gave a prodigious yawn) sleeping die.

So he sought Orlando in his room, and explained that he had not been able to sleep a wink all night because of the silence. (Indeed, the house was surrounded by a park fifteen miles in circumference and a wall ten feet high.) Silence, he said, was of all things the most oppressive to his nerves. He would end his visit, by Orlando's leave, that very morning. Orlando felt some relief at this, yet also a great reluctance to let him go. The house, he thought, would seem very dull without him. On parting (for he had never yet liked to mention the subject), he had the temerity to press his play upon the Death of Hercules upon the poet and ask his opinion of it. The poet took it; muttered something about Glawr and Cicero, which Orlando cut short by promising to pay the pension quarterly; whereupon Greene, with many protestations of affection, jumped into the coach and was gone.

The great hall had never seemed so large, so splendid, or so empty as the chariot rolled away. Orlando knew that he would never have the heart to make toasted cheese in the Italian fireplace again. He would never have the wit to crack jokes about Italian pictures; never have the skill to mix punch as it should be mixed; a thousand good quips and cranks would be lost to him. Yet what a relief to be out of the sound of that querulous voice, what a luxury to be alone once more, so he could not help reflecting, as he unloosed the mastiff which had been tied up these six weeks because it never saw the poet without biting him.

Nick Greene was set down at the corner of Fetter Lane that same afternoon, and found things going on much as he had left them. Mrs Greene, that is to say, was giving birth to a baby in one room; Tom Fletcher was drinking gin in another. Books were tumbled all about the floor; dinner – such as it was – was set on a dressing-table where the children had been making mud pies. But this, Greene felt, was the atmosphere for writing; here he could write, and write he did. The subject was made for him. A noble Lord at home. A visit to a Nobleman in the country – his new poem was to have some such title as that. Seizing the pen with which his little boy was tickling the cat's ears, and dipping it in the egg-cup which served for inkpot, Greene dashed off a very spirited satire there and then. It was so done to a turn that no one could doubt that the young Lord who was roasted was Orlando; his most private sayings and doings, his enthusiasms and follies, down to the very colour of his hair and the foreign way he had of rolling his r's, were there to the life. And if there had been any doubt about it, Greene clinched the matter by introducing, with scarcely any disguise, passages from that aristocratic tragedy, the Death of Hercules, which he found as he expected, wordy and bombastic in the extreme.

The pamphlet, which ran at once into several editions, and paid the expenses of Mrs Greene's tenth lying-in, was soon sent by friends who take care of such matters to Orlando himself. When he had read it, which he did with deadly composure from start to finish, he rang for the footman; delivered the document to him at the end of a pair of tongs; bade him drop it in the filthiest heart of the foulest midden on the estate. Then, when the man was turning to go he stopped him, 'Take the swiftest horse in the stable,' he said, 'ride for dear life to Harwich. There embark upon a ship which you will find bound for Norway. Buy for me from the King's own kennels the finest elk-hounds of the Royal strain, male and female. Bring them back without delay. For', he murmured, scarcely above his breath as he turned to his books, 'I have done with men.'

The footman, who was perfectly trained in his duties, bowed and disappeared. He fulfilled his task so efficiently that he was back that day three weeks, leading in his hand a leash of the finest elk-hounds, one of whom, a female, gave birth that very night under the dinner-table to a litter of eight fine puppies. Orlando had them brought to his bedchamber.

'For,' he said, 'I have done with men.'
Nevertheless, he paid the pension quarterly.

Thus, at the age of thirty, or thereabouts, this young Nobleman had not only had every experience that life has to offer, but had seen the worthlessness of them all. Love and ambition, women and poets were all equally vain. Literature was a farce. The night after reading Greene's Visit to a Nobleman in the Country, he burnt in a great conflagration fifty-seven poetical works, only retaining 'The Oak Tree', which was his boyish dream and very short. Two things alone remained to him in which he now put any trust: dogs and nature; an elk-hound and a rose bush. The world, in all its variety, life in all its complexity, had shrunk to that. Dogs and a bush were the whole of it. So feeling quit of a vast mountain of illusion, and very naked in consequence, he called his hounds to him and strode through the Park.

So long had he been secluded, writing and reading, that he had half forgotten the amenities of nature, which in June can be great. When he reached that high mound whence on fine days half of England with a slice of Wales and Scotland thrown in can be seen, he flung himself under his favourite oak tree and felt that if he need never speak to another man or woman so long as he lived; if his dogs did not develop the faculty of speech; if he never met a poet or a Princess again, he might make out what years remained to him in tolerable content.

Here he came then, day after day, week after week, month after month, year after year. He saw the beech trees turn golden and the young ferns unfurl; he saw the moon sickle and then circular; he saw – but probably the reader can imagine the passage which should follow and how every tree and plant in the neighbourhood is described first green, then golden; how moons rise and suns set; how spring follows winter and autumn summer; how night succeeds day and day night; how there is first a storm and then fine weather; how things remain much as they are for two or three hundred years or so, except for a little dust and a few cobwebs which one old woman can sweep up in half an hour; a conclusion which, one cannot help feeling, might have been reached more quickly by the simple statement that 'Time passed' (here the exact amount could be indicated in brackets) and nothing whatever happened.

But Time, unfortunately, though it makes animals and vegetables bloom and fade with amazing punctuality, has no such simple effect upon the mind of man. The mind of man, moreover, works with equal strangeness upon the body of time. An hour, once it lodges in the queer element of the human spirit, may be stretched to fifty or a hundred times its clock length; on the other hand, an hour may be accurately represented on the timepiece of the mind by one second. This extraordinary discrepancy between time on the clock and time in the mind is less known than it should be and deserves fuller investigation. But the biographer, whose interests are, as we have said, highly restricted, must confine himself to one simple statement: when a man has reached the age of thirty, as Orlando now had, time when he is thinking becomes inordinately long; time when he is doing becomes inordinately short. Thus Orlando gave his orders and did the business of his vast estates in a flash; but directly he was alone on the mound under the oak tree, the seconds began to round and fill until it seemed as if they would never fall. They filled themselves, moreover, with the strangest variety of objects. For not only did he find himself confronted by problems which have puzzled the wisest of men, such as What is love? What friendship? What truth? but directly he came to think about them, his whole past, which seemed to him of extreme length and variety, rushed into the falling second, swelled it a dozen times its natural size, coloured it a thousand tints, and filled it with all the odds and ends in the universe.

In such thinking (or by whatever name it should be called) he spent months and years of his life. It would be no exaggeration to say that he would go out after breakfast a man of thirty and come home to dinner a man of fifty-five at least. Some weeks added a century to his age, others no more than three seconds at most. Altogether, the task of estimating the length of human life (of the animals' we presume not to speak) is beyond our capacity, for directly we say that it is ages long, we are reminded that it is briefer than the fall of a rose leaf to the ground. Of the two forces which alternately, and what is more confusing still, at the same moment, dominate our unfortunate numbskulls – brevity and diuturnity – Orlando was sometimes under the influence of the elephant-footed deity, then of the gnat-winged fly. Life seemed to him of prodigious length. Yet even so, it went like a flash. But even when it stretched longest and the moments swelled biggest and he seemed to wander alone in deserts of vast eternity, there was no time for the smoothing out and deciphering of those thickly scored parchments which thirty years among men and women had rolled tight in his heart and brain. Long before he had done thinking about Love (the oak tree had put forth its leaves and shaken them to the ground a dozen times in the process) Ambition would jostle it off the field, to be replaced by Friendship or Literature. And as the first question had not been settled – What is Love? – back it would come at the least provocation or none, and hustle Books or Metaphors or What one lives for into the margin, there to wait till they saw their chance to rush into the field again. What made the process still longer was that it was profusely illustrated, not only with pictures, as that of old Queen Elizabeth, laid on her tapestry couch in rose-coloured brocade with an ivory snuff-box in her hand and a gold-hilted sword by her side, but with scents – she was strongly perfumed – and with sounds; the stags were barking in Richmond Park that winter's day. And so, the thought of love would be all ambered over with snow and winter; with log fires burning; with Russian women, gold swords, and the bark of stags; with old King James' slobbering and fireworks and sacks of treasure in the holds of Elizabethan sailing ships. Every single thing, once he tried to dislodge it from its place in his mind, he found thus cumbered with other matter like the lump of glass which, after a year at the bottom of the sea, is grown about with bones and dragonflies, and coins and the tresses of drowned women.

'Another metaphor by Jupiter!' he would exclaim as he said this (which will show the disorderly and circuitous way in which his mind worked and explain why the oak tree flowered and faded so often before he came to any conclusion about Love). 'And what's the point of it?' he would ask himself. 'Why not say simply in so many words – ' and then he would try to think for half an hour – or was it two years and a half? – how to say simply in so many words what love is. 'A figure like that is manifestly untruthful,' he argued, 'for no dragonfly, unless under very exceptional circumstances, could live at the bottom of the sea. And if literature is not the Bride and Bedfellow of Truth, what is she? Confound it all,' he cried, 'why say Bedfellow when one's already said Bride? Why not simply say what one means and leave it?'

So then he tried saying the grass is green and the sky is blue and so to propitiate the austere spirit of poetry whom still, though at a great distance, he could not help reverencing. 'The sky is blue,' he said, 'the grass is green.' Looking up, he saw that, on the contrary, the sky is like the veils which a thousand Madonnas have let fall from their hair; and the grass fleets and darkens like a flight of girls fleeing the embraces of hairy satyrs from enchanted woods. 'Upon my word,' he said (for he had fallen into the bad habit of speaking aloud), 'I don't see that one's more true than another. Both are utterly false.' And he despaired of being able to solve the problem of what poetry is and what truth is and fell into a deep dejection.

And here we may profit by a pause in his soliloquy to reflect how odd it was to see Orlando stretched there on his elbow on a June day and to reflect that this fine fellow with all his faculties about him and a healthy body, witness cheeks and limbs – a man who never thought twice about heading a charge or fighting a duel – should be so subject to the lethargy of thought, and rendered so susceptible by it, that when it came to a question of poetry, or his own competence in it, he was as shy as a little girl behind her mother's cottage door. In our belief, Greene's ridicule of his tragedy hurt him as much as the Princess's ridicule of his love. But to return –

Orlando went on thinking. He kept looking at the grass and at the sky and trying to bethink him what a true poet, who has his verses published in London, would say about them. Memory meanwhile (whose habits have already been described) kept steady before his eyes the face of Nicholas Greene, as if that sardonic loose-lipped man, treacherous as he had proved himself, were the Muse in person, and it was to him that Orlando must do homage. So Orlando, that summer morning, offered him a variety of phrases, some plain, others figured, and Nick Greene kept shaking his head and sneering and muttering something about Glawr and Cicero and the death of poetry in our time. At length, starting to his feet (it was now winter and very cold) Orlando swore one of the most remarkable oaths of his lifetime, for it bound him to a servitude than which none is stricter. 'I'll be blasted,' he said, 'if I ever write another word, or try to write another word, to please Nick Greene or the Muse. Bad, good, or indifferent, I'll write, from this day forward, to please myself'; and here he made as if he were tearing a whole budget of papers across and tossing them in the face of that sneering loose-lipped man. Upon which, as a cur ducks if you stoop to shy a stone at him, Memory ducked her effigy of Nick Greene out of sight; and substituted for it – nothing whatever.

But Orlando, all the same, went on thinking. He had indeed much to think of. For when he tore the parchment across, he tore, in one rending, the scrolloping, emblazoned scroll which he had made out in his own favour in the solitude of his room appointing himself, as the King appoints Ambassadors, the first poet of his race, the first writer of his age, conferring eternal immortality upon his soul and granting his body a grave among laurels and the intangible banners of a people's reverence perpetually. Eloquent as this all was, he now tore it up and threw it in the dustbin. 'Fame,' he said, 'is like' (and since there was no Nick Greene to stop him, he went on to revel in images of which we will choose only one or two of the quietest) 'a braided coat which hampers the limbs; a jacket of silver which curbs the heart; a painted shield which covers a scarecrow,' etc. etc. The pith of his phrases was that while fame impedes and constricts, obscurity wraps about a man like a mist; obscurity is dark, ample, and free; obscurity lets the mind take its way unimpeded. Over the obscure man is poured the merciful suffusion of darkness. None knows where he goes or comes. He may seek the truth and speak it; he alone is free; he alone is truthful; he alone is at peace. And so he sank into a quiet mood, under the oak tree, the hardness of whose roots, exposed above the ground, seemed to him rather comfortable than otherwise.

Sunk for a long time in profound thoughts as to the value of obscurity, and the delight of having no name, but being like a wave which returns to the deep body of the sea; thinking how obscurity rids the mind of the irk of envy and spite; how it sets running in the veins the free waters of generosity and magnanimity; and allows giving and taking without thanks offered or praise given; which must have been the way of all great poets, he supposed (though his knowledge of Greek was not enough to bear him out), for, he thought, Shakespeare must have written like that, and the church builders built like that, anonymously, needing no thanking or naming, but only their work in the daytime and a little ale perhaps at night – 'What an admirable life this is,' he thought, stretching his limbs out under the oak tree. 'And why not enjoy it this very moment?' The thought struck him like a bullet. Ambition dropped like a plummet. Rid of the heart-burn of rejected love, and of vanity rebuked, and all the other stings and pricks which the nettle-bed of life had burnt upon him when ambitious of fame, but could no longer inflict upon one careless of glory, he opened his eyes, which had been wide open all the time, but had seen only thoughts, and saw, lying in the hollow beneath him, his house.

There it lay in the early sunshine of spring. It looked a town rather than a house, but a town built, not hither and thither, as this man wished or that, but circumspectly, by a single architect with one idea in his head. Courts and buildings, grey, red, plum colour, lay orderly and symmetrical; the courts were some of them oblong and some square; in this was a fountain; in that a statue; the buildings were some of them low, some pointed; here was a chapel, there a belfry; spaces of the greenest grass lay in between and clumps of cedar trees and beds of bright flowers; all were clasped – yet so well set out was it that it seemed that every part had room to spread itself fittingly – by the roll of a massive wall; while smoke from innumerable chimneys curled perpetually into the air. This vast, yet ordered building, which could house a thousand men and perhaps two thousand horses, was built, Orlando thought, by workmen whose names are unknown. Here have lived, for more centuries than I can count, the obscure generations of my own obscure family. Not one of these Richards, Johns, Annes, Elizabeths has left a token of himself behind him, yet all, working together with their spades and their needles, their love-making and their child-bearing, have left this.

Never had the house looked more noble and humane.

Why, then, had he wished to raise himself above them? For it seemed vain and arrogant in the extreme to try to better that anonymous work of creation; the labours of those vanished hands. Better was it to go unknown and leave behind you an arch, a potting shed, a wall where peaches ripen, than to burn like a meteor and leave no dust. For after all, he said, kindling as he looked at the great house on the greensward below, the unknown lords and ladies who lived there never forgot to set aside something for those who come after; for the roof that will leak; for the tree that will fall. There was always a warm corner for the old shepherd in the kitchen; always food for the hungry; always their goblets were polished, though they lay sick; and their windows were lit though they lay dying. Lords though they were, they were content to go down into obscurity with the molecatcher and the stonemason. Obscure noblemen, forgotten builders – thus he apostrophised them with a warmth that entirely gainsaid such critics as called him cold, indifferent, slothful (the truth being that a quality often lies just on the other side of the wall from where we seek it) – thus he apostrophised his house and race in terms of the most moving eloquence; but when it came to the peroration – and what is eloquence that lacks a peroration? – he fumbled. He would have liked to have ended with a flourish to the effect that he would follow in their footsteps and add another stone to their building. Since, however, the building already covered nine acres, to add even a single stone seemed superfluous. Could one mention furniture in a peroration? Could one speak of chairs and tables and mats to lie beside people's beds? For whatever the peroration wanted, that was what the house stood in need of. Leaving his speech unfinished for the moment, he strode down hill again resolved henceforward to devote himself to the furnishing of the mansion. The news – that she was to attend him instantly – brought tears to the eyes of good old Mrs Grimsditch, now grown somewhat old. Together they perambulated the house.

The towel horse in the King's bedroom ('and that was King Jamie, my Lord,' she said, hinting that it was many a day since a King had slept under their roof; but the odious Parliament days were over and there was now a Crown in England again) lacked a leg; there were no stands to the ewers in the little closet leading into the waiting room of the Duchess's page; Mr Greene had made a stain on the carpet with his nasty pipe smoking, which she and Judy, for all their scrubbing, had never been able to wash out. Indeed, when Orlando came to reckon up the matter of furnishing with rosewood chairs and cedar-wood cabinets, with silver basins, china bowls, and Persian carpets, every one of the three hundred and sixty-five bedrooms which the house contained, he saw that it would be no light one; and if some thousands of pounds of his estate remained over, these would do little more than hang a few galleries with tapestry, set the dining hall with fine, carved chairs and provide mirrors of solid silver and chairs of the same metal (for which he had an inordinate passion) for the furnishing of the royal bedchambers.

He now set to work in earnest, as we can prove beyond a doubt if we look at his ledgers. Let us glance at an inventory of what he bought at this time, with the expenses totted up in the margin – but these we omit.

'To fifty pairs of Spanish blankets, ditto curtains of crimson and white taffeta; the valence to them of white satin embroidered with crimson and white silk . . .
'To seventy yellow satin chairs and sixty stools, suitable with their buckram covers to them all . . .
'To sixty-seven walnut tree tables . . .
'To seventeen dozen boxes containing each dozen five dozen of Venice glasses . . .
'To one hundred and two mats, each thirty yards long . . .
'To ninety-seven cushions of crimson damask laid with silver parchment lace and footstools of cloth of tissue and chairs suitable . . .
'To fifty branches for a dozen lights apiece . . . '

Already – it is an effect lists have upon us – we are beginning to yawn. But if we stop, it is only that the catalogue is tedious, not that it is finished. There are ninety-nine pages more of it and the total sum disbursed ran into many thousands – that is to say millions of our money. And if his day was spent like this, at night again, Lord Orlando might be found reckoning out what it would cost to level a million molehills, if the men were paid tenpence an hour; and again, how many hundredweight of nails at 5½d. a gill were needed to repair the fence round the park, which was fifteen miles in circumference. And so on and so on.

The tale, we say, is tedious, for one cupboard is much like another, and one molehill not much different from a million. Some pleasant journeys it cost him; and some fine adventures. As, for instance, when he set a whole city of blind women near Bruges to stitch hangings for a silver canopied bed; and the story of his adventure with a Moor in Venice of whom he bought (but only at the sword's point) his lacquered cabinet, might, in other hands, prove worth the telling. Nor did the work lack variety; for here would come, drawn by teams from Sussex, great trees, to be sawn across and laid along the gallery for flooring; and then a chest from Persia, stuffed with wool and sawdust, from which, at last, he would take a single plate, or one topaz ring.

At length, however, there was no room in the galleries for another table; no room on the tables for another cabinet; no room in the cabinet for another rose-bowl; no room in the bowl for another handful of pot-pourri; there was no room for anything anywhere; in short the house was furnished. In the garden snowdrops, crocuses, hyacinths, magnolias, roses, lilies, asters, the dahlia in all its varieties, pear trees and apple trees and cherry trees and mulberry trees, with an enormous quantity of rare and flowering shrubs, of trees evergreen and perennial, grew so thick on each other's roots that there was no plot of earth without its bloom, and no stretch of sward without its shade. In addition, he had imported wild fowl with gay plumage; and two Malay bears, the surliness of whose manners concealed, he was certain, trusty hearts.

All now was ready; and when it was evening and the innumerable silver sconces were lit and the light airs which for ever moved about the galleries stirred the blue and green arras, so that it looked as if the huntsmen were riding and Daphne flying; when the silver shone and lacquer glowed and wood kindled; when the carved chairs held their arms out and dolphins swam upon the walls with mermaids on their backs; when all this and much more than all this was complete and to his liking, Orlando walked through the house with his elk-hounds following and felt content. He had matter now, he thought, to fill out his peroration. Perhaps it would be well to begin the speech all over again. Yet, as he paraded the galleries he felt that still something was lacking. Chairs and tables, however richly gilt and carved, sofas, resting on lions' paws with swans' necks curving under them, beds even of the softest swansdown are not by themselves enough. People sitting in them, people lying in them improve them amazingly. Accordingly Orlando now began a series of very splendid entertainments to the nobility and gentry of the neighbourhood. The three hundred and sixty-five bed-rooms were full for a month at a time. Guests jostled each other on the fifty-two staircases. Three hundred servants bustled about the pantries. Banquets took place almost nightly. Thus, in a very few years, Orlando had worn the nap off his velvet, and spent the half of his fortune; but he had earned the good opinion of his neighbours, held a score of offices in the county, and was annually presented with perhaps a dozen volumes dedicated to his Lordship in rather fulsome terms by grateful poets. For though he was careful not to consort with writers at that time and kept himself always aloof from ladies of foreign blood, still, he was excessively generous both to women and to poets, and both adored him.

But when the feasting was at its height and his guests were at their revels, he was apt to take himself off to his private room alone. There when the door was shut, and he was certain of privacy, he would have out an old writing book, stitched together with silk stolen from his mother's workbox, and labelled in a round schoolboy hand, 'The Oak Tree, A Poem'. In this he would write till midnight chimed and long after. But as he scratched out as many lines as he wrote in, the sum of them was often, at the end of the year, rather less than at the beginning, and it looked as if in the process of writing the poem would be completely unwritten. For it is for the historian of letters to remark that he had changed his style amazingly. His floridity was chastened; his abundance curbed; the age of prose was congealing those warm fountains. The very landscape outside was less stuck about with garlands and the briars themselves were less thorned and intricate. Perhaps the senses were a little duller and honey and cream less seductive to the palate. Also that the streets were better drained and the houses better lit had its effect upon the style, it cannot be doubted.

One day he was adding a line or two with enormous labour to 'The Oak Tree, A Poem', when a shadow crossed the tail of his eye. It was no shadow, he soon saw, but the figure of a very tall lady in riding hood and mantle crossing the quadrangle on which his room looked out. As this was the most private of the courts, and the lady was a stranger to him, Orlando marvelled how she had got there. Three days later the same apparition appeared again; and on Wednesday noon appeared once more. This time, Orlando was determined to follow her, nor apparently was she afraid to be found, for she slackened her steps as he came up and looked him full in the face. Any other woman thus caught in a Lord's private grounds would have been afraid; any other woman with that face, headdress, and aspect would have thrown her mantilla across her shoulders to hide it. For this lady resembled nothing so much as a hare; a hare startled, but obdurate; a hare whose timidity is overcome by an immense and foolish audacity; a hare that sits upright and glowers at its pursuer with great, bulging eyes; with ears erect but quivering, with nose pointed, but twitching. This hare, moreover, was six feet high and wore a headdress into the bargain of some antiquated kind which made her look still taller. Thus confronted, she stared at Orlando with a stare in which timidity and audacity were most strangely combined.

First, she asked him, with a proper, but somewhat clumsy curtsey, to forgive her her intrusion. Then, rising to her full height again, which must have been something over six feet two, she went on to say – but with such a cackle of nervous laughter, so much tee-heeing and haw-hawing that Orlando thought she must have escaped from a lunatic asylum – that she was the Archduchess Harriet Griselda of Finster-Aarhorn and Scandop-Boom in the Roumanian territory. She desired above all things to make his acquaintance, she said. She had taken lodging over a baker's shop at the Park Gates. She had seen his picture and it was the image of a sister of hers who was – here she guffawed – long since dead. She was visiting the English court. The Queen was her Cousin. The King was a very good fellow but seldom went to bed sober. Here she tee-heed and haw-hawed again. In short, there was nothing for it but to ask her in and give her a glass of wine.

Indoors, her manners regained the hauteur natural to a Roumanian Arch-duchess; and had she not shown a knowledge of wines rare in a lady, and made some observations upon firearms and the customs of sportsmen in her country, which were sensible enough, the talk would have lacked spontaneity. Jumping to her feet at last, she announced that she would call the following day, swept another prodigious curtsey and departed. The following day, Orlando rode out. The next, he turned his back; on the third he drew his curtain. On the fourth it rained, and as he could not keep a lady in the wet, nor was altogether averse to company, he invited her in and asked her opinion whether a suit of armour, which belonged to an ancestor of his, was the work of Jacobi or of Topp. He inclined to Topp. She held another opinion – it matters very little which. But it is of some importance to the course of our story that, in illustrating her argument, which had to do with the working of the tie pieces, the Archduchess Harriet took the golden shin case and fitted it to Orlando's leg.

That he had a pair of the shapeliest legs that any Nobleman has ever stood upright upon has already been said.

Perhaps something in the way she fastened the ankle buckle; or her stooping posture; or Orlando's long seclusion; or the natural sympathy which is between the sexes; or the Burgundy; or the fire – any of these causes may have been to blame; for certainly blame there is on one side or another, when a Nobleman of Orlando's breeding, entertaining a lady in his house, and she his elder by many years, with a face a yard long and staring eyes, dressed somewhat ridiculously too, in a mantle and riding cloak though the season was warm – blame there is when such a Nobleman is so suddenly and violently overcome by passion of some sort that he has to leave the room.

But what sort of passion, it may well be asked, could this be? And the answer is double faced as Love herself. For Love – but leaving Love out of the argument for a moment, the actual event was this:

When the Archduchess Harriet Griselda stooped to fasten the buckle, Orlando heard, suddenly and unaccountably, far off the beating of Love's wings. The distant stir of that soft plumage roused in him a thousand memories of rushing waters, of loveliness in the snow and faithlessness in the flood; and the sound came nearer; and he blushed and trembled; and he was moved as he had thought never to be moved again; and he was ready to raise his hands and let the bird of beauty alight upon his shoulders, when – horror! – a creaking sound like that the crows make tumbling over the trees

The Archduchess Harriet

began to reverberate; the air seemed dark with coarse black wings; voices croaked; bits of straw, twigs, and feathers dropped; and there pitched down upon his shoulders the heaviest and foulest of the birds; which is the vulture. Thus he rushed from the room and sent the footman to see the Archduchess Harriet to her carriage.

For Love, to which we may now return, has two faces; one white, the other black; two bodies; one smooth, the other hairy. It has two hands, two feet, two tails, two, indeed, of every member and each one is the exact opposite of the other. Yet, so strictly are they joined together that you cannot separate them. In this case, Orlando's love began her flight towards him with her white face turned, and her smooth and lovely body outwards. Nearer and nearer she came wafting before her airs of pure delight. All of a sudden (at the sight of the Archduchess presumably) she wheeled about, turned the other way round; showed herself black, hairy, brutish; and it was Lust the vulture, not Love, the Bird of Paradise, that flopped, foully and disgustingly, upon his shoulders. Hence he ran; hence he fetched the footman.

But the harpy is not so easily banished as all that. Not only did the Archduchess continue to lodge at the Baker's, but Orlando was haunted every day and night by phantoms of the foulest kind. Vainly, it seemed, had he furnished his house with silver and hung the walls with arras, when at any moment a dung-bedraggled fowl could settle upon his writing-table. There she was, flopping about among the chairs; he saw her waddling ungracefully across the galleries. Now, she perched, top heavy upon a fire screen. When he chased her out, back she came and pecked at the glass till she broke it.

Thus realising that his home was uninhabitable, and that steps must be taken to end the matter instantly, he did what any other young man would have done in his place, and asked King Charles to send him as Ambassador Extraordinary to Constantinople. The King was walking in Whitehall. Nell Gwyn was on his arm. She was pelting him with hazel nuts. 'Twas a thousand pities, that amorous lady sighed, that such a pair of legs should leave the country.

Howbeit, the Fates were hard; she could do no more than toss one kiss over her shoulder before Orlando sailed.

Chapter 3

It is, indeed, highly unfortunate, and much to be regretted that at this stage of Orlando's career, when he played a most important part in the public life of his country, we have least information to go upon. We know that he discharged his duties to admiration – witness his Bath and his Dukedom. We know that he had a finger in some of the most delicate negotiations between King Charles and the Turks – to that, treaties in the vault of the Record Office bear testimony. But the revolution which broke out during his period of office, and the fire which followed, have so damaged or destroyed all those papers from which any trustworthy record could be drawn, that what we can give is lamentably incomplete. Often the paper was scorched a deep brown in the middle of the most important sentence. Just when we thought to elucidate a secret that has puzzled historians for a hundred years, there was a hole in the manuscript big enough to put your finger through. We have done our best to piece out a meagre summary from the charred fragments that remain; but often it has been necessary to speculate, to surmise, and even to use the imagination.

Orlando's day was passed, it would seem, somewhat in this fashion. About seven, he would rise, wrap himself in a long Turkish cloak, light a cheroot, and lean his elbows on the parapet. Thus he would stand, gazing at the city beneath him, apparently entranced. At this hour the mist would lie so thick that the domes of Santa Sofia and the rest would seem to be afloat; gradually the mist would uncover them; the bubbles would be seen to be firmly fixed; there would be the river; there the Galata Bridge; there the green-turbaned pilgrims without eyes or noses, begging alms; there the pariah dogs picking up offal; there the shawled women; there the innumerable donkeys; there men on horses carrying long poles. Soon, the whole town would be astir with the cracking of whips, the beating of gongs, cryings to prayer, lashing of mules, and rattle of brass-bound wheels, while sour odours, made from bread fermenting and incense, and spice, rose even to the heights of Pera itself and seemed the very breath of the strident multicoloured and barbaric population.

Nothing, he reflected, gazing at the view which was now sparkling in the sun, could well be less like the counties of Surrey and Kent or the towns of London and Tunbridge Wells. To the right and left rose in bald and stony prominence the inhospitable Asian mountains, to which the arid castle of a robber chief or two might hang; but parsonage there was none, nor manor house, nor cottage, nor oak, elm, violet, ivy, or wild eglantine. There were no hedges for ferns to grow on, and no fields for sheep to graze. The houses were white as eggshells and as bald. That he, who was English root and fibre, should yet exult to the depths of his heart in this wild panorama, and gaze and gaze at those passes and far heights planning journeys there alone on foot where only the goat and shepherd had gone before; should feel a passion of affection for the bright, unseasonable flowers, love the unkempt, pariah dogs beyond even his elk-hounds at home, and snuff the acrid, sharp smell of the streets eagerly into his nostrils, surprised him. He wondered if, in the season of the Crusades, one of his ancestors had taken up with a Circassian peasant woman; thought it possible; fancied a certain darkness in his complexion; and, going indoors again, withdrew to his bath.

An hour later, properly scented, curled, and anointed, he would receive visits from secretaries and other high officials carrying, one after another, red boxes which yielded only to his own golden key. Within were papers of the highest importance, of which only fragments, here a flourish, there a seal firmly attached to a piece of burnt silk, now remain. Of their contents then, we cannot speak, but can only testify that Orlando was kept busy, what with his wax and seals, his various coloured ribbons which had to be diversely attached, his engrossing of titles and making of flourishes round capital letters, till luncheon came – a splendid meal of perhaps thirty courses.

After luncheon, lackeys announced that his coach and six was at the door, and he went, preceded by purple Janissaries running on foot and waving great ostrich-feather fans above their heads, to call upon the other ambassadors and dignitaries of state. The ceremony was always the same. On reaching the courtyard, the Janissaries struck with their fans upon the main portal, which immediately flew open revealing a large chamber, splendidly furnished. Here were seated two figures, generally of the opposite sexes. Profound bows and curtseys were exchanged. In the first room, it was permissible only to mention the weather. Having said that it was fine or wet, hot or cold, the Ambassador then passed on to the next chamber, where again, two figures rose to greet him. Here it was only permissible to compare Constantinople as a place of residence with London; and – the Ambassador naturally said that he preferred Constantinople, and his hosts naturally said, though they had not seen it, that they preferred London. In the next chamber, King Charles's and the Sultan's healths had to be discussed at some length. In the next were discussed the Ambassador's health and that of his host's wife, but more briefly. In the next the Ambassador complimented his host upon his furniture, and the host complimented the Ambassador upon his dress. In the next, sweetmeats were offered, the host deploring their badness, the Ambassador extolling their goodness. The ceremony ended at length with the smoking of a hookah and the drinking of a glass of coffee; but though the motions of smoking and drinking were gone through punctiliously there was neither tobacco in the pipe nor coffee in the glass, as, had either smoke or drink been real, the human frame would have sunk beneath the surfeit. For, no sooner had the Ambassador despatched one such visit, than another had to be under-taken. The same ceremonies were gone through in precisely the same order six or seven times over at the houses of the other great officials, so that it was often late at night before the Ambassador reached home. Though Orlando performed these tasks to admiration and never denied that they are, perhaps, the most important part of a diplomatist's duties, he was undoubtedly fatigued by them, and often depressed to such a pitch of gloom that he preferred to take his dinner alone with his dogs. To them, indeed, he might be heard talking in his own tongue. And sometimes, it is said, he would pass out of his own gates late at night so disguised that the sentries did not know him. Then he would mingle with the crowd on the Galata Bridge; or stroll through the bazaars; or throw aside his shoes and join the worshippers in the Mosques. Once, when it was given out that he was ill of a fever, shepherds, bringing their goats to market, reported that they had met an English Lord on the mountain top and heard him praying to his God. This was thought to be Orlando himself, and his prayer was, no doubt, a poem said aloud, for it was known that he still carried about with him, in the bosom of his cloak, a much scored manuscript; and servants, listening at the door, heard the Ambassador chanting something in an odd, singsong voice when he was alone.

It is with fragments such as these that we must do our best to make up a picture of Orlando's life and character at this time. There exist, even to this day, rumours, legends, anecdotes of a floating and unauthenticated kind about Orlando's life in Constantinople – (we have quoted but a few of them) which go to prove that he possessed, now that he was in the prime of life, the power to stir the fancy and rivet the eye which will keep a memory green long after all that more durable qualities can do to preserve it is forgotten. The power is a mysterious one compounded of beauty, birth, and some rarer gift, which we may call glamour and have done with it. 'A million candles', as Sasha had said, burnt in him without his being at the trouble of lighting a single one. He moved like a stag, without any need to think about his legs. He spoke in his ordinary voice and echo beat a silver gong. Hence rumours gathered round him. He became the adored of many women and some men. It was not necessary that they should speak to him or even that they should see him; they conjured up before them especially when the scenery was romantic, or the sun was setting, the figure of a noble gentleman in silk stockings. Upon the poor and uneducated, he had the same power as upon the rich. Shepherds, gypsies, donkey drivers, still sing songs about the English Lord 'who dropped his emeralds in the well', which undoubtedly refer to Orlando, who once, it seems, tore his jewels from him in a moment of rage or intoxication and flung them in a fountain; whence they were fished by a page boy. But this romantic power, it is well known, is often associated with a nature of extreme reserve. Orlando seems to have made no friends. As far as is known, he formed no attachments. A certain great lady came all the way from England in order to be near him, and pestered him with her attentions, but he continued to discharge his duties so indefatigably that he had not been Ambassador at the Horn more than two years and a half before King Charles signified his intention of raising him to the highest rank in the peerage. The envious said that this was Nell Gwyn's tribute to the memory of a leg. But, as she had seen him once only, and was then busily engaged in pelting her royal master with nutshells, it is likely that it was his merits that won him his Dukedom, not his calves.

Here we must pause, for we have reached a moment of great significance in his career. For the conferring of the Dukedom was the occasion of a very famous, and indeed, much disputed incident, which we must now describe, picking our way among burnt papers and little bits of tape as best we may. It was at the end of the great fast of Ramadan that the Order of the Bath and the patent of nobility arrived in a frigate commanded by Sir Adrian Scrope; and Orlando made this the occasion for an entertainment more splendid than any that has been known before or since in Constantinople. The night was fine; the crowd immense, and the windows of the Embassy brilliantly illuminated. Again, details are lacking, for the fire had its way with all such records, and has left only tantalising fragments which leave the most important points obscure. From the diary of John Fenner Brigge, however, an English naval officer, who was among the guests, we gather that people of all nationalities 'were packed like herrings in a barrel' in the courtyard. The crowd pressed so unpleasantly close that Brigge soon climbed into a Judas tree, the better to observe the proceedings. The rumour had got about among the natives (and here is additional proof of Orlando's mysterious power over the imagination) that some kind of miracle was to be performed. 'Thus,' writes Brigge (but his manuscript is full of burns and holes, some sentences being quite illegible), 'when the rockets began to soar into the air, there was considerable uneasiness among us lest the native population should be seized . . . fraught with unpleasant consequences to all . . . English ladies in the company, I own that my hand went to my cutlass. Happily,' he continues in his somewhat long-winded style, 'these fears seemed, for the moment, groundless and, observing the demeanour of the natives . . . I came to the conclusion that this demonstration of our skill in the art of pyrotechny was valuable, if only because it impressed upon them . . . the superiority of the British . . . Indeed, the sight was one of indescribable magnificence. I found myself alternately praising the Lord that he had permitted . . . and wishing that my poor, dear mother . . . By the Ambassador's orders, the long windows, which are so imposing a feature of Eastern architecture, for though ignorant in many ways . . . were thrown wide; and within, we could see a tableau vivant or theatrical display in which English ladies and gentlemen . . . represented a masque the work of one . . . The words were inaudible, but the sight of so many of our countrymen and women, dressed with the highest elegance and distinction . . . moved me to emotions of which I am certainly not ashamed, though unable . . . I was intent upon observing the astonishing conduct of Lady – which was of a nature to fasten the eyes of all upon her, and to bring discredit upon her sex and country, when' – unfortunately a branch of the Judas tree broke, Lieutenant Brigge fell to the ground, and the rest of the entry records only his gratitude to Providence (who plays a very large part in the diary) and the exact nature of his injuries.

Happily, Miss Penelope Hartopp, daughter of the General of that name, saw the scene from inside and carries on the tale in a letter, much defaced too, which ultimately reached a female friend at Tunbridge Wells. Miss Penelope was no less lavish in her enthusiasm than the gallant officer. 'Ravishing,' she exclaims ten times on one page, 'wondrous . . . utterly beyond description . . . gold plate . . . candelabras . . . negroes in plush breeches . . . pyramids of ice . . . fountains of negus . . . jellies made to represent His Majesty's ships . . . swans made to represent water lilies . . . birds in golden cages . . . gentlemen in slashed crimson velvet . . . Ladies' headdresses *at least six* foot high . . . musical boxes . . . Mr Peregrine said I looked *quite* lovely which I only repeat to you, my dearest, because I know . . . Oh! how I longed for you all! . . . surpassing anything we have seen at the Pantiles . . . oceans to drink . . . some gentlemen overcome . . . Lady Betty ravishing . . . Poor Lady Bonham made the unfortunate mistake of sitting down without a chair beneath her . . . Gentlemen all very gallant . . . wished a thousand times for you and dearest Betsy . . . But the sight of all others, the cynosure of all eyes . . . as all admitted, for none could be so vile as to deny it, was the Ambassador himself. Such a leg! Such a countenance!! Such princely manners!!! To see him come into the room! To see him go out again! And something *interesting* in the expression, which makes one feel, one scarcely knows why, that he has *suffered!* They say a lady was the cause of it. The heartless monster!!! How can one of our *reputed tender sex* have had the effrontery!!! He is unmarried, and half the ladies in the place are wild for love of him . . . A thousand, thousand kisses to Tom, Gerry, Peter, and dearest Mew' [presumably her cat].

From the Gazette of the time, we gather that 'as the clock struck twelve, the Ambassador appeared on the centre Balcony which was hung with priceless rugs. Six Turks of the Imperial Body Guard, each over six foot in height, held torches to his right and left. Rockets rose into the air at his appearance, and a great shout went up from the people, which the Ambassador acknowledged, bowing deeply, and speaking a few words of thanks in the Turkish language, which it was one of his accomplishments to speak with fluency. Next, Sir Adrian Scrope, in the full dress of a British Admiral, advanced; the Ambassador knelt on one knee; the Admiral placed the Collar of the Most Noble Order of the Bath round his neck, then pinned the Star to his breast; after which another gentleman of the diplomatic corps advancing in a stately manner placed on his shoulders the ducal robes, and handed him on a crimson cushion, the ducal coronet.'

At length, with a gesture of extraordinary majesty and grace, first bowing profoundly, then raising himself proudly erect, Orlando took the golden

Orlando as ambassador

circlet of strawberry leaves and placed it, with a gesture which none that saw it ever forgot, upon his brows. It was at this point that the first disturbance began. Either the people had expected a miracle – some say a shower of gold was prophesied to fall from the skies – which did not happen, or this was the signal chosen for the attack to begin; nobody seems to know; but as the coronet settled on Orlando's brows a great uproar rose. Bells began ringing; the harsh cries of the prophets were heard above the shouts of the people; many Turks fell flat to the ground and touched the earth with their foreheads. A door burst open. The natives pressed into the banqueting-rooms. Women shrieked. A certain lady, who was said to be dying for love of Orlando, seized a candelabra and dashed it to the ground. What might not have happened, had it not been for the presence of Sir Adrian Scrope and a squad of British blue-jackets, nobody can say. But the Admiral ordered the bugles to be sounded; a hundred blue-jackets stood instantly at attention; the disorder was quelled, and quiet, at least for the time being, fell upon the scene.

So far, we are on the firm, if rather narrow, ground of ascertained truth. But nobody has ever known exactly what took place later that night. The testimony of the sentries and others seems, however, to prove that the Embassy was empty of company, and shut up for the night in the usual way by two a.m. The Ambassador was seen to go to his room, still wearing the insignia of his rank, and shut the door. Some say he locked it, which was against his custom. Others maintain that they heard music of a rustic kind, such as shepherds play, later that night in the courtyard under the Ambassador's window. A washerwoman, who was kept awake by a toothache, said that she saw a man's figure, wrapped in a cloak or dressing gown, come out upon the balcony. Then, she said, a woman, much muffled, but apparently of the peasant class, was drawn up by means of a rope which the man let down to her on to the balcony. There, the washerwoman said, they embraced passionately 'like lovers', and went into the room together, drawing the curtains so that no more could be seen.

Next morning, the Duke, as we must now call him, was found by his secretaries sunk in profound slumber amid bed clothes that were much tumbled. The room was in some disorder, his coronet having rolled on the floor, and his cloak and garter being flung all of a heap on a chair. The table was littered with papers. No suspicion was felt at first, as the fatigues of the night had been great. But when afternoon came and he still slept, a doctor was summoned. He applied remedies which had been used on the previous occasion, plasters, nettles, emetics, etc., but without success. Orlando slept on. His secretaries then thought it their duty to examine the papers on the table. Many were scribbled over with poetry, in which frequent mention was made of an oak tree. There were also various state papers and others of a private nature concerning the management of his estates in England. But at length they came upon a document of far greater significance. It was nothing less, indeed, than a deed of marriage, drawn up, signed, and witnessed between his Lordship, Orlando, Knight of the Garter, etc., etc., etc., and Rosina Pepita, a dancer, father unknown, but reputed a gypsy, mother also unknown but reputed a seller of old iron in the marketplace over against the Galata Bridge. The secretaries looked at each other in dismay. And still Orlando slept. Morning and evening they watched him, but, save that his breathing was regular and his cheeks still flushed their habitual deep rose, he gave no sign of life. Whatever science or ingenuity could do to waken him they did. But still he slept.

On the seventh day of his trance (Thursday, May the 10th) the first shot was fired of that terrible and bloody insurrection of which Lieutenant Brigge had detected the first symptoms. The Turks rose against the Sultan, set fire to the town, and put every foreigner they could find, either to the sword or to the bastinado. A few English managed to escape; but, as might have been expected, the gentlemen of the British Embassy preferred to die in defence of their red boxes, or, in extreme cases, to swallow bunches of keys rather than let them fall into the hands of the Infidel. The rioters broke into Orlando's room, but seeing him stretched to all appearance dead they left him untouched, and only robbed him of his coronet and the robes of the Garter.

And now again obscurity descends, and would indeed that it were deeper! Would, we almost have it in our hearts to exclaim, that it were so deep that we could see nothing whatever through its opacity! Would that we might here take the pen and write Finis to our work! Would that we might spare the reader what is to come and say to him in so many words, Orlando died and was buried. But here, alas, Truth, Candour, and Honesty, the austere Gods who keep watch and ward by the inkpot of the biographer, cry No! Putting their silver trumpets to their lips they demand in one blast, Truth! And again they cry Truth! and sounding yet a third time in concert they peal forth, The Truth and nothing but the Truth!

At which – Heaven be praised! for it affords us a breathing space – the doors gently open, as if a breath of the gentlest and holiest zephyr had wafted them apart, and three figures enter. First, comes our Lady of Purity; whose brows are bound with fillets of the whitest lamb's wool; whose hair is as an avalanche of the driven snow; and in whose hand reposes the white quill of a virgin goose. Following her, but with a statelier step, comes our Lady of Chastity; on whose brow is set like a turret of burning but unwasting fire a diadem of icicles; her eyes are pure stars, and her fingers, if they touch you, freeze you to the bone. Close behind her, sheltering indeed in the shadow of her more stately sisters, comes our Lady of Modesty, frailest and fairest of the three; whose face is only shown as the young moon shows when it is thin and sickle shaped and half hidden among clouds. Each advances towards the centre of the room where Orlando still lies sleeping; and with gestures at once appealing and commanding, *Our Lady of Purity* speaks first:

'I am the guardian of the sleeping fawn; the snow is dear to me; and the moon rising; and the silver sea. With my robes I cover the speckled hen's eggs and the brindled sea shell; I cover vice and poverty. On all things frail or dark or doubtful, my veil descends. Wherefore, speak not, reveal not. Spare, O spare!'

Here the trumpets peal forth.

'Purity Avaunt! Begone Purity!'

Then *Our Lady Chastity* speaks: 'I am she whose touch freezes and whose glance turns to stone. I have stayed the star in its dancing, and the wave as it falls. The highest Alps are my dwelling place; and when I walk, the lightnings flash in my hair; where my eyes fall, they kill. Rather than let Orlando wake, I will freeze him to the bone. Spare, O spare!'

Here the trumpets peal forth.

'Chastity Avaunt! Begone Chastity!'

Then *Our Lady of Modesty* speaks, so low that one can hardly hear: 'I am she that men call Modesty. Virgin I am and ever shall be. Not for me the fruitful fields and the fertile vineyard. Increase is odious to me; and when the apples burgeon or the flocks breed, I run, I run; I let my mantle fall. My hair covers my eyes. I do not see. Spare, O spare!'

Again the trumpets peal forth: 'Modesty Avaunt! Begone Modesty!'

With gestures of grief and lamentation the three sisters now join hands and dance slowly, tossing their veils and singing as they go: 'Truth come not out from your horrid den. Hide deeper, fearful Truth. For you flaunt in the brutal gaze of the sun things that were better unknown and undone; you unveil the shameful; the dark you make clear, Hide! Hide! Hide!'

Here they make as if to cover Orlando with their draperies. The trumpets, meanwhile, still blare forth,

'The Truth and nothing but the Truth.'

At this the Sisters try to cast their veils over the mouths of the trumpets so as to muffle them, but in vain, for now all the trumpets blare forth together,

'Horrid Sisters, go!'

The sisters become distracted and wail in unison, still circling and flinging their veils up and down.

'It has not always been so! But men want us no longer; the women detest us. We go; we go. I *(Purity says this)* to the hen roost. I *(Chastity says)* to the still unravished heights of Surrey. I *(Modesty says this)* to any cosy nook where there are ivy and curtains in plenty.'

'For there, not here (all speak together joining hands and making gestures of farewell and despair towards the bed where Orlando lies sleeping) dwell still in nest and boudoir, office and lawcourt those who love us; those who honour us, virgins and city men; lawyers and doctors; those who prohibit; those who deny; those who reverence without knowing why; those who praise without understanding; the still very numerous (Heaven be praised) tribe of the respectable; who prefer to see not; desire to know not; love the darkness; those still worship us, and with reason; for we have given them Wealth, Prosperity, Comfort, Ease. To them we go, you we leave. Come, Sisters, come! This is no place for us here.'

They retire in haste, waving their draperies over their heads, as if to shut out something that they dare not look upon and close the door behind them.

We are, therefore, now left entirely alone in the room with the sleeping Orlando and the trumpeters. The trumpeters, ranging themselves side by side in order, blow one terrific blast –

'The Truth!'

at which Orlando woke.

He stretched himself. He rose. He stood upright in complete nakedness before us, and while the trumpets pealed Truth! Truth! Truth! we have no choice left but confess – he was a woman.

*　　*　　*

The sound of the trumpets died away and Orlando stood stark naked. No human being, since the world began, has ever looked more ravishing. His form combined in one the strength of a man and a woman's grace. As he stood there, the silver trumpets prolonged their note, as if reluctant to leave the lovely sight which their blast had called forth; and Chastity, Purity, and Modesty, inspired, no doubt, by Curiosity, peeped in at the door and threw a garment like a towel at the naked form which, unfortunately, fell short by several inches. Orlando looked himself up and down in a long looking-glass, without showing any signs of discomposure, and went, presumably, to his bath.

We may take advantage of this pause in the narrative to make certain statements. Orlando had become a woman there is no denying it. But in every other respect, Orlando remained precisely as he had been. The change of sex, though it altered their future, did nothing whatever to alter their identity. Their faces remained, as their portraits prove, practically the same. His memory – but in future we must, for convention's sake, say 'her' for 'his', and 'she' for 'he' – her memory then, went back through all the events of her past life without encountering any obstacle. Some slight haziness there may have been, as if a few dark drops had fallen into the clear pool of memory; certain things had become a little dimmed; but that was all. The change seemed to have been accomplished painlessly and completely and in such a way that Orlando herself showed no surprise at it. Many people, taking this into account, and holding that such a change of sex is against nature, have been at great pains to prove (1) that Orlando had always been a woman, (2) that Orlando is at this moment a man. Let biologists and psychologists determine. It is enough for us to state the simple fact; Orlando was a man till the age of thirty; when he became a woman and has remained so ever since.

But let other pens treat of sex and sexuality; we quit such odious subjects as soon as we can. Orlando had now washed, and dressed herself in those Turkish coats and trousers which can be worn indifferently by either sex; and was forced to consider her position. That it was precarious and embarrassing in the extreme must be the first thought of every reader who has followed her story with sympathy. Young, noble, beautiful, she had woken to find herself in a position than which we can conceive none more delicate for a young lady of rank. We should not have blamed her had she rung the bell, screamed, or fainted. But Orlando showed no such signs of perturbation. All her actions were deliberate in the extreme, and might indeed have been thought to show tokens of premeditation. First, she carefully examined the papers on the table; took such as seemed to be written in poetry, and secreted them in her bosom; next she called her Seleuchi hound, which had never left her bed all these days, though half famished with hunger, fed and combed him; then stuck a pair of pistols in her belt; finally wound about her person several strings of emeralds and pearls of the finest orient which had formed part of her Ambassadorial wardrobe. This done, she leant out of the window, gave one low whistle, and descended the shattered and blood-stained staircase, now strewn with the litter of wastepaper baskets, treaties, despatches, seals, sealing wax, etc., and so entered the courtyard. There, in the shadow of a giant fig tree, waited an old gypsy on a donkey. He led another by the bridle. Orlando swung her leg over it; and thus, attended by a lean dog, riding a donkey, in company of a gypsy, the Ambassador of Great Britain at the Court of the Sultan left Constantinople.

They rode for several days and nights and met with a variety of adventures, some at the hands of men, some at the hands of nature, in all of which Orlando acquitted herself with courage. Within a week they reached the high ground outside Broussa, which was then the chief camping ground of the gypsy tribe to which Orlando had allied herself. Often she had looked at those mountains from her balcony at the Embassy; often had longed to be there; and to find oneself where one has longed to be always, to a reflective mind, gives food for thought. For some time, however, she was too well pleased with the change to spoil it by thinking. The pleasure of having no documents to seal or sign, no flourishes to make, no calls to pay, was enough. The gypsies followed the grass; when it was grazed down, on they moved again. She washed in streams if she washed at all; no boxes, red, blue, or green, were presented to her; there was not a key, let alone a golden key, in the whole camp; as for 'visiting', the word was unknown. She milked the goats; she collected brushwood; she stole a hen's egg now and then, but always put a coin or a pearl in place of it; she herded cattle; she stripped vines; she trod the grape; she filled the goatskin and drank from it; and when she remembered how, at about this time of day, she should have been making the motions of drinking and smoking over an empty coffee-cup and a pipe which lacked tobacco, she laughed aloud, cut herself another hunch of bread, and begged for a puff from old Rustum's pipe, filled though it was with cow dung.

The gypsies, with whom it is obvious that she must have been in secret communication before the revolution, seem to have looked upon her as one of themselves (which is always the highest compliment a people can pay), and her dark hair and dark complexion bore out the belief that she was, by birth, one of them and had been snatched by an English Duke from a nut tree when she was a baby and taken to that barbarous land where people live in houses because they are too feeble and diseased to stand the open air. Thus, though in many ways inferior to them, they were willing to help her to become more like them; taught her their arts of cheese-making and basket-weaving, their science of stealing and bird-snaring, and were even prepared to consider letting her marry among them.

But Orlando had contracted in England some of the customs or diseases (whatever you choose to consider them) which cannot, it seems, be expelled. One evening, when they were all sitting round the camp fire and the sunset was blazing over the Thessalian hills, Orlando exclaimed: 'How good to eat!' (The gypsies have no word for 'beautiful'. This is the nearest.)

All the young men and women burst out laughing uproariously. The sky good to eat, indeed! The elders, however, who had seen more of foreigners than they had, became suspicious. They noticed that Orlando often sat for whole hours doing nothing whatever, except look here and then there; they would come upon her on some hilltop staring straight in front of her, no matter whether the goats were grazing or straying. They began to suspect that she had other beliefs than their own, and the older men and women thought it probable that she had fallen into the clutches of the vilest and cruellest among all the Gods, which is Nature. Nor were they far wrong. The English disease, a love of Nature, was inborn in her, and here, where Nature was so much larger and more powerful than in England, she fell into its hands as she had never done before. The malady is too well known, and has been, alas, too often described to need describing afresh, save very briefly. There were mountains; there were valleys; there were streams. She climbed the mountains; roamed the valleys; sat on the banks of the streams. She likened the hills to ramparts, to the breasts of doves, and the flanks of kine. She compared the flowers to enamel and the turf to Turkey rugs worn thin. Trees were withered hags, and sheep were grey boulders. Everything, in fact, was something else. She found the tarn on the mountain-top and almost threw herself in to seek the wisdom she thought lay hid there; and when, from the mountain-top, she beheld far off, across the Sea of Marmara, the plains of Greece, and made out (her eyes were admirable) the Acropolis with a white streak or two which must, she thought, be the Parthenon, her soul expanded with her eyeballs, and she prayed that she might share the majesty of the hills, know the serenity of the plains, etc. etc., as all such believers do. Then, looking down, the red hyacinth, the purple iris wrought her to cry out in ecstasy at the goodness, the beauty of nature; raising her eyes again, she beheld the eagle soaring, and imagined its raptures and made them her own. Returning home, she saluted each star, each peak, and each watch-fire as if they signalled to her alone; and at last, when she flung herself upon her mat in the gypsies' tent, she could not help bursting out again, How good to eat! How good to eat! (For it is a curious fact that though human beings have such imperfect means of communication, that they can only say 'good to eat' when they mean 'beautiful' and the other way about, they will yet endure ridicule and misunderstanding rather than keep any experience to themselves.) All the young gypsies laughed. But Rustum el Sadi, the old man who had brought Orlando out of Constantinople on his donkey, sat silent. He had a nose like a scimitar; his cheeks were furrowed as if from the age-long descent of iron hail; he was brown and keen-eyed, and as he sat tugging at his hookah he observed Orlando narrowly. He had the deepest suspicion that her God was Nature. One day he found her in tears. Interpreting this to mean that her God had punished her, he told her that he was not surprised. He showed her the fingers of his left hand, withered by the frost; he showed her his right foot, crushed where a rock had fallen. This, he said, was what her God did to men. When she said, 'But so beautiful', using the English word, he shook his head; and when she repeated it he was angry. He saw that she did not believe what he believed, and that was enough, wise and ancient as he was, to enrage him.

This difference of opinion disturbed Orlando, who had been perfectly happy until now. She began to think, was Nature beautiful or cruel; and then she asked herself what this beauty was; whether it was in things themselves, or only in herself; so she went on to the nature of reality, which led her to truth, which in its turn led to Love, Friendship, Poetry (as in the days on the high mound at home); which meditations, since she could impart no word of them, made her long, as she had never longed before, for pen and ink.

'Oh! if only I could write!' she cried (for she had the odd conceit of those who write that words written are shared). She had no ink; and but little paper. But she made ink from berries and wine; and finding a few margins and blank spaces in the manuscript of 'The Oak Tree', managed, by writing a kind of shorthand, to describe the scenery in a long, blank verse poem, and to carry on a dialogue with herself about this Beauty and Truth concisely enough. This kept her extremely happy for hours on end. But the gypsies became suspicious. First, they noticed that she was less adept than before at milking and cheese-making; next, she often hesitated before replying; and once a gypsy boy who had been asleep, woke in a terror feeling her eyes upon him. Sometimes this constraint would be felt by the whole tribe, numbering some dozens of grown men and women. It sprang from the sense they had (and their senses are very sharp and much in advance of their vocabulary) that whatever they were doing crumbled like ashes in their hands. An old woman making a basket, a boy skinning a sheep, would be singing or crooning contentedly at their work, when Orlando would come into the camp, fling herself down by the fire and gaze into the flames. She need not even look at them, and yet they felt, here is someone who doubts; (we make a rough-and-ready translation from the gypsy language) here is someone who does not do the thing for the sake of doing; nor looks for looking's sake; here is someone who believes neither in sheepskin nor basket; but sees (here they looked apprehensively about the tent) something else. Then a vague but most unpleasant feeling would begin to work in the boy and in the old woman. They broke their withys; they cut their fingers. A great rage filled them. They wished Orlando would leave the tent and never come near them again. Yet she was of a cheerful and willing disposition, they owned; and one of her pearls was enough to buy the finest herd of goats in Broussa.

Slowly, she began to feel that there was some difference between her and the gypsies which made her hesitate sometimes to marry and settle down among them for ever. At first she tried to account for it by saying that she came of an ancient and civilised race, whereas these gypsies were an ignorant people, not much better than savages. One night when they were questioning her about England she could not help with some pride describing the house where she was born, how it had 365 bedrooms and had been in the possession of her family for four or five hundred years. Her ancestors were earls, or even dukes, she added. At this she noticed again that the gypsies were uneasy; but not angry as before when she had praised the beauty of nature. Now they were courteous, but concerned as people of fine breeding are when a stranger has been made to reveal his low birth or poverty. Rustum followed her out of the tent alone and said that she need not mind if her father were a Duke, and possessed all the bedrooms and furniture that she described. They would none of them think the worse of her for that. Then she was seized with a shame that she had never felt before. It was clear that Rustum and the other gypsies thought a descent of four or five hundred years only the meanest possible. Their own families went back at least two or three thousand years. To the gypsy whose ancestors had built the Pyramids centuries before Christ was born, the genealogy of Howards and Plantagenets was no better and no worse than that of the Smiths and the Joneses: both were negligible. Moreover, where the shepherd boy had a lineage of such antiquity, there was nothing specially memorable or desirable in ancient birth; vagabonds and beggars all shared it. And then, though he was too courteous to speak openly, it was clear that the gypsy thought that there was no more vulgar ambition than to possess bedrooms by the hundred (they were on top of a hill as they spoke; it was night; the mountains rose around them) when the whole earth is ours. Looked at from the gypsy point of view, a Duke, Orlando understood, was nothing but a profiteer or robber who snatched land and money from people who rated these things of little worth, and could think of nothing better to do than to build three hundred and sixty-five bedrooms when one was enough, and none was even better than one. She could not deny that her ancestors had accumulated field after field; house after house; honour after honour; yet had none of them been saints or heroes, or great benefactors of the human race. Nor could she counter the argument (Rustum was too much of a gentleman to press it, but she understood) that any man who did now what her ancestors had done three or four hundred years ago would be denounced – and by her own family most loudly – for a vulgar upstart, an adventurer, a *nouveau riche*.

She sought to answer such arguments by the familiar if oblique method of finding the gypsy life itself rude and barbarous; and so, in a short time, much bad blood was bred between them. Indeed, such differences of opinion are enough to cause bloodshed and revolution. Towns have been sacked for less, and a million martyrs have suffered at the stake rather than yield an inch upon any of the points here debated. No passion is stronger in the breast of man than the desire to make others believe as he believes. Nothing so cuts at the root of his happiness and fills him with rage as the sense that another rates low what he prizes high. Whigs and Tories, Liberal party and Labour party – for what do they battle except their own prestige? It is not love of truth but desire to prevail that sets quarter against quarter and makes parish desire the downfall of parish. Each seeks peace of mind and subserviency rather than the triumph of truth and the exaltation of virtue – but these moralities belong, and should be left to the historian, since they are as dull as ditch water.

'Four hundred and seventy-six bedrooms mean nothing to them,' sighed Orlando.

'She prefers a sunset to a flock of goats,' said the gypsies.

What was to be done, Orlando could not think. To leave the gypsies and become once more an Ambassador seemed to her intolerable. But it was equally impossible to remain for ever where there was neither ink nor writing paper, neither reverence for the Talbots nor respect for a multiplicity of bedrooms. So she was thinking, one fine morning on the slopes of Mount Athos, when minding her goats. And then Nature, in whom she trusted, either played her a trick or worked a miracle – again, opinions differ too much for it to be possible to say which. Orlando was gazing rather discon-solately at the steep hillside in front of her. It was now midsummer, and if we must compare the landscape to anything, it would have been to a dry bone; to a sheep's skeleton; to a gigantic skull picked white by a thousand vultures. The heat was intense, and the little fig tree under which Orlando lay only served to print patterns of fig-leaves upon her light burnous.

Suddenly a shadow, though there was nothing to cast a shadow, appeared on the bald mountain-side opposite. It deepened quickly and soon a green hollow showed where there had been barren rock before. As she looked, the hollow deepened and widened, and a great park-like space opened in the flank of the hill. Within, she could see an undulating and grassy lawn; she could see oak trees dotted here and there; she could see the thrushes hopping among the branches. She could see the deer stepping delicately from shade to shade, and could even hear the hum of insects and the gentle sighs and shivers of a summer's day in England. After she had gazed entranced for some time, snow began falling; soon the whole landscape was covered and marked with violet shades instead of yellow sunlight. Now she saw heavy carts coming along the roads, laden with tree trunks, which they were taking, she knew, to be sawn for firewood; and then there appeared the roofs and belfries and towers and courtyards of her own home. The snow was falling steadily, and she could now hear the slither and flop which it made as it slid down the roof and fell to the ground. The smoke went up from a thousand chimneys. All was so clear and minute that she could see a daw pecking for worms in the snow. Then, gradually, the violet shadows deepened and closed over the carts and the lawns and the great house itself. All was swallowed up. Now there was nothing left of the grassy hollow, and instead of the green lawns was only the blazing hillside which a thousand vultures seemed to have picked bare. At this, she burst into a passion of tears, and striding back to the gypsies' camp, told them that she must sail for England the very next day.

It was happy for her that she did so. Already the young men had plotted her death. Honour, they said, demanded it, for she did not think as they did. Yet they would have been sorry to cut her throat; and welcomed the news of her departure. An English merchant ship, as luck would have it, was already under sail in the harbour about to return to England; and Orlando, by breaking off another pearl from her necklace, not only paid her passage but had some bank-notes left over in her wallet. These she would have liked to present to the gypsies. But they despised wealth she knew; and she had to content herself with embraces, which on her part were sincere.

Chapter 4

With some of the guineas left from the sale of the tenth pearl of her string, Orlando had bought herself a complete outfit of such clothes as women then wore, and it was in the dress of a young Englishwoman of rank that she now sat on the deck of the *Enamoured Lady*. It is a strange fact, but a true one, that up to this moment she had scarcely given her sex a thought. Perhaps the Turkish trousers which she had hitherto worn had done something to distract her thoughts; and the gypsy women, except in one or two important particulars, differ very little from the gypsy men. At any rate, it was not until she felt the coil of skirts about her legs and the Captain offered, with the greatest politeness, to have an awning spread for her on deck, that she realised with a start the penalties and the privileges of her position. But that start was not of the kind that might have been expected.

It was not caused, that is to say, simply and solely by the thought of her chastity and how she could preserve it. In normal circumstances a lovely young woman alone would have thought of nothing else; the whole edifice of female government is based on that foundation stone; chastity is their jewel, their centrepiece, which they run mad to protect, and die when ravished of. But if one has been a man for thirty years or so, and an Ambassador into the bargain, if one has held a Queen in one's arms and one or two other ladies, if report be true, of less exalted rank, if one has married a Rosina Pepita, and so on, one does not perhaps give such a very great start about that. Orlando's start was of a very complicated kind, and not to be summed up in a trice. Nobody, indeed, ever accused her of being one of those quick wits who run to the end of things in a minute. It took her the entire length of the voyage to moralise out the meaning of her start, and so, at her own pace, we will follow her.

'Lord,' she thought, when she had recovered from her start, stretching herself out at length under her awning, 'this is a pleasant, lazy way of life, to be sure. But', she thought, giving her legs a kick, 'these skirts are plaguey things to have about one's heels. Yet the stuff (flowered paduasoy) is the loveliest in the world. Never have I seen my own skin (here she laid her hand on her knee) look to such advantage as now. Could I, however, leap over-board and swim in clothes like these? No! Therefore, I should have to trust to the protection of a blue-jacket. Do I object to that? Now do I?' she wondered, here encountering the first knot in the smooth skein of her argument.

Dinner came before she had untied it, and then it was the Captain himself – Captain Nicholas Benedict Bartolus, a sea-captain of distinguished aspect, who did it for her as he helped her to a slice of corned beef.

'A little of the fat, Ma'am?' he asked. 'Let me cut you just the tiniest little slice the size of your finger nail.' At those words a delicious tremor ran through her frame. Birds sang; the torrents rushed. It recalled the feeling of indescribable pleasure with which she had first seen Sasha, hundreds of years ago. Then she had pursued, now she fled. Which is the greater ecstasy? The man's or the woman's? And are they not perhaps the same? No, she thought, this is the most delicious (thanking the Captain but refusing), to refuse, and see him frown. Well, she would, if he wished it, have the very thinnest, smallest shiver in the world. This was the most delicious of all, to yield and see him smile. 'For nothing', she thought, regaining her couch on deck, and continuing the argument, 'is more heavenly than to resist and to yield; to yield and to resist. Surely it throws the spirit into such a rapture as nothing else can. So that I'm not sure', she continued, 'that I won't throw myself overboard, for the mere pleasure of being rescued by a blue-jacket after all.'

(It must be remembered that she was like a child entering into possession of a pleasaunce or toy cupboard; her arguments would not commend themselves to mature women, who have had the run of it all their lives.)

'But what used we young fellows in the cockpit of the *Marie Rose* to say about a woman who threw herself overboard for the pleasure of being rescued by a blue-jacket?' she said. 'We had a word for them. Ah! I have it . . . ' (But we must omit that word; it was disrespectful in the extreme and passing strange on a lady's lips.) 'Lord! Lord!' she cried again at the conclusion of her thoughts, 'must I then begin to respect the opinion of the other sex, however monstrous I think it? If I wear skirts, if I can't swim, if I have to be rescued by a blue-jacket, by God!' she cried, 'I must!' Upon which a gloom fell over her. Candid by nature, and averse to all kinds of equivocation, to tell lies bored her. It seemed to her a roundabout way of going to work. Yet, she reflected, the flowered paduasoy – the pleasure of being rescued by a blue-jacket – if these were only to be obtained by roundabout ways, roundabout one must go, she supposed. She remembered how, as a young man, she had insisted that women must be obedient, chaste, scented, and exquisitely apparelled. 'Now I shall have to pay in my own person for those desires,' she reflected; 'for women are not (judging by my own short experience of the sex) obedient, chaste, scented, and exquisitely apparelled by nature. They can only attain these graces, without which they may enjoy none of the delights of life, by the most tedious discipline. There's the hairdressing,' she thought, 'that alone will take an hour of my morning; there's looking in the looking-glass, another hour; there's staying and lacing; there's washing and powdering; there's changing from silk to lace and from lace to paduasoy; there's being chaste year in year out . . . ' Here she tossed her foot impatiently, and showed an inch or two of calf. A sailor on the mast, who happened to look down at the moment, started so violently that he missed his footing and only saved himself by the skin of his teeth. 'If the sight of my ankles means death to an honest fellow who, no doubt, has a wife and family to support, I must, in all humanity, keep them covered,' Orlando thought. Yet her legs were among her chiefest beauties. And she fell to thinking what an odd pass we have come to when all a woman's beauty has to be kept covered lest a sailor may fall from a mast-head. 'A pox on them!' she said, realising for the first time what, in other circumstances, she would have been taught as a child, that is to say, the sacred responsibilities of womanhood.

'And that's the last oath I shall ever be able to swear,' she thought; 'once I set foot on English soil. And I shall never be able to crack a man over the head, or tell him he lies in his teeth, or draw my sword and run him through the body, or sit among my peers, or wear a coronet, or walk in procession, or sentence a man to death, or lead an army, or prance down Whitehall on a charger, or wear seventy-two different medals on my breast. All I can do, once I set foot on English soil, is to pour out tea and ask my lords how they like it. D'you take sugar. D'you take cream?' And mincing out the words, she was horrified to perceive how low an opinion she was forming of the other sex, the manly, to which it had once been her pride to belong. 'To fall from a mast-head,' she thought, 'because you see a woman's ankles; to dress up like a Guy Fawkes and parade the streets, so that women may praise you; to deny a woman teaching lest she may laugh at you; to be the slave of the frailest chit in petticoats, and yet to go about as if you were the Lords of creation – Heavens!' she thought, 'what fools they make of us – what fools we are!' And here it would seem from some ambiguity in her terms that she was censuring both sexes equally, as if she belonged to neither; and indeed, for the time being, she seemed to vacillate; she was man; she was woman; she knew the secrets, shared the weaknesses of each. It was a most bewildering and whirligig state of mind to be in. The comforts of ignorance seemed utterly denied her. She was a feather blown on the gale. Thus it is no great wonder, as she pitted one sex against the other, and found each alternately full of the most deplorable infirmities, and was not sure to which she belonged – it was no great wonder that she was about to cry out that she would return to Turkey and become a gypsy again when the anchor fell with a great splash into the sea; the sails came tumbling on deck, and she perceived (so sunk had she been in thought that she had seen nothing for several days) that the ship was anchored off the coast of Italy. The Captain at once sent to ask the honour of her company ashore with him in the long-boat.

When she returned the next morning, she stretched herself on her couch under the awning and arranged her draperies with the greatest decorum about her ankles.

'Ignorant and poor as we are compared with the other sex,' she thought, continuing the sentence which she had left unfinished the other day, 'armoured with every weapon as they are, while they debar us even from a knowledge of the alphabet' (and from these opening words it is plain that something had happened during the night to give her a push towards the female sex, for she was speaking more as a woman speaks than as a man, yet with a sort of content after all), 'still – they fall from the mast-head.' Here she gave a great yawn and fell asleep. When she woke, the ship was sailing before a fair breeze so near the shore that towns on the cliffs' edge seemed only kept from slipping into the water by the interposition of some great rock or the twisted roots of some ancient olive tree. The scent of oranges wafted from a million trees, heavy with the fruit, reached her on deck. A score of blue dolphins, twisting their tails, leapt high now and again into the air. Stretching her arms out (arms, she had learnt already, have no such fatal effects as legs), she thanked Heaven that she was not prancing down Whitehall on a war-horse, nor even sentencing a man to death. 'Better is it,' she thought, 'to be clothed with poverty and ignorance, which are the dark garments of the female sex; better to leave the rule and discipline of the world to others; better be quit of martial ambition, the love of power, and all the other manly desires if so one can more fully enjoy the most exalted raptures known to the human spirit, which are,' she said aloud, as her habit was when deeply moved, 'contemplation, solitude, love.'

'Praise God that I'm a woman!' she cried, and was about to run into the extreme folly – than which none is more distressing in woman or man either – of being proud of her sex, when she paused over the singular word, which, for all we can do to put it in its place, has crept in at the end of the last sentence: Love. 'Love,' said Orlando. Instantly – such is its impetuosity – love took a human shape – such is its pride. For where other thoughts are content to remain abstract, nothing will satisfy this one but to put on flesh and blood, mantilla and petticoats, hose and jerkin. And as all Orlando's loves had been women, now, through the culpable laggardry of the human frame to adapt itself to convention, though she herself was a woman, it was still a woman she loved; and if the consciousness of being of the same sex had any effect at all, it was to quicken and deepen those feelings which she had had as a man. For now a thousand hints and mysteries became plain to her that were then dark. Now, the obscurity, which divides the sexes and lets linger innumerable impurities in its gloom, was removed, and if there is anything in what the poet says about truth and beauty, this affection gained in beauty what it lost in falsity. At last, she cried, she knew Sasha as she was, and in the ardour of this discovery, and in the pursuit of all those treasures which were now revealed, she was so rapt and enchanted that it was as if a cannon ball had exploded at her ear when a man's voice said, 'Permit me, Madam,' a man's hand raised her to her feet; and the fingers of a man with a three-masted sailing ship tattooed on the middle finger pointed to the horizon.

'The cliffs of England, Ma'am,' said the Captain, and he raised the hand which had pointed at the sky to the salute. Orlando now gave a second start, even more violent than the first.

'Christ Jesus!' she cried.

Happily, the sight of her native land after long absence excused both start and exclamation, or she would have been hard put to it to explain to Captain Bartolus the raging and conflicting emotions which now boiled within her. How tell him that she, who now trembled on his arm, had been a Duke and an Ambassador? How explain to him that she, who had been lapped like a lily in folds of paduasoy, had hacked heads off, and lain with loose women among treasure sacks in the holds of pirate ships on summer nights when the tulips were abloom and the bees buzzing off Wapping Old Stairs? Not even to herself could she explain the giant start she gave, as the resolute right hand of the sea-captain indicated the cliffs of the British Islands.

'To refuse and to yield,' she murmured, 'how delightful; to pursue and to conquer, how august; to perceive and to reason, how sublime.' Not one of these words so coupled together seemed to her wrong; nevertheless, as the chalky cliffs loomed nearer, she felt culpable; dishonoured; unchaste, which, for one who had never given the matter a thought, was strange. Closer and closer they drew, till the samphire gatherers, hanging halfway down the cliff, were plain to the naked eye. And watching them, she felt, scampering up and down within her, like some derisive ghost who in another instant will pick up her skirts and flaunt out of sight, Sasha the lost, Sasha the memory, whose reality she had proved just now so surprisingly – Sasha, she felt, mopping and mowing and making all sorts of disrespectful gestures towards the cliffs and the samphire gatherers; and when the sailors began chanting, 'So goodbye and adieu to you, Ladies of Spain,' the words echoed in Orlando's sad heart, and she felt that however much landing there meant comfort, meant opulence, meant consequence and state (for she would doubtless pick up some noble Prince and reign, his consort, over half Yorkshire), still, if it meant conventionality, meant slavery, meant deceit, meant denying her love, fettering her limbs, pursing her lips, and restraining her tongue, then she would turn about with the ship and set sail once more for the gypsies.

Among the hurry of these thoughts, however, there now rose, like a dome of smooth, white marble, something which, whether fact or fancy, was so impressive to her fevered imagination that she settled upon it as one has seen a swarm of vibrant dragonflies alight, with apparent satisfaction, upon the glass bell which shelters some tender vegetable. The form of it, by the hazard of fancy, recalled that earliest, most persistent memory – the man with the big forehead in Twitchett's sitting-room, the man who sat writing, or rather looking, but certainly not at her, for he never seemed to see her poised there in all her finery, lovely boy though she must have been, she could not deny it – and whenever she thought of him, the thought spread round it, like the risen moon on turbulent waters, a sheet of silver calm. Now her hand went to her bosom (the other was still in the Captain's keeping), where the pages of her poem were hidden safe. It might have been a talisman that she kept there. The distraction of sex, which hers was, and what it meant, subsided; she thought now only of the glory of poetry, and

the great lines of Marlowe, Shakespeare, Ben Jonson, Milton began booming and reverberating, as if a golden clapper beat against a golden bell in the
cathedral tower which was her mind. The truth was that the image of the
marble dome which her eyes had first discovered so faintly that it suggested
a poet's forehead and thus started a flock of irrelevant ideas, was no figment,
but a reality; and as the ship advanced down the Thames before a favouring
gale, the image with all its associations gave place to the truth, and revealed
itself as nothing more and nothing less than the dome of a vast cathedral
rising among a fretwork of white spires.

'St Paul's,' said Captain Bartolus, who stood by her side. 'The Tower of
London,' he continued. 'Greenwich Hospital, erected in memory of Queen
Mary by her husband, his late majesty, William the Third. Westminster
Abbey. The Houses of Parliament.' As he spoke, each of these famous
buildings rose to view. It was a fine September morning. A myriad of little
water-craft plied from bank to bank. Rarely has a gayer, or more interesting,
spectacle presented itself to the gaze of a returned traveller. Orlando hung
over the prow, absorbed in wonder. Her eyes had been used too long to
savages and nature not to be entranced by these urban glories. That, then,
was the dome of St Paul's which Mr Wren had built during her absence.
Near by, a shock of golden hair burst from a pillar – Captain Bartolus was at
her side to inform her that that was the Monument; there had been a plague
and a fire during her absence, he said. Do what she would to restrain them,
the tears came to her eyes, until, remembering that it is becoming in a
woman to weep, she let them flow. Here, she thought, had been the great
carnival. Here, where the waves slapped briskly, had stood the Royal Pavilion. Here she had first met Sasha. About here (she looked down into the
sparkling waters) one had been used to see the frozen bumboat woman with
her apples on her lap. All that splendour and corruption was gone. Gone,
too, was the dark night, the monstrous downpour, the violent surges of the
flood. Here, where yellow icebergs had raced circling with a crew of terror-
stricken wretches on top, a covey of swans floated, orgulous, undulant,
superb. London itself had completely changed since she had last seen it.
Then, she remembered, it had been a huddle of little black, beetle-browed
houses. The heads of rebels had grinned on pikes at Temple Bar. The
cobbled pavements had reeked of garbage and ordure. Now, as the ship
sailed past Wapping, she caught glimpses of broad and orderly thoroughfares. Stately coaches drawn by teams of well-fed horses stood at the doors
of houses whose bow windows, whose plate glass, whose polished knockers,
testified to the wealth and modest dignity of the dwellers within. Ladies in
flowered silk (she put the Captain's glass to her eye) walked on raised
footpaths. Citizens in broidered coats took snuff at street corners under
lamp-posts. She caught sight of a variety of painted signs swinging in the
breeze and could form a rapid notion from what was painted on them of the
tobacco, of the stuff, of the silk, of the gold, of the silver ware, of the gloves,

Orlando on her return to England

of the perfumes, and of a thousand other articles which were sold within. Nor could she do more as the ship sailed to its anchorage by London Bridge than glance at coffee-house windows where, on balconies, since the weather was fine, a great number of decent citizens sat at ease, with china dishes in front of them, clay pipes by their sides, while one among them read from a news sheet, and was frequently interrupted by the laughter or the comments of the others. Were these taverns, were these wits, were these poets? she asked of Captain Bartolus, who obligingly informed her that even now if she turned her head a little to the left and looked along the line of his first finger – so – they were passing the Cocoa Tree, where – yes, there he was – one might see Mr Addison taking his coffee; the other two gentlemen – 'there, Ma'am, a little to the right of the lamp-post, one of 'em humped, t'other much the same as you or me' – were Mr Dryden and Mr Pope.* 'Sad dogs,' said the Captain, by which he meant that they were Papists, 'but men of parts, none the less,' he added, hurrying aft to superintend the arrangements for landing.

'Addison, Dryden, Pope,' Orlando repeated as if the words were an incantation. For one moment she saw the high mountains above Broussa, the next, she had set her foot upon her native shore.

But now Orlando was to learn how little the most tempestuous flutter of excitement avails against the iron countenance of the law; how harder than the stones of London Bridge it is, and than the lips of a cannon more severe. No sooner had she returned to her home in Blackfriars than she was made aware by a succession of Bow Street runners and other grave emissaries from the Law Courts that she was a party to three major suits which had been preferred against her during her absence, as well as innumerable minor litigations, some arising out of, others depending on them. The chief charges against her were (1) that she was dead, and therefore could not hold any property whatsoever; (2) that she was a woman, which amounts to much the same thing; (3) that she was an English Duke who had married one Rosina Pepita, a dancer; and had had by her three sons, which sons now declaring that their father was deceased, claimed that all his property descended to them. Such grave charges as these would, of course, take time and money to dispose of. All her estates were put in Chancery and her titles pronounced in abeyance while the suits were under litigation. Thus it was in a highly ambiguous condition, uncertain whether she was alive or dead, man or woman, Duke or nonentity, that she posted down to her country seat, where, pending the legal judgment, she had the Law's permission to reside in a state of incognito or incognita, as the case might turn out to be.

It was a fine evening in December when she arrived and the snow was

---

* The Captain must have been mistaken, as a reference to any textbook of literature will show; but the mistake was a kindly one, and so we let it stand.

falling and the violet shadows were slanting much as she had seen them from the hilltop at Broussa. The great house lay more like a town than a house, brown and blue, rose and purple in the snow, with all its chimneys smoking busily as if inspired with a life of their own. She could not restrain a cry as she saw it there tranquil and massive, couched upon the meadows. As the yellow coach entered the park and came bowling along the drive between the trees, the red deer raised their heads as if expectantly, and it was observed that instead of showing the timidity natural to their kind, they followed the coach and stood about the courtyard when it drew up. Some tossed their antlers, others pawed the ground as the step was let down and Orlando alighted. One, it is said, actually knelt in the snow before her. She had not time to reach her hand towards the knocker before both wings of the great door were flung open, and there, with lights and torches held above their heads, were Mrs Grimsditch, Mr Dupper, and a whole retinue of servants come to greet her. But the orderly procession was interrupted first by the impetuosity of Canute, the elk-hound, who threw himself with such ardour upon his mistress that he almost knocked her to the ground; next, by the agitation of Mrs Grimsditch, who, making as if to curtsey, was overcome with emotion and could do no more than gasp Milord! Milady! Milady! Milord! until Orlando comforted her with a hearty kiss upon both her cheeks. After that, Mr Dupper began to read from a parchment, but the dogs barking, the huntsmen winding their horns, and the stags, who had come into the courtyard in the confusion, baying the moon, not much progress was made, and the company dispersed within after crowding about their Mistress, and testifying in every way to their great joy at her return.

No one showed an instant's suspicion that Orlando was not the Orlando they had known. If any doubt there was in the human mind the action of the deer and the dogs would have been enough to dispel it, for the dumb creatures, as is well known, are far better judges both of identity and character than we are. Moreover, said Mrs Grimsditch, over her dish of china tea, to Mr Dupper that night, if her Lord was a Lady now, she had never seen a lovelier one, nor was there a penny piece to choose between them; one was as well-favoured as the other; they were as like as two peaches on one branch; which, said Mrs Grimsditch, becoming confidential, she had always had her suspicions (here she nodded her head very mysteriously), which it was no surprise to her (here she nodded her head very knowingly), and for her part, a very great comfort; for what with the towels wanting mending and the curtains in the chaplain's parlour being moth-eaten round the fringes, it was time they had a Mistress among them.

'And some little masters and mistresses to come after her,' Mr Dupper added, being privileged by virtue of his holy office to speak his mind on such delicate matters as these.

So, while the old servants gossiped in the servants' hall, Orlando took a silver candle in her hand and roamed once more through the halls, the galleries, the courts, the bedrooms; saw loom down at her again the dark visage of this Lord Keeper, that Lord Chamberlain, among her ancestors; sat now in this chair of state, now reclined on that canopy of delight; observed the arras, how it swayed; watched the huntsmen riding and Daphne flying; bathed her hand, as she had loved to do as a child, in the yellow pool of light which the moonlight made falling through the heraldic Leopard in the window; slid along the polished planks of the gallery, the other side of which was rough timber; touched this silk, that satin; fancied the carved dolphins swam; brushed her hair with King James' silver brush; buried her face in the pot-pourri, which was made as the Conqueror had taught them many hundred years ago and from the same roses; looked at the garden and imagined the sleeping crocuses, the dormant dahlias; saw the frail nymphs gleaming white in the snow and the great yew hedges, thick as a house, black behind them; saw the orangeries and the giant medlars; – all this she saw, and each sight and sound, rudely as we write it down, filled her heart with such a lust and balm of joy, that at length, tired out, she entered the Chapel and sank into the old red armchair in which her ancestors used to hear service. There she lit a cheroot ('twas a habit she had brought back from the East) and opened the Prayer Book.

It was a little book bound in velvet, stitched with gold, which had been held by Mary Queen of Scots on the scaffold, and the eye of faith could detect a brownish stain, said to be made of a drop of the Royal blood. But what pious thoughts it roused in Orlando, what evil passions it soothed asleep, who dare say, seeing that of all communions this with the deity is the most inscrutable? Novelist, poet, historian all falter with their hand on that door; nor does the believer himself enlighten us, for is he more ready to die than other people, or more eager to share his goods? Does he not keep as many maids and carriage horses as the rest? and yet with it all, holds a faith he says which should make goods a vanity and death desirable. In the Queen's prayer book, along with the blood-stain, was also a lock of hair and a crumb of pastry; Orlando now added to these keepsakes a flake of tobacco, and so, reading and smoking, was moved by the humane jumble of them all – the hair, the pastry, the bloodstain, the tobacco – to such a mood of contemplation as gave her a reverent air suitable in the circumstances, though she had, it is said, no traffic with the usual God. Nothing, however, can be more arrogant, though nothing is commoner than to assume that of Gods there is only one, and of religions none but the speaker's. Orlando, it seemed, had a faith of her own. With all the religious ardour in the world, she now reflected upon her sins and the imperfections that had crept into her spiritual state. The letter S, she reflected, is the serpent in the poet's Eden. Do what she would there were still too many of these sinful reptiles in the first stanzas of 'The Oak Tree'. But 'S' was nothing, in her opinion, compared with the termination 'ing'. The present participle is the Devil himself, she thought (now that we are in the place for believing in Devils). To evade such temptations is the first duty of the poet, she concluded, for as the ear is the antechamber to the soul, poetry can adulterate and destroy more surely than lust or gunpowder. The poet's, then, is the highest office of all, she continued. His words reach where others fall short. A silly song of Shakespeare's has done more for the poor and the wicked than all the preachers and philanthropists in the world. No time, no devotion, can be too great, therefore, which makes the vehicle of our message less distorting. We must shape our words till they are the thinnest integument for our thoughts. Thoughts are divine, etc. Thus it is obvious that she was back in the confines of her own religion which time had only strengthened in her absence, and was rapidly acquiring the intolerance of belief.

'I am growing up,' she thought, taking her taper at last. 'I am losing some illusions,' she said, shutting Queen Mary's book, 'perhaps to acquire others,' and she descended among the tombs where the bones of her ancestors lay.

But even the bones of her ancestors, Sir Miles, Sir Gervase, and the rest, had lost something of their sanctity since Rustum el Sadi had waved his hand that night in the Asian mountains. Somehow the fact that only three or four hundred years ago these skeletons had been men with their way to make in the world like any modern upstart, and that they had made it by acquiring houses and offices, garters and ribbands, as any other upstart does, while poets, perhaps, and men of great mind and breeding had preferred the quietude of the country, for which choice they paid the penalty by extreme poverty, and now hawked broadsheets in the Strand, or herded sheep in the fields, filled her with remorse. She thought of the Egyptian pyramids and what bones lie beneath them as she stood in the crypt; and the vast, empty hills which lie above the Sea of Marmara seemed, for the moment, a finer dwelling-place than this many-roomed mansion in which no bed lacked its quilt and no silver dish its silver cover.

'I am growing up,' she thought, taking her taper. 'I am losing my illusions, perhaps to acquire new ones,' and she paced down the long gallery to her bedroom. It was a disagreeable process, and a troublesome. But it was interesting, amazingly, she thought, stretching her legs out to her log fire (for no sailor was present), and she reviewed, as if it were an avenue of great edifices, the progress of her own self along her own past.

How she had loved sound when she was a boy, and thought the volley of tumultuous syllables from the lips the finest of all poetry. Then – it was the effect of Sasha and her disillusionment perhaps – into this high frenzy was let fall some black drop, which turned her rhapsody to sluggishness. Slowly there had opened within her something intricate and many-chambered, which one must take a torch to explore, in prose not verse; and she remembered how passionately she had studied that doctor at Norwich, Browne, whose book was at her hand there. She had formed here in solitude after her affair with Greene, or tried to form, for Heaven knows these growths are age long in coming, a spirit capable of resistance. 'I will write,' she had said, 'what I enjoy writing'; and so had scratched out twenty-six volumes. Yet still, for all her travels and adventures and profound thinkings and turnings this way and that, she was only in process of fabrication. What the future might bring, Heaven only knew. Change was incessant, and change perhaps would never cease. High battlements of thought, habits that had seemed durable as stone, went down like shadows at the touch of another mind and left a naked sky and fresh stars twinkling in it. Here she went to the window, and in spite of the cold could not help unlatching it. She leant out into the damp night air. She heard a fox bark in the woods, and the clutter of a pheasant trailing through the branches. She heard the snow slither and flop from the roof to the ground. 'By my life,' she exclaimed, 'this is a thousand times better than Turkey. Rustum,' she cried, as if she were arguing with the gypsy (and in this new power of bearing an argument in mind and continuing it with someone who was not there to contradict she showed again the development of her soul), 'you were wrong. This is better than Turkey. Hair, pastry, tobacco – of what odds and ends are we compounded,' she said (thinking of Queen Mary's prayer book). 'What a phantasmagoria the mind is and meeting-place of dissemblables! At one moment we deplore our birth and state and aspire to an ascetic exaltation; the next we are overcome by the smell of some old garden path and weep to hear the thrushes sing.' And so bewildered as usual by the multitude of things which call for explanation and imprint their message without leaving any hint as to their meaning, she threw her cheroot out of the window and went to bed.

Next morning, in pursuance of these thoughts, she had out her pen and paper, and started afresh upon 'The Oak Tree', for to have ink and paper in plenty when one has made do with berries and margins is a delight not to be conceived. Thus she was now striking out a phrase in the depths of despair, now in the heights of ecstasy writing one in, when a shadow darkened the page. She hastily hid her manuscript.

As her window gave on to the most central of the courts, as she had given orders that she would see no one, as she knew no one and was herself legally unknown, she was first surprised at the shadow, then indignant at it, then (when she looked up and saw what caused it) overcome with merriment. For it was a familiar shadow, a grotesque shadow, the shadow of no less a personage than the Archduchess Harriet Griselda of Finster-Aarhorn and Scand-op-Boom in the Roumanian territory. She was loping across the court in her old black riding-habit and mantle as before. Not a hair of her head was changed. This then was the woman who had chased her from England! This was the eyrie of that obscene vulture – this the fatal fowl herself! At the thought that she had fled all the way to Turkey to avoid her seductions (now become excessively flat), Orlando laughed aloud. There was something inexpressibly comic in the sight. She resembled, as Orlando had thought before, nothing so much as a monstrous hare. She had the staring eyes, the lank cheeks, the high headdress of that animal. She stopped now, much as a hare sits erect in the corn when thinking itself unobserved, and stared at Orlando, who stared back at her from the window. After they had stared like this for a certain time, there was nothing for it but to ask her in, and soon the two ladies were exchanging compliments while the Archduchess struck the snow from her mantle.

'A plague on women,' said Orlando to herself, going to the cupboard to fetch a glass of wine, 'they never leave one a moment's peace. A more ferreting, inquisiting, busybodying set of people don't exist. It was to escape this Maypole that I left England, and now' – here she turned to present the Archduchess with the salver, and behold – in her place stood a tall gentleman in black. A heap of clothes lay in the fender. She was alone with a man.

Recalled thus suddenly to a consciousness of her sex, which she had completely forgotten, and of his, which was now remote enough to be equally upsetting, Orlando felt seized with faintness.

'La!' she cried, putting her hand to her side, 'how you frighten me!'

'Gentle creature,' cried the Archduchess, falling on one knee and at the same time pressing a cordial to Orlando's lips, 'forgive me for the deceit I have practised on you!'

Orlando sipped the wine and the Archduke knelt and kissed her hand.

In short, they acted the parts of man and woman for ten minutes with great vigour and then fell into natural discourse. The Archduchess (but she must in future be known as the Archduke) told his story – that he was a man and always had been one; that he had seen a portrait of Orlando and fallen hopelessly in love with him; that to compass his ends, he had dressed as a woman and lodged at the Baker's shop; that he was desolated when he fled to Turkey; that he had heard of her change and hastened to offer his services (here he teed and heed intolerably). For to him, said the Archduke Harry, she was and would ever be the Pink, the Pearl, the Perfection of her sex. The three p's would have been more persuasive if they had not been interspersed with tee-hees and haw-haws of the strangest kind. 'If this is love,' said Orlando to herself, looking at the Archduke on the other side of the fender, and now from the woman's point of view, 'there is something highly ridiculous about it.'

Falling on his knees, the Archduke Harry made the most passionate declaration of his suit. He told her that he had something like twenty million ducats in a strong box at his castle. He had more acres than any nobleman in England. The shooting was excellent: he could promise her a mixed bag of ptarmigan and grouse such as no English moor, or Scotch either, could rival. True, the pheasants had suffered from the gape in his absence, and the does had slipped their young, but that could be put right, and would be with her help when they lived in Roumania together.

As he spoke, enormous tears formed in his rather prominent eyes and ran down the sandy tracts of his long and lanky cheeks.

That men cry as frequently and as unreasonably as women, Orlando knew

from her own experience as a man; but she was beginning to be aware that
women should be shocked when men display emotion in their presence, and
so, shocked she was.

The Archduke apologised. He commanded himself sufficiently to say that
he would leave her now, but would return on the following day for his
answer.

That was a Tuesday. He came on Wednesday; he came on Thursday; he
came on Friday; and he came on Saturday. It is true that each visit began,
continued, or concluded with a declaration of love, but in between there
was much room for silence. They sat on either side of the fireplace and
sometimes the Archduke knocked over the fire-irons and Orlando picked
them up again. Then the Archduke would bethink him how he had shot an
elk in Sweden, and Orlando would ask, was it a very big elk, and the
Archduke would say that it was not as big as the reindeer which he had shot
in Norway; and Orlando would ask, had he ever shot a tiger, and the
Archduke would say he had shot an albatross, and Orlando would say (half
hiding her yawn) was an albatross as big as an elephant, and the Archduke
would say – something very sensible, no doubt, but Orlando heard it not,
for she was looking at her writing-table, out of the window, at the door.
Upon which the Archduke would say, 'I adore you', at the very same
moment that Orlando said 'Look, it's beginning to rain', at which they were
both much embarrassed, and blushed scarlet, and could neither of them
think what to say next. Indeed, Orlando was at her wit's end what to talk
about and had she not bethought her of a game called Fly Loo, at which
great sums of money can be lost with very little expense of spirit, she would
have had to marry him, she supposed; for how else to get rid of him
she knew not. By this device, however, and it was a simple one, needing
only three lumps of sugar and a sufficiency of flies, the embarrassment of
conversation was overcome and the necessity of marriage avoided. For now,
the Archduke would bet her five hundred pounds to a tester that a fly would
settle on this lump and not on that. Thus, they would have occupation for a
whole morning watching the flies (who were naturally sluggish at this
season and often spent an hour or so circling round the ceiling) until at
length some fine bluebottle made his choice and the match was won. Many
hundreds of pounds changed hands between them at this game, which the
Archduke, who was a born gambler, swore was every bit as good as horse
racing, and vowed he could play at for ever. But Orlando soon began to
weary.

'What's the good of being a fine young woman in the prime of life', she
asked, 'if I have to pass all my mornings watching bluebottles with an
Archduke?'

She began to detest the sight of sugar; flies made her dizzy. Some way out
of the difficulty there must be, she supposed, but she was still awkward in the
arts of her sex, and as she could no longer knock a man over the head or run

him through the body with a rapier, she could think of no better method than this. She caught a bluebottle, gently pressed the life out of it (it was half dead already, or her kindness for the dumb creatures would not have permitted it) and secured it by a drop of gum arabic to a lump of sugar. While the Archduke was gazing at the ceiling, she deftly substituted this lump for the one she had laid her money on, and crying 'Loo Loo!' declared that she had won her bet. Her reckoning was that the Archduke, with all his knowledge of sport and horse-racing, would detect the fraud and, as to cheat at Loo is the most heinous of crimes, and men have been banished from the society of mankind to that of apes in the tropics for ever because of it, she calculated that he would be manly enough to refuse to have anything further to do with her. But she misjudged the simplicity of the amiable nobleman. He was no nice judge of flies. A dead fly looked to him much the same as a living one. She played the trick twenty times on him and he paid her over £17,250 (which is about £40,885 6s. 8d. of our own money) before Orlando cheated so grossly that even he could be deceived no longer. When he realised the truth at last, a painful scene ensued. The Archduke rose to his full height. He coloured scarlet. Tears rolled down his cheeks one by one. That she had won a fortune from him was nothing – she was welcome to it; that she had deceived him was something – it hurt him to think her capable of it; but that she had cheated at Loo was everything. To love a woman who cheated at play was, he said, impossible. Here he broke down completely. Happily, he said, recovering slightly, there were no witnesses. She was, after all, only a woman, he said. In short, he was preparing in the chivalry of his heart to forgive her and had bent to ask her pardon for the violence of his language, when she cut the matter short, as he stooped his proud head, by dropping a small toad between his skin and his shirt.

In justice to her, it must be said that she would infinitely have preferred a rapier. Toads are clammy things to conceal about one's person a whole morning. But if rapiers are forbidden, one must have recourse to toads. Moreover toads and laughter between them sometimes do what cold steel cannot. She laughed. The Archduke blushed. She laughed. The Archduke cursed. She laughed. The Archduke slammed the door.

'Heaven be praised!' cried Orlando still laughing. She heard the sound of chariot wheels driven at a furious pace down the courtyard. She heard them rattle along the road. Fainter and fainter the sound became. Now it faded away altogether.

'I am alone,' said Orlando, aloud since there was no one to hear.

That silence is more profound after noise still wants the confirmation of science. But that loneliness is more apparent directly after one has been made love to, many women would take their oath. As the sound of the Archduke's chariot wheels died away, Orlando felt drawing further from her and further from her an Archduke (she did not mind that), a fortune (she did not mind that), a title (she did not mind that), the safety and circumstance of married life (she did not mind that), but life she heard going from her, and a lover. 'Life and a lover,' she murmured; and going to her writing-table she dipped her pen in the ink and wrote: 'Life and a lover' – a line which did not scan and made no sense with what went before – something about the proper way of dipping sheep to avoid the scab. Reading it over she blushed and repeated, 'Life and a lover.' Then laying her pen aside she went into her bedroom, stood in front of her mirror, and arranged her pearls about her neck. Then since pearls do not show to advantage against a morning gown of sprigged cotton, she changed to a dove-grey taffeta; thence to one of peach bloom; thence to a wine-coloured brocade. Perhaps a dash of powder was needed, and if her hair were disposed – so – about her brow, it might become her. Then she slipped her feet into pointed slippers, and drew an emerald ring upon her finger. 'Now,' she said when all was ready and lit the silver sconces on either side of the mirror. What woman would not have kindled to see what Orlando saw then burning in the snow – for all about the looking-glass were snowy lawns, and she was like a fire, a burning bush, and the candle flames about her head were silver leaves; or again, the glass was green water, and she a mermaid, slung with pearls, a siren in a cave, singing so that oarsmen leant from their boats and fell down, down to embrace her; so dark, so bright, so hard, so soft, was she, so astonishingly seductive that it was a thousand pities that there was no one there to put it in plain English, and say outright, 'Damn it, Madam, you are loveliness incarnate,' which was the truth. Even Orlando (who had no conceit of her person) knew it, for she smiled the involuntary smile which women smile when their own beauty, which seems not their own, forms like a drop falling or a fountain rising and confronts them all of a sudden in the glass – this smile she smiled and then she listened for a moment and heard only the leaves blowing and the sparrows twittering, and then she sighed, 'Life, a lover,' and then she turned on her heel with extraordinary rapidity; whipped her pearls from her neck, stripped the satins from her back, stood erect in the neat black silk knicker-bockers of an ordinary nobleman, and rang the bell. When the servant came, she told him to order a coach and six to be in readiness instantly. She was summoned by urgent affairs to London. Within an hour of the Archduke's departure, off she drove.

And as she drove, we may seize the opportunity, since the landscape was of a simple English kind which needs no description, to draw the reader's attention more particularly than we could at the moment to one or two remarks which have slipped in here and there in the course of the narrative. For example, it may have been observed that Orlando hid her manuscripts when interrupted. Next, that she looked long and intently in the glass; and now, as she drove to London, one might notice her starting and suppressing a cry when the horses galloped faster than she liked. Her modesty as to her writing, her vanity as to her person, her fears for her safety all seem to hint that what was said a short time ago about there being no change in Orlando the man and Orlando the woman, was ceasing to be altogether true. She was becoming a little more modest, as women are, of her brains, and a little more vain, as women are, of her person. Certain susceptibilities were asserting themselves, and others were diminishing. The change of clothes had, some philosophers will say, much to do with it. Vain trifles as they seem, clothes have, they say, more important offices than merely to keep us warm. They change our view of the world and the world's view of us. For example, when Captain Bartolus saw Orlando's skirt, he had an awning stretched for her immediately, pressed her to take another slice of beef, and invited her to go ashore with him in the long-boat. These compliments would certainly not have been paid her had her skirts, instead of flowing, been cut tight to her legs in the fashion of breeches. And when we are paid compliments, it behoves us to make some return. Orlando curtseyed; she complied; she flattered the good man's humours as she would not have done had his neat breeches been a woman's skirts, and his braided coat a woman's satin bodice. Thus, there is much to support the view that it is clothes that wear us and not we them; we may make them take the mould of arm or breast, but they mould our hearts, our brains, our tongues to their liking. So, having now worn skirts for a considerable time, a certain change was visible in Orlando, which was to be found, even in her face. If we compare the picture of Orlando as a man with that of Orlando as a woman we shall see that though both are undoubtedly one and the same person, there are certain changes. The man has his hand free to seize his sword, the woman must use hers to keep the satins from slipping from her shoulders. The man looks the world full in the face, as if it were made for his uses and fashioned to his liking. The woman takes a sidelong glance at it, full of subtlety, even of suspicion. Had they both worn the same clothes, it is possible that their outlook might have been the same.

That is the view of some philosophers and wise ones, but on the whole, we incline to another. The difference between the sexes is, happily, one of great profundity. Clothes are but a symbol of something hid deep beneath. It was a change in Orlando herself that dictated her choice of a woman's dress and of a woman's sex. And perhaps in this she was only expressing rather more openly than usual – openness indeed was the soul of her nature – something that happens to most people without being thus plainly expressed. For here again, we come to a dilemma. Different though the sexes are, they intermix. In every human being a vacillation from one sex to the other takes place, and often it is only the clothes that keep the male or female likeness, while underneath the sex is the very opposite of what it is above. Of the complications and confusions which thus result everyone has had experience; but here we leave the general question and note only the odd effect it had in the particular case of Orlando herself.

For it was this mixture in her of man and woman, one being uppermost and then the other, that often gave her conduct an unexpected turn. The curious of her own sex would argue, for example, if Orlando was a woman, how did she never take more than ten minutes to dress? And were not her clothes chosen rather at random, and sometimes worn rather shabby? And then they would say, still, she has none of the formality of a man, or a man's love of power. She is excessively tender-hearted. She could not endure to see a donkey beaten or a kitten drowned. Yet again, they noted, she detested household matters, was up at dawn and out among the fields in summer before the sun had risen. No farmer knew more about the crops than she did. She could drink with the best and liked games of hazard. She rode well and drove six horses at a gallop over London Bridge. Yet again, though bold and active as a man, it was remarked that the sight of another in danger brought on the most womanly palpitations. She would burst into tears on slight provocation. She was unversed in geography, found mathematics intolerable, and held some caprices which are more common among women than men, as for instance that to travel south is to travel downhill. Whether, then, Orlando was most man or woman, it is difficult to say and cannot now be decided. For her coach was now rattling on the cobbles. She had reached her home in the city. The steps were being let down; the iron gates were being opened. She was entering her father's house at Blackfriars, which, though fashion was fast deserting that end of the town, was still a pleasant, roomy mansion, with gardens running down to the river, and a pleasant grove of nut trees to walk in.

Here she took up her lodging and began instantly to look about her for what she had come in search of – that is to say, life and a lover. About the first there might be some doubt; the second she found without the least difficulty two days after her arrival. It was a Tuesday that she came to town. On Thursday she went for a walk in the Mall, as was then the habit of persons of quality. She had not made more than a turn or two of the avenue before she was observed by a little knot of vulgar people who go there to spy upon their betters. As she came past them, a common woman carrying a child at her breast stepped forward, peered familiarly into Orlando's face, and cried out, 'Lawk upon us, if it ain't the Lady Orlando!' Her companions came crowding round, and Orlando found herself in a moment the centre of a mob of staring citizens and tradesmen's wives, all eager to gaze upon the heroine of the celebrated lawsuit. Such was the interest that the case excited in the minds of the common people. She might, indeed, have found herself gravely discommoded by the pressure of the crowd – she had forgotten that ladies are not supposed to walk in public places alone – had not a tall gentleman at once stepped forward and offered her the protection of his arm. It was the Archduke. She was overcome with distress and yet with some amusement at the sight. Not only had this magnanimous nobleman forgiven her, but in order to show that he took her levity with the toad in good part, he had procured a jewel made in the shape of that reptile which he pressed upon her with a repetition of his suit as he handed her to her coach.

What with the crowd, what with the Duke, what with the jewel, she drove home in the vilest temper imaginable. Was it impossible then to go for a walk without being half-suffocated, presented with a toad set in emeralds, and asked in marriage by an Archduke? She took a kinder view of the case next day when she found on her breakfast table half a dozen billets from some of the greatest ladies in the land – Lady Suffolk, Lady Salisbury, Lady Chesterfield, Lady Tavistock, and others who reminded her in the politest manner of old alliances between their families and her own, and desired the honour of her acquaintance. Next day, which was a Saturday, many of these great ladies waited on her in person. On Tuesday, about noon, their footmen brought cards of invitation to various routs, dinners, and assemblies in the near future; so that Orlando was launched without delay, and with some splash and foam at that, upon the waters of London society.

To give a truthful account of London society at that or indeed at any other time, is beyond the powers of the biographer or the historian. Only those who have little need of the truth, and no respect for it – the poets and the novelists – can be trusted to do it, for this is one of the cases where the truth does not exist. Nothing exists. The whole thing is a miasma – a mirage. To make our meaning plain – Orlando would come home from one of these routs at three or four in the morning with cheeks like a Christmas tree and eyes like stars. She would untie a lace, pace the room a score of times, untie another lace, stop, and pace the room again. Often the sun would be blazing over Southwark chimneys before she could persuade herself to get into bed, and there she would lie, pitching and tossing, laughing and sighing for an hour or longer before she slept at last. And what was all this stir about? Society. And what had society said or done to throw a reasonable lady into such an excitement? In plain language, nothing. Rack her memory as she would, next day Orlando could never remember a single word to magnify into the name something. Lord O. had been gallant. Lord A. polite. The Marquis of C. charming. Mr M. amusing. But when she tried to recollect in what their gallantry, politeness, charm, or wit had consisted, she was bound to suppose her memory at fault, for she could not name a thing. It was the same always. Nothing remained over the next day, yet the excitement of the moment was intense. Thus we are forced to conclude that society is one of those brews such as skilled housekeepers serve hot about Christmas time, whose flavour depends upon the proper mixing and stirring of a dozen different ingredients. Take one out, and it is in itself insipid. Take away Lord O., Lord A., Lord C., or Mr M. and separately each is nothing. Stir them all together and they combine to give off the most intoxicating of flavours, the most seductive of scents. Yet this intoxication, this seductiveness, entirely evade our analysis. At one and the same time, therefore, society is everything and society is nothing. Society is the most powerful concoction in the world and society has no existence whatsoever. Such monsters the poets and the novelists alone can deal with; with such something-nothings their works are stuffed out to prodigious size; and to them with the best will in the world we are content to leave it.

Following the example of our predecessors, therefore, we will only say that society in the reign of Queen Anne was of unparalleled brilliance. To have the entry there was the aim of every well-bred person. The graces were supreme. Fathers instructed their sons, mothers their daughters. No education was complete for either sex which did not include the science of deportment, the art of bowing and curtseying, the management of the sword and the fan, the care of the teeth, the conduct of the leg, the flexibility of the knee, the proper methods of entering and leaving the room, with a thousand etceteras, such as will immediately suggest themselves to anybody who has himself been in society. Since Orlando had won the praise of Queen Elizabeth for the way she handed a bowl of rose water as a boy, it must be supposed that she was sufficiently expert to pass muster. Yet it is true that there was an absent-mindedess about her which sometimes made her clumsy; she was apt to think of poetry when she should have been thinking of taffeta; her walk was a little too much of a stride for a woman, perhaps, and her gestures, being abrupt, might endanger a cup of tea on occasion.

Whether this slight disability was enough to counterbalance the splen-dour of her bearing, or whether she inherited a drop too much of that black humour which ran in the veins of all her race, certain it is that she had not been in the world more than a score of times before she might have been heard to ask herself, had there been anybody but her spaniel Pippin to hear her, 'What the devil is the matter with me?' The occasion was Tuesday, the 16th of June 1712; she had just returned from a great ball at Arlington House; the dawn was in the sky, and she was pulling off her stockings. 'I don't care if I never meet another soul as long as I live,' cried Orlando, bursting into tears. Lovers she had in plenty, but life, which is, after all, of some importance in its way, escaped her. 'Is this,' she asked but there was none to answer, 'Is this,' she finished her sentence all the same, 'what people call life?' The spaniel raised her forepaw in token of sympathy. The spaniel licked Orlando with her tongue. Orlando stroked the spaniel with her hand. Orlando kissed the spaniel with her lips. In short, there was the truest sympathy between them that can be between a dog and its mistress, and yet it cannot be denied that the dumbness of animals is a great impediment to the refinements of intercourse. They wag their tails; they bow the front part of the body and elevate the hind; they roll, they jump, they paw, they whine, they bark, they slobber, they have all sorts of ceremonies and artifices of their own, but the whole thing is of no avail, since speak they cannot. Such was her quarrel, she thought, setting the dog gently on to the floor, with the great people at Arlington House. They, too, wag their tails, bow, roll, jump, paw, and slobber, but talk they cannot. 'All these months that I've been out in the world,' said Orlando, pitching one stocking across the room, 'I've heard nothing but what Pippin might have said. I'm cold. I'm happy. I'm hungry. I've caught a mouse. I've buried a bone. Please kiss my nose.' And it was not enough.

How, in so short a time, she had passed from intoxication to disgust we will only seek to explain by supposing that this mysterious composition which we call society, is nothing absolutely good or bad in itself, but has a spirit in it, volatile but potent, which either makes you drunk when you think it, as Orlando thought it, delightful, or gives you a headache when you think it, as Orlando thought it, repulsive. That the faculty of speech has much to do with it either way, we take leave to doubt. Often a dumb hour is the most ravishing of all; brilliant wit can be tedious beyond description. But to the poets we leave it, and so on with our story.

Orlando threw the second stocking after the first and went to bed dismally enough, determined that she would forswear society for ever. But again as it turned out, she was too hasty in coming to her conclusions. For the very next morning she woke to find, among the usual cards of invitation upon her table, one from a certain great Lady, the Countess of R. Having determined overnight that she would never go into society again, we can only explain Orlando's behaviour – she sent a messenger hot-foot to R— House to say that she would attend her Ladyship with all the pleasure in the world – by the fact that she was still suffering from the effect of three honeyed words dropped into her ear on the deck of the *Enamoured Lady* by Captain Nicholas Benedict Bartolus as they sailed down the Thames. Addison, Dryden, Pope, he had said, pointing to the Cocoa Tree, and Addison, Dryden, Pope had chimed in her head like an incantation ever since. Who can credit such folly? but so it was. All her experience with Nick Greene had taught her nothing. Such names still exercised over her the most powerful fascination. Something, perhaps, we must believe in, and as Orlando, we have said, had no belief in the usual divinities she bestowed her credulity upon great men – yet with a distinction. Admirals, soldiers, statesmen, moved her not at all. But the very thought of a great writer stirred her to such a pitch of belief that she almost believed him to be invisible. Her instinct was a sound one. One can only believe entirely, perhaps, in what one cannot see. The little glimpse she had of these great men from the deck of the ship was of the nature of a vision. That the cup was china, or the gazette paper, she doubted. When Lord O. said one day that he had dined with Dryden the night before, she flatly disbelieved him. Now, the Lady R.'s reception room had the reputation of being the antechamber to the presence room of genius; it was the place where men and women met to swing censers and chant hymns to the bust of genius in a niche in the wall. Sometimes the God himself vouchsafed his presence for a moment. Intellect alone admitted the suppliant, and nothing (so the report ran) was said inside that was not witty.

It was thus with great trepidation that Orlando entered the room. She found a company already assembled in a semicircle round the fire. Lady R., an oldish lady, of dark complexion, with a black lace mantilla on her head, was seated in a great armchair in the centre. Thus being somewhat deaf, she could control the conversation on both sides of her. On both sides of her sat men and women of the highest distinction. Every man, it was said, had been a Prime Minister and every woman, it was whispered, had been the mistress of a king. Certain it is that all were brilliant, and all were famous. Orlando took her seat with a deep reverence in silence . . . After three hours, she curtseyed profoundly and left.

But what, the reader may ask with some exasperation, happened in between? In three hours, such a company must have said the wittiest, the profoundest, the most interesting things in the world. So it would seem indeed. But the fact appears to be that they said nothing. It is a curious characteristic which they share with all the most brilliant societies that the world has seen. Old Madame du Deffand and her friends talked for fifty years without stopping. And of it all, what remains? Perhaps three witty sayings. So that we are at liberty to suppose either that nothing was said, or that nothing witty was said, or that the fraction of three witty sayings lasted eighteen thousand two hundred and fifty nights, which does not leave a liberal allowance of wit for any one of them.

The truth would seem to be – if we dare use such a word in such a connection – that all these groups of people lie under an enchantment. The hostess is our modern Sibyl. She is a witch who lays her guests under a spell. In this house they think themselves happy; in that witty; in a third profound. It is all an illusion (which is nothing against it, for illusions are the most valuable and necessary of all things, and she who can create one is among the world's greatest benefactors), but as it is notorious that illusions are shattered by conflict with reality, so no real happiness, no real wit, no real profundity are tolerated where the illusion prevails. This serves to explain why Madame du Deffand said no more than three witty things in the course of fifty years. Had she said more, her circle would have been destroyed. The witticism, as it left her lips, bowled over the current conversation as a cannon ball lays low the violets and the daisies. When she made her famous 'mot de Saint Denis' the very grass was singed. Disillusionment and desolation followed. Not a word was uttered. 'Spare us another such, for Heaven's sake, Madame!' her friends cried with one accord. And she obeyed. For almost seventeen years she said nothing memorable and all went well. The beautiful counterpane of illusion lay unbroken on her circle as it lay unbroken on the circle of Lady R. The guests thought that they were happy, thought that they were witty, thought that they were profound, and, as they thought this, other people thought it still more strongly; and so it got about that nothing was more delightful than one of Lady R.'s assemblies; everyone envied those who were admitted; those who were admitted envied themselves because other people envied them; and so there seemed no end to it – except that which we have now to relate.

For about the third time Orlando went there a certain incident occurred. She was still under the illusion that she was listening to the most brilliant epigrams in the world, though, as a matter of fact, old General C. was only saying, at some length, how the gout had left his left leg and gone to his right, while Mr L. interrupted when any proper name was mentioned, 'R.? Oh! I know Billy R. as well as I know myself. S.? My dearest friend. T.? Stayed with him a fortnight in Yorkshire' – which, such is the force of illusion, sounded like the wittiest repartee, the most searching comment upon human life, and kept the company in a roar; when the door opened and a little gentleman entered whose name Orlando did not catch. Soon a curiously disagreeable sensation came over her. To judge from their faces, the rest began to feel it as well. One gentleman said there was a draught. The Marchioness of C. feared a cat must be under the sofa. It was as if their eyes were being slowly opened after a pleasant dream and nothing met them but a cheap wash-stand and a dirty counterpane. It was as if the fumes of some delicious wine were slowly leaving them. Still the General talked and still Mr L. remembered. But it became more and more apparent how red the General's neck was, how bald Mr L.'s head was. As for what they said – nothing more tedious and trivial could be imagined. Everybody fidgeted and those who had fans yawned behind them. At last Lady R. rapped with hers upon the arm of her great chair. Both gentlemen stopped talking.

Then the little gentleman said,

He said next,

He said finally,*

Here, it cannot be denied, was true wit, true wisdom, true profundity. The company was thrown into complete dismay. One such saying was bad enough; but three, one after another, on the same evening! No society could survive it.

'Mr Pope,' said old Lady R. in a voice trembling with sarcastic fury, 'you are pleased to be witty.' Mr Pope flushed red. Nobody spoke a word. They sat in dead silence some twenty minutes. Then, one by one, they rose and slunk from the room. That they would ever come back after such an experience was doubtful. Link-boys could be heard calling their coaches all down South Audley Street. Doors were slammed and carriages drove off. Orlando found herself near Mr Pope on the staircase. His lean and misshapen frame was shaken by a variety of emotions. Darts of malice, rage, triumph, wit, and terror (he was shaking like a leaf) shot from his eyes. He looked like some squat reptile set with a burning topaz in its forehead. At the same time, the strangest tempest of emotion seized now upon the luckless Orlando. A

---

* These sayings are too well known to require repetition, and besides, they are all to be found in his published works.

disillusionment so complete as that inflicted not an hour ago leaves the mind rocking from side to side. Everything appears ten times more bare and stark than before. It is a moment fraught with the highest danger for the human spirit. Women turn nuns and men priests in such moments. In such moments, rich men sign away their wealth; and happy men cut their throats with carving knives. Orlando would have done all willingly, but there was a rasher thing still for her to do, and this she did. She invited Mr Pope to come home with her.

For if it is rash to walk into a lion's den unarmed, rash to navigate the Atlantic in a rowing boat, rash to stand on one foot on the top of St Paul's, it is still more rash to go home alone with a poet. A poet is Atlantic and lion in one. While one drowns us the other gnaws us. If we survive the teeth, we succumb to the waves. A man who can destroy illusions is both beast and flood. Illusions are to the soul what atmosphere is to the earth. Roll up that tender air and the plant dies, the colour fades. The earth we walk on is a parched cinder. It is marl we tread and fiery cobbles scorch our feet. By the truth we are undone. Life is a dream. 'Tis waking that kills us. He who robs us of our dreams robs us of our life – (and so on for six pages if you will, but the style is tedious and may well be dropped).

On this showing, however, Orlando should have been a heap of cinders by the time the chariot drew up at her house in Blackfriars. That she was still flesh and blood, though certainly exhausted, is entirely due to a fact to which we drew attention earlier in the narrative. The less we see the more we believe. Now the streets that lie between Mayfair and Blackfriars were at that time very imperfectly lit. True, the lighting was a great improvement upon that of the Elizabethan age. Then the benighted traveller had to trust to the stars or the red flame of some night watchman to save him from the gravel pits at Park Lane or the oak woods where swine rootled in the Tottenham Court Road. But even so it wanted much of our modern efficiency. Lamp-posts lit with oil-lamps occurred every two hundred yards or so, but between lay a considerable stretch of pitch darkness. Thus for ten minutes Orlando and Mr Pope would be in blackness; and then for about half a minute again in the light. A very strange state of mind was thus bred in Orlando. As the light faded, she began to feel steal over her the most delicious balm. 'This is indeed a very great honour for a young woman, to be driving with Mr Pope,' she began to think, looking at the outline of his nose. 'I am the most blessed of my sex. Half an inch from me – indeed, I feel the knot of his knee ribbons pressing against my thigh – is the greatest wit in Her Majesty's dominions. Future ages will think of us with curiosity and envy me with fury.' Here came the lamp-post again. 'What a foolish wretch I am!' she thought. 'There is no such thing as fame and glory. Ages to come will never cast a thought on me or on Mr Pope either. What's an "age", indeed? What are "we"?' and their progress through Berkeley Square seemed the groping of two blind ants, momentarily thrown together without interest or concern in common, across a blackened desert. She shivered. But here again was darkness. Her illusion revived. 'How noble his brow is,' she thought (mistaking a hump on a cushion for Mr Pope's forehead in the darkness). 'What a weight of genius lives in it! What wit, wisdom, and truth – what a wealth of all those jewels, indeed, for which people are ready to barter their lives! Yours is the only light that burns for ever. But for you the human pilgrimage would be performed in utter darkness' (here the coach gave a great lurch as it fell into a rut in Park Lane); 'without genius we should be upset and undone. Most august, most lucid of beams' – thus she was apostrophising the hump on the cushion when they drove beneath one of the street lamps in Berkeley Square and she realised her mistake. Mr Pope had a forehead no bigger than another man's. 'Wretched man,' she thought, 'how you have deceived me! I took that hump for your forehead. When one sees you plain, how ignoble, how despicable you are! Deformed and weakly, there is nothing to venerate in you, much to pity, most to despise.'

Again they were in darkness and her anger became modified directly she could see nothing but the poet's knees.

'But it is I that am a wretch,' she reflected, once they were in complete obscurity again, 'for base as you may be, am I not still baser? It is you who nourish and protect me, you who scare the wild beast, frighten the savage, make me clothes of the silkworm's wool, and carpets of the sheep's. If I want to worship, have you not provided me with an image of yourself and set it in the sky? Are not evidences of your care everywhere? How humble, how grateful, how docile, should I not be, therefore? Let it be all my joy to serve, honour, and obey you.'

Here they reached the big lamp-post at the corner of what is now Piccadilly Circus. The light blazed in her eyes, and she saw, besides some degraded creatures of her own sex, two wretched pigmies on a stark desert land. Both were naked, solitary, and defenceless. The one was powerless to help the other. Each had enough to do to look after itself. Looking Mr Pope full in the face, 'It is equally vain,' she thought, 'for you to think you can protect me, or for me to think I can worship you. The light of truth beats upon us without shadow, and the light of truth is damnably unbecoming to us both.'

All this time, of course, they went on talking agreeably, as people of birth and education use, about the Queen's temper and the Prime Minister's gout, while the coach went from light to darkness down the Haymarket, along the Strand, up Fleet Street, and reached, at length, her house in Blackfriars. For some time the dark spaces between the lamps had been becoming brighter and the lamps themselves less bright – that is to say, the sun was rising, and it was in the equable but confused light of a summer's morning in which everything is seen but nothing is seen distinctly that they alighted, Mr Pope handing Orlando from her carriage and Orlando curtseying Mr Pope to precede her into her mansion with the most scrupulous attention to the rites of the Graces.

From the foregoing passage, however, it must not be supposed that genius (but the disease is now stamped out in the British Isles, the late Lord Tennyson, it is said, being the last person to suffer from it) is constantly alight, for then we should see everything plain and perhaps should be scorched to death in the process. Rather it resembles the lighthouse in its working, which sends one ray and then no more for a time; save that genius is much more capricious in its manifestations and may flash six or seven beams in quick succession (as Mr Pope did that night) and then lapse into darkness for a year or for ever. To steer by its beams is therefore impossible, and when the dark spell is on them men of genius are, it is said, much like other people.

It was happy for Orlando, though at first disappointing, that this should be so, for she now began to live much in the company of men of genius. Nor were they so different from the rest of us as one might have supposed. Addison, Pope, Swift, proved, she found, to be fond of tea. They liked arbours. They collected little bits of coloured glass. They adored grottos. Rank was not distasteful to them. Praise was delightful. They wore plum-coloured suits one day and grey another. Mr Swift had a fine malacca cane. Mr Addison scented his handkerchiefs. Mr Pope suffered with his head. A piece of gossip did not come amiss. Nor were they without their jealousies. (We are jotting down a few reflections that came to Orlando higgledy-piggledy.) At first, she was annoyed with herself for noticing such trifles, and kept a book in which to write down their memorable sayings, but the page remained empty. All the same, her spirits revived, and she took to tearing up her cards of invitation to great parties; kept her evenings free; began to look forward to Mr Pope's visit, to Mr Addison's, to Mr Swift's – and so on and so on. If the reader will here refer to the *Rape of the Lock*, to the *Spectator*, to *Gulliver's Travels*, he will understand precisely what these mysterious words may mean. Indeed, biographers and critics might save themselves all their labours if readers would only take this advice. For when we read:

> Whether the Nymph shall break Diana's Law,
> Or some frail China Jar receive a Flaw,
> Or stain her Honour, or her new Brocade,
> Forget her Pray'rs or miss a Masquerade,
> Or lose her Heart, or Necklace, at a Ball.

– we know as if we heard him how Mr Pope's tongue flickered like a lizard's, how his eyes flashed, how his hand trembled, how he loved, how he lied, how he suffered. In short, every secret of a writer's soul, every experience of his life, every quality of his mind is written large in his works, yet we require critics to explain the one and biographers to expound the other. That time hangs heavy on people's hands is the only explanation of the monstrous growth.

So, now that we have read a page or two of the *Rape of the Lock*, we know exactly why Orlando was so much amused and so much frightened and so very bright-cheeked and bright-eyed that afternoon.

Mrs Nelly then knocked at the door to say that Mr Addison waited on her Ladyship. At this, Mr Pope got up with a wry smile, made his congee, and limped off. In came Mr Addison. Let us, as he takes his seat, read the following passage from the *Spectator*:

I consider woman as a beautiful, romantic animal, that may be adorned with furs and feathers, pearls and diamonds, ores and silks. The lynx shall cast its skin at her feet to make her a tippet, the peacock, parrot and swan shall pay contributions to her muff; the sea shall be searched for shells, and the rocks for gems, and every part of nature furnish out its share towards the embellishment of a creature that is the most consummate work of it. All this, I shall indulge them in, but as for the petticoat I have been speaking of, I neither can, nor will allow it.

We hold that gentleman, cocked hat and all, in the hollow of our hands. Look once more into the crystal. Is he not clear to the very wrinkle in his stocking? Does not every ripple and curve of his wit lie exposed before us, and his benignity and his timidity and his urbanity and the fact that he would marry a Countess and die very respectably in the end? All is clear. And when Mr Addison has said his say, there is a terrific rap at the door, and Mr Swift, who had these arbitrary ways with him, walks in unannounced. One moment, where is *Gulliver's Travels*? Here it is! Let us read a passage from the voyage to the Houyhnhnms:

I enjoyed perfect Health of Body and Tranquillity of Mind; I did not find the Treachery or Inconstancy of a Friend, nor the Injuries of a secret or open Enemy. I had no occasion of bribing, flattering or pimping, to procure the Favour of any great Man or of his Minion. I wanted no Fence against Fraud or Oppression; Here was neither Physician to destroy my Body, nor Lawyer to ruin my Fortune; No Informer to watch my Words, and Actions, or forge Accusations against me for Hire: Here were no Gibers, Censurers, Backbiters, Pickpockets, Highwaymen, Housebreakers, Attorneys, Bawds, Buffoons, Gamesters, Politicians, Wits, splenetick tedious Talkers . . .

But stop, stop your iron pelt of words, lest you flay us all alive, and yourself too! Nothing can be plainer than that violent man. He is so coarse and yet so clean; so brutal, yet so kind; scorns the whole world, yet talks baby language to a girl, and will die, can we doubt it? in a madhouse.

So Orlando poured out tea for them all; and sometimes, when the weather was fine, she carried them down to the country with her, and feasted them royally in the Round Parlour, which she had hung with their pictures all in a circle, so that Mr Pope could not say that Mr Addison came before him, or the other way about. They were very witty, too (but their wit is all in their books), and taught her the most important part of style, which is the natural run of the voice in speaking – a quality which none that has not heard it can imitate, not Greene even, with all his skill; for it is born of the air, and breaks like a wave on the furniture, and rolls and fades away, and is never to be recaptured, least of all by those who prick up their ears, half a century later, and try. They taught her this, merely by the cadence of their voices in speech; so that her style changed somewhat, and she wrote some very pleasant, witty verses and characters in prose. And so she lavished her wine on them and put bank-notes, which they took very kindly, beneath their plates at dinner, and accepted their dedications, and thought herself highly honoured by the exchange.

Thus time ran on, and Orlando could often be heard saying to herself with an emphasis which might, perhaps, make the hearer a little suspicious, 'Upon my soul, what a life this is!' (For she was still in search of that commodity.) But circumstances soon forced her to consider the matter more narrowly.

One day she was pouring out tea for Mr Pope while, as anyone can tell from the verses quoted above, he sat very bright-eyed, observant, and all crumpled up in a chair by her side.

'Lord,' she thought, as she raised the sugar tongs, 'how women in ages to come will envy me! And yet – ' she paused; for Mr Pope needed her attention. And yet – let us finish her thought for her – when anybody says, 'How future ages will envy me,' it is safe to say that they are extremely uneasy at the present moment. Was this life quite so exciting, quite so flattering, quite so glorious as it sounds when the memoir writer has done his work upon it? For one thing, Orlando had a positive hatred of tea; for another, the intellect, divine as it is, and all-worshipful, has a habit of lodging in the most seedy of carcases, and often, alas, acts the cannibal among the other faculties so that often, where the Mind is biggest, the Heart, the Senses, Magnanimity, Charity, Tolerance, Kindliness, and the rest of them scarcely have room to breathe. Then the high opinion poets have of themselves; then the low one they have of others; then the enmities, injuries, envies, and repartees in which they are constantly engaged; then the volubility with which they impart them; then the rapacity with which they demand sympathy for them; all this, one may whisper, lest the wits may overhear us, makes pouring out tea a more precarious and, indeed, arduous occupation than is generally allowed. Added to which (we whisper again lest the women may overhear us), there is a little secret which men share among them; Lord Chesterfield whispered it to his son with strict injunctions to secrecy, 'Women are but children of a larger growth . . . A man of sense only trifles with them, plays with them, humours and flatters them,' which, since children always hear what they are not meant to, and sometimes, even, grow up, may have somehow leaked out, so that the whole ceremony of pouring out tea is a curious one. A woman knows very well that, though a wit sends her his poems, praises her judgement, solicits her criticism, and drinks her tea, this by no means signifies that he respects her opinions, admires her understanding, or will refuse, though the rapier is denied him, to run her through the body with his pen. All this, we say, whisper it as low as we can, may have leaked out by now; so that even with the cream jug suspended and the sugar tongs distended the ladies may fidget a little, look out of the window a little, yawn a little, and so let the sugar fall with a great plop – as Orlando did now – into Mr Pope's tea. Never was any mortal so ready to suspect an insult or so quick to avenge one as Mr Pope. He turned to Orlando and presented her instantly with the rough draught of a certain famous line in the 'Characters of Women'. Much polish was afterwards bestowed on it, but even in the original it was striking enough. Orlando received it with a curtsey. Mr Pope left her with a bow. Orlando, to cool her cheeks, for really she felt as if the little man had struck her, strolled in the nut grove at the bottom of the garden. Soon the cool breezes did their work. To her amazement she found that she was hugely relieved to find herself alone. She watched the merry boatloads rowing up the river. No doubt the sight put her in mind of one or two incidents in her past life. She sat herself down in profound meditation beneath a fine willow tree. There she sat till the stars were in the sky. Then she rose, turned, and went into the house, where she sought her bedroom and locked the door. Now she opened a cupboard in which hung still many of the clothes she had worn as a young man of fashion, and from among them she chose a black velvet suit richly trimmed with Venetian lace. It was a little out of fashion, indeed, but it fitted her to perfection and dressed in it she looked the very figure of a noble Lord. She took a turn or two before the mirror to make sure that her petticoats had not lost her the freedom of her legs, and then let herself secretly out of doors.

It was a fine night early in April. A myriad stars mingling with the light of a sickle moon, which again was enforced by the street lamps, made a light infinitely becoming to the human countenance and to the architecture of Mr Wren. Everything appeared in its tenderest form, yet, just as it seemed on the point of dissolution, some drop of silver sharpened it to animation. Thus it was that talk should be, thought Orlando (indulging in foolish reverie); that society should be, that friendship should be, that love should be. For, Heaven knows why, just as we have lost faith in human intercourse some random collocation of barns and trees or a haystack and a waggon presents us with so perfect a symbol of what is unattainable that we begin the search again.

She entered Leicester Square as she made these observations. The buildings had an airy yet formal symmetry not theirs by day. The canopy of the sky seemed most dexterously washed in to fill up the outline of roof and chimney. A young woman who sat dejectedly with one arm drooping by her side, the other reposing in her lap, on a seat beneath a plane tree in the middle of the square seemed the very figure of grace, simplicity, and desolation. Orlando swept her hat off to her in the manner of a gallant

paying his addresses to a lady of fashion in a public place. The young
woman raised her head. It was of the most exquisite shapeliness. The
young woman raised her eyes. Orlando saw them to be of a lustre such as is
sometimes seen on teapots but rarely in a human face. Through this silver
glaze the young woman looked up at him (for a man he was to her)
appealing, hoping, trembling, fearing. She rose; she accepted his arm. For –
need we stress the point? – she was of the tribe which nightly burnishes
their wares, and sets them in order on the common counter to wait the
highest bidder. She led Orlando to the room in Gerrard Street which was
her lodging. To feel her hanging lightly yet like a suppliant on her arm,
roused in Orlando all the feelings which become a man. She looked, she
felt, she talked like one. Yet, having been so lately a woman herself, she
suspected that the girl's timidity and her hesitating answers and the very
fumbling with the key in the latch and the fold of her cloak and the droop of
her wrist were all put on to gratify her masculinity. Upstairs they went, and
the pains which the poor creature had been at to decorate her room and
hide the fact that she had no other deceived Orlando not a moment. The
deception roused her scorn; the truth roused her pity. One thing showing
through the other bred the oddest assortment of feeling, so that she did not
know whether to laugh or to cry. Meanwhile Nell, as the girl called herself,
unbuttoned her gloves; carefully concealed the left-hand thumb, which
wanted mending; then drew behind a screen, where, perhaps, she rouged
her cheeks, arranged her clothes, fixed a new kerchief round her neck – all
the time prattling as women do, to amuse her lover, though Orlando could
have sworn, from the tone of her voice, that her thoughts were elsewhere.
When all was ready, out she came, prepared – but here Orlando could stand
it no longer. In the strangest torment of anger, merriment, and pity she
flung off all disguise and admitted herself a woman.

At this, Nell burst into such a roar of laughter as might have been heard
across the way.

'Well, my dear,' she said, when she had somewhat recovered, 'I'm by no
means sorry to hear it. For the plain Dunstable of the matter is' (and it was
remarkable how soon, on discovering that they were of the same sex, her
manner changed and she dropped her plaintive, appealing ways), 'the plain
Dunstable of the matter is, that I'm not in the mood for the society of the
other sex tonight. Indeed, I'm in the devil of a fix.' Whereupon, drawing up
the fire and stirring a bowl of punch, she told Orlando the whole story of
her life. Since it is Orlando's life that engages us at present, we need not
relate the adventures of the other lady, but it is certain that Orlando had
never known the hours speed faster or more merrily, though Mistress Nell
had not a particle of wit about her, and when the name of Mr Pope came up
in talk asked innocently if he were connected with the perruque maker of
that name in Jermyn Street. Yet, to Orlando, such is the charm of ease and
the seduction of beauty, this poor girl's talk, larded though it was with the

commonest expressions of the street corners, tasted like wine after the fine phrases she had been used to, and she was forced to the conclusion that there was something in the sneer of Mr Pope, in the condescension of Mr Addison, and in the secret of Lord Chesterfield which took away her relish for the society of wits, deeply though she must continue to respect their works.

These poor creatures, she ascertained, for Nell brought Prue, and Prue Kitty, and Kitty Rose, had a society of their own of which they now elected her a member. Each would tell the story of the adventures which had landed her in her present way of life. Several were the natural daughters of earls and one was a good deal nearer than she should have been to the King's person. None was too wretched or too poor but to have some ring or handkerchief in her pocket which stood her in lieu of pedigree. So they would draw round the punch-bowl which Orlando made it her business to furnish generously, and many were the fine tales they told and many the amusing observations they made, for it cannot be denied that when women get together – but hist – they are always careful to see that the doors are shut and that not a word of it gets into print. All they desire is – but hist again – is that not a man's step on the stair? All they desire, we were about to say when the gentleman took the very words out of our mouths. Women have no desires, says this gentleman, coming into Nell's parlour; only affectations. Without desires (she has served him and he is gone) their conversation cannot be of the slightest interest to anyone. 'It is well known,' says Mr S. W., 'that when they lack the stimulus of the other sex, women can find nothing to say to each other. When they are alone, they do not talk, they scratch.' And since they cannot talk together and scratching cannot continue without interruption and it is well known (Mr T. R. has proved it) 'that women are incapable of any feeling of affection for their own sex and hold each other in the greatest aversion', what can we suppose that women do when they seek out each other's society?

As that is not a question that can engage the attention of a sensible man, let us, who enjoy the immunity of all biographers and historians from any sex whatever, pass it over, and merely state that Orlando professed great enjoyment in the society of her own sex, and leave it to the gentlemen to prove, as they are very fond of doing, that this is impossible.

But to give an exact and particular account of Orlando's life at this time becomes more and more out of the question. As we peer and grope in the ill-lit, ill-paved, ill-ventilated courtyards that lay about Gerrard Street and Drury Lane at that time, we seem now to catch sight of her and then again to lose it. The task is made still more difficult by the fact that she found it convenient at this time to change frequently from one set of clothes to another. Thus she often occurs in contemporary memoirs as 'Lord' So-and-so, who was in fact her cousin; her bounty is ascribed to him, and it is he who is said to have written the poems that were really hers. She had, it seems, no difficulty in sustaining the different parts, for her sex changed far more frequently than those who have worn only one set of clothing can conceive; nor can there be any doubt that she reaped a twofold harvest by this device; the pleasures of life were increased and its experiences multiplied. For the probity of breeches she exchanged the seductiveness of petticoats and enjoyed the love of both sexes equally.

So then one may sketch her spending her morning in a China robe of ambiguous gender among her books; then receiving a client or two (for she had many scores of suppliants) in the same garment; then she would take a turn in the garden and clip the nut trees – for which knee-breeches were convenient; then she would change into a flowered taffeta which best suited a drive to Richmond and a proposal of marriage from some great nobleman; and so back again to town, where she would don a snuff-coloured gown like a lawyer's and visit the courts to hear how her cases were doing – for her fortune was wasting hourly and the suits seemed no nearer consummation than they had been a hundred years ago; and so, finally, when night came, she would more often than not become a nobleman complete from head to toe and walk the streets in search of adventure.

Returning from some of these junketings – of which there were many stories told at the time, as, that she fought a duel, served on one of the King's ships as a captain, was seen to dance naked on a balcony, and fled with a certain lady to the Low Countries where the lady's husband followed them – but of the truth or otherwise of these stories, we express no opinion – returning from whatever her occupation may have been, she made a point sometimes of passing beneath the windows of a coffee house, where she could see the wits without being seen, and thus could fancy from their gestures what wise, witty, or spiteful things they were saying without hearing a word of them; which was perhaps an advantage; and once she stood half an hour watching three shadows on the blind drinking tea together in a house in Bolt Court.

Never was any play so absorbing. She wanted to cry out, Bravo! Bravo! For, to be sure, what a fine drama it was – what a page torn from the thickest volume of human life! There was the little shadow with the pouting lips, fidgeting this way and that on his chair, uneasy, petulant, officious; there was the bent female shadow, crooking a finger in the cup to feel how deep the tea was, for she was blind; and there was the Roman-looking rolling shadow in the big armchair – he who twisted his fingers so oddly and jerked his head from side to side and swallowed down the tea in such vast gulps. Dr Johnson, Mr Boswell, and Mrs Williams – those were the shadows' names. So absorbed was she in the sight, that she forgot to think how other ages would have envied her, though it seems probable that on this occasion they would. She was content to gaze and gaze. At length Mr Boswell rose. He saluted the old woman with tart asperity. But with what humility did he not abase himself before the great Roman shadow, who now rose to its full height and rocking somewhat as he stood there rolled out the most magnificent phrases that ever left human lips; so Orlando thought them, though she never heard a word that any of the three shadows said as they sat there drinking tea.

At length she came home one night after one of these saunterings and mounted to her bedroom. She took off her laced coat and stood there in shirt and breeches looking out of the window. There was something stirring in the air which forbade her to go to bed. A white haze lay over the town, for it was a frosty night in midwinter and a magnificent vista lay all round her. She could see St Paul's, the Tower, Westminster Abbey, with all the spires and domes of the city churches, the smooth bulk of its banks, the opulent and ample curves of its halls and meeting-places. On the north rose the smooth, shorn heights of Hampstead, and in the west the streets and squares of Mayfair shone out in one clear radiance. Upon this serene and orderly prospect the stars looked down, glittering, positive, hard, from a cloudless sky. In the extreme clearness of the atmosphere the line of every roof, the cowl of every chimney was perceptible; even the cobbles in the streets showed distinct one from another, and Orlando could not help comparing this orderly scene with the irregular and huddled purlieus which had been the city of London in the reign of Queen Elizabeth. Then, she remembered, the city, if such one could call it, lay crowded, a mere huddle and conglomeration of houses, under her windows at Blackfriars. The stars reflected themselves in deep pits of stagnant water which lay in the middle of the streets. A black shadow at the corner where the wine shop used to stand was, as likely as not, the corpse of a murdered man. She could remember the cries of many a one wounded in such night brawlings, when she was a little boy, held to the diamond-paned window in her nurse's arms. Troops of ruffians, men and women, unspeakably interlaced, lurched down the streets, trolling out wild songs with jewels flashing in their ears, and knives gleaming in their fists. On such a night as this the impermeable tangle of the forests on Highgate and Hampstead would be outlined, writhing in contorted intricacy against the sky. Here and there, on one of the hills which rose above London, was a stark gallows tree, with a corpse nailed to rot or parch on its cross; for danger and insecurity, lust and violence, poetry and filth swarmed over the tortuous Elizabethan highways and buzzed and stank – Orlando could remember even now the smell of them on a hot night – in the little rooms and narrow pathways of the city. Now – she leant out of her window – all was light, order, and serenity. There was the faint rattle of a coach on the cobbles. She heard the far-away cry of the night watchman – 'Just twelve o'clock on a frosty morning.' No sooner had the words left his lips than the first stroke of midnight sounded. Orlando then for the first time noticed a small cloud gathered behind the dome of St Paul's. As the strokes sounded, the cloud increased, and she saw it darken and spread with extraordinary speed. At the same time a light breeze rose and by the time the sixth stroke of midnight had struck the whole of the eastern sky was covered with an irregular moving darkness, though the sky to the west and north stayed clear as ever. Then the cloud spread north. Height upon height above the city was engulfed by it. Only Mayfair, with all its lights shining, burnt more brilliantly than ever by contrast. With the eighth stroke, some hurrying tatters of cloud sprawled over Piccadilly. They seemed to mass themselves and to advance with extraordinary rapidity towards the west end. As the ninth, tenth, and eleventh strokes struck, a huge blackness sprawled over the whole of London. With the twelfth stroke of midnight, the darkness was complete. A turbulent welter of cloud covered the city. All was darkness; all was doubt; all was confusion. The eighteenth century was over; the nineteenth century had begun.

The great cloud which hung, not only over London, but over the whole of the British Isles on the first day of the nineteenth century stayed, or rather, did not stay, for it was buffeted about constantly by blustering gales, long enough to have extraordinary consequences upon those who lived beneath its shadow. A change seemed to have come over the climate of England. Rain fell frequently, but only in fitful gusts, which were no sooner over than they began again. The sun shone, of course, but it was so girt about with clouds and the air was so saturated with water, that its beams were discoloured and purples, oranges, and reds of a dull sort took the place of the more positive landscapes of the eighteenth century. Under this bruised and sullen canopy the green of the cabbages was less intense, and the white of the snow was muddied. But what was worse, damp now began to make its way into every house – damp, which is the most insidious of all enemies, for while the sun can be shut out by blinds, and the frost roasted by a hot fire, damp steals in while we sleep; damp is silent, imperceptible, ubiquitous. Damp swells the wood, furs the kettle, rusts the iron, rots the stone. So gradual is the process, that it is not until we pick up some chest of drawers, or coal scuttle, and the whole thing drops to pieces in our hands, that we suspect even that the disease is at work.

Thus, stealthily and imperceptibly, none marking the exact day or hour of the change, the constitution of England was altered and nobody knew it. Everywhere the effects were felt. The hardy country gentleman, who had sat down gladly to a meal of ale and beef in a room designed, perhaps by the brothers Adam, with classic dignity, now felt chilly. Rugs appeared; beards were grown; trousers were fastened tight under the instep. The chill which he felt in his legs the country gentleman soon transferred to his house; furniture was muffled; walls and tables were covered; nothing was left bare. Then a change of diet became essential. The muffin was invented and the crumpet. Coffee supplanted the after-dinner port, and, as coffee led to a drawing-room in which to drink it, and a drawing-room to glass cases, and glass cases to artificial flowers, and artificial flowers to mantelpieces, and mantelpieces to pianofortes, and pianofortes to drawing-room ballads, and drawing-room ballads (skipping a stage or two) to innumerable little dogs, mats, and china ornaments, the home – which had become extremely important – was completely altered.

Outside the house – it was another effect of the damp – ivy grew in unparalleled profusion. Houses that had been of bare stone were smothered in greenery. No garden, however formal its original design, lacked a shrubbery, a wilderness, a maze. What light penetrated to the bedrooms where children were born was naturally of an obfusc green, and what light penetrated to the drawing-rooms where grown men and women lived came through curtains of brown and purple plush. But the change did not stop at outward things. The damp struck within. Men felt the chill in their hearts; the damp in their minds. In a desperate effort to snuggle their feelings into some sort of warmth one subterfuge was tried after another. Love, birth, and death were all swaddled in a variety of fine phrases. The sexes drew further and further apart. No open conversation was tolerated. Evasions and concealments were sedulously practised on both sides. And just as the ivy and the evergreen rioted in the damp earth outside, so did the same fertility show itself within. The life of the average woman was a succession of childbirths. She married at nineteen and had fifteen or eighteen children by the time she was thirty; for twins abounded. Thus the British Empire came into existence; and thus – for there is no stopping damp; it gets into the inkpot as it gets into the woodwork – sentences swelled, adjectives multiplied, lyrics became epics, and little trifles that had been essays a column long were now encyclopaedias in ten or twenty volumes. But Eusebius Chubb shall be our witness to the effect this all had upon the mind of a sensitive man who could do nothing to stop it. There is a passage towards the end of his memoirs where he describes how, after writing thirty-five folio pages one morning 'all about nothing' he screwed the lid on his inkpot and went for a turn in his garden. Soon he found himself involved in the shrubbery. Innumerable leaves creaked and glistened above his head. He seemed to himself 'to crush the mould of a million more under his feet'. Thick smoke exuded from a damp bonfire at the end of the garden. He reflected that no fire on earth could ever hope to consume that vast vegetable encumbrance. Wherever he looked, vegetation was rampant. Cucumbers 'came scrolloping across the grass to his feet'. Giant cauliflowers towered deck above deck till they rivalled, to his disordered imagination, the elm trees themselves. Hens laid incessantly eggs of no special tint. Then, remembering with a sigh his own fecundity and his poor wife Jane, now in the throes of her fifteenth confinement indoors, how, he asked himself, could he blame the fowls? He looked upwards into the sky. Did not heaven itself, or that great frontispiece of heaven, which is the sky, indicate the assent, indeed, the instigation of the heavenly hierarchy? For there, winter or summer, year in year out, the clouds turned and tumbled, like whales, he pondered, or elephants rather; but no, there was no escaping the simile which was pressed upon him from a thousand airy acres; the whole sky itself as it spread wide above the British Isles was nothing but a vast feather bed; and the undistinguished fecundity of the garden, the bedroom and the hen-roost was copied there. He went indoors, wrote the passage quoted above, laid his head in a gas oven, and when they found him later he was past revival.

While this went on in every part of England, it was all very well for Orlando to mew herself in her house at Blackfriars and pretend that the climate was the same; that one could still say what one liked and wear knee-breeches or skirts as the fancy took one. Even she, at length, was forced to acknowledge that times were changed. One afternoon in the early part of the century she was driving through St James's Park in her old panelled coach when one of those sunbeams, which occasionally, though not often, managed to come to earth, struggled through, marbling the clouds with strange prismatic colours as it passed. Such a sight was sufficiently strange after the clear and uniform skies of the eighteenth century to cause her to pull the window down and look at it. The puce and flamingo clouds made her think with a pleasurable anguish, which proves that she was insensibly afflicted with the damp already, of dolphins dying in Ionian seas. But what was her surprise when, as it struck the earth, the sunbeam seemed to call forth, or to light up, a pyramid, hecatomb, or trophy (for it had something of a banquet-table air) – a conglomeration at any rate of the most hetero-geneous and ill-assorted objects, piled higgledy-piggledy in a vast mound where the statue of Queen Victoria now stands! Draped about a vast cross of fretted and floriated gold were widow's weeds and bridal veils; hooked on to other excrescences were crystal palaces, bassinettes, military helmets, memorial wreaths, trousers, whiskers, wedding cakes, cannon, Christmas trees, telescopes, extinct monsters, globes, maps, elephants, and mathematical instruments – the whole supported like a gigantic coat of arms on the right side by a female figure clothed in flowing white; on the left, by a portly gentleman wearing a frock-coat and sponge-bag trousers. The incongruity of the objects, the association of the fully clothed and the partly draped, the garishness of the different colours and their plaid-like juxtapositions afflicted Orlando with the most profound dismay. She had never, in all her life, seen anything at once so indecent, so hideous, and so monumental. It might, and indeed it must be, the effect of the sun on the waterlogged air; it would vanish with the first breeze that blew; but for all that, it looked, as she drove past, as if it were destined to endure for ever. Nothing, she felt, sinking back into the corner of her coach, no wind, rain, sun, or thunder, could ever demolish that garish erection. Only the noses would mottle and the trumpets would rust; but there they would remain, pointing east, west, south, and north, eternally. She looked back as her coach swept up Constitution Hill. Yes, there it was, still beaming placidly in a light which – she pulled her watch out of her fob – was, of course, the light of twelve o'clock midday. None other could be so prosaic, so matter-of-fact, so impervious to any hint of dawn or sunset, so seemingly calculated to last for ever. She was determined not to look again. Already she felt the tides of her blood run sluggishly. But what was more peculiar, a blush, vivid and singular, over-spread her cheeks as she passed Buckingham Palace and her eyes seemed forced by a superior power down upon her knees. Suddenly she saw with a start that she was wearing black breeches. She never ceased blushing till she had reached her country house, which, considering the time it takes four

Orlando about the year 1840

horses to trot thirty miles, will be taken, we hope, as a signal proof of her chastity.

Once there, she followed what had now become the most imperious need of her nature and wrapped herself as well as she could in a damask quilt which she snatched from her bed. She explained to the Widow Bartholomew (who had succeeded good old Grimsditch as housekeeper) that she felt chilly.

'So do we all, m'lady,' said the Widow, heaving a profound sigh. 'The walls is sweating,' she said, with a curious, lugubrious complacency, and sure enough, she had only to lay her hand on the oak panels for the finger prints to be marked there. The ivy had grown so profusely that many windows were now sealed up. The kitchen was so dark that they could scarcely tell a kettle from a cullender. A poor black cat had been mistaken for coals and shovelled on the fire. Most of the maids were already wearing three or four red-flannel petticoats, though the month was August.

'But is it true, m'lady,' the good woman asked, hugging herself, while the golden crucifix heaved on her bosom, 'that the Queen, bless her, is wearing a what d'you call it, a – ' the good woman hesitated and blushed.

'A crinoline,' Orlando helped her out with it (for the word had reached Blackfriars). Mrs Bartholomew nodded. The tears were already running down her cheeks, but as she wept she smiled. For it was pleasant to weep. Were they not all of them weak women? wearing crinolines the better to conceal the fact; the great fact; the only fact; but, nevertheless, the deplorable fact; which every modest woman did her best to deny until denial was impossible; the fact that she was about to bear a child? to bear fifteen or twenty children indeed, so that most of a modest woman's life was spent, after all, in denying what, on one day at least of every year, was made obvious.

'The muffins is keepin' 'ot,' said Mrs Bartholomew, mopping up her tears, 'in the liberry.'

And wrapped in a damask bed quilt, to a dish of muffins Orlando now sat down.

'The muffins is keepin' 'ot in the liberry' – Orlando minced out the horrid cockney phrase in Mrs Bartholomew's refined cockney accents as she drank but no, she detested the mild fluid – her tea. It was in this very room, she remembered, that Queen Elizabeth had stood astride the fireplace with a flagon of beer in her hand, which she suddenly dashed on the table when Lord Burghley tactlessly used the imperative instead of the subjunctive. 'Little man, little man' – Orlando could hear her say – 'is "must" a word to be addressed to princes?' And down came the flagon on the table: there was the mark of it still.

But when Orlando leapt to her feet, as the mere thought of that great Queen commanded, the bed quilt tripped her up, and she fell back in her armchair with a curse. Tomorrow she would have to buy twenty yards or more of black bombazine, she supposed, to make a skirt. And then (here she blushed), she would have to buy a crinoline, and then (here she blushed) a bassinette, and then another crinoline, and so on . . . The blushes came and went with the most exquisite iteration of modesty and shame imaginable. One might see the spirit of the age blowing, now hot, now cold, upon her cheeks. And if the spirit of the age blew a little unequally, the crinoline being blushed for before the husband, her ambiguous position must excuse her (even her sex was still in dispute) and the irregular life she had lived before.

At length the colour on her cheeks resumed its stability and it seemed as if the spirit of the age – if such indeed it were – lay dormant for a time. Then Orlando felt in the bosom of her shirt as if for some locket or relic of lost affection, and drew out no such thing, but a roll of paper, sea-stained, blood-stained, travel-stained – the manuscript of her poem, 'The Oak Tree'. She had carried this about with her for so many years now, and in such hazardous circumstances, that many of the pages were stained, some were torn, while the straits she had been in for writing paper when with the gypsies, had forced her to overscore the margins and cross the lines till the manuscript looked like a piece of darning most conscientiously carried out. She turned back to the first page and read the date, 1586, written in her own boyish hand. She had been working at it for close on three hundred years now. It was time to make an end. Meanwhile she began turning and dipping and reading and skipping and thinking as she read, how very little she had changed all these years. She had been a gloomy boy, in love with death, as boys are; and then she had been amorous and florid; and then she had been sprightly and satirical; and sometimes she had tried prose and sometimes she had tried drama. Yet through all these changes she had remained, she reflected, fundamentally the same. She had the same brooding meditative temper, the same love of animals and nature, the same passion for the country and the seasons.

'After all,' she thought, getting up and going to the window, 'nothing has changed. The house, the garden are precisely as they were. Not a chair has been moved, not a trinket sold. There are the same walks, the same lawns, the same trees, and the same pool, which, I dare say, has the same carp in it. True, Queen Victoria is on the throne and not Queen Elizabeth, but what difference . . . '

No sooner had the thought taken shape, than, as if to rebuke it, the door was flung wide and in marched Basket, the butler, followed by Bartholomew, the housekeeper, to clear away tea. Orlando, who had just dipped her pen in the ink, and was about to indite some reflection upon the eternity of all things, was much annoyed to be impeded by a blot, which spread and meandered round her pen. It was some infirmity of the quill, she supposed; it was split or dirty. She dipped it again. The blot increased. She tried to go on with what she was saying; no words came. Next she began to decorate the blot with wings and whiskers, till it became a round-headed monster, something between a bat and a wombat. But as for writing poetry with Basket and Bartholomew in the room, it was impossible. No sooner had she said 'Impossible' than, to her astonishment and alarm, the pen began to curve and caracole with the smoothest possible fluency. Her page was written in the neatest sloping Italian hand with the most insipid verse she had ever read in her life:

> I am myself but a vile link
> Amid life's weary chain,
> But I have spoken hallow'd words,
> Oh, do not say in vain!
>
> Will the young maiden, when her tears,
> Alone in moonlight shine,
> Tears for the absent and the loved,
> Murmur –

she wrote without a stop as Bartholomew and Basket grunted and groaned about the room, mending the fire, picking up the muffins.

Again she dipped her pen and off it went –

> She was so changed, the soft carnation cloud
> Once mantling o'er her cheek like that which eve
> Hangs o'er the sky, glowing with roseate hue,
> Had faded into paleness, broken by
> Bright burning blushes, torches of the tomb,

but here, by an abrupt movement she spilt the ink over the page and blotted it from human sight she hoped for ever. She was all of a quiver, all of a stew. Nothing more repulsive could be imagined than to feel the ink flowing thus in cascades of involuntary inspiration. What had happened to her? Was it the damp, was it Bartholomew, was it Basket, what was it? she demanded. But the room was empty. No one answered her, unless the dripping of the rain in the ivy could be taken for an answer.

Meanwhile, she became conscious, as she stood at the window, of an extraordinary tingling and vibration all over her, as if she were made of a thousand wires upon which some breeze or errant fingers were playing scales. Now her toes tingled; now her marrow. She had the queerest sensations about the thigh bones. Her hairs seemed to erect themselves. Her arms sang and twanged as the telegraph wires would be singing and twanging in twenty years or so. But all this agitation seemed at length to concentrate in her hands; and then in one hand, and then in one finger of that hand, and then finally to contract itself so that it made a ring of quivering sensibility about the second finger of the left hand. And when she raised it to see what caused this agitation, she saw nothing – nothing but the vast solitary emerald which Queen Elizabeth had given her. And was that not enough? she asked. It was of the finest water. It was worth ten thousand pounds at least. The vibration seemed, in the oddest way (but remember we are dealing with some of the darkest manifestations of the human soul) to say No, that is not enough; and, further, to assume a note of interrogation, as though it were asking, what did it mean, this hiatus, this strange oversight? till poor Orlando felt positively ashamed of the second finger of her left hand without in the least knowing why. At this moment, Bartholomew came in to ask which dress she should lay out for dinner, and Orlando, whose senses were much quickened, instantly glanced at Bartholomew's left hand, and instantly perceived what she had never noticed before – a thick ring of rather jaundiced yellow circling the third finger where her own was bare.

'Let me look at your ring, Bartholomew,' she said, stretching her hand to take it.

At this, Bartholomew made as if she had been struck in the breast by a rogue. She started back a pace or two, clenched her hand and flung it away from her with a gesture that was noble in the extreme. 'No,' she said, with resolute dignity, her Ladyship might look if she pleased, but as for taking off her wedding ring, not the Archbishop nor the Pope nor Queen Victoria on her throne could force her to do that. Her Thomas had put it on her finger twenty-five years, six months, three weeks ago; she had slept in it; worked in it; washed in it; prayed in it; and proposed to be buried in it. In fact, Orlando understood her to say, but her voice was much broken with emotion, that it was by the gleam on her wedding ring that she would be assigned her station among the angels and its lustre would be tarnished for ever if she let it out of her keeping for a second.

'Heaven help us,' said Orlando, standing at the window and watching the pigeons at their pranks, 'what a world we live in! What a world to be sure!' Its complexities amazed her. It now seemed to her that the whole world was ringed with gold. She went in to dinner. Wedding rings abounded. She went to church. Wedding rings were everywhere. She drove out. Gold, or pinchbeck, thin, thick, plain, smooth, they glowed dully on every hand. Rings filled the jewellers' shops, not the flashing pastes and diamonds of Orlando's recollection, but simple bands without a stone in them. At the same time, she began to notice a new habit among the town people. In the old days, one would meet a boy trifling with a girl under a hawthorn hedge frequently enough. Orlando had flicked many a couple with the tip of her whip and laughed and passed on. Now, all that was changed. Couples trudged and plodded in the middle of the road indissolubly linked together. The woman's right hand was invariably passed through the man's left and her fingers were firmly gripped by his. Often it was not till the horses' noses were on them that they budged, and then, though they moved it was all in one piece, heavily, to the side of the road. Orlando could only suppose that some new discovery had been made about the race; that they were somehow stuck together, couple after couple, but who had made it, and when, she could not guess. It did not seem to be Nature. She looked at the doves and the rabbits and the elk-hounds and she could not see that Nature had changed her ways or mended them, since the time of Elizabeth at least. There was no indissoluble alliance among the brutes that she could see. Could it be Queen Victoria then, or Lord Melbourne? Was it from them that the great discovery of marriage proceeded? Yet the Queen, she pondered, was said to be fond of dogs, and Lord Melbourne, she had heard, was said to be fond of women. It was strange – it was distasteful; indeed, there was something in this indissolubility of bodies which was repugnant to her sense of decency and sanitation. Her ruminations, however, were accompanied by such a tingling and twangling of the afflicted finger that she could scarcely keep her ideas in order. They were languishing and ogling like a house-maid's fancies. They made her blush. There was nothing for it but to buy one of those ugly bands and wear it like the rest. This she did, slipping it, overcome with shame, upon her finger in the shadow of a curtain; but without avail. The tingling persisted more violently, more indignantly than ever. She did not sleep a wink that night. Next morning when she took up the pen to write, either she could think of nothing, and the pen make one large lachrymose blot after another, or it ambled off, more alarmingly still, into mellifluous fluencies about early death and corruption, which were worse than no thinking at all. For it would seem – her case proved it – that we write, not with the fingers, but with the whole person. The nerve which controls the pen winds itself about every fibre of our being, threads the heart, pierces the liver. Though the seat of her trouble seemed to be the left hand, she could feel herself poisoned through and through, and was forced at length to consider the most desperate of remedies, which was to yield completely and submissively to the spirit of the age, and take a husband.

That this was much against her natural temperament has been sufficiently made plain. When the sound of the Archduke's chariot wheels died away, the cry that rose to her lips was 'Life! A Lover!' not 'Life! A Husband!' and it was in pursuit of this aim that she had gone to town and run about the world as has been shown in the previous chapter. Such is the indomitable nature of the spirit of the age, however, that it batters down anyone who tries to make stand against it far more effectually than those who bend its own way. Orlando had inclined herself naturally to the Elizabethan spirit, to the Restoration spirit, to the spirit of the eighteenth century, and had in consequence scarcely been aware of the change from one age to the other. But the spirit of the nine-teenth century was antipathetic to her in the extreme, and thus it took her and broke her, and she was aware of her defeat at its hands as she had never been before. For it is probable that the human spirit has its place in time assigned to it; some are born of this age, some of that; and now that Orlando was grown a woman, a year or two past thirty indeed, the lines of her character were fixed, and to bend them the wrong way was intolerable.

So she stood mournfully at the drawing-room window (Bartholomew had so christened the library) dragged down by the weight of the crinoline which she had submissively adopted. It was heavier and more drab than any dress she had yet worn. None had ever so impeded her movements. No longer could she stride through the garden with her dogs, or run lightly to the high mound and fling herself beneath the oak tree. Her skirts collected damp leaves and straw. The plumed hat tossed on the breeze. The thin shoes were quickly soaked and mud-caked. Her muscles had lost their pliancy. She became nervous lest there should be robbers behind the wainscot and afraid, for the first time in her life, of ghosts in the corridors. All these things inclined her, step by step, to submit to the new discovery, whether Queen Victoria's or another's, that each man and each woman has another allotted to it for life, whom it supports, by whom it is supported, till death them do part. It would be a comfort, she felt, to lean; to sit down; yes, to lie down; never, never to get up again. Thus did the spirit work upon her, for all her past pride, and as she came sloping down the scale of emotion to this lowly and unaccustomed lodging-place, those twanglings and tinglings which had been so captious and so interrogative modulated into the sweetest melodies, till it seemed as if angels were plucking harp-strings with white fingers and her whole being was pervaded by a seraphic harmony.

But whom could she lean upon? She asked that question of the wild autumn winds. For it was now October, and wet as usual. Not the Archduke; he had married a very great lady and had hunted hares in Roumania these many years now; nor Mr M.; he was become a Catholic; nor the Marquis of C.; he made sacks in Botany Bay; nor the Lord O.; he had long been food for fishes. One way or another, all her old cronies were gone now, and the Nells and the Kits of Drury Lane, much though she favoured them, scarcely did to lean upon.

'Whom', she asked, casting her eyes upon the revolving clouds, clasping her hands as she knelt on the window-sill, and looking the very image of appealing womanhood as she did so, 'can I lean upon?' Her words formed themselves, her hands clasped themselves, involuntarily, just as her pen had written of its own accord. It was not Orlando who spoke, but the spirit of the age. But whichever it was, nobody answered it. The rooks were tumbling pell-mell among the violet clouds of autumn. The rain had stopped at last and there was an iridescence in the sky which tempted her to put on her plumed hat and her little stringed shoes and stroll out before dinner.

'Everyone is mated except myself,' she mused, as she trailed disconsolately across the courtyard. There were the rooks; Canute and Pippin even – transitory as their alliances were, still each this evening seemed to have a partner. 'Whereas, I, who am mistress of it all,' Orlando thought, glancing as she passed at the innumerable emblazoned windows of the hall, 'am single, am mateless, am alone.'

Such thoughts had never entered her head before. Now they bore her down unescapably. Instead of thrusting the gate open, she tapped with a

Marmaduke Bonthrop Shelmerdine, Esquire

gloved hand for the porter to unfasten it for her. One must lean on someone, she thought, if it is only on a porter; and half wished to stay behind and help him to grill his chop on a bucket of fiery coals, but was too timid to ask it. So she strayed out into the park alone, faltering at first and apprehensive lest there might be poachers or gamekeepers or even errand-boys to marvel that a great lady should walk alone.

At every step she glanced nervously lest some male form should be hiding behind a furze bush or some savage cow be lowering its horns to toss her. But there were only the rooks flaunting in the sky. A steel-blue plume from one of them fell among the heather. She loved wild birds' feathers. She had used to collect them as a boy. She picked it up and stuck it in her hat. The air blew upon her spirit somewhat and revived it. As the rooks went whirling and wheeling above her head and feather after feather fell gleaming through the purplish air, she followed them, her long cloak floating behind her, over the moor, up the hill. She had not walked so far for years. Six feathers had she picked from the grass and drawn between her finger tips and pressed to her lips to feel their smooth, glinting plumage, when she saw, gleaming on the hillside, a silver pool, mysterious as the lake into which Sir Bedivere flung the sword of Arthur. A single feather quivered in the air and fell into the middle of it. Then, some strange ecstasy came over her. Some wild notion she had of following the birds to the rim of the world and flinging herself on the spongy turf and there drinking forgetfulness, while the rooks' hoarse laughter sounded over her. She quickened her pace; she ran; she tripped; the tough heather roots flung her to the ground. Her ankle was broken. She could not rise. But there she lay content. The scent of the bog myrtle and the meadow-sweet was in her nostrils. The rooks' hoarse laughter was in her ears. 'I have found my mate,' she murmured. 'It is the moor. I am nature's bride,' she whispered, giving herself in rapture to the cold embraces of the grass as she lay folded in her cloak in the hollow by the pool. 'Here will I lie. (A feather fell upon her brow.) I have found a greener laurel than the bay. My forehead will be cool always. There are wild birds' feathers – the owl's, the nightjar's. I shall dream wild dreams. My hands shall wear no wedding ring,' she continued, slipping it from her finger. 'The roots shall twine about them. Ah!' she sighed, pressing her head luxuriously on its spongy pillow, 'I have sought happiness through many ages and not found it; fame and missed it; love and not known it; life – and behold, death is better. I have known many men and many women,' she continued; 'none have I understood. It is better that I should lie at peace here with only the sky above me – as the gypsy told me years ago. That was in Turkey.' And she looked straight up into the marvellous golden foam into which the clouds had churned themselves, and saw next moment a track in it, and camels passing in single file through the rocky desert among clouds of red dust; and then, when the camels had passed, there were only mountains, very high and full of clefts and with pinnacles of rock, and she fancied she heard goat bells ringing in their passes, and in their folds were fields of irises and gentian. So the sky changed and her eyes slowly lowered themselves down and down till they came to the rain-darkened earth and saw the great hump of the South Downs, flowing in one wave along the coast; and where the land parted, there was the sea, the sea with ships passing; and she fancied she heard a gun far out at sea, and thought at first, 'That's the Armada,' and then thought, 'No, it's Nelson,' and then remembered how those wars were over and the ships were busy merchant ships; and the sails on the winding river were those of pleasure boats. She saw, too, cattle sprinkled on the dark fields, sheep and cows, and she saw the lights coming here and there in farmhouse windows, and lanterns moving among the cattle as the shepherd went his rounds and the cowman; and then the lights went out and the stars rose and tangled themselves about the sky. Indeed, she was falling asleep with the wet feathers on her face and her ear pressed to the ground when she heard, deep within, some hammer on an anvil, or was it a heart beating? Tick-tock, tick-tock, so it hammered, so it beat, the anvil, or the heart in the middle of the earth; until, as she listened, she thought it changed to the trot of a horse's hoofs; one, two, three, four, she counted; then she heard a stumble; then, as it came nearer and nearer, she could hear the crack of a twig and the suck of the wet bog in its hoofs. The horse was almost on her. She sat upright. Towering dark against the yellow-slashed sky of dawn, with the plovers rising and falling about him, she saw a man on horseback. He started. The horse stopped.

'Madam,' the man cried, leaping to the ground, 'you're hurt!'

'I'm dead, sir!' she replied.

A few minutes later, they became engaged.

The morning after, as they sat at breakfast, he told her his name. It was Marmaduke Bonthrop Shelmerdine, Esquire.

'I knew it!' she said, for there was something romantic and chivalrous, passionate, melancholy, yet determined about him which went with the wild, dark-plumed name – a name which had, in her mind, the steel-blue gleam of rooks' wings, the hoarse laughter of their caws, the snakelike twisting descent of their feathers in a silver pool, and a thousand other things which will be described presently.

'Mine is Orlando,' she said. He had guessed it. For if you see a ship in full sail coming with the sun on it proudly sweeping across the Mediterranean from the South Seas, one says at once, 'Orlando,' he explained.

In fact, though their acquaintance had been so short, they had guessed, as always happens between lovers, everything of any importance about each other in two seconds at the utmost, and it now remained only to fill in such unimportant details as what they were called; where they lived; and whether they were beggars or people of substance. He had a castle in the Hebrides, but it was ruined, he told her. Gannets feasted in the banqueting-hall. He had been a soldier and a sailor, and had explored the East. He was on his way now to join his brig at Falmouth, but the wind had fallen and it was only when the gale blew from the South-west that he could put out to sea. Orlando looked hastily from the breakfast-room window at the gilt leopard on the weather vane. Mercifully its tail pointed due east and was steady as a rock. 'Oh! Shel, don't leave me!' she cried. 'I'm passionately in love with you,' she said. No sooner had the words left her mouth than an awful suspicion rushed into both their minds simultaneously,

'You're a woman, Shel!' she cried.

'You're a man, Orlando!' he cried.

Never was there such a scene of protestation and demonstration as then took place since the world began. When it was over and they were seated again she asked him, what was this talk of a South-west gale? Where was he bound for?

'For the Horn,' he said briefly, and blushed. (For a man had to blush as a woman had, only at rather different things.) It was only by dint of great pressure on her side and the use of much intuition that she gathered that his life was spent in the most desperate and splendid of adventures which is to voyage round Cape Horn in the teeth of a gale. Masts had been snapped off; sails torn to ribbons (she had to drag the admission from him). Sometimes the ship had sunk, and he had been left the only survivor on a raft with a biscuit.

'It's about all a fellow can do nowadays,' he said sheepishly, and helped himself to great spoonfuls of strawberry jam. The vision which she had thereupon of this boy (for he was little more) sucking peppermints, for which he had a passion, while the masts snapped and the stars reeled and he roared brief orders to cut this adrift, to heave that overboard, brought the tears to her eyes, tears, she noted, of a finer flavour than any she had cried before. 'I am a woman,' she thought, 'a real woman, at last.' She thanked Bonthrop from the bottom of her heart for having given her this rare and unexpected delight. Had she not been lame in the left foot, she would have sat upon his knee.

'Shel, my darling,' she began again, 'tell me . . . ' and so they talked two hours or more, perhaps about Cape Horn, perhaps not, and really it would profit little to write down what they said, for they knew each other so well that they could say anything, which is tantamount to saying nothing, or saying such stupid, prosy things as how to cook an omelette, or where to buy the best boots in London, things which have no lustre taken from their setting, yet are positively of amazing beauty within it. For it has come about, by the wise economy of nature, that our modern spirit can almost dispense with language; the commonest expressions do, since no expressions do; hence the most ordinary conversation is often the most poetic, and the most poetic is precisely that which cannot be written down. For which reasons we leave a great blank here, which must be taken to indicate that the space is filled to repletion.

After some days more of this kind of talk,

'Orlando, my dearest,' Shel was beginning, when there was a scuffling outside, and Basket the butler entered with the information that there was a couple of Peelers downstairs with a warrant from the Queen.

'Show 'em up,' said Shelmerdine briefly, as if on his own quarterdeck, taking up, by instinct, a stand with his hands behind him in front of the fireplace. Two officers in bottle-green uniforms with truncheons at their hips then entered the room and stood at attention. Formalities being over, they gave into Orlando's own hands, as their commission was, a legal document of some very impressive sort, judging by the blobs of sealing wax, the ribbons, the oaths, and the signatures, which were all of the highest importance.

Orlando ran her eyes through it and then, using the first finger of her right hand as pointer, read out the following facts as being most germane to the matter.

'The lawsuits are settled,' she read out . . . 'some in my favour, as for example . . . others not. Turkish marriage annulled (I was ambassador in Constantinople, Shel,' she explained). 'Children pronounced illegitimate (they said I had three sons by Pepita, a Spanish dancer). So they don't inherit, which is all to the good . . . Sex? Ah! what about sex? My sex', she read out with some solemnity, 'is pronounced indisputably, and beyond the shadow of a doubt (what was I telling you a moment ago, Shel?), female. The estates which are now desequestrated in perpetuity descend and are tailed and entailed upon the heirs male of my body, or in default of marriage' – but here she grew impatient with this legal verbiage, and said, 'but there won't be any default of marriage, nor of heirs either, so the rest can be taken as read.' Whereupon she appended her own signature beneath Lord Palmerston's and entered from that moment into the undisturbed possession of her titles, her house, and her estate – which was now so much shrunk, for the cost of the lawsuits had been prodigious, that, though she was infinitely noble again, she was also excessively poor.

When the result of the lawsuit was made known (and rumour flew much quicker than the telegraph which has supplanted it), the whole town was filled with rejoicings.

[Horses were put into carriages for the sole purpose of being taken out. Empty barouches and landaus were trundled up and down the High Street incessantly. Addresses were read from the Bull. Replies were made from the Stag. The town was illuminated. Gold caskets were securely sealed in glass cases. Coins were well and duly laid under stones. Hospitals were founded. Rat and Sparrow clubs were inaugurated. Turkish women by the dozen were burnt in effigy in the marketplace, together with scores of peasant boys with the label 'I am a base Pretender', lolling from their mouths. The Queen's cream-coloured ponies were soon seen trotting up the avenue with a command to Orlando to dine and sleep at the Castle, that very same night. Her table, as on a previous occasion, was snowed under with invitations from the Countess of R., Lady Q., Lady Palmerston, the Marchioness of P., Mrs W. E. Gladstone, and others, beseeching the pleasure of her company, reminding her of ancient alliances between their family and her own, etc.] – all of which is properly enclosed in square brackets, as above, for the good reason that a parenthesis it was without any importance in Orlando's life. She skipped it, to get on with the text. For when the bonfires were blazing in the marketplace, she was in the dark woods with Shelmerdine alone. So fine was the weather that the trees stretched their branches motionless above them, and if a leaf fell, it fell, spotted red and gold, so slowly that one could watch it for half an hour fluttering and falling till it came to rest at last, on Orlando's foot.

'Tell me, Mar,' she would say (and here it must be explained, that when she called him by the first syllable of his first name, she was in a dreamy, amorous, acquiescent mood, domestic, languid a little, as if spiced logs were burning, and it was evening, yet not time to dress, and a thought wet perhaps outside, enough to make the leaves glisten, but a nightingale might be singing even so among the azaleas, two or three dogs barking at distant farms, a cock crowing – all of which the reader should imagine in her voice) – 'Tell me, Mar,' she would say, 'about Cape Horn.' Then Shelmerdine would make a little model on the ground of the Cape with twigs and dead leaves and an empty snail shell or two.

'Here's the north,' he would say. 'There's the south. The wind's coming from hereabouts. Now the brig is sailing due west; we've just lowered the top-boom mizzen; and so you see – here, where this bit of grass is, she enters the current which you'll find marked – where's my map and compasses, Bo'sun? – Ah! thanks, that'll do, where the snail shell is. The current catches her on the starboard side, so we must rig the jib-boom or we shall be carried to the larboard, which is where that beech leaf – is for you must understand my dear – ' and so he would go on, and she would listen to every word; interpreting them rightly, so as to see, that is to say, without his having to tell her, the phosphorescence on the waves; the icicles clanking in the shrouds; how he went to the top of the mast in a gale; there reflected on the destiny of man; came down again; had a whisky and soda; went on shore; was trapped by a black woman; repented; reasoned it out; read Pascal; determined to write philosophy; bought a monkey; debated the true end of life; decided in favour of Cape Horn, and so on. All this and a thousand other things she understood him to say, and so when she replied, Yes, negresses are seductive, aren't they? he having told her that the supply of biscuits now gave out, he was surprised and delighted to find how well she had taken his meaning.

'Are you positive you aren't a man?' he would ask anxiously, and she would echo,

'Can it be possible you're not a woman?' and then they must put it to the proof without more ado. For each was so surprised at the quickness of the other's sympathy, and it was to each such a revelation that a woman could be as tolerant and free-spoken as a man, and a man as strange and subtle as a woman, that they had to put the matter to the proof at once.

And so they would go on talking or rather, understanding, which has become the main art of speech in an age when words are growing daily so scanty in comparison with ideas that 'the biscuits ran out' has to stand for kissing a negress in the dark when one has just read Bishop Berkeley's philosophy for the tenth time. (And from this it follows that only the most profound masters of style can tell the truth, and when one meets a simple one-syllabled writer, one may conclude, without any doubt at all, that the poor man is lying.)

So they would talk; and then, when her feet were fairly covered with spotted autumn leaves, Orlando would rise and stroll away into the heart of the woods in solitude, leaving Bonthrop sitting there among the snail shells, making models of Cape Horn. 'Bonthrop,' she would say, 'I'm off,' and when she called him by his second name, 'Bonthrop', it should signify to the reader that she was in a solitary mood, felt them both as specks on a desert, was desirous only of meeting death by herself, for people die daily, die at dinner-tables, or like this, out of doors in the autumn woods; and with the bonfires blazing and Lady Palmerston or Lady Derby asking her out every night to dinner, the desire for death would overcome her, and so saying 'Bonthrop', she said in effect, 'I'm dead', and pushed her way as a spirit might through the spectre-pale beech trees, and so oared herself deep into solitude as if the little flicker of noise and movement were over and she were free now to take her way – all of which the reader should hear in her voice when she said 'Bonthrop'; and should also add, the better to illumine the word, that for him too the same word signified, mystically, separation and isolation and the disembodied pacing the deck of his brig in unfathomable seas.

After some hours of death, suddenly a jay shrieked 'Shelmerdine', and stooping, she picked one of those autumn crocuses which to some people signify that very word, and put it with the jay's feather that came tumbling blue through the beech woods, in her breast. Then she called 'Shelmerdine' and the word went shooting this way and that way through the woods and struck him where he sat, making models out of snail shells in the grass. He saw her, and heard her coming to him with the crocus and the jay's feather in her breast, and cried 'Orlando', which meant (and it must be remembered that when bright colours like blue and yellow mix themselves in our eyes, some of it rubs off on our thoughts) first the bowing and swaying of bracken as if something were breaking through; which proved to be a ship in full sail, heaving and tossing a little dreamily, rather as if she had a whole year of summer days to make her voyage in; and so the ship bears down, heaving this way, heaving that way, nobly, indolently, and rides over the crest of this wave and sinks into the hollow of that one, and so, suddenly stands over you (who are in a little cockle shell of a boat, looking up at her) with all her sails quivering, and then, behold, they drop all of a heap on deck – as Orlando dropped now into the grass beside him.

Eight or nine days had been spent thus, but on the tenth, which was the 26th of October, Orlando was lying in the bracken, while Shelmerdine recited Shelley (whose entire works he had by heart), when a leaf which had started to fall slowly enough from a tree-top whipped briskly across Orlando's foot. A second leaf followed and then a third. Orlando shivered and turned pale. It was the wind. Shelmerdine – but it would be more proper now to call him Bonthrop – leapt to his feet.

'The wind!' he cried.

Together they ran through the woods, the wind plastering them with leaves as they ran, to the great court and through it and the little courts, frightened servants leaving their brooms and their saucepans to follow after till they reached the Chapel, and there a scattering of lights was lit as fast as could be, one knocking over this bench, another snuffing out that taper. Bells were rung. People were summoned. At length there was Mr Dupper catching at the ends of his white tie and asking where was the prayer book. And they thrust Queen Mary's prayer book in his hands and he searched hastily fluttering the pages, and said, 'Marmaduke Bonthrop Shelmerdine, and Lady Orlando, kneel down'; and they knelt down, and now they were bright and now they were dark as the light and shadow came flying helter-skelter through the painted windows; and among the banging of innumerable doors and a sound like brass pots beating, the organ sounded, its growl coming loud and faint alternately, and Mr Dupper, who was grown a very old man, tried now to raise his voice above the uproar and could not be heard and then all was quiet for a moment, and one word – it might be 'the jaws of death' – rang out clear, while all the estate servants kept pressing in with rakes and whips still in their hands to listen, and some sang aloud and others prayed, and now a bird was dashed against the pane, and now there was a clap of thunder, so that no one heard the word Obey spoken or saw, except as a golden flash, the ring pass from hand to hand. All was movement and confusion. And up they rose with the organ booming and the lightning playing and the rain pouring, and the Lady Orlando, with her ring on her finger, went out into the court in her thin dress and held the swinging stirrup, for the horse was bitted and bridled and the foam was still on his flank, for her husband to mount, which he did with one bound, and the horse leapt forward and Orlando, standing there, cried out Marmaduke Bonthrop Shelmerdine! and he answered her Orlando! and the words went dashing and circling like wild hawks together among the belfries and higher and higher, further and further, faster and faster they circled, till they crashed and fell in a shower of fragments to the ground; and she went in.

Chapter 6

Orlando went indoors. It was completely still. It was very silent. There was the inkpot: there was the pen; there was the manuscript of her poem, broken off in the middle of a tribute to eternity. She had been about to say, when Basket and Bartholomew interrupted with the tea things, nothing changes. And then, in the space of three seconds and a half, everything had changed – she had broken her ankle, fallen in love, married Shelmerdine.

There was the wedding ring on her finger to prove it. It was true that she had put it there herself before she met Shelmerdine, but that had proved worse than useless. She now turned the ring round and round, with superstitious reverence, taking care lest it should slip past the joint of her finger.

'The wedding ring has to be put on the third finger of the left hand,' she said, like a child cautiously repeating its lesson, 'for it to be of any use at all.'

She spoke thus, aloud and rather more pompously than was her wont, as if she wished someone whose good opinion she desired to overhear her. Indeed, she had in mind, now that she was at last able to collect her thoughts, the effect that her behaviour would have had upon the spirit of the age. She was extremely anxious to be informed whether the steps she had taken in the matter of getting engaged to Shelmerdine and marrying him met with its approval. She was certainly feeling more herself. Her finger had not tingled once, or nothing to count, since that night on the moor. Yet, she could not deny that she had her doubts. She was married, true; but if one's husband was always sailing round Cape Horn, was it marriage? If one liked him, was it marriage? If one liked other people, was it marriage? And finally, if one still wished, more than anything in the whole world, to write poetry, was it marriage? She had her doubts.

But she would put it to the test. She looked at the ring. She looked at the inkpot. Did she dare? No, she did not. But she must. No, she could not. What should she do then? Faint, if possible. But she had never felt better in her life.

'Hang it all!' she cried, with a touch of her old spirit, 'Here goes!'

And she plunged her pen neck deep in the ink. To her enormous surprise, there was no explosion. She drew the nib out. It was wet, but not dripping. She wrote. The words were a little long in coming, but come they did. Ah! but did they make sense? she wondered, a panic coming over her lest the pen might have been at some of its involuntary pranks again. She read,

> And then I came to a field where the springing grass
> Was dulled by the hanging cups of fritillaries,
> Sullen and foreign-looking, the snaky flower,
> Scarfed in dull purple, like Egyptian girls –

As she wrote she felt some power (remember we are dealing with the most obscure manifestations of the human spirit) reading over her shoulder, and when she had written 'Egyptian girls', the power told her to stop. Grass, the power seemed to say, going back with a ruler such as governesses use to the beginning, is all right; the hanging cups of fritillaries – admirable; the snaky flower – a thought, strong from a lady's pen, perhaps, but Wordsworth, no doubt, sanctions it; but – girls? Are girls necessary? You have a husband at the Cape, you say? Ah, well, that'll do.

And so the spirit passed on.

Orlando now performed in spirit (for all this took place in spirit) a deep obeisance to the spirit of her age, such as – to compare great things with small – a traveller, conscious that he has a bundle of cigars in the corner of his suitcase, makes to the customs officer who has obligingly made a scribble of white chalk on the lid. For she was extremely doubtful whether, if the spirit had examined the contents of her mind carefully, it would not have found something highly contraband for which she would have had to pay the full fine. She had only escaped by the skin of her teeth. She had just managed, by some dexterous deference to the spirit of the age, by putting on a ring and finding a man on a moor, by loving nature and being no satirist, cynic, or psychologist – any one of which goods would have been discovered at once – to pass its examination successfully. And she heaved a deep sigh of relief, as, indeed, well she might, for the transaction between a writer and the spirit of the age is one of infinite delicacy, and upon a nice arrangement between the two the whole fortune of his works depends. Orlando had so ordered it that she was in an extremely happy position; she need neither fight her age, nor submit to it; she was of it, yet remained herself. Now, therefore, she could write, and write she did. She wrote. She wrote. She wrote.

It was now November. After November, comes December. Then January, February, March, and April. After April comes May. June, July, August follow. Next is September. Then October, and so, behold, here we are back at November again, with a whole year accomplished.

This method of writing biography, though it has its merits, is a little bare, perhaps, and the reader, if we go on with it, may complain that he could recite the calendar for himself and so save his pocket whatever sum the Hogarth Press may think proper to charge for this book. But what can the biographer do when his subject has put him in the predicament into which Orlando has now put us? Life, it has been agreed by everyone whose opinion is worth consulting, is the only fit subject for novelist or biographer; life, the same authorities have decided, has nothing whatever to do with sitting still in a chair and thinking. Thought and life are as the poles asunder. Therefore – since sitting in a chair and thinking is precisely what Orlando is doing now – there is nothing for it but to recite the calendar, tell one's beads, blow one's nose, stir the fire, look out of the window, until she has done. Orlando sat so still that you could have heard a pin drop. Would, indeed, that a pin had dropped! That would have been life of a kind. Or if a butterfly had fluttered through the window and settled on her chair, one could write about that. Or suppose she had got up and killed a wasp. Then, at once, we could out with our pens and write. For there would be bloodshed, if only the blood of a wasp. Where there is blood there is life. And if killing a wasp is the merest trifle compared with killing a man, still it is a fitter subject for novelist or biographer than this mere wool-gathering; this thinking; this sitting in a chair day in, day out, with a cigarette and a sheet of paper and a pen and an inkpot. If only subjects, we might complain (for our patience is wearing thin), had more consideration for their biographers! What is more irritating than to see one's subject, on whom one has lavished so much time and trouble, slipping out of one's grasp altogether and indulging – witness her sighs and gasps, her flushing, her palings, her eyes now bright as lamps, now haggard as dawns – what is more humiliating than to see all this dumb show of emotion and excitement gone through before our eyes when we know that what causes it – thought and imagination – are of no importance whatsoever?

But Orlando was a woman – Lord Palmerston had just proved it. And when we are writing the life of a woman, we may, it is agreed, waive our demand for action, and substitute love instead. Love, the poet has said, is woman's whole existence. And if we look for a moment at Orlando writing at her table, we must admit that never was there a woman more fitted for that calling. Surely, since she is a woman, and a beautiful woman, and a woman in the prime of life, she will soon give over this pretence of writing and thinking and begin at least to think of a gamekeeper (and as long as she thinks of a man, nobody objects to a woman thinking). And then she will write him a little note (and as long as she writes little notes nobody objects to a woman writing either) and make an assignation for Sunday dusk and Sunday dusk will come; and the gamekeeper will whistle under the window – all of which is, of course, the very stuff of life and the only possible subject for fiction. Surely Orlando must have done one of these things? Alas – a thousand times, alas, Orlando did none of them. Must it then be admitted that Orlando was one of those monsters of iniquity who do not love? She was kind to dogs, faithful to friends, generosity itself to a dozen starving poets, had a passion for poetry. But love -as the male novelists define it – and who, after all, speak with greater authority? – has nothing whatever to do with kindness, fidelity, generosity, or poetry. Love is slipping off one's petticoat and – But we all know what love is. Did Orlando do that? Truth compels us to say no, she did not. If then, the subject of one's biography will neither love nor kill, but will only think and imagine, we may conclude that he or she is no better than a corpse and so leave her.

The only resource now left us is to look out of the window. There were sparrows; there were starlings; there were a number of doves, and one or two rooks, all occupied after their fashion. One finds a worm, another a snail. One flutters to a branch, another takes a little run on the turf. Then a servant crosses the courtyard, wearing a green baize apron. Presumably he is engaged on some intrigue with one of the maids in the pantry, but as no visible proof is offered us, in the courtyard, we can but hope for the best and leave it. Clouds pass, thin or thick, with some disturbance of the colour of the grass beneath. The sundial registers the hour in its usual cryptic way. One's mind begins tossing up a question or two, idly, vainly, about this same life. Life, it sings, or croons rather, like a kettle on a hob, Life, life, what art thou? Light or darkness, the baize apron of the under footman or the shadow of the starling on the grass?

Let us go, then, exploring, this summer morning, when all are adoring the plum blossom and the bee. And humming and hawing, let us ask of the starling (who is a more sociable bird than the lark) what he may think on the brink of the dustbin, whence he picks among the sticks combings of scullion's hair. What's life, we ask, leaning on the farmyard gate; Life, Life, Life! cries the bird, as if he had heard, and knew precisely, what we meant by this bothering prying habit of ours of asking questions indoors and out and peeping and picking at daisies as the way is of writers when they don't know what to say next. Then they come here, says the bird, and ask me what life is; Life, Life, Life!

We trudge on then by the moor path, to the high brow of the wine-blue purple-dark hill, and fling ourselves down there, and dream there and see there a grasshopper, carting back to his home in the hollow, a straw. And he says (if sawings like his can be given a name so sacred and tender) Life's labour, or so we interpret the whirr of his dust-choked gullet. And the ant agrees and the bees, but if we lie here long enough to ask the moths, when they come at evening, stealing among the paler heather bells, they will breathe in our ears such wild nonsense as one hears from telegraph wires in snow storms; tee-hee, haw-haw. Laughter, Laughter! the moths say.

Having asked then of man and of bird and the insects, for fish, men tell us, who have lived in green caves, solitary for years to hear them speak, never, never say, and so perhaps know what life is – having asked them all and grown no wiser, but only older and colder (for did we not pray once in a way to wrap up in a book something so hard, so rare, one could swear it was life's meaning?) back we must go and say straight out to the reader who waits a-tiptoe to hear what life is – alas, we don't know.

At this moment, but only just in time to save the book from extinction, Orlando pushed away her chair, stretched her arms, dropped her pen, came to the window, and exclaimed, 'Done!'

She was almost felled to the ground by the extraordinary sight which now met her eyes. There was the garden and some birds. The world was going on as usual. All the time she was writing the world had continued.

'And if I were dead, it would be just the same!' she exclaimed.

Such was the intensity of her feelings that she could even imagine that she had suffered dissolution, and perhaps some faintness actually attacked her. For a moment she stood looking at the fair, indifferent spectacle with staring eyes. At length she was revived in a singular way. The manuscript which reposed above her heart began shuffling and beating as if it were a living thing, and, what was still odder, and showed how fine a sympathy was between them, Orlando, by inclining her head, could make out what it was that it was saying. It wanted to be read. It must be read. It would die in her bosom if it were not read. For the first time in her life she turned with violence against nature. Elkhounds and rose bushes were about her in profusion. But elkhounds and rose bushes can none of them read. It is a lamentable oversight on the part of Providence which had never struck her before. Human beings alone are thus gifted. Human beings had become necessary. She rang the bell. She ordered the carriage to take her to London at once.

'There's just time to catch the eleven forty-five, M'Lady,' said Basket. Orlando had not yet realised the invention of the steam engine, but such was her absorption in the sufferings of a being, who, though not herself, yet entirely depended on her, that she saw a railway train for the first time, took her seat in a railway carriage, and had the rug arranged about her knees without giving a thought to 'that stupendous invention, which had (the historians say) completely changed the face of Europe in the past twenty years' (as, indeed, happens much more frequently than historians suppose). She noticed only that it was extremely smutty; rattled horribly; and the windows stuck. Lost in thought, she was whirled up to London in something less than an hour and stood on the platform at Charing Cross, not knowing where to go.

The old house at Blackfriars, where she had spent so many pleasant days in the eighteenth century, was now sold, part to the Salvation Army, part to an umbrella factory. She had bought another in Mayfair which was sanitary, convenient, and in the heart of the fashionable world, but was it in Mayfair that her poem would be relieved of its desire? Pray God, she thought, remembering the brightness of their ladyships' eyes and the symmetry of their lordships' legs, they haven't taken to reading there. For that would be a thousand pities. Then there was Lady R.'s. The same sort of talk would be going on there still, she had no doubt. The gout might have shifted from the General's left leg to his right, perhaps. Mr L. might have stayed ten days with R. instead of T. Then Mr Pope would come in. Oh! but Mr Pope was dead. Who were the wits now, she wondered – but that was not a question one could put to a porter, and so she moved on. Her ears were now distracted by the jingling of innumerable bells on the heads of innumerable horses. Fleets of the strangest little boxes on wheels were drawn up by the pavement. She walked out into the Strand. There the uproar was even worse. Vehicles of all sizes, drawn by blood horses and by dray horses, conveying one solitary dowager or crowded to the top by whiskered men in silk hats, were inextricably mixed. Carriages, carts, and omnibuses seemed to her eyes, so long used to the look of a plain sheet of foolscap, alarmingly at loggerheads; and to her ears, attuned to a pen scratching, the uproar of the street sounded violently and hideously cacophonous. Every inch of the pavement was crowded. Streams of people, threading in and out between their own bodies and the lurching and lumbering traffic with incredible agility, poured incessantly east and west. Along the edge of the pavement stood men, holding out trays of toys, and bawled. At corners, women sat beside great baskets of spring flowers and bawled. Boys running in and out of the horses' noses, holding printed sheets to their bodies, bawled too, Disaster! Disaster! At first Orlando supposed that she had arrived at some moment of national crisis; but whether it was happy or tragic, she could not tell. She looked anxiously at people's faces. But that confused her still more. Here would come by a man sunk in despair, muttering to himself as if he knew some terrible sorrow. Past him would nudge a fat, jolly-faced fellow, shouldering his way along as if it were a festival for all the world. Indeed, she came to the conclusion that there was neither rhyme nor reason in any of it. Each man and each woman was bent on his own affairs. And where was she to go?

She walked on without thinking, up one street and down another, by vast windows piled with handbags, and mirrors, and dressing gowns, and flowers, and fishing rods, and luncheon baskets; while stuff of every hue and pattern, thickness or thinness, was looped and festooned and ballooned across and across. Sometimes she passed down avenues of sedate mansions, soberly numbered 'one', 'two', 'three', and so on right up to two or three hundred, each the copy of the other, with two pillars and six steps and a pair of curtains neatly drawn and family luncheons laid on tables, and a parrot looking out of one window and a man servant out of another, until her mind was dizzied with the monotony. Then she came to great open squares with black, shiny, tightly buttoned statues of fat men in the middle, and war-horses prancing, and columns rising and fountains falling and pigeons fluttering. So she walked and walked along pavements between houses until she felt very hungry, and something fluttering above her heart rebuked her with having forgotten all about it. It was her manuscript, 'The Oak Tree'.

She was confounded at her own neglect. She stopped dead where she stood. No coach was in sight. The street, which was wide and handsome, was singularly empty. Only one elderly gentleman was approaching. There was something vaguely familiar to her in his walk. As he came nearer, she felt certain that she had met him at some time or other. But where? Could it be that this gentleman, so neat, so portly, so prosperous, with a cane in his hand and a flower in his buttonhole, with a pink, plump face, and combed white moustaches, could it be, Yes, by jove, it was! – her old, her very old friend, Nick Greene!

At the same time he looked at her; remembered her; recognised her. 'The Lady Orlando!' he cried, sweeping his silk hat almost in the dust.

'Sir Nicholas!' she exclaimed. For she was made aware intuitively by something in his bearing that the scurrilous penny-a-liner, who had lampooned her and many another in the time of Queen Elizabeth, was now risen in the world and become certainly a Knight and doubtless a dozen other fine things into the bargain.

With another bow, he acknowledged that her conclusion was correct; he was a Knight; he was a Litt.D.; he was a Professor. He was the author of a score of volumes. He was, in short, the most influential critic of the Victorian age.

A violent tumult of emotion besieged her at meeting the man who had caused her, years ago, so much pain. Could this be the plaguey, restless fellow who had burnt holes in her carpets, and toasted cheese in the Italian fireplace and told such merry stories of Marlowe and the rest that they had seen the sun rise nine nights out of ten? He was now sprucely dressed in a grey morning suit, had a pink flower in his buttonhole, and grey suede gloves to match. But even as she marvelled, he made another profound bow, and asked her whether she would honour him by lunching with him? The bow was a thought overdone perhaps, but the imitation of fine breeding was creditable. She followed him, wondering, into a superb restaurant, all red plush, white tablecloths, and silver cruets, as unlike as could be the old tavern or coffee house with its sanded floor, its wooden benches, its bowls of punch and chocolate, and its broadsheets and spittoons. He laid his gloves neatly on the table beside him. Still she could hardly believe that he was the same man. His nails were clean; where they used to be an inch long. His chin was shaved; where a black beard used to sprout. He wore gold sleeve-links; where his ragged linen used to dip in the broth. It was not, indeed, until he had ordered the wine, which he did with a care that reminded her of his taste in Malmsey long ago, that she was convinced he was the same man. 'Ah!' he said, heaving a little sigh, which was yet comfortable enough, 'ah! my dear lady, the great days of literature are over. Marlowe, Shakespeare, Ben Jonson – those were the giants. Dryden, Pope, Addison – those were the heroes. All, all are dead now. And whom have they left us? Tennyson, Browning, Carlyle!' – he threw an immense amount of scorn into his voice. 'The truth of it is,' he said, pouring himself a glass of wine, 'that all our young writers are in the pay of booksellers. They turn out any trash that serves to pay their tailor's bills. It is an age,' he said, helping himself to hors-d'oeuvres, 'marked by precious conceits and wild experiments – none of which the Elizabethans would have tolerated for an instant.'

'No, my dear lady,' he continued, passing with approval the turbot au gratin, which the waiter exhibited for his sanction, 'the great days are over. We live in degenerate times. We must cherish the past; honour those writers – there are still a few left of 'em – who take antiquity for their model and write, not for pay but – ' Here Orlando almost shouted 'Glawr!' Indeed she could have sworn that she had heard him say the very same things three hundred years ago. The names were different, of course, but the spirit was the same. Nick Greene had not changed, for all his knighthood. And yet, some change there was. For while he ran on about taking Addison as one's model (it had been Cicero once, she thought) and lying in bed of a morning (which she was proud to think her pension paid quarterly enabled him to do) rolling the best works of the best authors round and round on one's tongue for an hour, at least, before setting pen to paper, so that the vulgarity of the present time and the deplorable condition of our native tongue (he had lived long in America, she believed) might be purified – while he ran on in much the same way that Greene had run on three hundred years ago, she had time to ask herself, how was it then that he had changed? He had grown plump; but he was a man verging on seventy. He had grown sleek: literature had been a prosperous pursuit evidently; but somehow the old restless, uneasy vivacity had gone. His stories, brilliant as they were, were no longer quite so free and easy. He mentioned, it is true, 'my dear friend Pope' or 'my illustrious friend Addison' every other second, but he had an air of respectability about him which was depressing, and he preferred, it seemed, to enlighten her about the doings and sayings of her own blood relations rather than tell her, as he used to do, scandal about the poets.

Orlando was unaccountably disappointed. She had thought of literature all these years (her seclusion, her rank, her sex must be her excuse) as something wild as the wind, hot as fire, swift as lightning; something errant, incalculable, abrupt, and behold, literature was an elderly gentleman in a grey suit talking about duchesses. The violence of her disillusionment was such that some hook or button fastening the upper part of her dress burst open, and out upon the table fell 'The Oak Tree', a poem.

'A manuscript!' said Sir Nicholas, putting on his gold pince-nez. 'How interesting, how excessively interesting! Permit me to look at it.' And once more, after an interval of some three hundred years, Nicholas Greene took Orlando's poem and, laying it down among the coffee cups and the liqueur glasses, began to read it. But now his verdict was very different from what it had been then. It reminded him, he said as he turned over the pages, of Addison's *Cato*. It compared favourably with Thomson's *Seasons*. There was no trace in it, he was thankful to say, of the modern spirit. It was composed with a regard to truth, to nature, to the dictates of the human heart, which was rare indeed, in these days of unscrupulous eccentricity. It must, of course, be published instantly.

Really Orlando did not know what he meant. She had always carried her manuscripts about with her in the bosom of her dress. The idea tickled Sir Nicholas considerably.

'But what about royalties?' he asked.

Orlando's mind flew to Buckingham Palace and some dusky potentates who happened to be staying there.

Sir Nicholas was highly diverted. He explained that he was alluding to the fact that Messrs — (here he mentioned a well-known firm of publishers) would be delighted, if he wrote them a line, to put the book on their list. He could probably arrange for a royalty of ten per cent on all copies up to two thousand; after that it would be fifteen. As for the reviewers, he would himself write a line to Mr —, who was the most influential; then a compliment – say a little puff of her own poems – addressed to the wife of the editor of the — never did any harm. He would call — . So he ran on. Orlando understood nothing of all this, and from old experience did not altogether trust his good nature, but there was nothing for it but to submit to what was evidently his wish and the fervent desire of the poem itself. So Sir Nicholas made the blood-stained packet into a neat parcel; flattened it into his breast pocket, lest it should disturb the set of his coat; and with many compliments on both sides, they parted.

Orlando walked up the street. Now that the poem was gone – and she felt a bare place in her breast where she had been used to carry it – she had nothing to do but reflect upon whatever she liked – the extraordinary chances it might be of the human lot. Here she was in St James's Street; a married woman; with a ring on her finger; where there had been a coffee house once there was now a restaurant; it was about half-past three in the afternoon; the sun was shining; there were three pigeons; a mongrel terrier dog; two hansom cabs and a barouche landau. What then, was Life? The thought popped into her head violently, irrelevantly (unless old Greene were somehow the cause of it). And it may be taken as a comment, adverse or favourable, as the reader chooses to consider it upon her relations with her husband (who was at the Horn), that whenever anything popped violently into her head, she went straight to the nearest telegraph office and wired to him. There was one, as it happened, close at hand. 'My God Shel,' she wired; 'life literature Greene toady – ' here she dropped into a cypher language which they had invented between them so that a whole spiritual state of the utmost complexity might be conveyed in a word or two without the telegraph clerk being any the wiser, and added the words 'Rattigan Glumphoboo', which summed it up precisely. For not only had the events of the morning made a deep impression on her, but it cannot have escaped the reader's attention that Orlando was growing up – which is not necessarily growing better – and 'Rattigan Glumphoboo' described a very complicated spiritual state – which if the reader puts all his intelligence at our service he may discover for himself.

There could be no answer to her telegram for some hours; indeed, it was probable, she thought, glancing at the sky, where the upper clouds raced swiftly past, that there was a gale at Cape Horn, so that her husband would be at the mast-head, as likely as not, or cutting away some tattered spar, or even alone in a boat with a biscuit. And so, leaving the post office, she turned to beguile herself into the next shop, which was a shop so common in our day that it needs no description, yet, to her eyes, strange in the extreme; a shop where they sold books. All her life long Orlando had known manuscripts; she had held in her hands the rough brown sheets on which Spenser had written in his little crabbed hand; she had seen Shakespeare's script and Milton's. She owned, indeed, a fair number of quartos and folios, often with a sonnet in her praise in them and sometimes a lock of hair. But these innumerable little volumes, bright, identical, ephemeral, for they seemed bound in cardboard and printed on tissue paper, surprised her infinitely. The whole works of Shakespeare cost half a crown and could be put in your pocket. One could hardly read them, indeed, the print was so small, but it was a marvel, none the less. 'Works' – the works of every writer she had known or heard of and many more stretched from end to end of the long shelves. On tables and chairs, more 'works' were piled and tumbled, and these she saw, turning a page or two, were often works about other works by Sir Nicholas and a score of others whom, in her ignorance, she supposed, since they were bound and printed, to be very great writers too. So she gave an astounding order to the bookseller to send her everything of any importance in the shop and left.

She turned into Hyde Park, which she had known of old (beneath that cleft tree, she remembered, the Duke of Hamilton fell run through the body by Lord Mohun), and her lips, which are often to blame in the matter, began framing the words of her telegram into a senseless singsong: life literature Greene toady Rattigan Glumphoboo; so that several park keepers looked at her with suspicion and were only brought to a favourable opinion of her sanity by noticing the pearl necklace which she wore. She had carried off a sheaf of papers and critical journals from the book shop, and at length, flinging herself on her elbow beneath a tree, she spread these pages round her and did her best to fathom the noble art of prose composition as these masters practised it. For still the old credulity was alive in her; even the blurred type of a weekly newspaper had some sanctity in her eyes. So she read, lying on her elbow, an article by Sir Nicholas on the collected works of a man she had once known – John Donne. But she had pitched herself, without knowing it, not far from the Serpentine. The barking of a thousand dogs sounded in her ears. Carriage wheels rushed ceaselessly in a circle. Leaves sighed overhead. Now and again a braided skirt and a pair of tight scarlet trousers crossed the grass within a few steps of her. Once a gigantic rubber ball bounced on the newspaper. Violets, oranges, reds, and blues broke through the interstices of the leaves and sparkled in the emerald on her finger. She read a sentence and looked up at the sky; she looked up at the sky and looked down at the newspaper. Life? Literature? One to be made into the other? But how monstrously difficult! For – here came by a pair of tight scarlet trousers – how would Addison have put that? Here came two dogs dancing on their hind legs. How would Lamb have described that? For reading Sir Nicholas and his friends (as she did in the intervals of looking about her), she somehow got the impression – here she rose and walked – they made one feel – it was an extremely uncomfortable feeling – one must never, never say what one thought. (She stood on the banks of the Serpentine. It was a bronze colour; spider-thin boats were skimming from side to side.) They made one feel, she continued, that one must always, always write like somebody else. (The tears formed themselves in her eyes.) For really, she thought, pushing a little boat off with her toe, I don't think I could (here the whole of Sir Nicholas' article came before her as articles do, ten minutes after they are read, with the look of his room, his head, his cat, his writing-table, and the time of the day thrown in), I don't think I could, she continued, considering the article from this point of view, sit in a study, no, it's not a study, it's a mouldy kind of drawing-room, all day long, and talk to pretty young men, and tell them little anecdotes, which they mustn't repeat, about what Tupper said about Smiles; and then, she continued, weeping bitterly, they're all so manly; and then, I do detest Duchesses; and I don't like cake; and though I'm spiteful enough, I could never learn to be as spiteful as all that, so how can I be a critic and write the best English prose of my time? Damn it all! she exclaimed, launching a penny steamer so vigorously that the poor little boat almost sank in the bronze-coloured waves.

Now, the truth is that when one has been in a state of mind (as nurses call it) and the tears still stood in Orlando's eyes – the thing one is looking at becomes, not itself, but another thing, which is bigger and much more important and yet remains the same thing. If one looks at the Serpentine in this state of mind, the waves soon become just as big as the waves on the Atlantic; the toy boats become indistinguishable from ocean liners. So Orlando mistook the toy boat for her husband's brig; and the wave she had made with her toe for a mountain of water off Cape Horn; and as she watched the toy boat climb the ripple, she thought she saw Bonthrop's ship climb up and up a glassy wall; up and up it went, and a white crest with a thousand deaths in it arched over it; and through the thousand deaths it went and disappeared – 'It's sunk!' she cried out in an agony – and then, behold, there it was again sailing along safe and sound among the ducks on the other side of the Atlantic.

'Ecstasy!' she cried. 'Ecstasy! Where's the post office?' she wondered. 'For I must wire at once to Shel and tell him . . .' And repeating 'A toy boat on the Serpentine', and 'Ecstasy', alternately, for the thoughts were interchangeable and meant exactly the same thing, she hurried towards Park Lane.

'A toy boat, a toy boat, a toy boat,' she repeated, thus enforcing upon herself the fact that it is not articles by Nick Greene on John Donne nor eight-hour bills nor covenants nor factory acts that matter; it's something useless, sudden, violent; something that costs a life; red, blue, purple; a spirt; a splash; like those hyacinths (she was passing a fine bed of them); free from taint, dependence, soilure of humanity or care for one's kind; something rash, ridiculous, like my hyacinth, husband I mean, Bonthrop: that's what it is – a toy boat on the Serpentine, ecstasy – it's ecstasy that matters. Thus she spoke aloud, waiting for the carriages to pass at Stanhope Gate, for the consequence of not living with one's husband, except when the wind is sunk, is that one talks nonsense aloud in Park Lane. It would no doubt have been different had she lived all the year round with him as Queen Victoria recommended. As it was the thought of him would come upon her in a flash. She found it absolutely necessary to speak to him instantly. She did not care in the least what nonsense it might make, or what dislocation it might inflict on the narrative. Nick Greene's article had plunged her in the depths of despair; the toy boat had raised her to the heights of joy. So she repeated: 'Ecstasy, ecstasy,' as she stood waiting to cross.

But the traffic was heavy that spring afternoon, and kept her standing there, repeating, ecstasy, ecstasy, or a toy boat on the Serpentine, while the wealth and power of England sat, as if sculptured, in hat and cloak, in four-in-hand, victoria and barouche landau. It was as if a golden river had coagulated and massed itself in golden blocks across Park Lane. The ladies held card-cases between their fingers; the gentlemen balanced gold-mounted canes between their knees. She stood there gazing, admiring, awestruck. One thought only disturbed her, a thought familiar to all who behold great elephants, or whales of an incredible magnitude, and that is how do these leviathans to whom obviously stress, change, and activity are repugnant, propagate their kind? Perhaps, Orlando thought, looking at the stately, still faces, their time of propagation is over; this is the fruit; this is the consummation. What she now beheld was the triumph of an age. Portly and splendid there they sat. But now, the policeman let fall his hand; the stream became liquid; the massive conglomeration of splendid objects moved, dispersed, and disappeared into Piccadilly.

So she crossed Park Lane and went to her house in Curzon Street where, when the meadow-sweet blew there, she could remember curlew calling and one very old man with a gun.

She could remember, she thought, stepping across the threshold of her house, how Lord Chesterfield had said – but her memory was checked. Her discreet eighteenth-century hall, where she could see Lord Chesterfield putting his hat down here and his coat down there with an elegance of deportment which it was a pleasure to watch, was now completely littered with parcels. While she had been sitting in Hyde Park the bookseller had delivered her order, and the house was crammed – there were parcels slipping down the staircase – with the whole of Victorian literature done up in grey paper and neatly tied with string. She carried as many of these packets as she could to her room, ordered footmen to bring the others, and, rapidly cutting innumerable strings, was soon surrounded by innumerable volumes.

Accustomed to the little literatures of the sixteenth, seventeenth, and eighteenth centuries, Orlando was appalled by the consequences of her order. For, of course, to the Victorians themselves Victorian literature meant not merely four great names separate and distinct but four great names sunk and embedded in a mass of Alexander Smiths, Dixons, Blacks, Milmans, Buckles, Taines, Paynes, Tuppers, Jamesons – all vocal, clamorous, prominent, and requiring as much attention as anybody else. Orlando's reverence for print had a tough job set before it, but drawing her chair to the window to get the benefit of what light might filter between the high houses of Mayfair, she tried to come to a conclusion.

And now it is clear that there are only two ways of coming to a conclusion upon Victorian literature – one is to write it out in sixty volumes octavo, the other is to squeeze it into six lines of the length of this one. Of the two courses, economy, since time runs short, leads us to choose the second; and so we proceed. Orlando then came to the conclusion (opening half a dozen books) that it was very odd that there was not a single dedication to a nobleman among them; next (turning over a vast pile of memoirs) that several of these writers had family trees half as high as her own; next, that it would be impolitic in the extreme to wrap a ten-pound note round the sugar tongs when Miss Christina Rossetti came to tea; next (here were half a dozen invitations to celebrate centenaries by dining) that literature since it ate all these dinners must be growing very corpulent; next (she was invited to a score of lectures on the Influence of this upon that; the Classical revival; the Romantic survival, and other titles of the same engaging kind) that literature since it listened to all these lectures must be growing very dry; next (here she attended a reception given by a peeress) that literature since it wore all those fur tippets must be growing very respectable; next (here she visited Carlyle's sound-proof room at Chelsea) that genius since it needed all this coddling must be growing very delicate; and so at last she reached her final conclusion, which was of the highest importance but which, as we have already much overpassed our limit of six lines, we must omit.

Orlando, having come to this conclusion, stood looking out of the window for a considerable space of time. For, when anybody comes to a conclusion it is as if they had tossed the ball over the net and must wait for the unseen antagonist to return it to them. What would be sent her next from the colourless sky above Chesterfield House, she wondered? And with her hands clasped, she stood for a considerable space of time wondering. Suddenly she started – and here we could only wish that, as on a former occasion, Purity, Chastity, and Modesty would push the door ajar and provide, at least, a breathing space in which we could think how to wrap up what now has to be told delicately, as a biographer should. But no! Having thrown their white garment at the naked Orlando and seen it fall short by several inches, these ladies had given up all intercourse with her these many years; and were now otherwise engaged. Is nothing then, going to happen this pale March morning to mitigate, to veil, to cover, to conceal, to shroud this undeniable event whatever it may be? For after giving that sudden, violent start, Orlando – but Heaven be praised, at this very moment there struck up outside one of these frail, reedy, fluty, jerky, old-fashioned barrel-organs which are still sometimes played by Italian organ-grinders in back streets. Let us accept the intervention, humble though it is, as if it were the music of the spheres, and allow it, with all its gasps and groans, to fill this page with sound until the moment comes which it is impossible to deny is coming; which the footman has seen coming and the maidservant; and the reader will have to see too; for Orlando herself is clearly unable to ignore it any longer – let the barrel-organ sound and transport us on thought, which is no more than a little boat, when music sounds, tossing on the waves; on thought, which is, of all carriers, the most clumsy, the most erratic, over the roof tops and the back gardens where washing is hanging to – what is this place? Do you recognise the Green and in the middle the steeple, and the gates with a lion couchant on either side? Oh yes, it is Kew! Well, Kew will do. So here then we are at Kew, and I will show you today (the second of March) under the plum tree, a grape hyacinth, and a crocus, and a bud too, on the almond tree; so that to walk there is to be thinking of bulbs, hairy and red, thrust into the earth in October; flowering now; and to be dreaming of more than can rightly be said, and to be taking from its case a cigarette or cigar even, and to be flinging a cloak under (as the rhyme requires) an oak, and there to sit, waiting the kingfisher, which, it is said, was seen once to cross in the evening from bank to bank.

Wait! Wait! The kingfisher comes; the kingfisher comes not.

Behold, meanwhile, the factory chimneys, and their smoke; behold the city clerks flashing by in their outrigger. Behold the old lady taking her dog for a walk and the servant girl wearing her new hat for the first time not at the right angle. Behold them all. Though Heaven has mercifully decreed that the secrets of all hearts are hidden so that we are lured on for ever to suspect something, perhaps, that does not exist; still through our cigarette smoke, we see blaze up and salute the splendid fulfilment of natural desires for a hat, for a boat, for a rat in a ditch; as once one saw blazing – such silly hops and skips the mind takes when it slops like this all over the saucer and the barrel-organ plays – saw blazing a fire in a field against minarets near Constantinople.

Hail! natural desire! Hail! happiness! divine happiness! and pleasure of all sorts, flowers and wine, though one fades and the other intoxicates; and half-crown tickets out of London on Sundays, and singing in a dark chapel hymns about death, and anything, anything that interrupts and confounds the tapping of typewriters and filing of letters and forging of links and chains, binding the Empire together. Hail even the crude, red bows on shop girls' lips (as if Cupid, very clumsily, dipped his thumb in red ink and scrawled a token in passing). Hail, happiness! kingfisher flashing from bank to bank, and all fulfilment of natural desire, whether it is what the male novelist says it is; or prayer; or denial; hail! in whatever form it comes, and may there be more forms, and stranger. For dark flows the stream – would it were true, as the rhyme hints 'like a dream' – but duller and worser than that is our usual lot; without dreams, but alive, smug, fluent, habitual, under trees whose shade of an olive green drowns the blue of the wing of the vanishing bird when he darts of a sudden from bank to bank.

Hail, happiness, then, and after happiness, hail not those dreams which bloat the sharp image as spotted mirrors do the face in a country-inn parlour; dreams which splinter the whole and tear us asunder and wound us and split us apart in the night when we would sleep; but sleep, sleep, so deep that all shapes are ground to dust of infinite softness, water of dimness inscrutable, and there, folded, shrouded, like a mummy, like a moth, prone let us lie on the sand at the bottom of sleep.

But wait! but wait! we are not going, this time, visiting the blind land. Blue, like a match struck right in the ball of the innermost eye, he flies, burns, bursts the seal of sleep; the kingfisher; so that now floods back refluent like a tide, the red, thick stream of life again; bubbling, dripping; and we rise, and our eyes (for how handy a rhyme is to pass us safe over the awkward transition from death to life) fall on – (here the barrel-organ stops playing abruptly).

'It's a very fine boy, M'Lady,' said Mrs Banting, the midwife, putting her first-born child into Orlando's arms. In other words Orlando was safely delivered of a son on Thursday, March the 20th, at three o'clock in the morning.

*   *   *

Once more Orlando stood at the window, but let the reader take courage; nothing of the same sort is going to happen today, which is not, by any means, the same day. No – for if we look out of the window, as Orlando was doing at the moment, we shall see that Park Lane itself has considerably changed. Indeed one might stand there ten minutes or more, as Orlando stood now, without seeing a single barouche landau. 'Look at that!' she exclaimed, some days later when an absurd truncated carriage without any horses began to glide about of its own accord. A carriage without any horses indeed! She was called away just as she said that, but came back again after a time and had another look out of the window. It was odd sort of weather nowadays. The sky itself, she could not help thinking, had changed. It was no longer so thick, so watery, so prismatic now that King Edward – see, there he was, stepping out of his neat brougham to go and visit a certain lady opposite – had succeeded Queen Victoria. The clouds had shrunk to a thin gauze; the sky seemed made of metal, which in hot weather tarnished verdigris, copper colour or orange as metal does in a fog. It was a little alarming – this shrinkage. Everything seemed to have shrunk. Driving past

Buckingham Palace last night, there was not a trace of that vast erection which she had thought everlasting; top hats, widows' weeds, trumpets, telescopes, wreaths, all had vanished and left not a stain, not a puddle even, on the pavement. But it was now – after another interval she had come back again to her favourite station in the window – now, in the evening, that the change was most remarkable. Look at the lights in the houses! At a touch, a whole room was lit; hundreds of rooms were lit; and one was precisely the same as the other. One could see everything in the little square-shaped boxes; there was no privacy; none of those lingering shadows and odd corners that there used to be; none of those women in aprons carrying wobbly lamps which they put down carefully on this table and on that. At a touch, the whole room was bright. And the sky was bright all night long; and the pavements were bright; everything was bright. She came back again at midday. How narrow women had grown lately! They looked like stalks of corn, straight, shining, identical. And men's faces were as bare as the palm of one's hand. The dryness of the atmosphere brought out the colour in everything and seemed to stiffen the muscles of the cheeks. It was harder to cry now. Water was hot in two seconds. Ivy had perished or been scraped off houses. Vegetables were less fertile; families were much smaller. Curtains and covers had been frizzled up and the walls were bare so that new brilliantly coloured pictures of real things like streets, umbrellas, apples, were hung in frames, or painted upon the wood. There was something definite and distinct about the age, which reminded her of the eighteenth century, except that there was a distraction, a desperation – as she was thinking this, the immensely long tunnel in which she seemed to have been travelling for hundreds of years widened; the light poured in; her thoughts became mysteriously tightened and strung up as if a piano tuner had put his key in her back and stretched the nerves very taut; at the same time her hearing quickened; she could hear every whisper and crackle in the room so that the clock ticking on the mantelpiece beat like a hammer. And so for some seconds the light went on becoming brighter and brighter, and she saw everything more and more clearly and the clock ticked louder and louder until there was a terrific explosion right in her ear. Orlando leapt as if she had been violently struck on the head. Ten times she was struck. In fact it was ten o'clock in the morning. It was the eleventh of October. It was 1928. It was the present moment.

No one need wonder that Orlando started, pressed her hand to her heart, and turned pale. For what more terrifying revelation can there be than that it is the present moment? That we survive the shock at all is only possible because the past shelters us on one side and the future on another. But we have no time now for reflections; Orlando was terribly late already. She ran downstairs, she jumped into her motor car, she pressed the self-starter and was off. Vast blue blocks of building rose into the air; the red cowls of chimneys were spotted irregularly across the sky; the road shone like silver-headed nails; omnibuses bore down upon her with sculptured white-faced drivers; she noticed sponges, birdcages, boxes of green American cloth. But she did not allow these sights to sink into her mind even the fraction of an inch as she crossed the narrow plank of the present, lest she should fall into the raging torrent beneath. 'Why don't you look where you're going to? . . . Put your hand out, can't you?' – that was all she said sharply, as if the words were jerked out of her. For the streets were immensely crowded; people crossed without looking where they were going. People buzzed and hummed round the plate-glass windows within which one could see a glow of red, a blaze of yellow, as if they were bees, Orlando thought – but her thought that they were bees was violently snipped off and she saw, regaining perspective with one flick of her eye, that they were bodies. 'Why don't you look where you're going?' she snapped out.

At last, however, she drew up at Marshall & Snelgrove's and went into the shop. Shade and scent enveloped her. The present fell from her like drops of scalding water. Light swayed up and down like thin stuffs puffed out by a summer breeze. She took a list from her bag and began reading in a curious stiff voice at first as if she were holding the words – boys' boots, bath salts, sardines – under a tap of many-coloured water. She watched them change as the light fell on them. Bath and boots became blunt, obtuse; sardines serrated itself like a saw. So she stood in the ground-floor department of Messrs. Marshall & Snelgrove; looked this way and that; snuffed this smell and that and thus wasted some seconds. Then she got into the lift, for the good reason that the door stood open; and was shot smoothly upwards. The very fabric of life now, she thought as she rose, is magic. In the eighteenth century, we knew how everything was done; but here I rise through the air; I listen to voices in America; I see men flying – but how it's done, I can't even begin to wonder. So my belief in magic returns. Now the lift gave a little jerk as it stopped at the first floor; and she had a vision of innumerable coloured stuffs flaunting in a breeze from which came distinct, strange smells; and each time the lift stopped and flung its doors open, there was another slice of the world displayed with all the smells of that world clinging to it. She was reminded of the river off Wapping in the time of Elizabeth, where the treasure ships and the merchant ships used to anchor. How richly and curiously they had smelt! How well she remembered the feel of rough rubies running through her fingers when she dabbled them in a treasure sack! And then lying with Sukey – or whatever her name was – and having Cumberland's lantern flashed on them! The Cumberlands had a house in Portland Place now and she had lunched with them the other day and ventured a little joke with the old man about almshouses in the Sheen Road. He had winked. But here as the lift could go no higher, she must get out – Heaven knows into what 'department' as they called it. She stood still to consult her shopping list, but was blessed if she could see, as the list bade her, bath salts, or boy's boots anywhere about. And indeed, she was about to descend again, without buying anything, but was saved from that outrage by saying aloud automatically the last item on her list; which happened to be 'sheets for a double bed'.

'Sheets for a double bed,' she said to a man at a counter and, by a dispensation of Providence, it was sheets that the man at that particular counter happened to sell. For Grimsditch, no, Grimsditch was dead; Bartholomew, no, Bartholomew was dead; Louise then – Louise had come to her in a great taking the other day, for she had found a hole in the bottom of the sheet in the royal bed. Many kings and queens had slept there – Elizabeth; James; Charles; George; Victoria; Edward; no wonder the sheet had a hole in it. But Louise was positive she knew who had done it. It was the Prince Consort.

'*Sale bosch!*' she said (for there had been another war; this time against the Germans).

'Sheets for a double bed,' Orlando repeated dreamily, for a double bed with a silver counterpane in a room fitted in a taste which she now thought perhaps a little vulgar – all in silver; but she had furnished it when she had a passion for that metal. While the man went to get sheets for a double bed, she took out a little looking-glass and a powder puff. Women were not nearly as roundabout in their ways, she thought, powdering herself with the greatest unconcern, as they had been when she herself first turned woman and lay on the deck of the *Enamoured Lady*. She gave her nose the right tint deliberately. She never touched her cheeks. Honestly, though she was now thirty-six, she scarcely looked a day older. She looked just as pouting, as sulky, as handsome, as rosy (like a million-candled Christmas tree, Sasha had said) as she had done that day on the ice, when the Thames was frozen and they had gone skating –

'The best Irish linen, Ma'am,' said the shopman, spreading the sheets on the counter – and they had met an old woman picking up sticks. Here, as she was fingering the linen abstractedly, one of the swing-doors between the departments opened and let through, perhaps from the fancy-goods department, a whiff of scent, waxen, tinted as if from pink candles, and the scent curved like a shell round a figure – was it a boy's or was it a girl's? – young, slender, seductive – a girl, by God! furred, pearled, in Russian trousers; but faithless, faithless!

'Faithless!' cried Orlando (the man had gone) and all the shop seemed to pitch and toss with yellow water and far off she saw the masts of the Russian ship standing out to sea, and then, miraculously (perhaps the door opened again) the conch which the scent had made became a platform, a dais, off which stepped a fat, furred woman, marvellously well preserved, seductive, diademed, a Grand Duke's mistress; she who, leaning over the banks of the Volga, eating sandwiches, had watched men drown; and began walking down the shop towards her.

'Oh Sasha!' Orlando cried. Really, she was shocked that she should have come to this; she had grown so fat; so lethargic; and she bowed her head over the linen so that this apparition of a grey woman in fur, and a girl in Russian trousers, with all these smells of wax candles, white flowers, and old ships that it brought with it might pass behind her back unseen.

'Any napkins, towels, dusters today, Ma'am?' the shopman persisted. And it is enormously to the credit of the shopping list, which Orlando now consulted, that she was able to reply with every appearance of composure, that there was only one thing in the world she wanted and that was bath salts; which was in another department.

But descending in the lift again – so insidious is the repetition of any scene – she was again sunk far beneath the present moment; and thought when the lift bumped on the ground, that she heard a pot broken against a river bank. As for finding the right department, whatever it might be, she stood engrossed among the handbags, deaf to the suggestions of all the polite, black, combed, sprightly shop assistants, who descending as they did equally and some of them, perhaps, as proudly, even from such depths of the past as she did, chose to let down the impervious screen of the present so that today they appeared shop assistants in Marshall & Snelgrove's merely. Orlando stood there hesitating. Through the great glass doors she could see the traffic in Oxford Street. Omnibus seemed to pile itself upon omnibus and then to jerk itself apart. So the ice blocks had pitched and tossed that day on the Thames. An old nobleman in furred slippers had sat astride one of them. There he went – she could see him now – calling down maledictions upon the Irish rebels. He had sunk there, where her car stood.

'Time has passed over me,' she thought, trying to collect herself; 'this is the oncome of middle age. How strange it is! Nothing is any longer one thing. I take up a handbag and I think of an old bumboat woman frozen in the ice. Someone lights a pink candle and I see a girl in Russian trousers. When I step out of doors – as I do now,' here she stepped on to the pavement of Oxford Street, 'what is it that I taste? Little herbs. I hear goat bells. I see mountains. Turkey? India? Persia?' Her eyes filled with tears.

That Orlando had gone a little too far from the present moment will, perhaps, strike the reader who sees her now preparing to get into her motor car with her eyes full of tears and visions of Persian mountains. And indeed, it cannot be denied that the most successful practitioners of the art of life, often unknown people by the way, somehow contrive to synchronise the sixty or seventy different times which beat simultaneously in every normal human system so that when eleven strikes, all the rest chime in unison, and the present is neither a violent disruption nor completely forgotten in the past. Of them we can justly say that they live precisely the sixty-eight or seventy-two years allotted them on the tombstone. Of the rest some we know to be dead though they walk among us; some are not yet born though they go through the forms of life; others are hundreds of years old though they call themselves thirty-six. The true length of a person's life, whatever the *Dictionary of National Biography* may say, is always a matter of dispute. For it is a difficult business – this timekeeping; nothing more quickly disorders it than contact with any of the arts; and it may have been her love of poetry that was to blame for making Orlando lose her shopping list and start home without the sardines, the bath salts, or the boots. Now as she stood with her hand on the door of her motor car, the present again struck her on the head. Eleven times she was violently assaulted.

'Confound it all!' she cried, for it is a great shock to the nervous system, hearing a clock strike – so much so that for some time now there is nothing to be said of her save that she frowned slightly, changed her gears admirably, and cried out, as before, 'Look where you're going!' 'Don't you know your own mind?' 'Why didn't you say so then?' while the motor car shot, swung, squeezed, and slid, for she was an expert driver, down Regent Street, down Haymarket, down Northumberland Avenue, over Westminster Bridge, to the left, straight on, to the right, straight on again . . .

The Old Kent Road was very crowded on Thursday, the eleventh of October 1928. People spilt off the pavement. There were women with shopping bags. Children ran out. There were sales at drapers' shops. Streets widened and narrowed. Long vistas steadily shrunk together. Here was a market. Here a funeral. Here a procession with banners upon which was written 'Ra— Un—', but what else? Meat was very red. Butchers stood at the door. Women almost had their heels sliced off. Amor Vin— that was over a porch. A woman looked out of a bedroom window, profoundly contemplative, and very still. Applejohn and Applebed, Undert—. Nothing could be seen whole or read from start to finish. What was seen begun – like two friends starting to meet each other across the street – was never seen ended. After twenty minutes the body and mind were like scraps of torn paper tumbling from a sack and, indeed, the process of motoring fast out of London so much resembles the chopping up small of identity which precedes unconsciousness and perhaps death itself that it is an open question in what sense Orlando can be said to have existed at the present moment. Indeed we should have given her over for a person entirely disassembled were it not that here, at last, one green screen was held out on the right, against which the little bits of paper fell more slowly; and then another was held out on the left so that one could see the separate scraps now turning over by themselves in the air; and then green screens were held continuously on either side, so that her mind regained the illusion of holding things within itself and she saw a cottage, a farmyard and four cows, all precisely life-size.

When this happened, Orlando heaved a sigh of relief, lit a cigarette, and puffed for a minute or two in silence. Then she called hesitatingly, as if the person she wanted might not be there, 'Orlando?' For if there are (at a venture) seventy-six different times all ticking in the mind at once, how many different people are there not – Heaven help us – all having lodgment at one time or another in the human spirit? Some say two thousand and fifty-two. So that it is the most usual thing in the world for a person to call, directly they are alone, Orlando? (if that is one's name) meaning by that, Come, come! I'm sick to death of this particular self. I want another. Hence, the astonishing changes we see in our friends. But it is not altogether plain sailing, either, for though one may say, as Orlando said (being out in the country and needing another self presumably) Orlando? still the Orlando she needs may not come; these selves of which we are built up, one on top of another, as plates are piled on a waiter's hand, have attachments elsewhere, sympathies, little constitutions and rights of their own, call them what you will (and for many of these things there is no name) so that one will only come if it is raining, another in a room with green curtains, another when Mrs Jones is not there, another if you can promise it a glass of wine and so on; for everybody can multiply from his own experience the different terms which his different selves have made with him and some are too wildly ridiculous to be mentioned in print at all.

So Orlando, at the turn by the barn, called 'Orlando?' with a note of interrogation in her voice and waited. Orlando did not come.

'All right then,' Orlando said, with the good humour people practise on these occasions; and tried another. For she had a great variety of selves to call upon, far more than we have been able to find room for, since a biography is considered complete if it merely accounts for six or seven selves, whereas a person may well have as many thousand. Choosing then, only those selves we have found room for, Orlando may now have called on the boy who cut the nigger's head down; the boy who strung it up again; the boy who sat on the hill; the boy who saw the poet; the boy who handed the Queen the bowl of rose water; or she may have called upon the young man who fell in love with Sasha; or upon the Courtier; or upon the Ambassador; or upon the Soldier; or upon the Traveller; or she may have wanted the woman to come to her; the Gipsy; the Fine Lady; the Hermit; the girl in love with life; the Patroness of Letters; the woman who called Mar (meaning hot baths and evening fires) or Shelmerdine (meaning crocuses in autumn woods) or Bonthrop (meaning the death we die daily) or all three together – which meant more things than we have space to write out – all were different and she may have called upon any one of them.

Perhaps; but what appeared certain (for we are now in the region of 'perhaps' and 'appears') was that the one she needed most kept aloof, for she was, to hear her talk, changing her selves as quickly as she drove – there was a new one at every corner – as happens when, for some unaccountable reason, the conscious self, which is the uppermost, and has the power to desire, wishes to be nothing but one self. This is what some people call the true self, and it is, they say, compact of all the selves we have it in us to be; commanded and locked up by the Captain self, the Key self, which amalgamates and controls them all. Orlando was certainly seeking this self as the reader can judge from overhearing her talk as she drove (and if it is rambling talk, disconnected, trivial, dull, and sometimes unintelligible, it is the reader's fault for listening to a lady talking to herself; we only copy her words as she spoke them, adding in brackets which self in our opinion is speaking, but in this we may well be wrong).

'What then? Who then?' she said. 'Thirty-six; in a motor car; a woman. Yes, but a million other things as well. A snob am I? The garter in the hall? The leopards? My ancestors? Proud of them? Yes! Greedy, luxurious, vicious? Am I? (here a new self came in). Don't care a damn if I am. Truthful? I think so. Generous? Oh, but that don't count (here a new self came in). Lying in bed of a morning listening to the pigeons on fine linen; silver dishes; wine; maids; footmen. Spoilt? Perhaps. Too many things for nothing. Hence my books (here she mentioned fifty classical titles; which represented, so we think, the early romantic works that she tore up). Facile, glib, romantic. But (here another self came in) a duffer, a fumbler. More clumsy I couldn't be. And – and – (here she hesitated for a word and if we suggest 'love' we may be wrong, but certainly she laughed and blushed and then cried out -) A toad set in emeralds! Marry the Archduke! Bluebottles on the ceiling! (here another self came in). But Nell, Kit, Sasha? (she was sunk in gloom: tears actually shaped themselves and she had long given over crying). Trees, she said. (Here another self came in.) I love trees (she was passing a clump) growing there a thousand years. And barns (she passed a tumbledown barn at the edge of the road). And sheep dogs (here one came trotting across the road. She carefully avoided it). And the night. But people (here another self came in). People? (She repeated it as a question.) I don't know. Chattering, spiteful, always telling lies. (Here she turned into the High Street of her native town, which was crowded, for it was market day, with farmers, and shepherds, and old women with hens in baskets.) I like peasants. I understand crops. But (here another self came skipping over the top of her mind like the beam from a lighthouse). Fame! (She laughed.) Fame! Seven editions. A prize. Photographs in the evening papers (here she alluded to the 'Oak Tree' and 'The Burdett Coutts' Memorial Prize which she had won; and we must snatch space to remark how discomposing it is for her biographer that this culmination to which the whole book moved, this peroration with which the book was to end, should be dashed from us on a laugh casually like this; but the truth is that when we write of a woman, everything is out of place – culminations and perorations; the accent never falls where it does with a man). Fame! she repeated. A poet – a charlatan; both every morning as regularly as the post comes in. To dine, to meet; to meet, to dine; fame fame! (She had here to slow down to pass through the crowd of market people. But no one noticed her. A porpoise in a fishmonger's shop attracted far more attention than a lady who had won a prize and might, had she chosen, have worn three coronets one on top of another on her brow.) Driving very slowly she now hummed as if it were part of an old song, 'With my guineas I'll buy flowering trees, flowering trees, flowering trees and walk among my flowering trees and tell my sons what fame is.' So she hummed, and now all her words began to sag here and there like a barbaric necklace of heavy beads. 'And walk among my flowering trees', she sang, accenting the words strongly, 'and see the moon rise slow, the waggons go . . . ' Here she stopped short, and looked ahead of her intently at the bonnet of the car in profound meditation.

'He sat at Twitchett's table,' she mused, 'with a dirty ruff on . . . Was it old Mr Baker come to measure the timber? Or was it Sh–p–re?' (for when we speak names we deeply reverence to ourselves we never speak them whole). She gazed for ten minutes ahead of her, letting the car come almost to a standstill.

'Haunted!' she cried, suddenly pressing the accelerator. 'Haunted! ever since I was a child. There flies the wild goose. It flies past the window out to sea. Up I jumped (she gripped the steering-wheel tighter) and stretched after it. But the goose flies too fast. I've seen it, here – there – there – England, Persia, Italy. Always it flies fast out to sea and always I fling after it words like nets (here she flung her hand out) which shrivel as I've seen nets shrivel drawn on deck with only seaweed in them; and sometimes there's an inch of silver – six words – in the bottom of the net. But never the great fish who lives in the coral groves.' Here she bent her head, pondering deeply.

And it was at this moment, when she had ceased to call 'Orlando' and was deep in thoughts of something else, that the Orlando whom she had called came of its own accord; as was proved by the change that now came over her (she had passed through the lodge gates and was entering the park).

The whole of her darkened and settled, as when some foil whose addition makes the round and solidity of a surface is added to it, and the shallow becomes deep and the near distant; and all is contained as water is contained by the sides of a well. So she was now darkened, stilled, and become, with the addition of this Orlando, what is called; rightly or wrongly, a single self, a real self. And she fell silent. For it is probable that when people talk aloud, the selves (of which there may be more than two thousand) are conscious of disseverment, and are trying to communicate, but when communication is established they fall silent.

Masterfully, swiftly, she drove up the curving drive between the elms and oaks through the falling turf of the park whose fall was so gentle that had it been water it would have spread the beach with a smooth green tide. Planted here and in solemn groups were beech trees and oak trees. The deer stepped among them, one white as snow, another with its head on one side, for some wire netting had caught in its horns. All this, the trees, deer, and turf, she observed with the greatest satisfaction as if her mind had become a fluid that flowed round things and enclosed them completely. Next minute she drew up in the courtyard where, for so many hundred years she had come, on horseback or in coach and six, with men riding before or coming after;

where plumes had tossed, torches flashed, and the same flowering trees that let their leaves drop now had shaken their blossoms. Now she was alone. The autumn leaves were falling. The porter opened the great gates. 'Morning, James,' she said, 'there're some things in the car. Will you bring 'em in?' words of no beauty, interest, or significance themselves, it will be conceded, but now so plumped out with meaning that they fell like ripe nuts from a tree, and proved that when the shrivelled skin of the ordinary is stuffed out with meaning it satisfies the senses amazingly. This was true indeed of every movement and action now, usual though they were; so that to see Orlando change her skirt for a pair of whipcord breeches and leather jacket, which she did in less than three minutes, was to be ravished with the beauty of movement as if Madame Lopokova were using her highest art. Then she strode into the dining-room where her old friends Dryden, Pope, Swift, Addison regarded her demurely at first as who should say Here's the prize winner! but when they reflected that two hundred guineas was in question, they nodded their heads approvingly. Two hundred guineas, they seemed to say; two hundred guineas are not to be sniffed at. She cut herself a slice of bread and ham, clapped the two together and began to eat, striding up and down the room, thus shedding her company habits in a second, without thinking. After five or six such turns, she tossed off a glass of red Spanish wine, and, filling another which she carried in her hand, strode down the long corridor and through a dozen drawing-rooms and so began a perambulation of the house, attended by such elk-hounds and spaniels as chose to follow her.

This, too, was all in the day's routine. As soon would she come home and leave her own grandmother without a kiss as come back and leave the house unvisited. She fancied that the rooms brightened as she came in; stirred, opened their eyes as if they had been dozing in her absence. She fancied, too, that, hundreds and thousands of times as she had seen them, they never looked the same twice, as if so long a life as theirs had stored in them a myriad moods which changed with winter and summer, bright weather and dark, and her own fortunes and the people's characters who visited them. Polite, they always were to strangers, but a little wary; with her, they were entirely open and at their ease. Why not indeed? They had known each other for close on four centuries now. They had nothing to conceal. She knew their sorrows and joys. She knew what age each part of them was and its little secrets – a hidden drawer, a concealed cupboard, or some deficiency perhaps, such as a part made up, or added later. They, too, knew her in all her moods and changes. She had hidden nothing from them; had come to them as boy and woman, crying and dancing, brooding and gay. In this window-seat, she had written her first verses; in that chapel, she had been married. And she would be buried here, she reflected, kneeling on the window-sill in the long gallery and sipping her Spanish wine. Though she could hardly fancy it, the body of the heraldic leopard would be making yellow pools on the floor the day they lowered her to lie among her ancestors. She, who believed in no immortality, could not help feeling that her soul would come and go forever with the reds on the panels and the greens on the sofa. For the room – she had strolled into the Ambassador's bedroom – shone like a shell that has lain at the bottom of the sea for centuries and has been crusted over and painted a million tints by the water; it was rose and yellow, green and sand-coloured. It was frail as a shell, as iridescent and as empty. No Ambassador would ever sleep there again. Ah, but she knew where the heart of the house still beat. Gently opening a door, she stood on the threshold so that (as she fancied) the room could not see her and watched the tapestry rising and falling on the eternal faint breeze which never failed to move it. Still the hunter rode; still Daphne flew. The heart still beat, she thought, however faintly, however far withdrawn; the frail indomitable heart of the immense building.

Now, calling her troop of dogs to her she passed down the gallery whose floor was laid with whole oak trees sawn across. Rows of chairs with all their velvets faded stood ranged against the wall holding their arms out for Elizabeth, for James, for Shakespeare it might be, for Cecil, who never came. The sight made her gloomy. She unhooked the rope that fenced them off. She sat on the Queen's chair; she opened a manuscript book lying on Lady Betty's table; she stirred her fingers in the aged rose leaves; she brushed her short hair with King James' silver brushes; she bounced up and down upon his bed (but no King would ever sleep there again, for all Louise's new sheets) and pressed her cheek against the worn silver counter- pane that lay upon it. But everywhere were little lavender bags to keep the moth out and printed notices, 'Please do not touch', which, though she had put them there herself, seemed to rebuke her. The house was no longer hers entirely, she sighed. It belonged to time now; to history; was past the touch and control of the living. Never would beer be spilt here any more, she thought (she was in the bedroom that had been old Nick Greene's), or holes burnt in the carpet. Never two hundred servants come running and brawling down the corridors with warming pans and great branches for the great fireplaces. Never would ale be brewed and candles made and saddles fashioned and stone shaped in the workshops outside the house. Hammers and mallets were silent now. Chairs and beds were empty; tankards of silver and gold were locked in glass cases. The great wings of silence beat up and down the empty house.

So she sat at the end of the gallery with her dogs couched round her, in Queen Elizabeth's hard armchair. The gallery stretched far away to a point where the light almost failed. It was as a tunnel bored deep into the past. As her eyes peered down it, she could see people laughing and talking; the great men she had known; Dryden, Swift, and Pope; and statesmen in colloquy; and lovers dallying in the window-seats; and people eating and drinking at the long tables; and the wood smoke curling round their heads and making them sneeze and cough. Still further down, she saw sets of splendid dancers formed for the quadrille. A fluty, frail, but nevertheless stately music began to play. An organ boomed. A coffin was borne into the chapel. A marriage procession came out of it. Armed men with helmets left for the wars. They brought banners back from Flodden and Poitiers and stuck them on the wall. The long gallery filled itself thus, and still peering further, she thought she could make out at the very end, beyond the Elizabethans and the Tudors, some one older, further, darker, a cowled figure, monastic, severe, a monk, who went with his hands clasped, and a book in them, murmuring –

Like thunder, the stable clock struck four. Never did any earthquake so demolish a whole town. The gallery and all its occupants fell to powder. Her own face, that had been dark and sombre as she gazed, was lit as by an explosion of gunpowder. In this same light everything near her showed with extreme distinctness. She saw two flies circling round and noticed the blue sheen on their bodies; she saw a knot in the wood where her foot was, and her dog's ear twitching. At the same time, she heard a bough creaking in the garden, a sheep coughing in the park, a swift screaming past the window. Her own body quivered and tingled as if suddenly stood naked in a hard frost. Yet, she kept, as she had not done when the clock struck ten in London, complete composure (for she was now one and entire, and presented, it may be, a larger surface to the shock of time). She rose, but without precipitation, called her dogs, and went firmly but with great alertness of movement down the staircase and out into the garden. Here the shadows of the plants were miraculously distinct. She noticed the separate grains of earth in the flowerbeds as if she had a microscope stuck to her eye. She saw the intricacy of the twigs of every tree. Each blade of grass was distinct and the marking of veins and petals. She saw Stubbs, the gardener, coming along the path, and every button on his gaiters was visible; she saw Betty and Prince, the cart horses, and never had she marked so clearly the white star on Betty's fore-head, and the three long hairs that fell down below the rest on Prince's tail. Out in the quadrangle the old grey walls of the house looked like a scraped new photograph; she heard the loud speaker condensing on the terrace a dance tune that people were listening to in the red-velvet opera house at Vienna. Braced and strung up by the present moment she was also strangely afraid, as if whenever the gulf of time gaped and let a second through some unknown danger might come with it. The tension was too relentless and too rigorous to be endured long without discomfort. She walked more briskly than she liked, as if her legs were moved for her, through the garden and out into the park. Here she forced herself, by a great effort, to stop by the carpenter's shop, and to stand stock-still watching Joe Stubbs fashion a cart wheel. She was standing with her eye fixed on his hand when the quarter struck. It hurtled through her like a meteor, so hot that no fingers can hold it. She saw with disgusting vividness that the thumb on Joe's right hand was without a finger nail and there was a raised saucer of pink flesh where the nail should have been. The sight was so repulsive that she felt faint for a moment, but in that moment's darkness, when her eyelids flickered, she was relieved of the pressure of the present. There was something strange in the shadow that the flicker of her eyes cast, something which (as anyone can test for himself by looking now at the sky) is always absent from the present – whence its terror, its nondescript character – something one trembles to pin through the body with a name and call beauty, for it has no body, is as a shadow without substance or quality of its own, yet has the power to change whatever it adds itself to. This shadow now, while she flickered her eye in her faintness in the carpenter's shop, stole out, and attaching itself to the innumerable sights she had been receiving, composed them into something tolerable, comprehensible. Her mind began to toss like the sea. Yes, she thought, heaving a deep sigh of relief, as she turned from the carpenter's shop to climb the hill, I can begin to live again. I am by the Serpentine, she thought, the little boat is climbing through the white arch of a thousand deaths. I am about to understand . . .

Those were her words, spoken quite distinctly, but we cannot conceal the fact that she was now a very indifferent witness to the truth of what was before her and might easily have mistaken a sheep for a cow, or an old man called Smith for one who was called Jones and was no relation of his whatever. For the shadow of faintness which the thumb without a nail had cast had deepened now, at the back of her brain (which is the part furthest from sight), into a pool where things dwell in darkness so deep that what they are we scarcely know. She now looked down into this pool or sea in which everything is reflected – and, indeed, some say that all our most violent passions, and art and religion, are the reflections which we see in the dark hollow at the back of the head when the visible world is obscured for the time. She looked there now, long, deeply, profoundly, and immediately the ferny path up the hill along which she was walking became not entirely a path, but partly the Serpentine; the hawthorn bushes were partly ladies and gentlemen sitting with card-cases and gold-mounted canes; the sheep were partly tall Mayfair houses; everything was partly something else, as if her mind had become a forest with glades branching here and there; things came nearer, and further, and mingled and separated and made the strangest alliances and combinations in an incessant chequer of light and shade. Except when Canute, the elk-hound, chased a rabbit and so reminded her that it must be about half-past four– it was indeed twenty-three minutes to six – she forgot the time.

The ferny path led, with many turns and windings, higher and higher to the oak tree, which stood on the top. The tree had grown bigger, sturdier, and more knotted since she had known it, somewhere about the year 1588, but it was still in the prime of life. The little sharply frilled leaves were still fluttering thickly on its branches. Flinging herself on the ground, she felt the bones of the tree running out like ribs from a spine this way and that

Orlando at the present time

beneath her. She liked to think that she was riding the back of the world. She liked to attach herself to something hard. As she flung herself down a little square book bound in red cloth fell from the breast of her leather jacket – her poem 'The Oak Tree'. 'I should have brought a trowel,' she reflected. The earth was so shallow over the roots that it seemed doubtful if she could do as she meant and bury the book here. Besides, the dogs would dig it up. No luck ever attends these symbolical celebrations, she thought. Perhaps it would be as well then to do without them. She had a little speech on the tip of her tongue which she meant to speak over the book as she buried it. (It was a copy of the first edition, signed by author and artist.) 'I bury this as a tribute,' she was going to have said, 'a return to the land of what the land has given me,' but Lord! once one began mouthing words aloud, how silly they sounded! She was reminded of old Greene getting upon a platform the other day comparing her with Milton (save for his blindness) and handing her a cheque for two hundred guineas. She had thought then, of the oak tree here on its hill, and what has that got to do with this, she had wondered? What has praise and fame to do with poetry? What has seven editions (the book had already gone into no less) got to do with the value of it? Was not writing poetry a secret transaction, a voice answering a voice? So that all this chatter and praise and blame and meeting people who admired one and meeting people who did not admire one was as ill suited as could be to the thing itself – a voice answering a voice. What could have been more secret, she thought, more slow, and like the intercourse of lovers, than the stammering answer she had made all these years to the old crooning song of the woods, and the farms and the brown horses standing at the gate, neck to neck, and the smithy and the kitchen and the fields, so laboriously bearing wheat, turnips, grass, and the garden blowing irises and fritillaries?

So she let her book lie unburied and dishevelled on the ground, and watched the vast view, varied like an ocean floor this evening with the sun lightening it and the shadows darkening it. There was a village with a church tower among elm trees; a grey domed manor house in a park; a spark of light burning on some glasshouse; a farmyard with yellow corn stacks. The fields were marked with black tree clumps, and beyond the fields stretched long woodlands, and there was the gleam of a river, and then hills again. In the far distance Snowdon's crags broke white among the clouds; she saw the far Scottish hills and the wild tides that swirl about the Hebrides. She listened for the sound of gun-firing out at sea. No – only the wind blew. There was no war today. Drake had gone; Nelson had gone. 'And there,' she thought, letting her eyes, which had been looking at these far distances, drop once more to the land beneath her, 'was my land once: that Castle between the downs was mine; and all that moor running almost to the sea was mine.' Here the landscape (it must have been some trick of the fading light) shook itself, heaped itself, let all this encumbrance of houses, castles, and woods slide off its tent-shaped sides. The bare mountains of Turkey were before her. It was blazing noon. She looked straight at the baked hillside. Goats cropped the sandy tufts at her feet. An eagle soared above her. The raucous voice of old Rustum, the gypsy, croaked in her ears, 'What is your antiquity and your race, and your possessions compared with this? What do you need with four hundred bedrooms and silver lids on all your dishes, and house-maids dusting?'

At this moment some church clock chimed in the valley. The tent-like landscape collapsed and fell. The present showered down upon her head once more, but now that the light was fading, gentlier than before, calling into view nothing detailed, nothing small, but only misty fields, cottages with lamps in them, the slumbering bulk of a wood, and a fan-shaped light pushing the darkness before it along some lane. Whether it had struck nine, ten, or eleven, she could not say. Night had come – night that she loved of all times, night in which the reflections in the dark pool of the mind shine more clearly than by day. It was not necessary to faint now in order to look deep into the darkness where things shape themselves and to see in the pool of the mind now Shakespeare, now a girl in Russian trousers, now a toy boat on the Serpentine, and then the Atlantic itself, where it storms in great waves past Cape Horn. She looked into the darkness. There was her husband's brig, rising to the top of the wave! Up, it went, and up and up. The white arch of a thousand deaths rose before it. Oh rash, oh ridiculous man, always sailing, so uselessly, round Cape Horn in the teeth of a gale! But the brig was through the arch and out on the other side; it was safe at last!

'Ecstasy!' she cried, 'ecstasy!' And then the wind sank, the waters grew calm; and she saw the waves rippling peacefully in the moonlight.

'Marmaduke Bonthrop Shelmerdine!' she cried, standing by the oak tree.

The beautiful, glittering name fell out of the sky like a steel-blue feather. She watched it fall, turning and twisting like a slow-falling arrow that cleaves the deep air beautifully. He was coming, as he always came, in moments of dead calm; when the wave rippled and the spotted leaves fell slowly over her foot in the autumn woods; when the leopard was still; the moon was on the waters, and nothing moved between sky and sea. Then he came.

All was still now. It was near midnight. The moon rose slowly, over the weald. Its light raised a phantom castle upon earth. There stood the great house with all its windows robed in silver. Of wall or substance there was none. All was phantom. All was still. All was lit as for the coming of a dead Queen. Gazing below her, Orlando saw dark plumes tossing in the courtyard, and torches flickering and shadows kneeling. A Queen once more stepped from her chariot.

'The house is at your service, Ma'am,' she cried, curtseying deeply. 'Nothing has been changed. The dead Lord, my father, shall lead you in.'

As she spoke, the first stroke of midnight sounded. The cold breeze of the present brushed her face with its little breath of fear. She looked anxiously into the sky. It was dark with clouds now. The wind roared in her ears. But in the roar of the wind she heard the roar of an aeroplane coming nearer and nearer.

'Here! Shel, here!' she cried, baring her breast to the moon (which now showed bright) so that her pearls glowed like the eggs of some vast moon-spider. The aeroplane rushed out of the clouds and stood over her head. It hovered above her. Her pearls burnt like a phosphorescent flare in the darkness.

And as Shelmerdine, now grown a fine sea-captain, hale, fresh-coloured, and alert, leapt to the ground, there sprang up over his head a single wild bird.

'It is the goose!' Orlando cried. 'The wild goose . . . '

And the twelfth stroke of midnight sounded; the twelfth stroke of midnight, Thursday, the eleventh of October, Nineteen Hundred and Twenty-Eight.

A ROOM OF ONE'S OWN

A Room of One's Own

This essay is based upon two papers
presented by

VIRGINIA WOOLF

to the Arts Society at Newnham and
the Odtaa at Girton in October 1928.
The papers were too long to be read in full,
and have since been altered and expanded.

Chapter 1

But, you may say, we asked you to speak about women and fiction – what has that got to do with a room of one's own? I will try to explain. When you asked me to speak about women and fiction I sat down on the banks of a river and began to wonder what the words meant. They might mean simply a few remarks about Fanny Burney; a few more about Jane Austen; a tribute to the Brontës and a sketch of Haworth Parsonage under snow; some witticisms if possible about Miss Mitford; a respectful allusion to George Eliot; a reference to Mrs Gaskell and one would have done. But at second sight the words seemed not so simple. The title women and fiction might mean, and you may have meant it to mean, women and what they are like, or it might mean women and the fiction that they write; or it might mean women and the fiction that is written about them, or it might mean that somehow all three are inextricably mixed together and you want me to consider them in that light. But when I began to consider the subject in this last way, which seemed the most interesting, I soon saw that it had one fatal drawback. I should never be able to come to a conclusion. I should never be able to fulfil what is, I understand, the first duty of a lecturer – to hand you after an hour's discourse a nugget of pure truth to wrap up between the pages of your notebooks and keep on the mantelpiece for ever. All I could do was to offer you an opinion upon one minor point – a woman must have money and a room of her own if she is to write fiction; and that, as you will see, leaves the great problem of the true nature of woman and the true nature of fiction unsolved. I have shirked the duty of coming to a conclusion upon these two questions – women and fiction remain, so far as I am concerned, unsolved problems. But in order to make some amends I am going to do what I can to show you how I arrived at this opinion about the room and the money. I am going to develop in your presence as fully and freely as I can the train of thought which led me to think this. Perhaps if I lay bare the ideas, the prejudices, that lie behind this statement you will find that they have some bearing upon women and some upon fiction. At any rate, when a subject is highly controversial – and any question about sex is that – one cannot hope to tell the truth. One can only show how one came to hold whatever opinion one does hold. One can only give one's audience the chance of drawing their own conclusions as they observe the limitations, the prejudices, the idiosyncrasies of the speaker. Fiction here is likely to contain more truth than fact. Therefore I propose, making use of all the liberties and licences of a novelist, to tell you the story of the two days that preceded my coming here – how, bowed down by the weight of the subject which you have laid upon my shoulders, I pondered it, and made it work in and out of my daily life. I need not say that what I am about to describe has no existence; Oxbridge is an invention; so is Fernham; 'I' is only a convenient term for somebody who has no real being. Lies will flow from my lips, but there may perhaps be some truth mixed up with them; it is for you to seek out this truth and to decide whether any part of it is worth keeping. If not, you will of course throw the whole of it into the wastepaper basket and forget all about it.

Here then was I (call me Mary Beton, Mary Seton, Mary Carmichael or by any name you please – it is not a matter of any importance) sitting on the banks of a river a week or two ago in fine October weather, lost in thought. That collar I have spoken of, women and fiction, the need of coming to some conclusion on a subject that raises all sorts of prejudices and passions, bowed my head to the ground. To the right and left bushes of some sort, golden and crimson, glowed with the colour, even it seemed burnt with the heat, of fire. On the farther bank the willows wept in perpetual lamentation, their hair about their shoulders. The river reflected whatever it chose of sky and bridge and burning tree, and when the undergraduate had oared his boat through the reflections they closed again, completely, as if he had never been. There one might have sat the clock round lost in thought. Thought – to call it by a prouder name than it deserved – had let its line down into the stream. It swayed, minute after minute, hither and thither among the reflections and the weeds, letting the water lift it and sink it until – you know the little tug – the sudden conglomeration of an idea at the end of one's line: and then the cautious hauling of it in, and the careful laying of it out? Alas, laid on the grass how small, how insignificant this thought of mine looked; the sort of fish that a good fisherman puts back into the water so that it may grow fatter and be one day worth cooking and eating. I will not trouble you with that thought now, though if you look carefully you may find it for yourselves in the course of what I am going to say.

But however small it was, it had, nevertheless, the mysterious property of its kind – put back into the mind, it became at once very exciting, and important; and as it darted and sank, and flashed hither and thither, set up such a wash and tumult of ideas that it was impossible to sit still. It was thus that I found myself walking with extreme rapidity across a grass plot. Instantly a man's figure rose to intercept me. Nor did I at first understand that the gesticulations of a curious-looking object, in a cut-away coat and evening shirt, were aimed at me. His face expressed horror and indignation. Instinct rather than reason came to my help; he was a beadle; I was a woman. This was the turf; there was the path. Only the Fellows and Scholars are allowed here; the gravel is the place for me. Such thoughts were the work of a moment. As I regained the path the arms of the beadle sank, his face assumed its usual repose, and though turf is better walking than gravel, no very great harm was done. The only charge I could bring against the Fellows and Scholars of whatever the college might happen to be was that in protection of their turf, which has been rolled for three hundred years in succession, they had sent my little fish into hiding.

What idea it had been that had sent me so audaciously trespassing I could not now remember. The spirit of peace descended like a cloud from heaven, for if the spirit of peace dwells anywhere, it is in the courts and quadrangles of Oxbridge on a fine October morning. Strolling through those colleges past those ancient halls the roughness of the present seemed smoothed away; the body seemed contained in a miraculous glass cabinet through which no sound could penetrate, and the mind, freed from any contact with facts (unless one trespassed on the turf again), was at liberty to settle down upon whatever meditation was in harmony with the moment. As chance would have it, some stray memory of some old essay about revisiting Oxbridge in the long vacation brought Charles Lamb to mind – Saint Charles, said Thackeray, putting a letter of Lamb's to his forehead. Indeed, among all the dead (I give you my thoughts as they came to me), Lamb is one of the most congenial; one to whom one would have liked to say, Tell me then how you wrote your essays? For his essays are superior even to Max Beerbohm's, I thought, with all their perfection, because of that wild flash of imagination, that lightning crack of genius in the middle of them which leaves them flawed and imperfect, but starred with poetry. Lamb then came to Oxbridge perhaps a hundred years ago. Certainly he wrote an essay – the name escapes me – about the manuscript of one of Milton's poems which he saw here. It was *Lycidas* perhaps, and Lamb wrote how it shocked him to think it possible that any word in *Lycidas* could have been different from what it is. To think of Milton changing the words in that poem seemed to him a sort of sacrilege. This led me to remember what I could of *Lycidas* and to amuse myself with guessing which word it could have been that Milton had altered, and why. It then occurred to me that the very manuscript itself which Lamb had looked at was only a few hundred yards away, so that one could follow Lamb's footsteps across the quadrangle to that famous library where the treasure is kept. Moreover, I recollected, as I put this plan into execution, it is in this famous library that the manuscript of Thackeray's *Esmond* is also preserved. The critics often say that *Esmond* is Thackeray's most perfect novel. But the affectation of the style, with its imitation of the eighteenth century, hampers one, so far as I can remember; unless indeed the eighteenth-century style was natural to Thackeray – a fact that one might prove by looking at the manuscript and seeing whether the alterations were for the benefit of the style or of the sense. But then one would have to decide what is style and what is meaning, a question which – but here I was actually at the door which leads into the library itself. I must have opened it, for instantly there issued, like a guardian angel barring the way with a flutter of black gown instead of white wings, a deprecating, silvery, kindly gentleman, who regretted in a low voice as he waved me back that ladies are only admitted to the library if accompanied by a Fellow of the College or furnished with a letter of introduction.

That a famous library has been cursed by a woman is a matter of complete indifference to a famous library. Venerable and calm, with all its treasures safe locked within its breast, it sleeps complacently and will, so far as I am concerned, so sleep for ever. Never will I wake those echoes, never will I ask for that hospitality again, I vowed as I descended the steps in anger. Still an hour remained before luncheon, and what was one to do? Stroll on the meadows? sit by the river? Certainly it was a lovely autumn morning; the leaves were fluttering red to the ground; there was no great hardship in doing either. But the sound of music reached my ear. Some service or celebration was going forward. The organ complained magnificently as I passed the chapel door. Even the sorrow of Christianity sounded in that serene air more like the recollection of sorrow than sorrow itself; even the groanings of the ancient organ seemed lapped in peace. I had no wish to enter had I the right, and this time the verger might have stopped me, demanding perhaps my baptismal certificate, or a letter of introduction from the Dean. But the outside of these magnificent buildings is often as beautiful as the inside. Moreover, it was amusing enough to watch the congregation assembling, coming in and going out again, busying themselves at the door of the chapel like bees at the mouth of a hive. Many were in cap and gown; some had tufts of fur on their shoulders; others were wheeled in bath-chairs; others, though not past middle age, seemed creased and crushed into shapes so singular that one was reminded of those giant crabs and crayfish who heave with difficulty across the sand of an aquarium. As I leant against the wall the university indeed seemed a sanctuary in which are preserved rare types which would soon be obsolete if left to fight for existence on the pavement of the Strand. Old stories of old deans and old dons came back to mind, but before I had summoned up courage to whistle – it used to be said that at the sound of a whistle old Professor — instantly broke into a gallop – the venerable congregation had gone inside. The outside of the chapel remained. As you know, its high domes and pinnacles can be seen, like a sailing-ship always voyaging never arriving, lit up at night and visible for miles, far away across the hills. Once, presumably, this quadrangle with its smooth lawns, its massive buildings and the chapel itself was marsh too, where the grasses waved and the swine rootled. Teams of horses and oxen, I thought, must have hauled the stone in wagons from far countries, and then with infinite labour the grey blocks in whose shade I was now standing were poised in order one on top of another, and then the painters brought their glass for the windows, and the masons were busy for centuries up on that roof with putty and cement, spade and trowel. Every Saturday somebody must have poured gold and silver out of a leathern purse into their ancient fists, for they had their beer and skittles presumably of an evening. An unending stream of gold and silver, I thought, must have flowed into this court perpetually to keep the stones coming and the masons working; to level, to ditch, to dig and to drain. But it was then the age of faith, and money was poured liberally to set these stones on a deep foundation, and when the stones were raised, still more money was poured in from the coffers of kings and queens and great nobles to ensure that hymns should be sung here and scholars taught. Lands were granted; tithes were paid. And when the age of faith was over and the age of reason had come, still the same flow of gold and silver went on; fellowships were founded; lectureships endowed; only the gold and silver flowed now not from the coffers of the king but from the chests of merchants and manufacturers, from the purses of men who had made, say, a fortune from industry, and returned, in their wills, a bounteous share of it to endow more chairs, more lectureships, more fellowships in the university where they had learnt their craft. Hence the libraries and laboratories; the observatories; the splendid equipment of costly and delicate instruments which now stands on glass shelves, where centuries ago the grasses waved and the swine rooted. Certainly, as I strolled round the court, the foundation of gold and silver seemed deep enough; the pavement laid solidly over the wild grasses. Men with trays on their heads went busily from staircase to staircase. Gaudy blossoms flowered in window-boxes. The strains of the gramophone blared out from the rooms within. It was impossible not to reflect – the reflection whatever it may have been was cut short. The clock struck. It was time to find one's way to luncheon.

It is a curious fact that novelists have a way of making us believe that luncheon parties are invariably memorable for something very witty that was said, or for something very wise that was done. But they seldom spare a word for what was eaten. It is part of the novelist's convention not to mention soup and salmon and ducklings, as if soup and salmon and ducklings were of no importance whatsoever, as if nobody ever smoked a cigar or drank a glass of wine. Here, however, I shall take the liberty to defy that convention and to tell you that the lunch on this occasion began with soles, sunk in a deep dish, over which the college cook had spread a counterpane of the whitest cream, save that it was branded here and there with brown spots like the spots on the flanks of a doe. After that came the partridges, but if this suggests a couple of bald, brown birds on a plate you are mistaken. The partridges, many and various, came with all their retinue of sauces and salads, the sharp and the sweet, each in its order; their potatoes, thin as coins but not so hard; their sprouts, foliated as rosebuds but more succulent. And no sooner had the roast and its retinue been done with than the silent servingman, the beadle himself perhaps in a milder manifestation, set before us, wreathed in napkins, a confection which rose all sugar from the waves. To call it pudding and so relate it to rice and tapioca would be an insult. Meanwhile the wine glasses had flushed yellow and flushed crimson; had been emptied; had been filled. And thus by degrees was lit, halfway down the spine, which is the seat of the soul, not that hard little electric light which we call brilliance, as it pops in and out upon our lips, but the more profound, subtle and subterranean glow which is the rich yellow flame of rational intercourse. No need to hurry. No need to sparkle. No need to be anybody but oneself. We are all going to heaven and Van Dyck is of the company – in other words, how good life seemed, how sweet its rewards, how trivial this grudge or that grievance, how admirable friendship and the society of one's kind, as, lighting a good cigarette, one sank among the cushions in the window-seat.

If by good luck there had been an ashtray handy, if one had not knocked the ash out of the window in default, if things had been a little different from what they were, one would not have seen, presumably, a cat without a tail. The sight of that abrupt and truncated animal padding softly across the quadrangle changed by some fluke of the subconscious intelligence the emotional light for me. It was as if someone had let fall a shade. Perhaps the excellent hock was relinquishing its hold. Certainly, as I watched the Manx cat pause in the middle of the lawn as if it too questioned the universe, something seemed lacking, something seemed different. But what was lacking, what was different, I asked myself, listening to the talk? And to answer that question I had to think myself out of the room, back into the past, before the war indeed, and to set before my eyes the model of another luncheon party held in rooms not very far distant from these; but different. Everything was different. Meanwhile the talk went on among the guests, who were many and young, some of this sex, some of that; it went on swimmingly, it went on agreeably, freely, amusingly. And as it went on I set it against the background of that other talk, and as I matched the two together I had no doubt that one was the descendant, the legitimate heir of the other. Nothing was changed; nothing was different save only here I listened with all my ears not entirely to what was being said, but to the murmur or current behind it. Yes, that was it – the change was there. Before the war at a luncheon party like this people would have said precisely the same things but they would have sounded different, because in those days they were accompanied by a sort of humming noise, not articulate, but musical, exciting, which changed the value of the words themselves. Could one set that humming noise to words? Perhaps with the help of the poets one could. A book lay beside me and, opening it, I turned casually enough to Tennyson. And here I found Tennyson was singing:

> There has fallen a splendid tear
>   From the passion-flower at the gate.
> She is coming, my dove, my dear;
>   She is coming, my life, my fate;
> The red rose cries, 'She is near, she is near';
>   And the white rose weeps, 'She is late';
> The larkspur listens, 'I hear, I hear';
>   And the lily whispers, 'I wait.'

Was that what men hummed at luncheon parties before the war? And the women?

> My heart is like a singing bird
>   Whose nest is in a water'd shoot;
> My heart is like an apple tree
>   Whose boughs are bent with thick-set fruit;
> My heart is like a rainbow shell
>   That paddles in a halcyon sea;
> My heart is gladder than all these
>   Because my love is come to me.

Was that what women hummed at luncheon parties before the war?

There was something so ludicrous in thinking of people humming such things even under their breath at luncheon parties before the war that I burst out laughing, and had to explain my laughter by pointing at the Manx cat, who did look a little absurd, poor beast, without a tail, in the middle of the lawn. Was he really born so, or had he lost his tail in an accident? The tailless cat, though some are said to exist in the Isle of Man, is rarer than one thinks. It is a queer animal, quaint rather than beautiful. It is strange what a difference a tail makes – you know the sort of things one says as a lunch party breaks up and people are finding their coats and hats.

This one, thanks to the hospitality of the host, had lasted far into the afternoon. The beautiful October day was fading and the leaves were falling from the trees in the avenue as I walked through it. Gate after gate seemed to close with gentle finality behind me. Innumerable beadles were fitting innumerable keys into well-oiled locks; the treasure-house was being made secure for another night. After the avenue one comes out upon a road – I forget its name – which leads you, if you take the right turning, along to Fernham. But there was plenty of time. Dinner was not till half-past seven. One could almost do without dinner after such a luncheon. It is strange how a scrap of poetry works in the mind and makes the legs move in time to it along the road. Those words –

> There has fallen a splendid tear
>   From the passion-flower at the gate.
> She is coming, my dove, my dear –

sang in my blood as I stepped quickly along towards Headingley. And then, switching off into the other measure, I sang, where the waters are churned up by the weir:

> My heart is like a singing bird
>   Whose nest is in a water'd shoot;
> My heart is like an apple tree . . .

What poets, I cried aloud, as one does in the dusk, what poets they were!

In a sort of jealousy, I suppose, for our own age, silly and absurd though these comparisons are, I went on to wonder if honestly one could name two living poets now as great as Tennyson and Christina Rossetti were then. Obviously it is impossible, I thought, looking into those foaming waters, to compare them. The very reason why that poetry excites one to such abandonment, such rapture, is that it celebrates some feeling that one used to have (at luncheon parties before the war perhaps), so that one responds easily, familiarly, without troubling to check the feeling, or to compare it with any that one has now. But the living poets express a feeling that is actually being made and torn out of us at the moment. One does not recognise it in the first place; often for some reason one fears it; one watches it with keenness and compares it jealously and suspiciously with the old feeling that one knew. Hence the difficulty of modern poetry; and it is because of this difficulty that one cannot remember more than two consecutive lines of any good modern poet. For this reason – that my memory failed me – the argument flagged for want of material. But why, I continued, moving on towards Headingley, have we stopped humming under our breath at luncheon parties? Why has Alfred ceased to sing

> She is coming, my dove, my dear.

Why has Christina ceased to respond

> My heart is gladder than all these
> Because my love is come to me?

Shall we lay the blame on the war? When the guns fired in August 1914, did the faces of men and women show so plain in each other's eyes that romance was killed? Certainly it was a shock (to women in particular with their illusions about education, and so on) to see the faces of our rulers in the light of the shellfire. So ugly they looked – German, English, French – so stupid. But lay the blame where one will, on whom one will, the illusion which inspired Tennyson and Christina Rossetti to sing so passionately about the coming of their loves is far rarer now than then. One has only to read, to look, to listen, to remember. But why say 'blame'? Why, if it was an illusion, not praise the catastrophe, whatever it was, that destroyed illusion and put truth in its place? For truth . . . those dots mark the spot where, in search of truth, I missed the turning up to Fernham. Yes indeed, which was truth and which was illusion? I asked myself. What was the truth about these houses, for example, dim and festive now with their red windows in the dusk, but raw and red and squalid, with their sweets and their bootlaces, at nine o'clock in the morning? And the willows and the river and the gardens that run down to the river, vague now with the mist stealing over them, but gold and red in the sunlight – which was the truth, which was the illusion about them? I spare you the twists and turns of my cogitations, for no conclusion was found on the road to Headingley, and I ask you to suppose that I soon found out my mistake about the turning and retraced my steps to Fernham.

As I have said already that it was an October day, I dare not forfeit your respect and imperil the fair name of fiction by changing the season and describing lilacs hanging over garden walls, crocuses, tulips and other flowers of spring. Fiction must stick to facts, and the truer the facts the better the fiction – so we are told. Therefore it was still autumn and the leaves were still yellow and falling, if anything, a little faster than before, because it was now evening (seven twenty-three to be precise) and a breeze (from the south-west to be exact) had risen. But for all that there was something odd at work:

> My heart is like a singing bird
>> Whose nest is in a water'd shoot;
> My heart is like an apple tree
>> Whose boughs are bent with thick-set fruit –

perhaps the words of Christina Rossetti were partly responsible for the folly of the fancy – it was nothing of course but a fancy – that the lilac was shaking its flowers over the garden walls, and the brimstone butterflies were scudding hither and thither, and the dust of the pollen was in the air. A wind blew, from what quarter I know not, but it lifted the half-grown leaves so that there was a flash of silver grey in the air. It was the time between the lights when colours undergo their intensification and purples and golds burn in window-panes like the beat of an excitable heart; when for some reason the beauty of the world revealed and yet soon to perish (here I pushed into the garden, for, unwisely, the door was left open and no beadles seemed about), the beauty of the world which is so soon to perish, has two edges, one of laughter, one of anguish, cutting the heart asunder. The gardens of Fernham lay before me in the spring twilight, wild and open, and in the long grass, sprinkled and carelessly flung, were daffodils and bluebells, not orderly perhaps at the best of times, and now wind-blown and waving as they tugged at their roots. The windows of the building, curved like ships' windows among generous waves of red brick, changed from lemon to silver under the flight of the quick spring clouds. Somebody was in a hammock, somebody, but in this light they were phantoms only, half guessed, half seen, raced across the grass – would no one stop her? – and then on the terrace, as if popping out to breathe the air, to glance at the garden, came a bent figure, formidable yet humble, with her great forehead and her shabby dress – could it be the famous scholar, could it be J— H— herself? All was dim, yet intense too, as if the scarf which the dusk had flung over the garden were torn asunder by star or sword – the gash of some terrible reality leaping, as its way is, out of the heart of the spring. For youth –

Here was my soup. Dinner was being served in the great dining-hall. Far from being spring it was in fact an evening in October. Everybody was assembled in the big dining-room. Dinner was ready. Here was the soup. It was a plain gravy soup. There was nothing to stir the fancy in that. One could have seen through the transparent liquid any pattern that there might have been on the plate itself. But there was no pattern. The plate was plain. Next came beef with its attendant greens and potatoes – a homely trinity, suggesting the rumps of cattle in a muddy market, and sprouts curled and yellowed at the edge, and bargaining and cheapening and women with string bags on Monday morning. There was no reason to complain of human nature's daily food, seeing that the supply was sufficient and coal-miners doubtless were sitting down to less. Prunes and custard followed. And if anyone complains that prunes, even when mitigated by custard, are an uncharitable vegetable (fruit they are not), stringy as a miser's heart and exuding a fluid such as might run in misers' veins who have denied themselves wine and warmth for eighty years and yet not given to the poor, he should reflect that there are people whose charity embraces even the prune. Biscuits and cheese came next, and here the water-jug was liberally passed round, for it is the nature of biscuits to be dry, and these were biscuits to the core. That was all. The meal was over. Everybody scraped their chairs back; the swing-doors swung violently to and fro; soon the hall was emptied of every sign of food and made ready no doubt for breakfast next morning. Down corridors and up staircases the youth of England went banging and singing. And was it for a guest, a stranger (for I had no more right here in Fernham than in Trinity or Somerville or Girton or Newnham or Christchurch), to say, 'The dinner was not good,' or to say (we were now, Mary Seton and I, in her sitting-room), 'Could we not have dined up here alone?' for if I had said anything of the kind I should have been prying and searching into the secret economies of a house which to the stranger wears so fine a front of gaiety and courage. No, one could say nothing of the sort. Indeed, conversation for a moment flagged. The human frame being what it is, heart, body and brain all mixed together, and not contained in separate compartments as they will be no doubt in another million years, a good dinner is of great importance to good talk. One cannot think well, love well, sleep well, if one has not dined well. The lamp in the spine does not light on beef and prunes. We are all *probably* going to heaven, and Van Dyck is, we *hope*, to meet us round the next corner – that is the dubious and qualifying state of mind that beef and prunes at the end of the day's work breed between them. Happily my friend, who taught science, had a cupboard where there was a squat bottle and little glasses – (but there should have been sole and partridge to begin with) – so that we were able to draw up to the fire and repair some of the damages of the day's living. In a minute or so we were slipping freely in and out among all those objects of curiosity and interest which form in the mind in the absence of a particular person, and are naturally to be discussed on coming together again – how somebody has married, another has not; one thinks this, another that; one has improved out of all knowledge, the other most amazingly gone to the bad – with all those speculations upon human nature and the character of the amazing world we live in which spring naturally from such beginnings. While these things were being said, however, I became shamefacedly aware of a current setting in of its own accord and carrying everything forward to an end of its own. One might be talking of Spain or Portugal, of book or racehorse, but the real interest of whatever was said was none of those things, but a scene of masons on a high roof some five centuries ago. Kings and nobles brought treasure in huge sacks and poured it under the earth. This scene was forever coming alive in my mind and placing itself by another of lean cows and a muddy market and withered greens and the stringy hearts of old men – these two pictures, disjointed and disconnected and nonsensical as they were, were forever coming together and combating each other and had me entirely at their mercy. The best course, unless the whole talk was to be distorted, was to expose what was in my mind to the air, when with good luck it would fade and crumble like the head of the dead king when they opened the coffin at Windsor. Briefly, then, I told Miss Seton about the masons who had been all those years on the roof of the chapel, and about the kings and queens and nobles bearing sacks of gold and silver on their shoulders, which they shovelled into the earth; and then how the great financial magnates of our own time came and laid cheques and bonds, I suppose, where the others had laid ingots and rough lumps of gold. All that lies beneath the colleges down there, I said; but this college, where we are now sitting, what lies beneath its gallant red brick and the wild unkempt grasses of the garden? What force is behind that plain china off which we dined, and (here it popped out of my mouth before I could stop it) the beef, the custard and the prunes?

Well, said Mary Seton, about the year 1860 – Oh, but you know the story, she said, bored, I suppose, by the recital. And she told me – rooms were hired. Committees met. Envelopes were addressed. Circulars were drawn up. Meetings were held; letters were read out; so-and-so has promised so much; on the contrary, Mr— won't give a penny. The *Saturday Review* has been very rude. How can we raise a fund to pay for offices? Shall we hold a bazaar? Can't we find a pretty girl to sit in the front row? Let us look up what John Stuart Mill said on the subject. Can anyone persuade the editor of the — to print a letter? Can we get Lady — to sign it? Lady — is out of town. That was the way it was done, presumably, sixty years ago, and it was a prodigious effort, and a great deal of time was spent on it. And it was only after a long struggle and with the utmost difficulty that they got thirty thousand pounds together.* So obviously we cannot have wine and

* 'We are told that we ought to ask for £30,000 at least . . . It is not a large sum, considering that there is to be but one college of this sort for Great Britain, Ireland and the Colonies, and considering how easy it is to raise immense sums for boys' schools. But considering how few people really wish women to be educated, it is a good deal.' – LADY STEPHEN, *Emily Davies and Girton College*

partridges and servants carrying tin dishes on their heads, she said. We cannot have sofas and separate rooms. 'The amenities,' she said, quoting from some book or other, 'will have to wait.'*

At the thought of all those women working year after year and finding it hard to get two thousand pounds together, and as much as they could do to get thirty thousand pounds, we burst out in scorn at the reprehensible poverty of our sex. What had our mothers been doing then that they had no wealth to leave us? Powdering their noses? Looking in at shop windows? Flaunting in the sun at Monte Carlo? There were some photographs on the mantelpiece. Mary's mother – if that was her picture – may have been a wastrel in her spare time (she had thirteen children by a minister of the church), but if so her gay and dissipated life had left too few traces of its pleasures on her face. She was a homely body; an old lady in a plaid shawl which was fastened by a large cameo; and she sat in a basket-chair, encouraging a spaniel to look at the camera, with the amused, yet strained expression of one who is sure that the dog will move directly the bulb is pressed. Now if she had gone into business; had become a manufacturer of artificial silk or a magnate on the Stock Exchange; if she had left two or three hundred thousand pounds to Fernham, we could have been sitting at our ease tonight and the subject of our talk might have been archaeology, botany, anthropology, physics, the nature of the atom, mathematics, astronomy, relativity, geography. If only Mrs Seton and her mother and her mother before her had learnt the great art of making money and had left their money, like their fathers and their grandfathers before them, to found fellowships and lectureships and prizes and scholarships appropriated to the use of their own sex, we might have dined very tolerably up here alone off a bird and a bottle of wine; we might have looked forward without undue confidence to a pleasant and honourable lifetime spent in the shelter of one of the liberally endowed professions. We might have been exploring or writing; mooning about the venerable places of the earth; sitting contemplative on the steps of the Parthenon, or going at ten to an office and coming home comfortably at half-past four to write a little poetry. Only, if Mrs Seton and her like had gone into business at the age of fifteen, there would have been – that was the snag in the argument – no Mary. What, I asked, did Mary think of that? There between the curtains was the October night, calm and lovely, with a star or two caught in the yellowing trees. Was she ready to resign her share of it and her memories (for they had been a happy family, though a large one) of games and quarrels up in Scotland, which she is never tired of praising for the fineness of its air and the quality of its cakes, in order that Fernham might have been endowed with fifty thousand pounds or so by a stroke of the pen? For, to endow a college would necessitate the suppression

* Every penny which could be scraped together was set aside for building, and the amenities had to be postponed. – R. STRACHEY, *The Cause*

of families altogether. Making a fortune and bearing thirteen children – no human being could stand it. Consider the facts, we said. First there are nine months before the baby is born. Then the baby is born. Then there are three or four months spent in feeding the baby. After the baby is fed there are certainly five years spent in playing with the baby. You cannot, it seems, let children run about the streets. People who have seen them running wild in Russia say that the sight is not a pleasant one. People say, too, that human nature takes its shape in the years between one and five. If Mrs Seton, I said, had been making money, what sort of memories would you have had of games and quarrels? What would you have known of Scotland, and its fine air and cakes and all the rest of it? But it is useless to ask these questions, because you would never have come into existence at all. Moreover, it is equally useless to ask what might have happened if Mrs Seton and her mother and her mother before her had amassed great wealth and laid it under the foundations of college and library, because, in the first place, to earn money was impossible for them, and in the second, had it been possible, the law denied them the right to possess what money they earned. It is only for the last forty-eight years that Mrs Seton has had a penny of her own. For all the centuries before that it would have been her husband's property – a thought which, perhaps, may have had its share in keeping Mrs Seton and her mothers off the Stock Exchange. Every penny I earn, they may have said, will be taken from me and disposed of according to my husband's wisdom – perhaps to found a scholarship or to endow a fellowship in Balliol or Kings, so that to earn money, even if I could earn money, is not a matter that interests me very greatly. I had better leave it to my husband.

At any rate, whether or not the blame rested on the old lady who was looking at the spaniel, there could be no doubt that for some reason or other our mothers had mismanaged their affairs very gravely. Not a penny could be spared for 'amenities'; for partridges and wine, beadles and turf, books and cigars, libraries and leisure. To raise bare walls out of bare earth was the utmost they could do.

So we talked standing at the window and looking, as so many thousands look every night, down on the domes and towers of the famous city beneath us. It was very beautiful, very mysterious in the autumn moonlight. The old stone looked very white and venerable. One thought of all the books that were assembled down there; of the pictures of old prelates and worthies hanging in the panelled rooms; of the painted windows that would be throwing strange globes and crescents on the pavement; of the tablets and memorials and inscriptions; of the fountains and the grass; of the quiet rooms looking across the quiet quadrangles. And (pardon me the thought) I thought, too, of the admirable smoke and drink and the deep armchairs and the pleasant carpets; of the urbanity, the geniality, the dignity which are the offspring of luxury and privacy and space. Certainly our mothers had not provided us with anything comparable to all this – our mothers who found it difficult to scrape together thirty thousand pounds, our mothers who bore thirteen children to ministers of religion at St Andrews.

So I went back to my inn, and as I walked through the dark streets I pondered this and that, as one does at the end of the day's work. I pondered why it was that Mrs Seton had no money to leave us; and what effect poverty has on the mind; and what effect wealth has on the mind; and I thought of the queer old gentlemen I had seen that morning with tufts of fur upon their shoulders; and I remembered how if one whistled one of them ran; and I thought of the organ booming in the chapel and of the shut doors of the library; and I thought how unpleasant it is to be locked out; and I thought how it is worse perhaps to be locked in; and, thinking of the safety and prosperity of the one sex and of the poverty and insecurity of the other and of the effect of tradition and of the lack of tradition upon the mind of a writer, I thought at last that it was time to roll up the crumpled skin of the day, with its arguments and its impressions and its anger and its laughter, and cast it into the hedge. A thousand stars were flashing across the blue wastes of the sky. One seemed alone with an inscrutable society. All human beings were laid asleep – prone, horizontal, dumb. Nobody seemed stirring in the streets of Oxbridge. Even the door of the hotel sprang open at the touch of an invisible hand – not a boots was sitting up to light me to bed, it was so late.

Chapter 2

The scene, if I may ask you to follow me, was now changed. The leaves were still falling, but in London now, not Oxbridge; and I must ask you to imagine a room, like many thousands, with a window looking across people's hats and vans and motor cars to other windows, and on the table inside the room a blank sheet of paper on which was written in large letters *Women and Fiction*, but no more. The inevitable sequel to lunching and dining at Oxbridge seemed, unfortunately, to be a visit to the British Museum. One must strain off what was personal and accidental in all these impressions and so reach the pure fluid, the essential oil of truth. For that visit to Oxbridge and the luncheon and the dinner had started a swarm of questions. Why did men drink wine and women water? Why was one sex so prosperous and the other so poor? What effect has poverty on fiction? What conditions are necessary for the creation of works of art? – a thousand questions at once suggested themselves. But one needed answers, not questions; and an answer was only to be had by consulting the learned and the unprejudiced, who have removed themselves above the strife of tongue and the confusion of body and issued the result of their reasoning and research in books which are to be found in the British Museum. If truth is not to be found on the shelves of the British Museum, where, I asked myself, picking up a notebook and a pencil, is truth?

Thus provided, thus confident and enquiring, I set out in the pursuit of truth. The day, though not actually wet, was dismal, and the streets in the neighbourhood of the museum were full of open coal-holes, down which sacks were showering; four-wheeled cabs were drawing up and depositing on the pavement corded boxes containing, presumably, the entire wardrobe of some Swiss or Italian family seeking fortune or refuge or some other desirable commodity which is to be found in the boarding-houses of Bloomsbury in the winter. The usual hoarse-voiced men paraded the streets with plants on barrows. Some shouted; others sang. London was like a workshop. London was like a machine. We were all being shot backwards and forwards on this plain foundation to make some pattern. The British Museum was another department of the factory. The swing-doors swung open; and there one stood under the vast dome, as if one were a thought in the huge bald forehead which is so splendidly encircled by a band of famous names. One went to the counter; one took a slip of paper; one opened a volume of the catalogue, and . . . . . – the five dots here indicate five separate minutes of stupefaction, wonder and bewilderment. Have you any notion how many books are written about women in the course of one year? Have you any notion how many are written by men? Are you aware that you are, perhaps, the most discussed animal in the universe? Here had I come with a notebook and a pencil proposing to spend a morning reading, supposing that at the end of the morning I should have transferred the truth to my notebook. But I should need to be a herd of elephants, I thought, and a wilderness of spiders, desperately referring to the animals that are reputed longest lived and most multitudinously eyed, to cope with all this. I should need claws of steel and beak of brass even to penetrate the husk. How shall I ever find the grains of truth embedded in all this mass of paper? I asked myself, and in despair began running my eye up and down the long list of titles. Even the names of the books gave me food for thought. Sex and its nature might well attract doctors and biologists; but what was surprising and difficult of explanation was the fact that sex – woman, that is to say – also attracts agreeable essayists, light-fingered novelists, young men who have taken the M.A. degree; men who have taken no degree; men who have no apparent qualification save that they are not women. Some of these books were, on the face of it, frivolous and facetious; but many, on the other hand, were serious and prophetic, moral and hortatory. Merely to read the titles suggested innumerable schoolmasters, innumerable clergymen mounting their platforms and pulpits and holding forth with loquacity which far exceeded the hour usually allotted to such discourse on this one subject. It was a most strange phenomenon; and apparently – here I consulted the letter M – one confined to the male sex. Women do not write books about men – a fact that I could not help welcoming with relief, for if I had first to read all that men have written about women, then all that women have written about men, the aloe that flowers once in a hundred years would flower twice before I could set pen to paper. So, making a perfectly arbitrary choice of a dozen volumes or so, I sent my slips of paper to lie in the wire tray, and waited in my stall, among the other seekers for the essential oil of truth.

What could be the reason, then, of this curious disparity, I wondered, drawing cartwheels on the slips of paper provided by the British taxpayer for other purposes. Why are women, judging from this catalogue, so much more interesting to men than men are to women? A very curious fact it seemed, and my mind wandered to picture the lives of men who spend their time in writing books about women: whether they were old or young, married or unmarried, red-nosed or hump-backed – anyhow, it was flattering, vaguely, to feel oneself the object of such attention provided that it was not entirely bestowed by the crippled and the infirm – so I pondered until all such frivolous thoughts were ended by an avalanche of books sliding down on to the desk in front of me. Now the trouble began. The student who has been trained in research at Oxbridge has no doubt some method of shepherding his question past all distractions till it runs into his answer as a sheep runs into its pen. The student by my side, for instance, who was copying assiduously from a scientific manual, was, I felt sure, extracting pure nuggets of the essential ore every ten minutes or so. His little grunts of satisfaction indicated so much. But if, unfortunately, one has had no training in a university, the question far from being shepherded to its pen flies like a frightened flock hither and thither, helter-skelter, pursued by a whole pack of hounds. Professors, schoolmasters, sociologists, clergymen, novelists, essayists, journalists, men who had no qualification save that they were not women, chased my simple and single question – Why are some women poor? – until it became fifty questions; until the fifty questions leapt frantically into midstream and were carried away. Every page in my notebook was scribbled over with notes. To show the state of mind I was in, I will read you a few of them, explaining that the page was headed quite simply WOMEN AND POVERTY, in block letters; but what followed was something like this:

> Condition in Middle Ages of,
> Habits in the Fiji Islands of,
> Worshipped as goddesses by,
> Weaker in moral sense than,
> Idealism of,
> Greater conscientiousness of,
> South Sea Islanders, age of puberty among,
> Attractiveness of,
> Offered as sacrifice to,
> Small size of brain of,
> Profounder subconsciousness of,
> Less hair on the body of,
> Mental, moral and physical inferiority of,
> Love of children of,
> Greater length of life of,
> Weaker muscles of,
> Strength of affections of,
> Vanity of,
> Higher education of,
> Shakespeare's opinion of,
> Lord Birkenhead's opinion of,
> Dean Inge's opinion of,
> La Bruyère's opinion of,
> Dr Johnson's opinion of,
> Mr Oscar Browning's opinion of, . . .

Here I drew breath and added, indeed, in the margin, Why does Samuel Butler say, 'Wise men never say what they think of women'? Wise men never say anything else apparently. But, I continued, leaning back in my chair and looking at the vast dome in which I was a single but by now somewhat harassed thought, what is so unfortunate is that wise men never think the same thing about women. Here is Pope:

> Most women have no character at all.

And here is La Bruyère:

> Les femmes sont extrêmes; elles sont meilleures ou
>   pires que les hommes –

a direct contradiction by keen observers who were contemporary. Are they capable of education or incapable? Napoleon thought them incapable. Dr Johnson thought the opposite.* Have they souls or have they not souls? Some savages say they have none. Others, on the contrary, maintain that women are half divine and worship them on that account.† Some sages hold that they are shallower in the brain; others that they are deeper in the consciousness. Goethe honoured them; Mussolini despises them. Wherever one looked men thought about women and thought differently. It was impossible to make head or tail of it all, I decided, glancing with envy at the reader next door who was making the neatest abstracts, headed often with an A or a B or a C, while my own notebook rioted with the wildest scribble of contradictory jottings. It was distressing, it was bewildering, it was humiliating. Truth had run through my fingers. Every drop had escaped.

I could not possibly go home, I reflected, and add as a serious contribution to the study of women and fiction that women have less hair on their bodies than men, or that the age of puberty among the South Sea Islanders is nine – or is it ninety? – even the handwriting had become in its distraction indecipherable. It was disgraceful to have nothing more weighty or respectable to show after a whole morning's work. And if I could not grasp the truth about W (as for brevity's sake I had come to call her) in the past, why bother about W in the future? It seemed pure waste of time to consult all those gentlemen who specialise in woman and her effect on whatever it may be – politics, children, wages, morality – numerous and learned as they are. One might as well leave their books unopened.

But while I pondered I had unconsciously, in my listlessness, in my desperation, been drawing a picture where I should, like my neighbour, have been writing a conclusion. I had been drawing a face, a figure. It was the face and the figure of Professor von X, engaged in writing his monumental work entitled *The Mental, Moral and Physical Inferiority of the Female Sex*. He was not in my picture a man attractive to women. He was heavily built; he had a great jowl; to balance that he had very small eyes; he was very red in the face. His expression suggested that he was labouring under some emotion that

---

* 'Men know that women are an overmatch for them, and therefore they choose the weakest or the most ignorant. If they did not think so, they never could be afraid of women knowing as much as themselves' . . . In justice to the sex, I think it but candid to acknowledge that, in a subsequent conversation, he told me that he was serious in what he said. – BOSWELL, *The Journal of a Tour to the Hebrides*
† The ancient Germans believed that there was something holy in women, and accordingly consulted them as oracles. – FRAZER, *The Golden Bough*

made him jab his pen on the paper as if he were killing some noxious insect as he wrote, but even when he had killed it that did not satisfy him; he must go on killing it; and even so, some cause for anger and irritation remained. Could it be his wife, I asked, looking at my picture? Was she in love with a cavalry officer? Was the cavalry officer slim and elegant and dressed in astrakhan? Had he been laughed at, to adopt the Freudian theory, in his cradle by a pretty girl? For even in his cradle the professor, I thought, could not have been an attractive child. Whatever the reason, the professor was made to look very angry and very ugly in my sketch, as he wrote his great book upon the mental, moral and physical inferiority of women. Drawing pictures was an idle way of finishing an unprofitable morning's work. Yet it is in our idleness, in our dreams, that the submerged truth sometimes comes to the top. A very elementary exercise in psychology, not to be dignified by the name of psychoanalysis, showed me, on looking at my notebook, that the sketch of the angry professor had been made in anger. Anger had snatched my pencil while I dreamt. But what was anger doing there? Interest, confusion, amusement, boredom – all these emotions I could trace and name as they succeeded each other throughout the morning. Had anger, the black snake, been lurking among them? Yes, said the sketch, anger had. It referred me unmistakably to the one book, to the one phrase, which had roused the demon; it was the professor's statement about the mental, moral and physical inferiority of women. My heart had leapt. My cheeks had burnt. I had flushed with anger. There was nothing specially remarkable, however foolish, in that. One does not like to be told that one is naturally the inferior of a little man – I looked at the student next me – who breathes hard, wears a ready-made tie, and has not shaved this fortnight. One has certain foolish vanities. It is only human nature, I reflected, and began drawing cartwheels and circles over the angry professor's face till he looked like a burning bush or a flaming comet – anyhow, an apparition without human semblance or significance. The professor was nothing now but a faggot burning on the top of Hampstead Heath. Soon my own anger was explained and done with; but curiosity remained. How explain the anger of the professors? Why were they angry? For when it came to analysing the impression left by these books there was always an element of heat. This heat took many forms: it showed itself in satire, in sentiment, in curiosity, in reprobation. But there was another element which was often present and could not immediately be identified. Anger, I called it. But it was anger that had gone underground and mixed itself with all kinds of other emotions. To judge from its odd effects, it was anger disguised and complex, not anger simple and open.

Whatever the reason, all these books, I thought, surveying the pile on the desk, are worthless for my purposes. They were worthless scientifically, that is to say, though humanly they were full of instruction, interest, boredom, and very queer facts about the habits of the Fiji Islanders. They had been written in the red light of emotion and not in the white light of truth.

Therefore they must be returned to the central desk and restored each to his own cell in the enormous honeycomb. All that I had retrieved from that morning's work had been the one fact of anger. The professors – I lumped them together thus – were angry. But why, I asked myself, having returned the books, why, I repeated, standing under the colonnade among the pigeons and the prehistoric canoes, why are they angry? And, asking myself this question, I strolled off to find a place for luncheon. What is the real nature of what I call for the moment their anger? I asked. Here was a puzzle that would last all the time that it takes to be served with food in a small restaurant somewhere near the British Museum. Some previous luncher had left the lunch edition of the evening paper on a chair, and, waiting to be served, I began idly reading the headlines. A ribbon of very large letters ran across the page. Somebody had made a big score in South Africa. Lesser ribbons announced that Sir Austen Chamberlain was at Geneva. A meat axe with human hair on it had been found in a cellar. Mr Justice — commented in the divorce courts upon the Shamelessness of Women. Sprinkled about the paper were other pieces of news. A film actress had been lowered from a peak in California and hung suspended in midair. The weather was going to be foggy. The most transient visitor to this planet, I thought, who picked up this paper could not fail to be aware, even from this scattered testimony, that England is under the rule of a patriarchy. Nobody in their senses could fail to detect the dominance of the professor. His was the power and the money and the influence. He was the proprietor of the paper and its editor and sub-editor. He was the Foreign Secretary and the judge. He was the cricketer; he owned the racehorses and the yachts. He was the director of the company that pays two hundred per cent to its shareholders. He left millions to charities and colleges that were ruled by himself. He suspended the film actress in midair. He will decide if the hair on the meat axe is human; he it is who will acquit or convict the murderer, and hang him, or let him go free. With the exception of the fog he seemed to control everything. Yet he was angry. I knew that he was angry by this token. When I read what he wrote about women, I thought not of what he was saying but of himself. When an arguer argues dispassionately he thinks only of the argument; and the reader cannot help thinking of the argument too. If he had written dispassionately about women, had used indisputable proofs to establish his argument and had shown no trace of wishing that the result should be one thing rather than another, one would not have been angry either. One would have accepted the fact, as one accepts the fact that a pea is green or a canary yellow. So be it, I should have said. But I had been angry because he was angry. Yet it seemed absurd, I thought, turning over the evening paper, that a man with all this power should be angry. Or is anger, I wondered, some-how the familiar, the attendant sprite on power? Rich people, for example, are often angry because they suspect that the poor want to seize their wealth. The professors, or patriarchs, as it might be more accurate to call them, might be angry for that reason partly, but partly for one that lies a little less obviously on the surface. Possibly they were not 'angry' at all; often, indeed, they were admiring, devoted, exemplary in the relations of private life. Possibly when the professor insisted a little too emphatically upon the inferiority of women, he was concerned not with their inferiority, but with his own superiority. That was what he was protecting rather hot-headedly and with too much emphasis, because it was a jewel to him of the rarest price. Life for both sexes – and I looked at them, shouldering their way along the pavement – is arduous, difficult, a perpetual struggle. It calls for gigantic courage and strength. More than anything, perhaps, creatures of illusion as we are, it calls for confidence in oneself. Without self-confidence we are as babes in the cradle. And how can we generate this imponderable quality, which is yet so invaluable, most quickly? By thinking that other people are inferior to one-self. By feeling that one has some innate superiority – it may be wealth, or rank, a straight nose, or the portrait of a grandfather by Romney, for there is no end to the pathetic devices of the human imagination – over other people. Hence the enormous importance to a patriarch who has to conquer, who has to rule, of feeling that great numbers of people, half the human race indeed, are by nature inferior to himself. It must indeed be one of the chief sources of his power. But let me turn the light of this observation on to real life, I thought. Does it help to explain some of those psychological puzzles that one notes in the margin of daily life? Does it explain my astonishment of the other day when Z, most humane, most modest of men, taking up some book by Rebecca West and reading a passage in it, exclaimed, 'The arrant feminist! She says that men are snobs!' The exclamation, to me so surprising – for why was Miss West an arrant feminist for making a possibly true if uncomplimentary statement about the other sex? – was not merely the cry of wounded vanity; it was a protest against some infringement of his power to believe in himself. Women have served all these centuries as looking-glasses possessing the magic and delicious power of reflecting the figure of man at twice its natural size. Without that power probably the earth would still be swamp and jungle. The glories of all our wars would be unknown. We should still be scratching the outlines of deer on the remains of mutton bones and bartering flints for sheepskins or whatever simple ornament took our unsophisticated taste. Supermen and Fingers of Destiny would never have existed. The Czar and the Kaiser would never have worn crowns or lost them. Whatever may be their use in civilised societies, mirrors are essential to all violent and heroic action. That is why Napoleon and Mussolini both insist so emphatically upon the inferiority of women, for if they were not inferior, they would cease to enlarge. That serves to explain in part the necessity that women so often are to men. And it serves to explain how restless they are under her criticism; how impossible it is for her to say to them this book is bad, this picture is feeble, or whatever it may be, without giving far more pain and rousing far more anger than a man would do who gave the same criticism. For if she begins to tell the truth, the figure in the looking-glass shrinks; his fitness for life is diminished. How is he to go on giving judgment, civilising natives, making laws, writing books, dressing up and speechifying at banquets, unless he can see himself at breakfast and at dinner at least twice the size he really is? So I reflected, crumbling my bread and stirring my coffee and now and again looking at the people in the street. The looking-glass vision is of supreme importance because it charges the vitality; it stimulates the nervous system. Take it away and man may die, like the drug fiend deprived of his cocaine. Under the spell of that illusion, I thought, looking out of the window, half the people on the pavement are striding to work. They put on their hats and coats in the morning under its agreeable rays. They start the day confident, braced, believing themselves desired at Miss Smith's tea party; they say to themselves as they go into the room, I am the superior of half the people here, and it is thus that they speak with that self-confidence, that self-assurance, which have had such profound consequences in public life and lead to such curious notes in the margin of the private mind.

But these contributions to the dangerous and fascinating subject of the psychology of the other sex – it is one, I hope, that you will investigate when you have five hundred a year of your own – were interrupted by the necessity of paying the bill. It came to five shillings and ninepence. I gave the waiter a ten-shilling note and he went to bring me change. There was another ten-shilling note in my purse; I noticed it, because it is a fact that still takes my breath away – the power of my purse to breed ten-shilling notes automatically. I open it and there they are. Society gives me chicken and coffee, bed and lodging, in return for a certain number of pieces of paper which were left me by an aunt, for no other reason than that I share her name.

My aunt, Mary Beton, I must tell you, died by a fall from her horse when she was riding out to take the air in Bombay. The news of my legacy reached me one night about the same time that the act was passed that gave votes to women. A solicitor's letter fell into the postbox and when I opened it I found that she had left me five hundred pounds a year for ever. Of the two – the vote and the money – the money, I own, seemed infinitely the more important. Before that I had made my living by cadging odd jobs from newspapers, by reporting a donkey show here or a wedding there; I had earned a few pounds by addressing envelopes, reading to old ladies, making artificial flowers, teaching the alphabet to small children in a kindergarten. Such were the chief occupations that were open to women before 1918. I need not, I am afraid, describe in any detail the hardness of the work, for you know perhaps women who have done it; nor the difficulty of living on the money when it was earned, for you may have tried. But what still remains with me as a worse infliction than either was the poison of fear and bitterness which those days bred in me. To begin with, always to be doing work that one did not wish to do, and to do it like a slave, flattering and fawning, not always necessarily perhaps, but it seemed necessary and the stakes were too great to run risks; and then the thought of that one gift which it was death to hide – a small one but dear to the possessor – perishing and with it my self, my soul – all this became like a rust eating away the bloom of the spring, destroying the tree at its heart. However, as I say, my aunt died; and whenever I change a ten-shilling note a little of that rust and corrosion is rubbed off, fear and bitterness go. Indeed, I thought, slipping the silver into my purse, it is remarkable, remembering the bitterness of those days, what a change of temper a fixed income will bring about. No force in the world can take from me my five hundred pounds. Food, house and clothing are mine for ever. Therefore not merely do effort and labour cease, but also hatred and bitterness. I need not hate any man; he cannot hurt me. I need not flatter any man; he has nothing to give me. So imperceptibly I found myself adopting a new attitude towards the other half of the human race. It was absurd to blame any class or any sex, as a whole. Great bodies of people are never responsible for what they do. They are driven by instincts which are not within their control. They too, the patriarchs, the professors, had endless difficulties, terrible drawbacks to contend with. Their education had been in some ways as faulty as my own. It had bred in them defects as great. True, they had money and power, but only at the cost of harbouring in their breasts an eagle, a vulture, forever tearing the liver out and plucking at the lungs – the instinct for possession, the rage for acquisition which drives them to desire other people's fields and goods perpetually; to make frontiers and flags; battleships and poison gas; to offer up their own lives and their children's lives. Walk through the Admiralty Arch (I had reached that monument), or any other avenue given up to trophies and cannon, and reflect upon the kind of glory celebrated there. Or watch in the spring sunshine the stockbroker and the great barrister going indoors to make money and more money and more money when it is a fact that five hundred pounds a year will keep one alive in the sunshine. These are unpleasant instincts to harbour, I reflected. They are bred of the conditions of life; of the lack of civilisation, I thought, looking at the statue of the Duke of Cambridge, and in particular at the feathers in his cocked hat, with a fixity that they have scarcely ever received before. And, as I realised these drawbacks, by degrees fear and bitterness modified themselves into pity and toleration; and then in a year or two, pity and toleration went, and the greatest release of all came, which is freedom to think of things in themselves. That building, for example, do I like it or not? Is that picture beautiful or not? Is that in my opinion a good book or a bad? Indeed my aunt's legacy unveiled the sky to me, and substituted for the large and imposing figure of a gentleman, which Milton recommended for my perpetual adoration, a view of the open sky.

So thinking, so speculating I found my way back to my house by the river. Lamps were being lit and an indescribable change had come over London since the morning hour. It was as if the great machine after labouring all day had made with our help a few yards of something very exciting and beautiful – a fiery fabric flashing with red eyes, a tawny monster roaring with hot breath. Even the wind seemed flung like a flag as it lashed the houses and rattled the hoardings.

In my little street, however, domesticity prevailed. The house painter was descending his ladder; the nursemaid was wheeling the perambulator carefully in and out back to nursery tea; the coal-heaver was folding his empty sacks on top of each other; the woman who keeps the greengrocer's shop was adding up the day's takings with her hands in red mittens. But so engrossed was I with the problem you have laid upon my shoulders that I could not see even these usual sights without referring them to one centre. I thought how much harder it is now than it must have been even a century ago to say which of these employments is the higher, the more necessary. Is it better to be a coal-heaver or a nursemaid; is the charwoman who has brought up eight children of less value to the world than the barrister who has made a hundred thousand pounds? It is useless to ask such questions for nobody can answer them. Not only do the comparative values of charwomen and lawyers rise and fall from decade to decade, but we have no rods with which to measure them even as they are at the moment. I had been foolish to ask my professor to furnish me with 'indisputable proofs' of this or that in his argument about women. Even if one could state the value of any one gift at the moment, those values will change; in a century's time very possibly they will have changed completely. Moreover, in a hundred years, I thought, reaching my own doorstep, women will have ceased to be the protected sex. Logically they will take part in all the activities and exertions that were once denied them. The nursemaid will heave coal. The shopwoman will drive an engine. All assumptions founded on the facts observed when women were the protected sex will have disappeared – as, for example (here a squad of soldiers marched down the street), that women and clergymen and gardeners live longer than other people. Remove that protection, expose them to the same exertions and activities, make them soldiers and sailors and engine-drivers and dock labourers, and will not women die off so much younger, so much quicker, than men that one will say, 'I saw a woman today', as one used to say, 'I saw an aeroplane'? Anything may happen when womanhood has ceased to be a protected occupation, I thought, opening the door. But what bearing has all this upon the subject of my paper, Women and Fiction? I asked, going indoors.

Chapter 3

It was disappointing not to have brought back in the evening some important statement, some authentic fact. Women are poorer than men because – this or that. Perhaps now it would be better to give up seeking for the truth, and receiving on one's head an avalanche of opinion hot as lava, discoloured as dishwater. It would be better to draw the curtains; to shut out distractions; to light the lamp; to narrow the enquiry and to ask the historian, who records not opinions but facts, to describe under what conditions women lived, not throughout the ages, but in England, say, in the time of Elizabeth.

For it is a perennial puzzle why no woman wrote a word of that extraordinary literature when every other man, it seemed, was capable of song or sonnet. What were the conditions in which women lived? I asked myself; for fiction, imaginative work that is, is not dropped like a pebble upon the ground, as science may be; fiction is like a spider's web, attached ever so lightly perhaps, but still attached to life at all four corners. Often the attachment is scarcely perceptible; Shakespeare's plays, for instance, seem to hang there complete by themselves. But when the web is pulled askew, hooked up at the edge, torn in the middle, one remembers that these webs are not spun in midair by incorporeal creatures, but are the work of suffering human beings, and are attached to grossly material things, like health and money and the houses we live in.

I went, therefore, to the shelf where the histories stand and took down one of the latest, Professor Trevelyan's *History of England*. Once more I looked up Women, found 'position of' and turned to the pages indicated. 'Wife-beating,' I read, 'was a recognised right of man, and was practised without shame by high as well as low . . . Similarly,' the historian goes on, 'the daughter who refused to marry the gentleman of her parents' choice was liable to be locked up, beaten and flung about the room, without any shock being inflicted on public opinion. Marriage was not an affair of personal affection, but of family avarice, particularly in the "chivalrous" upper classes . . . Betrothal often took place while one or both of the parties was in the cradle, and marriage when they were scarcely out of the nurses' charge.' That was about 1470, soon after Chaucer's time. The next reference to the position of women is some two hundred years later, in the time of the Stuarts. 'It was still the exception for women of the upper and middle class to choose their own husbands, and when the husband had been assigned, he was lord and master, so far at least as law and custom could make him. Yet even so,' Professor Trevelyan concludes, 'neither Shakespeare's women nor those of authentic seventeenth-century memoirs, like the Verneys and the Hutchinsons, seem wanting in personality and character.' Certainly, if we consider it, Cleopatra must have had a way with her; Lady Macbeth, one would suppose, had a will of her own; Rosalind, one might conclude, was an attractive girl. Professor Trevelyan is speaking no more than the truth when he remarks that Shakespeare's women do not seem wanting in personality and character. Not being a historian, one might go even further and say that women have burnt like beacons in all the works of all the poets from the beginning of time – Clytemnestra, Antigone, Cleopatra, Lady Macbeth, Phèdre, Cressida, Rosalind, Desdemona, the Duchess of Malfi, among the dramatists; then among the prose writers: Millamant, Clarissa, Becky Sharp, Anna Karenina, Emma Bovary, Madame de Guermantes – the names flock to mind, nor do they recall women 'lacking in personality and character'. Indeed, if woman had no existence save in the fiction written by men, one would imagine her a person of the utmost importance; very various; heroic and mean; splendid and sordid; infinitely beautiful and hideous in the extreme; as great as a man, some think even greater.* But this is woman in fiction. In fact, as Professor Trevelyan points out, she was locked up, beaten and flung about the room.

A very queer, composite being thus emerges. Imaginatively she is of the highest importance; practically she is completely insignificant. She pervades poetry from cover to cover; she is all but absent from history. She dominates the lives of kings and conquerors in fiction; in fact she was the slave of any boy whose parents forced a ring upon her finger. Some of the most inspired words, some of the most profound thoughts in literature fall from her lips; in real life she could hardly read, could scarcely spell, and was the property of her husband.

It was certainly an odd monster that one made up by reading the historians first and the poets afterwards – a worm winged like an eagle; the spirit of life and beauty in a kitchen chopping up suet. But these monsters, however amusing to the imagination, have no existence in fact. What one must do to bring her to life was to think poetically and prosaically at one and the same

---

* It remains a strange and almost inexplicable fact that in Athena's city, where women were kept in almost Oriental suppression as odalisques or drudges, the stage should yet have produced figures like Clytemnestra and Cassandra, Atossa and Antigone, Phèdre and Medea, and all the other heroines who dominate play after play of the 'misogynist' Euripides. But the paradox of this world, where in real life a respectable woman could hardly show her face alone in the street and yet on the stage woman equals or surpasses man, has never been satisfactorily explained. In modern tragedy the same predominance exists. At all events, a very cursory survey of Shakespeare's work (similarly with Webster, though not with Marlowe or Jonson) suffices to reveal how this dominance, this initiative of women, persists from Rosalind to Lady Macbeth. So too in Racine: six of his tragedies bear their heroines' names; and what male characters of his shall we set against Hermione and Andromaque, Bérénice and Roxane, Phèdre and Athalie? So again with Ibsen: what men shall we match with Solveig and Nora, Hedda and Hilda Wangel and Rebecca West? – F. L. LUCAS, *Tragedy*, pp. 114–15

moment, thus keeping in touch with fact – that she is Mrs Martin, aged thirty-six, dressed in blue, wearing a black hat and brown shoes; but not losing sight of fiction either – that she is a vessel in which all sorts of spirits and forces are coursing and flashing perpetually. The moment, however, that one tries this method with the Elizabethan woman, one branch of illumination fails: one is held up by the scarcity of facts. One knows nothing detailed, nothing perfectly true and substantial about her. History scarcely mentions her. And I turned to Professor Trevelyan again to see what history meant to him. I found by looking at his chapter headings that it meant – 'The Manor Court and the Methods of Open-field Agriculture . . . The Cistercians and Sheep-farming . . . The Crusades . . . The University . . . The House of Commons . . . The Hundred Years' War . . . The Wars of the Roses . . . The Renaissance Scholars . . . The Dissolution of the Monasteries . . . Agrarian and Religious Strife . . . The Origin of English Sea-power. . . The Armada. . . ' and so on. Occasionally an individual woman is mentioned, an Elizabeth, or a Mary; a queen or a great lady. But by no possible means could middle-class women with nothing but brains and character at their command have taken part in any one of the great movements which, brought together, constitute the historian's view of the past. Nor shall we find her in any collection of anecdotes. Aubrey hardly mentions her. She never writes her own life and scarcely keeps a diary; there are only a handful of her letters in existence. She left no plays or poems by which we can judge her. What one wants, I thought – and why does not some brilliant student at Newnham or Girton supply it? – is a mass of information; at what age did she marry; how many children had she as a rule; what was her house like, had she a room to herself; did she do the cooking; would she be likely to have a servant? All these facts lie somewhere, presumably, in parish registers and account books; the life of the average Elizabethan woman must be scattered about somewhere, could one collect it and make a book of it. It would be ambitious beyond my daring, I thought, looking about the shelves for books that were not there, to suggest to the students of those famous colleges that they should rewrite history, though I own that it often seems a little queer as it is, unreal, lop-sided; but why should they not add a supplement to history, calling it, of course, by some in conspicuous name so that women might figure there without impropriety? For one often catches a glimpse of them in the lives of the great, whisking away into the background, concealing, I sometimes think, a wink, a laugh, perhaps a tear. And, after all, we have lives enough of Jane Austen; it scarcely seems necessary to consider again the influence of the tragedies of Joanna Baillie upon the poetry of Edgar Allan Poe; as for myself, I should not mind if the homes and haunts of Mary Russell Mitford were closed to the public for a century at least. But what I find deplorable, I continued, looking about the bookshelves again, is that nothing is known about women before the eighteenth century. I have no model in my mind to turn about this way and that. Here am I asking why women did not write poetry in the Elizabethan age, and I am not sure how they were educated; whether they were taught to write; whether they had sitting-rooms to themselves; how many women had children before they were twenty-one; what, in short, they did from eight in the morning till eight at night. They had no money evidently; according to Professor Trevelyan they were married whether they liked it or not before they were out of the nursery, at fifteen or sixteen very likely. It would have been extremely odd, even upon this showing, had one of them suddenly written the plays of Shakespeare, I concluded, and I thought of that old gentleman, who is dead now, but was a bishop, I think, who declared that it was impossible for any woman, past, present, or to come, to have the genius of Shakespeare. He wrote to the papers about it. He also told a lady who applied to him for information that cats do not as a matter of fact go to heaven, though they have, he added, souls of a sort. How much thinking those old gentlemen used to save one! How the borders of ignorance shrank back at their approach! Cats do not go to heaven. Women cannot write the plays of Shakespeare.

Be that as it may, I could not help thinking, as I looked at the works of Shakespeare on the shelf, that the bishop was right at least in this: it would have been impossible, completely and entirely, for any woman to have written the plays of Shakespeare in the age of Shakespeare. Let me imagine, since facts are so hard to come by, what would have happened had Shakespeare had a wonderfully gifted sister, called Judith, let us say. Shakespeare himself went, very probably (his mother was an heiress), to the grammar school, where he may have learnt Latin – Ovid, Virgil and Horace – and the elements of grammar and logic. He was, it is well known, a wild boy who poached rabbits, perhaps shot a deer, and had, rather sooner than he should have done, to marry a woman in the neighbourhood, who bore him a child rather quicker than was right. That escapade sent him to seek his fortune in London. He had, it seemed, a taste for the theatre; he began by holding horses at the stage door. Very soon he got work in the theatre, became a successful actor, and lived at the hub of the universe, meeting everybody, knowing everybody, practising his art on the boards, exercising his wits in the streets, and even getting access to the palace of the queen. Meanwhile his extraordinarily gifted sister, let us suppose, remained at home. She was as adventurous, as imaginative, as agog to see the world as he was. But she was not sent to school. She had no chance of learning grammar and logic, let alone of reading Horace and Virgil. She picked up a book now and then, one of her brother's perhaps, and read a few pages. But then her parents came in and told her to mend the stockings or mind the stew and not moon about with books and papers. They would have spoken sharply but kindly, for they were substantial people who knew the conditions of life for a woman and loved their daughter – indeed, more likely than not she was the apple of her father's eye. Perhaps she scribbled some pages up in an apple loft on the sly but was careful to hide them or set fire to them. Soon, however, before she was out of her teens, she was to be betrothed to the son of a neighbouring wool-stapler. She cried out that marriage was hateful to her, and for that she was severely beaten by her father. Then he ceased to scold her. He begged her instead not to hurt him, not to shame him in this matter of her marriage. He would give her a chain of beads or a fine petticoat, he said; and there were tears in his eyes. How could she disobey him? How could she break his heart? The force of her own gift alone drove her to it. She made up a small parcel of her belongings, let herself down by a rope one summer's night and took the road to London. She was not seventeen. The birds that sang in the hedge were not more musical than she was. She had the quickest fancy, a gift like her brother's, for the tune of words. Like him, she had a taste for the theatre. She stood at the stage door; she wanted to act, she said. Men laughed in her face. The manager – a fat, loose-lipped man – guffawed. He bellowed something about poodles dancing and women acting – no woman, he said, could possibly be an actress. He hinted – you can imagine what. She could get no training in her craft. Could she even seek her dinner in a tavern or roam the streets at midnight? Yet her genius was for fiction and lusted to feed abundantly upon the lives of men and women and the study of their ways. At last – for she was very young, oddly like Shakespeare the poet in her face, with the same grey eyes and rounded brows – at last Nick Greene the actor-manager took pity on her; she found herself with child by that gentleman and so – who shall measure the heat and violence of the poet's heart when caught and tangled in a woman's body? – killed herself one winter's night and lies buried at some crossroads where the omnibuses now stop outside the Elephant and Castle.

That, more or less, is how the story would run, I think, if a woman in Shakespeare's day had had Shakespeare's genius. But for my part, I agree with the deceased bishop, if such he was – it is unthinkable that any woman in Shakespeare's day should have had Shakespeare's genius. For genius like Shakespeare's is not born among labouring, uneducated, servile people. It was not born in England among the Saxons and the Britons. It is not born today among the working classes. How, then, could it have been born among women whose work began, according to Professor Trevelyan, almost before they were out of the nursery, who were forced to it by their parents and held to it by all the power of law and custom? Yet genius of a sort must have existed among women as it must have existed among the working classes. Now and again an Emily Brontë or a Robert Burns blazes out and proves its presence. But certainly it never got itself on to paper. When, however, one reads of a witch being ducked, of a woman possessed by devils, of a wise woman selling herbs, or even of a very remarkable man who had a mother, then I think we are on the track of a lost novelist, a suppressed poet, of some mute and inglorious Jane Austen, some Emily Brontë who dashed her brains out on the moor or mopped and mowed about the highways crazed with the torture that her gift had put her to. Indeed, I would venture to guess that Anon, who wrote so many poems without signing them, was often a woman. It was a woman Edward Fitzgerald, I think, suggested who made the ballads and the folk-songs, crooning them to her children, beguiling her spinning with them, or the length of the winter's night.

This may be true or it may be false – who can say? – but what is true in it, so it seemed to me, reviewing the story of Shakespeare's sister as I had made it, is that any woman born with a great gift in the sixteenth century would certainly have gone crazed, shot herself, or ended her days in some lonely cottage outside the village, half-witch, half-wizard, feared and mocked at. For it needs little skill in psychology to be sure that a highly gifted girl who had tried to use her gift for poetry would have been so thwarted and hindered by other people, so tortured and pulled asunder by her own contrary instincts, that she must have lost her health and sanity to a certainty. No girl could have walked to London and stood at a stage door and forced her way into the presence of actor-managers without doing herself a violence and suffering an anguish which may have been irrational – for chastity may be a fetish invented by certain societies for unknown reasons – but were none the less inevitable. Chastity had then, it has even now, a religious importance in a woman's life, and has so wrapped itself round with nerves and instincts that to cut it free and bring it to the light of day demands courage of the rarest. To have lived a free life in London in the sixteenth century would have meant for a woman who was poet and playwright a nervous stress and dilemma which might well have killed her. Had she survived, whatever she had written would have been twisted and deformed, issuing from a strained and morbid imagination. And un-doubtedly, I thought, looking at the shelf where there are no plays by women, her work would have gone unsigned. That refuge she would have sought certainly. It was the relic of the sense of chastity that dictated anonymity to women even so late as the nineteenth century. Currer Bell, George Eliot, George Sand, all the victims of inner strife as their writings prove, sought ineffectively to veil themselves by using the name of a man. Thus they did homage to the convention, which if not implanted by the other sex was liberally encouraged by them (the chief glory of a woman is not to be talked of, said Pericles, himself a much-talked-of man), that publicity in women is detestable. Anonymity runs in their blood. The desire to be veiled still possesses them. They are not even now as concerned about the health of their fame as men are, and, speaking generally, will pass a tombstone or a signpost without feeling an irresistible desire to cut their names on it, as Alf, Bert or Chas must do in obedience to their instinct, which murmurs if it sees a fine woman go by, or even a dog, Ce chien est à moi. And, of course, it may not be a dog, I thought, remembering Parliament Square, the Sièges Allée and other avenues; it may be a piece of land or a man with curly black hair. It is one of the great advantages of being a woman that one can pass even a very fine negress without wishing to make an Englishwoman of her.

That woman, then, who was born with a gift of poetry in the sixteenth century, was an unhappy woman, a woman at strife against herself. All the conditions of her life, all her own instincts, were hostile to the state of mind which is needed to set free whatever is in the brain. But what is the state of mind that is most propitious to the act of creation? I asked. Can one come by any notion of the state that furthers and makes possible that strange activity? Here I opened the volume containing the tragedies of Shakespeare. What was Shakespeare's state of mind, for instance, when he wrote *Lear* and *Antony and Cleopatra*? It was certainly the state of mind most favourable to poetry that there has ever existed. But Shakespeare himself said nothing about it. We only know casually and by chance that he 'never blotted a line'. Nothing indeed was ever said by the artist himself about his state of mind until the eighteenth century perhaps. Rousseau perhaps began it. At any rate, by the nineteenth century self-consciousness had developed so far that it was the habit for men of letters to describe their minds in confessions and autobiographies. Their lives also were written, and their letters were printed after their deaths. Thus, though we do not know what Shakespeare went through when he wrote *Lear*, we do know what Carlyle went through when he wrote the *French Revolution*; what Flaubert went through when he wrote *Madame Bovary*; what Keats was going through when he tried to write poetry against the coming of death and the indifference of the world.

And one gathers from this enormous modern literature of confession and self-analysis that to write a work of genius is almost always a feat of prodigious difficulty. Everything is against the likelihood that it will come from the writer's mind whole and entire. Generally material circumstances are against it. Dogs will bark; people will interrupt; money must be made; health will break down. Further, accentuating all these difficulties and making them harder to bear is the world's notorious indifference. It does not ask people to write poems and novels and histories; it does not need them. It does not care whether Flaubert finds the right word or whether Carlyle scrupulously verifies this or that fact. Naturally, it will not pay for what it does not want. And so the writer – Keats, Flaubert, Carlyle – suffers, especially in the creative years of youth, every form of distraction and discouragement. A curse, a cry of agony, rises from those books of analysis and confession. 'Mighty poets in their misery dead' – that is the burden of their song. If anything comes through in spite of all this, it is a miracle, and probably no book is born entire and uncrippled as it was conceived.

But for women, I thought, looking at the empty shelves, these difficulties were infinitely more formidable. In the first place, to have a room of her own, let alone a quiet room or a soundproof room, was out of the question, unless her parents were exceptionally rich or very noble, even up to the beginning of the nineteenth century. Since her pin money, which depended on the goodwill of her father, was only enough to keep her clothed, she was debarred from such alleviations as came even to Keats or Tennyson or Carlyle, all poor men, from a walking tour, a little journey to France, from the separate lodging which, even if it were miserable enough, sheltered them from the claims and tyrannies of their families. Such material difficulties were formidable; but much worse were the immaterial. The indifference of the world which Keats and Flaubert and other men of genius have found so hard to bear was in her case not indifference but hostility. The world did not say to her as it said to them, Write if you choose; it makes no difference to me. The world said with a guffaw, Write? What's the good of your writing? Here the psychologists of Newnham and Girton might come to our help, I thought, looking again at the blank spaces on the shelves. For surely it is time that the effect of discouragement upon the mind of the artist should be measured, as I have seen a dairy company measure the effect of ordinary milk and Grade A milk upon the body of the rat. They set two rats in cages side by side, and of the two one was furtive, timid and small, and the other was glossy, bold and big. Now what food do we feed women as artists upon? I asked, remembering, I suppose, that dinner of prunes and custard. To answer that question I had only to open the evening paper and to read that Lord Birkenhead is of opinion – but really I am not going to trouble to copy out Lord Birkenhead's opinion upon the writing of women. What Dean Inge says I will leave in peace. The Harley Street specialist may be allowed to rouse the echoes of Harley Street with his vociferations without raising a hair on my head. I will quote, however, Mr Oscar Browning, because Mr Oscar Browning was a great figure in Cambridge at one time, and used to examine the students at Girton and Newnham. Mr Oscar Browning was wont to declare 'that the impression left on his mind, after looking over any set of examination papers, was that, irrespective of the marks he might give, the best woman was intellectually the inferior of the worst man'. After saying that Mr Browning went back to his rooms – and it is this sequel that endears him and makes him a human figure of some bulk and majesty – he went back to his rooms and found a stable-boy lying on the sofa – 'a mere skeleton, his cheeks were cavernous and sallow, his teeth were black, and he did not appear to have the full use of his limbs. "That's Arthur" [said Mr Browning]. "He's a dear boy really and most high-minded."' The two pictures always seem to me to complete each other. And happily in this age of biography the two pictures often do complete each other, so that we are able to interpret the opinions of great men not only by what they say, but by what they do.

But though this is possible now, such opinions coming from the lips of important people must have been formidable enough even fifty years ago. Let us suppose that a father from the highest motives did not wish his daughter to leave home and become writer, painter or scholar. 'See what

Mr Oscar Browning says,' he would say; and there was not only Mr Oscar Browning; there was the *Saturday Review*; there was Mr Greg – the 'essentials of a woman's being,' said Mr Greg emphatically, 'are that *they are supported by, and they minister to, men*' – there was an enormous body of masculine opinion to the effect that nothing could be expected of women intellectually. Even if her father did not read out loud these opinions, any girl could read them for herself; and the reading, even in the nineteenth century, must have lowered her vitality, and told profoundly upon her work. There would always have been that assertion – you cannot do this, you are incapable of doing that – to protest against, to overcome. Probably for a novelist this germ is no longer of much effect; for there have been women novelists of merit. But for painters it must still have some sting in it; and for musicians, I imagine, is even now active and poisonous in the extreme. The woman composer stands where the actress stood in the time of Shakespeare. Nick Greene, I thought, remembering the story I had made about Shakespeare's sister, said that a woman acting put him in mind of a dog dancing. Johnson repeated the phrase two hundred years later of women preaching. And here, I said, opening a book about music, we have the very words used again in this year of grace, 1928, of women who try to write music. 'Of Mlle Germaine Tailleferre one can only repeat Dr Johnson's dictum concerning a woman preacher, transposed into terms of music. "Sir, a woman's composing is like a dog's walking on his hind legs. It is not done well, but you are surprised to find it done at all." '* So accurately does history repeat itself.

Thus, I concluded, shutting Mr Oscar Browning's life and pushing away the rest, it is fairly evident that even in the nineteenth century a woman was not encouraged to be an artist. On the contrary, she was snubbed, slapped, lectured and exhorted. Her mind must have been strained and her vitality lowered by the need of opposing this, of disproving that. For here again we come within range of that very interesting and obscure masculine complex which has had so much influence upon the woman's movement: that deep-seated desire, not so much that *she* shall be inferior as that *he* shall be superior, which plants him wherever one looks, not only in front of the arts but barring the way to politics too, even when the risk to himself seems infinitesimal and the suppliant humble and devoted. Even Lady Bessborough, I remembered, with all her passion for politics, must humbly bow herself and write to Lady Granville Leveson-Gower: ' . . . notwithstanding all my violence in politicks and talking so much on that subject, I perfectly agree with you that no woman has any business to meddle with that or any other serious business, further than giving her opinion (if she is ask'd)'. And so she goes on to spend her enthusiasm where it meets with no obstacle whatsoever, upon that immensely important subject, Lord Granville's maiden speech in the House of Commons. The spectacle is certainly a strange one, I thought.

* *A Survey of Contemporary Music*, Cecil Gray, p. 246

The history of men's opposition to women's emancipation is more interesting perhaps than the story of that emancipation itself. An amusing book might be made of it if some young student at Girton or Newnham would collect examples and deduce a theory – but she would need thick gloves on her hands and bars to protect her of solid gold.

But what is amusing now, I recollected, shutting Lady Bessborough, had to be taken in desperate earnest once. Opinions that one now pastes in a book labelled cock-a-doodle-dum and keeps for reading to select audiences on summer nights once drew tears, I can assure you. Among your grand-mothers and great-grandmothers there were many that wept their eyes out. Florence Nightingale shrieked aloud in her agony.* Moreover, it is all very well for you, who have got yourselves to college and enjoy sitting-rooms – or is it only bed-sitting-rooms? – of your own to say that genius should disregard such opinions; that genius should be above caring what is said of it. Unfortunately, it is precisely the men or women of genius who mind most what is said of them. Remember Keats. Remember the words he had cut on his tombstone. Think of Tennyson; think – but I need hardly multiply instances of the undeniable, if very unfortunate, fact that it is the nature of the artist to mind excessively what is said about him. Literature is strewn with the wreckage of men who have minded beyond reason the opinions of others.

And this susceptibility of theirs is doubly unfortunate, I thought, returning again to my original enquiry into what state of mind is most propitious for creative work, because the mind of an artist, in order to achieve the prodigious effort of freeing whole and entire the work that is in him, must be incandescent, like Shakespeare's mind, I conjectured, looking at the book which lay open at *Antony and Cleopatra*. There must be no obstacle in it, no foreign matter unconsumed.

For though we say that we know nothing about Shakespeare's state of mind, even as we say that, we are saying something about Shakespeare's state of mind. The reason perhaps why we know so little of Shakespeare – compared with Donne or Ben Jonson or Milton – is that his grudges and spites and antipathies are hidden from us. We are not held up by some 'revelation' which reminds us of the writer. All desire to protest, to preach, to proclaim an injury, to pay off a score, to make the world the witness of some hardship or grievance was fired out of him and consumed. Therefore his poetry flows from him free and unimpeded. If ever a human being got his work expressed completely, it was Shakespeare. If ever a mind was incandescent, unimpeded, I thought, turning again to the bookcase, it was Shakespeare's mind.

* See *Cassandra* by Florence Nightingale, printed in *The Cause* by R. Strachey.

Chapter 4

That one would find any woman in that state of mind in the sixteenth century was obviously impossible. One has only to think of the Elizabethan tombstones with all those children kneeling with clasped hands; and their early deaths; and to see their houses with their dark, cramped rooms, to realise that no woman could have written poetry then. What one would expect to find would be that rather later perhaps some great lady would take advantage of her comparative freedom and comfort to publish something with her name to it and risk being thought a monster. Men, of course, are not snobs, I continued, carefully eschewing 'the arrant feminism' of Miss Rebecca West; but they appreciate with sympathy for the most part the efforts of a countess to write verse. One would expect to find a lady of title meeting with far greater encouragement than an unknown Miss Austen or a Miss Brontë at that time would have met with. But one would also expect to find that her mind was disturbed by alien emotions like fear and hatred and that her poems showed traces of that disturbance. Here is Lady Winchilsea, for example, I thought, taking down her poems. She was born in the year 1661; she was noble both by birth and by marriage; she was childless; she wrote poetry, and one has only to open her poetry to find her bursting out in indignation against the position of women:

> How we are fallen! fallen by mistaken rules,
> And Education's more than Nature's fools;
> Debarred from all improvements of the mind,
> And to be dull, expected and designed;
> And if someone would soar above the rest,
> With warmer fancy, and ambition pressed,
> So strong the opposing faction still appears,
> The hopes to thrive can ne'er outweigh the fears.

Clearly her mind has by no means 'consumed all impediments and become incandescent'. On the contrary, it is harassed and distracted with hates and grievances. The human race is split up for her into two parties. Men are the 'opposing faction'; men are hated and feared, because they have the power to bar her way to what she wants to do – which is to write.

> Alas! a woman that attempts the pen,
> Such a presumptuous creature is esteemed,
> The fault can by no virtue be redeemed.
> They tell us we mistake our sex and way;
> Good breeding, fashion, dancing, dressing, play,

> Are the accomplishments we should desire;
> To write, or read, or think, or to enquire,
> Would cloud our beauty, and exhaust our time,
> And interrupt the conquests of our prime.
> Whilst the dull manage of a servile house
> Is held by some our utmost art and use.

Indeed she has to encourage herself to write by supposing that what she writes will never be published; to soothe herself with the sad chant:

> To some few friends, and to thy sorrows sing,
> For groves of laurel thou wert never meant;
> Be dark enough thy shades, and be thou there content.

Yet it is clear that could she have freed her mind from hate and fear and not heaped it with bitterness and resentment, the fire was hot within her. Now and again words issue of pure poetry:

> Nor will in fading silks compose,
> Faintly the inimitable rose.

– they are rightly praised by Mr Murry, and Pope, it is thought, remembered and appropriated those others:

> Now the jonquille o'ercomes the feeble brain;
> We faint beneath the aromatic pain.

It was a thousand pities that the woman who could write like that, whose mind was tuned to nature and reflection, should have been forced to anger and bitterness. But how could she have helped herself? I asked, imagining the sneers and the laughter, the adulation of the toadies, the scepticism of the professional poet. She must have shut herself up in a room in the country to write, and been torn asunder by bitterness and scruples perhaps, though her husband was of the kindest, and their married life perfection. She 'must have', I say, because when one comes to seek out the facts about Lady Winchilsea, one finds, as usual, that almost nothing is known about her. She suffered terribly from melancholy, which we can explain at least to some extent when we find her telling us how in the grip of it she would imagine:

> My lines decried, and my employment thought
> An useless folly or presumptuous fault.

The employment which was thus censured was, as far as one can see, the harmless one of rambling about the fields and dreaming:

> My hand delights to trace unusual things,
> And deviates from the known and common way,
> Nor will in fading silks compose,
> Faintly the inimitable rose.

Naturally, if that was her habit and that was her delight, she could only expect to be laughed at; and, accordingly, Pope or Gay is said to have satirised her 'as a blue-stocking with an itch for scribbling'. Also it is thought that she offended Gay by laughing at him. She said that his *Trivia* showed that 'he was more proper to walk before a chair than to ride in one'. But this is all 'dubious gossip' and, says Mr Murry, 'uninteresting'. But there I do not agree with him, for I should have liked to have had more even of dubious gossip so that I might have found out or made up some image of this melancholy lady, who loved wandering in the fields and thinking about unusual things and scorned, so rashly, so unwisely, 'the dull manage of a servile house'. But she became diffuse, Mr Murry says. Her gift is all grown about with weeds and bound with briars. It had no chance of showing itself for the fine distinguished gift it was.

And so, putting her back on the shelf, I turned to the other great lady, the duchess whom Lamb loved, hare-brained, fantastical Margaret of Newcastle, her elder, but her contemporary. They were very different, but alike in this – that both were noble and both childless and both were married to the best of husbands. In both burnt the same passion for poetry and both are disfigured and deformed by the same causes. Open the duchess and one finds the same outburst of rage: 'Women live like Bats or Owls, labour like Beasts, and die like Worms . . . ' Margaret too might have been a poet; in our day all that activity would have turned a wheel of some sort. As it was, what could bind, tame or civilise for human use that wild, generous, untutored intelligence? It poured itself out, higgledy-piggledy, in torrents of rhyme and prose, poetry and philosophy which stand congealed in quartos and folios that nobody ever reads. She should have had a microscope put in her hand. She should have been taught to look at the stars and reason scientifically. Her wits were turned with solitude and freedom. No one checked her. No one taught her. The professors fawned on her. At Court they jeered at her. Sir Egerton Brydges complained of her coarseness – 'as flowing from a female of high rank brought up in the Courts'. She shut herself up at Welbeck alone.

What a vision of loneliness and riot the thought of Margaret Cavendish brings to mind! as if some giant cucumber had spread itself over all the roses and carnations in the garden and choked them to death. What a waste that the woman who wrote 'the best bred women are those whose minds are civilest' should have frittered her time away scribbling nonsense and plunging ever deeper into obscurity and folly till the people crowded round her coach when she issued out. Evidently the crazy duchess became a bogey to frighten clever girls with. Here, I remembered, putting away the duchess and opening Dorothy Osborne's letters, is Dorothy writing to Temple about the duchess's new book. 'Sure the poore woman is a little distracted, shee could never bee soe rediculous else as to venture at writeing book's and in verse too, if I should not sleep this fortnight I should not come to that.'

And so, since no woman of sense and modesty could write books, Dorothy, who was sensitive and melancholy, the very opposite of the duchess in temper, wrote nothing. Letters did not count. A woman might write letters while she was sitting by her father's sick-bed. She could write them by the fire whilst the men talked without disturbing them. The strange thing is, I thought, turning over the pages of Dorothy's letters, what a gift that untaught and solitary girl had for the framing of a sentence, for the fashioning of a scene. Listen to her running on:

> After dinner wee sitt and talk till Mr B. com's in question and then I am gon. the heat of the day is spent in reading or working and about sixe or seven a Clock, I walke out into a Common that lyes hard by the house where a great many young wenches keep Sheep and Cow's and sitt in the shades singing of Ballads; I goe to them and compare their voyces and Beauty's to some Ancient Shepherdesses that I have read of and finde a vaste difference there, but trust mee I think these are as innocent as those could bee. I talke to them, and finde they want nothing to make them the happiest People in the world, but the knoledge that they are soe. most commonly when we are in the middest of our discourse one looks aboute her and spyes her Cow's goeing into the Corne and then away they all run, as if they had wing's at theire heels. I that am not soe nimble stay behinde, and when I see them driveing home theire Cattle I think tis time for mee to retyre too. when I have supped I goe into the Garden and soe to the syde of a small River that runs by it where I sitt downe and wish you with mee . . .

One could have sworn that she had the makings of a writer in her. But 'if I should not sleep this fortnight I should not come to that' – one can measure the opposition that was in the air to a woman writing when one finds that even a woman with a great turn for writing has brought herself to believe that to write a book was to be ridiculous, even to show oneself distracted. And so we come, I continued, replacing the single short volume of Dorothy Osborne's letters upon the shelf, to Mrs Behn.

And with Mrs Behn we turn a very important corner on the road. We leave behind, shut up in their parks among their folios, those solitary great ladies who wrote without audience or criticism, for their own delight alone. We come to town and rub shoulders with ordinary people in the streets. Mrs Behn was a middle-class woman with all the plebeian virtues of humour, vitality and courage; a woman forced by the death of her husband and some unfortunate adventures of her own to make her living by her wits. She had to work on equal terms with men. She made, by working very hard, enough to live on. The importance of that fact outweighs anything that she actually wrote, even the splendid 'A Thousand Martyrs I have made', or 'Love in Fantastic Triumph sat', for here begins the freedom of the mind, or rather the possibility that in the course of time the mind will be free to write what it likes. For now that Aphra Behn had done it, girls could go to their parents and say, You need not give me an allowance; I can make money by my pen. Of course the answer for many years to come was, Yes, by living the life of Aphra Behn! Death would be better! and the door was slammed faster than ever. That profoundly interesting subject, the value that men set upon women's chastity and its effect upon their education, here suggests itself for discussion, and might provide an interesting book if any student at Girton or Newnham cared to go into the matter. Lady Dudley, sitting in diamonds among the midges of a Scottish moor, might serve for frontispiece. Lord Dudley, *The Times* said when Lady Dudley died the other day, 'a man of cultivated taste and many accomplishments, was benevolent and bountiful, but whimsically despotic. He insisted upon his wife's wearing full dress, even at the remotest shooting-lodge in the Highlands; he loaded her with gorgeous jewels', and so on, 'he gave her everything – always excepting any measure of responsibility'. Then Lord Dudley had a stroke and she nursed him and ruled his estates with supreme competence for ever after. That whimsical despotism was in the nineteenth century too.

But to return. Aphra Behn proved that money could be made by writing at the sacrifice, perhaps, of certain agreeable qualities; and so by degrees writing became not merely a sign of folly and a distracted mind, but was of practical importance. A husband might die, or some disaster overtake the family. Hundreds of women began as the eighteenth century drew on to add to their pin money, or to come to the rescue of their families by making translations or writing the innumerable bad novels which have ceased to be recorded even in textbooks, but are to be picked up in the fourpenny boxes in the Charing Cross Road. The extreme activity of mind which showed itself in the later eighteenth century among women – the talking, and the meeting, the writing of essays on Shakespeare, the translating of the classics – was founded on the solid fact that women could make money by writing. Money dignifies what is frivolous if unpaid for. It might still be well to sneer at 'blue stockings with an itch for scribbling', but it could not be denied that they could put money in their purses. Thus, towards the end of the eighteenth century a change came about which, if I were rewriting history, I should describe more fully and think of greater importance than the Crusades or the Wars of the Roses.

The middle-class woman began to write. For if *Pride and Prejudice* matters, and *Middlemarch* and *Villette* and *Wuthering Heights* matter, then it matters far more than I can prove in an hour's discourse that women generally, and not merely the lonely aristocrat shut up in her country house among her folios and her flatterers, took to writing. Without those forerunners, Jane Austen and the Brontës and George Eliot could no more have written than Shakespeare could have written without Marlowe, or Marlowe without Chaucer, or Chaucer without those forgotten poets who paved the ways and tamed the natural savagery of the tongue. For masterpieces are not single and solitary births; they are the outcome of many years of thinking in common, of thinking by the body of the people, so that the experience of the mass is behind the single voice. Jane Austen should have laid a wreath upon the grave of Fanny Burney, and George Eliot done homage to the robust shade of Eliza Carter – the valiant old woman who tied a bell to her bedstead in order that she might wake early and learn Greek. All women together ought to let flowers fall upon the tomb of Aphra Behn, which is, most scandalously but rather appropriately, in Westminster Abbey, for it was she who earned them the right to speak their minds. It is she – shady and amorous as she was – who makes it not quite fantastic for me to say to you tonight: Earn five hundred a year by your wits.

Here, then, one had reached the early nineteenth century. And here, for the first time, I found several shelves given up entirely to the works of women. But why, I could not help asking, as I ran my eyes over them, were they, with very few exceptions, all novels? The original impulse was to poetry. The 'supreme head of song' was a poetess. Both in France and in England the women poets precede the women novelists. Moreover, I thought, looking at the four famous names, what had George Eliot in common with Emily Brontë? Did not Charlotte Brontë fail entirely to understand Jane Austen? Save for the possibly relevant fact that not one of them had a child, four more incongruous characters could not have met together in a room – so much so that it is tempting to invent a meeting and a dialogue between them. Yet by some strange force they were all compelled, when they wrote, to write novels. Had it something to do with being born of the middle class, I asked; and with the fact, which Miss Emily Davies a little later was so strikingly to demonstrate, that the middle-class family in the early nineteenth century was possessed only of a single sitting-room between them? If a woman wrote, she would have to write in the common sitting-room. And, as Miss Nightingale was so vehemently to complain – 'women never have an half-hour . . . that they can call their own' – she was always interrupted. Still it would be easier to write prose and fiction there than to write poetry or a play. Less concentration is required. Jane Austen wrote like that to the end of her days. 'How she was able to effect all this,' her nephew writes in his memoir, 'is surprising, for she had no separate study to repair to, and most of the work must have been done in the general sitting-room, subject to all kinds of casual interruptions. She was careful that her occupation should not be suspected by servants or visitors or any persons beyond her own family party.'* Jane Austen hid her manuscripts or covered them with a piece of blotting-paper. Then, again, all the literary training that a woman had in the early nineteenth century was training in the observation of character, in the analysis of emotion. Her sensibility had been educated for centuries by the influences of the common sitting-room. People's feelings were impressed on her; personal relations were always

*Memoir of Jane Austen by her nephew, James Edward Austen-Leigh

before her eyes. Therefore, when the middle-class woman took to writing, she naturally wrote novels, even though, as seems evident enough, two of the four famous women here named were not by nature novelists. Emily Brontë should have written poetic plays; the overflow of George Eliot's capacious mind should have spread itself when the creative impulse was spent upon history or biography. They wrote novels, however; one may even go further, I said, taking *Pride and Prejudice* from the shelf, and say that they wrote good novels. Without boasting or giving pain to the opposite sex, one may say that *Pride and Prejudice* is a good book. At any rate, one would not have been ashamed to have been caught in the act of writing *Pride and Prejudice*. Yet Jane Austen was glad that a hinge creaked, so that she might hide her manuscript before anyone came in. To Jane Austen there was something discreditable in writing *Pride and Prejudice*. And, I wondered, would *Pride and Prejudice* have been a better novel if Jane Austen had not thought it necessary to hide her manuscript from visitors? I read a page or two to see, but I could not find any signs that her circumstances had harmed her work in the slightest. That, perhaps, was the chief miracle about it. Here was a woman about the year 1800 writing without hate, without bitterness, without fear, without protest, without preaching. That was how Shakespeare wrote, I thought, looking at *Antony and Cleopatra*; and when people compare Shakespeare and Jane Austen, they may mean that the minds of both had consumed all impediments; and for that reason we do not know Jane Austen and we do not know Shakespeare, and for that reason Jane Austen pervades every word that she wrote, and so does Shakespeare. If Jane Austen suffered in any way from her circumstances it was in the narrowness of life that was imposed upon her. It was impossible for a woman to go about alone. She never travelled; she never drove through London in an omnibus or had luncheon in a shop by herself. But perhaps it was the nature of Jane Austen not to want what she had not. Her gift and her circumstances matched each other completely. But I doubt whether that was true of Charlotte Brontë, I said, opening *Jane Eyre* and laying it beside *Pride and Prejudice*.

I opened it at Chapter Twelve and my eye was caught by the phrase, 'Anybody may blame me who likes.' What were they blaming Charlotte Brontë for? I wondered. And I read how Jane Eyre used to go up on to the roof when Mrs Fairfax was making jellies and looked over the fields at the distant view. And then she longed – and it was for this that they blamed her –

> I longed for a power of vision which might overpass that limit; which might reach the busy world, towns, regions full of life I had heard of but never seen: that then I desired more of practical experience than I possessed; more of intercourse with my kind, of acquaintance with variety of character than was here within my reach. I valued what was good in Mrs Fairfax, and what was good in Adèle; but I believed in the existence of other and more vivid kinds of goodness, and what I believed in I wished to behold.

Who blames me? Many, no doubt, and I shall be called discontented. I could not help it: the restlessness was in my nature; it agitated me to pain sometimes . . .

It is vain to say human beings ought to be satisfied with tranquillity: they must have action; and they will make it if they cannot find it. Millions are condemned to a stiller doom than mine, and millions are in silent revolt against their lot. Nobody knows how many rebellions ferment in the masses of life which people earth. Women are supposed to be very calm generally: but women feel just as men feel; they need exercise for their faculties and a field for their efforts as much as their brothers do; they suffer from too rigid a restraint, too absolute a stagnation, precisely as men would suffer; and it is narrow-minded in their more privileged fellow-creatures to say that they ought to confine themselves to making puddings and knitting stockings, to playing on the piano and embroidering bags. It is thoughtless to condemn them, or laugh at them, if they seek to do more or learn more than custom has pronounced necessary for their sex.

When thus alone I not unfrequently heard Grace Poole's laugh . . .

That is an awkward break, I thought. It is upsetting to come upon Grace Poole all of a sudden. The continuity is disturbed. One might say, I continued, laying the book down beside *Pride and Prejudice*, that the woman who wrote those pages had more genius in her than Jane Austen; but if one reads them over and marks that jerk in them, that indignation, one sees that she will never get her genius expressed whole and entire. Her books will be deformed and twisted. She will write in a rage where she should write calmly. She will write foolishly where she should write wisely. She will write of herself where she should write of her characters. She is at war with her lot. How could she help but die young, cramped and thwarted?

One could not but play for a moment with the thought of what might have happened if Charlotte Brontë had possessed say three hundred a year – but the foolish woman sold the copyright of her novels outright for fifteen hundred pounds; had somehow possessed more knowledge of the busy world, and towns and regions full of life; more practical experience, and intercourse with her kind and acquaintance with a variety of character. In those words she puts her finger exactly not only upon her own defects as a novelist but upon those of her sex, at that time. She knew, no one better, how enormously her genius would have profited if it had not spent itself in solitary visions over distant fields; if experience and intercourse and travel had been granted her. But they were not granted; they were withheld; and we must accept the fact that all those good novels, *Villette*, *Emma*, *Wuthering Heights*, *Middlemarch*, were written by women without more experience of life than could enter the house of a respectable clergyman; written too in the common sitting-room of that respectable house and by women so poor that they could not afford to buy more than a few quires of paper at a time upon which to write *Wuthering Heights* or *Jane Eyre*. One of them, it is true, George Eliot, escaped after much tribulation, but only to a secluded villa in St John's Wood. And there she settled down in the shadow of the world's disapproval. 'I wish it to be understood,' she wrote, 'that I should never invite anyone to come and see me who did not ask for the invitation'; for was she not living in sin with a married man and might not the sight of her damage the chastity of Mrs Smith or whoever it might be that chanced to call? One must submit to the social convention, and be 'cut off from what is called the world'. At the same time, on the other side of Europe, there was a young man living freely with this gypsy or with that great lady; going to the wars; picking up unhindered and uncensored all that varied experience of human life which served him so splendidly later when he came to write his books. Had Tolstoy lived at the Priory in seclusion with a married lady, 'cut off from what is called the world', however edifying the moral lesson, he could scarcely, I thought, have written *War and Peace*.

But one could perhaps go a little deeper into the question of novel-writing and the effect of sex upon the novelist. If one shuts one's eyes and thinks of the novel as a whole, it would seem to be a creation owning a certain looking-glass likeness to life, though of course with simplifications and distortions innumerable. At any rate, it is a structure leaving a shape on the mind's eye, built now in squares, now pagoda shaped, now throwing out wings and arcades, now solidly compact and domed like the Cathedral of St Sofia at Constantinople. This shape, I thought, thinking back over certain famous novels, starts in one the kind of emotion that is appropriate to it. But that emotion at once blends itself with others, for the 'shape' is not made by the relation of stone to stone, but by the relation of human being to human being. Thus a novel starts in us all sorts of antagonistic and opposed emotions. Life conflicts with something that is not life. Hence the difficulty of coming to any agreement about novels, and the immense sway that our private prejudices have upon us. On the one hand we feel You – John the hero – must live, or I shall be in the depths of despair. On the other, we feel, Alas, John, you must die, because the shape of the book requires it. Life conflicts with something that is not life. Then since life it is in part, we judge it as life. James is the sort of man I most detest, one says. Or, This is a farrago of absurdity. I could never feel anything of the sort myself. The whole structure, it is obvious, thinking back on any famous novel, is one of infinite complexity, because it is thus made up of so many different judgements, of so many different kinds of emotion. The wonder is that any book so composed holds together for more than a year or two, or can possibly mean to the English reader what it means for the Russian or the Chinese. But they do hold together occasionally very remarkably. And what holds them together in these rare instances of survival (I was thinking of *War and Peace*) is something that one calls integrity, though it has nothing to do with paying one's bills or behaving honourably in an emergency. What one means by integrity, in the case of the novelist, is the conviction that he gives one that this is the truth. Yes, one feels, I should never have thought that this could be so; I have never known people behaving like that. But you have convinced me that so it is, so it happens. One holds every phrase, every scene to the light as one reads – for Nature seems, very oddly, to have provided us with an inner light by which to judge of the novelist's integrity or disintegrity. Or perhaps it is rather that Nature, in her most irrational mood, has traced in invisible ink on the walls of the mind a premonition which these great artists confirm; a sketch which only needs to be held to the fire of genius to become visible. When one so exposes it and sees it come to life one exclaims in rapture, But this is what I have always felt and known and desired! And one boils over with excitement, and, shutting the book even with a kind of reverence as if it were something very precious, a stand-by to return to as long as one lives, one puts it back on the shelf, I said, taking *War and Peace* and putting it back in its place. If, on the other hand, these poor sentences that one takes and tests rouse first a quick and eager response with their bright colouring and their dashing gestures but there they stop: something seems to check them in their development; or if they bring to light only a faint scribble in that corner and a blot over there, and nothing appears whole and entire, then one heaves a sigh of disappointment and says, Another failure. This novel has come to grief somewhere.

And for the most part, of course, novels do come to grief somewhere. The imagination falters under the enormous strain. The insight is confused; it can no longer distinguish between the true and the false, it has no longer the strength to go on with the vast labour that calls at every moment for the use of so many different faculties. But how would all this be affected by the sex of the novelist, I wondered, looking at *Jane Eyre* and the others. Would the fact of her sex in any way interfere with the integrity of a woman novelist – that integrity which I take to be the backbone of the writer? Now, in the passages I have quoted from *Jane Eyre*, it is clear that anger was tampering with the integrity of Charlotte Brontë the novelist. She left her story, to which her entire devotion was due, to attend to some personal grievance. She remembered that she had been starved of her proper due of experience – she had been made to stagnate in a parsonage mending stockings when she wanted to wander free over the world. Her imagination swerved from indignation and we feel it swerve. But there were many more influences than anger tugging at her imagination and deflecting it from its path. Ignorance, for instance. The portrait of Rochester is drawn in the dark. We feel the influence of fear in it; just as we constantly feel an acidity which is the result of oppression, a buried suffering smouldering beneath her passion, a rancour which contracts those books, splendid as they are, with a spasm of pain.

And since a novel has this correspondence to real life, its values are to some extent those of real life. But it is obvious that the values of women differ very often from the values which have been made by the other sex; naturally, this is so. Yet it is the masculine values that prevail. Speaking crudely, football and sport are 'important'; the worship of fashion, the buying of clothes 'trivial'. And these values are inevitably transferred from life to fiction. This is an important book, the critic assumes, because it deals with war. This is an insignificant book because it deals with the feelings of women in a drawing-room. A scene in a battlefield is more important than a scene in a shop – everywhere and much more subtly the difference of value persists. The whole structure, therefore, of the early nineteenth-century novel was raised, if one was a woman, by a mind which was slightly pulled from the straight, and made to alter its clear vision in deference to external authority. One has only to skim those old forgotten novels and listen to the tone of voice in which they are written to divine that the writer was meeting criticism; she was saying this by way of aggression, or that by way of conciliation. She was admitting that she was 'only a woman', or protesting that she was 'as good as a man'. She met that criticism as her temperament dictated, with docility and diffidence, or with anger and emphasis. It does not matter which it was; she was thinking of something other than the thing itself. Down comes her book upon our heads. There was a flaw in the centre of it. And I thought of all the women's novels that lie scattered, like small pock-marked apples in an orchard, about the second-hand bookshops of London. It was the flaw in the centre that had rotted them. She had altered her values in deference to the opinion of others.

But how impossible it must have been for them not to budge either to the right or to the left. What genius, what integrity it must have required in face of all that criticism, in the midst of that purely patriarchal society, to hold fast to the thing as they saw it without shrinking. Only Jane Austen did it and Emily Brontë. It is another feather, perhaps the finest, in their caps. They wrote as women write, not as men write. Of all the thousand women who wrote novels then, they alone entirely ignored the perpetual admonitions of the eternal pedagogue – write this, think that. They alone were deaf to that persistent voice, now grumbling, now patronising, now domineering, now grieved, now shocked, now angry, now avuncular, that voice which cannot let women alone, but must be at them, like some too-conscientious governess, adjuring them, like Sir Egerton Brydges, to be refined; dragging even into the criticism of poetry criticism of sex;* admonishing them, if they would be good and win, as I suppose, some shiny prize, to keep within certain limits which the gentleman in question thinks suitable – ' . . . female novelists should only aspire to excellence by courageously acknowledging

* '[She] has a metaphysical purpose, and that is a dangerous obsession, especially with a woman, for women rarely possess men's healthy love of rhetoric. It is a strange lack in the sex which is in other things more primitive and more materialistic.' *New Criterion*, June 1928

the limitations of their sex'.[†] That puts the matter in a nutshell, and when I tell you, rather to your surprise, that this sentence was written not in August 1828 but in August 1928, you will agree, I think, that however delightful it is to us now, it represents a vast body of opinion – I am not going to stir those old pools; I take only what chance has floated to my feet – that was far more vigorous and far more vocal a century ago. It would have needed a very stalwart young woman in 1828 to disregard all those snubs and chidings and promises of prizes. One must have been something of a firebrand to say to oneself, Oh, but they can't buy literature too. Literature is open to every-body. I refuse to allow you, beadle though you are, to turn me off the grass. Lock up your libraries if you like; but there is no gate, no lock, no bolt, that you can set upon the freedom of my mind.

But whatever effect discouragement and criticism had upon their writing – and I believe that they had a very great effect – that was unimportant compared with the other difficulty which faced them (I was still considering those early nineteenth-century novelists) when they came to set their thoughts on paper – that is that they had no tradition behind them, or one so short and partial that it was of little help. For we think back through our mothers if we are women. It is useless to go to the great men writers for help, however much one may go to them for pleasure. Lamb, Browne, Thackeray, Newman, Sterne, Dickens, De Quincey – whoever it may be – never helped a woman yet, though she may have learnt a few tricks of them and adapted them to her use. The weight, the pace, the stride of a man's mind are too unlike her own for her to lift anything substantial from him successfully. The ape is too distant to be sedulous. Perhaps the first thing she would find, setting pen to paper, was that there was no common sentence ready for her use. All the great novelists like Thackeray and Dick-ens and Balzac have written a natural prose, swift but not slovenly, expres-sive but not precious, taking their own tint without ceasing to be common property. They have based it on the sentence that was current at the time. The sentence that was current at the beginning of the nineteenth century ran something like this perhaps: 'The grandeur of their works was an argument with them, not to stop short, but to proceed. They could have no higher excitement or satisfaction than in the exercise of their art and endless generations of truth and beauty. Success prompts to exertion; and habit facilitates success.' That is a man's sentence; behind it one can see Johnson, Gibbon and the rest. It was a sentence that was unsuited for a woman's use. Charlotte Brontë, with all her splendid gift for prose, stumbled and fell with that clumsy weapon in her hands. George Eliot committed atrocities with it

---

† 'If, like the reporter, you believe that female novelists should only aspire to excellence by courageously acknowledging the limitations of their sex, Jane Austen [has] demonstrated how gracefully this gesture can be accomplished . . . ' *Life and Letters*, August 1928

that beggar description. Jane Austen looked at it and laughed at it and devised a perfectly natural, shapely sentence proper for her own use and never departed from it. Thus, with less genius for writing than Charlotte Brontë, she got infinitely more said. Indeed, since freedom and fullness of expression are of the essence of the art, such a lack of tradition, such a scarcity and inadequacy of tools, must have told enormously upon the writing of women. Moreover, a book is not made of sentences laid end to end, but of sentences built, if an image helps, into arcades or domes. And this shape too has been made by men out of their own needs for their own uses. There is no reason to think that the form of the epic or of the poetic play suit a woman any more than the sentence suits her. But all the older forms of literature were hardened and set by the time she became a writer. The novel alone was young enough to be soft in her hands – another reason, perhaps, why she wrote novels. Yet who shall say that even now 'the novel' (I give it inverted commas to mark my sense of the words' inadequacy), who shall say that even this most pliable of all forms is rightly shaped for her use? No doubt we shall find her knocking that into shape for herself when she has the free use of her limbs; and providing some new vehicle, not necessarily in verse, for the poetry in her. For it is the poetry that is still denied outlet. And I went on to ponder how a woman nowadays would write a poetic tragedy in five acts. Would she use verse? – would she not use prose rather?

But these are difficult questions which lie in the twilight of the future. I must leave them, if only because they stimulate me to wander from my subject into trackless forests where I shall be lost and, very likely, devoured by wild beasts. I do not want, and I am sure that you do not want me, to broach that very dismal subject, the future of fiction, so that I will only pause here one moment to draw your attention to the great part which must be played in that future so far as women are concerned by physical conditions. The book has somehow to be adapted to the body, and at a venture one would say that women's books should be shorter, more concentrated, than those of men, and framed so that they do not need long hours of steady and uninterrupted work. For interruptions there will always be. Again, the nerves that feed the brain would seem to differ in men and women, and if you are going to make them work their best and hardest, you must find out what treatment suits them – whether these hours of lectures, for instance, which the monks devised, presumably, hundreds of years ago, suit them – what alternations of work and rest they need, interpreting rest not as doing nothing but as doing something but something that is different; and what should that difference be? All this should be discussed and discovered; all this is part of the question of women and fiction. And yet, I continued, approaching the bookcase again, where shall I find that elaborate study of the psychology of women by a woman? If through their incapacity to play football women are not going to be allowed to practise medicine –

Happily my thoughts were now given another turn.

Chapter 5

I had come at last, in the course of this rambling, to the shelves which hold books by the living; by women and by men; for there are almost as many books written by women now as by men. Or if that is not yet quite true, if the male is still the voluble sex, it is certainly true that women no longer write novels solely. There are Jane Harrison's books on Greek archaeology; Vernon Lee's books on aesthetics; Gertrude Bell's books on Persia. There are books on all sorts of subjects which a generation ago no woman could have touched. There are poems and plays and criticism; there are histories and biographies, books of travel and books of scholarship and research; there are even a few philosophies and books about science and economics. And though novels predominate, novels themselves may very well have changed from association with books of a different feather. The natural simplicity, the epic age of women's writing, may have gone. Reading and criticism may have given her a wider range, a greater subtlety. The impulse towards autobiography may be spent. She may be beginning to use writing as an art, not as a method of self-expression. Among these new novels one might find an answer to several such questions.

I took down one of them at random. It stood at the very end of the shelf, was called *Life's Adventure*, or some such title, by Mary Carmichael, and was published in this very month of October. It seems to be her first book, I said to myself, but one must read it as if it were the last volume in a fairly long series, continuing all those other books that I have been glancing at – Lady Winchilsea's poems and Aphra Behn's plays and the novels of the four great novelists. For books continue each other, in spite of our habit of judging them separately. And I must also consider her – this unknown woman – as the descendant of all those other women whose circumstances I have been glancing at and see what she inherits of their characteristics and restrictions. So, with a sigh, because novels so often provide an anodyne and not an antidote, glide one into torpid slumbers instead of rousing one with a burning brand, I settled down with a notebook and a pencil to make what I could of Mary Carmichael's first novel, *Life's Adventure*.

To begin with, I ran my eye up and down the page. I am going to get the hang of her sentences first, I said, before I load my memory with blue eyes and brown and the relationship that there may be between Chloe and Roger. There will be time for that when I have decided whether she has a pen in her hand or a pickaxe. So I tried a sentence or two on my tongue. Soon it was obvious that something was not quite in order. The smooth gliding of sentence after sentence was interrupted. Something tore, something scratched; a single word here and there flashed its torch in my eyes. She was 'unhanding' herself as they say in the old plays. She is like a person striking a match that will not light, I thought. But why, I asked her as if she were present, are Jane Austen's sentences not of the right shape for you? Must they all be scrapped because Emma and Mr Woodhouse are dead? Alas, I sighed, that it should be so. For while Jane Austen breaks from melody to melody as Mozart from song to song, to read this writing was like being out at sea in an open boat. Up one went, down one sank. This terseness, this short-windedness, might mean that she was afraid of something; afraid of being called 'sentimental' perhaps; or she remembers that women's writing has been called flowery and so provides a superfluity of thorns; but until I have read a scene with some care, I cannot be sure whether she is being herself or someone else. At any rate, she does not lower one's vitality, I thought, reading more carefully. But she is heaping up too many facts. She will not be able to use half of them in a book of this size (it was about half the length of *Jane Eyre*). However, by some means or other she succeeded in getting us all – Roger, Chloe, Olivia, Tony and Mr Bigham – in a canoe up the river. Wait a moment, I said, leaning back in my chair, I must consider the whole thing more carefully before I go any further.

I am almost sure, I said to myself, that Mary Carmichael is playing a trick on us. For I feel as one feels on a switchback railway when the car, instead of sinking, as one has been led to expect, swerves up again. Mary is tampering with the expected sequence. First she broke the sentence; now she has broken the sequence. Very well, she has every right to do both these things if she does them not for the sake of breaking, but for the sake of creating. Which of the two it is I cannot be sure until she has faced herself with a situation. I will give her every liberty, I said, to choose what that situation shall be; she shall make it of tin cans and old kettles if she likes; but she must convince me that she believes it to be a situation; and then when she has made it she must face it. She must jump. And, determined to do my duty by her as reader if she would do her duty by me as writer, I turned the page and read . . . I am sorry to break off so abruptly. Are there no men present? Do you promise me that behind that red curtain over there the figure of Sir Charles Biron is not concealed? We are all women you assure me? Then I may tell you that the very next words I read were these – 'Chloe liked Olivia . . . ' Do not start. Do not blush. Let us admit in the privacy of our own society that these things sometimes happen. Sometimes women do like women.

'Chloe liked Olivia,' I read. And then it struck me how immense a change was there. Chloe liked Olivia perhaps for the first time in literature. Cleopatra did not like Octavia. And how completely *Antony and Cleopatra* would have been altered had she done so! As it is, I thought, letting my mind, I am afraid, wander a little from *Life's Adventure*, the whole thing is simplified, conventionalised, if one dared say it, absurdly. Cleopatra's only feeling about Octavia is one of jealousy. Is she taller than I am? How does she do her hair? The play, perhaps, required no more. But how interesting it would have been if the relationship between the two women had been more complicated. All these relationships between women, I thought, rapidly recalling the splendid gallery of fictitious women, are too simple. So much has been left out, unattempted. And I tried to remember any case in the course of my reading where two women are represented as friends. There is an attempt at it in *Diana of the Crossways*. They are confidantes, of course, in Racine and the Greek tragedies. They are now and then mothers and daughters. But almost without exception they are shown in their relation to men. It was strange to think that all the great women of fiction were, until Jane Austen's day, not only seen by the other sex, but seen only in relation to the other sex. And how small a part of a woman's life is that; and how little can a man know even of that when he observes it through the black or rosy spectacles which sex puts upon his nose. Hence, perhaps, the peculiar nature of woman in fiction; the astonishing extremes of her beauty and horror; her alternations between heavenly goodness and hellish depravity – for so a lover would see her as his love rose or sank, was prosperous or unhappy. This is not so true of the nineteenth-century novelists, of course. Woman becomes much more various and complicated there. Indeed it was the desire to write about women perhaps that led men by degrees to abandon the poetic drama which, with its violence, could make so little use of them, and to devise the novel as a more fitting receptacle. Even so it remains obvious, even in the writing of Proust, that a man is terribly hampered and partial in his knowledge of women, as a woman in her knowledge of men.

Also, I continued, looking down at the page again, it is becoming evident that women, like men, have other interests besides the perennial interests of domesticity. 'Chloe liked Olivia. They shared a laboratory together. . . ' I read on and discovered that these two young women were engaged in mincing liver, which is, it seems, a cure for pernicious anaemia; although one of them was married and had – I think I am right in stating – two small children. Now all that, of course, has had to be left out, and thus the splendid portrait of the fictitious woman is much too simple and much too monotonous. Suppose, for instance, that men were only represented in literature as the lovers of women, and were never the friends of men, soldiers, thinkers, dreamers; how few parts in the plays of Shakespeare could be allotted to them; how literature would suffer! We might perhaps have most of Othello; and a good deal of Antony; but no Caesar, no Brutus, no Hamlet, no Lear, no Jaques – literature would be incredibly impoverished, as indeed literature is impoverished beyond our counting by the doors that have been shut upon women. Married against their will, kept in one room, and to one occupation, how could a dramatist give a full or interesting or truthful account of them? Love was the only possible interpreter. The poet was forced to be passionate or bitter, unless indeed he chose to 'hate women', which meant more often than not that he was unattractive to them.

Now if Chloe likes Olivia and they share a laboratory, which of itself will make their friendship more varied and lasting because it will be less personal; if Mary Carmichael knows how to write, and I was beginning to enjoy some quality in her style; if she has a room to herself, of which I am not quite sure; if she has five hundred a year of her own – but that remains to be proved – then I think that something of great importance has happened.

For if Chloe likes Olivia and Mary Carmichael knows how to express it she will light a torch in that vast chamber where nobody has yet been. It is all half lights and profound shadows like those serpentine caves where one goes with a candle peering up and down, not knowing where one is stepping. And I began to read the book again, and read how Chloe watched Olivia put a jar on a shelf and say how it was time to go home to her children. That is a sight that has never been seen since the world began, I exclaimed. And I watched too, very curiously. For I wanted to see how Mary Carmichael set to work to catch those unrecorded gestures, those unsaid or half-said words, which form themselves, no more palpably than the shadows of moths on the ceiling, when women are alone, unlit by the capricious and coloured light of the other sex. She will need to hold her breath, I said, reading on, if she is to do it; for women are so suspicious of any interest that has not some obvious motive behind it, so terribly accustomed to concealment and suppression, that they are off at the flicker of an eye turned observingly in their direction. The only way for you to do it, I thought, addressing Mary Carmichael as if she were there, would be to talk of something else, looking steadily out of the window, and thus note, not with a pencil in a notebook, but in the shortest of shorthand, in words that are hardly syllabled yet, what happens when Olivia – this organism that has been under the shadow of the rock these million years – feels the light fall on it, and sees coming her way a piece of strange food – knowledge, adventure, art. And she reaches out for it, I thought, again raising my eyes from the page, and has to devise some entirely new combination of her resources, so highly developed for other purposes, so as to absorb the new into the old without disturbing the infinitely intricate and elaborate balance of the whole.

But, alas, I had done what I had determined not to do; I had slipped unthinkingly into praise of my own sex. 'Highly developed' – 'infinitely intricate' – such are undeniably terms of praise, and to praise one's own sex is always suspect, often silly; moreover, in this case, how could one justify it? One could not go to the map and say Columbus discovered America and Columbus was a woman; or take an apple and remark, Newton discovered the laws of gravitation and Newton was a woman; or look into the sky and say aeroplanes are flying overhead and aeroplanes were invented by women. There is no mark on the wall to measure the precise height of women. There are no yard measures, neatly divided into the fractions of an inch, that one can lay against the qualities of a good mother, or the devotion of a daughter, or the fidelity of a sister, or the capacity of a housekeeper. Few women even now have been graded at the universities; the great trials of the professions, army and navy, trade, politics and diplomacy have hardly tested them. They remain even at this moment almost unclassified. But if I want to know all that a human being can tell me about Sir Hawley Butts, for instance, I have only to open Burke or Debrett and I shall find that he took such and such a degree; owns a hall; has an heir; was Secretary to a Board; represented Great Britain in Canada; and has received a certain number of degrees, offices, medals and other distinctions by which his merits are stamped upon him indelibly. Only Providence can know more about Sir Hawley Butts than that.

When, therefore, I say 'highly developed', 'infinitely intricate' of women, I am unable to verify my words either in Whitaker, Debrett or the University Calendar. In this predicament what can I do? And I looked at the bookcase again. There were the biographies: Johnson and Goethe and Carlyle and Sterne and Cowper and Shelley and Voltaire and Browning and many others. And I began thinking of all those great men who have for one reason or another admired, sought out, lived with, confided in, made love to, written of, trusted in, and shown what can only be described as some need of and dependence upon certain persons of the opposite sex. That all these relationships were absolutely Platonic I would not affirm, and Sir William Joynson Hicks would probably deny. But we should wrong these illustrious men very greatly if we insisted that they got nothing from these alliances but comfort, flattery and the pleasures of the body. What they got, it is obvious, was something that their own sex was unable to supply; and it would not be rash, perhaps, to define it further, without quoting the doubtless rhapsodical words of the poets, as some stimulus; some renewal of creative power which is in the gift only of the opposite sex to bestow. He would open the door of drawing-room or nursery, I thought, and find her among her children perhaps, or with a piece of embroidery on her knee – at any rate, the centre of some different order and system of life, and the contrast between this world and his own, which might be the law courts or the House of Commons, would at once refresh and invigorate; and there would follow, even in the simplest talk, such a natural difference of opinion that the dried ideas in him would be fertilised anew; and the sight of her creating in a different medium from his own would so quicken his creative power that insensibly his sterile mind would begin to plot again, and he would find the phrase or the scene which was lacking when he put on his hat to visit her. Every Johnson has his Thrale, and holds fast to her for some such reasons as these, and when the Thrale marries her Italian music master Johnson goes half mad with rage and disgust, not merely that he will miss his pleasant evenings at Streatham, but that the light of his life will be 'as if gone out'.

And without being Dr Johnson or Goethe or Carlyle or Voltaire, one may feel, though very differently from these great men, the nature of this intricacy and the power of this highly developed creative faculty among women.

One goes into the room – but the resources of the English language would be much put to the stretch, and whole flights of words would need to wing their way illegitimately into existence before a woman could say what happens when she goes into a room. The rooms differ so completely: they are calm or thunderous; open on to the sea, or, on the contrary, give on to a prison yard; are hung with washing; or alive with opals and silks; are hard as horsehair or soft as feathers – one has only to go into any room in any street for the whole of that extremely complex force of femininity to fly in one's face. How should it be otherwise? For women have sat indoors all these millions of years, so that by this time the very walls are permeated by their creative force, which has, indeed, so overcharged the capacity of bricks and mortar that it must needs harness itself to pens and brushes and business and politics. But this creative power differs greatly from the creative power of men. And one must conclude that it would be a thousand pities if it were hindered or wasted, for it was won by centuries of the most drastic discipline, and there is nothing to take its place. It would be a thousand pities if women wrote like men, or lived like men, or looked like men, for if two sexes are quite inadequate, considering the vastness and variety of the world, how should we manage with one only? Ought not education to bring out and fortify the differences rather than the similarities? For we have too much likeness as it is, and if an explorer should come back and bring word of other sexes looking through the branches of other trees at other skies, nothing would be of greater service to humanity; and we should have the immense pleasure into the bargain of watching Professor X rush for his measuring-rods to prove himself 'superior'.

Mary Carmichael, I thought, still hovering at a little distance above the page, will have her work cut out for her merely as an observer. I am afraid indeed that she will be tempted to become, what I think the less interesting branch of the species – the naturalist-novelist, and not the contemplative. There are so many new facts for her to observe. She will not need to limit herself any longer to the respectable houses of the upper middle classes. She will go without kindness or condescension, but in the spirit of fellowship, into those small, scented rooms where sit the courtesan, the harlot and the lady with the pug dog. There they still sit in the rough and ready-made clothes that the male writer has had perforce to clap upon their shoulders. But Mary Carmichael will have out her scissors and fit them close to every hollow and angle. It will be a curious sight, when it comes, to see these women as they are, but we must wait a little, for Mary Carmichael will still be encumbered with that self-consciousness in the presence of 'sin' which is the legacy of our sexual barbarity. She will still wear the shoddy old fetters of class on her feet.

However, the majority of women are neither harlots nor courtesans; nor do they sit clasping pug dogs to dusty velvet all through the summer afternoon. But what do they do then? and there came to my mind's eye one of those long streets somewhere south of the river whose infinite rows are innumerably populated. With the eye of the imagination I saw a very ancient lady crossing the street on the arm of a middle-aged woman, her daughter, perhaps, both so respectably booted and furred that their dressing in the afternoon must be a ritual, and the clothes themselves put away in cupboards with camphor, year after year, throughout the summer months. They cross the road when the lamps are being lit (for the dusk is their favourite hour), as they must have done year after year. The elder is close on eighty; but if one asked her what her life has meant to her, she would say that she remembered the streets lit for the battle of Balaclava, or had heard the guns fire in Hyde Park for the birth of King Edward VII. And if one asked her, longing to pin down the moment with date and season, but what were you doing on the fifth of April 1868, or the second of November 1875, she would look vague and say that she could remember nothing. For all the dinners are cooked; the plates and cups washed; the children sent to school and gone out into the world. Nothing remains of it all. All has vanished. No biography or history has a word to say about it. And the novels, without meaning to, inevitably lie.

All these infinitely obscure lives remain to be recorded, I said, addressing Mary Carmichael as if she were present; and went on in thought through the streets of London feeling in imagination the pressure of dumbness, the accumulation of unrecorded life, whether from the women at the street corners with their arms akimbo, and the rings embedded in their fat swollen fingers, talking with a gesticulation like the swing of Shakespeare's words; or from the violet-sellers and match-sellers and old crones stationed under doorways; or from drifting girls whose faces, like waves in sun and cloud, signal the coming of men and women and the flickering lights of shop windows. All that you will have to explore, I said to Mary Carmichael, holding your torch firm in your hand. Above all, you must illumine your own soul with its profundities and its shallows, and its vanities and its generosities, and say what your beauty means to you or your plainness, and what is your relation to the ever-changing and turning world of gloves and shoes and stuffs swaying up and down among the faint scents that come through chemists' bottles down arcades of dress material over a floor of pseudo-marble. For in imagination I had gone into a shop; it was laid with black and white paving; it was hung, astonishingly beautifully, with coloured ribbons. Mary Carmichael might well have a look at that in passing, I thought, for it is a sight that would lend itself to the pen as fittingly as any snowy peak or rocky gorge in the Andes. And there is the girl behind the counter too – I would as soon have her true history as the hundred and fiftieth life of Napoleon or seventieth study of Keats and his use of Miltonic inversion which old Professor Z and his like are now inditing. And then I went on very warily, on the very tips of my toes (so cowardly am I, so afraid of the lash that was once almost laid on my own shoulders), to murmur that she should also learn to laugh, without bitterness, at the vanities – say rather at the peculiarities, for it is a less offensive word – of the other sex. For there is a spot the size of a shilling at the back of the head which one can never see for oneself. It is one of the good offices that sex can discharge for sex – to describe that spot the size of a shilling at the back of the head. Think how much women have profited by the comments of Juvenal; by the criticism of Strindberg. Think with what humanity and brilliancy men, from the earliest ages, have pointed out to women that dark place at the back of the head! And if Mary were very brave and very honest, she would go behind the other sex and tell us what she found there. A true picture of man as a whole can never be painted until a woman has described that spot the size of a shilling. Mr Woodhouse and Mr Casuabon are spots of that size and nature. Not of course that anyone in their senses would counsel her to hold up to scorn and ridicule of set purpose – literature shows the futility of what is written in that spirit. Be truthful, one would say, and the result is bound to be amazingly interesting. Comedy is bound to be enriched. New facts are bound to be discovered.

However, it was high time to lower my eyes to the page again. It would be better, instead of speculating what Mary Carmichael might write and should write, to see what in fact Mary Carmichael did write. So I began to read again. I remembered that I had certain grievances against her. She had broken up Jane Austen's sentence, and thus given me no chance of pluming myself upon my impeccable taste, my fastidious ear. For it was useless to say, 'Yes, yes, this is very nice; but Jane Austen wrote much better than you do', when I had to admit that there was no point of likeness between them. Then she had gone further and broken the sequence – the expected order. Perhaps she had done this unconsciously, merely giving things their natural order, as a woman would, if she wrote like a woman. But the effect was somehow baffling; one could not see a wave heaping itself, a crisis coming round the next corner. Therefore I could not plume myself either upon the depths of my feelings and my profound knowledge of the human heart. For whenever I was about to feel the usual things in the usual places, about love, about death, the annoying creature twitched me away, as if the important point were just a little further on. And thus she made it impossible for me to roll out my sonorous phrases about 'elemental feelings', the 'common stuff of humanity', 'the depths of the human heart', and all those other phrases which support us in our belief that, however clever we may be on top, we are very serious, very profound and very humane underneath. She made me feel, on the contrary, that instead of being serious and profound and humane, one might be – and the thought was far less seductive – merely lazy minded and conventional into the bargain.

But I read on, and noted certain other facts. She was no 'genius' that was evident. She had nothing like the love of nature, the fiery imagination, the wild poetry, the brilliant wit, the brooding wisdom of her great predecessors, Lady Winchilsea, Charlotte Brontë, Emily Brontë, Jane Austen and George

Eliot; she could not write with the melody and the dignity of Dorothy Osborne – indeed she was no more than a clever girl whose books will no doubt be pulped by the publishers in ten years' time. But, nevertheless, she had certain advantages which women of far greater gift lacked even half a century ago. Men were no longer to her 'the opposing faction'; she need not waste her time railing against them; she need not climb on to the roof and ruin her peace of mind longing for travel, experience and a knowledge of the world and character that were denied her. Fear and hatred were almost gone, or traces of them showed only in a slight exaggeration of the joy of freedom, a tendency to the caustic and satirical, rather than to the romantic, in her treatment of the other sex. Then there could be no doubt that as a novelist she enjoyed some natural advantages of a high order. She had a sensibility that was very wide, eager and free. It responded to an almost imperceptible touch on it. It feasted like a plant newly stood in the air on every sight and sound that came its way. It ranged, too, very subtly and curiously, among almost unknown or unrecorded things; it lighted on small things and showed that perhaps they were not small after all. It brought buried things to light and made one wonder what need there had been to bury them. Awkward though she was and without the unconscious bearing of long descent which makes the least turn of the pen of a Thackeray or a Lamb delightful to the ear, she had – I began to think – mastered the first great lesson: she wrote as a woman, but as a woman who has forgotten that she is a woman, so that her pages were full of that curious sexual quality which comes only when sex is unconscious of itself.

All this was to the good. But no abundance of sensation or fineness of perception would avail unless she could build up out of the fleeting and the personal the lasting edifice which remains unthrown. I had said that I would wait until she faced herself with 'a situation'. And I meant by that until she proved by summoning, beckoning and getting together that she was not a skimmer of surfaces merely, but had looked beneath into the depths. Now is the time, she would say to herself at a certain moment, when without doing anything violent I can show the meaning of all this. And she would begin – how unmistakable that quickening is! – beckoning and summoning, and there would rise up in memory, half forgotten, perhaps quite trivial things in other chapters dropped by the way. And she would make their presence felt while someone sewed or smoked a pipe as naturally as possible, and one would feel, as she went on writing, as if one had gone to the top of the world and seen it laid out, very majestically, beneath.

At any rate, she was making the attempt. And as I watched her lengthening out for the test, I saw, but hoped that she did not see, the bishops and the deans, the doctors and the professors, the patriarchs and the pedagogues all at her shouting warning and advice. You can't do this and you shan't do that! Fellows and scholars only allowed on the grass! Ladies not admitted without a letter of introduction! Aspiring and graceful female novelists this way! So they kept at her like the crowd at a fence on the racecourse, and it was her trial to take her fence without looking to right or to left. If you stop to curse you are lost, I said to her; equally, if you stop to laugh. Hesitate or fumble and you are done for. Think only of the jump, I implored her, as if I had put the whole of my money on her back; and she went over it like a bird. But there was a fence beyond that and a fence beyond that. Whether she had the staying power I was doubtful, for the clapping and the crying were fraying to the nerves. But she did her best. Considering that Mary Carmichael was no genius, but an unknown girl writing her first novel in a bed-sitting-room, without enough of those desirable things, time, money and idleness, she did not do so badly, I thought.

Give her another hundred years, I concluded, reading the last chapter – people's noses and bare shoulders showed naked against a starry sky, for someone had twitched the curtain in the drawing-room – give her a room of her own and five hundred a year, let her speak her mind and leave out half that she now puts in, and she will write a better book one of these days. She will be a poet, I said, putting *Life's Adventure* by Mary Carmichael at the end of the shelf, in another hundred years' time.

Chapter 6

Next day the light of the October morning was falling in dusty shafts through the uncurtained windows, and the hum of traffic rose from the street. London then was winding itself up again; the factory was astir; the machines were beginning. It was tempting, after all this reading, to look out of the window and see what London was doing on the morning of the 26th of October 1928. And what was London doing? Nobody, it seemed, was reading *Antony and Cleopatra*. London was wholly indifferent, it appeared, to Shakespeare's plays. Nobody cared a straw – and I do not blame them – for the future of fiction, the death of poetry or the development by the average woman of a prose style completely expressive of her mind. If opinions upon any of these matters had been chalked on the pavement, nobody would have stooped to read them. The nonchalance of the hurrying feet would have rubbed them out in half an hour. Here came an errand-boy; here a woman with a dog on a lead. The fascination of the London street is that no two people are ever alike; each seems bound on some private affair of his own. There were the businesslike, with their little bags; there were the drifters rattling sticks upon area railings; there were affable characters to whom the streets serve for clubroom, hailing men in carts and giving information without being asked for it. Also there were funerals to which men, thus suddenly reminded of the passing of their own bodies, lifted their hats. And then a very distinguished gentleman came slowly down a doorstep and paused to avoid collision with a bustling lady who had, by some means or other, acquired a splendid fur coat and a bunch of Parma violets. They all seemed separate, self-absorbed, on business of their own.

At this moment, as so often happens in London, there was a complete lull and suspension of traffic. Nothing came down the street; nobody passed. A single leaf detached itself from the plane tree at the end of the street, and in that pause and suspension fell. Somehow it was like a signal falling, a signal pointing to a force in things which one had overlooked. It seemed to point to a river, which flowed past, invisibly, round the corner, down the street, and took people and eddied them along, as the stream at Oxbridge had taken the undergraduate in his boat and the dead leaves. Now it was bringing from one side of the street to the other diagonally a girl in patent-leather boots, and then a young man in a maroon overcoat; it was also bringing a taxicab; and it brought all three together at a point directly beneath my window; where the taxi stopped; and the girl and the young man stopped; and they got into the taxi; and then the cab glided off as if it were swept on by the current elsewhere.

The sight was ordinary enough; what was strange was the rhythmical order with which my imagination had invested it; and the fact that the ordinary sight of two people getting into a cab had the power to communicate something of their own seeming satisfaction. The sight of two people coming down the street and meeting at the corner seems to ease the mind of some strain, I thought, watching the taxi turn and make off. Perhaps to think, as I had been thinking these two days, of one sex as distinct from the other is an effort. It interferes with the unity of the mind. Now that effort had ceased and that unity had been restored by seeing two people come together and get into a taxicab. The mind is certainly a very mysterious organ, I reflected, drawing my head in from the window, about which nothing whatever is known, though we depend upon it so completely. Why do I feel that there are severances and oppositions in the mind, as there are strains from obvious causes on the body? What does one mean by 'the unity of the mind'? I pondered, for clearly the mind has so great a power of concentrating at any point at any moment that it seems to have no single state of being. It can separate itself from the people in the street, for example, and think of itself as apart from them, at an upper window looking down on them. Or it can think with other people spontaneously, as, for instance, in a crowd waiting to hear some piece of news read out. It can think back through its fathers or through its mothers, as I have said that a woman writing thinks back through her mothers. Again if one is a woman one is often surprised by a sudden splitting off of consciousness, say in walking down Whitehall, when from being the natural inheritor of that civilisation, she becomes, on the contrary, outside of it, alien and critical. Clearly the mind is always altering its focus, and bringing the world into different perspectives. But some of these states of mind seem, even if adopted spontaneously, to be less comfortable than others. In order to keep oneself continuing in them one is unconsciously holding something back, and gradually the repression becomes an effort. But there may be some state of mind in which one could continue without effort because nothing is required to be held back. And this perhaps, I thought, coming in from the window, is one of them. For certainly when I saw the couple get into the taxicab the mind felt as if, after being divided, it had come together again in a natural fusion. The obvious reason would be that it is natural for the sexes to co-operate. One has a profound, if irrational, instinct in favour of the theory that the union of man and woman makes for the greatest satisfaction, the most complete happiness. But the sight of the two people getting into the taxi and the satisfaction it gave me made me also ask whether there are two sexes in the mind corresponding to the two sexes in the body, and whether they also require to be united in order to get complete satisfaction and happiness? And I went on amateurishly to sketch a plan of the soul so that in each of us two powers preside, one male, one female; and in the man's brain the man predominates over the woman, and in the woman's brain the woman predominates over the man. The normal and comfortable state of being is that when the two live in harmony together, spiritually co-operating. If one is a man, still the woman part of his brain must have effect; and a woman also must have intercourse with the man in her. Coleridge perhaps meant this when he said that a great mind is androgynous. It is when this fusion takes place that the mind is fully fertilised and uses all its faculties. Perhaps a mind that is purely masculine cannot create, any more than a mind that is purely feminine, I thought. But it would be well to test what one meant by man-womanly, and conversely by woman-manly, by pausing and looking at a book or two.

Coleridge certainly did not mean, when he said that a great mind is androgynous, that it is a mind that has any special sympathy with women; a mind that takes up their cause or devotes itself to their interpretation. Perhaps the androgynous mind is less apt to make these distinctions than the single-sexed mind. He meant, perhaps, that the androgynous mind is resonant and porous; that it transmits emotion without impediment; that it is naturally creative, incandescent and undivided. In fact one goes back to Shakespeare's mind as the type of the androgynous, of the man-womanly mind, though it would be impossible to say what Shakespeare thought of women. And if it be true that it is one of the tokens of the fully developed mind that it does not think specially or separately of sex, how much harder it is to attain that condition now than ever before. Here I came to the books by living writers, and there paused and wondered if this fact were not at the root of something that had long puzzled me. No age can ever have been as stridently sex-conscious as our own; those innumerable books by men about women in the British Museum are a proof of it. The Suffrage campaign was no doubt to blame. It must have roused in men an extraordinary desire for self-assertion; it must have made them lay an emphasis upon their own sex and its characteristics which they would not have troubled to think about had they not been challenged. And when one is challenged, even by a few women in black bonnets, one retaliates, if one has never been challenged before, rather excessively. That perhaps accounts for some of the character-istics that I remember to have found here, I thought, taking down a new novel by Mr A, who is in the prime of life and very well thought of, apparently, by the reviewers. I opened it. Indeed, it was delightful to read a man's writing again. It was so direct, so straightforward after the writing of women. It indicated such freedom of mind, such liberty of person, such confidence in himself. One had a sense of physical well-being in the presence of this well-nourished, well-educated, free mind, which had never been thwarted or opposed, but had had full liberty from birth to stretch itself in whatever way it liked. All this was admirable. But after reading a chapter or two a shadow seemed to lie across the page. It was a straight dark bar, a shadow shaped something like the letter 'I'. One began dodging this way and that to catch a glimpse of the landscape behind it. Whether that was indeed a tree or a woman walking I was not quite sure. Back one was always hailed to the letter 'I'. One began to be tired of 'I'. Not but what this 'I' was a most respectable 'I'; honest and logical; as hard as a nut, and polished for centuries by good teaching and good feeding. I respect and admire that 'I' from the bottom of my heart. But – here I turned a page or two, looking for something or other – the worst of it is that in the shadow of the letter 'I' all is shapeless as mist. Is that a tree? No, it is a woman. But . . . she has not a bone in her body, I thought, watching Phoebe, for that was her name, coming across the beach. Then Alan got up and the shadow of Alan at once obliterated Phoebe. For Alan had views and Phoebe was quenched in the flood of his views. And then Alan, I thought, has passions; and here I turned page after page very fast, feeling that the crisis was approaching, and so it was. It took place on the beach under the sun. It was done very openly. It was done very vigorously. Nothing could have been more indecent. But . . . I had said 'but' too often. One cannot go on saying 'but'. One must finish the sentence somehow, I rebuked myself. Shall I finish it, 'But – I am bored!' But why was I bored? Partly because of the dominance of the letter 'I' and the aridity, which, like the giant beech tree, it casts within its shade. Nothing will grow there. And partly for some more obscure reason. There seemed to be some obstacle, some impediment in Mr A's mind which blocked the fountain of creative energy and shored it within narrow limits. And remembering the lunch party at Oxbridge, and the cigarette ash and the Manx cat and Tennyson and Christina Rossetti all in a bunch, it seemed possible that the impediment lay there. As he no longer hums under his breath, 'There has fallen a splendid tear from the passion-flower at the gate', when Phoebe crosses the beach, and she no longer replies, 'My heart is like a singing bird whose nest is in a water'd shoot', when Alan approaches what can he do? Being honest as the day and logical as the sun, there is only one thing he can do. And that he does, to do him justice, over and over (I said turning the pages) and over again. And that, I added, aware of the awful nature of the confession, seems somehow dull. Shakespeare's indecency uproots a thousand other things in one's mind, and is far from being dull. But Shakespeare does it for pleasure; Mr A, as the nurses say, does it on purpose. He does it in protest. He is protesting against the equality of the other sex by asserting his own superiority. He is therefore impeded and inhibited and self-conscious as Shakespeare might have been if he too had known Miss Clough and Miss Davies. Doubtless Elizabethan literature would have been very different from what it is if the women's movement had begun in the sixteenth century and not in the nineteenth.

What, then, it amounts to, if this theory of the two sides of the mind holds good, is that virility has now become self-conscious – men, that is to say, are now writing only with the male side of their brains. It is a mistake for a woman to read them, for she will inevitably look for something that she will not find. It is the power of suggestion that one most misses, I thought, taking Mr B the critic in my hand and reading, very carefully and very dutifully, his remarks upon the art of poetry. Very able they were, acute and full of learning; but the trouble was that his feelings no longer communicated; his mind seemed separated into different chambers; not a sound carried from one to the other. Thus, when one takes a sentence of Mr B into the mind it falls plump to the ground – dead; but when one takes a sentence of Coleridge into the mind, it explodes and gives birth to all kinds of other ideas, and that is the only sort of writing of which one can say that it has the secret of perpetual life.

But whatever the reason may be, it is a fact that one must deplore. For it means – here I had come to rows of books by Mr Galsworthy and Mr Kipling – that some of the finest works of our greatest living writers fall upon deaf ears. Do what she will a woman cannot find in them that fountain of perpetual life which the critics assure her is there. It is not only that they celebrate male virtues, enforce male values and describe the world of men; it is that the emotion with which these books are permeated is to a woman incomprehensible. It is coming, it is gathering, it is about to burst on one's head, one begins saying long before the end. That picture will fall on old Jolyon's head; he will die of the shock; the old clerk will speak over him two or three obituary words; and all the swans on the Thames will simultaneously burst out singing. But one will rush away before that happens and hide in the gooseberry bushes, for the emotion which is so deep, so subtle, so symbolical to a man moves a woman to wonder. So with Mr Kipling's officers who turn their backs; and his Sowers who sow the Seed; and his Men who are alone with their Work; and the Flag – one blushes at all these capital letters as if one had been caught eavesdropping at some purely masculine orgy. The fact is that neither Mr Galsworthy nor Mr Kipling has a spark of the woman in him. Thus all their qualities seem to a woman, if one may generalise, crude and immature. They lack suggestive power. And when a book lacks suggestive power, however hard it hits the surface of the mind it cannot penetrate within.

And in that restless mood in which one takes books out and puts them back again without looking at them I began to envisage an age to come of pure, of self-assertive virility, such as the letters of professors (take Sir Walter Raleigh's letters, for instance) seem to forebode, and the rulers of Italy have already brought into being. For one can hardly fail to be impressed in Rome by the sense of unmitigated masculinity; and whatever the value of unmitigated masculinity upon the state, one may question the effect of it upon the art of poetry. At any rate, according to the newspapers, there is a certain anxiety about fiction in Italy. There has been a meeting of academicians whose object it is 'to develop the Italian novel'. 'Men famous by birth, or in finance, industry or the Fascist corporations' came together the other day and discussed the matter, and a telegram was sent to the Duce expressing the hope 'that the Fascist era would soon give birth to a poet worthy of it'. We may all join in that pious hope, but it is doubtful whether poetry can come out of an incubator. Poetry ought to have a mother as well as a father. The Fascist poem, one may fear, will be a horrid little abortion such as one sees in a glass jar in the museum of some county town. Such monsters never live long, it is said; one has never seen a prodigy of that sort cropping grass in a field. Two heads on one body do not make for length of life.

However, the blame for all this, if one is anxious to lay blame, rests no more upon one sex than upon the other. All seducers and reformers are responsible: Lady Bessborough when she lied to Lord Granville; Miss Davies when she told the truth to Mr Greg. All who have brought about a state of sex-consciousness are to blame, and it is they who drive me, when I want to stretch my faculties on a book, to seek it in that happy age, before Miss Davies and Miss Clough were born, when the writer used both sides of his mind equally. One must turn back to Shakespeare then, for Shakespeare was androgynous; and so were Keats and Sterne and Cowper and Lamb and Coleridge. Shelley perhaps was sexless. Milton and Ben Jonson had a dash too much of the male in them. So had Wordsworth and Tolstoy. In our time Proust was wholly androgynous, if not perhaps a little too much of a woman. But that failing is too rare for one to complain of it, since without some mixture of the kind the intellect seems to predominate and the other faculties of the mind harden and become barren. However, I consoled myself with the reflection that this is perhaps a passing phase; much of what I have said in obedience to my promise to give you the course of my thoughts will seem out of date; much of what flames in my eyes will seem dubious to you who have not yet come of age.

Even so, the very first sentence that I would write here, I said, crossing over to the writing-table and taking up the page headed Women and Fiction, is that it is fatal for anyone who writes to think of their sex. It is fatal to be a man or woman pure and simple; one must be woman-manly or man-womanly. It is fatal for a woman to lay the least stress on any grievance; to plead even with justice any cause; in any way to speak consciously as a woman. And fatal is no figure of speech, for anything written with that conscious bias is doomed to death. It ceases to be fertilised. Brilliant and effective, powerful and masterly, as it may appear for a day or two, it must wither at nightfall; it cannot grow in the minds of others. Some collaboration has to take place in the mind between the woman and the man before the art of creation can be accomplished. Some marriage of opposites has to be consummated. The whole of the mind must lie wide open if we are to get the sense that the writer is communicating his experience with perfect fullness. There must be freedom and there must be peace. Not a wheel must grate, not a light glimmer. The curtains must be close drawn. The writer, I thought, once his experience is over, must lie back and let his mind celebrate its nuptials in darkness. He must not look or question what is being done. Rather, he must pluck the petals from a rose or watch the swans float calmly down the river. And I saw again the current which took the boat and the undergraduate and the dead leaves; and the taxi took the man and the woman, I thought, seeing them come together across the street, and the current swept them away, I thought, hearing far off the roar of London's traffic, into that tremendous stream.

Here, then, Mary Beton ceases to speak. She has told you how she reached the conclusion – the prosaic conclusion – that it is necessary to have five hundred a year and a room with a lock on the door if you are to write fiction or poetry. She has tried to lay bare the thoughts and impressions that led her to think this. She has asked you to follow her flying into the arms of a beadle, lunching here, dining there, drawing pictures in the British Museum, taking books from the shelf, looking out of the window. While she has been doing all these things, you no doubt have been observing her failings and foibles and deciding what effect they have had on her opinions. You have been contradicting her and making whatever additions and deductions seem good to you. That is all as it should be, for in a question like this truth is only to be had by laying together many varieties of error. And I will end now in my own person by anticipating two criticisms, so obvious that you can hardly fail to make them.

No opinion has been expressed, you may say, upon the comparative merits of the sexes even as writers. That was done purposely, because, even if the time had come for such a valuation – and it is far more important at the moment to know how much money women have and how many rooms than to theorise about their capacities – even if the time had come I do not believe that gifts, whether of mind or character, can be weighed like sugar and butter, not even in Cambridge, where they are so adept at putting people into classes and fixing caps on their heads and letters after their names. I do not believe that even the Table of Precedency which you will find in Whitaker's *Almanack* represents a final order of values, or that there is any sound reason to suppose that a Commander of the Bath will ultimately walk in to dinner behind a Master in Lunacy. All this pitting of sex against sex, of quality against quality; all this claiming of superiority and imputing of inferiority, belong to the private-school stage of human existence where there are 'sides', and it is necessary for one side to beat another side, and of the utmost importance to walk up to a platform and receive from the hands of the headmaster himself a highly ornamental pot. As people mature they cease to believe in sides or in headmasters or in highly ornamental pots. At any rate, where books are concerned, it is notoriously difficult to fix labels of merit in such a way that they do not come off. Are not reviews of current literature a perpetual illustration of the difficulty of judgement? 'This great book', 'this worthless book', the same book is called by both names. Praise and blame alike mean nothing. No, delightful as the pastime of measuring may be, it is the most futile of all occupations, and to submit to the decrees of the measurers the most servile of attitudes. So long as you write what you wish to write, that is all that matters; and whether it matters for ages or only for hours, nobody can say. But to sacrifice a hair of the head of your vision, a shade of its colour, in deference to some headmaster with a silver pot in his hand or to some professor with a measuring-rod up his sleeve, is the most abject treachery, and the sacrifice of wealth and chastity which used to be said to be the greatest of human disasters, a mere flea bite in comparison.

Next I think that you may object that in all this I have made too much of the importance of material things. Even allowing a generous margin for symbolism, that five hundred a year stands for the power to contemplate, that a lock on the door means the power to think for oneself, still you may say that the mind should rise above such things; and that great poets have often been poor men. Let me then quote to you the words of your own Professor of Literature, who knows better than I do what goes to the making of a poet. Sir Arthur Quiller-Couch writes:

> What are the great poetical names of the last hundred years or so? Coleridge, Wordsworth, Byron, Shelley, Landor, Keats, Tennyson, Browning, Arnold, Morris, Rossetti, Swinburne – we may stop there. Of these, all but Keats, Browning, Rossetti were University men, and of these three, Keats, who died young, cut off in his prime, was the only one not fairly well to do. It may seem a brutal thing to say, and it is a sad thing to say: but, as a matter of hard fact, the theory that poetical genius bloweth where it listeth, and equally in poor and rich, holds little truth. As a matter of hard fact, nine out of those twelve were University men: which means that somehow or other they procured the means to get the best education England can give. As a matter of hard fact, of the remaining three you know that Browning was well to do, and I challenge you that, if he had not been well to do, he would no more have attained to write *Saul* or *The Ring and the Book* than Ruskin would have attained to writing *Modern Painters* if his father had not dealt prosperously in business. Rossetti had a small private income; and, moreover, he painted. There remains but Keats; whom Atropos slew young, as she slew John Clare in a madhouse, and James Thomson by the laudanum he took to drug disappointment. These are dreadful facts, but let us face them. It is – however dishonouring to us as a nation – certain that, by some fault in our commonwealth, the poor poet has not in these days, nor has had for two hundred years, a dog's chance. Believe me – and I have spent a great part of ten years in watching some three hundred and twenty elementary schools – we may prate of democracy, but actually, a poor child in England has little more hope than had the son of an Athenian slave to be emancipated into that intellectual freedom of which great writings are born.*

Nobody could put the point more plainly. 'The poor poet has not in these

---

* *The Art of Writing* by Sir Arthur Quiller-Couch

days, nor has had for two hundred years, a dog's chance . . . a poor child in England has little more hope than had the son of an Athenian slave to be emancipated into that intellectual freedom of which great writings are born.' That is it. Intellectual freedom depends upon material things. Poetry depends upon intellectual freedom. And women have always been poor, not for two hundred years merely, but from the beginning of time. Women have had less intellectual freedom than the sons of Athenian slaves. Women, then, have not had a dog's chance of writing poetry. That is why I have laid so much stress on money and a room of one's own. However, thanks to the toils of those obscure women in the past, of whom I wish we knew more, thanks, curiously enough to two wars, the Crimean which let Florence Nightingale out of her drawing-room, and the European War which opened the doors to the average woman some sixty years later, these evils are in the way to be bettered. Otherwise you would not be here tonight, and your chance of earning five hundred pounds a year, precarious as I am afraid that it still is, would be minute in the extreme.

Still, you may object, why do you attach so much importance to this writing of books by women when, according to you, it requires so much effort, leads perhaps to the murder of one's aunts, will make one almost certainly late for luncheon, and may bring one into very grave disputes with certain very good fellows? My motives, let me admit, are partly selfish. Like most uneducated Englishwomen, I like reading – I like reading books in the bulk. Lately my diet has become a trifle monotonous: history is too much about wars; biography too much about great men; poetry has shown, I think, a tendency to sterility; and fiction – but I have sufficiently exposed my disabilities as a critic of modern fiction and will say no more about it. Therefore I would ask you to write all kinds of books, hesitating at no subject however trivial or however vast. By hook or by crook, I hope that you will possess yourselves of money enough to travel and to idle, to contemplate the future or the past of the world, to dream over books and loiter at street corners and let the line of thought dip deep into the stream. For I am by no means confining you to fiction. If you would please me – and there are thousands like me – you would write books of travel and adventure, and research and scholarship, and history and biography, and criticism and philosophy and science. By so doing you will certainly profit the art of fiction. For books have a way of influencing each other. Fiction will be much the better for standing cheek by jowl with poetry and philosophy. Moreover, if you consider any great figure of the past, like Sappho, like the Lady Murasaki, like Emily Brontë, you will find that she is an inheritor as well as an originator, and has come into existence because women have come to have the habit of writing naturally; so that even as a prelude to poetry such activity on your part would be invaluable.

But when I look back through these notes and criticise my own train of thought as I made them, I find that my motives were not altogether selfish.

There runs through these comments and discursions the conviction – or is it the instinct? – that good books are desirable and that good writers, even if they show every variety of human depravity, are still good human beings. Thus when I ask you to write more books I am urging you to do what will be for your good and for the good of the world at large. How to justify this instinct or belief I do not know, for philosophic words, if one has not been educated at a university, are apt to play one false. What is meant by 'reality'? It would seem to be something very erratic, very undependable – now to be found in a dusty road, now in a scrap of newspaper in the street, now a daffodil in the sun. It lights up a group in a room and stamps some casual saying. It overwhelms one walking home beneath the stars and makes the silent world more real than the world of speech – and then there it is again in an omnibus in the uproar of Piccadilly. Sometimes, too, it seems to dwell in shapes too far away for us to discern what their nature is. But whatever it touches, it fixes and makes permanent. That is what remains over when the skin of the day has been cast into the hedge; that is what is left of past time and of our loves and hates. Now the writer, as I think, has the chance to live more than other people in the presence of this reality. It is his business to find it and collect it and communicate it to the rest of us. So at least I infer from reading *Lear* or *Emma* or *La Recherché du Temps Perdu*. For the reading of these books seems to perform a curious couching operation on the senses; one sees more intensely afterwards; the world seems bared of its covering and given an intenser life. Those are the enviable people who live at enmity with unreality; and those are the pitiable who are knocked on the head by the thing done without knowing or caring. So that when I ask you to earn money and have a room of your own, I am asking you to live in the presence of reality, an invigorating life, it would appear, whether one can impart it or not.

Here I would stop, but the pressure of convention decrees that every speech must end with a peroration. And a peroration addressed to women should have something, you will agree, particularly exalting and ennobling about it. I should implore you to remember your responsibilities, to be higher, more spiritual; I should remind you how much depends upon you, and what an influence you can exert upon the future. But those exhortations can safely, I think, be left to the other sex, who will put them, and indeed have put them, with far greater eloquence than I can compass. When I rummage in my own mind I find no noble sentiments about being companions and equals and influencing the world to higher ends. I find myself saying briefly and prosaically that it is much more important to be oneself than anything else. Do not dream of influencing other people, I would say, if I knew how to make it sound exalted. Think of things in themselves.

And again I am reminded by dipping into newspapers and novels and biographies that when a woman speaks to women she should have something

SELECTED WORKS OF VIRGINIA WOOLF

very unpleasant up her sleeve. Women are hard on women. Women dislike women. Women – but are you not sick to death of the word? I can assure you that I am. Let us agree, then, that a paper read by a woman to women should end with something particularly disagreeable.

But how does it go? What can I think of? The truth is, I often like women. I like their unconventionality. I like their completeness. I like their anonymity. I like – but I must not run on in this way. That cupboard there – you say it holds clean table-napkins only; but what if Sir Archibald Bodkin were concealed among them? Let me then adopt a sterner tone. Have I, in the preceding words, conveyed to you sufficiently the warnings and reprobation of mankind? I have told you the very low opinion in which you were held by Mr Oscar Browning. I have indicated what Napoleon once thought of you and what Mussolini thinks now. Then, in case any of you aspire to fiction, I have copied out for your benefit the advice of the critic about courageously acknowledging the limitations of your sex. I have referred to Professor X and given prominence to his statement that women are intellectually, morally and physically inferior to men. I have handed on all that has come my way without going in search of it, and here is a final warning – from Mr John Langdon Davies.* Mr John Langdon Davies warns women 'that when children cease to be altogether desirable, women cease to be altogether necessary'. I hope you will make a note of it.

How can I further encourage you to go about the business of life? Young women, I would say, and please attend, for the peroration is beginning, you are, in my opinion, disgracefully ignorant. You have never made a discovery of any sort of importance. You have never shaken an empire or led an army into battle. The plays of Shakespeare are not by you, and you have never introduced a barbarous race to the blessings of civilisation. What is your excuse? It is all very well for you to say, pointing to the streets and squares and forests of the globe swarming with black and white and coffee-coloured inhabitants, all busily engaged in traffic and enterprise and love making, we have had other work on our hands. Without our doing, those seas would be unsailed and those fertile lands a desert. We have borne and bred and washed and taught, perhaps to the age of six or seven years, the one thousand six hundred and twenty-three million human beings who are, according to statistics, at present in existence, and that, allowing that some had help, takes time.

There is truth in what you say – I will not deny it. But at the same time may I remind you that there have been at least two colleges for women in existence in England since the year 1866; that after the year 1880 a married woman was allowed by law to possess her own property; and that in 1919 – which is a whole nine years ago she was given a vote? May I also remind you that most of the professions have been open to you for close on ten years now? When you reflect upon these immense privileges and the length of

* *A Short History of Women* by John Langdon Davies

time during which they have been enjoyed, and the fact that there must be at this moment some two thousand women capable of earning over five hundred a year in one way or another, you will agree that the excuse of lack of opportunity, training, encouragement, leisure and money no longer holds good. Moreover, the economists are telling us that Mrs Seton has had too many children. You must, of course, go on bearing children, but, so they say, in twos and threes, not in tens and twelves.

Thus, with some time on your hands and with some book learning in your brains – you have had enough of the other kind, and are sent to college partly, I suspect, to be uneducated – surely you should embark upon another stage of your very long, very laborious and highly obscure career. A thousand pens are ready to suggest what you should do and what effect you will have. My own suggestion is a little fantastic, I admit; I prefer, therefore, to put it in the form of fiction.

I told you in the course of this paper that Shakespeare had a sister; but do not look for her in Sir Sidney Lee's life of the poet. She died young – alas, she never wrote a word. She lies buried where the omnibuses now stop, opposite the Elephant and Castle. Now my belief is that this poet who never wrote a word and was buried at the crossroads still lives. She lives in you and in me, and in many other women who are not here tonight, for they are washing up the dishes and putting the children to bed. But she lives; for great poets do not die; they are continuing presences; they need only the opportunity to walk among us in the flesh. This opportunity, as I think, it is now coming within your power to give her. For my belief is that if we live another century or so – I am talking of the common life which is the real life and not of the little separate lives which we live as individuals – and have five hundred a year each of us and rooms of our own; if we have the habit of freedom and the courage to write exactly what we think; if we escape a little from the common sitting-room and see human beings not always in their relation to each other but in relation to reality; and the sky, too, and the trees or whatever it may be in themselves; if we look past Milton's bogey, for no human being should shut out the view; if we face the fact, for it is a fact, that there is no arm to cling to, but that we go alone and that our relation is to the world of reality and not only to the world of men and women, then the opportunity will come and the dead poet who was Shakespeare's sister will put on the body which she has so often laid down. Drawing her life from the lives of the unknown who were her forerunners, as her brother did before her, she will be born. As for her coming without that preparation, without that effort on our part, without that determination that when she is born again she shall find it possible to live and write her poetry, that we cannot expect, for that would be impossible. But I maintain that she would come if we worked for her, and that so to work, even in poverty and obscurity, is worth while.

THE WAVES

The Waves

A novel by
VIRGINIA WOOLF
first published in 1931

The sun had not yet risen. The sea was indistinguishable from the sky, except that the sea was slightly creased as if a cloth had wrinkles in it. Gradually as the sky whitened a dark line lay on the horizon dividing the sea from the sky and the grey cloth became barred with thick strokes moving, one after another, beneath the surface, following each other, pursuing each other, perpetually.

As they neared the shore each bar rose, heaped itself, broke and swept a thin veil of white water across the sand. The wave paused, and then drew out again, sighing like a sleeper whose breath comes and goes unconsciously. Gradually the dark bar on the horizon became clear as if the sediment in an old wine-bottle had sunk and left the glass green. Behind it, too, the sky cleared as if the white sediment there had sunk, or as if the arm of a woman couched beneath the horizon had raised a lamp and flat bars of white, green and yellow spread across the sky like the blades of a fan. Then she raised her lamp higher and the air seemed to become fibrous and to tear away from the green surface flickering and flaming in red and yellow fibres like the smoky fire that roars from a bonfire. Gradually the fibres of the burning bonfire were fused into one haze, one incandescence which lifted the weight of the woollen grey sky on top of it and turned it to a million atoms of soft blue. The surface of the sea slowly became transparent and lay rippling and sparkling until the dark stripes were almost rubbed out. Slowly the arm that held the lamp raised it higher and then higher until a broad flame became visible; an arc of fire burnt on the rim of the horizon, and all round it the sea blazed gold.

The light struck upon the trees in the garden, making one leaf transparent and then another. One bird chirped high up; there was a pause; another chirped lower down. The sun sharpened the walls of the house, and rested like the tip of a fan upon a white blind and made a blue fingerprint of shadow under the leaf by the bedroom window. The blind stirred slightly, but all within was dim and unsubstantial. The birds sang their blank melody outside.

'I see a ring,' said Bernard, 'hanging above me. It quivers and hangs in a loop of light.'

'I see a slab of pale yellow,' said Susan, 'spreading away until it meets a purple stripe.'

'I hear a sound,' said Rhoda, 'cheep, chirp; cheep, chirp; going up and down.'

'I see a globe,' said Neville, 'hanging down in a drop against the enormous flanks of some hill.'

'I see a crimson tassel,' said Jinny, 'twisted with gold threads.'

'I hear something stamping,' said Louis. 'A great beast's foot is chained. It stamps, and stamps, and stamps.'

'Look at the spider's web on the corner of the balcony,' said Bernard. 'It has beads of water on it, drops of white light.'

'The leaves are gathered round the window like pointed ears,' said Susan.

'A shadow falls on the path,' said Louis, 'like an elbow bent.'

'Islands of light are swimming on the grass,' said Rhoda. 'They have fallen through the trees.'

'The birds' eyes are bright in the tunnels between the leaves,' said Neville.

'The stalks are covered with harsh, short hairs,' said Jinny, 'and drops of water have stuck to them.'

'A caterpillar is curled in a green ring,' said Susan, 'notched with blunt feet.'

'The grey-shelled snail draws across the path and flattens the blades behind him,' said Rhoda.

'And burning lights from the window-panes flash in and out on the grasses,' said Louis.

'Stones are cold to my feet,' said Neville. 'I feel each one, round or pointed, separately.'

'The back of my hand burns,' said Jinny, 'but the palm is clammy and damp with dew.'

'Now the cock crows like a spurt of hard, red water in the white tide,' said Bernard.

'Birds are singing up and down and in and out all round us,' said Susan.

'The beast stamps; the elephant with its foot chained; the great brute on the beach stamps,' said Louis.

'Look at the house,' said Jinny, 'with all its windows white with blinds.'

'Cold water begins to run from the scullery tap,' said Rhoda, 'over the mackerel in the bowl.'

'The walls are cracked with gold cracks,' said Bernard, 'and there are blue, finger-shaped shadows of leaves beneath the windows.'

'Now Mrs Constable pulls up her thick black stockings,' said Susan.

'When the smoke rises, sleep curls off the roof like a mist,' said Louis.

'The birds sang in chorus first,' said Rhoda. 'Now the scullery door is unbarred. Off they fly. Off they fly like a fling of seed. But one sings by the bedroom window alone.'

'Bubbles form on the floor of the saucepan,' said Jinny. 'Then they rise, quicker and quicker, in a silver chain to the top.'

'Now Biddy scrapes the fish-scales with a jagged knife on to a wooden board,' said Neville.

'The dining-room window is dark blue now,' said Bernard, 'and the air ripples above the chimneys.'

'A swallow is perched on the lightning-conductor,' said Susan. 'And Biddy has smacked down the bucket on the kitchen flags.'

'That is the first stroke of the church bell,' said Louis. 'Then the others follow: one, two; one, two; one, two.'

'Look at the tablecloth, flying white along the table,' said Rhoda. 'Now there are rounds of white china, and silver streaks beside each plate.'

'Suddenly a bee booms in my ear,' said Neville. 'It is here; it is past.'

'I burn, I shiver,' said Jinny, 'out of this sun, into this shadow.'

'Now they have all gone,' said Louis. 'I am alone. They have gone into the house for breakfast, and I am left standing by the wall among the flowers. It is very early, before lessons. Flower after flower is specked on the depths of green. The petals are harlequins. Stalks rise from the black hollows beneath. The flowers swim like fish made of light upon the dark, green waters. I hold a stalk in my hand. I am the stalk. My roots go down to the depths of the world, through earth dry with brick, and damp earth, through veins of lead and silver. I am all fibre. All tremors shake me, and the weight of the earth is pressed to my ribs. Up here my eyes are green leaves, unseeing. I am a boy in grey flannels with a belt fastened by a brass snake up here. Down there my eyes are the lidless eyes of a stone figure in a desert by the Nile. I see women passing with red pitchers to the river; I see camels swaying and men in turbans. I hear tramplings, tremblings, stirrings round me.

'Up here Bernard, Neville, Jinny and Susan (but not Rhoda) skim the flowerbeds with their nets. They skim the butterflies from the nodding tops of the flowers. They brush the surface of the world. Their nets are full of fluttering wings. "Louis! Louis! Louis!" they shout. But they cannot see me. I am on the other side of the hedge. There are only little eyeholes among the leaves. O Lord, let them pass. Lord, let them lay their butterflies on a pocket-handkerchief on the gravel. Let them count out their tortoiseshells, their red admirals and cabbage whites. But let me be unseen. I am green as a yew tree in the shade of the hedge. My hair is made of leaves. I am rooted to the middle of the earth. My body is a stalk. I press the stalk. A drop oozes from the hole at the mouth and slowly, thickly, grows larger and larger. Now something pink passes the eyehole. Now an eye-beam is slid through the chink. Its beam strikes me. I am a boy in a grey flannel suit. She has found me. I am struck on the nape of the neck. She has kissed me. All is shattered.'

'I was running,' said Jinny, 'after breakfast. I saw leaves moving in a hole in the hedge. I thought, "That is a bird on its nest." I parted them and looked; but there was no bird on a nest. The leaves went on moving. I was frightened. I ran past Susan, past Rhoda, and Neville and Bernard in the tool-house talking. I cried as I ran, faster and faster. What moved the leaves? What moves my heart, my legs? And I dashed in here, seeing you green as a bush, like a branch, very still, Louis, with your eyes fixed. "Is he dead?" I thought, and kissed you, with my heart jumping under my pink frock like the leaves, which go on moving, though there is nothing to move them. Now I smell geraniums; I smell earth mould. I dance. I ripple. I am thrown over you like a net of light. I lie quivering flung over you.'

'Through the chink in the hedge,' said Susan, 'I saw her kiss him. I raised my head from my flowerpot and looked through a chink in the hedge. I saw her kiss him. I saw them, Jinny and Louis, kissing. Now I will wrap my agony inside my pocket-handkerchief. It shall be screwed tight into a ball. I will go to the beech wood alone, before lessons. I will not sit at a table, doing sums. I will not sit next Jinny and next Louis. I will take my anguish and lay it upon the roots under the beech trees. I will examine it and take it between my fingers. They will not find me. I shall eat nuts and peer for eggs through the brambles and my hair will be matted and I shall sleep under hedges and drink water from ditches and die there.'

'Susan has passed us,' said Bernard. 'She has passed the tool-house door with her handkerchief screwed into a ball. She was not crying, but her eyes, which are so beautiful, were narrow as cats' eyes before they spring. I shall follow her, Neville. I shall go gently behind her, to be at hand, with my curiosity, to comfort her when she bursts out in a rage and thinks, "I am alone."

'Now she walks across the field with a swing, nonchalantly, to deceive us. Then she comes to the dip; she thinks she is unseen; she begins to run with her fists clenched in front of her. Her nails meet in the ball of her pocket-handkerchief. She is making for the beech woods out of the light. She spreads her arms as she comes to them and takes to the shade like a swimmer. But she is blind after the light and trips and flings herself down on the roots under the trees, where the light seems to pant in and out, in and out. The branches heave up and down. There is agitation and trouble here. There is gloom. The light is fitful. There is anguish here. The roots make a skeleton on the ground, with dead leaves heaped in the angles. Susan has spread her anguish out. Her pocket-handkerchief is laid on the roots of the beech trees and she sobs, sitting crumpled where she has fallen.'

'I saw her kiss him,' said Susan. 'I looked between the leaves and saw her. She danced in flecked with diamonds light as dust. And I am squat, Bernard,

I am short. I have eyes that look close to the ground and see insects in the grass. The yellow warmth in my side turned to stone when I saw Jinny kiss Louis. I shall eat grass and die in a ditch in the brown water where dead leaves have rotted.'

'I saw you go,' said Bernard. 'As you passed the door of the tool-house I heard you cry, "I am unhappy." I put down my knife. I was making boats out of firewood with Neville. And my hair is untidy, because when Mrs Constable told me to brush it there was a fly in a web, and I asked, "Shall I free the fly? Shall I let the fly be eaten?" So I am late always. My hair is unbrushed and these chips of wood stick in it. When I heard you cry I followed you, and saw you put down your handkerchief, screwed up, with its rage, with its hate, knotted in it. But soon that will cease. Our bodies are close now. You hear me breathe. You see the beetle too carrying off a leaf on its back. It runs this way, then that way, so that even your desire while you watch the beetle, to possess one single thing (it is Louis now), must waver, like the light in and out of the beech leaves; and then words, moving darkly in the depths of your mind, will break up this knot of hardness screwed in your pocket-handkerchief.'

'I love,' said Susan, 'and I hate. I desire one thing only. My eyes are hard. Jinny's eyes break into a thousand lights. Rhoda's are like those pale flowers to which moths come in the evening. Yours grow full and brim and never break. But I am already set on my pursuit. I see insects in the grass. Though my mother still knits white socks for me and hems pinafores and I am a child, I love and I hate.'

'But when we sit together, close,' said Bernard, 'we melt into each other with phrases. We are edged with mist. We make an unsubstantial territory.'

'I see the beetle,' said Susan. 'It is black, I see; it is green, I see; I am tied down with single words. But you wander off; you slip away; you rise up higher, with words and words in phrases.'

'Now,' said Bernard, 'let us explore. There is the white house lying among the trees. It lies down there ever so far beneath us. We shall sink like swimmers just touching the ground with the tips of their toes. We shall sink through the green air of the leaves, Susan. We sink as we run. The waves close over us, the beech leaves meet above our heads. There is the stable clock with its gilt hands shining. Those are the flats and heights of the roofs of the great house. There is the stable-boy clattering in the yard in rubber boots. That is Elvedon.

'Now we have fallen through the tree-tops to the earth. The air no longer rolls its long, unhappy, purple waves over us. We touch earth; we tread ground. That is the close-clipped hedge of the ladies' garden. There they walk at noon, with scissors, clipping roses. Now we are in the ringed wood with the wall round it. This is Elvedon. I have seen signposts at the cross-roads with one arm pointing "To Elvedon". No one has been there. The ferns smell very strong, and there are red funguses growing beneath them.

Now we wake the sleeping daws who have never seen a human form; now we tread on rotten oak apples, red with age and slippery. There is a ring of wall round this wood; nobody comes here. Listen! That is the flop of a giant toad in the undergrowth; that is the patter of some primeval fir-cone falling to rot among the ferns.

'Put your foot on this brick. Look over the wall. That is Elvedon. The lady sits between the two long windows, writing. The gardeners sweep the lawn with giant brooms. We are the first to come here. We are the discoverers of an unknown land. Do not stir; if the gardeners saw us they would shoot us. We should be nailed like stoats to the stable door. Look! Do not move. Grasp the ferns tight on the top of the wall.'

'I see the lady writing. I see the gardeners sweeping,' said Susan. 'If we died here, nobody would bury us.'

'Run!' said Bernard. 'Run! The gardener with the black beard has seen us! We shall be shot! We shall be shot like jays and pinned to the wall! We are in a hostile country. We must escape to the beech wood. We must hide under the trees. I turned a twig as we came. There is a secret path. Bend as low as you can. Follow without looking back. They will think we are foxes. Run!'

'Now we are safe. Now we can stand upright again. Now we can stretch our arms in this high canopy, in this vast wood. I hear nothing. That is only the murmur of the waves in the air. That is a wood-pigeon breaking cover in the tops of the beech trees. The pigeon beats the air; the pigeon beats the air with wooden wings.'

'Now you trail away,' said Susan, 'making phrases. Now you mount like an air-ball's string, higher and higher through the layers of the leaves, out of reach. Now you lag. Now you tug at my skirts, looking back, making phrases. You have escaped me. Here is the garden. Here is the hedge. Here is Rhoda on the path rocking petals to and fro in her brown basin.'

'All my ships are white,' said Rhoda. 'I do not want red petals of hollyhocks or geranium. I want white petals that float when I tip the basin up. I have a fleet now swimming from shore to shore. I will drop a twig in as a raft for a drowning sailor. I will drop a stone in and see bubbles rise from the depths of the sea. Neville has gone and Susan has gone; Jinny is in the kitchen garden picking currants with Louis perhaps. I have a short time alone, while Miss Hudson spreads our copybooks on the schoolroom table. I have a short space of freedom. I have picked all the fallen petals and made them swim. I have put raindrops in some. I will plant a lighthouse here, a head of Sweet Alice. And I will now rock the brown basin from side to side so that my ships may ride the waves. Some will founder. Some will dash themselves against the cliffs. One sails alone. That is my ship. It sails into icy caverns where the sea-bear barks and stalactites swing green chains. The waves rise; their crests curl; look at the lights on the mastheads. They have scattered, they have foundered, all except my ship, which mounts the wave and sweeps before the gale and reaches the islands where the parrots chatter and the creepers . . .'

'Where is Bernard?' said Neville. 'He has my knife. We were in the tool-shed making boats, and Susan came past the door. And Bernard dropped his boat and went after her taking my knife, the sharp one that cuts the keel. He is like a dangling wire, a broken bell-pull, always twangling. He is like the seaweed hung outside the window, damp now, now dry. He leaves me in the lurch; he follows Susan; and if Susan cries he will take my knife and tell her stories. The big blade is an emperor; the broken blade a Negro. I hate dangling things; I hate dampish things. I hate wandering and mixing things together. Now the bell rings and we shall be late. Now we must drop our toys. Now we must go in together. The copybooks are laid out side by side on the green baize table.'

'I will not conjugate the verb,' said Louis, 'until Bernard has said it. My father is a banker in Brisbane and I speak with an Australian accent. I will wait and copy Bernard. He is English. They are all English. Susan's father is a clergyman. Rhoda has no father. Bernard and Neville are the sons of gentlemen. Jinny lives with her grandmother in London. Now they suck their pens. Now they twist their copybooks, and looking sideways at Miss Hudson, count the purple buttons on her bodice. Bernard has a chip in his hair. Susan has a red look in her eyes. Both are flushed. But I am pale; I am neat, and my knickerbockers are drawn together by a belt with a brass snake. I know the lesson by heart. I know more than they will ever know. I know my cases and my genders; I could know everything in the world if I wished. But I do not wish to come to the top and say my lesson. My roots are threaded, like fibres in a flowerpot, round and round about the world. I do not wish to come to the top and live in the light of this great clock, yellow-faced, which ticks and ticks. Jinny and Susan, Bernard and Neville bind themselves into a thong with which to lash me. They laugh at my neatness, at my Australian accent. I will now try to imitate Bernard softly lisping Latin.'

'Those are white words,' said Susan, 'like stones one picks up by the seashore.'

'They flick their tails right and left as I speak them,' said Bernard. 'They wag their tails; they flick their tails; they move through the air in flocks, now this way, now that way, moving all together, now dividing, now coming together.'

'Those are yellow words, those are fiery words,' said Jinny. 'I should like a fiery dress, a yellow dress, a fulvous dress to wear in the evening.'

'Each tense,' said Neville, 'means differently. There is an order in this world; there are distinctions, there are differences in this world, upon whose verge I step. For this is only a beginning.'

'Now Miss Hudson,' said Rhoda, 'has shut the book. Now the terror is beginning. Now taking her lump of chalk she draws figures, six, seven, eight, and then a cross and then a line on the blackboard. What is the answer? The others look; they look with understanding. Louis writes; Susan writes; Neville writes; Jinny writes; even Bernard has now begun to write. But I cannot write. I see only figures. The others are handing in their answers, one by one. Now it is my turn. But I have no answer. The others are allowed to go. They slam the door. Miss Hudson goes. I am left alone to find an answer. The figures mean nothing now. Meaning has gone. The clock ticks. The two hands are convoys marching through a desert. The black bars on the clock face are green oases. The long hand has marched ahead to find water. The other painfully stumbles among hot stones in the desert. It will die in the desert. The kitchen door slams. Wild dogs bark far away. Look, the loop of the figure is beginning to fill with time; it holds the world in it. I begin to draw a figure and the world is looped in it, and I myself am outside the loop; which I now join – so – and seal up, and make entire. The world is entire, and I am outside of it, crying, "Oh save me, from being blown for ever outside the loop of time!" '

'There Rhoda sits staring at the blackboard,' said Louis, 'in the school-room, while we ramble off, picking here a bit of thyme, pinching here a leaf of southernwood, while Bernard tells a story. Her shoulder-blades meet across her back like the wings of a small butterfly. And as she stares at the chalk figures, her mind lodges in those white circles; it steps through those white loops into emptiness, alone. They have no meaning for her. She has no answer for them. She has no body as the others have. And I, who speak with an Australian accent, whose father is a banker in Brisbane, do not fear her as I fear the others.'

'Let us now crawl,' said Bernard, 'under the canopy of the currant leaves, and tell stories. Let us inhabit the underworld. Let us take possession of our secret territory, which is lit by pendant currants like candelabra, shining red on one side, black on the other. Here, Jinny, if we curl up close, we can sit under the canopy of the currant leaves and watch the censers swing. This is our universe. The others pass down the carriage-drive. The skirts of Miss Hudson and Miss Curry sweep by like candle extinguishers. Those are Susan's white socks. Those are Louis's neat sandshoes firmly printing the gravel. Here come warm gusts of decomposing leaves, of rotting vegetation. We are in a swamp now; in a malarial jungle. There is an elephant white with maggots, killed by an arrow shot dead in its eye. The bright eyes of hopping birds – eagles, vultures – are apparent. They take us for fallen trees. They pick at a worm – that is a hooded cobra – and leave it with a festering brown scar to be mauled by lions. This is our world, lit with crescents and stars of light; and great petals half transparent block the openings like purple windows. Everything is strange. Things are huge and very small. The stalks of flowers are thick as oak trees. Leaves are high as the domes of vast cathedrals. We are giants, lying here, who can make forests quiver.'

'This is here,' said Jinny, 'this is now. But soon we shall go. Soon Miss Curry will blow her whistle. We shall walk. We shall part. You will go to school. You will have masters wearing crosses with white ties. I shall have a mistress in a school on the East Coast who sits under a portrait of Queen Alexandra. That is where I am going, and Susan and Rhoda. This is only here: this is only now. Now we lie under the currant bushes and every time the breeze stirs we are mottled all over. My hand is like a snake's skin. My knees are pink floating islands. Your face is like an apple tree netted under.'

'The heat is going,' said Bernard, 'from the Jungle. The leaves flap black wings over us. Miss Curry has blown her whistle on the terrace. We must creep out from the awning of the currant leaves and stand upright. There are twigs in your hair, Jinny. There is a green caterpillar on your neck. We must form, two by two. Miss Curry is taking us for a brisk walk, while Miss Hudson sits at her desk settling her accounts.'

'It is dull,' said Jinny, 'walking along the high road with no windows to look at, with no bleared eyes of blue glass let into the pavement.'

'We must form into pairs,' said Susan, 'and walk in order, not shuffling our feet, not lagging, with Louis going first to lead us, because Louis is alert and not a woolgatherer.'

'Since I am supposed,' said Neville, 'to be too delicate to go with them, since I get so easily tired and then am sick, I will use this hour of solitude, this reprieve from conversation, to coast round the purlieus of the house and recover, if I can, by standing on the same stair halfway up the landing, what I felt when I heard about the dead man through the swing-door last night when cook was shoving in and out the dampers. He was found with his throat cut. The apple-tree leaves became fixed in the sky; the moon glared; I was unable to lift my foot up the stair. He was found in the gutter. His blood gurgled down the gutter. His jowl was white as a dead codfish. I shall call this stricture, this rigidity, "death among the apple trees" for ever. There were the floating, pale-grey clouds; and the immitigable tree; the implacable tree with its greaved silver bark. The ripple of my life was unavailing. I was unable to pass by. There was an obstacle. "I cannot surmount this unintelligible obstacle," I said. And the others passed on. But we are doomed, all of us, by the apple trees, by the immitigable tree which we cannot pass.

'Now the stricture and rigidity are over; and I will continue to make my survey of the purlieus of the house in the late afternoon, in the sunset, when the sun makes oleaginous spots on the linoleum, and a crack of light kneels on the wall, making the chair legs look broken.'

'I saw Florrie in the kitchen garden,' said Susan, 'as we came back from our walk, with the washing blown out round her, the pyjamas, the drawers, the nightgowns blown tight. And Ernest kissed her. He was in his green baize apron, cleaning silver; and his mouth was sucked like a purse in wrinkles and he seized her with the pyjamas blown out hard between them. He was blind as a bull, and she swooned in anguish, only little veins streaking her white cheeks red. Now though they pass plates of bread and butter and cups of milk at tea-time I see a crack in the earth and hot steam hisses up;

and the urn roars as Ernest roared, and I am blown out hard like the pyjamas, even while my teeth meet in the soft bread and butter, and I lap the sweet milk. I am not afraid of heat, nor of the frozen winter. Rhoda dreams, sucking a crust soaked in milk; Louis regards the wall opposite with snail-green eyes; Bernard moulds his bread into pellets and calls them "people". Neville with his clean and decisive ways has finished. He has rolled his napkin and slipped it through the silver ring. Jinny spins her fingers on the tablecloth, as if they were dancing in the sunshine, pirouetting. But I am not afraid of the heat or of the frozen winter.'

'Now,' said Louis, 'we all rise; we all stand up. Miss Curry spreads wide the black book on the harmonium. It is difficult not to weep as we sing, as we pray that God may keep us safe while we sleep, calling ourselves little children. When we are sad and trembling with apprehension it is sweet to sing together, leaning slightly, I towards Susan, Susan towards Bernard, clasping hands, afraid of much, I of my accent, Rhoda of figures; yet resolute to conquer.'

'We troop upstairs like ponies,' said Bernard, 'stamping, clattering one behind another to take our turns in the bathroom. We buffet, we tussle, we spring up and down on the hard white beds. My turn has come. I come now.

'Mrs Constable, girt in a bath-towel, takes her lemon-coloured sponge and soaks it in water; it turns chocolate-brown; it drips; and holding it high above me, shivering beneath her, she squeezes it. Water pours down the runnel of my spine. Bright arrows of sensation shoot on either side. I am covered with warm flesh. My dry crannies are wetted; my cold body is warmed; it is sluiced and gleaming. Water descends and sheets me like an eel. Now hot towels envelop me, and their roughness, as I rub my back, makes my blood purr. Rich and heavy sensations form on the roof of my mind; down showers the day – the woods; and Elvedon; Susan and the pigeon. Pouring down the walls of my mind, running together, the day falls copious, resplendent. Now I tie my pyjamas loosely round me, and lie under this thin sheet afloat in the shallow light which is like a film of water drawn over my eyes by a wave. I hear through it far off, far away, faint and far, the chorus beginning; wheels; dogs; men shouting; church bells; the chorus beginning.'

'As I fold up my frock and my chemise,' said Rhoda, 'so I put off my hopeless desire to be Susan, to be Jinny. But I will stretch my toes so that they touch the rail at the end of the bed; I will assure myself, touching the rail, of something hard. Now I cannot sink; cannot altogether fall through the thin sheet now. Now I spread my body on this frail mattress and hang suspended. I am above the earth now. I am no longer upright, to be knocked against and damaged. All is soft, and bending. Walls and cupboards whiten and bend their yellow squares on top of which a pale glass gleams. Out of me now my mind can pour. I can think of my armadas sailing on the high waves. I am relieved of hard contacts and collisions. I sail on alone under white cliffs. Oh, but I sink, I fall! That is the corner of the cupboard; that is the nursery looking-glass. But they stretch, they elongate. I sink down on the black plumes of sleep; its thick wings are pressed to my eyes. Travelling through darkness I see the stretched flowerbeds, and Mrs Constable runs from behind the corner of the pampas-grass to say my aunt has come to fetch me in a carriage. I mount; I escape; I rise on spring-heeled boots over the tree-tops. But I am now fallen into the carriage at the hall door, where she sits nodding yellow plumes with eyes hard like glazed marbles. Oh, to awake from dreaming! Look, there is the chest of drawers. Let me pull myself out of these waters. But they heap themselves on me; they sweep me between their great shoulders; I am turned; I am tumbled; I am stretched, among these long lights, these long waves, these endless paths, with people pursuing, pursuing.'

The sun rose higher. Blue waves, green waves swept a quick fan over the beach, circling the spike of sea-holly and leaving shallow pools of light here and there on the sand. A faint black rim was left behind them. The rocks which had been misty and soft hardened and were marked with red clefts.

Sharp stripes of shadow lay on the grass, and the dew dancing on the tips of the flowers and leaves made the garden like a mosaic of single sparks not yet formed into one whole. The birds, whose breasts were specked canary and rose, now sang a strain or two together, wildly, like skaters rollicking arm in arm, and were suddenly silent, breaking asunder.

The sun laid broader blades upon the house. The light touched something green in the window corner and made it a lump of emerald, a cave of pure green like stoneless fruit. It sharpened the edges of chairs and tables and stitched white tablecloths with fine gold wires. As the light increased a bud here and there split asunder and shook out flowers, green veined and quivering, as if the effort of opening had set them rocking, and pealing a faint carillon as they beat their frail clappers against their white walls. Everything became softly amorphous, as if the china of the plate flowed and the steel of the knife were liquid. Meanwhile the concussion of the waves breaking fell with muffled thuds, like logs falling, on the shore.

'Now,' said Bernard, 'the time has come. The day has come. The cab is at the door. My huge box bends George's bandy-legs even wider. The horrible ceremony is over, the tips, and the goodbyes in the hall. Now there is this gulping ceremony with my mother, this hand-shaking ceremony with my father; now I must go on waving, I must go on waving, till we turn the corner. Now that ceremony is over. Heaven be praised, all ceremonies are over. I am alone; I am going to school for the first time.

'Everybody seems to be doing things for this moment only; and never again. Never again. The urgency of it all is fearful. Everybody knows I am going to school, going to school for the first time. "That boy is going to school for the first time," says the housemaid, cleaning the steps. I must not cry. I must behold them indifferently. Now the awful portals of the station gape; "the moon-faced clock regards me". I must make phrases and phrases and so interpose something hard between myself and the stare of house-maids, the stare of clocks, staring faces, indifferent faces, or I shall cry. There is Louis, there is Neville, in long coats, carrying hand-bags, by the booking-office. They are composed. But they look different.'

'Here is Bernard,' said Louis. 'He is composed; he is easy. He swings his bag as he walks. I will follow Bernard, because he is not afraid. We are drawn through the booking-office on to the platform as a stream draws twigs and straws round the piers of a bridge. There is the very powerful, bottle-green engine without a neck, all back and thighs, breathing steam. The guard blows his whistle; the flag is dipped; without an effort, of its own momentum, like an avalanche started by a gentle push, we start forward. Bernard spreads a rug and plays knucklebones. Neville reads. London crumbles. London heaves and surges. There is a bristling of chimneys and towers. There a white church; there a mast among the spires. There a canal. Now there are open spaces with asphalt paths upon which it is strange that people should now be walking. There is a hill striped with red houses. A man crosses a bridge with a dog at his heels. Now the red boy begins firing at a pheasant. The blue boy shoves him aside. "My uncle is the best shot in England. My cousin is Master of Foxhounds." Boasting begins. And I cannot boast, for my father is a banker in Brisbane, and I speak with an Australian accent.'

'After all this hubbub,' said Neville, 'all this scuffling and hubbub, we have arrived. This is indeed a moment – this is indeed a solemn moment. I come, like a lord to his halls appointed. That is our founder; our illustrious founder, standing in the courtyard with one foot raised. I salute our founder. A noble Roman air hangs over these austere quadrangles. Already the lights are lit in the form rooms. Those are laboratories perhaps; and that a library, where I shall explore the exactitude of the Latin language, and step firmly upon the well-laid sentences, and pronounce the explicit, the sonorous hexameters of Virgil, of Lucretius; and chant with a passion that is never obscure or formless the loves of Catullus, reading from a big book, a quarto with margins. I shall lie, too, in the fields among the tickling grasses. I shall lie with my friends under the towering elm trees.

'Behold, the headmaster. Alas, that he should excite my ridicule. He is too sleek, he is altogether too shiny and black, like some statue in a public garden. And on the left side of his waistcoat, his taut, his drum-like waistcoat, hangs a crucifix.'

'Old Crane,' said Bernard, 'now rises to address us. Old Crane, the headmaster, has a nose like a mountain at sunset, and a blue cleft in his chin, like a wooded ravine, which some tripper has fired; like a wooded ravine seen from the train window. He sways slightly, mouthing out his tremendous and sonorous words. I love tremendous and sonorous words. But his words are too hearty to be true. Yet he is by this time convinced of their truth. And when he leaves the room, lurching rather heavily from side to side, and hurls his way through the swing-doors, all the masters, lurching rather heavily from side to side, hurl themselves also through the swing-doors. This is our first night at school, apart from our sisters.'

'This is my first night at school,' said Susan, 'away from my father, away from my home. My eyes swell; my eyes prick with tears. I hate the smell of pine and linoleum. I hate the wind-bitten shrubs and the sanitary tiles. I hate the cheerful jokes and the glazed look of everyone. I left my squirrel and my doves for the boy to look after. The kitchen door slams, and shot patters among the leaves when Percy fires at the rooks. All here is false; all is meretricious. Rhoda and Jinny sit far off in brown serge, and look at Miss Lambert who sits under a picture of Queen Alexandra reading from a book before her. There is also a blue scroll of needlework embroidered by some old girl. If I do not purse my lips, if I do not screw my handkerchief, I shall cry.'

'The purple light,' said Rhoda, 'in Miss Lambert's ring passes to and fro across the black stain on the white page of the Prayer Book. It is a vinous, it is an amorous light. Now that our boxes are unpacked in the dormitories, we sit herded together under maps of the entire world. There are desks with wells for the ink. We shall write our exercises in ink here. But here I am nobody. I have no face. This great company, all dressed in brown serge, has robbed me of my identity. We are all callous, unfriended. I will seek out a face, a composed, a monumental face, and will endow it with omniscience, and wear it under my dress like a talisman and then (I promise this) I will find some dingle in a wood where I can display my assortment of curious treasures. I promise myself this. So I will not cry.'

'That dark woman,' said Jinny, 'with high cheekbones, has a shiny dress, like a shell, veined, for wearing in the evening. That is nice for summer, but for winter I should like a thin dress shot with red threads that would gleam in the firelight. Then when the lamps were lit, I should put on my red dress and it would be thin as a veil, and would wind about my body, and billow out as I came into the room, pirouetting. It would make a flower shape as I sank down, in the middle of the room, on a gilt chair. But Miss Lambert wears an opaque dress, that falls in a cascade from her snow-white ruffle as she sits under a picture of Queen Alexandra pressing one white finger firmly on the page. And we pray.'

'Now we march, two by two,' said Louis, 'orderly, processional, into chapel. I like the dimness that falls as we enter the sacred building. I like the orderly progress. We file in; we seat ourselves. We put off our distinctions as we enter. I like it now, when, lurching slightly, but only from his momentum, Dr Crane mounts the pulpit and reads the lesson from a Bible spread on the back of the brass eagle. I rejoice; my heart expands in his bulk, in his authority. He lays the whirling dust clouds in my tremulous, my ignominiously agitated mind – how we danced round the Christmas tree and handing parcels they forgot me, and the fat woman said, "This little boy has no present," and gave me a shiny Union Jack from the top of the tree, and I cried with fury – to be remembered with pity. Now all is laid by his authority, his crucifix, and I feel come over me the sense of the earth under me, and my roots going down and down till they wrap themselves round some hardness at the centre. I recover my continuity, as he reads. I become a figure in the procession, a spoke in the huge wheel that, turning, at last erects me, here and now. I have been in the dark; I have been hidden; but when the wheel turns (as he reads) I rise into this dim light where I just perceive, but scarcely, kneeling boys, pillars and memorial brasses. There is no crudity here, no sudden kisses.'

'The brute menaces my liberty,' said Neville, 'when he prays. Unwarmed by imagination, his words fall cold on my head like paving-stones, while the gilt cross heaves on his waistcoat. The words of authority are corrupted by those who speak them. I gibe and mock at this sad religion, at these tremulous, grief-stricken figures advancing, cadaverous and wounded, down a white road shadowed by fig trees where boys sprawl in the dust – naked boys; and goatskins distended with wine hang at the tavern door. I was in Rome travelling with my father at Easter; and the trembling figure of Christ's mother was borne niddle-noddling along the streets; there went by also the stricken figure of Christ in a glass case.

'Now I will lean sideways as if to scratch my thigh. So I shall see Percival. There he sits, upright among the smaller fry. He breathes through his straight nose rather heavily. His blue and oddly inexpressive eyes are fixed with pagan indifference upon the pillar opposite. He would make an admirable churchwarden. He should have a birch and beat little boys for misdemeanours. He is allied with the Latin phrases on the memorial brasses. He sees nothing; he hears nothing. He is remote from us all in a pagan universe. But look – he flicks his hand to the back of his neck. For such gestures one falls hopelessly in love for a lifetime. Dalton, Jones, Edgar and Bateman flick their hands to the backs of their necks likewise. But they do not succeed.'

'At last,' said Bernard, 'the growl ceases. The sermon ends. He has minced the dance of the white butterflies at the door to powder. His rough and hairy voice is like an unshaven chin. Now he lurches back to his seat like a drunken sailor. It is an action that all the other masters will try to imitate; but, being flimsy, being floppy, wearing grey trousers, they will only succeed in making themselves ridiculous. I do not despise them. Their antics seem pitiable in my eyes. I note the fact for future reference with many others in my notebook. When I am grown up I shall carry a notebook – a fat book with many pages, methodically lettered. I shall enter my phrases. Under B shall come "Butterfly powder". If, in my novel, I describe the sun on the windowsill, I shall look under B and find butterfly powder. That will be useful. The tree "shades the window with green fingers". That will be useful. But alas! I am so soon distracted – by a hair like twisted candy, by Celia's prayer-book, ivory covered. Louis can contemplate nature, unwinking, by the hour. Soon I fail, unless talked to. "The lake of my mind, unbroken by oars, heaves placidly and soon sinks into an oily somnolence." That will be useful.'

'Now we move out of this cool temple, into the yellow playing-fields,' said Louis. 'And, as it is a half-holiday (the duke's birthday), we will settle among the long grasses while they play cricket. Could I be "they" I would choose it; I would buckle on my pads and stride across the playing-field at the head of the batsmen. Look now, how everybody follows Percival. He is heavy. He walks clumsily down the field, through the long grass, to where the great elm trees stand. His magnificence is that of some medieval commander. A wake of light seems to lie on the grass behind him. Look at us trooping after him, his faithful servants, to be shot like sheep, for he will certainly attempt some forlorn enterprise and die in battle. My heart turns rough; it abrades my side like a file with two edges: one, that I adore his magnificence; the other, I despise his slovenly accents – I who am so much his superior – and am jealous.'

'And now,' said Neville, 'let Bernard begin. Let him burble on, telling us stories, while we lie recumbent. Let him describe what we have all seen so that it becomes a sequence. Bernard says there is always a story. I am a story. Louis is a story. There is the story of the boot-boy, the story of the man with one eye, the story of the woman who sells winkles. Let him burble on with his story while I lie back and regard the stiff-legged figures of the padded batsmen through the trembling grasses. It seems as if the whole world were flowing and curving – on the earth the trees, in the sky the clouds. I look up, through the trees, into the sky. The match seems to be played up there. Faintly among the soft white clouds I hear the cry "Run", I hear the cry "How's that?" The clouds lose tufts of whiteness as the breeze dishevels them. If that blue could stay for ever; if that hole could remain for ever; if this moment could stay for ever –

'But Bernard goes on talking. Up they bubble – images. "Like a camel" . . . "a vulture". The camel is a vulture; the vulture a camel: for Bernard is a dangling wire, loose, but seductive. Yes, for when he talks, when he makes his foolish comparisons, a lightness comes over one. One floats, too, as if one were that bubble; one is freed; I have escaped, one feels. Even the chubby little boys (Dalton, Larpent and Baker) feel the same abandonment. They like this better than the cricket. They catch the phrases as they bubble. They let the feathery grasses tickle their noses. And then we all feel Percival lying heavy among us. His curious guffaw seems to sanction our laughter. But now he has rolled himself over in the long grass. He is, I think, chewing a stalk between his teeth. He feels bored; I too feel bored. Bernard at once perceives that we are bored. I detect a certain effort, an extravagance in his phrase, as if he said, "Look!" but Percival says, "No." For he is always the first to detect insincerity; and is brutal in the extreme. The sentence tails off feebly. Yes, the appalling moment has come when Bernard's power fails him and there is no longer any sequence and he sags and twiddles a bit of string and falls silent, gaping as if about to burst into tears. Among the tortures and devastations of life is this then – our friends are not able to finish their stories.'

'Now let me try,' said Louis, 'before we rise, before we go to tea, to fix the moment in one effort of supreme endeavour. This shall endure. We are parting; some to tea; some to the nets; I to show my essay to Mr Barker. This will endure. From discord, from hatred (I despise dabblers in imagery – I resent the power of Percival intensely), my shattered mind is pieced together by some sudden perception. I take the trees, the clouds, to be witnesses of my complete integration. I, Louis, I, who shall walk the earth these seventy years, am born entire, out of hatred, out of discord. Here on this ring of grass we have sat together, bound by the tremendous power of some inner compulsion. The trees wave, the clouds pass. The time approaches when these soliloquies shall be shared. We shall not always give out a sound like a beaten gong as one sensation strikes and then another. Children, our lives have been gongs striking; clamour and boasting; cries of despair; blows on the nape of the neck in gardens.

'Now grass and trees, the travelling air blowing empty spaces in the blue which they then recover, shaking the leaves which then replace themselves, and our ring here, sitting, with our arms binding our knees, hint at some other order, and better, which makes a reason everlastingly. This I see for a second, and shall try tonight to fix in words, to forge in a ring of steel, though Percival destroys it, as he blunders off, crushing the grasses, with the small fry trotting subservient after him. Yet it is Percival I need; for it is Percival who inspires poetry.'

'For how many months,' said Susan, 'for how many years, have I run up these stairs, in the dismal days of winter, in the chilly days of spring? Now it is midsummer. We go upstairs to change into white frocks to play tennis – Jinny and I with Rhoda following after. I count each step as I mount, counting each step something done with. So each night I tear off the old day from the calendar, and screw it tight into a ball. I do this vindictively, while Betty and Clara are on their knees. I do not pray. I revenge myself upon the day. I wreak my spite upon its image. You are dead now, I say, school day, hated day. They have made all the days of June – this is the twenty-fifth – shiny and orderly, with gongs, with lessons, with orders to wash, to change, to work, to eat. We listen to missionaries from China. We drive off in brakes, along the asphalt pavement, to attend concerts in halls. We are shown galleries and pictures.

'At home the hay waves over the meadows. My father leans upon the stile, smoking. In the house one door bangs and then another, as the summer air puffs along the empty passages. Some old picture perhaps swings on the wall. A petal drops from the rose in the jar. The farm wagons strew the hedges with tufts of hay. All this I see, I always see, as I pass the looking-glass on the landing, with Jinny in front and Rhoda lagging behind. Jinny dances. Jinny always dances in the hall on the ugly, the encaustic tiles; she turns cartwheels in the playground; she picks some flower forbiddenly, and sticks it behind her ear so that Miss Perry's dark eyes smoulder with admiration, for Jinny, not me. Miss Perry loves Jinny; and I could have loved her, but now love no one, except my father, my doves and the squirrel whom I left in the cage at home for the boy to look after.'

'I hate the small looking-glass on the stairs,' said Jinny. 'It shows our heads only; it cuts off our heads. And my lips are too wide, and my eyes are too close together; I show my gums too much when I laugh. Susan's head, with its fell look, with its grass-green eyes which poets will love, Bernard said, because they fall upon close white stitching, puts mine out; even Rhoda's face, mooning, vacant, is completed, like those white petals she used to swim in her bowl. So I skip up the stairs past them, to the next landing where the long glass hangs and I see myself entire. I see my body and head in one now; for even in this serge frock they are one, my body and my head. Look, when I move my head I ripple all down my narrow body; even my thin legs ripple like a stalk in the wind. I flicker between the set face of Susan and Rhoda's vagueness; I leap like one of those flames that run between the cracks of the earth; I move, I dance; I never cease to move and to dance. I move like the leaf that moved in the hedge as a child and frightened me. I dance over these streaked, these impersonal, distempered walls with their yellow skirting as firelight dances over teapots. I catch fire even from women's cold eyes. When I read, a purple rim runs round the black edge of the textbook. Yet I cannot follow any word through its changes. I cannot follow any thought from present to past. I do not stand lost, like Susan, with tears in my eyes remembering home; or lie, like Rhoda, crumpled among the ferns, staining my pink cotton green, while I dream of plants that flower under the sea, and rocks through which the fish swim slowly. I do not dream.

'Now let us be quick. Now let me be the first to pull off these coarse clothes. Here are my clean white stockings. Here are my new shoes. I bind my hair with a white ribbon, so that when I leap across the court the ribbon will stream out in a flash, yet curl round my neck, perfectly in its place. Not a hair shall be untidy.'

'That is my face,' said Rhoda, 'in the looking-glass behind Susan's shoulder – that face is my face. But I will duck behind her to hide it, for I am not here. I have no face. Other people have faces; Susan and Jinny have faces; they are here. Their world is the real world. The things they lift are heavy. They say Yes, they say No; whereas I shift and change and am seen through in a second. If they meet a housemaid she looks at them without laughing. But she laughs at me. They know what to say if spoken to. They laugh really; they get angry really; while I have to look first and do what other people do when they have done it.

'See now with what extraordinary certainty Jinny pulls on her stockings, simply to play tennis. That I admire. But I like Susan's way better, for she is more resolute, and less ambitious of distinction than Jinny. Both despise me for copying what they do; but Susan sometimes teaches me, for instance, how to tie a bow, while Jinny has her own knowledge but keeps it to herself. They have friends to sit by. They have things to say privately in corners. But I attach myself only to names and faces; and hoard them like amulets against disaster. I choose out across the hall some unknown face and can hardly drink my tea when she whose name I do not know sits opposite. I choke. I am rocked from side to side by the violence of my emotion. I imagine these nameless, these immaculate people, watching me from behind bushes. I leap high to excite their admiration. At night, in bed, I excite their complete wonder. I often die pierced with arrows to win their tears. If they should say, or I should see from a label on their boxes, that they were in Scarborough last holidays, the whole town runs gold, the whole pavement is illuminated. Therefore I hate looking-glasses which show me my real face. Alone, I often fall down into nothingness. I must push my foot stealthily lest I should fall off the edge of the world into nothingness. I have to bang my hand against some hard door to call myself back to the body.'

'We are late,' said Susan. 'We must wait our turn to play. We will pitch here in the long grass and pretend to watch Jinny and Clara, Betty and Mavis. But we will not watch them. I hate watching other people play games. I will make images of all the things I hate most and bury them in the ground. This shiny pebble is Madame Carlo, and I will bury her deep because of her fawning and ingratiating manners, because of the sixpence she gave me for keeping my knuckles flat when I played my scales. I buried her sixpence. I would bury the whole school: the gymnasium; the classroom;

the dining-room that always smells of meat; and the chapel. I would bury the red-brown tiles and the oily portraits of old men – benefactors, founders of schools. There are some trees I like; the cherry tree with lumps of clear gum on the bark; and one view from the attic towards some far hills. Save for these, I would bury it all as I bury these ugly stones that are always scattered about this briny coast, with its piers and its trippers. At home, the waves are mile-long. On winter nights we hear them booming. Last Christmas a man was drowned sitting alone in his cart.'

'When Miss Lambert passes,' said Rhoda, 'talking to the clergyman, the others laugh and imitate her hunch behind her back; yet everything changes and becomes luminous. Jinny leaps higher too when Miss Lambert passes. Suppose she saw that daisy, it would change. Wherever she goes, things are changed under her eyes; and yet when she has gone is not the thing the same again? Miss Lambert is taking the clergyman through the wicket-gate to her private garden; and when she comes to the pond, she sees a frog on a leaf, and that will change. All is solemn, all is pale where she stands, like a statue in a grove. She lets her tasselled silken cloak slip down, and only her purple ring still glows, her vinous, her amethystine ring. There is this mystery about people when they leave us. When they leave us I can companion them to the pond and make them stately. When Miss Lambert passes, she makes the daisy change; and everything runs like streaks of fire when she carves the beef. Month by month things are losing their hardness; even my body now lets the light through; my spine is soft like wax near the flame of the candle. I dream; I dream.'

'I have won the game,' said Jinny. 'Now it is your turn. I must throw myself on the ground and pant. I am out of breath with running, with triumph. Everything in my body seems thinned out with running and triumph. My blood must be bright red, whipped up, slapping against my ribs. My soles tingle, as if wire rings opened and shut in my feet. I see every blade of grass very clear. But the pulse drums so in my forehead, behind my eyes, that everything dances – the net, the grass; your faces leap like butterflies; the trees seem to jump up and down. There is nothing staid, nothing settled, in this universe. All is rippling, all is dancing; all is quickness and triumph. Only, when I have lain alone on the hard ground, watching you play your game, I begin to feel the wish to be singled out; to be summoned, to be called away by one person who comes to find me, who is attracted towards me, who cannot keep himself from me, but comes to where I sit on my gilt chair, with my frock billowing round me like a flower. And withdrawing into an alcove, sitting alone on a balcony we talk together.

'Now the tide sinks. Now the trees come to earth; the brisk waves that slap my ribs rock more gently, and my heart rides at anchor, like a sailing-boat whose sails slide slowly down on to the white deck. The game is over. We must go to tea now.'

'The boasting boys,' said Louis, 'have gone now in a vast team to play cricket. They have driven off in their great brake, singing in chorus. All their heads turn simultaneously at the corner by the laurel bushes. Now they are boasting. Larpent's brother played football for Oxford; Smith's father made a century at Lord's. Archie and Hugh; Parker and Dalton; Larpent and Smith; then again Archie and Hugh; Parker and Dalton; Larpent and Smith – the names repeat themselves; the names are the same always. They are the volunteers; they are the cricketers; they are the officers of the Natural History Society. They are always forming into fours and marching in troops with badges on their caps; they salute simultaneously passing the figure of their general. How majestic is their order, how beautiful is their obedience! If I could follow, if I could be with them, I would sacrifice all I know. But they also leave butterflies trembling with their wings pinched off; they throw dirty pocket-handkerchiefs clotted with blood screwed up into corners. They make little boys sob in dark passages. They have big red ears that stand out under their caps. Yet that is what we wish to be, Neville and I. I watch them go with envy. Peeping from behind a curtain, I note the simultaneity of their movements with delight. If my legs were reinforced by theirs, how they would run! If I had been with them and won matches and rowed in great races, and galloped all day, how I should thunder out songs at midnight! In what a torrent the words would rush from my throat!'

'Percival has gone now,' said Neville. 'He is thinking of nothing but the match. He never waved his hand as the brake turned the corner by the laurel bush. He despises me for being too weak to play (yet he is always kind to my weakness). He despises me for not caring if they win or lose except that he cares. He takes my devotion; he accepts my tremulous, no doubt abject offering, mixed with contempt as it is for his mind. For he cannot read. Yet when I read Shakespeare or Catullus, lying in the long grass, he understands more than Louis. Not the words – but what are words? Do I not know already how to rhyme, how to imitate Pope, Dryden, even Shakespeare? But I cannot stand all day in the sun with my eyes on the ball; I cannot feel the flight of the ball through my body and think only of the ball. I shall be a clinger to the outsides of words all my life. Yet I could not live with him and suffer his stupidity. He will coarsen and snore. He will marry and there will be scenes of tenderness at breakfast. But now he is young. Not a thread, not a sheet of paper lies between him and the sun, between him and the rain, between him and the moon as he lies naked, tumbled, hot, on his bed. Now as they drive along the high road in their brake his face is mottled red and yellow. He will throw off his coat and stand with his legs apart, with his hands ready, watching the wicket. And he will pray, "Lord, let us win"; he will think of one thing only, that they should win.

'How could I go with them in a brake to play cricket? Only Bernard could go with them, but Bernard is too late to go with them. He is always too late.

He is prevented by his incorrigible moodiness from going with them. He stops, when he washes his hands, to say, "There is a fly in that web. Shall I rescue that fly; shall I let the spider eat it?" He is shaded with innumerable perplexities, or he would go with them to play cricket, and would lie in the grass watching the sky, and would start when the ball was hit. But they would forgive him; for he would tell them a story.'

'They have bowled off,' said Bernard, 'and I am too late to go with them. The horrid little boys, who are also so beautiful, whom you and Louis, Neville, envy so deeply, have bowled off with their heads all turned the same way. But I am unaware of these profound distinctions. My fingers slip over the keyboard without knowing which is black and which white. Archie makes easily a hundred; I by a fluke make sometimes fifteen. But what is the difference between us? Wait though, Neville; let me talk. The bubbles are rising like the silver bubbles from the floor of a saucepan; image on top of image. I cannot sit down to my book, like Louis, with ferocious tenacity. I must open the little trap-door and let out these linked phrases in which I run together whatever happens, so that instead of incoherence there is perceived a wandering thread, lightly joining one thing to another. I will tell you the story of the doctor.

'When Dr Crane lurches through the swing-doors after prayers he is convinced, it seems, of his immense superiority; and indeed, Neville, we cannot deny that his departure leaves us not only with a sense of relief, but also with a sense of something removed, like a tooth. Now let us follow him as he heaves through the swing-door to his own apartments. Let us imagine him in his private room over the stables undressing. He unfastens his sock suspenders (let us be trivial, let us be intimate). Then with a characteristic gesture (it is difficult to avoid these ready-made phrases, and they are, in his case, somehow appropriate) he takes the silver, he takes the coppers from his trouser pockets and places them there, and there, on his dressing-table. With both arms stretched on the arms of his chair he reflects (this is his private moment; it is here we must try to catch him): shall he cross the pink bridge into his bedroom or shall he not cross it? The two rooms are united by a bridge of rosy light from the lamp at the bedside where Mrs Crane lies with her hair on the pillow reading a French memoir. As she reads, she sweeps her hand with an abandoned and despairing gesture over her fore-head, and sighs, "Is this all?" comparing herself with some French duchess. Now, says the doctor, in two years I shall retire. I shall clip yew hedges in a west-country garden. An admiral I might have been; or a judge; not a schoolmaster. What forces, he asks, staring at the gas-fire with his shoulders hunched up more hugely than we know them (he is in his shirtsleeves remember), have brought me to this? What vast forces? he thinks, getting into the stride of his majestic phrases as he looks over his shoulder at the window. It is a stormy night; the branches of the chestnut trees are plough-ing up and down. Stars flash between them. What vast forces of good and evil have brought me here? he asks, and sees with sorrow that his chair has worn a little hole in the pile of the purple carpet. So there he sits, swinging his braces. But stories that follow people into their private rooms are difficult. I cannot go on with this story. I twiddle a piece of string; I turn over four or five coins in my trouser pocket.'

'Bernard's stories amuse me,' said Neville, 'at the start. But when they tail off absurdly and he gapes, twiddling a bit of string, I feel my own solitude. He sees everyone with blurred edges. Hence I cannot talk to him of Percival. I cannot expose my absurd and violent passion to his sympathetic under-standing. It too would make a "story". I need someone whose mind falls like a chopper on a block; to whom the pitch of absurdity is sublime, and a shoestring adorable. To whom can I expose the urgency of my own passion? Louis is too cold, too universal. There is nobody – here among these grey arches, and moaning pigeons, and cheerful games and tradition and emulation, all so skilfully organised to prevent feeling alone. Yet I am struck still as I walk by sudden premonitions of what is to come. Yesterday, passing the open door leading into the private garden, I saw Fenwick with his mallet raised. The steam from the tea-urn rose in the middle of the lawn. There were banks of blue flowers. Then suddenly descended upon me the obscure, the mystic sense of adoration, of completeness that triumphed over chaos. Nobody saw my poised and intent figure as I stood at the open door. Nobody guessed the need I had to offer my being to one god; and perish, and disappear. His mallet descended; the vision broke.

'Should I seek out some tree? Should I desert these form rooms and libraries, and the broad yellow page in which I read Catullus, for woods and fields? Should I walk under beech trees, or saunter along the river bank, where the trees meet united like lovers in the water? But nature is too vegetable, too vapid. She has only sublimities and vastitudes and water and leaves. I begin to wish for firelight, privacy, and the limbs of one person.'

'I begin to wish,' said Louis, 'for night to come. As I stand here with my hand on the grained oak panel of Mr Wickham's door I think myself the friend of Richelieu, or the Duke of St Simon holding out a snuffbox to the king himself. It is my privilege. My witticisms "run like wildfire through the court". Duchesses tear emeralds from their earrings out of admiration – but these rockets rise best in darkness, in my cubicle at night. I am now a boy only with a colonial accent holding my knuckles against Mr Wickham's grained oak door. The day has been full of ignominies and triumphs concealed from fear of laughter. I am the best scholar in the school. But when darkness comes I put off this unenviable body – my large nose, my thin lips, my colonial accent – and inhabit space. I am then Virgil's companion, and Plato's. I am then the last scion of one of the great houses of France. But I am also one who will force himself to desert these windy and moonlit territories, these midnight wanderings, and confront grained oak doors. I will achieve in my life – heaven grant that it be not long – some gigantic amalgamation between the two discrepancies so hideously apparent to me. Out of my suffering I will do it. I will knock. I will enter.'

'I have torn off the whole of May and June,' said Susan, 'and twenty days of July. I have torn them off and screwed them up so that they no longer exist, save as a weight in my side. They have been crippled days, like moths with shrivelled wings unable to fly. There are only eight days left. In eight days' time I shall get out of the train and stand on the platform at six twenty-five. Then my freedom will unfurl, and all these restrictions that wrinkle and shrivel – hours and order and discipline, and being here and there exactly at the right moment – will crack asunder. Out the day will spring, as I open the carriage-door and see my father in his old hat and gaiters. I shall tremble. I shall burst into tears. Then next morning I shall get up at dawn. I shall let myself out by the kitchen door. I shall walk on the moor. The great horses of the phantom riders will thunder behind me and stop suddenly. I shall see the swallow skim the grass. I shall throw myself on a bank by the river and watch the fish slip in and out among the reeds. The palms of my hands will be printed with pine-needles. I shall there unfold and take out whatever it is I have made here; something hard. For something has grown in me here, through the winters and summers, on staircases, in bedrooms. I do not want, as Jinny wants, to be admired. I do not want people, when I come in, to look up with admiration. I want to give, to be given, and solitude in which to unfold my possessions.

'Then I shall come back through the trembling lanes under the arches of the nut leaves. I shall pass an old woman wheeling a perambulator full of sticks; and the shepherd. But we shall not speak. I shall come back through the kitchen garden, and see the curved leaves of the cabbages pebbled with dew, and the house in the garden, blind with curtained windows. I shall go upstairs to my room, and turn over my own things, locked carefully in the wardrobe: my shells; my eggs; my curious grasses. I shall feed my doves and my squirrel. I shall go to the kennel and comb my spaniel. So gradually I shall turn over the hard thing that has grown here in my side. But here bells ring; feet shuffle perpetually.'

'I hate darkness and sleep and night,' said Jinny, 'and lie longing for the day to come. I long that the week should be all one day without divisions. When I wake early – and the birds wake me – I lie and watch the brass handles on the cupboard grow clear; then the basin; then the towel-horse. As each thing in the bedroom grows clear, my heart beats quicker. I feel my body harden, and become pink, yellow brown. My hands pass over my legs and body. I feel its slopes, its thinness. I love to hear the gong roar through the house and the stir begin – here a thud, there a patter. Doors slam; water rushes. Here is another day, here is another day, I cry, as my feet touch the floor. It may be a bruised day, an imperfect day. I am often scolded. I am often in disgrace for idleness, for laughing; but even as Miss Matthews grumbles at my feather-headed carelessness, I catch sight of something moving – a speck of sun perhaps on a picture; or the donkey drawing the mowing machine across the lawn; or a sail that passes between the laurel leaves, so that I am never cast down. I cannot be prevented from pirouetting behind Miss Matthews into prayers.

'Now, too, the time is coming when we shall leave school and wear long skirts. I shall wear necklaces and a white dress without sleeves at night. There will be parties in brilliant rooms; and one man will single me out and will tell me what he has told no other person. He will like me better than Susan or Rhoda. He will find in me some quality, some peculiar thing. But I shall not let myself be attached to one person only. I do not want to be fixed, to be pinioned. I tremble, I quiver, like the leaf in the hedge, as I sit dangling my feet, on the edge of the bed, with a new day to break open. I have fifty years, I have sixty years to spend. I have not yet broken into my hoard. This is the beginning.'

'There are hours and hours,' said Rhoda, 'before I can put out the light and lie suspended on my bed above the world, before I can let the day drop down, before I can let my tree grow, quivering in green pavilions above my head. Here I cannot let it grow. Somebody knocks through it. They ask questions, they interrupt, they throw it down.

'Now I will go to the bathroom and take off my shoes and wash; but as I wash, as I bend my head down over the basin, I will let the Russian Empress's veil flow about my shoulders. The diamonds of the imperial crown blaze on my forehead. I hear the roar of the hostile mob as I step out on to the balcony. Now I dry my hands, vigorously, so that Miss, whose name I forget, cannot suspect that I am waving my fist at an infuriated mob. "I am your Empress, people." My attitude is one of defiance. I am fearless. I conquer.

'But this is a thin dream. This is a papery tree. Miss Lambert blows it down. Even the sight of her vanishing down the corridor blows it to atoms. It is not solid; it gives me no satisfaction – this Empress dream. It leaves me, now that it has fallen, here in the passage rather shivering. Things seem paler. I will go now into the library and take out some book, and read and look; and read again and look. Here is a poem about a hedge. I will wander down it and pick flowers, green cowbind and the moonlight-coloured may, wild roses and ivy serpentine. I will clasp them in my hands and lay them on the desk's shiny surface. I will sit by the river's trembling edge and look at the water-lilies, broad and bright, which lit the oak that overhung the hedge with moonlight beams of their own watery light. I will pick flowers; I will bind flowers in one garland and clasp them and present them – Oh! to whom? There is some check in the flow of my being; a deep stream presses on some obstacle; it jerks; it tugs; some knot in the centre resists. Oh, this is pain, this is anguish! I faint, I fail. Now my body thaws; I am unsealed, I am incandescent. Now the stream pours in a deep tide fertilising, opening the shut, forcing the tight-folded, flooding free. To whom shall I give all that now flows through me, from my warm, my porous body? I will gather my flowers and present them – Oh! to whom?

'Sailors loiter on the parade, and amorous couples; the omnibuses rattle along the sea front to the town. I will give; I will enrich; I will return to the world this beauty. I will bind my flowers in one garland and advancing with my hand outstretched will present them – Oh! to whom?'

'Now we have received,' said Louis, 'for this is the last day of the last term – Neville's and Bernard's and my last day – whatever our masters have had to give us. The introduction has been made; the world presented. They stay, we depart. The great Doctor, whom of all men I most revere, swaying a little from side to side among the tables, the bound volumes, has dealt out Horace, Tennyson, the complete works of Keats and Matthew Arnold, suitably inscribed. I respect the hand which gave them. He speaks with complete conviction. To him his words are true, though not to us. Speaking in the gruff voice of deep emotion, fiercely, tenderly, he has told us that we are about to go. He has bid us "quit ourselves like men". (On his lips quotations from the Bible, from *The Times*, seem equally magnificent.) Some will do this; others that. Some will not meet again. Neville, Bernard and I shall not meet here again. Life will divide us. But we have formed certain ties. Our boyish, our irresponsible years are over. But we have forged certain links. Above all, we have inherited traditions. These stone flags have been worn for six hundred years. On these walls are inscribed the names of men of war, of statesmen, of some unhappy poets (mine shall be among them). Blessings be on all traditions, on all safeguards and circumscriptions! I am most grateful to you men in black gowns, and you, dead, for your leading, for your guardianship; yet after all, the problem remains. The differences are not yet solved. Flowers toss their heads outside the window. I see wild birds and impulses wilder than the wildest birds strike from my wild heart. My eyes are wild; my lips tight pressed. The bird flies; the flower dances; but I hear always the sullen thud of the waves; and the chained beast stamps on the beach. It stamps and stamps.'

'This is the final ceremony,' said Bernard. 'This is the last of all our ceremonies. We are overcome by strange feelings. The guard holding his flag is about to blow his whistle; the train breathing steam in another moment is about to start. One wants to say something, to feel something, absolutely appropriate to the occasion. One's mind is primed; one's lips are pursed. And then a bee drifts in and hums round the flowers in the bouquet which Lady Hampton, the wife of the General, keeps smelling to show her appreciation of the compliment. If the bee were to sting her nose? We are all deeply moved; yet irreverent; yet penitent; yet anxious to get it over; yet reluctant to part. The bee distracts us; its casual flight seems to deride our intensity. Humming vaguely, skimming widely, it is settled now on the carnation. Many of us will not meet again. We shall not enjoy certain pleasures again, when we are free to go to bed, or to sit up, when I need no longer smuggle in bits of candle-ends and immoral literature. The bee now hums round the head of the great Doctor. Larpent, John, Archie, Percival, Baker and Smith – I have liked them enormously. I have known one mad boy only. I have hated one mean boy only. I enjoy in retrospect my terribly awkward breakfasts at the headmaster's table with toast and marmalade. He alone does not notice the bee. If it were to settle on his nose he would flick it off with one magnificent gesture. Now he has made his joke; now his voice has almost broken but not quite. Now we are dismissed – Louis, Neville and I for ever. We take our highly polished books, scholastically inscribed in a little crabbed hand. We rise, we disperse; the pressure is removed. The bee has become an insignificant, a disregarded insect, flown through the open window into obscurity. Tomorrow we go.'

'We are about to part,' said Neville. 'Here are the boxes; here are the cabs. There is Percival in his billycock hat. He will forget me. He will leave my letters lying about among guns and dogs unanswered. I shall send him poems and he will perhaps reply with a picture postcard. But it is for that that I love him. I shall propose meeting – under a clock, by some Cross; and shall wait, and he will not come. It is for that that I love him. Oblivious, almost entirely ignorant, he will pass from my life. And I shall pass, incredible as it seems, into other lives; this is only an escapade perhaps, a prelude only. I feel already, though I cannot endure the Doctor's pompous mummery and faked emotions, that things we have only dimly perceived draw near. I shall be free to enter the garden where Fenwick raises his mallet. Those who have despised me shall acknowledge my sovereignty. But, by some inscrutable law of my being, sovereignty and the possession of power will not be enough; I shall always push through curtains to privacy, and want some whispered words alone. Therefore I go, dubious, but elate; apprehensive of intolerable pain; yet I think bound in my adventuring to conquer after huge suffering, bound, surely, to discover my desire in the end. There, for the last time, I see the statue of our pious founder with the doves about his head. They will wheel for ever about his head, whitening it, while the organ moans in the chapel. So I take my seat; and, when I have found my place in the corner of our reserved compartment, I will shade my eyes with a book to hide one tear; I will shade my eyes to observe; to peep at one face. It is the first day of the summer holidays.'

'It is the first day of the summer holidays,' said Susan. 'But the day is still rolled up. I will not examine it until I step out on to the platform in the evening. I will not let myself even smell it until I smell the cold green air off the fields. But already these are not school fields; these are not school hedges; the men in these fields are doing real things; they fill carts with real hay; and those are real cows, not school cows. But the carbolic smell of corridors and the chalky smell of schoolrooms is still in my nostrils. The glazed, shiny look of matchboard is still in my eyes. I must wait for fields and hedges, and woods and fields, and steep railway cuttings, sprinkled with gorse bushes, and trucks in sidings, and tunnels and suburban gardens with women hanging out washing, and then fields again and children swinging on gates, to cover it over, to bury it deep, this school that I have hated.

'I will not send my children to school nor spend a night all my life in London. Here in this vast station everything echoes and booms hollowly. The light is like the yellow light under an awning. Jinny lives here. Jinny takes her dog for walks on these pavements. People here shoot through the streets silently. They look at nothing but shop-windows. Their heads bob up and down all at about the same height. The streets are laced together with telegraph wires. The houses are all glass, all festoons and glitter; now all front doors and lace curtains, all pillars and white steps. But now I pass on, out of London again; the fields begin again; and the houses, and women hanging washing, and trees and fields. London is now veiled, now vanished, now crumbled, now fallen. The carbolic and the pitch-pine begin to lose their savour. I smell corn and turnips. I undo a paper packet tied with a piece of white cotton. The egg shells slide into the cleft between my knees. Now we stop at station after station, rolling out milk cans. Now women kiss each other and help with baskets. Now I will let myself lean out of the window. The air rushes down my nose and throat – the cold air, the salt air with the smell of turnip fields in it. And there is my father, with his back turned, talking to a farmer. I tremble. I cry. There is my father in gaiters. There is my father.'

'I sit snug in my own corner going north,' said Jinny, 'in this roaring express which is yet so smooth that it flattens hedges, lengthens hills. We flash past signal-boxes; we make the earth rock slightly from side to side. The distance closes for ever in a point; and we forever open the distance wide again. The telegraph poles bob up incessantly; one is felled, another rises. Now we roar and swing into a tunnel. The gentleman pulls up the window. I see reflections on the shining glass which lines the tunnel. I see him lower his paper. He smiles at my reflection in the tunnel. My body instantly of its own accord puts forth a frill under his gaze. My body lives a life of its own. Now the black window glass is green again. We are out of the tunnel. He reads his paper. But we have exchanged the approval of our bodies. There is then a great society of bodies, and mine is introduced; mine has come into the room where the gilt chairs are. Look – all the windows of the villas and their white-tented curtains dance; and the men sitting in the hedges in the cornfields with knotted blue handkerchiefs are aware too, as I am aware, of heat and rapture. One waves as we pass him. There are bowers and arbours in these villa gardens and young men in shirtsleeves on ladders trimming roses. A man on a horse canters over the field. His horse plunges as we pass. And the rider turns to look at us. We roar again through blackness. And I lie back; I give myself up to rapture; I think that at the end of the tunnel I enter a lamp-lit room with chairs, into one of which I sink, much admired, my dress billowing round me. But behold, looking up, I meet the eyes of a sour woman, who suspects me of rapture. My body shuts in her face, impertinently, like a parasol. I open my body, I shut my body at my will. Life is beginning. I now break into my hoard of life.'

'It is the first day of the summer holidays,' said Rhoda. 'And now, as the train passes by these red rocks, by this blue sea, the term, done with, forms itself into one shape behind me. I see its colour. June was white. I see the fields white with daisies, and white with dresses; and tennis courts marked with white. Then there was wind and violent thunder. There was a star riding through clouds one night, and I said to the star, "Consume me." That was at midsummer, after the garden party and my humiliation at the garden party. Wind and storm coloured July. Also, in the middle, cadaverous, awful, lay the grey puddle in the courtyard, when, holding an envelope in my hand, I carried a message. I came to the puddle. I could not cross it. Identity failed me. We are nothing, I said, and fell. I was blown like a feather. I was wafted down tunnels. Then very gingerly, I pushed my foot across. I laid my hand against a brick wall. I returned very painfully, drawing myself back into my body over the grey, cadaverous space of the puddle. This is life then to which I am committed.

'So I detach the summer term. With intermittent shocks, sudden as the springs of a tiger, life emerges heaving its dark crest from the sea. It is to this we are attached; it is to this we are bound, as bodies to wild horses. And yet we have invented devices for filling up the crevices and disguising these fissures. Here is the ticket collector. Here are two men; three women; there is a cat in a basket; myself with my elbow on the windowsill – this is here and now. We draw on, we make off, through whispering fields of golden corn. Women in the fields are surprised to be left behind there, hoeing. The train now stamps heavily, breathes stertorously, as it climbs up and up. At last we are on the top of the moor. Only a few wild sheep live here; a few shaggy ponies; yet we are provided with every comfort; with tables to hold our newspapers, with rings to hold our tumblers. We come carrying these appliances with us over the top of the moor. Now we are on the summit. Silence will close behind us. If I look back over that bald head, I can see silence already closing and the shadows of clouds chasing each other over the empty moor; silence closes over our transient passage. This I say is the present moment; this is the first day of the summer holidays. This is part of the emerging monster to whom we are attached.'

'Now we are off,' said Louis. 'Now I hang suspended without attachments. We are nowhere. We are passing through England in a train. England slips by the window, always changing from hill to wood, from rivers and willows to towns again. And I have no firm ground to which I go. Bernard and Neville, Percival, Archie, Larpent and Baker go to Oxford or Cambridge, to

Edinburgh, Rome, Paris, Berlin, or to some American University. I go vaguely, to make money vaguely. Therefore a poignant shadow, a keen accent, falls on these golden bristles, on these poppy-red fields, this flowing corn that never overflows its boundaries; but runs rippling to the edge. This is the first day of a new life, another spoke of the rising wheel. But my body passes vagrant as a bird's shadow. I should be transient as the shadow on the meadow, soon fading, soon darkening and dying there where it meets the wood, were it not that I coerce my brain to form in my forehead; I force myself to state, if only in one line of unwritten poetry, this moment; to mark this inch in the long, long history that began in Egypt, in the time of the Pharaohs, when women carried red pitchers to the Nile. I seem already to have lived many thousand years. But if I now shut my eyes, if I fail to realise the meeting-place of past and present, that I sit in a third-class railway carriage full of boys going home for the holidays, human history is defrauded of a moment's vision. Its eye, that would see through me, shuts – if I sleep now, through slovenliness, or cowardice, burying myself in the past, in the dark; or acquiesce, as Bernard acquiesces, telling stories; or boast, as Percival, Archie, John, Walter, Lathom, Larpent, Roper, Smith boast – the names are the same always, the names of the boasting boys. They are all boasting, all talking, except Neville, who slips a look occasionally over the edge of a French novel, and so will always slip into cushioned firelit rooms, with many books and one friend, while I tilt on an office chair behind a counter. Then I shall grow bitter and mock at them. I shall envy them their continuance down the safe traditional ways under the shade of old yew trees while I consort with cockneys and clerks, and tap the pavements of the city.

'But now disembodied, passing over fields without lodgment – (there is a river; a man fishes; there is a spire, there is the village street with its bow-windowed inn) – all is dreamlike and dim to me. These hard thoughts, this envy, this bitterness, make no lodgment in me. I am the ghost of Louis, an ephemeral passer-by, in whose mind dreams have power, and garden sounds when in the early morning petals float on fathomless depths and the birds sing. I dash and sprinkle myself with the bright waters of childhood. Its thin veil quivers. But the chained beast stamps and stamps on the shore.'

'Louis and Neville,' said Bernard, 'both sit silent. Both are absorbed. Both feel the presence of other people as a separating wall. But if I find myself in company with other people, words at once make smoke rings – see how phrases at once begin to wreathe off my lips. It seems that a match is set to a fire; something burns. An elderly and apparently prosperous man, a traveller, now gets in. And I at once wish to approach him; I instinctively dislike the sense of presence, cold, unassimilated, among us. I do not believe in separation. We are not single. Also I wish to add to my collection of valuable observations upon the true nature of human life. My book will certainly run to many volumes, embracing every known variety of man and woman. I fill my mind with whatever happens to be the contents of a room or a railway carriage as one fills a fountain-pen in an inkpot. I have a steady unquenchable thirst. Now I feel by imperceptible signs, which I cannot yet interpret but will later, that his defiance is about to thaw. His solitude shows signs of cracking. He has passed a remark about a country house. A smoke ring issues from my lips (about crops) and circles him, bringing him into contact. The human voice has a disarming quality – (we are not single, we are one). As we exchange these few but amiable remarks about country houses, I furbish him up and make him concrete. He is indulgent as a husband but not faithful; a small builder who employs a few men. In local society he is important; is already a councillor, and perhaps in time will be mayor. He wears a large ornament, like a double tooth torn up by the roots, made of coral, hanging at his watch-chain. Walter J. Trumble is the sort of name that would fit him. He has been in America, on a business trip with his wife, and a double room in a smallish hotel cost him a whole month's wages. His front tooth is stopped with gold.

'The fact is that I have little aptitude for reflection. I require the concrete in everything. It is so only that I lay hands upon the world. A good phrase, however, seems to me to have an independent existence. Yet I think it is likely that the best are made in solitude. They require some final refrigeration which I cannot give them, dabbling always in warm soluble words. My method, nevertheless, has certain advantages over theirs. Neville is repelled by the grossness of Trumble. Louis, glancing, tripping with the high step of a disdainful crane, picks up words as if in sugar-tongs. It is true that his eyes – wild, laughing, yet desperate – express something that we have not gauged. There is about both Neville and Louis a precision, an exactitude, that I admire and shall never possess. Now I begin to be aware that action is demanded. We approach a junction; at a junction I have to change. I have to board a train for Edinburgh. I cannot precisely lay fingers on this fact – it lodges loosely among my thoughts like a button, like a small coin. Here is the jolly old boy who collects tickets. I had one – I had one certainly. But it does not matter. Either I shall find it, or I shall not find it. I examine my notecase. I look in all my pockets. These are the things that forever interrupt the process upon which I am eternally engaged of finding some perfect phrase that fits this very moment exactly.'

'Bernard has gone,' said Neville, 'without a ticket. He has escaped us, making a phrase, waving his hand. He talked as easily to the horse-breeder or to the plumber as to us. The plumber accepted him with devotion. "If he had a son like that," he was thinking, "he would manage to send him to Oxford." But what did Bernard feel for the plumber? Did he not only wish to continue the sequence of the story which he never stops telling himself? He began it when he rolled his bread into pellets as a child. One pellet was a man, one was a woman. We are all pellets. We are all phrases in Bernard's story, things he writes down in his notebook under A or under B. He tells our story with extraordinary understanding, except of what we most feel.

For he does not need us. He is never at our mercy. There he is, waving his arms on the platform. The train has gone without him. He has missed his connection. He has lost his ticket. But that does not matter. He will talk to the barmaid about the nature of human destiny. We are off; he has forgotten us already; we pass out of his view; we go on, filled with lingering sensations, half bitter, half sweet, for he is somehow to be pitied, breasting the world with half-finished phrases, having lost his ticket: he is also to be loved.

'Now I pretend again to read. I raise my book, till it almost covers my eyes. But I cannot read in the presence of horse-dealers and plumbers. I have no power of ingratiating myself. I do not admire that man; he does not admire me. Let me at least be honest. Let me denounce this piffling, trifling, self-satisfied world; these horsehair seats; these coloured photographs of piers and parades. I could shriek aloud at the smug self-satisfaction, at the mediocrity of this world, which breeds horse-dealers with coral ornaments hanging from their watch-chains. There is that in me which will consume them entirely. My laughter shall make them twist in their seats; shall drive them howling before me. No; they are immortal. They triumph. They will make it impossible for me always to read Catullus in a third-class railway carriage. They will drive me in October to take refuge in one of the universities, where I shall become a don; and go with schoolmasters to Greece; and lecture on the ruins of the Parthenon. It would be better to breed horses and live in one of those red villas than to run in and out of the skulls of Sophocles and Euripides like a maggot, with a high-minded wife, one of those university women. That, however, will be my fate. I shall suffer. I am already at eighteen capable of such contempt that horse-breeders hate me. That is my triumph; I do not compromise. I am not timid; I have no accent. I do not finick about fearing what people think of "my father a banker at Brisbane" like Louis.

'Now we draw near the centre of the civilised world. There are the familiar gasometers. There are the public gardens intersected by asphalt paths. There are the lovers lying shamelessly mouth to mouth on the burnt grass. Percival is now almost in Scotland; his train draws through the red moors; he sees the long line of the Border hills and the Roman wall. He reads a detective novel, yet understands everything.

'The train slows and lengthens, as we approach London, the centre, and my heart draws out too, in fear, in exultation. I am about to meet – what? What extraordinary adventure waits me, among these mail vans, these porters, these swarms of people calling taxis? I feel insignificant, lost, but exultant. With a soft shock we stop. I will let the others get out before me. I will sit still one moment before I emerge into that chaos, that tumult. I will not anticipate what is to come. The huge uproar is in my ears. It sounds and resounds under this glass roof like the surge of a sea. We are cast down on the platform with our hand-bags. We are whirled asunder. My sense of self almost perishes; my contempt. I become drawn in, tossed down, thrown sky-high. I step out on to the platform, grasping tightly all that I possess – one bag.'

The sun rose. Bars of yellow and green fell on the shore, gilding the ribs of the eaten-out boat and making the sea-holly and its mailed leaves gleam blue as steel. Light almost pierced the thin swift waves as they raced fan-shaped over the beach. The girl who had shaken her head and made all the jewels, the topaz, the aquamarine, the water-coloured jewels with sparks of fire in them, dance, now bared her brows and with wide-opened eyes drove a straight pathway over the waves. Their quivering mackerel sparkling was darkened; they massed themselves; their green hollows deepened and darkened and might be traversed by shoals of wandering fish. As they splashed and drew back they left a black rim of twigs and cork on the shore and straws and sticks of wood, as if some light shallop had foundered and burst its sides and the sailor had swum to land and bounded up the cliff and left his frail cargo to be washed ashore.

In the garden the birds that had sung erratically and spasmodically in the dawn on that tree, on that bush, now sang together in chorus, shrill and sharp; now together, as if conscious of companionship, now alone as if to the pale blue sky. They swerved, all in one flight, when the black cat moved among the bushes, when the cook threw cinders on the ash heap and startled them. Fear was in their song, and apprehension of pain, and joy to be snatched quickly now at this instant. Also they sang emulously in the clear morning air, swerving high over the elm tree, singing together as they chased each other, escaping, pursuing, pecking each other as they turned high in the air. And then tiring of pursuit and light, lovelily they came descending, delicately declining, dropped down and sat silent on the tree, on the wall, with their bright eyes glancing, and their heads turned this way, that way; aware, awake; intensely conscious of one thing, one object in particular.

Perhaps it was a snail shell, rising in the grass like a grey cathedral, a swelling building burnt with dark rings and shadowed green by the grass. Or perhaps they saw the splendour of the flowers making a light of flowing purple over the beds, through which dark tunnels of purple shade were driven between the stalks. Or they fixed their gaze on the small bright apple leaves, dancing yet withheld, stiffly sparkling among the pink-tipped blossoms. Or they saw the rain drop on the hedge, pendent but not falling, with a whole house bent in it, and towering elms; or, gazing straight at the sun, their eyes became gold beads.

Now glancing this side, that side, they looked deeper, beneath the flowers, down the dark avenues into the unlit world where the leaf rots and the flower has fallen. Then one of them, beautifully darting, accurately alighting, spiked the soft, monstrous body of the defenceless worm, pecked again and yet again, and left it to fester. Down there among the roots where the flowers decayed, gusts of dead smells were wafted; drops formed on the bloated sides of swollen things. The skin of rotten fruit broke, and matter oozed too thick to run. Yellow excretions were exuded by slugs, and now and again an amorphous body with a head at either end swayed slowly from side to side. The gold-eyed birds darting in between the leaves observed

SELECTED WORKS OF VIRGINIA WOOLF

that purulence, that wetness, quizzically. Now and then they plunged the tips of their beaks savagely into the sticky mixture.

Now, too, the rising sun came in at the window, touching the red-edged curtain, and began to bring out circles and lines. Now in the growing light its whiteness settled in the plate; the blade condensed its gleam. Chairs and cupboards loomed behind so that though each was separate they seemed inextricably involved. The looking-glass whitened its pool upon the wall. The real flower on the windowsill was attended by a phantom flower. Yet the phantom was part of the flower, for when a bud broke free the paler flower in the glass opened a bud too.

The wind rose. The waves drummed on the shore, like turbaned warriors, like turbaned men with poisoned assegais who, whirling their arms on high, advance upon the feeding flocks, the white sheep.

'The complexity of things becomes more close,' said Bernard, 'here at college, where the stir and pressure of life are so extreme, where the excitement of mere living becomes daily more urgent. Every hour something new is unburied in the great bran pie. What am I? I ask. This? No, I am that. Especially now, when I have left a room, and people talking, and the stone flags ring out with my solitary footsteps, and I behold the moon rising, sublimely, indifferently, over the ancient chapel – then it becomes clear that I am not one and simple, but complex and many. Bernard in public, bubbles; in private, is secretive. That is what they do not understand, for they are now undoubtedly discussing me, saying I escape them, am evasive. They do not understand that I have to effect different transitions; have to cover the entrances and exits of several different men who alternately act their parts as Bernard. I am abnormally aware of circumstances. I can never read a book in a railway carriage without asking, Is he a builder? Is she unhappy? I was aware today acutely that poor Simes, with his pimple, was feeling, how bitterly, that his chance of making a good impression upon Billy Jackson was remote. Feeling this painfully, I invited him to dinner with ardour. This he will attribute to an admiration which is not mine. That is true. But "joined to the sensibility of a woman" (I am here quoting my own biographer), "Bernard possessed the logical sobriety of a man". Now people who make a single impression, and that, in the main, a good one (for there seems to be a virtue in simplicity), are those who keep their equilibrium in midstream. (I instantly see fish with their noses one way, the stream rushing past another.) Canon, Lycett, Peters, Hawkins, Larpent, Neville – all fish in midstream. But *you* understand, *you*, my self, who always comes at a call (that would be a harrowing experience to call and for no one to come; that would make the midnight hollow, and explains the expression of old men in clubs – they have given up calling for a self who does not come), you understand that I am only superficially represented by what I was saying tonight. Underneath, and at the moment when I am most disparate, I am also integrated. I sympathise effusively; I also sit like a toad in a hole, receiving with perfect coldness whatever comes. Very few of you who are now discussing me have the double capacity to feel, to reason. Lycett, you see, believes in running after hares; Hawkins has spent a most industrious afternoon in the library. Peters has his young lady at the circulating library. You are all engaged, involved, drawn in, and absolutely energised to the top of your bent – all save Neville, whose mind is far too complex to be roused by any single activity. I also am too complex. In my case something remains floating, unattached.

'Now, as a proof of my susceptibility to atmosphere, here, as I come into my room, and turn on the light, and see the sheet of paper, the table, my gown lying negligently over the back of the chair, I feel that I am that dashing yet reflective man, that bold and deleterious figure, who, lightly throwing off his cloak, seizes his pen and at once flings off the following letter to the girl with whom he is passionately in love.

'Yes, all is propitious. I am now in the mood. I can write the letter straight off which I have begun ever so many times. I have just come in; I have flung down my hat and my stick; I am writing the first thing that comes into my head without troubling to put the paper straight. It is going to be a brilliant sketch which, she must think, was written without a pause, without an erasure. Look how unformed the letters are – there is a careless blot. All must be sacrificed to speed and carelessness. I will write a quick, running, small hand, exaggerating the down stroke of the y and crossing the t thus – with a dash. The date shall be only Tuesday, the 17th, and then a question mark. But also I must give her the impression that though he – for this is not myself – is writing in such an offhand, such a slapdash way, there is some subtle suggestion of intimacy and respect. I must allude to talks we have had together – bring back some remembered scene. But I must seem to her (this is very important) to be passing from thing to thing with the greatest ease in the world. I shall pass from the service for the man who was drowned (I have a phrase for that) to Mrs Moffat and her sayings (I have a note of them), and so to some reflections apparently casual but full of profundity (profound criticism is often written casually) about some book I have been reading, some out-of-the-way book. I want her to say as she brushes her hair or puts out the candle, "Where did I read that? Oh, in Bernard's letter." It is the speed, the hot, molten effect, the laval flow of sentence into sentence that I need. Who am I thinking of? Byron of course. I am, in some ways, like Byron. Perhaps a sip of Byron will help to put me in the vein. Let me read a page. No; this is dull; this is scrappy. This is rather too formal. Now I am getting the hang of it. Now I am getting his beat into my brain (the rhythm is the main thing in writing). Now, without pausing I will begin, on the very lilt of the stroke –

'Yet it falls flat. It peters out. I cannot get up steam enough to carry me over the transition. My true self breaks off from my assumed. And if I begin to rewrite it, she will feel, "Bernard is posing as a literary man; Bernard is thinking of his biographer" (which is true). No, I will write the letter tomorrow directly after breakfast.

'Now let me fill my mind with imaginary pictures. Let me suppose that I am asked to stay at Restover, King's Laughton, Station Langley three miles. I arrive in the dusk. In the courtyard of this shabby but distinguished house there are two or three dogs, slinking, long-legged. There are faded rugs in the hall; a military gentleman smokes a pipe as he paces the terrace. The note is of distinguished poverty and military connections. A hunter's hoof on the writing-table – a favourite horse. "Do you ride?" "Yes, sir, I love riding." "My daughter expects us in the drawing-room." My heart pounds against my ribs. She is standing at a low table; she has been hunting; she munches sandwiches like a tomboy. I make a fairly good impression on the colonel. I am not too clever, he thinks; I am not too raw. Also I play billiards. Then the nice maid who has been with the family thirty years comes in. The pattern on the plates is of Oriental long-tailed birds. Her mother's portrait in muslin hangs over the fireplace. I can sketch the surroundings up to a point with extraordinary ease. But can I make it work? Can I hear her voice – the precise tone with which, when we are alone, she says "Bernard"? And then what next?

'The truth is that I need the stimulus of other people. Alone, over my dead fire, I tend to see the thin places in my own stories. The real novelist, the perfectly simple human being, could go on, indefinitely, imagining. He would not integrate, as I do. He would not have this devastating sense of grey ashes in a burnt-out grate. Some blind flaps in my eyes. Everything becomes impervious. I cease to invent.

'Let me recollect. It has been on the whole a good day. The drop that forms on the roof of the soul in the evening is round, many-coloured. There was the morning, fine; there was the afternoon, walking. I like views of spires across grey fields. I like glimpses between people's shoulders. Things kept popping into my head. I was imaginative, subtle. After dinner, I was dramatic. I put into concrete form many things that we had dimly observed about our common friends. I made my transitions easily. But now let me ask myself the final question, as I sit over this grey fire, with its naked promontories of black coal, which of these people am I? It depends so much upon the room. When I say to myself, "Bernard", who comes? A faithful, sardonic man, disillusioned, but not embittered. A man of no particular age or calling. Myself, merely. It is he who now takes the poker and rattles the cinders so that they fall in showers through the grate. "Lord," he says to himself, watching them fall, "what a pother!" and then he adds, lugubriously but with some sense of consolation, "Mrs Moffat will come and sweep it all up – " I fancy I shall often repeat to myself that phrase, as I rattle and bang through life, hitting first this side of the carriage, then the other, "Oh, yes, Mrs Moffat will come and sweep it all up." And so to bed.'

'In a world which contains the present moment,' said Neville, 'why discriminate? Nothing should be named lest by so doing we change it. Let it exist, this bank, this beauty, and I, for one instant, steeped in pleasure. The sun is hot. I see the river. I see trees specked and burnt in the autumn sunlight. Boats float past, through the red, through the green. Far away a bell tolls, but not for death. There are bells that ring for life. A leaf falls, from joy. Oh, I am in love with life! Look how the willow shoots its fine sprays into the air! Look how through them a boat passes, filled with indolent, with unconscious, with powerful young men. They are listening to the gramophone; they are eating fruit out of paper bags. They are tossing the skins of bananas, which then sink eel-like, into the river. All they do is beautiful. There are cruets behind them and ornaments; their rooms are full of oars and oleographs but they have turned all to beauty. That boat passes under the bridge. Another comes. Then another. That is Percival, lounging on the cushions, monolithic, in giant repose. No, it is only one of his satellites, imitating his monolithic, his giant repose. He alone is unconscious of their tricks, and when he catches them at it he buffets them good-humouredly with a blow of his paw. They, too, have passed under the bridge through "the fountains of the pendent trees", through its fine strokes of yellow and plum colour. The breeze stirs; the curtain quivers; I see behind the leaves the grave yet eternally joyous buildings, which seem porous, not gravid; light, though set so immemorially on the ancient turf. Now begins to rise in me the familiar rhythm; words that have lain dormant now lift, now toss their crests, and fall and rise, and fall and rise again. I am a poet, yes. Surely I am a great poet. Boats and youth passing and distant trees, "the falling fountains of the pendent trees". I see it all. I feel it all. I am inspired. My eyes fill with tears. Yet even as I feel this, I lash my frenzy higher and higher. It foams. It becomes artificial, insincere. Words and words and words, how they gallop – how they lash their long manes and tails, but for some fault in me I cannot give myself to their backs; I cannot fly with them, scattering women and string bags. There is some flaw in me – some fatal hesitancy, which, if I pass it over, turns to foam and falsity. Yet it is incredible that I should not be a great poet. What did I write last night if it was not poetry? Am I too fast, too facile? I do not know. I do not know myself sometimes, or how to measure and name and count out the grains that make me what I am.

'Something now leaves me; something goes from me to meet that figure who is coming, and assures me that I know him before I see who it is. How curiously one is changed by the addition, even at a distance, of a friend. How useful an office one's friends perform when they recall us. Yet how painful to be recalled, to be mitigated, to have one's self adulterated, mixed up, become part of another. As he approaches I become not myself but Neville mixed with somebody – with whom? – with Bernard? Yes, it is Bernard, and it is to Bernard that I shall put the question, Who am I?'

'How strange,' said Bernard, 'the willow looks seen together. I was Byron, and the tree was Byron's tree, lachrymose, down-showering, lamenting. Now that we look at the tree together, it has a combed look, each branch distinct, and I will tell you what I feel, under the compulsion of your clarity.

'I feel your disapproval, I feel your force. I became, with you, an untidy, an impulsive human being whose bandanna handkerchief is forever stained with the grease of crumpets. Yes, I hold Gray's *Elegy* in one hand; with the other I scoop out the bottom crumpet that has absorbed all the butter and sticks to the bottom of the plate. This offends you; I feel your distress acutely. Inspired by it and anxious to regain your good opinion, I proceed to tell you how I have just pulled Percival out of bed; I describe his slippers, his table, his guttered candle; his surly and complaining accents as I pull the blanket off his feet; he burrowing like some vast cocoon meanwhile. I describe all this in such a way that, centred as you are upon some private sorrow (for a hooded shape presides over our encounter), you give way, you laugh and delight in me. My charm and flow of language, unexpected and spontaneous as it is, delights me too. I am astonished, as I draw the veil off things with words, how much, how infinitely more than I can say, I have observed. More and more bubbles into my mind as I talk, images and images. This, I say to myself, is what I need; why, I ask, can I not finish the letter that I am writing? For my room is always scattered with unfinished letters. I begin to suspect, when I am with you, that I am among the most gifted of men. I am filled with the delight of youth, with potency, with the sense of what is to come. Blundering, but fervid, I see myself buzzing round flowers, humming down scarlet cups, making blue funnels resound with my prodigious booming. How richly I shall enjoy my youth (you make me feel). And London. And freedom. But stop. You are not listening. You are making some protest, as you slide, with an inexpressibly familiar gesture, your hand along your knee. By such signs we diagnose our friends' diseases. "Do not, in your affluence and plenty," you seem to say, "pass me by." "Stop," you say. "Ask me what I suffer."

'Let me then create you. (You have done as much for me.) You lie on this hot bank, in this lovely, this fading, this still bright October day, watching boat after boat float through the combed-out twigs of the willow tree. And you wish to be a poet; and you wish to be a lover. But the splendid clarity of your intelligence, and the remorseless honesty of your intellect (these Latin words I owe you; these qualities of yours make me shift a little uneasily and see the faded patches, the thin strands in my own equipment) bring you to a halt. You indulge in no mystifications. You do not fog yourself with rosy clouds, or yellow.

'Am I right? Have I read the little gesture of your left hand correctly? If so, give me your poems; hand over the sheets you wrote last night in such a fervour of inspiration that you now feel a little sheepish. For you distrust inspiration, yours or mine. Let us go back together, over the bridge, under the elm trees, to my room, where, with walls round us and red serge curtains drawn, we can shut out these distracting voices, scents and savours of lime trees, and other lives; these pert shop-girls, disdainfully tripping, these shuffling, heavy-laden old women; these furtive glimpses of some vague and vanishing figure – it might be Jinny, it might be Susan, or was that Rhoda disappearing down the avenue? Again, from some slight twitch I guess your feeling; I have escaped you; I have gone buzzing like a swarm of bees, endlessly vagrant, with none of your power of fixing remorselessly upon a single object. But I will return.'

'When there are buildings like these,' said Neville, 'I cannot endure that there should be shop-girls. Their titter, their gossip, offends me; breaks into my stillness, and nudges me, in moments of purest exultation, to remember our degradation.

'But now we have regained our territory after that brief brush with the bicycles and the lime scent and the vanishing figures in the distracted street. Here we are masters of tranquillity and order; inheritors of proud tradition. The lights are beginning to make yellow slits across the square. Mists from the river are filling these ancient spaces. They cling gently to the hoary stone. The leaves now are thick in country lanes, sheep cough in the damp fields; but here in your room we are dry. We talk privately. The fire leaps and sinks, making some knob bright.

'You have been reading Byron. You have been marking the passages that seem to approve of your own character. I find marks against all those sentences which seem to express a sardonic yet passionate nature; a mothlike impetuosity dashing itself against hard glass. You thought, as you drew your pencil there, "I too throw off my cloak like that. I too snap my fingers in the face of destiny." Yet Byron never made tea as you do, who fill the pot so that when you put the lid on the tea spills over. There is a brown pool on the table – it is running among your books and papers. Now you mop it up, clumsily, with your pocket-handkerchief. You then stuff your handkerchief back into your pocket – that is not Byron; that is you; that is so essentially you that if I think of you in twenty years' time, when we are both famous, gouty and intolerable, it will be by that scene: and if you are dead, I shall weep. Once you were Tolstoy's young man; now you are Byron's young man; perhaps you will be Meredith's young man; then you will visit Paris in the Easter vacation and come back wearing a black tie for some detestable Frenchman whom nobody has ever heard of. Then I shall drop you.

'I am one person – myself. I do not impersonate Catullus, whom I adore. I am the most slavish of students, with here a dictionary, there a notebook in which I enter curious uses of the past participle. But one cannot go on for ever cutting these ancient inscriptions clearer with a knife. Shall I always draw the red serge curtain close and see my book, laid like a block of marble, pale under the lamp? That would be a glorious life, to addict oneself to perfection; to follow the curve of the sentence wherever it might lead, into deserts, under drifts of sand, regardless of lures, of seductions; to be poor always and unkempt; to be ridiculous in Piccadilly.

'But I am too nervous to end my sentence properly. I speak quickly, as I pace up and down, to conceal my agitation. I hate your greasy handker-chiefs – you will stain your copy of Don Juan. You are not listening to me. You are making phrases about Byron. And while you gesticulate, with your cloak, your cane, I am trying to expose a secret told to nobody yet; I am asking you (as I stand with my back to you) to take my life in your hands and tell me whether I am doomed always to cause repulsion in those I love?

'I stand with my back to you fidgeting. No, my hands are now perfectly still. Precisely, opening a space in the bookcase, I insert Don Juan; there. I would rather be loved, I would rather be famous than follow perfection through the sand. But am I doomed to cause disgust? Am I a poet? Take it. The desire which is loaded behind my lips, cold as lead, fell as a bullet, the thing I aim at shop-girls, women, the pretence, the vulgarity of life (because I love it) shoots at you as I throw – catch it – my poem.'

'He has shot like an arrow from the room,' said Bernard. 'He has left me his poem. O friendship, I too will press flowers between the pages of Shakespeare's sonnets! O friendship, how piercing are your darts – there, there, again there. He looked at me, turning to face me; he gave me his poem. All mists curl off the roof of my being. That confidence I shall keep to my dying day. Like a long wave, like a roll of heavy waters, he went over me, his devastating presence – dragging me open, laying bare the pebbles on the shore of my soul. It was humiliating; I was turned to small stones. All semblances were rolled up. "You are not Byron; you are your self." To be contracted by another person into a single being – how strange.

'How strange to feel the line that is spun from us lengthening its fine filament across the misty spaces of the intervening world. He is gone; I stand here, holding his poem. Between us is this line. But now, how comfortable, how reassuring to feel that alien presence removed, that scrutiny darkened and hooded over! How grateful to draw the blinds, and admit no other presence; to feel, returning from the dark corners in which they took refuge, those shabby inmates, those familiars, whom, with his superior force, he drove into hiding. The mocking, the observant spirits who, even in the crisis and stab of the moment, watched on my behalf now come flocking home again. With their addition, I am Bernard; I am Byron; I am this, that and the other. They darken the air and enrich me, as of old, with their antics, their comments, and cloud the fine simplicity of my moment of emotion. For I am more selves than Neville thinks. We are not simple as our friends would have us to meet their needs. Yet love is simple.

'Now they have returned, my inmates, my familiars. Now the stab, the rent in my defences that Neville made with his astonishing fine rapier, is repaired. I am almost whole now; and see how jubilant I am, bringing into play all that Neville ignores in me. I feel, as I look from the window, parting the curtains, "That would give him no pleasure; but it rejoices me." (We use our friends to measure our own stature.) My scope embraces what Neville never reaches. They are shouting hunting-songs over the way. They are celebrating some run with the beagles. The little boys in caps who always turned at the same moment when the brake went round the corner are clapping each other on the shoulder and boasting. But Neville, delicately avoiding interference, stealthily, like a conspirator, hastens back to his room. I see him sunk in his low chair gazing at the fire which has assumed for the moment an architectural solidity. If life, he thinks, could wear that permanence, if life could have that order – for above all he desires order, and detests my Byronic untidiness; and so draws his curtain; and bolts his door. His eyes (for he is in love; the sinister figure of love presided at our encounter) fill with longing; fill with tears. He snatches the poker and with one blow destroys that momentary appearance of solidity in the burning coals. All changes. And youth and love. The boat has floated through the arch of the willows and is now under the bridge. Percival, Tony, Archie, or another, will go to India. We shall not meet again. Then he stretches his hand for his copybook – a neat volume bound in mottled paper – and writes feverishly long lines of poetry, in the manner of whomever he admires most at the moment.

'But I want to linger; to lean from the window; to listen. There again comes that rollicking chorus. They are now smashing china – that also is the convention. The chorus, like a torrent jumping rocks, brutally assaulting old trees, pours with splendid abandonment headlong over precipices. On they roll; on they gallop; after hounds, after footballs; they pump up and down attached to oars like sacks of flour. All divisions are merged – they act like one man. The gusty October wind blows the uproar in bursts of sound and silence across the court. Now again they are smashing the china – that is the convention. An old, unsteady woman carrying a bag trots home under the fire-red windows. She is half afraid that they will fall on her and tumble her into the gutter. Yet she pauses as if to warm her knobbed, her rheumaticky hands at the bonfire which flares away with streams of sparks and bits of blown paper. The old woman pauses against the lit window. A contrast. That I see and Neville does not see; that I feel and Neville does not feel. Hence he will reach perfection, and I shall fail and shall leave nothing behind me but imperfect phrases littered with sand.

'I think of Louis now. What malevolent yet searching light would Louis throw upon this dwindling autumn evening, upon this china-smashing and trolling of hunting-songs, upon Neville, Byron and our life here? His thin lips are somewhat pursed; his cheeks are pale; he pores in an office over some obscure commercial document. "My father, a banker at Brisbane" – being ashamed of him he always talks of him – failed. So he sits in an office, Louis the best scholar in the school. But I seeking contrasts often feel his eye on us, his laughing eye, his wild eye, adding us up like insignificant items in some grand total which he is forever pursuing in his office. And one day, taking a fine pen and dipping it in red ink, the addition will be complete; our total will be known; but it will not be enough.

'Bang! They have thrown a chair now against the wall. We are damned then. My case is dubious too. Am I not indulging in unwarranted emotions? Yes, as I lean out of the window and drop my cigarette so that it twirls lightly to the ground, I feel Louis watching even my cigarette. And Louis says, "That means something. But what?" '

'People go on passing,' said Louis. 'They pass the window of this eating-shop incessantly. Motor-cars, vans, motor-omnibuses; and again motor-omnibuses, vans, motor-cars – they pass the window. In the background

I perceive shops and houses; also the grey spires of a city church. In the foreground are glass shelves set with plates of buns and ham sandwiches. All is somewhat obscured by steam from a tea-urn. A meaty, vapourish smell of beef and mutton, sausages and mash, hangs down like a damp net in the middle of the eating-house. I prop my book against a bottle of Worcester sauce and try to look like the rest.

'Yet I cannot. (They go on passing, they go on passing in disorderly procession.) I cannot read my book, or order my beef, with conviction. I repeat, "I am an average Englishman; I am an average clerk", yet I look at the little men at the next table to be sure that I do what they do. Supple-faced, with rippling skins, that are always twitching with the multiplicity of their sensations, prehensile like monkeys, greased to this particular moment, they are discussing with all the right gestures the sale of a piano. It blocks up the hall; so he would take a tenner. People go on passing; they go on passing against the spires of the church and the plates of ham sandwiches. The streamers of my consciousness waver out and are perpetually torn and distressed by their disorder. I cannot therefore concentrate on my dinner. "I would take a tenner. The case is handsome; but it blocks up the hall." They dive and plunge like guillemots whose feathers are slippery with oil. All excesses beyond that norm are vanity. That is the mean; that is the average. Meanwhile the hats bob up and down; the door perpetually shuts and opens. I am conscious of flux, of disorder; of annihilation and despair. If this is all, this is worthless. Yet I feel, too, the rhythm of the eating-house. It is like a waltz tune, eddying in and out, round and round. The waitresses, balancing trays, swing in and out, round and round, dealing plates of greens, of apricots and custard, dealing them at the right time, to the right customers. The average men, including her rhythm in their rhythm ("I would take a tenner; for it blocks up the hall"), take their greens, take their apricots and custard. Where then is the break in this continuity? What the fissure through which one sees disaster? The circle is unbroken; the harmony complete. Here is the central rhythm; here the common mainspring. I watch it expand, contract; and then expand again. Yet I am not included. If I speak, imitating their accent, they prick their ears, waiting for me to speak again, in order that they may place me – if I come from Canada or Australia, I, who desire above all things to be taken to the arms with love, am alien, external. I, who would wish to feel close over me the protective waves of the ordinary, catch with the tail of my eye some far horizon; am aware of hats bobbing up and down in perpetual disorder. To me is addressed the plaint of the wandering and distracted spirit (a woman with bad teeth falters at the counter), "Bring us back to the fold, we who pass so disjectedly, bobbing up and down, past windows with plates of ham sandwiches in the foreground." Yes; I will reduce you to order.

'I will read in the book that is propped against the bottle of Worcester sauce. It contains some forged rings, some perfect statements, a few words, but poetry. You, all of you, ignore it. What the dead poet said, you have forgotten. And I cannot translate it to you so that its binding power ropes you in, and makes it clear to you that you are aimless; and the rhythm is cheap and worthless; and so remove that degradation which, if you are unaware of your aimlessness, pervades you, making you senile, even while you are young. To translate that poem so that it is easily read is to be my endeavour. I, the companion of Plato, of Virgil, will knock at the grained oak door. I oppose to what is passing this ramrod of beaten steel. I will not submit to this aimless passing of billycock hats and Homburg hats and all the plumed and variegated head-dresses of women. (Susan, whom I respect, would wear a plain straw hat on a summer's day.) And the grinding and the steam that runs in unequal drops down the window-pane; and the stopping and the starting with a jerk of motor-omnibuses; and the hesitations at counters; and the words that trail drearily without human meaning; I will reduce you to order.

'My roots go down through veins of lead and silver, through damp, marshy places that exhale odours, to a knot made of oak roots bound together in the centre. Sealed and blind, with earth stopping my ears, I have yet heard rumours of wars; and the nightingale; have felt the hurrying of many troops of men flocking hither and thither in quest of civilisation like flocks of birds migrating seeking the summer; I have seen women carrying red pitchers to the banks of the Nile. I woke in a garden, with a blow on the nape of my neck, a hot kiss, Jinny's; remembering all this as one remembers confused cries and toppling pillars and shafts of red and black in some nocturnal conflagration. I am forever sleeping and waking. Now I sleep; now I wake. I see the gleaming tea-urn; the glass cases full of pale-yellow sandwiches; the men in round coats perched on stools at the counter; and also behind them, eternity. It is a stigma burnt on my quivering flesh by a cowled man with a red-hot iron. I see this eating-shop against the packed and fluttering birds' wings, many feathered, folded, of the past. Hence my pursed lips, my sickly pallor; my distasteful and uninviting aspect as I turn my face with hatred and bitterness upon Bernard and Neville, who saunter under yew trees; who inherit armchairs; and draw their curtains close, so that lamplight falls on their books.

'Susan, I respect; because she sits stitching. She sews under a quiet lamp in a house where the corn sighs close to the window and gives me safety. For I am the weakest, the youngest of them all. I am a child looking at his feet and the little runnels that the stream has made in the gravel. That is a snail, I say; that is a leaf. I delight in the snails; I delight in the leaf. I am always the youngest, the most innocent, the most trustful. You are all protected. I am naked. When the waitress with the plaited wreaths of hair swings past, she deals you your apricots and custard unhesitatingly, like a sister. You are her brothers. But when I get up, brushing the crumbs from my waistcoat, I slip too large a tip, a shilling, under the edge of my plate, so that she may not find it till I am gone, and her scorn, as she picks it up with laughter, may not strike on me till I am past the swing-doors.'

'Now the wind lifts the blind,' said Susan. 'Jars, bowls, matting and the shabby armchair with the hole in it are now become distinct. The usual faded ribbons sprinkle the wallpaper. The bird chorus is over, only one bird now sings close to the bedroom window. I will pull on my stockings and go quietly past the bedroom doors, and down through the kitchen, out through the garden past the greenhouse into the field. It is still early morning. The mist is on the marshes. The day is stark and stiff as a linen shroud. But it will soften; it will warm. At this hour, this still early hour, I think I am the field, I am the barn, I am the trees; mine are the flocks of birds, and this young hare who leaps, at the last moment when I step almost on him. Mine is the heron that stretches its vast wings lazily; and the cow that creaks as it pushes one foot before another munching; and the wild, swooping swallow; and the faint red in the sky, and the green when the red fades; the silence and the bell; the call of the man fetching cart-horses from the fields – all are mine.

'I cannot be divided, or kept apart. I was sent to school; I was sent to Switzerland to finish my education. I hate linoleum; I hate fir trees and mountains. Let me now fling myself on this flat ground under a pale sky where the clouds pace slowly. The cart grows gradually larger as it comes along the road. The sheep gather in the middle of the field. The birds gather in the middle of the road – they need not fly yet. The wood smoke rises. The starkness of the dawn is going out of it. Now the day stirs. Colour returns. The day waves yellow with all its crops. The earth hangs heavy beneath me.

'But who am I, who lean on this gate and watch my setter nose in a circle? I think sometimes (I am not twenty yet) I am not a woman, but the light that falls on this gate, on this ground. I am the seasons, I think sometimes, January, May, November; the mud, the mist, the dawn. I cannot be tossed about, or float gently, or mix with other people. Yet now, leaning here till the gate prints my arm, I feel the weight that has formed itself in my side. Something has formed, at school, in Switzerland, some hard thing. Not sighs and laughter; not circling and ingenious phrases; not Rhoda's strange communications when she looks past us, over our shoulders; nor Jinny's pirouetting, all of a piece, limbs and body. What I give is fell. I cannot float gently, mixing with other people. I like best the stare of shepherds met in the road; the stare of gypsy women beside a cart in a ditch suckling their children as I shall suckle my children. For soon in the hot midday when the bees hum round the hollyhocks my lover will come. He will stand under the cedar tree. To his one word I shall answer my one word. What has formed in me I shall give him. I shall have children; I shall have maids in aprons; men with pitchforks; a kitchen where they bring the ailing lambs to warm in baskets, where the hams hang and the onions glisten. I shall be like my mother, silent in a blue apron locking up the cupboards.

'Now I am hungry. I will call my setter. I think of crusts and bread and butter and white plates in a sunny room. I will go back across the fields. I will walk along this grass path with strong, even strides, now swerving to avoid the puddle, now leaping lightly to a clump. Beads of wet form on my rough skirt; my shoes become supple and dark. The stiffness has gone from the day; it is shaded with grey, green and umber. The birds no longer settle on the high road.

'I return, like a cat or fox returning, whose fur is grey with rime, whose pads are hardened by the coarse earth. I push through the cabbages, making their leaves squeak and their drops spill. I sit waiting for my father's foot-steps as he shuffles down the passage pinching some herb between his fingers. I pour out cup after cup while the unopened flowers hold them-selves erect on the table among the pots of jam, the loaves and the butter. We are silent.

'I go then to the cupboard, and take the damp bags of rich sultanas; I lift the heavy flour on to the clean scrubbed kitchen table. I knead; I stretch; I pull, plunging my hands in the warm inwards of the dough. I let the cold water stream fanwise through my fingers. The fire roars; the flies buzz in a circle. All my currants and rices, the silver bags and the blue bags, are locked again in the cupboard. The meat is stood in the oven; the bread rises in a soft dome under the clean towel. I walk in the afternoon down to the river. All the world is breeding. The flies are going from grass to grass. The flowers are thick with pollen. The swans ride the stream in order. The clouds, warm now, sun-spotted, sweep over the hills, leaving gold in the water, and gold on the necks of the swans. Pushing one foot before the other, the cows munch their way across the field. I feel through the grass for the white-domed mushroom; and break its stalk and pick the purple orchid that grows beside it and lay the orchid by the mushroom with the earth at its root, and so home to make the kettle boil for my father among the just reddened roses on the tea-table.

'But evening comes and the lamps are lit. And when evening comes and the lamps are lit they make a yellow fire in the ivy. I sit with my sewing by the table. I think of Jinny; of Rhoda; and hear the rattle of wheels on the pavement as the farm horses plod home; I hear traffic roaring in the evening wind. I look at the quivering leaves in the dark garden and think "They dance in London. Jinny kisses Louis." '

'How strange,' said Jinny, 'that people should sleep, that people should put out the lights and go upstairs. They have taken off their dresses, they have put on white nightgowns. There are no lights in any of these houses. There is a line of chimney-pots against the sky; and a street lamp or two burning, as lamps burn when nobody needs them. The only people in the streets are poor people hurrying. There is no one coming or going in this street; the day is over. A few policemen stand at the corners. Yet night is beginning. I feel myself shining in the dark. Silk is on my knee. My silk legs rub smoothly together. The stones of a necklace lie cold on my throat. My feet feel the pinch of shoes. I sit bolt upright so that my hair may not touch the back of the seat. I am arrayed, I am prepared. This is the momentary pause; the dark moment. The fiddlers have lifted their bows.

'Now the car slides to a stop. A strip of pavement is lighted. The door is opening and shutting. People are arriving; they do not speak; they hasten in. There is the swishing sound of cloaks falling in the hall. This is the prelude, this is the beginning. I glance, I peep, I powder. All is exact, prepared. My hair is swept in one curve. My lips are precisely red. I am ready now to join men and women on the stairs, my peers. I pass them, exposed to their gaze, as they are to mine. Like lightning we look but do not soften or show signs of recognition. Our bodies communicate. This is my calling. This is my world. All is decided and ready; the servants, standing here, and again here, take my name, my fresh, my unknown name, and toss it before me. I enter.

'Here are gilt chairs in the empty, the expectant rooms, and flowers, stiller, statelier, than flowers that grow, spread green, spread white, against the walls. And on one small table is one bound book. This is what I have dreamt; this is what I have foretold. I am native here. I tread naturally on thick carpets. I slide easily on smooth-polished floors. I now begin to unfurl, in this scent, in this radiance, as a fern when its curled leaves unfurl. I stop. I take stock of this world. I look among the groups of unknown people. Among the lustrous green, pink, pearl-grey women stand upright the bodies of men. They are black and white; they are grooved beneath their clothes with deep rills. I feel again the reflection in the window of the tunnel; it moves. The black-and-white figures of unknown men look at me as I lean forward; as I turn aside to look at a picture, they turn too. Their hands go fluttering to their ties. They touch their waistcoats, their pocket-handkerchiefs. They are very young. They are anxious to make a good impression. I feel a thousand capacities spring up in me. I am arch, gay, languid, melancholy by turns. I am rooted, but I flow. All gold, flowing that way, I say to this one, "Come." Rippling black, I say to that one, "No." One breaks off from his station under the glass cabinet. He approaches. He makes towards me. This is the most exciting moment I have ever known. I flutter. I ripple. I stream like a plant in the river, flowing this way, flowing that way but rooted, so that he may come to me. "Come," I say, "come." Pale, with dark hair, the one who is coming is melancholy, romantic. And I am arch and fluent and capricious; for he is melancholy, he is romantic. He is here; he stands at my side.

'Now with a little jerk, like a limpet broken from a rock, I am broken off: I fall with him; I am carried off. We yield to this slow flood. We go in and out of this hesitating music. Rocks break the current of the dance; it jars, it shivers. In and out, we are swept now into this large figure; it holds us together; we cannot step outside its sinuous, its hesitating, its abrupt, its perfectly encircling walls. Our bodies, his hard, mine flowing, are pressed together within its body; it holds us together; and then lengthening out, in smooth, in sinuous folds, rolls us between it, on and on. Suddenly the music breaks. My blood runs on but my body stands still. The room reels past my eyes. It stops.

'Come, then, let us wander whirling to the gilt chairs. The body is stronger than I thought. I am dizzier than I supposed. I do not care for anything in the world. I do not care for anybody save this man whose name I do not know. Are we not acceptable, moon? Are we not lovely sitting together here, I in my satin; he in black and white? My peers may look at me now. I look straight back at you, men and women. I am one of you. This is my world. Now I take this thin-stemmed glass and sip. Wine has a drastic, an astringent taste. I cannot help wincing as I drink. Scent and flowers, radiance and heat, are distilled here to a fiery, to a yellow liquid. Just behind my shoulder-blades some dry thing, wide-eyed, gently closes, gradually lulls itself to sleep. This is rapture; this is relief. The bar at the back of my throat lowers itself. Words crowd and cluster and push forth one on top of another. It does not matter which. They jostle and mount on each other's shoulders. The single and the solitary mate, tumble and become many. It does not matter what I say. Crowding, like a fluttering bird, one sentence crosses the empty space between us. It settles on his lips. I fill my glass again. I drink. The veils drop between us. I am admitted to the warmth and privacy of another soul. We are together, high up, on some Alpine pass. He stands melancholy on the crest of the road. I stoop. I pick a blue flower and fix it, standing on tiptoe to reach him, in his coat. There! That is my moment of ecstasy. Now it is over.

'Now slackness and indifference invade us. Other people brush past. We have lost consciousness of our bodies uniting under the table. I also like fair-haired men with blue eyes. The door opens. The door goes on opening. Now I think, next time it opens the whole of my life will be changed. Who comes? But it is only a servant, bringing glasses. That is an old man – I should be a child with him. That is a great lady – with her I should dissemble. There are girls of my own age, for whom I feel the drawn swords of an honourable antagonism. For these are my peers. I am a native of this world. Here is my risk, here is my adventure. The door opens. O come, I say to this one, rippling gold from head to heels. "Come," and he comes towards me.'

'I shall edge behind them,' said Rhoda, 'as if I saw someone I know. But I know no one. I shall twitch the curtain and look at the moon. Draughts of oblivion shall quench my agitation. The door opens; the tiger leaps. The door opens; terror rushes in; terror upon terror, pursuing me. Let me visit furtively the treasures I have laid apart. Pools lie on the other side of the world reflecting marble columns. The swallow dips her wing in dark pools. But here the door opens and people come; they come towards me. Throwing faint smiles to mask their cruelty, their indifference, they seize me. The swallow dips her wings; the moon rides through blue seas alone. I must take his hand; I must answer. But what answer shall I give? I am thrust back to stand burning in this clumsy, this ill-fitting body, to receive the shafts of his indifference and his scorn, I who long for marble columns and pools on the other side of the world where the swallow dips her wings.

'Night has wheeled a little further over the chimney-pots. I see out of the window over his shoulder some unembarrassed cat, not drowned in light, not trapped in silk, free to pause, to stretch, and to move again. I hate all details of the individual life. But I am fixed here to listen. An immense pressure is on me. I cannot move without dislodging the weight of centuries. A million arrows pierce me. Scorn and ridicule pierce me. I, who could beat my breast against the storm and let the hail choke me joyfully, am pinned down here; am exposed. The tiger leaps. Tongues with their whips are upon me. Mobile, incessant, they flicker over me. I must prevaricate and fence them off with lies. What amulet is there against this disaster? What face can I summon to lay cool upon this heat? I think of names on boxes; of mothers from whose wide knees skirts descend; of glades where the many-backed steep hills come down. Hide me, I cry, protect me, for I am the youngest, the most naked of you all. Jinny rides like a gull on the wave, dealing her looks adroitly here and there, saying this, saying that with truth. But I lie; I prevaricate.

'Alone, I rock my basins; I am mistress of my fleet of ships. But here, twisting the tassels of this brocaded curtain in my hostess's window, I am broken into separate pieces; I am no longer one. What then is the knowledge that Jinny has as she dances; the assurance that Susan has as, stooping quietly beneath the lamplight, she draws the white cotton through the eye of her needle? They say, Yes; they say, No; they bring their fists down with a bang on the table. But I doubt; I tremble; I see the wild thorn tree shake its shadow in the desert.

'Now I will walk, as if I had an end in view, across the room, to the balcony under the awning. I see the sky, softly feathered with its sudden effulgence of moon. I also see the railings of the square, and two people without faces, leaning like statues against the sky. There is, then, a world immune from change. When I have passed through this drawing-room flickering with tongues that cut me like knives, making me stammer, making me lie, I find faces rid of features, robed in beauty. The lovers crouch under the plane tree. The policeman stands sentinel at the corner. A man passes. There is, then, a world immune from change. But I am not composed enough, standing on tiptoe on the verge of fire, still scorched by the hot breath, afraid of the door opening and the leap of the tiger, to make even one sentence. What I say is perpetually contradicted. Each time the door opens I am interrupted. I am not yet twenty-one. I am to be broken. I am to be derided all my life. I am to be cast up and down among these men and women, with their twitching faces, with their lying tongues, like a cork on a rough sea. Like a ribbon of weed I am flung far every time the door opens. I am the foam that sweeps and fills the uttermost rims of the rocks with whiteness; I am also a girl, here in this room.'

The sun, risen, no longer couched on a green mattress darting a fitful glance through watery jewels, bared its face and looked straight over the waves. They fell with a regular thud. They fell with the concussion of horses' hooves on the turf. Their spray rose like the tossing of lances and assegais over the riders' heads. They swept the beach with steel blue and diamond-tipped water. They drew in and out with the energy, the muscularity, of an engine which sweeps its force out and in again. The sun fell on cornfields and woods. Rivers became blue and many-plaited, lawns that sloped down to the water's edge became green as birds' feathers softly ruffling their plumes. The hills, curved and controlled, seemed bound back by thongs, as a limb is laced by muscles; and the woods which bristled proudly on their flanks were like the curt, clipped mane on the neck of a horse.

In the garden where the trees stood thick over flowerbeds, ponds and greenhouses the birds sang in the hot sunshine, each alone. One sang under the bedroom window; another on the topmost twig of the lilac bush; another on the edge of the wall. Each sang stridently, with passion, with vehemence, as if to let the song burst out of it, no matter if it shattered the song of another bird with harsh discord. Their round eyes bulged with brightness; their claws gripped the twig or rail. They sang, exposed without shelter, to the air and the sun, beautiful in their new plumage, shell-veined or brightly mailed, here barred with soft blues, here splashed with gold or striped with one bright feather. They sang as if the song were urged out of them by the pressure of the morning. They sang as if the edge of being were sharpened and must cut, must split the softness of the blue-green light, the dampness of the wet earth; the fumes and steams of the greasy kitchen vapour; the hot breath of mutton and beef; the richness of pastry and fruit; the damp shreds and peelings thrown from the kitchen bucket, from which a slow steam oozed on the rubbish heap. On all the sodden, the damp-spotted, the curled with wetness, they descended, dry-beaked, ruthless, abrupt. They swooped suddenly from the lilac bough or the fence. They spied a snail and tapped the shell against a stone. They tapped furiously, methodically, until the shell broke and something slimy oozed from the crack. They swept and soared sharply in fights high into the air, twittering short, sharp notes, and perched in the upper branches of some tree, and looked down upon leaves and spires beneath, and the country white with blossom, flowing with grass, and the sea which beat like a drum that raises a regiment of plumed and turbaned soldiers. Now and again their songs ran together in swift scales like the interlacings of a mountain stream whose waters, meeting, foam and then mix, and hasten quicker and quicker down the same channel, brushing the same broad leaves. But there is a rock; they sever.

The sun fell in sharp wedges inside the room. Whatever the light touched became dowered with a fanatical existence. A plate was like a white lake. A knife looked like a dagger of ice. Suddenly tumblers revealed themselves upheld by streaks of light. Tables and chairs rose to the surface as if they had been sunk under water and rose, filmed with red, orange, purple like the bloom on the skin of ripe fruit. The veins on the glaze of the china, the grain of the wood, the fibres of the matting became more and more finely engraved. Everything was without shadow. A jar was so green that the eye seemed sucked up through a funnel by its intensity and stuck to it like a limpet. Then shapes took on mass and edge. Here was the boss of a chair; here the bulk of a cupboard. And as the light increased, flocks of shadow were driven before it and conglomerated and hung in many-pleated folds in the background.

'How fair, how strange,' said Bernard, 'glittering, many-pointed and many-domed London lies before me under mist. Guarded by gasometers, by factory chimneys, she lies sleeping as we approach. She folds the ant-heap to her breast. All cries, all clamour, are softly enveloped in silence. Not Rome herself looks more majestic. But we are aimed at her. Already her maternal somnolence is uneasy. Ridges fledged with houses rise from the mist. Factories, cathedrals, glass domes, institutions and theatres erect themselves. The early train from the north is hurled at her like a missile. We draw a curtain as we pass. Blank expectant faces stare at us as we rattle and flash through stations. Men clutch their newspapers a little tighter, as our wind sweeps them, envisaging death. But we roar on. We are about to explode in the flank of the city like a shell in the side of some ponderous, maternal, majestic animal. She hums and murmurs; she awaits us.

'Meanwhile, as I stand looking from the train window, I feel strangely, persuasively, that because of my great happiness (being engaged to be married) I am become part of this speed, this missile hurled at the city. I am numbed to tolerance and acquiescence. My dear sir, I could say, why do you fidget, taking down your suitcase and pressing into it the cap that you have worn all night? Nothing we can do will avail. Over us all broods a splendid unanimity. We are enlarged and solemnised and brushed into uniformity as with the grey wing of some enormous goose (it is a fine but colourless morning) because we have only one desire – to arrive at the station. I do not want the train to stop with a thud. I do not want the connection which has bound us together sitting opposite each other all night long to be broken. I do not want to feel that hate and rivalry have resumed their sway; and different desires. Our community in the rushing train, sitting together with only one wish to arrive at Euston, was very welcome. But behold! It is over. We have attained our desire. We have drawn up at the platform. Hurry and confusion and the wish to be first through the gate into the lift assert themselves. But I do not wish to be first through the gate, to assume the burden of individual life. I, who have been since Monday, when she accepted me, charged in every nerve with a sense of identity, who could not see a toothbrush in a glass without saying, "*My* toothbrush", now wish to unclasp my hands and let fall my possessions, and merely stand here in the street, taking no part, watching the omnibuses, without desire; without envy; with what would be boundless curiosity about human destiny if there were any longer an edge to my mind. But it has none. I have arrived; am accepted. I ask nothing.

'Having dropped off satisfied like a child from the breast, I am at liberty now to sink down, deep, into what passes, this omnipresent, general life. (How much, let me note, depends upon trousers; the intelligent head is entirely handicapped by shabby trousers.) One observes curious hesitations at the door of the lift. This way, that way, the other? Then individuality asserts itself. They are off. They are all impelled by some necessity. Some miserable affair of keeping an appointment, of buying a hat, severs these beautiful human beings once so united. For myself, I have no aim. I have no ambition. I will let myself be carried on by the general impulse. The surface of my mind slips along like a pale-grey stream reflecting what passes. I cannot remember my past, my nose, or the colour of my eyes, or what my general opinion of myself is. Only in moments of emergency, at a crossing, at a kerb, the wish to preserve my body springs out and seizes me and stops me, here, before this omnibus. We insist, it seems, on living. Then again, indifference descends. The roar of the traffic, the passage of undifferentiated faces, this way and that way, drugs me into dreams; rubs the features from faces. People might walk through me. And, what is this moment of time, this particular day in which I have found myself caught? The growl of traffic might be any uproar – forest trees or the roar of wild beasts. Time has whizzed back an inch or two on its reel; our short progress has been cancelled. I think also that our bodies are in truth naked. We are only lightly covered with buttoned cloth; and beneath these pavements are shells, bones and silence.

'It is, however, true that my dreaming, my tentative advance like one carried beneath the surface of a stream, is interrupted, torn, pricked and plucked at by sensations, spontaneous and irrelevant, of curiosity, greed, desire, irresponsible as in sleep. (I covet that bag – etc.) No, but I wish to go under; to visit the profound depths; once in a while to exercise my prerogative not always to act, but to explore; to hear vague, ancestral sounds of boughs creaking, of mammoths; to indulge impossible desires to embrace the whole world with the arms of understanding – impossible to those who act. Am I not, as I walk, trembling with strange oscillations and vibrations of sympathy, which, unmoored as I am from a private being, bid me embrace these engrossed flocks; these starers and trippers; these errand-boys and furtive and fugitive girls who, ignoring their doom, look in at shop-windows? But I am aware of our ephemeral passage.

'It is, however, true that I cannot deny a sense that life for me is now mysteriously prolonged. Is it that I may have children, may cast a fling of seed wider, beyond this generation, this doom-encircled population, shuffling each other in endless competition along the street? My daughters shall come here, in other summers; my sons shall turn new fields. Hence we are not raindrops, soon dried by the wind; we make gardens blow and forests roar; we come up differently, for ever and ever. This, then, serves to explain my confidence, my central stability, otherwise so monstrously absurd as I breast the stream of this crowded thoroughfare, making always a passage for myself between people's bodies, taking advantage of safe moments to cross. It is not vanity; for I am emptied of ambition; I do not remember my special gifts, or idiosyncrasy, or the marks I bear on my person; eyes, nose or mouth. I am not, at this moment, myself.

'Yet behold, it returns. One cannot extinguish that persistent smell. It steals in through some crack in the structure – one's identity. I am not part of the street – no, I observe the street. One splits off, therefore. For instance, up that back street a girl stands waiting; for whom? A romantic story. On the wall of that shop is fixed a small crane, and for what reason, I ask, was that crane fixed there? and invent a purple lady swelling, circumambient, hauled from a barouche landau by a perspiring husband sometime in the sixties. A grotesque story. That is, I am a natural coiner of words, a blower of bubbles through one thing and another. And, striking off these observations spontaneously, I elaborate myself; differentiate myself and, listening to the voice that says as I stroll past, "Look! Take note of that!" I conceive myself called upon to provide, some winter's night, a meaning for all my observations – a line that runs from one to another, a summing up that completes. But soliloquies in back streets soon pall. I need an audience. That is my downfall. That always ruffles the edge of the final statement and prevents it from forming. I cannot seat myself in some sordid eating-house and order the same glass day after day and imbue myself entirely in one fluid – this life. I make my phrase and run off with it to some furnished room where it will be lit by dozens of candles. I need eyes on me to draw out these frills and furbelows. To be myself (I note) I need the illumination of other people's eyes, and therefore cannot be entirely sure what is my self. The authentics, like Louis, like Rhoda, exist most completely in solitude. They resent illumination, reduplication. They toss their pictures once painted face downward on the field. On Louis's words the ice is packed thick. His words issue pressed, condensed, enduring.

'I wish, then, after this somnolence to sparkle many-faceted under the light of my friends' faces. I have been traversing the sunless territory of non-identity. A strange land. I have heard in my moment of appeasement, in my moment of obliterating satisfaction, the sigh, as it goes in, comes out, of the tide that draws beyond this circle of bright light, this drumming of insensate fury. I have had one moment of enormous peace. This perhaps is happiness. Now I am drawn back by pricking sensations; by curiosity, greed (I am hungry) and the irresistible desire to be myself. I think of people to whom I could say things: Louis, Neville, Susan, Jinny and Rhoda. With them I am many-sided. They retrieve me from darkness. We shall meet tonight, thank heaven. Thank heaven, I need not be alone. We shall dine together. We shall say goodbye to Percival, who goes to India. The hour is still distant, but I feel already those harbingers, those outriders, figures of one's friends in absence. I see Louis, stone-carved, sculpturesque; Neville, scissor-cutting, exact; Susan with eyes like lumps of crystal; Jinny dancing like a flame, febrile, hot, over dry earth; and Rhoda the nymph of the fountain always wet. These are fantastic pictures – these are figments, these visions of friends in absence, grotesque, dropsical, vanishing at the first touch of the toe of a real boot. Yet they drum me alive. They brush off these vapours. I begin to be impatient of solitude – to feel its draperies hang sweltering, unwholesome about me. Oh, to toss them off and be active! Anybody will do. I am not fastidious. The crossing-sweeper will do; the postman; the waiter in this French restaurant; better still the genial proprietor, whose geniality seems reserved for oneself. He mixes the salad with his own hands for some privileged guest. Which is the privileged guest, I ask, and why? And what is he saying to the lady in earrings; is she a friend or a customer? I feel at once, as I sit down at a table, the delicious jostle of confusion, of uncertainty, of possibility, of speculation. Images breed instantly. I am embarrassed by my own fertility. I could describe every chair, table, luncher here copiously, freely. My mind hums hither and thither with its veil of words for everything. To speak, about wine even to the waiter, is to bring about an explosion. Up goes the rocket. Its golden grain falls, fertilising, upon the rich soil of my imagination. The entirely unexpected nature of this explosion – that is the joy of intercourse. I, mixed with an unknown Italian waiter – what am I? There is no stability in this world. Who is to say what meaning there is in anything? Who is to foretell the flight of a word? It is a balloon that sails over tree-tops. To speak of knowledge is futile. All is experiment and adventure. We are forever mixing ourselves with unknown quantities. What is to come? I know not. But as I put down my glass I remember: I am engaged to be married. I am to dine with my friends tonight. I am Bernard, myself.'

'It is now five minutes to eight,' said Neville. 'I have come early. I have taken my place at the table ten minutes before the time in order to taste every moment of anticipation; to see the door open and to say, "Is it Percival? No, it is not Percival." There is a morbid pleasure in saying: "No, it is not Percival." I have seen the door open and shut twenty times already; each time the suspense sharpens. This is the place to which he is coming. This is the table at which he will sit. Here, incredible as it seems, will be his actual body. This table, these chairs, this metal vase with its three red flowers are about to undergo an extraordinary transformation. Already the room, with its swing-doors, its tables heaped with fruit, with cold joints, wears the wavering, unreal appearance of a place where one waits expecting something to happen. Things quiver as if not yet in being. The blankness of the white tablecloth glares. The hostility, the indifference of other people dining here is oppressive. We look at each other; see that we do not know each other, stare, and go off. Such looks are lashes. I feel the whole cruelty and indifference of the world in them. If he should not come I could not bear it. I should go. Yet somebody must be seeing him now. He must be in some cab; he must be passing some shop. And every moment he seems to pump into this room this prickly light, this intensity of being, so that things have lost their normal uses – this knife-blade is only a flash of light, not a thing to cut with. The normal is abolished.

'The door opens, but he does not come. That is Louis hesitating there. That is his strange mixture of assurance and timidity. He looks at himself in the looking-glass as he comes in; he touches his hair; he is dissatisfied with his appearance. He says, "I am a duke – the last of an ancient race." He is acrid, suspicious, domineering, difficult (I am comparing him with Percival). At the same time he is formidable, for there is laughter in his eyes. He has seen me. Here he is.'

'There is Susan,' said Louis. 'She does not see us. She has not dressed, because she despises the futility of London. She stands for a moment at the swing-door, looking about her like a creature dazed by the light of a lamp. Now she moves. She has the stealthy yet assured movements (even among tables and chairs) of a wild beast. She seems to find her way by instinct in and out among these little tables, touching no one, disregarding waiters, and comes straight to our table in the corner. When she sees us (Neville and myself) her face assumes a certainty which is alarming, as if she had what she wanted. To be loved by Susan would be to be impaled by a bird's sharp beak, to be nailed to a barnyard door. Yet there are moments when I could wish to be speared by a beak, to be nailed to a barnyard door, positively, once and for all.

Rhoda comes now, from nowhere, having slipped in while we were not looking. She must have made a tortuous course, taking cover now behind a waiter, now behind some ornamental pillar, so as to put off as long as possible the shock of recognition, so as to be secure for one more moment to rock her petals in her basin. We wake her. We torture her. She dreads us, she despises us, yet comes cringing to our sides because for all our cruelty there is always some name, some face, which sheds a radiance, which lights up her pavements and makes it possible for her to replenish her dreams.'

'The door opens, the door goes on opening,' said Neville, 'yet he does not come.'

'There is Jinny,' said Susan. 'She stands in the door. Everything seems stayed. The waiter stops. The diners at the table by the door look. She seems to centre everything; round her tables, lines of doors, windows, ceilings, ray themselves, like rays round the star in the middle of a smashed window-pane. She brings things to a point, to order. Now she sees us, and moves, and all the rays ripple and flow and waver over us, bringing in new tides of sensation. We change. Louis puts his hand to his tie. Neville, who sits waiting with agonised intensity, nervously straightens the forks in front of him. Rhoda sees her with surprise, as if on some far horizon a fire blazed. And I, though I pile my mind with damp grass, with wet fields, with the sound of rain on the roof and the gusts of wind that batter at the house in winter and so protect my soul against her, feel her derision steal round me, feel her laughter curl its tongues of fire round me and light up unsparingly my shabby dress, my square-tipped fingernails, which I at once hide under the tablecloth.'

'He has not come,' said Neville. 'The door opens and he does not come. That is Bernard. As he pulls off his coat he shows, of course, the blue shirt under his armpits. And then, unlike the rest of us, he comes in without pushing open a door, without knowing that he comes into a room full of strangers. He does not look in the glass. His hair is untidy, but he does not know it. He has no perception that we differ, or that this table is his goal. He hesitates on his way here. Who is that? he asks himself, for he half knows a woman in an opera cloak. He half knows everybody; he knows nobody (I compare him with Percival). But now, perceiving us, he waves benevolent salute; he bears down with such benignity, with such love of mankind (crossed with humour at the futility of "loving mankind"), that if it were not for Percival, who turns all this to vapour, one would feel, as the others already feel: Now is our festival; now we are together. But without Percival there is no solidity. We are silhouettes, hollow phantoms moving mistily without a background.'

'The swing-door goes on opening,' said Rhoda. 'Strangers keep on coming, people we shall never see again, people who brush us disagreeably with their familiarity, their indifference, and the sense of a world continuing without us. We cannot sink down, we cannot forget our faces. Even I who have no face, who make no difference when I come in (Susan and Jinny change bodies and faces), flutter unattached, without anchorage anywhere, unconsolidated, incapable of composing any blankness or continuity or wall against which these bodies move. It is because of Neville and his misery. The sharp breath of his misery scatters my being. Nothing can settle; nothing can subside. Every time the door opens he looks fixedly at the table – he dare not raise his eyes – then looks for one second and says, "He has not come." But here he is.'

'Now,' said Neville, 'my tree flowers. My heart rises. All oppression is relieved. All impediment is removed. The reign of chaos is over. He has imposed order. Knives cut again.'

'Here is Percival,' said Jinny. 'He has not dressed.'

'Here is Percival,' said Bernard, 'smoothing his hair, not from vanity (he does not look in the glass), but to propitiate the god of decency. He is conventional; he is a hero. The little boys trooped after him across the playing-fields. They blew their noses as he blew his nose, but unsuccessfully, for he is Percival. Now, when he is about to leave us, to go to India, all these trifles come together. He is a hero. Oh yes, that is not to be denied, and when he takes his seat by Susan, whom he loves, the occasion is crowned. We who yelped like jackals biting at each other's heels now assume the sober and confident air of soldiers in the presence of their captain. We who have been separated by our youth (the oldest is not yet twenty-five), who have sung like eager birds each his own song and tapped with the remorseless and savage egotism of the young our own snail-shell till it cracked (I am engaged), or perched solitary outside some bedroom window and sang of love, of fame and other single experiences so dear to the callow bird with a yellow tuft on its beak, now come nearer; and shuffling closer on our perch in this restaurant where everybody's interests are at variance, and the incessant passage of traffic chafes us with distractions and the door opening perpetually its glass cage solicits us with myriad temptations and offers insults and wounds to our confidence – sitting together here we love each other and believe in our own endurance.'

'Now let us issue from the darkness of solitude,' said Louis.

'Now let us say, brutally and directly, what is in our minds,' said Neville. 'Our isolation, our preparation, is over. The furtive days of secrecy and hiding, the revelations on staircases, moments of terror and ecstasy.'

'Old Mrs Constable lifted her sponge and warmth poured over us,' said Bernard. 'We became clothed in this changing, this feeling garment of flesh.'

'The boot-boy made love to the scullery maid in the kitchen garden,' said Susan, 'among the blown-out washing.'

'The breath of the wind was like a tiger panting,' said Rhoda.

'The man lay livid with his throat cut in the gutter,' said Neville. 'And going upstairs I could not raise my foot against the immitigable apple tree with its silver leaves held stiff.'

'The leaf danced in the hedge without anyone to blow it,' said Jinny.

'In the sun-baked corner,' said Louis, 'the petals swam on depths of green.'

'At Elvedon the gardeners swept and swept with their great brooms, and the woman sat at a table writing,' said Bernard.

'From these close-furled balls of string we draw now every filament,' said Louis, 'remembering, when we meet.'

'And then,' said Bernard, 'the cab came to the door, and, pressing our new bowler hats tightly over our eyes to hide our unmanly tears, we drove through streets in which even the housemaids looked at us, and our names painted in white letters on our boxes proclaimed to all the world that we were going to school with the regulation number of socks and drawers, on which our mothers for some nights previously had stitched our initials, in our boxes. A second severance from the body of our mother.'

'And Miss Lambert, Miss Cutting and Miss Bard,' said Jinny, 'monumental ladies, white-ruffed, stone-coloured, enigmatic, with amethyst rings moving like virginal tapers, dim glow-worms over the pages of French, geography and arithmetic, presided; and there were maps, green-baize boards, and rows of shoes on a shelf.'

'Bells rang punctually,' said Susan, 'maids scuffled and giggled. There was a drawing in of chairs and a drawing out of chairs on the linoleum. But from one attic there was a blue view, a distant view of a field unstained by the corruption of this regimented, unreal existence.'

'Down from our heads veils fell,' said Rhoda. 'We clasped the flowers with their green leaves rustling in garlands.'

'We changed, we became unrecognisable,' said Louis. 'Exposed to all these different lights, what we had in us (for we are all so different) came intermittently, in violent patches, spaced by blank voids, to the surface as if some acid had dropped unequally on the plate. I was this, Neville that, Rhoda different again, and Bernard too.'

'Then canoes slipped through palely tinted willow branches,' said Neville, 'and Bernard, advancing in his casual way against breadths of green, against houses of very ancient foundation, tumbled in a heap on the ground beside me. In an access of emotion – winds are not more raving, nor lightning more sudden – I took my poem, I flung my poem, I slammed the door behind me.'

'I, however,' said Louis, 'losing sight of you, sat in my office and tore the date from the calendar, and announced to the world of ship-brokers, corn-chandlers and actuaries that Friday the tenth, or Tuesday the eighteenth, had dawned on the city of London.'

'Then,' said Jinny, 'Rhoda and I, exposed in bright dresses, with a few precious stones nestling on a cold ring round our throats, bowed, shook hands and took a sandwich from a plate with a smile.'

'The tiger leapt, and the swallow dipped her wings in dark pools on the other side of the world,' said Rhoda.

'But here and now we are together,' said Bernard. 'We have come together, at a particular time, to this particular spot. We are drawn into this communion by some deep, some common emotion. Shall we call it, conveniently, "love"? Shall we say "love of Percival", because Percival is going to India?

'No, that is too small, too particular a name. We cannot attach the width and spread of our feelings to so small a mark. We have come together (from the north, from the south, from Susan's farm, from Louis's house of business) to make one thing, not enduring – for what endures? – but seen by many eyes simultaneously. There is a red carnation in that vase. A single flower as we sat here waiting, but now a seven-sided flower, many-petalled, red, puce, purple-shaded, stiff with silver-tinted leaves – a whole flower to which every eye brings its own contribution.'

'After the capricious fires, the abysmal dullness of youth,' said Neville, 'the light falls upon real objects now. Here are knives and forks. The world is displayed, and we too, so that we can talk.'

'We differ, it may be too profoundly,' said Louis, 'for explanation. But let us attempt it. I smoothed my hair when I came in, hoping to look like the rest of you. But I cannot, for I am not single and entire as you are. I have lived a thousand lives already. Every day I unbury – I dig up. I find relics of myself in the sand that women made thousands of years ago, when I heard songs by the Nile and the chained beast stamping. What you see beside you, this man, this Louis, is only the cinders and refuse of something once splendid. I was an Arab prince; behold my free gestures. I was a great poet in the time of Elizabeth. I was a duke at the court of Louis the Fourteenth. I am very vain, very confident; I have an immeasurable desire that women should sigh in sympathy. I have eaten no lunch today in order that Susan may think me cadaverous and that Jinny may extend to me the exquisite balm of her sympathy. But while I admire Susan and Percival, I hate the others, because it is for them that I do these antics, smoothing my hair, concealing my accent. I am the little ape who chatters over a nut, and you are the dowdy women with shiny bags of stale buns; I am also the caged tiger, and you are the keepers with red-hot bars. That is, I am fiercer and stronger than you are, yet the apparition that appears above ground after ages of nonentity will be spent in terror lest you should laugh at me, in veerings with the wind against the soot storms, in efforts to make a steel ring of clear poetry that shall connect the gulls and the women with bad teeth, the church spire and the bobbing billycock hats as I see them when I take my luncheon and prop my poet – is it Lucretius? – against a cruet and the gravy-splashed bill of fare.'

'But you will never hate me,' said Jinny. 'You will never see me, even across a room full of gilt chairs and ambassadors, without coming to me across the room to seek my sympathy. When I came in just now everything stood still in a pattern. Waiters stopped, diners raised their forks and held them. I had the air of being prepared for what would happen. When I sat down you put your hands to your ties, you hid them under the table. But I hide nothing. I am prepared. Every time the door opens I cry, "More!" But my imagination is the bodies. I can imagine nothing beyond the circle cast by my body. My body goes before me, like a lantern down a dark lane, bringing one thing after another out of darkness into a ring of light. I dazzle you; I make you believe that this is all.'

'But when you stand in the door,' said Neville, 'you inflict stillness, demanding admiration, and that is a great impediment to the freedom of intercourse. You stand in the door making us notice you. But none of you saw me approach. I came early; I came quickly and directly, *here*, to sit by the person whom I love. My life has a rapidity that yours lack. I am like a hound on the scent. I hunt from dawn to dusk. Nothing, not the pursuit of perfection through the sand, nor fame, nor money, has meaning for me. I shall have riches; I shall have fame. But I shall never have what I want, for I lack bodily grace and the courage that comes with it. The swiftness of my mind is too strong for my body. I fail before I reach the end and fall in a heap, damp, perhaps disgusting. I excite pity in the crises of life, not love. Therefore I suffer horribly. But I do not suffer, as Louis does, to make myself a spectacle. I have too fine a sense of fact to allow myself these juggleries, these pretences. I see everything – except one thing – with complete clarity. That is my saving. That is what gives my suffering an unceasing excitement. That is what makes me dictate, even when I am silent. And since I am, in one respect, deluded, since the person is always changing, though not the desire, and I do not know in the morning by whom I shall sit at night, I am never stagnant; I rise from my worst disasters, I turn, I change. Pebbles bounce off the mail of my muscular, my extended body. In this pursuit I shall grow old.'

'If I could believe,' said Rhoda, 'that I should grow old in pursuit and change, I should be rid of my fear: nothing persists. One moment does not lead to another. The door opens and the tiger leaps. You did not see me come. I circled round the chairs to avoid the horror of the spring. I am afraid of you all. I am afraid of the shock of sensation that leaps upon me, because I cannot deal with it as you do – I cannot make one moment merge in the next. To me they are all violent, all separate; and if I fall under the shock of the leap of the moment you will be on me, tearing me to pieces. I have no end in view. I do not know how to run minute to minute and hour to hour, solving them by some natural force until they make the whole and indivisible mass that you call life. Because you have an end in view – one person, is it, to sit beside, an idea is it, your beauty is it? I do not know – your days and hours pass like the boughs of forest trees and the smooth green of forest rides to a hound running on the scent. But there is no single scent, no single body for me to follow. And I have no face. I am like the foam that races over the beach or the moonlight that falls arrowlike here on a tin can, here on a spike of the mailed sea-holly, or a bone or a half-eaten boat. I am whirled down caverns, and flap like paper against endless corridors, and must press my hand against the wall to draw myself back.

'But since I wish above all things to have lodgment, I pretend, as I go upstairs lagging behind Jinny and Susan, to have an end in view. I pull on my stockings as I see them pull on theirs. I wait for you to speak and then speak like you. I am drawn here across London to a particular spot, to a particular place, not to see you or you or you, but to light my fire at the general blaze of you who live wholly, indivisibly and without caring.'

'When I came into the room tonight,' said Susan, 'I stopped, I peered about like an animal with its eyes near to the ground. The smell of carpets and furniture and scent disgusts me. I like to walk through wet fields alone, or to stop at a gate and watch my setter nose in a circle, and to ask, Where is the hare? I like to be with people who twist herbs, and spit into the fire and shuffle down long passages in slippers like my father. The only sayings I understand are cries of love, hate, rage and pain. This talking is undressing an old woman whose dress had seemed to be part of her, but now, as we talk, she turns pinkish underneath, and has wrinkled thighs and sagging breasts. When you are silent you are again beautiful. I shall never have anything but natural happiness. It will almost content me. I shall go to bed tired. I shall lie like a field bearing crops in rotation; in the summer heat will dance over me; in the winter I shall be cracked with the cold. But heat and cold will follow each other naturally without my willing or unwilling. My children will carry me on; their teething, their crying, their going to school and coming back will be like the waves of the sea under me. No day will be without its movement. I shall be lifted higher than any of you on the backs of the seasons. I shall possess more than Jinny, more than Rhoda, by the time I die. But on the other hand, where you are various and dimple a million times to the ideas and laughter of others, I shall be sullen, storm-tinted and all one purple. I shall be debased and hidebound by the bestial and beautiful passion of maternity. I shall push the fortunes of my children unscrupulously. I shall hate those who see their faults. I shall lie basely to help them. I shall let them wall me away from you, from you and from you. Also, I am torn with jealousy. I hate Jinny because she shows me that my hands are red, my nails bitten. I love with such ferocity that it kills me when the object of my love shows by a phrase that he can escape. He escapes, and I am left clutching at a string that slips in and out among the leaves on the tree-tops. I do not understand phrases.'

'Had I been born,' said Bernard, 'not knowing that one word follows another I might have been, who knows, perhaps anything. As it is, finding sequences everywhere, I cannot bear the pressure of solitude. When I cannot see words curling like rings of smoke round me I am in darkness – I am nothing. When I am alone I fall into lethargy, and say to myself dismally as I poke the cinders through the bars of the grate, Mrs Moffat will come. She will come and sweep it all up. When Louis is alone he sees with astonishing intensity, and will write some words that may outlast us all. Rhoda loves to be alone. She fears us because we shatter the sense of being which is so extreme in solitude – see how she grasps her fork – her weapon against us. But I only come into existence when the plumber, or the horse-dealer, or whoever it may be, says something which sets me alight. Then how lovely the smoke of my phrase is, rising and falling, flaunting and falling, upon red lobsters and yellow fruit, wreathing them into one beauty. But observe how meretricious the phrase is – made up of what evasions and old lies. Thus my character is in part made of the stimulus which other people provide, and is not mine, as yours are. There is some fatal streak, some wandering and irregular vein of silver, weakening it. Hence the fact that used to enrage Neville at school, that I left him. I went with the boasting boys with little caps and badges, driving off in big brakes – there are some here tonight, dining together, correctly dressed, before they go off in perfect concord to the music hall; I loved them. For they bring me into existence as certainly as you do. Hence, too, when I am leaving you and the train is going, you feel that it is not the train that is going, but I, Bernard, who does not care, who does not feel, who has no ticket, and has lost perhaps his purse. Susan, staring at the string that slips in and out among the leaves of the beech trees, cries: "He is gone! He has escaped me!" For there is nothing to lay hold of. I am made and remade continually. Different people draw different words from me.

'Thus there is not one person but fifty people whom I want to sit beside tonight. But I am the only one of you who is at home here without taking liberties. I am not gross; I am not a snob. If I lie open to the pressure of society I often succeed with the dexterity of my tongue in putting something difficult into the currency. See my little toys, twisted out of nothing in a second, how they entertain. I am no hoarder – I shall leave only a cupboard of old clothes when I die – and am almost indifferent to the minor vanities of life which cause Louis so much torture. But I have sacrificed much. Veined as I am with iron, with silver and streaks of common mud, I cannot contract into the firm fist which those clench who do not depend upon stimulus. I am incapable of the denials, the heroisms of Louis and Rhoda. I shall never succeed, even in talk, in making a perfect phrase. But I shall have contributed more to the passing moment than any of you; I shall go into more rooms, more different rooms, than any of you. But because there is something that comes from outside and not from within I shall be forgotten; when my voice is silent you will not remember me, save as the echo of a voice that once wreathed the fruit into phrases.'

'Look,' said Rhoda; 'listen. Look how the light becomes richer, second by second, and bloom and ripeness lie everywhere; and our eyes, as they range round this room with all its tables, seem to push through curtains of colour, red, orange, umber and queer ambiguous tints, which yield like veils and close behind them, and one thing melts into another.'

'Yes,' said Jinny, 'our senses have widened. Membranes, webs of nerve that lay white and limp, have filled and spread themselves and float round us like filaments, making the air tangible and catching in them faraway sounds unheard before.'

'The roar of London,' said Louis, 'is round us. Motor-cars, vans, omnibuses pass and repass continuously. All are merged in one turning wheel of single sound. All separate sounds – wheels, bells, the cries of drunkards, of merrymakers – are churned into one sound, steel blue, circular. Then a siren hoots. At that shores slip away, chimneys flatten themselves, the ship makes for the open sea.'

'Percival is going,' said Neville. 'We sit here, surrounded, lit up, many coloured; all things – hands, curtains, knives and forks, other people dining – run into each other. We are walled in here. But India lies outside.'

'I see India,' said Bernard. 'I see the low, long shore; I see the tortuous lanes of stamped mud that lead in and out among ramshackle pagodas; I see the gilt and crenellated buildings which have an air of fragility and decay as if they were temporarily run up buildings in some Oriental exhibition. I see a pair of bullocks who drag a low cart along the sun-baked road. The cart sways incompetently from side to side. Now one wheel sticks in the rut, and at once innumerable natives in loincloths swarm round it, chattering excitedly. But they do nothing. Time seems endless, ambition vain. Over all broods a sense of the uselessness of human exertion. There are strange sour smells. An old man in a ditch continues to chew betel and to contemplate his navel. But now, behold, Percival advances; Percival rides a flea-bitten mare, and wears a sun helmet. By applying the standards of the West, by using the violent language that is natural to him, the bullock-cart is righted in less than five minutes.

The Oriental problem is solved. He rides on; the multitude cluster round him, regarding him as if he were – what indeed he is – a god.'

'Unknown, with or without a secret, it does not matter,' said Rhoda, 'he is like a stone fallen into a pond round which minnows swarm. Like minnows, we who had been shooting this way, that way, all shot round him when he came. Like minnows, conscious of the presence of a great stone, we undulate and eddy contentedly. Comfort steals over us. Gold runs in our blood. One, two; one, two; the heart beats in serenity, in confidence, in some trance of well-being, in some rapture of benignity; and look – the outermost parts of the earth – pale shadows on the utmost horizon, India for instance, rise into our purview. The world that had been shrivelled, rounds itself; remote provinces are fetched up out of darkness; we see muddy roads, twisted jungle, swarms of men, and the vulture that feeds on some bloated carcass as within our scope, part of our proud and splendid province, since Percival, riding alone on a flea-bitten mare, advances down a solitary path, has his camp pitched among desolate trees, and sits alone, looking at the enormous mountains.'

'It is Percival,' said Louis, 'sitting silent as he sat among the tickling grasses when the breeze parted the clouds and they formed again, who makes us aware that these attempts to say, "I am this, I am that," which we make, coming together like separated parts of one body and soul, are false. Something has been left out from fear. Something has been altered, from vanity. We have tried to accentuate differences. From the desire to be separate we have laid stress upon our faults, and what is particular to us. But there is a chain whirling round, round, in a steel-blue circle beneath.'

'It is hate, it is love,' said Susan. 'That is the furious coal-black stream that makes us dizzy if we look down into it. We stand on a ledge here, but if we look down we turn giddy.'

'It is love,' said Jinny, 'it is hate, such as Susan feels for me because I kissed Louis once in the garden; because equipped as I am, I make her think when I come in, "My hands are red," and hide them. But our hatred is almost indistinguishable from our love.'

'Yet these roaring waters,' said Neville, 'upon which we build our crazy platforms are more stable than the wild, the weak and inconsequent cries that we utter when, trying to speak, we rise; when we reason and jerk out these false sayings, "I am this; I am that!" Speech is false.

'But I eat. I gradually lose all knowledge of particulars as I eat. I am becoming weighed down with food. These delicious mouthfuls of roast duck, fitly piled with vegetables, following each other in exquisite rotation of warmth, weight, sweet and bitter, past my palate, down my gullet, into my stomach, have stabilised my body. I feel quiet, gravity, control. All is solid now. Instinctively my palate now requires and anticipates sweetness and lightness, something sugared and evanescent; and cool wine, fitting glovelike over those finer nerves that seem to tremble from the roof of my mouth and make it spread (as I drink) into a domed cavern, green with vine leaves, musk-scented, purple with grapes. Now I can look steadily into the mill-race that foams beneath. By what particular name are we to call it? Let Rhoda speak, whose face I see reflected mistily in the looking-glass opposite; Rhoda whom I interrupted when she rocked her petals in a brown basin, asking for the pocket-knife that Bernard had stolen. Love is not a whirlpool to her. She is not giddy when she looks down. She looks far away over our heads, beyond India.'

'Yes, between your shoulders, over your heads, to a landscape,' said Rhoda, 'to a hollow where the many-backed steep hills come down like birds' wings folded. There, on the short, firm turf, are bushes, dark leaved, and against their darkness I see a shape, white, but not of stone, moving, perhaps alive. But it is not you, it is not you, it is not you; not Percival, Susan, Jinny, Neville or Louis. When the white arm rests upon the knee it is a triangle; now it is upright – a column; now a fountain, falling. It makes no sign, it does not beckon, it does not see us. Behind it roars the sea. It is beyond our reach. Yet there I venture. There I go to replenish my emptiness, to stretch my nights and fill them fuller and fuller with dreams. And for a second even now, even here, I reach my object and say, "Wander no more. All else is trial and make-believe. Here is the end." But these pilgrimages, these moments of departure, start always in your presence, from this table, these lights, from Percival and Susan, here and now. Always I see the grove over your heads, between your shoulders, or from a window when I have crossed the room at a party and stand looking down into the street.'

'But his slippers?' said Neville. 'And his voice downstairs in the hall? And catching sight of him when he does not see one? One waits and he does not come. It gets later and later. He has forgotten. He is with someone else. He is faithless, his love meant nothing. Oh, then the agony – then the intolerable despair! And then the door opens. He is here.'

'Rippling gold, I say to him, "Come," ' said Jinny. 'And he comes; he crosses the room to where I sit, with my dress like a veil billowing round me on the gilt chair. Our hands touch, our bodies burst into fire. The chair, the cup, the table – nothing remains unlit. All quivers, all kindles, all burns clear.'

('Look, Rhoda,' said Louis, 'they have become nocturnal, rapt. Their eyes are like moth's wings moving so quickly that they do not seem to move at all.'

'Horns and trumpets,' said Rhoda, 'ring out. Leaves unfold; the stags blare in the thicket. There is a dancing and a drumming, like the dancing and the drumming of naked men with assegais.'

'Like the dance of savages,' said Louis, 'round the campfire. They are savage; they are ruthless. They dance in a circle, flapping bladders. The flames leap over their painted faces, over the leopard skins and the bleeding limbs which they have torn from the living body.'

'The flames of the festival rise high,' said Rhoda. 'The great procession passes, flinging green boughs and flowering branches. Their horns spill blue smoke; their skins are dappled red and yellow in the torchlight. They throw violets. They deck the beloved with garlands and with laurel leaves, there on the ring of turf where the steep-backed hills come down. The procession passes. And while it passes, Louis, we are aware of downfalling, we forebode decay. The shadow slants. We who are conspirators, withdrawn together to lean over some cold urn, note how the purple flame flows downwards.'

'Death is woven in with the violets,' said Louis. 'Death and again death.')

'How proudly we sit here,' said Jinny, 'we who are not yet twenty-five! Outside the trees flower; outside the women linger; outside the cabs swerve and sweep. Emerged from the tentative ways, the obscurities and dazzle of youth, we look straight in front of us, ready for what may come (the door opens, the door keeps on opening). All is real; all is firm without shadow or illusion. Beauty rides our brows. There is mine, there is Susan's. Our flesh is firm and cool. Our differences are clear-cut as the shadows of rocks in full sunlight. Beside us lie crisp rolls, yellow-glazed and hard; the tablecloth is white; and our hands lie half curled, ready to contract. Days and days are to come; winter days, summer days; we have scarcely broken into our hoard. Now the fruit is swollen beneath the leaf. The room is golden, and I say to him, "Come." '

'He has red ears,' said Louis, 'and the smell of meat hangs down in a damp net while the city clerks take snacks at the lunch bar.'

'With infinite time before us,' said Neville, 'we ask what shall we do? Shall we loiter down Bond Street, looking here and there, and buying perhaps a fountain-pen because it is green, or asking how much is the ring with the blue stone? Or shall we sit indoors and watch the coals turn crimson? Shall we stretch our hands for books and read here a passage and there a passage? Shall we shout with laughter for no reason? Shall we push through flowering meadows and make daisy chains? Shall we find out when the next train starts for the Hebrides and engage a reserved compartment? All is to come.'

'For you,' said Bernard, 'but yesterday I walked bang into a pillar-box. Yesterday I became engaged.'

'How strange,' said Susan, 'the little heaps of sugar look by the side of our plates. Also the mottled peelings of pears, and the plush rims to the looking-glasses. I had not seen them before. Everything is now set; everything is fixed. Bernard is engaged. Something irrevocable has happened. A circle has been cast on the waters; a chain is imposed. We shall never flow freely again.'

'For one moment only,' said Louis. 'Before the chain breaks, before disorder returns, see us fixed, see us displayed, see us held in a vice.

'But now the circle breaks. Now the current flows. Now we rush faster than before. Now passions that lay in wait down there in the dark weeds which grow at the bottom rise and pound us with their waves. Pain and jealousy, envy and desire, and something deeper than they are, stronger than love and more subterranean. The voice of action speaks. Listen, Rhoda (for we are conspirators, with our hands on the cold urn), to the casual, quick, exciting voice of action, of hounds running on the scent. They speak now without troubling to finish their sentences. They talk a little language such as lovers use. An imperious brute possesses them. The nerves thrill in their thighs. Their hearts pound and churn in their sides. Susan screws her pocket-handkerchief. Jinny's eyes dance with fire.'

'They are immune,' said Rhoda, 'from picking fingers and searching eyes. How easily they turn and glance; what poses they take of energy and pride! What life shines in Jinny's eyes; how fell, how entire Susan's glance is, searching for insects at the roots! Their hair shines lustrous. Their eyes burn like the eyes of animals brushing through leaves on the scent of the prey. The circle is destroyed. We are thrown asunder.'

'But soon, too soon,' said Bernard, 'this egotistic exultation fails. Too soon the moment of ravenous identity is over, and the appetite for happiness, and happiness, and still more happiness is glutted. The stone is sunk; the moment is over. Round me there spreads a wide margin of indifference. Now open in my eyes a thousand eyes of curiosity. Anyone now is at liberty to murder Bernard, who is engaged to be married, so long as they leave untouched this margin of unknown territory, this forest of the unknown world. Why, I ask (whispering discreetly), do women dine alone together there? Who are they? And what has brought them on this particular evening to this particular spot? The youth in the corner, judging from the nervous way in which he puts his hand from time to time to the back of his head, is from the country. He is suppliant, and so anxious to respond suitably to the kindness of his father's friend, his host, that he can scarcely enjoy now what he will enjoy very much at about half-past eleven tomorrow morning. I have also seen that lady powder her nose three times in the midst of an absorbing conversation – about love perhaps, about the unhappiness of their dearest friend perhaps. "Ah, but the state of my nose!" she thinks, and out comes her powder-puff, obliterating in its passage all the most fervent feelings of the human heart. There remains, however, the insoluble problem of the solitary man with the eyeglass; of the elderly lady drinking champagne alone. Who and what are these unknown people? I ask. I could make a dozen stories of what he said, of what she said – I can see a dozen pictures. But what are stories? Toys I twist, bubbles I blow, one ring passing through another. And sometimes I begin to doubt if there are stories. What is my story? What is Rhoda's? What is Neville's? There are facts, as, for example: "The handsome young man in the grey suit, whose reserve contrasted so strangely with the loquacity of the others, now brushed the crumbs from his waistcoat and, with a characteristic gesture at once commanding and benign, made a sign to the waiter, who came instantly and returned a moment later with the bill discreetly folded upon a plate." That is the truth; that is the fact, but beyond it all is darkness and conjecture.'

'Now once more,' said Louis, 'as we are about to part, having paid our bill, the circle in our blood, broken so often, so sharply, for we are so different, closes in a ring. Something is made. Yes, as we rise and fidget, a little nervously, we pray, holding in our hands this common feeling, "Do not move, do not let the swing-door cut to pieces the thing that we have made, that globes itself here, among these lights, these peelings, this litter of bread crumbs and people passing. Do not move, do not go. Hold it for ever." '

'Let us hold it for one moment,' said Jinny; 'love, hatred, by whatever name we call it, this globe whose walls are made of Percival, of youth and beauty, and something so deep sunk within us that we shall perhaps never make this moment out of one man again.'

'Forests and far countries on the other side of the world,' said Rhoda, 'are in it; seas and jungles; the howlings of jackals and moonlight falling upon some high peak where the eagle soars.'

'Happiness is in it,' said Neville, 'and the quiet of ordinary things. A table, a chair, a book with a paperknife stuck between the pages. And the petal falling from the rose, and the light flickering as we sit silent, or, perhaps, bethinking us of some trifle, suddenly speak.'

'Weekdays are in it,' said Susan, 'Monday, Tuesday, Wednesday; the horses going up to the fields, and the horses returning; the rooks rising and falling, and catching the elm trees in their net, whether it is April, whether it is November.'

'What is to come is in it,' said Bernard. 'That is the last drop and the brightest that we let fall like some supernal quicksilver into the swelling and splendid moment created by us from Percival. What is to come? I ask, brushing the crumbs from my waistcoat, what is outside? We have proved, sitting eating, sitting talking, that we can add to the treasury of moments. We are not slaves bound to suffer incessantly unrecorded petty blows on our bent backs. We are not sheep either, following a master. We are creators. We too have made something that will join the innumerable congregations of past time. We too, as we put on our hats and push open the door, stride not into chaos, but into a world that our own force can subjugate and make part of the illumined and everlasting road.

'Look, Percival, while they fetch the taxi, at the prospect which you are so soon to lose. The street is hard and burnished with the churning of innumerable wheels. The yellow canopy of our tremendous energy hangs like a burning cloth above our heads. Theatres, music halls and lamps in private houses make that light.'

'Peaked clouds,' said Rhoda, 'voyage over a sky dark like polished whalebone.'

'Now the agony begins; now the horror has seized me with its fangs,' said Neville. 'Now the cab comes; now Percival goes. What can we do to keep him? How bridge the distance between us? How fan the fire so that it blazes for ever? How signal to all time to come that we, who stand in the street, in the lamplight, loved Percival? Now Percival is gone.'

The sun had risen to its full height. It was no longer half seen and guessed at, from hints and gleams, as if a girl couched on her green-sea mattress tired her brows with water-globed jewels that sent lances of opal-tinted light falling and flashing in the uncertain air like the flanks of a dolphin leaping, or the flash of a falling blade. Now the sun burnt uncompromising, undeniable. It struck upon the hard sand, and the rocks became furnaces of red heat, it searched each pool and caught the minnow hiding in the cranny, and showed the rusty cartwheel, the white bone, or the boot without laces stuck, black as iron, in the sand. It gave to everything its exact measure of colour; to the sandhills their innumerable glitter, to the wild grasses their glancing green; or it fell upon the arid waste of the desert, here wind-scourged into furrows, here swept into desolate cairns, here sprinkled with stunted dark-green jungle trees. It lit up the smooth gilt mosque, the frail pink-and-white card houses of the southern village, and the long-breasted, white-haired women who knelt in the riverbed beating wrinkled cloths upon stones. Steamers thudding slowly over the sea were caught in the level stare of the sun, and it beat through the yellow awnings upon passengers who dozed or paced the deck, shading their eyes to look for the land, while day after day, compressed in its oily throbbing sides, the ship bore them on monotonously over the waters.

The sun beat on the crowded pinnacles of southern hills and glared into deep, stony riverbeds where the water was shrunk beneath the high slung bridge so that washer-women kneeling on hot stones could scarcely wet their linen; and lean mules went picking their way among the chattering grey stones with panniers slung across their narrow shoulders. At midday the heat of the sun made the hills grey as if shaved and singed in an explosion, while, further north, in cloudier and rainier countries, hills smoothed into slabs as with the back of a spade had a light in them as if a warder, deep within, went from chamber to chamber carrying a green lamp. Through atoms of grey-blue air the sun struck at English fields and lit up marshes and pools, a white gull on a stake, the slow sail of shadows over blunt-headed woods and young corn and flowing hayfields. It beat on the orchard wall, and every pit and grain of the brick was silver pointed, purple, fiery as if soft to touch, as if touched it must melt into hot-baked grains of dust. The currants hung against the wall in ripples and cascades of polished red; plums swelled out their leaves, and all the blades of the grass were run together in one fluent green blaze. The trees' shadow was sunk to a dark pool at the root. Light descending in floods dissolved the separate foliation into one green mound.

The birds sang passionate songs addressed to one ear only and then stopped. Bubbling and chuckling they carried little bits of straw and twig to the dark knots in the higher branches of the trees. Gilt and purpled they perched in the garden, where cones of laburnum and purple shook down gold and lilac, for now at midday the garden was all blossom and profusion and even the tunnels under the plants were green and purple and tawny as the sun beat through the red petal, or the broad yellow petal, or was barred by some thickly furred green stalk.

The sun struck straight upon the house, making the white walls glare between the dark windows. Their panes, woven thickly with green branches, held circles of impenetrable darkness. Sharp-edged wedges of light lay upon the windowsill and showed inside the room plates with blue rings, cups with curved handles, the bulge of a great bowl, the crisscross pattern in the rug and the formidable corners and lines of cabinets and bookcases. Behind their conglomeration hung a zone of shadow in which might be a further shape to be disencumbered of shadow or still denser depths of darkness.

The waves broke and spread their waters swiftly over the shore. One after another they massed themselves and fell; the spray tossed itself back with the energy of their fall. The waves were steeped deep-blue save for a pattern of diamond-pointed light on their backs which rippled as the backs of great horses ripple with muscles as they move. The waves fell; withdrew and fell again, like the thud of a great beast stamping.

'He is dead,' said Neville. 'He fell. His horse tripped. He was thrown. The sails of the world have swung round and caught me on the head. All is over. The lights of the world have gone out. There stands the tree which I cannot pass.

'Oh, to crumple this telegram in my fingers – to let the light of the world flood back – to say this has not happened! But why turn one's head hither and thither? This is the truth. This is the fact. His horse stumbled; he was thrown. The flashing trees and white rails went up in a shower. There was a surge; a drumming in his ears. Then the blow; the world crashed; he breathed heavily. He died where he fell.

'Barns and summer days in the country, rooms where we sat – all now lie in the unreal world which is gone. My past is cut from me. They came running. They carried him to some pavilion, men in riding-boots, men in sun helmets; among unknown men he died. Loneliness and silence often surrounded him. He often left me. And then, returning, "See where he comes!" I said.

'Women shuffle past the window as if there were no gulf cut in the street; no tree with stiff leaves which we cannot pass. We deserve then to be tripped by molehills. We are infinitely abject, shuffling past with our eyes shut. But why should I submit? Why try to lift my foot and mount the stair? This is where I stand; here holding the telegram. The past, summer days and rooms where we sat, stream away like burnt paper with red eyes in it. Why meet and resume? Why talk and eat and make up other combinations with other people? From this moment I am solitary. No one will know me now. I have three letters, "I am about to play quoits with a colonel so no more," thus he ends our friendship, shouldering his way through the crowd with a wave of his hand. This farce is worth no more formal celebration. Yet if someone had but said: "Wait"; had pulled the strap three holes tighter – he would have done justice for fifty years, and sat in court and ridden alone at the head of troops and denounced some monstrous tyranny, and come back to us.

'Now I say there is a grinning, there is a subterfuge. There is something sneering behind our backs. That boy almost lost his footing as he leapt on the bus. Percival fell; was killed; is buried; and I watch people passing; holding tight to the rails of omnibuses; determined to save their lives.

'I will not lift my foot to climb the stair. I will stand for one moment beneath the immitigable tree, alone with the man whose throat is cut, while downstairs the cook shoves in and out the dampers. I will not climb the stair. We are doomed, all of us. Women shuffle past with shopping-bags. People keep on passing. Yet you shall not destroy me. For this moment, this one moment, we are together. I press you to me. Come, pain, feed on me. Bury your fangs in my flesh. Tear me asunder. I sob, I sob.'

'Such is the incomprehensible combination,' said Bernard, 'such is the complexity of things, that as I descend the staircase I do not know which is sorrow, which joy. My son is born; Percival is dead. I am upheld by pillars, shored up on either side by stark emotions; but which is sorrow, which is joy? I ask, and do not know, only that I need silence, and to be alone and to go out, and to save one hour to consider what has happened to my world, what death has done to my world.

'This then is the world that Percival sees no longer. Let me look. The butcher delivers meat next door; two old men stumble along the pavement; sparrows alight. The machine then works; I note the rhythm, the throb, but as a thing in which I have no part, since he sees it no longer. (He lies pale and bandaged in some room.) Now then is my chance to find out what is of great importance, and I must be careful, and tell no lies. About him my feeling was: he sat there in the centre. Now I go to that spot no longer. The place is empty.

'Oh yes, I can assure you, men in felt hats and women carrying baskets – you have lost something that would have been very valuable to you. You have lost a leader whom you would have followed; and one of you has lost happiness and children. He is dead who would have given you that. He lies on a camp-bed, bandaged, in some hot Indian hospital, while coolies squat-ted on the floor agitate those fans – I forget how they call them. But this is important: "You are well out of it," I said, while the doves descended over the roofs and my son was born, as if it were a fact. I remember, as a boy, his curious air of detachment. And I go on to say (my eyes fill with tears and then are dry), "But this is better than one had dared to hope." I say, addressing what is abstract, facing me eyeless at the end of the avenue, in the sky, "Is this the utmost you can do?" Then we have triumphed. You have done your utmost, I say, addressing that blank and brutal face (for he was twenty-five and should have lived to be eighty) without avail. I am not going to lie down and weep away a life of care. (An entry to be made in my pocket-book; contempt for those who inflict meaningless death.) Further, this is important; that I should be able to place him in trifling and ridiculous situations, so that he may not feel himself absurd, perched on a great horse. I must be able to say, "Percival, a ridiculous name." At the same time let me tell you, men and women, hurrying to the tube station, you would have had to respect him. You would have had to form up and follow behind him. How strange to oar one's way through crowds seeing life through hollow eyes, burning eyes.

'Yet already signals begin, beckonings, attempts to lure me back. Curiosity is knocked out only for a short time. One cannot live outside the machine for more perhaps than half an hour. Bodies, I note, already begin to look ordinary; but what is behind them differs – the perspective. Behind that newspaper placard is the hospital; the long room with black men pulling ropes; and then they bury him. Yet since it says a famous actress has been divorced, I ask instantly, Which? Yet I cannot take out my penny; I cannot buy a paper; I cannot suffer interruption yet.

'I ask, if I shall never see you again and fix my eyes on that solidity, what form will our communication take? You have gone across the court, further and further, drawing finer and finer the thread between us. But you exist somewhere. Something of you remains. A judge. That is, if I discover a new vein in myself I shall submit it to you privately. I shall ask, What is your verdict? You shall remain the arbiter. But for how long? Things will become too difficult to explain: there will be new things; already my son. I am now at the zenith of an experience. It will decline. Already I no longer cry with conviction, "What luck!" Exaltation, the flight of doves descending, is over. Chaos, detail, return. I am no longer amazed by names written over shop-windows. I do not feel Why hurry? Why catch trains? The sequence returns; one thing leads to another – the usual order.

'Yes, but I still resent the usual order. I will not let myself be made yet to accept the sequence of things. I will walk; I will not change the rhythm of my mind by stopping, by looking; I will walk. I will go up these steps into the gallery and submit myself to the influence of minds like mine outside the sequence. There is little time left to answer the question; my powers flag; I become torpid. Here are pictures. Here are cold madonnas among their pillars. Let them lay to rest the incessant activity of the mind's eye, the bandaged head, the men with ropes, so that I may find something unvisual beneath. Here are gardens; and Venus among her flowers; here are saints and blue madonnas. Mercifully these pictures make no reference; they do not nudge; they do not point. Thus they expand my consciousness of him and bring him back to me differently. I remember his beauty. "Look, where he comes," I said.

'Lines and colours almost persuade me that I too can be heroic, I, who make phrases so easily, am so soon seduced, love what comes next, and cannot clench my fist, but vacillate weakly making phrases according to my circumstances. Now, through my own infirmity, I recover what he was to me: my opposite. Being naturally truthful, he did not see the point of these exaggerations, and was borne on by a natural sense of the fitting, was indeed a great master of the art of living so that he seems to have lived long, and to have spread calm round him, indifference one might almost say, certainly to his own advancement, save that he had also great compassion. A child playing – a summer evening – doors will open and shut, will keep opening and shutting, through which I see sights that make me weep. For they cannot be imparted. Hence our loneliness; hence our desolation. I turn to that spot in my mind and find it empty. My own infirmities oppress me. There is no longer him to oppose them.

'Behold, then, the blue madonna streaked with tears. This is my funeral service. We have no ceremonies, only private dirges, and no conclusions, only violent sensations, each separate. Nothing that has been said meets our case. We sit in the Italian room at the National Gallery picking up fragments. I doubt that Titian ever felt this rat gnaw. Painters live lives of methodical absorption, adding stroke to stroke. They are not like poets – scapegoats; they are not chained to the rock. Hence the silence, the sublimity. Yet that crimson must have burnt in Titian's gizzard. No doubt he rose with the great arms holding the cornucopia, and fell, in that descent. But the silence weighs on me – the perpetual solicitation of the eye. The pressure is intermittent and muffled. I distinguish too little and too vaguely. The bell is pressed and I do not ring or give out irrelevant clamours all jangled. I am titillated inordinately by some splendour; the ruffled crimson against the green lining; the march of pillars; the orange light behind the black, pricked ears of the olive trees. Arrows of sensation strike from my spine, but without order.

'Yet something is added to my interpretation. Something lies deeply buried. For one moment I thought to grasp it. But bury it, bury it; let it breed, hidden in the depths of my mind some day to fructify. After a long lifetime, loosely, in a moment of revelation, I may lay hands on it, but now the idea breaks in my hand. Ideas break a thousand times for once that they globe themselves entire. They break; they fall over me. "Line and colours they survive, therefore . . . "

'I am yawning. I am glutted with sensations. I am exhausted with the strain and the long, long time – twenty-five minutes, half an hour – that I have held myself alone outside the machine. I grow numb; I grow stiff. How shall I break up this numbness which discredits my sympathetic heart? There are others suffering – multitudes of people suffering. Neville suffers. He loved Percival. But I can no longer endure extremities; I want someone with whom to laugh, with whom to yawn, with whom to remember how he scratched his head; someone he was at ease with and liked (not Susan, whom he loved, but Jinny rather). In her room also I could do penance. I could ask, Did he tell you how I refused him when he asked me to go to Hampton Court that day? Those are the thoughts that will wake me leaping in anguish in the middle of the night – the crimes for which one would do penance in all the markets of the world bareheaded; that one did not go to Hampton Court that day.

'But now I want life round me, and books and little ornaments, and the usual sounds of tradesmen calling on which to pillow my head after this exhaustion, and shut my eyes after this revelation. I will go straight, then, down the stairs, and hail the first taxi and drive to Jinny.'

'There is the puddle,' said Rhoda, 'and I cannot cross it. I hear the rush of the great grindstone within an inch of my head. Its wind roars in my face. All palpable forms of life have failed me. Unless I can stretch and touch something hard, I shall be blown down the eternal corridors for ever. What, then, can I touch? What brick, what stone? and so draw myself across the enormous gulf into my body safely?

'Now the shadow has fallen and the purple light slants downwards. The figure that was robed in beauty is now clothed in ruin. The figure that stood in the grove where the steep-backed hills come down falls in ruin, as I told them when they said they loved his voice on the stair, and his old shoes and moments of being together.

'Now I will walk down Oxford Street envisaging a world rent by lightning; I will look at oaks cracked asunder and red where the flowering branch has fallen. I will go to Oxford Street and buy stockings for a party. I will do the usual things under the lightning flash. On the bare ground I will pick violets and bind them together and offer them to Percival, something given him by me. Look now at what Percival has given me. Look at the street now that Percival is dead. The houses are lightly founded to be puffed over by a breath of air. Reckless and random the cars race and roar and hunt us to death like bloodhounds. I am alone in a hostile world. The human face is hideous. This is to my liking. I want publicity and violence and to be dashed like a stone on the rocks. I like factory chimneys and cranes and lorries. I like the passing of face and face and face, deformed, indifferent. I am sick of prettiness; I am sick of privacy. I ride rough waters and shall sink with no one to save me.

'Percival, by his death, has made me this present, has revealed this terror, has left me to undergo this humiliation – faces and faces, served out like soup-plates by scullions; coarse, greedy, casual; looking in at shop-windows with pendent parcels; ogling, brushing, destroying everything, leaving even our love impure, touched now by their dirty fingers.

'Here is the shop where they sell stockings. And I could believe that beauty is once more set flowing. Its whisper comes down these aisles, through these laces, breathing among baskets of coloured ribbons. There are then warm hollows grooved in the heart of the uproar; alcoves of silence where we can shelter under the wing of beauty from truth which I desire. Pain is suspended as a girl silently slides open a drawer. And then, she speaks; her voice wakes me. I shoot to the bottom among the weeds and see envy, jealousy, hatred and spite scuttle like crabs over the sand as she speaks. These are our companions. I will pay my bill and take my parcel.

'This is Oxford Street. Here are hate, jealousy, hurry and indifference frothed into the wild semblance of life. These are our companions. Consider the friends with whom we sit and eat. I think of Louis, reading the sporting column of an evening newspaper, afraid of ridicule; a snob. He says, looking at the people passing, he will shepherd us if we will follow. If we submit he will reduce us to order. Thus he will smooth out the death of Percival to his satisfaction, looking fixedly over the cruet, past the houses at the sky. Bernard, meanwhile, flops red-eyed into some armchair. He will have out his notebook; under D, he will enter "Phrases to be used on the deaths of friends". Jinny, pirouetting across the room, will perch on the arm of his chair and ask, "Did he love me?" "More than he loved Susan?" Susan, engaged to her farmer in the country, will stand for a second with the telegram before her, holding a plate; and then, with a kick of her heel, slam to the oven door. Neville, after staring at the window through his tears, will see through his tears, and ask, "Who passes the window?" – "What lovely boy?" This is my tribute to Percival: withered violets, blackened violets.

'Where shall I go then? To some museum, where they keep rings under glass cases, where there are cabinets, and the dresses that queens have worn? Or shall I go to Hampton Court and look at the red walls and courtyards and the seemliness of herded yew trees making black pyramids symmetrically on the grass among flowers? There shall I recover beauty, and impose order upon my raked, my dishevelled soul? But what can one make in loneliness? Alone I should stand on the empty grass and say, Rooks fly; somebody passes with a bag; there is a gardener with a wheelbarrow. I should stand in a queue and smell sweat, and scent as horrible as sweat; and be hung with other people like a joint of meat among other joints of meat.

'Here is a hall where one pays money and goes in, where one hears music among somnolent people who have come here after lunch on a hot afternoon. We have eaten beef and pudding enough to live for a week without tasting food. Therefore we cluster like maggots on the back of something that will carry us on. Decorous, portly – we have white hair waved under our hats; slim shoes; little bags; clean-shaven cheeks; here and there a military moustache; not a speck of dust has been allowed to settle anywhere on our broadcloth. Swaying and opening programmes, with a few words of greeting to friends, we settle down, like walruses stranded on rocks, like heavy bodies incapable of waddling to the sea, hoping for a wave to lift us, but we are too heavy, and too much dry shingle lies between us and the sea. We lie gorged with food, torpid in the heat. Then, swollen but contained in slippery satin, the sea-green woman comes to our rescue. She sucks in her lips, assumes an air of intensity, inflates herself and hurls herself precisely at the right moment, as if she saw an apple and her voice was the arrow into the note, "Ah!"

'An axe has split a tree to the core; the core is warm; sound quivers within the bark. "Ah!" cried a woman to her lover, leaning from her window in Venice. "Ah, ah!" she cried, and again she cries "Ah!" She has provided us with a cry. But only a cry. And what is a cry? Then the beetle-shaped men come with their violins; wait; count; nod; down come their bows. And there is ripple and laughter like the dance of olive trees and their myriad-tongued grey leaves when a seafarer, biting a twig between his lips where the many-backed steep hills come down, leaps on shore.

' "Like" and "like" and "like" – but what is the thing that lies beneath the semblance of the thing. Now that lightning has gashed the tree and the flowering branch has fallen and Percival, by his death, has made me this gift, let me see the thing. There is a square; there is an oblong. The players take the square and place it upon the oblong. They place it very accurately; they make a perfect dwelling-place. Very little is left outside. The structure is now visible; what is inchoate is here stated; we are not so various or so mean;

we have made oblongs and stood them upon squares. This is our triumph; this is our consolation.

'The sweetness of this content overflowing runs down the walls of my mind, and liberates understanding. Wander no more, I say; this is the end. The oblong has been set upon the square; the spiral is on top. We have been hauled over the shingle, down to the sea. The players come again. But they are mopping their faces. They are no longer so spruce or so debonair. I will go. I will set aside this afternoon. I will make a pilgrimage. I will go to Greenwich. I will fling myself fearlessly into trams, into omnibuses. As we lurch down Regent Street, and I am flung upon this woman, upon this man, I am not injured, I am not outraged by the collision. A square stands upon an oblong. Here are mean streets where chaffering goes on in street markets, and every sort of iron rod, bolt and screw is laid out, and people swarm off the pavement, pinching raw meat with thick fingers. The structure is visible. We have made a dwelling-place.

'These, then, are the flowers that grow among the rough grasses of the field which the cows trample, wind-bitten, almost deformed, without fruit or blossom. These are what I bring, torn up by the roots from the pavement of Oxford Street, my penny bunch, my penny bunch of violets. Now from the window of the tram I see masts among chimneys; there is the river; there are ships that sail to India. I will walk by the river. I will pace this embankment, where an old man reads a newspaper in a glass shelter. I will pace this terrace and watch the ships bowling down the tide. A woman walks on deck, with a dog barking round her. Her skirts are blown; her hair is blown; they are going out to sea; they are leaving us; they are vanishing this summer evening. Now I will relinquish: now I will let loose. Now I will at last free the checked, the jerked-back desire to be spent, to be consumed. We will gallop together over desert hills where the swallow dips her wings in dark pools and the pillars stand entire. Into the wave that dashes upon the shore, into the wave that flings its white foam to the uttermost corners of the earth, I throw my violets, my offering to Percival.'

The sun no longer stood in the middle of the sky. Its light slanted, falling obliquely. Here it caught on the edge of a cloud and burnt it into a slice of light, a blazing island on which no foot could rest. Then another cloud was caught in the light and another and another, so that the waves beneath were arrow-struck with fiery feathered darts that shot erratically across the quivering blue.

The topmost leaves of the tree were crisped in the sun. They rustled stiffly in the random breeze. The birds sat still save that they flicked their heads sharply from side to side. Now they paused in their song as if glutted with sound, as if the fullness of midday had gorged them. The dragonfly poised motionless over a reed, then shot its blue stitch further through the air. The far hum in the distance seemed made of the broken tremor of fine wings dancing up and down on the horizon. The river water held the reeds now fixed as if glass had hardened round them; and then the glass wavered and the reeds swept low. Pondering, sunken headed, the cattle stood in the fields and cumbrously moved one foot and then another. In the bucket near the house the tap stopped dripping, as if the bucket were full, and then the tap dripped one, two, three separate drops in succession.

The windows showed erratically spots of burning fire, the elbow of one branch, and then some tranquil space of pure clarity. The blind hung red at the window's edge and within the room daggers of light fell upon chairs and tables making cracks across their lacquer and polish. The green pot bulged enormously, with its white window elongated in its side. Light driving darkness before it spilt itself profusely upon the corners and bosses; and yet heaped up darkness in mounds of unmoulded shape.

The waves massed themselves, curved their backs and crashed. Up spurted stones and shingle. They swept round the rocks, and the spray, leaping high, spattered the walls of a cave that had been dry before, and left pools inland, where some fish stranded lashed its tail as the wave drew back.

'I have signed my name,' said Louis, 'already twenty times. I, and again I, and again I. Clear, firm, unequivocal, there it stands, my name. Clear-cut and unequivocal am I too. Yet a vast inheritance of experience is packed in me. I have lived thousands of years. I am like a worm that has eaten its way through the wood of a very old oak beam. But now I am compact; now I am gathered together this fine morning.

'The sun shines from a clear sky. But twelve o'clock brings neither rain nor sunshine. It is the hour when Miss Johnson brings me my letters in a wire tray. Upon these white sheets I indent my name. The whisper of leaves, water running down gutters, green depths flecked with dahlias or zinnias; I, now a duke, now Plato, companion of Socrates; the tramp of dark men and yellow men migrating east, west, north and south; the eternal procession, women going with attaché cases down the Strand as they went once with pitchers to the Nile; all the furled and close-packed leaves of my many-folded life are now summed in my name; incised cleanly and barely on the sheet. Now a full-grown man; now upright standing in sun or rain, I must drop heavy as a hatchet and cut the oak with my sheer weight, for if I deviate, glancing this way, or that way, I shall fall like snow and be wasted.

'I am half in love with the typewriter and the telephone. With letters and cables and brief but courteous commands on the telephone to Paris, Berlin, New York, I have fused my many lives into one; I have helped by my assiduity and decision to score those lines on the map there by which the different parts of the world are laced together. I love punctually at ten to come into my room; I love the purple glow of the dark mahogany; I love the table and its sharp edge and the smooth-running drawers. I love the telephone with its lip stretched to my whisper, and the date on the wall; and the engagement book. Mr Prentice at four; Mr Eyres sharp at four-thirty.

'I like to be asked to come to Mr Burchard's private room and report on our commitments to China. I hope to inherit an armchair and a Turkey carpet. My shoulder is to the wheel; I roll the dark before me, spreading commerce where there was chaos in the far parts of the world. If I press on, from chaos making order, I shall find myself where Chatham stood, and Pitt, Burke and Sir Robert Peel. Thus I expunge certain stains, and erase old defilements; the woman who gave me a flag from the top of the Christmas tree; my accent; beatings and other tortures; the boasting boys; my father, a banker at Brisbane.

'I have read my poet in an eating-house, and, stirring my coffee, listened to the clerks making bets at the little tables, watched the women hesitating at the counter. I said that nothing should be irrelevant, like a piece of brown paper dropped casually on the floor. I said their journeys should have an end in view; they should earn their two pound ten a week at the command of an august master; some hand, some robe, should fold us about in the evening.

When I have healed these fractures and comprehended these monstrosities so that they need neither excuse nor apology, which both waste our strength, I shall give back to the street and the eating-shop what they lost when they fell on these hard times and broke on these stony beaches. I shall assemble a few words and forge round us a hammered ring of beaten steel.

'But now I have not a moment to spare. There is no respite here, no shadow made of quivering leaves, or alcove to which one can retreat from the sun, to sit, with a lover, in the cool of the evening. The weight of the world is our shoulders; its vision is through our eyes; if we blink or look aside, or turn back to finger what Plato said or remember Napoleon and his conquests, we inflict on the world the injury of some obliquity. This is life; Mr Prentice at four; Mr Eyres at four-thirty. I like to hear the soft rush of the lift and the thud with which it stops on my landing and the heavy male tread of responsible feet down the corridors. So by dint of our united exertions we send ships to the remotest parts of the globe; replete with lavatories and gymnasiums. The weight of the world is on our shoulders. This is life. If I press on, I shall inherit a chair and a rug; a place in Surrey with glass houses, and some rare conifer, melon or flowering tree which other merchants will envy.

'Yet I still keep my attic room. There I open the usual little book; there I watch the rain glisten on the tiles till they shine like a policeman's waterproof; there I see the broken windows in poor people's houses; the lean cats; some slattern squinting in a cracked looking-glass as she arranges her face for the street corner; there Rhoda sometimes comes. For we are lovers.

'Percival has died (he died in Egypt; he died in Greece; all deaths are one death). Susan has children; Neville mounts rapidly to the conspicuous heights. Life passes. The clouds change perpetually over our houses. I do this, do that, and again do this and then that. Meeting and parting, we assemble different forms, make different patterns. But if I do not nail these impressions to the board and out of the many men in me make one; exist here and now and not in streaks and patches, like scattered snow wreaths on far mountains; and ask Miss Johnson as I pass through the office about the movies and take my cup of tea and accept also my favourite biscuit, then I shall fall like snow and be wasted.

'Yet when six o'clock comes and I touch my hat to the commissionaire, being always too effusive in ceremony since I desire so much to be accepted; and struggle, leaning against the wind, buttoned up, with my jaws blue and my eyes running water, I wish that a little typist would cuddle on my knees; I think that my favourite dish is liver and bacon; and so am apt to wander to the river, to the narrow streets where there are frequent public-houses, and the shadows of ships passing at the end of the street, and women fighting. But I say to myself, recovering my sanity, Mr Prentice at four; Mr Eyres at four-thirty. The hatchet must fall on the block; the oak must be cleft to the centre. The weight of the world is on my shoulders. Here is the pen and the paper; on the letters in the wire basket I sign my name, I, I, and again I.'

'Summer comes, and winter,' said Susan. 'The seasons pass. The pear fills itself and drops from the tree. The dead leaf rests on its edge. But steam has obscured the window. I sit by the fire watching the kettle boil. I see the pear tree through the streaked steam on the window-pane.

'Sleep, sleep, I croon, whether it is summer or winter, May or November. Sleep I sing – I am unmelodious and hear no music save rustic music when a dog barks, a bell tinkles, or wheels crunch upon the gravel. I sing my song by the fire like an old shell murmuring on the beach. Sleep, sleep, I say, warning off with my voice all who rattle milk-cans, fire at rooks, shoot rabbits, or in any way bring the shock of destruction near this wicker cradle, laden with soft limbs, curled under a pink coverlet.

'I have lost my indifference, my blank eyes, my pear-shaped eyes that saw to the root. I am no longer January, May or any other season, but am all spun to a fine thread round the cradle, wrapping in a cocoon made of my own blood the delicate limbs of my baby. Sleep, I say, and feel within me uprush some wilder, darker violence, so that I would fell down with one blow any intruder, any snatcher, who should break into this room and wake the sleeper.

'I pad about the house all day long in apron and slippers, like my mother who died of cancer. Whether it is summer, whether it is winter, I no longer know by the moor grass, and the heath flower; only by the steam on the window-pane, or the frost on the window-pane. When the lark peels high his ring of sound and it falls through the air like an apple paring, I stoop; I feed my baby. I, who used to walk through beech woods noting the jay's feather turning blue as it falls, past the shepherd and the tramp, who stared at the woman squatted beside a tilted cart in a ditch, go from room to room with a duster. Sleep, I say, desiring sleep to fall like a blanket of down and cover these weak limbs; demanding that life shall sheathe its claws and gird its lightning and pass by, making of my own body a hollow, a warm shelter for my child to sleep in. Sleep, I say, sleep. Or I go to the window, I look at the rook's high nest; and the pear tree. "His eyes will see when mine are shut," I think. "I shall go mixed with them beyond my body and shall see India. He will come home, bringing trophies to be laid at my feet. He will increase my possessions.

'But I never rise at dawn and see the purple drops in the cabbage leaves; the red drops in the roses. I do not watch the setter nose in a circle, or lie at night watching the leaves hide the stars and the stars move and the leaves hang still. The butcher calls; the milk has to be stood under a shade lest it should sour.

'Sleep, I say, sleep, as the kettle boils and its breath comes thicker and thicker issuing in one jet from the spout. So life fills my veins. So life pours through my limbs. So I am driven forward, till I could cry, as I move from dawn to dusk opening and shutting, "No more. I am glutted with natural happiness." Yet more will come, more children; more cradles, more baskets in the kitchen and hams ripening; and onions glistening; and more beds of lettuce and potatoes. I am blown like a leaf by the gale: now brushing the wet grass, now whirled up. I am glutted with natural happiness; and wish sometimes that the fullness would pass from me and the weight of the sleeping house rise, when we sit reading, and I stay the thread at the eye of my needle. The lamp kindles a fire in the dark pane. A fire burns in the heart of the ivy. I see a lit-up street in the evergreens. I hear traffic in the brush of the wind down the lane, and broken voices, and laughter, and Jinny who cries as the door opens, "Come, Come!"

'But no sound breaks the silence of our house, where the fields sigh close to the door. The wind washes through the elm trees; a moth hits the lamp; a cow lows; a crack of sound starts in the rafter, and I push my thread through the needle and murmur, "Sleep." '

'Now is the moment,' said Jinny. 'Now we have met, and have come together. Now let us talk, let us tell stories. Who is he? Who is she? I am infinitely curious and do not know what is to come. If you, whom I meet for the first time, were to say to me, "The coach starts at four from Piccadilly," I would not stay to fling a few necessaries in a band box, but would come at once.

'Let us sit here under the cut flowers, on the sofa by the picture. Let us decorate our Christmas tree with facts and again with facts. People are so soon gone; let us catch them. That man there, by the cabinet; he lives, you say, surrounded by china pots. Break one and you shatter a thousand pounds. And he loved a girl in Rome and she left him. Hence the pots, old junk found in lodging-houses or dug from the desert sands. And since beauty must be broken daily to remain beautiful, and he is static, his life stagnates in a china sea. It is strange though; for once, as a young man, he sat on damp ground and drank rum with soldiers.

'One must be quick and add facts deftly, like toys to a tree, fixing them with a twist of the fingers. He stoops, how he stoops, even over an azalea. He stoops over the old woman even, because she wears diamonds in her ears, and, bundling about her estate in a pony carriage, directs who is to be helped, what tree felled, and who turned out tomorrow. (I have lived my life, I must tell you, all these years, and I am now past thirty, perilously, like a mountain goat leaping from crag to crag; I do not settle long anywhere; I do not attach myself to one person in particular; but you will find that if I raise my arm, some figure at once breaks off and will come.) And that man is a judge; and that man is a millionaire; and that man, with the eyeglass, shot his governess through the heart with an arrow when he was ten years old. Afterwards he rode through deserts with dispatches, took part in revolutions and now collects materials for a history of his mother's family, long settled in Norfolk. That little man with a blue chin has a right hand that is withered. But why? We do not know. That woman, you whisper discreetly, with the pearl pagodas hanging from her ears, was the pure flame who lit the life of one of our statesmen; now since his death she sees ghosts, tells fortunes, and has adopted a coffee-coloured youth whom she calls the Messiah. That man with the drooping moustache, like a cavalry officer, lived a life of the utmost debauchery (it is all in some memoir) until one day he met a stranger in a train who converted him between Edinburgh and Carlisle by reading the Bible.

'Thus, in a few seconds, deftly, adroitly, we decipher the hieroglyphs written on other people's faces. Here, in this room, are the abraded and battered shells cast on the shore. The door goes on opening. The room fills and fills with knowledge, anguish, many kinds of ambition, much indifference, some despair. Between us, you say, we could build cathedrals, dictate policies, condemn men to death, and administer the affairs of several public offices. The common fund of experience is very deep. We have between us scores of children of both sexes, whom we are educating, going to see at school with the measles, and bringing up to inherit our houses. In one way or another we make this day, this Friday, some by going to the Law Courts; others to the City; others to the nursery; others by marching and forming fours. A million hands stitch, raise hods with bricks. The activity is endless. And tomorrow it begins again, tomorrow we make Saturday. Some take train for France; others ship for India. Some will never come into this room again. One may die tonight. Another will beget a child. From us every sort of building, policy, venture, picture, poem, child, factory, will spring. Life comes; life goes; we make life. So you say.

'But we who live in the body see with the body's imagination things in outline. I see rocks in bright sunshine. I cannot take these facts into some cave and, shading my eyes, grade their yellows, blues, umbers into one substance. I cannot remain seated for long. I must jump up and go. The coach may start from Piccadilly. I drop all these facts – diamonds, withered hands, china pots and the rest of it – as a monkey drops nuts from its naked paws. I cannot tell you if life is this or that. I am going to push out into the heterogeneous crowd. I am going to be buffeted; to be flung up, and flung down, among men, like a ship on the sea.

'For now my body, my companion, which is always sending its signals, the rough black "No", the golden "Come", in rapid running arrows of sensation, beckons. Someone moves. Did I raise my arm? Did I look? Did my yellow scarf with the strawberry spots float and signal? He has broken from the wall. He follows. I am pursued through the forest. All is rapt, all is nocturnal, and the parrots go screaming through the branches. All my senses stand erect. Now I feel the roughness of the fibre of the curtain through which I push; now I feel the cold iron railing and its blistered paint beneath my palm. Now the cool tide of darkness breaks its waters over me. We are out of doors. Night opens, night traversed by wandering moths; night hiding lovers roaming to adventure. I smell roses; I smell violets; I see red and blue just hidden. Now gravel is under my shoes; now grass. Up reel the tall backs of houses guilty with lights. All London is uneasy with flashing lights. Now let us sing our love song – Come, come, come. Now my gold signal is like a dragonfly flying taut. Jug, jug, jug, I sing like the nightingale whose melody is crowded in the too narrow passage of her throat. Now I hear the crash and rending of boughs and the crack of antlers as if the beasts of the forest were all hunting, all rearing high and plunging down among the thorns. One has pierced me. One is driven deep within me.

'And velvet flowers and leaves whose coolness has been stood in water wash me round, and sheathe me, embalming me.'

'Why, look,' said Neville, 'at the clock ticking on the mantelpiece? Time passes, yes. And we grow old. But to sit with you, alone with you, here in London, in this firelit room, you there, I here, is all. The world ransacked to its uttermost ends, and all its heights stripped and gathered of their flowers, holds no more. Look at the firelight running up and down the gold thread in the curtain. The fruit it circles droops heavy. It falls on the toe of your boot, it gives your face a red rim – I think it is the firelight and not your face; I think those are books against the wall, and that a curtain, and that perhaps an armchair. But when you come everything changes. The cups and saucers changed when you came in this morning. There can be no doubt, I thought, pushing aside the newspaper, that our mean lives, unsightly as they are, put on splendour and have meaning only under the eyes of love.

'I rose. I had done my breakfast. There was the whole day before us, and as it was fine, tender, noncommittal, we walked through the Park to the Embankment, along the Strand to St Paul's, then to the shop where I bought an umbrella, always talking, and now and then stopping to look. But can this last? I said to myself, by a lion in Trafalgar Square, by the lion seen once and for ever. So I revisit my past life, scene by scene; there is an elm tree, and there lies Percival. For ever and ever, I swore. Then darted in the usual doubt. I clutched your hand. You left me. The descent into the Tube was like death. We were cut up, we were dissevered by all those faces and the hollow wind that seemed to roar down there over desert boulders. I sat staring in my own room. By five I knew that you were faithless. I snatched the telephone and the buzz, buzz, buzz of its stupid voice in your empty room battered my heart down, when the door opened and there you stood. That was the most perfect of our meetings. But these meetings, these partings, finally destroy us.

'Now this room seems to me central, something scooped out of the eternal night. Outside lines twist and intersect, but round us, wrapping us about. Here we are centred. Here we can be silent, or speak without raising our voices. Did you notice that and then that? we say. He said that, meaning . . . She hesitated, and I believe suspected. Anyhow, I heard voices, a sob on the stair late at night. It is the end of their relationship. Thus we spin round us infinitely fine filaments and construct a system. Plato and Shakespeare are included, also quite obscure people, people of no importance whatsoever. I hate men who wear crucifixes on the left side of their waistcoats. I hate ceremonies and lamentations and the sad figure of Christ trembling beside another trembling and sad figure. Also the pomp and the indifference and the emphasis, always on the wrong place, of people holding forth under chandeliers in full evening dress, wearing stars and decorations. Some spray in a hedge, though, or a sunset over a flat winter field, or again the way some old woman sits, arms akimbo, in an omnibus with a basket – those we point at for the other to look at. It is so vast an alleviation to be able to point for another to look at. And then not to talk. To follow the dark paths of the mind and enter the past, to visit books, to brush aside their branches and break off some fruit. And you take it and marvel, as I take the careless movements of your body and marvel at its ease, its power – how you fling open windows and are dexterous with your hands. For alas! my mind is a little impeded, it soon tires; I fall damp, perhaps disgusting, at the goal.

'Alas! I could not ride about India in a sun helmet and return to a bungalow. I cannot tumble, as you do, like half-naked boys on the deck of a ship, squirting each other with hose-pipes. I want this fire, I want this chair. I want someone to sit beside after the day's pursuit and all its anguish, after its listenings, and its waitings, and its suspicions. After quarrelling and reconciliation I need privacy – to be alone with you, to set this hubbub in order. For I am as neat as a cat in my habits. We must oppose the waste and deformity of the world, its crowds eddying round and round disgorged and trampling. One must slip paper-knives, even, exactly through the pages of novels, and tie up packets of letters neatly with green silk, and brush up the cinders with a hearth broom. Everything must be done to rebuke the horror of deformity. Let us read writers of Roman severity and virtue; let us seek perfection through the sand. Yes, but I love to slip the virtue and severity of the noble Romans under the grey light of your eyes, and dancing grasses and summer breezes and the laughter and shouts of boys at play – of naked cabin-boys squirting each other with hose-pipes on the decks of ships. Hence I am not a disinterested seeker, like Louis, after perfection through the sand. Colours always stain the page; clouds pass over it. And the poem, I think, is only your voice speaking. Alcibiades, Ajax, Hector and Percival are also you. They loved riding, they risked their lives wantonly, they were not great readers either. But you are not Ajax or Percival. They did not wrinkle their noses and scratch their foreheads with your precise gesture. You are you. That is what consoles me for the lack of many things – I am ugly, I am weak – and the depravity of the world, and the flight of youth and Percival's death, and bitterness and rancour and envies innumerable.

'But if one day you do not come after breakfast, if one day I see you in some looking-glass perhaps looking after another, if the telephone buzzes and buzzes in your empty room, I shall then, after unspeakable anguish, I shall then – for there is no end to the folly of the human heart – seek another, find another, you. Meanwhile, let us abolish the ticking of time's clock with one blow. Come closer.'

The sun had now sunk lower in the sky. The islands of cloud had gained in density and drew themselves across the sun so that the rocks went suddenly black, and trembling sea-holly lost its blue and turned silver, and shadows were blown like grey cloths over the sea. The waves no longer visited the farther pools or reached the dotted black line which lay irregularly marked upon the beach. The sand was pearl white, smoothed and shining.

Birds swooped and circled high up in the air. Some raced in the furrows of the wind and turned and sliced through them as if they were one body cut into a thousand shreds. Birds fell like a net descending on the tree-tops. Here one bird taking its way alone made wing for the marsh and sat solitary on a white stake, opening its wings and shutting them.

Some petals had fallen in the garden. They lay shell-shaped on the earth. The dead leaf no longer stood upon its edge, but had been blown, now running, now pausing, against some stalk. Through all the flowers the same wave of light passed in a sudden flaunt and flash as if a fin cut the green glass of a lake. Now and again some level and masterly blast blew the multitudinous leaves up and down and then, as the wind flagged, each blade regained its identity. The flowers, burning their bright discs in the sun, flung aside the sunlight as the wind tossed them, and then some heads too heavy to rise again dropped slightly.

The afternoon sun warmed the fields, poured blue into the shadows and reddened the corn. A deep varnish was laid like a lacquer over the fields. A cart, a horse, a flock of rooks – whatever moved in it was rolled round in gold. If a cow moved a leg it stirred ripples of red gold, and its horns seemed lined with light. Sprays of flaxen-haired corn lay on the hedges, brushed from the shaggy carts that came up from the meadows short legged and primeval looking. The round-headed clouds never dwindled as they bowled along, but kept every atom of their rotundity. Now, as they passed, they caught a whole village in the fling of their net and, passing, let it fly free again. Far away on the horizon, among the million grains of blue-grey dust, burnt one pane, or stood the single line of one steeple or one tree.

The red curtains and the white blinds blew in and out, flapping against the edge of the window, and the light which entered by flaps and breadths unequally had in some brown tinge, and some abandonment as it blew through the blowing curtains in gusts. Here it browned a cabinet, there reddened a chair, here it made the window waver in the side of the green jar.

All for a moment wavered and bent in uncertainty and ambiguity, as if a great moth sailing through the room had shadowed the immense solidity of chairs and tables with floating wings.

'And time,' said Bernard, 'lets fall its drop. The drop that has formed on the roof of the soul falls. On the roof of my mind time, forming, lets fall its drop. Last week, as I stood shaving, the drop fell. I, standing with my razor in my hand, became suddenly aware of the merely habitual nature of my action (this is the drop forming) and congratulated my hands, ironically, for keeping at it. Shave, shave, shave, I said. Go on shaving. The drop fell. All through the day's work, at intervals, my mind went to any empty place, saying, "What is lost? What is over?" And "Over and done with," I muttered, "over and done with," solacing myself with words. People noticed the vacuity of my face and the aimlessness of my conversation. The last words of my sentence tailed away. And as I buttoned on my coat to go home I said more dramatically. "I have lost my youth."

'It is curious how, at every crisis, some phrase which does not fit insists upon coming to the rescue – the penalty of living in an old civilisation with a notebook. This drop falling has nothing to do with losing my youth. This drop falling is time tapering to a point. Time, which is a sunny pasture covered with a dancing light, time, which is widespread as a field at midday, becomes pendent. Time tapers to a point. As a drop falls from a glass heavy with some sediment, time falls. These are the true cycles, these are the true events. Then as if all the luminosity of the atmosphere were withdrawn I see to the bare bottom. I see what habit covers. I lie sluggish in bed for days. I dine out and gape like a codfish. I do not trouble to finish my sentences, and my actions, usually so uncertain, acquire a mechanical precision. On this occasion, passing an office, I went in and bought, with all the composure of a mechanical figure, a ticket for Rome.

'Now I sit on a stone seat in these gardens surveying the eternal city, and the little man who was shaving in London five days ago looks already like a heap of old clothes. London has also crumbled. London consists of fallen factories and a few gasometers. At the same time I am not involved in this pageantry. I see the violet-sashed priests and the picturesque nursemaids; I notice externals only. I sit here like a convalescent, like a very simple man who knows only words of one syllable. "The sun is hot," I say. "The wind is cold." I feel myself carried round like an insect on top of the earth and could swear that, sitting here, I feel its hardness, its turning movement. I have no desire to go the opposite way from the earth. Could I prolong this sense another six inches I have a foreboding that I should touch some queer territory. But I have a very limited proboscis. I never wish to prolong these states of detachment; I dislike them; I also despise them. I do not wish to be a man who sits for fifty years on the same spot thinking of his navel. I wish to be harnessed to a cart, a vegetable-cart that rattles over the cobbles.

'The truth is that I am not one of those who find their satisfaction in one person, or in infinity. The private room bores me, also the sky. My being only glitters when all its facets are exposed to many people. Let them fail and I am full of holes, dwindling like burnt paper. Oh, Mrs Moffat, Mrs Moffat, I say, come and sweep it all up. Things have dropped from me. I have outlived certain desires; I have lost friends, some by death – Percival – others through sheer inability to cross the street. I am not so gifted as at one time seemed likely. Certain things lie beyond my scope. I shall never understand the harder problems of philosophy. Rome is the limit of my travelling. As I drop asleep at night it strikes me sometimes with a pang that I shall never see savages in Tahiti spearing fish by the light of a blazing cresset, or a lion spring in the jungle, or a naked man eating raw flesh. Nor shall I learn Russian or read the Vedas. I shall never again walk bang into the pillar-box. (But still a few stars fall through my night, beautifully, from the violence of that concussion.) But as I think, truth has come nearer. For many years I crooned complacently, "My children... my wife... my house ... my dog." As I let myself in with my latchkey I would go through that familiar ritual and wrap myself in those warm coverings. Now that lovely veil has fallen. I do not want possessions now. (Note: an Italian washerwoman stands on the same rung of physical refinement as the daughter of an English duke.)

'But let me consider. The drop falls; another stage has been reached. Stage upon stage. And why should there be an end of stages? and where do they lead? To what conclusion? For they come wearing robes of solemnity. In these dilemmas the devout consult those violet-sashed and sensual-looking gentry who are trooping past me. But for ourselves, we resent teachers. Let a man get up and say, "Behold, this is the truth," and instantly I perceive a sandy cat filching a piece of fish in the background. Look, you have forgotten the cat, I say. So Neville, at school, in the dim chapel, raged at the sight of the Doctor's crucifix. I, who am always distracted, whether by a cat or by a bee buzzing round the bouquet that Lady Hampden keeps so diligently pressed to her nose, at once make up a story and so obliterate the angles of the crucifix. I have made up thousands of stories; I have filled innumerable notebooks with phrases to be used when I have found the true story, the one story to which all these phrases refer. But I have never yet found that story. And I begin to ask, Are there stories?

'Look now from this terrace at the swarming population beneath. Look at the general activity and clamour. That man is in difficulties with his mule. Half a dozen good-natured loafers offer their services. Other pass by without looking. They have as many interests as there are threads in a skein. Look at the sweep of the sky, bowled over by round white clouds. Imagine the leagues of level land and the aqueducts and the broken Roman pavement and the tombstones in the Campagna, and beyond the Campagna, the sea, then again more land, then the sea. I could break off any detail in all that prospect – say the mule-cart – and describe it with the greatest ease. But why describe a man in trouble with his mule? Again, I could invent stories about that girl coming up the steps. "She met him under the dark archway . . . 'It is over,' he said, turning from the cage where the china parrot hangs." Or simply, "That was all." But why impose my arbitrary design? Why stress this and shape that and twist up little figures like the toys men sell in trays in the street? Why select this, out of all that – one detail?

'Here am I shedding one of my life-skins, and all they will say is, "Bernard is spending ten days in Rome." Here am I marching up and down this terrace alone, unoriented. But observe how dots and dashes are beginning, as I walk, to run themselves into continuous lines, how things are losing the bald, the separate identity that they had as I walked up those steps. The great red pot is now a reddish streak in a wave of yellowish green. The world is beginning to move past me like the banks of a hedge when the train starts, like the waves of the sea when a steamer moves. I am moving too, am becoming involved in the general sequence when one thing follows another and it seems inevitable that the tree should come, then the telegraph-pole, then the break in the hedge. And as I move, surrounded, included and taking part, the usual phrases begin to bubble up, and I wish to free these bubbles from the trap-door in my head, and direct my steps therefore towards that man, the back of whose head is half familiar to me. We were together at school. We shall undoubtedly meet. We shall certainly lunch together. We shall talk. But wait, one moment wait.

'These moments of escape are not to be despised. They come too seldom. Tahiti becomes possible. Leaning over this parapet I see far out a waste of water. A fin turns. This bare visual impression is unattached to any line of reason, it springs up as one might see the fin of a porpoise on the horizon. Visual impressions often communicate thus briefly statements that we shall in time to come uncover and coax into words. I note under F, therefore, "Fin in a waste of waters". I, who am perpetually making notes in the margin of my mind for some final statement, make this mark, waiting for some winter's evening.

'Now I shall go and lunch somewhere, I shall hold my glass up, I shall look through the wine, I shall observe with more than my usual detachment, and when a pretty woman enters the restaurant and comes down the room between the tables I shall say to myself, "Look where she comes against a waste of waters." A meaningless observation, but to me, solemn, slate-coloured, with a fatal sound of ruining worlds and waters falling to destruction.

'So, Bernard (I recall you, you the usual partner in my enterprises), let us begin this new chapter, and observe the formation of this new, this unknown, strange, altogether unidentified and terrifying experience – the new drop – which is about to shape itself. Larpent is that man's name.'

'In this hot afternoon,' said Susan, 'here in this garden, here in this field where I walk with my son, I have reached the summit of my desires. The hinge of the gate is rusty; he heaves it open. The violent passions of childhood, my tears in the garden when Jinny kissed Louis, my rage in the schoolroom, which smelt of pine, my loneliness in foreign places, when the mules came clattering in on their pointed hoofs and the Italian women chattered at the fountain, shawled, with carnations twisted in their hair, are rewarded by security, possession, familiarity. I have had peaceful, productive years. I possess all I see. I have grown trees from the seed. I have made ponds in which goldfish hide under the broad-leaved lilies. I have netted over strawberry beds and lettuce beds, and stitched the pears and the plums into white bags to keep them safe from the wasps. I have seen my sons and daughters, once netted over like fruit in their cots, break the meshes and walk with me, taller than I am, casting shadows on the grass.

'I am fenced in, planted here like one of my own trees. I say, "My son", I say, "My daughter", and even the ironmonger looking up from his counter strewn with nails, paint and wire-fencing respects the shabby car at the door with butterfly nets, pads and beehives. We hang mistletoe over the clock at Christmas, weigh our blackberries and mushrooms, count out jam-pots, and stand year by year to be measured against the shutter in the drawing-room window. I also make wreaths of white flowers, twisting silver-leaved plants among them for the dead, attaching my card with sorrow for the dead shepherd, with sympathy for the wife of the dead carter; and sit by the beds of dying women, who murmur their last terrors, who clutch my hand; frequenting rooms intolerable except to one born as I was and early acquainted with the farmyard and the dung-heap and the hens straying in and out, and the mother with two rooms and growing children. I have seen the windows run with heat, I have smelt the sink.

'I ask now, standing with my scissors among my flowers, Where can the shadow enter? What shock can loosen my laboriously gathered, relentlessly pressed-down life? Yet sometimes I am sick of natural happiness, and fruit growing, and children scattering the house with oars, guns, skulls, books won for prizes and other trophies. I am sick of the body, I am sick of my own craft, industry and cunning, of the unscrupulous ways of the mother who protects, who collects under her jealous eyes at one long table her own children, always her own.

'It is when spring comes, cold, showery, with sudden yellow flowers – then as I look at the meat under the blue shade and press the heavy silver bags of tea, of sultanas, I remember how the sun rose, and the swallows skimmed the grass, and phrases that Bernard made when we were children, and the leaves shook over us, many-folded, very light, breaking the blue of the sky, scattering wandering lights upon the skeleton roots of the beech trees where I sat, sobbing. The pigeon rose. I jumped up and ran after the words that trailed like the dangling string from an air ball, up and up, from branch to branch escaping. Then like a cracked bowl the fixity of my morning broke, and putting down the bag of flour I thought, Life stands round me like glass round the imprisoned reed.

'I hold scissors and snip off hollyhocks, who went to Elvedon and trod on rotten oak-apples, and saw the lady writing and the gardeners with their great brooms. We ran back panting lest we should be shot and nailed like stoats to the wall. Now I measure, I preserve. At night I sit in the armchair and stretch my arm for my sewing; and hear my husband snore; and look up when the light from a passing car dazzles the windows and feel the waves of my life tossed, broken, round me who am rooted; and hear cries, and see others' lives eddying like straws round the piers of a bridge while I push my needle in and out and draw my thread through the calico.

'I think sometimes of Percival who loved me. He rode and fell in India. I think sometimes of Rhoda. Uneasy cries wake me at dead of night. But for the most part I walk content with my sons. I cut the dead petals from hollyhocks. Rather squat, grey before my time, but with clear eyes, pear-shaped eyes, I pace my fields.'

'Here I stand,' said Jinny, 'in the Tube station where everything that is desirable meets – Piccadilly South Side, Piccadilly North Side, Regent Street and the Haymarket. I stand for a moment under the pavement in the heart of London. Innumerable wheels rush and feet press just over my head. The great avenues of civilisation meet here and strike this way and that. I am in the heart of life. But look – there is my body in that looking-glass. How solitary, how shrunk, how aged! I am no longer young. I am no longer part of the procession. Millions descend those stairs in a terrible descent. Great wheels churn inexorably urging them downwards. Millions have died. Percival died. I still move. I still live. But who will come if I signal?

'Little animal that I am, sucking my flanks in and out with fear, I stand here, palpitating, trembling. But I will not be afraid. I will bring the whip down on my flanks. I am not a whimpering little animal making for the shadow. It was only for a moment, catching sight of myself before I had time to prepare myself as I always prepare myself for the sight of myself, that I quailed. It is true; I am not young – I shall soon raise my arm in vain and my scarf will fall to my side without having signalled. I shall not hear the sudden sigh in the night and feel through the dark someone coming. There will be no reflections in window-panes in dark tunnels. I shall look into faces, and I shall see them seek some other face. I admit, for one moment the soundless flight of upright bodies down the moving stairs like the pinioned and terrible descent of some army of the dead downwards and the churning of the great engines remorselessly forwarding us, all of us, onwards, made me cower and run for shelter.

'But now I swear, making deliberately in front of the glass those slight preparations that equip me, I will not be afraid. Think of the superb omni-buses, red and yellow, stopping and starting, punctually in order. Think of the powerful and beautiful cars that now slow to a foot's pace and now shoot forward; think of men, think of women, equipped, prepared, driving onward. This is the triumphant procession; this is the army of victory with banners and brass eagles and heads crowned with laurel-leaves won in battle. They are better than savages in loincloths, and women whose hair is dank, whose long breasts sag, with children tugging at their long breasts. These broad thoroughfares – Piccadilly South, Piccadilly North, Regent Street and the Haymarket – are sanded paths of victory driven through the jungle. I too, with my little patent-leather shoes, my handkerchief that is but a film of gauze, my reddened lips and my finely pencilled eyebrows, march to victory with the band.

'Look how they show off clothes here even underground in a perpetual radiance. They will not let the earth even lie wormy and sodden. There are gauzes and silks illumined in glass cases and underclothes trimmed with a million close stitches of fine embroidery. Crimson, green, violet, they are dyed all colours. Think how they organise, roll out, smooth, dip in dyes, and drive tunnels blasting the rock. Lifts rise and fall; trains stop, trains start as regularly as the waves of the sea. This is what has my adhesion. I am a native of this world, I follow its banners. How could I run for shelter when they are so magnificently adventurous, daring, curious, too, and strong enough in the midst of effort to pause and scrawl with a free hand a joke upon the wall? Therefore I will powder my face and redden my lips. I will make the angle of my eyebrows sharper than usual. I will rise to the surface, standing erect with the others in Piccadilly Circus. I will sign with a sharp gesture to a cab whose driver will signify by some indescribable alacrity his understanding of my signals. For I still excite eagerness. I still feel the bowing of men in the street like the silent stoop of the corn when the light wind blows, ruffling it red.

'I will drive to my own house. I will fill the vases with lavish, with luxurious, with extravagant flowers nodding in great bunches. I will place one chair there, another here. I will put ready cigarettes, glasses and some gaily covered new unread book in case Bernard comes, or Neville or Louis. But perhaps it will not be Bernard, Neville or Louis, but somebody new, somebody unknown, somebody I passed on a staircase and, just turning as we passed, I murmured, "Come." He will come this afternoon; somebody I do not know, somebody new. Let the silent army of the dead descend. I march forward.'

'I no longer need a room now,' said Neville, 'or walls and firelight. I am no longer young. I pass Jinny's house without envy, and smile at the young man who arranges his tie a little nervously on the doorstep. Let the dapper young man ring the bell; let him find her. I shall find her if I want her; if not, I pass on. The old corrosion has lost its bite – envy, intrigue and bitterness have been washed out. We have lost our glory too. When we were young we sat anywhere, on bare benches in draughty halls with the doors always banging. We tumbled about half-naked like boys on the deck of a ship squirting each other with hose-pipes. Now I could swear that I like people pouring profusely out of the Tube when the day's work is done, unanimous, indiscriminate, uncounted. I have picked my own fruit. I look dispassionately.

'After all, we are not responsible. We are not judges. We are not called upon to torture our fellows with thumbscrews and irons; we are not called upon to mount pulpits and lecture them on pale Sunday afternoons. It is better to look at a rose, or to read Shakespeare as I read him here in Shaftesbury Avenue. Here's the fool, here's the villain, here in a car comes Cleopatra, burning on her barge. Here are figures of the damned too, noseless men by the police-court wall, standing with their feet in fire, howling. This is poetry if we do not write it. They act their parts infallibly, and almost before they open their lips I know what they are going to say, and wait the divine moment when they speak the word that must have been written. If it were only for the sake of the play, I could walk Shaftesbury Avenue for ever.

'Then coming from the street, entering some room, there are people talking, or hardly troubling to talk. He says, she says, somebody else says things have been said so often that one word is now enough to lift a whole weight. Argument, laughter, old grievances – they fall through the air, thickening it. I take a book and read half a page of anything. They have not mended the spout of the teapot yet. The child dances, dressed in her mother's clothes.

'But then Rhoda, or it may be Louis, some fasting and anguished spirit, passes through and out again. They want a plot, do they? They want a reason? It is not enough for them, this ordinary scene. It is not enough to wait for the thing to be said as if it were written; to see the sentence lay its dab of clay precisely on the right place, making character; to perceive, suddenly, some group in outline against the sky. Yet if they want violence, I have seen death and murder and suicide all in one room. One comes in, one goes out. There are sobs on the staircase. I have heard threads broken and knots tied and the quiet stitching of white cambric going on and on on the knees of a woman. Why ask, like Louis, for a reason, or fly, like Rhoda, to some far grove and part the leaves of the laurels and look for statues? They say that one must beat one's wings against the storm in the belief that beyond this welter the sun shines; the sun falls sheer into pools that are fledged with willows. (Here it is November; the poor hold out matchboxes in wind-bitten fingers.) They say truth is to be found there entire, and virtue, that shuffles along here, down blind alleys, is to be had there perfect. Rhoda flies with her neck outstretched and blind fanatic eyes, past us. Louis, now so opulent, goes to his attic window among the blistered roofs and gazes where she has vanished, but must sit down in his office among the typewriters and the telephones and work it all out for our instruction, for our regeneration, and the reform of an unborn world.

'But now in this room, which I enter without knocking, things are said as if they had been written. I go to the bookcase. If I choose, I read half a page of anything. I need not speak. But I listen. I am marvellously on the alert. Certainly, one cannot read this poem without effort. The page is often corrupt and mud-stained, and torn and stuck together with faded leaves, with scraps of verbena or geranium. To read this poem one must have myriad eyes, like one of those lamps that turn on slabs of racing water at midnight in the Atlantic, when perhaps only a spray of seaweed pricks the surface, or suddenly the waves gape and up shoulders a monster. One must put aside antipathies and jealousies and not interrupt. One must have patience and infinite care and let the light sound, whether of spiders' delicate feet on a leaf or the chuckle of water in some irrelevant drainpipe, unfold too. Nothing is to be rejected in fear or horror. The poet who has written this page (what I read with people talking) has withdrawn. There are no commas or semicolons. The lines do not run in convenient lengths. Much is sheer nonsense. One must be sceptical, but throw caution to the winds and when the door opens accept absolutely. Also sometimes weep; also cut away ruthlessly with a slice of the blade soot, bark, hard accretions of all sorts. And so (while they talk) let down one's net deeper and deeper and gently draw in and bring to the surface what he said and she said and make poetry.

'Now I have listened to them talking. They have gone now. I am alone. I could be content to watch the fire burn for ever, like a dome, like a furnace; now some spike of wood takes the look of a scaffold, or pit, or happy valley; now it is a serpent curled crimson with white scales. The fruit on the curtain swells beneath the parrot's beak. Cheep, cheep, creaks the fire, like the cheep of insects in the middle of a forest. Cheep, cheep, it clicks while out there the branches thrash the air, and now, like a volley of shot, a tree falls. These are the sounds of a London night. Then I hear the one sound I wait for. Up and up it comes, approaches, hesitates, stops at my door. I cry, "Come in. Sit by me. Sit on the edge of the chair." Swept away by the old hallucination, I cry, "Come closer, closer." '

'I come back from the office,' said Louis. 'I hang my coat here, place my stick there – I like to fancy that Richelieu walked with such a cane. Thus I divest myself of my authority. I have been sitting at the right hand of a director at a varnished table. The maps of our successful undertakings confront us on the wall. We have laced the world together with our ships. The globe is strung with our lines. I am immensely respectable. All the young ladies in the office acknowledge my entrance. I can dine where I like now, and without vanity may suppose that I shall soon acquire a house in Surrey, two cars, a conservatory and some rare species of melon. But I still return, I still come back to my attic, hang up my hat and resume in solitude that curious attempt which I have made since I brought down my fist on my master's grained oak door. I open a little book. I read one poem. One poem is enough.

O western wind . . .

O western wind, you are at enmity with my mahogany table and spats, and also, alas, with the vulgarity of my mistress, the little actress who has never been able to speak English correctly –

O western wind, when wilt thou blow . . .

Rhoda, with her intense abstraction, with her unseeing eyes the colour of snail's flesh, does not destroy you, western wind, whether she comes at midnight when the stars blaze or at the most prosaic hour of midday. She stands at the window and looks at the chimney-pots and the broken windows in the houses of poor people –

O western wind, when wilt thou blow . . .

'My task, my burden, has always been greater than other people's. A pyramid has been set on my shoulders. I have tried to do a colossal labour. I have driven a violent, an unruly, a vicious team. With my Australian accent I have sat in eating-shops and tried to make the clerks accept me, yet never forgotten my solemn and severe convictions and the discrepancies and incoherences that must be resolved. As a boy I dreamt of the Nile, was reluctant to awake, yet brought down my fist on the grained oak door. It would have been happier to have been born without a destiny, like Susan, like Percival, whom I most admire.

O western wind, when wilt thou blow,
That the small rain down can rain?

'Life has been a terrible affair for me. I am like some vast sucker, some glutinous, some adhesive, some insatiable mouth. I have tried to draw from the living flesh the stone lodged at the centre. I have known little natural happiness, though I chose my mistress in order that, with her cockney accent, she might make me feel at my ease. But she only tumbled the floor with dirty under-linen, and the charwoman and the shop-boys called after me a dozen times a day, mocking my prim and supercilious gait.

O western wind, when wilt thou blow,
That the small rain down can rain?

'What has my destiny been, the sharp-pointed pyramid that has pressed on my ribs all the years? That I remember the Nile and the women carrying pitchers on their heads; that I feel myself woven in and out of the long summers and winters that have made the corn flow and have frozen the streams. I am not a single and passing being. My life is not a moment's bright spark like that on the surface of a diamond. I go beneath ground tortuously, as if a warder carried a lamp from cell to cell. My destiny has been that I remember and must weave together, must plait into one cable the many threads, the thin, the thick, the broken, the enduring of our long history, of our tumultuous and varied day. There is always more to be understood; a discord to be listened for; a falsity to be reprimanded. Broken and soot-stained are these roofs with their chimney cowls, their loose slates, their slinking cats and attic windows. I pick my way over broken glass, among blistered tiles, and see only vile and famished faces.

'Let us suppose that I make reason of it all – one poem on a page, and then die. I can assure you it will not be unwillingly. Percival died. Rhoda left me. But I shall live to be gaunt and sere, to tap my way, much respected, with my gold-headed cane along the pavements of the city. Perhaps I shall never die, shall never attain even that continuity and permanence –

O western wind, when wilt thou blow,
That the small rain down can rain?

'Percival was flowering with green leaves and was laid in the earth with all his branches still sighing in the summer wind. Rhoda, with whom I shared silence when the others spoke, she who hung back and turned aside when the herd assembled and galloped with orderly, sleek backs over the rich pastures, has gone now like the desert heat. When the sun blisters the roofs of the city I think of her; when the dry leaves patter to the ground; when the old men come with pointed sticks and pierce little bits of paper as we pierced her –

O western wind, when wilt thou blow,
That the small rain down can rain?
Christ, that my love were in my arms,
And I in my bed again!

I return now to my book; I return now to my attempt.'

'Oh, life, how I have dreaded you,' said Rhoda, 'oh, human beings, how I have hated you! How you have nudged, how you have interrupted, how hideous you have looked in Oxford Street, how squalid sitting opposite each other staring in the Tube! Now as I climb this mountain, from the top of which I shall see Africa, my mind is printed with brown-paper parcels and your faces. I have been stained by you and corrupted. You smelt so unpleasant too, lining up outside doors to buy tickets. All were dressed in indeterminate shades of grey and brown, never even a blue feather pinned to a hat. None had the courage to be one thing rather than another. What dissolution of the soul you demanded in order to get through one day, what lies, bowings, scrapings, fluency and servility! How you chained me to one spot, one hour, one chair and sat yourselves down opposite! How you snatched from me the white spaces that lie between hour and hour and rolled them into dirty pellets and tossed them into the wastepaper basket with your greasy paws. Yet those were my life.

'But I yielded. Sneers and yawns were covered with my hand. I did not go out into the street and break a bottle in the gutter as a sign of rage. Trembling with ardour, I pretended that I was not surprised. What you did, I did. If Susan and Jinny pulled up their stockings like that, I pulled mine up like that also. So terrible was life that I held up shade after shade. Look at life through this, look at life through that; let there be rose leaves, let there be vine leaves – I covered the whole street, Oxford Street, Piccadilly Circus, with the blaze and ripple of my mind, with vine leaves and rose leaves. There were boxes too, standing in the passage when the school broke up. I stole secretly to read the labels and dream of names and faces. Harrogate, perhaps, Edinburgh, perhaps, was ruffled with golden glory where some girl whose name I forget stood on the pavement. But it was the name only. I left Louis; I feared embraces. With fleeces, with vestments, I have tried to cover the blue-black blade. I implored day to break into night. I have longed to see the cupboard dwindle, to feel the bed soften, to float suspended, to perceive lengthened trees, lengthened faces, a green bank on a moor and two figures in distress saying goodbye. I flung words in fans like those the sower throws over the ploughed fields when the earth is bare. I desired always to stretch the night and fill it fuller and fuller with dreams.

'Then in some Hall I parted the boughs of music and saw the house we have made; the square stood upon the oblong. "The house which contains all," I said, lurching against people's shoulders in an omnibus after Percival died; yet I went to Greenwich. Walking on the embankments, I prayed that I might thunder for ever on the verge of the world where there is no vegetation, but here and there a marble pillar. I threw my bunch into the spreading wave. I said, "Consume me, carry me to the furthest limit." The wave has broken; the bunch is withered. I seldom think of Percival now.

'Now I climb this Spanish hill; and I will suppose that this mule-back is my bed and that I lie dying. There is only a thin sheet between me now and the infinite depths. The lumps in the mattress soften beneath me. We stumble up – we stumble on. My path has been up and up towards some solitary tree with a pool beside it on the very top. I have sliced the waters of beauty in the evening when the hills close themselves like birds' wings folded. I have picked sometimes a red carnation, and wisps of hay. I have sunk alone on the turf and fingered some old bone and thought: When the wind stoops to brush this height, may there be nothing found but a pinch of dust.

'The mule stumbles up and on. The ridge of the hill rises like mist, but from the top I shall see Africa. Now the bed gives under me. The sheets spotted with yellow holes let me fall through. The good woman with a face like a white horse at the end of the bed makes a valedictory movement and turns to go. Who then comes with me? Flowers only, the cowbind and the moonlight-coloured May. Gathering them loosely in a sheaf I made of them a garland and gave them – Oh, to whom? We launch out now over the precipice. Beneath us lie the lights of the herring fleet. The cliffs vanish. Rippling small, rippling grey, innumerable waves spread beneath us. I touch nothing. I see nothing. We may sink and settle on the waves. The sea will drum in my ears. The white petals will be darkened with sea water. They will float for a moment and then sink. Rolling me over the waves will shoulder me under. Everything falls in a tremendous shower, dissolving me.

'Yet that tree has bristling branches; that is the hard line of a cottage roof. Those bladder shapes painted red and yellow are faces. Putting my foot to the ground I step gingerly and press my hand against the hard door of a Spanish inn.'

The sun was sinking. The hard stone of the day was cracked and light poured through its splinters. Red and gold shot through the waves, in rapid running arrows, feathered with darkness. Erratically rays of light flashed and wandered, like signals from sunken islands, or darts shot through laurel groves by shameless, laughing boys. But the waves, as they neared the shore, were robbed of light, and fell in one long concussion, like a wall falling, a wall of grey stone, unpierced by any chink of light.

A breeze rose; a shiver ran through the leaves; and thus stirred they lost their brown density and became grey or white as the tree shifted its mass, winked and lost its domed uniformity. The hawk poised on the topmost branch flicked its eyelids and rose and sailed and soared far away. The wild plover cried in the marshes, evading, circling, and crying farther off in loneliness. The smoke of trains and chimneys was stretched and torn and became part of the fleecy canopy that hung over the sea and the fields.

Now the corn was cut. Now only a brisk stubble was left of all its flowing and waving. Slowly a great owl launched itself from the elm tree and swung and rose, as if on a line that dipped, to the height of the cedar. On the hills the slow shadows now broadened, now shrank, as they passed over. The pool on the top of the moor lay blank. No furry face looked there, or hoof splashed, or hot muzzle seethed in the water. A bird, perched on an ash-coloured twig, sipped a beak full of cold water. There was no sound of cropping, and no sound of wheels, but only the sudden roar of the wind letting its sails fill and brushing the tops of the grasses. One bone lay rain-pocked and sun-bleached till it shone like a twig that the sea has polished. The tree, that had burnt foxy red in spring and in midsummer bent pliant leaves to the south wind, was now black as iron, and as bare.

The land was so distant that no shining roof or glittering window could be any longer seen. The tremendous weight of the shadowed earth had engulfed such frail fetters, such snail-shell encumbrances. Now there was only the liquid shadow of the cloud, the buffeting of the rain, a single darting spear of sunshine, or the sudden bruise of the rainstorm. Solitary trees marked distant hills like obelisks.

The evening sun, whose heat had gone out of it and whose burning spot of intensity had been diffused, made chairs and tables mellower and inlaid them with lozenges of brown and yellow. Lined with shadows their weight seemed more ponderous, as if colour, tilted, had run to one side. Here lay knife, fork and glass, but lengthened, swollen, and made portentous. Rimmed in a gold circle the looking-glass held the scene immobile as if everlasting in its eye.

Meanwhile the shadows lengthened on the beach; the blackness deepened. The iron black boot became a pool of deep blue. The rocks lost their hardness. The water that stood round the old boat was dark as if mussels had been steeped in it. The foam had turned livid and left here and there a white gleam of pearl on the misty sand.

'Hampton Court,' said Bernard. 'Hampton Court. This is our meeting-place. Behold the red chimneys, the square battlements of Hampton Court. The tone of my voice as I say "Hampton Court" proves that I am middle-aged. Ten years, fifteen years ago, I should have said "Hampton Court?" with interrogation – what will it be like? Will there be lakes, mazes? Or with anticipation, What is going to happen to me here? Whom shall I meet? Now, Hampton Court – Hampton Court – the words beat a gong in the space which I have so laboriously cleared with half a dozen telephone messages and postcards, give off ring after ring of sound, booming, sonorous: and pictures rise – summer afternoons, boats, old ladies holding their skirts up, one urn in winter, some daffodils in March – these all float to the top of the waters that now lie deep on every scene.

'There at the door by the inn, our meeting-place, they are already standing – Susan, Louis, Rhoda, Jinny and Neville. They have come together already. In a moment, when I have joined them, another arrangement will form, another pattern. What now runs to waste, forming scenes profusely, will be checked, stated. I am reluctant to suffer that compulsion. Already at fifty yards distance I feel the order of my being changed. The tug of the magnet of their society tells upon me. I come nearer. They do not see me. Now Rhoda sees me, but she pretends, with her horror of the shock of meeting, that I am a stranger. Now Neville turns. Suddenly, raising my hand, saluting Neville, I cry, "I too have pressed flowers between the pages of Shakespeare's sonnets," and am churned up. My little boat bobs unsteadily upon the chopped and tossing waves. There is no panacea (let me note) against the shock of meeting.

'It is uncomfortable too, joining ragged edges, raw edges; only gradually, as we shuffle and trample into the inn, taking coats and hats off, does meeting become agreeable. Now we assemble in the long, bare dining-room that overlooks some park, some green space still fantastically lit by the setting sun so that there is a gold bar between the trees, and sit ourselves down.'

'Now sitting side by side,' said Neville, 'at this narrow table, now before the first emotion is worn smooth, what do we feel? Honestly now, openly and directly as befits old friends meeting with difficulty, what do we feel on meeting? Sorrow. The door will not open; he will not come. And we are laden. Being now all of us middle-aged, loads are on us. Let us put down our loads. What have you made of life, we ask, and I? You, Bernard; you, Susan; you, Jinny; and Rhoda and Louis? The lists have been posted on the doors. Before we break these rolls, and help ourselves to fish and salad, I feel in my private pocket and find my credentials – what I carry to prove my superiority. I have passed. I have papers in my private pocket that prove it. But your eyes,

Susan, full of turnips and cornfields, disturb me. These papers in my private pocket – the clamour that proves that I have passed – make a faint sound like that of a man clapping in an empty field to scare away rooks. Now it has died down altogether, under Susan's stare (the clapping, the reverberation that I have made), and I hear only the wind sweeping over the ploughed land and some bird singing – perhaps some intoxicated lark. Has the waiter heard of me, or those furtive everlasting couples, now loitering, now holding back and looking at the trees which are not yet dark enough to shelter their prostrate bodies? No; the sound of clapping has failed.

'What then remains, when I cannot pull out my papers and make you believe by reading aloud my credentials that I have passed? What remains is what Susan brings to light under the acid of her green eyes, her crystal, pear-shaped eyes. There is always somebody, when we come together, and the edges of meeting are still sharp, who refuses to be submerged; whose identity therefore one wishes to make crouch beneath one's own. For me now, it is Susan. I talk to impress Susan. Listen to me, Susan.

'When someone comes in at breakfast, even the embroidered fruit on my curtain swells so that parrots can peck it; one can break it off between one's thumb and finger. The thin skimmed milk of early morning turns opal, blue rose. At that hour your husband – the man who slapped his gaiters, pointing with his whip at the barren cow – grumbles. You say nothing. You see nothing. Custom blinds your eyes. At that hour your relationship is mute, null, dun-coloured. Mine at that hour is warm and various. There are no repetitions for me. Each day is dangerous. Smooth on the surface, we are all bone beneath like snakes coiling. Suppose we read *The Times*; suppose we argue. It is an experience. Suppose it is winter. The snow falling loads down the roof and seals us together in a red cave. The pipes have burst. We stand a yellow tin bath in the middle of the room. We rush helter-skelter for basins. Look there – it has burst again over the bookcase. We shout with laughter at the sight of ruin. Let solidity be destroyed. Let us have no possessions. Or is it summer? We may wander to a lake and watch Chinese geese waddling flat-footed to the water's edge, or see a bone-like city church with young green trembling before it. (I choose at random; I choose the obvious.) Each sight is an arabesque scrawled suddenly to illustrate some hazard and marvel of intimacy. The snow, the burst pipe, the tin bath, the Chinese goose – these are signs swung high aloft upon which, looking back, I read the character of each love; how each was different.

'You meanwhile – for I want to diminish your hostility, your green eyes fixed on mine, and your shabby dress, your rough hands, and all the other emblems of your maternal splendour – have stuck like a limpet to the same rock. Yet it is true, I do not want to hurt you; only to refresh and furbish up my own belief in myself that failed at your entry. Change is no longer possible. We are committed. Before, when we met in a restaurant in London with Percival, all simmered and shook; we could have been anything. We have chosen now, or sometimes it seems the choice was made for us – a pair of tongs pinched us between the shoulders. I chose. I took the print of life not outwardly, but inwardly upon the raw, the white, the unprotected fibre. I am clouded and bruised with the print of minds and faces and things so subtle that they have smell, colour, texture, substance, but no name. I am merely "Neville" to you, who see the narrow limits of my life and the line it cannot pass. But to myself I am immeasurable; a net whose fibres pass imperceptibly beneath the world. My net is almost indistinguishable from that which it surrounds. It lifts whales – huge leviathans and white jellies, what is amorphous and wandering; I detect, I perceive. Beneath my eyes opens – a book; I see to the bottom; the heart – I see to the depths. I know what loves are trembling into fire; how jealousy shoots its green flashes hither and thither; how intricately love crosses love; love makes knots; love brutally tears them apart. I have been knotted; I have been torn apart.

'But there was another glory once, when we watched for the door to open, and Percival came; when we flung ourselves unattached on the edge of a hard bench in a public room.'

'There was the beech wood,' said Susan, 'Elvedon, and the gilt hands of the clock sparkling among the trees. The pigeons broke the leaves. The changing travelling lights wandered over me. They escaped me. Yet look, Neville, whom I discredit in order to be myself, at my hand on the table. Look at the gradations of healthy colour here on the knuckles, here on the palm. My body has been used daily, rightly, like a tool by a good workman, all over. The blade is clean, sharp, worn in the centre. (We battle together like beasts fighting in a field, like stags making their horns clash.) Seen through your pale and yielding flesh, even apples and bunches of fruit must have a filmed look as if they stood under glass. Lying deep in a chair with one person, one person only, but one person who changes, you see one inch of flesh only; its nerves, fibres, the sullen or quick flow of blood on it; but nothing entire. You do not see a house in a garden; a horse in a field; a town laid out, as you bend like an old woman straining her eyes over her darning. But I have seen life in blocks, substantial, huge; its battlements and towers, factories and gasometers; a dwelling place made from time immemorial after an hereditary pattern. These things remain square, prominent, undissolved in my mind. I am not sinuous or suave; I sit among you abrading your softness with my hardness, quenching the silver-grey flickering moth-wing quiver of words with the green spurt of my clear eyes.

'Now we have clashed our antlers. This is the necessary prelude; the salute of old friends.'

'The gold has faded between the trees,' said Rhoda, 'and a slice of green lies behind them, elongated like the blade of a knife seen in dreams, or some tapering island on which nobody sets foot. Now the cars begin to wink and flicker, coming down the avenue. Lovers can draw into the darkness now; the boles of the trees are swollen, are obscene with lovers.'

'It was different once,' said Bernard. 'Once we could break the current as we chose. How many telephone calls, how many postcards, are now needed to cut this hole through which we come together, united, at Hampton Court? How swift life runs from January to December! We are all swept on by the torrent of things grown so familiar that they cast no shade; we make no comparisons; think scarcely ever of I or of you; and in this unconsciousness attain the utmost freedom from friction and part the weeds that grow over the mouths of sunken channels. We have to leap like fish, high in the air, in order to catch the train from Waterloo. And however high we leap we fall back again into the stream. I shall never now take ship for the South Sea Islands. A journey to Rome is the limit of my travelling. I have sons and daughters. I am wedged into my place in the puzzle.

'But it is only my body – this elderly man here whom you call Bernard – that is fixed irrevocably – so I desire to believe. I think more disinterestedly than I could when I was young and must dig furiously like a child rummaging in a bran-pie to discover my self. "Look, what is this? And this? Is this going to be a fine present? Is that all?" and so on. Now I know what the parcels hold; and do not care much. I throw my mind out in the air as a man throws seeds in great fan-flights, falling through the purple sunset, falling on the pressed and shining ploughland which is bare.

'A phrase. An imperfect phrase. And what are phrases? They have left me very little to lay on the table, beside Susan's hand; to take from my pocket, with Neville's credentials. I am not an authority on law, or medicine, or finance. I am wrapped round with phrases, like damp straw; I glow, phosphorescent. And each of you feels when I speak, "I am lit up. I am glowing." The little boys used to feel, "That's a good one, that's a good one," as the phrases bubbled up from my lips under the elm trees in the playing fields. They too bubbled up; they also escaped with my phrases. But I pine in solitude. Solitude is my undoing.

'I pass from house to house like the friars in the Middle Ages who cozened the wives and girls with beads and ballads. I am a traveller, a pedlar, paying for my lodging with a ballad; I am all indiscriminate, an easily pleased guest; often putting up in the best room in a four-poster; then lying in a barn on a haystack. I don't mind the fleas and find no fault with silk either. I am very tolerant. I am not a moralist. I have too great a sense of the shortness of life and its temptations to rule red lines. Yet I am not so indiscriminate as you think, judging me – as you judge me – from my fluency. I have a little dagger of contempt and severity hidden up my sleeve. But I am apt to be deflected. I make stories. I twist up toys out of anything. A girl sits at a cottage door; she is waiting; for whom? Seduced, or not seduced? The headmaster sees the hole in the carpet. He sighs. His wife, drawing her fingers through the waves of her still abundant hair, reflects – et cetera. Waves of hands, hesitations at street corners, someone dropping a cigarette into the gutter – all are stories. But which is the true story? That I do not know. Hence I keep my phrases hung like clothes in a cupboard, waiting for someone to wear them. Thus waiting, thus speculating, making this note and then another, I do not cling to life. I shall be brushed like a bee from a sunflower. My philosophy, always accumulating, welling up moment by moment, runs like quicksilver a dozen ways at once. But Louis, wild-eyed but severe, in his attic, in his office, has formed unalterable conclusions upon the true nature of what is to be known.'

'It breaks,' said Louis, 'the thread I try to spin; your laughter breaks it, your indifference, also your beauty. Jinny broke the thread when she kissed me in the garden years ago. The boasting boys mocked me at school for my Australian accent and broke it. "This is the meaning," I say; and then start with a pang – vanity. "Listen," I say, "to the nightingale, who sings among the trampling feet; the conquests and migrations. Believe – " and then am twitched asunder. Over broken tiles and splinters of glass I pick my way. Different lights fall, making the ordinary leopard-spotted and strange. This moment of reconciliation, when we meet together united, this evening moment, with its wine and shaking leaves, and youth coming up from the river in white flannels, carrying cushions, is to me black with the shadows of dungeons and the tortures and infamies practised by man upon man. So imperfect are my senses that they never blot out with one purple the serious charge that my reason adds and adds against us, even as we sit here. What is the solution, I ask myself, and the bridge? How can I reduce these dazzling, these dancing apparitions to one line capable of linking all in one? So I ponder; and you meanwhile observe maliciously my pursed lips, my sallow cheeks and my invariable frown.

'But I beg you also to notice my cane and my waistcoat. I have inherited a desk of solid mahogany in a room hung with maps. Our steamers have won an enviable reputation for their cabins replete with luxury. We supply swimming-baths and gymnasiums. I wear a white waistcoat now and consult a little book before I make an engagement.

'This is the arch and ironical manner in which I hope to distract you from my shivering, my tender, and infinitely young and unprotected soul. For I am always the youngest; the most naïvely surprised; the one who runs in advance in apprehension and sympathy with discomfort or ridicule – should there be a smut on a nose or a button undone. I suffer for all humiliations. Yet I am also ruthless, marmoreal. I do not see how you can say that it is fortunate to have lived. Your little excitements, your childish transports, when a kettle boils, when the soft air lifts Jinny's spotted scarf and it floats weblike, are to me like silk streamers thrown in the eyes of the charging bull. I condemn you. Yet my heart yearns towards you. I would go with you through the fires of death. Yet am happiest alone. I luxuriate in gold and purple vestments. Yet I prefer a view over chimney-pots; cats scraping their mangy sides upon blistered chimney-stacks; broken windows; and the hoarse clangour of bells from the steeple of some brick chapel.'

'I see what is before me,' said Jinny. 'This scarf, these wine-coloured spots. This glass. This mustard pot. This flower. I like what one touches, what one tastes. I like rain when it has turned to snow and become palpable. And being rash, and much more courageous than you are, I do not temper my beauty with meanness lest it should scorch me. I gulp it down entire. It is made of flesh; it is made of stuff. My imagination is the body's. Its visions are not finespun and white with purity like Louis's. I do not like your lean cats and your blistered chimney-pots. The scrannel beauties of your roof-tops repel me. Men and women, in uniforms, wigs and gowns, bowler hats and tennis shirts beautifully open at the neck, the infinite variety of women's dresses (I note all clothes always) delight me. I eddy with them, in and out, in and out, into rooms, into halls, here, there, everywhere, wherever they go. This man lifts the hoof of a horse. This man shoves in and out the drawers of his private collection. I am never alone. I am attended by a regiment of my fellows. My mother must have followed the drum, my father the sea. I am like a little dog that trots down the road after the regimental band, but stops to snuff a tree-trunk, to sniff some brown stain, and suddenly careers across the street after some mongrel cur and then holds one paw up while it sniffs an entrancing whiff of meat from the butcher's shop. My traffics have led me into strange places. Men, how many, have broken from the wall and come to me. I have only to hold my hand up. Straight as a dart they have come to the place of assignation – perhaps a chair on a balcony, perhaps a shop at a street corner. The torments, the divisions of your lives have been solved for me night after night, sometimes only by the touch of a finger under the tablecloth as we sat dining – so fluid has my body become, forming even at the touch of a finger into one full drop, which fills itself, which quivers, which flashes, which falls in ecstasy.

'I have sat before a looking-glass as you sit writing, adding up figures at desks. So, before the looking-glass in the temple of my bedroom, I have judged my nose and my chin; my lips that open too wide and show too much gum. I have looked. I have noted. I have chosen what yellow or white, what shine or dullness, what loop or straightness suits. I am volatile for one, rigid for another, angular as an icicle in silver, or voluptuous as a candle flame in gold. I have run violently like a whip flung out to the extreme end of my tether. His shirt front, there in the corner, has been white; then purple; smoke and flame have wrapped us about; after a furious conflagration – yet we scarcely raised our voices, sitting on the hearth-rug, as we murmured all the secrets of our hearts as into shells so that nobody might hear in the sleeping-house, but I heard the cook stir once, and once we thought the ticking of the clock was a footfall – we have sunk to ashes, leaving no relics, no unburnt bones, no wisps of hair to be kept in lockets such as your intimacies leave behind them. Now I turn grey; now I turn gaunt; but I look at my face at midday sitting in front of the looking-glass in broad daylight, and note precisely my nose, my chin, my lips that open too wide and show too much gum. But I am not afraid.'

'There were lamp-posts,' said Rhoda, 'and trees that had not yet shed their leaves on the way from the station. The leaves might have hidden me still. But I did not hide behind them. I walked straight up to you instead of circling round to avoid the shock of sensation as I used. But it is only that I have taught my body to do a certain trick. Inwardly I am not taught; I fear, I hate, I love, I envy and despise you, but I never join you happily. Coming up from the station, refusing to accept the shadow of the trees and the pillar-boxes, I perceived, from your coats and umbrellas, even at a distance, how you stand embedded in a substance made of repeated moments run together; are committed, have an attitude, with children, authority, fame, love, society; where I have nothing. I have no face.

'Here in this dining-room you see the antlers and the tumblers; the salt-cellars; the yellow stains on the tablecloth. "Waiter!" says Bernard. "Bread!" says Susan. And the waiter comes; he brings bread. But I see the side of a cup like a mountain and only parts of antlers, and the brightness on the side of that jug like a crack in darkness with wonder and terror. Your voices sound like trees creaking in a forest. So with your faces and their prominences and hollows. How beautiful, standing at a distance immobile at midnight against the railings of some square! Behind you is a white crescent of foam, and fishermen on the erge of the world are drawing in nets and casting them. A wind ruffles the topmost leaes of primeval trees. (Yet here we sit at Hampton Court.) Parrots shrieking break the intense stillness of the jungle. (Here the trams start.) The swallow dips her wings in midnight pools. (Here we talk.) That is the circumference that I try to grasp as we sit together. Thus I must undergo the penance of Hampton Court at seven-thirty precisely.

'But since these rolls of bread and wine bottles are needed by me, and your faces with their hollows and prominences are beautiful, and the table-cloth and its yellow stains, far from being allowed to spread in wider and wider circles of understanding that may at last (so I dream, falling off the edge of the earth at night when my bed floats suspended) embrace the entire world, I must go through the antics of the individual. I must start when you pluck at me with your children, your poems, your chilblains or whatever it is that you do and suffer. But I am not deluded. After all these callings hither and thither, these pluckings and searchings, I shall fall alone through this thin sheet into gulfs of fire. And you will not help me. More cruel than the old torturers, you will let me fall, and will tear me to pieces when I am fallen. Yet there are moments when the walls of the mind grow thin; when nothing is unabsorbed, and I could fancy that we might blow so vast a bubble that the sun might set and rise in it and we might take the blue of midday and the black of midnight and be cast off and escape from here and now.'

'Drop upon drop,' said Bernard, 'silence falls. It forms on the roof of the mind and falls into pools beneath. For ever alone, alone, alone – hear silence fall and sweep its rings to the farthest edges. Gorged and replete, solid with middle-aged content, I, whom loneliness destroys, let silence fall, drop by drop.

'But now silence falling pits my face, wastes my nose like a snowman stood out in a yard in the rain. As silence falls I am dissolved utterly and become featureless and scarcely to be distinguished from another. It does not matter. What matters? We have dined well. The fish, the veal cutlets, the wine have blunted the sharp tooth of egotism. Anxiety is at rest. The vainest of us, Louis perhaps, does not care what people think. Neville's tortures are at rest. Let others prosper – that is what he thinks. Susan hears the breathing of all her children safe asleep. Sleep, sleep, she murmurs. Rhoda has rocked her ships to shore. Whether they have foundered, whether they have anchored, she cares no longer. We are ready to consider any suggestion that the world may offer quite impartially. I reflect now that the earth is only a pebble flicked off accidentally from the face of the sun and that there is no life anywhere in the abysses of space.'

'In this silence,' said Susan, 'it seems as if no leaf would ever fall, or bird fly.'

'As if the miracle had happened,' said Jinny, 'and life were stayed here and now.'

'And,' said Rhoda, 'we had no more to live.'

'But listen,' said Louis, 'to the world moving through abysses of infinite space. It roars; the lighted strip of history is past and our kings and queens; we are gone; our civilisation; the Nile; and all life. Our separate drops are dissolved; we are extinct, lost in the abysses of time, in the darkness.'

'Silence falls; silence falls,' said Bernard. 'But now listen; tick, tick; hoot, hoot; the world has hailed us back to it. I heard for one moment the howling winds of darkness as we passed beyond life. Then tick, tick (the clock); then hoot, hoot (the cars). We are landed; we are on shore; we are sitting, six of us, at a table. It is the memory of my nose that recalls me. I rise; "Fight," I cry, "fight!" remembering the shape of my own nose, and strike with this spoon upon this table pugnaciously.'

'Oppose ourselves to this illimitable chaos,' said Neville, 'this formless imbecility. Making love to a nursemaid behind a tree, that soldier is more admirable than all the stars. Yet sometimes one trembling star comes in the clear sky and makes me think the world beautiful and we maggots deforming even the trees with our lust.'

('Yet, Louis,' said Rhoda, 'how short a time silence lasts. Already they are beginning to smooth their napkins by the side of their plates. "Who comes?" says Jinny; and Neville sighs, remembering that Percival comes no more. Jinny has taken out her looking-glass. Surveying her face like an artist, she draws a powder-puff down her nose, and after one moment of deliberation has given precisely that red to the lips that the lips need. Susan, who feels scorn and fear at the sight of these preparations, fastens the top button of her coat, and unfastens it. What is she making ready for? For something, but something different.'

'They are saying to themselves,' said Louis, ' "It is time. I am still vigorous," they are saying. "My face shall be cut against the black of infinite space." They do not finish their sentences. "It is time," they keep saying. "The gardens will be shut." And going with them, Rhoda, swept into their current, we shall perhaps drop a little behind.'

'Like conspirators who have something to whisper,' said Rhoda.)

'It is true, and I know for a fact,' said Bernard, 'as we walk down this avenue, that a king, riding, fell over a molehill here. But how strange it seems to set against the whirling abysses of infinite space a little figure with a golden teapot on his head. Soon one recovers belief in figures: but not at once in what they put on their heads. Our English past – one inch of light. Then people put teapots on their heads and say, "I am a king!" No, I try to recover, as we walk, the sense of time, but with that streaming darkness in my eyes I have lost my grip. This palace seems light as a cloud set for a moment on the sky. It is a trick of the mind – to put kings on their thrones, one following another, with crowns on their heads. And we ourselves, walking six abreast, what do we oppose, with this random flicker of light in us that we call brain and feeling, how can we do battle against this flood; what has permanence? Our lives too stream away, down the unlighted avenues, past the strip of time, unidentified. Once Neville threw a poem at my head. Feeling a sudden conviction of immortality, I said, "I too know what Shakespeare knew." But that has gone.'

'Unreasonably, ridiculously,' said Neville, 'as we walk, time comes back. A dog does it, prancing. The machine works. Age makes hoary that gateway. Three hundred years now seem more than a moment vanished against that dog. King William mounts his horse wearing a wig, and the court ladies sweep the turf with their embroidered panniers. I am beginning to be convinced, as we walk, that the fate of Europe is of immense importance, and, ridiculous as it still seems, that all depends upon the battle of Blenheim. Yes; I declare, as we pass through this gateway, it is the present moment; I am become a subject of King George.'

'While we advance down this avenue,' said Louis, 'I leaning slightly upon Jinny, Bernard arm-in-arm with Neville, and Susan with her hand in mine, it is difficult not to weep, calling ourselves little children, praying that God may keep us safe while we sleep. It is sweet to sing together, clasping hands, afraid of the dark, while Miss Curry plays the harmonium.'

'The iron gates have rolled back,' said Jinny. 'Time's fangs have ceased their devouring. We have triumphed over the abysses of space, with rouge, with powder, with flimsy pocket-handkerchiefs.'

'I grasp, I hold fast,' said Susan. 'I hold firmly to this hand, anyone's, with love, with hatred; it does not matter which.'

'The still mood, the disembodied mood is on us,' said Rhoda, 'and we enjoy this momentary alleviation (it is not often that one has no anxiety) when the walls of the mind become transparent. Wren's palace, like the quartet played to the dry and stranded people in the stalls, makes an oblong. A square is stood upon the oblong and we say, "This is our dwelling place. The structure is now visible. Very little is left outside." '

'The flower,' said Bernard, 'the red carnation that stood in the vase on the table of the restaurant when we dined together with Percival, is become a six-sided flower; made of six lives.'

'A mysterious illumination,' said Louis, 'visible against those yew trees.'

'Built up with much pain, many strokes,' said Jinny.

'Marriage, death, travel, friendship,' said Bernard; 'town and country; children and all that; a many-sided substance cut out of this dark; a many-faceted flower. Let us stop for a moment; let us behold what we have made. Let it blaze against the yew trees. One life. There. It is over. Gone out.'

'Now they vanish,' said Louis. 'Susan with Bernard. Neville with Jinny. You and I, Rhoda, stop for a moment by this stone urn. What song shall we hear now that these couples have sought the groves, and Jinny, pointing with her gloved hand, pretends to notice the water-lilies, and Susan, who has always loved Bernard, says to him, "My ruined life, my wasted life." And Neville, taking Jinny's little hand, with the cherry-coloured finger-nails, by the lake, by the moonlit water, cries, "Love, love," and she answers, imitating the bird, "Love, love?" What song do we hear?'

'They vanish, towards the lake,' said Rhoda. 'They slink away over the grass furtively, yet with assurance as if they asked of our pity their ancient privilege – not to be disturbed. The tide in the soul, tipped, flows that way; they cannot help deserting us. The dark has closed over their bodies. What song do we hear – the owl's, the nightingale's, the wren's? The steamer hoots; the light on the electric rails flashes, the trees gravely bow and bend. The flare hangs over London. Here is an old woman, quietly returning, and a man, a late fisherman, comes down the terrace with his rod. Not a sound, not a movement must escape us.'

'A bird flies homeward,' said Louis. 'Evening opens her eyes and gives one quick glance among the bushes before she sleeps. How shall we put it together, the confused and composite message that they send back to us, and not they only, but many dead, boys and girls, grown men and women, who have wandered here, under one king or another?'

'A weight has dropped into the night,' said Rhoda, 'dragging it down. Every tree is big with a shadow that is not the shadow of the tree behind it. We hear a drumming on the roofs of a fasting city when the Turks are hungry and uncertain tempered. We hear them crying with sharp, stag-like barks, "Open, open." Listen to the trams squealing and to the flashes from the electric rails. We hear the beech trees and the birch trees raise their branches as if the bride had let her silken nightdress fall and come to the doorway saying, "Open, open." '

'All seems alive,' said Louis. 'I cannot hear death anywhere tonight. Stupidity, on that man's face, age, on that woman's, would be strong enough, one would think, to resist the incantation, and bring in death. But where is death tonight? All the crudity, odds and ends, this and that, have been crushed like glass splinters into the blue, the red-fringed tide, which, drawing into the shore, fertile with innumerable fish, breaks at our feet.'

'If we could mount together, if we could perceive from a sufficient height,' said Rhoda, 'if we could remain untouched without any support – but you, disturbed by faint clapping sounds of praise and laughter, and I, resenting compromise and right and wrong on human lips, trust only in solitude and the violence of death and thus are divided.'

'For ever,' said Louis, 'divided. We have sacrificed the embrace among the ferns, and love, love, love by the lake, standing, like conspirators who have drawn apart to share some secret, by the urn. But now look, as we stand here, a ripple breaks on the horizon. The net is raised higher and higher. It comes to the top of the water. The water is broken by silver, by quivering little fish. Now leaping, now lashing, they are laid on shore. Life tumbles its catch upon the grass. There are figures coming towards us. Are they men or are they women? They still wear the ambiguous draperies of the flowing tide in which they have been immersed.'

'Now,' said Rhoda, 'as they pass that tree, they regain their natural size. They are only men, only women. Wonder and awe change as they put off the draperies of the flowing tide. Pity returns, as they emerge into the moonlight, like the relics of an army, our representatives, going every night (here or in Greece) to battle, and coming back every night with their wounds, their ravaged faces. Now light falls on them again. They have faces. They become Susan and Bernard, Jinny and Neville, people we know. Now what a shrinkage takes place! Now what a shrivelling, what a humiliation! The old shivers run through me, hatred and terror, as I feel myself grappled to one spot by these hooks they cast on us; these greetings, recognitions, pluckings of the finger and searchings of the eyes. Yet they have only to speak, and their first words, with the remembered tone and the perpetual deviation from what one expects, and their hands moving and making a thousand past days rise again in the darkness, shake my purpose.'

'Something flickers and dances,' said Louis. 'Illusion returns as they approach down the avenue. Rippling and questioning begin. What do I think of you – what do you think of me? Who are you? Who am I? – that quivers again its uneasy air over us, and the pulse quickens and the eye brightens and all the insanity of personal existence without which life would fall flat and die, begins again. They are on us. The southern sun flickers over this urn; we push off into the tide of the violent and cruel sea. Lord help us to act our parts as we greet them returning – Susan and Bernard, Neville and Jinny.'

'We have destroyed something by our presence,' said Bernard, 'a world perhaps.'

'Yet we scarcely breathe,' said Neville, 'spent as we are. We are in that passive and exhausted frame of mind when we only wish to rejoin the body of our mother from whom we have been severed. All else is distasteful, forced and fatiguing. Jinny's yellow scarf is moth-coloured in this light; Susan's eyes are quenched. We are scarcely to be distinguished from the river. One cigarette end is the only point of emphasis among us. And sadness tinges our content, that we should have left you, torn the fabric; yielded to the desire to press out, alone, some bitterer, some blacker juice, which was sweet too. But now we are worn out.'

'After our fire,' said Jinny, 'there is nothing left to put in lockets.'

'Still I gape,' said Susan, 'like a young bird, unsatisfied, for something that has escaped me.'

'Let us stay for a moment,' said Bernard, 'before we go. Let us pace the terrace by the river almost alone. It is nearly bedtime. People have gone home. Now how comforting it is to watch the lights coming out in the bedrooms of small shopkeepers on the other side of the river. There is one – there is another. What do you think their takings have been today? Only just enough to pay for the rent, for light and food and the children's clothing. But just enough. What a sense of the tolerableness of life the lights in the bedrooms of small shopkeepers give us! Saturday comes, and there is just enough to pay perhaps for seats at the pictures. Perhaps before they put out the light they go into the little garden and look at the giant rabbit couched in its wooden hut. That is the rabbit they will have for Sunday dinner. Then they put out the light. Then they sleep. And for thousands of people sleep is nothing but warmth and silence and one moment's sport with some fantastic dream. "I have posted my letter," the greengrocer thinks, "to the Sunday newspaper. Suppose I win five hundred pounds in the football competition? And we shall kill the rabbit. Life is pleasant. Life is good. I have posted the letter. We shall kill the rabbit." And he sleeps.

'That goes on. Listen. There is a sound like the knocking of railway trucks in a siding. That is the happy concatenation of one event following another in our lives. Knock, knock, knock. Must, must, must. Must go, must sleep, must wake, must get up – sober, merciful word which we pretend to revile, which we press tight to our hearts, without which we should be undone. How we worship that sound like the knocking together of trucks in a siding!

'Now far off down the river I hear the chorus; the song of the boasting boys, who are coming back in large charabancs from a day's outing on the decks of crowded steamers. Still they are singing as they used to sing, across the court, on winters' nights, or with the windows open in summer, getting drunk, breaking the furniture, wearing little striped caps, all turning their heads the same way as the brake rounded the corner; and I wished to be with them.

'What with the chorus and the spinning water and the just perceptible murmur of the breeze we are slipping away. Little bits of ourselves are crumbling. There! Something very important fell then. I cannot keep myself together. I shall sleep. But we must go; must catch our train; must walk back to the station – must, must, must. We are only bodies jogging along side by side. I exist only in the soles of my feet and in the tired muscles of my thighs. We have been walking for hours it seems. But where? I cannot remember. I am like a log slipping smoothly over some waterfall. I am not a judge. I am not called upon to give my opinion. Houses and trees are all the same in this grey light. Is that a post? Is that a woman walking? Here is the station, and if the train were to cut me in two, I should come together on the farther side, being one, being indivisible. But what is odd is that I still clasp the return half of my ticket to Waterloo firmly between the fingers of my right hand, even now, even sleeping.'

Now the sun had sunk. Sky and sea were indistinguishable. The waves breaking spread their white fans far out over the shore, sent white shadows into the recesses of sonorous caves and then rolled back sighing over the shingle.

The tree shook its branches and a scattering of leaves fell to the ground. There they settled with perfect composure on the precise spot where they would await dissolution. Black and grey were shot into the garden from the broken vessel that had once held red light. Dark shadows blackened the tunnels between the stalks. The thrush was silent and the worm sucked itself back into its narrow hole. Now and again a whitened and hollow straw was blown from an old nest and fell into the dark grasses among the rotten apples. The light had faded from the tool-house wall and the adder's skin hung from the nail empty. All the colours in the room had over-flown their banks. The precise brushstroke was swollen and lopsided; cupboards and chairs melted their brown masses into one huge obscurity. The height from floor to ceiling was hung with vast curtains of shaking darkness. The looking-glass was pale as the mouth of a cave shadowed by hanging creepers.

The substance had gone from the solidity of the hills. Travelling lights drove a plumy wedge among unseen and sunken roads, but no lights opened among the folded wings of the hills, and there was no sound save the cry of a bird seeking some lonelier tree. At the cliff's edge there was an equal murmur of air that had been brushed through forests, of water that had been cooled in a thousand glassy hollows of mid-ocean.

As if there were waves of darkness in the air, darkness moved on, covering houses, hills, trees, as waves of water wash round the sides of some sunken ship. Darkness washed down streets, eddying round single figures, engulfing them; blotting out couples clasped under the showery darkness of elm trees in full summer foliage. Darkness rolled its waves along grassy rides and over the wrinkled skin of the turf, enveloping the solitary thorn tree and the empty snail shells at its foot. Mounting higher, darkness blew along the bare upland slopes, and met the fretted and abraded pinnacles of the mountain where the snow lodges for ever on the hard rock even when the valleys are full of running streams and yellow vine leaves, and girls, sitting on verandahs, look up at the snow, shading their faces with their fans. Them, too, darkness covered.

'Now to sum up,' said Bernard. 'Now to explain to you the meaning of my life. Since we do not know each other (though I met you once, I think, on board a ship going to Africa), we can talk freely. The illusion is upon me that something adheres for a moment, has roundness, weight, depth, is completed. This, for the moment, seems to be my life. If it were possible, I would hand it you entire. I would break it off as one breaks off a bunch of grapes. I would say, "Take it. This is my life."

'But unfortunately, what I see (this globe, full of figures) you do not see. You see me, sitting at a table opposite you, a rather heavy, elderly man, grey at the temples. You see me take my napkin and unfold it. You see me pour myself out a glass of wine. And you see behind me the door opening, and people passing. But in order to make you understand, to give you my life, I must tell you a story – and there are so many, and so many – stories of childhood, stories of school, love, marriage, death, and so on; and none of them are true. Yet like children we tell each other stories, and to decorate them we make up these ridiculous, flamboyant, beautiful phrases. How tired I am of stories, how tired I am of phrases that come down beautifully with all their feet on the ground! Also, how I distrust neat designs of life that are drawn upon half-sheets of notepaper. I begin to long for some little language such as lovers use, broken words, inarticulate words, like the shuffling of feet on the pavement. I begin to seek some design more in accordance with those moments of humiliation and triumph that come now and then undeniably. Lying in a ditch on a stormy day, when it has been raining, then enormous clouds come marching over the sky, tattered clouds, wisps of cloud. What delights me then is the confusion, the height, the indifference and the fury. Great clouds always changing, and movement; something sulphurous and sinister, bowled up, helter-skelter; towering, trailing, broken off, lost, and I forgotten, minute, in a ditch. Of story, of design, I do not see a trace then.

'But meanwhile, while we eat, let us turn over these scenes as children turn over the pages of a picture-book and the nurse says, pointing: "That's a cow. That's a boat." Let us turn over the pages, and I will add, for your amusement, a comment in the margin.

'In the beginning, there was the nursery, with windows opening on to a garden, and beyond that the sea. I saw something brighten – no doubt the brass handle of a cupboard. Then Mrs Constable raised the sponge above her head, squeezed it, and out shot, right, left, all down the spine, arrows of sensation. And so, as long as we draw breath, for the rest of time, if we knock against a chair, a table, or a woman, we are pierced with arrows of sensation – if we walk in a garden, if we drink this wine. Sometimes indeed, when I pass a cottage with a light in the window where a child has been born, I could implore them not to squeeze the sponge over that new body. Then, there was the garden and the canopy of the currant leaves which seemed to enclose everything; flowers, burning like sparks upon the depths of green; a rat wreathing with maggots under a rhubarb leaf; the fly going buzz, buzz, buzz upon the nursery ceiling, and plates upon plates of innocent bread and butter. All these things happen in one second and last for ever. Faces loom. Dashing round the corner, "Hallo," one says, "there's Jinny. That's Neville. That's Louis in grey flannels with a snake belt. That's Rhoda." She had a basin in which she sailed petals of white flowers. It was Susan who cried, that day when I was in the tool-house with Neville; and I felt my indifference melt. Neville did not melt. "Therefore," I said, "I am myself, not Neville," a wonderful discovery. Susan cried and I followed her. Her wet pocket-hand-kerchief, and the sight of her little back heaving up and down like a pump-handle, sobbing for what was denied her, screwed my nerves up. "This is not to be borne," I said, as I sat beside her on the roots that were hard as skeletons. I then first became aware of the presence of those enemies who change, but are always there; the forces we fight against. To let oneself be carried on passively is unthinkable. "That's your course, world," one says, "mine is this." So, "Let's explore," I cried, and jumped up, and ran downhill with Susan and saw the stable-boy clattering about the yard in great boots. Down below, through the depths of the leaves, the gardeners swept the lawns with great brooms. The lady sat writing. Transfixed, stopped dead, I thought, "I cannot interfere with a single stroke of those brooms. They sweep and they sweep. Nor with the fixity of that woman writing." It is strange that one cannot stop gardeners sweeping nor dislodge a woman. There they have remained all my life. It is as if one had woken in Stone-henge surrounded by a circle of great stones, these enemies, these presences. Then a wood-pigeon flew out of the trees. And being in love for the first time, I made a phrase – a poem about a wood-pigeon – a single phrase, for a hole had been knocked in my mind, one of those sudden transparencies through which one sees everything. Then more bread and butter and more flies droning round the nursery ceiling on which quivered islands of light, ruffled, opalescent, while the pointed fingers of the lustre dripped blue pools on the corner of the mantelpiece. Day after day as we sat at tea we observed these sights.

'But we were all different. The wax – the virginal wax that coats the spine melted in different patches for each of us. The growl of the boot-boy making love to the tweeny among the gooseberry bushes; the clothes blown out hard on the line; the dead man in the gutter; the apple tree, stark in the moonlight; the rat swarming with maggots; the lustre dripping blue – our white wax was streaked and stained by each of these differently. Louis was disgusted by the nature of human flesh; Rhoda by our cruelty; Susan could not share; Neville wanted order; Jinny love; and so on. We suffered terribly as we became separate bodies.

'Yet I was preserved from these excesses and have survived many of my friends, am a little stout, grey, rubbed on the thorax as it were, because it is the panorama of life, seen not from the roof, but from the third-storey window, that delights me, not what one woman says to one man, even if that man is myself. How could I be bullied at school therefore? How could they make things hot for me? There was the Doctor lurching into chapel, as if he trod a battleship in a gale of wind, shouting out his commands through a megaphone, since people in authority always become melodramatic – I did not hate him like Neville, or revere him like Louis. I took notes as we sat together in chapel. There were pillars, shadows, memorial brasses, boys scuffling and swopping stamps behind prayer-books; the sound of a rusty pump; the Doctor booming, about immortality and quitting ourselves like men; and Percival scratching his thigh. I made notes for stories; drew portraits in the margin of my pocket-book and thus became still more separate. Here are one or two of the figures I saw.

'Percival sat staring straight ahead of him that day in chapel. He also had a way of flicking his hand to the back of his neck. His movements were always remarkable. We all flicked our hands to the backs of our heads – unsuccessfully. He had the kind of beauty which defends itself from any caress. As he was not in the least precocious, he read whatever was written up for our edification without any comment, and thought, with that magnificent equanimity (Latin words come naturally) that was to preserve him from so many meannesses and humiliations, that Lucy's flaxen pigtails and pink cheeks were the height of female beauty. Thus preserved, his taste later was of extreme fineness. But there should be music, some wild carol. Through the window should come a hunting-song from some rapid unapprehended life – a sound that shouts among the hills and dies away. What is startling, what is unexpected, what we cannot account for, what turns symmetry to nonsense – that comes suddenly to my mind thinking of him. The little apparatus of observation is unhinged. Pillars go down; the Doctor floats off; some sudden exaltation possesses me. He was thrown, riding in a race, and when I came along Shaftesbury Avenue tonight, those insignificant and scarcely formulated faces that bubble up out of the doors of the Tube, and many obscure Indians, and people dying of famine and disease, and women who have been cheated, and whipped dogs and crying children – all these seemed to me bereft. He would have done justice. He would have protected. About the age of forty he would have shocked the authorities. No lullaby has ever occurred to me capable of singing him to rest.

'But let me dip again and bring up in my spoon another of these minute objects which we call optimistically, "characters of our friends" – Louis. He sat staring at the preacher. His being seemed conglobulated in his brow, his lips were pressed; his eyes were fixed, but suddenly they flashed with laughter. Also he suffered from chilblains, the penalty of an imperfect circulation. Unhappy, unfriended, in exile, he would sometimes, in moments of confidence, describe how the surf swept over the beaches of his home. The remorseless eye of youth fixed itself upon his swollen joints. Yes, but we were also quick to perceive how cutting, how apt, how severe he was, how naturally, when we lay under the elm trees pretending to watch cricket, we waited his approval, seldom given. His ascendancy was resented, as Percival's was adored. Prim, suspicious, lifting his feet like a crane, there was yet a legend that he had smashed a door with his naked fist. But his peak was too bare, too stony for that kind of mist to cling to it. He was without those simple attachments by which one is connected with another. He remained aloof; enigmatic; a scholar capable of that inspired accuracy which has something formidable about it. My phrases (how to describe the moon) did not meet with his approval. On the other hand, he envied me to the point of desperation for being at my ease with servants. Not that the sense of his own deserts failed him. That was commensurate with his respect for discipline. Hence his success, finally. His life, though, was not happy. But look – his eye turns white as he lies in the palm of my hand. Suddenly the sense of what people are leaves one. I return him to the pool where he will acquire lustre.

'Neville next – lying on his back staring up at the summer sky. He floated among us like a piece of thistledown, indolently haunting the sunny corner of the playing-field, not listening, yet not remote. It was through him that I have nosed round without ever precisely touching the Latin classics and have also derived some of those persistent habits of thought which make us irredeemably lopsided – for instance about crucifixes, that they are the mark of the devil. Our half-loves and half-hates and ambiguities on these points were to him indefensible treacheries. The swaying and sonorous Doctor, whom I made to sit swinging his braces over a gas-fire, was to him nothing but an instrument of the Inquisition. So he turned with a passion that made up for his indolence upon Catullus, Horace, Lucretius, lying lazily dormant, yes, but regardant, noticing, with rapture, cricketers, while with a mind like the tongue of an anteater, rapid, dexterous, glutinous, he searched out every curl and twist of those Roman sentences, and sought out one person, always one person to sit beside.

'And the long skirts of the master's wives would come swishing by, mountainous, menacing; and our hands would fly to our caps. And immense dullness would descend unbroken, monotonous. Nothing, nothing, nothing broke with its fin that leaden waste of waters. Nothing would happen to lift that weight of intolerable boredom. The terms went on. We grew; we changed; for, of course, we are animals. We are not always aware by any means; we breathe, eat, sleep automatically. We exist not only separately but in undifferentiated blobs of matter. With one scoop a whole brakeful of boys is swept up and goes cricketing, footballing. An army marches across Europe. We assemble in parks and halls and sedulously oppose any renegade (Neville, Louis, Rhoda) who sets up a separate existence. And I am so made that, while I hear one or two distinct melodies, such as Louis sings, or

Neville, I am also drawn irresistibly to the sound of the chorus chanting its old, chanting its almost wordless, almost senseless song that comes across courts at night; which we hear now booming round us as cars and omnibuses take people to theatres. (Listen; the cars rush past this restaurant; now and then, down the river, a siren hoots, as a steamer makes for the sea.) If a bagman offers me snuff in a train, I accept. I like the copious, shapeless, warm, not so very clever, but extremely easy and rather coarse aspect of things; the talk of men in clubs and public-houses, of miners half-naked in drawers – the forthright, perfectly unassuming, and without end in view except dinner, love, money and getting along tolerably; that which is without great hopes, ideals or anything of that kind; what is unassuming except to make a tolerably good job of it. I like all that. So I joined them, when Neville sulked or Louis, as I quite agree sublimely, turned on his heel.

'Thus, not equally by any means or with order, but in great streaks my waxen waistcoat melted, here one drop, there another. Now through this transparency became visible those wondrous pastures, at first so moon-white, radiant, where no foot has been; meadows of the rose, the crocus, of the rock and the snake too; of the spotted and swart; the embarrassing, the binding and tripping up. One leaps out of bed, throws up the window; with what a whirr the birds rise! You know that sudden rush of wings, that exclamation, carol, and confusion; the riot and babble of voices; and all the drops are sparkling, trembling, as if the garden were a splintered mosaic, vanishing, twinkling; not yet formed into one whole; and a bird sings close to the window. I heard those songs. I followed those phantoms. I saw Joans, Dorothys, Miriams, I forget their names, passing down avenues, stopping on the crest of bridges to look down into the river. And from among them rise one or two distinct figures, birds who sang with the rapt egotism of youth by the window; broke their snails on stones, dipped their beaks in sticky, viscous matter; hard, avid, remorseless; Jinny, Susan, Rhoda. They had been educated on the east coast or on the south coast. They had grown long pigtails and acquired the look of startled foals, which is the mark of adolescence.

'Jinny was the first to come sidling up to the gate to eat sugar. She nipped it off the palms of one's hands very cleverly, but her ears were laid back as if she might bite. Rhoda was wild – Rhoda one never could catch. She was both frightened and clumsy. It was Susan who first became wholly woman, purely feminine. It was she who dropped on my face those scalding tears which are terrible, beautiful; both, neither. She was born to be the adored of poets, since poets require safety; someone who sits sewing, who says, "I hate, I love," who is neither comfortable nor prosperous, but has some quality in accordance with the high but unemphatic beauty of pure style which those who create poetry so particularly admire. Her father trailed from room to room and down flagged corridors in his flapping dressing-gown and worn slippers. On still nights a wall of water fell with a roar a mile off. The ancient dog could scarcely heave himself up on to his chair. And some witless servant could be heard laughing at the top of the house as she whirred the wheel of the sewing-machine round and round.

'That I observed even in the midst of my anguish when, twisting her pocket-handkerchief, Susan cried, "I love; I hate." "A worthless servant," I observed, "laughs upstairs in the attic," and that little piece of dramatisation shows how incompletely we are merged in our own experiences. On the outskirts of every agony sits some observant fellow who points; who whispers as he whispered to me that summer morning in the house where the corn comes up to the window, "The willow grows on the turf by the river. The gardeners sweep with great brooms and the lady sits writing." Thus he directed me to that which is beyond and outside our own predicament; to that which is symbolic, and thus perhaps permanent, if there is any permanence in our sleeping, eating, breathing, so animal, so spiritual and tumultuous lives.

'The willow tree grew by the river. I sat on the smooth turf with Neville, with Larpent, with Baker, Romsey, Hughes, Percival and Jinny. Through its fine plumes specked with little pricked ears of green in spring, of orange in autumn, I saw boats; buildings; I saw hurrying, decrepit women. I buried match after match in the turf decidedly to mark this or that stage in the process of understanding (it might be philosophy; science; it might be myself), while the fringe of my intelligence floating unattached caught those distant sensations which after a time the mind draws in and works upon; the chime of bells; general murmurs; vanishing figures; one girl on a bicycle who, as she rode, seemed to lift the corner of a curtain concealing the populous undifferentiated chaos of life which surged behind the outlines of my friends and the willow tree.

'The tree alone resisted our eternal flux. For I changed and changed; was Hamlet, was Shelley, was the hero, whose name I now forget, of a novel by Dostoevsky; was for a whole term, incredibly, Napoleon; but was Byron chiefly. For many weeks at a time it was my part to stride into rooms and fling gloves and coat on the back of chairs, scowling slightly. I was always going to the bookcase for another sip of the divine specific. Therefore, I let fly my tremendous battery of phrases upon somebody quite inappropriate – a girl now married, now buried; every book, every window-seat was littered with the sheets of my unfinished letters to the woman who made me Byron. For it is difficult to finish a letter in somebody else's style. I arrived all in a lather at her house; exchanged tokens but did not marry her, being no doubt unripe for that intensity.

'Here again there should be music. Not that wild hunting-song, Percival's music; but a painful, guttural, visceral, also soaring, lark-like, pealing song to replace these flagging, foolish transcripts – how much too deliberate! how much too reasonable! – which attempt to describe the flying moment of first love. A purple slide is slipped over the day. Look at a room before she comes and after. Look at the innocents outside pursuing their way. They neither see nor hear; yet on they go. Moving oneself in this radiant yet gummy atmosphere, how conscious one is of every movement – something adheres, something sticks to one's hands, taking up a newspaper even. Then there is the being eviscerated – drawn out, spun like a spider's web and twisted in agony round a thorn. Then a thunderclap of complete indifference; the light blown out; then the return of measureless irresponsible joy; certain fields seem to glow green for ever, and innocent landscapes appear as if in the light of the first dawn – one patch of green, for example, up at Hampstead; and all faces are lit up, all conspire in a hush of tender joy; and then the mystic sense of completion and then that rasping, dogfish-skinlike roughness – those black arrows of shivering sensation, when she misses the post, when she does not come. Out rush a bristle of horned suspicions, horror, horror, horror – but what is the use of painfully elaborating these consecutive sentences when what one needs is nothing consecutive but a bark, a groan? And years later to see a middle-aged woman in a restaurant taking off her cloak.

'But to return. Let us again pretend that life is a solid substance, shaped like a globe, which we turn about in our fingers. Let us pretend that we can make out a plain and logical story, so that when one matter is dispatched – love for instance – we go on, in an orderly manner, to the next. I was saying there was a willow tree. Its shower of falling branches, its creased and crooked bark had the effect of what remains outside our illusions yet cannot stay them, is changed by them for the moment, yet shows through stable, still, and with a sternness that our lives lack. Hence the comment it makes; the standard it supplies, and the reason why, as we flow and change, it seems to measure. Neville, for example, sat with me on the turf. But can anything be as clear as all that, I would say, following his gaze, through the branches, to a punt on the river, and a young man eating bananas from a paper bag? The scene was cut out with such intensity and so permeated with the quality of his vision that for a moment I could see it too; the punt, the bananas, the young man, through the branches of the willow tree. Then it faded.

'Rhoda came wandering vaguely. She would take advantage of any scholar in a blowing gown, or donkey rolling the turf with slippered feet to hide behind. What fear wavered and hid itself and blew to a flame in the depths of her grey, her startled, her dreaming eyes? Cruel and vindictive as we are, we are not bad to that extent. We have our fundamental goodness surely or to talk as I talk freely to someone I hardly know would be impossible – we should cease. The willow as she saw it grew on the verge of a grey desert where no bird sang. The leaves shrivelled as she looked at them, tossed in agony as she passed them. The trams and omnibuses roared hoarse in the street, ran over rocks and sped foaming away. Perhaps one pillar, sunlit, stood in her desert by a pool where wild beasts come down stealthily to drink.

'Then Jinny came. She flashed her fire over the tree. She was like a crinkled poppy, febrile, thirsty with the desire to drink dry dust. Darting, angular, not in the least impulsive, she came prepared. So little flames zigzag over the cracks in the dry earth. She made the willows dance, but not with illusion; for she saw nothing that was not there. It was a tree; there was the river; it was afternoon; here we were; I in my serge suit; she in green. There was no past, no future; merely the moment in its ring of light, and our bodies; and the inevitable climax, the ecstasy.

'Louis, when he let himself down on the grass, cautiously spreading (I do not exaggerate) a mackintosh square, made one acknowledge his presence. It was formidable. I had the intelligence to salute his integrity; his research with bony fingers wrapped in rags because of chilblains for some diamond of indissoluble veracity. I buried boxes of burnt matches in holes in the turf at his feet. His grim and caustic tongue reproved my indolence. He fascinated me with his sordid imagination. His heroes wore bowler-hats and talked about selling pianos for tenners. Through his landscape the tram squealed; the factory poured its acrid fumes. He haunted mean streets and towns where women lay drunk, naked, on counterpanes on Christmas day. His words falling from a shot-tower hit the water and up it spurted. He found one word, one only for the moon. Then he got up and went; we all got up; we all went. But I, pausing, looked at the tree, and as I looked in autumn at the fiery and yellow branches, some sediment formed; I formed; a drop fell; I fell – that is, from some completed experience I had emerged.

'I rose and walked away – I, I, I; not Byron, Shelley, Dostoevsky, but I, Bernard. I even repeated my own name once or twice. I went, swinging my stick, into a shop, and bought – not that I love music – a picture of Beethoven in a silver frame. Not that I love music, but because the whole of life, its masters, its adventurers, then appeared in long ranks of magnificent human beings behind me; and I was the inheritor; I, the continuer; I, the person miraculously appointed to carry it on. So, swinging my stick, with my eyes filmed, not with pride, but with humility rather, I walked down the street. The first whirr of wings had gone up, the carol, the exclamation; and now one enters; one goes into the house, the dry, uncompromising, inhabited house, the place with all its traditions, its objects, its accumulations of rubbish, and treasures displayed upon tables. I visited the family tailor, who remembered my uncle. People turned up in great quantities, not cut out, like the first faces (Neville, Louis, Jinny, Susan, Rhoda), but confused, featureless, or changed their features so fast that they seemed to have none. And blushing yet scornful, in the oddest condition of raw rapture and scepticism, I took the blow; the mixed sensations; the complex and disturbing and utterly unprepared for impacts of life all over, in all places at the same time. How upsetting! How humiliating never to be sure what to say next, and those painful silences, glaring as dry deserts, with every pebble apparent; and then to say what one ought not to have said, and then to be conscious of a ramrod of incorruptible sincerity which one would willingly exchange for a shower of – smooth pence, but could not, there at that party, where Jinny sat quite at her ease, rayed out on a gilt chair.

'Then says some lady with an impressive gesture, "Come with me." She leads one into a private alcove and admits one to the honour of her intimacy. Surnames change to Christian names; Christian names to nicknames. What is to be done about India, Ireland or Morocco? Old gentlemen answer the question standing decorated under chandeliers. One finds oneself surprisingly supplied with information. Outside the undifferentiated forces roar; inside we are very private, very explicit, have a sense indeed, that it is here, in this little room, that we make whatever day of the week it may be. Friday or Saturday. A shell forms upon the soft soul, nacreous, shiny, upon which sensations tap their beaks in vain. On me it formed earlier than on most. Soon I could carve my pear when other people had done dessert. I could bring my sentence to a close in a hush of complete silence. It is at that season too that perfection has a lure. One can learn Spanish, one thinks, by tying a string to the right toe and waking early. One fills up the little compartments of one's engagement book with dinner at eight; luncheon at one-thirty. One has shirts, socks, ties laid out on one's bed.

'But it is a mistake, this extreme precision, this orderly and military progress; a convenience, a lie. There is always deep below it, even when we arrive punctually at the appointed time with our white waistcoats and polite formalities, a rushing stream of broken dreams, nursery rhymes, street cries, half-finished sentences and sights – elm trees, willow trees, gardeners sweeping, women writing – that rise and sink even as we hand a lady down to dinner. While one straightens the fork so precisely on the tablecloth, a thousand faces mop and mow. There is nothing one can fish up in a spoon; nothing one can call an event. Yet it is alive too and deep, this stream. Immersed in it, I would stop between one mouthful and the next, and look intently at a vase, perhaps with one red flower, while a reason struck me, a sudden revelation. Or I would say, walking along the Strand, "That's the phrase I want," as some beautiful, fabulous phantom bird, fish or cloud with fiery edges swam up to enclose once and for all some notion haunting me, after which on I trotted taking stock with renewed delight of ties and things in shop-windows.

'The crystal, the globe of life as one calls it, far from being hard and cold to the touch, has walls of thinnest air. If I press them all will burst. Whatever sentence I extract whole and entire from this cauldron is only a string of six little fish that let themselves be caught while a million others leap and sizzle, making the cauldron bubble like boiling silver, and slip through my fingers. Faces recur, faces and faces – they press their beauty to the walls of my bubble – Neville, Susan, Louis, Jinny, Rhoda and a thousand others. How impossible to order them rightly; to detach one separately, or to give the effect of the whole – again like music. What a symphony with its concord and its discord, and its tunes on top and its complicated bass beneath, then grew up! Each played his own tune, fiddle, flute, trumpet, drum or whatever the instrument might be. With Neville, "Let's discuss *Hamlet*." With Louis, science. With Jinny, love. Then suddenly, in a moment of exasperation, off to Cumberland with a quiet man for a whole week in an inn, with the rain running down the window-panes and nothing but mutton and mutton and again mutton for dinner. Yet that week remains a solid stone in the welter of unrecorded sensation. It was then we played dominoes; then we quarrelled about tough mutton. Then we walked on the fell. And a little girl, peeping round the door, gave me that letter, written on blue paper, in which I learnt that the girl who had made me Byron was to marry a squire. A man in gaiters, a man with a whip, a man who made speeches about fat oxen at dinner – I exclaimed derisively and looked at the racing clouds, and felt my own failure; my desire to be free; to escape; to be bound; to make an end; to continue; to be Louis; to be myself; and walked out in my mackintosh alone, and felt grumpy under the eternal hills and not in the least sublime; and came home and blamed the meat and packed and so back again to the welter; to the torture.

'Nevertheless, life is pleasant, life is tolerable. Tuesday follows Monday; then comes Wednesday. The mind grows rings; the identity becomes robust; pain is absorbed in growth. Opening and shutting, shutting and opening, with increasing hum and sturdiness, the haste and fever of youth are drawn into service until the whole being seems to expand in and out like the mainspring of a clock. How fast the stream flows from January to December! We are swept on by the torrent of things grown so familiar that they cast no shadow. We float, we float . . .

'However, since one must leap (to tell you this story), I leap, here, at this point, and alight now upon some perfectly commonplace object – say the poker and tongs, as I saw them some time later, after that lady who had made me Byron had married, under the light of one whom I will call the third Miss Jones. She is the girl who wears a certain dress expecting one at dinner, who picks a certain rose, who makes one feel, "Steady, steady, this is a matter of some importance," as one shaves. Then one asks, "How does she behave to children?" One observes that she is a little clumsy with her umbrella; but minded when the mole was caught in the trap; and finally, would not make the loaf at breakfast (I was thinking of the interminable breakfasts of married life as I shaved) altogether prosaic – it would not surprise one sitting opposite this girl to see a dragonfly perched on the loaf at breakfast. Also she inspired me with a desire to rise in the world; also she made me look with curiosity at the hitherto repulsive faces of newborn babies. And the little fierce beat – tick-tack, tick-tack – of the pulse of one's mind took on a more majestic rhythm. I roamed down Oxford Street. We are the continuers, we are the inheritors, I said, thinking of my sons and daughters; and if the feeling is so grandiose as to be absurd and one conceals it by jumping on to a bus or buying the evening paper, it is still a curious element in the ardour with which one laces up one's boots, with which one now addresses old friends committed to different careers. Louis, the attic dweller; Rhoda, the nymph of the fountain always wet; both contradicted what was then so positive to me; both gave the other side of what seemed to me so evident (that we marry, that we domesticate); for which I loved them, pitied them, and also deeply envied them their different lot.

'Once I had a biographer, dead long since, but if he still followed my footsteps with his old flattering intensity he would here say, "About this time Bernard married and bought a house . . . His friends observed in him a growing tendency to domesticity . . . The birth of children made it highly desirable that he should augment his income." That is the biographic style, and it does to tack together torn bits of stuff, stuff with raw edges. After all, one cannot find fault with the biographic style if one begins letters "Dear sir", ends them "yours faithfully"; one cannot despise these phrases laid like Roman roads across the tumult of our lives, since they compel us to walk in step like civilised people with the slow and measured tread of policemen though one may be humming any nonsense under one's breath at the same time – "Hark, hark, the dogs do bark", "Come away, come away, death", "Let me not to the marriage of true minds", and so on. "He attained some success in his profession . . . " "He inherited a small sum of money from an uncle" – that is how the biographer continues, and if one wears trousers and hitches them up with braces, one has to say that, though it is tempting now and then to go blackberrying; tempting to play ducks and drakes with all these phrases. But one has to say that.

'I became, I mean, a certain kind of man, scoring my path across life as one treads a path across the fields. My boots became worn a little on the left side. When I came in, certain rearrangements took place. "Here's Bernard!" How differently different people say that! There are many rooms – many Bernards. There was the charming, but weak; the strong, but supercilious; the brilliant, but remorseless; the very good fellow, but, I make no doubt, the awful bore; the sympathetic, but cold; the shabby, but – go into the next room – the foppish, worldly, and too well dressed. What I was to myself was different; was none of these. I am inclined to pin myself down most firmly there before the loaf at breakfast with my wife who, being now entirely my wife and not at all the girl who wore when she hoped to meet me a certain rose, gave me that feeling of existing in the midst of unconsciousness such as the tree-frog must have, couched on the right shade of green leaf. "Pass" . . . I would say. "Milk" . . . she might answer, or "Mary's coming" . . . simple words for those who have inherited the spoils of all the ages but not as said then, day after day, in the full tide of life, when one feels complete, entire, at breakfast. Muscles, nerves, intestines, blood-vessels, all that makes the coil and spring of our being, the unconscious hum of the engine, as well as the dart and flicker of the tongue, functioned superbly. Opening, shutting; shutting, opening; eating, drinking; sometimes speaking – the whole mechanism seemed to expand, to contract, like the mainspring of a clock. Toast and butter, coffee and bacon, *The Times* and letters – suddenly the telephone rang with urgency and I rose deliberately and went to the telephone. I took up the black mouth. I marked the ease with which my mind adjusted itself to assimilate the message – it might be (one has these fancies) to assume command of the British Empire; I observed my composure; I remarked with what magnificent vitality the atoms of my attention dispersed, swarmed round the interruption, assimilated the message, adapted themselves to a new state of affairs and had created, by the time I put back the receiver, a richer, a stronger, a more complicated world in which I was called upon to act my part and had no doubt whatever that I could do it. Clapping my hat on my head, I strode into a world inhabited by vast numbers of men who had also clapped their hats on their heads, and as we jostled and encountered in trains and tubes we exchanged the knowing wink of competitors and comrades braced with a thousand snares and dodges to achieve the same end – to earn our livings.

'Life is pleasant. Life is good. The mere process of life is satisfactory. Take the ordinary man in good health. He likes eating and sleeping. He likes the snuff of fresh air and walking at a brisk pace down the Strand. Or in the country there's a cock crowing on a gate; there's a foal galloping round a field. Something always has to be done next. Tuesday follows Monday; Wednesday Tuesday. Each spreads the same ripple of well-being, repeats the same curve of rhythm; covers fresh sand with a chill or ebbs a little slackly without. So the being grows rings; identity becomes robust. What was fiery and furtive like a fling of grain cast into the air and blown hither and thither by wild gusts of life from every quarter is now methodical and orderly and flung with a purpose – so it seems.

'Lord, how pleasant! Lord, how good! How tolerable is the life of little shopkeepers, I would say, as the train drew through the suburbs and one saw lights in bedroom windows. Active, energetic as a swarm of ants, I said, as I stood at the window and watched workers, bag in hand, stream into town. What hardness, what energy and violence of limb, I thought, seeing men in white drawers scouring after a football on a patch of snow in January. Now being grumpy about some small matter – it might be the meat – it seemed luxurious to disturb with a little ripple the enormous stability, whose quiver, for our child was about to be born, increased its joy, of our married life. I snapped at dinner. I spoke unreasonably as if, being a millionaire, I could throw away five shillings; or, being a perfect steeplejack, stumbled over a footstool on purpose. Going up to bed we settled our quarrel on the stairs, and standing by the window looking at a sky clear like the inside of a blue stone, "Heaven be praised," I said, "we need not whip this prose into poetry. The little language is enough." For the space of the prospect and its clarity seemed to offer no impediment whatsoever, but to allow our lives to spread out and out beyond all bristling of roofs and chimneys to the flawless verge.

'Into this crashed death – Percival's. "Which is happiness?" I said (our child had been born), "which pain?" referring to the two sides of my body, as

I came downstairs, making a purely physical statement. Also I made note of the state of the house; the curtain blowing; the cook singing; the wardrobe showing through the half-opened door. I said, "Give him (myself) another moment's respite," as I went downstairs. "Now in this drawing-room he is going to suffer. There is no escape." But for pain words are lacking. There should be cries, cracks, fissures, whiteness passing over chintz covers, interference with the sense of time, of space; the sense also of extreme fixity in passing objects; and sounds very remote and then very close; flesh being gashed and blood spurting, a joint suddenly twisted – beneath all of which appears something very important, yet remote, to be just held in solitude. So I went out. I saw the first morning he would never see – the sparrows were like toys dangled from a string by a child. To see things without attachment, from the outside, and to realise their beauty in itself – how strange! And then the sense that a burden has been removed; pretence and make-believe and unreality are gone, and lightness has come with a kind of transparency, making oneself invisible and things seen through as one walks – how strange. "And now what other discovery will there be?" I said, and in order to hold it tight ignored newspaper placards and went and looked at pictures. Madonnas and pillars, arches and orange trees, still as on the first day of creation, but acquainted with grief, there they hung, and I gazed at them. "Here," I said, "we are together without interruption." This freedom, this immunity, seemed then a conquest, and stirred in me such exaltation that I sometimes go there, even now, to bring back exaltation and Percival. But it did not last. What torments one is the horrible activity of the mind's eye – how he fell, how he looked, where they carried him; men in loincloths, pulling ropes; the bandages and the mud. Then comes the terrible pounce of memory, not to be foretold, not to be warded off – that I did not go with him to Hampton Court. That claw scratched; that fang tore; I did not go. In spite of his impatiently protesting that it did not matter; why interrupt, why spoil our moment of uninterrupted community? – Still, I repeated sullenly, I did not go, and so, driven out of the sanctuary by these officious devils, went to Jinny because she had a room; a room with little tables, with little ornaments scattered on little tables. There I confessed, with tears – I had not gone to Hampton Court. And she, remembering other things, to me trifles but torturing to her, showed me how life withers when there are things we cannot share. Soon, too, a maid came in with a note, and as she turned to answer it and I felt my own curiosity to know what she was writing and to whom, I saw the first leaf fall on his grave. I saw us push beyond this moment, and leave it behind us for ever. And then sitting side by side on the sofa we remembered inevitably what had been said by others; "the lily of the day is fairer far in May"; we compared Percival to a lily – Percival whom I wanted to lose his hair, to shock the authorities, to grow old with me; he was already covered over with lilies.

'So the sincerity of the moment passed; so it became symbolical; and that

I could not stand. Let us commit any blasphemy of laughter and criticism rather than exude this lily-sweet glue and cover him with phrases, I cried. Therefore I broke off, and Jinny, who was without future, or speculation, but respected the moment with complete integrity, gave her body a flick with the whip, powdered her face (for which I loved her), and waved to me as she stood on the doorstep, pressing her hand to her hair so that the wind might not disorder it, a gesture for which I honoured her, as if it confirmed our determination – not to let lilies grow.

'I observed with disillusioned clarity the despicable nonentity of the street; its porches; its window curtains; the drab clothes, the cupidity and complacency of shopping women; and old men taking the air in comforters; the caution of people crossing; the universal determination to go on living, when really, fools and gulls that you are, I said, any slate may fly from a roof, any car may swerve, for there is neither rhyme nor reason when a drunk man staggers about with a club in his hand – that is all. I was like one admitted behind the scenes: like one shown how the effects are produced. I returned, however, to my own snug home and was warned by the parlourmaid to creep upstairs in my stockings. The child was asleep. I went to my room.

'Was there no sword, nothing with which to batter down these walls, this protection, this begetting of children and living behind curtains, and becoming daily more involved and committed, with books and pictures? Better burn one's life out like Louis, desiring perfection; or like Rhoda leave us, flying past us to the desert; or choose one out of millions and one only like Neville; better be like Susan and love and hate the heat of the sun or the frostbitten grass; or be like Jinny, honest, an animal. All had their rapture; their common feeling with death; something that stood them in stead. Thus I visited each of my friends in turn, trying, with fumbling fingers, to prise open their locked caskets. I went from one to the other holding my sorrow – no, not my sorrow but the incomprehensible nature of this our life – for their inspection. Some people go to priests; others to poetry; I to my friends, I to my own heart, I to seek among phrases and fragments something unbroken – I to whom there is not beauty enough in moon or tree; to whom the touch of one person with another is all, yet who cannot grasp even that, who am so imperfect, so weak, so unspeakably lonely. There I sat.

'Should this be the end of the story? a kind of sigh? a last ripple of the wave? A trickle of water to some gutter where, burbling, it dies away? Let me touch the table – so – and thus recover my sense of the moment. A sideboard covered with cruets; a basket full of rolls; a plate of bananas – these are comfortable sights. But if there are no stories, what end can there be, or what beginning? Life is not susceptible perhaps to the treatment we give it when we try to tell it. Sitting up late at night it seems strange not to have more control. Pigeon-holes are not then very useful. It is strange how force ebbs away and away into some dry creek. Sitting alone, it seems we are spent; our waters can only just surround feebly that spike of sea-holly; we cannot reach that further pebble so as to wet it. It is over, we are ended. But wait – I sat all night waiting – an impulse again runs through us; we rise, we toss back a mane of white spray; we pound on the shore; we are not to be confined. That is, I shaved and washed; did not wake my wife, and had breakfast; put on my hat, and went out to earn my living. After Monday, Tuesday comes.

'Yet some doubt remained, some note of interrogation. I was surprised, opening a door, to find people thus occupied; I hesitated, taking a cup of tea, whether one said milk or sugar. And the light of the stars falling, as it falls now, on my hand after travelling for millions upon millions of years – I could get a cold shock from that for a moment – not more, my imagination is too feeble. But some doubt remained. A shadow flitted through my mind like moths' wings among chairs and tables in a room in the evening. When, for example, I went to Lincolnshire that summer to see Susan and she advanced towards me across the garden with the lazy movement of a half-filled sail, with the swaying movement of a woman with child, I thought, "It goes on; but why?" We sat in the garden; the farm carts came up dripping with hay; there was the usual country gabble of rooks and doves; fruit was netted and covered over; the gardener dug. Bees boomed down the purple tunnels of flowers; bees embedded themselves on the golden shields of sunflowers. Little twigs were blown across the grass. How rhythmical and half conscious and like something wrapped in mist it was; but to me hateful, like a net folding one's limbs in its meshes, cramping. She who had refused Percival lent herself to this, to this covering over.

'Sitting down on a bank to wait for my train, I thought then how we surrender, how we submit to the stupidity of nature. Woods covered in thick green leafage lay in front of me. And by some flick of a scent or a sound on a nerve, the old image – the gardeners sweeping, the lady writing – returned. I saw the figures beneath the beech trees at Elvedon. The gardeners swept; the lady at the table sat writing. But I now made the contribution of maturity to childhood's intuitions – satiety and doom; the sense of what is unescapable in our lot; death; the knowledge of limitations; how life is more obdurate than one had thought it. Then, when I was a child, the presence of an enemy had asserted itself; the need for opposition had stung me. I had jumped up and cried, "Let's explore." The horror of the situation was ended.

'Now what situation was there to end? Dullness and doom. And what to explore? The leaves and the wood concealed nothing. If a bird rose I should no longer make a poem – I should repeat what I had said before. Thus if I had a stick with which to point to indentations in the curve of being, this is the lowest; here it coils useless on the mud where no tide comes – here, where I sat with my back to a hedge, and my hat over my eyes, while the sheep advanced remorselessly in that wooden way of theirs, step by step on stiff, pointed legs. But if you hold a blunt blade to a grindstone long enough, something spurts – a jagged edge of fire; so held to lack of reason, aimlessness, the usual, all massed together, out spurted in one flame hatred, contempt. I took my mind, my being, the old dejected, almost inanimate object, and lashed it about among these odds and ends, sticks and straws, detestable little bits of wreckage, flotsam and jetsam, floating on the oily surface. I jumped up. I said, "Fight! Fight!" I repeated. It is the effort and the struggle, it is the perpetual warfare, it is the shattering and piecing together – this is the daily battle, defeat or victory, the absorbing pursuit. The trees, scattered, put on order; the thick green of the leaves thinned itself to a dancing light. I netted them under with a sudden phrase. I retrieved them from formlessness with words.

'The train came in. Lengthening down the platform, the train came to a stop. I caught my train. And so back to London in the evening. How satisfactory, the atmosphere of common sense and tobacco; old women clambering into the third-class carriage with their baskets; the sucking at pipes; the good-nights and see you tomorrows of friends parting at wayside stations, and then the lights of London – not the flaring ecstasy of youth, not that tattered violet banner, but still the lights of London all the same: hard electric lights, high up in offices; street lamps laced along dry pavements; flares roaring above street markets. I like all this when I have dispatched the enemy for a moment.

'Also I like to find the pageant of existence roaring, in a theatre for instance. The clay-coloured, earthy nondescript animal of the field here erects himself and with infinite ingenuity and effort puts up a fight against the green woods and green fields and sheep advancing with measured tread, munching. And, of course, windows in the long grey streets were lit up; strips of carpet cut the pavement; there were swept and garnished rooms, fire, food, wine, talk. Men with withered hands, women with pearl pagodas hanging from their ears, came in and went out. I saw old men's faces carved into wrinkles and sneers by the work of the world; beauty cherished so that it seemed newly sprung even in age; and youth so apt for pleasure that pleasure, one thought, must exist; it seemed that grasslands must roll for it; and the sea be chopped up into little waves; and the woods rustle with bright-coloured birds for youth, for youth expectant. There one met Jinny and Hal, Tom and Betty; there we had our jokes and shared our secrets; and never parted in the doorway without arranging to meet again in some other room as the occasion, as the time of the year, suggested. Life is pleasant; life is good. After Monday comes Tuesday, and Wednesday follows.

'Yes, but after a time with a difference. It may be that something in the look of the room one night, in the arrangement of the chairs, suggests it. It seems comfortable to sink down on a sofa in a corner, to look, to listen. Then it happens that two figures standing with their backs to the window appear against the branches of a spreading tree. With a shock of emotion one feels, "There are figures without features robed in beauty." In the pause that follows while the ripples spread, the girl to whom one should be talking says to herself, "He is old." But she is wrong. It is not age; it is that a drop has fallen; another drop. Time has given the arrangement another shake. Out we creep from the arch of the currant leaves, out into a wider world. The true order of things – this is our perpetual illusion – is now apparent. Thus in a moment, in a drawing-room, our life adjusts itself to the majestic march of day across the sky.

'It was for this reason that instead of pulling on my patent-leather shoes and finding a tolerable tie, I sought Neville. I sought my oldest friend, who had known me when I was Byron; when I was Meredith's young man, and also that hero in a book by Dostoevsky whose name I have forgotten. I found him alone reading. A perfectly neat table; a curtain pulled methodically straight; a paperknife dividing a French volume – nobody, I thought, ever changes the attitude in which we saw them first, or the clothes. Here he has sat in this chair, in these clothes, ever since we first met. Here was freedom; here was intimacy; the firelight broke off some round apple on the curtain. There we talked; sat talking; sauntered down that avenue, the avenue which runs under the trees, under the thick-leaved murmuring trees, the trees that are hung with fruit, which we have trodden so often together, so that now the turf is bare round some of those trees, round certain plays and poems, certain favourites of ours – the turf is trodden bare by our incessant unmethodical pacing. If I have to wait, I read; if I wake in the night, I feel along the shelf for a book. Swelling, perpetually augmented, there is a vast accumulation of unrecorded matter in my head. Now and then I break off a lump, Shakespeare it may be, it may be some old woman called Peck; and say to myself, smoking a cigarette in bed, "That's Shakespeare. That's Peck" – with a certainty of recognition and a shock of knowledge which is endlessly delightful, though not to be imparted. So we shared our Pecks, our Shakespeares; compared each other's versions; allowed each other's insight to set our own Peck or Shakespeare in a better light; and then sank into one of those silences which are now and again broken by a few words, as if a fin rose in the wastes of silence; and then the fin, the thought, sinks back into the depths, spreading round it a little ripple of satisfaction, content.

'Yes, but suddenly one hears a clock tick. We who had been immersed in this world became aware of another. It is painful. It was Neville who changed our time. He, who had been thinking with the unlimited time of the mind, which stretches in a flash from Shakespeare to ourselves, poked the fire and began to live by that other clock which marks the approach of a particular person. The wide and dignified sweep of his mind contracted. He became on the alert. I could feel him listening to sounds in the street. I noted how he touched a cushion. From the myriads of mankind and all time past he had chosen one person, one moment in particular. A sound was heard in the hall. What he was saying wavered in the air like an uneasy flame. I watched him disentangle one footstep from other footsteps; wait for some particular mark of identification and glance with the swiftness of a snake at the handle of the door. (Hence the astonishing acuteness of his perceptions; he has been trained always by one person.) So concentrated a passion shot out others like foreign matter from a still, sparkling fluid. I became aware of my own vague and cloudy nature full of sediment, full of doubt, full of phrases and notes to be made in pocket-books. The folds of the curtain became still, statuesque; the paperweight on the table hardened; the threads on the curtain sparkled; everything became definite, external, a scene in which I had no part. I rose, therefore; I left him.

'Heavens! how they caught me as I left the room, the fangs of that old pain! the desire for someone not there. For whom? I did not know at first; then remembered Percival. I had not thought of him for months. Now to laugh with him, to laugh with him at Neville – that was what I wanted, to walk off arm in arm together laughing. But he was not there. The place was empty.

'It is strange how the dead leap out on us at street corners, or in dreams.

'This fitful gust blowing so sharp and cold upon me sent me that night across London to visit other friends, Rhoda and Louis, desiring company, certainty, contact. I wondered, as I mounted the stairs, what was their relationship? What did they say alone? I figured her awkward with the tea-kettle. She gazed over the slate roofs – the nymph of the fountain always wet, obsessed with visions, dreaming. She parted the curtain to look at the night. "Away!" she said. "The moor is dark beneath the moon." I rang; I waited. Louis perhaps poured out milk in a saucer for the cat; Louis, whose bony hands shut like the sides of a dock closing themselves with a slow anguish of effort upon an enormous tumult of waters, who knew what has been said by the Egyptian, the Indian, by men with high cheekbones and solitaries in hair shirts. I knocked: I waited; there was no answer. I tramped down the stone stairs again. Our friends – how distant, how mute, how seldom visited and little known. And I, too, am dim to my friends and unknown; a phantom, sometimes seen, often not. Life is a dream surely. Our flame, the will-o'-the-wisp that dances in a few eyes, is soon to be blown out and all will fade. I recalled my friends. I thought of Susan. She had bought fields. Cucumbers and tomatoes ripened in her hothouses. The vine that had been killed by last year's frost was putting out a leaf or two. She walked heavily with her sons across her meadows. She went about the land attended by men in gaiters, pointing with her stick at a roof, at hedges, at walls fallen into disrepair. The pigeons followed her, waddling, for the grain that she let fall from her capable, earthy fingers. "But I no longer rise at dawn," she said. Then Jinny – entertaining, no doubt, some new young man. They reached the crisis of the usual conversation. The room would be darkened; chairs arranged. For she still sought the moment. Without illusions, hard and clear as crystal, she rode at the day with her breast bared. She let its spikes pierce her. When the lock whitened on her forehead she twisted it fearlessly among the rest. So when they come to bury her nothing will be out of order. Bits of ribbons will be found curled up. But still the door opens. Who is coming in? she asks, and rises to meet him, prepared, as on those first spring nights when the tree under the big London houses where respectable citizens were going soberly to bed scarcely sheltered her love; and the squeak of trams mixed with her cry of delight and the rippling of leaves had to shade her languor, her delicious lassitude as she sank down cooled by all the sweetness of nature satisfied. Our friends, how seldom visited, how little known – it is true; and yet, when I meet an unknown person, and try to break off, here at this table, what I call "my life", it is not one life that I look back upon; I am not one person; I am many people; I do not altogether know who I am – Jinny, Susan, Neville, Rhoda or Louis: or how to distinguish my life from theirs.

'So I thought that night in early autumn when we came together and dined once more at Hampton Court. Our discomfort was at first considerable, for each by that time was committed to a statement, and the other person coming along the road to the meeting-place dressed like this or that, with a stick or without, seemed to contradict it. I saw Jinny look at Susan's earthy fingers and then hide her own; I, considering Neville, so neat and exact, felt the nebulosity of my own life blurred with all these phrases. He then boasted, because he was ashamed of one room and one person and his own success. Louis and Rhoda, the conspirators, the spies at table, who take notes, felt, "After all, Bernard can make the waiter fetch us rolls – a contact denied us." We saw for a moment laid out among us the body of the complete human being whom we have failed to be, but at the same time cannot forget. All that we might have been we saw; all that we had missed; and we grudged for a moment the other's claim, as children when the cake is cut, the one cake, the only cake, watch their slice diminishing.

'However, we had our bottle of wine, and under that seduction lost our enmity, and stopped comparing. And, half way through dinner, we felt enlarge itself round us the huge blackness of what is outside us, of what we are not. The wind, the rush of wheels, became the roar of time, and we rushed – where? And who were we? We were extinguished for a moment, went out like sparks in burnt paper and the blackness roared. Past time, past history we went. For me this lasts but one second. It is ended by my own pugnacity. I strike the table with a spoon. If I could measure things with compasses I would, but since my only measure is a phrase, I make phrases – I forget what, on this occasion. We became six people at a table in Hampton Court. We rose and walked together down the avenue. In the thin, the unreal twilight, fitfully like the echo of voices laughing down some alley, geniality returned to me and flesh. Against the gateway, against some cedar tree I saw blaze bright, Neville, Jinny, Rhoda, Louis, Susan and myself, our life, our identity. Still King William seemed an unreal monarch and his crown mere tinsel. But we – against the brick, against the branches, we six, out of how many million millions, for one moment out of what measureless abundance of past time and time to come, burnt there triumphant. The moment was all; the moment was enough. And then Neville, Jinny, Susan and I, as a wave breaks, burst asunder, surrendered – to the next leaf, to the precise bird, to a child with a hoop, to a prancing dog, to the warmth that is hoarded in woods after a hot day, to the lights twisted like white ribbon on rippled waters. We drew apart; we were consumed in the darkness of the trees, leaving Rhoda and Louis to stand on the terrace by the urn.

'When we returned from that immersion – how sweet, how deep! – and came to the surface and saw the conspirators still standing there it was with some compunction. We had lost what they had kept. We interrupted. But we were tired, and whether it had been good or bad, accomplished or left undone, the dusky veil was falling upon our endeavours; the lights were sinking as we paused for a moment upon the terrace that overlooks the river. The steamers were landing their trippers on the bank; there was a distant cheering, the sound of singing, as if people waved their hats and joined in some last song. The sound of the chorus came across the water and I felt leap up that old impulse, which has moved me all my life, to be thrown up and down on the roar of other people's voices, singing the same song; to be tossed up and down on the roar of almost senseless merriment, sentiment, triumph, desire. But not now. No! I could not collect myself; I could not distinguish myself; I could not help letting fall the things that had made me a minute ago eager, amused, jealous, vigilant and hosts of other things, into the water. I could not recover myself from that endless throwing away, dissipation, flooding forth without our willing it and rushing soundlessly away out there under the arches of the bridge, round some clump of trees or an island, out where sea-birds sit on stakes, over the roughened water to become waves in the sea – I could not recover myself from that dissipation. So we parted.

'Was this, then, this streaming away mixed with Susan, Jinny, Neville, Rhoda, Louis, a sort of death? A new assembly of elements? Some hint of what was to come? The note was scribbled, the book shut, for I am an intermittent student. I do not say my lessons by any means at the stated hour. Later, walking down Fleet Street at the rush hour, I recalled that moment; I continued it. "Must I for ever," I said, "beat my spoon on the tablecloth? Shall I not, too, consent?" The omnibuses were clogged; one came up behind another and stopped with a click, like a link added to a stone chain. People passed.

'Multitudinous, carrying attaché cases, dodging with incredible celerity in and out, they went past like a river in spate. They went past roaring like a train in a tunnel. Seizing my chance I crossed; dived down a dark passage and entered the shop where they cut my hair. I leant my head back and was swathed in a sheet. Looking-glasses confronted me in which I could see my pinioned body and people passing; stopping, looking and going on indifferent. The hairdresser began to move his scissors to and fro. I felt myself powerless to stop the oscillations of the cold steel. So we are cut and laid in swaths, I said; so we lie side by side on the damp meadows, withered branches and flowering. We have no more to expose ourselves on the bare hedges to the wind and snow; no more to carry ourselves erect when the gale sweeps, to bear our burden upheld; or stay, unmurmuring, on those pallid noon days when the bird creeps close to the bough and the damp whitens the leaf. We are cut, we are fallen. We are become part of that unfeeling universe that sleeps when we are at our quickest and burns red when we lie asleep. We have renounced our station and lie now flat, withered and how soon forgotten! Upon which I saw an expression in the tail of the eye of the hairdresser as if something interested him in the street.

'What interested the hairdresser? What did the hairdresser see in the street? It is thus that I am recalled. (For I am no mystic; something always plucks at me – curiosity, envy, admiration, interest in hairdressers and the like bring me to the surface.) While he brushed the fluff from my coat I took pains to assure myself of his identity, and then, swinging my stick, I went into the Strand, and evoked to serve as opposite to myself the figure of Rhoda, always so furtive, always with fear in her eyes, always seeking some pillar in the desert, to find which she had gone; she had killed herself. "Wait," I said, putting my arm in imagination (thus we consort with our friends) through her arm. "Wait until these omnibuses have gone by. Do not cross so dangerously. These men are your brothers." In persuading her I was also persuading my own soul. For this is not one life; nor do I always know if I am man or woman, Bernard or Neville, Louis, Susan, Jinny or Rhoda – so strange is the contact of one with another.

'Swinging my stick, with my hair newly cut and the nape of my neck tingling, I went past all those trays of penny toys imported from Germany that men hold out in the street by St Paul's – St Paul's, the brooding hen with spread wings from whose shelter run omnibuses and streams of men and women at the rush hour. I thought how Louis would mount those steps in his neat suit with his cane in his hand and his angular, rather detached gait. With his Australian accent ("My father, a banker at Brisbane") he would come, I thought, with greater respect to these old ceremonies than I do, who have heard the same lullabies for a thousand years. I am always impressed, as I enter, by the rubbed noses; the polished brasses; the flapping and the chanting, while one boy's voice wails round the dome like some lost and wandering dove. The recumbency and the peace of the dead impress me – warriors at rest under their old banners. Then I scoff at the floridity and absurdity of some scrolloping tomb; and the trumpets and the victories and the coats of arms and the certainty, so sonorously repeated, of resurrection, of eternal life. My wandering and inquisitive eye then shows me an awe-stricken child; a shuffling pensioner; or the obeisances of tired shop-girls burdened with heaven knows what strife in their poor thin breasts come to solace themselves in the rush hour. I stray and look and wonder, and sometimes, rather furtively, try to rise on the shaft of somebody else's prayer into the dome, out, beyond, wherever they go. But then like the lost and wailing dove, I find myself failing, fluttering, descending and perching upon some curious gargoyle, some battered nose or absurd tombstone, with humour, with wonder, and so again watch the sightseers with their Baedekers shuffling past, while the boy's voice soars in the dome and the organ now and then indulges in a moment of elephantine triumph. How then, I asked, would Louis roof us all in? How would he confine us, make us one, with his red ink, with his very fine nib? The voice petered out in the dome, wailing.

'So into the street again, swinging my stick, looking at wire trays in stationers' shop-windows, at baskets of fruit grown in the colonies, murmuring Pillicock sat on Pillicock's hill, or Hark, hark, the dogs do bark, or The World's great age begins anew, or Come away, come away, death – mingling nonsense and poetry, floating in the stream. Something always has to be done next. Tuesday follows Monday; Wednesday, Tuesday. Each spreads the same ripple. The being grows rings, like a tree. Like a tree, leaves fall.

'For one day as I leant over a gate that led into a field, the rhythm stopped: the rhymes and the hummings, the nonsense and the poetry. A space was cleared in my mind. I saw through the thick leaves of habit. Leaning over the gate I regretted so much litter, so much unaccomplishment and separation, for one cannot cross London to see a friend, life being so full of engage-ments; nor take ship to India and see a naked man spearing fish in blue water. I said life had been imperfect, an unfinished phrase. It had been impossible for me, taking snuff as I do from any bagman met in a train, to keep coherency – that sense of the generations, of women carrying red pitchers to the Nile, of the nightingale who sings among conquests and migrations. It had been too vast an undertaking, I said, and how can I go on lifting my foot perpetually to climb the stair? I addressed my self as one would speak to a companion with whom one is voyaging to the North Pole.

'I spoke to that self who has been with me in many tremendous adventures; the faithful man who sits over the fire when everybody has gone to bed, stirring the cinders with a poker; the man who has been so mysteriously and with sudden accretions of being built up, in a beech wood, sitting by a willow tree on a bank, leaning over a parapet at Hampton Court; the man who has collected himself in moments of emergency and banged his spoon on the table, saying, "I will not consent."

'This self now as I leant over the gate looking down over fields rolling in waves of colour beneath me made no answer. He threw up no opposition. He attempted no phrase. His fist did not form. I waited. I listened. Nothing came, nothing. I cried then with a sudden conviction of complete desertion, Now there is nothing. No fin breaks the waste of this immeasurable sea. Life has destroyed me. No echo comes when I speak, no varied words. This is more truly death than the death of friends, than the death of youth. I am the swathed figure in the hairdresser's shop taking up only so much space.

'The scene beneath me withered. It was like the eclipse when the sun went out and left the earth, flourishing in full summer foliage, withered, brittle, false. Also I saw on a winding road in a dust dance the groups we had made, how they came together, how they ate together, how they met in this room or that. I saw my own indefatigable busyness – how I had rushed from one to the other, fetched and carried, travelled and returned, joined this group and that, here kissed, here withdrawn; always kept hard at it by some extraordinary purpose, with my nose to the ground like a dog on the scent; with an occasional toss of the head, an occasional cry of amazement, despair and then back again with my nose to the scent. What a litter – what a confusion; with here birth, here death; succulence and sweetness; effort and anguish; and myself always running hither and thither. Now it was done with. I had no more appetites to glut; no more stings in me with which to poison people; no more sharp teeth and clutching hands or desire to feel the pear and the grape and the sun beating down from the orchard wall.

'The woods had vanished; the earth was a waste of shadow. No sound broke the silence of the wintry landscape. No cock crowed; no smoke rose; no train moved. A man without a self, I said. A heavy body leaning on a gate. A dead man. With dispassionate despair, with entire disillusionment, I surveyed the dust dance; my life, my friends' lives, and those fabulous presences, men with brooms, women writing, the willow tree by the river – clouds and phantoms made of dust too, of dust that changed, as clouds lose and gain and take gold or red and lose their summits and billow this way and that, mutable, vain. I, carrying a notebook, making phrases, had recorded merely changes; a shadow, I had been sedulous to take note of shadows. How can I proceed now, I said, without a self, weightless and visionless, through a world weightless, without illusion?

'The heaviness of my despondency thrust open the gate I leant on and pushed me, an elderly man, a heavy man with grey hair, through the colourless field, the empty field. No more to hear echoes, no more to see phantoms, to conjure up no opposition, but to walk always unshadowed, making no impress upon the dead earth. If even there had been sheep munching, pushing one foot after another, or a bird, or a man driving a spade into the earth, had there been a bramble to trip me, or a ditch, damp with soaked leaves, into which to fall – but no, the melancholy path led along the level, to more wintriness and pallor and the equal and uninteresting view of the same landscape.

'How then does light return to the world after the eclipse of the sun? Miraculously. Frailly. In thin stripes. It hangs like a glass cage. It is a hoop to be fractured by a tiny jar. There is a spark there. Next moment a flush of dun. Then a vapour as if earth were breathing in and out, once, twice, for the first time. Then under the dullness someone walks with a green light.

Then off twists a white wraith. The woods throb blue and green, and gradually the fields drink in red, gold, brown. Suddenly a river snatches a blue light. The earth absorbs colour like a sponge slowly drinking water. It puts on weight; rounds itself; hangs pendent; settles and swings beneath our feet.

'So the landscape returned to me; so I saw fields rolling in waves of colour beneath me but now with this difference; I saw but was not seen. I walked unshadowed; I came unheralded. From me had dropped the old cloak, the old response; the hollowed hand that beats back sounds. Thin as a ghost, leaving no trace where I trod, perceiving merely, I walked alone in a new world, never trodden; brushing new flowers, unable to speak save in a child's words of one syllable; without shelter from phrases – I who have made so many; unattended, I who have always gone with my kind; solitary, I who have always had someone to share the empty grate or the cupboard with its hanging loop of gold.

'But how describe the world seen without a self? There are no words. Blue, red – even they distract, even they hide with thickness instead of letting the light through. How describe or say anything in articulate words again? – save that it fades, save that it undergoes a gradual transformation, becomes, even in the course of one short walk, habitual – this scene also. Blindness returns as one moves and one leaf repeats another. Loveliness returns as one looks, with all its train of phantom phrases. One breathes in and out substantial breath; down in the valley the train draws across the fields lop-eared with smoke.

'But for a moment I had sat on the turf somewhere high above the flow of the sea and the sound of the woods, had seen the house, the garden, and the waves breaking. The old nurse who turns the pages of the picture-book had stopped and had said, "Look. This is the truth."

'So I was thinking as I came along Shaftesbury Avenue tonight. I was thinking of that page in the picture-book. And when I met you in the place where one goes to hang up one's coat I said to myself, "It does not matter whom I meet. All this little affair of 'being' is over. Who this is I do not know; nor care; we will dine together." So I hung up my coat, tapped you on the shoulder, and said, "Sit with me."

'Now the meal is finished; we are surrounded by peelings and breadcrumbs. I have tried to break off this bunch and hand it you; but whether there is substance or truth in it I do not know. Nor do I know exactly where we are. What city does that stretch of sky look down upon? Is it Paris, is it London where we sit, or some southern city of pink-washed houses lying under cypresses, under high mountains, where eagles soar? I do not at this moment feel certain.

'I begin now to forget; I begin to doubt the fixity of tables, the reality of here and now, to tap my knuckles smartly upon the edges of apparently solid objects and say, "Are you hard?" I have seen so many different things, have made so many different sentences. I have lost in the process of eating and drinking and rubbing my eyes along surfaces that thin, hard shell which cases the soul, which, in youth, shuts one in – hence the fierceness, and the tap, tap, tap of the remorseless beaks of the young. And now I ask, "Who am I?" I have been talking of Bernard, Neville, Jinny, Susan, Rhoda and Louis. Am I all of them? Am I one and distinct? I do not know. We sat here together. But now Percival is dead, and Rhoda is dead; we are divided; we are not here. Yet I cannot find any obstacle separating us. There is no division between me and them. As I talked I felt, "I am you." This difference we make so much of, this identity we so feverishly cherish, was overcome. Yes, ever since old Mrs Constable lifted her sponge and pouring warm water over me covered me with flesh I have been sensitive, percipient. Here on my brow is the blow I got when Percival fell. Here on the nape of my neck is the kiss Jinny gave Louis. My eyes fill with Susan's tears. I see far away, quivering like a gold thread, the pillar Rhoda saw and feel the rush of the wind of her flight when she leapt.

'Thus when I come to shape here at this table between my hands the story of my life and set it before you as a complete thing, I have to recall things gone far, gone deep, sunk into this life or that and become part of it; dreams, too, things surrounding me, and the inmates, those old half-articulate ghosts who keep up their hauntings by day and night; who turn over in their sleep, who utter their confused cries, who put out their phantom fingers and clutch at me as I try to escape – shadows of people one might have been; unborn selves. There is the old brute, too, the savage, the hairy man who dabbles his fingers in ropes of entrails; and gobbles and belches; whose speech is guttural, visceral – well, he is here. He squats in me. Tonight he has been feasted on quails, salad, and sweetbread. He now holds a glass of fine old brandy in his paw. He brindles, purrs and shoots warm thrills all down my spine as I sip. It is true, he washes his hands before dinner, but they are still hairy. He buttons on trousers and waistcoats, but they contain the same organs. He jibs if I keep him waiting for dinner. He mops and mows perpetually, pointing with his half-idiot gestures of greed and covetousness at what he desires. I assure you, I have great difficulty sometimes in controlling him. That man, the hairy, the apelike, has contributed his part to my life. He has given a greener glow to green things, has held his torch with its red flames, its thick and smarting smoke, behind every leaf. He has lit up the cool garden even. He has brandished his torch in murky by-streets where girls suddenly seem to shine with a red and intoxicating translucency. Oh, he has tossed his torch high! He has led me wild dances!

'But no more. Now, tonight, my body rises tier upon tier like some cool temple whose floor is strewn with carpets and murmurs rise and the altars stand smoking; but up above, here in my serene head, come only fine gusts of melody, waves of incense, while the lost dove wails, and the banners tremble above tombs, and the dark airs of midnight shake trees outside the open windows. When I look down from this transcendency, how beautiful are even the crumbled relics of bread! What shapely spirals the peelings of pears make – how thin, and mottled like some sea-bird's egg. Even the forks laid straight side by side appear lucid, logical, exact; and the horns of the rolls which we have left are glazed, yellow-plated, hard. I could worship my hand even, with its fan of bones laced by blue mysterious veins and its astonishing look of aptness, suppleness and ability to curl softly or suddenly crush – its infinite sensibility.

'Immeasurably receptive, holding everything, trembling with fullness, yet clear, contained – so my being seems, now that desire urges it no more out and away; now that curiosity no longer dyes it a thousand colours. It lies deep, tideless, immune, now that he is dead, the man I called "Bernard", the man who kept a book in his pocket in which he made notes – phrases for the moon, notes of features; how people looked, turned, dropped their cigarette ends; under B, butterfly powder, under D, ways of naming death. But now let the door open, the glass door that is for ever turning on its hinges. Let a woman come, let a young man in evening-dress with a moustache sit down; is there anything that they can tell me? No! I know all that, too. And if she suddenly gets up and goes, "My dear," I say, "you no longer make me look after you." The shock of the falling wave which has sounded all my life, which woke me so that I saw the gold loop on the cupboard, no longer makes quiver what I hold.

'So now, taking upon me the mystery of things, I could go like a spy without leaving this place, without stirring from my chair. I can visit the remote verges of the desert lands where the savage sits by the campfire. Day rises; the girl lifts the watery fire-hearted jewels to her brow; the sun levels his beams straight at the sleeping house; the waves deepen their bars; they fling themselves on shore; back blows the spray; sweeping their waters they surround the boat and the sea-holly. The birds sing in chorus; deep tunnels run between the stalks of flowers; the house is whitened; the sleeper stretches; gradually all is astir. Light floods the room and drives shadow beyond shadow to where they hang in folds inscrutable. What does the central shadow hold? Something? Nothing? I do not know.

'Oh, but there is your face. I catch your eye. I, who had been thinking myself so vast, a temple, a church, a whole universe, unconfined and capable of being everywhere on the verge of things and here too, am now nothing but what you see – an elderly man, rather heavy, grey above the ears, who (I see myself in the glass) leans one elbow on the table and holds in his left hand a glass of old brandy. That is the blow you have dealt me. I have walked bang into the pillar-box. I reel from side to side. I put my hands to my head. My hat is off – I have dropped my stick. I have made an awful ass of myself and am justly laughed at by any passer-by.

'Lord, how unutterably disgusting life is! What dirty tricks it plays us: one moment free; the next, this. Here we are among the breadcrumbs and the stained napkins again. That knife is already congealing with grease. Disorder, sordidity and corruption surround us. We have been taking into our mouths the bodies of dead birds. It is with these greasy crumbs, slobbered-over napkins, and little corpses that we have to build. Always it begins again; always there is the enemy; eyes meeting ours; fingers twitching ours; the effort waiting. Call the waiter. Pay the bill. We must pull ourselves up out of our chairs. We must find our coats. We must go. Must, must, must – detestable word. Once more, I who had thought myself immune, who had said, "Now I am rid of all that," find that the wave has tumbled me over, head over heels, scattering my possessions, leaving me to collect, to assemble, to heap together, summon my forces, rise and confront the enemy.

'It is strange that we, who are capable of so much suffering, should inflict so much suffering. Strange that the face of a person, whom I scarcely know save that I think we met once on the gangway of a ship bound for Africa – a mere a umbration of eyes, cheeks, nostrils – should have power to inflict this insu t. You look, eat, smile, are bored, pleased, annoyed – that is all I know. Yet this shadow which has sat by me for an hour or two, this mask from which peep two ey s, has power to drive me back, to pinion me down among all those other faces, to shu me in a hot room; to send me dashing like a moth from candle to candle.

'But wait. While they add up the bill behind the screen, wait one moment. Now that I have reviled you for the blow that sent me staggering among peelings and crumblings and old scraps of meat, I will record in words of one syllable how also under your gaze with that compulsion on me I begin to perceive this, that and the other. The clock ticks; the woman sneezes; the waiter comes – there is a gradual coming together, running into one, acceleration and unification. Listen: a whistle sounds, wheels rush, the door creaks on its hinges. I regain the sense of the complexity and the reality and the struggle, for which I thank you. And with some pity, some envy and much good will, take your hand and bid you good-night.

'Heaven be praised for solitude! I am alone now. That almost unknown person has gone, to catch some train, to take some cab, to go to some place or person whom I do not know. The face looking at me has gone. The pressure is removed. Here are empty coffee-cups. Here are chairs turned but nobody sits on them. Here are empty tables and nobody any more coming to dine at them tonight.

'Let me now raise my song of glory. Heaven be praised for solitude. Let me be alone. Let me cast and throw away this veil of being, this cloud that changes with the least breath, night and day, and all night and all day. While I sat here I have been changing. I have watched the sky change. I have seen clouds cover the stars, then free the stars, then cover the stars again. Now I look at their changing no more. Now no one sees me and I change no more. Heaven be praised for solitude that has removed the pressure of the eye, the solicitation of the body, and all need of lies and phrases.

'My book, stuffed with phrases, has dropped to the floor. It lies under the table, to be swept up by the charwoman when she comes wearily at dawn looking for scraps of paper, old tram tickets, and here and there a note screwed into a ball and left with the litter to be swept up. What is the phrase for the moon? And the phrase for love? By what name are we to call death? I do not know. I need a little language such as lovers use, words of one syllable such as children speak when they come into the room and find their mother sewing and pick up some scrap of bright wool, a feather or a shred of chintz. I need a howl; a cry. When the storm crosses the marsh and sweeps over me where I lie in the ditch unregarded I need no words. Nothing neat. Nothing that comes down with all its feet on the floor. None of those resonances and lovely echoes that break and chime from nerve to nerve in our breasts, making wild music, false phrases. I have done with phrases.

'How much better is silence; the coffee-cup, the table. How much better to sit by myself like the solitary sea-bird that opens its wings on the stake. Let me sit here for ever with bare things, this coffee-cup, this knife, this fork, things in themselves, myself being myself. Do not come and worry me with your hints that it is time to shut the shop and be gone. I would willingly give all my money that you should not disturb me but let me sit on and on, silent, alone.

'But now the head waiter, who has finished his own meal, appears and frowns; he takes his muffler from his pocket and ostentatiously makes ready to go. They must go; must put up the shutters, must fold the tablecloths and give one brush with a wet mop under the tables.

'Curse you then. However beat and done with it all I am, I must haul myself up, and find the particular coat that belongs to me; must push my arms into the sleeves; must muffle myself up against the night air and be off. I, I, I, tired as I am, spent as I am, and almost worn out with all this rubbing of my nose along the surfaces of things, even I, an elderly man who is getting rather heavy and dislikes exertion, must take myself off and catch some last train.

'Again I see before me the usual street. The canopy of civilisation is burnt out. The sky is dark as polished whalebone. But there is a kindling in the sky whether of lamplight or of dawn. There is a stir of some sort – sparrows on plane trees somewhere chirping. There is a sense of the break of day. I will not call it dawn. What is dawn in the city to an elderly man standing in the street looking up rather dizzily at the sky? Dawn is some sort of whitening of the sky; some sort of renewal. Another day; another Friday; another twentieth of March, January or September. Another general awakening. The stars draw back and are extinguished. The bars deepen themselves between the waves. The film of mist thickens on the fields. A redness gathers on the roses, even on the pale rose that hangs by the bedroom window. A bird chirps. Cottagers light their early candles. Yes, this is the eternal renewal, the incessant rise and fall and fall and rise again.

'And in me too the wave rises. It swells; it arches its back. I am aware once more of a new desire, something rising beneath me like the proud horse whose rider first spurs and then pulls him back. What enemy do we now perceive advancing against us, you whom I ride now, as we stand pawing this stretch of pavement? It is death. Death is the enemy. It is death against whom I ride with my spear couched and my hair flying back like a young man's, like Percival's, when he galloped in India. I strike spurs into my horse. Against you I will fling myself, unvanquished and unyielding, O Death!'

The waves broke on the shore.

THREE GUINEAS

Three Guineas

A reply framed by
VIRGINIA WOOLF
to a letter posing the question
'How are we to prevent war?'
1938

Chapter 1

Three years is a long time to leave a letter unanswered, and your letter has been lying without an answer even longer than that. I had hoped that it would answer itself, or that other people would answer it for me. But there it is with its question – How in your opinion are we to prevent war? – still unanswered.

It is true that many answers have suggested themselves, but none that would not need explanation, and explanations take time. In this case, too, there are reasons why it is particularly difficult to avoid misunderstanding. A whole page could be filled with excuses and apologies; declarations of unfitness, incompetence, lack of knowledge and experience: and they would be true. But even when they were said there would still remain some difficulties so fundamental that it may well prove impossible for you to understand or for us to explain. But one does not like to leave so remarkable a letter as yours – a letter perhaps unique in the history of human correspondence, since when before has an educated man asked a woman how in her opinion war can be prevented? – unanswered. Therefore let us make the attempt; even if it is doomed to failure.

In the first place let us draw what all letter-writers instinctively draw, a sketch of the person to whom the letter is addressed. Without someone warm and breathing on the other side of the page, letters are worthless. You, then, who ask the question, are a little grey on the temples; the hair is no longer thick on the top of your head. You have reached the middle years of life, not without effort, at the Bar; but on the whole your journey has been prosperous. There is nothing parched, mean or dissatisfied in your expression. And without wishing to flatter you, your prosperity – wife, children, house – has been deserved. You have never sunk into the contented apathy of middle life, for, as your letter from an office in the heart of London shows, instead of turning on your pillow and prodding your pigs, pruning your pear trees – you have a few acres in Norfolk – you are writing letters, attending meetings, presiding over this and that, asking questions, with the sound of the guns in your ears. For the rest, you began your education at one of the great public schools and finished it at the university.

It is now that the first difficulty of communication between us appears. Let us rapidly indicate the reason. We both come of what, in this hybrid age when, though birth is mixed, classes still remain fixed, it is convenient to call the educated class. When we meet in the flesh we speak with the same accent; use knives and forks in the same way; expect maids to cook dinner and wash up after dinner; and can talk during dinner without much difficulty about politics and people; war and peace; barbarism and civilisation – all the questions indeed suggested by your letter. Moreover, we both earn our livings. But . . . those three dots mark a precipice, a gulf so deeply cut between us that for three years and more I have been sitting on my side of it wondering whether it is any use to try to speak across it. Let us then ask someone else – it is Mary Kingsley – to speak for us. 'I don't know if I ever revealed to you the fact that being allowed to learn German was *all* the paid-for education I ever had. Two thousand pounds was spent on my brother's, I still hope not in vain.'[1]* Mary Kingsley is not speaking for herself alone; she is speaking, still, for many of the daughters of educated men. And she is not merely speaking for them; she is also pointing to a very important fact about them, a fact that must profoundly influence all that follows: the fact of Arthur's Education Fund. You who have read *Pendennis* will remember how the mysterious letters A.E.F. figured in the household ledgers. Ever since the thirteenth century English families have been paying money into that account. From the Pastons to the Pendennises, all educated families from the thirteenth century to the present moment have paid money into that account. It is a voracious receptacle. Where there were many sons to educate it required a great effort on the part of the family to keep it full. For your education was not merely in book-learning; games educated your body; friends taught you more than books or games. Talk with them broadened your outlook and enriched your mind. In the holidays you travelled; acquired a taste for art; a knowledge of foreign politics; and then, before you could earn your own living, your father made you an allowance upon which it was possible for you to live while you learnt the profession which now entitles you to add the letters K.C. to your name. All this came out of Arthur's Education Fund. And to this your sisters, as Mary Kingsley indicates, made their contribution. Not only did their own education, save for such small sums as paid the German teacher, go into it; but many of those luxuries and trimmings which are, after all, an essential part of education – travel, society, solitude, a lodging apart from the family house – they were paid into it too. It was a voracious receptacle, a solid fact – Arthur's Education Fund – a fact so solid indeed that it cast a shadow over the entire landscape. And the result is that though we look at the same things, we see them differently. What is that congregation of buildings there, with a semi-monastic look, with chapels and halls and green playing-fields? To you it is your old school, Eton or Harrow; your old university, Oxford or Cambridge; the source of memories and of traditions innumerable. But to us, who see it through the shadow of Arthur's Education Fund, it is a schoolroom table; an omnibus going to a class; a little woman with a red nose who is not well educated herself but has an invalid mother to support; an allowance of £50 a year with which to buy clothes, give presents and take journeys on coming to maturity. Such is the effect that Arthur's Education Fund has had upon us. So magically

* See Notes and References to *Three Guineas*, pp. 873–907.

does it change the landscape that the noble courts and quadrangles of Oxford and Cambridge often appear to educated men's daughters[2] like petticoats with holes in them, cold legs of mutton, and the boat train starting for abroad while the guard slams the door in their faces.

The fact that Arthur's Education Fund changes the landscape – the halls, the playing grounds, the sacred edifices – is an important one; but that aspect must be left for future discussion. Here we are only concerned with the obvious fact, when it comes to considering this important question – how we are to help you prevent war – that education makes a difference. Some knowledge of politics, of international relations, of economics, is obviously necessary in order to understand the causes which lead to war. Philosophy, theology even, might come in usefully. Now you the uneducated, you with an untrained mind, could not possibly deal with such questions satisfactorily. War, as the result of impersonal forces, is you will agree beyond the grasp of the untrained mind. But war as the result of human nature is another thing. Had you not believed that human nature, the reasons, the emotions of the ordinary man and woman, lead to war, you would not have written asking for our help. You must have argued, men and women, here and now, are able to exert their wills; they are not pawns and puppets dancing on a string held by invisible hands. They can act, and think for themselves. Perhaps even they can influence other people's thoughts and actions. Some such reasoning must have led you to apply to us; and with justification. For happily there is one branch of education which comes under the heading 'unpaid-for education' – that understanding of human beings and their motives which, if the word is rid of its scientific associations, might be called psychology. Marriage, the one great profession open to our class since the dawn of time until the year 1919; marriage, the art of choosing the human being with whom to live life successfully, should have taught us some skill in that. But here again another difficulty confronts us. For though many instincts are held more or less in common by both sexes, to fight has always been the man's habit, not the woman's. Law and practice have developed that difference, whether innate or accidental. Scarcely a human being in the course of history has fallen to a woman's rifle; the vast majority of birds and beasts have been killed by you, not by us; and it is difficult to judge what we do not share.[3]

How then are we to understand your problem, and if we cannot, how can we answer your question, how to prevent war? The answer based upon our experience and our psychology – Why fight? – is not an answer of any value. Obviously there is for you some glory, some necessity, some satisfaction in fighting which we have never felt or enjoyed. Complete understanding could only be achieved by blood transfusion and memory transfusion – a miracle still beyond the reach of science. But we who live now have a substitute for blood transfusion and memory transfusion which must serve at a pinch. There is that marvellous, perpetually renewed, and as yet largely untapped aid to the understanding of human motives which is provided in our age by biography and autobiography. Also there is the daily paper, history in the raw. There is thus no longer any reason to be confined to the minute span of actual experience which is still, for us, so narrow, so circumscribed. We can supplement it by looking at the picture of the lives of others. It is of course only a picture at present, but as such it must serve. It is to biography then that we will turn first, quickly and briefly, in order to attempt to understand what war means to you. Let us extract a few sentences from a biography. First, this from a soldier's life:

I have had the happiest possible life, and have always been working for war, and have now got into the biggest in the prime of life for a soldier . . . Thank God, we are off in an hour. Such a magnificent regiment! Such men, such horses! Within ten days I hope Francis and I will be riding side by side straight at the Germans.[4]

To which the biographer adds:

From the first hour he had been supremely happy, for he had found his true calling.

To that let us add this from an airman's life:

We talked of the League of Nations and the prospects of peace and disarmament. On this subject he was not so much militarist as martial. The difficulty to which he could find no answer was that if permanent peace were ever achieved, and armies and navies ceased to exist, there would be no outlet for the manly qualities which fighting developed, and that human physique and human character would deteriorate.[5]

Here, immediately, are three reasons which lead your sex to fight: war is a profession; a source of happiness and excitement; and it is also an outlet for manly qualities, without which men would deteriorate. But that these feelings and opinions are by no means universally held by your sex is proved by the following extract from another biography, the life of a poet who was killed in the European war: Wilfred Owen.

Already I have comprehended a light which never will filter into the dogma of any national church: namely, that one of Christ's essential commands was: Passivity at any price! Suffer dishonour and disgrace, but never resort to arms. Be bullied, be outraged, be killed; but do not kill . . . Thus you see how pure Christianity will not fit in with pure patriotism.

And among some notes for poems that he did not live to write are these:

The unnaturalness of weapons . . . Inhumanity of war . . . The insupportability of war . . . Horrible beastliness of war . . . Foolishness of war.[6]

From these quotations it is obvious that the same sex holds very different opinions about the same thing. But also it is obvious, from today's newspaper, that however many dissentients there are, the great majority of your sex are today in favour of war. The Scarborough Conference of educated men and the Bournemouth Conference of working men are both agreed that to spend £300,000,000 annually upon arms is a necessity. They are of opinion that Wilfred Owen was wrong; that it is better to kill than to be killed. Yet since biography shows that differences of opinion are many, it is plain that there must be some one reason which prevails in order to bring about this over-powering unanimity. Shall we call it, for the sake of brevity, 'patriotism'? What then, we must ask next, is this 'patriotism' which leads you to go to war? Let the Lord Chief Justice of England interpret it for us:

> Englishmen are proud of England. For those who have been trained in English schools and universities, and who have done the work of their lives in England, there are few loves stronger than the love we have for our country. When we consider other nations, when we judge the merits of the policy of this country or of that, it is the standard of our own country that we apply . . . Liberty has made her abode in England. England is the home of democratic institutions . . . It is true that in our midst there are many enemies of liberty – some of them, perhaps, in rather unexpected quarters. But we are standing firm. It has been said that an Englishman's Home is his Castle. The home of Liberty is in England. And it is a castle indeed – a castle that will be defended to the last. . . Yes, we are greatly blessed, we Englishmen.[7]

That is a fair general statement of what patriotism means to an educated man and what duties it imposes upon him. But the educated man's sister – what does 'patriotism' mean to her? Has she the same reasons for being proud of England, for loving England, for defending England? Has she been 'greatly blessed' in England? History and biography when questioned would seem to show that her position in the home of freedom has been different from her brother's; and psychology would seem to hint that history is not without its effect upon mind and body. Therefore her interpretation of the word 'patriotism' may well differ from his. And that difference may make it extremely difficult for her to understand his definition of patriotism and the duties it imposes. If then our answer to your question, 'How in your opinion are we to prevent war?' depends upon understanding the reasons, the emotions, the loyalties which lead men to go to war, this letter had better be torn across and thrown into the wastepaper basket. For it seems plain that we cannot understand each other because of these differences. It seems plain that we think differently according as we are born differently; there is a Grenfell point of view; a Knebworth point of view; a Wilfred Owen point of view; a Lord Chief Justice's point of view and the point of view of an educated man's daughter. All differ. But is there no absolute point of view? Can we not find somewhere written up in letters of fire or gold, 'This is right. This wrong'? – a moral judgement which we must all, whatever our differences, accept? Let us then refer the question of the rightness or wrongness of war to those who make morality their profession – the clergy. Surely if we ask the clergy the simple question: 'Is war right or is war wrong?' they will give us a plain answer which we cannot deny. But no – the Church of England, which might be supposed able to abstract the question from its worldly confusions, is of two minds also. The bishops themselves are at loggerheads. The Bishop of London maintained that 'the real danger to the peace of the world today were the pacifists. Bad as war was, dishonour was far worse.'[8] On the other hand, the Bishop of Birmingham[9] described himself as an 'extreme pacifist . . . I cannot see myself that war can be regarded as consonant with the spirit of Christ.' So the Church itself gives us divided counsel – in some circumstances it is right to fight; in no circumstances is it right to fight. It is distressing, baffling, confusing, but the fact must be faced: there is no certainty in heaven above or on earth below. Indeed the more lives we read, the more speeches we listen to, the more opinions we consult, the greater the confusion becomes and the less possible it seems, since we cannot understand the impulses, the motives, or the morality which lead you to go to war, to make any suggestion that will help you to prevent war.

But besides these pictures of other people's lives and minds – these biographies and histories – there are also other pictures – pictures of actual facts; photographs. Photographs, of course, are not arguments addressed to the reason; they are simply statements of fact addressed to the eye. But in that very simplicity there may be some help. Let us see then whether when we look at the same photographs we feel the same things. Here then on the table before us are photographs. The Spanish Government sends them with patient pertinacity about twice a week.* They are not pleasant photographs to look upon. They are photographs of dead bodies for the most part. This morning's collection contains the photograph of what might be a man's body, or a woman's; it is so mutilated that it might, on the other hand, be the body of a pig. But those certainly are dead children, and that undoubtedly is the section of a house. A bomb has torn open the side; there is still a birdcage hanging in what was presumably the sitting-room, but the rest of the house looks like nothing so much as a bunch of spillikins suspended in mid air.

Those photographs are not an argument; they are simply a crude statement of fact addressed to the eye. But the eye is connected with the brain; the brain with the nervous system. That system sends its messages in a flash through every past memory and present feeling. When we look at those photographs some fusion takes place within us; however different the education, the traditions behind us, our sensations are the same; and they are violent. You, sir, call them 'horror and disgust'. We also call them horror and disgust. And the same words rise to our lips. War, you say, is an abomination; a barbarity; war must be stopped at whatever cost. And we

* written in the winter of 1936–7

echo your words. War is an abomination; a barbarity; war must be stopped. For now at last we are looking at the same picture; we are seeing with you the same dead bodies, the same ruined houses.

Let us then give up, for the moment, the effort to answer your question, how we can help you to prevent war, by discussing the political, the patriotic or the psychological reasons which lead you to go to war. The emotion is too positive to suffer patient analysis. Let us concentrate upon the practical suggestions which you bring forward for our consideration. There are three of them. The first is to sign a letter to the newspapers; the second is to join a certain society; the third is to subscribe to its funds. Nothing on the face of it could sound simpler. To scribble a name on a sheet of paper is easy; to attend a meeting where pacific opinions are more or less rhetorically Σreiterated to people who already believe in them is also easy; and to write a cheque in support of those vaguely acceptable opinions, though not so easy, is a cheap way of quieting what may conveniently be called one's conscience. Yet there are reasons which make us hesitate; reasons into which we must enter, less superficially, later on. Here it is enough to say that though the three measures you suggest seem plausible, yet it also seems that, if we did what you ask, the emotion caused by the photographs would still remain unappeased. That emotion, that very positive emotion, demands something more positive than a name written on a sheet of paper; an hour spent listening to speeches; a cheque written for whatever sum we can afford – say one guinea. Some more energetic, some more active method of expressing our belief that war is barbarous, that war is inhuman, that war, as Wilfred Owen put it, is insupportable, horrible and beastly seems to be required. But, rhetoric apart, what active method is open to us? Let us consider and compare. You, of course, could once more take up arms – in Spain, as before in France – in defence of peace. But that presumably is a method that having tried you have rejected. At any rate that method is not open to us; both the Army and the Navy are closed to our sex. We are not allowed to fight. Nor again are we allowed to be members of the Stock Exchange. Thus we can use neither the pressure of force nor the pressure of money. The less direct but still effective weapons which our brothers, as educated men, possess in the diplomatic service, in the Church, are also denied to us. We cannot preach sermons or negotiate treaties. Then again although it is true that we can write articles or send letters to the Press, the control of the Press – the decision what to print, what not to print – is entirely in the hands of your sex. It is true that for the past twenty years we have been admitted to the Civil Service and to the Bar; but our position there is still very precarious and our authority of the slightest. Thus all the weapons with which an educated man can enforce his opinion are either beyond our grasp or so nearly beyond it that even if we used them we could scarcely inflict one scratch. If the men in your profession were to unite in any demand and were to say: 'If it is not granted we will stop work,' the laws of England would cease to be administered. If the women in your profession said the same thing it would make no difference to the laws of England whatever. Not only are we incomparably weaker than the men of our own class; we are weaker than the women of the working class. If the working women of the country were to say: 'If you go to war, we will refuse to make munitions or to help in the production of goods,' the difficulty of war-making would be seriously increased. But if all the daughters of educated men were to down tools tomorrow, nothing essential either to the life or to the war-making of the community would be embarrassed. Our class is the weakest of all the classes in the state. We have no weapon with which to enforce our will.[10]

The answer to that is so familiar that we can easily anticipate it. The daughters of educated men have no direct influence, it is true; but they possess the greatest power of all; that is, the influence that they can exert upon educated men. If this is true, if, that is, influence is still the strongest of our weapons and the only one that can be effective in helping you to prevent war, let us, before we sign your manifesto or join your society, consider what that influence amounts to. Clearly it is of such immense importance that it deserves profound and prolonged scrutiny. Ours cannot be profound; nor can it be prolonged; it must be rapid and imperfect – still, let us attempt it.

What influence then have we had in the past upon the profession that is most closely connected with war – upon politics? There again are the innumerable, the invaluable biographies, but it would puzzle an alchemist to extract from the massed lives of politicians that particular strain which is the influence upon them of women. Our analysis can only be slight and super-ficial; still if we narrow our inquiry to manageable limits, and run over the memoirs of a century and a half we can hardly deny that there have been women who have influenced politics. The famous Duchess of Devonshire, Lady Palmerston, Lady Melbourne, Madame de Lieven, Lady Holland, Lady Ashburton – to skip from one famous name to another – were all undoubtedly possessed of great political influence. Their famous houses and the parties that met in them play so large a part in the political memoirs of the time that we can hardly deny that English politics, even perhaps English wars, would have been different had those houses and those parties never existed. But there is one characteristic that all those memoirs possess in common: the names of the great political leaders – Pitt, Fox, Burke, Sheridan, Peel, Canning, Palmerston, Disraeli, Gladstone – are sprinkled on every page; but you will not find either at the head of the stairs receiving the guests, or in the more private apartments of the house, any daughter of an educated man. It may be that they were deficient in charm, in wit, in rank, or in clothing. Whatever the reason, you may turn page after page, volume after volume, and though you will find their brothers and husbands – Sheridan at Devonshire House, Macaulay at Holland House, Matthew Arnold at Lansdowne House, Carlyle even at Bath House, the names of Jane Austen, Charlotte Brontë and George Eliot do not occur; and though Mrs

Carlyle went, Mrs Carlyle seems on her own showing to have found herself ill at ease.

But, as you will point out, the daughters of educated men may have possessed another kind of influence – one that was independent of wealth and rank, of wine, food, dress and all the other amenities that make the great houses of the great ladies so seductive. Here indeed we are on firmer ground, for there was of course one political cause which the daughters of educated men had much at heart during the past hundred and fifty years: the franchise. But when we consider how long it took them to win that cause, and what labour, we can only conclude that influence has to be combined with wealth in order to be effective as a political weapon, and that influence of the kind that can be exerted by the daughters of educated men is very low in power, very slow in action, and very painful in use.[11] Certainly the one great political achievement of the educated man's daughter cost her over a century of the most exhausting and menial labour; kept her trudging in processions, working in offices, speaking at street corners; finally, because she used force, sent her to prison, and would very likely still keep her here, had it not been, paradoxically enough, that the help she gave her brothers when they used force at last gave her the right to call herself, if not a full daughter, still a stepdaughter of England.[12] Influence then wh n put to the test would seem to be only fully effective when combined with rank, wealth and great houses. The influential are Žthe daughters of nobl men, not the daughters of educated men. And that influence is of the ki d described by a distinguished member of your own profession, the late Sir Er est Wild.

> He claimed that the great influence which women exerted over men always had been, and always ought to be, an indirect influence. Man liked to think he was doing his job himself when, in fact, he was doing just what the woman wanted, but the wise woman always let him think he was running the show when he was not. Any woman who chose to take an interest in politics had an immensely greater power without the vote than with it, because she could influence many voters. His feeling was that it was not right to bring women down to the level of men. He looked up to women, and wanted to continue to do so. He desired that the age of chivalry should not pass, because every man who had a woman to care about him liked to shine in her eyes.[13]

And so on.

If such is the real nature of our influence, and we all recognise the description and have noted the effects, it is either beyond our reach, for many of us are plain, poor and old; or beneath our contempt, for many of us would prefer to call ourselves prostitutes simply and to take our stand openly under the lamps of Piccadilly Circus rather than use it. If such is the real nature, the indirect nature, of this celebrated weapon, we must do without it;

add our pigmy impetus to your more substantial forces, and have recourse, as you suggest, to letter signing, society joining and the drawing of an occasional exiguous cheque. Such would seem to be the inevitable, though depressing, conclusion of our inquiry into the nature of influence, were it not that for some reason, never satisfactorily explained, the right to vote,[14] in itself by no means negligible, was mysteriously connected with another right of such immense value to the daughters of educated men that almost every word in the dictionary has been changed by it, including the word 'influence'. You will not think these words exaggerated if we explain that they refer to the right to earn one's living.

That, sir, was the right that was conferred upon us less than twenty years ago, in the year 1919, by an Act which unbarred the professions. The door of the private house was thrown open. In every purse there was, or might be, one bright new sixpence in whose light every thought, every sight, every action looked different. Twenty years is not, as time goes, a long time; nor is a sixpenny bit a very important coin; nor can we yet draw upon biography to supply us with a picture of the lives and minds of the new-sixpenny owners. But in imagination perhaps we can see the educated man's daughter, as she issues from the shadow of the private house, and stands on the bridge which lies between the old world and the new, and asks, as she twirls the sacred coin in her hand, 'What shall I do with it? What do I see with it?' Through that light we may guess everything she saw looked different – men and women, cars and churches. The moon even, scarred as it is in fact with forgotten craters, seemed to her a white sixpence, a chaste sixpence, an altar upon which she vowed never to side with the servile, the signers-on, since it was hers to do what she liked with – the sacred sixpence that she had earned with her own hands herself. And if checking imagination with prosaic good sense, you object that to depend upon a profession is only another form of slavery, you will admit from your own experience that to depend upon a profession is a less odious form of slavery than to depend upon a father. Recall the joy with which you received your first guinea for your first brief, and the deep breath of freedom that you drew when you realised that your days of dependence upon Arthur's Education Fund were over. From that guinea, as from one of the magic pellets to which children set fire and a tree rises, all that you most value – wife, children, home – and above all that influence which now enables you to influence other men, have sprung. What would that influence be if you were still drawing forty pounds a year from the family purse, and for any addition to that income were dependent even upon the most benevolent of fathers? But it is needless to expatiate. Whatever the reason, whether pride, or love of freedom, or hatred of hypocrisy, you will understand the excitement with which in 1919 your sisters began to earn not a guinea but a sixpenny bit, and will not scorn that pride, or deny that it was justly based, since it meant that they need no longer use the influence described by Sir Ernest Wild.

The word 'influence' then has changed. The educated man's daughter has now at her disposal an influence which is different from any influence that she has possessed before. It is not the influence which the great lady, the Siren, possesses; nor is it the influence which the educated man's daughter possessed when she had no vote; nor is it the influence which she possessed when she had a vote but was debarred from the right to earn her living. It differs, because it is an influence from which the charm element has been removed; it is an influence from which the money element has been removed. She need no longer use her charm to procure money from her father or brother. Since it is beyond the power of her family to punish her financially she can express her own opinions. In place of the admirations and antipathies which were often unconsciously dictated by the need of money she can declare her genuine likes and dislikes. In short, she need not acquiesce; she can criticise. At last she is in posses sion of an influence that is disinterested.

Such in rough and rapid outlines is the nature of our new weapon, the influence which the educated man's daughter can exert now that she is able to earn her own living. The question that has next to be discussed, therefore, is how can she use this new weapon to help you to prevent war? And it is immediately plain that if there is no difference between men who earn their livings in the professions and women who earn their livings, then this letter can end; for if our point of view is the same as yours then we must add our sixpence to your guinea; follow your methods and repeat your words. But, whether fortunately or unfortunately, that is not true. The two classes still differ enormously. And to prove this, we need not have recourse to the dangerous and uncertain theories of psychologists and biologists; we can appeal to facts. Take the fact of education. Your class has been educated at public schools and universities for five or six hundred years, ours for sixty. Take the fact of property.[15] Your class possesses in its own right and not through marriage practically all the capital, all the land, all the valuables, and all the patronage in England. Our class possesses in its own right and not through marriage practically none of the capital, none of the land, none of the valuables, and none of the patronage in England. That such differences make for very considerable differences in mind and body, no psychologist or biologist would deny. It would seem to follow then as an indisputable fact that 'we' – meaning by 'we' a whole made up of body, brain and spirit, influenced by memory and tradition – must still differ in some essential respects from 'you', whose body, brain and spirit have been so differently trained and are so differently influenced by memory and tradition. Though we see the same world, we see it through different eyes. Any help we can give you must be different from that you can give yourselves, and perhaps the value of that help may lie in the fact of that difference. Therefore before we agree to sign your manifesto or join your society, it might be well to discover where the difference lies, because then we may discover where the help lies also. Let us then by way of a very elementary beginning lay before you a photograph – a crudely coloured photograph – of your world as it appears to us who see it from the threshold of the private house; through the shadow of the veil that St Paul still lays upon our eyes; from the bridge which connects the private house with the world of public life.

Your world, then, the world of professional, of public life, seen from this angle undoubtedly looks queer. At first sight it is enormously impressive. Within quite a small space are crowded together St Paul's, the Bank of England, the Mansion House, the massive if funereal battlements of the Law Courts; and on the other side, Westminster Abbey and the Houses of Parliament. There, we say to ourselves, pausing in this moment of transition on the bridge, our fathers and brothers have spent their lives. All these hundreds of years they have been mounting those steps, passing in and out of those doors, ascending those pulpits, preaching, money-making, administering justice. It is from this world that the private house (somewhere, roughly speaking, in the West End) has derived its creeds, its laws, its clothes and carpets, its beef and mutton. And then, as is now permissible, cautiously pushing aside the swing doors of one of these temples, we enter on tiptoe and survey the scene in greater detail. The first sensation of colossal size, of majestic masonry is broken up into a myriad points of mazement mixed with interrogation. Your clothes in the first place make u gape with astonishment.[16] How many, how splendid, how extremely ornate they a e – the clothes worn by the educated man in his public capacity! Now you dre s in violet; a jewelled crucifix swings on your breast; now your shoulders are overed with lace; now furred with ermine; now slung with many linked chains et with precious stones. Now you wear wigs on your heads; rows of grad ated curls descend to your necks. Now your hats are boat-shaped, or cocked now they mount in cones of black fur; now they are made of brass and scutt e shaped; now plumes of red, now of blue hair surmount them. Sometimes gowns cover your legs; sometimes gaiters. ŽTabards embroidered with lions and unicorn swing from your shoulders; metal objects cut in star shapes or in circl s glitter and twinkle upon your breasts. Ribbons of all colours – blue, purpl , crimson – cross from shoulder to shoulder. After the comparative simplic ty of your dress at home, the splendour of your public attire is dazzling. But far stranger are two other facts that grad

ally reveal themselves when our eyes have recovered from their first amazement. Not only are whole bodies of men dressed alike summer and winter – a strange characteristic to a sex which changes its clothes according to the season, and for reasons of private taste and comfort – but every button, rosette and stripe seems to have some symbolical meaning. Some have the right to wear plain buttons only; others rosettes; some may wear a single stripe; others three, four, five or six. And each curl or stripe is sewn on at precisely the right distance apart; it may be one inch for one man, one inch and a quarter for another. Rules again regulate the gold wire on the shoulders, the braid on the trousers, the cockades on the hats – but no single pair of eyes can observe all these distinctions, let alone account for them accurately.

Even stranger, however, than the symbolic splendour of your clothes are the ceremonies that take place when you wear them. Here you kneel; there you bow; here you advance in procession behind a man carrying a silver poker; here you mount a carved chair; here you appear to do homage to a piece of painted wood; here you abase yourselves before tables covered with richly worked tapestry. And whatever these ceremonies may mean you perform them always together, always in step, always in the uniform proper to the man and the occasion.

Apart from the ceremonies, such decorative apparel appears to us at first sight strange in the extreme. For dress, as we use it, is comparatively simple. Besides the prime function of covering the body, it has two other offices – that it creates beauty for the eye, and that it attracts the admiration of your sex. Since marriage until the year 1919 – less than twenty years ago – was the only profession open to us, the enormous importance of dress to a woman can hardly be exaggerated. It was to her what clients are to you – dress was her chief, perhaps her only, method of becoming Lord Chancellor. But your dress in its immense elaboration has obviously another function. It not only covers nakedness, gratifies vanity, and creates pleasure for the eye, but it serves to advertise the social, professional or intellectual standing of the wearer. If you will excuse the humble illustration, your dress fulfils the same function as the tickets in a grocer's shop. But, here, instead of saying, 'This is margarine; this pure butter; this is the finest butter in the market,' it says, 'This man is a clever man – he is Master of Arts; this man is a very clever man – he is Doctor of Letters; this man is a most clever man – he is a Member of the Order of Merit.' It is this function – the advertisement function – of your dress that seems to us most singular. In the opinion of St Paul, such advertisement, at any rate for our sex, was unbecoming and immodest; until a very few years ago we were denied the use of it. And still the tradition, or belief, lingers among us that to express worth of any kind, whether intellectual or moral, by wearing pieces of metal, or ribbon, coloured hoods or gowns, is a barbarity which deserves the ridicule which we bestow upon the rites of savages. A woman who advertised her motherhood by a tuft of horsehair on the left shoulder would scarcely, you will agree, be a venerable object.

But what light does our difference here throw upon the problem before us? What connection is there between the sartorial splendours of the educated man and the photograph of ruined houses and dead bodies? Obviously the connection between dress and war is not far to seek: your finest clothes are those that you wear as soldiers. Since the red and the gold, the brass and the feathers are discarded upon active service, it is plain that their expensive and not, one might suppose, hygienic splendour is invented partly in order to impress the beholder with the majesty of the military office, partly in order through their vanity to induce young men to become soldiers. Here, then, our influence and our difference might have some effect: we, who are forbidden to wear such clothes ourselves, can express the opinion that the wearer is not to us a pleasing or an impressive spectacle. He is on the contrary a ridiculous, a barbarous, a displeasing spectacle. But as the daughters of educated men we can use our influence more effectively in another direction, upon our own class – the class of educated men. For there, in courts and universities, we find the same love of dress. There, too, are velvet and silk, fur and ermine. We can say that for educated men to emphasise their superiority over other people, either in birth or intellect, by dressing differently, or by adding titles before, or letters after their names are acts that rouse competition and jealousy – emotions which, as we need scarcely draw upon biography to prove, nor ask psychology to show, have their share in encouraging a disposition towards war. If then we express the opinion that such distinctions make those who possess them ridiculous and learning contemptible we should do something, indirectly, to discourage the feelings that lead to war. Happily we can now do more than express an opinion; we can refuse all such distinctions and all such uniforms for ourselves. This would be a slight but definite contribution to the problem before us – how to prevent war; and one that a different training and a different tradition puts more easily within our reach than within yours.[17]

But our bird's-eye view of the outside of things is not altogether encouraging. The coloured photograph that we have been looking at presents some remarkable features, it is true; but it serves to remind us that there are many inner and secret chambers that we cannot enter. What real influence can we bring to bear upon law or business, religion or politics – we to whom many doors are still locked, or at best ajar, we who have neither capital nor force behind us? It seems as if our influence must stop short at the surface. When we have expressed an opinion upon the surface we have done all that we can do. It is true that the surface may have some connection with the depths, but if we are to help you to prevent war we must try to penetrate deeper beneath the skin. Let us then look in another direction – in a direction natural to educated men's daughters, in the direction of education itself.

Here, fortunately, the year, the sacred year 1919, comes to our help. Since that year put it into the power of educated men's daughters to earn their livings they have at last some real influence upon education. They have money. They have money to subscribe to causes. Honorary treasurers invoke their help. To prove it, here, opportunely, cheek by jowl with your letter, is a letter from one such treasurer asking for money with which to rebuild a women's college. And when honorary treasurers invoke help, it stands to reason that they can be bargained with. We have the right to say to her, 'You shall only have our guinea with which to help you rebuild your college if you will help this gentleman whose letter also lies before us to prevent war.' We can say to her, 'You must educate the young to hate war. You must teach them to feel the inhumanity, the beastliness, the insupportability of war.' But what kind of education shall we bargain for? What sort of education will teach the young to hate war?

That is a question that is difficult enough in itself; and may well seem unanswerable by those who are of Mary Kingsley's persuasion – those who have had no direct experience of university education themselves. Yet the part that education plays in human life is so important, and the part that it might play in answering your question is so considerable that to shirk any attempt to see how we can influence the young through education against war would be craven. Let us therefore turn from our station on the bridge across the Thames to another bridge over another river, this time in one of the great universities; for both have rivers, and both have bridges, too, for us to stand upon. Once more, how strange it looks, this world of domes and spires, of lecture rooms and laboratories, from our vantage point! How different it looks to us from what it must look to you! To those who behold it from Mary Kingsley's angle – 'being allowed to learn German was *all* the paid education I ever had' – it may well appear a world so remote, so formidable, so intricate in its ceremonies and traditions that any criticism or comment may well seem futile. Here, too, we marvel at the brilliance of your clothes; here, too, we watch maces erect themselves and processions form, and note with eyes too dazzled to record the differences, let alone to explain them, the subtle distinctions of hats and hoods, of purples and crimsons, of velvet and cloth, of cap and gown. It is a solemn spectacle. The words of Arthur's song in *Pendennis* rise to our lips:

> Although I enter not,
> Yet round about the spot
> Sometimes I hover,
> And at the sacred gate,
> With longing eyes I wait,
> Expectant . . .

and again,

> I will not enter there,
> To sully your pure prayer
> With thoughts unruly.

> But suffer me to pace
> Round the forbidden place,
> Lingering a minute,
> Like outcast spirits, who wait
> And see through Heaven's gate
> Angels within it.

But, since both you, sir, and the honorary treasurer of the college re-building fund are waiting for answers to your letters, we must cease to hang over old bridges humming old songs; we must attempt to deal with the question of education, however imperfectly.

What, then, is this 'university education' of which Mary Kingsley's sister-hood have heard so much and to which they have contributed so painfully? What is this mysterious process that takes about three years to accomplish, costs a round sum in hard cash, and turns the crude and raw human being into the finished product – an educated man or woman? There can be no doubt in the first place of its supreme value. The witness of biography – that witness which anyone who can read English can consult on the shelves of any public library – is unanimous upon this point; the value of education is among the greatest of all human values. Biography proves this in two ways. First, there is the fact that the great majority of the men who have ruled England for the past five hundred years, who are now ruling England in Parliament and the Civil Service, have received a university education. Second, there is the fact, which is even more impressive if you consider what toil, what privation it implies – and of this, too, there is ample proof in biography – the fact of the immense sum of money that has been spent upon education in the past five hundred years. The income of Oxford University is £435,656 (1933–4), the income of Cambridge University is £212,000 (1930). In addition to the univer-sity income each college has its own separate income, which, judging only from the gifts and bequests announced from time to time in the newspapers, must in some cases be of fabulous proportions.[18] If we add further the in-comes enjoyed by the great public schools – Eton, Harrow, Winchester, Rugby, to name the largest only – so huge a sum of money is reached that there can be no doubt of the enormous value that human beings place upon education. And the study of biography – the lives of the poor, of the obscure, of the uneducated – proves that they will make any effort, any sacrifice to procure an education at one of the great universities.[19]

But perhaps the greatest testimony to the value of education with which biography provides us is the fact that the sisters of educated men not only made the sacrifices of comfort and pleasure, which were needed in order to educate their brothers, but actually desired to be educated themselves. When we consider the ruling of the Church on this subject, a ruling which we learn from biography was in force only a few years ago – ' . . . I was told that desire for learning in women was against the will of God . . . '[20] – we must allow that their desire must have been strong. And if we reflect that all the professions for which a university education fitted her brothers were closed to her, her belief in the value of education must appear still stronger, since she must have believed in education for itself. And if we reflect further that the one profession that was open to her – marriage – was held to need no education, and indeed was of such a nature that education unfitted women to practise it, then it would have been no surprise to find that she had renounced any wish or attempt to be educated herself, but had contented herself with providing education for her brothers – the vast majority of women, the nameless, the poor, by cutting down household expenses; the minute minority, the titled, the rich, by founding or endowing colleges for men. This indeed they did. But so innate in human nature is the desire for education that you will find, if you consult biography, that the same desire, in spite of all the impediments that tradition, poverty and ridicule could put in its way, existed too among women. To prove this let us examine one life only – the life of Mary Astell.[21] Little is known about her, but enough to show that almost two hundred and fifty years ago this obstinate and perhaps irreligious desire was alive in her; she actually proposed to found a college for women. What is almost as remarkable, the Princess Anne was ready to give her £10,000 – a very considerable sum then, and, indeed, now, for any woman to have at her disposal – towards the expenses. And then – then we meet with a fact which is of extreme interest, both historically and psychologically: the Church intervened. Bishop Burnet was of opinion that to educate the sisters of educated men would be to encourage the wrong branch, that is to say, the Roman Catholic branch, of the Christian faith. The money went elsewhere; the college was never founded.

But these facts, as facts so often do, prove double-faced; for though they establish the value of education, they also prove that education is by no means a positive value; it is not good in all circumstances, and good for all people; it is only good for some people and for some purposes. It is good if it produces a belief in the Church of England, bad if it produces a belief in the Church of Rome; it is good for one sex and for some professions, but bad for another sex and for another profession.

Such at least would seem to be the answer of biography – the oracle is not dumb, but it is dubious. As, however, it is of great importance that we should use our influence through education to affect the young against war we must not be baffled by the evasions of biography or seduced by its charm. We must try to see what kind of education an educated man's sister receives at present, in order that we may do our utmost to use our influence in the universities where it properly belongs, and where it will have most chance of penetrating beneath the skin. Now happily we need no longer depend upon biography, which inevitably, since it is concerned with the private life, bristles with innumerable conflicts of private opinion. We have now to help us that record of the public life which is history. Even outsiders can consult the annals of those public bodies which record not the day-to-day opinions of private people, but use a larger accent and convey through the mouths of Parliaments and Senates the considered opinions of bodies of educated men.

History at once informs us that there are now, and have been since about 1870, colleges for the sisters of educated men both at Oxford and at Cambridge. But history also informs us of facts of such a nature about those colleges that all attempt to influence the young against war through the education they receive there must be abandoned. In face of them it is mere waste of time and breath to talk of 'influencing the young'; useless to lay down terms, before allowing the honorary treasurer to have her guinea; better to take the first train to London than to haunt the sacred gates. But, you will interpose, what are these facts? these historical but deplorable facts? Therefore let us place them before you, warning you that they are taken only from such records as are available to an outsider and from the annals of the university which is not your own – Cambridge. Your judgement, therefore, will be undistorted by loyalty to old ties, or gratitude for benefits received, but it will be impartial and disinterested.

To begin then where we left off: Queen Anne died and Bishop Burnet died and Mary Astell died; but the desire to found a college for her own sex did not die. Indeed, it became stronger and stronger. By the middle of the nineteenth century it became so strong that a house was taken at Cambridge to lodge the students. It was not a nice house; it was a house without a garden in the middle of a noisy street. Then a second house was taken, a better house this time, though it is true that the water rushed through the dining-room in stormy weather and there was no playground. But that house was not sufficient; the desire for education was so urgent that more rooms were needed, a garden to walk in, a playground to play in. Therefore another house was needed. Now history tells us that in order to build this house, money was needed. You will not question that fact but you may well question the next – that the money was borrowed. It will seem to you more probable that the money was given. The other colleges, you will say, were rich; all derived their incomes indirectly, some directly, from their sisters. There is Gray's *Ode* to prove it. And you will quote the song with which he hails the benefactors: the Countess of Pembroke who founded Pembroke; the Countess of Clare who founded Clare; Margaret of Anjou who founded Queens'; the Countess of Richmond and Derby who founded St John's and Christ's.

> What is grandeur, what is power?
> Heavier toil, superior pain.
> What the bright reward we gain?
> The grateful memory of the good.
> Sweet is the breath of vernal shower,
> The bee's collected treasures sweet,
> Sweet music's melting fall, but sweeter yet
> The still small voice of gratitude.[22]

Here, you will say in sober prose, was an opportunity to repay the debt. For what sum was needed? A beggarly £10,000 – the very sum that the bishop intercepted about two centuries previously. That £10,000 surely was disgorged by the Church that had swallowed it? But churches do not easily disgorge what they have swallowed. Then the colleges, you will say, which had benefited, they must have given it gladly in memory of their noble benefactresses? What could £10,000 mean to St John's or Clare or Christ's? And the land belonged to St John's. But the land, history says, was leased; and the £10,000 was not given; it was collected laboriously from private purses. Among them one lady must be for ever remembered because she gave £1,000; and Anon. must receive whatever thanks Anon. will consent to receive, because she gave sums ranging from £20 to £100. And another lady was able, owing to a legacy from her mother, to give her services as mistress without salary. And the students themselves subscribed – so far as students can – by making beds and washing dishes, by forgoing amenities and living on simple fare. Ten thousand pounds is not at all a beggarly sum when it has to be collected from the purses of the poor, from the bodies of the young. It takes time, energy, brains, to collect it, sacrifice to give it. Of course, several educated men were very kind; they lectured to their sisters; others were not so kind; they refused to lecture to their sisters. Some educated men were very kind and encouraged their sisters; others were not so kind, they discouraged their sisters.[23] Nevertheless, by hook or by crook, the day came at last, history tells us, when somebody passed an examination. And then the mistresses, principals or whatever they called themselves – for the title that should be worn by a woman who will not take a salary must be a matter of doubt – asked the Chancellors and the Masters about whose titles there need be no doubt, at any rate upon that score, whether the girls who had passed examinations might advertise the fact as those gentlemen themselves did by putting letters after their names. This was advisable, because, as the present Master of Trinity, Sir J. J. Thomson, O.M., F.R.S., after poking a little justifiable fun at the 'pardonable vanity' of those who put letters after their names, informs us, 'the general public who have not taken a degree themselves attach much more importance to B.A. after a person's name than those who have. Headmistresses of schools therefore prefer a belettered staff, so that students of Newnham and Girton, since they could not put B.A. after their name, were at a disadvantage in obtaining appointments.' And in heaven's name, we may both ask, what conceivable reason could there be for preventing them from putting the letters B.A. after their names if it helped them to obtain appointments? To that question history supplies no answer; we must look for it in psychology, in biography; but history supplies us with the fact. 'The proposal, however,' the Master of Trinity continues – the proposal, that is, that those who had passed examinations might call themselves B.A. – 'met with the most determined opposition . . . On the day of the voting there was a great influx of non-residents and the proposal was thrown out by the crushing majority of 1707 to 661. I believe the number of voters has never been equalled . . . The behaviour of some of the undergraduates after the poll was declared in the Senate House was exceptionally deplorable and disgraceful. A large band of them left the Senate House, proceeded to Newnham and damaged the bronze gates which had been put up as a memorial to Miss Clough, the first Principal.'[24]

Is that not enough? Need we collect more facts from history and bio-graphy to prove our statement that all attempt to influence the young against war through the education they receive at the universities must be aban-doned? For do they not prove that education, the finest education in the world, does not teach people to hate force, but to use it? Do they not prove that education, far from teaching the educated generosity and magnanimity, makes them on the contrary so anxious to keep their possessions, that 'grandeur and power' of which the poet speaks, in their own hands, that they will use not force but much subtler methods than force when they are asked to share them? And are not force and possessiveness very closely connected with war? Of what use then is a university education in influencing people to prevent war? But history goes on of course; year succeeds to year. The years change things; slightly but imperceptibly they change them. And history tells us that at last, after spending time and strength whose value is immeasurable in repeatedly soliciting the authorities with the humility expected of our sex and proper to suppliants, the right to impress headmistresses by putting the letters B.A. after the name was granted. But that right, history tells us, was only a titular right. At Cambridge, in the year 1937, the women's colleges – you will scarcely believe it, sir, but once more it is the voice of fact that is speaking, not of fiction – the women's colleges are not allowed to be mem-bers of the university;[25] and the number of educated men's daughters who are allowed to receive a university education is still strictly limited, though both sexes contribute to the university funds.[26] As for poverty, *The Times* news-paper supplies us with figures; any ironmonger will provide us with a foot-rule; if we measure the money available for scholarships at the men's colleges with the money available for their sisters at the women's colleges, we shall save ourselves the trouble of adding up; and come to the conclusion that the colleges for the sisters of educated men are, compared with their brothers' colleges, unbelievably and shamefully poor.[27]

Proof of that last fact comes pat to hand in the honorary treasurer's letter, asking for money with which to rebuild her college. She has been asking for some time; she is still asking, it seems. But there is nothing, after what has been said above, that need puzzle us, either in the fact that she is poor, or in the fact that her college needs rebuilding. What is puzzling, and has become still more puzzling, in view of the facts given above, is this: What answer ought we to make her when she asks us to help her to rebuild her college? History, biography, and the daily paper between them make it difficult either to answer her letter or to dictate terms. For between them they have raised many questions. In the first place, what reason is there to think that a university education makes the educated against war? Again, if we help an educated man's daughter to go to Cambridge are we not forcing her to think not about education but about war? – not how she can learn, but how she can fight in order that she may win the same advantages as her brothers? Further, since the daughters of educated men are not members of Cambridge University they have no say in that education, therefore how can they alter that education even if we ask them to? And then, of course, other questions arise – questions of a practical nature, which will easily be understood by a busy man, an honorary treasurer, like yourself, sir. You will be the first to agree that to ask people who are so largely occupied in raising funds with which to rebuild a college to consider the nature of education and what effect it can have upon war is to heap another straw upon an already overburdened back. From an outsider, moreover, who has no right to speak, such a request may well deserve, and perhaps receive, a reply too forcible to be quoted. But we have sworn that we will do all we can to help you to prevent war by using our influence – our earned money influence. And education is the obvious way. Since she is poor, since she is asking for money, and since the giver of money is entitled to dictate terms, let us risk it and draft a letter to her, laying down the terms upon which she shall have our money to help rebuild her college. Here, then, is an attempt:

Your letter, madam, has been waiting some time without an answer. But certain doubts and questions have arisen. May we put them to you, ignorantly as an outsider must, but frankly as an outsider should when asked to contribute money? You say, then, that you are asking for £100,000 with which to rebuild your college. But how can you be so foolish? Or are you so secluded among the nightingales and the willows, or so busy with profound questions of caps and gowns, and which is to walk first into the Provost's drawing-room – the Master's pug or the Mistress's pom – that you have no time to read the daily papers? Or are you so harassed with the problem of drawing £100,000 gracefully from an indifferent public that you can only think of appeals and committees, bazaars and ices, strawberries and cream?

Let us then inform you: we are spending three hundred millions annually upon the army and navy; for, according to a letter that lies cheek by jowl with your own, there is grave danger of war. How then can you seriously ask us to provide you with money with which to rebuild your college? If you reply that the college was built on the cheap, and that the college needs rebuilding, that may be true. But when you go on to say that the public is generous, and that the public is still capable of providing large sums for rebuilding colleges, let us draw your attention to a significant passage in the Master of Trinity's memoirs. It is this: 'Fortunately, however, soon after the beginning of this century the University began to receive a succession of very handsome bequests and donations, and these, aided by a liberal grant from the Government, have put the finances of the University in such a good position that it has been quite unnecessary to ask for any increase in the contribution from the Colleges. The income of the University from all sources has increased from about £60,000 in

1900 to £212,000 in 1930. It is not a very wild hypothesis to suppose that this has been to a large extent due to the important and very interesting discoveries which have been made in the University, and Cambridge may be quoted as an example of the practical results which come from Research for its own sake.'

Consider only that last sentence: ' . . . Cambridge may be quoted as an example of the practical results which come from Research for its own sake.' What has your college done to stimulate great manufacturers to endow it? Have you taken a leading part in the invention of the implements of war? How far have your students succeeded in business as capitalists? How then can you expect 'very handsome bequests and donations' to come your way? Again, are you a member of Cambridge University? You are not. How then can you fairly ask for any say in their distribution? You cannot. Therefore, madam, it is plain that you must stand at the door, cap in hand, giving parties, spending your strength and your time in soliciting subscriptions. That is plain. But it is also plain that outsiders who find you thus occupied must ask themselves, when they receive a request for a contribution towards rebuilding your college, Shall I send it or shan't I? If I send it, what shall I ask them to do with it? Shall I ask them to rebuild the college on the old lines? Or shall I ask them to rebuild it, but differently? Or shall I ask them to buy rags and petrol and Bryant & May's matches and burn the college to the ground?

These are the questions, madam, that have kept your letter so long unanswered. They are questions of great difficulty and perhaps they are useless questions. But can we leave them unasked in view of this gentleman's questions? He is asking how can we help him to prevent war? He is asking us how we can help him to defend liberty; to defend culture? Also consider these photographs: they are pictures of dead bodies and ruined houses. Surely in view of these questions and pictures you must consider very carefully before you begin to rebuild your college what is the aim of education, what kind of society, what kind of human being it should seek to produce. At any rate I will only send you a guinea with which to rebuild your college if you can satisfy me that you will use it to produce the kind of society, the kind of people that will help to prevent war.

Let us then discuss as quickly as we can the sort of education that is needed. Now since history and biography – the only evidence available to an outsider – seem to prove that the old education of the old colleges breeds neither a particular respect for liberty nor a particular hatred of war it is clear that you must rebuild your college differently. It is young and poor; let it therefore take advantage of those qualities and be founded on poverty and youth. Obviously, then, it must be an experimental college, an adventurous college. Let it be built on lines of its own. It must be built not of carved stone and stained glass, but of some cheap, easily combustible material which does not hoard dust and perpetrate traditions. Do not have chapels.[28] Do not have museums and libraries with chained books and first editions under glass cases. Let the pictures and the books be new and always changing. Let it be decorated afresh by each generation with their own hands cheaply. The work of the living is cheap; often they will give it for the sake of being allowed to do it. Next, what should be taught in the new college, the poor college? Not the arts of dominating other people; not the arts of ruling, of killing, of acquiring land and capital. They require too many overhead expenses: salaries and uniforms and ceremonies. The poor college must teach only the arts that can be taught cheaply and practised by poor people; such as medicine, mathematics, music, painting and literature. It should teach the arts of human inter-course: the art of understanding other people's lives and minds, and the little arts of talk, of dress, of cookery that are allied with them. The aim of the new college, the cheap college, should be not to segregate and specialise, but to combine. It should explore the ways in which mind and body can be made to cooperate; discover what new combinations make good wholes in human life. The teachers should be drawn from the good livers as well as from the good thinkers. There should be no difficulty in attracting them. For there would be none of the barriers of wealth and ceremony, of advertisement and competition which now make the old and rich universities such uneasy dwelling-places – cities of strife, cities where this is locked up and that is chained down; where nobody can walk freely or talk freely for fear of transgressing some chalk mark, of displeasing some dignitary. But if the college were poor it would have nothing to offer; competition would be abolished. Life would be open and easy. People who love learning for itself would gladly come there. Musicians, painters, writers, would teach there, because they would learn. What could be of greater help to a writer than to discuss the art of writing with people who were thinking not of examinations or degrees or of what honour or profit they could make literature give them but of the art itself?

And so with the other arts and artists. They would come to the poor college and practise their arts there because it would be a place where society was free; not parcelled out into the miserable distinctions of rich and poor, of clever and stupid; but where all the different degrees and kinds of mind, body and soul merit cooperated. Let us then found this new college; this poor college; in which learning is sought for itself; where advertisement is abolished; and there are no degrees; and lectures are not given, and sermons are not preached, and the old poisoned vanities and parades which breed competition and jealousy . . .

The letter broke off there. It was not from lack of things to say; the peroration indeed was only just beginning. It was because the face on the other side of the page – the face that a letter-writer always sees – appeared to be fixed with a certain melancholy upon a passage in the book from which quotation has already been made: 'Headmistresses of schools therefore prefer a belettered staff, so that students of Newnham and Girton, since they could not put B.A. after their name, were at a disadvantage in obtaining appointments.' The honorary treasurer of the Rebuilding Fund had her eyes fixed on that. 'What is the use of thinking how a college can be different,' she seemed to say, 'when it must be a place where students are taught to obtain appointments?' 'Dream your dreams,' she seemed to add, turning, rather wearily, to the table which she was arranging for some festival, a bazaar presumably, 'but we have to face realities.'

That then was the 'reality' on which her eyes were fixed: students must be taught to earn their livings. And since that reality meant that she must rebuild her college on the same lines as the others, it followed that the college for the daughters of educated men must also make research produce practical results which will induce bequests and donations from rich men; it must encourage competition; it must accept degrees and coloured hoods; it must accumulate great wealth; it must exclude other people from a share of its wealth; and, therefore, in five hundred years or so, that college, too, must ask the same question that you, sir, are asking now: 'How in your opinion are we to prevent war?'

An undesirable result that seemed; why then subscribe a guinea to procure it? That question at any rate was answered. No guinea of earned money should go to rebuilding the college on the old plan; just as certainly none could be spent upon building a college upon a new plan; therefore the guinea should be earmarked 'Rags. Petrol. Matches'. And this note should be attached to it. 'Take this guinea and with it burn the college to the ground. Set fire to the old hypocrisies. Let the light of the burning building scare the nightingales and incarnadine the willows. And let the daughters of educated men dance round the fire and heap armful upon armful of dead leaves upon the flames. And let their mothers lean from the upper windows and cry, "Let it blaze! Let it blaze! For we have done with this 'education'!" '

That passage, sir, is not empty rhetoric, for it is based upon the respectable opinion of the late headmaster of Eton, the present Dean of Durham.[29] Nevertheless, there is something hollow about it, as is shown by a moment's conflict with fact. We have said that the only influence which the daughters of educated men can at present exert against war is the disinterested influence that they possess through earning their livings. If there were no means of training them to earn their livings, there would be an end of that influence. They could not obtain appointments. If they could not obtain appointments they would again be dependent upon their fathers and brothers; and if they were again dependent upon their fathers and brothers they would again be consciously and unconsciously in favour of war. History would seem to put that beyond doubt. Therefore we must send a guinea to the honorary treasurer of the college rebuilding fund, and let her do what she can with it. It is useless as things are to attach conditions as to the way in which that guinea is to be spent.

Such then is the rather lame and depressing answer to our question whether we can ask the authorities of the colleges for the daughters of educated men to use their influence through education to prevent war. It appears that we can ask them to do nothing; they must follow the old road to the old end; our own influence as outsiders can only be of the most indirect sort. If we are asked to teach, we can examine very carefully into the aim of such teaching, and refuse to teach any art or science that encourages war. Further, we can pour mild scorn upon chapels, upon degrees, and upon the value of examinations. We can intimate that a prize poem can still have merit in spite of the fact that it has won a prize; and maintain that a book may still be worth reading in spite of the fact that its author took a first class with honours in the English tripos. If we are asked to lecture we can refuse to bolster up the vain and vicious system of lecturing by refusing to lecture.[30] And, of course, if we are offered offices and honours for ourselves we can refuse them – how, indeed, in view of the facts, could we possibly do otherwise? But there is no blinking the fact that in the present state of things the most effective way in which we can help you through education to prevent war is to subscribe as generously as possible to the colleges for the daughters of educated men. For, to repeat, if those daughters are not going to be educated, they are not going to earn their livings; if they are not going to earn their livings, they are going once more to be restricted to the education of the private house; and if they are going to be restricted to the education of the private house they are going, once more, to exert all their influence both consciously and unconsciously in favour of war. Of that there can be little doubt. Should you doubt it, should you ask proof, let us once more consult biography. Its testimony upon this point is so conclusive, but so voluminous, that we must try to condense many volumes into one story. Here, then, is the narrative of the life of an educated man's daughter who was dependent upon father and brother in the private house of the nineteenth century.

The day was hot, but she could not go out. 'How many a long dull summer's day have I passed immured indoors because there was no room for me in the family carriage and no lady's maid who had time to walk out with me.' The sun set; and out she went at last, dressed as well as could be managed upon an allowance of from £40 to £100 a year.[31] But 'to any sort of entertainment she must be accompanied by father or mother or by some married woman'. Whom did she meet at those entertainments thus dressed, thus accompanied? Educated men – 'cabinet ministers, ambassadors, famous soldiers and the like, all splendidly dressed, wearing decorations'. What did they talk about? Whatever refreshed the minds of busy men who wanted to forget their own work – 'the gossip of the dancing world' did very well. The days passed. Saturday came. On Saturday 'MPs and other busy men had leisure to enjoy society'; they came to tea and they came to dinner. Next day was Sunday. On Sundays 'the great majority of us went as a matter of course to morning church'. The seasons changed. It was summer. In the summer they entertained visitors, 'mostly relatives', in the country. Now it was winter. In the winter 'they studied history and literature and music, and tried to draw and paint. If they did not produce anything remarkable they learnt much in the process.' And so with some visiting the sick and teaching the poor the years passed. And what was the great end and aim of these years, of that education? Marriage, of course. ' . . . it was not a question of *whether* we should marry, but simply of *whom* we should marry,' says one of them. It was with a view to marriage that her mind was taught. It was with a view to marriage that she tinkled on the piano, but was not allowed to join an orchestra; sketched innocent domestic scenes, but was not allowed to study from the nude; read this book, but was not allowed to read that; charmed and talked. It was with a view to marriage that her body was educated; a maid was provided for her; that the streets were shut to her; that the fields were shut to her; that solitude was denied her – all this was enforced upon her in order that she might preserve her body intact for her husband. In short, the thought of marriage influenced what she said, what she thought, what she did. How could it be otherwise? Marriage was the only profession open to her.[32]

The sight is so curious for what it shows of the educated man as well as of his daughter that it is tempting to linger. The influence of the pheasant upon love alone deserves a chapter to itself.[33] But we are not asking now the interesting question, what was the effect of that education upon the race? We are asking why did such an education make the person so educated consciously and unconsciously in favour of war? Because consciously, it is obvious, she was forced to use whatever influence she possessed to bolster up the system which provided her with maids; with carriages; with fine clothes; with fine parties – it was by these means that she achieved marriage. Consciously she must use whatever charm or beauty she possessed to flatter and cajole the busy men, the soldiers, the lawyers, the ambassadors, the cabinet ministers who wanted recreation after their day's work. Consciously she must accept their views, and fall in with their decrees because it was only so that she could wheedle them into giving her the means to marry or marriage itself.[34] In short, all her conscious effort must be in favour of what Lady Lovelace called 'our splendid Empire' . . . 'the price of which,' she added, 'is mainly paid by women'. And who can doubt her, or that the price was heavy?

But her unconscious influence was even more strongly perhaps in favour of war. How else can we explain that amazing outburst in August 1914, when the daughters of educated men who had been educated thus rushed into hospitals, some still attended by their maids, drove lorries, worked in fields and munition factories, and used all their immense stores of charm, of sympathy, to persuade young men that to fight was heroic, and that the wounded in battle deserved all her care and all her praise? The reason lies in that same education. So profound was her unconscious loathing for the education of the private house with its cruelty, its poverty, its hypocrisy, its immorality, its inanity that she would undertake any task however menial, exercise any fascination however fatal that enabled her to escape. Thus consciously she desired 'our splendid Empire'; unconsciously she desired our splendid war.

So, sir, if you want us to help you to prevent war the conclusion seems to be inevitable; we must help to rebuild the college which, imperfect as it may be, is the only alternative to the education of the private house. We must hope that in time that education may be altered. That guinea must be given before we give you the guinea that you ask for your own society. But it is contributing to the same cause – the prevention of war. Guineas are rare; guineas are valuable; but let us send one without any condition attached to the honorary treasurer of the building fund, because by so doing we are making a positive contribution to the prevention of war.

Now that we have given one guinea towards rebuilding a college we must consider whether there is not more that we can do to help you to prevent war. And it is at once obvious, if what we have said about influence is true, that we must turn to the professions, because if we could persuade those who can earn their livings, and thus actually hold in their hands this new weapon, our only weapon, the weapon of independent opinion based upon independent income, to use that weapon against war, we should do more to help you than by appealing to those who must teach the young to earn their livings; or by lingering, however long, round the forbidden places and sacred gates of the universities where they are thus taught. This, therefore, is a more important question than the other.

Let us then lay your letter asking for help to prevent war, before the independent, the mature, those who are earning their livings in the professions. There is no need of rhetoric; hardly, one would suppose, of argument. 'Here is a man,' one has only to say, 'whom we all have reason to respect; he tells us that war is possible; perhaps probable; he asks us, who can earn our livings, to help him in any way we can to prevent war.' That surely will be enough without pointing to the photographs that are all this time piling up on the table – photographs of more dead bodies, of more ruined houses, to call forth an answer, and an answer that will give you, sir, the very help that you require. But . . . it seems that there is some hesitation, some doubt – not certainly that war is horrible, that war is beastly, that war is insupportable and that war is inhuman, as Wilfred Owen said, or that we wish to do all we can to help you to prevent war. Nevertheless, doubts and hesitations there are; and the quickest way to understand them is to place before you another letter, a letter as genuine as your own, a letter that happens to lie beside it on the table.[35]

It is a letter from another honorary treasurer, and it is again asking for money. 'Will you,' she writes, 'send a subscription to [a society to help the daughters of educated men to obtain employment in the professions] in order to help us to earn our livings? Failing money,' she goes on, 'any gift will be acceptable – books, fruit or cast-off clothing that can be sold in a bazaar.' Now that letter has so much bearing upon the doubts and hesitations referred to above, and upon the help we can give you, that it seems impossible either to send her a guinea or to send you a guinea until we have considered the questions which it raises.

The first question is obviously, Why is she asking for money? Why is she so poor, this representative of professional women, that she must beg for cast-off clothing for a bazaar? That is the first point to clear up, because if

she is as poor as this letter indicates, then the weapon of independent
opinion upon which we have been counting to help you to prevent war is
not, to put it mildly, a very powerful weapon. On the other hand, poverty
has its advantages; for if she is poor, as poor as she pretends to be, then we
can bargain with her, as we bargained with her sister at Cambridge, and
exercise the right of potential givers to impose terms. Let us then question
her about her financial position and certain other facts before we give her a
guinea, or lay down the terms upon which she is to have it. Here is the draft
of such a letter:

Accept a thousand apologies, madam, for keeping you waiting so long
for an answer to your letter. The fact is, certain questions have arisen, to
which we must ask you to reply before we send you a subscription. In
the first place you are asking for money – money with which to pay your
rent. But how can it be, how can it possibly be, my dear madam, that you
are so terribly poor? The professions have been open to the daughters of
educated men for almost twenty years. Therefore, how can it be that
you, whom we take to be their representative, are standing, like your
sister at Cambridge, hat in hand, pleading for money, or failing money,
for fruit, books, or cast-off clothing to sell at a bazaar? How can it be, we
repeat? Surely there must be some very grave defect, of common humanity, of common justice or of common sense. Or can it simply be that
you are pulling a long face and telling a tall story like the beggar at the
street corner who has a stocking full of guineas safely hoarded under her
bed at home? In any case, this perpetual asking for money and pleading
of poverty is laying you open to very grave rebukes, not only from
indolent outsiders who dislike thinking about practical affairs almost as
much as they dislike signing cheques, but from educated men. You are
drawing upon yourselves the censure and contempt of men of established
reputation as philosophers and novelists – of men like Mr Joad and Mr
Wells. Not only do they deny your poverty, but they accuse you of
apathy and indifference. Let me draw your attention to the charges that
they bring against you. Listen, in the first place, to what Mr C. E. M.
Joad has to say of you. He says: 'I doubt whether at any time during the
last fifty years young women have been more politically apathetic, more
socially indifferent than at the present time.' That is how he begins. And
he goes on to say, very rightly, that it is not his business to tell you what
you ought to do; but he adds, very kindly, that he will give you an
example of what you might do. You might imitate your sisters in
America. You might found 'a society for the advertisement of peace'.
He tells us that their society declared – 'I know not with what truth – that
the number of pounds spent by the world on armaments in the current
year was exactly equal to the number of minutes (or was it seconds?)
which had elapsed since the death of Christ, who taught that war is

unchristian . . . ' Now why should not you, too, follow their example and create such a society in England? It would need money, of course; but – and this is the point that I wish particularly to emphasise – there can be no doubt that you have the money. Mr Joad provides the proof. 'Before the war money poured into the coffers of the WSPU in order that women might win the vote which, it was hoped, would enable them to make war a thing of the past. The vote is won,' Mr Joad continues, 'but war is very far from being a thing of the past.' That I can corroborate myself – witness this letter from a gentleman asking for help to prevent war, and there are certain photographs of dead bodies and ruined houses – but let Mr Joad continue. 'Is it unreasonable,' he goes on, 'to ask that contemporary women should be prepared to give as much energy and money, to suffer as much obloquy and insult in the cause of peace, as their mothers gave and suffered in the cause of equality?' And again, I cannot help but echo, is it unreasonable to ask women to go on, from generation to generation, suffering obloquy and insult first from their brothers and then for their brothers? Is it not both perfectly reasonable and on the whole for their physical, moral and spiritual welfare? But let us not interrupt Mr Joad. 'If it is, then the sooner they give up the pretence of playing with public affairs and return to private life the better. If they cannot make a job of the House of Commons, let them at least make something of their own houses. If they cannot learn to save men from the destruction which incurable male mischievousness bids fair to bring upon them, let women at least learn to feed them, before they destroy themselves.'[36] Let us not pause to ask how even with a vote they can cure what Mr Joad himself admits to be incurable, for the point is how, in the face of that statement, you have the effrontery to ask me for a guinea towards your rent? According to Mr Joad you are not only extremely rich; you are also extremely idle; and so given over to the eating of peanuts and ice cream that you have not learnt how to cook him a dinner before he destroys himself, let alone how to prevent that fatal act. But more serious charges are to follow. Your lethargy is such that you will not fight even to protect the freedom which your mothers won for you. That charge is made against you by the most famous of living English novelists – Mr H. G. Wells. Mr H. G. Wells says, 'There has been no perceptible woman's movement to resist the practical obliteration of their freedom by Fascists or Nazis.'[37] Rich, idle, greedy and lethargic as you are, how have you the effrontery to ask me to subscribe to a society which helps the daughters of educated men to make their livings in the professions? For as these gentlemen prove, in spite of the vote and the wealth which that vote must have brought with it, you have not ended war; in spite of the vote and the power which that vote must have brought with it, you have not resisted the practical obliteration of your freedom by Fascists or Nazis. What other conclusion then can one come to but that the whole of what was called 'the woman's movement' has proved itself a failure; and the guinea which I am sending you herewith is to be devoted not to paying your rent but to burning your building. And when that is burnt, retire once more to the kitchen, madam, and learn, if you can, to cook the dinner which you may not share . . . [38]

There, sir, the letter stopped; for on the face at the other side of the letter – the face that a letter-writer always sees – was an expression, of boredom was it, or was it of fatigue? The honorary treasurer's glance seemed to rest upon a little scrap of paper upon which were written two dull little facts which, since they have some bearing upon the question we are discussing, how the daughters of educated men who are earning their livings in the professions can help you to prevent war, may be copied here. The first fact was that the income of the WSPU upon which Mr Joad has based his estimate of their wealth was (in the year 1912 at the height of their activity) £42,000.[39] The second fact was that: 'To earn £250 a year is quite an achievement even for a highly qualified woman with years of experience.'[40] The date of that statement is 1934.

Both facts are interesting; and since both have a direct bearing upon the question before us, let us examine them. To take the first fact first – that is interesting because it shows that one of the greatest political changes of our times was accomplished upon the incredibly minute income of £42,000 a year. 'Incredibly minute' is, of course, a comparative term; it is incredibly minute, that is to say, compared with the income which the Conservative party, or the Liberal party – the parties to which the educated woman's brother belonged – had at their disposal for their political causes. It is considerably less than the income which the Labour party – the party to which the working woman's brother belongs – has at their disposal.[41] It is incredibly minute compared with the sums that a society like the Society for the Abolition of Slavery for example had at its disposal for the abolition of that slavery. It is incredibly minute compared with the sums which the educated man spends annually, not upon political causes, but upon sports and pleasure. But our amazement, whether at the poverty of educated men's daughters or at their economy, is a decidedly unpleasant emotion in this case, for it forces us to suspect that the honorary treasurer is telling the sober truth; she is poor; and it forces us to ask once more how, if £42,000 was all that the daughters of educated men could collect after many years of indefatigable labour for their own cause, they can help you to win yours? How much peace will £42,000 a year buy at the present moment when we are spending £300,000,000 annually upon arms?

But the second fact is the more startling and the more depressing of the two – the fact that now, almost twenty years, that is, after they have been admitted to the money-making professions 'to earn £250 a year is quite an achievement even for a highly qualified woman with years of experience'.

Indeed, that fact, if it is a fact, is so startling and has so much bearing upon the question before us that we must pause for a moment to examine it. It is so important that it must be examined, moreover, by the white light of facts, not by the coloured light of biography. Let us have recourse then to some impersonal and impartial authority who has no more axe to grind or dinner to cook than Cleopatra's Needle – *Whitaker's Almanack*, for example.

Whitaker, needless to say, is not only one of the most dispassionate of authors, but one of the most methodical. There, in his *Almanack* he has collected all the facts about all, or almost all, of the professions that have been opened to the daughters of educated men. In a section called 'Government and Public Offices' he provides us with a plain statement of whom the Government employs professionally, and of what the Government pays those whom it employs. Since Whitaker adopts the alphabetical system, let us follow his lead and examine the first six letters of the alphabet. Under A there are the Admiralty, the Air Ministry and Ministry of Agriculture. Under B there is the British Broadcasting Corporation; under C the Colonial Office and the Charity Commissioners; under D the Dominions Office and Development Commission; under E there are the Ecclesiastical Commissioners and the Board of Education; and so we come to the sixth letter F under which we find the Ministry of Fisheries, the Foreign Office, the Friendly Societies and the Fine Arts. These then are some of the professions which are now, as we are frequently reminded, open to both men and women equally. And the salaries paid to those employed in them come out of public money which is supplied by both sexes equally. And the income tax which supplies those salaries (among other things) now stands at about five shillings in the pound. We have all, therefore, an interest in asking how that money is spent, and upon whom. Let us look at the salary list of the Board of Education, since that is the class to which we both, sir, though in very different degrees, have the honour to belong. The President, Whitaker says, of the Board of Education gets £2,000; his principal Private Secretary gets from £847 to £1,058; his Assistant Private Secretary gets from £277 to £634. Then there is the Permanent Secretary of the Board of Education. He gets £3,000; his Private Secretary gets from £277 to £634. The Parliamentary Secretary gets £1,200; his Private Secretary gets from £277 to £634. The Deputy Secretary gets £2,200. The Permanent Secretary of the Welsh Department gets £1,650. And then there are Principal Assistant Secretaries and Assistant Secretaries, there are Directors of Establishments, Accountants-General, principal Finance Officers, Finance Officers, Legal Advisers, Assistant Legal Advisers – all these ladies and gentlemen, the impeccable and impartial Whitaker informs us, get incomes which run into four figures or over. Now an income which is over or about a thousand a year is a nice round sum when it is paid yearly and paid punctually; but when we consider that the work is a whole-time job and a skilled job we shall not grudge these ladies and gentlemen their salaries, even though our income tax does stand at five shillings in the pound, and our incomes are by no means paid punctually or paid annually. Men and women who spend every day and all day in an office from the age of about 23 to the age of 60 or so deserve every penny they get. Only, the reflection will intrude itself, if these ladies are drawing £1,000, £2,000 and £3,000 a year, not only in the Board of Education but in all the other boards and offices which are now open to them, from the Admiralty at the beginning of the alphabet to the Board of Works at the end, the statement that '£250 is quite an achievement, even for a highly qualified woman with years of experience' must be, to put it plainly, an unmitigated lie. Why, we have only to walk down Whitehall and consider how many boards and offices are housed there; reflect that each is staffed and officered by a flock of secretaries and under-secretaries so many and so nicely graded that their very names make our heads spin; and remember that each has his or her own sufficient salary, to exclaim that the statement is impossible, inexplicable. How can we explain it? Only by putting on a stronger pair of glasses. Let us read down the list, farther and farther and farther down. At last we come to a name to which the prefix 'Miss' is attached. Can it be that all the names on top of hers, all the names to which the big salaries are attached, are the names of gentlemen? It seems so. So then it is not the salaries that are lacking; it is the daughters of educated men.

Now three good reasons for this curious deficiency or disparity lie upon the surface. Dr Robson supplies us with the first – 'The Administrative Class, which occupies all the controlling positions in the Home Civil Service, consists to an overwhelming extent of the fortunate few who can manage to get to Oxford and Cambridge; and the entrance examination has always been expressly designed for that purpose.'[42] The fortunate few in our class, the daughters of educated men class, are very, very few. Oxford and Cambridge, as we have seen, strictly limit the number of educated men's daughters who are allowed to receive a university education. Secondly, many more daughters stay at home to look after old mothers than sons stay at home to look after old fathers. The private house, we must remember, is still a going concern. Hence fewer daughters than sons enter for the Civil Service Examination. In the third place, we may fairly assume that 60 years of examination passing are not so effective as 500. The Civil Service Examination is a stiff one; we may reasonably expect more sons to pass it than daughters. We have nevertheless to explain the curious fact that though a certain number of daughters enter for the examination and pass the examination those to whose names the word 'Miss' is attached do not seem to enter the four-figure zone. The sex distinction seems, according to Whitaker, possessed of a curious leaden quality, liable to keep any name to which it is fastened circling in the lower spheres. Plainly the reason for this may lie not upon the surface, but within. It may be, to speak bluntly, that the daughters are in themselves deficient; that they have proved themselves untrustworthy; unsatisfactory; so lacking in the necessary ability that it is to the public interest to keep them to the lower grades where, if they are paid less, they have less chance of impeding the transaction of public business. This solution would be easy but, unfortunately, it is denied to us. It is denied to us by the Prime Minister himself. Women in the Civil Services are not untrustworthy, Mr Baldwin informed us the other day. 'Many of them,' he said, 'are in positions in the course of their daily work to amass secret information. Secret information has a way of leaking very often, as we politicians know to our cost. I have never known a case of such a leakage being due to a woman, and I have known cases of leakage coming from men who should have known a great deal better.'* So they are not so loose-lipped and fond of gossip as the tradition would have it? A useful contribution in its way to psychology and a hint to novelists; but still there may be other objections to women's employment as civil servants.

Intellectually, they may not be so able as their brothers. But here again the Prime Minister will not help us out. 'He was not prepared to say that any conclusion had been formed – or was even necessary – whether women were as good as, or better than, men, but he believed that women had worked in the Civil Service to their own content, and certainly to the complete satisfaction of everybody who had anything to do with them.' Finally, as if to cap what must necessarily be an inconclusive statement by expressing a personal opinion which might rightly be more positive, he said, 'I should like to pay my personal tribute to the industry, capacity, ability and loyalty of the women I have come across in Civil Service positions.' And he went on to express the hope that businessmen would make more use of those very valuable qualities.[43]

Now if anyone is in a position to know the facts it is the Prime Minister; and if anyone is able to speak the truth about them it is the same gentleman. Yet Mr Baldwin says one thing; Mr Whitaker says another. If Mr Baldwin is well informed, so is Mr Whitaker. Nevertheless, they contradict each other. The issue is joined; Mr Baldwin says that women are first-class civil servants; Mr Whitaker says that they are third-class civil servants. It is, in short, a case of *Baldwin v. Whitaker*, and since it is a very important case, for upon it depends the answer to many questions which puzzle us, not only about the poverty of educated men's daughters but about the psychology of educated men's sons, let us try the case of the *Prime Minister v. the Almanack*.

For such a trial you, sir, have definite qualifications; as a barrister you have first-hand knowledge of one profession, and as an educated man second-hand knowledge of many more. And if it is true that the daughters of educated men who are of Mary Kingsley's persuasion have no direct knowledge, still through fathers and uncles, cousins and brothers they may claim some

* Since these words were written Mr Baldwin has ceased to be prime minister and become an earl.

indirect knowledge of professional life – it is a photograph that they have often looked upon – and this indirect knowledge they can improve, if they have a mind, by peeping through doors, taking notes, and asking questions discreetly. If, then, we pool our first-hand, second-hand, direct and indirect knowledge of the professions with a view to trying the important case of *Baldwin v. Whitaker* we shall agree at the outset that professions are very queer things. It by no means follows that a clever man gets to the top or that a stupid man stays at the bottom. This rising and falling is by no means a cut-and-dried clear-cut rational process, we shall both agree. After all, as we both have reason to know, Judges are fathers; and Permanent Secretaries have sons. Judges require marshals; Permanent Secretaries, private secretaries. What is more natural than that a nephew should be a marshal or the son of an old school friend a private secretary? To have such perquisites in their gift is as much the due of the public servant as a cigar now and then or a cast-off dress here and there are perquisites of the private servant. But the giving of such perquisites, the exercise of such influence, queers the professions. Success is easier for some, harder for others, however equal the brain power may be, so that some rise unexpectedly; some fall unexpectedly; some remain strangely stationary; with the result that the professions are queered. Often indeed it is to the public advantage that they should be queered. Since nobody, from the Master of Trinity downwards (bating, presumably, a few headmistresses), believes in the infallibility of examiners, a certain degree of elasticity is to the public advantage; since the impersonal is fallible, it is well that it should be supplemented by the personal. Happily for us all, therefore, we may conclude, a board is not made literally of oak, nor a division of iron. Both boards and divisions transmit human sympathies and reflect human antipathies, with the result that the imperfections of the examination system are rectified; the public interest is served; and the ties of blood and friendship are recognised. Thus it is quite possible that the name 'Miss' transmits through the board or division some vibration which is not registered in the examination room. 'Miss' transmits sex; and sex may carry with it an aroma. 'Miss' may carry with it the swish of petticoats, the savour of scent or other odour perceptible to the nose on the farther side of the partition and obnoxious to it. What charms and consoles in the private house may distract and exacerbate in the public office. The Archbishops' Commission assures us that this is so in the pulpit.[44] Whitehall may be equally susceptible. At any rate since Miss is a woman, Miss was not educated at Eton or Christ Church. Since Miss is a woman, Miss is not a son or a nephew. We are hazarding our way among imponderables. We can scarcely proceed too much on tiptoe. We are trying, remember, to discover what flavour attaches itself to sex in a public office; we are sniffing most delicately not facts but savours. And therefore it would be well not to depend on our own private noses, but to call in evidence from outside. Let us turn to the public press and see if we can discover from the opinions aired there any hint that will guide us in our attempt to decide the delicate and difficult question as to the aroma, the atmosphere that surrounds the word 'Miss' in Whitehall. We will consult the newspapers.

First:

I think your correspondent . . . correctly sums up this discussion in the observation that woman has too much liberty. It is probable that this so-called liberty came with the war, when women assumed responsibilities so far unknown to them. They did splendid service during those days. Unfortunately, they were praised and petted out of all proportion to the value of their performances.[45]

That does very well for a beginning. But let us proceed:

I am of the opinion that a considerable amount of the distress which is prevalent in this section of the community [the clerical] could be relieved by the policy of employing men instead of women, wherever possible. There are today in Government offices, post offices, insurance companies, banks and other offices, thousands of women doing work which men could do. At the same time there are thousands of qualified men, young and middle-aged, who cannot get a job of any sort. There is a large demand for woman labour in the domestic arts, and in the process of regrading a large number of women who have drifted into clerical service would become available for domestic service.[46]

The odour thickens, you will agree.
Then once more:

I am certain I voice the opinion of thousands of young men when I say that if men were doing the work that thousands of young women are now doing the men would be able to keep those same women in decent homes. Homes are the real places of the women who are now compelling men to be idle. It is time the Government insisted upon employers giving work to more men, thus enabling them to marry the women they cannot now approach.[47]

There! There can be no doubt of the odour now. The cat is out of the bag; and it is a Tom.

After considering the evidence contained in those three quotations, you will agree that there is good reason to think that the word 'Miss', however delicious its scent in the private house, has a certain odour attached to it in Whitehall which is disagreeable to the noses on the other side of the partition; and that it is likely that a name to which 'Miss' is attached will, because of this odour, circle in the lower spheres where the salaries are small rather than mount to the higher spheres where the salaries are substantial. As for 'Mrs', it is a contaminated word; an obscene word. The less said about that word the better. Such is the smell of it, so rank does it stink in the nostrils of Whitehall, that Whitehall excludes it entirely. In Whitehall as in heaven, there is neither marrying nor giving in marriage.[48]

Odour then – or shall we call it 'atmosphere'? – is a very important element in professional life, in spite of the fact that like other important elements it is impalpable. It can escape the noses of examiners in examination rooms, yet penetrate boards and divisions and affect the senses of those within. Its bearing upon the case before us is undeniable. For it allows us to decide in the case of *Baldwin v. Whitaker* that both the Prime Minister and the *Almanack* are telling the truth. It is true that women civil servants deserve to be paid as much as men; but it is also true that they are not paid as much as men. The discrepancy is due to atmosphere.

Atmosphere plainly is a very mighty power. Atmosphere not only changes the sizes and shapes of things; it affects solid bodies, like salaries, which might have been thought impervious to atmosphere. An epic poem might be written about atmosphere, or a novel in ten or fifteen volumes. But since this is only a letter, and you are pressed for time, let us confine ourselves to the plain statement that atmosphere is one of the most powerful, partly because it is one of the most impalpable, of the enemies with which the daughters of educated men have to fight. If you think that statement exaggerated, look once more at the samples of atmosphere contained in those three quotations. We shall find there not only the reason why the pay of the professional woman is still so small, but something more dangerous, something which, if it spreads, may poison both sexes equally. There, in those quotations, is the egg of the very same worm that we know under other names in other countries. There we have in embryo the creature, Dictator as we call him when he is Italian or German, who believes that he has the right, whether given by God, nature, sex or race is immaterial, to dictate to other human beings how they shall live; what they shall do. Let us quote again: 'Homes are the real places of the women who are now compelling men to be idle. It is time the Government insisted upon employers giving work to more men, thus enabling them to marry the women they cannot now approach.' Place beside it another quotation: 'There are two worlds in the life of the nation, the world of men and the world of women. Nature has done well to entrust the man with the care of his family and the nation. The woman's world is her family, her husband, her children and her home.' One is written in English, the other in German. But where is the difference? Are they not both saying the same thing? Are they not both the voices of Dictators, whether they speak English or German, and are we not all agreed that the dictator when we meet him abroad is a very dangerous as well as a very ugly animal? And he is here among us, raising his ugly head, spitting his poison, small still, curled up like a caterpillar on a leaf, but in the heart of England. Is it not from this egg, to quote Mr Wells again, that 'the practical obliteration of [our] freedom by Fascists or Nazis' will spring? And is not the woman who has to breathe that poison and to fight that insect, secretly and without arms, in her office, fighting the Fascist or the Nazi as surely as those who fight him with arms in the limelight of publicity? And must not that fight wear down her strength and exhaust her spirit? Should we not help her to crush him in our own country before we ask her to help us to crush him abroad? And what right have we, sir, to trumpet our ideals of freedom and justice to other countries when we can shake out from our most respectable newspapers any day of the week eggs like these?

Here, rightly, you will check what has all the symptoms of becoming a peroration by pointing out that though the opinions expressed in these letters are not altogether agreeable to our national self-esteem they are the natural expression of fear and a jealousy which we must understand before we condemn them. It is true, you will say, that these gentlemen seem a little unduly concerned with their own salaries and their own security, but that is comprehensible, given the traditions of their sex, and even compatible with a genuine love of freedom and a genuine hatred of dictatorship. For these gentlemen are, or wish to become, husbands and fathers, and in that case the support of the family will depend upon them. In other words, sir, I take you to mean that the world as it is at present is divided into two services: one the public and the other the private. In one world the sons of educated men work as civil servants, judges, soldiers and are paid for that work; in the other world, the daughters of educated men work as wives, mothers, daughters – but are they not paid for that work? Is the work of a mother, of a wife, of a daughter, worth nothing to the nation in solid cash? That fact, if it be a fact, is so astonishing that we must confirm it by appealing once more to the impeccable Whitaker. Let us turn to his pages again. We may turn them, and turn them again. It seems incredible, yet it seems undeniable. Among all those offices there is no such office as a mother's; among all those salaries there is no such salary as a mother's. The work of an archbishop is worth £15,000 a year to the state; the work of a judge is worth £5,000 a year; the work of a permanent secretary is worth £3,000 a year; the work of an army captain, of a sea captain, of a sergeant of dragoons, of a policeman, of a postman – all these works are worth paying out of the taxes, but wives and mothers and daughters who work all day and every day, without whose work the state would collapse and fall to pieces, without whose work your sons, sir, would cease to exist, are paid nothing whatever. Can it be possible? Or have we convicted Whitaker, the impeccable, of errata?

Ah, you will interpose, here is another misunderstanding. Husband and wife are not only one flesh; they are also one purse. The wife's salary is half the husband's income. The man is paid more than the woman for that very reason – because he has a wife to support. The bachelor then is paid at the same rate as the unmarried woman? It appears not – another queer effect of atmosphere, no doubt; but let it pass. Your statement that the wife's salary is half the husband's income seems to be an equitable arrangement, and no doubt, since it is equitable, it is confirmed by law. Your reply that the law leaves these private matters to be decided privately is less satisfactory, for it means that the wife's half-share of the common income is not paid legally into her hands, but into her husband's. But still a spiritual right may be as binding as a legal right; and if the wife of an educated man has a spiritual right to half her husband's income, then we may assume that the wife of an educated man has as much money to spend, once the common household bills are met, upon any cause that appeals to her as her husband. Now her husband, witness Whitaker, witness the wills in the daily paper, is often not merely well paid by his profession, but is master of a very considerable capital sum. Therefore this lady who asserts that £250 a year is all that a woman can earn today in the professions is evading the question; for the profession of marriage in the educated class is a highly paid one, since she has a right, a spiritual right, to half her husband's salary. The puzzle deepens; the mystery thickens. For if the wives of rich men are themselves rich women, how does it come about that the income of the WSPU was only £42,000 a year; how does it come about that the honorary treasurer of the college rebuilding fund is still asking for £100,000; how does it come about that the treasurer of a society for helping professional women to obtain employment is asking not merely for money to pay her rent but will be grateful for books, fruit or cast-off clothing? It stands to reason that if the wife has a spiritual right to half her husband's income because her own work as his wife is unpaid, then she must have as much money to spend upon such causes as appeal to her as he has. And since those causes are standing hat in hand a-begging we are forced to conclude that they are causes that do not take the fancy of the educated man's wife. The charge against her is a very serious one. For consider – there is the money – that surplus fund that can be devoted to education, to pleasure, to philanthropy when the household dues are met; she can spend her share as freely as her husband can spend his. She can spend it upon whatever causes she likes; and yet she will not spend it upon the causes that are dear to her own sex. There they are, hat in hand a-begging. That is a terrible charge to bring against her.

But let us pause for a moment before we decide that charge against her. Let us ask what are the causes, the pleasures, the philanthropies upon which the educated man's wife does in fact spend her share of the common surplus fund. And here we are confronted with facts which, whether we like them or not, we must face. The fact is that the tastes of the married woman in our class are markedly virile. She spends vast sums annually upon party funds; upon sport; upon grouse moors; upon cricket and football. She lavishes money upon clubs – Brooks', White's, the Travellers', the Reform, the Athenaeum – to mention only the most prominent. Her expenditure upon these causes, pleasures and philanthropies must run into many millions every year. And yet by far the greater part of this sum is spent upon pleasures which she does not share. She lays out thousands and thousands of pounds upon clubs to which her own sex is not admitted;[49] upon racecourses where she may not ride; upon colleges from which her own sex is excluded. She pays a huge bill annually for wine which she does not drink and for cigars which she does not smoke. In short, there are only two conclusions to which we can come about the educated man's wife – the first is that she is the most altruistic of beings who prefers to spend her share of the common fund upon his pleasures and causes; the second, and more probable, if less creditable, is not that she is the most altruistic of beings, but that her spiritual right to a share of half her husband's income peters out in practice to an actual right to board, lodging and a small annual allowance for pocket money and dress. Either of these conclusions is possible; the evidence of public institutions and subscription lists puts any other out of the question. For consider how nobly the educated man supports his old school, his old college; how splendidly he subscribes to party funds; how munificently he contributes to all those institutions and sports by which he and his sons educate their minds and develop their bodies – the daily papers bear daily witness to those indisputable facts. But the absence of her name from subscription lists, and the poverty of the institutions which educate her mind and her body seem to prove that there is something in the atmosphere of the private house which deflects the wife's spiritual share of the common income impalpably but irresistibly towards those causes which her husband approves and those pleasures which he enjoys. Whether creditable or discreditable, that is the fact. And that is the reason why those other causes stand a-begging.

With Whitaker's facts and the facts of the subscription lists before us, we seem to have arrived at three facts which are indisputable and must have great influence upon our inquiry how we can help you to prevent war. The first is that the daughters of educated men are paid very little from the public funds for their public services; the second is that they are paid nothing at all from the public funds for their private services; and the third is that their share of the husband's income is not a flesh-and-blood share but a spiritual or nominal share, which means that when both are clothed and fed the surplus fund that can be devoted to causes, pleasures or philanthropies gravitates mysteriously but indisputably towards those causes, pleasures and philanthropies which the husband enjoys, and of which the husband approves. It seems that the person to whom the salary is actually paid is the person who has the actual right to decide how that salary shall be spent.

These facts then bring us back in a chastened mood and with rather altered views to our starting point. For we were going, you may remember, to lay your appeal for help in the prevention of war before the women who earn their livings in the professions. It is to them, we said, to whom we must appeal, because it is they who have our new weapon, the influence of an independent opinion based upon an independent income, in their possession. But the facts once more are depressing. They make it clear in the first place that we must rule out, as possible helpers, that large group to whom marriage is a profession, because it is an unpaid profession, and because the spiritual share of half the husband's salary is not, facts seem to show, an actual share. Therefore, her disinterested influence founded upon an independent income is nil. If he is in favour of force, she too will be in favour of force. In the second place, facts seem to prove that the statement, 'To earn £250 a year is quite an achievement even for a highly qualified woman with years of experience,' is not an unmitigated lie but a highly probable truth. Therefore, the influence which the daughters of educated men have at present from their money-earning power cannot be rated very highly. Yet since it has become more than ever obvious that it is to them that we must look for help, for they alone can help us, it is to them that we must appeal. This conclusion then brings us back to the letter from which we quoted above – the honorary treasurer's letter, the letter asking for a subscription to the society for helping the daughters of educated men to obtain employment in the professions. You will agree, sir, that we have strong selfish motives for helping her – there can be no doubt about that. For to help women to earn their livings in the professions is to help them to possess that weapon of independent opinion which is still their most powerful weapon. It is to help them to have a mind of their own and a will of their own with which to help you to prevent war. But . . . – here again, in those dots, doubts and hesitations assert themselves – can we, considering the facts given above, send her our guinea without laying down very stringent terms as to how that guinea shall be spent?

For the facts which we have discovered in checking her statement as to her financial position have raised questions which make us wonder whether we are wise to encourage people to enter the professions if we wish to prevent war. You will remember that we are using our psychological insight (for that is our only qualification) to decide what kind of qualities in human nature are likely to lead to war. And the facts disclosed above are of a kind to make us ask, before we write our cheque, whether if we encourage the daughters of educated men to enter the professions we shall not be encouraging the very qualities that we wish to prevent? Shall we not be doing our guinea's worth to ensure that in two or three centuries not only the educated men in the professions but the educated women in the professions will be asking – oh, of whom? as the poet says – the very question that you are asking us now: How can we prevent war? If we encourage the daughters to enter the professions without making any conditions as to the way in which the professions are to be practised shall we not be doing our best to stereotype the old tune which human nature, like a gramophone whose needle has stuck, is now grinding out with such disastrous unanimity? 'Here we go round the mulberry tree, the mulberry tree, the mulberry tree. Give it all to me, give it all to me, all to me. Three hundred millions spent upon war.' With that song, or something like it, ringing in our ears we cannot send our guinea to the honorary treasurer without warning her that she shall only have it on condition that she shall swear that the professions in future shall be practised so that they shall lead to a different song and a different conclusion. She shall only have it if she can satisfy us that our guinea shall be spent in the cause of peace. It is difficult to formulate such conditions; in our present psychological ignorance perhaps impossible. But the matter is so serious, war is so insupportable, so horrible, so inhuman, that an attempt must be made. Here then is another letter to the same lady.

Your letter, madam, has waited a long time for an answer, but we have been examining into certain charges made against you and making certain enquiries. We have acquitted you, madam, you will be relieved to learn, of telling lies. It would seem to be true that you are poor. We have acquitted you further, of idleness, apathy and greed. The number of causes that you are championing, however secretly and ineffectively, is in your favour. If you prefer ice creams and peanuts to roast beef and beer the reason would seem to be economic rather than gustatory. It would seem probable that you have not much money to spend upon food or much leisure to spend upon eating it in view of the circulars and leaflets you issue, the meetings you arrange, the bazaars you organise. Indeed, you would appear to be working, without a salary too, rather longer hours than the Home Office would approve. But though we are willing to deplore your poverty and to commend your industry we are not going to send you a guinea to help you to help women to enter the professions unless you can assure us that they will practise those professions in such a way as to prevent war. That, you will say, is a vague statement, an impossible condition. Still, since guineas are rare and guineas are valuable you will listen to the terms we wish to impose if, you intimate, they can be stated briefly. Well then, madam, since you are pressed for time, what with the Pensions Bill, what with shepherding the peers into the House of Lords so that they may vote on it as instructed by you, what with reading Hansard and the newspapers – though that should not take much time; you will find no mention of your activities there;[50] a conspiracy of silence seems to be the rule; what with plotting still for equal pay for equal work in the Civil Service, while at the same time you are arranging hares and old coffee-pots so as to seduce people into paying more for them than they are strictly worth at a bazaar – since, in one word, it is obvious that you are busy, let us be quick; make a rapid survey; discuss a few passages in the books in your library; in the papers on your table, and then see if we can make the statement less vague, the conditions more clear.

Let us then begin by looking at the outside of things, at the general aspect. Things have outsides let us remember as well as insides. Close at hand is a bridge over the Thames, an admirable vantage ground for such a survey. The river flows beneath; barges pass, laden with timber, bursting with corn; there on one side are the domes and spires of the city; on the other, Westminster and the Houses of Parliament. It is a place to stand on by the hour, dreaming. But not now. Now we are pressed for time. Now we are here to consider facts; now we must fix our eyes upon the procession – the procession of the sons of educated men.

There they go, our brothers who have been educated at public schools and universities, mounting those steps, passing in and out of those doors, ascending those pulpits, preaching, teaching, administering justice, practising medicine, transacting business, making money. It is a solemn sight always – a procession, like a caravanserai crossing a desert. Great-grandfathers, grandfathers, fathers, uncles – they all went that way, wearing their gowns, wearing their wigs, some with ribbons across their breasts, others without. One was a bishop. Another a judge. One was an admiral. Another a general. One was a professor. Another a doctor. And some left the procession and were last heard of doing nothing in Tasmania; were seen, rather shabbily dressed, selling newspapers at Charing Cross. But most of them kept in step, walked according to rule, and by hook or by crook made enough to keep the family house, somewhere, roughly speaking, in the West End, supplied with beef and mutton for all, and with education for Arthur. It is a solemn sight, this procession, a sight that has often caused us, you may remember, looking at it sidelong from an upper window, to ask ourselves certain questions. But now, for the past twenty years or so, it is no longer a sight merely, a photograph, or fresco scrawled upon the walls of time, at which we can look with merely an aesthetic appreciation. For there, trapesing along at the tail end of the procession, we go ourselves. And that makes a difference. We who have looked so long at the pageant in books, or from a curtained window watched educated men leaving the house at about nine-thirty to go to an office, returning to the house at about six-thirty from an office, need look passively no longer. We too can leave the house, can mount those steps, pass in and out of those doors, wear wigs and gowns, make money, administer justice. Think – one of these days, you may wear a judge's wig on your head, an ermine cape on your shoulders; sit under the lion and the unicorn; draw a salary of five thousand a year with a pension on retiring. We who now agitate these humble pens may in another century or two speak from a pulpit. Nobody will dare contradict us then; we shall be the mouthpieces of the divine spirit – a solemn thought, is it not? Who can say whether, as time goes on, we may not dress in military uniform, with gold lace on our breasts, swords at our sides, and something like the old family coal-scuttle on our heads, save that that venerable object was never decorated with plumes of white horsehair. You laugh – indeed the shadow of the private house still makes those dresses look a little queer. We have worn private clothes so long – the veil that St Paul recommended. But we have not come here to laugh, or to talk of fashions – men's and women's. We are here, on the bridge, to ask ourselves certain questions. And they are very important questions; and we have very little time in which to answer them. The questions that we have to ask and to answer about that procession during this moment of transition are so important that they may well change the lives of all men and women for ever. For we have to ask ourselves, here and now, do we wish to join that procession, or don't we? On what terms shall we join that procession? Above all, where is it leading us, the procession of educated men? The moment is short: it may last five years, ten years, or perhaps only a matter of a few months longer. But the questions must be answered; and they are so important that if all the daughters of educated men did nothing, from morning to night, but consider that procession from every angle, if they did nothing but ponder it and analyse it, and think about it and read about it and pool their thinking and reading, and what they see and what they guess, their time would be better spent than in any other activity now open to them. But, you will object, you have no time to think; you have your battles to fight, your rent to pay, your bazaars to organise. That excuse shall not serve you, madam. As you know from your own experience, and there are facts that prove it, the daughters of educated men have always done their thinking from hand to mouth; not under green lamps at study tables in the cloisters of secluded colleges. They have thought while they stirred the pot, while they rocked the cradle. It was thus that they won us the right to our brand-new sixpence. It falls to us now to go on thinking; how are we to spend that sixpence? Think we must. Let us think in offices; in omnibuses; while we are standing in the crowd watching Coronations and Lord Mayor's Shows; let us think as we pass the Cenotaph; and in Whitehall; in the gallery of the House of Commons; in the Law Courts; let us think at baptisms and marriages and funerals. Let us never cease from thinking – what is this 'civilisation' in which we find ourselves? What are these ceremonies and why should we take part in them? What are these professions and why should we make money out of them? Where in short is it leading us, the procession of the sons of educated men?

But you are busy; let us return to facts. Come indoors then, and open the books on your library shelves. For you have a library, and a good one. A working library, a living library; a library where nothing is chained down and nothing is locked up; a library where the songs of the singers rise naturally from the lives of the livers. There are the poems, here the biographies. And what light do they throw upon the professions, these biographies? How far do they encourage us to think that if we help the daughters to become professional women we shall discourage war? The answer to that question is scattered all about these volumes; and is legible to anyone who can read plain English. And the answer, one must admit, is extremely queer. For almost every biography we read of professional men in the nineteenth century, to limit ourselves to that not distant and fully documented age, is largely concerned with war. They were great fighters, it seems, the professional men in the age of Queen Victoria. There was the battle of Westminster. There was the battle of the universities. There was the battle of Whitehall. There was the battle of Harley Street. There was the battle of the Royal Academy. Some of these battles, as you can testify, are still in progress. In fact the only profession which does not seem to have fought a fierce battle during the nineteenth century is the profession of literature. All the other professions, according to the testimony of biography, seem to be as bloodthirsty as the profession of arms itself. It is true that the combatants did not inflict flesh wounds;[51] chivalry forbade; but you will agree that a battle that wastes time is as deadly as a battle that wastes blood. You will agree that a battle that costs money is as deadly as a battle that costs a leg or an arm. You will agree that a battle that forces youth to spend its strength haggling in committee rooms, soliciting favours, assuming a mask of reverence to cloak its ridicule, inflicts wounds upon the human spirit which no surgery can heal. Even the battle of equal pay for equal work is not without its timeshed, its spiritshed, as you yourself, were you not unaccountably reticent on certain matters, might agree. Now the books in your library record so many of these battles that it is impossible to go into them all; but as they all seem to have been fought on much the same plan, and by the same combatants, that is by professional men v. their sisters and daughters, let us, since time presses, glance at one of these campaigns only and examine the battle of Harley Street, in order that we may understand what effect the professions have upon those who practise them.

The campaign was opened in the year 1869 under the leadership of Sophia Jex-Blake. Her case is so typical an instance of the great Victorian fight between the victims of the patriarchal system and the patriarchs, of the daughters against the fathers, that it deserves a moment's examination. Sophia's father was an admirable specimen of the Victorian educated man, kindly, cultivated and well-to-do. He was a proctor of Doctors' Commons. He could afford to keep six servants, horses and carriages, and could provide his daughter not only with food and lodging but with 'handsome furniture' and 'a cosy fire' in her bedroom. For salary, 'for dress and private money', he gave her £40 a year. For some reason she found this sum insufficient. In 1859, in view of the fact that she had only nine shillings and ninepence left to last her till next quarter, she wished to earn money herself. And she was offered a tutorship with the pay of five shillings an hour. She told her father of the offer. He replied, 'Dearest, I have only this moment heard that you contemplate being *paid* for the tutorship. It would be quite beneath you, darling, and *I cannot consent to it.*' She argued: 'Why should I not take it? You as a man did your work and received your payment, and no one thought it any degradation, but a fair exchange . . . Tom is doing on a large scale what I am doing on a small one.' He replied: 'The cases you cite, darling, are not to the point . . . T. W . . . feels bound as a *man* . . . to support his wife and family, and his position is a high one, which can only be filled by a first-class man of character, and yielding him nearer two than one thousand a year . . . How entirely different is my darling's case! You want for nothing, and know that (humanly speaking) you will want for nothing. If you married tomorrow – to my liking – and I don't believe you would ever marry otherwise – I should give you a good fortune.' Upon which her comment, in a private diary, was: 'Like a fool I have consented to give up the fees for this term only – though I am miserably poor. It was foolish. It only defers the struggle.'[52]

There she was right. The struggle with her own father was over. But the struggle with fathers in general, with the patriarchy itself, was deferred to another place and another time. The second fight was at Edinburgh in 1869. She had applied for admission to the Royal College of Surgeons. Here is a newspaper account of the first skirmish. 'A disturbance of a very unbecoming nature took place yesterday afternoon in front of the Royal College of Surgeons . . . Shortly before four o'clock . . . nearly 200 students assembled in front of the gate leading to the building . . . ' the medical students howled and sang songs. 'The gate was closed in their [the women's] faces . . . Dr Handyside found it utterly impossible to begin his demonstration . . . a pet sheep was introduced into the room . . . ' and so on. The methods were much the same as those that were employed at Cambridge during the battle of the Degree. And again, as on that occasion, the authorities deplored those downright methods and employed others, more astute and more effective, of their own. Nothing would induce the authorities encamped within the sacred gates to allow the women to enter. They said that God was on their side, Nature was on their side, Law was on their side and Property was on their side. The college was founded for the benefit of men only; men only were entitled by law to benefit from its endowments. The usual committees were formed. The usual petitions were signed. The humble appeals were made. The usual bazaars were held. The usual questions of tactics were debated. As usual it was asked, ought we to attack now, or is it wiser to wait? Who are our friends and who are our enemies? There were the usual differences of opinion, the usual divisions among the counsellors. But why particularise? The whole proceeding is so familiar that the battle of Harley Street in the year 1869 might well be the battle of Cambridge University at the present moment. On both occasions there is the same waste of strength, waste of temper, waste of time, and waste of money. Almost the same daughters ask almost the same brothers for almost the same privileges. Almost the same gentlemen intone the same refusals for almost the same reasons. It seems as if there were no progress in the human race, but only repetition. We can almost hear them if we listen singing the same old song, 'Here we go round the mulberry tree, the mulberry tree, the mulberry tree', and if we add, 'of property, of property, of property', we shall fill in the rhyme without doing violence to the facts.

But we are not here to sing old songs or to fill in missing rhymes. We are here to consider facts. And the facts which we have just extracted from biography seem to prove that the professions have a certain undeniable effect upon the professors. They make the people who practise them possessive, jealous of any infringement of their rights and highly combative if anyone dares dispute them. Are we not right then in thinking that if we enter the same professions we shall acquire the same qualities? And do not such qualities lead to war? In another century or so if we practise the professions in the same way, shall we not be just as possessive, just as jealous, just as pugnacious, just as positive as to the verdict of God, Nature, Law and Property as these gentlemen are now? Therefore this guinea, which is to help you to help women to enter the professions, has this condition as a first condition attached to it. You shall swear that you will do all in your power to insist that any woman who enters any profession shall in no way hinder any other human being, whether man or woman, white or black, provided that he or she is qualified to enter that profession, from entering it; but shall do all in her power to help them.

You are ready to put your hand to that, here and now, you say, and at the same time stretch out that hand for the guinea. But wait. Other conditions are attached to it before it is yours. For consider once more the procession of the sons of educated men; ask yourself once more, where is it leading us? One answer suggests itself instantly. To incomes, it is obvious, that seem, to us at least, extremely handsome. Whitaker puts that beyond a doubt. And besides the evidence of Whitaker, there is the evidence of the daily paper – the evidence of the wills, of the subscription lists that we have considered already. In one issue of one paper, for example, it is stated that three educated men died: and one left £1,193,251; another £1,010,288; another £1,404,132. These are large sums for private people to amass, you will admit. And why should we not amass them too in course of time? Now that the Civil Service is open to us we may well earn from one thousand to three thousand a year; now that the Bar is open to us we may well earn five thousand a year as judges, and any sum up to forty or fifty thousand a year as barristers. When the Church is open to us we may draw salaries of fifteen thousand, five thousand, three thousand yearly, with palaces and deaneries attached. When the Stock Exchange is open to us we may die worth as many millions as Pierpont Morgan, or as Rockefeller himself. As doctors we may make anything from two thousand to fifty thousand a year. As editors even we may earn salaries that are by no means despicable. One has a thousand a year; another two thousand; it is rumoured that the editor of a great daily paper has a salary of five thousand yearly. All this wealth may in the course of time come our way if we follow the professions. In short, we may change our position from being the victims of the patriarchal system, paid on the truck system, with £30 or £40 a year in cash and board and lodging thrown in, to being the champions of the capitalist system, with a yearly income in our own possession of many thousands which, by judicious investment, may leave us when we die possessed of a capital sum of more millions than we can count.

It is a thought not without its glamour. Consider what it would mean if among us there were now a woman motor-car manufacturer who, with a stroke of the pen, could endow the women's colleges with two or three hundred thousand pounds apiece. The honorary treasurer of the rebuilding fund, your sister at Cambridge, would have her labours considerably lightened then. There would be no need of appeals and committees, of strawberries and cream and bazaars. And suppose that there were not merely one rich woman, but that rich women were as common as rich men. What could you not do? You could shut up your office at once. You could finance a woman's party in the House of Commons. You could run a daily newspaper committed to a conspiracy, not of silence, but of speech. You could get pensions for spinsters, those victims of the patriarchal system whose allowance is insufficient and whose board and lodging are no longer thrown in. You could get equal pay for equal work. You could provide every mother with chloroform when her child is born;[53] bring down the maternal death-rate from four in every thousand to none at all, perhaps. In one session you could pass Bills that will now take you perhaps a hundred years of hard and continuous labour to get through the House of Commons. There seems at first sight nothing that you could not do, if you had the same capital at your disposal that your brothers have at theirs. Why not, then, you exclaim, help us to take the first step towards possessing it? The professions are the only way in which we can earn money. Money is the only means by which we can achieve objects that are immensely desirable. Yet here you are, you seem to protest, haggling and bargaining over conditions. But consider this letter from a professional man asking us to help him to prevent war. Look also at the photographs of dead bodies and ruined houses that the Spanish Government sends almost weekly. That is why it is necessary to haggle and to bargain over conditions.

For the evidence of the letter and of the photographs when combined with the facts with which history and biography provide us about the professions seem together to throw a certain light, a red light, shall we say, upon those same professions. You make money in them; that is true; but how far is money in view of those facts in itself a desirable possession? A great authority upon human life, you will remember, held over two thousand years ago that great possessions were undesirable. To which you reply, and with some heat as if you suspected another excuse for keeping

the purse-string tied, that Christ's words about the rich and the Kingdom
of Heaven are no longer helpful to those who have to face different facts
in a different world. You argue that as things are now in England extreme
poverty is less desirable than extreme wealth. The poverty of the Christian
who should give away all his possessions produces, as we have daily and
abundant proof, the crippled in body, the feeble in mind. The unemployed,
to take the obvious example, are not a source of spiritual or intellectual
wealth to their country. These are weighty arguments; but consider for a
moment the life of Pierpont Morgan. Do you not agree with that evidence
before us that extreme wealth is equally undesirable, and for the same
reasons? If extreme wealth is undesirable and extreme poverty is undesirable, it is arguable that there is some mean between the two which is
desirable. What then is that mean – how much money is needed to live
upon in England today? How should that money be spent? What is the
kind of life, the kind of human being, you propose to aim at if you succeed
in extracting this guinea? Those, madam, are the questions that I am
asking you to consider and you cannot deny that those are questions of
the utmost importance. But alas, they are questions that would lead us far
beyond the solid world of actual fact to which we are here confined. So let
us shut the New Testament, Shakespeare, Shelley, Tolstoy and the rest,
and face the fact that stares us in the face at this moment of transition –
the fact of the procession; the fact that we are trapesing along somewhere
in the rear and must consider that fact before we can fix our eyes upon the
vision on the horizon.

There it is then, before our eyes, the procession of the sons of educated men, ascending those pulpits, mounting those steps, passing in and
out of those doors, preaching, teaching, administering justice, practising
medicine, making money. And it is obvious that if you are going to make
the same incomes from the same professions that those men make you will
have to accept the same conditions that they accept. Even from an upper
window and from books we know or can guess what those conditions are.
You will have to leave the house at nine and come back to it at six. That
leaves very little time for fathers to know their children. You will have to
do this daily from the age of twenty-one or so to the age of about sixty-
five. That leaves very little time for friendship, travel or art. You will
have to perform some duties that are very arduous, others that are very
barbarous. You will have to wear certain uniforms and profess certain
loyalties. If you succeed in your profession the words 'For God and
Empire' will very likely be written, like the address on a dog-collar, round
your neck.54 And if words have meaning, as words perhaps should have
meaning, you will have to accept that meaning and do what you can to
enforce it. In short, you will have to lead the same lives and profess the
same loyalties that professional men have professed for many centuries.
There can be no doubt of that.

If you retaliate, what harm is there in that? Why should we hesitate to do what our fathers and grandfathers have done before us? Let us go into greater detail and consult the facts which are nowadays open to the inspection of all who can read their mother tongue in biography. There they are, those innumerable and invaluable works upon the shelves of your own library. Let us glance again rapidly at the lives of professional men who have succeeded in their professions. Here is an extract from the life of a great lawyer: 'He went to his chambers about half-past nine . . . He took briefs home with him . . . so that he was lucky if he got to bed about one or two o'clock in the morning.'[55] That explains why most successful barristers are hardly worth sitting next to at dinner – they yawn so. Next, here is a quotation from a famous politician's speech: ' . . . since 1914 I have never seen the pageant of the blossom from the first damson to the last apple – never once have I seen that in Worcestershire since 1914, and if that is not a sacrifice I do not know what is.'[56] A sacrifice indeed, and one that explains the perennial indifference of the Government to art – why, these unfortunate gentlemen must be as blind as bats. Take the religious profession next. Here is a quotation from the life of a great bishop: 'This is an awful mind-and-soul-destroying life. I really do not know how to live it. The arrears of important work accumulate and crush.'[57] That bears out what so many people are saying now about the Church and the nation. Our bishops and deans seem to have no soul with which to preach and no mind with which to write. Listen to any sermon in any church; read the journalism of Dean Alington or Dean Inge in any newspaper. Take the doctor's profession next. 'I have taken a good deal over £13,000 during the year, but this cannot possibly be maintained, and while it lasts it is slavery. What I feel most is being away from Eliza and the children so frequently on Sundays, and again at Christmas.'[58] That is the complaint of a great doctor; and his patient might well echo it, for what Harley Street specialist has time to understand the body, let alone the mind, or both in combination, when he is a slave to thirteen thousand a year? But is the life of a professional writer any better? Here is a sample taken from the life of a highly successful journalist: 'On another day at this time he wrote a 1,600-words article on Nietzsche, a leader of equal length on the railway strike for the *Standard*, 600 words for the *Tribune* and in the evening was at Shoe Lane.'[59] That explains among other things why the public reads its politics with cynicism, and authors read their reviews with foot-rules – it is the advertisement that counts; praise or blame have ceased to have any meaning. And with one more glance at the politician's life, for his profession after all is the most important practically, let us have done. 'Lord Hugh *loitered in the lobby* . . . The bill [the Deceased Wife's Sister Bill] was in consequence dead, and the further chances of the cause were relegated to the chances and mischances of another year.'[60] That not only serves to explain a certain prevalent distrust of politicians, but also reminds us that since you have the Pensions Bill to steer through the lobbies of so just and humane an institution as the House of Commons, we must not loiter too long ourselves among these delightful biographies, but must try to sum up the information which we have gained from them.

What then do these quotations from the lives of successful professional men prove, you ask? They prove, as Whitaker proves things, nothing whatever. If Whitaker, that is, says that a bishop is paid five thousand a year, that is a fact; it can be checked and verified. But if Bishop Gore says that the life of a bishop is 'an awful mind- and soul-destroying life' he is merely giving us his opinion; the next bishop on the bench may flatly contradict him. These quotations then prove nothing that can be checked and verified; they merely cause us to hold opinions. And those opinions cause us to doubt and criticise and question the value of professional life – not its cash value; that is great; but its spiritual, its moral, its intellectual value. They make us of the opinion that if people are highly successful in their professions they lose their senses. Sight goes. They have no time to look at pictures. Sound goes. They have no time to listen to music. Speech goes. They have no time for conversation. They lose their sense of proportion – the relations between one thing and another. Humanity goes. Money-making becomes so important that they must work by night as well as by day. Health goes. And so competitive do they become that they will not share their work with others though they have more than they can do themselves. What then remains of a human being who has lost sight, and sound, and sense of proportion? Only a cripple in a cave.

That of course is a figure, and fanciful; but that it has some connection with figures that are statistical and not fanciful – with the three hundred millions spent upon arms – seems possible. Such at any rate would seem to be the opinion of disinterested observers whose position gives them every opportunity for judging widely, and for judging fairly. Let us examine two such opinions only. The Marquess of Londonderry said:

> We seem to hear a babel of voices among which direction and guidance are lacking, and the world appears to be marking time . . . During the last century gigantic forces of scientific discovery had been unloosed, while at the same time we could discern no corresponding advance in literary or scientific achievement . . . The question we are asking ourselves is whether man is capable of enjoying these new fruits of scientific knowledge and discovery, or whether by their misuse he will bring about the destruction of himself and the edifice of civilisation.[61]

Mr Churchill said:

> Certain it is that while men are gathering knowledge and power with ever-increasing and measureless speed, their virtues and their wisdom

have not shown any notable improvement as the centuries have rolled. The brain of a modern man does not differ in essentials from that of the human beings who fought and loved here millions of years ago. The nature of man has remained hitherto practically unchanged. Under sufficient stress – starvation, terror, warlike passion or even cold intellectual frenzy, the modern man we know so well will do the most terrible deeds, and his modern woman will back him up.[62]

Those are two quotations only from a great number to the same effect. And to them let us add another, from a less impressive source but worth your reading since it too bears upon our problem, from Mr Cyril Chaventry of North Wembley.

A woman's sense of values [he writes] is indisputably different from that of a man. Obviously therefore a woman is at a disadvantage and under suspicion when in competition in a man-created sphere of activity. More than ever today women have the opportunity to build a new and better world, but in this slavish imitation of men they are wasting their chance.[63]

That opinion, too, is a representative opinion, one from a great number to the same effect provided by the daily papers. And the three quotations taken together are highly instructive. The first two seem to prove that the enormous professional competence of the educated man has not brought about an altogether desirable state of things in the civilised world; and the last, which calls upon professional women to use 'their different sense of values' to 'build a new and better world', not only implies that those who have built that world are dissatisfied with the results, but by calling upon the other sex to remedy the evil imposes a great responsibility and implies a great compliment. For if Mr Chaventry and the gentlemen who agree with him believe that 'at a disadvantage and under suspicion' as she is, with little or no political or professional training and upon a salary of about £250 a year, the professional woman can yet 'build a new and better world', they must credit her with powers that might almost be called divine. They must agree with Goethe:

> The things that must pass
> Are only symbols;
> Here shall all failure
> Grow to achievement,
> Here, the Untellable
> Work all fulfilment,
> The woman in woman
> Lead forward for ever – [64]

another very great compliment, and from a very great poet you will agree.

But you do not want compliments; you are pondering quotations. And since your expression is decidedly downcast, it seems as if these quotations about the nature of professional life have brought you to some melancholy conclusion. What can it be? Simply, you reply, that we, daughters of educated men, are between the devil and the deep sea. Behind us lies the patriarchal system: the private house, with its nullity, its immorality, its hypocrisy, its servility. Before us lies the public world, the professional system, with its possessiveness, its jealousy, its pugnacity, its greed. The one shuts us up like slaves in a harem; the other forces us to circle, like caterpillars head to tail, round and round the mulberry tree, the sacred tree, of property. It is a choice of evils. Each is bad. Had we not better plunge off the bridge into the river; give up the game; declare that the whole of human life is a mistake and so end it?

But before you take that step, madam, a decisive one, unless you share the opinion of the professors of the Church of England that death is the gate of life – *Mors Janua Vitae* is written upon an arch in St Paul's – in which case there is, of course, much to recommend it, let us see if another answer is not possible.

Another answer may be staring us in the face on the shelves of your own library, once more in the biographies. Is it not possible that by considering the experiments that the dead have made with their lives in the past we may find some help in answering the very difficult question that is now forced upon us? At any rate, let us try. The question that we will now put to biography is this: For reasons given above we are agreed that we must earn money in the professions. For reasons given above those professions seem to us highly undesirable. The questions we put to you, lives of the dead, is how can we enter the professions and yet remain civilised human beings; human beings, that is, who wish to prevent war?

This time let us turn to the lives not of men but of women in the nineteenth century – to the lives of professional women. But there would seem to be a gap in your library, madam. There are no lives of professional women in the nineteenth century. A Mrs Tomlinson, the wife of a Mr Tomlinson, F.R.S., F.C.S., explains the reason. This lady, who wrote a book 'advocating the employment of young ladies as nurses for children', says: ' . . . it seemed as if there were no way in which an unmarried lady could earn a living but by taking a situation as governess, for which post she was often unfit by nature and education, or want of education."[65] That was written in 1859 – less than a hundred years ago. That explains the gap on your shelves. There were no professional women, except governesses, to have lives written of them. And the lives of governesses, that is the written lives, can be counted on the fingers of one hand. What then can we learn about the lives of professional women from studying the lives of governesses? Happily old boxes are beginning to give up their old secrets. Out the other day crept one such document written about the year 1811. There was, it appears, an obscure Miss Weeton, who used to scribble down her thoughts upon professional life among other things when her pupils were in bed. Here is one such thought. 'Oh! how I have burned to learn Latin, French, the Arts, the Sciences, anything rather than the dogtrot way of sewing, teaching, writing copies, and washing dishes every day . . . Why are not females permitted to study physics, divinity, astronomy, etc., etc., with their attendants, chemistry, botany, logic, mathematics, &c.?'[66] That comment upon the lives of governesses, that question from the lips of governesses, reaches us from the darkness. It is illuminating, too. But let us go on groping; let us pick up a hint here and a hint there as to the professions as they were practised by women in the nineteenth century. Next we find Anne Clough, the sister of Arthur Clough, pupil of Dr Arnold, Fellow of Oriel, who, though she served without a salary, was the first principal of Newnham, and thus may be called a professional woman in embryo – we find her training for her profession by 'doing much of the housework' . . . 'earning money to pay off what had been lent by their friends', 'pressing for leave to keep a small school', reading books her brother lent her, and exclaiming, 'If I were a man, I would not work for riches, to make myself a name or to leave a wealthy family behind me. No, I think I would work for my country, and make its people my heirs.'[67] The nineteenth-century women were not without ambition it seems. Next we find Josephine Butler, who, though not strictly speaking a professional woman, led the campaign against the Contagious Diseases Act to victory, and then the campaign against the sale and purchase of children 'for infamous purposes' – we find Josephine Butler refusing to have a life of herself written, and saying of the women who helped her in those campaigns: 'The utter absence in them of any desire for recognition, of any vestige of egotism in any form, is worthy of remark. In the purity of their motives they shine out "clear as crystal".'[68] That, then, was one of the qualities that the Victorian woman praised and practised – a negative one, it is true; not to be recognised; not to be egotistical; to do the work for the sake of doing the work.[69] An interesting contribution to psychology in its way. And then we come closer to our own time; we find Gertrude Bell, who, though the diplomatic service was and is shut to women, occupied a post in the East which almost entitled her to be called a pseudo-diplomat – we find rather to our surprise that 'Gertrude could never go out in London without a female friend or, failing that, a maid[70] . . . when it seemed unavoidable for Gertrude to drive in a hansom with a young man from one tea party to another, she feels obliged to write and confess it to my mother.'[71] So they were chaste, the women pseudo-diplomats of the Victorian Age?[72] And not merely in body; in mind also. 'Gertrude was not allowed to read Bourget's *The Disciple*' for fear of contracting whatever disease that book may disseminate. Dissatisfied but ambitious, ambitious but austere, chaste yet adventurous – such are some of the qualities that we have discovered. But let us go on looking – if not at the lines, then between the lines of biography. And we find, between the lines of their husbands' biographies, so many women practising – but what are we to call the profession that consists in bringing nine or ten children into the world, the profession which consists in running a house, nursing an invalid, visiting the poor and the sick, tending here an old father, there an old mother? – there is no name and there is no pay for that profession; but we find so many mothers, sisters and daughters of educated men practising it in the nineteenth century that we must lump them and their lives together behind their husbands' and brothers', and leave them to deliver their message to those who have the time to extract it and the imagination with which to decipher it. Let us ourselves, who as you hint are pressed for time, sum up these random hints and reflections upon the professional life of women in the nineteenth century by quoting once more the highly significant words of a woman who was not a professional woman in the strict sense of the word, but had some nondescript reputation as a traveller nevertheless – Mary Kingsley:

> I don't know if I ever revealed the fact to you that being allowed to learn German was *all* the paid-for education I ever had. Two thousand pounds was spent on my brother's. I still hope not in vain.

That statement is so suggestive that it may save us the bother of groping and searching between the lines of professional men's lives for the lives of their sisters. If we develop the suggestions we find in that statement, and connect it with the other hints and fragments that we have uncovered, we may arrive at some theory or point of view that may help us to answer the very difficult question which now confronts us. For when Mary Kingsley says, ' . . . being allowed to learn German was *all* the paid-for education I ever had,' she suggests that she had an unpaid-for education. The other lives that we have been examining corroborate that suggestion. What then was the nature of that 'unpaid-for education' which, whether for good or for evil, has been ours for so many centuries? If we mass the lives of the obscure behind four lives that were not obscure, but were so successful and distinguished that they were actually written, the lives of Florence Nightingale, Miss Clough, Mary Kingsley and Gertrude Bell, it seems undeniable that they were all educated by the same teachers. And those teachers, biography indicates, obliquely and indirectly, but emphatically and indisputably none the less, were poverty, chastity, derision and – but what word covers 'lack of rights and privileges'? Shall we press the old word 'freedom' once more into service? 'Freedom from unreal loyalties', then, was the fourth of their teachers; that freedom from loyalty to old schools, old colleges, old churches, old ceremonies, old countries which all those women enjoyed, and which, to a great extent, we still enjoy by the law and custom of England. We have no time to coin new words, greatly though the language is in need of them. Let 'freedom from unreal loyalties' then stand as the fourth great teacher of the daughters of educated men.

Biography thus provides us with the fact that the daughters of educated men received an unpaid-for education at the hands of poverty, chastity, derision and freedom from unreal loyalties. It was this unpaid-for education, biography informs us, that fitted them, aptly enough, for the unpaid-for professions. And biography also informs us that those unpaid-for professions had their laws, traditions and labours no less certainly than the paid-for professions. Further, the student of biography cannot possibly doubt from the evidence of biography that this education and these professions were in many ways bad in the extreme, both for the unpaid themselves and for their descendants. The intensive childbirth of the unpaid wife, the intensive money-making of the paid husband in the Victorian age had terrible results, we cannot doubt, upon the mind and body of the present age. To prove it we need not quote once more the famous passage in which Florence Nightingale denounced that education and its results; nor stress the natural delight with which she greeted the Crimean War; nor illustrate from other sources – they are, alas, innumerable – the inanity, the pettiness, the spite, the tyranny, the hypocrisy, the immorality which it engendered as the lives of both sexes so abundantly testify. Final proof of its harshness upon one sex at any rate can be found in the annals of our 'great war', when hospitals, harvest fields and munition works were largely staffed by refugees flying from its horrors to their comparative amenity.

But biography is many-sided; biography never returns a single and simple answer to any question that is asked of it. Thus the biographies of those who had biographies – say Florence Nightingale, Anne Clough, Emily Brontë, Christina Rossetti, Mary Kingsley – prove beyond a doubt that this same education, the unpaid for, must have had great virtues as well as great defects, for we cannot deny that these, if not educated, still were civilised women. We cannot, when we consider the lives of our uneducated mothers and grandmothers, judge education simply by its power to 'obtain appointments', to win honour, to make money. We must, if we are honest, admit that some who had no paid-for education, no salaries and no appointments were civilised human beings – whether or not they can rightly be called 'English' women is matter for dispute; and thus admit that we should be extremely foolish if we threw away the results of that education or gave up the knowledge that we have obtained from it for any bribe or decoration whatsoever. Thus biography, when asked the question we have put to it – how can we enter the professions and yet remain civilised human beings, human beings who discourage war? – would seem to reply: If you refuse to be separated from the four great teachers of the daughters of educated men – poverty, chastity, derision and freedom from unreal loyalties – but combine them with some wealth, some knowledge and some service to real loyalties, then you can enter the professions and escape the risks that make them undesirable.

Such being the answer of the oracle, such are the conditions attached to this guinea. You shall have it, to recapitulate, on condition that you help all properly qualified people, of whatever sex, class or colour, to enter your profession; and further on condition that in the practice of your profession you refuse to be separated from poverty, chastity, derision and freedom from unreal loyalties. Is the statement now more positive, have the conditions been made more clear and do you agree to the terms? You hesitate. Some of the conditions, you seem to suggest, need further discussion. Let us take them, then, in order. By poverty is meant enough money to live upon. That is, you must earn enough to be independent of any other human being and to buy that modicum of health, leisure, knowledge and so on that is needed for the full development of body and mind. But no more. Not a penny more.

By chastity is meant that when you have made enough to live on by your profession you must refuse to sell your brain for the sake of money. That is you must cease to practise your profession, or practise it for the sake of research and experiment; or, if you are an artist, for the sake of the art; or give the knowledge acquired professionally to those who need it for nothing. But directly the mulberry tree begins to make you circle, break off. Pelt the tree with laughter.

By derision – a bad word, but once again the English language is much in need of new words – is meant that you must refuse all methods of advertising merit, and hold that ridicule, obscurity and censure are preferable, for psychological reasons, to fame and praise. Directly badges, orders or degrees are offered you, fling them back in the giver's face.

By freedom from unreal loyalties is meant that you must rid yourself of pride of nationality in the first place; also of religious pride, college pride, school pride, family pride, sex pride and those unreal loyalties that spring from them. Directly the seducers come with their seductions to bribe you into captivity, tear up the parchments; refuse to fill up the forms.

And if you still object that these definitions are both too arbitrary and too general, and ask how anybody can tell how much money and how much knowledge are needed for the full development of body and mind, and which are the real loyalties which we must serve and which the unreal which we must despise, I can only refer you – time presses – to two authorities. One is familiar enough. It is the psychometer that you carry on your wrist, the little instrument upon which you depend in all personal relationships. If it were visible it would look something like a thermometer. It has a vein of quicksilver in it which is affected by any body or soul, house or society in whose presence it is exposed. If you want to find out how much wealth is desirable, expose it in a rich man's presence; how much learning is desirable expose it in a learned man's presence. So with patriotism, religion and the rest. The conversation need not be interrupted while you consult it; nor its amenity disturbed. But if you object that this is too personal and fallible a method to employ without risk of mistake, witness the fact that the private psychometer has led to many unfortunate marriages and broken friendships, then there is the other authority now easily within the reach even of the poorest of the daughters of educated men. Go to the public galleries and look at pictures; turn on the wireless and rake down music from the air; enter any of the public libraries which are now free to all. There you will be able to consult the findings of the public psychometer for yourself. To take one example, since we are pressed for time. The *Antigone* of Sophocles has been done into English prose or verse by a man whose name is immaterial.[73] Consider the character of Creon. There you have a most profound analysis by a poet, who is a psychologist in action, of the effect of power and wealth upon the soul. Consider Creon's claim to absolute rule over his subjects. That is a far more instructive analysis of tyranny than any our politicians can offer us. You want to know which are the unreal loyalties which we must despise, which are the real loyalties which we must honour? Consider Antigone's distinction between the laws and the Law. That is a far more profound statement of the duties of the individual to society than any our sociologists can offer us. Lame as the English rendering is, Antigone's five words are worth all the sermons of all the archbishops.[74] But to enlarge would be impertinent. Private judgement is still free in private and that freedom is the essence of freedom.

For the rest, though the conditions may seem many and the guinea, alas, is single, they are not for the most part as things are at present very difficult of fulfilment. With the exception of the first – that we must earn enough money to live upon – they are largely ensured us by the laws of England. The law of England sees to it that we do not inherit great possessions; the law of England denies us, and let us hope will long continue to deny us, the full stigma of nationality. Then we can scarcely doubt that our brothers will provide us for many centuries to come, as they have done for many centuries past, with what is so essential for sanity, and so invaluable in preventing the great modern sins of vanity, egotism, megalomania – that is to say ridicule, censure and contempt.[75] And so long as the Church of England refuses our services – long may she exclude us! – and the ancient schools and colleges refuse to admit us to a share of their endowments and privileges we shall be immune without any trouble on our part from the particular loyalties and fealties which such endowments and privileges engender. Further, madam, the traditions of the private house, that ancestral memory which lies behind the present moment, are there to help you. We have seen in the quotations given above how great a part chastity, bodily chastity, has played in the unpaid education of our sex. It should not be difficult to transmute the old ideal of bodily chastity into the new ideal of mental chastity – to hold that if it was wrong to sell the body for money it is much more wrong to sell the mind for money, since the mind, people say, is nobler than the body. Then again, are we not greatly fortified in resisting the seductions of the most powerful of all seducers – money – by those same traditions? For how many centuries have we not enjoyed the right of working all day and every day for £40 a year with board and lodging thrown in? And does not Whitaker prove that half the work of educated men's daughters is still unpaid-for work? Finally, honour, fame, consequence – is it not easy for us to resist that seduction, we who have worked for centuries without other honour than that which is reflected from the coronets and badges on our father's or husband's brows and breasts?

Thus, with law on our side, and property on our side, and ancestral memory to guide us, there is no need of further argument; you will agree that the conditions upon which this guinea is yours are, with the exception of the first, comparatively easy to fulfil. They merely require that you should develop, modify and direct by the findings of the two psychometers the traditions and the education of the private house which have been in existence these two thousand years. And if you will agree to do that, there can be an end of bargaining between us. Then the guinea with which to pay the rent of your house is yours – would that it were a thousand! For if you agree to these terms then you can join the professions and yet remain uncontaminated by them; you can rid them of their possessiveness, their jealousy, their pugnacity, their greed. You can use them to have a mind of your own and a will of your own. And you can use that mind and will to abolish the inhumanity, the beastliness, the horror, the folly of war. Take this guinea then and use it, not to burn the house down, but to make its windows blaze. And let the daughters of uneducated women dance round the new house, the poor house, the house that stands in a narrow street where omnibuses pass and the street hawkers cry their wares, and let them sing, 'We have done with war! We have done with tyranny!' And their mothers will laugh from their graves, 'It was for this that we suffered obloquy and contempt! Light up the windows of the new house, daughters! Let them blaze!'

Those then are the terms upon which I give you this guinea with which to help the daughters of uneducated women to enter the professions. And by cutting short the peroration let us hope that you will be able to give the finishing touches to your bazaar, arrange the hare and the coffee-pot, and receive the Right Honourable Sir Sampson Legend, O.M., K.C.B., LL.D., D.C.L., P.C., etc., with that air of smiling deference which befits the daughter of an educated man in the presence of her brother.

Such then, sir, was the letter finally sent to the honorary treasurer of the society for helping the daughters of educated men to enter the professions.

Those are the conditions upon which she is to have her guinea. They have been framed, so far as possible, to ensure that she shall do all that a guinea can make her do to help you to prevent war. Whether the conditions have been rightly laid down, who shall say? But as you will see, it was necessary to answer her letter and the letter from the honorary treasurer of the college rebuilding fund, and to send them both guineas before answering your letter, because unless they are helped, first to educate the daughters of educated men, and then to earn their living in the professions, those daughters cannot possess an independent and disinterested influence with which to help you to prevent war. The causes it seems are connected. But having shown this to the best of our ability, let us return to your own letter and to your request for a subscription to your own society.

Chapter 3

Here then is your own letter. In that, as we have seen, after asking for an opinion as to how to prevent war, you go on to suggest certain practical measures by which we can help you to prevent it. These are it appears that we should sign a manifesto, pledging ourselves 'to protect culture and intellectual liberty';[76] that we should join a certain society, devoted to certain measures whose aim is to preserve peace; and, finally, that we should subscribe to that society which like the others is in need of funds.

First, then, let us consider how we can help you to prevent war by protecting culture and intellectual liberty, since you assure us that there is a connection between those rather abstract words and these very positive photographs – the photographs of dead bodies and ruined houses.

But if it was surprising to be asked for an opinion how to prevent war, it is still more surprising to be asked to help you in the rather abstract terms of your manifesto to protect culture and intellectual liberty. Consider, sir, in the light of the facts given above, what this request of yours means. It means that in the year 1938 the sons of educated men are asking the daughters to help them to protect culture and intellectual liberty. And why, you may ask, is that so surprising? Suppose that the Duke of Devonshire, in his star and garter, stepped down into the kitchen and said to the maid who was peeling potatoes with a smudge on her cheek: 'Stop your potato peeling, Mary, and help me to construe this rather difficult passage in Pindar,' would not Mary be surprised and run screaming to Louisa the cook, 'Lawks, Louie, master must be mad!' That, or something like it, is the cry that rises to our lips when the sons of educated men ask us, their sisters, to protect intellectual liberty and culture. But let us try to translate the kitchen-maid's cry into the language of educated people.

Once more we must beg you, sir, to look from our angle, from our point of view, at Arthur's Education Fund. Try once more, difficult though it is to twist your head in that direction, to understand what it has meant to us to keep that receptacle filled all these centuries so that some ten thousand of our brothers may be educated every year at Oxford and Cambridge. It has meant that we have already contributed to the cause of culture and intellectual liberty more than any other class in the community. For have not the daughters of educated men paid into Arthur's Education Fund from the year 1262 to the year 1870 all the money that was needed to educate themselves, bating such miserable sums as went to pay the governess, the German teacher, and the dancing master? Have they not paid with their own education for Eton and Harrow, Oxford and Cambridge, and all the great schools and universities on the continent – the Sorbonne and Heidelberg, Salamanca and Padua and Rome? Have they not paid so generously and lavishly if so indirectly, that when at last, in the nineteenth century, they won the right to some paid-for education for themselves, there was not a single woman who had received enough paid-for education to be able to teach them?[77] And now, out of the blue, just as they were hoping that they might filch not only a little of that same university education for themselves but some of the trimmings – travel, pleasure, liberty – for themselves, here is your letter informing them that the whole of that vast, that fabulous sum – for whether counted directly in cash, or indirectly in things done without, the sum that filled Arthur's Education Fund is vast – has been wasted or wrongly applied. With what other purpose were the universities of Oxford and Cambridge founded, save to protect culture and intellectual liberty? For what other object did your sisters go without teaching or travel or luxuries themselves except that with the money so saved their brothers should go to schools and universities and there learn to protect culture and intellectual liberty? But now since you proclaim them in danger and ask us to add our voice to yours, and our sixpence to your guinea, we must assume that the money so spent was wasted and that those societies have failed. Yet, the reflection must intrude, if the public schools and universities with their elaborate machinery for mind-training and body-training have failed, what reason is there to think that your society, sponsored though it is by distinguished names, is going to succeed, or that your manifesto, signed though it is by still more distinguished names, is going to convert? Ought you not, before you lease an office, hire a secretary, elect a committee and appeal for funds, to consider why those schools and universities have failed?

That, however, is a question for you to answer. The question which concerns us is what possible help we can give you in protecting culture and intellectual liberty – we, who have been shut out from the universities so repeatedly, and are only now admitted so restrictedly; we who have received no paid-for education whatsoever, or so little that we can only read our own tongue and write our own language, we who are, in fact, members not of the intelligentsia but of the ignorantsia? To confirm us in our modest estimate of our own culture and to prove that you in fact share it there is Whitaker with his facts. Not a single educated man's daughter, Whitaker says, is thought capable of teaching the literature of her own language at either university. Nor is her opinion worth asking, Whitaker informs us, when it comes to buying a picture for the National Gallery, a portrait for the Portrait Gallery or a mummy for the British Museum. How then can it be worth your while to ask us to protect culture and intellectual liberty when, as Whitaker proves with his cold facts, you have no belief that our advice is worth having when it comes to spending the money, to which we have contributed, in buying culture and intellectual liberty for the state? Do you wonder that the unexpected compliment takes us by surprise? Still, there is your letter. There are facts in that letter, too. In it you say that war is imminent; and you go on to say, in more languages than one – here is the French version:[78] Seule la culture désintéressée peut garder le monde de sa ruine – you go on to say that by protecting intellectual liberty and our inheritance of culture we can help you to prevent war. And since the first statement at least is indisputable and any kitchen-maid even if her French is defective can read and understand the meaning of 'Air Raid Precautions' when written in large letters upon a blank wall, we cannot ignore your request on the plea of ignorance or remain silent on the plea of modesty. Just as any kitchen-maid would attempt to construe a passage in Pindar if told that her life depended on it, so the daughters of educated men, however little their training qualifies them, must consider what they can do to protect culture and intellectual liberty if by so doing they can help you to prevent war. So let us by all means in our power examine this further method of helping you, and see, before we consider your request that we should join your society, whether we can sign this manifesto in favour of culture and intellectual liberty with some intention of keeping our word.

What, then, is the meaning of those rather abstract words? If we are to help you to protect them it would be well to define them in the first place. But like all honorary treasurers you are pressed for time, and to ramble through English literature in search of a definition, though a delightful pastime in its way, might well lead us far. Let us agree, then, for the present, that we know what they are, and concentrate upon the practical question how we can help you to protect them. Now the daily paper with its provision of facts lies on the table; and a single quotation from it may save time and limit our inquiry. 'It was decided yesterday at a conference of headmasters that women were not fit teachers for boys over the age of fourteen.' That fact is of instant help to us here, for it proves that certain kinds of help are beyond our reach. For us to attempt to reform the education of our brothers at public schools and universities would be to invite a shower of dead cats, rotten eggs and broken gates from which only street scavengers and locksmiths would benefit, while the gentlemen in authority, history assures us, would survey the tumult from their study windows without taking the cigars from their lips or ceasing to sip, slowly as its bouquet deserves, their admirable claret.[79] The teaching of history, then, reinforced by the teaching of the daily paper, drives us to a more restricted position. We can only help you to defend culture and intellectual liberty by defending our own culture and our own intellectual liberty. That is to say, we can hint, if the treasurer of one of the women's colleges asks us for a subscription, that some change might be made in that satellite body when it ceases to be satellite; or again, if the treasurer of some society for obtaining professional employment for women asks us for a subscription, suggest that some change might be desirable, in the interests of culture and intellectual liberty, in the practice of the professions. But as paid-for education is still raw and young, and as the number of those allowed to enjoy it at Oxford and Cambridge is still strictly limited, culture for the great majority of educated men's daughters must still be that which is acquired outside the sacred gates, in public libraries or in private libraries, whose doors by some unaccountable oversight have been left unlocked. It must still, in the year 1938, largely consist in reading and writing our own tongue. The question thus becomes more manageable. Shorn of its glory it is easier to deal with. What we have to do now, then, sir, is to lay your request before the daughters of educated men and to ask them to help you to prevent war, not by advising their brothers how they shall protect culture and intellectual liberty, but simply by reading and writing their own tongue in such a way as to protect those rather abstract goddesses themselves.

This would seem, on the face of it, a simple matter, and one that needs neither argument nor rhetoric. But we are met at the outset by a new difficulty. We have already noted the fact that the profession of literature, to give it a simple name, is the only profession which did not fight a series of battles in the nineteenth century. There has been no battle of Grub Street. That profession has never been shut to the daughters of educated men. This was due of course to the extreme cheapness of its professional requirements. Books, pens and paper are so cheap, reading and writing have been, since the eighteenth century at least, so universally taught in our class, that it was impossible for any body of men to corner the necessary knowledge or to refuse admittance, except on their own terms, to those who wished to read books or to write them. But it follows, since the profession of literature is open to the daughters of educated men, that there is no honorary treasurer of the profession in such need of a guinea with which to prosecute her battle that she will listen to our terms, and promise to do what she can to observe them. This places us, you will agree, in an awkward predicament. For how then can we bring pressure upon them – what can we do to persuade them to help us? The profession of literature differs, it would seem, from all the other professions. There is no head of the profession; no Lord Chancellor as in your own case: no official body with the power to lay down rules and enforce them.[80] We cannot debar women from the use of libraries;[81] or forbid them to buy ink and paper; or rule that metaphors shall only be used by one sex, as the male only in art schools was allowed to study from the nude; or rule that rhyme shall be used by one sex only as the male only in academies of music was allowed to play in orchestras. Such is the inconceivable licence of the profession of letters that any daughter of an educated man may use a man's name – say George Eliot or George Sand – with the result that an editor or a publisher, unlike the authorities in Whitehall, can detect no difference in the scent or savour of a manuscript, or even know for certain whether the writer is married or not.

Thus, since we have very little power over those who earn their livings by reading and writing, we must go to them humbly without bribes or penalties. We must go to them cap in hand, like beggars, and ask them of their goodness to spare time to listen to our request that they shall practise the profession of reading and writing in the interests of culture and intellectual liberty.

And now, clearly, some further definition of 'culture and intellectual liberty' would be useful. Fortunately, it need not be, for our purposes, exhaustive or elaborate. We need not consult Milton, Goethe or Matthew Arnold; for their definition would apply to paid-for culture – the culture which, in Miss Weeton's definition, includes physics, divinity, astronomy, chemistry, botany, logic and mathematics, as well as Latin, Greek and French. We are appealing in the main to those whose culture is the unpaid-for culture, that which consists in being able to read and write their own tongue. Happily your manifesto is at hand to help us to define the terms further; 'disinterested' is the word you use. Therefore let us define culture for our purposes as the disinterested pursuit of reading and writing the English language. And intellectual liberty may be defined for our purposes as the right to say or write what you think in your own words, and in your own way. These are very crude definitions, but they must serve. Our appeal then might begin: 'O daughters of educated men, this gentleman, whom we all respect, says that war is imminent; by protecting culture and intellectual liberty he says that we can help him to prevent war. We entreat you, therefore, who earn your livings by reading and writing . . . ' But here the words falter on our lips, and the prayer peters out into three separate dots because of facts again – because of facts in books, facts in biographies, facts which make it difficult, perhaps impossible, to go on.

What are those facts then? Once more we must interrupt our appeal in order to examine them. And there is no difficulty in finding them. Here, for example, is an illuminating document before us, a most genuine and indeed moving piece of work, the autobiography of Mrs Oliphant, which is full of facts. She was an educated man's daughter who earned her living by reading and writing. She wrote books of all kinds. Novels, biographies, histories, handbooks of Florence and Rome, reviews, newspaper articles innumerable came from her pen. With the proceeds she earned her living and educated her children. But how far did she protect culture and intellectual liberty? That you can judge for yourself by reading first a few of her novels: *The Duke's Daughter, Diana Trelawny, Harry Joscelyn*, say; continue with the lives of Sheridan and Cervantes; go on to *Makers of Florence and Rome*; conclude by sousing yourself in the innumerable faded articles, reviews, sketches of one kind and another which she contributed to literary papers. When you have done, examine the state of your own mind, and ask yourself whether that reading has led you to respect disinterested culture and intellectual liberty. Has it not on the contrary smeared your mind and dejected your imagination, and led you to deplore the fact that Mrs Oliphant sold her brain, her very admirable brain, prostituted her culture and enslaved her intellectual liberty in order that she might earn her living and educate her children?[82] Inevitably, considering the damage that poverty inflicts upon mind and body, the necessity that is laid upon those who have children to see that they are fed and clothed, nursed and educated, we have to applaud her choice and to admire her courage. But if we applaud the choice and admire the courage of those who do what she did, we can spare ourselves the trouble of addressing our appeal to them, for they will no more be able to protect disinterested culture and intellectual liberty than she was. To ask them to sign your manifesto would be to ask a publican to sign a manifesto in favour of temperance. He may himself be a total abstainer; but since his wife and children depend upon the sale of beer, he must continue to sell beer, and his signature to the manifesto would be of no value to the cause of temperance because directly he had signed it he must be at the counter inducing his customers to drink more beer. So to ask the daughters of educated men who have to earn their livings by reading and writing to sign your manifesto would be of no value to the cause of disinterested culture and intellectual liberty, because directly they had signed it they must be at the desk writing those books, lectures and articles by which culture is prostituted and intellectual liberty is sold into slavery. As an expression of opinion it may have value; but if what you need is not merely an expression of opinion but positive help, you must frame your request rather differently. Then you will have to ask them to pledge themselves not to write anything that denies culture, or to sign any contract that infringes intellectual liberty. And to that the answer given us by biography would be short but sufficient: Have I not to earn my living? Thus, sir, it becomes clear that we must make our appeal only to those daughters of educated men who have enough to live upon. To them we might address ourselves in this wise: 'Daughters of educated men who have enough to live upon . . . ' But again the voice falters: again the prayer peters out into separate dots. For how many of them are there? Dare we assume in the face of Whitaker, of the laws of property, of the wills in the newspapers, of facts in short, that 1,000, 500, or even 250 will answer when thus addressed? However that may be, let the plural stand and continue: 'Daughters of educated men who have enough to live upon, and read and write your own language for your own pleasure, may we very humbly entreat you to sign this gentleman's manifesto with some intention of putting your promise into practice?'

Here, if indeed they consent to listen, they might very reasonably ask us to be more explicit – not indeed to define culture and intellectual liberty, for they have books and leisure and can define the words for themselves. But what, they may well ask, is meant by this gentleman's 'disinterested' culture, and how are we to protect that and intellectual liberty in practice? Now as they are daughters, not sons, we may begin by reminding them of a compliment once paid them by a great historian. 'Mary's conduct,' says Macaulay, 'was really a signal instance of that perfect disinterestedness and self-devotion of which man seems to be incapable, but which is sometimes found in women.'[83] Compliments, when you are asking a favour, never come amiss. Next let us refer them to the tradition which has long been honoured in the private house – the tradition of chastity. 'Just as for many centuries, madam,' we might plead, 'it was thought vile for a woman to sell her body without love, but right to give it to the husband whom she loved, so it is wrong, you will agree, to sell your mind without love, but right to give it to the art which you love.' 'But what,' she may ask, 'is meant by "selling your mind without love"?' 'Briefly,' we might reply, 'to write at the command of another person what you do not want to write for the sake of money. But to sell a brain is worse than to sell a body, for when the body seller has sold her momentary pleasure she takes good care that the matter shall end there. But when a brain seller has sold her brain, its anaemic, vicious and diseased progeny are let loose upon the world to infect and corrupt and sow the seeds of disease in others. Thus we are asking you, madam, to pledge yourself not to commit adultery of the brain because it is a much more serious offence than the other.' 'Adultery of the brain,' she may reply, 'means writing what I do not want to write for the sake of money. Therefore you ask me to refuse all publishers, editors, lecture agents and so on who bribe me to write or to speak what I do not want to write or to speak for the sake of money?' 'That is so, madam; and we further ask that if you should receive proposals for such sales you will resent them and expose them as you would resent and expose such proposals for selling your body, both for your own sake and for the sake of others. But we would have you observe that the verb "to adulterate" means, according to the dictionary, "to falsify by admixture of baser ingredients". Money is not the only baser ingredient. Advertisement and publicity are also adulterers. Thus, culture mixed with personal charm, or culture mixed with advertisement and publicity, are also adulterated forms of culture. We must ask you to abjure them; not to appear on public platforms; not to lecture; not to allow your private face to be published, or details of your private life; not to avail yourself, in short, of any of the forms of brain prostitution which are so insidiously suggested by the pimps and panders of the brain-selling trade; or to accept any of those baubles and labels by which brain merit is advertised and certified – medals, honours, degrees – we must ask you to refuse them absolutely, since they are all tokens that culture has been prostituted and intellectual liberty sold into captivity.'

Upon hearing this definition, mild and imperfect as it is, of what it means, not merely to sign your manifesto in favour of culture and intellectual liberty, but to put that opinion into practice, even those daughters of educated men who have enough to live upon may object that the terms are too hard for them to keep. For they would mean loss of money, which is desirable, loss of fame which is universally held to be agreeable, and censure and ridicule which are by no means negligible. Each would be the butt of all who have an interest to serve or money to make from the sale of brains. And for what reward? Only, in the rather abstract terms of your manifesto, that they would thus 'protect culture and intellectual liberty', not by their opinion but by their practice.

Since the terms are so hard, and there is no body in existence whose ruling they need respect or obey, let us consider what other method of persuasion is left to us. Only, it would seem, to point to the photographs – the photographs of dead bodies and ruined houses. Can we bring out the connection between them and prostituted culture and intellectual slavery and make it so clear that the one implies the other, that the daughters of educated men will prefer to refuse money and fame and to be the objects of scorn and ridicule rather than suffer themselves, or allow others to suffer, the penalties there made visible? It is difficult in the short time at our disposal, and with the weak weapons in our possession, to make that connection clear, but if what you, sir, say is true, and there is a connection and a very real one between them, we must try to prove it.

Let us then begin by summoning, if only from the world of imagination, some daughter of an educated man who has enough to live upon and can read and write for her own pleasure and, taking her to be the representative of what may in fact be no class at all, let us ask her to examine the products of that reading and writing which lie upon her own table. 'Look, madam,' we might begin, 'at the newspapers on your table. Why, may we ask, do you take in three dailies and three weeklies?' 'Because,' she replies, 'I am interested in politics, and wish to know the facts.' 'An admirable desire, madam. But why three? Do they differ then about facts, and if so, why?' To which she replies, with some irony, 'You call yourself an educated man's daughter, and yet pretend not to know the facts – roughly that each paper is financed by a board; that each board has a policy; that each board employs writers to expound that policy, and if the writers do not agree with that policy, the writers, as you may remember after a moment's reflection, find themselves unemployed in the street. Therefore if you want to know any fact about politics you must read at least three different papers, compare at least three different versions of the same fact, and come in the end to your own conclusion. Hence the three daily papers on my table.' Now that we have discussed, very briefly, what may be called the literature of fact, let us turn to what may be called the literature of fiction. 'There are such things, madam,' we may remind her, 'as pictures, plays, music and books. Do you pursue the same rather extravagant policy there – glance at three daily papers and three weekly papers if you want to know the facts about pictures, plays, music and books, because those who write about art are in the pay of an editor, who is in the pay of a board, which has a policy to pursue, so that each paper takes a different view, so that it is only by comparing three different views that you can come to your own conclusion – what pictures to see, what play or concert to go to, which book to order from the library?' And to that she replies, 'Since I am an educated man's daughter, with a smattering of culture picked up from reading, I should no more dream, given the conditions of journalism at present, of taking my opinions of pictures, plays, music or books from the newspapers than I would take my opinion of politics from the newspapers.

Compare the views, make allowance for the distortions, and then judge for yourself. That is the only way. Hence the many newspapers on my table.'[84]

So then the literature of fact and the literature of opinion, to make a crude distinction, are not pure fact, or pure opinion, but adulterated fact and adulterated opinion, that is fact and opinion 'adulterated by the admixture of baser ingredients' as the dictionary has it. In other words you have to strip each statement of its money motive, of its power motive, of its advertisement motive, of its publicity motive, of its vanity motive, let alone of all the other motives which, as an educated man's daughter, are familiar to you, before you make up your mind which fact about politics to believe, or even which opinion about art? 'That is so,' she agrees. But if you were told by somebody who had none of those motives for wrapping up truth that the fact was in his or her opinion this or that, you would believe him or her, always allowing of course for the fallibility of human judgement which, in judging works of art, must be considerable? 'Naturally,' she agrees. If such a person said that war was bad, you would believe him; or if such a person said that some picture, symphony, play or poem were good you would believe him? 'Allowing for human fallibility, yes.' Now suppose, madam, that there were 250 or 50, or 25 such people in existence, people pledged not to commit adultery of the brain, so that it was unnecessary to strip what they said of its money motive, power motive, advertisement motive, publicity motive, vanity motive and so on before we unwrapped the grain of truth, might not two very remarkable consequences follow? Is it not possible that if we knew the truth about war, the glory of war would be scotched and crushed where it lies curled up in the rotten cabbage leaves of our prostituted fact-purveyors; and if we knew the truth about art instead of shuffling and shambling through the smeared and dejected pages of those who must live by prostituting culture, the enjoyment and practice of art would become so desirable that by comparison the pursuit of war would be a tedious game for elderly dilettantes in search of a mildly sanitary amusement – the tossing of bombs instead of balls over frontiers instead of nets? In short, if newspapers were written by people whose sole object in writing was to tell the truth about politics and the truth about art we should not believe in war and we should believe in art.

Hence there is a very clear connection between culture and intellectual liberty and those photographs of dead bodies and ruined houses. And to ask the daughters of educated men who have enough to live upon to commit adultery of the brain is to ask them to help in the most positive way now open to them – since the profession of literature is still that which stands widest open to them – to prevent war.

Thus, sir, we might address this lady – crudely, briefly it is true; but time passes and we cannot define further. And to this appeal she might well reply, if indeed she exists: 'What you say is obvious; so obvious that every educated man's daughter already knows it for herself, or if she does not, has only to read the newspapers to be sure of it. But suppose she were well enough off not merely to sign this manifesto in favour of disinterested culture and intellectual liberty but to put her opinion into practice, how could she set about it? And do not,' she may reasonably add, 'dream dreams about ideal worlds behind the stars; consider actual facts in the actual world.' Indeed, the actual world is much more difficult to deal with than the dream world. Still, madam, the private printing press is an actual fact, and not beyond the reach of a moderate income. Typewriters and duplicators are actual facts and even cheaper. By using these cheap and so far unforbidden instruments you can at once rid yourself of the pressure of boards, policies and editors. They will speak your own mind, in your own words, at your own time, at your own length, at your own bidding. And that, we are agreed, is our definition of 'intellectual liberty'. 'But,' she may say, ' "the public"? How can that be reached without putting my own mind through the mincing machine and turning it into sausage?' ' "The public", madam,' we may assure her, 'is very like ourselves; it lives in rooms; it walks in streets; it is said moreover to be tired of sausage. Fling leaflets down basements; expose them on stalls; trundle them along streets on barrows to be sold for a penny or given away. Find out new ways of approaching "the public"; single it into separate people instead of massing it into one monster, gross in body, feeble in mind. And then reflect – since you have enough to live on, you have a room, not necessarily "cosy" or "handsome" but still silent, private; a room where safe from publicity and its poison you could, even asking a reasonable fee for the service, speak the truth to artists, about pictures, music, books, without fear of affecting their sales, which are exiguous, or wounding their vanity, which is prodigious.[85] Such at least was the criticism that Ben Jonson gave Shakespeare at the Mermaid and there is no reason to suppose, with *Hamlet* as evidence, that literature suffered in consequence. Are not the best critics private people, and is not the only criticism worth having spoken criticism? Those then are some of the active ways in which you, as a writer of your own tongue, can put your opinion into practice. But if you are passive, a reader, not a writer, then you must adopt not active but passive methods of protecting culture and intellectual liberty.' 'And what may they be?' she will ask. 'To abstain, obviously. Not to subscribe to papers that encourage intellectual slavery; not to attend lectures that prostitute culture; for we are agreed that to write at the command of another what you do not want to write is to be enslaved, and to mix culture with personal charm or advertisement is to prostitute culture. By these active and passive measures you would do all in your power to break the ring, the vicious circle, the dance round and round the mulberry tree, the poison tree of intellectual harlotry. The ring once broken, the captives would be freed. For who can doubt that once writers had the chance of writing what they enjoy writing they would find it so much more pleasurable that they would refuse to write on any other terms; or that readers once they had the chance of reading what writers enjoy writing, would find it so much more nourishing than what is written for money that they would refuse to be palmed off with the stale substitute any longer? Thus the slaves who are now kept hard at work piling words into books, piling words into articles, as the old slaves piled stones into pyramids, would shake the manacles from their wrists and give up their loathsome labour. And "culture", that amorphous bundle, swaddled up as she now is in insincerity, emitting half truths from her timid lips, sweetening and diluting her message with whatever sugar or water serves to swell the writer's fame or his master's purse, would regain her shape and become, as Milton, Keats and other great writers assure us that she is in reality, muscular, adventurous, free. Whereas now, madam, at the very mention of culture the head aches, the eyes close, the doors shut, the air thickens; we are in a lecture room, rank with the fumes of stale print, listening to a gentleman who is forced to lecture or to write every Wednesday, every Sunday, about Milton or about Keats, while the lilac shakes its branches in the garden free, and the gulls, swirling and swooping, suggest with wild laughter that such stale fish might with advantage be tossed to them. That is our plea to you, madam; those are our reasons for urging it. Do not merely sign this manifesto in favour of culture and intellectual liberty; attempt at least to put your promise into practice.'

Whether the daughters of educated men who have enough to live upon and read and write their own tongue for their own pleasure will listen to this request or not, we cannot say, sir. But if culture and intellectual liberty are to be protected, not by opinions merely but by practice, this would seem to be the way. It is not an easy way, it is true. Nevertheless, such as it is, there are reasons for thinking that the way is easier for them than for their brothers. They are immune, through no merit of their own, from certain compulsions. To protect culture and intellectual liberty in practice would mean, as we have said, ridicule and chastity, loss of publicity and poverty. But those, as we have seen, are their familiar teachers. Further, Whitaker with his facts is at hand to help them; for since he proves that all the fruits of professional culture – such as directorships of art galleries and museums, professorships and lectureships and editorships – are still beyond their reach, they should be able to take a more purely disinterested view of culture than their brothers, without for a moment claiming, as Macaulay asserts, that they are by nature more disinterested. Thus helped by tradition and by facts as they are, we have not only some right to ask them to help us to break the circle, the vicious circle of prostituted culture, but some hope that if such people exist they will help us. To return then to your manifesto: we will sign it if we can keep these terms; if we cannot keep them, we will not sign it.

Now that we have tried to see how we can help you to prevent war by attempting to define what is meant by protecting culture and intellectual liberty let us consider your next and inevitable request: that we should subscribe to the funds of your society. For you, too, are an honorary treasurer, and like the other honorary treasurers in need of money. Since you, too, are asking for money it might be possible to ask you, also, to define your aims, and to bargain and to impose terms as with the other honorary treasurers. What then are the aims of your society? To prevent war, of course. And by what means? Broadly speaking, by protecting the rights of the individual; by opposing dictatorship; by ensuring the democratic ideals of equal opportunity for all. Those are the chief means by which as you say, 'the lasting peace of the world can be assured'. Then, sir, there is no need to bargain or to haggle. If those are your aims, and if, as it is impossible to doubt, you mean to do all in your power to achieve them, the guinea is yours – would that it were a million! The guinea is yours; and the guinea is a free gift, given freely.

But the word 'free' is used so often, and has come, like used words, to mean so little, that it may be well to explain exactly, even pedantically, what the word 'free' means in this context. It means here that no right or privilege is asked in return. The giver is not asking you to admit her to the priesthood of the Church of England; or to the Stock Exchange; or to the Diplomatic Service. The giver has no wish to be 'English' on the same terms that you yourself are 'English'. The giver does not claim in return for the gift admission to any profession; any honour, title, or medal; any professorship or lecture-ship; any seat upon any society, committee or board. The gift is free from all such conditions because the one right of paramount importance to all human beings is already won. You cannot take away her right to earn a living. Now then for the first time in English history an educated man's daughter can give her brother one guinea of her own making at his request for the purpose specified above without asking for anything in return. It is a free gift, given without fear, without flattery and without conditions. That, sir, is so momentous an occasion in the history of civilisation that some celebration seems called for. But let us have done with the old ceremonies – the Lord Mayor, with turtles and sheriffs in attendance, tapping nine times with his mace upon a stone while the Archbishop of Canterbury in full canonicals invokes a blessing. Let us invent a new ceremony for this new occasion. What more fitting than to destroy an old word, a vicious and corrupt word that has done much harm in its day and is now obsolete? The word 'feminist' is the word indicated. That word, according to the dictionary, means 'one who champions the rights of women'. Since the only right, the right to earn a living, has been won, the word no longer has a meaning. And a word without a meaning is a dead word, a corrupt word. Let us therefore celebrate this occasion by cremating the corpse. Let us write that word in large black letters on a sheet of foolscap; then solemnly apply a match to the paper. Look, how it burns! What a light dances over the world! Now let us bray the ashes in a mortar with a goose-feather pen, and declare in unison singing together that anyone who uses that word in future is a ring-the-bell-and-run-away-man,[86] a mischief maker, a groper among old bones, the proof of whose defilement is written in a smudge of dirty water upon his face. The smoke has died down; the word is destroyed. Observe, sir, what has happened as the result of our celebration.

The word 'feminist' is destroyed; the air is cleared; and in that clearer air what do we see? Men and women working together for the same cause. The cloud has lifted from the past too. What were they working for in the nineteenth century – those queer dead women in their poke bonnets and shawls? The very same cause for which we are working now. 'Our claim was no claim of women's rights only;' – it is Josephine Butler who speaks – 'it was larger and deeper; it was a claim for the rights of all – all men and women – to the respect in their persons of the great principles of Justice and Equality and Liberty.' The words are the same as yours; the claim is the same as yours. The daughters of educated men who were called, to their resentment, 'feminists' were in fact the advance guard of your own movement. They were fighting the same enemy that you are fighting and for the same reasons. They were fighting the tyranny of the patriarchal state as you are fighting the tyranny of the Fascist state. Thus we are merely carrying on the same fight that our mothers and grandmothers fought; their words prove it; your words prove it. But now with your letter before us we have your assurance that you are fighting with us, not against us. That fact is so inspiring that another celebration seems called for. What could be more fitting than to write more dead words, more corrupt words, upon more sheets of paper and burn them – the words, tyrant, dictator, for example? But, alas, those words are not yet obsolete. We can still shake out eggs from newspapers; still smell a peculiar and unmistakable odour in the region of Whitehall and Westminster. And abroad the monster has come more openly to the surface. There is no mistaking him there. He has widened his scope. He is interfering now with your liberty; he is dictating how you shall live; he is making distinctions not merely between the sexes, but between the races. You are feeling in your own persons what your mothers felt when they were shut out, when they were shut up, because they were women. Now you are being shut out, you are being shut up, because you are Jews, because you are democrats, because of race, because of religion. It is not a photograph that you look upon any longer; there you go, trapesing along in the procession yourselves. And that makes a difference. The whole iniquity of dictatorship, whether in Oxford or Cambridge, in Whitehall or Downing Street, against Jews or against women, in England or in Germany, in Italy or in Spain is now apparent to you. But now we are fighting together. The daughters and sons of educated men are fighting side by side. That fact is so inspiring, even if no celebration is possible, that if this one guinea could be multiplied a million times all those guineas should be at your service without any other conditions than those that you have imposed upon yourself. Take this one guinea then and use it to assert 'the rights of all – all men and women – to the respect in their persons of the great principles of Justice and Equality and Liberty'. Put this penny candle in the window of your new society, and may we live to see the day when in the blaze of our common freedom the words tyrant and dictator shall be burnt to ashes, because the words tyrant and dictator shall be obsolete.

That request then for a guinea answered, and the cheque signed, only one further request of yours remains to be considered – it is that we should fill up a form and become members of your society. On the face of it that seems a simple request, easily granted. For what can be simpler than to join the society to which this guinea has just been contributed? On the face of it, how easy, how simple; but in the depths, how difficult, how complicated . . . What possible doubts, what possible hesitations can those dots stand for? What reason or what emotion can make us hesitate to become members of a society whose aims we approve, to whose funds we have contributed? It may be neither reason nor emotion, but something more profound and fundamental than either. It may be difference. Different we are, as facts have proved, both in sex and in education. And it is from that difference, as we have already said, that our help can come, if help we can, to protect liberty, to prevent war. But if we sign this form which implies a promise to become active members of your society, it would seem that we must lose that difference and therefore sacrifice that help. To explain why this is so is not easy, even though the gift of a guinea has made it possible (so we have boasted), to speak freely without fear or flattery. Let us then keep the form unsigned on the table before us while we discuss, so far as we are able, the reasons and the emotions which make us hesitate to sign it. For those reasons and emotions have their origin deep in the darkness of ancestral memory; they have grown together in some confusion; it is very difficult to untwist them in the light.

To begin with an elementary distinction: a society is a conglomeration of people joined together for certain aims; while you, who write in your own person with your own hand, are single. You the individual are a man whom we have reason to respect; a man of the brotherhood, to which, as biography proves, many brothers have belonged. Thus Anne Clough, describing her brother, says: 'Arthur is my best friend and adviser . . . Arthur is the comfort and joy of my life; it is for him, and from him, that I am incited to seek after all that is lovely and of good report.'[87] To which William Wordsworth, speaking of his sister but answering the other as if one nightingale called to another in the forests of the past, replies:

> The Blessing of my later years
> Was with me when a Boy:
> She gave me eyes, she gave me ears;
> And humble cares, and delicate fears;
> A heart, the fountain of sweet tears;
> And love, and thought, and joy.[88]

Such was, such perhaps still is, the relationship of many brothers and sisters in private, as individuals. They respect each other and help each other and have aims in common. Why then, if such can be their private relationship, as biography and poetry prove, should their public relationship, as law and history prove, be so very different? And here, since you are a lawyer, with a lawyer's memory, it is not necessary to remind you of certain decrees of English law from its first records to the year 1919 by way of proving that the public, the society relationship of brother and sister has been very different from the private. The very word 'society' sets tolling in memory the dismal bells of a harsh music: shall not, shall not, shall not. You shall not learn; you shall not earn; you shall not own; you shall not – such was the society relationship of brother to sister for many centuries. And though it is possible, and to the optimistic credible, that in time a new society may ring a carillon of splendid harmony, and your letter heralds it, that day is far distant. Inevitably we ask ourselves, is there not something in the conglomeration of people into societies that releases what is most selfish and violent, least rational and humane in the individuals themselves? Inevitably we look upon society, so kind to you, so harsh to us, as an ill-fitting form that distorts the truth; deforms the mind; fetters the will. Inevitably we look upon societies as conspiracies that sink the private brother, whom many of us have reason to respect, and inflate in his stead a monstrous male, loud of voice, hard of fist, childishly intent upon scoring the floor of the earth with chalk marks, within whose mystic boundaries human beings are penned, rigidly, separately, artificially; where, daubed red and gold, decorated like a savage with feathers, he goes through mystic rites and enjoys the dubious pleasures of power and dominion while we, 'his' women, are locked in the private house without share in the many societies of which his society is composed. For such reasons compact as they are of many memories and emotions – for who shall analyse the complexity of a mind that holds so deep a reservoir of time past within it? – it seems both wrong for us rationally and impossible for us emotionally to fill up your form and join your society. For by so doing we should merge our identity in yours; follow and repeat and score still deeper the old worn ruts in which society, like a gramophone whose needle has stuck, is grinding out with intolerable unanimity 'Three hundred millions spent upon arms.' We should not give effect to a view which our own experience of 'society' should have helped us to envisage. Thus, sir, while we respect you as a private person and prove it by giving you a guinea to spend as you choose, we believe that we can help you most effectively by refusing to join your society; by working for our common ends – justice and equality and liberty for all men and women – outside your society, not within.

But this, you will say, if it means anything, can only mean that you, the daughters of educated men, who have promised us your positive help, refuse to join our society in order that you may make another of your own. And what sort of society do you propose to found outside ours, but in cooperation with it, so that we may both work together for our common ends? That is a question which you have every right to ask, and which we must try to answer in order to justify our refusal to sign the form you send. Let us then draw rapidly in outline the kind of society which the daughters of educated men might found and join outside your society but in cooperation with its ends. In the first place, this new society, you will be relieved to learn, would have no honorary treasurer, for it would need no funds. It would have no office, no committee, no secretary; it would call no meetings; it would hold no conferences. If name it must have, it could be called the Outsiders' Society. That is not a resonant name, but it has the advantage that it squares with facts – the facts of history, of law, of biography; even, it may be, with the still hidden facts of our still unknown psychology. It would consist of educated men's daughters working in their own class – how indeed can they work in any other?[89] – and by their own methods for liberty, equality and peace. Their first duty, to which they would bind themselves not by oath, for oaths and ceremonies have no part in a society which must be anonymous and elastic before everything, would be not to fight with arms. This is easy for them to observe, for in fact, as the papers inform us, 'the Army Council have no intention of opening recruiting for any women's corps'.[90] The country ensures it. Next they would refuse in the event of war to make munitions or nurse the wounded. Since in the last war both these activities were mainly discharged by the daughters of working men, the pressure upon them here too would be slight, though probably disagreeable. On the other hand the next duty to which they would pledge themselves is one of considerable difficulty, and calls not only for courage and initiative, but for the special knowledge of the educated man's daughter. It is, briefly, not to incite their brothers to fight, or to dissuade them, but to maintain an attitude of complete indifference. But the attitude expressed by the word 'indifference' is so complex and of such importance that it needs even here further definition. Indifference in the first place must be given a firm footing upon fact. As it is a fact that she cannot understand what instinct compels him, what glory, what interest, what manly satisfaction fighting provides for him – 'without war there would be no outlet for the manly qualities which fighting develops' – as fighting thus is a sex characteristic which she cannot share, the counterpart some claim of the maternal instinct which he cannot share, so is it an instinct which she cannot judge. The outsider therefore must leave him free to deal with this instinct by himself, because liberty of opinion must be respected, especially when it is based upon an instinct which is as foreign to her as centuries of tradition and education can make it.[91] This is a fundamental and instinctive distinction upon which indifference may be based. But the outsider will make it her duty not merely to base her indifference upon instinct, but upon reason. When he says, as history proves that he has said, and may say again, 'I am fighting to protect our country,' and thus seeks to rouse her patriotic emotion, she will ask herself, 'What does "our country" mean to me an outsider?' To decide this she will analyse the meaning of patriotism in her own case. She will inform herself of the position of her sex and her class in the past. She will inform herself of the amount of land, wealth and property in the possession of her own sex and class in the present – how much of 'England' in fact belongs to her. From the same sources she will inform herself of the legal protection which the law has given her in the past and now gives her. And if he adds that he is fighting to protect her body, she will reflect upon the degree of physical protection that she now enjoys when the words 'Air Raid Precautions' are written on blank walls. And if he says that he is fighting to protect England from foreign rule, she will reflect that for her there are no 'foreigners', since by law she becomes a foreigner if she marries a foreigner. And she will do her best to make this a fact, not by forced fraternity, but by human sympathy. All these facts will convince her reason (to put it in a nutshell) that her sex and class has very little to thank England for in the past; not much to thank England for in the present; while the security of her person in the future is highly dubious. But probably she will have imbibed, even from the governess, some romantic notion that Englishmen, those fathers and grandfathers whom she sees marching in the picture of history, are 'superior' to the men of other countries. This she will consider it her duty to check by comparing French historians with English; German with French; the testimony of the ruled – the Indians or the Irish, say – with the claims made by their rulers. Still some 'patriotic' emotion, some ingrained belief in the intellectual superiority of her own country over other countries may remain. Then she will compare English painting with French painting; English music with German music; English literature with Greek literature, for translations abound. When all these comparisons have been faithfully made by the use of reason, the outsider will find herself in possession of very good reasons for her indifference. She will find that she has no good reason to ask her brother to fight on her behalf to protect 'our' country. ' "Our country", ' she will say, 'throughout the greater part of its history has treated me as a slave; it has denied me education or any share in its possessions. "Our" country still ceases to be mine if I marry a foreigner. "Our" country denies me the means of protecting myself, forces me to pay others a very large sum annually to protect me, and is so little able, even so, to protect me that Air Raid Precautions are written on the wall. Therefore if you insist upon fighting to protect me, or "our" country, let it be understood, soberly and rationally between us, that you are fighting to gratify a sex instinct which I cannot share; to procure benefits which I have not shared and probably will not share; but not to gratify my instincts, or to protect either myself or my country. For,' the outsider will say, 'in fact, as a woman, I have no country. As a woman I want no country. As a woman my country is the whole world.' And if, when reason has said its say, still some obstinate emotion remains, some love of England dropped into a child's ears by the cawing of rooks in an elm tree, by the splash of waves on a beach, or by English voices murmuring nursery rhymes, this drop of pure, if irrational, emotion she will make serve her to give to England first what she desires of peace and freedom for the whole world.

Such then will be the nature of her 'indifference' and from this indifference certain actions must follow. She will bind herself to take no share in patriotic demonstrations; to assent to no form of national self-praise; to make no part of any claque or audience that encourages war; to absent herself from military displays, tournaments, tattoos, prize-givings and all such ceremonies as encourage the desire to impose 'our' civilisation or 'our' dominion upon other people. The psychology of private life, moreover, warrants the belief that this use of indifference by the daughters of educated men would help materially to prevent war. For psychology would seem to show that it is far harder for human beings to take action when other people are indifferent and allow them complete freedom of action, than when their actions are made the centre of excited emotion. The small boy struts and trumpets outside the window: implore him to stop; he goes on; say nothing; he stops. That the daughters of educated men then should give their brothers neither the white feather of cowardice nor the red feather of courage, but no feather at all; that they should shut the bright eyes that rain influence, or let those eyes look elsewhere when war is discussed – that is the duty to which outsiders will train themselves in peace before the threat of death inevitably makes reason powerless.

Such then are some of the methods by which the society, the anonymous and secret Society of Outsiders, would help you, sir, to prevent war and to ensure freedom. Whatever value you may attach to them you will agree that they are duties which your own sex would find it more difficult to carry out than ours; and duties moreover which are specially appropriate to the daughters of educated men. For they would need some acquaintance with the psychology of educated men, and the minds of educated men are more highly trained and their words subtler than those of working men.[92] There are other duties, of course – many have already been outlined in the letters to the other honorary treasurers. But at the risk of some repetition let us roughly and rapidly repeat them, so that they may form a basis for a society of outsiders to take its stand upon. First, they would bind themselves to earn their own livings. The importance of this as a method of ending war is obvious; sufficient stress has already been laid upon the superior cogency of an opinion based upon economic independence over an opinion based upon no income at all or upon a spiritual right to an income to make further proof unnecessary. It follows that an outsider must make it her business to press for a living wage in all the professions now open to her sex; further that she must create new professions in which she can earn the right to an independent opinion. Therefore she must bind herself to press for a money wage for the unpaid worker in her own class – the daughters and sisters of educated men who, as biographies have shown us, are now paid on the truck system, with food, lodging and a pittance of £40 a year. But above all she must press for a wage to be paid by the state legally to the mothers of educated men. The importance of this to our common fight is immeasurable; for it is the most effective way in which we can ensure that the large and very honourable class of married women shall have a mind and a will of their own, with which, if his mind and will are good in her eyes, to support her husband, if bad to resist him, in any case to cease to be 'his woman' and to be her self. You will agree, sir, without any aspersion upon the lady who bears your name, that to depend upon her for your income would effect a most subtle and undesirable change in your psychology. Apart from that, this measure is of such importance directly to yourselves, in your own fight for liberty and equality and peace, that if any condition were to be attached to the guinea it would be this: that you should provide a wage to be paid by the state to those whose profession is marriage and motherhood. Consider, even at the risk of a digression, what effect this would have upon the birth-rate, in the very class where the birth-rate is falling, in the very class where births are desirable – the educated class. Just as the increase in the pay of soldiers has resulted, the papers say, in additional recruits to the force of arms-bearers, so the same inducement would serve to recruit the child-bearing force, which we can hardly deny to be as necessary and as honourable, but which, because of its poverty, and its hardships, is now failing to attract recruits. That method might succeed where the one in use at present – abuse and ridicule – has failed. But the point which, at the risk of further digression, the outsiders would press upon you is one that vitally concerns your own lives as educated men and the honour and vigour of your professions. For if your wife were paid for her work, the work of bearing and bringing up children, a real wage, a money wage, so that it became an attractive profession instead of being as it is now an unpaid profession, an unpensioned profession, and therefore a precarious and dishonoured profession, your own slavery would be lightened.[93] No longer need you go to the office at nine-thirty and stay there till six. Work could be equally distributed. Patients could be sent to the patientless. Briefs to the briefless. Articles could be left unwritten. Culture would thus be stimulated. You could see the fruit trees flower in spring. You could share the prime of life with your children. And after that prime was over no longer need you be thrown from the machine on to the scrap heap without any life left or interests surviving to parade the environs of Bath or Cheltenham in the care of some unfortunate slave. No longer would you be the Saturday caller, the albatross on the neck of society, the sympathy addict, the deflated work slave calling for replenishment; or, as Herr Hitler puts it, the hero requiring recreation, or, as Signor Mussolini puts it, the wounded warrior requiring female dependants to bandage his wounds.[94] If the state paid your wife a living wage for her work which, sacred though it is, can scarcely be called more sacred than that of the clergyman, yet as his work is paid without derogation so may hers be – if this step which is even more essential to your freedom than to hers were taken, the old mill in which the professional man now grinds out his round, often so wearily, with so little pleasure to himself or profit to his profession, would be broken;

the opportunity of freedom would be yours; the most degrading of all servitudes, the intellectual servitude, would be ended; the half-man might become whole. But since three hundred millions or so have to be spent upon the arms-bearers, such expenditure is obviously, to use a convenient word supplied by the politicians, 'impracticable' and it is time to return to more feasible projects.

The outsiders then would bind themselves not only to earn their own livings, but to earn them so expertly that their refusal to earn them would be a matter of concern to the work master. They would bind themselves to obtain full knowledge of professional practices, and to reveal any instance of tyranny or abuse in their professions. And they would bind themselves not to continue to make money in any profession, but to cease all competition and to practise their profession experimentally, in the interests of research and for love of the work itself, when they had earned enough to live upon. Also they would bind themselves to remain outside any profession hostile to freedom, such as the making or the improvement of the weapons of war. And they would bind themselves to refuse to take office or honour from any society which, while professing to respect liberty, restricts it, like the universities of Oxford and Cambridge. And they would consider it their duty to investigate the claims of all public societies to which, like the Church and the universities, they are forced to contribute as taxpayers as carefully and fearlessly as they would investigate the claims of private societies to which they contribute voluntarily. They would make it their business to scrutinise the endowments of the schools and universities and the objects upon which that money is spent. As with the educational, so with the religious profession. By reading the New Testament in the first place and next those divines and historians whose works are all easily accessible to the daughters of educated men, they would make it their business to have some knowledge of the Christian religion and its history. Further they would inform themselves of the practice of that religion by attending church services; by analysing the spiritual and intellectual value of sermons; by criticising the opinions of men whose profession is religion as freely as they would criticise the opinions of any other body of men. Thus they would be creative in their activities, not merely critical. By criticising education they would help to create a civilised society which protects culture and intellectual liberty. By criticising religion they would attempt to free the religious spirit from its present servitude and would help, if need be, to create a new religion based it might well be upon the New Testament, but, it might well be, very different from the religion now erected upon that basis. And in all this, and in much more than we have time to particularise, they would be helped, you will agree, by their position as outsiders, that freedom from unreal loyalties, that freedom from interested motives which are at present assured them by the state.

It would be easy to define in greater number and more exactly the duties of those who belong to the Society of Outsiders, but not profitable. Elasticity is essential; and some degree of secrecy, as will be shown later, is at present even more essential; But the description thus loosely and imperfectly given is enough to show you, sir, that the Society of Outsiders has the same ends as your society – freedom, equality, peace; but that it seeks to achieve them by the means that a different sex, a different tradition, a different education and the different values which result from those differences have placed within our reach. Broadly speaking, the main distinction between us who are out-side society and you who are inside society must be that whereas you will make use of the means provided by your position – leagues, conferences, campaigns, great names, and all such public measures as your wealth and political influence place within your reach – we, remaining outside, will experiment not with public means in public but with private means in private. Those experiments will not be merely critical but creative. To take two obvious instances. The outsiders will dispense with pageantry not from any puritanical dislike of beauty. On the contrary, it will be one of their aims to increase private beauty; the beauty of spring, summer, autumn; the beauty of flowers, silks, clothes; the beauty which brims not only every field and wood but every barrow in Oxford Street; the scattered beauty which needs only to be combined by artists in order to become visible to all. But they will dispense with the dictated, regimented, official pageantry, in which only one sex takes an active part – those ceremonies, for example, which depend upon the deaths of kings or their coronations to inspire them. Again, they will dispense with personal distinctions – medals, ribbons, badges, hoods, gowns – not from any dislike of personal adornment, but because of the obvious effect of such distinctions to constrict, to stereotype and to destroy. Here, as so often, the example of the Fascist states is at hand to instruct us – for if we have no example of what we wish to be, we have, what is perhaps equally valuable, a daily and illuminating example of what we do not wish to be. With the example, then, that they give us of the power of medals, symbols, orders and even, it would seem, of decorated ink-pots[95] to hypnotise the human mind it must be our aim not to submit ourselves to such hypnotism. We must extinguish the coarse glare of advertisement and publicity, not merely because the limelight is apt to be held in incompetent hands, but because of the psychological effect of such illumination upon those who receive it. Consider next time you drive along a country road the attitude of a rabbit caught in the glare of a head-lamp – its glazed eyes, its rigid paws. Is there not good reason to think, without going outside our own country, that the 'attitudes', the false and unreal positions taken by the human form in England as well as in Germany, are due to the limelight which paralyses the free action of the human faculties and inhibits the human power to change and create new wholes, much as a strong head-lamp paralyses the little creatures who run out of the darkness into its beams? It is a guess; guessing is dangerous; yet we have some reason to guide us in the guess that ease and freedom, the power to change and the power to grow, can only be preserved by obscurity; and that if we wish to help the human mind to create, and to prevent it from scoring the same rut repeatedly, we must do what we can to shroud it in darkness.

But enough of guessing. To return to facts – what chance is there, you may ask, that such a Society of Outsiders, without office, meetings, leaders or any hierarchy, without so much as a form to be filled up, or a secretary to be paid, can be brought into existence, let alone work to any purpose? Indeed it would have been waste of time to write even so rough a definition of the Outsiders' Society were it merely a bubble of words, a covert form of sex or class glorification, serving, as so many such expressions do, to relieve the writer's emotion, lay the blame elsewhere, and then burst. Happily there is a model in being, a model from which the above sketch has been taken, furtively it is true, for the model, far from sitting still to be painted, dodges and disappears. That model then, the evidence that such a body, whether named or unnamed, exists and works, is provided not yet by history or biography, for the outsiders have only had a positive existence for twenty years – that is since the professions were opened to the daughters of educated men. But evidence of their existence is provided by history and biography in the raw – by the newspapers that is, sometimes openly in the lines, sometimes covertly between them. There, anyone who wishes to verify the existence of such a body can find innumerable proofs. Many, it is obvious, are of dubious value. For example, the fact that an immense amount of work is done by the daughters of educated men without pay or for very little pay need not be taken as a proof that they are experimenting of their own free will in the psychological value of poverty. Nor need the fact that many daughters of educated men do not 'eat properly'[96] serve as a proof that they are experimenting in the physical value of undernourishment. Nor need the fact that a very small proportion of women compared with men accept honours be held to prove that they are experimenting in the virtues of obscurity. Many such experiments are forced experiments and therefore of no positive value. But others of a much more positive kind are coming daily to the surface of the press. Let us examine three only, in order that we may prove our statement that the Society of Outsiders is in being. The first is straightforward enough.

> Speaking at a bazaar last week at the Plumstead Common Baptist Church the Mayoress of Woolwich said: ' . . . I myself would not even do as much as darn a sock to help in a war.' These remarks are resented by the majority of the Woolwich public, who hold that the Mayoress was, to say the least, rather tactless. Some 12,000 Woolwich electors are employed in Woolwich Arsenal on armament making.[97]

There is no need to comment upon the tactlessness of such a statement made publicly, in such circumstances; but the courage can scarcely fail to command our admiration, and the value of the experiment, from a practical point of view, should other mayoresses in other towns and other countries where the electors are employed in armament-making follow suit may well be immeasurable. At any rate, we shall agree that the Mayoress of Woolwich, Mrs Kathleen Rance, has made a courageous and effective experiment in the prevention of war by not knitting socks. For a second proof that the outsiders are at work let us choose another example from the daily paper, one that is less obvious, but still you will agree an outsider's experiment, a very original experiment, and one that may be of great value to the cause of peace.

Speaking of the work of the great voluntary associations for the playing of certain games, Miss Clarke [Miss E. R. Clarke of the Board of Education] referred to the women's organisations for hockey, lacrosse, netball, and cricket, and pointed out that under the rules there could be no cup or award of any kind to a successful team. The 'gates' for their matches might be a little smaller than for the men's games, but their players played the game for the love of it, and they seemed to be proving that cups and awards are not necessary to stimulate interest for each year the numbers of players steadily continued to increase.[98]

That, you will agree, is an extraordinarily interesting experiment, one that may well bring about a psychological change of great value in human nature, and a change that may be of real help in preventing war. It is further of interest because it is an experiment that outsiders, owing to their comparative freedom from certain inhibitions and persuasions, can carry out much more easily than those who are necessarily exposed to such influences inside. That statement is corroborated in a very interesting way by the following quotation:

Official football circles here [Wellingborough, Northants] regard with anxiety the growing popularity of girls' football. A secret meeting of the Northants Football Association's consultative committee was held here last night to discuss the playing of a girls' match on the Peterborough ground. Members of the Committee are reticent . . . One member, however, said today: 'The Northants Football Association is to forbid women's football. This popularity of girls' football comes when many men's clubs in the country are in a parlous state through lack of support. Another serious aspect is the possibility of grave injury to women players.'[99]

There we have proof positive of those inhibitions and persuasions which make it harder for your sex to experiment freely in altering current values than for ours; and without spending time upon the delicacies of psychological analysis even a hasty glance at the reasons given by this association for its decision will throw a valuable light upon the reasons which lead other and even more important associations to come to their decisions. But to return to the outsiders' experiments. For our third example let us choose what we may call an experiment in passivity.

A remarkable change in the attitude of young women to the Church was discussed by Canon F. A. Barry, vicar of St Mary the Virgin (the University Church), at Oxford last night . . . The task before the Church, he said, was nothing less than to make civilisation moral, and this was a great cooperative task which demanded all that Christians could bring to it. It simply could not be carried through by men alone. For a century, or a couple of centuries, women had predominated in the congregations in roughly the ratio of 75 per cent to 25 per cent. The whole situation was now changing, and what the keen observer would notice in almost any church in England was the paucity of young women . . . Among the student population the young women were, on the whole, farther away from the Church of England and the Christian faith than the young men.[100]

That again is an experiment of very great interest. It is, as we have said, a passive experiment. For while the first example was an outspoken refusal to knit socks in order to discourage war, and the second was an attempt to prove whether cups and awards are necessary to stimulate interest in games, the third is an attempt to discover what happens if the daughters of educated men absent themselves from church. Without being in itself more valuable than the others, it is of more practical interest because it is obviously the kind of experiment that great numbers of outsiders can practise with very little difficulty or danger. To absent yourself – that is easier than to speak aloud at a bazaar, or to draw up rules of an original kind for playing games. Therefore it is worth watching very carefully to see what effect the experiment of absenting oneself has had – if any. The results are positive and they are encouraging. There can be no doubt that the Church is becoming concerned about the attitude to the Church of educated men's daughters at the universities. The report of the Archbishops' Commission on the Ministry of Women is there to prove it. This document, which costs only one shilling and should be in the hands of all educated men's daughters, points out that 'one outstanding difference between men's colleges and women's colleges is the absence in the latter of a chaplain'. It reflects that, 'It is natural that in this period of their lives they [the students] exercise to the full their critical faculties.' It deplores the fact that, 'Very few women coming to the universities can now afford to offer continuous voluntary service either in social or in directly religious work.' And it concludes that, 'There are many special spheres in which such services are particularly needed, and the time has clearly come when the functions and position of women within the Church require further determination.'[101] Whether this concern is due to the empty churches at Oxford, or whether the voices of the 'older schoolgirls' at Isleworth expressing 'very grave dissatisfaction at the way in which organised religion was carried on' [102] have somehow penetrated to those august spheres where their sex is not supposed to

speak, or whether our incorrigibly idealistic sex is at last beginning to take
to heart Bishop Gore's warning, 'Men do not value ministrations which are
gratuitous,'[103] and to express the opinion that a salary of £150 a year – the
highest that the Church allows her daughters as deaconesses – is not
enough – whatever the reason, considerable uneasiness at the attitude of
educated men's daughters is apparent; and this experiment in passivity,
whatever our belief in the value of the Church of England as a spiritual
agency, is highly encouraging to us as outsiders. For it seems to show that
to be passive is to be active; those also serve who remain outside. By making
their absence felt their presence becomes desirable. What light this throws
upon the power of outsiders to abolish or modify other institutions of
which they disapprove, whether public dinners, public speeches, Lord
Mayors' banquets and other obsolete ceremonies are pervious to indifference and will yield to its pressure, are questions, frivolous questions, that
may well amuse our leisure and stimulate our curiosity. But that is not now
the object before us. We have tried to prove to you, sir, by giving three
different examples of three different kinds of experiment that the Society of
Outsiders is in being and at work. When you consider that these examples
have all come to the surface of the newspaper you will agree that they
represent a far greater number of private and submerged experiments of
which there is no public proof. Also you will agree that they substantiate the
model of the society given above, and prove that it was no visionary sketch
drawn at random but based upon a real body working by different means
for the same ends that you have set before us in your own society. Keen
observers, like Canon Barry, could, if they liked, discover many more
proofs that experiments are being made not only in the empty churches of
Oxford. Mr Wells even might be led to believe if he put his ear to the
ground that a movement is going forward, not altogether imperceptibly,
among educated men's daughters against the Nazi and the Fascist. But it is
essential that the movement should escape the notice even of keen observers
and of famous novelists.

Secrecy is essential. We must still hide what we are doing and thinking
even though what we are doing and thinking is for our common cause. The
necessity for this, in certain circumstances, is not hard to discover. When
salaries are low, as Whitaker proves that they are, and jobs are hard to get
and keep, as everybody knows them to be, it is, 'to say the least, rather
tactless', as the newspaper puts it, to criticise your master. Still, in country
districts, as you yourself may be aware, farm labourers will not vote Labour.
Economically, the educated man's daughter is much on a level with the farm
labourer. But it is scarcely necessary for us to waste time in searching out
what reason it is that inspires both his and her secrecy. Fear is a powerful
reason; those who are economically dependent have strong reasons for fear.
We need explore no further. But here you may remind us of a certain
guinea, and draw our attention to the proud boast that our gift, small though

it was, had made it possible not merely to burn a certain corrupt word, but to speak freely without fear or flattery. The boast it seems had an element of brag in it. Some fear, some ancestral memory prophesying war, still remains, it seems. There are still subjects that educated people, when they are of different sexes, even though financially independent, veil or hint at in guarded terms and then pass on. You may have observed it in real life; you may have detected it in biography. Even when they meet privately and talk, as we have boasted, about 'politics and people, war and peace, barbarism and civilisation', yet they evade and conceal. But it is so important to accustom ourselves to the duties of free speech, for without private there can be no public freedom, that we must try to uncover this fear and to face it. What then can be the nature of the fear that still makes concealment necessary between educated people and reduces our boasted freedom to a farce? . . . Again there are three dots; again they represent a gulf – of silence this time, of silence inspired by fear. And since we lack both the courage to explain it and the skill, let us lower the veil of St Paul between us, in other words take shelter behind an interpreter. Happily we have one at hand whose credentials are above suspicion. It is none other than the pamphlet from which quotation has already been made, the report of the Archbishops' Commission on the Ministry of Women – a document of the highest interest for many reasons. For not only does it throw light of a searching and scientific nature upon this fear, but it gives us an opportunity to consider that profession which since it is the highest of all may be taken as the type of all, the profession of religion, about which, purposely, very little has yet been said. And since it is the type of all it may throw light upon the other professions about which something has been said. You will pardon us therefore if we pause here to examine this report in some detail.

The Commission was appointed by the Archbishops of Canterbury and York 'in order to examine any theological or other relevant principles which have governed or ought to govern the Church in the development of the Ministry of Women'.[104] Now the profession of religion, for our purposes the Church of England, though it seems on the surface to resemble the others in certain respects – it enjoys, Whitaker says, a large income, owns much property, and has a hierarchy of officials drawing salaries and taking precedence one of the other – yet ranks above all the professions. The Archbishop of Canterbury precedes the Lord High Chancellor; the Archbishop of York precedes the Prime Minister. And it is the highest of all the professions because it is the profession of religion. But what, we may ask, is 'religion'? What the Christian religion is has been laid down once and for all by the founder of that religion in words that can be read by all in a translation of singular beauty; and whether or not we accept the interpretation that has been put on them we cannot deny them to be words of the most profound meaning. It can thus safely be said that whereas few people know what medicine is, or what law is, everyone who owns a copy of the New

Testament knows what religion meant in the mind of its founder. Therefore, when in the year 1935 the daughters of educated men said that they
wished to have the profession of religion opened to them, the priests of that
profession, who correspond roughly to the doctors and barristers in the
other professions, were forced not merely to consult some statute or charter
which reserves the right to practise that profession professionally to the
male sex; they were forced to consult the New Testament. They did so; and
the result, as the Commissioners point out, was that they found that 'the
Gospels show us that our Lord regarded men and women alike as members
of the same spiritual kingdom, as children of God's family, and as possessors
of the same spiritual capacities . . . ' In proof of this they quote: 'There is
neither male nor female: for ye are all one in Christ Jesus' (Galatians 3:28).
It would seem then that the founder of Christianity believed that neither
training nor sex was needed for this profession. He chose his disciples from
the working class from which he sprang himself. The prime qualification
was some rare gift which in those early days was bestowed capriciously upon
carpenters and fishermen, and upon women also. As the Commission points
out there can be no doubt that in those early days there were prophetesses –
women upon whom the divine gift had descended. Also they were allowed to
preach. St Paul, for example, lays it down that women, when praying in
public, should be veiled. 'The implication is that if veiled a woman might
prophesy [i.e. preach] and lead in prayer.' How then can they be excluded
from the priesthood since they were thought fit by the founder of the
religion and by one of his apostles to preach? That was the question, and the
Commission solved it by appealing not to the mind of the founder, but to
the mind of the Church. That, of course, involved a distinction. For the
mind of the Church had to be interpreted by another mind, and that mind
was St Paul's mind; and St Paul, in interpreting that mind, changed his
mind. For after summoning from the depths of the past certain venerable if
obscure figures – Lydia and Chloe, Euodia and Syntyche, Tryphoena
and Tryphosa and Persis, debating their status, and deciding what was the
difference between a prophetess and presbyteress, what the standing of a
deaconess in the pre-Nicene Church and what in the post-Nicene Church,
the Commissioners once more have recourse to St Paul, and say: 'In any case
it is clear that the author of the Pastoral Epistles, be he St Paul or another,
regarded woman as being debarred on the ground of her sex from the
position of an official "teacher" in the Church, or from any office involving
the exercise of a governmental authority over a man (1 Timothy 2:12).' That,
it may frankly be said, is not so satisfactory as it might be; for we cannot
altogether reconcile the ruling of St Paul, or another, with the ruling of
Christ himself who 'regarded men and women alike as members of the same
spiritual kingdom . . . and as possessors of the same spiritual capacities'. But
it is futile to quibble over the meaning of the words, when we are so soon in
the presence of facts. Whatever Christ meant, or St Paul meant, the fact was

that in the fourth or fifth century the profession of religion had become so highly organised that 'the deacon [unlike the deaconess] may, "after serving unto well-pleasing the ministry committed unto him", aspire to be appointed eventually to higher offices in the Church; whereas for the deaconess the Church prays simply that God "would grant unto her the Holy Spirit . . . that she may worthily accomplish the work committed to her".' In three or four centuries, it appears, the prophet or prophetess whose message was voluntary and untaught became extinct; and their places were taken by the three orders of bishops, priests and deacons, who are invariably men, and invariably, as Whitaker points out, paid men, for when the Church became a profession its professors were paid. Thus the profession of religion seems to have been originally much what the profession of literature is now.[105] It was originally open to anyone who had received the gift of prophecy. No training was needed; the professional requirements were simple in the extreme – a voice and a market-place, a pen and paper. Emily Brontë, for instance, who wrote:

> No coward soul is mine,
> No trembler in the world's storm-troubled sphere;
> I see Heaven's glories shine.
> And faith shines equal, arming me from fear.
>
> O God within my breast,
> Almighty, ever-present Deity!
> Life – that in me has rest,
> As I – undying Life – have power in Thee!

though not worthy to be a priest in the Church of England, is the spiritual descendant of some ancient prophetess who prophesied when prophecy was a voluntary and unpaid occupation. But when the Church became a profession, required special knowledge of its prophets and paid them for imparting it, one sex remained inside; the other was excluded. 'The deacons rose in dignity – partly no doubt from their close association with the bishops – and became subordinate ministers of worship and of the sacraments; but the deaconess shared only in the preliminary stages of this evolution.' How elementary that evolution has been is proved by the fact that in England in 1938 the salary of an archbishop is £15,000; the salary of a bishop is £10,000 and the salary of a dean is £3,000. But the salary of a deaconess is £150; and as for the 'parish worker', who 'is called upon to assist in almost every department of parish life', whose 'work is exacting and often solitary . . .' she is paid from £120 to £150 a year; nor is there anything to surprise us in the statement that 'prayer needs to be the very centre of her activities'. Thus we might even go further than the Commissioners and say that the evolution of the deaconess is not merely 'elementary', it is positively stunted; for though she is ordained, and 'ordination . . . conveys an indelible character, and involves the obligation of lifelong service', she must remain outside the

Church; and rank beneath the humblest curate. Such is the decision of the Church. For the Commission, having consulted the mind and tradition of the Church, reported finally: 'While the Commission as a whole would not give their positive assent to the view that a woman is inherently incapable of receiving the grace of Order, and consequently to admission to any of the three Orders, we believe that the general mind of the Church is still in accord with the continuous tradition of a male priesthood.'

By thus showing that the highest of all the professions has many points of similarity with the other professions our interpreter, you will admit, has thrown further light upon the soul or essence of those professions. We must now ask him to help us, if he will, to analyse the nature of that fear which still, as we have admitted, makes it impossible for us to speak freely as free people should. Here again he is of service. Though identical in many respects, one very profound difference between the religious profession and other professions has been noted above: the Church being a spiritual profession has to give spiritual and not merely historical reasons for its actions; it has to consult the mind, not the law. Therefore when the daughters of educated men wished to be admitted to the profession of the Church it seemed advisable to the Commissioners to give psychological and not merely historical reasons for their refusal to admit them. They therefore called in Professor Grensted, D. D., the Nolloth Professor of the Philosophy of the Christian Religion in the University of Oxford, and asked him 'to summarise the relevant psychological and physiological material', and to indicate 'the grounds for the opinions and recommendations put forward by the Commission'. Now psychology is not theology; and the psychology of the sexes, as the professor insisted, and 'its bearing upon human conduct, is still a matter for specialists . . . and . . . its interpretation remains controversial, in many respects obscure'. But he gave his evidence for what it was worth, and it is evidence that throws so much light upon the origin of the fear which we have admitted and deplored that we can do no better than follow his words exactly.

It was represented [he said] in evidence before the Commission that man has a natural precedence of woman. This view, in the sense intended, cannot be supported psychologically. Psychologists fully recognise the fact of male dominance, but this must not be confused with male superiority, still less with any type of precedence which could have a bearing upon questions as to the admissibility of one sex rather than the other to Holy Orders.

The psychologist, therefore, can only throw light upon certain facts. And this was the first fact that he investigated.

It is clearly a fact of the very greatest practical importance that strong feeling is aroused by any suggestion that women should be admitted to the status and functions of the threefold Order of the Ministry. The evidence before the Commission went to show that this feeling is predominantly hostile to such proposals . . . This strength of feeling, conjoined with a wide variety of rational explanations, is clear evidence of the presence of powerful and widespread subconscious motive. In the absence of detailed analytical material, of which there seems to be no record in this particular connection, it nevertheless remains clear that infantile fixation plays a predominant part in determining the strong emotion with which this whole subject is commonly approached.

The exact nature of this fixation must necessarily differ with different individuals, and suggestions which can be made as to its origin can only be general in character. But whatever be the exact value and interpretation of the material upon which theories of the 'Oedipus complex' and the 'castration complex' have been founded, it is clear that the general acceptance of male dominance, and still more of feminine inferiority, resting upon subconscious ideas of woman as 'man manqué', has its background in infantile conceptions of this type. These commonly, and even usually, survive in the adult, despite their irrationality, and betray their presence, below the level of conscious thought, by the strength of the emotions to which they give rise. It is strongly in support of this view that the admission of women to Holy Orders, and especially to the ministry of the sanctuary, is so commonly regarded as something shameful. This sense of shame cannot be regarded in any other light than as a non-rational sex-taboo.

Here we can take the professor's word for it that he has sought, and found, 'ample evidence of these unconscious forces', both in pagan religions and in the Old Testament, and so follow him to his conclusion:

At the same time it must not be forgotten that the Christian conception of the priesthood rests not upon these subconscious emotional factors, but upon the institution of Christ. It thus not only fulfils but supersedes the priesthoods of paganism and the Old Testament. So far as psychology is concerned there is no theoretical reason why this Christian priesthood should not be exercised by women as well as by men and in exactly the same sense. The difficulties which the psychologist foresees are emotional and practical only.[106]

With that conclusion we may leave him.

The Commissioners, you will agree, have performed the delicate and difficult task that we asked them to undertake. They have acted as interpreters between us. They have given us an admirable example of a profession in its purest state; and shown us how a profession bases itself upon mind and tradition. They have further explained why it is that educated people when they are of different sexes do not speak openly upon certain subjects. They have shown why the outsiders, even when there is no question of financial dependence, may still be afraid to speak freely or to experiment openly. And, finally, in words of scientific precision, they have revealed to us the nature of that fear. For as Professor Grensted gave his evidence, we, the daughters of educated men, seemed to be watching a surgeon at work – an impartial and scientific operator, who as he dissected the human mind by human means laid bare for all to see what cause, what root lies at the bottom of our fear. It is an egg. Its scientific name is 'infantile fixation'. We, being unscientific, have named it wrongly. An egg we called it; a germ. We smelt it in the atmosphere; we detected its presence in Whitehall, in the universities, in the Church. Now undoubtedly the professor has defined it and described it so accurately that no daughter of an educated man, however uneducated she may be, can miscall it or misinterpret it in future. Listen to the description. 'Strong feeling is aroused by any suggestion that women be admitted' – it matters not to which priesthood: the priesthood of medicine or the priesthood of science or the priesthood of the Church. Strong feeling, she can corroborate the professor, is undoubtedly shown should she ask to be admitted. 'This strength of feeling is clear evidence of the presence of powerful and subconscious motive.' She will take the professor's word for that, and even supply him with some motives that have escaped him. Let us draw attention to two only. There is the money motive for excluding her, to put it plainly. Are not salaries motives now, whatever they may have been in the time of Christ? The archbishop has £15,000, the deaconess £150; and the Church, so the Commissioners say, is poor. To pay women more would be to pay men less. Secondly, is there not a motive, a psychological motive, for excluding her, hidden beneath what the Commissioners call a 'practical consideration'? 'At present a married priest,' they tell us, 'is able to fulfil the requirements of the ordination service "to forsake and set aside all worldly cares and studies" largely because his wife can undertake the care of the household and the family, . . . '[107] To be able to set aside all worldly cares and studies and lay them upon another person is a motive, to some of great attractive force; for some undoubtedly wish to withdraw and study, as theology with its refinements, and scholarship with its subtleties, prove; to others, it is true, the motive is a bad motive, a vicious motive, the cause of that separation between the Church and the people; between literature and the people; between the husband and the wife which has had its part in putting the whole of our Commonwealth out of gear. But whatever the powerful and subconscious motives may be that lie behind the exclusion of women from the priesthoods, and plainly we cannot count them, let alone dig to the roots of them here, the educated man's daughter can testify from her own experience that they 'commonly, and even usually, survive in the adult and betray their presence, below the level of conscious thought, by the strength of the emotions to which they give rise'. And you will agree that to oppose strong emotion needs courage; and that when courage fails, silence and evasion are likely to manifest themselves.

But now that the interpreters have performed their task, it is time for us to raise the veil of St Paul and to attempt, face to face, a rough and clumsy analysis of that fear and of the anger which causes that fear; for they may have some bearing upon the question you put us, how we can help you to prevent war. Let us suppose, then, that in the course of that bi-sexual private conversation about politics and people, war and peace, barbarism and civilisation, some question has cropped up, about admitting, shall we say, the daughters of educated men to the Church or the Stock Exchange or the diplomatic service. The question is adumbrated merely; but we on our side of the table become aware at once of some 'strong emotion' on your side 'arising from some motive below the level of conscious thought' by the ringing of an alarm bell within us; a confused but tumultuous clamour: You shall not, shall not, shall not . . . The physical symptoms are unmistakable. Nerves erect themselves; fingers automatically tighten upon spoon or cigarette; a glance at the private psychometer shows that the emotional temperature has risen from ten to twenty degrees above normal. Intellectually, there is a strong desire either to be silent; or to change the conversation; to drag in, for example, some old family servant, called Crosby, perhaps, whose dog Rover has died . . . and so evade the issue and lower the temperature.

But what analysis can we attempt of the emotions on the other side of the table – your side? Often, to be candid, while we are talking about Crosby, we are asking questions – hence a certain flatness in the dialogue – about you. What are the powerful and subconscious motives that are raising the hackles on your side of the table? Is the old savage who has killed a bison asking the other old savage to admire his prowess? Is the tired professional man demanding sympathy and resenting competition? Is the patriach calling for the siren? Is dominance craving for submission? And, most persistent and difficult of all the questions that our silence covers, what possible satisfaction can dominance give to the dominator?[108] Now, since Professor Grensted has said that the psychology of the sexes is 'still a matter for specialists', while 'its interpretation remains controversial and in many respects obscure', it would be politic perhaps to leave these questions to be answered by specialists. But since, on the other hand, if common men and women are to be free they must learn to speak freely, we cannot leave the psychology of the sexes to the charge of specialists. There are two good reasons why we must try to analyse both our fear and your anger; first, because such fear and anger prevent real freedom in the private house; second, because such fear and anger may prevent real freedom in the public world: they may have a positive share in causing war. Let us then grope our way amateurishly enough among these very ancient and obscure emotions which we have known ever since the time of Antigone and Ismene and Creon at least; which St Paul himself seems to have felt; but which the professors have only lately brought to the surface and named 'infantile fixation', 'Oedipus complex', and the rest. We must try, however feebly, to analyse those emotions since you have asked us to help you in any way we can to protect liberty and to prevent war.

Let us then examine this 'infantile fixation', for such it seems is the proper name, in order that we may connect it with the question you have put to us. Once more, since we are generalists not specialists, we must rely upon such evidence as we can collect from history, biography, and from the daily paper – the only evidence that is available to the daughters of educated men. We will take our first example of infantile fixation from biography, and once more we will have recourse to Victorian biography because it is only in the Victorian age that biography becomes rich and representative. Now there are so many cases of infantile fixation as defined by Professor Grensted in Victorian biography that we scarcely know which to choose. The case of Mr Barrett of Wimpole Street is, perhaps, the most famous and the best authenticated. Indeed, it is so famous that the facts scarcely bear repetition. We all know the story of the father who would allow neither sons nor daughters to marry; we all know in greatest detail how his daughter Elizabeth was forced to conceal her lover from her father; how she fled with her lover from the house in Wimpole Street; and how her father never forgave her for that act of disobedience. We shall agree that Mr Barrett's emotions were strong in the extreme; and their strength makes it obvious that they had their origin in some dark place below the level of conscious thought. That is a typical, a classical case of infantile fixation which we can all bear in mind. But there are others less famous which a little investigation will bring to the surface and show to be of the same nature. There is the case of the Reverend Patrick Brontë. The Reverend Arthur Nicholls was in love with his daughter Charlotte; 'What his words were,' she wrote, when Mr Nicholls proposed to her, 'you can imagine; his manner you can hardly realise nor can I forget it . . . I asked if he had spoken to Papa. He said he dared not.' Why did he dare not? He was strong and young and passionately in love; the father was old. The reason is immediately apparent. 'He [the Reverend Patrick Brontë] always disapproved of marriages, and constantly talked against them. But he more than disapproved this time; he could not bear the idea of this attachment of Mr Nicholls to his daughter. Fearing the consequences . . . she made haste to give her father a promise that, on the morrow, Mr Nicholls should have a distinct refusal.'[109] Mr Nicholls left Haworth; Charlotte remained with her father. Her married life – it was to be a short one – was shortened still further by her father's wish.

For a third example of infantile fixation let us choose one that is less simple, but for that reason more illuminating. There is the case of Mr Jex-Blake. Here we have the case of a father who is not confronted with his daughter's marriage but with his daughter's wish to earn her living. That wish also would seem to have aroused in the father a very strong emotion and an emotion which also seems to have its origin in the levels below conscious thought. Again with your leave we will call it a case of infantile fixation. The daughter, Sophia, was offered a small sum for teaching mathematics; and she asked her father's permission to take it. That permission was instantly and heatedly refused. 'Dearest, I have only this moment heard that you contemplate being paid for the tutorship. It would be quite beneath you, darling, and *I cannot consent* to it. [The italics are the father's.] Take the post as one of honour and usefulness, and I shall be glad . . . But to be *paid* for the work would be to alter the thing *completely*, and would lower you sadly in the eyes of almost everybody.' That is a very interesting statement. Sophia, indeed, was led to argue the matter. Why was it beneath her, she asked, why should it lower her? Taking money for work did not lower Tom in anybody's eyes. That, Mr Jex-Blake explained, was quite a different matter; Tom was a man; Tom 'feels bound as a man . . . to support his wife and family'; Tom had therefore taken 'the *plain path* of duty'. Still Sophia was not satisfied. She argued – not only was she poor and wanted the money; but also she felt strongly 'the honest, and I believe perfectly justifiable pride of earning'. Thus pressed Mr Jex-Blake at last gave, under a semi-transparent cover, the real reason why he objected to her taking money. He offered to give her the money himself if she would refuse to take it from the college. It was plain, therefore, that he did not object to her taking money: what he objected to was her taking money from another man. The curious nature of his proposal did not escape Sophia's scrutiny. 'In that case,' she said, 'I must say to the Dean, not, "I am willing to work without payment," but, "My father prefers that I should receive payment from *him*, not from the College," and I think the Dean would think us both ridiculous, or at least foolish.' Whatever interpretation the Dean might have put upon Mr Jex-Blake's behaviour, we can have no doubt what emotion was at the root of it. He wished to keep his daughter in his own power. If she took money from him she remained in his power; if she took it from another man not only was she becoming independent of Mr Jex-Blake, she was becoming dependent upon another man. That he wished her to depend upon him and felt obscurely that this desirable dependence could only be secured by financial dependence is proved indirectly by another of his veiled statements. 'If you married tomorrow to my liking – and I don't believe you would ever marry otherwise – I should give you a good fortune.'[110] If she became a wage-earner, she could dispense with the fortune and marry whom she liked. The case of Mr Jex-Blake is very easily diagnosed, but it is a very important case because it is a normal case, a typical case. Mr Jex-Blake was no monster of Wimpole Street; he was an ordinary father; he was doing what thousands of other Victorian fathers whose cases remain unpublished were doing daily. It is a case, therefore, that explains much that lies at the root of Victorian psychology – that psychology of the sexes which is still, Professor Grensted tells us, so obscure. The case of Mr Jex-Blake shows that the daughter must not on any account be allowed to make money because if she makes money she will be independent of her father and free to marry any man she chooses. Therefore the daughter's desire to earn her living rouses two different forms of jealousy. Each is strong separately; together they are very strong. It is further significant that in order to justify this very strong emotion which has its origin below the levels of conscious thought Mr Jex-Blake had recourse to one of the commonest of all evasions; the argument which is not an argument but an appeal to the emotions. He appealed to the very deep, ancient and complex emotion which we may, as amateurs, call the womanhood emotion. To take money was beneath her he said; if she took money she would lower herself in the eyes of almost everybody. Tom being a man would not be lowered; it was her sex that made the difference. He appealed to her womanhood.

Whenever a man makes that appeal to a woman he rouses in her, it is safe to say, a conflict of emotions of a very deep and primitive kind which it is extremely difficult for her to analyse or to reconcile. It may serve to transmit the feeling if we compare it with the confused conflict of manhood emotions that is roused in you, sir, should a woman hand you a white feather.[111] It is interesting to see how Sophia, in the year 1859, tried to deal with this emotion. Her first instinct was to attack the most obvious form of woman-hood, that which lay uppermost in her consciousness and seemed to be responsible for her father's attitude – her ladyhood. Like other educated men's daughters Sophia Jex-Blake was what is called 'a lady'. It was the lady who could not earn money; therefore the lady must be killed. 'Do you honestly, father, think,' she asked, 'any lady lowered by the mere act of receiving money? Did you think the less of Mrs Teed because you paid her?' Then, as if aware that Mrs Teed, being a governess, was not on a par with herself, who came of an upper-middle-class family 'whose lineage will be found in *Burke's Landed Gentry*', she quickly called in to help her to kill the lady 'Mary Jane Evans . . . one of the proudest families of our relations', and then Miss Wodehouse, 'whose family is better and older than mine' – they both thought her right in wishing to earn money. And not only did Miss Wodehouse think her right in wishing to earn money; Miss Wodehouse 'showed she agreed with my opinions by her actions. She sees no meanness in earning, but in those that think it mean. When accepting Maurice's school, she said to him, most nobly, I think, "If you think it better that I should work as a paid mistress, I will take any salary you please; if not, I am willing to do the work freely and for nothing," ' The lady, sometimes, was a noble lady; and that lady it was hard to kill; but killed she must be, as Sophia realised, if Sophia were to enter that paradise where 'lots of girls walk about London when and where they please', that 'Elysium upon earth', which is (or was) Queen's College, Harley Street, where the daughters of educated men enjoy the happiness not of ladies 'but of queens – work and independ-ence!'[112] Thus Sophia's first instinct was to kill the lady;[113] but when the lady was killed the woman still remained. We can see her, concealing and excusing the disease of infantile fixation, more clearly in the other two cases. It was the woman, the human being whose sex made it her sacred duty to sacrifice herself to the father, whom Charlotte Brontë and Elizabeth Barrett had to kill. If it was difficult to kill the lady, it was even more difficult to kill the woman. Charlotte found it at first almost impossible. She refused her lover; ' . . . thus thoughtfully for her father, and unselfishly for herself, [she] put aside all consideration of how she should reply, excepting as he wished.' She loved Arthur Nicholls; but she refused him; ' . . . she held herself simply passive, as far as words and actions went, while she suffered acute pain from the strong expressions which her father used in speaking of Mr Nicholls.' She waited; she suffered; until 'the great conqueror Time', as Mrs Gaskell puts it, 'achieved his victory over strong prejudice and human resolve'. Her father consented. The great conqueror, however, had met his match in Mr Barrett; Elizabeth Barrett waited; Elizabeth suffered; at last Elizabeth fled.

The extreme force of the emotions to which the infantile fixation gives rise is proved by these three cases. It is remarkable, we may agree. It was a force that could quell not only Charlotte Brontë but Arthur Nicholls; not only Elizabeth Barrett but Robert Browning. It was a force thus that could do battle with the strongest of human passions – the love of men and women; and could compel the most brilliant and the boldest of Victorian sons and daughters to quail before it; to cheat the father, to deceive the father, and then to fly from the father. But to what did it owe this amazing force? Partly, as these cases make clear, to the fact that the infantile fixation was protected by society. Nature, law and property were all ready to excuse and conceal it. It was easy for Mr Barrett, Mr Jex-Blake and the Reverend Patrick Brontë to hide the real nature of their emotions from themselves. If they wished that their daughter should stay at home, society agreed that they were right. If the daughter protested, then nature came to their help. A daughter who left her father was an unnatural daughter; her womanhood was suspect. Should she persist further, then law came to his help. A daughter who left her father had no means of supporting herself. The lawful professions were shut to her. Finally, if she earned money in the one profession that was open to her, the oldest profession of all, she unsexed herself. There can be no question – the infantile fixation is powerful, even when a mother is infected. But when the father is infected it has a threefold power: he has nature to protect him, law to protect him and property to protect him. Thus protected it was perfectly possible for the Reverend Patrick Brontë to cause 'acute pain' to his daughter Charlotte for several months, and to steal several months of her short married happiness without incurring any censure from the society in which he practised the profession of a priest of the Church of England; though had he tortured a dog, or stolen a watch, that same society would have unfrocked him and cast him forth. Society it seems was a father, and afflicted with the infantile fixation too.

Since society protected and indeed excused the victims of the infantile fixation in the nineteenth century, it is not surprising that the disease, though unnamed, was rampant. Whatever biography we open we find almost always the familiar symptoms – the father is opposed to his daughter's marriage; the father is opposed to his daughter's earning her living. Her wish either to marry, or to earn her living, rouses strong emotion in him; and he gives the same excuses for that strong emotion; the lady will debase her ladyhood; the daughter will outrage her womanhood. But now and again, very rarely, we find a father who was completely immune from the disease. The results are then extremely interesting. There is the case of Mr Leigh Smith.[114] This gentleman was contemporary with Mr Jex-Blake, and came of the same social caste. He, too, had property in Sussex; he, too, had horses and carriages; and he, too, had children. But there the resemblance ends. Mr Leigh Smith was devoted to his children; he objected to schools; he kept his children at home. It would be interesting to discuss Mr Leigh Smith's educational methods; how he had masters to teach them; how, in a large carriage built like an omnibus, he took them with him on long journeys yearly all over England. But like so many experimentalists, Mr Leigh Smith remains obscure; and we must content ourselves with the fact that he 'held the unusual opinion that daughters should have an equal provision with sons'. So completely immune was he from the infantile fixation that 'he did not adopt the ordinary plan of paying his daughters' bills and giving them an occasional present, but when Barbara came of age in 1848 he gave her an allowance of £300 a year'. The results of that immunity from the infantile fixation were remarkable. For 'treating her money as a power to do good, one of the first uses to which Barbara put it was educational'. She founded a school; a school that was open not only to different sexes and different classes, but to different creeds: Roman Catholics, Jews and 'pupils from families of advanced free thought' were received in it. 'It was a most unusual school,' an outsiders' school. But that was not all that she attempted upon three hundred a year. One thing led to another. A friend, with her help, started a cooperative evening class for ladies 'for drawing from an undraped model'. In 1858 only one life class in London was open to ladies. And then a petition was got up to the Royal Academy; its schools were actually, though as so often happens only nominally, opened to women in 1861;[115] next Barbara went into the question of the laws concerning women; so that actually in 1871 married women were allowed to own their property; and finally she helped Miss Davies to found Girton. When we reflect what one father who was immune from infantile fixation could do by allowing one daughter £300 a year we need not wonder that most fathers firmly refused to allow their daughters more than £40 a year with bed and board thrown in.

The infantile fixation in the fathers then was, it is clear, a strong force, and all the stronger because it was a concealed force. But the fathers were met, as the nineteenth century drew on, by a force which had become so strong in its turn that it is much to be hoped that the psychologists will find some name for it. The old names as we have seen are futile and false. 'Feminism', we have had to destroy. 'The emancipation of women' is equally inexpressive and corrupt. To say that the daughters were inspired prematurely by the principles of anti-Fascism is merely to repeat the fashionable and hideous jargon of the moment. To call them champions of intellectual liberty and culture is to cloud the air with the dust of lecture halls and the damp dowdiness of public meetings. Moreover, none of these tags and labels express the real emotions that inspired the daughters' opposition to the infantile fixation of the fathers, because, as biography shows, that force had behind it many different emotions, and many that were contradictory. Tears were behind it, of course – tears, bitter tears: the tears of those whose desire for knowledge was frustrated. One daughter longed to learn chemistry; the books at home only taught her alchemy. She 'cried bitterly at not being taught things'. Also the desire for an open and rational love was behind it. Again there were tears – angry tears. 'She flung herself on the bed in tears . . . "Oh," she said, "Harry is on the roof." "Who's Harry?" said I; "which roof? Why?" "Oh, don't be silly," she said; "he had to go." '[116] But again the desire not to love, to lead a rational existence without love, was behind it. 'I make the confession humbly . . . I know nothing myself of love,'[117] wrote one of them. An odd confession from one of the class whose only profession for so many centuries had been marriage; but significant. Others wanted to travel; to explore Africa; to dig in Greece and Palestine. Some wanted to learn music, not to tinkle domestic airs, but to compose – operas, symphonies, quartets. Others wanted to paint, not ivy-clad cottages, but naked bodies. They all wanted – but what one word can sum up the variety of the things that they wanted, and had wanted, consciously or subconsciously, for so long? Josephine Butler's label – Justice, Equality, Liberty – is a fine one; but it is only a label, and in our age of innumerable labels, of multi-coloured labels, we have become suspicious of labels; they kill and constrict. Nor does the old word 'freedom' serve, for it was not freedom in the sense of licence that they wanted; they wanted, like Antigone, not to break the laws, but to find the law.[118] Ignorant as we are of human motives and ill supplied with words, let us then admit that no one word expresses the force which in the nineteenth century opposed itself to the force of the fathers. All we can safely say about that force was that it was a force of tremendous power. It forced open the doors of the private house. It opened Bond Street and Piccadilly; it opened cricket grounds and football grounds; it shrivelled flounces and stays; it made the oldest profession in the world (but Whitaker supplies no figures) unprofitable. In fifty years, in short, that force made the life lived by Lady Lovelace and Gertrude Bell unlivable, and almost incredible. The fathers, who had triumphed over the strongest emotions of strong men, had to yield.

If that full stop were the end of the story, the final slam of the door, we could turn at once to your letter, sir, and to the form which you have asked us to fill up. But it was not the end; it was the beginning. Indeed though we have used the past, we shall soon find ourselves using the present tense. The fathers in private, it is true, yielded; but the fathers in public, massed together in societies, in professions, were even more subject to the fatal disease than the fathers in private. The disease had acquired a motive, had connected itself with a right, a conception, which made it still more virulent outside the house than within. The desire to support wife and children – what motive could be more powerful, or deeply rooted? For it was connected with manhood itself – a man who could not support his family failed in his own conception of manliness. And was not that conception as deep in him as the conception of womanhood in his daughter? It was those motives, those rights and conceptions that were now challenged. To protect them, and from women, gave, and gives, rise it can scarcely be doubted to an emotion perhaps below the level of conscious thought but certainly of the utmost violence. The infantile fixation develops, directly the priest's right to practise his profession is challenged, to an aggravated and exacerbated emotion to which the name sex taboo is scientifically applied. Take two instances: one private, the other public. A scholar has 'to mark his disapproval of the admission of women to his university by refusing to enter his beloved college or city.'[119] A hospital has to decline an offer to endow a scholarship because it is made by a woman on behalf of women.[120] Can we doubt that both actions are inspired by that sense of shame which, as Professor Grensted says, 'cannot be regarded in any other light than as a non-rational sex taboo'? But since the emotion itself had increased in strength it became necessary to invoke the help of stronger allies to excuse and conceal it. Nature was called in; Nature it was claimed, who is not only omniscient but unchanging, had made the brain of woman of the wrong shape or size. 'Anyone,' writes Bertrand Russell, 'who desires amusement may be advised to look up the tergiversations of eminent craniologists in their attempts to prove from brain measurements that women are stupider than men.'[121] Science, it would seem, is not sexless; she is a man, a father, and infected too. Science, thus infected, produced measurements to order: the brain was too small to be examined. Many years were spent waiting before the sacred gates of the universities and hospitals for permission to have the brains that the professors said that Nature had made incapable of passing examinations examined. When at last permission was granted the examinations were passed. A long and dreary list of those barren if necessary triumphs lies presumably along with other broken records[122] in college archives, and harassed headmistresses still consult them, it is said, when desiring official proof of impeccable mediocrity. Still Nature held out. The brain that could pass examinations was not the creative brain, the brain that can bear responsibility and earn the higher salaries. It was a practical brain, a pettifogging brain, a brain fitted for routine work under the command of a superior. And since the professions were shut, it was undeniable – the daughters had not ruled empires, commanded fleets, or led armies to victory; only a few trivial books testified to their professional ability, for literature was the only profession that had been open to them. And, moreover, whatever the brain might do when the professions were opened to it, the body remained. Nature, the priests said, in her infinite wisdom, had laid down the unalterable law that man is the creator. He enjoys; she only passively endures. Pain was more beneficial than pleasure to the body that endures. 'The views of medical men on pregnancy, childbirth, and lactation were until fairly recently,' Bertrand Russell writes, 'impregnated with sadism. It required, for example, more evidence to persuade them that anaesthetics may be used in childbirth than it would have required to persuade them of the opposite.' So science argued, so the professors agreed. And when at last the daughters interposed: But are not brain and body affected by training? Does not the wild rabbit differ from the rabbit in the hutch? And must we not, and do we not change this unalterable nature? By setting a match to a fire frost is defied; Nature's decree of death is postponed. And the breakfast egg, they persisted, is it all the work of the cock? Without yolk, without white, how far would your breakfasts, O priests and professors, be fertile? Then the priests and professors in solemn unison intoned: But childbirth itself, that burden you cannot deny, is laid upon woman alone. Nor could they deny it, nor wish to renounce it. Still they declared, consulting the statistics in books, the time occupied by woman in childbirth is under modern conditions – remember we are in the twentieth century now – only a fraction.[123] Did that fraction incapacitate us from working in Whitehall, in fields and factories, when our country was in danger? To which the fathers replied: The war is over; we are in England now.

And if, sir, pausing in England now, we turn on the wireless of the daily press we shall hear what answer the fathers who are infected with infantile fixation now are making to those questions now. 'Homes are the real places of the women . . . Let them go back to their homes . . . The Government should give work to men . . . A strong protest is to be made by the Ministry of Labour . . . Women must not rule over men . . . There are two worlds, one for women, the other for men . . . Let them learn to cook our dinners . . . Women have failed . . . They have failed . . . They have failed . . . '

Even now the clamour, the uproar that infantile fixation is making even here is such that we can hardly hear ourselves speak; it takes the words out of our mouths; it makes us say what we have not said. As we listen to the voices we seem to hear an infant crying in the night, the black night that now covers Europe, and with no language but a cry, Ay, ay, ay, ay . . . But it is not a new cry, it is a very old cry. Let us shut off the wireless and listen to the past. We are in Greece now; Christ has not been born yet, nor St Paul either. But listen: 'Whomsoever the city may appoint, that man must be obeyed, in little things and great, in just things and unjust . . . disobedience is the worst of evils . . . We must support the cause of order, and in no wise suffer a woman to worst us . . . They must be women, and not range at large. Servants, take them within.' That is the voice of Creon, the dictator. To whom Antigone, who was to have been his daughter, answered, 'Not such are the laws set among men by the justice who dwells with the gods below.' But she had neither capital nor force behind her. And Creon said: 'I will take her where the path is loneliest, and hide her, living, in a rocky vault.' And he shut her not in Holloway or in a concentration camp but in a tomb. And Creon we read brought ruin on his house, and scattered the land with the bodies of the dead. It seems, sir, as we listen to the voices of the past, as if we were looking at the photograph again, at the picture of dead bodies and ruined houses that the Spanish Government sends us almost weekly. Things repeat themselves it seems. Pictures and voices are the same today as they were two thousand years ago.

Such then is the conclusion to which our inquiry into the nature of fear has brought us – the fear which forbids freedom in the private house. That fear, small, insignificant and private as it is, is connected with the other fear, the public fear, which is neither small nor insignificant, the fear which has led you to ask us to help you to prevent war. Otherwise we should not be looking at the picture again. But it is not the same picture that caused us at the beginning of this letter to feel the same emotions – you called them 'horror and disgust'; we called them horror and disgust. For as this letter has gone on, adding fact to fact, another picture has imposed itself upon the foreground. It is the figure of a man; some say, others deny, that he is Man himself,[124] the quintessence of virility, the perfect type of which all the others are imperfect adumbrations. He is a man certainly. His eyes are glazed; his eyes glare. His body, which is braced in an unnatural position, is tightly cased in a uniform. Upon the breast of that uniform are sewn several medals and other mystic symbols. His hand is upon a sword. He is called in German and Italian Führer or Duce; in our own language Tyrant or Dictator. And behind him lie ruined houses and dead bodies – men, women and children. But we have not laid that picture before you in order to excite once more the sterile emotion of hate. On the contrary it is in order to release other emotions such as the human figure, even thus crudely in a coloured photograph, arouses in us who are human beings. For it suggests a connection and for us a very important connection. It suggests that the public and the private worlds are inseparably connected; that the tyrannies and servilities of the one are the tyrannies and servilities of the other. But the human figure even in a photograph suggests other and more complex emotions. It suggests that we cannot dissociate ourselves from that figure but are ourselves that figure. It suggests that we are not passive spectators doomed to unresisting obedience but by our thoughts and actions can ourselves change that figure. A common interest unites us; it is one world, one life. How essential it is that we should realise that unity the dead bodies, the ruined houses prove. For such will be our ruin if you in the immensity of your public abstractions forget the private figure, or if we in the intensity of our private emotions forget the public world. Both houses will be ruined, the public and the private, the material and the spiritual, for they are inseparably connected. But with your letter before us we have reason to hope. For by asking our help you recognise that connection; and by reading your words we are reminded of other connections that lie far deeper than the facts on the surface. Even here, even now your letter tempts us to shut our ears to these little facts, these trivial details, to listen not to the bark of the guns and the bray of the gramophones but to the voices of the poets, answering each other, assuring us of a unity that rubs out divisions as if they were chalk marks only; to discuss with you the capacity of the human spirit to overflow boundaries and make unity out of multiplicity. But that would be to dream – to dream the recurring dream that has haunted the human mind since the beginning of time: the dream of peace, the dream of freedom. But, with the sound of the guns in your ears you have not asked us to dream. You have not asked us what peace is; you have asked us how to prevent war. Let us then leave it to the poets to tell us what the dream is; and fix our eyes upon the photograph again: the fact. Whatever the verdict of others may be upon the man in uniform – and opinions differ – there is your letter to prove that to you the picture is the picture of evil. And though we look upon that picture from different angles our conclusion is the same as yours – it is evil. We are both determined to do what we can to destroy the evil which that picture represents, you by your methods, we by ours. And since we are different, our help must be different. What ours can be we have tried to show – how imperfectly, how superficially there is no need to say.[125] But as a result the answer to your question must be that we can best help you to prevent war not by repeating your words and following your methods but by finding new words and creating new methods. We can best help you to prevent war not by joining your society but by remaining outside your society but in cooperation with its aim. That aim is the same for us both. It is to assert 'the rights of all – all men and women – to the respect in their persons of the great principles of Justice and Equality and Liberty'. To elaborate further is unnecessary, for we have every confidence that you interpret those words as we do. And excuses are unnecessary, for we can trust you to make allowances for those deficiencies which we foretold and which this letter has abundantly displayed.

To return then to the form that you have sent and ask us to fill up: for the reasons given we will leave it unsigned. But in order to prove as substantially as possible that our aims are the same as yours, here is the guinea, a free gift, given freely, without any other conditions than you choose to impose upon yourself. It is the third of three guineas; but the three guineas, you will observe, though given to three different treasurers are all given to the same cause, for the causes are the same and inseparable.

Now, since you are pressed for time, let me make an end – apologising three times over to the three of you, first for the length of this letter, second for the smallness of the contribution and thirdly for writing at all. The blame for that however rests upon you, for this letter would never have been written had you not asked for an answer to your own.

1 *The Life of Mary Kingsley*, Stephen Gwynn, p. 15. It is difficult to get exact figures of the sums spent on the education of educated men's daughters. About £20 or £30 presumably covered the entire cost of Mary Kingsley's education (b. 1862; d. 1900). A sum of £100 may be taken as about the average in the nineteenth century and even later. The women thus educated often felt the lack of education very keenly. 'I always feel the defects of my education most painfully when I go out,' wrote Anne J. Clough, the first principal of Newnham (*Life of Anne J. Clough*, B. A. Clough, p. 60). Elizabeth Haldane, who came, like Miss Clough, of a highly literate family, but was educated in much the same way, says that when she grew up, 'My first conviction was that I was not educated, and I thought of how this could be put right. I should have loved going to college, but college in those days was unusual for girls, and the idea was not encouraged. It was also expensive. For an only daughter to leave a widowed mother was indeed considered to be out of the question, and no one made the plan seem feasible. There was in those days a new movement for carrying on correspondence classes . . . ' (*From One Century to Another*, Elizabeth Haldane, p. 73). The efforts of such uneducated women to conceal their ignorance were often valiant, but not always successful. 'They talked agreeably on current topics, carefully avoiding controversial subjects. What impressed me was their ignorance and indifference concerning anything outside their own circle . . . no less a personage than the mother of the Speaker of the House of Commons believed that California belonged to us, part of our Empire!' (*Distant Fields*, H. A. Vachell, p. 109). That ignorance was often simulated in the nineteenth century owing to the current belief that educated men enjoyed it is shown by the energy with which Thomas Gisborne, in his instructive work *On the Duties of Women* (p. 278), rebuked those who recommend women 'studiously to refrain from discovering to their partners in marriage the full extent of their abilities and attainments'. 'This is not discretion but art. It is dissimulation, it is deliberate imposition . . . It could scarcely be practised long without detection.'

But the educated man's daughter in the nineteenth century was even more ignorant of life than of books. One reason for that ignorance is suggested by the following quotation: 'It was supposed that most men were not "virtuous", that is, that nearly all would be capable of accosting and annoying – or worse – any unaccompanied young woman whom they met' ('Society and the Season', Mary, Countess of Lovelace, in *Fifty Years: 1882–1932*, p. 37). She was therefore confined to a very narrow circle; and her 'ignorance and indifference' to anything outside it was excusable. The connection between that ignorance and the nineteenth-century conception of manhood, which – witness the Victorian hero – made 'virtue' and virility incompatible, is obvious. In a well-known passage Thackeray complains of the limitations which virtue and virility between them imposed upon his art.

2 Our ideology is still so inveterately anthropocentric that it has been necessary to coin this clumsy term – educated man's daughter – to describe the class whose fathers have been educated at public schools and universities. Obviously, if the term 'bourgeois' fits her brother, it is grossly incorrect to use it of one who differs so profoundly in the two prime characteristics of the bourgeoisie – capital and environment.

3 The number of animals killed in England for sport during the past century must be beyond computation; 1,212 head of game is given as the average for a day's shooting at Chatsworth in 1909 (*Men, Women and Things*, the Duke of Portland, p. 251). Little mention is made in sporting memoirs of women guns; and their appearance in the hunting field was the cause of much caustic comment. 'Skittles', the famous nineteenth-century horsewoman, was a lady of easy morals. It is highly probable that there was held to be some connection between sport and unchastity in women in the nineteenth century.

4 *Francis and Riversdale Grenfell*, John Buchan, pp. 189, 205

5 *Antony (Viscount Knebworth)*, the Earl of Lytton, p. 355

6 *The Poems of Wilfred Owen*, edited by Edmund Blunden, pp. 25, 41

7 Lord Hewart, proposing the toast of 'England' at the banquet of the Society of St George at Cardiff

8 *Daily Telegraph*, 5 February 1937

9 *Daily Telegraph*, 5 February 1937

10 There is of course one essential that the educated woman can supply: children. And one method by which she can help to prevent war is to refuse to bear children. Thus Mrs Helena Normanton is of opinion that: 'The only thing that women in any country can do to prevent war is to stop the supply of "cannon fodder" ' (Report of the Annual Council for Equal Citizenship, *Daily Telegraph*, 5 March 1937). Letters in the news-papers frequently support this view. 'I can tell Mr Harry Campbell why women refuse to have children in these times. When men have learnt how to run the lands they govern so that wars shall hit only those who make the quarrels, instead of mowing down those who do not, then women may again feel like having large families. Why should women bring children into such a world as this one is today?' (Edith Maturin-Porch, in the *Daily Telegraph*, 6 September 1937). The fact that the birth rate in the educated class is falling would seem to show that educated

women are taking Mrs Normanton's advice. It was offered them in very similar circumstances over two thousand years ago by Lysistrata.

11 There are of course innumerable kinds of influence besides those specified in the text. It varies from the simple kind described in the following passage: 'Three years later . . . we find her writing to him as Cabinet Minister to solicit his interest on behalf of a favourite parson for a Crown living . . . ' (*Henry Chaplin: A Memoir*, Lady Londonderry, p. 57), to the very subtle kind exerted by Lady Macbeth upon her husband. Somewhere between the two lies the influence described by D. H. Lawrence: 'It is hopeless for me to try to do anything without I have a woman at the back of me . . . I daren't sit in the world without I have a woman behind me . . . But a woman that I love sort of keeps me in direct communication with the unknown, in which otherwise I am a bit lost' (*Letters of D. H. Lawrence*, pp. 93–4), with which we may compare, though the collocation is strange, the famous and very similar definition given by the ex-king Edward VIII upon his abdication. Present political conditions abroad seem to favour a return to the use of interested influence. For example: 'A story serves to illustrate the present degree of women's influence in Vienna. During the past autumn a measure was planned to further diminish women's professional opportunities. Protests, pleas, letters, all were of no avail. Finally, in desperation, a group of well-known ladies of the city . . . got together and planned. For the next fortnight, for a certain number of hours per day, several of these ladies got on to the telephone to the ministers they knew personally, ostensibly to ask them to dinner at their homes. With all the charm of which the Viennese are capable, they kept the ministers talking, asking about this and that, and finally mentioning the matter that distressed them so much. When the ministers had been rung up by several ladies, all of whom they did not wish to offend, and kept from urgent state affairs by this manoeuvre, they decided on compromise – and so the measure was postponed' (*Women Must Choose*, Hilary Newitt, p. 129). Similar use of influence was often deliberately made during the battle for the franchise. But women's influence is said to be impaired by the possession of a vote. Thus Marshal von Bieberstein was of opinion that: 'Women led men always . . . but he did not wish them to vote' (*From One Century to Another*, Elizabeth Haldane, p. 258).

12 English women were much criticised for using force in the battle for the franchise. When in 1910 Mr Birrell had his hat 'reduced to pulp' and his shins kicked by suffragettes, Sir Almeric Fitzroy commented, 'an attack of this character upon a defenceless old man by an organised band of "janissaries" will, it is hoped, convince many people of the insane and anarchical spirit actuating the movement' (*Memoirs of Sir Almeric Fitzroy*, Vol. II, p. 425). These remarks did not apply apparently to the force in the European war. The vote indeed was given to English

women largely because of the help they gave to English men in using force in that war. 'On 14 August [1916], Mr Asquith himself gave up his opposition [to the franchise]. "It is true," he said, "[that women] cannot fight in the sense of going out with rifles and so forth, but . . . they have aided in the most effective way in the prosecution of the war" ' (*The Cause*, Ray Strachey, p. 354). This raises the difficult question whether those who did not aid in the prosecution of the war, but did what they could to hinder the prosecution of the war, ought to use the vote to which they are entitled chiefly because others 'aided in the prosecution of the war'? That they are stepdaughters, not full daughters, of England is shown by the fact that they change nationality on marriage. A woman, whether or not she helped to beat the Germans, becomes a German if she marries a German. Her political views must then be entirely reversed, and her filial piety transferred.

13 *Sir Ernest Wild, K.C.*, Robert J. Blackburn, pp. 174–5

14 That the right to vote has not proved negligible is shown by the facts published from time to time by the National Union of Societies for Equal Citizenship. 'This publication [*What the Vote Has Done*] was originally a single-page leaflet; it has now (1927) grown to a six-page pamphlet, and has to be constantly enlarged' (*Josephine Butler*, M. G. Fawcett and E. M. Turner, note, p. 101).

15 There are no figures available with which to check facts that must have a very important bearing upon the biology and psychology of the sexes. A beginning might be made in this essential but strangely neglected preliminary by chalking on a large-scale map of England property owned by men, red; by women, blue. Then the number of sheep and cattle consumed by each sex must be compared; the hogsheads of wine and beer; the barrels of tobacco; after which we must examine carefully their physical exercises; domestic employments; facilities for sexual intercourse, etc. Historians are of course mainly concerned with war and politics, but sometimes throw light upon human nature. Thus Macaulay, dealing with the English country gentleman in the seventeenth century, says: 'His wife and daughter were in tastes and acquirements below a housekeeper or still-room maid of the present day. They stitched and spun, brewed gooseberry wine, cured marigolds, and made the crust for the venison pasty.'

Again, 'The ladies of the house, whose business it had commonly been to cook the repast, retired as soon as the dishes had been devoured, and left the gentlemen to their ale and tobacco' (Macaulay, *History of England*, Chapter Three). But the gentlemen were still drinking and the ladies were still withdrawing a great deal later. 'In my mother's young days before her marriage, the old hard-drinking habits of the Regency and of the eighteenth century still persisted. At Woburn Abbey it was the custom for the trusted old family butler to make his nightly report to my grandmother in the drawing-room. 'The gentlemen have had a good deal tonight; it might be as well for the young ladies to retire,' or, 'The gentlemen have had very little tonight,' was announced according to circumstances by this faithful family retainer. Should the young girls be packed off upstairs, they liked standing on an upper gallery of the staircase 'to watch the shouting, riotous crowd issuing from the dining-room' (*The Days Before Yesterday*, Lord F. Hamilton, p. 322). It must be left to the scientist of the future to tell us what effect drink and property have had upon chromosomes.

16 The fact that both sexes have a very marked though dissimilar love of dress seems to have escaped the notice of the dominant sex owing largely it must be supposed to the hypnotic power of dominance. Thus the late Mr Justice MacCardie, in summing up the case of Mrs Frankau, remarked: 'Women cannot be expected to renounce an essential feature of femininity or to abandon one of nature's solaces for a constant and insuperable physical handicap . . . Dress, after all, is one of the chief methods of women's self-expression . . . In matters of dress women often remain children to the end. The psychology of the matter must not be overlooked. But whilst bearing the above matters in mind the law has rightly laid it down that the rule of prudence and proportion must be observed.' The judge who thus dictated was wearing a scarlet robe, an ermine cape, and a vast wig of artificial curls. Whether he was enjoying 'one of nature's solaces for a constant and insuperable physical handicap', whether again he was himself observing 'the rule of prudence and proportion' must be doubtful. But 'the psychology of the matter must not be overlooked'; and the fact that the singularity of his own appearance, together with that of admirals, generals, heralds, life guards, peers, beef-eaters, etc., was completely invisible to him so that he was able to lecture the lady without any consciousness of sharing her weakness, raises two questions: how often must an act be performed before it becomes tradition, and therefore venerable; and what degree of social prestige causes blindness to the remarkable nature of one's own clothes? Singularity of dress, when not associated with office, seldom escapes ridicule.

17 In the New Year's Honours List for 1937, 147 men accepted honours as against seven women. For obvious reasons this cannot be taken as a measure of their comparative desire for such advertisement. But that it should be easier, psychologically, for a woman to reject honours than for a man seems to be indisputable. For the fact that intellect (roughly speaking) is man's chief professional asset, and that stars and ribbons are his chief means of advertising intellect, suggests that stars and ribbons are identical with powder and paint, a woman's chief method of advertising her chief professional asset: beauty. It would therefore be as unreasonable to ask him to refuse a knighthood as to ask her to refuse a dress. The sum paid for a knighthood in 1901 would seem to

provide a very tolerable dress allowance: '21 April (Sunday) – To see Meynell, who was as usual full of gossip. It appears that the King's debts have been paid off privately by his friends, one of whom is said to have lent £100,000, and satisfies himself with £25,000 in repayment plus a Knighthood' (*My Diaries*, Wilfrid Scawen Blunt, Part II, p. 8).

18 What the precise figures are it is difficult for an outsider to know. But that the incomes are substantial can be conjectured from a delightful review some years ago by Mr J. M. Keynes in *The Nation* of a history of Clare College, Cambridge. The book 'it is rumoured cost six thousand pounds to produce'. Rumour has it also that a band of students returning at dawn from some festivity about that time saw a cloud in the sky; which as they gazed assumed the shape of a woman; who, being supplicated for a sign, let fall in a shower of radiant hail the one word 'Rats'. This was interpreted to signify what from another page of the same number of *The Nation* would seem to be the truth: that the students of one of the women's colleges suffered greatly from 'cold gloomy ground-floor bedrooms overrun with mice'. The apparition, it was supposed, took this means of suggesting that, if the gentlemen of Clare wished to do her honour, a cheque for £6,000 payable to the Principal of — would celebrate her better than a book, even though 'clothed in the finest dress of paper and black buckram . . . ' There is nothing mythical, however, about the fact recorded in the same number of *The Nation* that 'Somerville received with pathetic gratitude the £7,000 which went to it last year from the Jubilee gift and a private bequest.'

19 A great historian has thus described the origin and character of the universities, in one of which he was educated: 'The schools of Oxford and Cambridge were founded in a dark age of false and barbarous science; and they are still tainted by the vices of their origin . . . The legal incorporation of these societies by the charters of popes and kings had given them a monopoly of public instruction; and the spirit of monopolists is narrow, lazy, and oppressive: their work is more costly and less productive than that of independent artists; and the new improvements so eagerly grasped by the competition of freedom are admitted with slow and sullen reluctance in those proud corporations, above the fear of a rival, and below the confession of an error. We may scarcely hope that any reformation will be a voluntary act; and so deeply are they rooted in law and prejudice, that even the omnipotence of Parliament would shrink from an inquiry into the state and abuses of the two universities' (Edward Gibbon, *Memoirs of My Life and Writings*). 'The omnipotence of Parliament' did however institute an inquiry in the middle of the nineteenth century 'into the state of the University [of Oxford], its discipline, studies, and revenues. But there was so much passive resistance from the Colleges that the last item had to go by the board. It was ascertained however that out of 542 Fellowships in all the Colleges of Oxford only twenty-two were really

open to competition without restrictive conditions of patronage, place or kin . . . The Commissioners . . . found that Gibbon's indictment had been reasonable . . . ' (*Herbert Warren of Magdalen*, Laurie Magnus, pp. 47–9). Nevertheless the prestige of a university education remained high; and Fellowships were considered highly desirable. When Pusey became a Fellow of Oriel, 'The bells of the parish church at Pusey expressed the satisfaction of his father and family.' Again, when Newman was elected a Fellow, 'all the bells of the three towers [were] set pealing – at Newman's expense' (*Oxford Apostles*, Geoffrey Faber, pp. 131, 169). Yet both Pusey and Newman were men of a distinctly spiritual nature.

20 *The Crystal Cabinet*, Mary Butts, p. 138. The sentence in full runs: 'For just as I was told that desire for learning in woman was against the will of God, so were many innocent freedoms, innocent delights, denied in the same Name' – a remark which makes it desirable that we should have a biography from the pen of an educated man's daughter of the Deity in whose Name such atrocities have been committed. The influence of religion upon women's education, one way or another, can scarcely be overestimated. 'If, for example,' says Thomas Gisborne, 'the uses of music are explained, let not its effect in heightening devotion be over- looked. If drawing is the subject of remark, let the student be taught habitually to contemplate in the works of creation the power, the wisdom and the goodness of their Author' (*The Duties of the Female Sex*, Thomas Gisborne, p. 85). The fact that Mr Gisborne and his like – a numerous band – base their educational theories upon the teaching of St Paul would seem to hint that the female sex was to be 'taught habitually to contemplate, in the works of creation, the power and wisdom and the goodness', not so much of the Deity, but of Mr Gisborne. And from that we were led to conclude that a biography of the Deity would resolve itself into a *Dictionary of Clerical Biography*.

21 *Mary Astell*, Florence M. Smith. 'Unfortunately, the opposition to so new an idea [a college for women] was greater than the interest in it, and came not only from the satirists of the day, who, like the wits of all ages, found the progressive woman a source of laughter and made Mary Astell the subject of stock jokes in comedies of the *Femmes Savantes* type, but from churchmen, who saw in the plan an attempt to bring back popery. The strongest opponent of the idea was a celebrated bishop, who, as Ballard asserts, prevented a prominent lady from subscribing £10,000 to the plan. Elizabeth Elstob gave to Ballard the name of this celebrated bishop in reply to an inquiry from him. "According to Elizabeth Elstob . . . it was Bishop Burnet that prevented that good design by dissuading that lady from encouraging it" ' (op. cit., pp. 21–2). 'That lady' may have been Princess Ann, or Lady Elizabeth Hastings; but there seems reason to think that it was the Princess. That the Church swallowed the money is an assumption, but one perhaps justified by the history of the Church.

22 *Ode for Music*, performed in the Senate House at Cambridge, 1 July 1769

23 'I assure you I am not an enemy of women. I am very favourable to their employment as *laboureres* or in other *menial* capacity. I have, however, doubts as to the likelihood of their succeeding in business as capitalists. I am sure the nerves of most women would break down under the anxiety, and that most of them are utterly destitute of the disciplined reticence necessary to every sort of cooperation. Two thousand years hence you may have changed it all, but the present women will only flirt with men, and quarrel with one another' (extract from a letter from Walter Bagehot to Emily Davies, who had asked his help in founding Girton).

24 *Recollections and Reflections*, Sir J. J. Thomson, pp. 86–8, 296–7

25 'Cambridge University still refuses to admit women to the full rights of membership; it grants them only titular degrees and they have therefore no share in the government of the University' (*Memorandum on the Position of English Women in Relation to that of English Men*, Philippa Strachey, 1935, p. 26). Nevertheless, the Government makes a 'liberal grant' from public money to Cambridge University.

26 'The total number of students at recognised institutions for the higher education of women who are receiving instruction in the University or working in the University laboratories or museums shall not at any time exceed five hundred' (*The Student's Handbook to Cambridge*, 1934–5, p. 616). Whitaker informs us that the number of male students who were in residence at Cambridge in October 1935 was 5,328. Nor would there appear to be any limitation.

27 The men's scholarship list at Cambridge printed in *The Times* of 20 December 1937, measures roughly thirty-one inches; the women's scholarship list at Cambridge measures roughly five inches. There are, however, seventeen colleges for men and the list here measured includes only eleven. The thirty-one inches must therefore be increased. There are only two colleges for women; both are here measured.

28 Until the death of Lady Stanley of Alderley, there was no chapel at Girton. 'When it was proposed to build a chapel, she objected, on the ground that all the available funds should be spent on education. "So long as I live, there shall be no chapel at Girton," I heard her say. The present chapel was built immediately after her death.' (*The Amberley Papers*, Patricia and Bertrand Russell, Vol. I, p. 17). Would that her ghost had possessed the same influence as her body! But ghosts, it is said, have no cheque books.

29 'I have also a feeling that girls' schools have, on the whole, been content to take the general lines of their education from the older-established institutions for my own, the weaker sex. My own feeling is that the problem ought to be attacked by some original genius on quite different lines . . . ' (*Things Ancient and Modern*, C. A. Alington, pp. 216–17). It scarcely needs genius or originality to see that 'the lines', in the first

place, must be cheaper. But it would be interesting to know what meaning we are to attach to the word 'weaker' in the context. For since Dr Alington is a former headmaster of Eton he must be aware that his sex has not only acquired but retained the vast revenues of that ancient foundation – a proof, one would have thought, not of sexual weakness but of sexual strength. That Eton is not 'weak', at least from the material point of view, is shown by the following quotation from Dr Alington: 'Following out the suggestion of one of the Prime Minister's Committees on Education, the Provost and Fellows in my time decided that all scholarships at Eton should be of a fixed value, capable of being liberally augmented in case of need. So liberal has been this augmentation that there are several boys in College whose parents pay nothing towards either their board or education.' One of the benefactors was the late Lord Rosebery. 'He was a generous benefactor to the school,' Dr Alington informs us, 'and endowed a history scholarship, in connection with which a characteristic episode occurred. He asked me whether the endowment was adequate and I suggested that a further £200 would provide for the payment to the examiner. He sent a cheque for £2,000: his attention was called to the discrepancy, and I have in my scrapbook the reply in which he said that he thought a good round sum would be better than a fraction' (op. cit., pp. 163, 186). The entire sum spent at Cheltenham College for Girls in 1854 upon salaries and visiting teachers was £1,300; 'and the accounts in December showed a deficit of £400' (*Dorothea Beale of Cheltenham*, Elizabeth Raikes, p. 91).

30 The words 'vain and vicious' require qualification. No one would maintain that all lecturers and all lectures are 'vain and vicious'; many subjects can only be taught with diagrams and personal demonstration. The words in the text refer only to the sons and daughters of educated men who lecture their brothers and sisters upon English literature; and for the reasons that it is an obsolete practice dating from the Middle Ages when books were scarce; that it owes its survival to pecuniary motives; or to curiosity; that the publication in book form is sufficient proof of the evil effect of an audience upon the lecturer intellectually; and that psychologically eminence upon a platform encourages vanity and the desire to impose authority. Further, the reduction of English literature to an examination subject must be viewed with suspicion by all who have first-hand knowledge of the difficulty of the art, and therefore of the very superficial value of an examiner's approval or disapproval; and with profound regret by all who wish to keep one art at least out of the hands of middlemen and free, as long as may be, from all association with competition and money-making. Again, the violence with which one school of literature is now opposed to another, the rapidity with which one school of taste succeeds another, may not unreasonably be traced to the power which a mature mind lecturing immature minds has to infect

them with strong, if passing, opinions, and to tinge those opinions with personal bias. Nor can it be maintained that the standard of critical or of creative writing has been raised. A lamentable proof of the mental docility to which the young are reduced by lecturers is that the demand for lectures upon English literature steadily increases (as every writer can bear witness) and from the very class which should have learnt to read at home – the educated. If, as is sometimes urged in excuse, what is desired by college literary societies is not knowledge of literature but acquaintance with writers, there are cocktails, and there is sherry; both better unmixed with Proust. None of this applies of course to those whose homes are deficient in books. If the working class finds it easier to assimilate English literature by word of mouth they have a perfect right to ask the educated class to help them thus. But for the sons and daughters of that class after the age of eighteen to continue to sip English literature through a straw, is a habit that seems to deserve the terms vain and vicious; which terms can justly be applied with greater force to those who pander to them.

31 It is difficult to procure exact figures of the sums allowed the daughters of educated men before marriage. Sophia Jex-Blake had an allowance of from £30 to £40 annually; her father was an upper-middle-class man. Lady Lascelles, whose father was an earl, had, it seems, an allowance of about £100 in 1860; Mr Barrett, a rich merchant, allowed his daughter Elizabeth 'from forty to forty-five pounds . . . every three months, the income tax being first deducted'. But this seems to have been the interest upon £8,000, 'or more or less . . . it is difficult to ask about it', which she had 'in the funds', 'the money being in two different per cents', and apparently, though belonging to Elizabeth, under Mr Barrett's control. But these were unmarried women. Married women were not allowed to own property until the passing of the Married Woman's Property Act in 1870. Lady St Helier records that since her marriage settlements had been drawn up in conformity with the old law, 'What money I had was settled on my husband, and no part of it was reserved for my private use . . . I did not even possess a cheque book, nor was I able to get any money except by asking my husband. He was kind and generous but he acquiesced in the position then existing that a woman's property belonged to her husband . . . he paid all my bills, he kept my bank book, and gave me a small allowance for my personal expenses' (*Memories of Fifty Years*, Lady St Helier, p. 341). But she does not say what the exact sum was. The sums allowed to the sons of educated men were considerably larger. An allowance of £200 was considered to be only just sufficient for an undergraduate at Balliol, 'which still had traditions of frugality', about 1880. On that allowance 'they could not hunt and they could not gamble . . . But with care, and with a home to fall back on in the vacations, they could make this do' (*Anthony Hope and His Books*, Sir C. Mallet,

p. 38). The sum that is now needed is considerably more. Gino Watkins 'never spent more than the £400 yearly allowance with which he paid all his college and vacation bills' (*Gino Watkins*, J. M. Scott, p. 59). This was at Cambridge, a few years ago.

32 How incessantly women were ridiculed throughout the nineteenth century for attempting to enter their solitary profession, novel readers know, for those efforts provide half the stock-in-trade of fiction. But biography shows how natural it was, even in the present century, for the most enlightened of men to conceive of all women as spinsters, all desiring marriage. Thus: ' "Oh dear, what is to happen to them?" he [G. L. Dickinson] once murmured sadly as a stream of aspiring but uninspiring spinsters flowed round the front court of King's; "I don't know and they don't know." And then in still lower tones as if his bookshelves might overhear him, "Oh dear! What they want is a husband!" ' (*Goldsworthy Lowes Dickinson*, E. M. Forster, p. 106). 'What they wanted' might have been the Bar, the Stock Exchange or rooms in Gibbs's Buildings, had the choice been open to them. But it was not; and therefore Mr Dickinson's remark was a very natural one.

33 'Now and then, at least in the larger houses, there would be a set party, selected and invited long beforehand, and over these always one idol dominated – the pheasant. Shooting had to be used as a lure. At such times the father of the family was apt to assert himself. If his house was to be filled to bursting, his wines drunk in quantities, and his best shooting provided, then for that shooting he would have the best guns possible. What despair for the mother of daughters to be told that the one guest whom of all others she secretly desired to invite was a bad shot and totally inadmissible!' ('Society and the Season', Mary, Countess of Lovelace, in *Fifty Years: 1882–1932*, p. 29).

34 Some idea of what men hoped that their wives might say and do, at least in the nineteenth century, may be gathered from the following hints in a letter 'addressed to a young lady for whom he had a great regard a short time before her marriage' by John Bowdler. 'Above all, avoid everything which has the *least tendency* to indelicacy or indecorum. Few women have any *idea* how much men are disgusted at the slightest approach to these in any female, and especially in one to whom they are attached. By attending the nursery, or the sick bed, women are too apt to acquire a habit of conversing on such subjects in language which men of delicacy are shocked at' (*Life of John Bowdler*, p. 123). But though delicacy was essential, it could, after marriage, be disguised. 'In the 'seventies of last century, Miss Jex-Blake and her associates were vigorously fighting the battle for admission of women to the medical profession, and the doctors were still more vigorously resisting their entry, alleging that it must be improper and demoralising for a woman to have to study and deal with delicate and intimate medical questions. At that time Ernest Hart, the

editor of the *British Medical Journal*, told me that the majority of the contributions sent to him for publication in the *Journal* dealing with delicate and intimate medical questions were in the handwriting of the doctors' wives, to whom they had obviously been dictated. There were no typewriters or stenographers available in those days' (*The Doctor's Second Thoughts*, Sir J. Crichton-Browne, pp. 73–4).

The duplicity of delicacy was observed long before this, however. Thus Mandeville in *The Fable of the Bees* (1714) says: ' . . . I would have it first consider'd that the Modesty of Woman is the result of Custom and Education, by which all unfashionable Denudations and filthy Expressions are render'd frightful and abominable to them, and that notwithstanding this, the most Virtuous Young Woman alive will often, in spite of her Teeth, have Thoughts and confus'd Ideas of Things arise in her Imagination, which she would not reveal to some People for a Thousand Worlds.'

35 To quote the exact words of one such appeal: 'This letter is to ask you to set aside for us garments for which you have no further use . . . Stockings, of every sort, no matter how worn, are also most acceptable . . . The Committee find that by offering these clothes at bargain prices . . . they are performing a really useful service to women whose professions require that they should have presentable day and evening dresses which they can ill afford to buy' (extract from a letter received from the London and National Society for Women's Service, 1938).

36 *The Testament of Joad*, C. E. M. Joad, pp. 210–11. Since the number of societies run directly or indirectly by Englishwomen in the cause of peace is too long to quote (see *The Story of the Disarmament Declaration*, p. 15, for a list of the peace activities of professional, business and working-class women) it is unnecessary to take Mr Joad's criticism seriously, however illuminating psychologically.

37 *Experiment in Autobiography*, H. G. Wells, p. 486. The men's 'movement to resist the practical obliteration of their freedom by Nazis or Fascists' may have been more perceptible. But that it has been more successful is doubtful. 'Nazis now control the whole of Austria' (report in a daily paper, 12 March 1938).

38 'Women, I think, ought not to sit down to table with men; their presence ruins conversation, tending to make it trivial and genteel, or at best merely clever' (*Under the Fifth Rib*, C. E. M. Joad, p. 58). This is an admirably outspoken opinion, and if all who share Mr Joad's sentiments were to express them as openly, the hostess's dilemma – whom to ask, whom not to ask – would be lightened and her labour saved. If those who prefer the society of their own sex at table would signify the fact, the men, say, by wearing a red, the women by wearing a white rosette, while those who prefer the sexes mixed wore parti-coloured buttonholes of red and white blended, not only would much inconvenience and

misunderstanding be prevented, but it is possible that the honesty of the buttonhole would kill a certain form of social hypocrisy now all too prevalent. Meanwhile, Mr Joad's candour deserves the highest praise, and his wishes the most implicit observance.

39 According to Mrs H. M. Swanwick, the WSPU had 'an income from gifts, in the year 1912, of £42,000' (*I Have Been Young*, H. M. Swanwick, p. 189). The total spent in 1912 by the Women's Freedom League was £26,772 12s. 9d. (*The Cause*, Ray Strachey, p. 311). Thus the joint income of the two societies was £68,772 12s. 9d. But the two societies were, of course, opposed.

40 'But, exceptions apart, the general run of women's earnings is low, and £250 a year is quite an achievement, even for a highly qualified woman with years of experience' (*Careers and Openings for Women*, Ray Strachey, p. 70). Nevertheless, 'The numbers of women doing professional work have increased very fast in the last twenty years, and were about 400,000 in 1931, in addition to those doing secretarial work or employed in the Civil Service' (ibid., p. 44).

41 The income of the Labour Party in 1936 was £50,153 (*Daily Telegraph*, September 1937).

42 *The British Civil Servant: The Public Service*, William A. Robson, p. 16. Professor Ernest Barker suggests that there should be an alternative Civil Service Examination for 'men and women of an older growth' who have spent some years in social work and social service. 'Women candidates in particular might benefit. It is only a very small proportion of women students who succeed in the present open competition; indeed very few compete. On the alternative system here suggested it is possible, and indeed probable, that a much larger proportion of women would be candidates. Women have a genius and a capacity for social work and service. The alternative form of competition would give them a chance of showing that genius and that capacity. It might give them a new incentive to compete for entry into the administrative service of the state, in which their gifts and their presence are needed' ('The Home Civil Service', Professor Ernest Barker, in *The British Civil Servant*, p. 41). But while the home service remains as exacting as it is at present, it is difficult to see how an incentive can make women free to give 'their gifts and their presence' to the service of the state, unless the state will undertake the care of elderly parents; or make it a penal offence for elderly people of either sex to require the services of daughters at home.

43 Mr Baldwin, speaking at Downing Street, at a meeting on behalf of Newnham College Building Fund, 31 March 1936

44 The effect of a woman in the pulpit is thus defined in *Women and the Ministry: Some Considerations on the Report of the Archbishops' Commission on the Ministry of Women* (1936), p. 24: 'But we maintain that the ministration of women . . . will tend to produce a lowering of the spiritual tone of

Christian worship, such as is not produced by the ministrations of men before congregations largely or exclusively female. It is a tribute to the quality of Christian womanhood that it is possible to make this statement; but it would appear to be a simple matter of fact that in the thoughts and desires of that sex the natural is more easily made subordinate to the supernatural, the carnal to the spiritual than is the case with men; and that the ministrations of a male priesthood do not normally arouse that side of female human nature which should be quiescent during the times of the adoration of almighty God. We believe, on the other hand, that it would be impossible for the male members of the average Anglican congregation to be present at a service at which a woman ministered without becoming unduly conscious of her sex.'

In the opinion of the Commissioners, therefore, Christian women are more spiritually minded than Christian men – a remarkable, but no doubt adequate, reason for excluding them from the priesthood.

45 *Daily Telegraph*, 20 January 1936

46 *Daily Telegraph*, 1936

47 *Daily Telegraph*, 22 January 1936

48 'There are, so far as I know, no universal rules on this subject [i.e. sexual relations between civil servants]; but civil servants and municipal officers of both sexes are certainly expected to observe the conventional proprieties and to avoid conduct which might find its way into the newspapers and there be described as "scandalous". Until recently sexual relations between men and women officers of the Post Office were punishable with immediate dismissal of both parties . . . The problem of avoiding newspaper publicity is a fairly easy one to solve so far as court proceedings are concerned: but official restriction extends further so as to prevent women civil servants (who usually have to resign on marriage) from cohabiting openly with men if they desire to do so. The matter, therefore, takes on a different complexion' (*The British Civil Servant: The Public Service*, William A. Robson, pp. 14, 15).

49 Most men's clubs confine women to a special room, or annexe, and exclude them from other apartments, whether on the principle observed at St Sofia that they are impure, or whether on the principle observed at Pompeii that they are too pure, is matter for speculation.

50 The power of the press to burke discussion of any undesirable subject was, and still is, very formidable. It was one of the 'extraordinary obstacles' against which Josephine Butler had to fight in her campaign against the Contagious Diseases Act. 'Early in 1870 the London Press began to adopt that policy of silence with regard to the question, which lasted for many years, and called forth from the Ladies' Association the famous "Remonstrance against the Conspiracy of Silence", signed by Harriet Martineau and Josephine E. Butler, which concluded with the following words: "Surely, while such a conspiracy of silence is possible and practised

among leading journalists, we English greatly exaggerate our privileges as a free people when we profess to encourage a free press, and to possess the right to hear both sides in a momentous question of morality and legislation" ' (*Personal Reminiscences of a Great Crusade*, Josephine E. Butler, p. 49). Again, during the battle for the vote the Press used the boycott with great effect. And so recently as July 1937 Miss Philippa Strachey in a letter headed 'A Conspiracy of Silence', printed (to its honour) by the *Spectator*, almost repeats Mrs Butler's words: 'Many hundreds and thousands of men and women have been participating in an endeavour to induce the Government to abandon the provision in the new Contributory Pensions Bill for the black-coated workers which for the first time introduces a differential income limit for men and women entrants . . . In the course of the last month the Bill has been before the House of Lords, where this particular provision has met with strong and determined opposition from all sides of the Chamber . . . These are events one would have supposed to be of sufficient interest to be recorded in the daily Press. But they have been passed over in complete silence by the newspapers from *The Times* to the *Daily Herald* . . . The differential treatment of women under this Bill has aroused a feeling of resentment among them such as has not been witnessed since the granting of the franchise . . . How is one to account for this being completely concealed by the Press?'

51 Flesh wounds were of course inflicted during the battle of Westminster. Indeed the fight for the vote seems to have been more severe than is now recognised. Thus Flora Drummond says: 'Whether we won the vote by our agitation, as I believe, or whether we got it for other reasons, as some people say, I think many of the younger generation will find it hard to believe the fury and brutality aroused by our claim for votes for women less than thirty years ago.' (Flora Drummond in the *Listener*, 25 August 1937.) The younger generation is presumably so used to the fury and brutality that claims for liberty arouse that they have no emotion available for this particular instance. Moreover, that particular fight has not yet taken its place among the fights which have made England the home, and Englishmen the champions, of liberty. The fight for the vote is still generally referred to in terms of sour deprecation: ' . . . and the women . . . had not begun that campaign of burning, whipping, and picture-slashing which was finally to prove to both Front Benches their eligibility for the Franchise' (*Reflections and Memories*, Sir John Squire, p. 10). The younger generation therefore can be excused if they believe that there was nothing heroic about a campaign in which only a few windows were smashed, shins broken, and Sargent's portrait of Henry James damaged, but not irreparably, with a knife. Burning, whipping and picture-slashing only it would seem become heroic when carried out on a large scale by men with machine-guns.

52 *The Life of Sophia Jex-Blake*, Margaret Todd, M.D., p. 72

53 'Much has lately been said and written of the achievements and accomplishments of Sir Stanley Baldwin during his Premierships and too much would be impossible. Might I be permitted to call attention to what Lady Baldwin has done? When I first joined the committee of this hospital in 1929, analgesics (pain deadeners) for normal maternity cases in the wards were almost unknown, now their use is ordinary routine and they are availed of in practically 100 per cent of cases, and what is true of this hospital is true virtually for all similar hospitals. This remarkable change in so short a time is due to the inspiration and the tireless efforts and encouragement of Mrs Stanley Baldwin, as she then was . . . ' (letter to *The Times* from C. S. Wentworth Stanley, Chairman of the House Committee, the City of London Maternity Hospital, 1937). Since chloroform was first administered to Queen Victoria on the birth of Prince Leopold in April 1853 'normal maternity cases in the wards' have had to wait for seventy-six years and the advocacy of a prime minister's wife to obtain this relief.

54 According to *Debrett* the Knights and Dames of the Most Excellent Order of the British Empire wear a badge consisting of 'a cross patonce, enamelled pearl, fimbriated or, surmounted by a gold medallion with a representation of Britannia seated within a circle gules inscribed with the motto "For God and the Empire".' This is one of the few orders open to women, but their subordination is properly marked by the fact that the ribbon in their case is only two inches and one quarter in breadth; whereas the ribbon of the Knights is three inches and three quarters in breadth. The stars also differ in size. The motto, however, is the same for both sexes, and must be held to imply that those who thus ticket themselves see some connection between the Deity and the Empire, and hold themselves prepared to defend them. What happens if Britannia seated within a circle gules is opposed (as is conceivable) to the other authority whose seat is not specified on the medallion, *Debrett* does not say, and the Knights and Dames must themselves decide.

55 *Life of Sir Ernest Wild, K.C.*, R. J. Rackham, p. 91

56 Lord Baldwin, speech reported in *The Times*, 20 April 1936

57 *Life of Charles Gore*, G. L. Prestige, D.D., pp. 240–1

58 *Life of Sir William Broadbent, K.C.V.O., F.R.S.*, edited by his daughter, M. E. Broadbent, p. 242

59 *The Lost Historian: A Memoir of Sir Sidney Low*, Desmond Chapman-Huston, p. 198

60 *Thoughts and Adventures*, the Rt Hon. Winston Churchill, p. 57

61 Speech at Belfast, Lord Londonderry, reported in *The Times*, 11 July 1936

62 *Thoughts and Adventures*, op. cit., p. 279

63 *Daily Herald*, 13 February 1935

64 Goethe's *Faust*, translated by Melian Stawell and G. L. Dickinson

65 *The Life of Charles Tomlinson* by his niece, Mary Tomlinson, p. 30

66 *Miss Weeton: Journal of a Governess, 1807–1811*, edited by Edward Hall, pp. 14, xvii

67 *A Memoir of Anne Jemima Clough*, B. A. Clough, p. 32

68 *Personal Reminiscences of a Great Crusade*, op. cit., p. 189

69 'You and I know that it matters little if we have to be the out-of-sight piers driven deep into the marsh, on which the visible ones are carried, that support the bridge. We do not mind if, hereafter, people forget that there *are* any low down at all; if some have to be used up in trying experiments, before the best way of building the bridge is discovered. We are quite willing to be among these. The bridge is what we care for, and not our place in it, and we believe that, to the end, it may be kept in remembrance that this is alone to be our object' (letter from Octavia Hill to Mrs N. Senior, 20 September 1874, in *The Life of Octavia Hill*, C. Edmund Maurice, pp. 307–8). Octavia Hill (1838–1912) initiated the movement for 'securing better homes for the poor and open spaces for the public . . . The "Octavia Hill System" has been adopted over the whole planned extension of [Amsterdam]. In January 1928 no less than 28,648 dwellings had been built.' (*Octavia Hill*, from letters edited by Emily S. Maurice, pp. 10–11).

70 The maid played so important a part in English upper-class life from the earliest times until the year 1914, when the Hon. Monica Grenfell went to nurse wounded soldiers accompanied by a maid (*Bright Armour*, Monica Salmond, p. 20), that some recognition of her services seems to be called for. Her duties were peculiar. Thus she had to escort her mistress down Piccadilly 'where a few club men might have looked at her out of a window', but was unnecessary in Whitechapel, 'where malefactors were possibly lurking round every corner'. But her office was undoubtedly arduous. Wilson's part in Elizabeth Barrett's private life is well known to readers of the famous letters. Later in the century (about 1889–92), Gertrude Bell 'went with Lizzie, her maid, to picture exhibitions; she was fetched by Lizzie from dinner parties; she went with Lizzie to see the Settlement in Whitechapel where Mary Talbot was working . . . ' (*Early Letters of Gertrude Bell*, edited by Lady Richmond). We have only to consider the hours she waited in cloakrooms, the acres she toiled in picture galleries, the miles she trudged along West End pavements to conclude that if Lizzie's day is now almost over, it was in its day a long one. Let us hope that the thought that she was putting into practice the commands laid down by St Paul in his Letters to Titus and the Corinthians was a support; and the knowledge that she was doing her utmost to deliver her mistress's body intact to her master a solace. Even so in the weakness of the flesh and in the darkness of the beetle-haunted basement she must sometimes have bitterly reproached St Paul on the

one hand for his chastity, and the gentlemen of Piccadilly on the other for their lust. It is much to be regretted that no lives of maids, from which a more fully documented account could be constructed, are to be found in the *Dictionary of National Biography*.

71 *The Early Letters of Gertrude Bell*, collected and edited by Elsa Richmond, pp. 217–18

72 The question of chastity, both of mind and body, is of the greatest interest and complexity. The Victorian, Edwardian and much of the Fifth Georgian conception of chastity was based, to go no further back, upon the words of St Paul. To understand their meaning we should have to understand his psychology and environment – no light task in view of his frequent obscurity and the lack of biographical material. From internal evidence, it seems clear that he was a poet and a prophet, but lacked logical power, and was without that psychological training which forces even the least poetic or prophetic nowadays to subject their personal emotions to scrutiny. Thus his famous pronouncement on the matter of veils, upon which the theory of women's chastity seems to be based, is susceptible to criticism from several angles. In the Letter to the Corinthians his argument that a woman must be veiled when she prays or prophesies is based upon the assumption that to be unveiled 'is one and the same thing as if she were shaven'. That assumption granted, we must ask next: What shame is there in being shaven? Instead of replying, St Paul proceeds to assert, 'For a man indeed ought not to have his head veiled, forasmuch as he is the image and glory of God': from which it appears that it is not being shaven in itself that is wrong; but to be a woman and to be shaven. It is wrong, it appears, for the woman because 'the woman is the glory of the man'. If St Paul had said openly that he liked the look of women's long hair many of us would have agreed with him, and thought the better of him for saying so. But other reasons appeared to him preferable, as appears from his next remark: 'For the man is not of the woman; but the woman of the man; for neither was the man created for the woman; but the woman for the man: for this cause ought the woman to have a sign of authority on her head, because of the angels.' What view the angels took of long hair we have no means of knowing; and St Paul himself seems to have been doubtful of their support or he would not think it necessary to drag in the familiar accomplice nature. 'Doth not even nature itself teach you, that, if a man have long hair, it is a dishonour to him? But if a woman have long hair, it is a glory to her: for her hair is given her for a covering. But if any man seemeth to be contentious, we have no such custom, neither the churches of God.' The argument from nature may seem to us susceptible of amendment; nature, when allied with financial advantage, is seldom of divine origin; but if the basis of the argument is shifty, the conclusion is firm. 'Let the women keep silence in the churches: for it is not permitted unto them to speak;

but let them be in subjection, as also saith the law.' Having thus invoked
the familiar but always suspect trinity of accomplices, angels, nature and
law, to support his personal opinion, St Paul reaches the conclusion
which has been looming unmistakably ahead of us: 'And if they would
learn anything, let them ask their own husbands at home: for it is
shameful for a woman to speak in the church.' The nature of that
'shame', which is closely connected with chastity has, as the letter
proceeds, been considerably alloyed. For it is obviously compounded of
certain sexual and personal prejudices. St Paul, it is obvious, was not only
a bachelor (for his relations with Lydia, see Renan, *Saint Paul*, p. 149.
'Est-il cependant absolument impossible que Paul ait contracté avec
cette soeur une union plus intime? On ne saurait l'affirmer . . . ') and, like
many bachelors, suspicious of the other sex but a poet and, like many poets,
preferred to prophesy himself rather than to listen to the prophecies of
others. Also he was of the virile or dominant type, so familiar at present
in Germany, for whose gratification a subject race or sex is essential.
Chastity then as defined by St Paul is seen to be a complex conception,
based upon the love of long hair; the love of subjection; the love of an
audience; the love of laying down the law, and, subconsciously, upon a
very strong and natural desire that the woman's mind and body shall be
reserved for the use of one man and one only. Such a conception when
supported by the angels, nature, law, custom and the Church, and
enforced by a sex with a strong personal interest to enforce it, and the
economic means, was of undoubted power. The grip of its white if
skeleton fingers can be found upon whatever page of history we open
from St Paul to Gertrude Bell. Chastity was invoked to prevent her from
studying medicine; from painting from the nude; from reading Shakespeare; from playing in orchestras; from walking down Bond Street
alone. In 1848 it was 'an unpardonable solecism' for the daughters of a
gardener to drive down Regent Street in a hansom cab (*Paxton and the
Bachelor Duke*, Violet Markham, p. 288); that solecism became a crime,
of what magnitude theologians must decide, if the flaps were left open.
In the beginning of the present century the daughter of an ironmaster
(for let us not flout distinctions said today to be of prime importance),
Sir Hugh Bell, had 'reached the age of 27 and married without ever
having walked alone down Piccadilly . . . Gertrude, of course, would never
have dreamt of doing that . . . ' The West End was the contaminated
area. 'It was one's own class that was taboo . . . ' (*The Early Letters of
Gertrude Bell*, op. cit., pp. 217–18). But the complexities and incon-
sistencies of chastity were such that the same girl who had to be veiled,
i.e. accompanied by a male or a maid, in Piccadilly, could visit
Whitechapel or Seven Dials, then haunts of vice and disease, alone and
with her parents' approval. This anomaly did not altogether escape
comment. Thus Charles Kingsley as a boy exclaimed: ' . . . and the girls

908 SELECTED WORKS OF VIRGINIA WOOLF

have their heads crammed full of schools, and district visiting, and baby linen, and penny clubs. Confound!!! and going about among the most abominable scenes of filth and wretchedness, and indecency to visit the poor and read the Bible to them. My own mother says that the places they go into are fit for no girl to see, and that they should not know such things exist' (*Charles Kingsley*, Margaret Farrand Thorp, p. 12). Mrs Kingsley, however, was exceptional. Most of the daughters of educated men saw such 'abominable scenes', and knew that such things existed. That they concealed their knowledge is probable; what effect that concealment had psychologically it is impossible here to enquire. But that chastity, whether real or imposed, was an immense power, whether good or bad, it is impossible to doubt. Even today it is probable that a woman has to fight a psychological battle of some severity with the ghost of St Paul, before she can have intercourse with a man other than her husband. Not only was the social stigma strongly exerted on behalf of chastity, but the Bastardy Act did its utmost to impose chastity by financial pressure. Until women had the vote in 1918, 'the Bastardy Act of 1872 fixed the sum of 5s. a week as the maximum which a father, whatever his wealth, could be made to pay towards the maintenance of his child' (*Josephine Butler*, M. G. Fawcett and E. M. Turner, note, p. 101). Now that St Paul and many of his apostles have been unveiled themselves by modern science chastity has undergone considerable revision. Yet there is said to be a reaction in favour of some degree of chastity for both sexes. This is partly due to economic causes; the protection of chastity by maids is an expensive item in the bourgeois budget. The psychological argument in favour of chastity is well expressed by Mr Upton Sinclair: 'Nowadays we hear a great deal about mental troubles caused by sex repression; it is the mood of the moment. We do not hear anything about the complexes which may be caused by sex indulgence. But my observation has been that those who permit themselves to follow every sexual impulse are quite as miserable as those who repress every sexual impulse. I remember a class-mate in College; I said to him: "Did it ever occur to you to stop and look at your own mind? Everything that comes to you is turned into sex." He looked surprised, and I saw that it was a new idea to him; he thought it over, and said: "I guess you are right" ' (*Candid Reminiscences*, Upton Sinclair, p. 63). Further illustration is supplied by the following anecdote: 'In the splendid library of Columbia University were treasures of beauty, costly volumes of engravings, and in my usual greedy fashion I went at these, intending to learn all there was to know about Renaissance art in a week or two. But I found myself overwhelmed by this mass of nakedness; my senses reeled, and I had to quit' (ibid., pp. 62–3).

73 The translation here used is by Sir Richard Jebb (*Sophocles: The Plays and Fragments*, with critical notes, commentary and translation, in English prose). It is impossible to judge any book from a translation, yet even

when thus read *The Antigone* is clearly one of the great masterpieces of dramatic literature. Nevertheless, it could undoubtedly be made, if necessary, into anti-Fascist propaganda. Antigone herself could be transformed either into Mrs Pankhurst, who broke a window and was imprisoned in Holloway; or into Frau Pommer, the wife of a Prussian mines official at Essen, who said: ' "The thorn of hatred has been driven deep enough into the people by the religious conflicts, and it is high time that the men of today disappeared." . . . She has been arrested and is to be tried on a charge of insulting and slandering the State and the Nazi movement' (*The Times*, 12 August 1935). Antigone's crime was of much the same nature and was punished in much the same way. Her words, 'See what I suffer, and from whom, because I feared to cast away the fear of heaven! . . . And what law of heaven have I transgressed? Why, hapless one, should I look to the gods any more – what ally should I invoke – when by piety I have earned the name of impious?' could be spoken either by Mrs Pankhurst or by Frau Pommer; and are certainly topical. Creon, again, who 'thrust the children of the sunlight to the shades, and ruthlessly lodged a living soul in the grave'; who held that 'disobedience is the worst of evils', and that 'whomsoever the city may appoint, that man must be obeyed, in little things and great, in just things and unjust', is typical of certain politicians in the past, and of Herr Hitler and Signor Mussolini in the present. But though it is easy to squeeze these characters into up-to-date dress, it is impossible to keep them there. They suggest too much; when the curtain falls we sympathise, it may be noted, even with Creon himself. This result, to the propagandist undesirable, would seem to be due to the fact that Sophocles (even in a translation) uses freely all the faculties that can be possessed by a writer; and suggests, therefore, that if we use art to propagate political opinions, we must force the artist to clip and cabin his gift to do us a cheap and passing service. Literature will suffer the same mutilation that the mule has suffered; and there will be no more horses.

74 The five words of Antigone are: Οὔτοι συνέχθειν ἄλλα συμφίλειν ἔφυν – ' 'Tis not my nature to join in hating, but in loving' (*Antigone*, line 523, Jebb). To which Creon replied: 'Pass, then, to the world of the dead, and, if thou must needs love, love them. While I live, no woman shall rule me.'

75 Even at a time of great political stress like the present it is remarkable how much criticism is still bestowed upon women. The announcement, 'A shrewd, witty and provocative study of modern woman', appears on an average three times yearly in publishers' lists. The author, often a doctor of letters, is invariably of the male sex; and 'to mere man', as the blurb puts it (see *Times Literary Supplement*, 12 March 1938), 'this book will be an eye-opener.'

76 It is to be hoped that some methodical person has made a collection of the various manifestos and questionnaires issued broadcast during the years 1936–7. Private people of no political training were invited to sign

appeals asking their own and foreign governments to change their policy; artists were asked to fill up forms stating the proper relations of the artist to the state, to religion, to morality; pledges were required that the writer should use English grammatically and avoid vulgar expressions; and dreamers were invited to analyse their dreams. By way of inducement it was generally proposed to publish the results in the daily or weekly press. What effect this inquisition has had upon governments it is for the politician to say. Upon literature, since the output of books is unstaunched, and grammar would seem to be neither better nor worse, the effect is problematical. But the inquisition is of great psychological and social interest. Presumably it originated in the state of mind suggested by Dean Inge (The Rickman Godlee Lecture, reported in *The Times*, 23 November 1937), 'whether in our own interests we were moving in the right direction. If we went on as we were doing now, would the man of the future be superior to us or not? . . . Thoughtful people were beginning to realise that before congratulating ourselves on moving fast we ought to have some idea where we were moving to': a general self-dissatisfaction and desire 'to live differently'. It also points, indirectly, to the death of the Siren, that much ridiculed and often upper-class lady who by keeping open house for the aristocracy, plutocracy, intelligentsia, ignorantsia, etc., tried to provide all classes with a talking-ground or scratching-post where they could rub up minds, manners and morals more privately, and perhaps as usefully. The part that the Siren played in promoting culture and intellectual liberty in the eighteenth century is held by historians to be of some importance. Even in our own day she had her uses. Witness W. B. Yeats – 'How often I have wished that he [Synge] might live long enough to enjoy that communion with idle, charming, cultivated women which Balzac in one of his dedications calls "the chief consolation of genius"!' (*Dramatis Personae*, W. B. Yeats, p. 127). Lady St Helier who, as Lady Jeune, preserved the eighteenth-century tradition, informs us, however, that 'Plovers' eggs at 2s. 6d. apiece, forced strawberries, early asparagus, petits poussins . . . are now considered almost a necessity by anyone aspiring to give a good dinner' (1909); and her remark that the reception day was 'very fatiguing . . . how exhausted I felt when half-past seven came, and how gladly at eight o'clock I sat down to a peaceful tête-à-tête dinner with my husband!' (*Memories of Fifty Years*, Lady St Helier, pp. 3, 5, 182) may explain why such houses are shut, why such hostesses are dead, and why therefore the intelligentsia, the ignorantsia, the aristocracy, the bureaucracy, the bourgeoisie, etc., are driven (unless somebody will revive that society on an economic basis) to do their talking in public. But in view of the multitude of manifestos and questionnaires now in circulation it would be foolish to suggest another into the minds and motives of the Inquisitors.

77 'He did begin however on May 13th [1844] to lecture weekly at Queen's

College, which Maurice and other professors at King's had established a year before, primarily for the examination and training of governesses. Kingsley was ready to share in this unpopular task because he believed in the higher education of women' (*Charles Kingsley*, Margaret Farrand Thorp, p. 65).

78 The French, as the above quotation shows, are as active as the English in issuing manifestos. That the French, who refuse to allow the women of France to vote, and still inflict upon them laws whose almost medieval severity can be studied in *The Position of Women in Contemporary France*, Frances Clark, should appeal to Englishwomen to help them to protect liberty and culture must cause surprise.

79 Strict accuracy, here slightly in conflict with rhythm and euphony, requires the word 'port'. A photograph in the daily press of 'Dons in a Senior Common Room after dinner' (1937) showed 'a railed trolley in which the port decanter travels across a gap between diners at the fireplace, and thus continues its round without passing against the sun'. Another picture shows the 'sconce' cup in use. 'This old Oxford custom ordains that mention of certain subjects in Hall shall be punished by the offender drinking three pints of beer at one draught . . . ' Such examples are by themselves enough to prove how impossible it is for a woman's pen to describe life at a man's college without committing some unpardonable solecism. But the gentlemen whose customs are often, it is to be feared, travestied, will extend their indulgence when they reflect that the female novelist, however reverent in intention, works under grave physical drawbacks. Should she wish, for example, to describe a Feast at Trinity, Cambridge, she has to 'listen through the peephole in the room of Mrs Butler (the Master's wife) to the speeches taking place at the Feast which was held in Trinity College'. Miss Haldane's observation was made in 1907, when she reflected that, 'The whole surroundings seemed medieval' (*From One Century to Another*, E. Haldane, p. 235).

80 According to Whitaker there is a Royal Society of Literature and also the British Academy, both presumably, since they have offices and officers, official bodies, but what their powers are it is impossible to say, since if Whitaker had not vouched for their existence it would scarcely have been suspected.

81 Women were apparently excluded from the British Museum Reading-Room in the eighteenth century. Thus: '*Miss Chudleigh* solicits permission to be received into the reading-room. The only female student who as yet has honoured us was *Mrs Macaulay*; and your Lordship may recollect what an untoward event offended her delicacy' (Daniel Wray to Lord Harwicke, 22 October 1768, in Nichols, *Literary Anecdotes of the Eighteenth Century*, Vol. I, p. 137). The editor adds in a footnote: 'This alludes to the indelicacy of a gentleman there, in Mrs Macaulay's presence; of which the particulars will not bear to be repeated.'

82 *The Autobiography and Letters of Mrs M. O. W. Oliphant*, arranged and edited by Mrs Harry Coghill. Mrs Oliphant (1825–97) 'lived in perpetual embarrassment owing to her undertaking education and maintenance of her widowed brother's children in addition to her own two sons . . . ' (*Dictionary of National Biography*).

83 Macaulay's *History of England*, Vol. III, p. 278 (standard edition)

84 Mr Littlewood, until recently dramatic critic of the *Morning Post*, described the condition of 'Journalism at Present' at a dinner given in his honour, 6 December 1937. Mr Littlewood said: 'that he had in season and out of season fought for more space for the theatre in the columns of the London daily papers. It was Fleet Street where, between eleven and half-past twelve, not to mention before and after, thousands of beautiful words and thoughts were systematically massacred. It had been his lot for at least two out of his four decades to return to that shambles every night with the sure and certain prospect of being told that the paper was already full with important news, and that there was no room for any sanguinary stuff about the theatre. It had been his luck to wake up the next morning to find himself answerable for the mangled remains of what was once a good notice . . . It was not the fault of the men in the office. Some of them put the blue pencil through with tears in their eyes. The real culprit was that huge public who knew nothing about the theatre and could not be expected to care' (*The Times*, 6 December 1937).

Mr Douglas Jerrold describes the treatment of politics in the press. 'In those few brief years [between 1928–33] truth had fled from Fleet Street. You could never tell all the truth all the time. You never will be able to do so. But you used at least to be able to tell the truth about other countries. By 1933, you did it at your peril. In 1928 there was no direct political pressure from advertisers. Today it is not only direct but effective.'

Literary criticism would seem to be in much the same case and for the same reason: 'There are no critics in whom the public have any more confidence. They trust, if at all, to the different Book Societies, and the selections of individual newspapers, and on the whole they are wise . . . The Book Societies are frankly booksellers, and the great national newspapers cannot afford to puzzle their readers. They must all choose books which have, at the prevailing level of public taste, a potentially large sale' (*Georgian Adventure*, Douglas Jerrold, pp. 282, 283, 298).

85 While it is obvious that under the conditions of journalism at present the criticism of literature must be unsatisfactory, it is also obvious that no change can be made without changing the economic structure of society and the psychological structure of the artist. Economically, it is necessary that the reviewer should herald the publication of a new book with his town-crier's shout, 'O yez, O yez, O yez, such and such a book has been published; its subject is this, that or the other.' Psychologically,

vanity and the desire for 'recognition' are still so strong among artists that to starve them of advertisement and to deny them frequent if contrasted shocks of praise and blame would be as rash as the introduction of rabbits into Australia: the balance of nature would be upset and the consequences might well be disastrous. The suggestion in the text is not to abolish public criticism; but to supplement it by a new service based on the example of the medical profession. A panel of critics recruited from reviewers (many of whom are potential critics of genuine taste and learning) would practise like doctors and in strictest privacy. Publicity removed, it follows that most of the distractions and corruptions which inevitably make contemporary criticism worthless to the writer would be abolished; all inducement to praise or blame for personal reasons would be destroyed; neither sales nor vanity would be affected; the author could attend to criticism without considering the effect upon public or friends; the critic could criticise without considering the editor's blue pencil or the public taste. Since criticism is much desired by the living, as the constant demand for it proves, and since fresh books are as essential for the critic's mind as fresh meat for his body, each would gain; literature even might benefit. The advantages of the present system of public criticism are mainly economic; the evil effects psychologically are shown by the two famous *Quarterly* reviews of Keats and Tennyson. Keats was deeply wounded; and 'the effect . . . upon Tennyson himself was penetrating and prolonged. His first act was at once to withdraw from the press *The Lover's Tale* . . . We find him thinking of leaving England altogether, of living abroad' (*Tennyson*, Harold Nicolson, p. 118). The effect of Mr Churton Collins upon Sir Edmund Gosse was much the same: 'His self-confidence was undermined, his personality reduced . . . was not everyone watching his struggles regarding him as doomed? . . . His own account of his sensations was that he went about feeling that he had been flayed alive' (*The Life and Letters of Sir Edmund Gosse*, Evan Charteris, p. 196).

86 'A-ring-the-bell-and-run-away-man.' This word has been coined in order to define those who make use of words with the desire to hurt but at the same time to escape detection. In a transitional age when many qualities are changing their value, new words to express new values are much to be desired. Vanity, for example, which would seem to lead to severe complications of cruelty and tyranny, judging from evidence supplied abroad, is still masked by a name with trivial associations. A supplement to the *Oxford English Dictionary* is indicated.

87 *Memoir of Anne J. Clough*, B. A. Clough, pp. 38, 67

88 'The Sparrow's Nest', William Wordsworth

89 In the nineteenth century much valuable work was done for the working class by educated men's daughters in the only way that was then open to them. But now that some of them at least have received an expensive

education, it is arguable that they can work much more effectively by remaining in their own class and using the methods of that class to improve a class which stands much in need of improvement. If on the other hand the educated (as so often happens) renounce the very qualities which education should have bought – reason, tolerance, knowledge – and play at belonging to the working class and adopting its cause, they merely expose that cause to the ridicule of the educated class, and do nothing to improve their own. But the number of books written by the educated about the working class would seem to show that the glamour of the working class and the emotional relief afforded by adopting its cause, are today as irresistible to the middle class as the glamour of the aristocracy was twenty years ago (see *A La Recherche du Temps Perdu*). Meanwhile it would be interesting to know what the true-born working man or woman thinks of the playboys and playgirls of the educated class who adopt the working-class cause without sacrificing middle-class capital, or sharing working-class experience. 'The average housewife,' according to Mrs Murphy, Home Service Director of the British Commercial Gas Association, 'washed an acre of dirty dishes, a mile of glass and three miles of clothes and scrubbed five miles of floor yearly' (*Daily Telegraph*, 29 September 1937). For a more detailed account of working-class life, see *Life as We Have Known It* by Cooperative Working Women, edited by Margaret Llewelyn Davies. *The Life of Joseph Wright* also gives a remarkable account of working-class life at first hand and not through pro-proletarian spectacles.

90 'It was stated yesterday at the War Office that the Army Council have no intention of opening recruiting for any women's corps' (*The Times*, 22 October 1937). This marks a prime distinction between the sexes. Pacifism is enforced upon women. Men are still allowed liberty of choice.

91 The following quotation shows, however, that if sanctioned the fighting instinct easily develops. 'The eyes deeply sunk into the sockets, the features acute, the amazon keeps herself very straight on the stirrups at the head of her squadron . . . Five English parlementaries look at this woman with the respectful and a bit restless admiration one feels for a "fauve" of an unknown species . . .

"Come nearer Amalia," orders the commandant. She pushes her horse towards us and salutes her chief with the sword. "Sergeant Amalia Bonilla," continues the chief of the squadron, "how old are you?"

"Thirty-six."

"Where were you born?"

"In Granada.'

"Why have you joined the army?"

"My two daughters were militiawomen. The younger has been killed in the Alto de Leon. I thought I had to supersede her and avenge her."

"And how many enemies have you killed to avenge her?"

"You know it, commandant, five. The sixth is not sure."

"No, but you have taken his horse."

The amazon Amalia rides in fact a magnificent dapple-grey horse, with glossy hair, which flatters like a parade horse . . . This woman who has killed five men – but who feels not sure about the sixth – was for the envoys of the House of Commons an excellent introducer to the Spanish war' (*The Martyrdom of Madrid: Inedited Witnesses*, Louis Delaprée, pp. 34– 6, Madrid, 1937).

92 By way of proof, an attempt may be made to elucidate the reasons given by various Cabinet Ministers in various Parliaments from about 1870 to 1918 for opposing the Suffrage Bill. An able effort has been made by Mrs Oliver Strachey (see chapter 'The Deceitfulness of Polities' in her *The Cause*).

93 'We have had women's civil and political status before the League only since 1935.' From reports sent in as to the position of the woman as wife, mother and homemaker, 'the sorry fact was discovered that her economic position in many countries (including Great Britain) was unstable. She is entitled neither to salary nor wages and has definite duties to perform. In England, though she may have devoted her whole life to husband and children, her husband, no matter how wealthy, can leave her destitute at his death and she has no legal redress. We must alter this – by legislation . . . ' (Linda P. Littlejohn, reported in the *Listener*, 10 November 1937).

94 This particular definition of woman's task comes not from an Italian but from a German source. There are so many versions and all are so much alike that it seems unnecessary to verify each separately. But it is curious to find how easy it is to cap them from English sources. Mr Gerhardi for example writes: 'Never yet have I committed the error of looking on women writers as serious fellow artists. I enjoy them rather as spiritual helpers who, endowed with a sensitive capacity for appreciation, may help the few of us afflicted with genius to bear our cross with good grace. Their true role, therefore, is rather to hold out the sponge to us, cool our brow, while we bleed. If their sympathetic understanding may indeed be put to a more romantic use, how we cherish them for it!' (*Memoirs of a Polyglot*, William Gerhardi, pp. 320, 321). This conception of woman's role tallies almost exactly with that quoted above.

95 To speak accurately, 'a large silver plaque in the form of the Reich eagle . . . was created by President Hindenburg for scientists and other distinguished civilians . . . It may not be worn. It is usually placed on the writing-desk of the recipient' (report in a daily paper, 21 April 1936).

96 'It is a common thing to see the business girl contenting herself with a bun or a sandwich for her midday meal; and though there are theories that this is from choice . . . the truth is that they often cannot afford to

eat properly' (*Careers and Openings for Women*, Ray Strachey, p. 74). Compare also Miss E. Turner: '. . . many offices had been wondering why they were unable to get through their work as smoothly as formerly. It had been found that junior typists were fagged out in the afternoons because they could afford only an apple and a sandwich for lunch. Employers should meet the increased cost of living by increased salaries' (*The Times*, 28 March 1938).

97 The Mayoress of Woolwich (Mrs Kathleen Rance) speaking at a bazaar, reported in the *Evening Standard*, 20 December 1937

98 Miss E. R. Clarke, reported in *The Times*, 24 September 1937

99 Reported in the *Daily Herald*, 15 August 1936

100 Canon F. R. Barry, speaking at a conference arranged by the Anglican Group at Oxford, reported in *The Times*, 10 January 1933

101 *The Ministry of Women: Report of the Archbishops' Commission*, VII, Secondary Schools and Universities, p. 65

102 'Miss D. Carruthers, headmistress of the Green School, Isleworth, said there was a "very grave dissatisfaction" among older schoolgirls at the way in which organised religion was carried on. "The churches seem somehow to be failing to supply the spiritual needs of young people," she said. "It is a fault that seems common to all churches" ' (*Sunday Times*, 21 November 1937).

103 *Life of Charles Gore*, G. L. Prestige, D.D., p. 353

104 *The Ministry of Women: Report of the Archbishops' Commission*, *passim*

105 Whether or not the gift of prophecy and the gift of poetry were originally the same, a distinction has been made between those gifts and professions for many centuries. But the fact that the Song of Songs, the work of a poet, is included among the sacred books, and that propagandist poems and novels, the works of prophets, are included among the secular, points to some confusion. Lovers of English literature can scarcely be too thankful that Shakespeare lived too late to be canonised by the Church. Had the plays been ranked among the sacred books they must have received the same treatment as the Old and New Testaments; we should have had them doled out on Sundays from the mouths of priests in snatches; now a soliloquy from *Hamlet*; now a corrupt passage from the pen of some drowsy reporter; now a bawdy song; now half a page from *Antony and Cleopatra*, as the Old and New Testaments have been sliced up and interspersed with hymns in the Church of England service; and Shakespeare would have been as unreadable as the Bible. Yet those who have not been forced from childhood to hear it thus dismembered weekly assert that the Bible is a work of the greatest interest, much beauty and deep meaning.

106 *The Ministry of Women*, Appendix I: 'Certain Psychological and Physiological Considerations', Professor Grensted, D.D., pp. 79–87

107 'At present a married priest is able to fulfil the requirements of the

ordination service, "to forsake and set aside all worldly cares and studies", largely because his wife can undertake the care of the household and the family . . . ' (*The Ministry of Women*, p. 32).

The Commissioners are here stating and approving a principle which is frequently stated and approved by the dictators. Herr Hitler and Signor Mussolini have both often in very similar words expressed the opinion that: 'There are two worlds in the life of the nation, the world of men and the world of women'; and proceeded to much the same definition of the duties. The effect which this division has had upon the woman: the petty and personal nature of her interests; her absorption in the practical; her apparent incapacity for the poetical and adventurous – all this has been made the staple of so many novels, the target for so much satire, has confirmed so many theorists in the theory that by the law of nature the woman is less spiritual than the man, that nothing more need be said to prove that she has carried out, willingly or unwillingly, her share of the contract. But very little attention has yet been paid to the intellectual and spiritual effect of this division of duties upon those who are enabled by it 'to forsake all worldly cares and studies'. Yet there can be no doubt that we owe to this segregation the immense elaboration of modern instruments and methods of war; the astonishing complexities of theology; the vast deposit of notes at the bottom of Greek, Latin and even English texts; the innumerable carvings, chasings and unnecessary ornamentations of our common furniture and crockery; the myriad distinctions of *Debrett* and *Burke*; and all those meaningless but highly ingenious turnings and twistings into which the intellect ties itself when rid of 'the cares of the household and the family'. The emphasis which both priests and dictators place upon the necessity for two worlds is enough to prove that it is essential to the domination.

108 Evidence of the complex nature of satisfaction of dominance is provided by the following quotation: 'My husband insists that I call him "Sir",' said a woman at the Bristol Police Court yesterday, when she applied for a maintenance order. 'To keep the peace I have complied with his request,' she added. 'I also have to clean his boots, fetch his razor when he shaves, and speak up promptly when he asks me questions.' In the same issue of the same paper Sir E. F. Fletcher is reported to have 'urged the House of Commons to stand up to dictators' (*Daily Herald*, 1 August 1926). This would seem to show that the common consciousness which includes husband, wife and House of Commons is feeling at one and the same moment the desire to dominate, the need to comply in order to keep the peace, and the necessity of dominating the desire for dominance – a psychological conflict which serves to explain much that appears inconsistent and turbulent in contemporary opinion. The pleasure of dominance is of course further complicated by the fact that

it is still, in the educated class, closely allied with the pleasures of wealth, social and professional prestige. Its distinction from the comparatively simple pleasures – e.g. the pleasure of a country walk – is proved by the fear of ridicule which great psychologists, like Sophocles, detect in the dominator; who is also peculiarly susceptible according to the same authority either to ridicule or defiance on the part of the female sex. An essential element in this pleasure therefore would seem to be derived not from the feeling itself but from the reflection of other people's feelings, and it would follow that it can be influenced by a change in those feelings. Laughter as an antidote to dominance is perhaps indicated.

109 *The Life of Charlotte Brontë*, Mrs Gaskell

110 *The Life of Sophia Jex-Blake*, op. cit., pp. 67–9, 70–1, 72

111 External observation would suggest that a man still feels it a peculiar insult to be taunted with cowardice by a woman in much the same way that a woman feels it a peculiar insult to be taunted with unchastity by a man. The following quotation supports this view. Mr Bernard Shaw writes: 'I am not forgetting the gratification that war gives to the instinct of pugnacity and admiration of courage that are so strong in women . . . In England on the outbreak of war civilised young women rush about handing white feathers to all young men who are not in uniform. This,' he continues, 'like other survivals from savagery, is quite natural,' and he points out that, 'in old days a woman's life and that of her children depended on the courage and killing capacity of her mate.' Since vast numbers of young men did their work all through the war in offices without any such adornment, and the number of 'civilised young women' who stuck feathers in coats must have been infinitesimal compared with those who did nothing of the kind, Mr Shaw's exaggeration is sufficient proof of the immense psychological impression that fifty or sixty feathers (no actual statistics are available) can still make. This would seem to show that the male still preserves an abnormal susceptibility to such taunts; therefore that courage and pugnacity are still among the prime attributes of manliness; therefore that he still wishes to be admired for possessing them; therefore that any derision of such qualities would have a proportionate effect. That 'the manhood emotion' is also connected with economic independence seems probable. 'We have never known a man who was not, openly or secretly, proud of being able to support women; whether they were his sisters or his mistresses. We have never known a woman who did not regard the change from economic independence on an employer to economic dependence on a man as an honourable promotion. What is the good of men and women lying to each other about these things? It is not we that have made them' (*A. H. Orage*, Philip Mairet, vii), an interesting statement, attributed by G. K. Chesterton to A. H. Orage.

112 Until the beginning of the 1880s, according to Miss Haldane, the sister of R. B. Haldane, no lady could work. 'I should, of course, have liked to study for a profession, but that was an impossible idea unless one were in the sad position of "having to work for one's bread" and that would have been a terrible state of affairs. Even a brother wrote of the melancholy fact after he had been to see Mrs Langtry act. "She was a lady and acted like a lady, but what a sad thing it was that she should have to do so!" ' (*From One Century to Another*, Elizabeth Haldane, pp. 73–4). Harriet Martineau earlier in the century was delighted when her family lost its money, for thus she lost her 'gentility' and was allowed to work.

113 *Life of Sophia Jex-Blake*, op. cit., pp. 69, 70

114 For an account of Mr Leigh Smith, see *The Life of Emily Davies*, Barbara Stephen. Barbara Leigh Smith became Madame Bodichon.

115 How nominal that opening was is shown by the following account of the actual conditions under which women worked in the Royal Academy Schools about 1900. 'Why the female of the species should never be given the same advantages as the male it is difficult to understand. At the Royal Academy Schools we women had to compete against men for all the prizes and medals that were given each year, and we were only allowed half the amount of tuition and less than half their opportunities for study . . . No nude model was allowed to be posed in the women's painting room at the R.A. Schools . . . The male students not only worked from nude models, both male and female, during the day, but they were given an evening class as well, at which they could make studies from the figure, the visiting Academician instructing.' This seemed to the women students 'very unfair indeed'; Miss Collyer had the courage and the social standing necessary to beard first Mr Franklin Dicksee, who argued that since girls marry, money spent on their teaching is money wasted; next Lord Leighton; and at length the thin edge of the wedge, that is the undraped figure, was allowed. But 'the advantages of the night class we never did succeed in obtaining . . . ' The women students therefore clubbed together and hired a photographer's studio in Baker Street. 'The money that we, as the committee, had to find, reduced our meals to near starvation diet' (*Life of an Artist*, Margaret Collyer, pp. 19–81, 82). The same rule was in force at the Nottingham Art School in the twentieth century. 'Women were not allowed to draw from the nude. If the men worked from the living figure I had to go into the Antique Room . . . the hatred of those plaster figures stays with me till this day. I never got any benefit out of their study' (*Oil Paint and Grease Paint*, Dame Laura Knight, p. 47). But the profession of art is not the only profession that is thus nominally open. The profession of medicine is 'open', but ' . . . nearly all the Schools attached to London Hospitals are barred to women students, whose training in London is mainly carried on at the London School of

Medicine' (*Memorandum on the Position of English Women in Relation to that of English Men*, Philippa Strachey, 1935, p. 26). 'Some of the girl "medicals" at Cambridge University have formed themselves into a group to ventilate the grievance' (*Evening News*, 25 March 1937). In 1922 women students were admitted to the Royal Veterinary College, Camden Town; ' . . . since then the profession has attracted so many women that the number has recently been restricted to 50' (*Daily Telegraph*, 1 October 1937).

116 and 117   *The Life of Mary Kingsley*, Stephen Gwyn, pp. 18, 26. In a fragment of a letter Mary Kingsley writes: 'I am useful occasionally, but that is all – very useful a few months ago when on calling on a friend she asked me to go up to her bedroom and see her new hat – a suggestion that staggered me, I knowing her opinion of mine in such matters.' 'The letter,' says Mr Gwyn, 'did not complete this adventure of an unauthorised fiancé, but I am sure she got him off the roof and enjoyed the experience riotously.'

118   According to Antigone there are two kinds of law, the written and the unwritten, and Mrs Drummond maintains that it may sometimes be necessary to improve the written law by breaking it. But the many and varied activities of the educated man's daughter in the nineteenth century were clearly not simply or even mainly directed towards breaking the laws. They were, on the contrary, endeavours of an experimental kind to discover what are the unwritten laws; that is the private laws that should regulate certain instincts, passions, mental and physical desires. That such laws exist and are observed by civilised people, is fairly generally allowed; but it is beginning to be agreed that they were not laid down by 'God', who is now very generally held to be a conception, of patriarchial origin, valid only for certain races, at certain stages and times; nor by nature, who is now known to vary greatly in her commands and to be largely under control; but have to be discovered afresh by successive generations, largely by their own efforts of reason and imagination. Since, however, reason and imagination are to some extent the product of our bodies, and there are two kinds of body, male and female, and since these two bodies have been proved within the past few years to differ fundamentally, it is clear that the laws that they perceive and respect must be differently interpreted. Thus Professor Julian Huxley says: ' . . . from the moment of fertilisation onwards, man and woman differ in every cell of their body in regard to the number of their chromosomes – those bodies which, for all the world's unfamiliarity, have been shown by the last decade's work to be the bearers of heredity, the determiners of our characters and qualities.' In spite of the fact, therefore, that 'the superstructure of intellectual and practical life is potentially the same in both sexes', and that 'the recent Board of Education Report of the Committee on the Differentiation of

the Curriculum for Boys and Girls in Secondary Schools (London, 1923) has established that the intellectual differences between the sexes are very much slighter than popular belief allows' (*Essays in Popular Science*, Julian Huxley, pp. 62–3), it is clear that the sexes now differ and will always differ. If it were possible not only for each sex to ascertain what laws hold good in its own case, and to respect each other's laws, but also to share the results of those discoveries, it might be possible for each sex to develop fully and improve in quality without surrendering its special characteristics. The old conception that one sex must 'dominate' another would then become not only obsolete but so odious that if it were necessary for practical purposes that a dominant power should decide certain matters, the repulsive task of coercion and dominion would be relegated to an inferior and secret society, much as the flogging and execution of criminals is now carried out by masked beings in profound obscurity. But this is to anticipate.

119 From *The Times* obituary notice of H. W. Greene, fellow of Magdalen College, Oxford, familiarly called 'Grugger', 6 February 1933

120 'In 1747 the quarterly court (of the Middlesex Hospital) decided to set apart some of the beds for lying-in cases under rules which precluded any woman from acting as midwife. The exclusion of women has remained the traditional attitude. In 1861 Miss Garrett, afterwards Dr Garrett Anderson, obtained permission to attend classes . . . and was permitted to visit the wards with the resident officers, but the students protested and the medical officers gave way. The Board declined an offer from her to endow a scholarship for women students' (*The Times*, 17 May 1935).

121 'There is, in the modern world, a great body of well-attested knowledge . . . . but as soon as any strong passion intervenes to warp the expert's judgement he becomes unreliable, whatever scientific equipment he may possess' (*The Scientific Outlook*, Bertrand Russell, p. 17).

122 One of the record-breakers, however, gave a reason for record-breaking which must compel respect: 'Then, too, there was my belief that now and then women should do for themselves what men have already done – and occasionally what men have not done – thereby establishing themselves as persons, and perhaps encouraging other women towards greater independence of thought and action . . . When they fail, their failure must be a challenge to others' (*The Last Flight*, Amelia Earhart, pp. 21, 65).

123 'In point of fact this process [childbirth] actually disables women only for a very small fraction in most of their lives – even a woman who has six children is only necessarily laid up for twelve months out of her whole lifetime' (*Careers and Openings for Women*, Ray Strachey, pp. 47–8). At present, however, she is necessarily occupied for much longer. The bold suggestion has been made that the occupation is not

exclusively maternal, but could be shared by both parents to the common good.

124   The nature of manhood and the nature of womanhood are frequently defined both by Italian and German dictators. Both repeatedly insist that it is the nature of man and indeed the essence of manhood to fight. Hitler, for example, draws a distinction between 'a nation of pacifists and a nation of men'. Both repeatedly insist that it is the nature of womanhood to heal the wounds of the fighter. Nevertheless a very strong movement is on foot towards emancipating man from the old 'natural and eternal law' that man is essentially a fighter; witness the growth of pacifism among the male sex today. Compare further Lord Knebworth's statement 'that if permanent peace were ever achieved, and armies and navies ceased to exist, there would be no outlet for the manly qualities which fighting developed', with the following statement by another young man of the same social caste a few months ago: ' . . . it is not true to say that every boy at heart longs for war. It is only other people who teach it us by giving us swords and guns, soldiers and uniforms to play with.' (*Conquest of the Past*, Prince Hubertus Loewenstein, p. 215). It is possible that the Fascist states by revealing to the younger generation at least the need for emancipation from the old conception of virility are doing for the male sex what the Crimean and the European wars did for their sisters. Professor Huxley, however, warns us that 'any considerable alteration of the hereditary constitution is an affair of millennia, not of decades'. On the other hand, as science also assures us that our life on earth is 'an affair of millennia, not of decades', some alteration in the hereditary constitution may be worth attempting.

125   Coleridge however expresses the views and aims of the outsiders with some accuracy in the following passage: 'Man must be *free* or to what purpose was he made a Spirit of Reason, and not a Machine of Instinct? Man must *obey*; or wherefore has he a conscience? The powers, which create this difficulty, contain its solution likewise; for *their* service is perfect freedom. And whatever law or system of law compels any other service, disennobles our nature, leagues itself with the animal against the godlike, kills in us the very principle of joyous well-doing, and fights against humanity . . . If therefore society is to be under a *rightful* constitution of government, and one that can impose on rational Beings a true and moral obligation to obey it, it must be framed on such principles that every individual follows his own Reason, while he obeys the laws of the constitution, and performs the will of the State while he follows the dictates of his own Reason. This is expressly asserted by Rousseau, who states the problem of a perfect constitution of government in the following words: Trouver une forme d'Association – par laquelle chacun s'unisant à tous, n'obeisse pourtant

qu'à lui même, et reste aussi libre qu'auparavant, i.e. To find a form of society according to which each one uniting with the whole shall yet obey himself only and remain as free as before' (*The Friend*, S. T. Coleridge, Vol. I, pp. 333, 334, 335, 1818 edition). To which may be added a quotation from Walt Whitman:

> Of Equality – as if it harm'd me, giving others the same chances and rights as myself – as if it were not indispensable to my own rights that others possess the same.

And finally the words of a half-forgotten novelist, George Sand, are worth considering:

> Toutes les existences sont solidaires les unes des autres, et tout être humain qui présenterait la sienne isolément, sans la rattacher à celle de ses semblables, n'offrirait qu'une énigme à débrouiller . . . Cette individualité n'a par elle seule ni signification ni importance aucune. Elle ne prend un sens quelconque qu'en devenant une parcelle de la vie générale, en se fondant avec l'individualité de chacun de mes semblables, et c'est par là qu'elle devient de l'histoire [*Histoire de ma Vie*, George Sand, pp. 240–1].

BETWEEN THE ACTS

Between the Acts

The last novel by
VIRGINIA WOOLF
1941

Note

The manuscript of this book had been completed, but had
not been finally revised for the printer, at the time of
Virginia Woolf's death. She would not, I believe, have
made any large or material alterations in it, though she
would probably have made a good many small corrections
or revisions before passing the final proofs.

LEONARD WOOLF

It was a summer's night and they were talking, in the big room with the windows open to the garden, about the cesspool. The county council had promised to bring water to the village, but they hadn't.

Mrs Haines, the wife of the gentleman farmer, a goose-faced woman with eyes protruding as if they saw something to gobble in the gutter, said affectedly: 'What a subject to talk about on a night like this!'

Then there was silence; and a cow coughed; and that led her to say how odd it was, as a child, she had never feared cows, only horses. But, then, as a small child in a perambulator, a great cart-horse had brushed within an inch of her face. Her family, she told the old man in the armchair, had lived near Liskeard for many centuries. There were the graves in the churchyard to prove it.

A bird chuckled outside. 'A nightingale?' asked Mrs Haines. No, nightingales didn't come so far north. It was a daylight bird, chuckling over the substance and succulence of the day, over worms, snails, grit, even in sleep.

The old man in the armchair – Mr Oliver, of the Indian Civil Service, retired – said that the site they had chosen for the cesspool was, if he had heard aright, on the Roman road. From an aeroplane, he said, you could still see, plainly marked, the scars made by the Britons; by the Romans; by the Elizabethan manor house; and by the plough, when they ploughed the hill to grow wheat in the Napoleonic wars.

'But you don't remember . . . ' Mrs Haines began. No, not that. Still he did remember – and he was about to tell them what, when there was a sound outside, and Isa, his son's wife, came in with her hair in pigtails; she was wearing a dressing-gown with faded peacocks on it. She came in like a swan swimming its way; then was checked and stopped; was surprised to find people there; and lights burning. She had been sitting with her little boy who wasn't well, she apologised. What had they been saying?

'Discussing the cesspool,' said Mr Oliver.

'What a subject to talk about on a night like this!' Mrs Haines exclaimed again.

What had *he* said about the cesspool; or indeed about anything? Isa wondered, inclining her head towards the gentleman farmer, Rupert Haines. She had met him at a bazaar; and at a tennis party. He had handed her a cup and a racquet – that was all. But in his ravaged face she always felt mystery; and in his silence, passion. At the tennis party she had felt this, and at the bazaar. Now a third time, if anything more strongly, she felt it again.

'I remember,' the old man interrupted, 'my mother . . . ' Of his mother he remembered that she was very stout; kept her tea-caddy locked; yet had given him in that very room a copy of Byron. It was over sixty years ago, he told them, that his mother had given him the works of Byron in that very room. He paused.

' "She walks in beauty like the night",' he quoted. Then again: ' "So we'll go no more a-roving by the light of the moon".'

Isa raised her head. The words made two rings, perfect rings, that floated them, herself and Haines, like two swans downstream. But his snow-white breast was circled with a tangle of dirty duckweed; and she, too, in her webbed feet was entangled, by her husband, the stockbroker. Sitting on her three-cornered chair she swayed, with her dark pigtails hanging, and her body like a bolster in its faded dressing-gown.

Mrs Haines was aware of the emotion circling them, excluding her. She waited, as one waits for the strain of an organ to die out before leaving church. In the car going home to the red villa in the cornfields, she would destroy it, as a thrush pecks the wings off a butterfly. Allowing ten seconds to intervene, she rose; paused; and then, as if she had heard the last strain die out, offered Mrs Giles Oliver her hand.

But Isa, though she should have risen at the same moment that Mrs Haines rose, sat on. Mrs Haines glared at her out of goose-like eyes, gobbling, 'Please, Mrs Giles Oliver, do me the kindness to recognise my existence . . . ' which she was forced to do, rising at last from her chair, in her faded dressing-gown, with the pigtails falling over each shoulder.

Pointz Hall was seen in the light of an early summer morning to be a middle-sized house. It did not rank among the houses that are mentioned in guide books. It was too homely. But this whitish house with the grey roof, and the wing thrown out at right angles, lying unfortunately low on the meadow with a fringe of trees on the bank above it so that smoke curled up to the nests of the rooks, was a desirable house to live in. Driving past, people said to each other: 'I wonder if that'll ever come into the market?' And to the chauffeur: 'Who lives there?'

The chauffeur didn't know. The Olivers, who had bought the place something over a century ago, had no connection with the Warings, the Elveys, the Mannerings or the Burnets; the old families who had all inter-married, and lay in their deaths intertwisted, like the ivy roots, beneath the churchyard wall.

Only something over a hundred and twenty years the Olivers had been there. Still, on going up the principal staircase – there was another, a mere ladder at the back for the servants – there was a portrait. A length of yellow brocade was visible halfway up; and, as one reached the top, a small powdered face, a great head-dress slung with pearls, came into view: an ancestress of sorts. Six or seven bedrooms opened out of the corridor. The butler had been a soldier; had married a lady's maid; and, under a glass case there was a watch that had stopped a bullet on the field of Waterloo.

It was early morning. The dew was on the grass. The church clock struck eight times. Mrs Swithin drew the curtain in her bedroom – the faded white chintz that so agreeably from the outside tinged the window with its green lining. There with her old hands on the hasp, jerking it open, she stood: old Oliver's married sister; a widow. She always meant to set up a house of her own; perhaps in Kensington, perhaps at Kew, so that she could have the benefit of the gardens. But she stayed on all through the summer; and when winter wept its damp upon the panes, and choked the gutters with dead leaves, she said: 'Why, Bart, did they build the house in the hollow, facing north?' Her brother said, 'Obviously to escape from nature. Weren't four horses needed to drag the family coach through the mud?' Then he told her the famous story of the great eighteenth-century winter; when for a whole month the house had been blocked by snow. And the trees had fallen. So every year, when winter came, Mrs Swithin retired to Hastings.

But it was summer now. She had been waked by the birds. How they sang! attacking the dawn like so many choirboys attacking an iced cake. Forced to listen, she had stretched for her favourite reading – an *Outline of History* – and had spent the hours between three and five thinking of rhododendron forests in Piccadilly; when the entire continent, not then, she understood, divided by a channel, was all one; populated, she understood, by elephant-bodied, seal-necked, heaving, surging, slowly writhing and, she supposed, barking monsters: the iguanodon, the mammoth and the mastodon; from whom presumably, she thought, jerking the window open, we descend.

It took her five seconds in actual time, in mind time ever so much longer, to separate Grace herself, with blue china on a tray, from the leather-covered grunting monster who was about, as the door opened, to demolish a whole tree in the green steaming undergrowth of the primeval forest. Naturally, she jumped as Grace put the tray down and said: 'Good-morning, ma'am.' 'Batty,' Grace called her, as she felt on her face the divided glance that was half meant for a beast in a swamp, half for a maid in a print frock and white apron.

'How those birds sing!' said Mrs Swithin, at a venture. The window was open now; the birds certainly were singing. An obliging thrush hopped across the lawn; a coil of pinkish rubber twisted in its beak. Tempted by the sight to continue her imaginative reconstruction of the past, Mrs Swithin paused; she was given to increasing the bounds of the moment by flights into past or future; or sidelong down corridors and alleys; but she remembered her mother – her mother in that very room rebuking her. 'Don't stand gaping, Lucy, or the wind'll change . . . ' How often her mother had rebuked her in that very room – 'but in a very different world', as her brother would remind her. So she sat down to morning tea, like any other old lady with a high nose, thin cheeks, a ring on her finger and the usual trappings of rather shabby but gallant old age, which included in her case a cross gleaming gold on her breast.

The nurses after breakfast were trundling the perambulator up and down the terrace; and as they trundled they were talking – not shaping pellets of information or handing ideas from one to another, but rolling words like sweets on their tongues; which, as they thinned to transparency, gave off pink, green, and sweetness. This morning that sweetness was: 'How cook had told 'im off about the asparagus; how when she rang I said: how it was a sweet costume with blouse to match;' and that was leading to something about a feller as they walked up and down the terrace rolling sweets, trundling the perambulator.

It was a pity that the man who had built Pointz Hall had pitched the house in a hollow, when beyond the flower garden and the vegetables there was this stretch of high ground. Nature had provided a site for a house; man had built his house in a hollow. Nature had provided a stretch of turf half a mile in length and level, till it suddenly dipped to the lily pool. The terrace was broad enough to take the entire shadow of one of the great trees laid flat. There you could walk up and down, up and down, under the shade of the trees. Two or three grew close together; then there were gaps. Their roots broke the turf, and among those bones were green waterfalls and cushions of grass in which violets grew in spring or in summer the wild purple orchis.

Amy was saying something about a feller when Mabel, with her hand on the pram, turned sharply, her sweet swallowed. 'Leave off grubbing,' she said sharply. 'Come along, George.'

The little boy had lagged and was grouting in the grass. Then the baby, Caro, thrust her fist out over the coverlet and the furry bear was jerked overboard. Amy had to stoop. George grubbed. The flower blazed between the angles of the roots. Membrane after membrane was torn. It blazed a soft yellow, a lambent light under a film of velvet; it filled the caverns behind the eyes with light. All that inner darkness became a hall, leaf smelling, earth smelling of yellow light. And the tree was beyond the flower; the grass, the flower and the tree were entire. Down on his knees grubbing he held the flower complete. Then there was a roar and a hot breath and a stream of coarse grey hair rushed between him and the flower. Up he leapt, toppling in his fright, and saw coming towards him a terrible peaked eyeless monster moving on legs, brandishing arms.

'Good-morning, sir,' a hollow voice boomed at him from a beak of paper.

The old man had sprung upon him from his hiding-place behind a tree.

'Say good-morning, George; say, "Good-morning, Grandpa",' Mabel urged him, giving him a push towards the man. But George stood gaping. George stood gazing. Then Mr Oliver crumpled the paper which he had cocked into a snout and appeared in person. A very tall old man, with gleaming eyes, wrinkled cheeks, and a head with no hair on it. He turned.

'Heel!' he bawled, 'heel, you brute!' And George turned; and the nurses turned holding the furry bear; they all turned to look at Sohrab the Afghan hound bounding and bouncing among the flowers.

'Heel!' the old man bawled, as if he were commanding a regiment. It was impressive, to the nurses, the way an old boy of his age could still bawl and make a brute like that obey him. Back came the Afghan hound, sidling, apologetic. And as he cringed at the old man's feet, a string was slipped over his collar; the noose that old Oliver always carried with him.

'You wild beast . . . you bad beast,' he grumbled, stooping. George looked at the dog only. The hairy flanks were sucked in and out; there was a blob of foam on its nostrils. He burst out crying.

Old Oliver raised himself, his veins swollen, his cheeks flushed; he was angry. His little game with the paper hadn't worked. The boy was a cry-baby. He nodded and sauntered on, smoothing out the crumpled paper and muttering, as he tried to find his line in the column, 'A cry-baby – a cry-baby.' But the breeze blew the great sheet out; and over the edge he surveyed the landscape – flowing fields, heath and woods. Framed, they became a picture. Had he been a painter, he would have fixed his easel here, where the country, barred by trees, looked like a picture. Then the breeze fell.

'M. Daladier,' he read finding his place in the column, 'has been successful in pegging down the franc . . .'

Mrs Giles Oliver drew the comb through the thick tangle of hair which, after giving the matter her best attention, she had never had shingled or bobbed; and lifted the heavily embossed silver brush that had been a wedding present and had its uses in impressing chambermaids in hotels. She lifted it and stood in front of the three-folded mirror, so that she could see three separate versions of her rather heavy, yet handsome, face; and also, outside the glass, a slip of terrace, lawn and tree tops.

Inside the glass, in her eyes, she saw what she had felt overnight for the ravaged, the silent, the romantic gentleman farmer. 'In love' was in her eyes. But outside, on the washstand, on the dressing-table, among the silver boxes and toothbrushes, was the other love: love for her husband, the stockbroker – 'The father of my children,' she added, slipping into the cliché conveniently provided by fiction. Inner love was in the eyes; outer love on the dressing-table. But what feeling was it that stirred in her now when above the looking-glass, out of doors, she saw coming across the lawn the perambulator; two nurses; and her little boy George, lagging behind?

She tapped on the window with her embossed hairbrush. They were too far off to hear. The drone of the trees was in their ears; the chirp of birds; other incidents of garden life, inaudible, invisible to her in the bedroom, absorbed them. Isolated on a green island, hedged about with snowdrops, laid with a counterpane of puckered silk, the innocent island floated under her window. Only George lagged behind.

She returned to her eyes in the looking-glass. 'In love' she must be; since the presence of his body in the room last night could so affect her; since the words he said, handing her a teacup, handing her a tennis racquet, could so attach themselves to a certain spot in her; and thus lie between them like a wire, tingling, tangling, vibrating – she groped, in the depths of the looking-glass, for a word to fit the infinitely quick vibrations of the aeroplane propeller that she had seen once at dawn at Croydon. Faster, faster, faster, it whizzed, whirred, buzzed, till all the flails became one flail and up soared the plane away and away . . .

'Where we know not, where we go not, neither know nor care,' she hummed. 'Flying, rushing through the ambient, incandescent, summer silent . . . '

The rhyme was 'air'. She put down her brush. She took up the telephone.

'Three, four, eight, Pyecombe,' she said. 'Mrs Oliver speaking . . . What fish have you this morning? Cod? Halibut? Sole? Plaice?'

'There to lose what binds us here,' she murmured. 'Soles. Filleted. In time for lunch please,' she said aloud. 'With a feather, a blue feather . . . flying mounting through the air . . . there to lose what binds us here . . . ' The words weren't worth writing in the book bound like an account book in case Giles suspected. 'Abortive', was the word that expressed her. She never came out of a shop, for example, with the clothes she admired; nor did her figure, seen against the dark roll of trousering in a shop window, please her. Thick of waist, large of limb, and, save for her hair, fashionable in the tight modern way, she never looked like Sappho, or one of the beautiful young men whose photographs adorned the weekly papers. She looked what she was: Sir Richard's daughter; and niece of the two old ladies at Wimbledon who were so proud, being O'Neils, of their descent from the kings of Ireland.

A foolish, flattering lady, pausing on the threshold of what she once called 'the heart of the house', the threshold of the library, had once said: 'Next to the kitchen, the library's always the nicest room in the house.' Then she added, stepping across the threshold: 'Books are the mirrors of the soul.'

In this case a tarnished, a spotted soul. For as the train took over three hours to reach this remote village in the very heart of England, no one ventured so long a journey without staving off possible mind-hunger, without buying a book on a bookstall. Thus the mirror that reflected the soul sublime, reflected also the soul bored. Nobody could pretend, as they looked at the shuffle of shilling shockers that weekenders had dropped, that the looking-glass always reflected the anguish of a queen or the heroism of King Harry.

At this early hour of a June morning the library was empty. Mrs Giles had to visit the kitchen. Mr Oliver still tramped the terrace. And Mrs Swithin was of course at church. The light but variable breeze, foretold by the weather expert, flapped the yellow curtain, tossing light, then shadow. The fire greyed, then glowed, and the tortoiseshell butterfly beat on the lower pane of the window; beat, beat, beat; repeating that if no human being ever came, never, never, never, the books would be mouldy, the fire out and the tortoiseshell butterfly dead on the pane.

Heralded by the impetuosity of the Afghan hound, the old man entered. He had read his paper; he was drowsy; and so sank down into the chintz-covered chair with the dog at his feet – the Afghan hound. His nose on his paws, his haunches drawn up, he looked a stone dog, a crusader's dog, guarding even in the realms of death the sleep of his master. But the master was not dead; only dreaming; drowsily, seeing as in a glass, its lustre spotted, himself, a young man helmeted; and a cascade falling. But no water; and the hills, like grey stuff pleated; and in the sand a hoop of ribs; a bullock maggot-eaten in the sun; and in the shadow of the rock, savages; and in his hand a gun. The dream hand clenched; the real hand lay on the chair arm, the veins swollen but only with a brownish fluid now.

The door opened.

'Am I,' Isa apologised, 'interrupting?'

Of course she was – destroying youth and India. It was his fault, since she had persisted in stretching his thread of life so fine, so far. Indeed he was grateful to her, watching her as she strolled about the room, for continuing.

Many old men had only their India – old men in clubs, old men in rooms off Jermyn Street. She in her striped dress continued him, murmuring, in front of the bookcases: 'The moor is dark beneath the moon, rapid clouds have drunk the last pale beams of even . . . I have ordered the fish,' she said aloud, turning, 'though whether it'll be fresh or not I can't promise. But veal is dear, and everybody in the house is sick of beef and mutton . . . Sohrab,' she said, coming to a standstill in front of them, 'what's *he* been doing?'

His tail never wagged. He never admitted the ties of domesticity. Either he cringed or he bit. Now his wild yellow eyes gazed at her, gazed at him. He could outstare them both.

Then Oliver remembered: 'Your little boy's a cry-baby,' he said scornfully.

'Oh,' she sighed, pegged down on a chair arm, like a captive balloon, by a myriad of hair-thin ties into domesticity. 'What's been happening?'

'I took the newspaper,' he explained, 'so . . . '

He took it and crumpled it into a beak over his nose. 'So,' he had sprung out from behind a tree on to the children.

'And he howled. He's a coward, your boy is.'

She frowned. He was not a coward, her boy wasn't. And she loathed the domestic, the possessive; the maternal. And he knew it and did it on purpose to tease her, the old brute, her father-in-law.

She looked away.

'The library's always the nicest room in the house,' she quoted, and ran her eyes along the books. 'The mirror of the soul' books were. *The Faerie*

Queene and Kinglake's *Crimea*; Keats and *The Kreutzer Sonata*. There they were, reflecting. What? What remedy was there for her at her age – the age of the century, thirty-nine – in books? Book-shy she was, like the rest of her generation; and gun-shy too. Yet as a person with a raging tooth runs her eye in a chemist's shop over green bottles with gilt scrolls on them lest one of them may contain a cure, she considered: Keats and Shelley; Yeats and Donne. Or perhaps not a poem; a life. The life of Garibaldi. The life of Lord Palmerston. Or perhaps not a person's life; a county's. *The Antiquities of Durham*; *The Proceedings of the Archaeological Society of Nottingham*. Or not a life at all, but science – Eddington, Darwin or Jeans.

None of them stopped her toothache. For her generation the newspaper was a book; and, as her father-in-law had dropped *The Times*, she took it and read: 'A horse with a green tail . . . ' which was fantastic. Next, 'The guard at Whitehall . . . ' which was romantic, and then, building word upon word, she read: 'The troopers told her the horse had a green tail; but she found it was just an ordinary horse. And they dragged her up to the barrack room where she was thrown upon a bed. Then one of the troopers removed part of her clothing, and she screamed and hit him about the face . . . '

That was real; so real that on the mahogany door panels she saw the Arch in Whitehall; through the Arch the barrack room; in the barrack room the bed; and on the bed the girl was screaming and hitting him about the face, when the door (for in fact it was a door) opened and in came Mrs Swithin carrying a hammer.

She advanced, sidling, as if the floor were fluid under her shabby garden shoes, and, advancing, pursed her lips and smiled, sidelong, at her brother. Not a word passed between them as she went to the cupboard in the corner and replaced the hammer, which she had taken without asking leave, together – she unclosed her fist – with a handful of nails.

'Cindy – Cindy,' he growled, as she shut the cupboard door.

Lucy, his sister, was three years younger than he was. The name Cindy, or Sindy, for it could be spelt either way, was short for Lucy. It was by this name that he had called her when they were children; when she had trotted after him as he fished, and had made the meadow flowers into tight little bunches, winding one long grass stalk round and round and round. Once, she remembered, he had made her take the fish off the hook herself. The blood had shocked her – 'Oh!' she had cried – for the gills were full of blood. And he had growled: 'Cindy!' The ghost of that morning in the meadow was in her mind as she replaced the hammer where it belonged on one shelf; and the nails where they belonged on another; and shut the cupboard about which, for he still kept his fishing tackle there, he was still so very particular.

'I've been nailing the placard on the barn,' she said, giving him a little pat on the shoulder.

The words were like the first peal of a chime of bells. As the first peals, you hear the second; as the second peals, you hear the third. So when Isa heard Mrs Swithin say: 'I've been nailing the placard to the barn,' she knew she would say next:

'For the pageant.'

And he would say:

'Today? By Jupiter! I'd forgotten!'

'If it's fine,' Mrs Swithin continued, 'they'll act on the terrace . . . '

'And if it's wet,' Bartholomew continued, 'in the barn.'

'And which will it be?' Mrs Swithin continued. 'Wet or fine?'

Then, for the seventh time in succession, they both looked out of the window.

Every summer, for seven summers now, Isa had heard the same words: about the hammer and the nails; the pageant and the weather. Every year they said, would it be wet or fine; and every year it was – one or the other. The same chime followed the same chime, only this year beneath the chime she heard: 'The girl screamed and hit him about the face with a hammer.'

'The forecast,' said Mr Oliver, turning the pages till he found it, 'says: variable winds; fair average temperature; rain at times.'

He put down the paper, and they all looked at the sky to see whether the sky obeyed the meteorologist. Certainly the weather was variable. It was green in the garden one moment; grey the next. Here came the sun – an illimitable rapture of joy, embracing every flower, every leaf. Then in compassion it withdrew, covering its face, as if it forebore to look on human suffering. There was a fecklessness, a lack of symmetry and order in the clouds as they thinned and thickened. Was it their own law, or no law, they obeyed? Some were wisps of white hair merely. One, high up, very distant, had hardened to golden alabaster; was made of immortal marble. Beyond that was blue, pure blue, black blue; blue that had never filtered down; that had escaped registration. It never fell as sun, shadow, or rain upon the world, but disregarded the little coloured ball of earth entirely. No flower felt it; no field; no garden.

Mrs Swithin's eyes glazed as she looked at it. Isa thought her gaze was fixed because she saw God there, God on his throne. But as a shadow fell next moment on the garden Mrs Swithin loosed and lowered her fixed look and said: 'It's very unsettled. It'll rain, I'm afraid. We can only pray,' she added, and fingered her crucifix.

'And provide umbrellas,' said her brother.

Lucy flushed. He had struck her faith. When she said 'pray', he added 'umbrellas'. She half covered the cross with her fingers. She shrank; she cowered; but next moment she exclaimed: 'Oh there they are – the darlings!'

The perambulator was passing across the lawn.

Isa looked too. What an angel she was – the old woman! Thus to salute the children; to beat up against those immensities and the old man's irreverences her skinny hands, her laughing eyes! How courageous to defy Bart and the weather!

'He looks blooming,' said Mrs Swithin.

'It's astonishing how they pick up,' said Isa.

'He ate his breakfast?' Mrs Swithin asked.

'Every scrap,' said Isa.

'And baby? No sign of measles?'

Isa shook her head. 'Touch wood,' she added, tapping the table.

'Tell me, Bart,' said Mrs Swithin turning to her brother, 'what's the origin of that? Touch wood . . . Antaeus, didn't he touch earth?'

She would have been, he thought, a very clever woman, had she fixed her gaze. But this led to that; that to the other. What went in at this ear, went out at that. And all were circled, as happens after seventy, by one recurring question. Hers was, should she live at Kensington or at Kew? But every year, when winter came, she did neither. She took lodgings at Hastings.

'Touch wood; touch earth; Antaeus,' he muttered, bringing the scattered bits together. Lemprière would settle it; or the *Encyclopaedia*. But it was not in books the answer to his question – why, in Lucy's skull, shaped so much like his own, there existed a prayable being? She didn't, he supposed, invest it with hair, teeth or toe-nails. It was, he supposed more of a force or a radiance, controlling the thrush and the worm; the tulip and the hound; and himself, too, an old man with swollen veins. It got her out of bed on a cold morning and sent her down the muddy path to worship it, whose mouth-piece was Streatfield. A good fellow, who smoked cigars in the vestry. He needed some solace, doling out preachments to asthmatic elders, perpetually repairing the perpetually falling steeple by means of placards nailed to barns. The love, he was thinking, that they should give to flesh and blood they give to the church . . . when Lucy rapping her fingers on the table said: 'What's the origin – the origin – of that?'

'Superstition,' he said.

She flushed, and the little breath too was audible that she drew in as once more he struck a blow at her faith. But, brother and sister, flesh and blood was not a barrier, but a mist. Nothing changed their affection; no argument; no fact; no truth. What she saw he didn't; what he saw she didn't – and so on, *ad infinitum*.

'Cindy,' he growled. And the quarrel was over.

The barn to which Lucy had nailed her placard was a great building in the farmyard. It was as old as the church, and built of the same stone, but it had no steeple. It was raised on cones of grey stone at the corners to protect it from rats and damp. Those who had been to Greece always said it reminded them of a temple. Those who had never been to Greece – the majority – admired it all the same. The roof was weathered red-orange; and inside it was a hollow hall, sun-shafted, brown, smelling of corn, dark when the doors were shut, but splendidly illuminated when the doors at the end stood open, as they did to let the wagons in – the long low wagons, like ships of the sea, breasting the corn, not the sea, returning in the evening shagged with hay. The lanes caught tufts where the wagons had passed.

Now benches were drawn across the floor of the barn. If it rained, the actors were to act in the barn; planks had been laid together at one end to form a stage. Wet or fine, the audience would take tea there. Young men and women – Jim, Iris, David, Jessica – were even now busy with garlands of red and white paper roses left over from the Coronation. The seeds and the dust from the sacks made them sneeze. Iris had a handkerchief bound round her forehead; Jessica wore breeches. The young men worked in shirt sleeves. Pale husks had stuck in their hair, and it was easy to run a splinter of wood into the fingers.

'Old Flimsy' (Mrs Swithin's nickname) had been nailing another placard on the barn. The first had been blown down, or the village idiot, who always tore down what had been nailed up, had done it, and was chuckling over the placard under the shade of some hedge. The workers were laughing too, as if old Swithin had left a wake of laughter behind her. The old girl with a wisp of white hair flying, knobbed shoes as if she had claws corned like a canary's, and black stockings wrinkled over the ankles, naturally made David cock his eye and Jessica wink back as she handed him a length of paper roses. Snobs they were; long enough stationed that is in that one corner of the world to have taken indelibly the print of some three hundred years of customary behaviour. So they laughed; but respected. If she wore pearls, pearls they were.

'Old Flimsy on the hop,' said David. She would be in and out twenty times, and finally bring them lemonade in a great jug and a plate of sandwiches. Jessie held the garland; he hammered. A hen strayed in; a file of cows passed the door; then a sheepdog; then the cowman, Bond, who stopped.

He contemplated the young people hanging roses from one rafter to another. He thought very little of anybody, simples or gentry. Leaning, silent, sardonic, against the door he was like a withered willow, bent over a stream, all its leaves shed, and in his eyes the whimsical flow of the waters.

'Hi – huh!' he cried suddenly. It was cow language presumably, for the parti-coloured cow, who had thrust her head in at the door, lowered her horns, lashed her tail and ambled off. Bond followed after.

'That's the problem,' said Mrs Swithin. While Mr Oliver consulted the *Encyclopaedia* searching under Superstition for the origin of the expression 'Touch wood', she and Isa discussed fish: whether, coming from a distance, it would be fresh.

They were so far from the sea. A hundred miles away, Mrs Swithin said; no, perhaps a hundred and fifty. 'But they do say,' she continued, 'one can hear the waves on a still night. After a storm, they say, you can hear a wave break . . . I like that story,' she reflected. ' "Hearing the waves in the middle of the night he saddled a horse and rode to the sea." Who was it, Bart, who rode to the sea?'

He was reading.

'You can't expect it brought to your door in a pail of water,' said Mrs Swithin, 'as I remember when we were children, living in a house by the sea. Lobsters, fresh from the lobster pots. How they pinched the stick cook gave them! And salmon. You know if they're fresh because they have lice in their scales.'

Bartholomew nodded. A fact that was. He remembered, the house by the sea. And the lobster.

They were bringing up nets full of fish from the sea; but Isa was seeing – the garden, variable as the forecast said, in the light breeze. Again, the children passed, and she tapped on the window and blew them a kiss. In the drone of the garden it went unheeded.

'Are we really,' she said, turning round, 'a hundred miles from the sea?'

'Thirty-five only,' her father-in-law said, as if he had whipped a tape-measure from his pocket and measured it exactly.

'It seems more,' said Isa. 'It seems from the terrace as if the land went on for ever and ever.'

'Once there was no sea,' said Mrs Swithin. 'No sea at all between us and the continent. I was reading that in a book this morning. There were rhododendrons in the Strand; and mammoths in Piccadilly.'

'When we were savages,' said Isa.

Then she remembered; her dentist had told her that savages could perform very skilful operations on the brain. Savages had false teeth, he said. False teeth were invented, she thought he said, in the time of the Pharaohs.

'At least so my dentist told me,' she concluded.

'Which man d'you go to now?' Mrs Swithin asked her.

'The same old couple: Batty and Bates in Sloane Street.'

'And Mr Batty told you they had false teeth in the time of the Pharaohs?' Mrs Swithin pondered.

'Batty? Oh not Batty. Bates,' Isa corrected her.

Batty, she recalled, only talked about royalty. Batty, she told Mrs Swithin, had a patient a princess. 'So he kept me waiting well over an hour. And you know, when one's a child, how long that seems.'

'Marriages with cousins,' said Mrs Swithin, 'can't be good for the teeth.'

Bart put his finger inside his mouth and projected the upper row outside his lips. They were false. Yet, he said, the Olivers hadn't married cousins. The Olivers couldn't trace their descent for more than two or three hundred years. But the Swithins could. The Swithins were there before the Conquest.

'The Swithins,' Mrs Swithin began. Then she stopped. Bart would crack another joke about saints if she gave him the chance. And she had had two jokes cracked at her already; one about an umbrella; another about superstition.

So she stopped and said, 'How did we begin this talk?' She counted on her fingers. 'The Pharaohs. Dentists. Fish . . . Oh yes, you were saying, Isa,

you'd ordered fish; and you were afraid it wouldn't be fresh. And I said,
"That's the problem . . ."'

The fish had been delivered. Mitchell's boy, holding them in the crook of his
arm, jumped off his motor bike. There was no feeding the pony with lumps
of sugar at the kitchen door, nor time for gossip, since his round had been
increased. He had to deliver right over the hill at Bickley; also go round by
Waythorn, Roddam and Pyeminster, whose names, like his own, were in
Domesday Book. But the cook – Mrs Sands she was called, but by old
friends Trixie – had never in all her fifty years been over the hill, nor
wanted to.

He dabbed them down on the kitchen table, the filleted soles, the semi-
transparent boneless fish. And before Mrs Sands had time to peel the paper
off, he was gone, giving a slap to the very fine yellow cat who rose majestically from the basket chair and advanced superbly to the table, winding the
fish.

Were they a bit whiffy? Mrs Sands held them to her nose. The cat rubbed
itself this way, that way against the table legs, against her legs. She would
save a slice for Sunny – his drawing-room name Sung-Yen had undergone a
kitchen change into Sunny. She took them, the cat attendant, to the larder,
and laid them on a plate in that semi-ecclesiastical apartment. For the house
before the Reformation, like so many houses in that neighbourhood, had a
chapel; and the chapel had become a larder, changing, like the cat's name, as
religion changed. The Master (his drawing-room name; in the kitchen they
called him Bartie) would bring gentlemen sometimes to see the larder –
often when cook wasn't dressed. Not to see the hams that hung from hooks,
or the butter on a blue slate, or the joint for tomorrow's dinner, but to see
the cellar that opened out of the larder and its carved arch. If you tapped –
one gentleman had a hammer – there was a hollow sound; a reverberation;
undoubtedly, he said, a concealed passage where once somebody had hid. So
it might be. But Mrs Sands wished they wouldn't come into her kitchen
telling stories with the girls about. It put ideas into their silly heads. They
heard dead men rolling barrels. They saw a white lady walking under the
trees. No one would cross the terrace after dark. If a cat sneezed, 'There's
the ghost!'

Sunny had his little bit off the fillet. Then Mrs Sands took an egg from
the brown basket full of eggs; some with yellow fluff sticking to the shells;
then a pinch of flour to coat those semi-transparent slips; and a crust from
the great earthenware crock full of crusts. Then, returning to the kitchen, she
made those quick movements at the oven, cinder raking, stoking, damping,
which sent strange echoes through the house, so that in the library, the
sitting-room, the dining-room and the nursery, whatever they were doing,
thinking, saying, they knew, they all knew, it was getting on for breakfast,
lunch or dinner.

'The sandwiches . . . ' said Mrs Swithin, coming into the kitchen. She refrained from adding 'Sands' to 'sandwiches', for Sands and sandwiches clashed. 'Never play,' her mother used to say, 'on people's names.' And Trixie was not a name that suited, as Sands did, the thin, acid woman, red-haired, sharp and clean, who never dashed off masterpieces, it was true; but then never dropped hairpins in the soup. 'What in the name of thunder?' Bart had said, raising a hairpin in his spoon, in the old days, fifteen years ago, before Sands came, in the time of Jessie Pook.

Mrs Sands fetched bread; Mrs Swithin fetched ham. One cut the bread; the other the ham. It was soothing, it was consolidating, this handwork together. The cook's hands cut, cut, cut. Whereas Lucy, holding the loaf, held the knife up. Why's stale bread, she mused, easier to cut than fresh? And so skipped, sidelong, from yeast to alcohol; so to fermentation; so to inebriation; so to Bacchus; and lay under purple lamps in a vineyard in Italy, as she had done, often; while Sands heard the clock tick; saw the cat; noted a fly buzz; and registered, as her lips showed, a grudge she mustn't speak against people making work in the kitchen while they had a high old time hanging paper roses in the barn.

'Will it be fine?' asked Mrs Swithin, her knife suspended. In the kitchen they humoured old Mother Swithin's fancies.

'Seems like it,' said Mrs Sands, giving her sharp look-out of the kitchen window.

'It wasn't last year,' said Mrs Swithin. 'D'you remember what a rush we had – when the rain came – getting in the chairs?' She cut again. Then she asked about Billy, Mrs Sands's nephew, apprenticed to the butcher.

'He's been doing,' Mrs Sands said, 'what boys shouldn't; cheeking the master.'

'That'll be all right,' said Mrs Swithin, half meaning the boy, half meaning the sandwich, as it happened a very neat one, trimmed, triangular. 'Mr Giles may be late,' she added, laying it, complacently, on top of the pile.

For Isa's husband, the stockbroker, was coming from London. And the local train, which met the express train, arrived by no means punctually, even if he caught the early train which was by no means certain. In which case it meant – but what it meant to Mrs Sands, when people missed their trains, and she, whatever she might want to do, must wait, by the oven, keeping meat hot, no one knew.

'There!' said Mrs Swithin, surveying the sandwiches, some neat, some not, 'I'll take 'em to the barn.' As for the lemonade, she assumed, without a flicker of doubt, that Jane the kitchenmaid would follow after.

Candish paused in the dining-room to move a yellow rose. Yellow, white, carnation red – he placed them. He loved flowers, and arranging them, and placing the green sword- or heart-shaped leaf that came, fitly, between them. Queerly, he loved them, considering his gambling and drinking. The yellow rose went there. Now all was ready – silver and white, forks and napkins, and in the middle the splashed bowl of variegated roses. So, with one last look, he left the dining-room.

Two pictures hung opposite the window. In real life they had never met, the long lady and the man holding his horse by the rein. The lady was a picture, bought by Oliver because he liked the picture; the man was an ancestor. He had a name. He held the rein in his hand. He had said to the painter: 'If you want my likeness, dang it, sir, take it when the leaves are on the trees.' There were leaves on the trees. He had said: 'Ain't there room for Colin as well as Buster?' Colin was his famous hound. But there was only room for Buster. It was, he seemed to say, addressing the company not the painter, a damned shame to leave out Colin whom he wished buried at his feet, in the same grave, about 1750; but that skunk the Reverend Whatshisname wouldn't allow it.

He was a talk producer, that ancestor. But the lady was a picture. In her yellow robe, leaning, with a pillar to support her, a silver arrow in her hand, and a feather in her hair, she led the eye up, down, from the curve to the straight, through glades of greenery and shades of silver, dun and rose into silence. The room was empty.

Empty, empty, empty; silent, silent, silent. The room was a shell, singing of what was before time was; a vase stood in the heart of the house, alabaster, smooth, cold, holding the still, distilled essence of emptiness, silence.

Across the hall a door opened. One voice, another voice, a third voice came wimpling and warbling: gruff – Bart's voice; quavering – Lucy's voice; middle-toned – Isa's voice. Their voices impetuously, impatiently, protestingly came across the hall saying: 'The train's late'; saying: 'Keep it hot'; saying: 'We won't, no Candish, we won't wait.'

Coming out from the library the voices stopped in the hall. They encountered an obstacle evidently: a rock. Utterly impossible was it, even in the heart of the country, to be alone? That was the shock. After that, the rock was raced round, embraced. If it was painful, it was essential. There must be society. Coming out of the library it was painful, but pleasant, to run slap into Mrs Manresa and an unknown young man with tow-coloured hair and a twisted face. No escape was possible; meeting was inevitable. Uninvited, unexpected, droppers-in, lured off the high road by the very same instinct that caused the sheep and the cows to desire propinquity, they had come. But they had brought a lunch basket. Here it was.

'We couldn't resist when we saw the name on the signpost,' Mrs Manresa began in her rich fluty voice. 'And this is a friend – William Dodge. We were going to sit all alone in a field. And I said: "Why not ask our dear friends," seeing the signpost, "to shelter us?" A seat at the table – that's all we want. We have our grub. We have our glasses. We ask nothing but – ' society apparently, to be with her kind.

And she waved her hand upon which there was a glove, and under the glove it seemed rings, at old Mr Oliver.

He bowed deep over her hand; a century ago, he would have kissed it. In all this sound of welcome, protestation, apology and again welcome, there was an element of silence, supplied by Isabella, observing the unknown young man. He was of course a gentleman: witness socks and trousers; brainy – tie spotted, waistcoat undone; urban, professional, that is putty coloured, unwholesome; very nervous, exhibiting a twitch at this sudden introduction, and fundamentally infernally conceited, for he deprecated Mrs Manresa's effusion, yet was her guest.

Isa felt antagonised, yet curious. But when Mrs Manresa added, to make all shipshape: 'He's an artist,' and when William Dodge corrected her: 'I'm a clerk in an office' – she thought he said Education or Somerset House – she had her finger on the knot which had tied itself so tightly, almost to the extent of squinting, certainly of twitching, in his face.

Then they went in to lunch, and Mrs Manresa bubbled up, enjoying her own capacity to surmount, without turning a hair, this minor social crisis – this laying of two more places. For had she not complete faith in flesh and blood? and aren't we all flesh and blood? and how silly to make bones of trifles when we're all flesh and blood under the skin – men and women too! But she preferred men – obviously.

'Or what are your rings for, and your nails, and that really adorable little straw hat?' said Isabella addressing Mrs Manresa silently and thereby making silence add its unmistakable contribution to talk. Her hat, her rings, her fingernails red as roses, smooth as shells, were there for all to see. But not her life history. That was only scraps and fragments to all of them, excluding perhaps William Dodge, whom she called 'Bill' publicly – a sign perhaps that he knew more than they did. Some of the things that he knew – that she strolled the garden at midnight in silk pyjamas, had the loudspeaker playing jazz, and a cocktail bar – of course they knew also. But nothing private; no strict biographical facts.

She had been born, but it was only gossip said so, in Tasmania: her grandfather had been exported for some hanky-panky mid-Victorian scandal; malversation of trusts was it? But the story got no further the only time Isabella heard it than 'exported', for the husband of the communicative lady – Mrs Blencowe of the Grange – took exception, pedantically, to 'exported', said 'expatriated' was more like it, but not the right word, which he had on the tip of his tongue, but couldn't get at. And so the story dwindled away. Sometimes she referred to an uncle, a bishop. But he was thought to have been a colonial bishop only. They forgot and forgave very easily in the colonies. Also it was said her diamonds and rubies had been dug out of the earth with his own hands by a 'husband' who was not Ralph Manresa. Ralph, a Jew, got up to look the very spit and image of the landed gentry, supplied from directing City companies – that was certain – tons of money; and they had no child. But surely with George VI on the throne it was old fashioned, dowdy, savoured of moth-eaten furs, bugles, cameos and black-edged notepaper, to go ferreting into people's pasts?

'All I need,' said Mrs Manresa ogling Candish, as if he were a real man, not a stuffed man, 'is a corkscrew.' She had a bottle of champagne, but no corkscrew.

'Look, Bill,' she continued, cocking her thumb – she was opening the bottle – 'at the pictures. Didn't I tell you you'd have a treat?'

Vulgar she was in her gestures, in her whole person, over-sexed, over-dressed for a picnic. But what a desirable, at least valuable, quality it was – for everybody felt, directly she spoke, 'She's said it, she's done it, not I,' and could take advantage of the breach of decorum, of the fresh air that blew in, to follow like leaping dolphins in the wake of an ice-breaking vessel. Did she not restore to old Bartholomew his spice islands, his youth?

'I told him,' she went on, ogling Bart now, 'that he wouldn't look at our things' (of which they had heaps and mountains) 'after yours. And I promised him you'd show him the – the – ' here the champagne fizzed up and she insisted upon filling Bart's glass first. 'What is it all you learned gentlemen rave about? An arch? Norman? Saxon? Who's the last from school? Mrs Giles?'

She ogled Isabella now, conferring youth upon her; but always when she spoke to women, she veiled her eyes, for they, being conspirators, saw through it.

So with blow after blow, with champagne and ogling, she staked out her claim to be a wild child of nature, blowing into this – she did give one secret smile – sheltered harbour; which did make her smile, after London; yet it did, too, challenge London. For on she went to offer them a sample of her life; a few gobbets of gossip; mere trash; but she gave it for what it was worth; how last Tuesday she had been sitting next so and so; and she added, very casually a Christian name; then a nickname; and he'd said – for, as a mere nobody, they didn't mind what they said to her – and 'in strict confidence, I needn't tell you,' she told them. And they all pricked their ears. And then, with a gesture of her hands as if tossing overboard that odious crackling-under-the-pot London life – so – she exclaimed, 'There! . . . And what's the first thing I do when I come down here?' They had only come last night, driving through June lanes, alone with Bill it was understood, leaving London, suddenly become dissolute and dirty, to sit down to dinner. 'What do I do? Can I say it aloud? Is it permitted, Mrs Swithin? Yes, everything can be said in this house. I take off my stays' (here she pressed her hands to her sides – she was stout) 'and roll in the grass. Roll – you'll believe that . . . ' She laughed wholeheartedly. She had given up dealing with her figure and thus gained freedom.

'That's genuine,' Isa thought. Quite genuine. And her love of the country too. Often when Ralph Manresa had to stay in town she came down alone;

wore an old garden hat; taught the village women *not* how to pickle and preserve; but how to weave frivolous baskets out of coloured straw. Pleasure's what they want she said. You often heard her, if you called, yodelling among the hollyhocks, 'Hoity te doity te ray do . . . '

A thorough good sort she was. She made old Bart feel young. Out of the corner of his eye, as he raised his glass, he saw a flash of white in the garden. Someone passing.

The scullery maid, before the plates came out, was cooling her cheeks by the lily pond.

There had always been lilies there, self-sown from wind-dropped seed, floating red and white on the green plates of their leaves. Water, for hundreds of years, had silted down into the hollow, and lay there four or five feet deep over a black cushion of mud. Under the thick plate of green water, glazed in their self-centred world, fish swam – gold, splashed with white, streaked with black or silver. Silently they manoeuvred in their water world, poised in the blue patch made by the sky, or shot silently to the edge where the grass, trembling, made a fringe of nodding shadow. On the water-pavement spiders printed their delicate feet. A grain fell and spiralled down; a petal fell, filled and sank. At that the fleet of boat-shaped bodies paused: poised; equipped; mailed; then with a waver of undulation off they flashed.

It was in that deep centre, in that black heart, that the lady had drowned herself. Ten years since the pool had been dredged and a thigh bone recovered. Alas, it was a sheep's, not a lady's. And sheep have no ghosts, for sheep have no souls. But, the servants insisted, they must have a ghost; the ghost must be a lady's; who had drowned herself for love. So none of them would walk by the lily pool at night, only now when the sun shone and the gentry still sat at table.

The flower petal sank; the maid returned to the kitchen; Bartholomew sipped his wine. Happy he felt as a boy; yet reckless as an old man; an unusual, an agreeable sensation. Fumbling in his mind for something to say to the adorable lady, he chose the first thing that came handy; the story of the sheep's thigh. 'Servants,' he said, 'must have their ghost.' Kitchen-maids must have their drowned lady.

'But so must I!' cried the wild child of nature, Mrs Manresa. She became, of a sudden, solemn as an owl. She *knew*, she said, pinching a bit of bread to make this emphatic, that Ralph, when he was at the war, couldn't have been killed without her seeing him – 'wherever I was, whatever I was doing,' she added, waving her hands so that the diamonds flashed in the sun.

'I don't feel that,' said Mrs Swithin, shaking her head.

'No,' Mrs Manresa laughed. 'You wouldn't. None of you would. You see I'm on a level with . . . ' she waited till Candish had retired, 'the servants. I'm nothing like so grown up as you are.'

She preened, approving her adolescence. Rightly or wrongly? A spring of feeling bubbled up through her mud. They had laid theirs with blocks of marble. Sheep's bones were sheep's bones to them, not the relics of the drowned Lady Ermyntrude.

'And which camp,' said Bartholomew turning to the unknown guest, 'd'you belong to? The grown, or the ungrown?'

Isabella opened her mouth, hoping that Dodge would open his, and so enable her to place him. But he sat staring. 'I beg your pardon, sir?' he said. They all looked at him. 'I was looking at the pictures.'

The picture looked at nobody. The picture drew them down the paths of silence.

Lucy broke it.

'Mrs Manresa, I'm going to ask you a favour – If it comes to a pinch this afternoon, will you sing?'

This afternoon? Mrs Manresa was aghast. Was it the pageant? She had never dreamt it was this afternoon. They would never have thrust themselves in – had they known it was this afternoon. And, of course, once more the chime pealed. Isa heard the first chime; and the second; and the third – If it was wet, it would be in the barn; if it was fine on the terrace. And which would it be, wet or fine? And they all looked out of the window. Then the door opened. Candish said Mr Giles had come. Mr Giles would be down in a moment.

Giles had come. He had seen the great silver-plated car at the door with the initials R. M. twisted so as to look at a distance like a coronet. Visitors, he had concluded, as he drew up behind; and had gone to his room to change. The ghost of convention rose to the surface, as a blush or a tear rises to the surface at the pressure of emotion; so the car touched his training. He must change. And he came into the dining-room looking like a cricketer, in flannels, wearing a blue coat with brass buttons; though he was enraged. Had he not read, in the morning paper, in the train, that sixteen men had been shot, others prisoned, just over there, across the gulf, in the flat land which divided them from the continent? Yet he changed. It was Aunt Lucy, waving her hand at him as he came in, who made him change. He hung his grievances on her, as one hangs a coat on a hook, instinctively. Aunt Lucy, foolish, free; always, since he had chosen, after leaving college, to take a job in the City, expressing her amazement, her amusement, at men who spent their lives, buying and selling – ploughs? glass beads was it? or stocks and shares? – to savages who wished most oddly – for were they not beautiful naked? – to dress and live like the English? A frivolous, a malignant statement hers was of a problem which, for he had no special gift, no capital, and had been furiously in love with his wife – he nodded to her across the table – had afflicted him for ten years. Given his choice, he would have chosen to farm. But he was not given his choice. So one thing led to another; and the conglomeration of things pressed you flat; held you fast, like a fish in water. So he came for the weekend, and changed.

'How d'you do?' he said all round; nodded to the unknown guest; took against him; and ate his fillet of sole.

He was the very type of all that Mrs Manresa adored. His hair curled; far from running away, as many chins did, his was firm; the nose straight, if short; the eyes, of course, with that hair, blue; and finally to make the type complete, there was something fierce, untamed, in the expression which incited her, even at forty-five, to furbish up her ancient batteries.

'He is my husband,' Isabella thought, as they nodded across the bunch of many-coloured flowers. 'The father of my children.' It worked, that old cliché; she felt pride; and affection; then pride again in herself, whom he had chosen. It was a shock to find, after the morning's look in the glass, and the arrow of desire shot through her last night by the gentleman farmer, how much she felt when he came in, not a dapper City gent, but a cricketer, of love; and of hate.

They had met first in Scotland, fishing – she from one rock, he from another. Her line had got tangled; she had given over, and had watched him with the stream rushing between his legs, casting, casting – until, like a thick ingot of silver bent in the middle, the salmon had leapt, had been caught, and she had loved him.

Bartholomew too loved him; and noted his anger – about what? But he remembered his guest. The family was not a family in the presence of strangers. He must, rather laboriously, tell them the story of the pictures at which the unknown guest had been looking when Giles came in.

'That,' he indicated the man with a horse, 'was my ancestor. He had a dog. The dog was famous. The dog has his place in history. He left it on record that he wished his dog to be buried with him.'

They looked at the picture.

'I always feel,' Lucy broke the silence, 'he's saying: "Paint my dog." '

'But what about the horse?' said Mrs Manresa.

'The horse,' said Bartholomew, putting on his glasses. He looked at the horse. The hindquarters were not satisfactory.

But William Dodge was still looking at the lady.

'Ah,' said Bartholomew who had bought that picture because he liked that picture, 'you're an artist.'

Dodge denied it, for the second time in half an hour, or so Isa noted.

What for did a good sort like the woman Manresa bring these half-breeds in her trail? Giles asked himself. And his silence made its contribution to talk – Dodge that is, shook his head. 'I like that picture.' That was all he could bring himself to say.

'And you're right,' said Bartholomew. 'A man – I forget his name – a man connected with some Institute, a man who goes about giving advice, gratis, to descendants like ourselves, degenerate descendants, said . . . said . . . ' He paused. They all looked at the lady. But she looked over their heads, looking at nothing. She led them down green glades into the heart of silence.

'Said it was by Sir Joshua?' Mrs Manresa broke the silence abruptly.

'No, no,' William Dodge said hastily, but under his breath.

'Why's he afraid?' Isabella asked herself. A poor specimen he was; afraid to stick up for his own beliefs – just as she was afraid, of her husband. Didn't she write her poetry in a book bound like an account book lest Giles might suspect? She looked at Giles.

He had finished his fish; he had eaten quickly, not to keep them waiting. Now there was cherry tart. Mrs Manresa was counting the stones.

'Tinker, tailor, soldier, sailor, apothecary, ploughboy . . . that's me!' she cried, delighted to have it confirmed by the cherry stones that she was a wild child of nature.

'You believe,' said the old gentleman, courteously chaffing her, 'in that too?'

'Of course, of course I do!' she cried. Now she was on the rails again. Now she was a thorough good sort again. And they too were delighted; now they could follow in her wake and leave the silver and dun shades that led to the heart of silence.

'I had a father,' said Dodge beneath his breath to Isa who sat next him, 'who loved pictures.'

'Oh, I too!' she exclaimed. Flurriedly, disconnectedly, she explained. She used to stay when she was a child, when she had the whooping cough, with an uncle, a clergyman; who wore a skull cap; and never did anything; didn't even preach; but made up poems, walking in his garden, saying them aloud.

'People thought him mad,' she said. 'I didn't . . . '

She stopped.

'Tinker, tailor, soldier, sailor, apothecary, ploughboy . . . It appears,' said old Bartholomew, laying down his spoon, 'that I am a thief. Shall we take our coffee in the garden?' He rose.

Isa dragged her chair across the gravel, muttering: 'To what dark antre of the unvisited earth, or wind-brushed forest, shall we go now? Or spin from star to star and dance in the maze of the moon? Or . . . '

She held her deckchair at the wrong angle. The frame with the notches was upside down.

'Songs my uncle taught me?' said William Dodge, hearing her mutter. He unfolded the chair and fixed the bar into the right notch.

She flushed, as if she had spoken in an empty room and someone had stepped out from behind a curtain.

'Don't you, if you're doing something with your hands, talk nonsense?' she stumbled. But what did he do with his hands, the white, the fine, the shapely?

Giles went back to the house and brought more chairs and placed them in a semi-circle, so that the view might be shared, and the shelter of the old wall.

For by some lucky chance a wall had been built continuing the house, it might be with the intention of adding another wing, on the raised ground in the sun. But funds were lacking; the plan was abandoned, and the wall remained, nothing but a wall. Later, another generation had planted fruit trees, which in time had spread their arms widely across the red-orange weathered brick. Mrs Sands called it a good year if she could make six pots of apricot jam from them – the fruit was never sweet enough for dessert. Perhaps three apricots were worth enclosing in muslin bags. But they were so beautiful, naked, with one flushed cheek, one green, that Mrs Swithin left them naked, and the wasps burrowed holes.

The ground sloped up so that, to quote Figgis's *Guide Book* (1833), 'it commanded a fine view of the surrounding country . . . The spire of Bolney Minster, Rough Norton woods, and on an eminence rather to the left, Hogben's Folly, so called because . . . '

The *Guide Book* still told the truth; 1833 was true in 1939. No house had been built; no town had sprung up. Hogben's Folly was still eminent; the very flat, field-parcelled land had changed only in this – the tractor had to some extent superseded the plough. The horse had gone; but the cow remained. If Figgis were here now, Figgis would have said the same. So they always said when in summer they sat there to drink coffee, if they had guests. When they were alone, they said nothing. They looked at the view; they looked at what they knew, to see if what they knew might perhaps be different today. Most days it was the same.

'That's what makes a view so sad,' said Mrs Swithin, lowering herself into the deckchair which Giles had brought her. 'And so beautiful. It'll be there,' she nodded at the strip of gauze laid upon the distant fields, 'when we're not.'

Giles nicked his chair into position with a jerk. Thus only could he show his irritation, his rage with old fogies who sat and looked at views over coffee and cream when the whole of Europe – over there – was bristling like . . . He had no command of metaphor. Only the ineffective word 'hedgehog' illustrated his vision of Europe, bristling with guns, poised with planes. At any moment guns would rake that land into furrows; planes splinter Bolney Minster into smithereens and blast the Folly. He, too, loved the view. And blamed Aunt Lucy, looking at views, instead of – doing what? What she had done was to marry a squire now dead; she had borne two children, one in Canada, the other, married, in Birmingham. His father, whom he loved, he exempted from censure; as for himself, one thing followed another; and so he sat, with old fogies, looking at views.

'Beautiful,' said Mrs Manresa, 'beautiful . . . ' she mumbled. She was lighting a cigarette. The breeze blew out her match. Giles hollowed his hand and lit another. She too was exempted – why, he could not say.

'Since you're interested in pictures,' said Bartholomew, turning to the silent guest, 'why, tell me, are we, as a race, so incurious, irresponsive and insensitive' – the champagne had given him a flow of unusual three-decker words – 'to that noble art, whereas, Mrs Manresa, if she'll allow me my old man's liberty, has her Shakespeare by heart?'

'Shakespeare by heart!' Mrs Manresa protested. She struck an attitude. ' "To be, or not to be, that is the question. Whether 'tis nobler . . . " Go on!' she nudged Giles, who sat next her.

' "Fade far away and quite forget what thou amongst the leaves hast never known . . . " ' Isa supplied the first words that came into her head by way of helping her husband out of his difficulty.

' "The weariness, the torture, and the fret . . . " ' William Dodge added, burying the end of his cigarette in a grave between two stones.

'There!' Bartholomew exclaimed, cocking his forefinger aloft. 'That proves it! What spring's touched, what secret drawer displays its treasures, if I say' – he raised more fingers – 'Reynolds! Constable! Crome!'

'Why called "Old"?' Mrs Manresa thrust in.

'We haven't the words – we haven't the words,' Mrs Swithin protested. 'Behind the eyes; not on the lips; that's all.'

'Thoughts without words,' her brother mused. 'Can that be?'

'Quite beyond me!' cried Mrs Manresa, shaking her head. 'Much too clever! May I help myself? I know it's wrong. But I've reached the age – and the figure – when I do what I like.'

She took the little silver cream jug and let the smooth fluid curl luxuriously into her coffee, to which she added a shovel full of brown sugar candy. Sensuously, rhythmically, she stirred the mixture round and round.

'Take what you like! Help yourself!' Bartholomew exclaimed. He felt the champagne withdrawing and hastened, before the last trace of geniality was withdrawn, to make the most of it, as if he cast one last look into a lit-up chamber before going to bed.

The wild child, afloat once more on the tide of the old man's benignity, looked over her coffee cup at Giles, with whom she felt in conspiracy. A thread united them – visible, invisible, like those threads, now seen, now not, that unite trembling grass blades in autumn before the sun rises. She had met him once only, at a cricket match. And then had been spun between them an early-morning thread before the twigs and leaves of real friendship emerge. She looked before she drank. Looking was part of drinking. Why waste sensation, she seemed to ask, why waste a single drop that can be pressed out of this ripe, this melting, this adorable world? Then she drank. And the air round her became threaded with sensation. Bartholomew felt it; Giles felt it. Had he been a horse, the thin brown skin would have twitched, as if a fly had settled. Isabella twitched too. Jealousy, anger pierced her skin.

'And now,' said Mrs Manresa, putting down her cup, 'about this entertainment – this pageant, into which we've gone and butted' – she made it, too, seem ripe like the apricot into which the wasps were burrowing. 'Tell me, what's it to be?' She turned. 'Don't I hear?' She listened. She heard laughter, down among the bushes, where the terrace dipped to the bushes.

Beyond the lily pool the ground sank again, and in that dip of the ground, bushes and brambles had mobbed themselves together. It was always shady; sun-flecked in summer, dark and damp in winter. In the summer there were always butterflies; fritillaries darting through; red admirals feasting and floating; cabbage whites unambitiously fluttering round a bush, like muslin milkmaids, content to spend a life there. Butterfly catching, for generation after generation, began there; for Bartholomew and Lucy; for Giles; for George it had began only the day before yesterday, when, in his little green net, he had caught a cabbage white.

It was the very place for a dressing-room, just as, obviously, the terrace was the very place for a play.

'The very place!' Miss La Trobe had exclaimed the first time she came to call and was shown the grounds. It was a winter's day. The trees were leafless then.

'That's the place for a pageant, Mr Oliver!' she had exclaimed. 'Winding in and out between the trees . . . ' She waved her hand at the trees standing bare in the clear light of January.

'There the stage; here the audience; and down there among the bushes a perfect dressing-room for the actors.'

She was always all agog to get things up. But where did she spring from? With that name she wasn't presumably pure English. From the Channel Islands perhaps? Only her eyes and something about her always made Mrs Bingham suspect that she had Russian blood in her. 'Those deep-set eyes; that very square jaw' reminded her – not that she had been to Russia – of the Tartars. Rumour said that she had kept a tea shop at Winchester; that had failed. She had been an actress. That had failed. She had bought a four-roomed cottage and shared it with an actress. They had quarrelled. Very little was actually known about her. Outwardly she was swarthy, sturdy and thick set; strode about the fields in a smock frock; sometimes with a cigarette in her mouth; often with a whip in her hand; and used rather strong language – perhaps, then, she wasn't altogether a lady? At any rate, she had a passion for getting things up.

The laughter died away.

'Are they going to act?' Mrs Manresa asked.

'Act; dance; sing; a little bit of everything,' said Giles.

'Miss La Trobe is a lady of wonderful energy,' said Mrs Swithin.

'She makes everyone do something,' said Isabella.

'Our part,' said Bartholomew, 'is to be the audience. And a very important part too.'

'Also, we provide the tea,' said Mrs Swithin.

'Shan't we go and help?' said Mrs Manresa. 'Cut up bread and butter?'

'No, no,' said Mr Oliver. 'We are the audience.'

'One year we had *Gammer Gurton's Needle*,' said Mrs Swithin. 'One year we wrote the play ourselves. The son of our blacksmith – Tony? Tommy? – had the loveliest voice. And Elsie at the Crossways – how she mimicked! Took us all off. Bart; Giles; Old Flimsy – that's me. People are gifted – very. The question is – how to bring it out? That's where she's so clever – Miss La Trobe. Of course, there's the whole of English literature to choose from. But how can one choose? Often on a wet day I begin counting up; what I've read; what I haven't read.'

'And leaving books on the floor,' said her brother. 'Like the pig in the story; or was it a donkey?'

She laughed, tapping him lightly on the knee.

'The donkey who couldn't choose between hay and turnips and so starved,' Isabella explained, interposing – anything – between her aunt and her husband, who hated this kind of talk this afternoon. Books open; no conclusion come to; and he sitting in the audience.

'We remain seated' – 'We are the audience.' Words this afternoon ceased to lie flat in the sentence. They rose, became menacing and shook their fists at you. This afternoon he wasn't Giles Oliver come to see the villagers act their annual pageant; manacled to a rock he was, and forced passively to behold indescribable horror. His face showed it; and Isa, not knowing what to say, abruptly, half purposely, knocked over a coffee cup.

William Dodge caught it as it fell. He held it for a moment. He turned it. From the faint blue mark, as of crossed daggers, in the glaze at the bottom he knew that it was English, made perhaps at Nottingham; date about 1760. His expression, considering the daggers, coming to this conclusion, gave Giles another peg on which to hang his rage as one hangs a coat on a peg, conveniently. A toady; a lickspittle; not a downright plain man of his senses but a teaser and twitcher; a fingerer of sensations; picking and choosing; dillying and dallying; not a man to have straightforward love for a woman – his head was close to Isa's head – but simply a — At this word, which he could not speak in public, he pursed his lips; and the signet-ring on his little finger looked redder, for the flesh next it whitened as he gripped the arm of his chair.

'Oh what fun!' cried Mrs Manresa in her fluty voice. 'A little bit of everything. A song; a dance; then a play acted by the villagers themselves. Only,' here she turned with her head on one side to Isabella, 'I'm sure *she's* written it. Haven't you, Mrs Giles?'

Isa flushed and denied it.

'For myself,' Mrs Manresa continued, 'speaking plainly, I can't put two words together. I don't know how it is – such a chatterbox as I am with my tongue, once I hold a pen – ' She made a face, screwed her fingers as if she held a pen in them. But the pen she held thus on the little table absolutely refused to move. 'And my handwriting – so huge – so clumsy – ' She made another face and dropped the invisible pen.

Very delicately William Dodge set the cup in its saucer. 'Now *he*,' said

Mrs Manresa, as if referring to the delicacy with which he did this, and imputing to him the same skill in writing, 'writes beautifully. Every letter perfectly formed.'

Again they all looked at him. Instantly he put his hands in his pockets.

Isabella guessed the word that Giles had not spoken. Well, was it wrong if he was that word? Why judge each other? Do we know each other? Not here, not now. But somewhere, this cloud, this crust, this doubt, this dust – She waited for a rhyme, it failed her; but somewhere surely one sun would shine and all, without a doubt, would be clear.

She started. Again, sounds of laughter reached her.

'I think I hear them,' she said. 'They're getting ready. They're dressing up in the bushes.'

Miss La Trobe was pacing to and fro between the leaning birch trees. One hand was deep stuck in her jacket pocket; the other held a foolscap sheet. She was reading what was written there. She had the look of a commander pacing his deck. The leaning graceful trees with black bracelets circling the silver bark were distant about a ship's length.

Wet would it be, or fine? Out came the sun; and, shading her eyes in the attitude proper to an admiral on his quarter-deck, she decided to risk the engagement out of doors. Doubts were over. All stage properties, she commanded, must be moved from the barn to the bushes. It was done. And the actors, while she paced, taking all responsibility and plumping for fine not wet, dressed among the brambles. Hence the laughter.

The clothes were strewn on the grass. Cardboard crowns, swords made of silver paper, turbans that were sixpenny dishcloths, lay on the grass or were flung on the bushes. There were pools of red and purple in the shade; flashes of silver in the sun. The dresses attracted the butterflies. Red and silver, blue and yellow gave off warmth and sweetness. Red admirals gluttonously absorbed richness from dishcloths, cabbage whites drank icy coolness from silver paper. Flitting, tasting, returning, they sampled the colours.

Miss La Trobe stopped her pacing and surveyed the scene. 'It has the makings . . . ' she murmured. For another play always lay behind the play she had just written. Shading her eyes, she looked. The butterflies circling; the light changing; the children leaping; the mothers laughing – 'No, I don't get it,' she muttered and resumed her pacing.

'Bossy' they called her privately, just as they called Mrs Swithin 'Flimsy'. Her abrupt manner and stocky figure; her thick ankles and sturdy shoes; her rapid decisions barked out in guttural accents – all this 'got their goat'. No one liked to be ordered about singly. But in little troops they appealed to her. Someone must lead. Then too they could put the blame on her. Suppose it poured?

'Miss La Trobe!' they hailed her now. 'What's the idea about this?'

She stopped. David and Iris each had a hand on the gramophone. It must be hidden; yet must be close enough to the audience to be heard. Well, hadn't she given orders? Where were the hurdles covered in leaves? Fetch them. Mr Streatfield had said he would see to it. Where was Mr Streatfield? No clergyman was visible. Perhaps he's in the barn? 'Tommy, cut along and fetch him.' 'Tommy's wanted in the first scene.' 'Beryl then . . . ' The mothers disputed. One child had been chosen; another not. Fair hair was unjustly preferred to dark. Mrs Ebury had forbidden Fanny to act because of the nettle-rash. There was another name in the village for nettle-rash.

Mrs Ball's cottage was not what you might call clean. In the last war Mrs Ball lived with another man while her husband was in the trenches. All this Miss La Trobe knew, but refused to be mixed up in it. She splashed into the fine mesh like a great stone into the lily pool. The criss-cross was shattered. Only the roots beneath the water were of use to her. Vanity, for example, made them all malleable. The boys wanted the big parts; the girls wanted the fine clothes. Expenses had to be kept down. Ten pounds was the limit. Thus conventions were outraged. Swathed in conventions, they couldn't see, as she could, that a dishcloth wound round a head in the open looked much richer than real silk. So they squabbled; but she kept out of it. Waiting for Mr Streatfield, she paced between the birch trees.

The other trees were magnificently straight. They were not too regular; but regular enough to suggest columns in a church; in a church without a roof; in an open-air cathedral, a place where swallows darting seemed, by the regularity of the trees, to make a pattern, dancing, like the Russians, only not to music but to the unheard rhythm of their own wild hearts.

The laughter died away.

'We must possess our souls in patience,' said Mrs Manresa again. 'Or could we help?' she suggested, glancing over her shoulder, 'with those chairs?'

Candish, a gardener and a maid were all bringing chairs – for the audience. There was nothing for the audience to do. Mrs Manresa suppressed a yawn. They were silent. They stared at the view, as if something might happen in one of those fields to relieve them of the intolerable burden of sitting silent, doing nothing, in company. Their minds and bodies were too close, yet not close enough. We aren't free, each one of them felt separately, to feel or think separately, nor yet to fall asleep. We're too close; but not close enough. So they fidgeted.

The heat had increased. The clouds had vanished. All was sun now. The view laid bare by the sun was flattened, silenced, stilled. The cows were motionless; the brick wall, no longer sheltering, beat back grains of heat. Old Mr Oliver sighed profoundly. His head jerked; his hand fell. It fell within an inch of the dog's head on the grass by his side. Then up he jerked it again on to his knee.

Giles glared. With his hands bound tight round his knees he stared at the flat fields. Staring, glaring, he sat silent.

Isabella felt prisoned. Through the bars of the prison, through the sleep haze that deflected them, blunt arrows bruised her; of love, then of hate. Through other people's bodies she felt neither love nor hate distinctly. Most consciously she felt – she had drunk sweet wine at luncheon – a desire for water. 'A beaker of cold water, a beaker of cold water,' she repeated, and saw water surrounded by walls of shining glass.

Mrs Manresa longed to relax and curl in a corner with a cushion, a picture paper and a bag of sweets.

Mrs Swithin and William surveyed the view aloofly, and with detachment.

How tempting, how very tempting, to let the view triumph; to reflect its ripple; to let their own minds ripple; to let outlines elongate and pitch over – so – with a sudden jerk.

Mrs Manresa yielded, pitched, plunged, then pulled herself up.

'What a view!' she exclaimed, pretending to dust the ashes of her cigarette, but in truth concealing her yawn. Then she sighed, pretending to express not her own drowsiness, but something connected with what she felt about views.

Nobody answered her. The flat fields glared green yellow, blue yellow, red yellow, then blue again. The repetition was senseless, hideous, stupefying.

'Then,' said Mrs Swithin, in a low voice, as if the exact moment for speech had come, as if she had promised, and it was time to fulfil her promise, 'come, come and I'll show you the house.'

She addressed no one in particular. But William Dodge knew she meant him. He rose with a jerk, like a toy suddenly pulled straight by a string.

'What energy!' Mrs Manresa half sighed, half yawned.

'Have I the courage to go too?' Isabella asked herself. They were going; above all things, she desired cold water, a beaker of cold water; but desire petered out, suppressed by the leaden duty she owed to others. She watched them go – Mrs Swithin tottering yet tripping; and Dodge unfurled and straightened, as he strode beside her along the blazing tiles under the hot wall, till they reached the shade of the house.

A matchbox fell – Bartholomew's. His fingers had loosed it; he had dropped it. He gave up the game; he couldn't be bothered. With his head on one side, his hand dangling above the dog's head he slept; he snored.

Mrs Swithin paused for a moment in the hall among the gilt-clawed tables.

'This,' she said, 'is the staircase. And now – up we go.'

She went up, two stairs ahead of her guest. Lengths of yellow satin unfurled themselves on a cracked canvas as they mounted.

'Not an ancestress,' said Mrs Swithin, as they came level with the head in the picture. 'But we claim her because we've known her – Oh, ever so many years. Who was she?' she gazed. 'Who painted her?' She shook her head. She looked lit up, as if for a banquet, with the sun pouring over her.

'But I like her best in the moonlight,' Mrs Swithin reflected, and mounted more stairs.

She panted slightly, going upstairs. Then she ran her hand over the sunk books in the wall on the landing, as if they were pan pipes.

'Here are the poets from whom we descend by way of the mind, Mr . . .' she murmured. She had forgotten his name. Yet she had singled him out.

'My brother says, they built the house north for shelter, not south for sun. So they're damp in the winter.' She paused. 'And now what comes next?'

She stopped. There was a door.

'The morning room.' She opened the door. 'Where my mother received her guests.'

Two chairs faced each other on either side of a fine fluted mantelpiece. He looked over her shoulder.

She shut the door.

'Now up, now up again.' Again they mounted. 'Up and up they went,' she panted, seeing, it seemed, an invisible procession, 'up and up to bed. A bishop; a traveller – I've forgotten even their names. I ignore. I forget.'

She stopped at a window in the passage and held back the curtain. Beneath was the garden, bathed in sun. The grass was sleek and shining. Three white pigeons were flirting and tiptoeing as ornate as ladies in ball dresses. Their elegant bodies swayed as they minced with tiny steps on their little pink feet upon the grass. Suddenly, up they rose in a flutter, circled, and flew away.

'Now,' she said, 'for the bedrooms.' She tapped twice very distinctly on a door. With her head on one side, she listened. 'One never knows,' she murmured, 'if there's somebody there.' Then she flung open the door.

He half expected to see somebody there, naked, or half dressed, or knelt in prayer. But the room was empty. The room was tidy as a pin, not slept in for months, a spare room. Candles stood on the dressing-table. The counterpane was straight. Mrs Swithin stopped by the bed.

'Here,' she said, 'yes, here,' she tapped the counterpane, 'I was born. In this bed.'

Her voice died away. She sank down on the edge of the bed. She was tired, no doubt, by the stairs, by the heat.

'But we have other lives, I think, I hope,' she murmured. 'We live in others, Mr . . . We live in things.'

She spoke simply. She spoke with an effort. She spoke as if she must overcome her tiredness out of charity towards a stranger, a guest. She had forgotten his name. Twice she had said 'Mr' and stopped.

The furniture was mid-Victorian, bought at Maples, perhaps, in the forties. The carpet was covered with small purple dots. And a white circle marked the place where the slop pail had stood by the washstand.

Could he say 'I'm William'? He wished to. Old and frail she had climbed the stairs. She had spoken her thoughts, ignoring – not caring – if he thought her, as he had, inconsequent, sentimental, foolish. She had lent him a hand to help him up a steep place. She had guessed his trouble. Sitting on the bed he heard her sing, swinging her little legs, 'Come and see my sea weeds, come and see my sea shells, come and see my dicky bird hop upon its perch' – an old child's nursery rhyme to help a child. Standing by the cupboard in the corner he saw her reflected in the glass. Cut off from their bodies, their eyes smiled, their bodiless eyes, at their eyes in the glass.

Then she slipped off the bed.

'Now,' she said, 'what comes next?' and pattered down the corridor. A door stood open. Everyone was out in the garden. The room was like a ship deserted by its crew. The children had been playing – there was a spotted horse in the middle of the carpet. The nurse had been sewing – there was a piece of linen on the table. The baby had been in the cot. The cot was empty.

'The nursery,' said Mrs Swithin.

Words raised themselves and became symbolical. 'The cradle of our race,' she seemed to say.

Dodge crossed to the fireplace and looked at the Newfoundland dog in the *Christmas Annual* that was pinned to the wall. The room smelt warm and sweet: of clothes drying; of milk; of biscuits and warm water. 'Good Friends' the picture was called. A rushing sound came in through the open door. He turned. The old woman had wandered out into the passage and leant against the window.

He left the door open for the crew to come back to and joined her.

Down in the courtyard beneath the window cars were assembling. Their narrow black roofs were laid together like the blocks of a floor. Chauffeurs were jumping down; here old ladies gingerly advanced black legs with silver-buckled shoes; old men striped trousers. Young men in shorts leapt out on one side; girls with skin-coloured legs on the other. There was a purring and a churning of the yellow gravel. The audience was assembling. But they, looking down from the window, were truants, detached. Together they leant half out of the window.

And then a breeze blew and all the muslin blinds fluttered out, as if some majestic goddess, rising from her throne among her peers, had tossed her amber-coloured raiment, and the other gods, seeing her rise and go, laughed, and their laughter floated her on.

Mrs Swithin put her hands to her hair, for the breeze had ruffled it.

'Mr . . .' she began.

'I'm William,' he interrupted.

At that she smiled a ravishing girl's smile, as if the wind had warmed the wintry blue in her eyes to amber.

'I took you,' she apologised, 'away from your friends, William, because I felt wound tight here . . .' She touched her bony forehead upon which a blue vein wriggled like a blue worm. But her eyes in their caves of bone were still lambent. He saw her eyes only. And he wished to kneel before her, to kiss her hand, and to say: 'At school they held me under a bucket of dirty water, Mrs Swithin; when I looked up, the world was dirty, Mrs Swithin; so I married; but my child's not my child, Mrs Swithin. I'm a half-man, Mrs Swithin; a flickering, mind-divided little snake in the grass, Mrs Swithin; as Giles saw; but you've healed me . . . ' So he wished to say; but said nothing; and the breeze went lolloping along the corridors, blowing the blinds out.

Once more he looked and she looked down on to the yellow gravel that made a crescent round the door. Pendant from her chain her cross swung as she leant out and the sun struck it. How could she weight herself down by that sleek symbol? How stamp herself, so volatile, so vagrant, with that image? As he looked at it, they were truants no more. The purring of the wheels became vocal. 'Hurry, hurry, hurry,' it seemed to say, 'or you'll be late. Hurry, hurry, hurry, or the best seats'll be taken.'

'Oh,' cried Mrs Swithin, 'there's Mr Streatfield!' And they saw a clergyman, a strapping clergyman, carrying a hurdle, a leafy hurdle. He was striding through the cars with the air of a person of authority, who is awaited, expected, and now comes.

'Is it time,' said Mrs Swithin, 'to go and join – ' She left the sentence unfinished, as if she were of two minds, and they fluttered to right and to left, like pigeons rising from the grass.

The audience was assembling. They came streaming along the paths and spreading across the lawn. Some were old; some were in the prime of life. There were children among them. Among them, as Mr Figgis might have observed, were representatives of our most respected families – the Dyces of Denton; the Wickhams of Owlswick; and so on. Some had been there for centuries, never selling an acre. On the other hand there were newcomers, the Manresas, bringing the old houses up to date, adding bathrooms. And a scatter of odds and ends, like Cobbet of Cobbs Corner, retired, it was understood, on a pension from a tea plantation. Not an asset. He did his own housework and dug in his garden. The building of a car factory and of an aerodrome in the neighbourhood had attracted a number of unattached floating residents. Also there was Mr Page, the reporter, representing the local paper. Roughly speaking, however, had Figgis been there in person and called a roll call, half the ladies and gentlemen present would have said: '*Adsum*; I'm here, in place of my grandfather or great-grandfather,' as the case might be. At this very moment, half-past three on a June day in 1939, they greeted each other, and as they took their seats, finding if possible a seat next one another, they said: 'That hideous new house at Pyes Corner! What an eyesore! And those bungalows! – have you seen 'em?'

Again, had Figgis called the names of the villagers, they too would have answered. Mrs Sands was born Iliffe; Candish's mother was one of the Perrys. The green mounds in the churchyard had been cast up by their molings, which for centuries had made the earth friable. True, there were absentees when Mr Streatfield called his roll call in the church. The motor bike, the motor bus and the movies – when Mr Streatfield called his roll call, he laid the blame on them.

Rows of chairs, deckchairs, gilt chairs, hired cane chairs and indigenous garden seats had been drawn up on the terrace. There were plenty of seats for everybody. But some preferred to sit on the ground. Certainly Miss La Trobe had spoken the truth when she said: 'The very place for a pageant!' The lawn was as flat as the floor of a theatre. The terrace, rising, made a natural stage. The trees barred the stage like pillars. And the human figure was seen to great advantage against a background of sky. As for the weather, it was turning out, against all expectation, a very fine day. A perfect summer afternoon.

'What luck!' Mrs Carter was saying. 'Last year . . . ' Then the play began. Was it, or was it not, the play? Chuff, chuff, chuff sounded from the bushes. It was the noise a machine makes when something has gone wrong. Some sat down hastily; others stopped talking guiltily. All looked at the bushes. For the stage was empty. Chuff, chuff, chuff, the machine buzzed in the bushes. While they looked apprehensively and some finished their sentences, a small girl, like a rosebud in pink, advanced, took her stand on a mat behind a conch hung with leaves, and piped:

Gentles and simples, I address you all . . .

So it was the play then. Or was it the prologue?

Come hither for our festival (she continued);

This is a pageant, all may see,

Drawn from our island history.

   England am I . . .

'She's England,' they whispered. 'It's begun. The prologue,' they added, looking down at the programme.

'*England am I*,' she piped again; and stopped.

She had forgotten her lines.

'Hear! Hear!' said an old man in a white waistcoat briskly. 'Bravo! Bravo!'

'Blast 'em!' cursed Miss La Trobe, hidden behind the tree. She looked along the front row. They glared as if they were exposed to a frost that nipped them and fixed them all at the same level. Only Bond the cowman looked fluid and natural.

'Music!' she signalled. 'Music!' But the machine continued: Chuff, chuff, chuff.

'*A child new born* . . . ' she prompted.

'*A child new born*,' Phyllis Jones continued,

Sprung from the sea,

Whose billows blown by mighty storm

Cut off from France and Germany

This isle.

She glanced back over her shoulder. Chuff, chuff, chuff, the machine buzzed. A long line of villagers in shirts made of sacking began passing in and out in single file behind her between the trees. They were singing, but not a word reached the audience.

England am I, Phyllis Jones continued, facing the audience,

Now weak and small,
A child, as all may see . . .

Her words peppered the audience as with a shower of hard little stones. Mrs Manresa in the very centre smiled; but she felt as if her skin cracked when she smiled. There was a vast vacancy between her, the singing villagers and the piping child.

Chuff, chuff, chuff went the machine like a corn-cutter on a hot day.

The villagers were singing, but half their words were blown away.

Cutting the roads . . . up to the hilltop . . . we climbed. Down in the valley . . . sow,
wild boar, hog, rhinoceros, reindeer . . . Dug ourselves into the hilltop . . . Ground
roots between stones . . . Ground corn . . . till we too . . . lay underg–r–o–u–n–d . . .

The words petered away. Chuff, chuff, chuff, the machine ticked. Then at last the machine ground out a tune!

Armed against fate,
The valiant Rhoderick,
Armed and valiant,
Bold and blatant,
Firm, elatant,
See the warriors – here they come . . .

The pompous popular tune brayed and blared. Miss La Trobe watched from behind the tree. Muscles loosened; ice cracked. The stout lady in the middle began to beat time with her hand on her chair. Mrs Manresa was humming:

My home is at Windsor, close to the Inn.

Royal George is the name of the pub.

And boys you'll believe me,

I don't want no asking . . .

She was afloat on the stream of the melody. Radiating royalty, complacency, good humour, the wild child was queen of the festival. The play had begun.

But there was an interruption. 'Oh,' Miss La Trobe growled behind her tree, 'the torture of these interruptions!'

'Sorry I'm so late,' said Mrs Swithin. She pushed her way through the chairs to a seat beside her brother. 'What's it all about? I've missed the prologue. England? That little girl? Now she's gone . . .'

Phyllis had slipped off her mat.

'And who's this?' asked Mrs Swithin.

It was Hilda, the carpenter's daughter. She now stood where England had stood.

'*Oh, England's grown . . .*' Miss La Trobe prompted her.

'*Oh, England's grown a girl now,*' Hilda sang out

('What a lovely voice!' someone exclaimed),

With roses in her hair,
Wild roses, red roses,

She roams the lanes and chooses
A garland for her hair.

'A cushion? Thank you so much,' said Mrs Swithin, stuffing the cushion behind her back. Then she leant forward.

'That's England in the time of Chaucer, I take it. She's been maying, nutting. She has flowers in her hair . . . But those passing behind her – ' she pointed. 'The Canterbury pilgrims? Look!'

All the time the villagers were passing in and out between the trees. They were singing; but only a word or two was audible ' . . . *wore ruts in the grass . . . built the house in the lane . . .* ' The wind blew away the connecting words of their chant, and then, as they reached the tree at the end, they sang: '*To the shrine of the saint . . . to the tomb . . . lovers . . . believers . . . we come . . .* '

They grouped themselves together.

Then there was a rustle and an interruption. Chairs were drawn back. Isa looked behind her. Mr and Mrs Rupert Haines, detained by a breakdown on the road, had arrived. He was sitting to the right, several rows back, the man in grey.

Meanwhile the pilgrims, having done their homage to the tomb, were, it appeared, tossing hay on their rakes.

I kissed a girl and let her go,
Another did I tumble
In the straw and in the hay . . .

– that was what they were singing, as they scooped and tossed the invisible hay, when she looked round again.

'Scenes from English history,' Mrs Manresa explained to Mrs Swithin. She spoke in a loud cheerful voice, as if the old lady were deaf. 'Merrie England.'

She clapped energetically.

The singers scampered away into the bushes. The tune stopped. Chuff, chuff, chuff, the machine ticked. Mrs Manresa looked at her programme. It would take till midnight unless they skipped. Early Briton; Plantagenets; Tudors; Stuarts – she ticked them off, but probably she had forgotten a reign or two.

'Ambitious, ain't it?' she said to Bartholomew, while they waited. Chuff, chuff, chuff went the machine. Could they talk? Could they move? No, for the play was going on. Yet the stage was empty; only the cows moved in the meadows; only the tick of the gramophone needle was heard. The tick, tick, tick seemed to hold them together, tranced. Nothing whatsoever appeared on the stage.

'I'd no notion we looked so nice,' Mrs Swithin whispered to William. Hadn't she? The children; the pilgrims; behind the pilgrims the trees, and behind them the fields – the beauty of the visible world took his breath away. Tick, tick, tick, the machine continued.

'Marking time,' said old Oliver beneath his breath.

'Which don't exist for us,' Lucy murmured. 'We've only the present.'

'Isn't that enough?' William asked himself. Beauty – isn't that enough? But here Isa fidgetted. Her bare brown arms went nervously to her head. She half turned in her seat. 'No, not for us, who've the future,' she seemed to say. The future disturbing our present. Who was she looking for? William, turning, following her eyes, saw only a man in grey.

The ticking stopped. A dance tune was put on the machine. In time to it, Isa hummed: 'What do I ask? To fly away, from night and day, and issue where – no partings are – but eye meets eye – and . . . Oh,' she cried aloud, 'look at her!'

Everyone was clapping and laughing. From behind the bushes issued Queen Elizabeth – Eliza Clark, licensed to sell tobacco. Could she be Mrs Clark of the village shop? She was splendidly made up. Her head, pearl-hung, rose from a vast ruff. Shiny satins draped her. Sixpenny brooches glared like cats' eyes and tigers' eyes; pearls looked down; her cape was made of cloth of silver – in fact swabs used to scour saucepans. She looked the age in person. And when she mounted the soap box in the centre, representing perhaps a rock in the ocean, her size made her appear gigantic. She could reach a flitch of bacon or haul a tub of oil with one sweep of her arm in the shop. For a moment she stood there, eminent, dominant, on the soap box with the blue and sailing clouds behind her. The breeze had risen.

The Queen of this great land . . .

– those were the first words that could be heard above the roar of laughter and applause.

Mistress of ships and bearded men (she bawled),
Hawkins, Frobisher, Drake,
Tumbling their oranges, ingots of silver,
Cargoes of diamonds, ducats of gold,
Down on the jetty, there in the west land –
(she pointed her fist at the blazing blue sky)
Mistress of pinnacles, spires and palaces –
(her arm swept towards the house)
For me Shakespeare sang –
(a cow mooed; a bird twittered)
The throstle, the mavis (she continued)
In the green wood, the wild wood,
Carolled and sang, praising England, the Queen.
Then there was heard too
On granite and cobble
From Windsor to Oxford
Loud laughter, low laughter
Of warrior and lover,
The fighter, the singer.
The ashen-haired babe

(she stretched out her swarthy, muscular arm)
Stretched his arm in contentment
As home from the Isles came
The seafaring men . . .

Here the wind gave a tug at her head dress. Loops of pearls made it top-heavy. She had to steady the ruffle which threatened to blow away.

'Laughter, loud laughter,' Giles muttered. The tune on the gramophone reeled from side to side as if drunk with merriment. Mrs Manresa began beating her foot and humming in time to it.

'Bravo! Bravo!' she cried. 'There's life in the old dog yet!' And she trolloped out the words of the song with an abandonment which, if vulgar, was a great help to the Elizabethan age. For the ruff had become unpinned and great Eliza had forgotten her lines. But the audience laughed so loud that it did not matter.

'I fear I am not in my perfect mind,' Giles muttered to the same tune. Words came to the surface – he remembered ' "a stricken deer in whose lean flank the world's harsh scorn has struck its thorn . . . Exiled from its festival, the music turned ironical . . . A churchyard haunter at whom the owl hoots and the ivy mocks tap-tap-tapping on the pane . . . For they are dead, and I . . . I . . . I," ' he repeated, forgetting the words, and glaring at his Aunt Lucy who sat craned forward, her mouth gaping, and her bony little hands clapping.

What were they laughing at?

At Albert, the village idiot, apparently. There was no need to dress him up. There he came, acting his part to perfection. He came ambling across the grass, mopping and mowing.

I know where the tit nests, he began –
In the hedgerow. I know, I know –
What don't I know?
All your secrets, ladies,
And yours too, gentlemen . . .

He skipped along the front row of the audience, leering at each in turn. Now he was picking and plucking at Great Eliza's skirts. She cuffed him on the ear. He tweaked her back. He was enjoying himself immensely.

'Albert having the time of his life,' Bartholomew muttered.

'Hope he don't have a fit,' Lucy murmured.

'*I know . . . I know . . .* ' Albert tittered, skipping round the soap box.

'The village idiot,' whispered a stout black lady – Mrs Elmhurst – who came from a village ten miles distant where they, too, had an idiot. It wasn't nice. Suppose he suddenly did something dreadful? There he was pinching the queen's skirts. She half covered her eyes, in case he did do – something dreadful.

Hoppety, jiggety, Albert resumed,
In at the window, out at the door,

What does the little bird hear? (he whistled on his fingers).

And see! There's a mouse . . . (he made as if chasing it through the grass).

Now the clock strikes! (he stood erect, puffing out his cheeks as if he were blowing a dandelion clock)

One, two, three, four . . .

And off he skipped, as if his turn was over.

'Glad that's over,' said Mrs Elmhurst, uncovering her face. 'Now what comes next? A tableau. . . ?'

For helpers, issuing swiftly from the bushes, carrying hurdles, had enclosed the queen's throne with screens papered to represent walls. They had strewn the ground with rushes. And the pilgrims who had continued their march and their chant in the background, now gathered round the figure of Eliza on her soap box as if to form the audience at a play.

Were they about to act a play in the presence of Queen Elizabeth? Was this, perhaps, the Globe Theatre?

'What does the programme say?' Mrs Herbert Winthrop asked, raising her lorgnettes. She mumbled through the blurred carbon sheet. Yes; it was a scene from a play.

'About a false duke; and a princess disguised as a boy; then the long lost heir turns out to be the beggar, because of a mole on his cheek; and Carinthia – that's the duke's daughter, only she's been lost in a cave – falls in love with Ferdinando who had been put into a basket as a baby by an aged crone. And they marry. That's I think what happens,' she said, looking up from the programme.

'*Play out the play*,' great Eliza commanded.

An aged crone tottered forward.

('Mrs Otter of the End House,' someone murmured.)

She sat herself on a packing case, and made motions, plucking her dishevelled locks and rocking herself from side to side as if she were an aged beldame in a chimney corner.

('The crone, who saved the rightful heir,' Mrs Winthrop explained.)

'Twas a winter's night (she croaked out),

I mind me that, I to whom all's one now, summer or winter.

You say the sun shines? I believe you, sir . . .

'Oh, but it's winter, and the fog's abroad,'

All's one to Elsbeth, summer or winter,

By the fireside, in the chimney corner, telling her beads.

I've cause to tell 'em.

Each bead (she held a bead between thumb and finger)

A crime!

'Twas a winter's night, before cockcrow,

Yet the cock did crow ere he left me –

The man with a hood on his face, and the bloody hands,

And the babe in the basket.

'Tee hee,' he mewed, as who should say, 'I want my toy.'
Poor witling!
'Tee hee, tee hee!' I could not slay him!
For that, Mary in heaven forgive me
The sins I've sinned before cockcrow!
Down to the creek i' the dawn I slipped,
Where the gull haunts and the heron stands
Like a stake on the edge of the marshes . . .
Who's here?
(Three young men swaggered on to the stage and accosted her.)
'Are you come to torture me, sirs?
There is little blood in this arm
(she extended her skinny forearm from her ragged shift),
Saints in heaven preserve me!
She bawled. They bawled. All together they bawled, and so loud that it was difficult to make out what they were saying: apparently it was: *Did she remember concealing a child in a cradle among the rushes some twenty years previously? A babe in a basket, crone! A babe in a basket?* they bawled. *The wind howls and the bittern shrieks*, she replied.

'There is little blood in my arm,' Isabella repeated.

That was all she heard. There was such a medley of things going on, what with the beldame's deafness, the bawling of the youths and the confusion of the plot, that she could make nothing of it.

Did the plot matter? She shifted and looked over her right shoulder. The plot was only there to beget emotion. There were only two emotions: love and hate. There was no need to puzzle out the plot. Perhaps Miss La Trobe meant that when she cut this knot in the centre?

Don't bother about the plot: the plot's nothing.

But what was happening? The prince had come.

Plucking up his sleeve, the beldame recognised the mole; and, staggering back in her chair, shrieked:

My child! My child!

Recognition followed. The young prince (Albert Perry) was almost smothered in the withered arms of the beldame. Then suddenly he started apart.

'Look where she comes!' he cried.

They all looked where she came – Sylvia Edwards in white satin.

Who came? Isa looked. The nightingale's song? The pearl in night's black ear? Love embodied.

All arms were raised; all faces stared.

'Hail, sweet Carinthia!' said the prince, sweeping his hat off.

And she to him, raising her eyes:

'My love! My lord!'

'It was enough. Enough. Enough,' Isa repeated.

All else was verbiage, repetition.

The beldame meanwhile, because that was enough, had sunk back on her chair, the beads dangling from her fingers.

'*Look to the beldame there – old Elsbeth's sick!*'

(They crowded round her.)

Dead, sirs!

She fell back lifeless. The crowd drew away. *Peace, let her pass. She to whom all's one now, summer or winter.*

Peace was the third emotion. Love. Hate. Peace. Three emotions made the ply of human life. Now the priest, whose cotton-wool moustache confused his utterance, stepped forward and pronounced benediction.

From the distaff of life's tangled skein, unloose her hands.

(They unloosed her hands.)

Of her frailty, let nothing now remembered be.

Call for the robin redbreast and the wren.

And roses fall your crimson pall.

(Petals were strewn from wicker baskets.)

Cover the corpse. Sleep well.

(They covered the corpse.)

On you, fair sirs (he turned to the happy couple),

Let heaven rain benediction!

Haste ere the envying sun

Night's curtain hath undone. Let music sound

And the free air of heaven waft you to your slumber!

Lead on the dance!

The gramophone blared. Dukes, priests, shepherds, pilgrims and serving men took hands and danced. The idiot scampered in and out. Hands joined, heads knocking, they danced round the majestic figure of the Elizabethan age personified by Mrs Clark, licensed to sell tobacco, on her soap box.

It was a mellay; a medley; an entrancing spectacle (to William) of dappled light and shade on half-clothed, fantastically coloured, leaping, jerking, swinging legs and arms. He clapped till his palms stung.

Mrs Manresa applauded loudly. Somehow she was the queen; and he (Giles) was the surly hero.

'Bravo! Bravo!' she cried, and her enthusiasm made the surly hero squirm on his seat. Then the great lady in the bath chair, the lady whose marriage with the local peer had obliterated in his trashy title a name that had been a name when there were brambles and briars where the church now stood – so indigenous was she that even her body, crippled by arthritis, resembled an uncouth, nocturnal animal, now nearly extinct – clapped and laughed loud – the sudden laughter of a startled jay.

'Ha, ha, ha!' she laughed and clutched the arms of her chair with ungloved twisted hands.

'A-maying, a-maying,' they bawled. 'In and out and round about, a-maying, a-maying . . .'

It didn't matter what the words were; or who sang what. Round and round they whirled, intoxicated by the music. Then, at a sign from Miss La Trobe behind the tree, the dance stopped. A procession formed. Great Eliza descended from her soap box. Taking her skirts in her hand, striding with long strides, surrounded by dukes and princes, followed by the lovers arm in arm, with Albert the idiot playing in and out, and the corpse on its bier concluding the procession, the Elizabethan age passed from the scene.

'Curse! Blast! Damn 'em!' Miss La Trobe in her rage stubbed her toe against a root. Here was her downfall; here was the Interval. Writing this skimble-skamble stuff in her cottage, she had agreed to cut the play here; a slave to her audience – to Mrs Sands's grumble about tea; about dinner – she had gashed the scene here. Just as she had brewed emotion, she spilt it. So she signalled: Phyllis! And, summoned, Phyllis popped up on the mat again in the middle.

Gentles and simples, I address you all (she piped).
Our act is done, our scene is over.
Past is the day of crone and lover.
The bud has flowered; the flower has fallen.
But soon will rise another dawning,
For time whose children small we be
Hath in his keeping, you shall see,
You shall see . . .

Her voice petered out. No one was listening. Heads bent, they read 'Interval' on the programme. And, cutting short her words, the megaphone announced in plain English: 'An interval.' Half an hour's interval, for tea. Then the gramophone blared out:

Armed against fate,
The valiant Rhoderick,
Bold and blatant,
Firm, elatant, etc., etc.

At that, the audience stirred. Some rose briskly; others stooped, retrieving walking-sticks, hats, bags. And then, as they raised themselves and turned about, the music modulated. The music chanted: *Dispersed are we*. It moaned: *Dispersed are we*. It lamented: *Dispersed are we*, as they streamed, spotting the grass with colour, across the lawns, and down the paths: *Dispersed are we*.

Mrs Manresa took up the strain. *Dispersed are we*. 'Freely, boldly, fearing no one' (she pushed a deckchair out of her way), 'youths and maidens' (she glanced behind her; but Giles had his back turned), 'follow, follow, follow me . . . Oh, Mr Parker, what a pleasure to see *you* here! I'm for tea!'

'Dispersed are we,' Isabella followed her, humming. 'All is over. The wave has broken. Left us stranded, high and dry. Single, separate on the shingle. Broken is the three-fold ply . . . Now I follow' (she pushed her chair back . . . The man in grey was lost in the crowd by the ilex) 'that old strumpet' (she invoked Mrs Manresa's tight, flowered figure in front of her) 'to have tea.'

Dodge remained behind. 'Shall I,' he murmured, 'go or stay? Slip out some other way? Or follow, follow, follow the dispersing company?'

Dispersed are we, the music wailed; *dispersed are we*. Giles remained like a stake in the tide of the flowing company.

'Follow?' He kicked his chair back. 'Whom? Where?' He stubbed his light tennis shoes on the wood. 'Nowhere. Anywhere.' Stark still he stood.

Here Cobbet of Cobbs Corner, alone under the monkey-puzzle tree, rose and muttered: 'What was in her mind, eh? What idea lay behind, eh? What made her indue the antique with this glamour – this sham lure, and set 'em climbing, climbing, climbing up the monkey-puzzle tree?'

Dispersed are we, the music wailed. *Dispersed are we*. He turned and sauntered slowly after the retreating company.

Now Lucy, retrieving her bag from beneath the seat, chirruped to her brother: 'Bart, my dear, come with me . . . D'you remember, when we were children, the play we acted in the nursery?'

He remembered. Red Indians the game was; a reed with a note wrapped up in a pebble.

'But for us, my old Cindy' – he picked up his hat – 'the game's over.' The glare and the stare and the beat of the tom-tom, he meant. He gave her his arm. Off they strolled. And Mr Page, the reporter, noted, 'Mrs Swithin, Mr B. Oliver,' then turning, added further, 'Lady Haslip, of Haslip Manor,' as he spied that old lady wheeled in her chair by her footman winding up the procession.

To the valediction of the gramophone hid in the bushes the audience departed. *Dispersed*, it wailed, *Dispersed are we*.

Now Miss La Trobe stepped from her hiding. Flowing, and streaming, on the grass, on the gravel, still for one moment she held them together – the dispersing company. Hadn't she, for twenty-five minutes, made them see? A vision imparted was relief from agony . . . for one moment . . . one moment. Then the music petered out on the last word *we*. She heard the breeze rustle in the branches. She saw Giles Oliver with his back to the audience. Also Cobbet of Cobbs Corner. She hadn't made them see. It was a failure, another damned failure! As usual. Her vision escaped her. And turning, she strode to the actors, undressing, down in the hollow, where butterflies feasted upon swords of silver paper; where the dishcloths in the shadow made pools of yellow.

Cobbet had out his watch. Three hours till seven, he noted; then water the plants. He turned.

Giles, nicking his chair into its notch, turned too, in the other direction.

He took the short cut by the fields to the barn. This dry summer the path was hard as brick across the fields. This dry summer the path was strewn with stones. He kicked – a flinty yellow stone, a sharp stone, edged as if cut by a savage for an arrow. A barbaric stone; a prehistoric. Stone-kicking was a child's game. He remembered the rules. By the rules of the game, one stone, the same stone, must be kicked to the goal. Say a gate, or a tree. He played it alone. The gate was a goal; to be reached in ten. The first kick was Manresa (lust). The second, Dodge (perversion). The third himself (coward). And the fourth and the fifth and all the others were the same.

He reached it in ten. There, couched in the grass, curled in an olive-green ring, was a snake. Dead? No, choked with a toad in its mouth. The snake was unable to swallow, the toad was unable to die. A spasm made the ribs contract; blood oozed. It was birth the wrong way round – a monstrous inversion. So, raising his foot, he stamped on them. The mass crushed and slithered. The white canvas on his tennis shoes was bloodstained and sticky. But it was action. Action relieved him. He strode to the barn, with blood on his shoes.

The barn, the Noble Barn, the barn that had been built over seven hundred years ago and reminded some people of a Greek temple, others of the middle ages, most people of an age before their own, scarcely anybody of the present moment, was empty.

The great doors stood open. A shaft of light like a yellow banner sloped from roof to floor. Festoons of paper roses, left over from the Coronation, drooped from the rafters. A long table, on which stood an urn, plates and cups, cakes and bread and butter, stretched across one end. The barn was empty. Mice slid in and out of holes or stood upright, nibbling. Swallows were busy with straw in pockets of earth in the rafters. Countless beetles and insects of various sorts burrowed in the dry wood. A stray bitch had made the dark corner where the sacks stood a lying-in ground for her puppies. All these eyes, expanding and narrowing, some adapted to light, others to darkness, looked from different angles and edges. Minute nibblings and rustlings broke the silence. Whiffs of sweetness and richness veined the air. A bluebottle had settled on the cake and stabbed its yellow rock with its short drill. A butterfly sunned itself sensuously on a sunlit yellow plate.

But Mrs Sands was approaching. She was pushing her way through the crowd. She had turned the corner. She could see the great open doors. But butterflies she never saw, mice were only black pellets in kitchen drawers; moths she bundled in her hands and put out of the window. Bitches suggested only servant girls misbehaving. Had there been a cat she would have seen it – any cat, a starved cat with a patch of mange on its rump opened the flood gates of her childless heart. But there was no cat. The barn was empty. And so running, panting, set upon reaching the barn and taking up her station behind the tea urn before the company came, she reached the barn. And the butterfly rose and the bluebottle.

Following her in a scud came the servants and helpers – David, John, Irene, Lois. Water boiled. Steam issued. Cake was sliced. Swallows swooped from rafter to rafter. And the company entered.

'This fine old barn . . . ' said Mrs Manresa, stopping in the doorway. It was not for her to press ahead of the villagers. It was for her, moved by the beauty of the barn, to stand still; to draw aside; to gaze; to let other people come first.

'We have one, much like it, at Lathom,' said Mrs Parker, stopping, for the same reasons. 'Perhaps,' she added, 'not quite so large.'

The villagers hung back. Then, hesitating, dribbled past.

'And the decorations . . . ' said Mrs Manresa, looking round for someone to congratulate. She stood smiling, waiting. Then old Mrs Swithin came in. She was gazing up too, but not at the decorations. At the swallows apparently.

'They come every year,' she said, 'the same birds.' Mrs Manresa smiled benevolently, humouring the old lady's whimsy. It was unlikely, she thought, that the birds were the same.

'The decorations, I suppose, are left over from the Coronation,' said Mrs Parker. 'We kept ours too. We built a village hall.'

Mrs Manresa laughed. She remembered. An anecdote was on the tip of her tongue, about a public lavatory built to celebrate the same occasion, and how the mayor . . . Could she tell it? No. The old lady, gazing at the swallows, looked too refined. 'Refeened' – Mrs Manresa qualified the word to her own advantage, thus confirming her approval of the wild child she was, whose nature was somehow 'just human nature'. Somehow she could span the old lady's 'refeenment', also the boy's fun – Where was that nice fellow Giles? She couldn't see him; nor Bill either. The villagers still hung back. They must have someone to start the ball rolling.

'Well, I'm dying for my tea!' she said in her public voice; and strode forward. She laid hold of a thick china mug. Mrs Sands giving precedence, of course, to one of the gentry, filled it at once. David gave her cake. She was the first to drink, the first to bite. The villagers still hung back. 'It's all my eye about democracy,' she concluded. So did Mrs Parker, taking her mug too. The people looked to them. They led; the rest followed.

'What delicious tea!' each exclaimed, disgusting though it was, like rust boiled in water, and the cake fly-blown. But they had a duty to society.

'They come every year,' said Mrs Swithin, ignoring the fact that she spoke to the empty air. 'From Africa.' As they had come, she supposed, when the barn was a swamp.

The barn filled. Fumes rose. China clattered; voices chattered. Isa pressed her way to the table.

'Dispersed are we,' she murmured. And held her cup out to be filled. She took it. 'Let me turn away,' she murmured, turning, 'from the array' – she looked desolately round her – 'of china faces, glazed and hard. Down the ride, that leads under the nut tree and the may tree, away, till I come to the wishing well, where the washerwoman's little boy – ' she dropped sugar, two lumps, into her tea, 'dropped a pin. He got his horse, so they say. But what wish should I drop into the well?' She looked round. She could not see the man in grey, the gentleman farmer; nor anyone known to her. 'That the waters should cover me,' she added, 'of the wishing well.'

The noise of china and chatter drowned her murmur. 'Sugar for you?' they were saying. 'Just a spot of milk? And you?' 'Tea without milk or sugar. That's the way I like it.' 'A bit too strong? Let me add water.'

'That's what I wished,' Isa added, 'when I dropped my pin. Water. Water . . . '

'I must say,' the voice said behind her, 'it's brave of the King and Queen. They're said to be going to India. She looks such a dear. Someone I know said his hair . . . '

'There,' Isa mused, 'would the dead leaf fall, when the leaves fall, on the water. Should I mind not again to see may tree or nut tree? Not again to hear on the trembling spray the thrush sing, or to see, dipping and diving as if he skimmed waves in the air, the yellow woodpecker?' She was looking at the canary-yellow festoons left over from the Coronation.

'I thought they said Canada, not India,' the voice said behind her back.

To which the other voice answered: 'D'you believe what the papers say? For instance, about the Duke of Windsor. He landed on the south coast. Queen Mary met him. She'd been buying furniture – that's a fact. And the papers say she met him . . . '

'Alone, under a tree, the withered tree that keeps all day murmuring of the sea and hears the Rider gallop . . . '

Isa filled in the phrase. Then she started. William Dodge was by her side.

He smiled. She smiled. They were conspirators; each murmuring some song my uncle taught me.

'It's the play,' she said. 'The play keeps running in my head.'

' "Hail, sweet Carinthia. My love. My life," ' he quoted.

' "My lord, my liege," ' she bowed ironically.

She was handsome. He wanted to see her, not against the tea urn, but with her glass-green eyes and thick body, the neck was broad as a pillar, against an arum lily or a vine. He wished she would say: 'Come along. I'll show you the greenhouse, the pig sty, or the stable.' But she said nothing, and they stood there holding their cups, remembering the play. Then he saw her face change, as if she had got out of one dress and put on another. A small boy battled his way through the crowd, striking against skirts and trousers as if he were swimming blindly.

'Here!' she cried raising her arm.

He made a bee-line for her. He was her little boy, apparently, her son, her George. She gave him cake; then a mug of milk. Then Nurse came up. Then again she changed her dress. This time, from the expression in her eyes, it was apparently something in the nature of a strait waistcoat. Hirsute, handsome, virile, the young man in blue jacket and brass buttons, standing in a beam of dusty light, was her husband. And she his wife. Their relations, as he had noted at lunch, were as people say in novels 'strained'. As he had noted at the play, her bare arm had raised itself nervously to her shoulder when she turned – looking for whom? But here he was; and the muscular, the hirsute, the virile plunged him into emotions in which the mind had no share. He forgot how she would have looked against vine leaf in a greenhouse. Only at Giles he looked; and looked and looked. Of whom was he thinking as he stood with his face turned? Not of Isa. Of Mrs Manresa?

Mrs Manresa halfway down the barn had gulped her cup of tea. How can I rid myself, she asked, of Mrs Parker? If they were of her own class, how they bored her – her own sex! Not the class below – cooks, shopkeepers, farmers' wives; nor the class above – peeresses, countesses; it was the women of her own class that bored her. So she left Mrs Parker, abruptly.

'Oh Mrs Moore,' she hailed the keeper's wife. 'What did you think of it? And what did baby think of it?' Here she pinched baby. 'I thought it every bit as good as anything I'd seen in London . . . But we mustn't be outdone. We'll have a play of our own. In *our* barn. We'll show 'em' (here she winked obliquely at the table; so many bought cakes, so few made at home) 'how *we* do it.'

Then cracking her jokes, she turned; saw Giles; caught his eye; and swept him in, beckoning. He came. And what – she looked down – had he done with his shoes? They were bloodstained. Vaguely some sense that he had proved his valour for her admiration flattered her. If vague it was sweet. Taking him in tow, she felt: I am the queen, he my hero, my sulky hero.

'That's Mrs Neale!' she exclaimed. 'A perfect marvel of a woman, aren't you, Mrs Neale! She runs our post office, Mrs Neale. She can do sums in her head, can't you, Mrs Neale? Twenty-five halfpenny stamps, two packets of stamped envelopes and a packet of postcards – how much does that come to, Mrs Neale?'

Mrs Neale laughed; Mrs Manresa laughed; Giles too smiled, and looked down at his shoes.

She drew him down the barn, in and out, from one to another. She knew 'em all. Everyone was a thorough good sort. No, she wouldn't allow it, not for a moment – Pinsent's bad leg. 'No, no. We're not going to take that for an excuse, Pinsent.' If he couldn't bowl, he could bat. Giles agreed. A fish on a line meant the same to him and Pinsent; also jays and magpies. Pinsent stayed on the land; Giles went to an office. That was all. And she was a thorough good sort, making him feel less of an audience, more of an actor, going round the barn in her wake.

Then, at the end by the door, they came upon the old couple, Lucy and Bartholomew, sitting on their Windsor chairs.

Chairs had been reserved for them. Mrs Sands had sent them tea. It would have caused more bother than it was worth – asserting the democratic principle; standing in the crowd at the table.

'Swallows,' said Lucy, holding her cup, looking at the birds. Excited by the company they were flitting from rafter to rafter. Across Africa, across France they had come to nest here. Year after year they came. Before there was a channel, when the earth, upon which the Windsor chair was planted, was a riot of rhododendrons, and humming birds quivered at the mouths of scarlet trumpets, as she had read that morning in her *Outline of History*, they had come . . . Here Bart rose from his chair.

But Mrs Manresa absolutely refused to take his seat. 'Go on sitting, go on sitting,' she pressed him down again. 'I'll squat on the floor.' She squatted. The surly knight remained in attendance.

'And what did you think of the play?' she asked.

Bartholomew looked at his son. His son remained silent.

'And you, Mrs Swithin?' Mrs Manresa pressed the old lady.

Lucy mumbled, looking at the swallows.

'I was hoping you'd tell me,' said Mrs Manresa. 'Was it an old play? Was it a new play?'

No one answered.

'Look!' Lucy exclaimed.

'The birds?' said Mrs Manresa, looking up.

There was a bird with a straw in its beak; and the straw dropped.

Lucy clapped her hands. Giles turned away. She was mocking him as usual, laughing.

'Going?' said Bartholomew. 'Time for the next act?'

And he heaved himself up from his chair. Regardless of Mrs Manresa and of Lucy, off he strolled too.

'Swallow, my sister, O sister swallow,' he muttered, feeling for his cigar case, following his son.

Mrs Manresa was nettled. What for had she squatted on the floor then? Were her charms fading? Both were gone. But, woman of action as she was, deserted by the male sex, she was not going to suffer tortures of boredom from the refeened old lady. Up she scrambled, putting her hands to her hair as if it were high time that she went too, though it was nothing of the kind and her hair was perfectly tidy. Cobbet in his corner saw through her little game. He had known human nature in the East. It was the same in the West. Plants remained – the carnation, the zinnia and the geranium. Automatically he consulted his watch; noted time to water at seven; and observed the little game of the woman following the man to the table in the West as in the East.

William at the table, now attached to Mrs Parker and Isa, watched him approach. Armed and valiant, bold and blatant, firm, elatant – the popular march tune rang in his head. And the fingers of William's left hand closed firmly, surreptitiously, as the hero approached.

Mrs Parker was deploring to Isa in a low voice the village idiot.

'Oh that idiot!' she was saying. But Isa was immobile, watching her husband. She could feel the Manresa in his wake. She could hear in the dusk in their bedroom the usual explanation. It made no difference, his infidelity – but hers did.

'The idiot?' William answered Mrs Parker for her. 'He's in the tradition.'

'But surely,' said Mrs Parker, and told Giles how creepy the idiot – 'We have one in our village' – had made her feel. 'Surely, Mr Oliver, we're more civilised?'

'*We*?' said Giles. '*We*?' He looked, once, at William. He knew not his name; but what his left hand was doing. It was a bit of luck – that he could despise him, not himself. Also Mrs Parker. But not Isa – not his wife. She had not spoken to him, not one word. Nor looked at him either.

'Surely,' said Mrs Parker, looking from one to the other. 'Surely we are?'

Giles then did what to Isa was his little trick; shut his lips; frowned; and took up the pose of one who bears the burden of the world's woe, making money for her to spend.

'No,' said Isa, as plainly as words could say it, 'I don't admire you,' and looked, not at his face, but at his feet. 'Silly little boy, with blood on his boots.'

Giles shifted his feet. Whom then did she admire? Not Dodge. That he could take for certain. Who else? Some man he knew. Some man, he was sure, in the barn. Which man? He looked round him.

Then Mr Streatfield, the clergyman, interrupted. He was carrying cups.

'So I shake hands with my heart!' he exclaimed, nodding his handsome, grizzled head and depositing his burden safely.

Mrs Parker took the tribute to herself.

'Mr Streatfield!' she exclaimed. 'Doing all the work! While we stand gossiping!'

'Like to see the greenhouse?' said Isa suddenly, turning to William Dodge.

Oh not now, he could have cried. But had to follow, leaving Giles to welcome the approaching Manresa, who had him in thrall.

The path was narrow. Isa went ahead. And she was broad; she fairly filled the path, swaying slightly as she walked, and plucking a leaf here and there from the hedge.

'Fly then, follow,' she hummed, 'the dappled herds in the cedar grove, who, sporting, play, the red with the roe, the stag with the doe. Fly, away. I grieving stay. Alone I linger. I pluck the bitter herb by the ruined wall, the churchyard wall, and press its sour, its sweet, its sour, long grey leaf, so, twixt thumb and finger . . .'

She threw away the shred of old man's beard that she had picked in passing and kicked open the greenhouse door. Dodge had lagged behind.

She waited. She picked up a knife from the plank. He saw her standing against the green glass, the fig tree and the blue hydrangea, knife in hand.

'She spake,' Isa murmured. 'And from her bosom's snowy antre drew the gleaming blade. "Plunge blade!" she said. And struck. "Faithless!" she cried. Knife, too! It broke. So too my heart,' she said.

She was smiling ironically as he came up.

'I wish the play didn't run in my head,' she said. Then she sat down on a plank under the vine. And he sat beside her. The little grapes above them were green buds; the leaves thin and yellow as the web between birds' claws.

'Still the play?' he asked. She nodded. 'That was your son,' he said, 'in the barn?'

She had a daughter too, she told him, in the cradle.

'And you – married?' she asked. From her tone he knew she guessed, as women always guessed, everything. They knew at once they had nothing to fear, nothing to hope. At first they resented – serving as statues in a greenhouse. Then they liked it. For then they could say – as she did – whatever came into their heads. And hand him, as she handed him, a flower.

'There's something for your buttonhole, Mr . . . ' she said, handing him a sprig of scented geranium.

'I'm William,' he said, taking the furry leaf and pressing it between thumb and finger.

'I'm Isa,' she answered. Then they talked as if they had known each other all their lives; which was odd, she said, as they always did, considering she'd known him perhaps one hour. Weren't they, though, conspirators, seekers after hidden faces? That confessed, she paused and wondered, as they always did, why they could speak so plainly to each other. And added: 'Perhaps because we've never met before, and never shall again.'

'The doom of sudden death hanging over us,' he said. 'There's no retreating and advancing' – he was thinking of the old lady showing him the house – 'for us as for them.'

The future shadowed their present, like the sun coming through the many-veined transparent vine leaf; a criss-cross of lines making no pattern.

They had left the greenhouse door open, and now music came through it. A B C, A B C, A B C – someone was practising scales. C A T, C A T, C A T . . . Then the separate letters made one word 'Cat'. Other words followed. It was a simple tune, like a nursery rhyme –

The king is in his counting house,
Counting out his money,
The queen is in her parlour,
Eating bread and honey.

They listened. Another voice, a third voice, was saying something simple. And they sat on in the greenhouse, on the plank with the vine over them, listening to Miss La Trobe, or whoever it was, practising her scales.

He could not find his son. He had lost him in the crowd. So old Bartholomew left the barn, and went to his own room, holding his cheroot and murmuring: 'O sister swallow, O sister swallow, How can thy heart be full of the spring?

'How can my heart be full of the spring?' he said aloud, standing in front of the bookcase. Books: the treasured life-blood of immortal spirits. Poets; the legislators of mankind. Doubtless, it was so. But Giles was unhappy. 'How can my heart, how can my heart,' he repeated, puffing at his cheroot. 'Condemned in life's infernal mine, condemned in solitude to pine . . . ' Arms akimbo, he stood in front of his country gentleman's library. Garibaldi; Wellington; Irrigation Officers' Reports; and Hibbert on *The Diseases of the Horse*. A great harvest the mind had reaped; but for all this, compared with his son, he did not care one damn.

'What's the use, what's the use,' he sank down into his chair muttering, 'O sister swallow, O sister swallow, of singing your song?' The dog, who had followed him, flopped down on to the floor at his feet. Flanks sucked in and out, the long nose resting on his paws, a fleck of foam on the nostril, there he was, his familiar spirit, his Afghan hound.

The door trembled and stood half open. That was Lucy's way of coming in – as if she did not know what she would find. Really! It was her brother! And his dog! She seemed to see them for the first time. Was it that she had no body? Up in the clouds, like an air ball, her mind touched ground now and then with a shock of surprise. There was nothing in her to weight a man like Giles to the earth.

She perched on the edge of a chair like a bird on a telegraph wire before starting for Africa.

'Swallow, my sister, O sister swallow . . . ' he murmured.

From the garden – the window was open – came the sound of someone practising scales. A B C, A B C, A B C. Then the separate letters formed one word 'Dog'. Then a phrase. It was a simple tune, another voice speaking.

'Hark, hark, the dogs do bark,
The beggars are coming to town . . . '

Then it languished and lengthened, and became a waltz. As they listened and looked – out into the garden – the trees tossing and the birds swirling seemed called out of their private lives, out of their separate avocations, and made to take part.

The lamp of love burns high, over the dark cedar groves,
The lamp of love shines clear, clear as a star in the sky . . .

Old Bartholomew tapped his fingers on his knee in time to the tune.

Leave your casement and come, lady, I love till I die,

He looked sardonically at Lucy, perched on her chair. How, he wondered, had she ever borne children?

For all are dancing, retreating and advancing,
The moth and the dragonfly . . .

She was thinking, he supposed, God is peace. God is love. For she belonged to the unifiers; he to the separatists.

Then the tune with its feet always on the same spot, became sugared, insipid; bored a hole with its perpetual invocation to perpetual adoration. Had it – he was ignorant of musical terms – gone into the minor key?

> For this day and this dance and this merry, merry May
> Will be over

he tapped his forefinger on his knee,

> With the cutting of the clover this retreating and advancing –

the swifts seemed to have shot beyond their orbits –

> Will be over, over, over,
> And the ice will dart its splinter, and the winter,
> Oh the winter, will fill the grate with ashes,
> And there'll be no glow, no glow on the log.

He knocked the ash off his cheroot and rose.

'So we must,' said Lucy; as if he had said aloud, 'It's time to go.'

The audience was assembling. The music was summoning them. Down the paths, across the lawns they were streaming again. There was Mrs Manresa, with Giles at her side, heading the procession. In taut plump curves her scarf blew round her shoulders. The breeze was rising. She looked, as she crossed the lawn to the strains of the gramophone, goddess-like, buoyant, abundant, her cornucopia running over. Bartholomew, following, blessed the power of the human body to make the earth fruitful. Giles would keep his orbit so long as she weighted him to the earth. She stirred the stagnant pool of his old heart even – where bones lay buried, but the dragonflies shot and the grass trembled as Mrs Manresa advanced across the lawn to the strains of the gramophone.

Feet crunched the gravel. Voices chattered. The inner voice, the other voice was saying: How can we deny that this brave music, wafted from the bushes, is expressive of some inner harmony? 'When we wake' (some were thinking) 'the day breaks us with its hard mallet blows.' 'The office' (some were thinking) 'compels disparity. Scattered, shattered, hither thither summoned by the bell. "Ping-ping-ping" that's the phone. "Forward!" "Serving!" – that's the shop.' So we answer to the infernal, age-long and eternal order issued from on high. And obey. 'Working, serving, pushing, striving, earning wages – to be spent – here? Oh dear no. Now? No, by and by. When ears are deaf and the heart is dry.'

Here Cobbet of Cobbs Corner who had stooped – there was a flower – was pressed on by people pushing from behind.

For I hear music, they were saying. Music wakes us. Music makes us see the hidden, join the broken. Look and listen. See the flowers, how they ray their redness, whiteness, silverness and blue. And the trees with their many-tongued much syllabling, their green and yellow leaves hustle us and shuffle us, and bid us, like the starlings, and the rooks, come together, crowd

together, to chatter and make merry while the red cow moves forward and
the black cow stands still.

The audience had reached their seats. Some sat down; others stood a
moment, turned, and looked at the view. The stage was empty; the actors
were still dressing up among the bushes. The audience turned to one another
and began to talk. Scraps and fragments reached Miss La Trobe where she
stood, script in hand, behind the tree.

'They're not ready . . . I hear 'em laughing' (they were saying). '. . .
Dressing up. That's the great thing, dressing up. And it's pleasant now, the
sun's not so hot . . . That's one good the war brought us – longer days . . .
Where did we leave off? D'you remember? The Elizabethans . . . Perhaps
she'll reach the present, if she skips . . . D'you think people change? Their
clothes, of course . . . But I meant ourselves . . . Clearing out a cupboard, I
found my father's old top hat . . . But ourselves – do we change?'

'No, I don't go by politicians. I've a friend who's been to Russia. He says . . .
And my daughter, just back from Rome, she says the common people, in the
cafés, hate dictators . . . Well, different people say different things . . . '

'Did you see it in the papers – the case about the dog? D'you believe dogs
can't have puppies? . . . And Queen Mary and the Duke of Windsor on the
south coast? . . . D'you believe what's in the papers? I ask the butcher or the
grocer . . . That's Mr Streatfield, carrying a hurdle . . . The good clergyman,
I say, does more work for less pay than all the lot . . . It's the wives that make
the trouble . . . '

'And what about the Jews? The refugees . . . the Jews . . . People like
ourselves, beginning life again . . . But it's always been the same . . . My old
mother, who's over eighty, can remember . . . Yes, she still reads without
glasses . . . How amazing! Well, don't they say, after eighty . . . Now they're
coming . . . No, that's nothing . . . I'd make it penal, leaving litter. But then,
who's, my husband says, to collect the fines? . . . Ah there she is, Miss La
Trobe, over there, behind that tree . . . '

Over there behind the tree Miss La Trobe gnashed her teeth. She crushed
her manuscript. The actors delayed. Every moment the audience slipped the
noose; split up into scraps and fragments.

'Music!' she signalled. 'Music!'

'What's the origin,' said a voice, 'of the expression "with a flea in
his ear"?'

Down came her hand peremptorily. 'Music, music,' she signalled.

And the gramophone began A B C, A B C.

> The king is in his counting house,
> Counting out his money,
> The queen is in her parlour,
> Eating bread and honey . . .

Miss La Trobe watched them sink down peacefully into the nursery rhyme. She watched them fold their hands and compose their faces. Then she beckoned. And at last, with a final touch to her head-dress, which had been giving trouble, Mabel Hopkins strode from the bushes, and took her place on the raised ground facing the audience.

Eyes fed on her as fish rise to a crumb of bread on the water. Who was she? What did she represent? She was beautiful – very. Her cheeks had been powdered; her colour glowed smooth and clear underneath. Her grey satin robe (a bedspread), pinned in stone-like folds, gave her the majesty of a statue. She carried a sceptre and a little round orb. England was she? Queen Anne was she? Who was she? She spoke too low at first; all they heard was . . . *reason holds sway.*

Old Bartholomew applauded. 'Hear! Hear!' he cried. 'Bravo! Bravo!'

Thus encouraged Reason spoke out.

Time, leaning on his sickle, stands amazed. While commerce from her cornucopia pours the mingled tribute of her different ores. In distant mines the savage sweats; and from the reluctant earth the painted pot is shaped. At my behest, the armed warrior lays his shield aside; the heathen leaves the altar steaming with unholy sacrifice. The violet and the eglantine over the riven earth their flowers entwine. No longer fears the unwary wanderer the poisoned snake. And in the helmet, yellow bees their honey make.

She paused. A long line of villagers in sacking were passing in and out of the trees behind her.

Digging and delving, ploughing and sowing they were singing, but the wind blew their words away.

Beneath the shelter of my flowing robe (she resumed, extending her arms) *the arts arise. Music for me unfolds her heavenly harmony. At my behest the miser leaves his hoard untouched; at peace the mother sees her children play . . . Her children play . . .* she repeated, and at the waving of her sceptre, figures advanced from the bushes.

Let swains and nymphs lead on the play, while Zephyr sleeps, and the unruly tribes of heaven confess my sway.

A merry little old tune was played on the gramophone. Old Bartholomew joined his fingertips; Mrs Manresa smoothed her skirts about her knees.

> *Young Damon said to Cynthia,*
> *Come out now with the dawn*
> *And don your azure tippet*
> *And cast your cares adown,*
> *For peace has come to England,*
> *And reason now holds sway.*
> *What pleasure lies in dreaming*
> *When blue and green's the day?*

> *Now cast your cares behind you.*
> *Night passes: here is day.*

Digging and delving, the villagers sang, passing in single file in and out between the trees, *for the earth is always the same, summer and winter and spring; and spring and winter again; ploughing and sowing, eating and growing; time passes* . . .

The wind blew the words away.

The dance stopped. The nymphs and swains withdrew. Reason held the centre of the stage alone. Her arms extended, her robes flowing, holding orb and sceptre, Mabel Hopkins stood sublimely looking over the heads of the audience. The audience gazed at her. She ignored the audience. Then while she gazed, helpers from the bushes arranged round her what appeared to be the three sides of a room. In the middle they stood a table. On the table they placed a china tea service. Reason surveyed this domestic scene from her lofty eminence unmoved. There was a pause.

'Another scene from another play, I suppose,' said Mrs Elmhurst, referring to her programme. She read out for the benefit of her husband, who was deaf: *'Where there's a Will there's a Way*. That's the name of the play. And the characters . . . ' She read out: 'Lady Harpy Harraden, in love with Sir Spaniel Lilyliver. Deb, her maid. Flavinda, her niece, in love with Valentine. Sir Spaniel Lilyliver, in love with Flavinda. Sir Smirking Peace-be-with-you-all, a clergyman. Lord and Lady Fribble. Valentine, in love with Flavinda. What names for real people! But look – here they come!'

Out they came from the bushes – men in flowered waistcoats, white waistcoats and buckled shoes; women wearing brocades tucked up, hooped and draped; glass stars, blue ribands and imitation pearls made them look the very image of lords and ladies.

'The first scene,' Mrs Elmhurst whispered into her husband's ear, 'is Lady Harraden's dressing-room . . . That's her . . . ' She pointed. 'Mrs Otter, I think, from the End House; but she's wonderfully made up. And that's Deb her maid. Who she is, I don't know.'

'Hush, hush, hush,' someone protested.

Mrs Elmhurst dropped her programme. The play had begun.

Lady Harpy Harraden entered her dressing-room, followed by Deb her maid.

LADY H. H. *Give me the pounce-box. Then the patch. Hand me the mirror, girl. So. Now my wig . . . A pox on the girl – she's dreaming!*

DEB . . . *I was thinking, my lady, what the gentleman said when he saw you in the Park.*

LADY H. H. (gazing in the glass) *So, so – what was it? Some silly trash! Cupid's dart – hah, hah! lighting his taper – tush – at my eyes . . . pooh! That was in milord's time, twenty years since . . . But now – what'll he say of me now?* (She looks in the mirror) *Sir Spaniel Lilyliver, I mean . . .* (a rap at the door) *Hark! That's his chaise at the door. Run child. Don't stand gaping.*

DEB (going to the door) *Say? He'll rattle his tongue as a gambler rattles dice in a box. He'll find no words to fit you. He'll stand like a pig in a poke . . . Your servant, Sir Spaniel.*

Enter Sir Spaniel.

SIR S. L. *Hail, my fair saint! What, out o' bed so early? Methought as I came along the Mall the air was something brighter than usual. Here's the reason . . . Venus, Aphrodite, upon my word a very galaxy, a constellation! As I'm a sinner, a very Aurora Borealis!* (He sweeps his hat off.)

LADY H. H. *Oh flatterer, flatterer! I know your ways. But come. Sit down . . . A glass of Aqua Vitae. Take this seat, Sir Spaniel. I've something very private and particular to say to you . . . You had my letter, sir?*

SIR S. L. *Pinned to my heart!* (He strikes his breast.)

LADY H. H. *I have a favour to ask of you, sir.*

SIR S. L. (singing) *What favour could fair Chloe ask that Damon would not get her? . . . A-done with rhymes. Rhymes are still a-bed. Let's speak prose. What can Asphodilla ask of her plain servant Lilyliver? Speak out, madam. An ape with a ring in his nose, or a strong young jackanapes to tell tales of us when we're no longer here to tell truth about ourselves?*

LADY H. H. (flirting her fan) *Fie, fie, Sir Spaniel. You make me blush – you do indeed. But come closer.* (She shifts her seat nearer to him.) *We don't want the whole world to hear us.*

SIR S. L. (aside) *Come closer? A pox on my life! The old hag stinks like a red herring that's been stood over head in a tar barrel!* (Aloud) *Your meaning, madam? You were saying?*

LADY H. H. *I have a niece, Sir Spaniel, Flavinda by name.*

SIR S. L. (aside) *Why that's the girl I love, to be sure!* (Aloud) *You have a niece, madam? I seem to remember hearing so. An only child, left by your brother, so I've heard, in your ladyship's charge – him that perished at sea.*

LADY H. H. *The very same, sir. She's of age now and marriageable. I've kept her close as a weevil, Sir Spaniel, wrapped in the sere cloths of her virginity. Only maids about her, never a man to my knowledge, save Clout the serving man, who has a wart on his nose and a face like a nutgrater. Yet some fool has caught her fancy. Some gilded fly – some Harry, Dick; call him what you will.*

SIR S. L. (aside) *That's young Valentine, I warrant. I caught 'em at the play together.* (Aloud) *Say you so, madam?*

LADY H. H. *She's not so ill favoured, Sir Spaniel – there's beauty in our line – but that a gentleman of taste and breeding like yourself now might take pity on her.*

SIR S. L. *Saving your presence, madam. Eyes that have seen the sun are not so easily dazzled by the lesser lights – the Cassiopeias, Aldebarans, Great Bears and so on – A fig for them when the sun's up!*

LADY H. H. (ogling him) *You praise my hairdresser, sir, or my ear-rings* (she shakes her head).

SIR S. L. (aside) *She jingles like a she-ass at a fair! She's rigged like a barber's pole of a May Day.* (Aloud) *Your commands, madam?*

LADY H. H. *Well, sir, t'was this way, sir. Brother Bob, for my father was a plain country gentleman and would have none of the fancy names the foreigners brought with 'em – Asphodilla I call myself, but my Christian name's plain Sue – brother Bob, as I was telling you, ran away to sea; and, so they say, became Emperor of the Indies; where the very stones are emeralds and the sheep-crop rubies. Which, for a tenderer-hearted man never lived, he would have brought back with him, sir, to mend the family fortunes, sir. But the brig, frigate or what they call it, for I've no head for sea terms – never crossed a ditch without saying the Lord's Prayer backwards – struck a rock. The whale had him. But the cradle was by the bounty of heaven washed ashore. With the girl in it; Flavinda here. What's more to the point, with the will in it; safe and sound; wrapped in parchment. Brother Bob's will. Deb, there! Deb, I say! Deb!*

(She hollas for Deb.)

SIR S. L. (aside) *Ah hah! I smell a rat! A will, quotha! Where there's a will there's a way.*

LADY H. H. (bawling) *The will, Deb! The will! In the ebony box by the right hand of the escritoire opposite the window . . . A pox on the girl! She's dreaming. It's these romances, Sir Spaniel – these romances. Can't see a candle gutter but its her heart that's melting, or snuff a wick without reciting all the names in Cupid's Calendar . . .*

Enter Deb carrying a parchment.

LADY H. H. *So . . . Give it here. The will. Brother Bob's will* (she mumbles over the will).

LADY H. H. *To cut the matter short, sir, for these lawyers even at the Antipodes are a long-winded race –*

SIR S. L. *To match their ears, ma'am –*

LADY H. H. *Very true, very true. To cut the matter short, sir, my brother Bob left all he died possessed of to his only child Flavinda; with this proviso, mark ye. That she marry to her aunt's liking. Her aunt; that's me. Otherwise, mark ye, all – to wit ten bushels of diamonds; item of rubies; item two hundred square miles of fertile territory bounding the River Amazon to the nor-nor-east; item his snuff box; item his flageolet – he was always one to love a tune, sir, brother Bob; item six macaws and as many concubines as he had with him at the time of his decease – all this with other trifles needless to specify he left, mark ye, should she fail to marry to her aunt's liking – that's me – to found a chapel, Sir Spaniel, where six poor virgins should sing hymns in perpetuity for the repose of his soul – which, to speak the truth, Sir Spaniel, poor brother Bob stands in need of, perambulating the Gulf Stream as he is and consorting with Sirens. But take it; read the will yourself, sir.*

SIR S. L. (reading) *'Must marry to her aunt's liking'. That's plain enough.*

LADY H. H. *Her aunt, sir. That's me. That's plain enough.*

SIR S. L. (aside) *She speaks the truth there!* (Aloud) *You would have me understand, madam . . . ?*

LADY H. H. *Hist! Come closer. Let me whisper in your ear . . . You and I have long entertained a high opinion of one another, Sir Spaniel. Played at ball together. Bound our wrists with daisy chains together. If I mind aright, you called me little bride – 'tis fifty years since. We might have made a match of it, Sir Spaniel, had fortune favoured . . . You take my meaning, sir?*

SIR S. L. *Had it been written in letters of gold, fifty feet high, visible from Paul's Churchyard to the Goat and Compasses at Peckham, it could have been no plainer . . . Hist, I'll whisper it. I, Sir Spaniel Lilyliver, do hereby bind myself to take thee – what's the name of the green girl that was cast up in a lobster pot covered with seaweed? Flavinda, eh? Flavinda, so – to be my wedded wife . . . Oh for a lawyer to have it all in writing!*

LADY H. H. *On condition, Sir Spaniel –*

SIR S. L. *On condition, Asphodilla –*

(both speak together)

that the money is shared between us.

LADY H. H. *We want no lawyer to certify that! Your hand on it, Sir Spaniel!*

SIR S. L. *Your lips, madam!*

(They embrace)

SIR S. L. *Pah! She stinks!*

'Ha! Ha! Ha!' laughed the indigenous old lady in her bath chair.

'Reason, begad! Reason!' exclaimed old Bartholomew, and looked at his son as if exhorting him to give over these womanish vapours and be a man, sir.

Giles sat straight as a dart, his feet tucked under him.

Mrs Manresa had out her mirror and lipstick and attended to her lips and nose.

The gramophone, while the scene was removed, gently stated certain facts which everybody knows to be perfectly true. The tune said, more or less, how Eve, gathering her robes about her, stands reluctant still to let her dewy mantle fall. The herded flocks, the tune continued, in peace repose. The poor man to his cot returns, and, to the eager ears of wife and child, the simple story of his toil relates: what yield the furrow bears; and how the team the plover on the nest has spared; while Wat her courses ran; and speckled eggs in the warm hollow lay. Meanwhile the good wife on the table spreads her simple fare; and to the shepherd's flute, from toil released, the nymphs and swains join hands and foot it on the green. Then Eve lets down her sombre tresses brown and spreads her lucent veil o'er hamlet, spire and mead, etc., etc. And the tune repeated itself once more.

The view repeated in its own way what the tune was saying. The sun was sinking; the colours were merging; and the view was saying how after toil men rest from their labours; how coolness comes; reason prevails; and having unharnessed the team from the plough, neighbours dig in cottage gardens and lean over cottage gates.

The cows, making a step forward, then standing still, were saying the same thing to perfection.

Folded in this triple melody, the audience sat gazing; and beheld gently and approvingly without interrogation, for it seemed inevitable, a box tree in a green tub take the place of the lady's dressing-room; while on what seemed to be a wall was hung a great clock face; the hands pointing to three minutes to the hour; which was seven.

Mrs Elmhurst roused herself from her reverie; and looked at her programme. 'Scene Two. The Mall,' she read out. 'Time; early morning. Enter Flavinda. Here she comes!'

Here came Millie Loder (shop assistant at Messrs Hunt and Dickson's, drapery emporium), in sprigged satin, representing Flavinda.

FLAV. *Seven he said, and there's the clock's word for it. But Valentine – where's Valentine? La! How my heart beats! Yet it's not the time o' day, for I'm often afoot before the sun's up in the meadows . . . See – the fine folk passing! All a-tiptoeing like peacocks with spread tails! And I in my petticoat that looked so fine by my aunt's cracked mirror. Why, here it's a dish clout . . . And they heap their hair up like a birthday cake stuck about with candles . . . That's a diamond – that's a ruby . . . Where's Valentine? The Orange Tree in the Mall, he said. The tree – there. Valentine – nowhere. That's a courtier, I'll warrant, that old fox with his tail between his legs. That's a serving wench out without her master's knowledge. That's a man with a broom to sweep paths for the fine ladies' flounces . . . La! the red in their cheeks! They never got that in the fields, I warrant! O faithless, cruel, hard-hearted Valentine. Valentine! Valentine.* (She wrings her hands, turning from side to side.) *Didn't I leave my bed a-tiptoe and steal like a mouse in the wainscot for fear of waking aunt? And lard my hair from her powder box? And scrub my cheeks to make 'em shine? And lie awake watching the stars climb the chimney pots? And give my gold guinea that Godfather hid behind the mistletoe last Twelfth Night to Deb so she shouldn't tell on me? And grease the key in the lock so that aunt shouldn't wake and shriek Flavvy! Flavvy! Val, I say, Val – That's him coming . . . No, I could tell him a mile off the way he strides the waves like what d'you call him in the picture book . . . That's not Val . . . That's a cit; that's a fop; raising his glass, prithee, to have his fill of me . . . I'll be home then . . . No, I won't . . . That's to play the green girl again and sew samplers . . . I'm of age, ain't I, come Michaelmas? Only three turns of the moon and I inherit . . . Didn't I read it in the will the day the ball bounced on top of the old chest where aunt keeps her furbelows, and the lid opened? . . . 'All I die possessed of to my daughter . . .' So far I'd read when the old lady came tapping down the passage like a blind man in an alley . . . I'm no castaway, I'd have you know, sir; no fishtailed mermaid with a robe of seaweed, at your mercy. I'm a match for any of 'em – the chits you dally with, and bid me meet you at the Orange Tree when you're drowsing the night off spent in their arms . . . Fie upon you, sir, making sport with a poor girl so . . . I'll not cry, I swear I won't. I'll not brew a drop of the salt liquid for a man who's served me so . . . Yet to think on't – how we hid in the dairy the day the cat jumped. And read romances under the holly tree. La! how I cried when the duke left poor Polly . . . And my aunt found me with eyes like red jellies. 'What stung, niece?' says she. And cried, 'Quick, Deb, the blue bag.' I told ye . . . La, to think I read it all in a book and cried for another! . . . Hist, what's there among the trees? It's come – it's gone. The breeze is it? In the shade now – in the sun now . . . Valentine on my life! It's he! Quick, I'll hide. Let the tree conceal me!* (Flavinda hides behind the tree.)

He's here . . . He turns . . . He casts about . . . He's lost the scent . . . He gazes – this way, that way . . . Let him feast his eyes on the fine faces – taste 'em, sample 'em, say: 'That's the fine lady I danced with . . . that I lay with . . . that I kissed under the mistletoe . . . ' Ha! How he spews 'em out! Brave Valentine! How he casts his eyes upon the ground! How his frowns become him! 'Where's Flavinda?' he sighs. 'She I love like the heart in my breast.' See him pull his watch out! 'O faithless wretch!' he sighs. See how he stamps the earth! Now turns on his heel . . . He sees me – no, the sun's in his eyes. Tears fill 'em . . . Lord, how he fingers his sword! He'll run it through his breast like the duke in the story book! . . . Stop, sir, stop! (She reveals herself.)

VALENTINE *Oh Flavinda, Oh!*

FLAVINDA *Oh Valentine, Oh!*

(They embrace as the clock strikes nine.)

'All that fuss about nothing!' a voice exclaimed. People laughed. The voice stopped. But the voice had seen; the voice had heard. For a moment Miss La Trobe behind her tree glowed with glory. The next, turning to the villagers who were passing in and out between the trees, she barked: 'Louder! Louder!'

For the stage was empty; the emotion must be continued; the only thing to continue the emotion was the song; and the words were inaudible.

'Louder! Louder!' She threatened them with her clenched fists.

Digging and delving (they sang), *hedging and ditching, we pass . . . Summer and winter, autumn and spring return . . . All passes but we, all changes . . . but we remain for ever the same . . .* (the breeze blew gaps between their words).

'Louder, louder!' Miss La Trobe vociferated.

Palaces tumble down (they resumed), *Babylon, Nineveh, Troy . . . And Caesar's great house . . . all fallen they lie . . . Where the plover nests was the arch . . . through which the Romans trod . . . Digging and delving we break with the share of the plough the clod . . . Where Clytemnestra watched for her lord . . . saw the beacons blaze on the hills . . . we see only the clod . . . Digging and delving we pass . . . and the queen and the watchtower fall . . . for Agamemnon has ridden away . . . Clytemnestra is nothing but . . .*

The words died away. Only a few great names – Babylon, Nineveh, Clytemnestra, Agamemnon, Troy – floated across the open space. Then the wind rose, and in the rustle of the leaves even the great words became inaudible; and the audience sat staring at the villagers, whose mouths opened, but no sound came.

And the stage was empty. Miss La Trobe leant against the tree, paralysed. Her power had left her. Beads of perspiration broke on her forehead. Illusion had failed. 'This is death,' she murmured, 'death.'

Then suddenly, as the illusion petered out, the cows took up the burden. One had lost her calf. In the very nick of time she lifted her great moon-eyed head and bellowed. All the great moon-eyed heads laid themselves back. From cow after cow came the same yearning bellow. The whole world was filled with dumb yearning. It was the primeval voice sounding loud in the ear of the present moment. Then the whole herd caught the infection. Lashing their tails, blobbed like pokers, they tossed their heads high, plunged and bellowed, as if Eros had planted his dart in their flanks and goaded them to fury. The cows annihilated the gap; bridged the distance; filled the emptiness and continued the emotion.

Miss La Trobe waved her hand ecstatically at the cows.

'Thank heaven!' she exclaimed.

Suddenly the cows stopped; lowered their heads, and began browsing. Simultaneously the audience lowered their heads and read their programmes.

'The producer,' Mrs Elmhurst read out for her husband's benefit, 'craves the indulgence of the audience. Owing to lack of time a scene has been omitted; and she begs the audience to imagine that in the interval Sir Spaniel Lilyliver has contracted an engagement with Flavinda; she had been about to plight her troth when Valentine, hidden inside the grandfather clock, steps forward; claims Flavinda as his bride; reveals the plot to rob her of her inheritance; and, during the confusion that ensues, the lovers fly together, leaving Lady Harpy and Sir Spaniel alone together.'

'We're asked to imagine all that,' she said, putting down her glasses.

'That's very wise of her,' said Mrs Manresa, addressing Mrs Swithin. 'If she'd put it all in, we should have been here till midnight. So we've got to imagine, Mrs Swithin.' She patted the old lady on the knee.

'Imagine?' said Mrs Swithin. 'How right! Actors show us too much. The Chinese, you know, put a dagger on the table and that's a battle. And so Racine . . . '

'Yes, they bore one stiff,' Mrs Manresa interrupted, scenting culture, resenting the snub to the jolly human heart. 'T'other day I took my nephew – such a jolly boy at Sandhurst – to *Pop Goes the Weasel*. Seen it?' She turned to Giles.

'Up and down the City Road,' he hummed by way of an answer.

'Did your nanny sing that!' Mrs Manresa exclaimed. 'Mine did. And when she said "Pop" she made a noise like a cork being drawn from a ginger-beer bottle. Pop!'

She made the noise.

'Hush, hush,' someone whispered.

'Now I'm being naughty and shocking your aunt,' she said. 'We must be good and attend. This is Scene Three. Lady Harpy Harraden's closet. The sound of horses' hooves is heard in the distance.'

The sound of horses' hooves, energetically represented by Albert the idiot with a wooden spoon on a tray, died away.

LADY H. H. *Halfway to Gretna Green already! Oh my deceitful niece! You that I rescued from the brine and stood on the hearthstone dripping! Oh that the whale had swallowed you whole! Perfidious porpoise, Oh! Didn't the hornbook teach you Honour thy Great Aunt? How have you misread it and misspelt it, learnt thieving and cheating and reading of wills in old boxes and hiding of rascals in honest time-pieces that have never missed a second since King Charles's day! Oh Flavinda! Oh porpoise, Oh!*

SIR S. L. (trying to pull on his jack boots) *Old – old – old. He called me 'old' – 'To your bed, old fool, and drink hot posset!'*

LADY H. H. *And she, stopping at the door and pointing the finger of scorn at me, said 'old', sir – 'woman', sir – I that am in the prime of life and a lady!*

SIR S. L. (tugging at his boots) *But I'll be even with him. I'll have the law on 'em! I'll run 'em to earth* . . . (He hobbles up and down, one boot on, one boot off.)

LADY H. H. (laying her hand on his arm) *Have mercy on your gout, Sir Spaniel. Bethink you, sir – let's not run mad, we that are on the sunny side of fifty. What's this youth they prate on? Nothing but a goose feather blown on a north wind. Sit you down, Sir Spaniel. Rest your leg – so* – (She pushes a cushion under his leg.)

SIR S. L. *'Old' he called me* . . . *jumping from the clock like a jack-in-the-box* . . . *And she, making mock of me, points to my leg and cries, 'Cupid's darts, sir Spaniel, Cupid's darts.' Oh that I could braise 'em in a mortar and serve 'em up smoking hot on the altar of – Oh my gout, Oh my gout!*

LADY H. H. *This talk, sir, ill befits a man of sense. Bethink you, sir, only t'other day you were invoking – ahem – the constellations. Cassiopeia; Aldebaran; the Aurora Borealis* . . . *It's not to be denied that one of 'em has left her sphere, has shot, has eloped, to put it plainly, with the entrails of a time-piece, the mere pendulum of a grandfather clock. But, Sir Spaniel, there are some stars that – ahem – stay fixed; that shine, to put it in a nutshell, never so bright as by a sea-coal fire on a brisk morning.*

SIR S. L. *Oh that I were five and twenty with a sharp sword at my side!*

LADY H. H. (bridling) *I take your meaning, sir. Te hee – To be sure, I regret it as you do. But youth's not all. To let you into a secret, I've passed the meridian myself. Am on t'other side of the equator too. Sleep sound o' nights without turning. The dog days are over* . . . *But bethink you, sir. Where there's a will there's a way.*

SIR S. L. *God's truth, ma'am* . . . *ah, my foot's like a burning, burning horseshoe on the devil's anvil, ah! – what's your meaning?*

LADY H. H. *My meaning, sir? Must I disrupt my modesty and unquilt that*

*which has been laid in lavender since, my lord, peace be to his name – 'tis twenty
years since – was lapped in lead? In plain words, sir, Flavinda's flown. The cage is
empty. But we that have bound our wrists with cowslips might join 'em with a
stouter chain. To have done with fallals and figures. Here am I, Asphodilla – but
my plain name is Sue. No matter what my name is – Asphodilla or Sue – here am
I, hale and hearty, at your service. Now that the plot's out, brother Bob's bounty
must go to the virgins. That's plain. Here's Lawyer Quill's word for it. 'Virgins . . .
in perpetuity . . . sing for his soul' And I warrant you, he has need of it . . . But no
matter. Though we have thrown that to the fishes that might have wrapped us in
lambswool, I'm no beggar. There's messuages; tenements; napery; cattle; my dowry;
an inventory, I'll show you, engrossed on parchment; enough I'll warrant you to
keep us handsomely, for what's to run of our time, as husband and wife.*

SIR S. L. *Husband and wife! So that's the plain truth of it! Why, madam, I'd
rather lash myself to a tar barrel, be bound to a thorn tree in a winter's gale. Faugh!*

LADY H. H. *A tar barrel, quotha! A thorn tree – quotha! You that were
harping on galaxies and milky ways! You that were swearing I outshone 'em all! A
pox on you – you faithless! You shark, you! You serpent in jack boots, you! So you
won't have me? Reject my hand, do you?* (She proffers her hand; he strikes it
from him.)

SIR S. L. *Hide your chalk stones in a woollen mit! pah! I'll none of 'em! Were
they diamond, pure diamond, and half the habitable globe and all its concubines
strung upon a string round your throat, I'd none of it . . . none of it. Unhand me,
scritch owl, witch, vampire! Let me go!*

LADY H. H. *So all your fine words were tinsel wrapped round a Christmas
cracker!*

SIR S. L. *Bells hung on an ass's neck! Paper roses on a barber's pole . . . Oh my
foot, my foot . . . Cupid's darts, she mocked me . . . Old, old, he called me old . . .* (He
hobbles away.)

LADY H. H. (left alone) *All gone. Following the wind. He's gone; she's gone;
and the old clock that the rascal made himself into a pendulum for is the only one of
'em all to stop. A pox on 'em – turning an honest woman's house into a brothel. I
that was Aurora Borealis am shrunk to a tar barrel. I that was Cassiopeia am
turned to a she-ass. My head turns. There's no trusting man nor woman; nor fine
speeches; nor fine looks. Off comes the sheep's skin; out creeps the serpent. Get ye to
Gretna Green; couch on the wet grass and breed vipers. My head spins . . . Tar
barrels, quotha. Cassiopeia . . . Chalk stones . . . Andromeda . . . Thorn trees . . .
Deb, I say, Deb!* (She holloas.) *Unlace me. I'm fit to burst . . . Bring me my green-
baize table and set the cards . . . And my fur-lined slippers, Deb. And a dish of
chocolate . . . I'll be even with 'em . . . I'll outlive 'em all. . . . Deb, I say! Deb! A pox
on the girl! Can't she hear me? Deb, I say, you gipsy's spawn that I snatched from
the hedge and taught to sew samplers! Deb! Deb!* (She throws open the door
leading to the maid's closet.) *Empty! She's gone too! . . . Hist, what's that on the
dresser?* (She picks up a scrap of paper and reads.) *'What care I for your goose-
feather bed? I'm off with the raggle-taggle gipsies, O! Signed: Deborah, one time*

your maid.' So! She that I fed on apple parings and crusts from my own table, she that I taught to play cribbage and sew chemises . . . she's gone too. O ingratitude, thy name is Deborah! Who's to wash the dishes now; who's to bring me my posset now, suffer my temper and unlace my stays? . . . All gone. I'm alone then. Sans niece, sans lover – and sans maid.

> *And so to end the play, the moral is*
> *The God of love is full of tricks;*
> *Into the foot his dart he sticks,*
> *But the way of the will is plain to see;*
> *Let holy virgins hymn perpetually:*
> *'Where there's a will there's a way.'*
> *Good people all, farewell.*

Dropping a curtsey, Lady H. H. withdrew.

The scene ended. Reason descended from her plinth. Gathering her robes about her, serenely acknowledging the applause of the audience, she passed across the stage; while lords and ladies in stars and garters followed after; Sir Spaniel limping escorted Lady Harraden smirking; and Valentine and Flavinda arm in arm bowed and curtsied.

'God's truth!' cried Bartholomew catching the infection of the language. 'There's a moral for you!'

He threw himself back in his chair and laughed, like a horse whinnying.

A moral. What? Giles supposed it was: Where there's a will there's a way. The words rose and pointed a finger of scorn at him. Off to Gretna Green with his girl; the deed done. Damn the consequences.

'Like to see the greenhouse?' he said abruptly, turning to Mrs Manresa.

'Love to!' she exclaimed, and rose.

Was there an interval? Yes, the programme said so. The machine in the bushes went chuff, chuff, chuff. And the next scene?

'The Victorian age,' Mrs Elmhurst read out. Presumably there was time then for a stroll round the gardens, even for a look over the house. Yet somehow they felt – how could one put it – a little not quite here or there. As if the play had jerked the ball out of the cup; as if what I call myself was still floating unattached, and didn't settle. Not quite themselves, they felt. Or was it simply that they felt clothes conscious? Skimpy out-of-date voile dresses; flannel trousers; panama hats; hats wreathed with raspberry-coloured net in the style of the royal duchess's hat at Ascot seemed flimsy somehow.

'How lovely the clothes were,' said someone, casting a last look at Flavinda disappearing. 'Most becoming. I wish . . . '

Chuff, chuff, chuff went the machine in the bushes, accurately, insistently.

Clouds were passing across the sky. The weather looked a little unsettled. Hogben's Folly was for a moment ashen white. Then the sun struck the gilt vane of Bolney Minster.

'Looks a little unsettled,' said someone.

'Up you get . . . Let's stretch our legs,' said another voice. Soon the lawns were floating with little moving islands of coloured dresses. Yet some of the audience remained seated.

'Major and Mrs Mayhew,' Page the reporter noted, licking his pencil. As for the play, he would collar Miss Whatshername and ask for a synopsis. But Miss La Trobe had vanished.

Down among the bushes she worked like a nigger. Flavinda was in her petticoats. Reason had thrown her mantle on a holly hedge. Sir Spaniel was tugging at his jack boots. Miss La Trobe was scattering and foraging.

'The Victorian mantle with the bead fringe . . . Where is the damned thing? Chuck it here . . . Now the whiskers . . . '

Ducking up and down she cast her quick bird's eye over the bushes at the audience. The audience was on the move. The audience was strolling up and down. They kept their distance from the dressing-room; they respected the conventions. But if they wandered too far, if they began exploring the grounds, going over the house, then . . . Chuff, chuff, chuff went the machine. Time was passing. How long would time hold them together? It was a gamble; a risk . . . And she laid about her energetically, flinging clothes on the grass.

Over the tops of the bushes came stray voices, voices without bodies, symbolical voices they seemed to her, half hearing, seeing nothing, but still, over the bushes, feeling invisible threads connecting the bodiless voices.

'It all looks very black.'

'No one wants it – save those damned Germans.'

There was a pause.

'I'd cut down those trees . . . '

'How they get their roses to grow!'

'They say there's been a garden here for five hundred years . . . '

'Why even old Gladstone, to do him justice . . . '

Then there was silence. The voices passed the bushes. The trees rustled. Many eyes, Miss La Trobe knew, for every cell in her body was absorbent, looked at the view. Out of the corner of her eye she could see Hogben's Folly; then the vane flashed.

'The glass is falling,' said a voice.

She could feel them slipping through her fingers, looking at the view.

'Where's that damned woman, Mrs Rogers? Who's seen Mrs Rogers?' she cried, snatching up a Victorian mantle.

Then, ignoring the conventions, a head popped up between the trembling sprays: Mrs Swithin's.

'Oh, Miss La Trobe!' she exclaimed; and stopped. Then she began again; 'Oh, Miss La Trobe, I do congratulate you!'

She hesitated. 'You've given me . . . ' She skipped, then alighted – 'Ever since I was a child I've felt . . . ' A film fell over her eyes, shutting off the present. She tried to recall her childhood; then gave it up; and, with a little wave of her hand, as if asking Miss La Trobe to help her out, continued: 'This daily round; this going up and down stairs; this saying, "What am I going for? My specs? I have 'em on my nose" . . . '

She gazed at Miss La Trobe with a cloudless old-aged stare. Their eyes met in a common effort to bring a common meaning to birth. They failed; and Mrs Swithin, laying hold desperately of a fraction of her meaning, said: 'What a small part I've had to play! But you've made me feel I could have played . . . Cleopatra!'

She nodded between the trembling bushes and ambled off.

The villagers winked. 'Batty' was the word for old Flimsy, breaking through the bushes.

' "I might have been – Cleopatra," ' Miss La Trobe repeated. 'You've stirred in me my unacted part, she meant. Now for the skirt, Mrs Rogers,' she said.

Mrs Rogers stood grotesque in her black stockings. Miss La Trobe pulled the voluminous flounces of the Victorian age over her head. She tied the tapes. 'You've twitched the invisible strings,' was what the old lady meant; and revealed – of all people – Cleopatra! Glory possessed her. Ah, but she was not merely a twitcher of individual strings; she was one who seethes wandering bodies and floating voices in a cauldron, and makes rise up from its amorphous mass a recreated world. Her moment was on her – her glory.

'There!' she said, tying the black ribbons under Mrs Rogers' chin. 'That's done it! Now for the gentleman. Hammond!'

She beckoned Hammond. Sheepishly he came forward, and submitted to the application of black side whiskers. With his eyes half shut, his head leant back, he looked, Miss La Trobe thought, like King Arthur – noble, knightly, thin.

'Where's the Major's old frock coat?' she asked, trusting to the effect of that to transform him.

Tick, tick, tick, the machine continued. Time was passing. The audience was wandering, dispersing. Only the tick, tick of the gramophone held them together. There, sauntering solitary far away by the flower-beds, was Mrs Giles escaping.

'The tune!' Miss La Trobe commanded. 'Hurry up! The tune! The next tune! Number Ten!'

'Now may I pluck,' Isa murmured, picking a rose, 'my single flower. The white or the pink? And press it so, twixt thumb and finger . . . '

She looked among the passing faces for the face of the man in grey. There he was for one second; but surrounded, inaccessible. And now vanished.

She dropped her flower. What single, separate leaf could she press? None. Nor stray by the beds alone. She must go on; and she turned in the direction of the stable.

'Where do I wander?' she mused. 'Down what draughty tunnels? Where the eyeless wind blows? And there grows nothing for the eye. No rose. To issue where? In some harvestless dim field where no evening lets fall her mantle; nor sun rises. All's equal there. Unblowing, ungrowing are the roses there. Change is not; nor the mutable and lovable; nor greetings, nor partings; nor furtive findings and feelings, where hand seeks hand and eye seeks shelter from the eye.'

She had come into the stable yard where the dogs were chained; where the buckets stood; where the great pear tree spread its ladder of branches against the wall. The tree whose roots went beneath the flags was weighted with hard green pears. Fingering one of them she murmured: 'How am I burdened with what they drew from the earth; memories; possessions. This is the burden that the past laid on me, last little donkey in the long caravanserai crossing the desert. "Kneel down," said the past. "Fill your pannier from our tree. Rise up, donkey. Go your way till your heels blister and your hoofs crack." '

The pear was hard as stone. She looked down at the cracked flags beneath which the roots spread . 'That was the burden,' she mused, 'laid on me in the cradle; murmured by waves; breathed by restless elm trees; crooned by singing women; what we must remember; what we would forget.'

She looked up. The gilt hands of the stable clock pointed inflexibly at two minutes to the hour. The clock was about to strike.

'Now comes the lightning,' she muttered, 'from the stone blue sky. The thongs are burst that the dead tied. Loosed are our possessions.'

Voices interrupted. People passed the stable yard, talking.

'It's a good day, some say, the day we are stripped naked. Others, it's the end of the day. They see the Inn and the Inn's keeper. But none speaks with a single voice. None with a voice free from the old vibrations. Always I hear corrupt murmurs; the chink of gold and metal. Mad music . . . '

More voices sounded. The audience was streaming back to the terrace. She roused herself. She encouraged herself. 'On little donkey, patiently stumble. Hear not the frantic cries of the leaders who in that they seek to lead desert us. Nor the chatter of china faces glazed and hard. Hear rather the shepherd, coughing by the farmyard wall; the withered tree that sighs when the Rider gallops; the brawl in the barrack room when they stripped her naked; or the cry which in London when I thrust the window open someone cries . . . ' She had come out on to the path that led past the greenhouse. The door was kicked open. Out came Mrs Manresa and Giles. Unseen, Isa followed them across the lawns to the front row of seats.

The chuff, chuff, chuff of the machine in the bushes had stopped. In obedience to Miss La Trobe's command, another tune had been put on the gramophone. Number Ten. London street cries it was called. 'A Pot Pourri'.

'Lavender, sweet lavender, who'll buy my sweet lavender' the tune trilled and tinkled, ineffectively shepherding the audience. Some ignored it. Some still wandered. Others stopped, but stood upright. Some, like Colonel and

Mrs Mayhew, who had never left their seats, brooded over the blurred carbon sheet which had been issued for their information.

'The Nineteenth Century.' Colonel Mayhew did not dispute the producer's right to skip two hundred years in less than fifteen minutes. But the choice of scenes baffled him.

'Why leave out the British Army? What's history without the army, eh?' he mused. Inclining her head, Mrs Mayhew protested after all one mustn't ask too much. Besides, very likely there would be a Grand Ensemble, round the Union Jack, to end with. Meanwhile, there was the view. They looked at the view.

'Sweet lavender . . . sweet lavender . . . ' Humming the tune old Mrs Lynn-Jones (of the Mount) pushed a chair forward. 'Here, Etty,' she said, and plumped down, with Etty Springett, with whom, since both were widows now, she shared a house.

'I remember . . . ' she nodded in time to the tune, 'you remember too – how they used to cry it down the streets.' They remembered – the curtains blowing, and the men crying: 'All a-blowing, all a-growing,' as they came with geraniums, sweet william, in pots, down the street.

'A harp, I remember, and a hansom and a growler. So quiet the street was then. Two for a hansom, was it? One for a growler? And Ellen, in cap and apron, whistling in the street? D'you remember? And the runners, my dear, who followed, all the way from the station, if one had a box.'

The tune changed. 'Any old iron, any old iron to sell?' 'D'you remember? That was what the men shouted in the fog. Seven Dials they came from. Men with red handkerchiefs. Garotters, did they call them? You couldn't walk – Oh, dear me, no – home from the play. Regent Street. Piccadilly. Hyde Park Corner. The loose women . . . And everywhere loaves of bread in the gutter. The Irish you know round Covent Garden . . . Coming back from a ball, past the clock at Hyde Park Corner, d'you remember the feel of white gloves? . . . My father remembered the old Duke in the Park. Two fingers like that – he'd touch his hat . . . I've got my mother's album. A lake and two lovers. She'd copied out Byron, I suppose, in what was called then the Italian hand . . . '

'What's that? "Knocked 'em in the Old Kent Road". I remember the bootboy whistled it. Oh, my dear, the servants . . . Old Ellen . . . Sixteen pound a year wages . . . And the cans of hot water! And the crinolines! And the stays! D'you remember the Crystal Palace, and the fireworks, and how Mira's slipper got lost in the mud?'

'That's young Mrs Giles . . . I remember her mother. She died in India . . . We wore, I suppose, a great many petticoats then. Unhygienic? I dare say . . . Well, look at my daughter. To the right, just behind you. Forty, but slim as a wand. Each flat has its refrigerator . . . It took my mother half the morning to order dinner . . . We were eleven. Counting servants, eighteen in family . . . Now they simply ring up the Stores . . . That's Giles coming, with Mrs

Manresa. She's a type I don't myself fancy. I may be wrong . . . And Colonel
Mayhew, as spruce as ever . . . And Mr Cobbet of Cobbs Corner, there, under
the monkey-puzzle tree. One don't see him often . . . That's what's so nice –
it brings people together. These days, when we're all so busy, that's what one
wants . . . The programme? Have you got it? Let's see what comes next . . .
The Nineteenth Century . . . Look, there's the chorus, the villagers, coming
on now, between the trees. First, there's a prologue . . . '

A great box, draped in red baize festooned with heavy gold tassels had
been moved into the middle of the stage. There was a swish of dresses, a stir
of chairs. The audience seated themselves, hastily, guiltily. Miss La Trobe's
eye was on them. She gave them ten seconds to settle their faces. Then she
flicked her hand. A pompous march tune brayed. 'Firm, elatant, bold and
blatant,' etc . . . And once more a huge symbolical figure emerged from the
bushes. It was Budge the publican; but so disguised that even cronies who
drank with him nightly failed to recognise him; and a little titter of enquiry
as to his identity ran about among the villagers. He wore a long black many-
caped cloak: waterproof; shiny; of the substance of a statue in Parliament
Square; a helmet which suggested a policeman; a row of medals crossed his
breast; and in his right hand he held extended a special-constable's baton
(loaned by Mr Willert of the Hall). It was his voice, husky and rusty, issuing
from a thick black cotton-wool beard that gave him away.

'Budge, Budge. That's Mr Budge,' the audience whispered.

Budge extended his truncheon and spoke: *It ain't an easy job, directing the
traffic at 'Yde Park Corner. Buses and 'ansom cabs. All a-clatter on the cobbles.
Keep to the right, can't you? Hi there, Stop!* (He waved his truncheon.)

There she goes, the old party with the umbrella right under the 'orse's nose. (The
truncheon pointed markedly at Mrs Swithin.)

She raised her skinny hand as if in truth she had fluttered off the pavement
on the impulse of the moment to the just rage of authority. Got her, Giles
thought, taking sides with authority against his aunt.

Fog or fine weather, I does my duty (Budge continued). *At Piccadilly Circus; at
'Yde Park Corner, directing the traffic of 'Er Majesty's Empire. The Shah of
Persia; Sultan of Morocco; or it may be 'Er Majesty in person; or Cook's tourists;
black men; white men; sailors, soldiers; crossing the ocean; to proclaim her Empire;
all of 'em Obey the Rule of my truncheon.* (He flourished it magnificently from
right to left.)

*But my job don't end there. I take under my protection and direction the purity
and security of all Her Majesty's minions; in all parts of her dominions; insist that
they obey the laws of God and Man.*

The laws of God and Man (he repeated and made as if to consult a statute,
engrossed on a sheet of parchment, which with great deliberation he now
produced from his trouser pocket.)

*Go to church on Sunday; on Monday, nine sharp, catch the City bus. On Tuesday
it may be, attend a meeting at the Mansion House for the redemption of the sinner;*

at dinner on Wednesday attend another – turtle soup. Some bother it may be in Ireland. Famine. Fenians. What not. On Thursday it's the natives of Peru require protection and correction; we give 'em what's due. But mark you, our rule don't end there. It's a Christian country, our Empire; under the White Queen Victoria. Over thought and religion; drink; dress; manners; marriage too, I wield my truncheon. Prosperity and respectability always go, as we know, 'and in 'and. The ruler of an Empire must keep his eye on the cot; spy too in the kitchen; drawing-room; library; wherever one or two, me and you, come together. Purity our watchword; prosperity and respectability. If not, why, let 'em fester in . . . (he paused – no, he had not forgotten his words) *Cripplegate; St Giles's; Whitechapel; the Minories. Let 'em sweat at the mines; cough at the looms; rightly endure their lot. That's the price of Empire; that's the white man's burden. And, I can tell you, to direct the traffic orderly, at 'Yde Park Corner, Piccadilly Circus, is a whole-time, white man's job.*

He paused, eminent, dominant, glaring from his pedestal. A very fine figure of a man he was, everyone agreed, his truncheon extended; his waterproof pendant. It only wanted a shower of rain, a flight of pigeons round his head and the pealing bells of St Paul's and the Abbey to transform him into the very spit and image of a Victorian constable; and to transport them to a foggy London afternoon, with the muffin bells ringing and the church bells pealing, at the very height of Victorian prosperity.

There was a pause. The voices of the pilgrims singing, as they wound in and out between the trees, could be heard; but the words were inaudible. The audience sat waiting.

'Tut-tut-tut,' Mrs Lynn-Jones expostulated. 'There were grand men among them . . . ' Why she did not know, yet somehow she felt that a sneer had been aimed at her father; therefore at herself.

Etty Springett tutted too. Yet, children did draw trucks in mines; there was the basement; yet papa read Walter Scott aloud after dinner; and divorced ladies were not received at court. How difficult to come to any conclusion! She wished they would hurry on with the next scene. She liked to leave a theatre knowing exactly what was meant. Of course this was only a village play . . . They were setting another scene, round the red-baize box. She read out from her programme: 'The Picnic Party. About 1860. Scene: A lake. Characters – '

She stopped. A sheet had been spread on the terrace. It was a lake apparently. Roughly painted ripples represented water. Those green stakes were bulrushes. Rather prettily, real swallows darted across the sheet.

'Look, Minnie!' she exclaimed. 'Those are real swallows!'

'Hush, hush,' she was admonished. For the scene had begun. A young man in peg-top trousers and side whiskers carrying a spiked stick appeared by the lake.

EDGAR T. *Let me help you, Miss Hardcastle! There!*
(he helps Miss Eleanor Hardcastle, a young lady in crinoline and mushroom hat to the top. They stand for a moment panting slightly, looking at the view.)

ELEANOR *How small the church looks down among the trees!*

EDGAR *So this is Wanderer's Well, the trysting-place.*

ELEANOR *Please, Mr Thorold, finish what you were saying before the others come. You were saying, 'Our aim in life . . .'*

EDGAR *Should be to help our fellow men.*

ELEANOR (sighing deeply) *How true – how profoundly true!*

EDGAR *Why sigh, Miss Hardcastle? – You have nothing to reproach yourself with – you whose whole life is spent in the service of others. It was of myself that I was thinking. I am no longer young. At twenty-four the best days of life are over. My life has passed* (he throws a pebble on to the lake) *like a ripple in water.*

ELEANOR *Oh Mr Thorold, you do not know me. I am not what I seem. I too –*

EDGAR *Do not tell me, Miss Hardcastle – no, I cannot believe it – You have doubted?*

ELEANOR *Thank heaven not that, not that . . . But safe and sheltered as I am, always at home, protected as you see me, as you think me . . . Oh what am I saying? But yes, I will speak the truth, before mama comes. I too have longed to convert the heathen!*

EDGAR *Miss Hardcastle . . . Eleanor . . . You tempt me! Dare I ask you? No – so young, so fair, so innocent. Think, I implore you, before you answer.*

ELEANOR *I have thought – on my knees!*

EDGAR (taking a ring from his pocket) *Then . . . My mother with her last breath charged me to give this ring only to one to whom a lifetime in the African desert among the heathens would be –*

ELEANOR (taking the ring) *Perfect happiness! But hist!* (She slips the ring into her pocket.) *Here's mama!* (They start asunder.)

(Enter Mrs Hardcastle, a stout lady in black bombazine, upon a donkey, escorted by an elderly gentleman in a deer-stalker's cap.)

MRS H. *So you stole a march upon us, young people. There was a time, Sir John, when you and I were always first on top. Now . . .*

(He helps her to alight. Children, young men, young women, some carrying hampers, others butterfly nets, others spy-glasses, others tin botanical cases arrive. A rug is thrown by the lake and Mrs H. and Sir John seat themselves on camp stools.)

MRS H. *Now who'll fill the kettles? Who'll gather the sticks? Alfred* (to a small boy), *don't run about chasing butterflies or you'll make yourself sick . . . Sir John and I will unpack the hampers, here where the grass is burnt, where we had the picnic last year.*

(The young people scatter off in different directions. Mrs H. and Sir John begin to unpack the hamper.)

MRS H. *Last year poor dear Mr Beach was with us. It was a blessed release.* (She takes out a black-bordered handkerchief and wipes her eyes.) *Every year one of us is missing. That's the ham . . . That's the grouse . . . There in that packet are the game pasties . . .* (She spreads the eatables on the grass.) *As I was saying, poor dear Mr Beach . . . I do hope the cream hasn't curdled. Mr Hardcastle is bringing the claret. I always leave that to him. Only when Mr Hardcastle gets talking with Mr Pigott about the Romans . . . last year they quite came to words . . . But it's nice for gentlemen to have a hobby, though they do gather the dust – those skulls and things . . . But I was saying – poor dear Mr Beach . . . I wanted to ask you* (she drops her voice), *as a friend of the family, about the new clergyman – they can't hear us, can they? No, they're picking up sticks . . . Last year, such a disappointment. Just got the things out . . . down came the rain. But I wanted to ask you about the new clergyman, the one who's come in place of dear Mr Beach. I'm told the name's Sibthorp. To be sure, I hope I'm right, for I had a cousin who married a girl of that name, and as a friend of the family, we don't stand on ceremony . . . And when one has daughters – I'm sure I quite envy you, with only one daughter, Sir John, and I have four! So I was asking you to tell me in confidence, about this young – if that's his name – Sibthorp, for I must tell you the day before yesterday our Mrs Potts happened to say, as she passed the Rectory, bringing our laundry, they were unpacking the furniture; and what did she see on top of the wardrobe? A tea cosy! But of course she might be mistaken . . . But it occurred to me to ask you, as a friend of the family, in confidence, has Mr Sibthorp a wife?*

Here a chorus composed of villagers in Victorian mantles, side whiskers and top hats sang in concert: *Oh has Mr Sibthorp a wife? Oh has Mr Sibthorp a wife? That is the hornet, the bee in the bonnet, the screw in the cork and the drill that whirling and twirling are for ever unfurling the folds of the motherly heart; for a mother must ask, if daughters she has, begot in the feathery billowy fourposter family bed, Oh did he unpack, with his prayer book and bands; his gown and his cane; his rod and his line; and the family album and gun; did he also display the connubial respectable tea-table token, a cosy with honeysuckle embossed. Has Mr Sibthorp a wife? Oh has Mr Sibthorp a wife?*

While the chorus was sung, the picnickers assembled. Corks popped. Grouse, ham, chickens were sliced. Lips munched. Glasses were drained. Nothing was heard but the chump of jaws and the chink of glasses.

'They did eat,' Mrs Lynn-Jones whispered to Mrs Springett. 'That's true. More than was good for them, I dare say.'

MR HARDCASTLE (brushing flakes of meat from his whiskers) *Now . . .*

'Now what?' whispered Mrs Springett, anticipating further travesty.

Now that we have gratified the inner man, let us gratify the desire of the spirit. I call upon one of the young ladies for a song.

CHORUS OF YOUNG LADIES *Oh not me . . . not me . . . I really couldn't . . . No, you cruel thing, you know I've lost my voice . . . I can't sing without the instrument . . . etc., etc.*

CHORUS OF YOUNG MEN *Oh bosh! Let's have 'The Last Rose of Summer'. Let's have 'I Never Loved a Dear Gazelle'.*

MRS H. (authoritatively) *Eleanor and Mildred will now sing 'I'd be a Butterfly'.*

(Eleanor and Mildred rise obediently and sing a duet: 'I'd be a Butterfly'.)

MRS H. *Thank you very much, my dears. And now gentlemen, Our Country!*

(Arthur and Edgar sing 'Rule Britannia'.)

Mrs H. *Thank you very much. Mr Hardcastle –*

Mr Hardcastle (rising to his feet, clasping his fossil) *Let us pray.*

(The whole company rise to their feet.)

'This is too much, too much,' Mrs Springett protested.

Mr H. *Almighty God, giver of all good things, we thank thee for our food and drink; for the beauties of nature; for the understanding with which thou hast enlightened us* (he fumbled with his fossil)*; and for thy great gift of peace. Grant us to be thy servants on earth; grant us to spread the light of thy . . .*

Here the hindquarters of the donkey, represented by Albert the idiot, became active. Intentional was it, or accidental? 'Look at the donkey! Look at the donkey!' A titter drowned Mr Hardcastle's prayer; and then he was heard saying:

. . . a happy homecoming with bodies refreshed by thy bounty, and minds inspired by thy wisdom. Amen.

Holding his fossil in front of him, Mr Hardcastle marched off. The donkey was captured; hampers were loaded; and forming into a procession, the picnickers began to disappear over the hill.

Edgar (winding up the procession with Eleanor) *To convert the heathen!*

Eleanor *To help our fellow men!*

(The actors disappeared into the bushes.)

Budge *It's time, gentlemen, time, ladies, time to pack up and be gone. From where I stand, truncheon in hand, guarding respectability, and prosperity, and the purity of Victoria's land, I see before me –* (he pointed: there was Pointz Hall; the rooks cawing; the smoke rising) *– 'Ome, Sweet 'Ome.*

The gramophone took up the strain: *Through pleasures and palaces, etc. there's no place like home.*

Budge *Home, gentlemen; home, ladies, it's time to pack up and go home. Don't I see the fire* (he pointed: one window blazed red) *blazing ever higher? In kitchen and nursery; drawing-room and library? That's the fire of 'Ome. And see! Our Jane has brought the tea. Now, children, where's the toys? Mama, your knitting, quick. For here* (he swept his truncheon at Cobbet of Cobbs Corner) *comes the breadwinner, home from the City, home from the counter, home from the shop. 'Mama, a cup o' tea.' 'Children, gather round my knee. I will read aloud. Which shall it be? Sindbad the sailor? Or some simple tale from the Scriptures? And show you the pictures? What none of 'em? Then out with the bricks. Let's build: a conservatory? a laboratory? a mechanics' institute? Or shall it be a tower; with our flag on top; where our widowed Queen, after tea, calls the royal orphans round her knee? For it's 'Ome, ladies, 'Ome, gentlemen. Be it never so humble, there's no place like 'Ome.'*

The gramophone warbled 'Home, Sweet Home', and Budge, swaying slightly, descended from his box and followed the procession off the stage.

There was an interval.

'Oh, but it was beautiful,' Mrs Lynn-Jones protested. Home she meant; the lamplit room; the ruby curtains; and papa reading aloud.

They were rolling up the lake and uprooting the bulrushes. Real swallows were skimming over real grass. But she still saw the home.

'It was . . . ' she repeated, referring to the home.

'Cheap and nasty, I call it,' snapped Etty Springett, referring to the play, and shot a vicious glance at Dodge's green trousers, yellow spotted tie and unbuttoned waistcoat.

But Mrs Lynn-Jones still saw the home. Was there, she mused, as Budge's red-baize pediment was rolled off, something – not impure, that wasn't the word – but perhaps 'unhygienic' about the home? Like a bit of meat gone sour, with whiskers, as the servants called it? Or why had it perished? Time went on and on like the hands of the kitchen clock. (The machine chuffed in the bushes.) If they had met with no resistance, she mused, nothing wrong, they'd still be going round and round and round. The home would have remained; and papa's beard, she thought, would have grown and grown; and mama's knitting – what did she do with all her knitting? Change had to come, she said to herself, or there'd have been yards and yards of papa's beard, of mama's knitting. Nowadays her son-in-law was clean-shaven. Her daughter had a refrigerator . . . Dear, how my mind wanders, she checked herself. What she meant was, change had to come, unless things were perfect; in which case she supposed they resisted time. Heaven was changeless.

'Were they like that?' Isa asked abruptly. She looked at Mrs Swithin as if she had been a dinosaur or a very diminutive mammoth. Extinct she must be, since she had lived in the reign of Queen Victoria.

Tick, tick, tick went the machine in the bushes.

'The Victorians,' Mrs Swithin mused. 'I don't believe' she said with her odd little smile, 'that there ever were such people. Only you and me and William dressed differently.'

'You don't believe in history,' said William.

The stage remained empty. The cows moved in the field. The shadows were deeper under the trees.

Mrs Swithin caressed her cross. She gazed vaguely at the view. She was off, they guessed, on a circular tour of the imagination – one-making. Sheep, cows, grass, trees, ourselves – all are one. If discordant, producing harmony – if not to us, to a gigantic ear attached to a gigantic head. And thus – she was smiling benignly – the agony of the particular sheep, cow or human being is necessary; and so – she was beaming seraphically at the gilt vane in the distance – we reach the conclusion that *all* is harmony, could we hear it. And we shall. Her eyes now rested on the white summit of a cloud. Well, if the thought gave her comfort, William and Isa smiled across her, let her think it.

Tick, tick, tick, the machine reiterated.

'D'you get her meaning?' said Mrs Swithin alighting suddenly. 'Miss La Trobe's?'

Isa, whose eyes had been wandering, shook her head.

'But you might say the same of Shakespeare,' said Mrs Swithin.

'Shakespeare and the musical glasses!' Mrs Manresa intervened. 'Dear, what a barbarian you all make me feel!'

She turned to Giles. She invoked his help against this attack upon the jolly human heart.

'Tosh,' Giles muttered.

Nothing whatever appeared on the stage.

Darts of red and green light flashed from the rings on Mrs Manresa's fingers. He looked from them at Aunt Lucy. From her to William Dodge. From him to Isa. She refused to meet his eyes. And he looked down at his blood-stained tennis shoes.

He said (without words), 'I'm damnably unhappy.'

'So am I,' Dodge echoed.

'And I too,' Isa thought.

They were all caught and caged; prisoners; watching a spectacle. Nothing happened. The tick of the machine was maddening.

'On, little donkey,' Isa murmured, 'crossing the desert . . . bearing your burden . . . '

She felt Dodge's eye upon her as her lips moved. Always some cold eye crawled over the surface like a winter bluebottle! She flicked him off.

'What a time they take!' she exclaimed irritably.

'Another interval,' Dodge read out, looking at the programme.

'And after that, what?' asked Lucy.

'Present time. Ourselves,' he read.

'Let's hope to God that's the end,' said Giles gruffly.

'Now you're being naughty,' Mrs Manresa reproved her little boy, her surly hero.

No one moved. There they sat, facing the empty stage, the cows, the meadows and the view, while the machine ticked in the bushes.

'What's the object,' said Bartholomew, suddenly rousing himself, 'of this entertainment?'

'The profits,' Isa read out from her blurred carbon copy, 'are to go to a fund for installing electric light in the church.'

'All our village festivals,' Mr Oliver snorted turning to Mrs Manresa, 'end with a demand for money.'

'Of course, of course,' she murmured, deprecating his severity, and the coins in her bead bag jingled.

'Nothing's done for nothing in England,' the old man continued.

Mrs Manresa protested. It might be true, perhaps, of the Victorians; but surely not of ourselves?

Did she really believe that we were disinterested? Mr Oliver demanded.

'Oh you don't know my husband!' the wild child exclaimed, striking an attitude.

Admirable woman! You could trust her to crow when the hour struck like an alarm clock; to stop like an old bus horse when the bell rang. Oliver said nothing.

Mrs Manresa had out her mirror and attended to her face.

All their nerves were on edge. They sat exposed. The machine ticked. There was no music. The horns of cars on the high road were heard. And the swish of trees. They were neither one thing nor the other; neither Victorians nor themselves. They were suspended, without being, in limbo. Tick, tick, tick went the machine.

Isa fidgeted; glancing to right and to left over her shoulder.

'Four and twenty blackbirds, strung upon a string,' she muttered.

'Down came an ostrich, an eagle, an executioner,
"Which of you is ripe," he said, "to bake in my pie?
Which of you is ripe, which of you is ready,
Come, my pretty gentleman,
Come, my pretty lady" . . . '

How long was she going to keep them waiting? 'The present time. Ourselves.' They read it on the programme. Then they read what came next: 'The profits are to go to a fund for installing electric light in the church.' Where was the church? Over there. You could see the spire among the trees.

'Ourselves . . . ' They returned to the programme. But what could she know about ourselves? The Elizabethans, yes; the Victorians, perhaps; but ourselves sitting here on a June day in 1939 – it was ridiculous. 'Myself' – it was impossible. Other people, perhaps . . . Cobbet of Cobbs Corner; the Major; old Bartholomew; Mrs Swithin – them, perhaps. But she won't get me – no, not me. The audience fidgeted. Sounds of laughter came from the bushes. But nothing whatsoever appeared on the stage.

'What's she keeping us waiting for?' Colonel Mayhew asked irritably. 'They don't need to dress up if it's present time.'

Mrs Mayhew agreed. Unless of course she was going to end with a Grand Ensemble. Army; Navy; Union Jack; and behind them perhaps – Mrs Mayhew sketched what she would have done had it been her pageant – the church. In cardboard. One window, looking east, brilliantly illuminated to symbolise – she could work that out when the time came.

'There she is, behind the tree,' she whispered, pointing at Miss La Trobe.

Miss La Trobe stood there with her eye on her script. 'After Vic.,' she had written, 'try ten mins of present time. Swallows, cows, etc.' She wanted to expose them, as it were, to douche them with present-time reality. But something was going wrong with the experiment. 'Reality too strong,' she muttered. 'Curse 'em!' She felt everything they felt. Audiences were the devil. Oh to write a play without an audience – the play. But here she was fronting her audience. Every second they were slipping the noose. Her little game had gone wrong. If only she'd a backcloth to hang between the trees – to shut out cows, swallows, present time! But she had nothing. She had forbidden music. Grating her fingers in the bark, she damned the audience. Panic seized her. Blood seemed to pour from her shoes. This is death, death, death she noted in the margin of her mind; when illusion fails. Unable to lift her hand, she stood facing the audience.

And then the shower fell, sudden, profuse.

No one had seen the cloud coming. There it was, black, swollen, on top of them. Down it poured like all the people in the world weeping. Tears, Tears. Tears.

'Oh that our human pain could here have ending!' Isa murmured. Looking up she received two great blots of rain full in her face. They trickled down her cheeks as if they were her own tears. But they were all people's tears, weeping for all people. Hands were raised. Here and there a parasol opened. The rain was sudden and universal. Then it stopped. From the grass rose a fresh earthy smell.

'That's done it,' sighed Miss La Trobe, wiping away the drops on her cheeks. Nature once more had taken her part. The risk she had run acting in the open air was justified. She brandished her script. Music began – A B C – A B C. The tune was as simple as could be. But now that the shower had fallen, it was the other voice speaking, the voice that was no one's voice. And the voice that wept for human pain unending said:

> The king is in his counting house,
> Counting out his money,
> The queen is in her parlour . . .

'Oh that my life could here have ending,' Isa murmured (taking care not to move her lips). Readily would she endow this voice with all her treasure if so be tears could be ended. The little twist of sound could have the whole of her. On the altar of the rain-soaked earth she laid down her sacrifice . . .

'Oh look!' she cried aloud.

That was a ladder. And that (a cloth roughly painted) was a wall. And that a man with a hod on his back. Mr Page the reporter, licking his pencil, noted: 'With the very limited means at her disposal, Miss La Trobe conveyed to the audience civilisation (the wall) in ruins; rebuilt (witness man with hod) by human effort; witness also woman handing bricks.' Any fool could grasp that. 'Now issued black man in fuzzy wig; coffee-coloured ditto in silver turban; they signify presumably the League of . . . '

A burst of applause greeted this flattering tribute to ourselves. Crude of course. But then she had to keep expenses down. A painted cloth must convey – what The Times and the Telegraph both said in their leaders that very morning.

The tune hummed:

> The king is in his counting house,
> Counting out his money,
> The queen is in her parlour,
> Eating . . .

Suddenly the tune stopped. The tune changed. A waltz, was it? Something half known, half not. The swallows danced it. Round and round, in and out they skimmed. Real swallows. Retreating and advancing. And the trees, oh the trees, how gravely and sedately like senators in council, or the spaced pillars of some cathedral church . . . Yes, they barred the music, and massed and hoarded; and prevented what was fluid from overflowing. The swallows – or martins were they? – The temple-haunting martins who come, have always come . . . Yes, perched on the wall, they seemed to foretell what after all *The Times* was saying yesterday. Homes will be built. Each flat with its refrigerator, in the crannied wall. Each of us a free man; plates washed by machinery; not an aeroplane to vex us; all liberated; made whole . . .

The tune changed; snapped; broke; jagged. Foxtrot was it? Jazz? Anyhow the rhythm kicked, reared, snapped short. What a jangle and a jingle! Well, with the means at her disposal, you can't ask too much. What a cackle, a cacophony! Nothing ended. So abrupt. And corrupt. Such an outrage; such an insult. And not plain. Very up to date, all the same. What is her game? To disrupt? Jog and trot? Jerk and smirk? Put the finger to the nose? Squint and pry? Peak and spy? Oh the irreverence of the generation which is only momentarily – thanks be – 'the young'. The young, who can't make, but only break; shiver into splinters the old vision; smash to atoms what was whole. What a cackle, what a rattle, what a yaffle – as they call the woodpecker, the laughing bird that flits from tree to tree.

Look! Out they come, from the bushes – the riff-raff. Children? Imps – elves – demons. Holding what? Tin cans? Bedroom candlesticks? Old jars? My dear, that's the cheval glass from the Rectory! And the mirror – that I lent her. My mother's. Cracked. What's the notion? Anything that's bright enough to reflect, presumably, ourselves?

Ourselves! Ourselves!

Out they leapt, jerked, skipped. Flashing, dazzling, dancing, jumping. Now old Bart . . . he was caught. Now Manresa. Here a nose . . . There a skirt . . . Then trousers only . . . Now perhaps a face . . . Ourselves? But that's cruel. To snap us as we are, before we've had time to assume . . . And only, too, in parts . . . That's what's so distorting and upsetting and utterly unfair.

Mopping, mowing, whisking, frisking, the looking glasses darted, flashed, exposed. People in the back rows stood up to see the fun. Down they sat, caught themselves . . . What an awful show-up! Even for the old who, one might suppose, hadn't any longer any care about their faces . . . And Lord! the jangle and the din! The very cows joined in. Walloping, tail lashing, the reticence of nature was undone, and the barriers which should divide Man the Master from the Brute were dissolved. Then the dogs joined in. Excited by the uproar, scurrying and worrying, here they came! Look at them! And the hound, the Afghan hound . . . look at him!

Then once more, in the uproar which by this time has passed quite beyond control, behold Miss Whatshername behind the tree summoned from the bushes – or was it *they* who broke away – Queen Bess; Queen Anne; and the girl in the Mall; and the Age of Reason; and Budge the policeman. Here they came. And the pilgrims. And the lovers. And the grandfather clock. And the old man with a beard. They all appeared. What's more, each declaimed some phrase or fragment from their parts . . . *I am not* (said one) *in my perfect mind . . . Another, Reason am I . . . And I? I'm the old top hat . . . Home is the hunter, home from the hill . . . Home? Where the miner sweats, and the maiden faith is rudely strumpeted . . . Sweet and low; sweet and low, wind of the western sea . . . Is that a dagger that I see before me? . . . The owl hoots and the ivy mocks tap-tap-tapping on the pane . . . Lady I love till I die, leave thy chamber and come . . . Where the worm weaves its winding sheet . . . I'd be a butterfly. I'd be a butterfly . . . In thy will is our peace . . . Here, papa, take your book and read aloud . . . Hark, hark, the dogs do bark and the beggars . . .*

It was the cheval glass that proved too heavy. Young Bonthorp for all his muscle couldn't lug the damned thing about any longer. He stopped. So did they all – hand glasses, tin cans, scraps of scullery glass, harness-room glass and heavily embossed silver mirrors – all stopped. And the audience saw themselves, not whole by any means, but at any rate sitting still.

The hands of the clock had stopped at the present moment. It was now. Ourselves.

So that was her little game! To show us up, as we are, here and how. All shifted, preened, minced; hands were raised, legs shifted. Even Bart, even Lucy, turned away. All evaded or shaded themselves – save Mrs Manresa who, facing herself in the glass, used it as a glass; had out her mirror; powdered her nose; and moved one curl, disturbed by the breeze, to its place.

'Magnificent!' cried old Bartholomew. Alone she preserved unashamed her identity, and faced without blinking herself. Calmly she reddened her lips.

The mirror bearers squatted: malicious; observant; expectant; expository.

'That's them,' the back rows were tittering. 'Must we submit passively to this malignant indignity?' the front row demanded. Each turned ostensibly to say – oh, whatever came handy – to his neighbour. Each tried to shift an inch or two beyond the inquisitive insulting eye. Some made as if to go.

'The play's over, I take it,' muttered Colonel Mayhew, retrieving his hat. 'It's time . . .'

But before they had come to any common conclusion, a voice asserted itself. Whose voice it was no one knew. It came from the bushes – a megaphonic, anonymous, loud-speaking affirmation. The voice said: *Before we part, ladies and gentlemen, before we go . . .* (Those who had risen sat down.) *. . . let's talk in words of one syllable, without larding, stuffing or cant. Let's break the rhythm and forget the rhyme. And calmly consider ourselves. Ourselves. Some bony. Some fat.* (The glasses confirmed this.) *Liars most of us. Thieves too.* (The glasses made no comment on that.) *The poor are as bad as*

*the rich are. Perhaps worse. Don't hide among rags. Or let our cloth protect us. Or
for the matter of that book learning; or skilful practice on pianos; or laying on of
paint. Or presume there's innocency in childhood. Consider the sheep. Or faith in
love. Consider the dogs. Or virtue in those that have grown white hairs. Consider
the gun slayers, bomb droppers here or there. They do openly what we do slyly. Take
for example* (here the megaphone adopted a colloquial, conversational tone)
*Mr M.'s bungalow. A view spoilt for ever. That's murder . . . Or Mrs E.'s lipstick
and blood-red nails . . . A tyrant, remember, is half a slave. Item the vanity of Mr
H. the writer, scraping in the dunghill for sixpenny fame . . . Then there's the
amiable condescension of the lady of the manor – the upper-class manner. And
buying shares in the market to sell 'em . . . Oh we're all the same. Take myself
now. Do I escape my own reprobation, simulating indignation, in the bush, among
the leaves? There's a rhyme, to suggest, in spite of protestation and the desire for
immolation, I too have had some, what's called, education . . . Look at ourselves,
ladies and gentlemen! Then at the wall; and ask how's this wall, the great wall,
which we call, perhaps miscall, civilisation, to be built by* (here the mirrors
flicked and flashed) *orts, scraps and fragments like ourselves?*

All the same here I change (by way of the rhyme mark ye) *to a loftier strain –
there's something to be said: for our kindness to the cat; note too in today's paper,
'Dearly loved by his wife'; and the impulse which leads us – mark you, when no
one's looking – to the window at midnight to smell the bean. Or the resolute refusal
of some pimpled dirty little scrub in sandals to sell his soul. There is such a thing –
you can't deny it. What? You can't descry it? All you can see of yourselves is scraps,
orts and fragments? Well then listen to the gramophone affirming . . .*

A hitch occurred here. The records had been mixed. Foxtrot; Sweet
lavender; Home, Sweet Home; Rule Britannia – sweating profusely, Jimmy,
who had charge of the music, threw them aside and fitted the right one –
was it Bach, Handel, Beethoven, Mozart or nobody famous, but merely a
traditional tune? Anyhow, thank heaven, it was somebody speaking after
the anonymous bray of the infernal megaphone.

Like quicksilver sliding, filings magnetised, the distracted united. The
tune began; the first note meant a second; the second a third. Then down
beneath a force was born in opposition; then another. On different levels
they diverged. On different levels ourselves went forward; flower gathering
some on the surface; others descending to wrestle with the meaning; but
all comprehending; all enlisted. The whole population of the mind's immeasurable profundity came flocking; from the unprotected, the unskinned;
and dawn rose; and azure; from chaos and cacophony measure; but not the
melody of surface sound alone controlled it; but also the warring battle-
plumed warriors straining asunder: To part? No. Compelled from the ends of
the horizon; recalled from the edge of appalling crevasses; they crashed;
solved; united. And some relaxed their fingers; and others uncrossed their legs.

Was that voice ourselves? Scraps, orts and fragments, are we, also, that?
The voice died away.

As waves withdrawing uncover; as mist uplifting reveals; so, raising their eyes (Mrs Manresa's were wet; for an instant tears ravaged her powder), they saw, as waters withdrawing leave visible a tramp's old boot, a man in a clergyman's collar surreptitiously mounting a soap-box.

'The Reverend G. W. Streatfield,' the reporter licked his pencil and noted, 'then spoke . . . '

All gazed. What an intolerable constriction, contraction and reduction to simplified absurdity he was to be sure! Of all incongruous sights a clergyman in the livery of his servitude to the summing up was the most grotesque and entire. He opened his mouth. O Lord, protect and preserve us from words the defilers, from words the impure! What need have we of words to remind us? Must I be Thomas, you Jane?

As if a rook had hopped unseen to a prominent bald branch, he touched his collar and hemmed his preliminary croak. One fact mitigated the horror: his forefinger, raised in the customary manner, was stained with tobacco juice. He wasn't such a bad fellow, the Reverend G. W. Streatfield; a piece of traditional church furniture; a corner cupboard; or the top beam of a gate, fashioned by generations of village carpenters after some lost-in-the-mists-of-antiquity model.

He looked at the audience; then up at the sky. The whole lot of them, gentles and simples, felt embarrassed, for him, for themselves. There he stood, their representative spokesman; their symbol; themselves; a butt, a clod, laughed at by looking-glasses; ignored by the cows; condemned by the clouds which continued their majestic rearrangement of the celestial landscape; an irrelevant forked stake in the flow and majesty of the summer silent world.

His first words (the breeze had risen; the leaves were rustling) were lost. Then he was heard saying: 'What.' To that word he added another: 'Message'; and at last a whole sentence emerged; not comprehensible; say rather audible. 'What message,' it seemed he was asking, 'was our pageant meant to convey?'

They folded their hands in the traditional manner as if they were seated in church.

'I have been asking myself' – the words were repeated – 'what meaning, or message, this pageant was meant to convey?'

If he didn't know, calling himself Reverend, also M.A., who after all could?

'As one of the audience,' he continued (words now put on meaning), 'I will offer, very humbly, for I am not a critic' – and he touched the white gate that enclosed his neck with a yellow forefinger – 'my interpretation. No, that is too bold a word. The gifted lady . . . ' He looked round. La Trobe was invisible. He continued: 'Speaking merely as one of the audience, I confess I was puzzled. For what reason, I asked, were we shown these scenes? Briefly, it is true. The means at our disposal this afternoon were limited. Still we were shown different groups. We were shown, unless I mistake, the effort renewed. A few were chosen; the many passed in the background. That surely we were shown. But again, were we not given to understand – am I too presumptuous? Am I treading, like angels, where as a fool I should absent myself? To me at least it was indicated that we are members one of another. Each is part of the whole. Yes, that occurred to me, sitting among you in the audience. Did I not perceive Mr Hardcastle here' (he pointed) 'at one time a Viking? And in Lady Harridan – excuse me, if I get the names wrong – a Canterbury pilgrim? We act different parts; but are the same. That I leave to you. Then again, as the play or pageant proceeded, my attention was distracted. Perhaps that too was part of the producer's intention? I thought I perceived that nature takes her part. Dare we, I asked myself, limit life to ourselves? May we not hold that there is a spirit that inspires, pervades . . . ' (the swallows were sweeping round him. They seemed cognisant of his meaning. Then they swept out of sight.) 'I leave that to you. I am not here to explain. That role has not been assigned me. I speak only as one of the audience, one of ourselves. I caught myself too reflected, as it happened in my own mirror . . . ' (Laughter) 'Scraps, orts and fragments! Surely, we should unite?'

'But' ('but' marked a new paragraph) 'I speak also in another capacity. As Treasurer of the Fund. In which capacity' (he consulted a sheet of paper) 'I am glad to be able to tell you that a sum of thirty-six pounds ten shillings and eightpence has been raised by this afternoon's entertainment towards our object: the illumination of our dear old church.'

'Applause,' the reporter reported.

Mr Streatfield paused. He listened. Did he hear some distant music?

He continued: 'But there is still a deficit' (he consulted his paper) 'of one hundred and seventy-five pounds odd. So that each of us who has enjoyed this pageant has still an opp . . . '

The word was cut in two. A zoom severed it. Twelve aeroplanes in perfect formation like a flight of wild duck came overhead. *That* was the music. The audience gaped; the audience gazed. Then zoom became drone. The planes had passed.

' . . . portunity,' Mr Streatfield continued, 'to make a contribution.' He signalled. Instantly collecting boxes were in operation. Hidden behind glasses they emerged. Coppers rattled. Silver jingled. But oh what a pity – how creepy it made one feel! Here came Albert, the idiot, jingling his collecting box – an aluminium saucepan without a lid. You couldn't very well deny him, poor fellow. Shillings were dropped. He rattled and sniggered; chattered and jibbered. As Mrs Parker made her contribution – half a crown as it happened – she appealed to Mr Streatfield to exorcise this evil, to extend the protection of his cloth.

The good man contemplated the idiot benignly. His faith had room, he indicated, for him too. He too, Mr Streatfield appeared to be saying, is part of ourselves. But not a part we like to recognise, Mrs Springett added silently, dropping her sixpence.

Contemplating the idiot, Mr Streatfield had lost the thread of his discourse. His command over words seemed gone. He twiddled the cross on his watch-chain. Then his hand sought his trouser pocket. Surreptitiously he extracted a small silver box. It was plain to all that the natural desire of the natural man was overcoming him. He had no further use for words.

'And now,' he resumed, cuddling the pipe lighter in the palm of his hand, 'for the pleasantest part of my duty. To propose a vote of thanks to the gifted lady . . . ' He looked round for an object corresponding to this description. None such was visible. '. . . who wishes it seems to remain anonymous.' He paused. 'And so . . . ' He paused again.

It was an awkward moment. How to make an end? Whom to thank? Every sound in nature was painfully audible: the swish of the trees; the gulp of a cow; even the skim of the swallows over the grass could be heard. But no one spoke. Whom could they make responsible? Whom could they thank for their entertainment? Was there no one?

Then there was a scuffle behind the bush; a preliminary premonitory scratching. A needle scraped a disc; chuff, chuff, chuff; then having found the rut, there was a roll and a flutter which portended God . . . they all rose to their feet . . . Save the King.

Standing, the audience faced the actors; who also stood, with their collecting boxes quiescent, their looking-glasses hidden, and the robes of their various parts hanging stiff.

> Happy and glorious,
> Long to reign over us,
> God save the King.

The notes died away.

Was that the end? The actors were reluctant to go. They lingered; they mingled. There was Budge the policeman talking to old Queen Bess. And the Age of Reason hobnobbed with the foreparts of the donkey. And Mrs Hardcastle patted out the folds of her crinoline. And little England, still a child, sucked a peppermint-drop out of a bag. Each still acted the unacted part conferred on them by their clothes. Beauty was on them. Beauty revealed them. Was it the light that did it? – the tender, the fading, the uninquisitive but searching light of evening that reveals depths in water and makes even the red-brick bungalow radiant?

'Look,' the audience whispered. 'Oh look, look, look – ' And once more they applauded; and the actors joined hands and bowed.

Old Mrs Lynn-Jones, fumbling for her bag, sighed, 'What a pity – must they change?'

But it was time to pack up and be off.

'Home, gentlemen; home ladies; it's time to pack up and be off,' the reporter whistled, snapping the band round his notebook.

And Mrs Parker was stooping. 'I'm afraid I've dropped my glove. I'm so sorry to trouble you. Down there, between the seats . . . '

The gramophone was affirming in tones there was no denying, triumphant yet valedictory: *Dispersed are we; who have come together. But*, the gramophone asserted, *let us retain whatever made that harmony*.

Oh let us, the audience echoed (stooping, peering, fumbling), keep together. For there is joy, sweet joy, in company.

Dispersed are we, the gramophone repeated.

And the audience turning saw the flaming windows, each daubed with golden sun; and murmured: 'Home, gentlemen; sweet. . . ' yet delayed a moment, seeing through the golden glory perhaps a crack in the boiler; perhaps a hole in the carpet; and hearing, perhaps, the daily drop of the daily bill.

Dispersed are we, the gramophone informed them. And dismissed them. So, straightening themselves for the last time, each grasping, it might be a hat, or a stick, or a pair of suede gloves, for the last time they applauded Budge and Queen Bess; the trees; the white road; Bolney Minster; and the Folly. One hailed another, and they dispersed, across lawns, down paths, past the house to the gravel-strewn crescent, where cars, push bikes and cycles were crowded together.

Friends hailed each other in passing.

'I do think,' someone was saying, 'Miss Whatshername should have come forward and not left it to the rector . . . After all, she wrote it . . . I thought it brilliantly clever . . . Oh my dear, I thought it utter bosh. Did *you* understand the meaning? Well, he said she meant we all act all parts . . . He said, too, if I caught his meaning, nature takes part . . . Then there was the idiot . . . Also, why leave out the army, as my husband was saying, if it's history? And if one spirit animates the whole, what about the aeroplanes? . . . Ah, but you're being too exacting. After all, remember, it was only a village play . . . For my part, I think they should have passed a vote of thanks to the owners. When we had our pageant, the grass didn't recover till autumn . . . Then we had tents . . . That's the man, Cobbet of Cobbs Corner, who wins all the prizes at all the shows. I don't myself admire prize flowers, nor yet prize dogs . . . '

Dispersed are we, the gramophone triumphed, yet lamented, *Dispersed are we* . . .

'But you must remember,' the old cronies chatted, 'they had to do it on the cheap. You can't get people, at this time o' year, to rehearse. There's the hay, let alone the movies . . . What we need is a centre. Something to bring us all together . . . The Brookes have gone to Italy, in spite of everything. Rather rash? . . . If the worst should come – let's hope it won't – they'd hire an aeroplane, so they said . . . What amused me was old Streatfield, feeling for his pouch. I like a man to be natural, not always on a perch . . . Then those voices from the bushes . . . Oracles? You're referring to the Greeks? Were the oracles, if I'm not being irreverent, a foretaste of our own religion? Which is what? . . . Crêpe soles? That's so sensible . . . They last much longer and protect the feet . . . But I was saying: can the Christian faith adapt itself? In times like these . . . At Larting no one goes to church . . . There's the dogs, there's the pictures . . . It's odd that science, so they tell me, is making things (so to speak) more spiritual . . . The very latest notion, so I'm told, is nothing's solid . . . There, you can get a glimpse of the church through the trees . . .

'Mr Umphelby! How nice to see you! Do come and dine . . . No, alas, we're going back to town. The House is sitting . . . I was telling them, the Brookes have gone to Italy. They've seen the volcano. Most impressive, so they say – they were lucky – in eruption. I agree – things look worse than ever on the continent. And what's the Channel, come to think of it, if they mean to invade us? The aeroplanes, I didn't like to say it, made one think . . . No, I thought it much too scrappy. Take the idiot. Did she mean, so to speak, something hidden, the unconscious as they call it? But why always drag in sex . . . It's true, there's a sense in which we all, I admit, are savages still. Those women with red nails. And dressing up – what's that? The old savage, I suppose . . . That's the bell. Ding dong. Ding . . . Rather a cracked old bell . . . And the mirrors! Reflecting us . . . I called that cruel. One feels such a fool, caught unprotected . . . There's Mr Streatfield, going, I suppose to take the evening service. He'll have to hurry or he won't have time to change . . . He said she meant we all act. Yes, but whose play? Ah, that's the question! And if we're left asking questions, isn't it a failure, as a play? I must say I like to feel sure if I go to the theatre that I've grasped the meaning . . . Or was that, perhaps, what she meant? . . . Ding dong. Ding . . . that if we don't jump to conclusions, if you think, and I think, perhaps one day, thinking differently, we shall think the same?

'There's dear old Mr Carfax . . . Can't we give you a lift, if you don't mind playing bodkin? We were asking questions, Mr Carfax, about the play. The looking-glasses now – did they mean the reflection is the dream; and the tune – was it Bach, Handel, or no one in particular – is the truth? Or was it t'other way about?

'Bless my soul, what a dither! Nobody seems to know one car from another. That's why I have a mascot, a monkey . . . But I can't see it . . . While we're waiting, tell me, did you feel when the shower fell someone wept for us all? There's a poem, *Tears tears tears*, it begins. And goes on *Oh then the unloosened ocean* . . . but I can't remember the rest.

'Then when Mr Streatfield said: One spirit animates the whole – the aeroplanes interrupted. That's the worst of playing out of doors . . . Unless of course she meant that very thing . . . Dear me, the parking arrangements are not what you might call adequate . . . I shouldn't have expected either so many Hispano-Suizas . . . That's a Rolls . . . That's a Bentley . . . That's the new type of Ford . . . To return to the meaning – Are machines the devil, or do they introduce a discord . . . Ding dong, ding . . . by means of which we reach the final . . . Ding dong . . . Here's the car with the monkey . . . Hop in . . . And goodbye, Mrs Parker . . . Ring us up. Next time we're down, don't forget . . . Next time . . . Next time . . . '

The wheels scrurred on the gravel. The cars drove off.

The gramophone gurgled *Unity–Dispersity*. It gurgled *Un* . . . *dis* . . . and ceased.

The little company who had come together at luncheon were left standing on the terrace. The pilgrims had bruised a lane on the grass. Also, the lawn would need a deal of clearing up. Tomorrow the telephone would ring: 'Did I leave my handbag? . . . A pair of spectacles in a red leather case? . . . A little old brooch of no value to anyone but me?' Tomorrow the telephone would ring. Now Mr Oliver said: 'Dear lady,' and, taking Mrs Manresa's gloved hand in his, pressed it, as if to say: 'You have given me what you now take from me.' He would have liked to hold on for a moment longer to the emeralds and rubies dug up, so people said, by thin Ralph Manresa in his ragamuffin days. But alas, sunset light was unsympathetic to her make-up; plated it looked, not deeply interfused. And he dropped her hand; and she gave him an arch roguish twinkle, as if to say – but the end of that sentence was cut short. For she turned, and Giles stepped forward; and the light breeze which the meteorologist had foretold fluttered her skirts; and she went, like a goddess, buoyant, abundant, with flower-chained captives following in her wake.

All were retreating, withdrawing and dispersing; and he was left with the ash grown cold and no glow, no glow on the log. What word expressed the sag at his heart, the effusion in his veins, as the retreating Manresa, with Giles attendant, admirable woman, all sensation, ripped the rag doll and let the sawdust stream from his heart?

The old man made a guttural sound, and turned to the right. On with the hobble, on with the limp, since the dance was over. He strolled alone past the trees. It was here, early that very morning, that he had destroyed the little boy's world. He had popped out with his newspaper; the child had cried.

Down in the dell, past the lily pool, the actors were undressing. He could see them among the brambles. In vests and trousers; unhooking; buttoning up; on all fours stuffing clothes into cheap attaché cases; with silver swords, beards and emeralds on the grass. Miss La Trobe in coat and skirt – too short, for her legs were stout – battled with the billows of a crinoline. He must respect the conventions. So he stopped, by the pool. The water was opaque over the mud.

Then, coming up behind him, 'Oughtn't we to thank her?' Lucy asked him. She gave him a light pat on the arm.

How imperceptive her religion made her! The fumes of that incense obscured the human heart. Skimming the surface, she ignored the battle in the mud. After La Trobe had been excruciated by the rector's interpretation, by the maulings and the manglings of the actors . . . 'She don't want our thanks, Lucy,' he said gruffly. What she wanted, like that carp (something moved in the water), was darkness in the mud; a whisky and soda at the pub; and coarse words descending like maggots through the waters.

'Thank the actors, not the author,' he said. 'Or ourselves, the audience.'

He looked over his shoulder. The old lady, the indigenous, the prehistoric, was being wheeled away by a footman. He rolled her through the arch. Now the lawn was empty. The line of the roof, the upright chimneys, rose hard and red against the blue of the evening. The house emerged; the house that had been obliterated. He was damned glad it was over – the scurry and the scuffle, the rouge and the rings. He stooped and raised a peony that had shed its petals. Solitude had come again. And reason and the lamplit paper . . . But where was his dog? Chained in a kennel? The little veins swelled with rage on his temples. He whistled. And here, released by Candish, racing across the lawn with a fleck of foam on the nostril, came his dog.

Lucy still gazed at the lily pool. 'All gone,' she murmured, 'under the leaves.' Scared by shadows passing, the fish had withdrawn. She gazed at the water. Perfunctorily she caressed her cross. But her eyes went water searching, looking for fish. The lilies were shutting: the red lily, the white lily, each on its plate of leaf. Above, the air rushed; beneath was water. She stood between two fluidities, caressing her cross. Faith required hours of kneeling in the early morning. Often the delight of the roaming eye seduced her – a sunbeam, a shadow. Now the jagged leaf at the corner suggested, by its contours, Europe. There were other leaves. She fluttered her eye over the surface, naming leaves India, Africa, America. Islands of security, glossy and thick.

'Bart . . . ' She spoke to him. She had meant to ask him about the dragon-fly – couldn't the blue thread settle, if we destroyed it here, then there? But he had gone into the house.

Then something moved in the water; her favourite fantail. The golden orfe followed. Then she had a glimpse of silver – the great carp himself, who came to the surface so very seldom. They slid on, in and out between the stalks – silver; pink; gold; splashed; streaked; pied.

'Ourselves,' she murmured. And retrieving some glint of faith from the grey waters, hopefully, without much help from reason, she followed the fish: the speckled, streaked and blotched; seeing in that vision beauty, power and glory in ourselves.

Fish had faith, she reasoned. They trust us because we've never caught 'em. But her brother would reply: 'That's greed.' 'Their beauty!' she protested. 'Sex,' he would say. 'Who makes sex susceptible to beauty?' she would argue. He shrugged who? Why? Silenced, she returned to her private vision: of beauty which is goodness; the sea on which we float. Mostly impervious, but surely every boat sometimes leaks?

He would carry the torch of reason till it went out in the darkness of the cave. For herself, every morning, kneeling, she protected her vision. Every night she opened the window and looked at leaves against the sky. Then slept. Then the random ribbons of birds' voices woke her.

The fish had come to the surface. She had nothing to give them – not a crumb of bread. 'Wait, my darlings,' she addressed them. She would trot into the house and ask Mrs Sands for a biscuit. Then a shadow fell. Off they flashed. How vexatious! Who was it? Dear me, the young man whose name she had forgotten; not Jones; nor Hodge . . .

Dodge had left Mrs Manresa abruptly. All over the garden he had been searching for Mrs Swithin. Now he found her; and she had forgotten his name.

'I'm William,' he said. At that she revived, like a girl in a garden in white, among roses, who came running to meet him – an unacted part.

'I was going to get a biscuit – no, to thank the actors,' she stumbled, virginal, blushing. Then she remembered her brother. 'My brother,' she added, 'says one mustn't thank the author, Miss La Trobe.'

It was always 'my brother . . . my brother' who rose from the depths of her lily pool.

As for the actors, Hammond had detached his whiskers and was now buttoning up his coat. When the chain was inserted between the buttons he was off.

Only Miss La Trobe remained, bending over something in the grass.

'The play's over,' he said. 'The actors have departed.'

'And we mustn't, my brother says, thank the author,' Mrs Swithin repeated, looking in the direction of Miss La Trobe.

'So I thank you,' he said. He took her hand and pressed it. Putting one thing with another, it was unlikely that they would ever meet again.

The church bells always stopped, leaving you to ask: Won't there be another note? Isa, halfway across the lawn, listened . . . Ding, dong, ding . . . There was not going to be another note. The congregation was assembled, on their knees, in the church. The service was beginning. The play was over; swallows skimmed the grass that had been the stage.

There was Dodge, the lip reader, her semblable, her conspirator, a seeker like her after hidden faces. He was hurrying to rejoin Mrs Manresa who had gone in front with Giles – 'the father of my children,' she muttered. The flesh poured over her, the hot, nerve-wired, now lit up, now dark as the grave, physical body. By way of healing the rusty fester of the poisoned dart she sought the face that all day long she had been seeking. Preening and peering, between backs, over shoulders, she had sought the man in grey. He had given her a cup of tea at a tennis party; handed her, once, a racquet. That was all. But, she was crying, had we met before the salmon leapt like a bar of silver . . . had we met, she was crying. And when her little boy came battling through the bodies in the barn, 'Had he been his son,' she had muttered . . . In passing, she stripped the bitter leaf that grew, as it happened, outside the nursery window. Old man's beard. Shrivelling the shreds in lieu of words, for no words grew there, nor roses either, she swept past her conspirator, her semblable, the seeker after vanished faces – 'like Venus,' he thought, making a rough translation, 'to her prey . . . ' – and followed after.

Turning the corner, they saw Giles attached to Mrs Manresa. She was standing at the door of her car. Giles had his foot on the edge of the running-board. Did they perceive the arrows about to strike them?

'Jump in, Bill,' Mrs Manresa chaffed him.

And the wheels scurred on the gravel, and the car drove off.

At last, Miss La Trobe could raise herself from her stooping position. It had been prolonged to avoid attention. The bells had stopped; the audience had gone; also the actors. She could straighten her back. She could open her arms. She could say to the world, You have taken my gift! Glory possessed her – for one moment. But what had she given? A cloud that melted into the other clouds on the horizon. It was in the giving that the triumph was. And the triumph faded. Her gift meant nothing. If they had understood her meaning; if they had known their parts; if the pearls had been real and the funds illimitable – it would have been a better gift. Now it had gone to join the others.

'A failure,' she groaned, and stooped to put away the records.

Then suddenly the starlings attacked the tree behind which she had hidden. In one flock they pelted it like so many winged stones. The whole tree hummed with the whizz they made, as if each bird plucked a wire. A whizz, a buzz rose from the bird-buzzing, bird-vibrant, bird-blackened tree. The tree became a rhapsody, a quivering cacophony, a whizz and vibrant rapture, branches, leaves, birds syllabling discordantly life, life, life, without measure, without stop, devouring the tree. Then up! Then off!

What interrupted? It was old Mrs Chalmers, creeping through the grass with a bunch of flowers – pinks apparently – to fill the vase that stood on her husband's grave. In winter it was holly, or ivy. In summer, a flower. It was she who had scared the starlings. Now she passed.

Miss La Trobe nicked the lock and hoisted the heavy case of gramophone records to her shoulder. She crossed the terrace and stopped by the tree where the starlings had gathered. It was here that she had suffered triumph, humiliation, ecstasy, despair – for nothing. Her heels had ground a hole in the grass.

It was growing dark. Since there were no clouds to trouble the sky, the blue was bluer, the green greener. There was no longer a view – no Folly, no spire of Bolney Minster. It was land merely, no land in particular. She put down her case and stood looking at the land. Then something rose to the surface.

'I should group them,' she murmured, 'here.' It would be midnight; there would be two figures, half concealed by a rock. The curtain would rise. What would the first words be? The words escaped her.

Again she lifted the heavy suitcase to her shoulder. She strode off across the lawn. The house was dormant; one thread of smoke thickened against the trees. It was strange that the earth, with all those flowers incandescent – the lilies, the roses, and clumps of white flowers and bushes of burning green – should still be hard. From the earth green waters seemed to rise over her. She took her voyage away from the shore, and, raising her hand, fumbled for the latch of the iron entrance gate.

She would drop her suitcase in at the kitchen window, and then go on up to the inn. Since the row with the actress who had shared her bed and her purse the need of drink had grown on her. And the horror and the terror of being alone. One of these days she would break – which of the village laws? Sobriety? Chastity? Or take something that did not properly belong to her?

At the corner she ran into old Mrs Chalmers returning from the grave. The old woman looked down at the dead flowers she was carrying and cut her. The women in the cottages with the red geraniums always did that. She was an outcast. Nature had somehow set her apart from her kind. Yet she had scribbled in the margin of her manuscript: 'I am the slave of my audience.'

She thrust her suitcase in at the scullery window and walked on, till at the corner she saw the red curtain at the bar window. There would be shelter; voices; oblivion. She turned the handle of the public-house door. The acrid smell of stale beer saluted her; and voices talking. They stopped. They had been talking about Bossy as they called her – it didn't matter. She took her chair and looked through the smoke at a crude glass painting of a cow in a stable; also at a cock and a hen. She raised her glass to her lips. And drank. And listened. Words of one syllable sank down into the mud. She drowsed; she nodded. The mud became fertile. Words rose above the intolerably laden dumb oxen plodding through the mud. Words without meaning – wonderful words.

The cheap clock ticked; smoke obscured the pictures. Smoke became tart on the roof of her mouth. Smoke obscured the earth-coloured jackets. She no longer saw them, yet they upheld her, sitting arms akimbo with her glass before her. There was the high ground at midnight; there the rock; and two scarcely perceptible figures. Suddenly the tree was pelted with starlings. She set down her glass. She heard the first words.

Down in the hollow, at Pointz Hall, beneath the trees, the table was cleared in the dining-room. Candish, with his curved brush, had swept the crumbs; had spared the petals and finally left the family to dessert. The play was over, the strangers gone, and they were alone – the family.

Still the play hung in the sky of the mind – moving, diminishing, but still there. Dipping her raspberry in sugar, Mrs Swithin looked at the play. She said, popping the berry into her mouth, 'What did it mean?' and added: 'The peasants; the kings; the fool; and' (she swallowed) 'ourselves?'

They all looked at the play: Isa, Giles and Mr Oliver. Each of course saw something different. In another moment it would be beneath the horizon, gone to join the other plays. Mr Oliver, holding out his cheroot, said: 'Too ambitious.' And, lighting his cheroot, he added: 'Considering her means.'

It was drifting away to join the other clouds: becoming invisible. Through the smoke Isa saw not the play but the audience dispersing. Some drove; others cycled. A gate swung open. A car swept up the drive to the red villa in the cornfields. Low hanging boughs of acacia brushed the roof. Acacia-petalled the car arrived.

'The looking-glasses and the voices in the bushes,' she murmured. 'What did she mean?'

'When Mr Streatfield asked her to explain, she wouldn't,' said Mrs Swithin.

Here, with its sheaf sliced in four, exposing a white cone, Giles offered his wife a banana. She refused it. He stubbed his match on the plate. Out it went with a little fizz in the raspberry juice.

'We should be thankful,' said Mrs Swithin, folding her napkin, 'for the weather, which was perfect, save for one shower.'

Here she rose, Isa followed her across the hall to the big room.

They never pulled the curtains till it was too dark to see, nor shut the windows till it was too cold. Why shut out the day before it was over? The flowers were still bright; the birds chirped. You could see more in the evening often when nothing interrupted, when there was no fish to order, no telephone to answer. Mrs Swithin stopped by the great picture of Venice – school of Canaletto. Possibly in the hood of the gondola there was a little figure – a woman, veiled; or a man?

Isa, sweeping her sewing from the table, sank, her knee doubled, into the chair by the window. Within the shell of the room she overlooked the summer night. Lucy returned from her voyage into the picture and stood silent. The sun made each pane of her glasses shine red. Silver sparkled on her black shawl. For a moment she looked like a tragic figure from another play.

Then she spoke in her usual voice. 'We made more this year than last, he said. But then last year it rained.'

'This year, last year, next year, never . . . ' Isa murmured. Her hand burnt in the sun on the window sill.

Mrs Swithin took her knitting from the table. 'Did you feel,' she asked, 'what he said: we act different parts but are the same?'

'Yes,' Isa answered. 'No,' she added. It was Yes, No. Yes, yes, yes, the tide rushed out embracing. No, no no, it contracted. The old boot appeared on the shingle.

'Orts, scraps and fragments,' she quoted what she remembered of the vanishing play.

· Lucy had just opened her lips to reply, and had laid her hand on her cross caressingly, when the gentlemen came in. She made her little chirruping sound of welcome. She shuffled her feet to clear a space. But in fact there was more space than was needed, and great hooded chairs.

They sat down, ennobled both of them by the setting sun. Both had changed. Giles now wore the black coat and white tie of the professional classes, which needed – Isa looked down at his feet – patent-leather pumps. 'Our representative, our spokesman,' she sneered. Yet he was extraordinarily handsome. 'The father of my children, whom I love and hate.' Love and hate – how they tore her asunder! Surely it was time someone invented a new plot, or that the author came out from the bushes . . .

Here Candish came in. He brought the second post on a silver salver. There were letters; bills; and the morning paper – the paper that obliterated the day before. Like a fish rising to a crumb of biscuit, Bartholomew snapped at the paper. Giles slit the flap of an apparently business document. Lucy read a criss-cross from an old friend at Scarborough. Isa had only bills.

The usual sounds reverberated through the shell: Sands making up the fire; Candish stoking the boiler. Isa had done with her bills. Sitting in the shell of the room, she watched the pageant fade. The flowers flashed before they faded. She watched them flash.

The paper crackled. The second hand jerked on. M. Daladier had pegged down the franc. The girl had gone skylarking with the troopers. She had screamed. She had hit him . . . What then?

When Isa looked at the flowers again, the flowers had faded.

Bartholomew flicked on the reading lamp. The circle of the readers, attached to white papers, was lit up. There in that hollow of the sun-baked field were congregated the grasshopper, the ant and the beetle, rolling pebbles of sun-baked earth through the glistening stubble. In that rosy corner of the sun-baked field, Bartholomew, Giles and Lucy polished and nibbled and broke off crumbs. Isa watched them.

Then the newspaper dropped.

'Finished?' said Giles, taking it from his father.

The old man relinquished his paper. He basked. One hand caressing the dog, resting on the rippled folds of skin towards the collar.

The clock ticked. The house gave little cracks as if it were very brittle, very dry. Isa's hand on the window felt suddenly cold. Shadow had obliterated the garden. Roses had withdrawn for the night.

Mrs Swithin folding her letter murmured to Isa: 'I looked in and saw the babies, sound asleep, under the paper roses.'

'Left over from the Coronation,' Bartholomew muttered, half asleep.

'But we needn't have been to all that trouble with the decorations,' Lucy added, 'for it didn't rain this year.'

'This year, last year, next year, never,' Isa murmured.

'Tinker, tailor, soldier, sailor,' Bartholomew echoed. He was talking in his sleep.

Lucy slipped her letter into its envelope. It was time to read now, her *Outline of History*. But she had lost her place. She turned the pages looking at pictures – mammoths, mastodons, prehistoric birds. Then she found the page where she had stopped.

The darkness increased. The breeze swept round the room. With a little shiver Mrs Swithin drew her sequined shawl about her shoulders. She was too deep in the story to ask for the window to be shut. 'England,' she was reading, 'was then a swamp. Thick forests covered the land. On the top of their matted branches birds sang . . . '

The great square of the open window showed only sky now. It was drained of light, severe, stone cold. Shadows fell. Shadows crept over Bartholomew's high forehead; over his great nose. He looked leafless, spectral, and his chair monumental. As a dog shudders its skin, his skin shuddered. He rose, shook himself, glared at nothing and stalked from the room. They heard the dog's paws padding on the carpet behind him.

Lucy turned the page, quickly, guiltily, like a child who will be told to go to bed before the end of the chapter.

'Prehistoric man,' she read, 'half-human, half-ape, roused himself from his semi-crouching position and raised great stones.'

She slipped the letter from Scarborough between the pages to mark the end of the chapter, rose, smiled and tiptoed silently out of the room.

The old people had gone up to bed. Giles crumpled the newspaper and turned out the light. Left alone together for the first time that day, they were silent. Alone, enmity was bared; also love. Before they slept, they must fight; after they had fought, they would embrace. From that embrace another life might be born. But first they must fight, as the dog fox fights with the vixen, in the heart of darkness, in the fields of night.

Isa let her sewing drop. The great hooded chairs had become enormous. And Giles too. And Isa too against the window. The window was all sky without colour. The house had lost its shelter. It was night before roads were made, or houses. It was the night that dwellers in caves had watched from some high place among rocks.

Then the curtain rose. They spoke.